Comprehensive Catalog and Encyclopedia of Morgan and Peace Dollars

Fourth Edition

Comprehensive Catalog and Encyclopedia of Morgan and Peace Dollars

By
Leroy C. Van Allen
A. George Mallis
(With research and contributions in Chapter Five by Pete R. Bishal)

REVISED EDITION OF
*Comprehensive Catlaogue and Encyclopedia of
U.S. Morgan and Peace Silver Dollars*

Containing

POPULARITY OF COLLECTING & INVESTING
BACKGROUND OF SILVER DOLLAR COINAGE
CONDITION AVAILABILITY
DETAILS OF MINTING PROCESSES
HISTORICAL LETTERS o 2100+ ILLUSTRATIONS
DESCRIPTIONS OF 1800 ERRORS/VARIETIES
GSA SALE OF CARSON CITY DOLLARS
SILVER DOLLAR HOARDS
DETECTING COUNTERFEITS
PRESERVATION & STORAGE
GRADING

Published by

Worldwide Ventures, Inc.
3107 Edgewater Dr.
Orlando, FL 32804

Bob Paul, Inc.
648 South St.
Philadelphia, PA 19147

Copyright © 1991 by Leroy C. Van Allen & A. George Mallis

All rights reserved. No part of this book may be reproduced, by any means, without written permission, except by a reviewer who wishes to quote brief excerpts in connection with a review in a magazine or newspaper.

Library of Congress Catalog Card Number: 97-61594

ISBN 0-9660168-0-7 (Leather Edition)
ISBN 0-9660168-1-5 (Hardbound Edition)
ISBN 0-9660168-2-3 (Paperback Edition)

Printed in the United States of America

THE HISTORY OF THE VAM BOOK

VAM book refers to the joint authorship book by Leroy Catlin Van Allen and A. George Mallis with a rather long title of *Comprehensive Catalog and Encyclopedia of Morgan and Peace Dollars*. The book had its genesis as independent efforts and books by both authors in the late 1950's and early 1960's. The following story briefly traces the development of these initial independent books and the later joint efforts to produce the various editions of the VAM book.

EARLY INDEPENDENT EFFORTS

In the mid-1950's, Mallis' collecting interests turned to Morgan dollars, since they were relatively inexpensive to collect and were in need of being catalogued. Beginning late 1958 as CEO of an architect firm, he made weekly trips to a job site at Bailey's Cross Roads in Alexandria, VA. Before returning home in Massachusetts, he would purchase a thousand dollar bag of silver dollars from the Treasury Department sales counter in Washington DC. Each bag was subsequently checked and recorded for dates, mint marks, and varieties. When the Treasury Department stopped issuing silver dollars in 1964, Mallis had examined some THIRTY-FIVE THOUSAND of them. When the Treasury released the scarce New Orleans Morgan dollars late in 1962, Van Allen became interested in them. From early 1963 through 1964, he examined some ten-thousand silver dollars from the Treasury Department in Washington, DC and the Baltimore Federal Reserve.

Mallis began preparing a pamphlet in 1962 of his recordings on the silver dollars he had examined. In mid-1963, Francis Kleas published a pamphlet entitled *Die Varieties of Morgan Silver Dollars*. This was a real eye opener with large clear photos of some major varieties. It was Klaes' pamphlet that started Van Allen writing an independent manuscript on Morgan varieties in late 1963. He thought Klaes' listings and photographs could be expanded with additional varieties.

Van Allen's first manuscript was sent to Neil Shafer of Whitman Publishing early in 1964. Shafer advised him that it was NOT READY for publication and that he needed to consult the mint records to explain the WHY of the varieties (as he had in several articles). Van Allen then spent a good deal of the spring of 1964 at the National Archives and Library of Congress in Washington, DC gathering material and studying additional coins.

In the spring of 1964, Mallis approached Klaes about collaborating on a revised list of Morgan dollar die varieties, but this partnership never developed. Mallis then continued his research alone. In October 1964, this effort was completed with his distribution of 50 free copies of a pamphlet entitled *List of Die Varieties of Morgan*

Head Silver Dollars. The pamphlets were distributed to interested numismatists and libraries.

By September 1964, Van Allen sent a completely revised manuscript of the Morgan dollar series varieties to Charles "Shotgun" Slade III (a prominent silver dollar dealer who owned a printing shop). Slade thought the manuscript was of interest but that a SHORTER pamphlet would be more suitable for him to publish. In October 1964, Van Allen submitted a new manuscript on the 1878 Morgan varieties to Slade. He then suggested a DIE CLASSIFICATION SYSTEM was needed and that Sheldon's *Penny Whimsy* should be studied. Taking his suggestion, Van Allen rewrote the 1878 dollar manuscript and resubmitted it to him late in November 1964. This book was not printed as scheduled in February 1965 and the manuscript was again revised and forwarded to Slade in March 1965.

After some negotiations in early 1965, Walter Breen agreed to act as consulting or collaborating author with Mallis on a new book, *United States Silver Dollars, Morgan Type*. Unfortunately, Breen suffered a lengthy illness and was unable to assist in the manuscript preparation. Mallis pressed on alone and copyrighted the complete manuscript in June 1965. He worked with Whitman Publishing in 1965 to prepare the book for publication, but the project was abandoned early in 1966 because of the efforts with Van Allen. Only THREE copies of this manuscript exist - one in the Library of Congress, one with Mallis and one with Van Allen (extensively marked up as a basis for the later collaboration effort).

At this point, Van Allen decided to publish his own book entitled *Morgan and Peace Dollar Varieties*. His wife, Ruth, typed the camera ready copy and 5,000 softbound and 100 hardbound copies were printed by December 1965. Izzy Fishman of Ace Coin Exchange in Baltimore, Maryland distributed the books which were sold out within about a year at a retail price of $2.50.

VAN ALLEN AND MALLIS JOINT EFFORTS

In January 1966, Mallis suggested to Van Allen that their two works and Shafer's efforts should be combined into ONE reference work. Mallis and Van Allen first met at Mallis' home in Massachusetts in April 1966 to discuss a joint book venture. Jim Johnson of Coin World's Collectors' Clearinghouse was very much in favor of such a project and endorsed it several times in Coin World in 1965. Walter Breen had also recommended the collaboration in his November 1964 column in Coin world.

In June 1966, Whitman Publishing was contacted concerning the publication of their joint book on silver dollar varieties. Whitman Publishing would not accept the project since it was not one hundred percent ready with each variety of silver dollar verified. The manuscript was completely ready in mid 1986. Then began a long string of publisher rejection notices! Twelve publishers declined offers to print the book.

Meanwhile, new varieties of silver dollars were pointed out to the authors by various coin collectors. This kept increasing the size of the manuscript.

In February 1971, the authors decided to finance the publication of the book and Van Allen's wife, Ruth, again typed the final text. Van Allen pasted the camera ready copy. By December 1971, 2,610 softbound and 205 hardbound copies were received from the printer with the title of *Guide to Morgan and Peace Dollars*. Frank and Louise Katen of Katen Coins in Silver Springs Maryland distributed the book. These books were sold in about a year and a half. By 1975, the book had become hard to find and the going price for a copy was two to three times its original price.

Collectors continued to point out new varieties to the authors. By mid 1975, enough new material had accumulated that it was time to revise the VAM book as it had become known. A publishing agreement was made with First Coinnvestors of Long Island, New York and Arco Publishing delivered 5,500 hardbound books in October 1976 followed by 2,800 hardbound and 50 leather bound books were delivered in December 1976. Minor changes were incorporated in the second printing of 4,500 hardbound books delivered in March 1977. The retail price of the initial printing of the book was $19.95 and the title was *Comprehensive Catalogue and Encyclopedia of U.S. Morgan and Peace Silver Dollars*. This second edition had four printings with the last one in 1981. There were more than 20,000 hardbound copies printed. In 1977, it received the Book of the Year award from the Numismatic Literary Guild.

A great many new varieties were reported by collectors after the 1976 book release and new material on silver dollars accumulated during the coin market boom of the late 1970's and early 1980's. The authors intended to publish a revised edition of the VAM book in the mid 1980's and the manuscript was ready by early 1986. Meanwhile, Arco Publishing had been sold and was no longer interested in publishing the book and First Coinvestors had moved and lost most of the negatives. The book had to be typeset again and Van Allen had to reprint the majority of the book photos from his old film negatives.

From 1986 through 1991, the authors were unable to find a publisher for the VAM book. In 1991, DLRC Press of Virginia Beach, Virginia agreed to republish the book. Further additions and revisions were made and the third edition was released in September 1992 at $49.95 retail with 4,400 softbound and 600 hardbound copies printed. The VAM book again received the Book of the Year award from the Numismatic Literary Guild in 1993, and had the title of *Comprehensive Catalog and Encyclopedia of Morgan and Peace Dollars*.

Leroy Van Allen

Glossary of Abbreviations

MINT MARKS:
- P   Philadelphia
- O   New Orleans
- S   San Francisco
- CC   Carson City
- D   Denver

OTHERS:
- Obv.   Obverse
- Rev.   Reverse
- TF   Tail Feathers
- PAF   Parallel Arrow Feathers
- SAF   Slanted Arrow Feathers
- I...IV   Type of Mint Mark or Obverse Design
- A...D   Type of Reverse Design
- O/O   O Repunched Over O
- O/S   O Repunched Over S
- O/CC   O Repunched Over CC
- II/I Obv.   Second Design Obverse Over First Design Obverse
- 7/8TF   Seven Over Eight Tail Feathers
- BU   Brilliant Uncirculated

RARITY SCALE:
- R-1   Common (Tens of Millions)
- R-2   Not so Common (Several Millions)
- R-3   Scarce (Hundreds of Thousands)
- R-4   Very Scarce (Tens of Thousands)
- R-5   Rare (Several Thousands)
- R-6   Very Rare (Several Hundred)
- R-7   Extremely Rare (Few Tens)
- R-8   Unique or Nearly Unique (Several)

INTEREST FACTOR:

I-1   Normal die variety with little interest to variety collectors.

I-2   Minor die variety with some interest to variety collectors.

I-3   Significant die variety with general interest to variety collectors.

I-4   Major die variety with universal interest to variety collectors.

I-5   Outstanding die variety with prime interest to variety collectors.

AMPLIFYING DESCRIPTIONS:

I-1   Normal die variety with no unusual die states. Can have hairline die cracks, small die chips, or minor clash marks which are normal as die wears or portions of the design may be weak due to polishing of the die.

I-2   Minor variations from normal die such as slight shifts in date or mint mark placement and orientation; micro doubling of date or mint mark; and slight abnormalities in die state such as fairly large die cracks or die chips (i.e., spiked dates). Such die variations may not be of interest to all collectors but they are identifiable using a medium power magnifying glass.

I-3   Significant variations from normal die such as changes in mint mark or date digit sizes; small die design changes; large shifts in date or mint mark placement and orientation; major doubling of date or mint mark; slight doubling of die design; small modifications of individual dies (touch ups, polishing, and weak overdates and over mint marks), and large abnormalities in die state such as big die cracks or gouges. These die variations are of general interest to many variety collectors and are usually noticeable with a low power magnifying glass.

I-4   Major variations from normal die such as large die design changes; unusually large doubling of date or mint mark; large doubled die design; and strong individual die modifications of date or mint mark (i.e., over dates and over mint marks). Most of these die variations are visible to the naked eye and are of universal interest to variety collectors.

I-5   An outstanding major die variation representing the best example of its type.

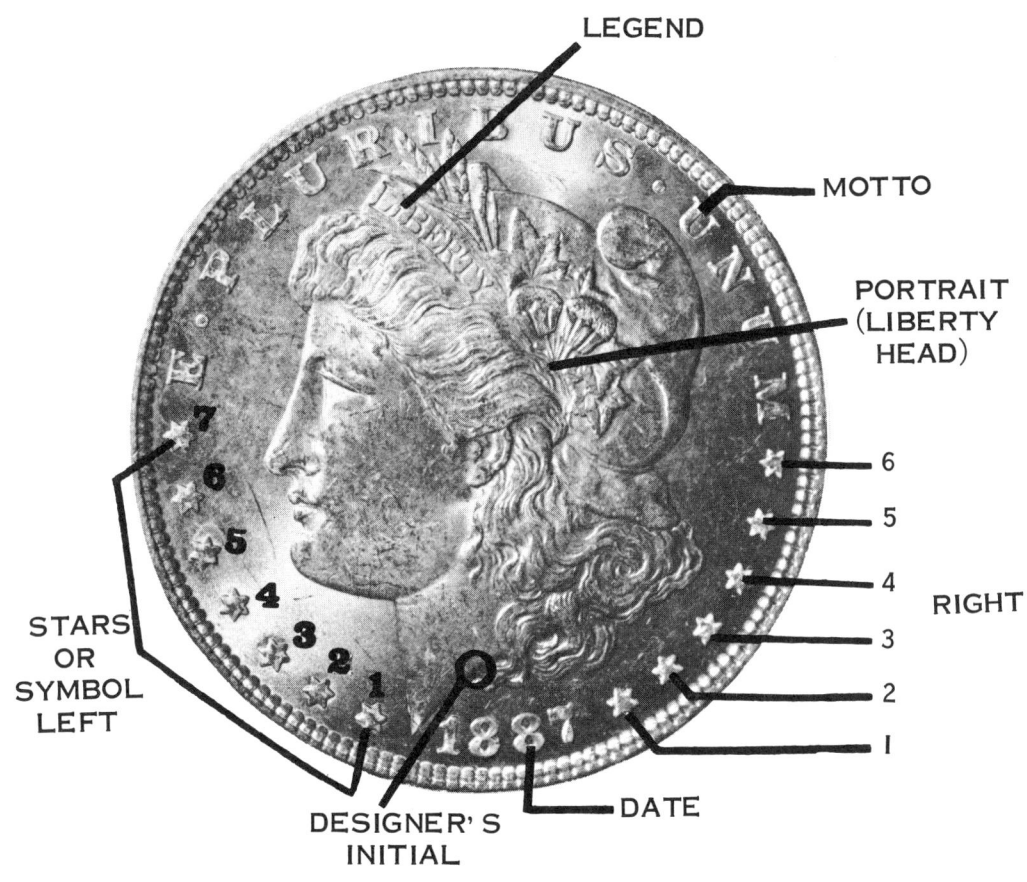
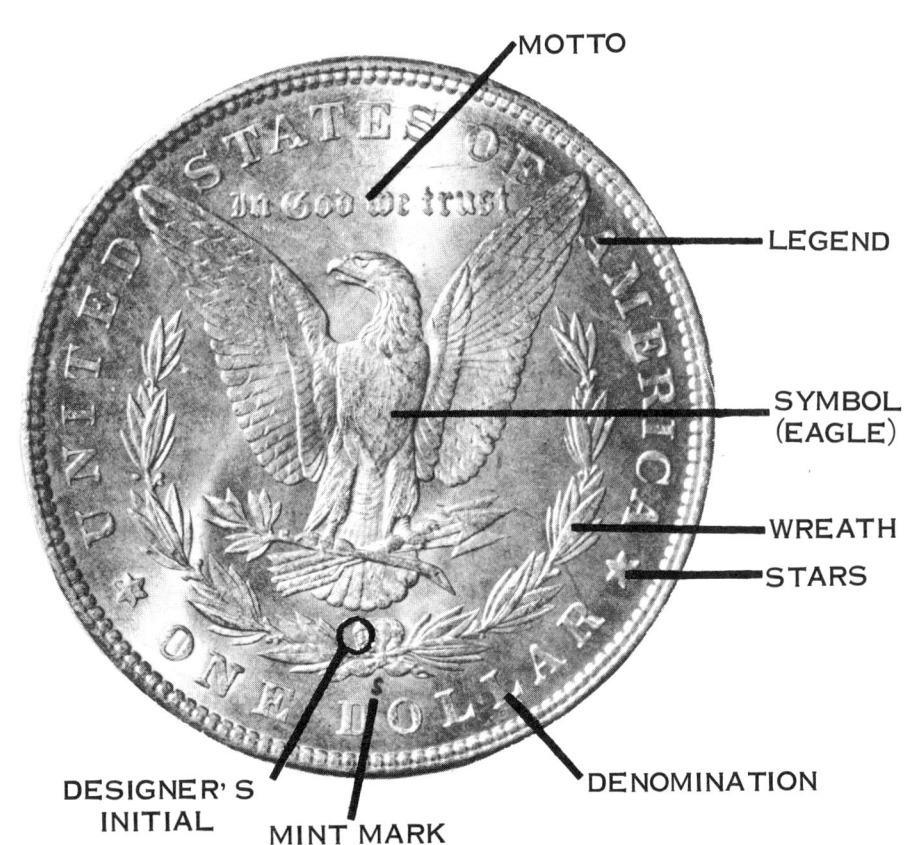

Table of Contents

Page

PART I

BACKGROUND ON THE SILVER DOLLAR 2

Chapter One...
POPULARITY OF COLLECTING/INVESTING IN
SILVER DOLLARS 3
- Availability
- Price
- Size and Design
- Appearance
- Relative Condition Availability

Chapter Two...
SILVER DOLLAR COINAGE 21
- Crime of '73
- Bland-Allison Act
- Sherman Silver Purchase Act
- Pittman Act
- Thomas Amendment
- Silver Purchase Act
- Public Law 88-36 of 1963
- Legislation of August 3, 1964
- Coinage Act of 1965
- Summary of Events
- Selected Bibliography

Chapter Three...
THE MINTING OF SILVER DOLLARS 39
- General Minting Operations
- Sources of Silver
- Mint Organization
- Receipt of Bullion
- Bullion Refining
- Ingot Preparation
- Preparation of Silver Strips
- Production of Planchets
- Die Preparation
- Coinage Operations
- Testing the Coins
- Selected Bibliography

Chapter Four...
PAST LITERATURE ON DOLLARS 65

Page

PART TWO

MORGAN SILVER DOLLARS 72

Chapter Five...
DEVELOPMENT OF THE DESIGN 73
- Morgan's Initial Work
- Initial Design of the Silver Dollar
- Design Changes in the Regular Coinage
- Design Changes After 1878
- Summary

Chapter Six...
DESCRIPTION OF THE DESIGNS 97
- Reverse Design Descriptions
- Obverse Design Descriptions
- Design Combinations
- Design Type Identification Summary

Chapter Seven...
DISCUSSION OF SIGNIFICANT VARIETIES 107
- Planchet Errors
- Re-engraved 1878-P 8 TF Reverses
- Re-engraved 1878-S and 1879-S Reverses
- Hub and Die Breaks and Cracks
- Doubled Dies
- Dual Hub Dies
- Date Position and Dashes
- Mispositioned Mint Marks
- Doubled Dates
- Doubled Mint Marks
- Overdates
- Dual Mint Marks
- Clashed Dies
- Die Scratches and Gouges
- Overpolished Dies
- Mint Mark Variations
- Date Variations
- Identifying Marks on Individual Dies
- Dots
- Edge Reeding
- 1878-P Die Marriages
- Master Hub and Die Doubling
- Striking Errors

Chapter Eight...
CONDITION ANALYSIS and
LIST OF DIE VARIETIES 139
- Key To Classification
- Die Descriptions

Chapter Nine...
GSA SALE OF CARSON CITY
DOLLARS...............97
    Background of the Sales
    Transfer of Dollars
    Initial Sorting
    GSA Holdings of Silver Dollars
    Packaging The Coins
    GSA Sales

Chapter Ten...
REDFIELD and
CONTINENTAL-ILLINOIS BANK
HOARDS..........403
    Redfield Hoard
    Continental-Illinois Bank Hoard

PART III
PEACE SILVER DOLLARS
.................408

Chapter Eleven...
DEVELOPMENT OF THE
DESIGN.....................409
    Initial Design
    Design Changes in the Regular Coinage

Chapter Twelve...
DESCRIPTION OF THE
DESIGNS.....................413
    Reverse Design Descriptions
    Obverse Design Descriptions
    Design Combinations

Chapter Thirteen..
DISCUSSION OF SIGNIFICANT
VARIETIES.........419
    Mint Mark Variations
    Mint Mark Placement
    Date Variations
    Clashed Dies
    Machine Doubling
    Die Breaks
    Doubled Dies
    Dots
    Rotated Dies
    Other Errors

Chapter Fourteen...
CONDITION ANALYSIS and
LIST OF DIE
VARIETIES.....................427

PART IV
WORKING WITH THE COINS 438

Chapter FIFTEEN...
DETECTING
COUNTERFEITS................................439
    General Detection Methods
    Cast coins
    False Dies
    Edges
    Coin Alterations

Chapter Sixteen...
SILVER DOLLAR PRESERVATION
and
STORAGE................................55
    Handling Silver Dollars
    Removal of Contaminants
    Storage

Chapter Seventeen...
GRADING................................461
    Grading Evolution
    Grading Factors
    Condition Availability Spectrum
    Mint State Grading Change Effects
    Grading Scale
    Examining Silver Dollars
    Abrasions/Wear
    Strike
    Luster
    Color
    Proof-Like Coins
    Proof Versus Proof-Like Coins
    Grading Proof Silver Dollars
    Grading Morgan Silver Dollars
    Grading Peace Silver Dollars

Chapter Eighteen...
PHOTOGRAPHING SILVER
DOLLARS.................493
    Cameras
    Lenses
    Setting Up The Camera
    Taking The Picture
    Processing The Film
    Making Your Own Print

Index...
....504

New Varieties and Errata list
.............................508

Part I
Background on the Silver Dollar

Chapter 1
Popularity of Collecting/Investing in Silver Dollars

Collecting and investing in Morgan and Peace silver dollars increased tremendously during the 1970s and 1980s. These are now one of the most widely collected of the entire U.S. series. This is particularly true of the Morgan silver dollar which is much more popular than the Peace silver dollar. Why has the silver dollar been thrust into the limelight of contemporary collecting and investing when, in the 1960s, few people seriously collected them? For an answer one must look at several factors.

AVAILABILITY

It is ironic that since silver dollars were generally unused by the public in years past because they were bulky and heavy, except for parts of the south and west, large quantities are now available in uncirculated condition. Some 570 million Morgan dollars were minted between 1878 and 1904. About 270 million of these were melted in 1918 and 1919 under the Pittman Act. Another 86 million Morgan dollars were minted in 1921 and 190 million Peace dollars were minted from 1921 to 1935. Over 52 million silver dollars were melted in 1943 and 1944 for wartime uses. About 10 million mutilated and damaged silver dollars were melted from 1945 to 1964 by the Treasury. Many more millions of circulated and some common 1921 Morgan and Peace uncirculated silver dollars were also melted commercially during late 1979 and early 1980 when the price of silver soared briefly to $50 per ounce. Over 340 million silver dollars were thus melted.

This would leave something like 250 million Morgan dollars still in existence, about 60 to 70 million 1921 Morgan dollars and about 150-160 million Peace dollars. The total stock of silver dollars was 484,722,100 in 1964[1] which was later reduced by perhaps 10 to 30 million during the 1979 and 1980 silver melts. The key question is, how many of these remaining silver dollars are in uncirculated condition?

For an answer one must look at Treasury Department records of silver dollars in circulation as shown in *Table 1-1*. During the coinage of the Morgan dollar from 1878 through 1904, only about one-fourth to one-eighth of the coins were in circulation at any one time. Most were held as backing for silver certificate paper money which was much preferred for use by the public and were stored in the various Mint and Treasury vaults. Even by the late 1950s only half of the silver dollars were in circulation by Treasury Department figures. Of these, most were not actually in circulation but were in various commercial bank vaults.

By 1961 only about 150 million silver dollars remained in the Treasury vaults. Then in early December, 1962, as the Treasury dug deeper into its vaults for the traditional Christmas time demands for silver dollars, bags of former scarce New Orleans "O" mint dollars were released including, 1898-O, 99-O, 00-O, 01-O, 02-O, 03-O, and 04-O. Their sudden availability sparked the interest of speculators, investors, and collectors to the common silver dollars. Also, the price of silver was increasing to over $1.00 per ounce and rapidly approaching $1.29 per ounce when the bullion value in a silver dollar would be equal to its face value. So, the public was increasingly hoarding silver dollars and other silver coins for their bullion value.

The demand for silver dollars kept accelerating and by the summer of 1963 the Treasury stock was down to about 50 million. Huge quantities of uncirculated 1921-P Morgan and 1922-P and 1923-P Peace dollars were being released. Then bags of uncirculated Morgan dollars dating mostly 1878 through 1888 started being distributed. Here were uncirculated coins 80 to 90 years old being released for the first time by the Treasury. The numismatic world went wild over them! Collecting silver dollars suddenly became very popular and investors and speculators were quick to cash in. Bags of uncirculated silver dollars were being bought up a tremendous rate. There were released thousands of bags of 1878-P,CC,S; 1879-P,O,S; 1880-P,O,S; 1881-P,O,S; 1882-P,O,S; 1883-P,O; 1884-P,O; 1885-P,O,S; 1886-P,O; 1887-P,O; 1888-P,O; 1889-P, 1890-P, 1891-P, 1896-P, 1897-P, 1898-P, 1900-P, 1902-P, and 1903-P. Many thousands of bags of circulated silver dollars containing all dates were released as well as a few bags of Seated Liberty dollars as the Treasury vaults were cleaned out.

By late February and early March 1964, lines of people waited to buy the last remaining bags of silver dollars using silver certificates with only about 3 million scarce Carson City silver dollars remaining in the vaults for later sale in the 1970s. The great silver dollar rush on the Treasury was over and the silver dollars were in the dealers, collectors, and investors hands.

Many of these silver dollars were shipped out West to the gambling centers where their use was high. The gambling casinos hoarded silver dollars for use in the casinos. Later, they even ground off the dates of the silver dollars in an attempt to keep them from slipping away to collectors and investors. But the continued advance of the price of silver eventually made the bullion value of the silver dollar greater than $1.00 in 1967, and even these mutilated silver dollars disappeared from use.

Based on the low quantities of silver dollars that reached circulation, probably something like one-sixth to one-fourth of the pre-1921 Morgan dollars never reached circulation and perhaps one-fifth to one-quarter of the 1921 Morgan and Peace dollars never circulated. This would mean around 40 to 50 million pre-1921 Morgans, 10 to 15 million 1921 Morgans, and 30 to 40 million Peace dollars exist today in uncirculated condition. It is estimated that there are a total of 80 to 100 million uncirculated Morgan and Peace dollars out of a total of about 450 to 470 million surviving silver dollars. This may seem high but the Treasury held back 3 million scarce CC dollars and many more times this of common dates were released.

Compared to Barber quarters and halves or coins of the 1920s this is a tremendous number of surviving uncirculated coins. Gold coins of the comparable time period were too expensive for many people to hoard. Subsidiary coins circulated extensively for commerce with few being held by the Treasury from year to year in uncirculated condition. Not many subsidiary coins were hoarded by rolls and bags throughout the silver dollar production time period. Only the U.S. Government could afford to store millions and millions of silver dollars unused for many decades to back silver certificates. And thus, only the Morgan and Peace silver dollars are available in such large quantities in uncirculated condition.

Even twenty-five years after the release of almost all of the silver dollars by the Treasury, uncirculated silver dollars were still being traded by the bags and rolls. No other contemporary U.S. coin has such availability in uncirculated condition. They are usually traded by individual coins only.

It is because of the widespread availability of uncirculated silver dollars that a tremendous market has grown around them. The volume of the coin market in silver dollars has recently grown to be one of the largest segments in the U.S. coin industry. Most collectors/investors prefer uncirculated specimens. The very availability of uncirculated silver dollars has provided the fuel for the dollar market. At an average price of $20 per uncirculated coin and $10 per circulated coin, the market values are about $2 billion in uncirculated and $4 billion in circulated condition.

Of course the availability of uncirculated silver dollars is not evenly distributed by date or mint. This relative availability will be discussed in a later section.

Table 1-1 SILVER DOLLARS IN CIRCULATION
(from the Annual Report of the Director of the Mint)

DATE	TOTAL COINAGE	Held for Payment of Certificates Outstanding	Held in Excess of Certificates Outstanding	IN CIRCULATION
1878				
1879				
1880				
1881				
1882				
1883				
1884(Dec)	189,561,994	114,865,911	31,636,954	43,059,129
1885(Oct)	210,759,431	93,656,716	71,827,005	45,275,710
1886(Nov)	244,433,386	100,306,800	82,624,431	61,502,155
1887	277,110,157	160,713,957	53,461,575	62,934,625
1888	309,750,890	229,783,152	20,196,288	59,771,450
1889	343,638,001	277,319,944	6,219,577	60,098,480
1890	380,988,466	308,206,177	7,072,725	65,709,564
1891	409,475,368	321,142,642	26,197,265	62,135,461
1892	416,412,835	324,552,532	30,187,848	61,672,455
1893	419,332,550	325,717,232	34,889,500	58,725,818
1894	421,776,408	331,143,301	34,189,437	56,443,670
1895	423,289,309	342,409,504	22,525,713	58,354,092
1896	439,552,141	366,463,504	14,897,835	58,190,802
1897	452,713,792	372,838,919	19,678,095	60,196,778
1898	466,836,597	398,753,504	4,645,838	63,437,255
1899(July)	480,251,231	406,085,504	10,783,976	63,381,751
1900	498,496,215	416,015,000	15,826,299	66,654,916
1901	522,795,065	435,014,000	18,688,931	69,092,134
1902				
1903				
1904				
1905	568,228,865	454,864,708	39,779,821	73,584,336

DATE	TOTAL STOCK	HELD IN TREASURY	HELD IN RESERVE BANKS	IN CIRCULATION
1957	488,435,800	229,200,021	6,628,920	252,606,859
1958	488,246,700	213,311,029	7,008,444	267,927,227
1959	488,046,100	194,411,064	8,143,867	285,491,169
1960	487,773,300	174,314,287	8,376,508	305,082,505
1961	487,589,300	149,172,946	9,745,018	328,671,336
1962	487,355,300	115,487,279	12,278,324	359,589,697
1963	486,017,400	65,760,615	8,768,069	411,488,716
1964	484,722,100	2,943,295	57,866	481,720,939

PRICE

Up until 1964 Morgan and Peace dollars were readily available at face value from most commercial banks. Once the price of silver advanced beyond the bullion value contained in a silver dollar ($1.29 per ounce), they naturally were hoarded and disappeared from circulation. From then on there has been an almost steady increase in the price of uncirculated silver dollars. The price of common circulated silver dollars has varied with the price of silver.

Table 1-2 summarizes the price history of the Morgan and Peace silver dollar, for the past forty years. The 1952 price is from the Whitman Blue book guide which list wholesale prices. These prices were indicative of the general prices of Morgan and Peace dollars for previous decades. Most dates brought only a small premium of 10 to 25 cents above face value because of their ready

Table 1-2 MORGAN AND PEACE DOLLAR PRICE HISTORY

DATE	1952 BLUE BOOK UNC	1963 RED BOOK UNC	1972 RED BOOK UNC	1977 RED BOOK UNC	SEP 79 MS 60	CDN BID MS 65	DEC 82 MS 60	CDN BID MS 65	MAY 86 MS 60	CDN BID MS 65	JUN 89 MS 60	CDN BID MS 65	NOV 91 MS 60	CDN BID MS 65
1878 P 8 TF	1.25	10.00	14.00	25	45	120	50	310	60	2,250	50	4,300	38	1,050
1878 P 7/8 TF	-	12.50	17.50	40	45	170	60	575	65	2,700	50	5,800	50	1,825
1878 P 7 TF	1.10	3.00	6.00	16	40	90	40	295	50	1,650	28	4,200	22	1,150
1878 CC	1.25	7.50	16.00	33	83	125	100	210	107	1,625	75	4,150	60	950
1878 S	1.10	3.00	5.00	14	39	43	42	140	52	1,125	26	875	18	195
1879 P	1.10	3.00	4.75	14	34	110	35	460	40	1,550	24	3,850	18	1,050
1879 CC	2.00	95.00	210.00	750	750	3,000	675	3,500	1,150	8,600	950	27,000	950	22,500
1879 O	1.50	9.50	7.00	17	50	300	50	900	48	2,450	40	7,200	25	3,700
1879 S	1.10	3.75	4.75	11	31	35	42	115	52	750	22	545	15	88
1880 P	1.10	2.75	5.00	14	35	90	35	340	38	1,250	23	6,200	18	1,350
1880 CC	1.50	25.00	75.00	100	140	190	150	315	170	2,100	120	2,550	103	585
1880 O	1.35	7.50	5.50	30	75	310	70	1,000	60	3,150	35	69,000	28	19,000
1880 S	1.10	3.00	4.25	10	30	35	40	110	51	725	21	545	15	85
1881 P	1.10	2.75	5.25	14	30	95	35	330	36	1,050	24	3,400	19	1,300
1881 CC	2.50	25.00	75.00	90	140	195	157	310	220	1,900	150	1,325	125	430
1881 O	1.25	5.00	4.75	12	28	75	34	380	28	1,050	20	5,350	15	2,125
1881 S	1.10	3.75	4.25	11	30	35	38	110	50	700	21	545	14	85
1882 P	1.10	2.75	4.50	12	30	95	35	315	34	1,075	23	1,875	18	400
1882 CC	1.25	12.00	35.00	30	77	85	62	155	98	1,075	72	1,075	46	215
1882 O	1.25	5.50	4.50	11	28	75	37	375	28	1,000	20	4,200	17	1,220
1882 S	1.10	3.00	4.50	11	31	38	42	150	51	800	22	545	17	85
1883 P	1.10	3.00	4.50	11	29	85	35	325	35	900	23	825	17	110
1883 CC	1.25	15.00	30.00	30	54	58	62	135	98	1,000	70	925	45	200
1883 O	1.10	4.50	4.50	11	22	25	26	155	26	850	18	675	11	110
1883 S	1.10	12.50	40.00	350	400	1,300	365	1,750	380	4,750	300	45,000	275	26,500
1884 P	1.10	3.50	4.50	12	50	140	43	375	35	1,125	21	1,175	15	200
1884 CC	1.15	17.50	40.00	30	54	58	62	135	98	1,000	71	925	46	250
1884 O	1.15	5.00	4.50	11	22	25	26	155	27	800	18	545	11	80
1884 S	1.35	20.00	85.00	850	900	9,500	825	9,500	1,400	22,500	3,500	110,000	3,000	100,000
1885 P	1.10	3.50	4.50	11	22	27	27	150	26	800	18	575	12	100
1885 CC	4.50	25.00	65.00	90	145	195	155	290	240	1,800	218	1,900	178	465
1885 O	1.10	4.50	4.50	11	22	25	26	155	26	800	18	545	11	80
1885 S	1.10	10.00	15.50	50	90	460	97	750	110	1,800	70	5,100	65	1,900
1886 P	1.10	4.50	4.50	11	22	25	27	127	26	750	18	545	12	80
1886 O	1.25	15.00	17.50	130	250	3,500	290	2,700	290	4,950	265	60,000	150	17,500
1886 S	1.10	20.00	37.50	125	155	400	95	550	145	2,150	80	6,300	75	2,300
1887 P	1.15	3.50	4.50	11	22	25	27	130	26	750	18	545	11	80
1887 O	1.35	6.50	6.00	18	40	375	44	620	46	1,650	31	11,850	24	4,500
1887 S	1.10	12.00	17.00	50	110	250	60	600	80	1,900	55	7,600	45	2,740
1888 P	1.10	5.00	4.50	12	26	65	31	290	26	900	23	925	13	181
1888 O	1.75	6.50	4.75	12	35	112	29	270	26	1,000	23	2,125	13	600
1888 S	1.10	25.00	37.50	135	250	600	100	575	160	2,300	80	6,900	80	3,100
1889 P	1.15	2.50	4.50	12	26	65	28	380	26	1,175	18	1,950	12	450
1889 CC	2.50	275.00	950.00	3,200	4,250	12,500	3,650	16,500	5,000	21,250	5,500	100,000	5,000	100,000
1889 O	1.35	9.00	15.00	42	120	600	75	1,650	75	3,100	55	6,100	55	3,260
1889 S	1.10	20.00	36.50	90	145	310	60	360	130	1,800	75	4,975	60	1,250
1890 P	1.15	3.50	5.00	15	32	100	36	485	28	1,450	21	7,200	17	3,150
1890 CC	1.15	10.00	30.00	85	165	300	182	660	200	2,000	170	10,500	150	3,900
1890 O	1.25	7.50	13.50	30	65	275	46	950	55	1,575	34	7,000	24	2,050
1890 S	1.10	5.00	8.00	33	72	190	37	175	70	1,100	35	2,150	28	740
1891 P	1.15	4.00	11.00	35	175	475	70	950	70	2,400	38	14,100	33	5,800
1891 CC	1.15	10.00	28.00	75	130	200	147	610	200	1,900	150	6,300	105	1,900
1891 O	1.35	10.00	15.00	42	145	1,150	64	2,100	64	4,250	45	11,100	45	6,000
1891 S	1.10	6.00	12.50	35	78	210	37	205	70	1,125	40	3,100	28	1,000
1892 P	1.25	12.50	31.50	75	100	615	120	1,250	120	2,925	70	6,700	75	2,700
1892 CC	1.25	30.00	65.00	225	300	725	250	800	325	2,550	270	10,000	235	3,200
1892 O	1.35	20.00	25.00	110	160	1,200	100	2,250	100	3,825	80	8,700	70	4,050
1892 S	2.00	175.00	2,200.00	12,500	5,000	15,500	3,400	18,000	3,750	32,250	6,750	100,000	7,600	45,000
1893 P	1.25	15.00	60.00	200	325	1,150	260	1,650	255	3,375	250	9,600	190	3,600
1893 CC	2.00	75.00	225.00	800	850	3,000	675	3,650	675	8,500	725	61,000	800	27,500
1893 O	1.75	50.00	220.00	775	900	6,650	850	10,000	850	19,250	875	60,000	875	160,000
1893 S	50.00	1,200.00	5,250.00	25,000	20,000	42,500	15,000	47,500	15,000	61,500	17,250	135,000	15,000	242,000
1894 P	1.25	75.00	21.00	630	750	5,000	775	3,800	800	9,000	725	24,000	600	9,000
1894 O	1.25	15.00	75.00	350	525	6,000	400	7,000	370	14,000	350	52,500	410	16,500
1894 S	1.25	25.00	55.00	250	285	1,150	285	1,650	285	2,925	270	7,600	235	3,800
1895 (Proof)	25.00	1,500.00	4,900.00	8,250	10,500	21,000	10,500	22,500	12,500	31,500	11,500	35,500	10,000	19,000
1895 O	1.50	75.00	400.00	1,850	1,650	15,500	1,500	25,000	1,750	40,500	2,500	68,600	3,850	75,000
1895 S	1.50	150.00	525.00	1,800	1,400	3,750	725	3,250	825	8,100	700	32,250	740	22,500
1896 P	1.25	2.50	4.50	12	27	75	30	245	26	925	18	975	13	145
1896 O	1.35	15.00	65.00	250	320	5,500	640	10,000	630	25,250	575	60,000	515	24,000
1896 S	1.25	60.00	225.00	500	775	1,750	350	1,500	470	5,200	475	20,000	500	11,000
1897 P	1.25	3.00	6.50	15	45	110	36	345	26	900	19	1,500	16	305
1897 O	1.25	12.50	46.00	225	265	4,300	320	5,000	320	9,000	400	27,750	320	32,500
1897 S	1.10	7.50	12.50	45	80	240	50	260	70	1,150	35	1,400	27	400
1898 P	1.15	4.50	5.00	13	26	65	36	265	26	900	18	1,275	14	165
1898 O	1.25	300.00	5.00	12	24	30	32	240	26	850	18	550	14	100
1898 S	1.10	15.00	33.50	150	290	600	115	650	155	2,200	125	3,750	95	1,400
1899 P	1.25	10.00	25.00	60	90	225	82	510	85	1,575	60	2,600	55	800
1899 O	1.25	10.00	4.50	11	24	30	33	250	26	900	19	565	12	100
1899 S	1.10	15.00	40.00	220	350	700	125	600	125	2,150	75	4,600	77	1,350
1900 P	1.10	3.50	4.50	12	24	65	35	295	26	1,000	18	1,050	14	140
1900 O	1.10	6.00	4.50	12	23	50	33	255	100	950	19	675	14	110
1900 S	1.10	15.00	33.50	135	100	250	105	650	105	1,600	70	3,625	70	1,600
1901 P	1.10	37.50	85.00	900	650	6,500	750	11,000	800	25,200	900	90,000	850	50,000
1901 O	1.50	7.50	4.50	11	35	100	37	315	26	1,100	20	1,125	15	210
1901 S	1.15	22.50	50.00	140	225	800	225	2,000	225	3,450	200	5,500	170	3,150
1902 P	1.15	3.50	9.00	35	55	290	50	850	50	1,800	28	1,875	30	490
1902 O	1.75	35.00	4.50	11	22	32	28	290	26	900	19	900	12	150
1902 S	1.15	25.00	100.00	250	175	600	185	1,000	190	2,500	100	5,900	120	2,550
1903 P	1.15	3.00	7.75	22	55	190	44	410	46	1,200	24	1,275	24	210
1903 O	60.00	1,500.00	40.00	65	250	400	190	685	230	1,350	167	1,675	130	370
1903 S	15.00	75.00	370.00	1,500	1,225	4,800	1,250	6,500	1,500	8,000	1,500	7,300	1,450	4,900
1904 P	1.10	10.00	19.00	55	150	900	95	1,300	80	2,700	50	8,300	45	3,750
1904 O	3.50	350.00	5.00	11	22	25	27	220	27	825	18	565	12	80
1904 S	1.15	50.00	200.00	550	685	3,000	700	3,000	750	4,500	650	13,000	650	8,250
1921 P	1.00	2.25	4.25	10	14	18	19	145	23	925	13	650	8	120
1921 D	1.00	2.50	5.50	17	32	150	23	550	37	1,125	22	1,625	20	260
1921 S	1.00	2.50	5.50	15	58	450	26	825	28	1,450	22	4,800	20	2,000

5

Table 1-2 *continued*

DATE	1952 BLUE BOOK UNC	1963 RED BOOK UNC	1972 RED BOOK UNC	1977 RED BOOK UNC	SEP 79 MS 60	CDN BID MS 65	DEC 82 MS 60	CDN BID MS 65	MAY 86 MS 60	CDN BID MS 65	JUN 89 MS 60	CDN BID MS 65	NOV 91 MS 60	CDN BID MS 65
1921 P	1.50	17.50	40.00	150	225	1,100	200	1,700	180	4,275	125	5,200	100	1,725
1922 P	1.05	2.50	4.25	9	14	18	18	140	23	750	12	800	8	135
1922 D	1.05	6.50	6.00	27	28	150	26	475	38	1,200	27	2,600	20	765
1922 S	1.05	4.50	6.00	27	50	375	27	575	40	1,600	27	7,600	21	2,375
1923 P	1.05	2.50	4.25	9	14	18	18	135	23	750	12	700	8	125
1923 D	1.05	8.00	12.50	27	45	240	28	700	40	2,000	27	3,450	18	1,700
1923 S	1.05	4.00	6.50	27	80	425	28	775	39	2,400	23	12,700	19	3,900
1924 P	1.05	3.00	5.00	12	18	55	24	320	35	900	17	900	12	150
1924 S	1.10	8.50	42.50	90	125	725	135	2,100	135	3,200	80	13,500	100	9,000
1925 P	2.00	2.50	4.50	11	18	32	22	230	35	850	17	700	12	126
1925 S	1.10	8.50	16.50	75	155	700	90	850	115	2,600	70	10,900	42	8,500
1926 P	1.05	8.00	11.00	23	32	145	41	550	45	1,250	25	1,450	18	300
1926 D	1.05	14.00	15.00	30	110	360	60	975	60	1,700	40	2,475	35	750
1926 S	1.05	10.00	8.50	28	37	175	41	440	45	1,450	35	3,250	22	975
1927 P	1.05	15.00	25.00	55	70	295	100	1,040	95	2,000	50	8,800	45	5,000
1927 D	1.05	22.50	42.00	95	240	1,100	195	2,500	195	3,825	125	10,700	120	4,700
1927 S	1.05	17.50	46.00	150	235	950	140	900	135	2,200	95	17,700	65	5,000
1928 P	1.50	40.00	100.00	185	260	775	200	1,325	200	3,150	170	8,775	145	3,300
1928 S	1.10	20.00	30.00	125	160	775	105	925	105	2,600	80	15,600	55	3,000
1934 P	1.15	12.00	24.00	52	70	340	82	1,000	83	2,100	65	3,600	55	1,525
1934 D	1.05	12.50	35.00	77	90	625	100	1,450	90	2,675	80	4,300	75	1,400
1934 S	3.00	85.00	270.00	820	1,250	6,250	1,100	4,200	1,200	8,150	1,050	12,550	900	5,850
1935 P	1.15	10.00	15.00	50	55	225	55	740	55	1,450	50	2,525	32	875
1935 S	1.15	17.50	45.00	135	120	600	140	1,350	140	2,525	85	4,175	75	1,050

---

availability from banks at face value. Only certain dates like the 1879-CC, 1881-CC, 1885-CC, 1889-CC brought a modest premium of a few dollars. And only the 1893-S, 1895 proof, 1903-O, and 1903-S had substantial premiums.

By 1963, prices for all dates and mints had advanced significantly as shown by the 1963 Whitman Red Book which gave the retail prices. Silver had begun its advance in price and collecting silver dollars had become more popular. Since the 1963 Red book prices had been compiled in 1962 it showed the 1903-O as the most valuable business strike Morgan or Peace dollar. The release of uncirculated 1898-O, 1903-O, 1904-O and other O-mint dollars around Christmas 1962 plummeted the value of these once scarce dates with the 1903-O value dropping from $1,500 to $15 and the 1898-O and the 1904-O from $300 to $2 in a few weeks. As the Treasury Department dug deeper into its vaults, bags of the scarcer dates would surface causing turmoil in their market value. But on the other hand, the release of the previously scarce O-mints late in 1962 made collectors, investors and speculators aware of the Treasury hoard of silver dollars. So the run on the Treasury began in earnest at that point for silver dollars.

Once the silver dollars held by the Treasury had been dis-

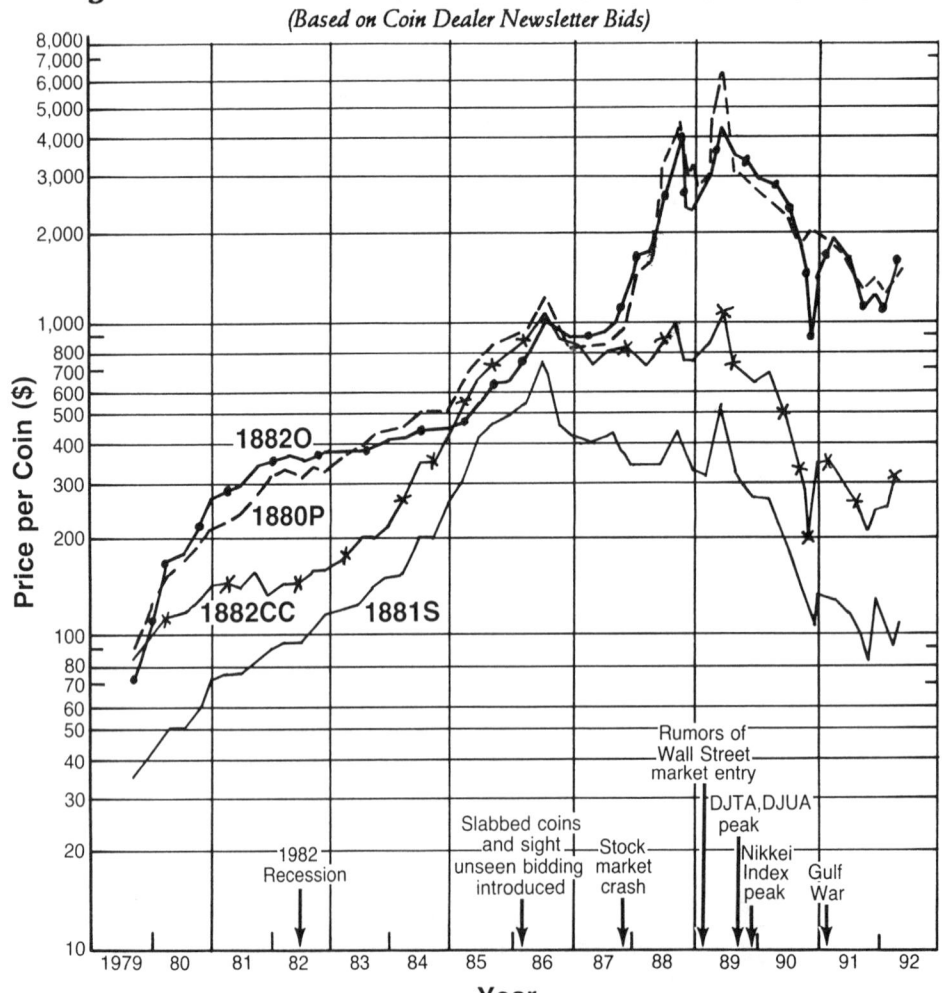

Figure 1-1 TYPICAL MORGAN DOLLAR MS65 PRICE TRENDS
(Based on Coin Dealer Newsletter Bids)

pensed prices climbed steadily as shown by the 1972 Red book prices. By then the uncirculated 1893-S had become the most valuable silver dollar and the most common silver dollar retailed for over four dollars. Prices continued to advance by 1977 with only the Treasury CC hoard dates showing a slight decline. The king of the Morgan and Peace dollars was the 1893-S at $25,000 in uncirculated condition and a number of dates were priced above $100 a coin.

By 1977 the single uncirculated grade had been divided into MS60 and MS65 with the release of the *Official A.N.A. Grading Standards for United States Coins*. *The Coin Dealer Newsletter* (CDN) of September 1979 reflected the continued increase in silver dollar prices, particularly in MS65. Many of the common dates showed little spread between MS60 and MS65 because of the wide availability. But by December 1982 there was a considerable spread in the MS60 and MS65 price for all dates because of collector/investor preference for MS65 and their lesser availability compared to MS60 coins. The minimum price for a MS65 dollar was over $100 by then — quite an increase from just over the face value of the 1950s.

It is this phenomenal price rise in the 1960s, 1970s and 1980s that helped spur investor and collector interest in Morgan and Peace dollars. In addition, the price of an uncirculated silver dollar during this time period was relatively low compared to other uncirculated coins of 50 to 100 years old. Simply put, Morgan and Peace dollars were seen as bargain priced

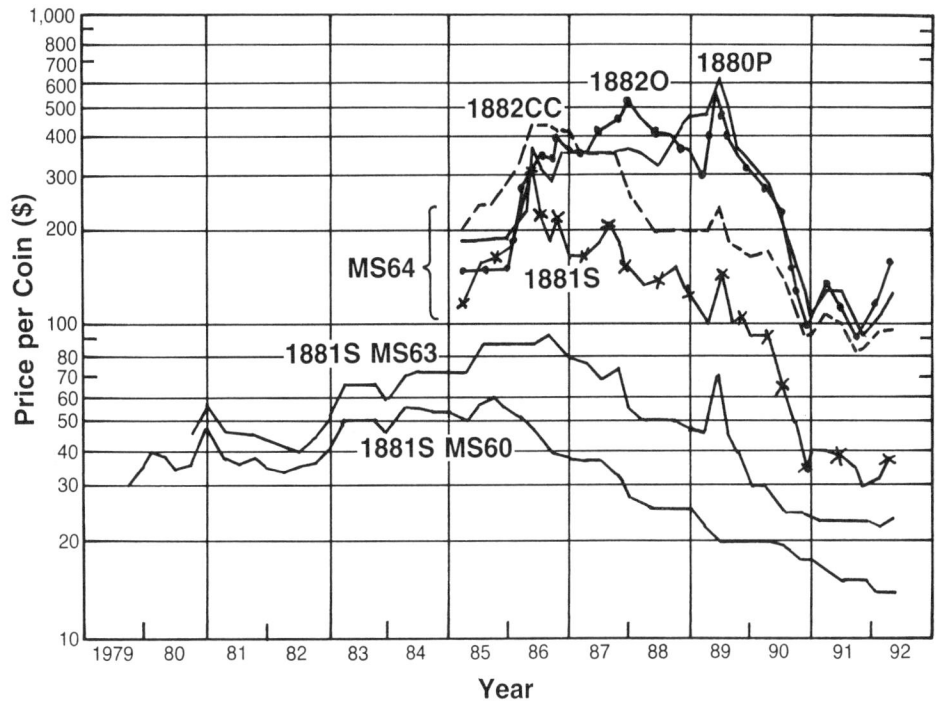

Figure 1-2 TYPICAL MORGAN DOLLAR MS60-64 PRICE TRENDS
(Based on Coin Dealer Newsletter Bids)

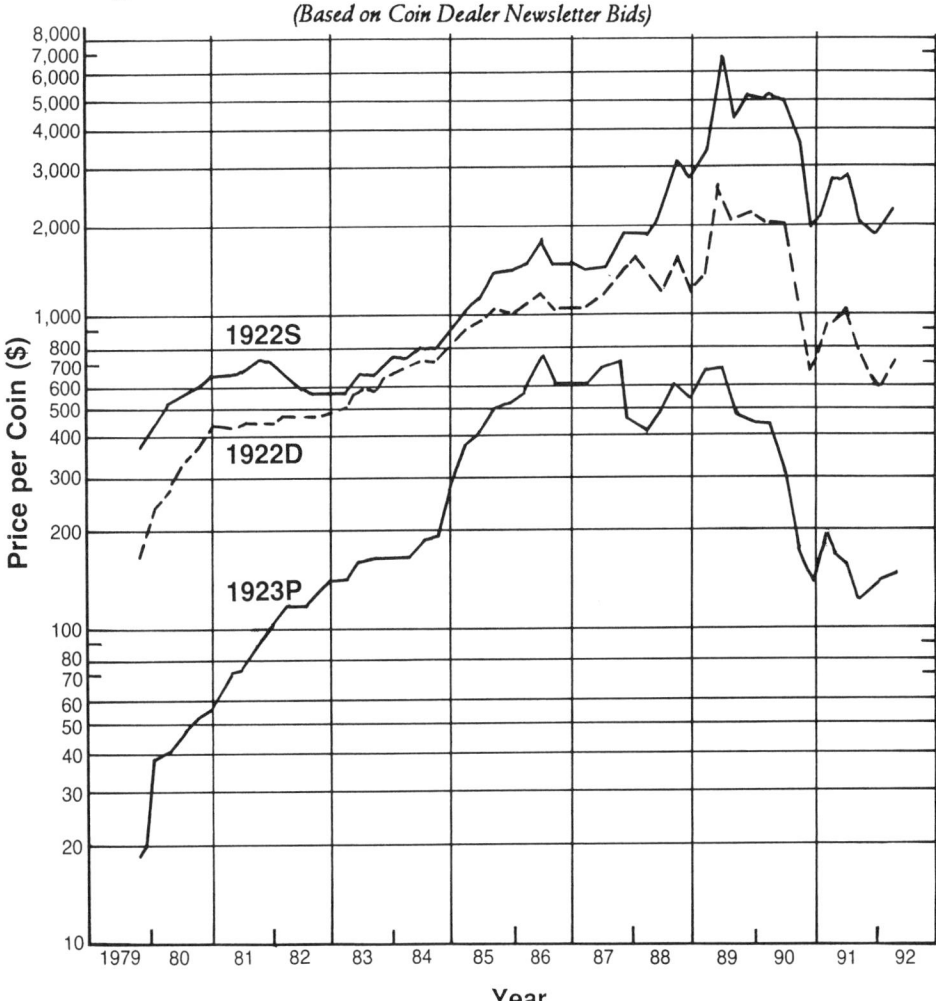

Figure 1-3 TYPICAL PEACE DOLLAR MS65 PRICE TRENDS
(Based on Coin Dealer Newsletter Bids)

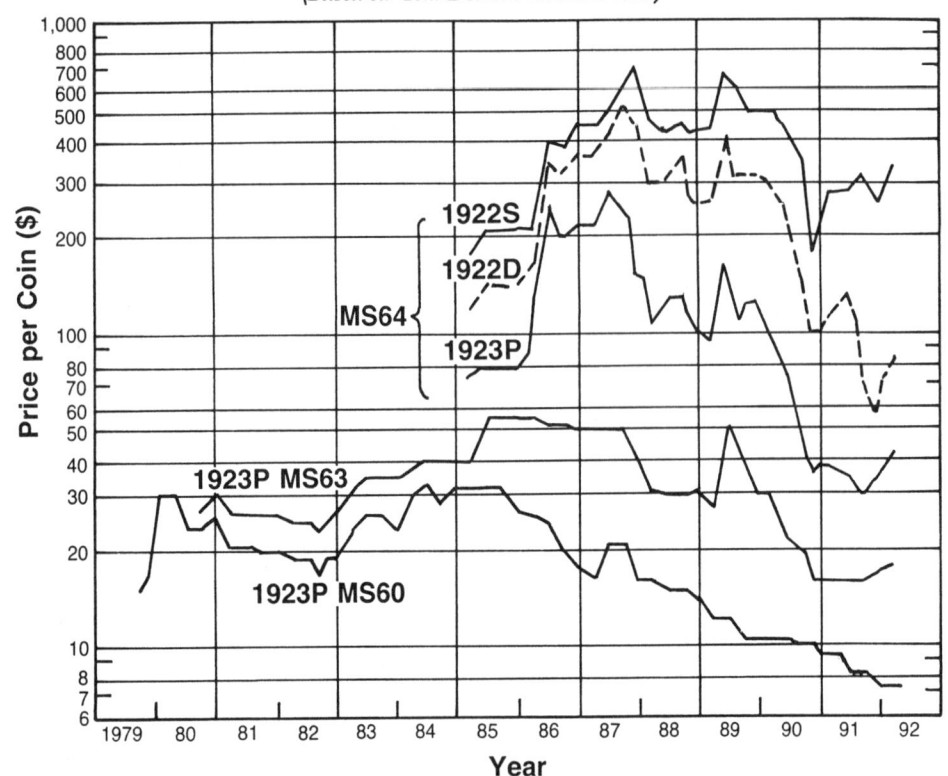

Figure 1-4 TYPICAL PEACE DOLLAR MS60-64 PRICE TRENDS
(Based on Coin Dealer Newsletter Bids)

with excellent price appreciation potential. The high inflation of 1970s and early 1980s caused many investors to see silver dollars as a good hedge against inflation. This interest helped drive their prices upward during the boom years of the 1980s. This spectacular rise and subsequent crash in Morgan and Peace dollar prices in the 1980s and early 1990s is treated in the following section.

Boom and Bust of the 1980s

Figures 1-1 through *1-4* show the Morgan and Peace dollar price trends from 1979 onward based on *The Coin Dealer Newsletter*, in grades MS60, MS63, MS64 and MS65 for select dates. For the grades MS60 and MS63, the common date 1881-S and 1923-P are shown. The MS63 grade started being reported in the Fall of 1980 in *The Coin Dealer Newsletter*. For MS64 and MS65, the common dates 1881-S and 1923-P are again shown and the somewhat scarcer dates of 1880-P, 1880-CC, 1882-O, 1922-D and 1922-S are also shown. The MS64 grade started being reported in the Spring of 1985 in *The Coin Dealer Newsletter*.

There are several different price trends depending upon the grade and whether the date is common or scarce. Apparent is the incredible price rise of the MS65 coins from 1979 to peaks in 1986 and 1989 and then the dramatic fall of price from these peaks to lows in late 1991. Similar price rise and falls occurred for MS64 coins from their first reporting early in 1985 to peaks in 1986 and 1989 and dramatic drop thereafter. These changes were much greater than those of the various New York stock market averages for example, during the same time period.

The common date 1881-S in MS65 rose from $35 in 1979 to $700 in 1986 and dropped to $85 late in 1991, while the 1923-P rose from $18 in 1979 to $750 in 1986 and $700 in 1989 and then dropped to $125 in late 1991. These are rises of 20 to 40 times within seven years and a drop to 1/6 to 1/8 of the peak values in two to five years. These are blow-offs and crashes in prices by anyone's definition.

The scarcer dates in MS65 generally peaked later in the middle of 1989 and dropped to lows in late 1990 and 1991. The rises from 1979 to 1989 were from $90 to $6,200 for the 1880-P, $85 to $1,075 for the 1882-CC, $75 to $4,200 for the 1882-O, $150 to $2,600 for the 1922-D and $375 to $7,600 for the 1922-D. These are rises of 13 to 60 times over ten years. Within one or two years, the 1880-P fell to $1,350, 1882-CC to $200, 1882-O to $950, 1922-D to $600 and 1922-S to $1,950. These are drops to 1/4 to 1/5 of the peak values within one to two years.

The MS64 grades did not have much time to participate in the great coin market rise of the early 1980's having been first reported on early in 1985.

The common date 1881-S rose from about $120 in MS64 to a peak of just over $300 in about one year and the 1923-P rose from $75 to a peak of about $280 in 1886 and 1987. These are increases of 3 to 4 times in one to two years. Thereafter, both prices fell steadily to lows in late 1991 of $30 for the 1881-S and 1923-P. This is a decrease to about 1/10 of the peak value in four to five years.

The scarcer date MS64 grade also had dramatic changes. The 1880-P rose from $185 to $625 in 1989, the 1882-CC from $200 to $460 in 1986, 1882-O from $140 to $550 in 1989, 1922-D from $125 to $520 in 1987 and 1922-S from $175 to $700 in 1987. These are increases of three to four times in one to three years. They also fell to lows in late 1990 or 1991 to $90 for the 1880-P, $87 for the 1882-CC, $85 for the 1882-O, $51 for the 1922-D and $260 for the 1922-S. These are decreases to 1/3 to 1/9 of their peak values in two to five years.

The common dates in MS60 and MS63 had some large changes in prices although generally more gradual. The 1881-S in MS63 was at a low of $40 in 1982 during the recession, rose to $90 in 1986 and fell to $23 in 1991, while the 1923-P in MS63 during those same years was priced at $22, $55 and $16 respectively. These are price rises of about two and one-half times and decreases to about 1/4 of the peak values. In MS60 there were steep rises in the prices of the 1881-S and 1923-P late in 1979 due to the rapid rise in the price of silver, with peaks in prices in 1985 and steady price declines thereafter. The 1881-S rose from $30 to a peak of $60 and to $13 early in 1992 while the 1923-P rose from $14 to $31 to $7.50. These are increases of two times and decreases to 1/4 to 1/5 their peak value.

From the charts it is obvious that the various grades and the common versus scarcer dates did not all follow the same price change patterns. There were different market forces that controlled them. These will be summarized in the following paragraphs starting with the lower grades and ending with the scarcer higher grades.

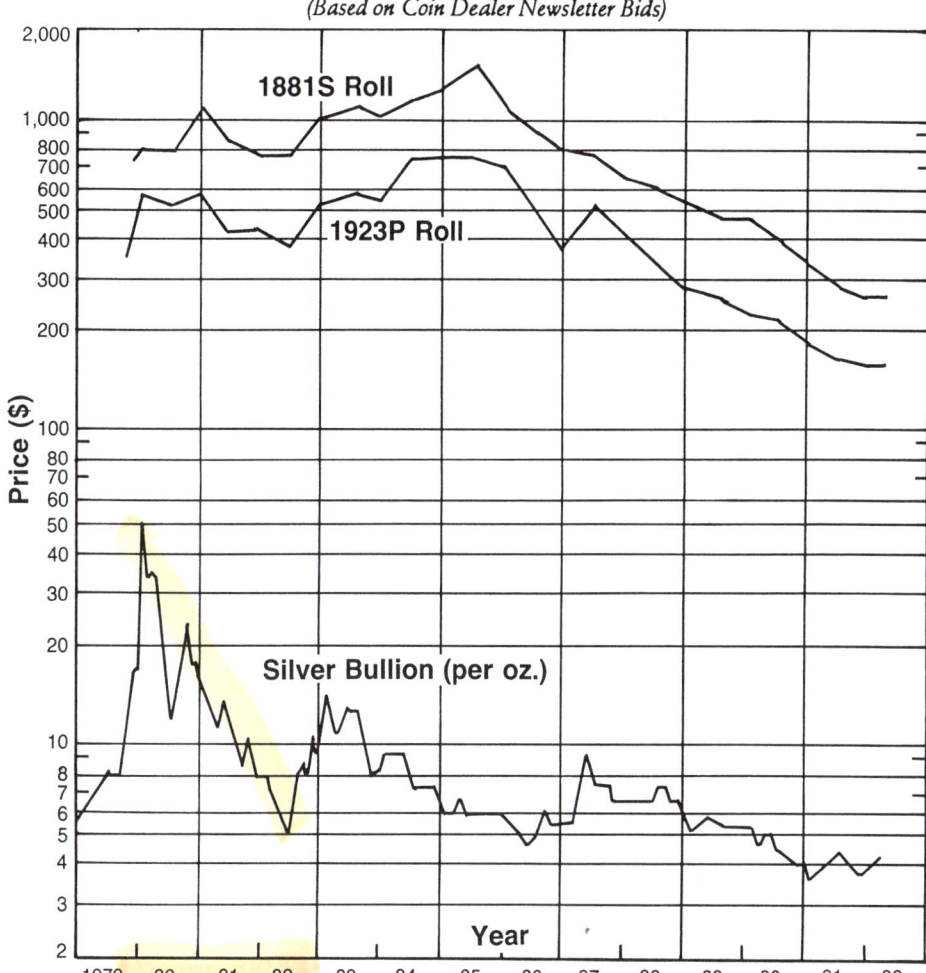

Figure 1-5 COMMON DATE MORGAN & PEACE DOLLAR ROLL & SILVER BULLION PRICE TRENDS
(Based on Coin Dealer Newsletter Bids)

Silver Bullion and Roll Related

Common date Morgan and Peace dollars in MS60 and MS63 are the predominant grades that make up the uncirculated silver dollar rolls. So the prices of these grades are tied to roll prices and vice-versa. Investor, dealer and collector interest in rolls therefore have a major affect on the low grade singles prices. Also, the price of silver bullion affects their price as it provides a base value or floor for the 90% silver dollars.

For the MS60 and MS63 common dollars, the rapid rise in their price late in 1979 was due to the corresponding rapid rise in the price of silver as shown in Chapter Two. The price of the common 1923-P in MS60 follows almost exactly the price variations in silver. Both declined from peaks in early 1980 to lows in early 1982. Both rose sharply to high values in 1983 and then declined to lows in early 1987. There was again a sharp rise for both later in 1987 and then steady declines to 1992.

The 1881-S in MS60 and MS63 and the 1923-P in MS63 did not decrease in price as significantly during the big fall in the price of silver bullion in 1980-82. They did rise when silver bullion rose in 1982, but did not follow silver bullion's immediate retreat in price. The 1881-S and 1923-P in MS60 both were fairly stable until late in 1985 while these dates in MS63 remained high until 1987. Their prices during these years were driven by silver dollar roll activity since vastly more coins traded as rolls rather than singles in these grades.

Figure 1-5 shows the price of 1881-S and 1923-P rolls during this time period. There was a general rise in roll prices from mid-1982 to mid-1985. The price of silver bullion at that time was fairly high during one of its bear market rallies. Thereafter, the roll market trend was downward from mid-1985 to 1992 with a slight rise in 1987 when silver bullion rallied briefly and then continued its downward trend. These rolls dropped to 1/5 their peak value in 1985 by 1992.

With the rapid rise in the price of common date MS65 singles during 1984 and 1985, the nice pieces in the rolls were naturally pulled out. By 1985, most of the rolls had been searched through and few so-called original rolls were left. This caused a price collapse of the roll market in mid-1985. Further declines in the price of silver bullion put downward pressure on roll prices. And investors, dealers and collectors turned their attention to the encapsulated graded coins introduced by PCGS early in 1986 and the sight unseen bidding market that developed from them.

Higher Grade Common Dates Rise and Fall

From 1979 to mid-1986, the common dates 1881-S and 1923-P in MS65 saw steady price increases with a few plateaus and no reversals. The definition of the MS65 was not very specific then, but as the prices increased, the market demanded a nicer coin. In other words, grading standards for MS65 continually tightened as coin prices rose. Fewer and fewer coins could meet the MS65 standards. Then when the MS64 grade was introduced in late 1984 and early 1985, more coins couldn't be graded as MS65, but instead fell into the lower MS64 grade. So during 1979 to 1986, the general perception was that common Morgan and Peace dollars in MS65 were becoming less and less available which in some ways helped push their price upward.

From mid-1986 to 1987, the 1881-S and 1923-P experienced their first price reversal in MS64 and MS65. This was due to a general peak in the coin market in mid-1986. It corresponded to a peak in the economic indicators as further discussed later for the scarcer dates. The economic indicators dropped sharply until mid-1987 which caused a general decline in the coin market. Thereafter the 1881-S and 1923-P prices to 1992 were quite volatile with many peaks and lows. This volatility was due to the introduction in early 1986 of the encapsulated coins by PCGS and simultaneously the sight unseen bidding by a network of dealers. Bid prices of coins were instantaneously available by electronic coin trading networks instead of the weekly *The Coin Dealer Newsletter*. A few market makers could raise and lower their bids and have a major impact on coin market prices instead of the wide sampling of price sources previously relied upon by *The Coin Dealer Newsletter*.

The 1881-S in grades MS64 and MS65 and the 1923-P in MS64 experienced almost a constant decrease in prices, except for short peaks, from the peak in mid-1986 to 1992. The scarcer dates didn't experience this downward price pressure until 1989 and 1990, although there was a small dip in prices during the latter part of 1986 and early 1987. As the number of available encapsulated coins increased quickly from zero in early 1986, there was increased financial pressure on the sight unseen bidders in absorbing more and more coins. Reduction in bids by the dealers resulted.

The continued price slide of the 1881-S in MS64 and MS65 and the 1923-P in MS64 was due to ever increasing population of the encapsulated grade coins. Instead of the market having a perception of increasing scarcity of those common dates that occurred from 1979 to 1986, the opposite was occurring with greater quantities of these common date coins being made available with the passage of time. The publishing of coin population and census reports by the grading services made it clear to everyone whether the dates were common or scarce. In addition, instead of the general tightening of grading from 1979 to 1986, the sight unseen bidders had to be prepared to accommodate the increasing quantities of the lowest examples offered in the grades. These market pressures drove the common high grade date prices down from mid-1986 to 1992.

The 1923-P in MS65 did not have its price slip constantly during 1986 to 1989. The so-called common Peace dollars were actually semi-scarce in MS65 and not as readily available as the common date Morgans in MS65. Their price movements were more related to that shown for the 1882-CC in MS65 that was not priced as a common date Morgan. The 1881-S and 1923-P both show a general sideways price movement from mid-1986 to mid-1989. This was because their population in grade MS65 was not increasing nearly as rapidly as the common date Morgans. The 1882-CC had a population of one-tenth that of any of the common date S mints in MS65 and the 1923-P population in MS65 was less than most of the common date Morgans in MS65.

Both the 1882-CC and 1923-P in MS65 had a precipitous drop starting in June 1989 where the coin market turned downward at the Long Beach convention. This downturn coincided with the last peak of the coin market during the decade which is more apparent in the price trends of the scarcer dates. It marked the end of the great bull coin market and the quick transition into the great coin market crash of the last half of 1989, all of 1990 and most of 1991. Both the 1881-S and 1923-P in grades MS64 and MS65 showed this crash in prices.

There was also a sharp drop in prices late in 1987 for the 1881-S and 1923-P in grades MS60, 63, 64 and 65. This coincided with the general stock market crash in November 1987 and the declining price in silver bullion after a sharp increase earlier in 1987. The overall economic market psychology turned negative for a short while which also apparently affected portions or the strength of the coin market.

Scarcer Dates Blow-off and Crash

The scarcer dates also experienced relatively steady price increases from 1979 to mid-1986 with few fluctuations down. There was some correction or adjustment downward in price for some scarce dates during the recession in 1982. But otherwise, like the higher grade common dates, grading standards gradually tightened and their availability was perceived to be lessening.

The scarcer dates tie-in with the nation's economy is quite close. Two of the economic indicators that are closely related to the past coin market peaks and bottoms are M2 growth and retail sales growth. *Figure 1-6* shows the M2 growth percentage variation from 1968 to 1992. M2 is all of the nation's money in cash, savings and checking accounts and various money market funds. The Federal Reserve has some control over this M2 money supply to stimulate or throttle back the nation's economy. The percent change in M2 growth is shown for 24-

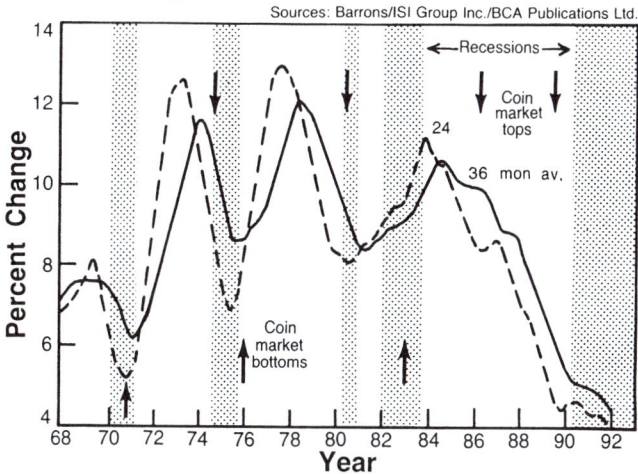

Figure 1-6 M2 GROWTH

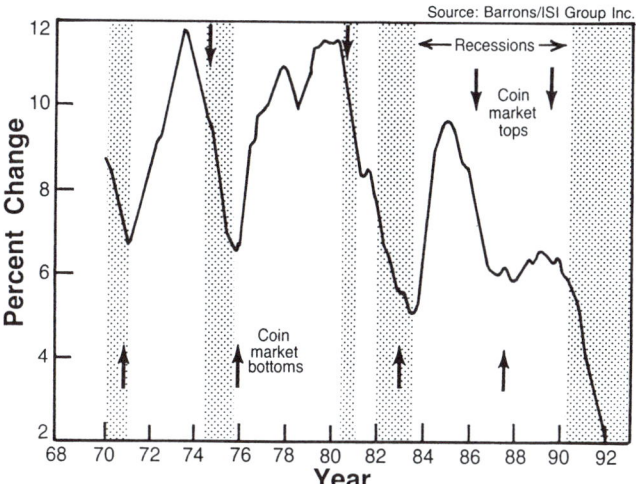

Figure 1-7 RETAIL SALES GROWTH

month and 36- month averages. This smoothes out the fluctuations and shifts the curves out in time which more nearly coincides with the effects of M2 growth on the economy. The coin market bottoms in 1970, 1976 and 1982 coincide with the lows in M2 growth. But the coin market tops in 1974, 1980, 1986 and 1989 only coincide with the 1974 and 1986 M2 growth peaks but not with the 1978 M2 growth peak. There is no M2 growth peak near the time of the 1989 coin market peak.

Figure 1-7 shows the percent change in the retail sales growth. The retail sales growth peaks just before the recessions shown on the chart and bottoms out at the end of each recession. In this chart of retail sales growth the coin market bottoms and tops coincide within a year of the retail sales growth peaks and lows. The mid-1986 peak in the scarcer high grade coin trends is within a year after the retail sales growth peak. The mid-1989 peak in the scarcer high grade coin trends is at the point in 1989 that the retail sales growth turned downward. The M2 growth also shows steep declines in 1990 and 1991.

Thus, the coin market cycles are very closely tied to the retail sales growth cycles which in turn is closely tied to M2 growth trends. It is logical that coin sales go down when the retail sales growth slows down and coin sales go up when retail sales growth picks up.

From mid-1985 to around mid-1987, the retail sales growth dropped sharply and the high grade MS65 Morgan and Peace dollars dropped from mid-1986 to mid-1987. Then retail sales growth leveled off and increased slightly from early 1988 to mid-1989. Scarce high grade Morgan and Peace dollars such as the 1880-P, 1882-O, 1922-D and 1922-S increased sharply during this time period to a peak in mid-1989. Thereafter, retail sales growth and these scarce high grade coin prices dropped precipitously throughout the second half of 1989 and all of 1990.

The flight to quality began in ernest after the market peak in mid-1986. Scarce high grade dates went on to higher peaks in mid-1989 while the somewhat scarce high grade dates such as 1882-CC and 1923-P generally had sideways price movements up until mid-1989. Common high grade dates such as the 1881-S had nearly constant price decreases from mid-1986 onwards.

Early in 1989 there were rumors of Wall Street and stock market brokerage firms planning to put money into the coin market. This contributed to the final blow-off in silver dollar prices in grades MS63-65 in mid-1989. Those rumors of Wall Street funds entering the coin market didn't happen to any significant extent. This contributed to the sharp turnaround in the coin market just prior to and early in the June 1989 Long Beach convention.

Also, in September 1989, the Dow Jones Transportation and Utility Averages peaked and then fell, and in December the same year, the Japanese Nikkei Index peaked and crashed in 1990. This signaled the end of the boom years of the 1980 decade and the start of a business and economic down cycle as a recession early in 1990. Real estate values and collectible prices including those for art, coins and antique cars began to tumble. Throughout 1990 coin prices in all grades fell. With the advent of the Gulf War early in 1991, the prices of MS64 and MS65 coin prices rose sharply. By the middle of 1991 the coin prices started decreasing again as the optimism of quickly winning the Gulf War wore off and the nation continued in an economic recession.

This shows that the overall coin market is driven in the directions of the fundamental economic and business cycles. The economic indicators best correlated to the coin market cycles are M2 growth and retail sales growth. On top of this, the coin market has its own integral trends and forces affecting coin prices. Bullion prices control the direction of the low priced bullion related grades. Common date higher grade coins can have different price trends than scarcer date higher grade coins, especially at market tops when there is a flight to quality. As a final word, the encapsulated coin and sight unseen bidding were not the prime causes of the boom and crash of the late 1980's. They made prices more volatile and made more evident which coins were common and scarce in the higher grades. But the basic economic forces that caused the boom in coin prices and subsequent crash have much more control of the coin market cycles than these special coin market tools.

SIZE AND DESIGN

At one and one half inches in diameter, the Morgan and Peace silver dollars are the largest business struck U. S. coins except for the very earliest silver dollars. This large size makes them more desirable to many collectors/investors.

Their composition of 90 percent silver also makes them more desirable to collector/investors than the comparable sized Eisenhower dollars. The precious metal in Morgan and Peace dollars gives them greater intrinsic worth than clad Ike dollars. The silver-copper composition also is easier to strike up fully to show all the design detail compared to the nickel — copper clad layers over a copper core of clad coinage. Thus, the Morgan and Peace dollar coins typically have more and sharper detail than Ike dollars. The luster of silver is also more attractive than the nickel-copper clad layer.

The design of the Morgan dollar shows a classic Liberty head. This seems to impart a solid and conservative feeling about the design compared to the more modern and youthful look of the Peace dollar Liberty head. There are far more collectors of the Morgan dollar than the Peace dollar. In addition to the greater number of date and mints of the Morgan series than the Peace, probably one of the main reasons for the Morgan dollars greater popularity is its very detailed design. There is much more fine detail in the hair of the Liberty Head and on the eagle. The lettering is sharp and raised with a very detailed wreath and denticles at the edge. It gives a more artistic and detailed appearance than the Peace dollar or most modern U. S. coin series.

APPEARANCE

Besides the attractive luster of silver, the Morgan dollar has other appearance items that are desired by collectors and investors. These are proof-like reflective surfaces of the field and frosted devices on some coins. The ultimate Morgan dollar in many collector/investors eyes is a deep mirror proof-like with white frosted head and eagle. This produces a cameo effect with the white devices placed on a dark and reflective field approaching the appearance of a proof specimen.

Silver is the most reflective of all metals. Few can resist the attractiveness of a dazzlingly reflective silver coin. The reflective fields of the Morgan dollars were caused by the polishing of the dies to achieve a field curvature to properly strike up the coins. This polished die field would last only a few thousand coins before it became dulled by die wear from striking of the coins. The Peace dollar did not have individual working dies polished since the field curvature was established in the master die. Thus, the Peace dollars do not have any proof-like or reflective fields.

The frosted effect on the coin devices is from the tooling of the master die. It becomes worn and brilliant as the working die wears from striking coins. Peace dollar dies tended to be used longer to strike coins than Morgan dollars so there would be fewer coins with frosted devices.

In addition, because the Peace dollar dies struck more coins, on the average, than Morgan dollar dies, the Peace dollars tend to have rougher surfaces in many instances. The Peace dollar design had shallower and more rounded edges to the design and lettering than the Morgan design. The Morgan dies were retired in many cases for die cracks around the letters before the die field had become very worn. This was due to higher stress concentrations in the sharper and more raised design. The Peace dollar dies, on the other hand, were generally retired because of die wear and roughness in the field instead of die cracks. So more Peace dollars have a mushy and rough appearance than Morgan dollars.

The highly prized and sought after deep mirror of cameo Morgan dollar represents to many the ultimate silver dollar. There are also deep mirror cameo subsidiary coins of the same period. But because of the much greater surviving numbers of uncirculated Morgan dollars than say Barber quarters and halves, cameo PL Morgans are much more available and thus collectable. And again, the larger size of the silver dollar shows off the cameo effect to better advantage.

RELATIVE CONDITION AVAILABILITY

The mintage figures of Morgan and Peace dollars given in Chapter Two does not indicate the true relative availability of the coins in uncirculated condition. First, the melting of almost one half of the Morgan dollars under the Pittman Act in 1918 and 1919 was not done evenly in proportion to mintages. Records were not kept by date or mint during the coin flattening and melting operations. Thus, certain dates would have been melted and destroyed more heavily than others changing the relative numbers of surviving coins.

Second, the melting of over 50 million silver dollar in 1943 and 1944 for wartime uses again devastated the silver dollar inventory. It is not known whether primarily Morgan or Peace silver dollars were melted or which dates or mints since records were not kept. But random selection of bags from the Treasury and Mint vaults would have again changed the relative surviving number of silver dollars

The great silver melt of 1979 and 1980 again saw many Morgan and Peace dollars hit the melting pot. This time most were common circulated coins since bullion and coin dealers kept the scarcer dates that were valued above bullion value. But some common uncirculated bags such as 1921-P Morgan and 1922-P and 1923-P Peace dollars were also melted.

A third imponderable factor is the actual release into circulation of the various dates and mints. The mints did not release a certain percentage each year into circulation. It varied depending upon the commerce needs and the requirements of the Treasury Department to back the outstanding silver certificates with silver dollars in stock. Many dates saw fairly extensive circulation and are common in that condition. Other dates like the 1880-O and 1886-O have large quantities of AU coins that barely saw circulation. They were released into circulation but soon returned to the bank and Treasury vaults because of little demand for their use. Other dates like the 1881-CC, 1885-CC and 1903-O saw very little circulation and are scare in circulated condition. Some dates like 1884 S and 1901-P are scare in uncirculated condition even though they had substantial mintages.

Some dates were not released extensively by the Treasury Department and mints until the final run on silver dollars in the early 1960s. These include: 1898-O, 1903-O, 1904-O, and to a lesser degree, the other late O mints. The 1881-1885-CC bags were held aside during the final run and later sold by the Government Services Administration in 1973-74 and 1980. Some of the CC dates had very large percentages of their original mintages sold by the GSA and so are relatively available in uncirculated condition even though their mintages were not high.

Another factor in the uncirculated availability is the availability in MS60 versus higher grades of MS63, 65 and 67. The New Orleans Mint produced many weakly struck coins that are not valued as MS65 for some years such as the 1886-O, 1892-O, 1894-O, and 1902-O. Likewise, the San Francisco Mint had problems with weakly struck coins for some years such as the 1902-S, 1922-S, 1923-S, and 1924-S. Some mints used the dies longer than others for some years which resulted in coins with rough fields and dull luster. Examples are the 1889-P, 1890-P, 1921-P and 1924-P. Some years and mints are notable for excessive bag marks such as many CC dates and the 1891-S and 1895-S. This is due to their handling in bags of 1000 coins and transportation via stagecoach, trains, boat, and later by car and truck. As a result, the distribution of available coins among the various uncirculated grades varies again by date and mint. For example, early Morgan S mints and the 1925-P Peace tend to be well struck, with few bag marks and good luster. Many other dates have a wide difference between the MS60 and MS65 availability.

The availability of proof-like Morgans is also variable from year to year because of die preparation differences, melts and release into circulation. Some dates like the 1884-S, 1892-S, 1893-S, 1894-O, 1901-P and 1903-S are extremely rare in proof-like. Other dates such as the early S mints are much more available.

Another factor affecting the availability is the collector and investor interest in particular dates and mints. Promotions by investment firms, newsletter and books can stimulate demand for certain dates and mints. This can decrease their availability as the supply is bought up and salted away. The market in silver dollars is very dynamic and the availability of the coins is constantly changing. Thus, an undervalued date may change to one that is overvalued as its price changes. Their availability changes as coins are put away, or bags, rolls and collections appear on the market.

During the 1960s and early 1970s the supply of silver dollars available to the general collecting and investing public was constantly changing from the release of the silver dollars by the Treasury, GSA CC hoard, Redfield hoard, Continental-Illinois Bank hoard, and other smaller private hoards. By the early 1980s, the silver dollar supply has been fairly widely distributed and the available hoards of bags and rolls considerably reduced. So the market price of silver dollars reflected by that time, a fairly accurate picture of relative availability. It is unlikely that large hoards will surface anymore to drastically change the availability and pricing structure overnight.

As a result of these factors, the relative availability of Morgan and Peace dollars in circulated and uncirculated condition does not closely follow their original mintage figures. However, the free market interplay of supply and demand tends to establish prices that reflect the availability by grades. Also, since the late 1980's, the various coin grading services have made available their population reports showing the quantities of coins graded for specific grades. For silver dollars, these population reports are statistically useful primarily for the higher uncirculated grades. Grading fee costs made submittal of lower grade uncirculated and circulated coins impractical because the fee was about equal to the coin's value for most dates and mints.

Use of the grading services census and population reports must also be tempered because the quantities of coins graded are increasing with time. A small and variable quantity of coins are resubmitted one or more times and the cut off point where coins are worth submitting constantly changes as market conditions fluctuate. Nevertheless, these population reports represent, for the first time, a statistically useful record on the relative condition availability for the higher uncirculated grades of all dates and mints.

Prior to the issuance of these population reports, the market price and the general feel of the market availability by various coin dealers, investors and collectors had to be relied upon. But the market price and hearsay speculation did not always reflect the true availability. The market prices could easily be manipulated and few individuals had access to the market in such depth that allowed an accurate assessment.

As of early 1992, the Professional Coin Grading Service and Numismatic Guaranty Corporation of

Table 1-3 RELATIVE AVAILABILITY ORDER OF MORGAN DOLLARS IN MINT STATE
(Based on January 1992 Grading Services Population Reports)

RANK ORDER	MS63 MS	MS63 PL	MS63 DM	MS64 MS	MS64 PL	MS64 DM	MS65 MS	MS65 PL	MS65 DM	MS66 MS	MS66 PL	MS66 DM
1 Common	81S	80S	83CC	81S	80S	80S	80S	80S	80S	81S	80S	80S
2	84O	81S	80S	80S	81S	84CC	81S	81S	81S	80S	81S	81S
3	85O	79S	84CC	85O	79S	83CC	79S	79S	83CC	79S	79S	79S
4	87P	83CC	85O	87P	82S	81S	82S	82S	84CC	82S	82S	83CC
5	80S	82S	84O	84O	04O	85P	85O	83CC	85P	86P	83CC	84CC
6	04O	04O	83O	79S	83CC	85O	86P	84CC	85O	85O	84CC	81CC
7	86P	84CC	85P	86P	84CC	82CC	87P	87P	79S	85P	98O	85CC
8	83O	83O	82CC	04O	87P	84O	84O	04O	84O	98O	04O	85P
9	79S	85O	81S	82S	82CC	83O	98O	82CC	82CC	83P	82CC	98O
10	82S	82CC	87P	98O	85O	87P	85P	84O	87P	87P	86P	84O
11	85P	84O	81CC	83O	84O	79S	04O	85O	85CC	83CC	87P	85O
12	98O	78S	85CC	85P	78S	04O	83O	98O	86P	99O	85P	87P
13	99O	87P	79S	99O	83O	85CC	99O	85P	98O	84O	85O	82CC
14	21P	85P	86P	21P	85P	81CC	83CC	01O	04O	81CC	81CC	99O
15	02O	78CC	04O	02O	98O	86P	83P	78S	83O	84CC	97S	86P
16	84CC	98O	83P	00O	01O	98O	84CC	97S	81CC	83O	78S	82S
17	78S	81CC	90CC	84CC	97S	96P	00O	83O	96P	85CC	84O	04O
18	00O	97S	78CC	83CC	85CC	82S	88P	85CC	99O	03P	85CC	83P
19	83CC	85CC	98O	88P	02O	88P	81CC	02O	82S	04O	88P	78S
20	88P	78P 7TF R78	88O	00P	81CC	78CC	78S	81CC	97S	82CC	80CC	83O
21	96P	02O	96P	78S	86P	98P	82CC	86P	83P	78S	83O	84P
22	89P	80CC	78P 7TF R78	83P	80CC	83P	02O	00O	99P	03O	84P	97S
23	00P	98P	82O	96P	98P	90CC	00P	80CC	88O	00O	96P	98P
24	82CC	86P	98P	82CC	96P	80CC	96P	98P	78CC	88P	99O	99P
25	01O	96P	80CC	01O	00O	90O	03P	78CC	98P	96P	01O	78CC
26	83P	78P 8TF	90O	81CC	78CC	78P 7TF R78	21P	96P	78S	02O	02P	88P
27	82O	01O	81O	89P	78P 7TF R78	99O	85CC	99O	88P	84P	02O	88O
28	88O	83P	84P	03P	88O	78S	84P	88O	80P	97S	03P	89O
29	78CC	82O	88S	98P	21P	88P	03O	99O	00O	02P	03O	02O
30	98P	00O	78S	85CC	83P	97S	98P	88P	84P	00P	78P 7TF R78	03O
31	82P	88O	91CC	84P	97P	84P	01O	97P	97P	80CC	78CC	81O
32	85CC	21P	82S	21D	99P	99P	80CC	78P 7TF R78	80CC	98P	81O	
33	81CC	90O	88P	88O	78P 8TF	82O	21D	99S	02O	90S	95S	
34	97P	97P	82P	00S	80P	97P	97P	00P	01O	21D	97P	
35	84P	86S	97S	03O	99O	87O	02P	83P	90CC	82P	99S	0
36	81O	91S	78P 7/8TF	82P	84P	97P	78CC	84P	90O	78CC	00S	
37	80P	78P 7/8TF	87O	82O	90O	82P	82P	80P	82O	21P	21P	
38	90P	91CC	02O	78CC	82O	02O	89P	00S	82P	97P		
39	03P	99P	89P	80CC	87O	88S	97S	03P	89P	99P		
40	21D	84P	90P	79S	82P	89P	88O	03O	92P	01O		
41	79P	89S	80P	80P	91S	79P	99P	21P	03O	89P		
42	90O	82P	97P	81P	00P	78P 8TF	79P	82P	78P 8TF	99S	0	
43	03O	81O	99P	02P	86S	01O	90S	90O	90S	91S		
44	81P	88P	78P 8TF	97S	80P	78P 7/8TF	81P	86P	78P 7TF R78	00S		
45	78P 7TF R78	00S	80O	99P	03P	81O	82O	91CC	79O	03S		
46	80CC	79P	79P	90O	78P 7/8TF	81P	80P	02P	81P	88O		
47	91CC	89P	99O	81O	91CC	80O	89S	78P 8TF	87O	80CC R78		
48	99P	88S	91S	21S	85S	90P	00S	78P 7/8TF	88S	81P		
49	21S	87O	89O	78P 7TF R78	88P	91S	91S	82O	91S	86S		
50	78P 8TF	92CC	81P	90P	79P	00O	78P 8TF	87O	93O	89S		
51	97S	90S	92CC	90S	92CC	03O	85S	92CC	00P	91CC		
52	90S	81P	90S	78P 8TF	99S	21P	78P 7TF R78	21D	03P	81O		
53	87O	85S	01O	91CC	89S	89O	99S	79P	78P 7/8TF	92CC		
54	92O	90P	98S	85S	89P	92CC	98S	89P	78P 7TF R79	00O/CC		
55	85S	99S	21P	78P 7/8TF	03O	99S	90O	90S	79P	85S		
56	78P 7/8TF	80P	78P 7TF R79	89S	21D	90S	81O	91S	80CC R78	02S		
57	79O	79O	89O	91S	02P	79O	91CC	81P	89O	89O		
58	89S	98S	79CC	00S	81P	91CC	00O/CC	85S	99S	78P 8TF		
59	91S	78P 7TF R79	87S	79O	81O	98S	80CC R78	89O	00S	79P		
60	02P	03O	79O	92O	88S	86S	86S	89S	21P	79O		
61	87S	79CC	92P	02S	79O	89S	02S	80CC R78	21D	01S		
62	91P	90CC	99S	87S	94S	80CC R78	92CC	87S	85S	78P 7TF R78		
63	90CC	00P	03O	87O	89O	78P 7TF R79	87S	88S	86S	82O		
64	04P	99S	89S	99S	98S	92P	79S	92P	87P 7/6	90O		
65	00S	21D	80CC R78	89O	90P	03P	78P 7/8TF	04S	90P	92S		
66	91O	79S R78	86S	00O/CC	90S	95S	79O	78P 7TF R79	91CC	94S		
67	80O	80O	91P	86S	78P 7TF R79	79CC	90CC	90P	91O	98S		
68	89O	03P	00O	78P 7TF R79	87S	91P	92P	90CC	92O	88S		
69	88S	87S	95S	90CC	90CC	87S	01S	98S	98S	90CC		
70	02S	89O	79CC capped	91P	92P	91O	88S	79O	02P	04P		
71	92CC	92P	00S	98S	04S	05S	78P 7TF R79	80O	79CC	78P 7/8TF		
72	86S	87P 7/6	01S	88S	80CC R78	21D	04P	81O	79CC capped	94P		
73	92P	91O	03P	91O	87P 7/6	89CC	90P	94S	79S R78	80P		
74	78P 7TF R79	94S	79S R78	92CC	79CC	01S	03S	80O	94S	87S		
75	99S	02P	91O	04P	91P	79CC capped	94S	96S	81O	90P		
76	98S	83S	21D	92P	80O	92P	89O	01S	82O/S	91P		
77	00O/CC	89CC	86O	80O	21S	93CC	93P	04P	83S	95O		
78	93P	91P	93CC	01S	95S	79S R78	92O	21S	84S	95S		
79	01S	80CC R78	93CC	80CC R78	92O	85S	91P	79CC	86O	96S		
80	94S	79CC capped	93O	93P	90O	86O	04S	79CC capped	87O 7/6	97O		
81	79S R78	04S	97O	94P	79CC capped	94P	91O	79S R78	87S	78P 7TF R79		
82	79CC	21S	85S	04S	79S R78	94S	87O	82O/S	89CC	79CC		
83	80CC R78	02S	83S	83S	83S	95O	96S	83S	89S	79CC capped		
84	83S	95S	96O	79CC	89CC	96O	87P 7/6	84S	91P	79S R78		
85	96S	93CC	00P	79S R78	93P	00P	79S R78	86O	92S	80O		
86	93CC	95O	02P	96S	93O	21S	79CC	87P 7/6	92O	82O/S		
87	04S	04P	04P	03P	95O	82O/S	94P	87O 7/6	93P	83S		
88	86O	01S	82O/S	95S	97O	83S	95S	89CC	93CC	84S		
89	95S	86O	83S	93CC	01S	84S	80O	91P	93S	86O		
90	87P 7/6	92S	84S	87P 7/6	82O/S	87P 7/6	97O	91O	94P	87P 7/6		
91	79CC capped	92O	87P 7/6	94P	84S	87O 7/6	83S	92O	94O	87O		
92	94O	93O	87O 7/6	94S	86O	92S	93CC	92S	94S	87O 7/6		
93	94P	84S	92S	79CC capped	87O 7/6	93P	93S	93P	95O	89CC		
94	03S	94P	93P	86O	92S	93O	92S	93CC	95S	91O		
95	97O	97O	93S	82O/S	93CC	93S	94O	93S	96O	92P		
96	93O	96S	94P	93O	93S	94O	79CC capped	94P	96S	92O		
97	01P	03S	94O	95O	94P	96S	89CC	94O	97O	93P		
98	89CC	82O/S	95O	97O	94O	94O	95O	95O	00O/CC	93CC		
99	87O 7/6	87O 7/6	96S	96O	96O	00O/CC	96O	95S	01P	93O		
100	96O	93P	00O/CC	89CC	96S	01P	84S	96O	01S	93S		
101	82O/S	93S	01P	84S	00O/CC	02P	93O	97O	02S	94O		
102	84S	94O	02S	87O 7/6	01P	03S	01P	00O/CC	03P	96O		
103	95O	96O	03S	92S	02S	03S	82O/S	01P	04P	01P		
104	93S	00O/CC	04S	01S	03S	04P	86O	02S	04S	04S		
105 Scarce	92S	01P	21S	93S	04P	04S	87O 7/6	03S	21S	21S		

America had graded almost a million uncirculated Morgan dollars and about 150,000 uncirculated Peace dollars. Of these, for the Morgan dollars, about 350,000 were MS64, 150,000 MS65 and 20,000 MS66. For the Peace dollars, about 60,000 were MS64, 15,000 MS65 and only 500 MS66. These quantities will continue to increase with time of course but they are sufficient to establish relative availability trends for most dates and mints. In some instances the quantities are not sufficient to establish trends such as many MS66 and some higher grade proof-like and deep mirror.

Using the PCGS and NGC population and census reports for early 1992, *Table 1-3* was prepared showing the relative availability for Morgan dollars by MS63 through MS66 for mint state, proof-like and deep mirror categories. The ranking is from the most common to the scarcest. Some of the most common had coin populations of 20,000 to 40,000 for MS63, MS64 and MS65. At the other end of the scale, the scarcest generally had many zero population coins. These scarcest dates could have their order changed radically with the addition of one or two coins. So the order of the scarcest end of the scale is not very firm. Those many dates with zero or one population are listed in chronological order for each category. On the other hand, the relative sequence for the most common will likely not change significantly since a sizeable quantity of coins had been graded for each date in each category except MS66.

Some of the observations to be made are, for the mint state category, the 1881-S is the most common for all four grades, as expected. The P, D and S common dates dominate the top dozen most common in MS63 and MS64. In MS65 and MS66 the 1879-S and 1882-S are in the top four positions. The common 1882-CC, 1883-CC and 1884-CC are in the top 24 in availability. In the grades MS65 and MS66, the 1881-CC is more available than the 1882-CC. There are other surprising trends such as the 1878-S being less available than many of the CC - dates, the 1879-P – 1882-P are grouped fairly close together. The 1891-CC is more available than the 1890-CC whereas the 1890-S is more available than the 1891-S. In grades MS65 and MS66, the 1892-CC is more available than the 1890-CC.

In the Proof-like category, the common date S mints are the most available. But the 1904-O is the 4th to 8th most available and the 1883-CC and 1884-CC occupy the 4th to 7th spot in all grades. The 1883-O, 1884-O and 1885-O are the 8th to 11th most common in MS63, but they steadily get scarcer in PL in the higher grades. In MS66, only about one-third the dates have had any coins graded PL.

The Deep Mirror category shows the 1883-CC and 1884-CC as the most common one in MS63, second most common in MS64, third most common in MS65 and fourth most common in MS66. The 1883-O to 1885-O are the fourth to sixth most common in MS63 but

drop down in ranking as the grade gets higher. The 1885-P and 1887-P are among the top dozen most common Deep Mirror in all grades and the 1881-CC and 1885-CC are in the 11th to 16th position in MS63 to MS65, but rise to the 5th and 7th position in MS66. One-third of the MS65 Deep Mirror and two-thirds of the MS66 Deep Mirror dates have yet to have any examples graded in those categories.

Table 1-4 shows the relative availability order of Peace dollars in grades MS63 through MS66 using the PCGS and NGC population and census reports. The 1923-P is the most common in grades MS63 through MS65 while the 1925-P is the most common in MS66. The 1925-P is the third most common in MS63 and MS64 and in the second position in MS65. The 1922-P which has the highest mintage is in second position for MS63 and MS64, third in MS65 and slips to fifth position in MS66. The 1921-P is surprisingly available in MS63 and MS64 and only slips to ninth and eighth position in MS65 and MS66.

At the other end of the availability scale for Peace dollars, the 1934-S is the scarcest date in MS63 and MS64, but increases in relative availability in the higher grades and is near the median in MS66. The 1928-P is only slightly below the median in grades MS63 and

Table 1-4
PEACE DOLLARS RELATIVE AVAILABILITY ORDER IN MINT STATE
(Based on January 1992 Grading Services Population Reports)

RANK ORDER	MS63	MS64	MS65	MS66
Most Common				
1	1923-P	1923-P	1923-P	1925-P
2	1922-P	1922-P	1925-P	1923-P
3	1925-P	1925-P	1922-P	1924-P
4	1924-P	1924-P	1924-P	1926-D
5	1921-P	1926-P	1926-P	1922-P
6	1926-P	1922-D	1922-D	1922-D
7	1922-D	1921-P	1926-D	1935-P
8	1935-P	1935-P	1935-P	1921-P
9	1922-S	1926-D	1921-P	1926-P
10	1925-S	1926-S	1935-S	1926-S
11	1923-S	1934-P	1926-S	1934-D
12	1926-S	1923-D	1934-P	1935-S
13	1927-P	1922-S	1923-D	1934-S
14	1827-S	1928-P	1934-D	1934-P
15	1928-P	1935-S	1922-S	1922-S
16	1934-P	1923-S	1928-P	1923-D
17	1923-D	1925-S	1927-P	1927-D
18	1928-S	1927-P	1934-S	1927-S
19	1926-D	1927-S	1923-S	1927-P (1)
20	1924-S	1934-D	1924-S	1928-P (1)
21	1934-D	1924-S	1927-D	1928-S (1)
22	1935-S	1927-D	1927-S	1923-S (0)
23	1927-D	1928-S	1925-S	1924-S (0)
24	1934-S	1934-S	1928-S	1925-S (0)
Scarcest				

MS65, but is at the lower end in MS66. The 1923-S, 1924-S, 1925-S and 1928-S are near the median or just below in MS63, but drop in availability ranking as the grade increases until they are the scarcest in grade MS66.

Figure 1-8 shows the relative condition availability of Morgan dollars in mint state again using the PCGS and NGC population and census reports. It shows grades MS63-66 for each date on one line. This visually depicts where the various grades for each date are in the availability scale from commonest to scarcest, and how the grades are grouped together or spread out. For example, the 1882-O relative availability decreases significantly as the grade increases, whereas the 1881-S has the same availability in all grades. It is easy to see that the 1878-P 8TF and 1878-P 7TF Rev. 78 are near the median in availability with the 1878-P 7/8TF becoming scarcer and the 1878-P 7TF Rev. 79 at about the one-quarter point from scarcest in MS63-65 and among the scarcest in MS66. The varieties 1882-O/S, 1887-P 7/6 and 1887-O 7/6 are among the scarcest in relative availability in all grades, but the 1900-O/CC becomes more available as the grade increases.

The common dates are readily apparent from their position on the left side of the chart. The scarce dates are also apparent on the right side with the 1879-CC capped, 1884-S, 1889-CC, 1892-S, 1893-CC, 1893-O, 1893-S, 1894-O, 1896-O and 1901-P scarcest in all grades. Other trends can be seen such as the 1898-O becoming relatively more available with increasing grade while the 1904-O does just the opposite. The 1887-P – 94-P become increasingly scarcer with each later year, while the years 1878-P – 86-P tend to become relatively more available with each year, except for the 1884-P which is between the 1882-P and 1883-P in scarcity. Of the later O Mints from 1898-O – 1904-O, the 1901-O and 1903-O are the scarcest with the 1901-O being relatively more available in MS63 and MS64, but scarcer than the 1903-O in grades MS65 and MS66.

Figure 1-9 shows the relative condition availability of Morgan dollar in Proof-like for grades MS63 – 66. The most common in all grades are the 1879-S through 1882-S, 1897-S, 1880-CC through 1885-CC, 1885-P through 1887-P, 1896-P, 1883-O through 1885-O, 1898-O, 1904-O and the 1898-P and 1902-O in grades MS63 - MS65. Many dates have MS66 at the scarcest end of the availability scale because no coins have been graded PL in that grade.

Figure 1-10 shows the relative condition availability of Morgan dollars in Deep Mirror. The groupings are similar to those in the Proof-like chart, except that even more dates are at the scarcest end of the availability scale in MS65 and MS66. The dates from 1878 through 1899 show very similar availability distributions in grades MS63-65 to those shown in the Proof-like chart. However, from 1900 through 1921, there is a general shift to the scarcer end of the availability scale of all grades when compared to the Proof-like chart except for the 1903-O. There could have been a change in the preparation of working dies or planchets from which the coins were struck around 1900 that caused fewer coins to be produced with deep mirrors. A likely cause would be less intense polishing of the die face for these years. This is discussed further in Chapter 3 on the minting process.

Figure 1-11 shows the relative condition availability of Peace Dollars in MS63-66. It clearly shows that the 1934-S is the scarcest of all dates in MS63 and MS64, but a number of other dates are scarcer in MS65 and MS66. It also shows that the 1927-P is slightly scarcer than the 1928-P in grades MS64 and MS65 and about the same in MS66. The 1922-D and 1926-D are the most readily available D mints in grades MS64-66 while the 1926-S and 1935-S are the most readily available S mints in these grades. The scarcest dates in MS64 and MS65 are the 1924-S, 1925-S, 1927-D, 1927-S, 1928-S and 1934-S. The 1923-S, 1924-S and 1925-S are scarcest in MS66 with no graded coins, but the 1927-P, 1928-P and 1928-S are very close with only one each graded so the order could change in the near future.

Figure 1-12 shows the relative condition availability of Morgan dollars in circulated and MS60 grades. The grading services do not have many Morgan dollars graded in these conditions so their availability is based primarily on price. In circulated conditions, most Morgan dollars are fairly common except for a few dates like 1879-CC, 1881-CC, 1885-CC, 1883-S, 1884-S, 1889-CC, the scarcer dates in the years 1892-1896, 1901-P and 1902-S through 1904-S. These same dates are the scarcer ones in MS60 with the 1884-S, 1889-CC, 1892-S, 1893-S and 1895-O being rare to very rare.

Generally the Peace dollars are common to readily available in circulated condition with only the 1928-P being somewhat scarce in the lower circulated grades. In AU, the 1921-P, 1924-S, 1927-D, 1927-S and 1935-S are somewhat scarce with the 1928-P scarce and the 1934-S scarcest. The same trends exist in the MS60 grade.

Footnote

[1] U. S. Department of the Treasury, *Annual Report of the Director of the Mint, Fiscal Year Ended June 30, 1964*.

Figure 1-8 MORGAN DOLLAR RELATIVE CONDITION AVAILABILITY FOR MINT STATE
(Based on January 1992 Grading Services Population Reports)
3, 4, 5, 6 = MS63, 64, 65, 66 Relative Within Each Grade

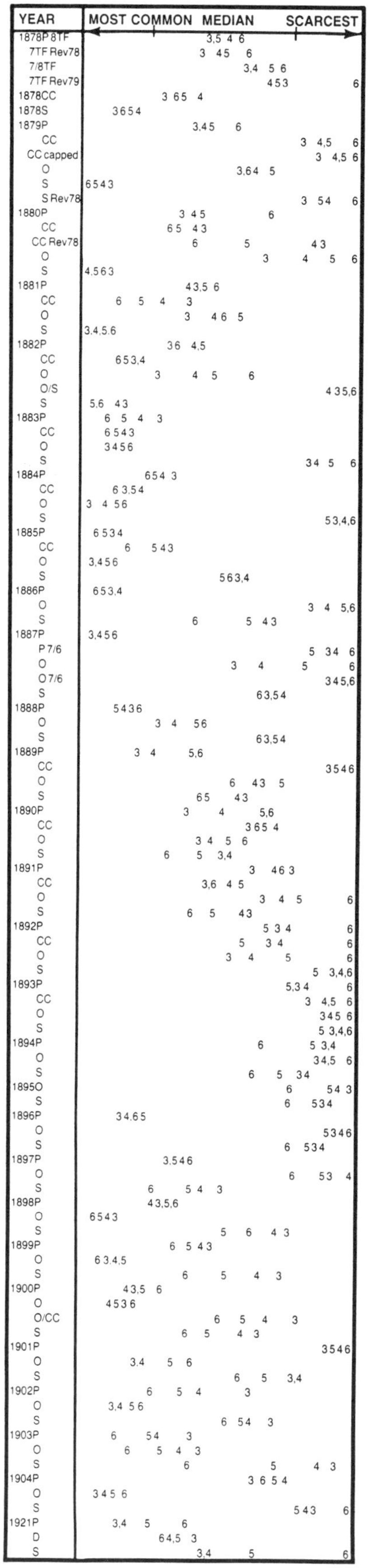

Figure 1-9 MORGAN DOLLAR RELATIVE CONDITION AVAILABILITY FOR MINT STATE PROOF-LIKE
(Based on January 1992 Grading Services Population Reports)
3, 4, 5, 6 = MS63 PL, 64 PL, 65 PL, 66 PL Relative Within Each Grade

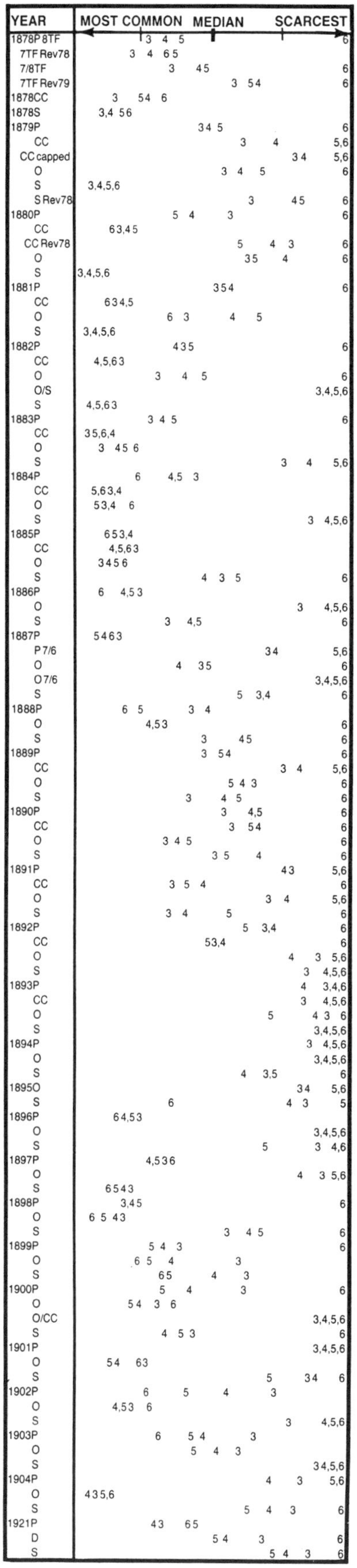

Figure 1-10 MORGAN DOLLAR RELATIVE CONDITION AVAILABILITY FOR MINT STATE DEEP MIRROR
(Based on January 1992 Grading Services Population Reports)
3, 4, 5, 6 = MS63 DM, 64 DM, 65 DM, 66 DM Relative Within Each Grade

YEAR	MOST COMMON — MEDIAN — SCARCEST
1878P 8TF	5 4 3 — 6
7TF Rev78	3 4 5 — 6
7/8TF	3 4 5 — 6
7TF Rev79	5 3 — 4 — 6
1878CC	3 4 5 6
1878S	6 5 4 3
1879P	4 3 5 — 6
CC	3 4 — 5,6
CC capped	5 3 4 — 5,6
O	5 3 4 — 6
S	6 5 4 3 — 6
S Rev78	3 4 — 5,6
1880P	5 4 3 — 6
CC	4 3 5 — 6
CC Rev78	5 4 3 — 6
O	3 4 — 5,6
S	4,5,6 3 — 6
1881P	5 4 3 — 6
CC	6 3 5 4 — 6
O	3 4 5 — 6
S	5,6 4 3 — 6
1882P	3 5 4 — 6
CC	4 3,5 6 — 6
O	3 4 5 — 6
O/S	— 3,4,5,6
S	6 5 4 3 — 6
1883P	3 6 5 4 — 6
CC	3 4,5 6
O	3 4 5 6
S	— 3,4,5,6
1884P	6 3,4 5 — 6
CC	4 3 6 5
O	3 5 4 6
S	— 3,4,5,6
1885P	4,5 3 6
CC	6 5 3 4
O	3 4,5 6
S	5 4 3 — 6
1886P	5 3 4,6
O	3 4 — 5,6
S	4 5 3 — 6
1887P	5 3,4 6
P 7/6	5 — 3,4,6
O	4 3 5 — 6
O 7/6	— 3,4,5,6
S	3 4 — 5,6
1888P	5 6 4 3
O	4 3 5 6
S	3 4 5 — 6
1889P	5 3 4 — 6
CC	3 4 — 5,6
O	6 3 4 5
S	4 3 — 5,6
1890P	3 4 5 — 6
CC	3 4 5 — 6
O	4 3 5 — 6
S	5 3 4 — 6
1891P	3 4 — 5,6
CC	3 4 5 — 6
O	5 4 3 — 6
S	5 3 4 — 6
1892P	5 3 4 — 6
CC	3 4 — 5,6
O	5 4 3 — 6
S	— 3,4,5,6
1893P	— 3,4,5,6
CC	4 3 — 5,6
O	5 3 4,6
S	— 3,4,5,6
1894P	4 3,5,6
O	— 3,4,5,6
S	3,4 — 5,6
1895O	4 3,5,6
S	4 3 — 5,6
1896P	5 4 3 — 6
O	3,4 — 5,6
S	— 3,4,5,6
1897P	5 4 3 — 6
O	3 4,5,6
S	5 6 4 3
1898P	4,5,6,3
O	6 5 4 3
S	3 4 5 — 6
1899P	5 6 4 3
O	5 6 4 3
S	4 5 3 — 6
1900P	5 3 4 — 6
O	5 4 3
O/CC	— 3,4,5,6
S	5 3,4 — 6
1901P	— 3,4,5,6
O	5 4 3
S	3 4 — 5,6
1902P	5 3 4,6
O	6 5 3,4
S	— 3,4,5,6
1903P	5 4 3 — 6
O	6 5 4 3
S	— 3,4,5,6
1904P	3 4,5,6
O	4,5 3 6
S	— 3,4,5,6
1921P	4 3 5 — 6
D	5 4 3 — 6
S	4 3,5,6

Figure 1-11 PEACE DOLLAR RELATIVE CONDITION AVAILABILITY FOR MINT STATE
(Based on January 1992 Grading Services Population Reports)
3, 4, 5, 6 = MS63, 64, 65, 66 Relative Within Each Grade

YEAR	MOST COMMON — MEDIAN — SCARCEST
1921P	3 4 6 5
1922P	3,4 5 6
1922D	4,5,6 3
1922S	3 4 5,6
1923P	3,4,5 6
1923D	4 5 6 3
1923S	3 4 5 6
1924P	6 3,4,5
1924S	3,5 4 6
1925P	6 5 3,4
1925S	3 4 5 6
1926P	4,5 3 6
1926D	6 5 4 3
1926S	4,6 5 3
1927P	3 5 4,6
1927D	6 5 4 3
1927S	3 6 4 5
1928P	4 3 5 6
1928S	3 6 4 5
1934P	4 5 6 3
1934D	6 5 4 3
1934S	6 5 3,4
1935P	6 3,4,5
1935S	5 6 4 3

18

# Figure 1-12 MORGAN DOLLAR RELATIVE CONDITION AVAILABILITY FOR CIRCULATED & MS60
C = Circulated; 60 = MS60

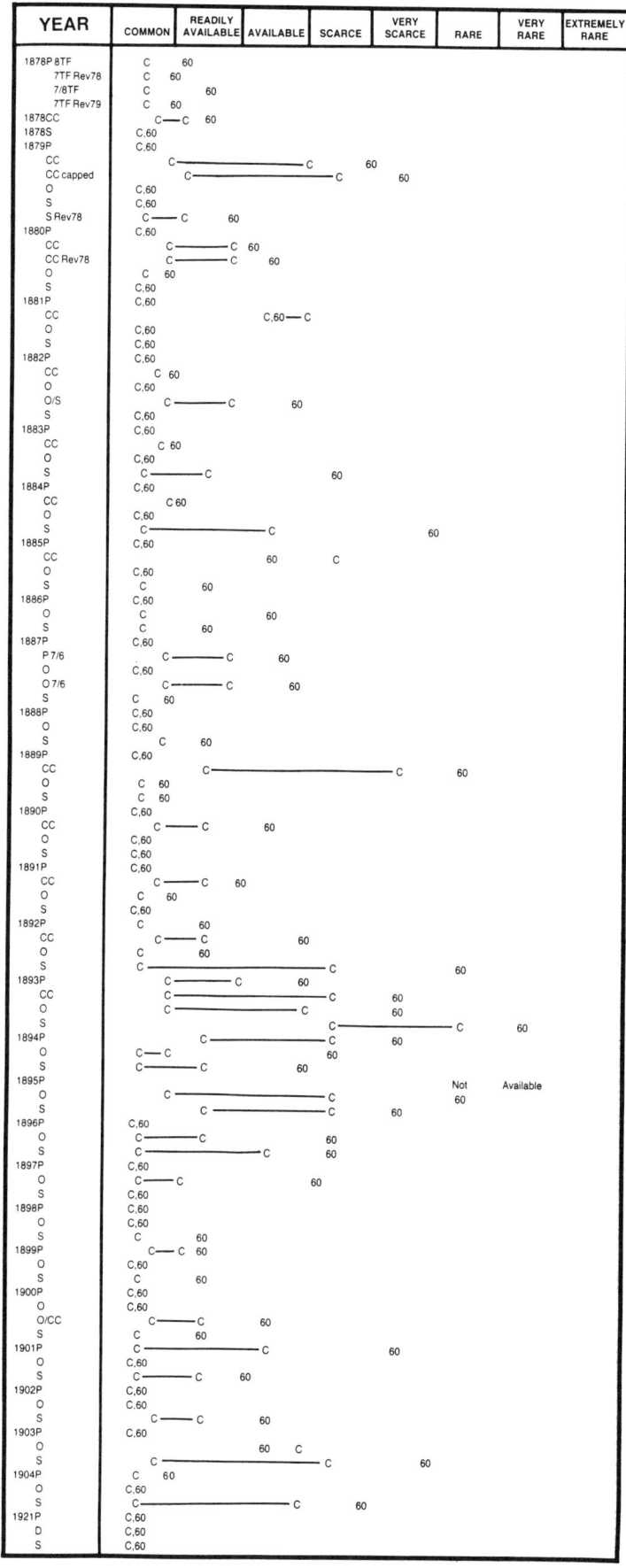

19

Chapter 2
Silver Dollar Coinage

Silver dollars, sometimes known as standards or cartwheels, have always had an unsettled existence. Even though Morgan silver dollars were coined continuously from 1878 to 1904, yearly mintage figures for dollars coined at each mint during that period varied from none to tens of millions *(see Table 2-1)*. The Carson City Mint had interruptions in its yearly coinage of silver dollars, and there was a large gap in mintage from 1904 to 1921 for all mints. Coinage of Peace dollars was also interrupted; they were struck from 1921 to 1928 and again in 1934 and 1935.

Philadelphia Mint, 1901
(U.S. Treasury Dept., 1902)

In order to determine why these interruptions in coinage occurred and why some years had very low mintage, one must look at the background of the silver dollar. The coinage of silver dollars was affected primarily by various Acts of Congress. Their existence was also affected by the political climate, the prevailing political party, the availability of silver bullion, and the coining costs at the various mints.

Important Acts of Congress and political background are cited in the discussion that follows to explain why silver dollar coinage has varied through the years.

CRIME OF '73

The United States had a bimetallic money standard until 1873. The government could coin the silver and gold bullion brought to the Treasury into gold and silver dollars as the standards. A value ratio of 15 ounces of silver to 1 ounce of gold was used until the 1830's. In accordance with Gresham's law, the metal with more intrinsic value – gold – was consistently driven out of monetary use, and this outflow of gold tended to make silver the nation's standard money. A revaluation of gold in the 1830's, resulting in a 16-to-1 mint ratio, caused a reversal of this situation and led to a disappearance of silver.

Gold production in the United States jumped significantly in 1848 with its discovery in California and remained around two million ounces annually from 1849 for many decades.[1] Silver production was very small until 1861 when the Western mines began significant production of 1.5 million ounces that year. By 1867 the United States produced more than 10 million ounces annually.

The Mint Director at that time, Dr. Henry Linderman, knew that silver production would rise significantly in the next few years because more mines would be opened with the completion of the transcontinental railroad in 1869. Linderman advocated demonetization of silver and suspension of the free coinage of silver before the market was flooded thus lowering its price and providing a cheap means of inflating the economy. By 1872 the silver production in the United States had jumped to over 22 million ounces. Nearly three years elapsed from the introduction of the proposition demonetizing silver till its final passage. The bill was considered at length by the Finance Committee of the Senate and the Coinage Committee of the House, during five different sessions of Congress. It was repeatedly read in full in both houses, printed in full eleven different times, and debated repeatedly in both the House and Senate.[2] The point was made that it was impossible to retain the double standard since the values of gold and silver continually fluctuated.

The Act to most legislators was merely to codify the 1792 legislation and later laws, and to appoint a responsible head of the Mint under the Secretary of the Treasury. The market price of silver had been high enough because of

Philadelphia Mint, 1833-1901
(Bureau of the Mint)

Table 2-1 MINTAGES OF MORGAN AND PEACE SILVER DOLLARS

1. Chronological Order (Proofs are in parentheses)

Morgan

Date	Proofs	Mintage
1878	(550)	10,509,550
1878CC		2,212,000
1878S		9,774,000
1879	(1,100)	14,807,100
1879CC		756,000
1879O		2,887,000
1879S		9,110,000
1880	(1,355)	12,601,355
1880CC		591,000
1880O		5,305,000
1880S		8,900,000
1881	(975)	9,163,975
1881CC		296,000
1881O		5,708,000
1881S		12,760,000
1882	(1,100)	11,101,100
1882CC		1,133,000
1882O		6,090,000
1882S		9,250,000
1883	(1,039)	12,291,039
1883CC		1,204,000
1883O		8,725,000
1883S		6,250,000
1884	(875)	14,070,875
1884CC		1,136,000
1884O		9,730,000
1884S		3,200,000
1885	(930)	17,787,767
1885CC		228,000
1885O		9,185,000
1885S		1,497,000
1886	(886)	19,963,886
1886O		10,710,000
1886S		750,000
1887	(710)	20,290,710
1887O		11,550,000
1887S		1,771,000
1888	(832)	19,183,832
1888O		12,150,000
1888S		657,000
1889	(811)	21,726,811
1889CC		350,000
1889O		11,875,000
1889S		700,000
1890	(590)	16,802,590
1890CC		2,309,041
1890O		10,701,000
1890S		8,230,373
1891	(650)	8,694,206
1891CC		1,618,000
1891O		7,954,529
1891S		5,296,000
1892	(1,245)	1,037,245
1892CC		1,352,000
1892O		2,744,000
1892S		1,200,000
1893	(792)	378,792
1893CC		677,000
1893O		300,000
1893S		100,000
1894	(972)	110,972
1894O		1,723,000
1894S		1,260,000
1895	(880)	12,880 *
1895O		450,000
1895S		400,000
1896	(762)	9,976,762
1896O		4,900,000
1896S		5,000,000
1897	(731)	2,822,731
1897O		4,004,000
1897S		5,825,000
1898	(735)	5,844,735
1898O		4,440,000
1898S		4,102,000
1899	(846)	330,846
1899O		12,290,000
1899S		2,562,000
1900	(912)	8,830,912
1900O		12,590,000
1900 S		3,540,000
1901	(813)	6,962,813
1901O		13,320,000
1901S		2,284,000
1902	(777)	7,994,777
1902O		8,636,000
1902S		1,530,000
1903	(755)	4,652,755
1903O		4,450,000
1903S		1,241,000
1904	(650)	2,788,650
1904O		3,720,000
1904S		2,304,000
1921		44,690,000
1921D		20,345,000
1921S		21,695,000

Peace

Date	Mintage
1921	1,006,473
1922	51,737,000
1922D	15,063,000
1922S	17,475,000
1923	30,800,000
1923D	6,811,000
1923S	19,020,000
1924	11,811,000
1924S	1,728,000
1925	10,198,000
1925S	1,610,000
1926	1,939,000
1926D	2,348,700
1926S	6,980,000
1927	848,000
1927D	1,268,900
1927S	866,000
1928	360,649
1928S	1,632,000
1934	954,057
1934D	1,569,500
1934S	1,011,000
1935	1,576,000
1935S	1,964,000

* The 12,000 1895P business strikes are not known to exist and were probably melted under the Pittman Act of 1918.

Table 2-1 *Continued*

2. In Order of Quantity Minted

Morgan

1895	12,880*
1893S	100,000
1894	110,972
1885CC	228,000
1881CC	296,000
1893O	300,000
1899	330,846
1889CC	350,000
1893	378,792
1895S	400,000
1895O	450,000
1880CC	591,000
1888S	657,000
1893CC	677,000
1889S	700,000
1886S	750,000
1879CC	756,000
1892	1,037,245
1882CC	1,133,000
1884CC	1,136,000
1892S	1,200,000
1883CC	1,204,000
1903S	1,241,000
1894S	1,260,000
1892CC	1,352,000
1885S	1,497,000
1902S	1,530,000
1891CC	1,618,000
1894O	1,723,000
1887S	1,771,000
1878CC	2,212,000
1901S	2,284,000
1904S	2,304,000
1890CC	2,309,041
1899S	2,562,000
1892O	2,744,000
1904	2,788,650
1897	2,822,731
1879O	2,887,000
1884S	3,200,000
1900S	3,540,000
1904O	3,720,000
1897O	4,004,000
1898S	4,102,000
1898O	4,440,000
1903O	4,450,000
1903	4,652,755
1896O	4,900,000
1896S	5,000,000
1891S	5,296,000
1880O	5,305,000
1881O	5,708,000
1897S	5,825,000
1898	5,884,735
1882O	6,090,000
1883S	6,250,000
1901	6,962,813
1891O	7,954,529
1902	7,994,777
1890S	8,230,373
1902O	8,636,000
1891	8,694,206
1883O	8,725,000
1900	8,830,912
1880S	8,900,000
1879S	9,110,000
1881	9,163,975
1885O	9,185,000
1882S	9,250,000
1884O	9,730,000
1878S	9,774,000
1896	9,976,762
1878	10,509,550
1890O	10,701,000
1886O	10,710,000
1882	11,101,100
1887O	11,550,000
1889O	11,875,000
1888O	12,150,000
1899O	12,290,000
1883	12,291,039
1900O	12,590,000
1880	12,601,355
1881S	12,760,000
1901O	13,320,000
1884	14,070,875
1879	14,807,100
1890	16,802,590
1885	17,787,767
1888	19,183,832
1886	19,963,886
1887	20,290,710
1921D	20,345,000
1921S	21,695,000
1889	21,726,811
1921	44,690,000

Peace

1928	360,649
1927	848,000
1927S	866,000
1934	954,057
1921	1,006,473
1934S	1,011,000
1927D	1,268,900
1934D	1,569,500
1935	1,576,000
1925S	1,610,000
1928S	1,632,000
1924S	1,728,000
1926	1,939,000
1935S	1,964,000
1926D	2,348,700
1923D	6,811,000
1926S	6,980,000
1925	10,198,000
1924	11,811,000
1922D	15,063,000
1922S	17,475,000
1923S	19,020,000
1923	30,800,000
1922	51,737,000

its 16-to-1 value ratio to gold so that the silver dollar had not been in wide circulation since 1836 (its bullion value was at or slightly higher than its face value). Demonetization of standard silver dollars to many simply would give legal recognition to that fact. In addition, Germany had in 1871 already decided to go on a single standard, gold.

The Coinage Act of 1873 was signed into law on February 12, 1873. It demonetized silver by only providing for deposits of gold bullion for coinage. Silver coinage was authorized only in Trade dollars, half dollars, quarters and dimes. Silver bullion producers could deposit the bullion, have it cast into bars, or coined into Trade dollars for a small fee. However, Trade dollars were not legal tender in the domestic United States. This prevented bullion producers from converting silver into coinage to make an additional profit as the price of silver fell due to increased production and the face value of the silver dollar became more than its bullion value.

Since the price of silver at the time of the Coinage Act passage was $1.30 per ounce (a silver dollar's bullion value is $1.00 when the price of silver is $1.2929) and had been above that level for decades, there was no public outcries when the silver dollar was dropped. However, a downward price trend for silver began in 1873 *(see Figure 2-1)*. It persisted, except for the silver purchase period around 1890 and during World War I, until the abandonment of the gold standard in 1932. From that time to 1980, the price trend had been upward, due to Treasury purchases in the 1930's and 1940's and to the greater industrial usage after World War II, inflationary trends and speculation at the end of the 1970's. Since 1980, when the speculation bubble burst, the trend has now been downward due to softening of commodity prices in the 1980's and deflationary trends in the early 1990's.

It was the steady decline in the price of silver during the late 1800's that caused the action taken by Congress in 1873 to be referred to as the "Crime of '73." This so-called "Crime of '73" was to dominate every national election between 1876 and 1896.

Actually there had been a progressive decline of the value of silver in relation to gold for a number of centuries. At the commencement of the sixteenth century the ratio of gold to silver was 1:10.75.[3] It was 1:12.25 during the first twenty years of the seventeenth century, 14.50 between 1641 and 1660, and 15.27 at the beginning of the eighteenth century. The ratio rose to 14.56 between 1751 and 1760 but fell afterwards to 15.83 by 1850 where it remained around that level until the early 1870's. A perceptible decline started again in 1871 and 1872 before Germany began to demonetize its silver coins.

The change from the bimetallic standard in 1873 came at a time of rapidly rising silver production. The price of silver began to fall in 1873 after the opening of mines in Nevada and Colorado and the earlier demonetization of silver in Germany. Mining interests wanted a return to free silver coinage to check the declining price of silver.

Several important eastern banks failed in September 1873, and a financial panic swept the country. Hardest hit by the panic were bankers, manufacturers, and farmers in the South and West. In an attempt to gain relief, the bankers and manufacturers formed the Greenback Party, which demanded redemption in paper money rather than gold, of war bonds which had been contracted in a period of inflation. The farmers organized the Grange movement and the Farmer's Alliance. These groups demanded an inflation of currency to ease the ever increasing financial depression that occurred after 1873.

The inflationists demanded "free silver," a return to the unlimited coinage of silver at the old ratio of 16 ounces of silver to 1 ounce of gold. They wanted the government to issue more paper and silver money, even though they could not be backed by large amounts of gold in the Treasury. Farm groups favored currency inflation because it would enable them to pay debts with cheaper money than they had borrowed. Free "Silverites" contended that, with more money in circulation, farmers would receive higher prices for their crops and workers would get higher wages. On the other hand, business

New Orleans Mint, Circa 1890
(Illustrated History of the U.S. Mint, George C. Evans)

leaders argued for the gold standard and against free silver, because inflation would cheapen the value of money.

BLAND-ALLISON ACT

In the summer of 1876 several bills came up in the House to coin the standard silver dollar and restore its legal tender character.[4] The following autumn the Kelley bill, slightly altered, was again introduced in the House by Richard P. Bland and passed. In the Senate the bill was under the charge of William B. Allison of the Committee on Finance who reported the bill with important amendments. The chief amendment took away from the House bill the provision granting free coinage and added a provision for silver certificates originated by Booth.

Bankers sent a memorial to Congress in January 1878 stating their reasons against passage of the so-called "Bland Bill." These included "that silver bullion sufficient to make a dollar of 412 1/2 grains, can today be had for a

Figure 2-1 HISTORICAL PRICE OF SILVER PER OUNCE

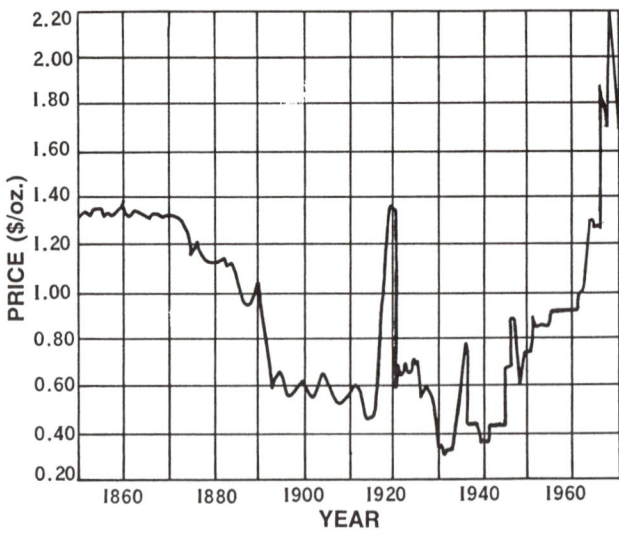
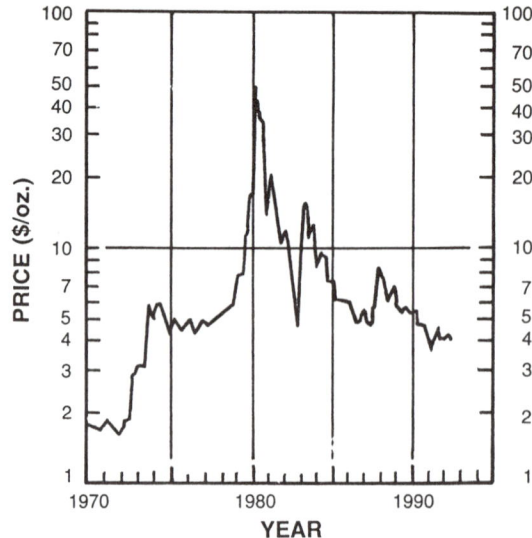

fraction less than 90 cents in gold, so that the dollars which the proposed law would create, would at once reduce the standard one-tenth, and strike that amount from the value of all outstanding debts and commercial obligations." They also stated that, "The great mass of the exchanges in all commercial countries are no longer affected by the use of coin, but by the issues of Banks and Bankers, representing capital in some form, and serving as instruments for its transfer. The tendency everywhere is constantly to a decreased use of metallic money."[5] Thus, the Bankers were afraid of the inflationary effect of the silver dollars and recognized that most commerce was carried out in paper money.

On the other side, those in favor of the remonitization of silver pointed out "that while the value of silver had fallen about 10 percent since 1872-73, as measured in gold, commercial commodities measured in the same way have fallen twice 10 percent."[6] They thus pointed out that silver could purchase more in commodities than five years prior and had only fallen in value relative to gold. There had been a depression in nearly every industry in this country with falling markets and universality of business disasters since 1873. Remonitization of silver was advocated to help check the rapidly spreading bankruptcy and poverty by increasing the money supply.

This Bland-Allison Act as it became known was passed by Congress on February 28, 1878, over the veto of Republican President Rutherford B. Hayes. He pointed out that the market value of the silver in the proposed silver dollar was from ninety to ninety-two cents as compared with the standard gold dollar. His main objection to the bill was "The capital deficit of the bill is that it contains no provision protecting from its operation pre-existing debts in case the coinage which it creates shall continue to be of less value than that which was the sole legal tender when they were contracted."[7] He concluded his veto statement with "A currency with less than it purports to be worth, will in the end defraud not only creditors, but all who are engaged in legitimate business, and none more surely than those who are dependent on their daily labor for their daily bread."

This Act restored legal tender character to silver money and required the Treasury to purchase at the market price $2,000,000 to $4,000,000 worth of silver per month and to coin it into silver dollars at a ratio to gold of 16 to 1. The coins were to be 412.5 grains in weight and 0.900 fine (nine-tenths pure silver), as provided in an Act of January 18, 1837. In its final form the Bland-Allison Act was a compromise between a bill for the free and unlimited coinage of silver, which Missouri Representative Richard P. Bland had forced through the House in 1877 and the "sound money" doctrines, espoused by Iowa's Senator William B. Allison, which prevailed in the Senate.

Never before in the history of the U. S. had the Government bought gold or silver bullion outright for gold and silver dollar coinage. Free coinage of gold or silver bullion from depositors had been previously made except for subsidiary coins. The Bland-Allison Act required sizable purchases of silver each month to be coined into silver dollars no matter what the commercial needs were or how the price of silver varied.

The Act of 1878 also introduced a new kind of paper money into the U.S. currency, the silver certificate. Although they were not full legal tender for all debts, in practice they were received equally with silver dollars because they were readily converted to silver dollars. These silver certificates circulated in much greater amounts than silver dollars because of the latter's heaviness and bulk.

Under the Bland-Allison Act, 291,272,018.56 fine ounces of silver were purchased at a cost of $308,279,260.71. This bullion was coined into 378,166,793 silver dollars (the standard silver dollar contains 0.77 ounces of pure silver). Purchases were continued under this Act until passage of the Sherman Act on July 14, 1890. These silver dollars were initially known as Bland dollars. Later, in the twentieth century, they became better known as Morgan dollars.

Soon after passage of the Bland-Allison Act, attempts were made to procure on the Pacific Coast the requisite silver bullion for the western mints (San Francisco and Carson City). It was found, however, that the producers and dealers there refused to sell silver to the government at the London rate unless they were paid, in addition, an amount equivalent to the cost of bringing silver from London to San Francisco.[8] These terms were deemed exorbitant and were rejected. The western mints had only limited stocks of silver at that time. Arrangements were immediately made to bring the Philadelphia Mint to its maximum capacity to meet the provisions of the law, which required 2 million silver dollars to be coined each month. Because the available domestic sources of silver were insufficient for coinage of this amount, the foreign market was indirectly resorted to.

The San Francisco and Carson City Mints began striking the new silver dollars in April 1878 when the requisite dies and collars arrived from the Philadelphia Mint using existing limited stocks of silver bullion. Coinage was suspended at these mints in early June during the annual settlement but could not resume because of the bullion shortage. In late July 1878, the principal holders of bullion on the Pacific Coast retreated from their position and accepted the equivalent of the London rate.[9] At this price, sufficient bullion was purchased to supply the San Francisco and Carson City Mints so silver dollar coinage could be resumed.

During the time the Bland-Allison Act was in force, enough silver bullion was required to be purchased yearly to allow coinage of over 25 million coins. In actuality, there were many years of reduced coinage for the western mints during the period from 1885 to 1889. Although the Carson City Mint had never coined more than about 2 million silver dollars in any one year because of its limited capacity, San Francisco had coined over 10 million in some years. Why then, was the output of these two mints reduced to a yearly output of hundreds of thousands or eliminated completely during the years 1885 to 1889? An examination of the operations of the Carson City Mint during these years will provide the answer.

For some time prior to March 1885, Assistant Secretary French, Treasurer Wyman, and Director Burchard of the U.S. Treasury had recommended that silver for delivery at Carson City be purchased only when the rates were such that the cost of transporting the resulting coin to the Atlantic coast, added to the price of bullion, would not exceed the cost of bullion at the Philadelphia and New Orleans Mints.

Because of the difficulty of procuring silver bullion for delivery at the Carson City Mint at reasonable rates, coinage was suspended there from the last week in March to the first week of August 1879; from November 15, 1879 to September 1, 1880; and from April 1 to October 1, 1881.[10] This accounts for the low silver dollar mintage at Carson City in 1879, 1880, and 1881.

Grover Cleveland, a Democrat and a strong anti-silver man, was elected President in November 1884. Thus, the political atmosphere in Washington had shifted against the silver interests of the western states and the San Francisco and Carson City Mints located there.

On March 8, 1885, the Superintendent of the Carson City Mint, James Crawford, died. Business was suspended and the mint was closed pending appointment and qualification of a successor. A new superintendent and new coiner assumed office on April 1. However, on March 28, the Director of the Mint, Horatio C. Burchard, with the approval of the Secretary of the Treasury, had ordered suspension of coinage (which had not yet been resumed) for the balance of fiscal 1885, because of the fact that only $7,200 of that year's appropriation for "wages of workmen" remained for 4 months of operation.[11] The force of working personnel was also reduced to the lowest possible limit. The Carson City Mint was subsequently ordered closed on November 6, 1885.[12] It was reopened on October 1, 1886, but with only enough appropriations to act as an assay office for the receipt and testing of bullion with an acid refinery. If bullion deposits were sufficient, coining could resume.[13]

The reduction in business at the Carson City Mint which led to its closing had two main causes: first, the practice of paying for depositions by draft instead of by cash; and second, the collection of a transportation charge from depositors for the cost of transporting refined bullion by express to the San Francisco Mint.[14] The Carson City Mint had at no period in its history received deposits in any great amount from the mines of the Nevada Comstock lode; their product was sent to the San Francisco Mint for coinage, just as it had been before the establishment of the Carson City Mint.

Comparison of the costs of coining each piece above the denomination of one cent shows that costs were considerably higher at the western mints at this time (see Table 2-2).

The cost of coinage was principally the cost of striking. These high coining costs contributed to the reduced operating appropriations that caused both the closing of the Carson City Mint in 1885 and the reduced coinage at the San Francisco Mint. The small number of Carson City silver dollars minted in 1885 was due to the suspension of coining operations on March 8 of that year.

By 1888 the Carson City Mint refinery was running at full capacity and a change from the nitric process to the sulfuric method of refining further increased the capacity. But, the mint was still not given the order from the U.S. Mint Director to proceed with coining. However, in November 1888, Benjamin Harrison, a Republican who supported silver interests, was elected President. Finally, the Carson City Mint budget was approved for fiscal year 1890 and the coinage department of the Carson City Mint was then reopened July 1, 1889. But due to the deterioration of the building and machinery after four years of idleness, repairs were first necessary. Therefore, coinage of the silver dollar was not commenced until October 1, 1889, which accounts for the low mintage that year.[15]

As a result of the anti-silver atmosphere and the relatively high coining costs of the western mints, coinage of silver at the San Francisco Mint was also discontinued in fiscal 1886.[16] There was small coinage of silver dollars at this mint until 1890 because of limited appropriations provided for the mint.

In order to meet the provisions of the Bland-Allison Act, a minimum of $2,000,000 worth of silver had to be purchased by the Treasury each month at market prices and coined into silver dollars. From 1878 to 1885 the market price of silver remained around $1.10 per ounce. Since one silver dollar contained 0.77 ounces of silver, this meant the Treasury had to coin a minimum of some 28,000,000 silver dollars per year. As shown in Table 2-3, the combined total of Morgan dollars minted each year from 1879 to 1885 was at this level. This was

Table 2-2 COINING COSTS

From Annual Report of the Director of the Mint, 1886.

	1884	1885
Philadelphia	$.0130	$.0189
New Orleans	$.0155	$.0149
San Francisco	$.0437	$.0580
Carson City	$.0728	$.0913

Table 2-3 MORGAN DOLLARS MINTED BY YEAR

Year	Mintage
1878	22,495,550
1879	27,560,100
1880	27,397,355
1881	27,927,975
1882	27,574,100
1883	28,470,039
1884	28,136,875
1885	28,697,767
1886	31,423,886
1887	33,611,710
1888	31,990,833
1889	34,651,811
1890	38,043,004
1891	23,562,735
1892	6,333,245
1893	1,455,792
1894	3,093,972
1895	862,880
1896	19,876,762
1897	12,651,731
1898	14,426,735
1899	15,182,846
1900	24,960,912
1901	22,566,813
1902	18,160,777
1903	10,343,755
1904	8,812,650
1921	86,730,000

because the Secretaries of the Treasury were generally unsympathetic to the cause of silver and bought only the minimum amount of silver per month.

From 1886 to 1890 the market price of silver fell steadily to below $0.90 per ounce which required the Treasury to increase quantities of Morgan dollars minted to 38,000,000 for 1890. This burden fell almost entirely on the Philadelphia and New Orleans Mints during this time period.

During Grover Cleveland's first term, from 1885 to 1889, dissension grew between the bankers and industrialists of the East and the farmers of the South and West. The industrialists wanted a high tariff to protect high prices and a "sound money" system based on gold. The farmers held heavy debts and wanted money to be cheap in comparison with goods; that is, they wanted inflation, so they could pay their debts with less farm produce.

The net increase in currency due to coinage of silver dollars during this period, however, merely met the normal growth in the Nation's money requirements. In addition, silver certificates simply took the place of normal bank notes, which were being retired with the current reduction of the national debt. Meanwhile new silver mines had been discovered, and the world price of silver continued to fall. The currency of the United States was based on gold, and limited amounts of silver could be sold to the Treasury for gold at the fixed proportion of 16 to 1. A profit could be made by buying silver on the open market and selling it to the Government for gold; as a result, gold was drained from the Treasury.

Cleveland, as a Democrat, believed in the gold standard and had asked Congress to repeal the Bland-Allison Act, but Congress refused. The government then issued bonds and sold them to banks for gold; but this helped matters for only a short time, and the drain in the Treasury's gold continued.

The election of Benjamin Harrison in November 1888, who was a silver supporter, resulted in an immediate advance in silver prices. Also increased appropriations for the two western mints were provided beginning fiscal year 1890. Thus, these two mints struck a considerable portion of the 38,000,000 Morgan dollars produced that year.

SHERMAN SILVER PURCHASE ACT

Farm prices continued to drop during the late 1880's and farmers believed that all their problems would be solved if the government would issue enough silver money. The owners of silver mines naturally favored a policy that would increase the price of silver and boost their own profits. Renewed agitation by inflationists during Republican President Benjamin Harrison's term (1889-1893) prompted the adoption of the Sherman Silver Purchase Act of July 14, 1890, which repealed the provisions of the Bland-Allison Act. It was passed because of a trade in which western Congressmen voted for a tariff bill which they disliked, while easterners voted for a silver bill which they feared.

This Act provided for purchase, at the current market price not exceeding $1.00 for 371.25 grains of pure silver, of 4,500,000 ounces of silver bullion each month. The government purchased this silver to be coined into standard silver dollars and paid for it with Treasury notes that could be redeemed in either silver or gold. Because most people chose to redeem their notes in gold, fear of a resulting drain on the Treasury's gold reserve helped cause the financial panic which occurred in 1893.

Under the Sherman Act, 168,674,682.53 fine ounces of silver were purchased at a cost of $155,931,002.25, for which Treasury notes were issued. Of the silver purchased, 144,653,722.68 fine ounces costing $134,192,285.02 were coined into 187,027,345 silver dollars. The balance was used for subsidiary silver coinage.

Acts of March 3, 1887, and March 3, 1891, authorized coinage from Trade dollar bullion and Trade dollars then in the Treasury. Under these Acts, 5,078,472 standard silver dollars were coined.

With the adoption of the Sherman Silver

Richard P. Bland
(Silver and Gold, Trumbull White)

William B. Allison
(Silver and Gold, Trumbull White)

Grover Cleveland
(Silver and Gold, Trumbull White)

John Sherman
(Silver and Gold, Trumbull White)

Benjamin Harrison
(Silver and Gold, Trumbull White)

William McKinley
(Silver and Gold, Trumbull White)

Purchase Act, and the repealing of the Bland-Allison Act, the Treasury was obliged to purchase $4,500,000 of silver per month and coin two million ounces of silver bullion into silver dollars each month until July 1, 1891. Thereafter, only as much needed to be coined to provide for redemption of the Treasury notes. Since the Treasury had huge stocks of uncirculated silver dollars at that time, the production of silver dollars fell in 1891 and 1892.

The price of silver rose slightly during the debate and passage of the Sherman Act, but fell sharply thereafter because of the high production of the metal. The United States then called an international monetary conference at Brussels on November 22, 1892, to find ways to increase the use of silver, but the delegates adjourned on December 17 without having passed any resolutions.[17] Because of the continued fall in the price of silver, India stopped coinage of silver in June 1893.

In November 1892, Grover Cleveland, who still opposed the silver interests was re-elected. During the second month of Grover Cleveland's second term (1893-1897), a severe financial panic swept the country. Its causes included a farm depression, a business slump abroad, and the drain on the Treasury's gold reserve. Cleveland felt that a basic cause of the panic was the Sherman Silver Purchase Act of Harrison's administration. The Act had failed to increase either the price of silver or the amount of money in circulation, and had not affected the steady decline in farm prices.

In June 1893, Cleveland called a special session of Congress to repeal the Sherman Act. Congress did so on November 1, 1893, but the nation's gold reserves had dwindled alarmingly. The government floated four bond issues during the next 3 years to replenish them. Silver dollar coinage remained very low during the first 3 years of Cleveland's second administration, since the Sherman Act had been repealed and Cleveland opposed the free coinage of silver.

Coinage of Morgan silver dollars fell to new lows in 1893 due to Cleveland's opposition to silver interests, the financial panic of that year, the repeal of the Sherman Act, and the large number of uncirculated Morgan dollars still on hand at the Treasury. The Carson City Mint was a major casualty of that year. Mine production of silver on the Comstock had fallen off and the San Francisco Mint could handle all the western mines output. The Treasury did not require coinage of large amounts of silver dollars at that time.[18] Thus, on June 1, 1893, Robert E. Preston, acting U.S. Mint Director, ordered suspension of coining at the Carson City Mint, with only its refining department to remain open.

The final blow to the Carson City Mint came in 1895 when it was discovered that some of the ingots were coming back from the melting rooms much lighter than the weight and value stamped on their faces. The resulting investigation found that $75,549.75 of gold was missing.[19] On April 18, 1895, the Carson City Mint operations (as a refinery) were suspended and most of the employees laid off. In January 1896, the Treasury ordered the minting of silver dollars at the Philadelphia, New Orleans, and San Francisco Mints. The Carson City Mint was missing from the list; it could not be trusted. The assistant melter and refiner, silver dissolver, and a refinery worker were charged and convicted by May 1, 1896 of the Carson City Mint gold theft. Only about one-third of the missing bullion had been accounted for and none had been recovered. The refining department reopened again on June 9, 1896. On July 1, 1899, the Carson City Mint status was officially changed to an assay office. Its three coining presses, remaining coin dies, and associated machinery were shipped to the Philadelphia Mint by the middle of September 1899.[20]

Meanwhile, silver interests grew stronger. By the time of the Democratic convention in 1896, the "Silverites" outnumbered the "Goldbugs". William Jennings Bryan won the Democratic presidential nomination and his famous "cross of gold" speech swung the party to the silver cause and thus elevated the currency issue to first place in the campaign.

The Republican financial platform stated "We are unalterably opposed to every measure calculated to debase our currency or impair the credit of our country. We are, therefore, opposed to the free coinage of silver, except by international agreement with the leading commercial nations of the world... All our silver and paper currency must be maintained at parity with gold..." The Democratic financial platform stated "We demand the free and unlimited coinage of both gold and silver at the present legal ratio of 16 to 1 without waiting for the aid or consent of any other nation. We demand that the standard silver dollar shall be full legal tender, equally with gold, for all debts, public and private...".

William McKinley won the election in November 1896. Although he had favored limited coinage of silver as a Republican Congressman, he took the opposite view during his term of office (1897-1901). He still, however, favored the gold standard.

An Act of June 13, 1898, directed coinage into standard dollars of all the remaining bullion in the Treasury which had been purchased under the Sherman Act. Of the silver dollars coined under the Sherman Act, 36,087,285 were coined before repeal of the silver purchase authority on November 1, 1893; 42,139,872 were coined between November 1, 1893, and June 12, 1898; and 108,800,188 were coined as directed by the Act of June 13, 1898.

In 1899 the general upturn of business created an increased demand for coinage. The Philadelphia Mint, besides turning out the usual supply of minor coins, bore the brunt of an exceptionally heavy demand for subsidiary silver.[21] To meet this demand, it had to run overtime shifts. As a result, only a small amount of silver dollars were struck in 1899 by the Philadelphia Mint. The

Carson City Mint, 1875
(Nevada Historical Society)

Denver Mint, 1906 to Present
(Bureau of the Mint)

San Francisco Mint, Circa 1890
(Illustrated History of the U.S. Mint, George G. Evans)

New Orleans Mint was employed chiefly for coinage of the silver dollar that year and it also ran overtime shifts.

Bryan's defeat heralded the end of free silver. In 1900, after the new Yukon mines had greatly increased the available supply of gold and a general inflationary trend had begun, the Republicans succeeded in passing the Gold Standard Act, making gold the single monetary standard. This Act provided that the dollar should be the standard unit of value and should consist of 25.8 grains of gold nine-tenths fine. It also directed the Secretary of the Treasury to keep all forms of money issued or coined by the United States at parity of value with this standard, and declared that nothing should affect the legal tender quality of the silver dollar or of any other money coined or issued by the United States.

Only a limited amount of the silver bullion purchased under the Sherman Act remained when the Act of 1898 authorized further coinage of silver dollars. By 1904, when this amount had been struck, coinage of silver dollars ended.

PITTMAN ACT

In the early spring of 1918 during WW I, the Germans started a propaganda campaign in India that the British government could not redeem its silver certificates. The Indian government, under British supervision, had spent many years teaching the Indians to accept paper silver certificates in lieu of silver rupees. These certificates were payable in silver on demand and the Indian government had established many agencies of redemption throughout India. The German propaganda had started a run on the Indian redemption agencies which threatened to start a revolution. At that time the great German drive against the Western Front was about to start and the allied forces could not afford to deplete their forces to quell an Indian revolution.

Later in the spring of 1918, the British ambassador met with U.S. Treasury officials and Senator Key Pittman who was a friend of President Wilson and represented Western silver interests.[22] Apparently India and Great Britain did not have enough silver rupee coins or silver bullion to satisfy the silver certificate redemptions and asked the United States to provide them with silver bullion to meet these demands. The U.S. Treasury Department had at that time over 400 million silver dollars held unused in reserve that were coined under the Bland-Allison and Sherman Acts.

On April 9, 1918, Senator Pittman introduced bill S.4292 which was passed on April 22, 1918 and signed by President Wilson the next day. It states that the purpose was: "That sales of silver bullion under authority of this act may be made for the purpose of conserving the existing stock of gold in the United States, of providing silver for subsidiary coinage and for commercial use, and of assisting foreign governments at war with the enemies of the United States."

The Pittman Act directed that not more than 350,000,000 standard silver dollars be converted into bullion and sold at a price not less than $1.00 per fine ounce or used for subsidiary silver coinage. It also authorized purchase of a like amount of silver, at a price of $1.00 per ounce, from American mine owners and the coining of the same number of dollars that had been melted.

Initially in 1918, Great Britain paid over the current market price of silver in order to obtain huge quantities quickly. In late 1919 the price of silver advanced to over $1.00 per ounce. But by then Great Britain had purchased all the silver it needed. The Treasury was obligated to pay $1.00 per ounce to buy replacement silver which was over the market price most of the time. Silver rose above $1.00 per ounce only briefly in November 1919 to early 1920 and thereafter fell to $0.70 per ounce.

The silver dollars immediately began being melted after passage and signing of the Pittman Act. The *London Times*, on May 4, 1918 reported that 25 million were already melted at New York and several consignments of silver bullion derived from the melting of silver dollars were on their way to the Calcutta Mint. And by June 30, 1918, 68,752,554 had been melted.

Under this Act, 270,232,722 standard silver dollars were converted into bullion by passing the coins through large greased rollers to flatten them and then melting them. A total of 259,121,554 dollars were melted and sold to Great Britain at $1.00 per fine ounce plus mint charges and 11,111,168 were converted into bullion for subsidiary coinage, the equivalent of about 209,000,000 fine ounces of silver. A charge of $0.015/oz. sufficient to cover the cost of coinage, together with the cost of copper for alloy, was collected in addition to the price of $1.00/oz. of silver. This additional amount was placed in a trust fund to pay labor and materials in recoinage of the silver dollars.[23]

Under the Pittman Act, 39,434,500 dollars came from the Philadelphia Mint, and 19,301,000 from the San Francisco Reserve during fiscal 1918.[24] In fiscal 1919, 158,620,554 dollars came from Philadelphia, 74,001,000 from San Francisco, and 26,500 from New York. Not all of these dollars were melted, however. No records were kept of the year or mint of the dollars melted. Almost half the total Morgan dollars minted were melted under this Act. Undoubtedly some years and mints were more heavily melted than others. This has caused a drastic change in the surviving number by date and mint from the original mintage figures which is reflected in the current supply and demand market prices.

War can be extremely wasteful as the Pittman Act shows. Great Britain paid a premium of $0.40 per ounce over the 1918 price of $0.60 per ounce or 67% in order to obtain the silver bullion quickly. Two hundred million ounces of silver was not immediately available from private suppliers. The United States, on the other hand, by selling the silver dollars for bullion for about $0.78 each, sold them for $0.22 each below face value. One dollar face value theoretically could have purchased 1.7 ounces of silver at the market price of $0.60 per ounce but the private suppliers could not have immediately provided the needed amount and the demand would have quickly forced the price of silver higher. Also, the Treasury paid a large premium to buy back replacement silver from American mines at $1.00 per ounce since the market price of silver was $0.70 per ounce after early 1920. Public funds were again used to protect and subsidize the private silver industry.

After WW I ended, the price of silver shot up rapidly from the 50 and 60 cents an ounce levels that had prevailed since the mid 1890's. Part of this increase may have been due to the provision of the Pittman Act that required repurchase of silver at $1.00 per ounce to replace the silver dollars melted. Speculator demands in other countries, principally China, caused the price of silver to rise to nearly $1.40 per ounce by November 1919. On November 26, 1919, the Treasury, acting in cooperation with the Federal Reserve Board and the Federal Reserve Banks, arranged to release silver dollars coined under the Sherman Act and held unused, to be employed to regulate the exchange with countries having a silver standard.[25] The price of silver had to be brought down below the bullion value of $1.38 per ounce in subsidiary coins and $1.29 per ounce in silver dollars so they would not be hoarded and melted.

The Treasury contracted with three American banks to sell silver dollars at $1.35 per ounce of silver delivered in China which had the greatest demand and price for silver. Initially 20 million silver dollars were allocated for this purpose, but this was later raised to 40 million in February 1920.[26] The 1920 Director of the Mint Report states that 13 million dollars of silver and 29 million silver dollars left the country to the Orient from November 1919 to May 1920.

As a result, the speculator bubble burst and the price of silver fell sharply early in 1920 to $0.70 per ounce. The 13 million dollars of silver mentioned in the 1920 Director of the Mint Report were undoubtedly from the silver dollars melted under the Pittman Act which included 10 million melted in FY 1920. There are no additional silver dollars reported melted by the U.S. Government in 1920 other than those 10 million included in the Pittman Act amounts. The 29 million silver dollars that left the country were in addition to those melted under the Pittman Act. However, these may not have been melted in the Orient since they were sold to the banks in China with the provision that they would be melted or that they would not be re-exported from China.

At any rate, it appears that 29 million Morgan silver dollars were shipped to China in late 1919 and early 1920 where they were either melted or went into commerce as silver bullion. Thus, they were lost to collectors if melted or became circulated coins. Of course, over the years, many additional silver dollars have gone to other countries through the efforts of private individuals, but these quantities are not known.

In addition to the silver dollars melted under the Pittman Act, some were melted each year, beginning in the 1880's, because they were mutilated or uncurrent. Besides the Seated Liberty and earlier dollars, many of these were probably mutilated Morgan dollars. Approximately 50,000,000 silver dollars were also melted under the World War II Silver Act of December 18, 1942. The resulting bullion was diverted to wartime uses, including the Manhattan Project. *Table 2-4* lists the number of silver dollars melted per year from 1883 to the present. These figures were obtained from the Director of the Mint's annual reports. None have been melted by the Treasury since FY 1964.

It is not known whether the dollars melted during World War II were primarily Morgan or Peace dollars. However, because of the Pittman Act, the World War II Silver Act, and the melting of uncurrent silver dollars, all totaling over 333,000,000, certainly less than one-half of the Morgan dollars and perhaps three-quarters of the Peace dollars remain.

In the early 1960's, the demand for silver dollars had been so great when the Treasury vaults were cleaned out that bags of uncurrent silver dollars were put back into circulation. These bags contained mostly coins with only partial rims, and a few coins had even been passed through the rollers and flattened!

The Pittman Act, since it specified replacement of the silver dollars that were melted, authorized coinage of 270,232,722 silver dollars. Under this authority, 86,730,000 of the 1921 Morgan dollars and 183,502,722 of the Peace dollars from 1921 to 1928 were struck.

Coinage of the Morgan silver dollar resumed on February 21, 1921. This was changed over to the new Peace dollar design commencing on December 29, 1921. All three mints at Philadelphia, San Francisco and Denver operated at full capacity in order to replace the silver dollars melted under the Pittman Act as speedily as possible. The reasons for this were stated in a 1924 memorandum by the Director of the Mint, Robert J. Grant:

The work of recoining the silver dollars melted under the terms of the Pittman Act of April 23, 1918 was of such magnitude as to require the full capacity of the three coinage mints of the U.S. for over two years time, if the coinage of all other denominations had been discontinued. It was impossible to discontinue the manufacture of other coins. The policy of the Department was to recoin as rapidly as possible the silver bullion being purchased in accordance with the Act, into dollars, because of the fact that the silver bullion, as such, was a dead asset which could not be used to pay the Government's expenses or debts nor as a reserve against other forms of money, while the Government must pay interest on many borrowed millions with which to buy the bullion.

...When the stocks of silver bullion were very large the operations of the mints were increased by the employment of additional men and by working 16 or more hours per day...[27]

These silver dollars were needed to back the silver certificate paper money and to pay debts incurred in buying the silver bullion. The silver bullion purchased was converted as fast as possible to silver dollars resulting in large mintages during 1921, 1922 and 1923. Subsidiary coinage was low during these years because of this.

However, coinage of silver dollars stretched out until 1928. The reason for this was the time required to refine some of the purchased bullion as related by Director of the Mint Grant. "...Part of the purchased silver bullion was combined with gold and other metals and must be separated therefrom before it can be coined. This separation involves mixing non-Pittman Act bullion, and will not be completed for a year or more."[28] Recoinage of the silver dollars melted under the Pittman Act was completed in April 1928 at the Philadelphia Mint. During April 1928, 360,649 silver dollars were coined at the Philadelphia Mint and was the total silver dollar output at that mint for 1928 because this coinage completed the replacement requirements of the Pittman Act. The coinage of the Peace series was temporarily suspended in 1928, when the 270,232,722 dollars had been replaced using bullion purchased from the output of American mines.

Again, few of these silver dollars were initially released for circulation but were kept in the Treasury vaults to back silver certificates. This was the policy as stated by the Director of the Mint to several private citizens who had requested some silver dollars:

"Silver dollars now being coined at Philadelphia Mint are not being put into circulation. For one or two of these coins, make application to Superintendent of Philadelphia Mint."[29]

"Treasury is not paying dollars out to banks or in quantities, but only for special occasions or in small amounts."[30] Because of this, large quantities of 1921 Morgans and 1922 and 1923 Peace dollars were never released for circulation until the final run on the Treasury in the early 1960's.

Table 2-4 SILVER DOLLARS MELTED

Fiscal Year (Ending June 30)	From U.S. Treasurer and Federal Reserve Banks and Branches	From Other Sources or Purchased*	Total Melted
1964	349,169	944,209	1,293,378
1963	464,983	615,741	1,080,724
1962	174,352	158,823	333,175
1961	136,982	59,538	196,520
1960	144,706	46,879	191,585
1959	194,745	127,924	332,669
1958	189,050	1,481	190,531
1957	212,176	4,305	216,481
1956	1,696,925	3,286	1,700,211
1955	665,327	3,990	669,317
1954	498,034		498,034
1953	378,993		378,993
1952	349,674	1,968	351,642
1951	333,292	1,147	334,439
1950	273,501	1,122	274,623
1949	241,740	926	242,666
1948	361,789	451	362,240
1947	684,170	4,776	688,946
1946	96,455	617	97,072
1945	393,881	436	394,317
1944	44,658,194	682	44,658,876
1943	8,080,739	244	8,080,983
1942		562	562
1941		407	407
1940		366	366
1939		629	629
1938		607	607
1937		339	339
1936		638	638
1935		649	649
1934		504	504
1933		513	513
1932		442	442
1931		1,193	1,193
1930		1,329	1,329
1929		852	852
1928		1,394	1,394
1927		3,638	3,638
1926		2,594	2,594
1925		1,773	1,773
1924		1,918	1,918
1923		2,635	2,635
1922		2,447	2,447
1921	112,116	948	113,064
1920	10,000,000	1,164	10,001,164
1919	191,369,000	1,031	191,370,031
1918	68,752,554	1,029	68,753,583
1917		961	961
1916		1,092	1,092
1915		823	823
1914		785	785
1913		4,757	4,757
1912		1,024	1,024
1911		1,320	1,320
1910		961	961
1909		1,293	1,293
1908		1,170	1,170
1907		1,548	1,548
1906		909	909

Table 2-4 *Continued*

Fiscal Year (Ending June 30)	From U.S. Treasurer and Federal Reserve Banks and Branches	From Other Sources or Purchased*	Total Melted
1905		2,298	2,298
1904		1,304	1,304
1903		1,777	1,777
1902		1,893	1,893
1901		1,786	1,786
1900		1,341	1,341
1899		1,734	1,734
1898		1,365	1,365
1897		1,898	1,898
1896		2,034	2,034
1895		18,580	18,580
1894		15,055	15,055
1893		10,500	10,500
1892		42,881	42,881
1891		10,800	10,800
1890		11,977	11,977
1889		31,642	31,642
1888		14,055	14,055
1887		8,292	8,929
1886			None
1885		1,850	1,850
1884			None
1883		621	621
		TOTAL	333,031,656

* Includes assay coins melted, mutilated coins received over the counter, and uncurrent coins withdrawn from monetary use.

THOMAS AMENDMENT

Silver interests revived once again during the depression of the early 1930's with the success of a movement aimed at halting the deflationary trend by restoring currency values to the level at which wartime and postwar debts had been contracted. Besides reduction in the gold content of the dollar, unlimited coinage of silver was eventually approved.

Under the Thomas Amendment to the Agricultural Adjustment Act approved May 12, 1933, President Roosevelt authorized, for a period of 5 months, acceptance of silver on war debt account at a maximum price of 50 cents an ounce, the total amount accepted not to exceed a value of $200,000,000.

Silver certificates were to be issued against the silver so received, to the total value at which the silver was accepted. The law further provided that the silver so accepted should be coined into standard silver dollars and subsidiary silver coins sufficient, in the opinion of the Secretary of the Treasury to meet any demands for redemption of the silver certificates issued.

A Presidential proclamation of December 21, 1933, called upon the mints to coin silver dollars for payment of newly purchased domestic silver. Under the Thomas Amendment and the Proclamation of 1933, 7,021,528 silver dollars were minted in 1934 and 1935.

SILVER PURCHASE ACT

Reduction in gold content of the dollar brought some inflation, but not as much as had been expected. Silver inflation was therefore introduced in the form of the Silver Purchase Act of June 18, 1934, as a supplement to the incomplete gold inflation. Under the terms of this Act, the Secretary of the Treasury was directed to purchase silver at home and abroad until the market price reached the monetary value of the silver in the dollar ($1.2929 an ounce) or until the monetary value of the Treasury's silver stock reached one-third of the monetary value of its gold stock.

Section 5 of the Silver Purchase Act provided that all the silver certificates issued thereunder should be redeemable on demand at the Treasury in standard silver dollars, and it gave the Secretary of the Treasury authority to coin dollars for such redemption. Further, a proclamation of August 9, 1934, nationalized silver, and provided that the silver received would be added to the monetary stocks of the United States and coined from time to time into standard silver dollars in amounts required to carry out the provisions of the proclamations. A total of 53,029 silver dollars were minted under these two authorities in 1934 and 1935; only a token amount, since some 500 million silver dollars were then on hand at the Treasury and the Federal Reserve Banks.

PUBLIC LAW 88-36 OF 1963

The silver certificates issued under the Silver Purchase Act state that one dollar in silver is payable to the bearer on demand. Public Law 88-36, approved June 4, 1963 provides: "Silver certificates shall be exchangeable on demand at the Treasury of the United States for silver dollars or at the option of the Secretary of the Treasury, at such places as he may designate, for silver bullion at a monetary value equal to the face amount of the certificates". Thus, silver dollars were no longer needed to back the silver certificates, since silver bullion could be used to back the outstanding silver certificates which remained. Silver certificates eventually went out of circulation in the late 1960's because they were withdrawn from circulation as they were redeemed for silver bullion.

Public law 88-36 also repealed the Silver Purchase Act of 1934 and later legislation dealing with silver, and authorized the issuance of $1.00 and $2.00 Federal Reserve Notes to eliminate the need for silver as a backing for these denominations.

LEGISLATION OF AUGUST 3, 1964

Legislation passed on August 3, 1964, provided for the mintage of 45 million 90 percent silver dollars of the Peace design. These were to be minted under the authorizing Acts of February 28, 1878, and April 23, 1918. An acute coin shortage prevented their mintage at that time, and President Lyndon Johnson again ordered them minted on May 15, 1965. To expedite production of the dollars, the Peace dollar design was utilized. A total of 316,076 trial coins were struck at the Denver Mint before the Treasury Department, with White House approval, reversed the order on May 24, 1965.[31]

The minting of the 1964 silver dollars had been spurred by a few western mining state senators. This was at a time of the silver shortage and the nation's silver coins were being phased over to clad coins. The new silver dollars would have benefitted only a few western states where the silver dollar was used to any great extent. It would have drained the Treasury's stockpile of silver by 33.9 million ounces. In addition, numismatists predicted widespread speculation in the new dollars with little chance of the dollars reaching the public's hands. Besides, the Treasury officials informed the groups of western mining senators that only five million silver dollars could be minted before the end of the fiscal year for which appropriations were provided. The group of congressmen therefore requested that the minting of the silver dollars be stopped. The Treasury announced on May 25, 1965, that it had decided against minting any new silver dollars at that time because of recommendations from members of Congress. Supposedly, all the trial dollars were subsequently melted down. None were issued by the mint's cashier as finished coins. Rumors persist that a few of the 1964-D Peace dollars still exist.

It was perhaps not unexpected that this final striking of the silver dollar was again due to political pressures. As is obvious, the Morgan and Peace silver dollars were made a political football throughout their unsettled existence like no other coins in American history! Produced as the result of self-serving political and economic interests, little used by the public and stored for many years unused in vaults, they finally found a permanent place in the hands of numismatists.

COINAGE ACT OF 1965

The Coinage Act of 1965 signed into law on July 23, 1965, provided in Sec. 101 (C) that, "no standard silver dollars may be minted during the five year period which begins on the date of enactment of this Act." Thus, no silver dollars could be minted until after July 23, 1970.

As the industrial demands for silver increased during the 1960's, the Treasury's stockpile of silver decreased. The Treasury lifted its price for silver of $1.29 per ounce on July 26, 1967. The price rose to over $2.00 per ounce soon afterward as was shown in *Figure 2-1*. Beginning August 21, 1967, silver was traded as a commodity on the open market. The silver content value of the Morgan and Peace silver dollars became greater than $1.00 when the price of silver rose above $1.2929 an ounce. A May 1967 Regulation made it unlawful for a private citizen to melt U. S. coinage. This Regulation was repealed in May 1969 and undoubtedly some silver dollars have since disappeared by meltage both in the U.S. and overseas.

During the rapid rise of the price of silver in late 1979 and early 1980 to $50.00 an ounce, the bullion value of most circulating silver dollars and some common uncirculated silver dollars became greater than their numismatic value. During this six month period until the crash of the price of silver in March 1980, there were long lines of people cashing in silver dollars to bullion dealers. Many millions of circulating Morgan and Peace dollars and uncirculated common dates such as 1921-P Morgan and 1922-P and 1923-P Peace dollars were carried by the bucketfull to the smelters. The exact number by date and mint or total will never be known since records were not kept.

The silver dollar was never widely used in circulation. Thus, the passing of the silver dollar from circulation in the mid-1960's will be permanent with no chance of high silver content dollar coins being minted for general circulation as long as the price of silver is high.

SUMMARY OF EVENTS

Table 2-5 lists the various acts and proclamations that affected coinage of the Morgan and Peace silver dollars and the corresponding silver dollars mintages.[32] *Figure 2-2* shows chronologically the important events affecting silver dollars from 1878 to 1984.

Table 2-5 AUTHORITIES FOR SILVER DOLLAR COINAGE

Act February 28, 1878 (Bland-Allison Act)	378,166,793
Act July 14, 1890 (Sherman Act) to date before repeal of purchasing clause, October 31, 1893	36,087,285
Act November 1, 1893, to June 12, 1898	42,139,872
Act June 13, 1898, War Revenue Bill	108,800,188
Act March 3, 1887, and March 3, 1891 Trade dollar conversion	5,078,472
Total Morgan Dollars to 1904	**570,272,610**
Act April 23, 1918 (Pittman Act) 270,232,722 pre-1904 Morgan dollars melted	
Morgan design since February 21, 1921	86,730,000
Peace design since December 29, 1921	183,502,722
	270,232,722
Act May 12, 1933 (Sec. 43), Executive proclamation, December 21, 1933	7,021,528
Act June 18, 1934 (Sec. 7), Executive proclamation, August 9, 1934	53,029
Total Peace Dollars	**190,577,279**

Selected Bibliography

1. "Silver Dollars Never Far Away From Attention of Lawmakers Over Years." *Coin World*, April 1, 1964, p. 85. (Summarizes various Acts of Congress affecting silver dollar coinage. From *A History of the Silver Dollar* by Bureau of the Mint.)
2. "Current Developments in Silver Send Historians Back To Days of 73." *Coin World*, February 10 and 17, 1965, p. 62. (Discusses the cause of the fluctuations of the price of silver in the late 1800's. A reprint from: Federal Reserve Bank of San Francisco *Monthly Review*. June 1964.)
3. Hickson, Howard. *Mint Mark: "CC,"* Carson City Nevada: The Nevada State Museum, 1972. (Gives the historical background of the Carson City mint operations.)
4. "Government Would Seize 1964 Dollars." *Coin World*, June 20, 1973, p. 1. (Reviews the events leading up to the striking of trial 1964 Peace silver dollars.)
5. Ganz, David. "For Numismatists, Crime of '73 (Silver Demonetization) Lives On." *Numismatic News Weekly*, August 7, 1973, p. 26. (Discusses the background of the Coinage Act of 1873.)
6. U.S. Department of the Treasury, Bureau of the Mint. *Domestic and Foreign Coins Manufactured by Mints of the United States 1793-1973*, 1974. (Lists quantities of silver dollars produced under the various Acts of Congress.)
7. White, Trumbull, ed. *Silver and Gold*. By the Editor, 1895. (Presents articles by leading statesman and economists of 1895 on pros and cons of bi-metalism along with their portraits.)
8. Julian, Robert W. "History of the Morgan Dollar." *Coin World*, Sept. 5, 12, 19, Oct. 10 and Nov. 7, 14, 21, 1984. (Extensive series of articles on history of silver coinage and development of Morgan dollar designs.)

Footnotes

[1] U. S. Department of the Treasury, Office of the Director of the Mint. *Twenty-fifth Annual Report of the Director of the Mint to the Secretary of the Treasury, for the Fiscal year ended June 30, 1897*, p. 51.
[2] *The Silver Question*, Memorial to Congress, January 1878 from Committee on behalf of Banks in New York, Boston, Philadelphia and Baltimore.
[3] *Annual Report of the Director of the Mint, 1897*, p. 115.
[4] *The History of Bimetallism in the United States* by J. Lawrence Laughlin, Ph.D., 1897, New York, D. Appleton & Co.
[5] *The Silver Bill*, Report of Meeting of Officers of Bank, Savings Banks, Trusts and Insurance Companies held in New York City, January 8, 1878.
[6] *Coinage of Silver Dollar*, Speech of Hon. John P. Jones of Nevada in the U.S. Senate, February 14, 1878.
[7] Veto of the Silver Bill, Message from the President of the United States, February 28, 1878.
[8] *Annual Report of the Director of the Mint, 1878*.
[9] Ibid.
[10] Howard Hickson, *Mint Mark: "CC,"* Carson City, Nevada: The Nevada State Museum, 1972, pp. 49 and 51.
[11] *Annual Report of the Director of the Mint, 1886*.
[12] Ibid.
[13] *Annual Report of the Director of the Mint, 1887*.
[14] *Annual Report of the Director of the Mint, 1886*.
[15] U.S. Department of the Treasury, Bureau of the Mint. *The Mint Story*, p. 17.
[16] *Annual Report of the Director of the Mint, 1886*.
[17] *Annual Report of the Director of the Mint, 1897*, p. 124.
[18] Because of the low demand for silver dollars for redemption of notes issued for silver purchased. *Annual Report of the Director of the Mint, 1893*.
[19] Hickson, p. 71.
[20] Hickson, pp. 75 and 97.
[21] *Annual Report of the Director of the Mint, 1899*.
[22] Stuckey, Dwight H., "Did German Intrigue Cause Pittman Act?," *Coin World*, November 13, 1985, p. 46.
[23] Letter from Director of the Mint, Raymond T. Baker, to Congressman Albert H. Vestal, Chairman of the Commission on Coinage, Weights and Measures, House of Representatives (1921), undated.
[24] Glasgow III, J.D. and T.J. Stevens, "Deep Fabulous Silver Dollar Study Reveals Coin Aesthetic, Profitable," *Coin World*, February 26, 1964, p. 26.
[25] Stuckey, Dwight H., "Silver Dollar Melt Part of War Intrigue", *Coin World*, November 13, 1985, p.1.
[26] Ibid.
[27] Memorandum from Robert J. Grant, Director of the Mint, to Mr. William M. Geldes, Office Comptroller General, U.S., July 15, 1924.
[28] Ibid.
[29] Letter from O'Reilly, Acting Director of Mint to Mr. J.W. Bisher, August 3, 1921.
[30] Letter from Baker, Dir. of Mint to Mr. A.T. Swanson, November 1, 1921.
[31] "Government Would Seize 1964 Dollars", *Coin World*, June 20, 1973, p. 1.
[32] U.S. Department of the Treasury, Bureau of the Mint. *Domestic and Foreign Coins Manufactured by the Mints of the United States 1793 -1973*, 1974, p. 7.

Figure 2-2 IMPORTANT EVENTS AFFECTING SILVER DOLLARS

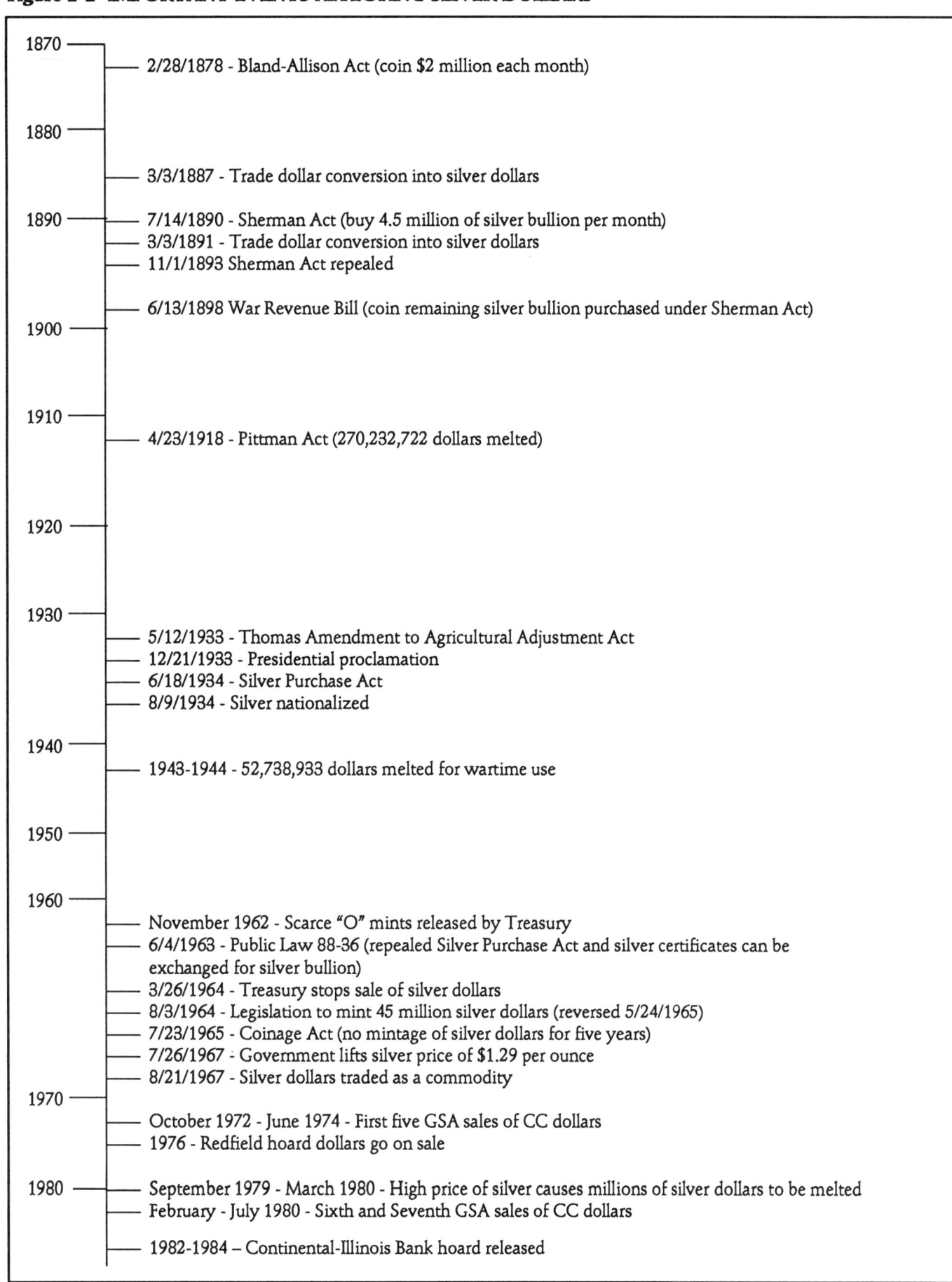

- 1870
  - 2/28/1878 - Bland-Allison Act (coin $2 million each month)
- 1880
  - 3/3/1887 - Trade dollar conversion into silver dollars
- 1890
  - 7/14/1890 - Sherman Act (buy 4.5 million of silver bullion per month)
  - 3/3/1891 - Trade dollar conversion into silver dollars
  - 11/1/1893 Sherman Act repealed
  - 6/13/1898 War Revenue Bill (coin remaining silver bullion purchased under Sherman Act)
- 1900
- 1910
  - 4/23/1918 - Pittman Act (270,232,722 dollars melted)
- 1920
- 1930
  - 5/12/1933 - Thomas Amendment to Agricultural Adjustment Act
  - 12/21/1933 - Presidential proclamation
  - 6/18/1934 - Silver Purchase Act
  - 8/9/1934 - Silver nationalized
- 1940
  - 1943-1944 - 52,738,933 dollars melted for wartime use
- 1950
- 1960
  - November 1962 - Scarce "O" mints released by Treasury
  - 6/4/1963 - Public Law 88-36 (repealed Silver Purchase Act and silver certificates can be exchanged for silver bullion)
  - 3/26/1964 - Treasury stops sale of silver dollars
  - 8/3/1964 - Legislation to mint 45 million silver dollars (reversed 5/24/1965)
  - 7/23/1965 - Coinage Act (no mintage of silver dollars for five years)
  - 7/26/1967 - Government lifts silver price of $1.29 per ounce
  - 8/21/1967 - Silver dollars traded as a commodity
- 1970
  - October 1972 - June 1974 - First five GSA sales of CC dollars
  - 1976 - Redfield hoard dollars go on sale
- 1980
  - September 1979 - March 1980 - High price of silver causes millions of silver dollars to be melted
  - February - July 1980 - Sixth and Seventh GSA sales of CC dollars
  - 1982-1984 – Continental-Illinois Bank hoard released

Chapter 3
The Minting of Silver Dollars

In order to better understand the causes and characteristics of the various types of silver dollar errors, the collector should be familiar with the major minting operations. This chapter provides a general background of the minting process used to strike the Morgan silver dollar in the late 1800's and in the 1920's for the Peace dollar. The minting operations and equipment used varied slightly from mint to mint for a given time period and of course changed through the years as more modern techniques were incorporated.

GENERAL MINTING OPERATIONS

The major minting operations for the silver dollar are illustrated in *Figure 3-1*. These operations began with the selection and weighing of the basic materials to make a "melt." "Fine" (pure) silver was generally used, mixed with copper to make it 900 parts per thousand of silver. Planchet clippings and condemned coins (coins with incorrect fineness or mechanical faults) were also frequently used. The correct portions of the basic materials for a melt were calculated by the assistant melter and refiner.

After the materials had been melted and thoroughly mixed, ingots were cast. Assay samples were taken at the beginning and end of each cast, and these were examined by the assay office to determine if the ingots were within the proper fineness tolerance: 0.898 to 0.901½. The accepted ingots were rolled to the proper thickness by passing them through the breaking down rolling operations about eight times and through the finishing rolling operations about three times. After both the breaking down and finishing rolling operations, the brittle silver strips were annealed to soften them by heating to a dull red heat and then cooling them.

Until 1901 the strips could not be rolled to a perfectly consistent thickness. A draw bench was used to achieve the final strip thickness up until that time. The silver strip was pulled through two parallel flat dies reducing the strip to its final thickness. The rough surfaces of the draw bench dies would cause parallel lines lengthwise along the silver strip. If the planchet with these lines on the surface was not fully struck up against the die surfaces, then so-called planchet striations would show on the cheek, hair and eagle's breast feathers (common on 1878's and early CC coins).

These silver strips were fed into a cutting press which punched out single rows of planchets (blank discs). The grease used in the draw bench operation was

Figure 3-1 MINTING OPERATIONS

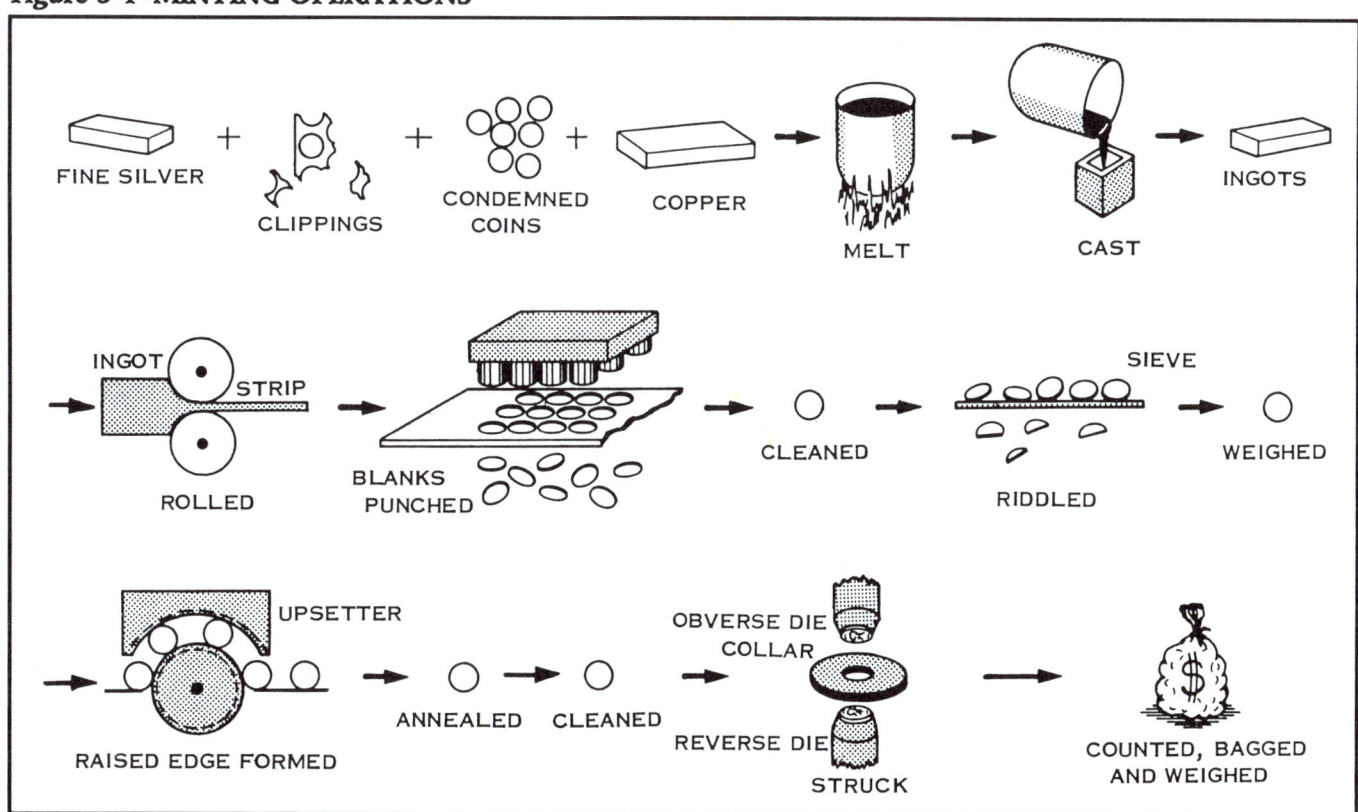

then removed from the planchets using a lye solution followed by rinsing and drying steps. Up until the early 1900's the perfect planchets were separated from the defective ones by hand at selecting tables. Later, sieves were used to separate out clippings and undersized planchets in a riddling operation. The hand sorting operation of the nineteenth century resulted in very few Morgan dollars with planchet defects.

The perfect planchets (in appearance) were then automatically weighed to determine those that were light, within tolerance (412.5 grains plus or minus 1.5 grains), and heavy. The light ones were returned to the melting pot and the heavy ones were sent to the adjusting room where the edges were filed off to bring them within the weight tolerance.

Acceptable planchets were then passed through an upsetting machine which raised the edge of the planchets by forcing them between a revolving grooved wheel and grooved stationary segment. This allowed easier handling of the planchets by the coining presses and also allowed a full coin rim when they were struck.

The upset planchets were next annealed by heating to a cherry red to soften them for easier striking in the coining presses. They were then whitened by being dipped in a weak solution of sulfuric acid to remove any tarnish. After being rinsed in boiling water they were dried and brightened in a revolving riddle with sawdust. Sometimes this sawdust clung to the planchets causing small indentations of wood in the finished coins (common on early O mints).

Dies to strike the obverse and reverse of the coins, plus collars to form the reeded edge were all manufactured at the Philadelphia mint. A plaster of Paris model was prepared from sketches of the design. After approval, the design was reduced from the plaster model to a master die using a special reducing lathe. For the Morgan dollar, the inscription lettering and stars were punched into the master die by hand. For the Peace dollar, the entire design with all lettering was reduced from the plaster model to the master die. The master die was impressed into other steel cylinders to produce working hubs which, in turn, were used to make working dies through a similar hubbing process.

Striking of the coins was performed by large coining presses at the rate of 90 coins per minute. An operator transferred the planchets into a vertical feeder tube on the press. Steel feeders carried the planchet over the collar and released it to settle on top of the lower die. The upper die came down upon the planchet resting on the lower die within the collar with a force of 150 tons. After the coin was struck, the end of the feeder fingers pushed the coin off the lower die into a box underneath the press.

The last operations were the counting, bagging and final weighing of the coins. The sensitivity of the scales used in the weighing process was sufficient that a single coin more or less than the normal 1,000 silver dollars per bag could be detected.

The minting steps for the production of Peace dollars was very similar to the Morgan dollars at the turn of the century. In general, the equipment was larger and was driven by electric motors instead of belts from a central steam-driven engine. The ingots were larger as were the rolling machines to flatten them into strips. Gang punches were used to punch out the planchets from the strips instead of a single punch. The planchets were moved about in larger bins and the press had bins to hold thousands of planchets which automatically

Mining, Circa 1870's
(Nevada Historical Society)

Ore Concentration Mill, Circa 1870's
(Frank Leslie's Illustrated Newspaper, April 20, 1878)

dropped into the feed tubes eliminating the need for individual operators at each press. Other than the addition of electric motors and automatic feeding of the planchets from a storage bin, the coining presses were the same as those used to strike the Morgan dollars.

SOURCES OF SILVER

Silver obtained by the mints for the production of silver dollars was purchased on the open market in the form of bars of silver and gold alloys. The silver used by the mints formerly came from Mexico and South America, but since the mid-1800's the supply has come from the mines of the Western United States.[1]

Silver also came from foreign coins, defaced U.S. coins issued before 1834 and U.S. coins abraded beyond one half per cent for twenty years circulation. No silver bullion was purchased for the Morgan silver dollar production after repeal of the Sherman Act on November 1, 1893 until 1920 after the Pittman Act.

The silver and gold were not found native in a pure state. They were always found in combination with each other whether in gold nuggets, silver ore, or other ores such as lead and copper. Thus, the mints had to put the bullion purchased through a parting and refining process to separate the gold from the silver and refine each of these precious metals to remove impurities.

The California nuggets contained, on an average, about 88 percent gold, the balance being chiefly silver.[2] Native silver has been found more nearly approaching purity; but even this contained enough gold to pay for parting. By far the largest domestic source of silver was the lead and copper ores of the West, in which it occurred with a small but valuable percentage of gold.

The most important silver ores are sulfides in which silver is chemically combined with sulfur and other small impurities such as arsenic or antimony. These silver ores generally occurred in veins which were mined in the early days by pick and shovel. Later, mechanized drills and loaders greatly speeded up the mining operations. Associated with the ore minerals in the veins were quartz, siderite, ankerite, or pyrite. The ore was concentrated by various milling processes. The ore was first taken through coarse crushing followed by grinding in water. Next, the particles of the finely ground ore were mixed with water and flotation reagents. The resulting frothy bubbles carried the silver compounds to the top of the vat where it was skimmed off and dried. The resulting concentrate was smelted by heating (roasting) in furnaces to cause the sulfur to escape as a gas (sulfur dioxide). Mercury was also sometimes used to

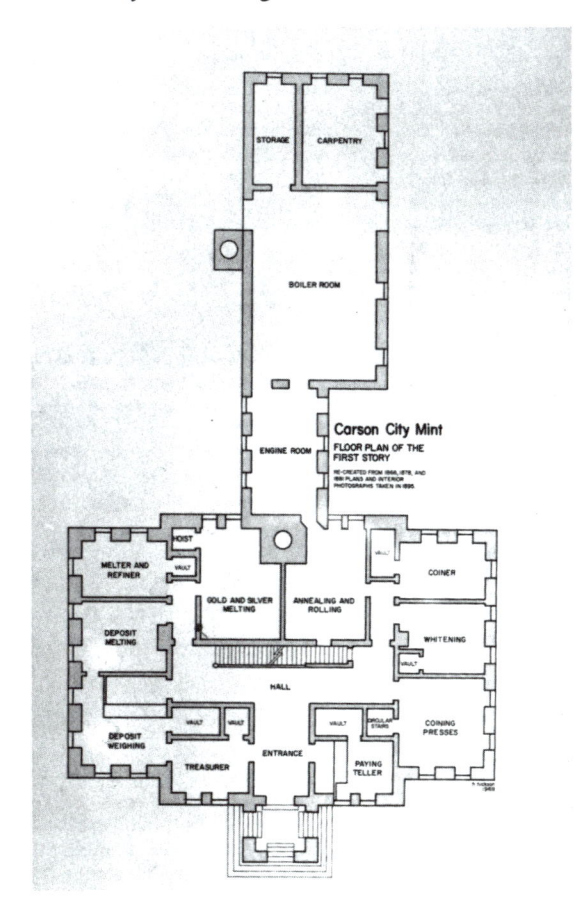

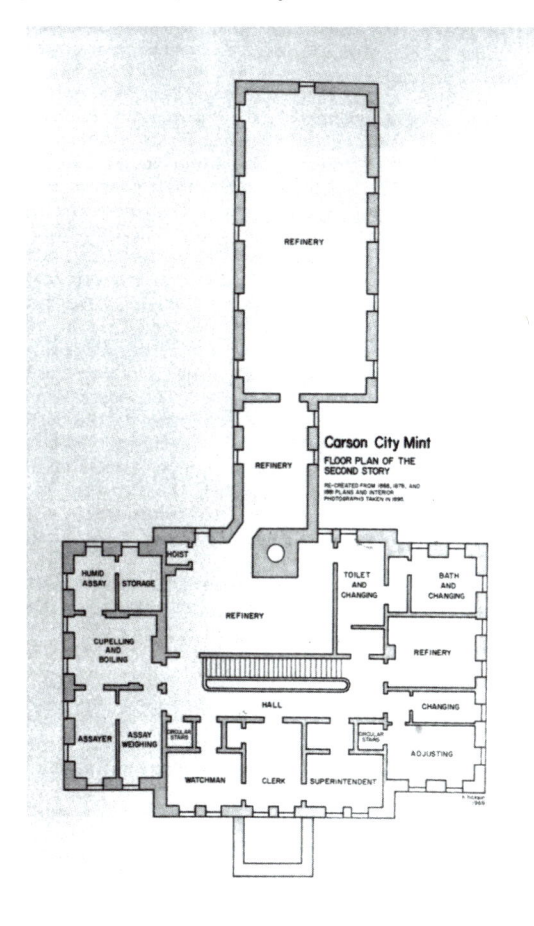

Carson City Mint Floor Plan
(Courtesy of the Nevada State Museum, Carson City, Nevada)

Table 3-1 CARSON CITY MINT STAFF – 1877

(Total 75 Employees)	
General Department	Dissolver
Superintendent-Treasurer	
Chief Clerk	**Melting and Refining Department**
Cashier	
Voucher Clerk	Melter and Refiner
Bookkeeper	Assistant Melter & Refiner
Weighing Clerk	Weigher
Computing Clerk	Foreman
Assistant Clerk	Melter
Recording Clerk	Melter's helper
Seamstress	Melter of Fine Metal
Assistant Seamstress	Day Foreman
Captain of the Watch	Night Foreman
Watchmen (7)	Refinery helpers (4)
Blacksmith	
Blacksmith's helper	**Coining Department**
Carpenter	Coiner
Engineer	Assistant Coiner
Day Firemen	Pressman
Sweep	Machinist
Conductor	Weigher
Coalman	Cutting Room Weigher
Messenger	Cutting Room Drawer
	Cutter
Assaying Department	Annealer
Assayer	Roller helper
Assistant Assayer	Whitener
Weigher	Forewoman of Adjusters
Humid Assayer	Adjusters (16)
Cupeller	

produce an amalgam (an alloy with the silver). Further heating in furnaces produced liquid silver which was cast into bars of silver bullion. These bars contained small amounts of gold plus various impurities which were separated and removed by the mint refineries.

The lead ores were also sulfides and often contained sulfides of silver. The lead ore was concentrated by crushing, grinding in water, and using a flotation process to separate the minerals from the rock. These ore concentrates were then smelted to basic bullion. Silver and gold were removed by adding zinc to the hot lead, cooling it to the melting point, and skimming off the zinc crust containing the silver and gold. This was further concentrated into doré bars which were silver carrying gold as its chief impurity. These bars went to the refinery for parting.

The copper minerals of Montana, Arizona, Utah and other western states carried silver and gold. As with lead ore, the copper ore was crushed, ground into fine particles in a water solution and separated from the rock by a flotation process. Smelting in a furnace and converter produced blister copper from 97 to 99.5 percent pure. This blister copper was then cast into cakes and electrolytically refined. The resulting sludge at the bottom of the electrolytic tank contained silver and gold plus other impurities. Processors used various methods to recover small amounts of silver, gold, and other metals from the sludge. The resulting bullion was subjected to one of the parting and refining processes at the mints.

MINT ORGANIZATION

At the Carson City Mint during the 1870's to 1890's there were four departments: General, Assaying, Melting and Refining, and Coining as shown in *Table 3-1*.[3] Other mints had a similar organization. The General Department under control of the superintendent kept the administrative records, performed general operations and maintenance, ordered supplies, and received and paid for the bullion. The superintendent doubled as the treasurer. It was the other three departments that performed the many steps in converting bullion to coins. Records were kept, receipts issued, and weighings made every time the metal changed hands in these departments to keep track of it — particularly the gold and silver.

RECEIPT OF BULLION

After the Coinage Act of 1873, depositors had to sell their silver bullion to the government at current market prices since it could no longer be deposited for coinage into standard silver dollars. In order to determine the value of a deposit, it had to be weighed and assayed by the mint.

Deposit Weighing

Upon receiving a bullion deposit, the weighing clerk weighed the bullion, prepared several preliminary records, and issued a certificate of weight to the depositor. Weights were given in the troy system in which 12 ounces equals one pound and a pound contains 5,760 grains. Large balance scales were used and the largest at the Philadelphia Mint in the 1880's had a capacity of 6,000 ounces with an accuracy to 5 grains troy.[4]

Deposit Melting

After being weighed, the bullion was transferred to the deposit melting room for melting into a homogeneous mixture and casting into a bar. Crucibles of black-lead pots were placed in the furnace empty, on a stand, which rested upon the grate that was filled with common coke dust to prevent adhesion of the pot to the stand. Coal fires were lighted and the crucibles gradually heated to prevent their cracking. The bullion was then introduced while the crucibles were in the furnace along with borax and other fluxing materials. A muffle of baked clay was then put over each pot and this was topped with a flat cover of black-lead. With this protection, the fire could entirely surround the vessel producing equally distributed heat that rendered the

Melting and Molding Bullion, Circa 1870s
(Frank Leslie's Illustrated Newspaper, April 20, 1878)

Melting Furnace, Philadelphia Mint, 1901
(U.S. Treasury Department, 1902)

Making Granulations, Circa 1870's
(Hutchings' California Magazine)

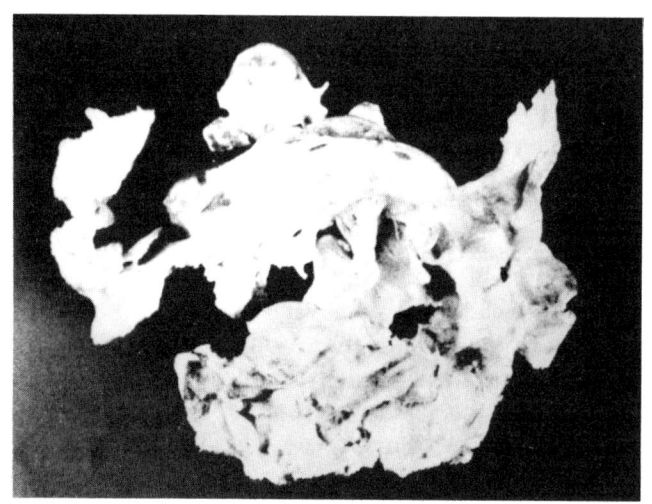

Cupel Furnaces, Philadelphia Mint, 1901
(U.S. Treasury Department, 1902)

Silver Granulation
(Courtesy of The Nevada State Museum, Carson City, Nevada)

melting uniform, producing a thorough mixture. When sufficiently fluid, the contents of a crucible was cast into a bar. The flux, appearing as a dark layer of glass, was knocked off and any foreign substances were then chipped off. The cast was then dipped into a weak solution of sulfuric acid to remove impurities and the deposit numbers stamped on it. The assayer determined, through tests of two small chips removed from opposite ends of these bars, the exact proportions of gold, silver, and other metals.

With the opening of the new mint at Philadelphia in October 1901, gas furnaces replaced the coal furnaces for the first time.[5] With coal, a fresh fire had to be made for each crucible, a time consuming process. The large quantities of ashes produced became impregnated with particles of the precious metals so they had to be treated as "sweeps". These sweeps were pulverized and valuable metals recovered through a rotary sifting machine. Gas furnaces eliminated these problems.

Assaying

If the exact proportions of gold and silver were to be determined in the bullion, then the "dry" or "furnace" assay or "cupellation" method was used. If only the exact proportion of silver was desired, then the "wet" or "humid" assay or the "volumetric" process was used.

Cupellation Assay

In the cupellation process, the sample bullion chip was rolled out and a piece weighing a half gram was cut out. This was then weighed and sufficient fine (pure) silver added to make about twice (according to one system) or three times (in an earlier quartation system) the amount of silver as gold. The bullion sample and silver were enclosed in a piece of lead foil about ten times the weight of the assay. A very little copper was added to assist the cupellation. The lead was rolled to form a hollow cone and inside were placed the assay piece, quartation silver, and copper with the lead then closed around this to form a ball.

The leaden ball was then placed into a cupel preheated in the cupel furnace and the furnace closed. The cupel was a small, shallow cup made from the ash of bones that had the quality of absorbing the oxides of the metals, but not the pure metals. The lead was rapidly changed to fluid vitreous oxide, which, exerting an oxidizing effect upon the base metals in the bullion sample, caused their absorption into the pores of the cupel. After all agitation ceased, the metal presented a bright surface indicating that all base metals had been oxidized and absorbed. It was then allowed to cool gradually and the resulting button was flattened by a hammer, heated to a red heat for annealing, and rolled into a thin strip to present a large surface for the acid used in the next step.

The addition of fine silver previous to the cupellation was to make an alloy in which the particles of gold would be so far separated from each other that it would not protect any of the silver from their dissolving by nitric acid. This strip was loosely coiled in a small roll called a cornet. The cornet was placed in a small glass flask or platinum vessel and boiled twice in nitric acid for ten minutes dissolving all the silver. The remaining cornet of fine gold was then washed, dried, annealed, and weighed to an accuracy of one thousandth of half a gram.[6] The weight of this remaining gold expressed in thousandths of a half gram gave the gold fineness of the original bullion sample. By subjecting the second bullion sample to the cupellation process without adding any silver, the base metals were removed, and the remaining metal weight included both the gold and original silver. The weight of fineness of silver was then determined by subtracting the known gold fineness.

Humid Assay

The cupellation assay for determining the proportion of silver of the bullion required a close regulation of the furnace temperature and other precautions in order to obtain a reasonably accurate measurement.[7] The humid assay provided a more accurate measurement of the proportion of silver in bullion, plate, or coin without measuring the exact proportions of the other metals. However, the approximate fineness of the silver must be known. In the humid assay, the proportion of fine silver in an alloy was determined by measuring the exact amount of a salt solution added to precipitate the silver from a nitric acid dissolving solution.

For a humid assay, when the silver alloy was melted, a small portion was dipped from the melting pot and poured into cold water. Upon hitting the water the metal solidified into granulations of uniform mixture (to prevent any copper present from separating) and large surface areas (to facilitate dissolving by acid). After drying the granulations by heat, a sample was hammered and rolled into a thin strip. Granulations and portions of the rolled strip were then weighed out so that the amount of pure silver in this sample was about one gram or slightly more. For example, silver of about 0.900 fineness would have required about 1.111 grams of total metal for the sample. This sample was then placed in a glass bottle and dissolved in 10 grams of nitric acid under gentle heat. Some of the foreign elements in the alloy, such as gold, tin, copper, antimony, the sulfide of silver, etc. are difficult to dissolve or do not dissolve at all, each showing characteristic differences that allow their detection.

The next step in the humid assay was the precipitation of the silver from the nitric acid mixture. For this, a solution of common salt, chloride of sodium, was used. Two solutions of different proportions were made; the first was known as the "normal solution" and the second as the "decimal solution." The normal solution consisted of 97.93 parts water and 2.07 parts of a saturated solution of salt in water by weight.[8] The decimal solution was only one-tenth as strong as the normal solution.

First, 100 cubic centimeters of the normal solution was added to the nitric acid mixture that had dissolved the silver granulations. This precipitated exactly 1 gram of pure silver in the form of chloride of silver which was a white flocculent substance, rendering the liquid in the bottle opaque. Agitation of the bottle for four or five minutes caused the precipitates to curdle and quickly settle to the bottom of the bottle.

Next, one cubic centimeter of the decimal solution was added which was capable of precipitating only one milligram of silver. If the normal solution was not sufficient to precipitate all of the silver, this decimal solution dose caused a white cloud to form upon the surface of the liquid. The bottle was charged with sufficient decimal solution doses until only a delicate trace of precipitate appeared on the surface proving the assay complete. If the assayer happened to overdose with the decimal solution, then decimal solutions of nitrate of silver was used to work backwards. The ratio of the normal solution plus parts of decimal solution (one-thousandth of the normal solution) to the weight of the granulations in grams gave the fineness of the silver. This assay method allowed the silver fineness to be determined to the one-fourth of a thousandth for most cases.[9]

Deposit Payment

Upon completion of the assay, the bullion bar was stamped with the degree of fineness (purity in parts per thousands) of gold or silver. The assayer reported the exact proportions of gold, silver, and other metals to the treasurer and the computing clerk calculated the standard fineness of the bar and its deposit value. From this, the cashier or paying teller paid the depositor for the bullion. The depositor was paid either fine gold or coin at his option for the full value of gold in his deposit and for any silver in the deposit, either pure silver bars or silver dollars or currency at the market value of silver. The bar was then placed into the deposit weighing vault until time for the refining process.

BULLION REFINING

Refining of the bullion was the responsibility of the melting and refining department of the mints. The refining process parted the gold and silver in the deposit bullion and prepared ingots of the proper composition for coining of silver dollars.

Parting

Three general methods were used at the mints for parting gold and silver, known as the nitric acid, sulfuric acid and electrolytic processes.[10] The nitric acid process was the oldest of the three having first been used on a large scale in the fifteenth century. The sulfuric acid process was introduced at the mints in the late 1880's and the electrolytic process at the new Philadelphia Mint when it opened in 1901. The acid parting processes depend upon the solubility of silver, copper, etc., in an acid which would not attack the gold. The mode of action and equipment required for the nitric acid and sulfuric acid processes were quite different however. The electrolytic process relied on an electric current to dissolve relatively high purity bullion in an electrolyte solution and redeposit pure metal on a conductor in this solution.

Preparing the Bullion Melt

When the bullion was ready for refining, the bars were taken from the deposit vaults and sent to the melting room. There the bullion deposits were sorted into melts of about 4,000 ounces each, preferably by mingling gold and silver deposits. If the latter was not on hand in sufficient quantity, fine silver was substituted.

For the nitric acid processes, it was originally thought that the proper proportion for parting was three parts silver to one part gold, hence the name quartation given to the process. Experience had shown, however, that a lesser proportion of silver was quite as effective and that any copper present could be considered as silver for the parting purposes. The Philadelphia Mint used two and one third parts silver to one part gold for the nitric acid process and from two to three parts of silver for each part of gold for the sulfuric acid process. In any proportions less than these, the silver is protected by the gold against dissolving by the acids.

The melt was brought to fusion in a large crucible and thoroughly mixed. The melter then dipped a cup into the molten metal and poured it out with a swirling, wavy motion about three feet above a vat of cold water. As the stream of molten metal struck the water, it broke up into leafy granules and hollow spheres. This granulation process was to create a large surface area on the metal to allow the dissolving acids to perform efficiently. These granulations were gathered from the water vat and sent to the refinery for the parting processes.

Nitric Acid Process

This process consisted of the following steps: (1) dissolving of the silver in nitric acid, (2) treatment of the gold residue, (3) precipitation of the silver as chloride, (4) reduction of the chloride by zinc to extract pure silver, and (5) washing, drying, and melting the parted metals.

The granulations were dissolved in porcelain vessels of about thirty-three gallons capacity. Twelve such vessels were placed in a large heated water vat lined with lead in the parting house. Each vessel received 190 pounds of granulations and 175 pounds of strong nitric acid. After the first strong action had subsided, steam was added to the water surrounding the vessels to gently boil the mixture for six hours. The vessel contents were thoroughly stirred with a wooden paddle every twenty minutes through raised doors on the side of the house.

After six hours most of the silver was dissolved as nitrate of silver leaving the gold as a granular sediment. Hot water was added to dilute the strong silver solution and this was siphoned off into small tubs and transferred to the precipitation tank.[11] Another 50 pounds of strong nitric acid was added to each vessel and boiled again for five or six hours. This solution and water used to wash the gold in a tub filter was also transferred to the precipitation tank. From the tub filter the gold was transferred to cast iron pots in which it received a boiling in strong sulfuric acid with a little niter added. This treatment extracted additional silver which was periodically recovered as residues from vessels partly filled with water. The gold was then washed, dried, and melted.

The silver solutions, together with the gold treatment wash waters, were transferred to a large precipitation tank with a capacity of 2,000 gallons. Salt water was added until a test showed that enough was added to convert all silver present into a curd-like chloride of silver. After stirring thoroughly, the contents were drawn off through a lead lined wooden tank with cotton cloths over a perforated bottom serving as a filter to catch the silver chloride. This was then washed with water to remove all traces of the acid.

The silver chloride was transferred to a wooden, lead-lined reducing vat. Hot water, granulated zinc and sulfuric acid to hasten the process was added to the vat. Action of the acid on the zinc and water produced hydrogen gas which combined with the chlorine of the chloride of silver to form muriatic acid and left pure powered metallic silver at the bottom of the vat. The resulting pure silver was washed with hot water and compacted into cakes of ten inches diameter and three inches thick by a hydraulic press under a pressure of eighty tons. These cakes were dried in hot air and melted without fluxes to produce bars with a fineness of 0.998 to 0.999.

Sulfuric Acid Process

The comparatively high price of nitric acid and the necessity of using either platinum or porcelain vessels for the nitric acid process led to its being superseded by the sulfuric acid parting process. Cast iron kettles could be used for the sulfuric acid process since strong sulfuric acid does not dissolve iron. Three to four hundred pounds of granulated bullion were placed into large iron kettles over a furnace and covered with three to four times its weight of sulfuric acid. Heat was applied and the boiling continued for several hours until all the silver was dissolved as silver sulfide and the gold was left as a sediment in the bottom of the dissolving kettle. The gold

Dissolving House, Filter on Truck at Left.
Nitric Acid Process, Philadelphia Mint, Circa 1890
(U.S. Treasury Dept, 1896)

Drawing Silver Nitric Acid Solution From Porcelain
Pots In Dissolving House, Circa 1870'S
(Hutchings' California Magazine)

Sulfuric Dissolving Furnaces and Precipitating House,
Carson City Mint Refinery, 1895
(Courtesy of the Nevada State Museum, Carson City, Nevada)

was boiled at least five times in fresh strong acid, then washed, dried, and melted into ingots.

The hot strongly acid silver solution was siphoned off from the dissolving kettles and placed into reducing vats lined with lead. Slabs or ingots of metallic copper lined the bottom and sides of these vats which were partly filled with cold water. A lively reaction resulted which produced a weak solution of silver sulfate. The copper plates precipitated the silver as a crystalline moss easily collectable after the process was completed in about twenty-four hours. These flaky crystals of silver were then washed, compacted into cakes by hydraulic presses, dried and melted in a black lead crucible without fluxes to give bullion 0.998 to 0.999 fine.

Electrolytic Process

This process was first used for large scale production of pure silver at lead smelting plants in the 1890's.[12] These smelting works refined the bullion in a cupel furnace until it contained not over two percent of impurities (lead, copper, bismuth, etc.). This bullion was cast into plates for the anodes and pure silver sheets were used for the cathodes. The solution was silver and copper nitrate with about one percent nitric acid to prevent deposition of copper with the silver. Electric current passing between the anode and cathode deposited pure silver on the cathode while removing metal from the anode. Undissolved metals from the anode such as gold, bismuth, lead peroxide, and other impurities were caught below the anode as the anode dissolved from the electric current.

The Philadelphia Mint began experimenting with the electrolytic refining process in 1898 for the refining of gold bullion carrying small portions of silver. A suitable process was developed and in use by the time the new mint was built in 1901.[13]

In the twentieth century, the electrolytic process eventually replaced the acid parting processes for bullion refining at the mints and assay offices. The advantage of this process was that it did not require the use of large quantities of silver and acids in the process and it was simpler and cheaper. Also, the silver bars containing small amounts of gold (doré bars) were parted at the smelter by the electrolytic process. As a result, less and less unrefined bullion reached the mints and eventually most of the silver bullion purchased by the mints had already been refined by other sources.

INGOT PREPARATION

Having a stock of nearly pure silver, the first step

Refinery-Acid Process, Philadelphia Mint, 1901
(U. S. Treasury Dept., 1902)

Refinery House, Philadelphia Mint, 1901
(U. S. Treasury Dept., 1902)

Electrolytic Refinery, Philadelphia Mint, 1901
(U.S. Treasury Dept., 1902)

toward conversion into coin was to make an alloy with copper in the correct proportion for the standard silver dollar. This proportion was 900 parts pure silver to 100 parts of pure copper. Although the correct fineness for silver was 0.900[14], for practical reasons in production, limits of about 0.898 to 0.901½ were used.[15] The following paragraphs describe the preparation of the silver ingots and the steps taken to check the fineness of the silver at the Carson City Mint during the early 1880's; similar operations were carried on at the other mints during that time period.

Melts for Ingots

The weighing clerk of the Melter and Refiner's Department weighed the fine and deposit silver and gave the weight figures to the assistant melter and refiner, who computed the amount of copper to be added for alloy. The weighing clerk weighed the copper and put it beside the silver with which it would be melted.

In making up melts of fine silver for ingots, the melter and refiner added from 1 to 1½ additional ounces of copper, after making calculations to bring the melt up to 0.900 fine to allow for copper oxidation. When clippings were used as one-half of a melt, the lower fineness of the clippings was considered equivalent to the copper added in other cases. In preparing a melt of all clippings, 6 to 10 ounces of fine silver were generally added to bring it to 0.899½. Melts were also frequently made from condemned coins and chips, which were melted two-thirds coins with one-third clippings. All melts were made as near to 0 0.899 and 0.899½ fine as possible.[16] This was because when the alloy cooled, it tended to segregate in the ingots with the center containing a higher concentration of silver than the outside. The ingots, when rolled flat, produced dollar planchets cut from the center that were slightly higher fineness than the total alloy. Thus, to produce dollar planchets of 0.900 fineness, from long experience the melts should not assay above 0.899 in silver.

When the melts were made up, they were brought to the melting room, each melt in a lot by itself. The melt was placed with a little borax, into a black lead crucible and melted at about 2,000 degrees Fahrenheit; it was then covered with charcoal and stirred. The flux was skimmed off and fresh charcoal was put on, then the melt was dipped out into ingot molds. An assay sample was taken after pouring the second ingot, and a second assay was taken after pouring the thirty-sixth ingot (38 ingots made a melt) at the Carson City Mint and when the crucible was nearly empty at the Philadelphia Mint in the early 1900's (were 70 ingots were made from one melt).[18]

The ingot mold of the 1890's produced ingots for silver dollar coinage one and five-eighths inches wide by one half inch thick and twelve and one half inches long.[19] As soon as a mold was filled it was removed by an attendant helper, and passed by him to another who opened it on an iron-covered table and threw out the red hot ingots. These were chilled in water and then immersed for a few minutes in very dilute sulfuric acid to remove the slight coating of copper oxide. The gate end of the ingot was then cut off and the parting line of the mold was removed by a file. Each ingot received the number of the melt from which it was made.

In 1901, the new Philadelphia Mint converted from the old coal furnaces for making melts to specially designed gas furnaces with several advantages as previously discussed. As technology for melting furnaces and rolling of the ingots improved, larger size melts and ingots were made. Later, the Philadelphia Mint used electrically heated and operated furnaces for smelting of the alloys which made melts of 640 pounds of silver alloy. Each melt produced two standard size ingots of nine and one half inches wide by one and one half inches thick and sixty inches long weighing 320 pounds.[20]

Casting Ingots, Circa 1880
(Visitors' Guide to The U. S. Mint, A.M. Smith)

Melting Furnace, Showing Crucible, Dipping Cup, Stirrer, Tongs, Ingot Molds And Metal Bars, 1896
(U.S. Treasury Department, 1896)

Melt Assays

The assay samples were taken from the melts rather than the ingots because of the slight variation of silver fineness within an ingot. These molten assay samples were immediately poured into copper water buckets to produce granulations. They were then removed and placed into drying pans with a tag and taken into the melter and refiner's office. The melts were identified by a number on the tag with each granulated sample. A corresponding number was stamped on the upper row of ingots in the box in which the melt was placed. Only one melt was placed in a box.

The granulations were dried in copper cups in the melting room and marked "1" and "2". They were taken into the office, examined, put into papers marked "A" and "B", numbered, and sent to the assay office on the second floor.[21] The humid assayer weighed the "A" and "B" samples under the supervision of the assayer or his assistant. The two samples were weighed consecutively and placed in numbered bottles, the numbers of which were also recorded. The weighed samples were then dissolved in nitric acid and charged with 100 cubic centimeters of normal salt solution. They were then shaken down and the "A" sample of each ingot was dosed with 1 cubic centimeter of decimal salt solution. The additional manipulations with the decimal salt solution was carried out under the personal direction of the assayer or his assistant. Records of this work were kept in the same book in which the original weights were recorded by the humid assayer.

Indication that a melt was of proper fineness for delivery was made by a copy of a certificate from the assayer in which the fineness was reported to the tenth of a thousandth. If a melt was not fit for delivery, the assayer stated on the certificate that the melt was condemned. Condemned ingots were cut in half, computations were made, and the ingots were again melted and numbered. (The top of an ingot may differ from the bottom by 0.0004 fine, with the top always higher.[22]) Ingots of the good melts were delivered, after weighing, to the Superintendent of the Mint, in the coiner's presence, by the weigh clerk of the Melter and Refiner's Department and were at once transferred to the coiner.

PREPARATION OF SILVER STRIPS

In order for the planchets to be punched out of the silver strips, the ingots first had to be rolled down to the proper thickness. Several annealing operations softened the metal which had been made brittle by the rolling operations. The last step was to pass the strips of silver through a draw bench to produce strips of uniform thickness. The following paragraphs discuss these operations for the time period 1880 to 1900.[23]

Rolling

The first act of rolling operations was called "breaking down" and formed the ingots into strips. The silver ingot was passed through the rolls about eight times. After each pass the rolls were tightened or brought together by means of wedges under the lower roll that were moved by a worm wheel. The settings were shown on a dial indicator.

After annealing, the silver strips were passed through the finishing rolls three times to bring the strip thickness just slightly more than that required for punching out planchets. Until 1901, the strips could not be rolled to a perfectly consistent thickness. These variations in the strip rolled thickness were removed by draw benches after being annealed again.

Annealing

After both the breaking down and finishing rolling operations, the brittle silver strips were annealed again by heating on an open hearth to a dull red heat. Upon cooling with a spray of water, the metal again became soft and pliable. The tarnished or oxidized surface produced by this annealing process was later removed from the silver planchets by immersing them in a weak solution of sulfuric acid.

Ingot Molds, Opened & Closed, 1896
(U.S. Treasury Dept., 1896)

Melting Room, Philadelphia Mint, 1901
(U.S. Treasury Dept., 1902)

In 1901, the new Philadelphia Mint converted from the old wood annealing furnaces to strip gas furnaces. The new strip gas furnaces produced more even annealing in half the time with much less oxidation. They were ten feet long with automatic conveyor belts that drew the strips slowly through the furnace. The strips were automatically sprayed with water to cool before entering the outside air.

Draw Benches

The strips upon leaving the finishing rolls were again annealed and cut in two for convenience in handling. About one and one-half inch of one end was pointed or flattened in special pointing rolls to permit their easy passage through the dies of the draw bench. The strips were then greased with tallow.

The draw benches were double, with each section having independent action. Each section had two dies regulated by set screws. The pointed end of the silver was passed edgewise between these two dies. When the end was between the jaws of the carriage, the operator touched a foot pedal which closed the jaws in a carriage firmly on the strip end. Upon pressing another pedal, a hook was forced down to catch an endless chain which drew the carriage away from the two dies pulling the strip through them. This reduced the strip to the correct thickness for producing silver dollar planchets. When the strip passed through the dies, the reduced tension on the jaws caused them to open, the hook disengaged from the carriage and the carriage returned back to its starting place near the dies.

Sample planchets were punched from either end and weighed to determine if the strip was of the correct thickness. If the strips were too thick they were re-drawn. If they were too thin they were returned to the melter and refiner to be again cast into ingots. The pointed ends of acceptable strips were then cut off to prevent defective planchets from being cut from them.

In 1901, the new Philadelphia Mint introduced

Drawing Benches, Circa 1880
(Illustrated History Of The U. S. Mint, George G. Evans)

Strip Annealing Furnaces, Philadelphia Mint, 1901
(U.S. Treasury Dept., 1902)

Rolling Machine, Circa 1880
(Illustrated History Of The U.S. Mint, George G. Evans)

Rolling Room
Philadelphia Mint, 1901
(U.S. Treasury Dept., 1902)

Drawing Bench, Philadelphia Mint, 1896
(U.S. Treasury Dept., 1896)

geared rolls which, when combined with new gas annealing furnaces, produced silver strips of sufficiently accurate thickness to allow planchets to be cut from them without the use of draw benches. This eliminated the labor involved in using the draw benches in addition to the application of tallow for greasing the strips for the draw benches and the cleaning with borax and soap to remove the tallow from the planchets.

PRODUCTION OF PLANCHETS

Production of planchets ready for coining from the silver strips consisted of cutting planchets from the strips, cleaning, weighing, adjusting their weight to within allowable tolerances, producing a raised edge in an upsetting machine, and a final cleaning and annealing before being struck by the coining presses.[24]

Cutting

The silver strips were fed into a cutting press which automatically advanced the silver strip between feed rolls. A steel punch, working into a matrix below, punched out the planchets in a single row at the rate of from 175 to 225 planchets per minute. The planchets fell into a box below along with any clippings.

These planchets together with the resulting perforated strips and chips were then taken to the wash or whitening room to be cleaned of grease by washing in a lye solution of soap, borax, and water. After rinsing in clean water, they were dried in a large copper pan that was heated by steam. Up until the early 1900's the perfect planchets were separated from the defective ones by hand at selecting tables. Later, sieves were used to separate out the clippings and other extraneous metal. All waste silver material was returned to the melter and refiner to be remelted.

Weighing

The "perfect" planchets (in appearance) were taken to the coining room where they were individually weighed on a Seyss automatic weighing machine. The standard or legal weight of the silver dollar was 412.5 grains with an allowed deviation of 1.5 grains above or below this weight.[25] The Seyss machine was introduced at the Philadelphia Mint in the late 1860's to automatically weigh and sort the planchets into those that exceeded the weight limit, those that fell into the weight limits, and those that were too light for coinage and were returned for the melting pot.[26] Each machine had ten scales for simultaneous weighing and sorting of the planchets. In the early 1880's these machines were arranged for making four divisions of planchets; light, light adjusted, heavy adjusted, and heavy.[27]

With the older process of using wood furnaces for annealing the silver strips and draw benches for producing the final strip thickness, the average number of silver dollar planchets obtained that were within the weight limits was only about 60 percent. In 1901, the Philadelphia Mint using the automatic gas annealing furnaces and rolling mills to produce the final silver strip thickness, was able to obtain better than 90 percent of the planchets within even stricter weight limits. These later weight limits were made stricter at one grain heavy or one grain light for practical reasons to eliminate the need to mix heavy adjusted and light adjusted coins in preparing $1,000 lots of standard dollars. These $1,000 lots had to weigh 859.375 troy ounces with a deviation of no more than two-hundredths of an ounce.

Adjusting

Those silver dollar planchets that were sorted out by the automatic weighing machine as heavy were then sent to the adjusting room. Here, mint employees individually weighed each planchet on an accurate balance scale. If a planchet was too heavy, but near the weight limit, it was filed off at the edges to bring the weight down to within the limit. Some were too heavy

Planchet Cutting Press And Drawing Bench, Circa 1870'S
(Hutchings' California Magazine)

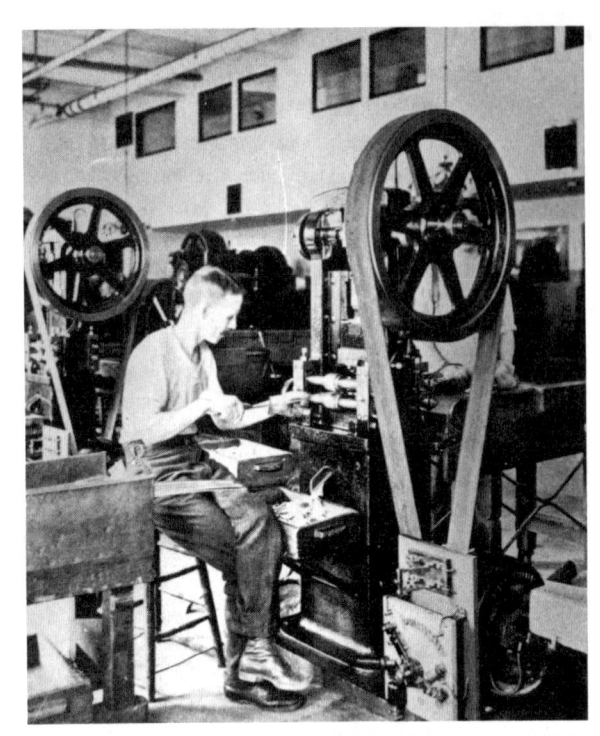

Planchet Cutting Machines, Philadelphia Mint, 1901
(U.S. Treasury Dept., 1902)

Punched Strip Emerging from Cutting Press, 1896
(U.S. Treasury Dept., 1896)

even for filing and these were set aside for later remelting.

Upsetting

All silver dollar planchets within the weight tolerances were then taken to the upsetting machines (previously referred to as milling machines in the earlier days) in the coining room. These machines raised the edge of the planchets to allow full coin rims to be produced when they were struck. The planchets were fed by hand into a vertical tube, and, one by one, were rotated and spun around in a horizontal plane in a groove on the inner revolving wheel. The other side of the planchet was pressed against a groove in a decreasing diameter outer cylinder of about a quarter segment. As the planchet rotated between the revolving wheel and fixed cylinder segment, its diameter was slightly reduced from 1$\frac{32}{64}$ inch to 1$\frac{30}{64}$ inch and its edge was raised.[28]

Earlier so-called "milling" machines could upset the edges of silver dollar planchets at the rate of about 120 per minute using two tubes for feeding.

Cleaning and Annealing

The upset planchets were then next taken to the cleaning or whitening room to be annealed and cleaned again. To facilitate the cleaning and to soften the planchets for striking by the coining press dies, they were again annealed by heating to a cherry red. They were then whitened by being dipped into a weak solution of sulfuric acid and water to remove any tarnish or oxidation caused by the heat of annealing. After a thorough rinsing in boiling water, they were dried and brightened in a revolving riddle with sawdust. They were then ready for striking by the coin presses.

DIE PREPARATION

The Philadelphia Mint produced all of the dies and collars used in the coin presses of all mints to strike the Morgan and Peace dollars. Die production was an exacting process since any imperfections would show on all the coins struck by them. The following paragraphs describe the die making steps and list the quantities of Morgan silver dollars dies produced.[29]

Master Die Preparation

There were differences in the master die preparation process for the Morgan and Peace dollars. This was summarized in a brief article in *The Numismatist*, July 1936, page 531, which contained a letter from Nellie Tayloe Ross, Director of the Mint:

The 1936 Proof Coins

Some dissatisfaction has been expressed by collectors over the new proof coins being struck without the mirror-like field and frosted design so much admired in the proofs before 1907. In reply to a request by the editor for a description of the process used on the new coins, the Director of the Mint has sent the following letter:

Your letter of June 13th, relative to proof coins, has been referred to this Bureau for attention. The Superintendent submits the following explanation in regard to the method of preparing proof coins:

Proof coins being struck at the mint at the present time are

Seyss Automatic Weighing Machine, Circa 1880's
(Illustrated History of the U.S. Mint, George C. Evans)

Milling (Upsetting) Machine, Circa 1880
(Visitors' Guide to the U.S. Mint, A. M. Smith)

Upsetting Machine, 1896
(U.S. Treasury Dept., 1896)

Adjusting Planchets, Circa 1870's
(Hutchings' California Magazine)

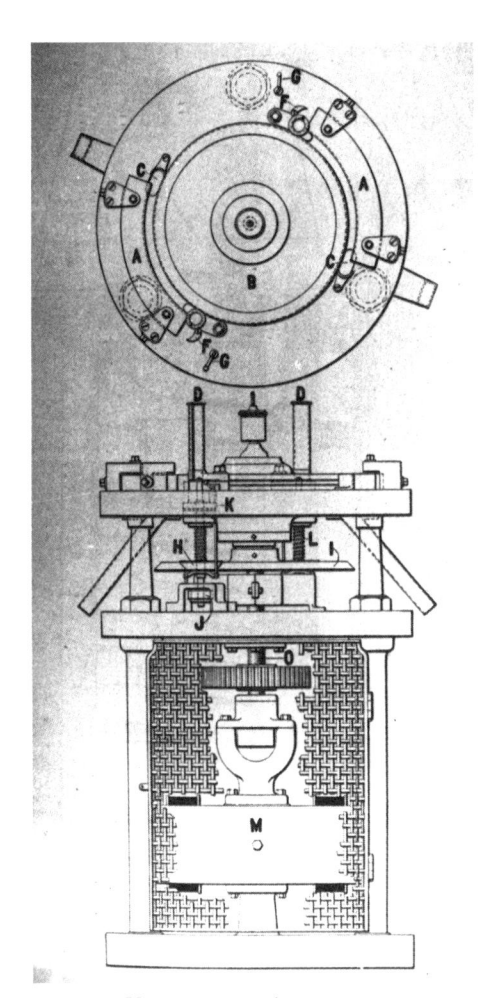

Upsetting Machine, 1901
(U.S. Treasury Dept., 1902)

Cleaning Room, Circa 1880
(Visitors' Guide to The U.S. Mint, A.M. Smith)

Revolving Riddle, 1896
(U.S. Treasury Dept., 1896)

Whitening Room, Philadelphia Mint, 1901
(U.S. Treasury Dept., 1902)

made in every detail exactly as they have been made in the past, namely, the planchets are carefully selected and each one struck individually on a hydraulic press, and handled so that one coin cannot mar another. The dies are polished to a mirror finish at frequent intervals.

The difference between the recent proofs and those struck in the past is due to the difference in the design and the method used in preparing the master dies. All the present coins are made from sculptured models without retouching with a graver in any way in order to preserve the exact quality and texture of the original sculptor's work. This gives a more or less uneven background with less sharpness in the details. In other words, they are produced the same as small medals might be struck.

The master dies for the gold coins struck previous to 1907, and the silver coins struck prior to 1916, were prepared in the older and entirely different method, being lower in relief and much greater sharpness in detail by re-engraving, even though the original design was reduced from a sculptured model. The inscriptions were usually put in the master dies by means of punches. In addition,

they were prepared with a "basined" background or field, that is, the field was polished to a perfect radius on a revolving disc, which again produced a much clearer definition between motif and field, and this gave an entirely different appearance to the coin.

With the present coins, the models were never prepared with the intention of "basining" and it could not be done without many radical alterations in the relief of the present designs.

Very truly yours,
NELLIE TAYLOE ROSS,
Director of the Mint.

The sculptured models of the designs from 1916 onwards were prepared with no intention of basining the working dies. In addition, the designs were not retouched with a graver in any way during the intermediate steps from sculptured plaster model through working hubs and working dies in order to preserve the exact quality and texture of the original sculptor's work. These changes in die preparation procedures resulted in a number of appearance differences between the Morgan and Peace dollars.

Design Preparation

Both the Morgan and Peace dollars utilized similar manufacturing steps from design to final coin. The Morgan dollar Liberty head, eagle, and wreath designs were first prepared in a wax model three to five times the size of the final coin. That the design elements were separately prepared and separate dies and hubs made is confirmed by the records of dies and hubs destroyed by the Philadelphia Mint on May 25, 1910. The October 1913 issue of *The Numismatist* included an official list of dies and hubs destroyed in 1910 and listed 15 designs for eagles, by Morgan, for dollar, half dollar and quarter dollar; 15 designs for Liberty heads, by Morgan, for dollar and subsidiary coins; and 3 wreath designs (Barber) dollar and half dollar size. It is possible that the wreath dies were made by directly engraving on a die face rather than using a wax model because of the relatively simple design.

A plaster of Paris negative cast was then made from the wax model. This cast was touched up, and from it a positive cast was made. The positive plaster of Paris cast was touched up and the design sharpened and modified until found suitable. From this a negative cast was made and again touched up and sharpened. This negative cast was dipped in hot beeswax and covered with powdered copper. It was electroplated with alternate layers of copper and nickel to a thickness of 1/16 inch and backed with lead to form a "Galvano" plate. Again, the Galvano design was touched up and sharpened.

Die Room, Philadelphia Mint, 1901
(U.S. Treasury Dept., 1902)

Cancelled CC Die
(Courtesy of the Nevada State Museum, Carson City, Nevada)

Design Reduction

The preparation of the designs in enlarged size allowed the sculptor to more easily develop the design and resulted in greater design sharpness when it was later reduced to the actual coin size. This reduction in design size was accomplished using a portrait lathe from the mid-1830's to 1867 when a Hill reducing lathe was acquired from Great Britain and used until 1907. A point traced the Galvano surface in concentric circles. This copper shell Galvano was necessary since the tracer point would have dug into and scratched the plaster of Paris models. A small graver on the other end of a lever arm from the tracer point carved out the reduced design into the end of a master hub cylinder. This process was very slow and required delicate handling by the operator.

Since the Hill reducing lathe was a rather crude machine, the engraver reduced only as much design as experience indicated would give the desired effect. Extensive engraving work was required at the time of the Morgan design development (1878) on the design hubs to complete and sharpen the Liberty head, eagle and wreath designs. Next, the design was transferred to a master die in a hubbing operation and the inscriptions or lettering and stars around the designs were added using individual letter and star punches. From the completed master die, the working hubs and working dies were made using the hubbing process.

In contrast, the Peace dollar design was not extensively touched up or sharpened at each design transfer step. The design proceeded through basically the same steps of wax model - negative cast - positive model - Galvano - master hub - master die - working hubs -

Transfer Lathe, Circa 1870's
(Illustrated History of the U.S. Mint, George G. Evans)

Medal Room, Philadelphia Mint, 1901
(U.S. Treasury Dept., 1902)

working die steps. In this case an outside sculptor, Anthony De Francisci, provided the positive plaster model whereas mint engravers developed the design and punched in the inscriptions of the Morgan design.

Use of outside sculptors to provide finished plaster models which the mint could then faithfully reduce to final coin size was made possible by the mint purchase in 1907 of a Janvier reducing machine from France. This machine was much more accurate than the old Hill portrait lathe and allowed, for the first time, a reduction of the entire design, including inscriptions, from model to master die without subsequent touch-up. This is the reason the gold coins were designed by outside sculptors starting in 1907 and that the design and the method used in preparing the master dies changed in 1907 as stated in the above letter from the Director of the Mint.

The mint did not touch up and sharpen the initial Peace dollar design during the manufacturing steps from the positive mold provided by De Francisci to the working dies. Only minor engraving work to remove tooling marks, chips and scratches was performed. The various design transfer steps would have each caused a reduction in the sharpness of the design detail. In particular, the reducing lathe transfer step would have smoothed off the sharp edges and radii because of the finite radius of the tracing point and the cutting tool. It should be noted that the mint engraver, George Morgan, did modify the Peace dollar design several times in 1922 to reduce its relief and change minor design details. But the basic design transfer steps remained the same.

Because of these differences in design transfer methods, the Morgan design is very detailed and with crisp, sharp detail because of the master die engraving work. The Morgan dollar has sharply defined lettering that is raised and generally squared off because the inscriptions were punched into the master die. There is a very sharp delineation between the Morgan dollar field and the design and lettering due to the basining process.

In contrast, the Peace dollar design of 1922 and later has a more rounded appearance with less detail because of the lack of design touch-up during the transfer process. The lettering appears shallow and rounded because it was part of the original plaster model and the sharpness was reduced primarily during the reducing lathe transfer process. In addition, the design and lettering meet the field with a radius rather than a sharp edge as in the Morgan dollar.

Another difference is the greater whiteness of the Morgan design parts compared to the Peace design. A frostiness or whiteness of the devices gives more contrast between the design and fields of the coin. To most people this has more eye appeal and is more desirable. This frostiness is due to roughness in the surface of the design. Extensive engraving work on the master die of the Morgan dollar left the design in the master die with a certain roughness. In addition, the lettering was punched into the master die which left a virgin roughness on the tops of the letters.

The design of the Peace dollar was not re-engraved or extensively touched-up on the master die to sharpen details (although the design was reduced in relief and minor changes added in 1922). The lettering was incorporated in the plaster model and did not have the surface roughness on the master die that was characteristic of the Morgan master die. Although some early strike Peace dollars do exhibit some frostiness in the Liberty head hair and on the eagle's feathers, it is nowhere near as white as on some of the early Morgan dollar devices. This is because of the additional amount of engraving work and the punching of inscription lettering and stars on the Morgan master die.

As the working dies struck coins, the surface roughness on the devices was gradually worn smooth by the constant friction of the planchet metal flow against the dies. Peace dollar dies struck more coins (upwards of 500,000 each) as opposed to Morgan dollar dies (100,000 to 200,000 coins each). Thus, the Peace dollar had a higher percentage of coins with the frostiness polished away because of this friction in striking coins than the Morgan dollars dies.

Over the years the Morgan dollar master die lost much of its frostiness due to the friction of the hubbing process in preparing working hubs. In addition, each working hub lost its frostiness in preparing the many working dies. So in the Morgan series, the frostiness of new working dies varied from year to year and within a given year due to the variances in the frostiness of a working hub during its lifetime. This explains the common occurrence of frosted coins of, say, the 1879-S and 1880-S and the relative scarcity for 1881-S and 1882-S (although these two years have some examples of deep cameos). Gradually over the years the frostiness of the Morgan series decreased so that by 1900 the deep cameos had disappeared and frosted coins are virtually unknown for 1904.

Hub Hardening

The steel used for the hubs and dies had to be of moderately fine grain and uniform texture so that, when they were polished, no spots or patches were visible even when inspected using a high power magnifying glass. A sufficiently large block of such steel was first annealed to make it quite soft. This was done by heating the steel to a bright red in an iron pot filled with carbon to exclude the air. It was then allowed to cool slowly and was faced flat and smooth in a lathe.

The design was then transferred to the face of this cylinder using the reducing machine as described previously to produce a master hub (or sometimes a die) with raised (positive) design. Because of the lengthy process and skill required to produce this first metal

Figure 3-2 DIE MAKING PROCESS

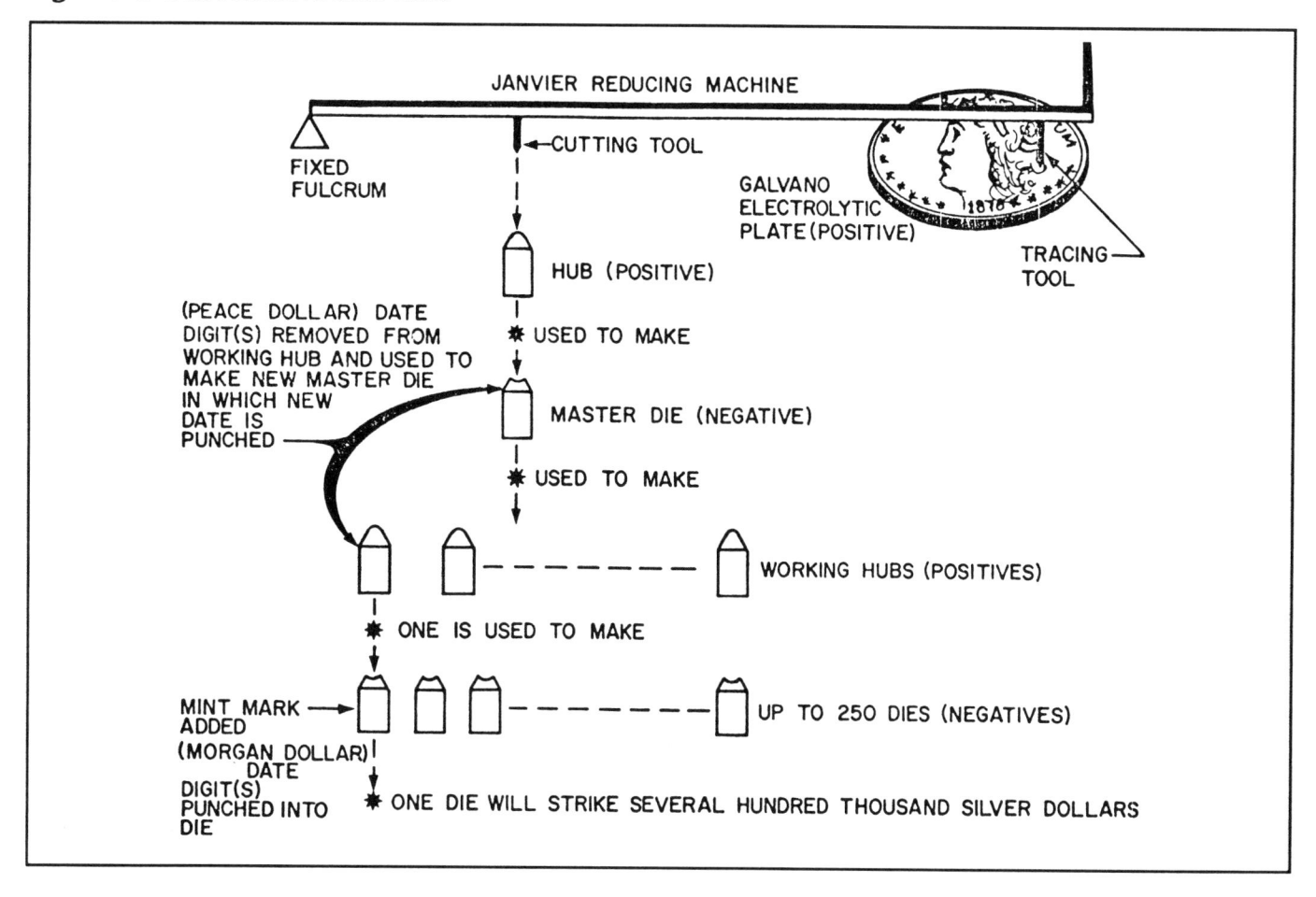

```
                    JANVIER REDUCING MACHINE
         △─────────────┬──────────────────────────●
        FIXED      ←CUTTING TOOL              GALVANO
       FULCRUM                               ELECTROLYTIC
                         ╷                   PLATE (POSITIVE)
                         ╵                              TRACING
                         ▯                                TOOL
                      HUB (POSITIVE)
  (PEACE DOLLAR) DATE
  DIGIT(S) REMOVED FROM  ✱ USED TO MAKE
  WORKING HUB AND USED TO        ╷
  MAKE NEW MASTER DIE            ╵
  IN WHICH NEW          ▯
  DATE IS               MASTER DIE (NEGATIVE)
  PUNCHED
                        ✱ USED TO MAKE
                              ╷
                              ╵
              ▯     ▯  ─ ─ ─ ─ ─ ─  ▯   WORKING HUBS (POSITIVES)

              ✱ ONE IS USED TO MAKE
  MINT MARK →  ▯  ▯  ▯  ─ ─ ─ ─ ─  ▯   UP TO 250 DIES (NEGATIVES)
  ADDED
  (MORGAN DOLLAR)
  DATE         ✱ ONE DIE WILL STRIKE SEVERAL HUNDRED THOUSAND SILVER DOLLARS
  DIGIT(S)
  PUNCHED INTO
  DIE
```

impression of the design, it was too valuable to be used to strike coins. Therefore, it served as a master hub from which other dies and hubs could be made having the exact same design.

In order to transfer the design from the master hub, it first had to be carefully hardened to withstand the operation of the transfer process without breaking or changing shape. To harden the steel hub, a mask of fixed oil, oil thickened with animal charcoal or linseed oil and lampblack was put on the hub face. It was packed in cast-iron boxes filled with animal charcoal and heated to a bright red. It was then plunged into a large tank of water and kept in rapid motion until all boiling had ceased and was left in the bath until quite cool. If there was any "piping" or "singing" it meant that there was a crack or other imperfection in the hub.

The flat field of the hub face design was then polished using an iron disc coated with successively finer emery grit compounds mixed with oil. The quenching of the hot hub in water left it too hard and brittle so they were apt to crack and break on the edges. Therefore, it had to be tempered by gently heating to a rich straw color or in some cases to a blue color with slow cooling.

Working Dies Preparation

Working dies were used to strike the coins in the coining presses. Since thousands of these working dies were used to strike the Morgan and Peace dollars, additional intermediate master die and working hubs had to be made so that the master hub did not deteriorate significantly over the years. Thus, the master hub was used to make a master die which, in turn, was used to make many working hubs that each could make up to 250 working dies. *Figure 3-2* shows this die-making process.

The process of transferring the design from one steel cylinder to another was called "hubbing". The blank steel cylinder was annealed and one end turned down into a shallow cone by a lathe to allow the metal to expand during the hubbing process without chipping or cracking. This cylinder of soft steel was placed under the plunger of a strong screw press. The hardened finished hub or die was placed on top of the soft steel cylinder and the plunger was brought down with a good sharp blow. In order to fully transfer the complete design, this hubbing procedure had to be repeated many times. Since the metal in the lower cylinder hardened with each blow, it had to be annealed between each hubbing operation. For the Peace dollar design, hydraulic presses were used for the hubbing operation with pressures of 50 to 150 tons per square inch.

For the Morgan dollar design, this hubbing was repeated from seven to ten times[30] and from three to five times for the Peace dollar design.[31] After the final hubbing operation, the cylinder was hardened and tempered as described previously for the master hub. The base of the finished working dies was ground to the proper height for the press, the excess spread metal was turned on a lathe to cylindrical shape, and it was given a neck with sloping shoulders, to fit into the collar that surrounded the coin during striking in the presses. The cylinder face was polished to polish the flat field of the die.

Any misalignment between blows into the cylinder will, of course, cause imperfections, mostly in the form of doubling part or all of the coin design. However, the hubs and dies were usually inspected carefully at each step.

In making the Morgan working dies, the date digits and the mint mark for dies to be used at branch mints were punched in by hand before the dies were polished and hardened.[32,33] Since it took several blows to punch the numerals or letters into the die, misalignment between blows frequently occurred. For Morgan dollars, this resulted in doubling of portions or all of the date digits and mint mark letters. Other common die varieties produced by punching in the date and mint mark included their off-center placement or rotated orientation.

For the Peace dollar, the last digit of the date was ground off a working hub at the end of each year and the hub was used to make a new master die.[34] The date digits were then punched into this master die. As a result, few doubled date die varieties are known for the Peace dollar.

Before the working dies were used in the coining presses, they were hardened and tempered. Each working die struck an average of 160,000 Morgan dollars An average of up to 500,000 Peace dollars were struck per working die, because of more advanced metal technology and because the design was shallower with rounded lettering.

Silver coins designed prior to 1916 were struck from basined dies. Since the 1921 Morgan dollar was similar to the design used up until 1904, it was also struck from basined dies. Thus, there are proof-like 1921 Morgans. However, there are relatively few proof-like 1921-D and 1921-S Morgans. At some point in 1921 the mints at Philadelphia, Denver and San Francisco probably discarded the basining step of the die. For the Morgan design this resulted in less than optimum striking of the coin as evidenced by many 1921-D and 1921-S with weakly struck wreath and other details. All three mints operated at full capacity in 1921 to replace the silver dollars melted in 1918 and 1919 under the Pittman Act. So production short-cuts were apparently taken to achieve the highest possible production.

Basining of the Morgan dollar working dies was performed at each mint just prior to their being placed into the presses. It consisted of putting the dies upright in a fixture which held the die face against a slightly dished disk. As this disk revolved it polished the die face making it slightly convex. The radius of this curvature varied with each mint and caused the planchet metal to flow more towards the coin rim or coin center in the extreme cases. This resulted in the weakly struck center coins with full rims typical of the New Orleans Mint or fully struck center design and rounded rims typical of the San Francisco Mint.

A polishing grit or compound was used in the basining process. The depth of mirror on the die face was a function of how fine a compound was used during the basining process and also if a final buffing of the die face was performed. Thus, the degree of mirror initially on the die varied from mint to mint over the years and at a particular mint with time because of the different workmen and practices enforced.

As the basined and polished die struck coins, the friction of the planchet metal moving against the die field would wear the die surfaces making them dull. The mirror surface would gradually be less and less reflective until it became semi-proof-like and finally dull with no reflection. Proof dies that are not chrome-plated can strike around 2,000 coins before they are discarded with too many dull spots on the field. So it is estimated that a proof-like Morgan die could have struck around 5,000 to 10,000 fully proof-like coins before it became semi-proof-like or non-reflective.

The condition of the planchet has only a secondary effect on the degree of mirror on a coin. The tremendous pressures of 150 tons used to strike the Morgan dollar caused the planchet metal to flow into the die cavities and against the die surfaces smoothing out any planchet surface imperfections. So, proof-like Morgans are the result of polished die fields and not just polished planchets.

Morgan dollar dies were also occasionally polished during their lifetime to remove severe die clash marks. If the dies accidently came together without a planchet between them, then some of the design of one die would be transferred to the other die. Polishing the dies to remove these clash marks resulted in mirror fields again on the dies. If the dies clashed early in the die's lifetime, some frosting may still have been present on the devices. Polishing the dies late in their lifetime would result in brilliant proof-likes.

In rare instances the Peace dollar dies were also polished to remove clash marks. This resulted in the few known weak proof-like Peace dollars such as the 1922-D, 1925-P, 1927-S, 1935-D, and 1935-S. Usually only part of the Peace dollar fields had any degree of reflection. Peace dollars frequently have die clash marks just as the

Philadelphia Mint Coining Room, Circa 1880
(Visitors' Guide To The U. S. Mint, A.M. Smith)

Philadelphia Mint Coining Room, 1901
(U.S. Treasury Dept., 1902)

Morgan dollars commonly show them. But the Peace dollar clash marks are not as evident or severe, perhaps due to the more rounded design next to the fields.

Collars

The collars were a thick cylinder which kept the planchet from expanding too far to the side when struck by the obverse and reverse dies in the coining presses. They also produced the edge reeding on the coins. For the Morgan dollar, the number of reeds around the edge varied from 157 to 194.[35] For the Peace dollar this was 189 for all years.

The collars were made with a slight slope from the top to the bottom so that the inside diameter was slightly larger at the top than the bottom.[36] This allowed the struck piece to be easily shoved up out of the collar by the lower die.

Morgan Dies Produced

The number of Morgan silver dollar dies produced during each fiscal year is shown in *Table 3-2*. *Table 3-3* shows the average number of pieces struck per die pair produced for each mint. The low figure of 62,441 for the Carson City Mint was probably due to an oversupply of dies, stemming from its limited coinage for most years. For the other mints, the figures are probably representative, even though some obverse dies may have been discarded at the end of the year without being used. The number of coins struck per die pair in any one year varied from about 120,000 for the San Francisco Mint to about 220,000 for the Philadelphia Mint.

COINAGE OPERATIONS

When the coin blanks or planchets were finally ready to be struck into coin they were put through the coinage operations. This consisted of striking the planchets in the coining presses to impress on them the obverse and reverse designs plus producing reeding on the coin edge by the collar; counting them into lots of 1,000 coins and placing them into canvas bags; and a final weighing.

Striking the Coins

After the planchets had been through the upsetting machines and cleaned, they were taken back to the coin pressroom. There they were poured into the bins near the front of the large coin presses. The press operator transferred the planchets to a vertical feeder tube on the press. Later presses in the twentieth century had hoppers above the vertical feeder tubes to automatically keep the feeder tube full of planchets.

The planchets worked their way down the feeder tube. As each piece reached the bottom, steel feeders carried it over between the dies and placed it in a steel collar on the top of the lower (reverse) die. The upper (obverse) die came down with a force of 150 tons upon the silver dollar planchet causing the metal to flow into the design of the dies.[37] The pressures upon the piece also caused the metal to expand sideways out into the inner rim of the collar which was reeded or fluted. The most important operation in the stamping of a piece was the adjustment of the dies in the press. This adjustment required great skill and long experience.[38]

The upper die rose first and then the lower die rose pushing the coin up out of the collar.[39] Then the end of the feeder fingers pushed the coin off the lower die into a box underneath the press.

There were various types of errors that could

Table 3-2 MORGAN SILVER DOLLAR DIES PRODUCED

(Sources: Annual Reports of Director of the Mint)

Mint

Fiscal Year (*)	Philadelphia	New Orleans	San Francisco	Carson City
1903	142	180	20	
1902	136	300	40	
1901	114	210	80	
1900	45	230	40	
1899	37	140	40	
1898	40	34	58	
1897	70	50	98	
1896	40	40	40	
1895	4	10	38	
1894	—	20	20	
1893	16	20	30	20
1892	15	30	33	30
1891	81	100	73	40
1890	95	60	80	50
1889	104	150	20	10
1888	116	136	80	—
1887	107	108	8	—
1886	161	80	—	—
1885	131	124	40	20
1884	128	60	80	20
1883	127	92	105	20
1882	92	50	80	30
1881	148	119	200	50
1880	199	80	110	25
1879	157	40	192	30
1878	92	—	192	100
TOTAL	**2,397**	**2,463**	**1,797**	**445**

(*) Since the fiscal year extends from July 1 of one year to June 30 of the next, the numbers only approximate the quantities of dies used to strike the coins in any given calendar year.

Table 3-3 AVERAGE PIECES STRUCK PER DIE PAIR PRODUCED

Morgan Silver Dollar less 1921

	Total Number of Pieces Struck	Die Pairs Produced	Average Number of Pieces Struck Per Die Pair
	260,779,667 P	1,198 P	217,679 P
	186,137,529 O	1,231 O	151,208 O
	109,493,373 S	898 S	121,930 S
	13,862,041 CC	222 CC	62,441 CC
Total	570,272,610	3,549	160,411

have occurred during the striking of the coins such as off centers, broadstrikes out of the collar, double strikes, partial collars, etc. Each one of these types of errors would produce unique error coins although there may be many coins of the same error type. Doubling of portions of the design during the striking process due to looseness in the press mechanism was common for Morgan and Peace dollars.

Descriptions of the Coin Presses

The coin presses used to strike the Morgan and Peace dollars over a fifty year time span were basically of the same design and construction. One of the significant changes came about at the turn of the century when the motive power was changed from belt driven to electric motors. By the time that the Morgan silver dollars were first struck in 1878, the design of the coin presses had reached a high degree of refinement. Their reliability and efficiency allowed them to be used for many years.[40]

One of the longest service records of a coin press was that of the number one coin press at the Carson City Mint.[41] It arrived there in 1869 as the first coin press for that mint. It was built by the firm of Morgan and Orr of Philadelphia and weighed six tons. On February 11, 1870, it struck the first coin, an 1870 Christian Gobrecht or Seated Liberty silver dollar. The press struck coins at the Carson City Mint from its opening in 1870 to the closing of the coining operations there in 1893. After the first month of striking the new Morgan dollars in 1878, the arch or frame developed a crack and had to be replaced. The 6,058 pound iron piece was cast by the Virginia and Truckee Railroad at a cost of $800. The press was transferred to the Philadelphia Mint in 1899 where it was used and later remodeled in 1930 to operate electrically. In 1945 it was transferred to the San Francisco Mint

Coining Press, Philadelphia Mint, 1901
(U.S. Treasury Dept., 1902)

Coining Press, Circa 1880
(Illustrated History of the U.S. Mint, George G. Evans)

No. 1 Press For Carson City Mint
(On Display At Nevada State Museum)

where it operated until that mint closed in 1955. It was rescued from a scrap pile fate in 1958 by becoming part of the Nevada State Museum mint exhibits at the old Carson City Mint. The press was again put back in service from 1964 to 1967 at the Denver Mint where it struck some 118,000,000 coins to help alleviate the severe coin shortage of that time. It now resides back at the Nevada State Museum.

In order to withstand the tremendous pressure of 150 tons needed to strike the silver dollars, the frame or arch of the coining presses was a massive piece of solid iron weighing about 3 tons. The arch rested on an iron support and table and it was braced at the back with two large iron girders. The larger presses had a total weight of 6 to 9 tons.

To develop the 150 tons of pressure on the dies used to strike the coins, a special lever and toggle joint mechanical leverage system was used. This relied on the very high leverage obtained when a bent toggle joint was straightened forcing the lower end down.

As shown in *Figures 3-3 and 3-4*, the top half of the toggle joint was a long lever moved up and down at the far end by an off-center crank on the flywheel shaft at the back of the press. The top of the toggle joint rotated around a pin and shoe, I and J. The lower half of the toggle joint was attached to a nearly round plate of brass, called a triangle, by a ball, F, and cup, E.

The whole toggle joint and triangle assembly was held in suspension by two long bolts, L, at the top and two stirrups between the triangle and lower toggle joint half. The triangle was attached to a locating arm whose other end was anchored by a bearing at the rear of the press. This allowed the triangle to move up and down. The impression on the coins was regulated by a wedge, K, which raised or lowered the entire toggle joint and triangle.

When the flywheel crank raised the back of the lever of the top half of the toggle joint, it caused the front of the lever to rotate around the pin and shoe at the top. This pulled the toggle joint middle back, straightening the joint and moving the triangle down. The obverse die, D, was fastened to the bottom of the triangle and moved up and down with it.

Beneath the triangle was a steel cup or "die stake" that rested on the solid foundation of the lower part of the arch. The reverse die, C, was fastened to the die stake. Over the die stake was the collar, B, or steel plate into which the planchet dropped and produced the reeding on the coin edges when it was struck.

The planchets dropped from tube, A, into steel feeder fingers, G. They were then carried between the dies and dropped into the collar when the steel feeder fingers expanded. The feeder fingers action was controlled by the friction block, H. The feeder was caused to slide back and forth over the dies by a bar following an eccentric wheel on the flywheel shaft. The feeder then slid back onto the small platform extending in front of the press and received another planchet. Next, the top arm of the toggle joint was raised causing the joint to straighten forcing the top (obverse) die onto the planchet resting on top of the lower (reverse) die.

The toggle joint was then bent raising the top die about one half inch above the collar. The die stake with the lower die was raised slightly later about one-eighth of an inch forcing the newly struck coin up out of the collar. This coin was forced off the lower die by the front of the advancing feeder fingers into a sloping channel where it slid into a box underneath the press. The presses that struck silver dollars were run at 90 revolutions per minute thus striking coins at 90 per minute.

Proof silver dollars were struck by a large screw press and, after 1901, by a 350-ton hydraulic press in the Philadelphia Mint medal department. These presses were capable of much higher striking pressures than the mechanical presses used to strike coins for circulation. Each proof coin was individually handled by the press operator. Highly polished planchets and dies were used and the planchets were each struck twice at high pressures to produce a proof coin with a perfect mirror finish on the coin field and sharply defined design detail.

Ringing

Before the coins were counted and weighed, they were given a ringing test. Every silver dollar was dropped by hand on a metal plate.[42] Defective ones with a bubble or hollow spot inside, or split, would give a dull sound and not a true ring. These defective coins were then set aside.

Counting and Weighing

Periodically, the coins were collected from the press boxes and taken to the reviewing room to be inspected and counted. The silver dollars were inspected for flaws and then counted by hand into piles of ten each. They were placed into canvas bags of $1,000 and sealed. The light and heavy planchets near the limits of the legal weight were kept separate in the coining operations. In making up drafts of 1,000 silver dollars the light, heavies, and standards were mixed so that the deviation from the legal weight of 859.375 troy ounces did not exceed two hundredths of an ounce. After preparing a bag of 1,000 silver dollars, it was weighed to check that it was within the legal limits and then placed in temporary storage in a vault.

TESTING THE COINS

The Coinage Act of 1873 had stated that each mint superintendent and assayer would select, indiscriminately, one coin from each lot of 2,000 coins. From each coin delivery by the coiner, the weigh clerk took one sample to be sent to the Director of the Mint at Washington, D.C., for special tests. One sample from each 2,000 pieces of every delivery was selected to be sent to the Philadelphia Mint for testing by the Annual Assay Commission. The selected coins were placed in envelopes, sealed, deposited in a pyx, and locked by two keys, one belonging to the superintendent and the other in the possession of the assayer.[43]

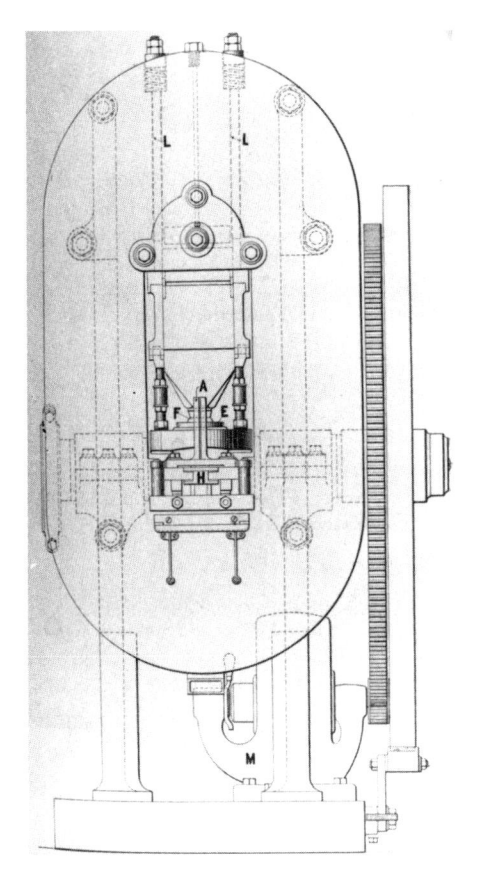

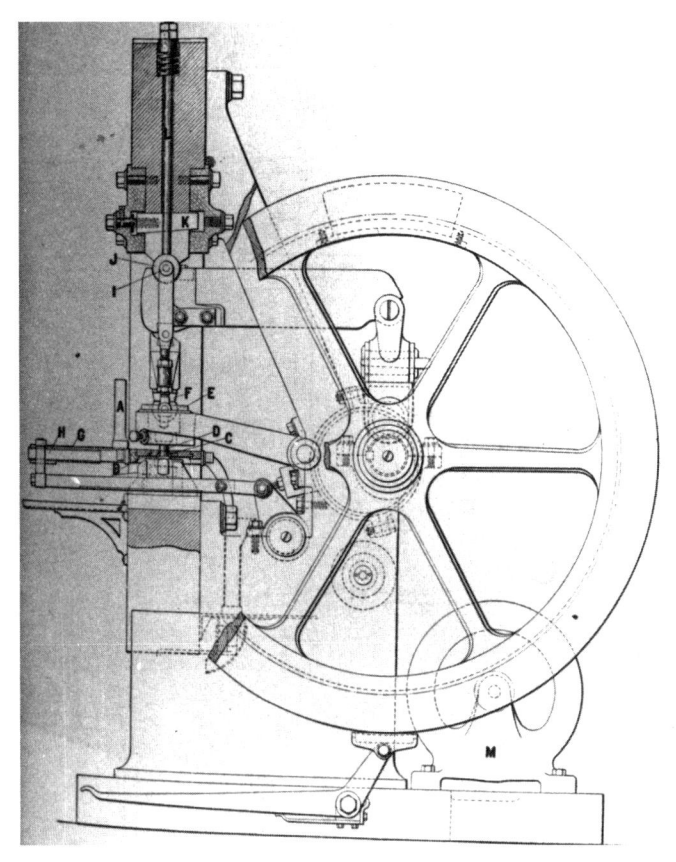

The cashier mailed the test pieces at the close of each month to the Director of the Mint where test coins from all the mints were assayed once a month. At the close of each quarter the pyx was opened, the coins were placed in wooden boxes and shipped to the Philadelphia Mint for the Annual Assay Commission. This Assay Commission met each February at the Philadelphia Mint to weigh and assay every sample coin.

Despite the checks made on the fineness of the melts, some standard silver dollars of defective fineness were coined and shipped at the Carson City Mint in 1880. This was discovered by the Annual Assay Commission in early 1881. The resulting investigation revealed that three melts (numbered 244, 245, and 246) made during 1880 had been of about 0.892 fineness[44], and that about 3,000 defective pieces had been struck from these melts.[45] The ingots from these low fineness melts were made into coins between July 23 and 31, 1880. The defective coins were delivered to the superintendent in the July 1880 deliveries numbered 10 and 11, the August 1880 delivery numbered 13, and the September 1880 deliveries numbered 14 and 15. It was the practice that when many "lights" or "heavies" occurred consecutively, part of them were held by the coiner for mixture with subsequent deliveries.[46] Thus, delivery of the defective coins was spread over a period of three months.

The deliveries containing the defective coins were located and melted as was recommended by the Director of the Mint, Horatio C. Burchard. Some 96,000 of the 1880 Carson City silver dollars were melted, since (in 1881) the 3,000 defective coins were mixed with other deliveries.[47]

Selected Bibliography

1. "Coining Money at the San Francisco Branch Mint," *Hutchings' California Magazine*, vol. 1, no. 4 (October 1856), pp. 145-153. (Describes and illustrates the minting operations and equipment used at the San Francisco Branch Mint in 1856.)
2. Smith, A.M., ed. *Visitor's Guide to U.S. Mint*. Philadelphia: By the Editor, 1885. (Describes and illustrates the Philadelphia Mint equipment and procedures in the early 1880's.)
3. Evans, George G., ed. *Illustrated History of the United States Mint*. Philadelphia: By the Editor, Various editions 1885 through 1901. (Describes and illustrates the Philadelphia Mint equipment and procedures of 1880's. An update of Smith, A.M., ed. *Illustrated History of the U.S. Mint*. Philadelphia: By the Editor, 1881.)
4. Hickson, Howard. *Mint Mark: "CC"*. Carson City, Nevada: The Nevada State Museum, 1972. (Describes and illustrates the minting operations of the Carson City Mint from 1860's to 1890's.)

Adjusting Room, Philadelphia Mint, 1901
(U. S. Treasury Dept., 1902)

5. U.S. Department of the Treasury. Office of the Director of the Mint. *Annual Report of the Director of the Mint to the Secretary of the Treasury for the Fiscal Year Ended June 30, 1896.* (Describes and illustrates the minting operations of the Philadelphia Mint in 1896.)
6. U.S. Department of the Treasury. Office of the Director of the Mint. *Annual Report of the Director of the Mint to the Secretary of the Treasury for the Fiscal Year Ended June 30, 1902.* (Describes and illustrates some equipment used in the then new Philadelphia Mint.)
7. Young, James Rankin. *The United States Mint at Philadelphia.* Philadelphia: 1903. (Describes and illustrates new Philadelphia Mint operation based on 1902 *Director of the Mint Report.*)
8. Thompson, Walter. *How United States Coins Are Made.* Chicago: Numismatic Scrapbook Magazine, 1962 (Describes and illustrates the minting operations and equipment used from 1900's to 1950's at the Philadelphia Mint.)

Footnotes

[1] George G. Evans, ed., *Illustrated History of the United States Mint.* Philadelphia: By the Editor, 1890 ed., p. 22.
[2] U.S. Department of the Treasury, Office of the Director of the Mint, *Annual Report of the Director of the Mint of the Secretary of the Treasury for the Fiscal Year Ended June 30, 1895,* p. 77.
[3] Howard Hickson, *Mint Mark: "CC",* Carson City, Nevada: The Nevada State Museum, 1972, p. 103.
[4] A. M. Smith, ed., *Illustrated History of The U.S. Mint,* Philadelphia: By the Editor, 1881, p. 15.
[5] *Annual Report of the Director of the Mint, 1902,* p. 120. Special gas furnaces for the mint were developed by the American Gas Furnace Co.
[6] *Annual Report of the Director of the Mint, 1896,* p. 144. The scale used for assays were sensitive to the fiftieth of a milligram.
[7] Ibid., p. 147. The cupellation assay was normally used to furnish an approximate silver fineness as a basis for more accurate humid assay.
[8] Ibid.
[9] Ibid., p. 149. It could be carried to a tenth of a thousand for higher grade silver fineness, if necessary.
[10] Material on the parting process is primarily from:
    a. *Annual Report of the Director of the Mint, 1895,* pp. 72-78.
    b. *Annual Report of the Director of the Mint, 1902,* pp. 121-122.
[11] A gold siphon worth $2,000 had to be used. See "Coining Money at the San Francisco Branch Mint," *Hutchings' California Magazine,* vol. 1, no. 4. October 1856, p. 147.
[12] It yielded silver of exceptional purity (0.9995).
[13] The Philadelphia Mint purchased the right to use the Wohlwill process developed in Germany.
[14] Coinage Act of 1873 allowed a deviation of three thousandths.
[15] Letter of A. Mason, Melter and Refiner of U.S. Assay office, to H. Burchard, Director of the Mint, May 5, 1881, Record Group 104, National Archives.
[16] Ibid.
[17] Ibid.
[18] *Annual Report of The Director of the Mint, 1896,* pp. 139 and 141.
[19] Ibid.
[20] Walter Thompson, *How United States Coins are Made,* Chicago: Numismatic Scrapbook Magazine, 1962, pp. 24 and 26.
[21] Letter of A. Mason. These assay procedures were for the Carson City Mint in 1880. Other mints had similar procedures.
[22] Ibid.
[23] Primary sources for data on preparation of silver strips are:
    a. *Annual Report of the Director of the Mint, 1896,* pp.152-154.
    b. *Annual Report of the Director of the Mint, 1902,* pp. 123-124.
    c. Evans, pp. 28-30.
[24] Data for the production of planchets is primarily from:
    a. *Annual Report of The Director of The Mint, 1896,* pp. 154-157.
    b. *Annual Report of The Director of The Mint, 1902,* pp. 123-124, 127, 131-135.
    c. Evans, pp. 30-37.
[25] As provided for by Section 37 of the Coinage Act of February 12, 1873, as re-enacted in section 3536 of the Revised Statutes. This allowable weight deviation remained effective until amended by the Act of June 14, 1947 which provided for an allowable deviation of six grains.
[26] Smith, *Illustrated History,* pp. 28 and 49.
[27] Ibid.
[28] Letter of O.C. Bosbyshell, Coiner, Philadelphia Mint, to R. A. Will, Supt. Operative Dept., Royal Mint, London, on November 23, 1877, Record Group 104, National Archives.
[29] Sources for data on die preparation are:
    a. Thompson, pp. 15-18.
    b. *Annual Report of the Director of The Mint, 1896,* p. 151.
    c. A. M. Smith ed., *Visitor's Guide to the U. S. Mint,* Philadelphia: By the Editor, 1885, p. 26.
[30] Letter from George T. Morgan, Special Engraver, Philadelphia Mint, to Dr. H.R. Linderman, Director of the Mint, on February 22, 1878, Record Group 104, National Archives.
[31] Thompson, p.18.
[32] "Making Money," *Harper's New Monthly Magazine,* New York: December 1861, p.25.
[33] Don Taxay, *The U.S. Mint and Coinage,* New York: Arco Publishing Co., 1966. p. 152.
[34] Taxay, p. 305.
[35] See Chapter Seven section on "Reeding Variations on Collars".
[36] Note of O.C. Bosbyshell, Coiner, Philadelphia Mint, to J. Pollock, Superintendent Philadelphia Mint, on February 7, 1878, Record Group 104, National Archives.
[37] *Annual Report of the Director of the Mint, 1896,* p. 156.
[38] Ibid., p. 155.
[39] Smith, *Visitor's Guide,* p. 21.
[40] Principal sources for this section are:
    a. *Annual Report of the Director of the Mint, 1902,* pp. 135 and 136.
    b. Evans. pp. 37-39.
    c. Smith, *Illustrated History,* pp. 24-26.
    d. Smith, *Visitor's Guide,* pp. 18-21.
[41] As related by Hickson, p. 97.
[42] James Rankin Young, *The Unites States Mint at Philadelphia,* Philadelphia: 1903. p. 52.
[43] Hickson, p. 46.
[44] Coinage Act of 1873 specified an allowed minimum fineness of 0.897.
[45] Letter of A. Mason.
[46] Ibid.
[47] *Annual Report of the Director of The Mint, 1881,* p. 10.

Chapter 4
Past Literature on Dollars

Since the first serious article on Morgan dollars by Newcomb in 1913 through the mid-1970's the emphasis was on dollar varieties in published material. Little was written that contained well researched articles from the original article in 1913 until the 1950's when a couple of articles surveyed Morgan varieties. The 1960's saw additional articles and a couple of early books, again slanted towards varieties. This reflected the limited interest of collectors and investors in these series.

Collectors and investor interest picked up in the late 1960's when most of the dollars had been dispersed by the Government and they were not so common anymore. From the mid-1970's the interest and prices of these series has skyrocketed with a corresponding flood of new books. Since 1976 no less than 25 books and their various editions have hit the market on Morgan and Peace dollars. This is by far more books than on any other U.S. series and reflects their great current popularity. The vast majority of them are from the investment viewpoint. Needless to say, some treatments are rather shallow while others are well documented and researched. The dollar collectors and investors of today are indeed fortunate to have such a wealth of material available from which to pick and choose.

The following is a brief review of the major articles and books on the silver dollars.

NEWCOMB

In the February 1913 issue of *The Numismatist*, an article by Howard R. Newcomb on "Standard Dollar Die Varieties of 1878-79-80" was the first published discussion of the major die varieties of those three years. Nineteen varieties were listed, together with illustrations of each. Six of the varieties were for the year 1878: the 1878-P 8 TF, the PAF and SAF 1878-P 7 TF, the 1878-CC, the 1878-S 7 TF PAF, and the 1878-S 7 TF PAF with the arm of the letter R in TRUST broken away.

McILVAINE

The American Numismatic Society published a pamphlet by Arthur D. McIlvaine in 1941 entitled *The Silver Dollars of the United States of America*. It treated dollar types and designs for all U. S. dollars from Draped Bust through the Peace dollar. The treatment of the Morgan and Peace dollars was brief with a mention of the 7 and 8 tailfeather 1878 and two types of 1921 Peace dollar designs.

CARMICHAEL

In the August 1951 issue of *The Numismatic Scrapbook Magazine*, Melvin O. Carmichael wrote an article entitled "Morgan Dollar Die Varieties." (In it he actually listed varieties for both the Morgan and Peace Dollars.)

Carmichael discussed some 60 varieties, many of them based on mint mark position. None of the varieties were illustrated. Among the eleven 1878 varieties listed, five appeared on Newcomb's list. These included the 1878-P 8 TF with re-engraved obverse stars, 1878-P 7 TF PAF with broken R, 1878-P 7/8 TF (The 1878-P 7/8 TF variety was first reported in the January 1948 issue of *The Numismatic Scrapbook Magazine*.), and two varieties of the 1878-CC mint mark position.

WALLACE

In the February 20 and April 20, 1959, issues of *The Numismatic Scrapbook Magazine*, Charles Wallace listed "Varieties of Morgan Silver Dollar." Again, most varieties (some 153 of them) were based on mint mark placement. Twenty-one varieties for the year 1878 were mentioned. The 1878-P 7/8 TF varieties with both the five tail feather and the eight tail feather ends showing were listed, and a die break in the word DOLLAR to form an open D was listed for the first time.

The April 1, 1970, issue of *Coin World* contained a later silver dollar variety listing by Wallace in the "Collectors' Clearinghouse" column. Some 339 varieties were given for the Morgan silver dollar. A short description was provided on each variety, but none were illustrated. Forty-eight varieties for the 1878 were mentioned. Included were one to eight tail feathers showing for the 1878-P 7/8 TF. Many examples were given on the later years for mint mark position, light strikes, die breaks, and filled die letters.

HURLBUT

A sixteen page full size pamphlet was prepared by Clarence J. Hurlbut in 1961 entitled *Relative Rarity of United States Silver Dollars*. After a short discussion of the authorities for coinage of U. S. silver dollars, each mint that struck the silver dollars was briefly described by giving the dates of operation and the mint mark used. There followed a series of tables giving the mintage of silver dollars from 1794 to 1935 for all series including the early Liberty Head, Liberty Seated, Trade, Morgan and Peace types. Relative rarity tables were given based on the entire series and also based on just the Morgan and Peace dollars. Although varieties were not treated, it was the first publication devoted exclusively to U.S. silver dollars and it provided some data on the background and legislative history.

KLAES

In 1963, Francis X. Klaes published a pamphlet on *Die Varieties of Morgan Silver Dollars*. Large, clear photographs were used to identify 55 varieties which included the more important varieties of mint mark size, clashed dies, design types and doubled design. Although there was very little discussion of the varieties, Klaes' pamphlet was a milestone because of the many new varieties, all expertly illustrated. Klaes listed 13 1878 varieties. Three doubled obverses with the 1878-P 8 TF reverses and two doubled 1878-P 8 TF reverses were illustrated. One doubled obverse was shown for the 1878-P 7/8 TF, two for the 1878-P 7 PAF, and one for the 1878-S. The other 1878 varieties had been mentioned by previous authors.

DROST

A short list of mint mark sizes and combinations for the Morgan series was given by Fred Drost in the "Collectors' Clearinghouse" section of the June 28, 1963, issue of *Coin World*. No new 1878 varieties were listed, but the O and S mint marks were classified by type for the first time.

SHAFER

The November 1964 issue of *The Whitman Numismatic Journal* included a lengthy article by Neil Shafer on "Morgan Silver Dollars of 1878-1921." This excellent article concentrated on the 1878-P varieties, although it also mentioned those of the 1878-S, 1878-CC, 1879-S, and 1880-CC dollars. It traced for the first time the evolution of the Morgan silver dollar design through the difficult period when it was being perfected. Shafer's discussion for the reason for the design changes was backed up by correspondence of the period obtained from the National Archives in Washington, D.C., and each design change was also illustrated to aid the reader in identifying the coins. This article was another major milestone in the study of dollar die varieties and, especially, in attempts to unravel the complexities of the 1878 series varieties.

Four obverse die varieties and five reverse die varieties for 1878 were discussed in Shafer's article. No new reverse varieties were included, except for a minor variety of the 1878-P 7 TF SAF. An attempt was also made to explain how the 1878-P 7/8 TF variety was caused (more will be said later about this, as well as about some new minor reverses varieties).

Over 50 years after the first discussion of reverse varieties by Newcomb, the fact that there were design changes in the obverse was finally discovered. This was another major contribution by Shafer. He pointed out that four different obverse designs had been used (there will be later comments on some of the obverse varieties) and that various design types of the obverse and reverse dies had occurred in a number of combinations. Eleven of these combinations were listed for the 1878-P.

MALLIS

Late in 1964, George Mallis printed a limited edition pamphlet entitled, *List of Die Varieties of Morgan Head Silver Dollars*. It listed and briefly described the obverse and reverse die varieties for the entire Morgan series including those discussed by Klaes' and the earlier editions of Spadone's books. Forty-seven of the 1878 variety and 274 of later varieties were briefly described and assigned designations according to the reverse design type. The obverse design types were not covered, leaving Shafer's article as the best treatment of the 1878 design types at that time. Mallis made a major contribution by listing the obverse and reverse die variety combinations of the series for the first time.

Early in 1966, Mallis made a limited printing of the second edition of his book. The list was greatly expanded with more detailed descriptions of each variety given. Obverse and reverse types were included in this edition based upon Shafer's article. A rarity table of the varieties was added based upon the sampling of 34,000 silver dollars. Sixty-five 1878 varieties and 458 later varieties were included.

MORANO

The February 1965 issue of *The Numismatic Scrapbook Magazine* included an article by Anthony J. and Dazelle Morano entitled "The 1878 Silver Dollar Story". Most of the article dealt with the 7/8 TF varieties concluding that they were the result of individually re-engraving dies. The basic reverse design types were illustrated and the minor design variety of the 7 TF PAF type, the extended center arrow feather, was pointed out for the first time.

VAN ALLEN

The April 1965 issue of *The Numismatic Scrapbook Magazine* included an article by Leroy C. Van Allen entitled, "1878 7/8 Tailfeather Silver Dollar: How and Why." The dual hub theory of the cause of the 7/8 tail feather 1878 reverse was first put forth through quotations of mint employee letters of the time. Twelve different 7/8 TF reverses were pictured and the dual hub 1878 obverse was pointed out for the first time.

Late in 1965, Van Allen authored a book entitled, *Morgan and Peace Dollar Varieties*. Its major contribution was the listing and illustration of additional 1878 die varieties and their combinations to bring the total number to 85 of different 1878-P coins. The evolution of the Morgan silver dollar design was traced by quoting correspondence among the Treasury officials. New minor obverse and reverse design types, together with a new major obverse type of reimpressed design were introduced. In addition, a discussion was included on how the 7/8 TF reverse originated.

New varieties of the remaining Morgan series and of the Peace series were listed and illustrated. The legislation, which evolved over the years affecting silver dollar production, was reviewed and the minting operations were summarized. In addition, the past literature on silver dollar varieties was described, grading standards were given, cleaning methods were outlined, and photographic techniques were also described.

The February 1972 issue of *Coins* magazine included an article by Van Allen entitled "Old Fashioned Treasure Hunt" which explored the die variety possibilities in the Treasury's CC dollar hoard. This was followed up in October 1973 issue of *Coins* by an article entitled "Pictorial Survey of GSA Silver Dollars" which showed the CC die varieties held by GSA. The June 1974 issue of *The Numismatic Scrapbook Magazine* included an article by Van Allen entitled "Survey of GSA silver Dollars" which presented the statistical survey of the die varieties held by the GSA.

The April 14, 1976 issue of "Collectors' Clearinghouse" in *Coin World* featured an article by Van Allen entitled "Date Positioning Reason for Morgan Dashes" that treated dashes under the date of Morgan dollars. Van Allen discussed and illustrated how Morgan overdates were made in an article "Van Allen Presents Theory on Overdates," in the October 27 and November 3, 1976, issues of the "Collectors' Clearinghouse" of *Coin World*. The October 17 and October 24, 1979 issues of *Coin World* "Collectors' Clearinghouse" featured an article by Van Allen entitled "Dollar Specialist Details Dot Varieties" which discussed dots found on 1921 Morgan dollars. In January 1979 Van Allen compiled a book entitled *Dollar Varieties and Errors Scrapbook* of VAM Club reports and other articles on dollar varieties and errors that appeared in the "Numismatic Error Collectors of America," monthly publication, *The Errorscope*.

CLARK

Ted F. Clark wrote a series of seven articles on the 1880 overdates in the "Collectors' Clearinghouse" column of the November and December 1970, issues of *Coin World*. Comprehensive descriptions and multiple photographs were given for each overdate variety. Five overdates were given for the 1880-CC, two for the 1880-S, five for the 1880-O, and four for the 1880-P. Many of these overdates were described for the first time in this excellent series of articles.

In a follow-up series of twelve articles in the "Collectors' Clearinghouse" column of the January to May 1973, issues of *Coin World,* Clark treated eighteen questions on the Morgan overdates and related deceptive selling practices. This was another interesting and well written series of articles that updated the knowledge of Morgan 1880 overdates by correcting some errors in the VAM book and presenting several new die varieties. Several articles treated the then newly discovered 1887/6 overdates.

MARGOLIS

In 1973 Arnold Margolis authored a pamphlet entitled, *Mint Errors on Carson City Silver Dollars*. This was a collection of several articles by Margolis in the 1973 issues *Error Trends Coin Magazine* on this subject plus historical material on the Carson City dollar sales by the GSA. Various types of error coins were discussed and illustrated that the author had examined from the GSA Carson City dollar hoard.

SPADONE

Included in the various editions of Frank G. Spadone's book, *Major Variety and Oddity Guide to United States Coins*, were Morgan and Peace silver dollar varieties.

The eighth edition in 1981 listed 136 Morgan varieties, of which 11 were of the 1878-P varieties. Thirty-three Peace varieties were also listed. There were ten pictures of Morgan varieties and one for the Peace varieties. The listings were essentially the same as the previous three editions.

BOWERS

In a series of articles in the "Numismatic Depth Study" column of October 30, 1974, to 15 January 1975 issues of *Coin World*, Q. David Bowers traced the history of the Morgan and Peace dollars. These articles were very well written and covered in narrative form the development of the design, legislation affecting their coinage, production difficulties, proof coin production and patterns for both these series.

DeLOREY

Tom DeLorey wrote a series of five articles in the "Collectors' Clearinghouse" column in the January to May 1975 issues of *Coin World* about some possible 1882/1881P and O overdates. Detailed descriptions of various obverse and reverse die states were given along with photographs of each die variety. Unfortunately, the possible remains of a 1 under a 2 were not as clear as some of the 1880/1879 or the 1887/1886 overdates and are not generally accepted. In the June 9, 1976, issue of "Collectors' Clearinghouse" in *Coin World*, DeLorey wrote an article entitled "New Overdate Theory Given for Morgan Dollars," in which he illustrated overdate remains on top of date digits. A series of articles by DeLorey in the June 14, 21, 28, July 26, August 2 and 9, 1978, in "Collectors' Clearinghouse" of *Coin World* treated the development of the Morgan dollar obverse and reverse designs and dies.

OSBON

A book by Jim Osbon entitled, *Silver Dollar Encyclopedia,* was published early in 1976. It was oriented primarily for the investor with emphasis on the Morgan and Peace dollars. A fifteen year price history and a three year price forecast plus the striking characteristics and condition availability were provided for each year and mint. In 1979 a second edition of Osbon's book was released. The price forecasts were updated and chapters on the GSA CC sales and Redfield hoard were added. It still remained a book oriented primarily for the investor.

MILLER

A book by Wayne Miller entitled, *An Analysis of Morgan and Peace Dollars*, was published in mid-1976. The emphasis was on a date by date analysis of the striking characteristics and condition availability. Rarity ratings of mint state and proof-like specimens were given. A separate section on grading included grading factors and illustrations for all conditions. Other topics treated included the supply and distribution of dollars, counterfeit detection, and major die varieties.

Late in 1982 Miller released the second edition of his book entitled *The Morgan and Peace Dollar Textbook*. It updated the condition availability by date and mint and added discussions on silver dollar hoards, market cycles, coin storage and Proofs. The first edition has become one of the standard books for silver dollar collectors and investors and the second edition continues that tradition.

FOX

In the summer of 1977 Les and Sue Fox published a book entitled, *Silver Dollar Fortune Telling*. Written in an easy going and readable style, the book was for investors and silver dollar collectors in general. Varieties were not treated except for the universally listed 1878 seven over eight tailfeather. Brief design development and legislative histories were provided along with an analysis of the Redfield hoard. Estimates were given on the total number of proof-like dollars in existence. Five lessons on grading were given accompanied by photographs of higher grade examples. The thrust of the book was contained in a date by date analysis of the estimated surviving specimens in various uncirculated categories, price projection of choice BU specimens in 1987, and brief descriptions, the general background, availability, distinguishing characteristics, location of surviving specimens and investment potential.

A second edition of this book was released in 1978, a third edition in 1979, and a fourth edition in 1981 under the title *Fight Inflation with Silver Dollars*. Additional chapters in these later editions included interviews with various dealers, CC dollars and an excellent examination of proof-like Morgans by Randy Campbell. Price projections were continually updated as the silver dollar market exploded during this time period. The book remained primarily oriented towards the investor.

LEMKE

The Morgan Dollar Centennial issue of *Numismatic News* on March 11, 1978, included an article by Robert Lemke entitled "Morgan Dollar Centennial Prompts New Striking Study". In it Lemke presents a contemporary newspaper account of the first striking of the Morgan dollar at the Philadelphia Mint which established that date as March 11, 1878.

JULIAN

A series of articles by Robert Julian in the August, October and December 1979 issues of *Coins* magazine traced the evolution of the Morgan dollar design. These excellent articles described in a very readable style the design changes of Morgan's dollar patterns and regular coinage. The personalities involved were identified and dates for the major design evolution changes were specified.

Robert Julian wrote a series of articles in the September 5, 12, 19, October 10, November 7, 14, and 21, 1984 *Coin World*, entitled "History of the Morgan Dollar." He again traced in detail the evolution of the design including the early fifty-cent patterns with Morgan's Liberty head and the complications in the refinement of the silver dollar design. These articles were an update and expansion of the previous articles in *Coins* magazine. Highly recommended reading.

LUDWIG

Richard Ludwig released a book entitled *Silver Dollars and Profit's* in 1979. A date by date analysis of Morgan and Peace dollars included price history charts, risk factor and investment. Other chapters covered silver dollars as investments, selecting a dealer, inflation and deflation, and investor's questions answered. This book was also aimed at the investor.

SPEER

A book entitled *Investing in Morgan and Peace Dollars* was written by Richard Speer in 1981. Another book for the investor, it included a price guide for ANACS certified coins by date and mint. Brief chapters covered the history of the dollar market and its future, grading and pricing, and investment recommendations.

ROUSSO

In 1982 Morris Rousso released an analysis of the price history of Morgan dollars from 1964 to 1978 and from 1978 to 1982. Charts and tables documented the price increases by date and mint along with commentary on the relation of coin price and number of coins available to the hobby.

HERBERT

Alan Herbert authored a book in 1982 entitled *Official Investors Guide, Buying - Selling, Silver Dollars*. This covered Morgan and Peace dollars as well as Flowing Hair, Draped Bust, Gobrecht, Liberty Seated, Trade, Eisenhower and Anthony dollars. The short chapters on

Morgan and Peace dollars covered their history, price histories, investment recommendations and varieties. Other chapters treated the minting process, varieties, buying and selling, grading, investment opportunities, timing your purchases, and storing and protecting silver dollars.

REED

Dick Reed authored a book entitled *The Complete Investor's Guide to Silver Dollar Investing* which was published in 1982. Yet another book for the investor, it briefly treated the minting of coins, history of the silver dollar, and grading of Morgan and Peace dollars. The major portion of the book is a date by date analysis that included approximate availability and investment desirability for various uncirculated grades.

SMITH

A booklet entitled *Date by Date Analysis of the Morgan Dollar*, by Roger Smith was published in 1983. It briefly covered such topics as great melt downs, the Redfield hoard, the Government hoard and grading. Each date and mint of the series was briefly treated on availability and condition.

CARTER

A small booklet entitled *The 1921 Morgan Dollar*, by Mike Carter, was also published in 1983. This was updated in 1986. As the title suggests, it treated the 1921 Morgan dollars only, including the Zerbe and Chapman proofs. Strike and proof-like condition were covered for each of the P, D and S mint issues and rarity and price comparison charts were included.

IVY AND HOWARD

In 1984, Steve Ivy and Ron Howard authored a book entitled *What Every Silver Dollar Buyer Should Know*. It described the Mint State grading standards and the technique for grading Mint State silver dollars. The major portion of the book was devoted to a date by date analysis of the Morgan and Peace dollar series. Each was treated on availability, rarity in prooflike (only Morgans), rarity in superb condition, whether it was in the Redfield hoard, proofs where applicable, and the investment potential. Contains a great deal of worthwhile information.

ZINK AND WOODRUFF

A booklet entitled *Correct Grading of Morgan Silver Dollars* was published in 1984 by Chuck Zink and Dave Woodruff. It covered some general topics of grading and the specifics for MS65, 63 and 60 and some circulated grades. Another section covered investment guidelines.

HAGER

In 1984, Alan Hager published two volumes of books entitled *The Accugrade System-A Comprehensive Guide to Morgan and Peace Dollars in Accugrade "Uncirculated"*, and *A Comprehensive Guide to Morgan and Peace Dollars in Accugrade "Prooflike and Proofs"*. These large books have separate pages of each date and mint and in each of three grades of MS60, 63, and 65. Each date analysis covered surviving numbers in the grade, price history, recommendation and history. Other separate topics covered include economics, grading, Morgan dollar history, future for the various grades, accugrade system of strike and luster factors for each grade, melts and hoards, Peace dollar history, proofs and branch mint proofs. There was some duplication of text between the two volumes.

HALPERIN

A book by James Halperin entitled *N.C.I Grading Guide* was published in 1984. It provided a step-by-step approach to the grading of uncirculated and proof coins. Although it covered all U.S. series coins, the Morgan dollar was used as the example for grading coins, using the factors of surface preservation, strike, luster and eye appeal. Excellent colored photographs indicated the coin areas of prime and secondary interest in grading.

HOWE

This booklet was published in 1988 by Dean Howe and was entitled *Morgan Dollars An In-Depth Study*. It consisted of a date and mint analysis covering estimated remaining population by grade, condition availability and special items of interest.

COIN INVESTORS' REPORT

This was a number of issues covering various coin series. One published in 1990 covered *Morgan Dollars and Peace Dollars*. Two charts were provided for each date and mint for two grades between MS63 and MS66 that showed the number of coins graded by PCGS per month from 1987-1990 and the sight unseen bid for PCGS certified coins.

HIGHFILL

A very large book entitled *The Comprehensive U.S. Silver Dollar Encyclopedia*, by John Highfill was published in 1992. It consisted of over 80 chapters with many of them written by contributing authors. A wide range of topics were covered including market cycles, reminiscing by various dealers, coin hoards, die varieties, counterfeit coins, notable collections, grading services, trading networks, Bust, Gobrecht, Liberty Seated, Trade, Morgan, Peace, Eisenhower and Susan B. Anthony dollars. A statistical section devoted two pages to each date and mint of the Morgan and Peace dollars that included color graphs and data. It was a very extensive compilation of information on all aspects of the silver dollar coin market.

THIS BOOK

The previous books of Van Allen and Mallis were combined in the first edition of this book in 1971 entitled *Guide to Morgan and Peace Dollars*. Mallis' book formed the basis for the listing and description of the Morgan varieties after 1878 in this book. In checking each of these varieties, their descriptions were revised, photographs of each were added, and they were assigned new identification numbers according to the Van Allen obverse and reverse design type nomenclature. The other chapters of this book were based on Van Allen's book. The list of 1878-P varieties was expanded to 92 and the Peace dollar varieties were put in a descriptive list form. A new chapter on detecting counterfeit silver dollars was added.

The 1976 second edition entitled *Comprehensive Catalogue and Encyclopedia of U.S. Morgan and Peace Silver Dollars* incorporated many new varieties discovered by various collectors to expand the descriptive listings to over 800 Morgan varieties. The number of 1878-P varieties was increased to 106. The discussion of significant Morgan varieties was revised into the planchet-die-striking format and the chapter on minting operations was expanded with more illustrations. Grading chapter was revised to conform to proposed A.N.A. grading standards and discussions on differences between proof and prooflike dollars plus the availability of proof-like dollars by date and mint were added. Photographing techniques were updated and new chapters on the sale, packaging, and survey of GSA Carson City dollars were added.

This third edition continues an emphasis on die varieties and historical background information of Morgan and Peace dollars. Over 900 new die variety descriptions have been added to bring the total to over 1,700. New chapters have been added on the popularity of collecting and investing, the GSA Carson City dollar sales, the Redfield and Continental-Illinois Bank hoards, and photographing dollars. New information has also been added to chapters on the minting process, past literature, development of the designs, discussions of significant varieties and preserving silver dollars. The chapter on grading was expanded to provide more detail on grading mint state coins and proofs.

Part II
Morgan Silver Dollars

Chapter 5
Development of the Design
"Efforts of Ingenuity"

Authors' Note: Much of this chapter has been revised to reflect new information based on the research and contributions of Pete R. Bishal.

The Morgan silver dollar, or the Bland silver dollar as it had been known earlier after its sponsor in Congress, was designed by an Englishman, George T. Morgan. An unusual set of circumstances led to this rather than it being designed in the normal procedure by the U.S. Mint Chief Engraver at that time, William Barber, or one of his assistant engravers.

Director of the Mint, Dr. Henry Richard Linderman, was responsible for this change in procedure for designing U.S. coins. He had been the U.S. Mint Director from 1867 to 1869 and was again in charge of that office from 1873 on until his death early in 1879. Linderman wanted to change the silver coinage designs in 1876 and needed additional engravers. He desired to improve the design and dies for U.S. coinage and wanted some new engraving talent at the Mint. In a June 13, 1876 letter to C. W. Fremantle, Deputy Master, Royal Mint, London, Linderman asked him to "find a first class die-sinker who would be willing to take the position of Assistant Engraver at the Mint at Philadelphia." He further remarked that "The engraving of coinage and medal dies has not been brought to much perfection in this country. In England it appears to have reached a standard equal if not superior to that of any other country."[1]

Fremantle replied to Linderman in a July 31, 1876 letter "My inquiries as to an Assistant Engraver lead me very strongly to recommend for the post Mr. George Morgan, age 30, who has made himself a considerable name, but for whom there is not much opening at present in this country. I send a letter from him... I may add that he is personally agreeable and gentlemanlike, and particularly modest and quiet in manner..."

He added in the letter "I have lost no time in taking steps to obtain for you designs in this country for the head of Liberty to be put upon your silver coin... I put myself in communication with Messrs. J.S. and A.B. Wyon, Mr. Leonard Wyon (Engraver of the Mint)..." A September 19, 1876 letter from Fremantle to Linderman mentioned sending "those designs in plaster of the head of Liberty for the obverse of your silver coinage... you will have already received the designs sent by Messrs. J. S. and A. B. Wyon." From this it was evident that Linderman was at this early point in time obtaining sample Liberty head designs for the U. S. coinage from the Mint in England.

George Morgan was born in 1845 in Birmingham, England. He served his apprenticeship to the Die Sinking at Birmingham School of Art, and won a national scholarship to South Kensington Art School where he studied for two years. There he obtained medals and prizes for models of heads from life, figures from life, heads from photographs and flowers from nature. Later he assisted J.S. and A.B. Wyon of the Royal Mint in London for several years.[2]

Morgan came to an agreement with Linderman to work at the Philadelphia Mint for a trial six-month appointment, reporting directly to Linderman, followed by a longer period if things worked out. Morgan was 31 when he left Liverpool, England, on September 27, 1876 on the steamship Illinois,[3] and arrived in Philadelphia on October 9, 1876. As it turned out, he served at the

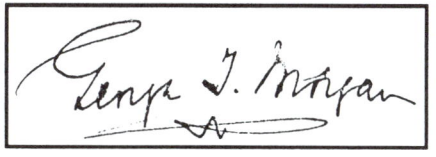

George T. Morgan, Engraver, 1910
with Signature (June 11, 1921)
(Bureau of the Mint)

Col. O.C. Bosbyshell
Philadelphia Mint Coiner 1878
(Illustrated History of the U.S. Mint, George G. Evans)

James Pollock
Superintendent of the Philadelphia Mint
1873-1879
(Illustrated History of the U.S. Mint, George G. Evans)

Dr. Henry R. Linderman
Director of the Mint 1873-1879
(Library of Congress)

Col. A. Loudon Snowden
Superintendent of the Philadelphia Mint
1879-1885
(Illustrated History of the U.S. Mint, George G. Evans)

Philadelphia Mint as an assistant engraver under William Barber until Barber's death in January 1879. He then served in the same capacity under William Barber's son, Charles Barber, until 1917, when he was appointed chief engraver upon Charles Barber's death. Morgan held this office until his own death on January 4, 1925, at the age of 79.

George Morgan was survived by his widow and three children: Miss Phyllis Morgan, Leonard P. Morgan, who was an electrolytic chemist in the U.S. Assay Office at New York, and Mrs. C.M. Graham. He had a love of the cricket sport and was one of the founders of the Belmont Cricket Club in West Philadelphia and an active member of the Germantown Cricket Club. He was also a life member of the Philadelphia Academy of the Fine Arts and a member of the Philadelphia Sketch Club. For many years he was vestryman of Christ Protestant Episcopal Church in Germantown and a superintendent of its Sunday School.[4]

His accomplishments as an engraver were many and included for commemoratives: the reverse of the 1892 Columbian Exposition half dollar, Lincoln-Illinois Centennial half obverse in 1918, McKinley Memorial gold dollar reverse of 1916 and 1917, Huguenot-Walloon Tercentenary half dollar and the 1915-S Panama-Pacific Exposition quarter eagle designed in collaboration with Charles Barber. The coiled-hair obverse for the Stella patterns were also designed by Morgan.

He was known for his portraits in the Mint's presidential series of medals and his designs included those of Rutherford Hayes, Woodrow Wilson and Warren Harding. Also working with Charles Barber, he designed medals of Abraham Lincoln, Martin Van Buren, James Garfield, Chester Arthur, Benjamin Harrison, William McKinley, Theodore Roosevelt and William Taft. His portraits of Presidents Hayes, Cleveland and Harrison appeared on the obverse of the Assay Commission medals of 1880, 1886 and 1893. Other portrait work included medals honoring Secretaries of the Treasury Alexander Hamilton, Daniel Manning, George Cortelyou, Franklin MacVeagh, William McAdoo and Carter Glass plus those of William Windom, John G. Carlisle, Lyman J. Gage and Leslie Shaw in collaboration with Barber. In addition, he designed four Director of the Mint medals and worked with Barber in designing four others.

Additional medals designed by Morgan included the Hayes Indian Peace, Pennsylvania Bicentennial, Lincoln Centennial and Wright Brothers plus others on David Roberts, Thomas Carlyle, Railway Exhibition in Chicago in 1883, and Henry Bessemer.

Although Morgan began his work at the Philadelphia Mint, he reported directly to Mint Director Linderman, who kept his office in Washington. D.C. As a result, there was considerable correspondence between them. Even in those days the mail service was quite fast with only a day required between the two cities and, if a shorter time was needed, the telegraph was available. These letters form a unique record of the timing of and reasons for the Morgan silver dollar design changes.

MORGAN'S INITIAL WORK[5]

Morgan did not begin working on the silver dollar until a year after he arrived at the Philadelphia Mint. However, his first year's work laid the foundation for the design of the silver dollar, since a number of pattern dies were made with devices similar to that of the silver dollar. These first designs were for pattern half dollar pieces.

After arriving in the United States, Morgan stayed at Mrs. Eckfeldt's boarding house at 1614 Mt. Vernon Street in Philadelphia.[6] He did his initial modeling work there because there was not sufficient space at the Mint. An August 16, 1876 letter from James Pollock, Superintendent of the Philadelphia Mint, to Linderman mentioned that "space and light in our Engraver's office are limited... I would be at a loss to know where to put Mr. Morgan that he could work to advantage." Chief Engraver, William T. Barber, and his assistant and son, Charles E. Barber, were probably not very cooperative with Morgan since he was an outsider who had the special privilege of reporting directly to Dr. Linderman. Thus Morgan was forced to not only develop his designs in the less-than-ideal place of his residence, but to also endure the hostile atmosphere of the Mint Engraving Department.

Because of the lack of privacy at the boarding house, in the spring of 1877 he moved to 3727 Chestnut Street where he could work better. Later in September 1877 he moved again to 436 South 40th Street where he stayed at least through the middle of 1878.

As preparation for designing the head of the Goddess of Liberty, Morgan enrolled in the fall of 1876 as a student at the Academy of Fine Arts in Philadelphia. There he made profile studies of Greek figures (Linderman had instructed Morgan on October 31, 1876 "to proceed with models according to his own judgement"). He also obtained studies from nature for the eagle.[7] By November 1, 1876 he had already started a design for the head of Liberty and prepared a design of an eagle and wreath for the reverse.

Morgan then sought a model to pose for the face of the Goddess of Liberty so it would look more like a representation of an American girl. The model he chose was introduced to him by a friend, Thomas Eakins, an independent artist with a wide reputation. She was Miss Anna Willess Williams, a fair haired girl of 19 who was the daughter of Henry Williams of Philadelphia. Although she was a modest young women, friends persuaded her to pose before the artist, and Morgan had five sittings with Miss Williams in November 1876.[8] He declared Miss Williams' profile the most perfect he had seen in England or America.

The identity of Morgan's model was kept secret until the summer of 1879 when a newspaper man discovered that her likeness, as good as a photograph, was on the silver dollar. Miss Williams, who later became a successful kindergarten school teacher and philosophical writer, received thousands of letters and visitors at her home and school. These attentions greatly troubled her and it was some time before the furor died down. She remained single and died unmarried in 1926 at the age of 68.

On November 1, 1876, Morgan took his first model of a reverse eagle to the mint for reduction. During November and December 1876, Morgan prepared additional models of the reverse eagle and obverse Liberty head for the half dollar. Morgan's letter of January 8, 1877 to Linderman stated he had forwarded wax impressions of three dies to Linderman for his criticism, "No. 1 is an impression from a wax mold taken from the working hub... and also shows the uneven surfaces where I have cut down the ground and round the body of the eagle, of course all this would be taken away when the die is made and the surface polished." Apparently there is no available pattern showing this eagle. "No. 2 is the same design with a different treatment of the wings – I have yet another in hand where I make the feathers of the wings as large as No. 1, but to radiate from a center as in No. 2." These eagles are shown in Judd patterns 1514 and 1516,[9] with outstretched but stubby wings and encircled by a ring of pearls. "In No. 3 you will notice that the outline of the

Philadelphia Mint Engravers, 1910
(Philadelphia Mint)

face is too bold. The working hub nearly up from this die. I shall cut down the relief on the outline and also get some more delicate modeling in the neck. I have the profile eagle so far advanced that I hope to be able to send you an impression this day week. The other head is being electroplated previous to reduction by the machine."

No. 3 impression mentioned in Morgan's letter was the obverse Liberty head shown in Judd 1514 and 1516 and very similar to that used on the Morgan dollar but encircled by a ring of pearls. The profile eagle also encircled by a ring of pearls that was ready a week later is Judd 1512. Specimen coins from these dies were struck and forwarded to Linderman early in February 1877.

All of these first half dollar specimens had the same Liberty head design on the obverse with identical stars, lettering, ring of pearls and denticles. The reverses had three different eagles each with a large scroll beneath it that was the same except for size. All had the same ring of pearls with 121 dots surrounding the center designs on each side and all have the same outer ring of 120 small denticles on both sides. So there are common design elements in all three specimens. Morgan seemed to prefer working with three design combinations at a time as this number repeats over and over again throughout his design refinement work.

At this point it is well to review the steps in preparing the hubs and dies during 1876-1878. According to a letter by then Director of the Mint Nellie Tayloe Ross in 1936,[10] the master dies for silver coins struck prior to 1916 were prepared with "the original design reduced from a sculptured model. The inscriptions were usually put in the master die by means of punches." These original designs included Liberty heads, eagles and wreathes but not the peripheral lettering, stars and dates. Some of the numerous dies and hubs destroyed at the Philadelphia Mint on May 25, 1910 included the following:[11]

- 15 designs for eagles, by Morgan, for dollar, half dollar and quarter dollar.
- 15 designs for Liberty heads, by Morgan, for dollar and subsidiary coins.
- 29 designs for Liberty heads, by W. Barber, for dollars, half dollars, quarter dollars and dimes.
- 15 designs for standing eagle, by W. Barber, for dollar, half dollars, quarter dollars and twenty cent piece.
- 3 wreath designs (Barber), dollar and half dollar size.

Clearly, many different dies and hubs of various Liberty heads, eagles and wreaths were prepared by Morgan and William Barber during the 1876-1878 time period.

Although the dies and hubs made by Morgan were all destroyed in 1910, the Philadelphia Mint still has a number of galvanoes of Morgan dollars. These include an eagle clutching a scroll, olive branch and arrows similar to that of Judd 1516, an eagle with outstretched wings similar to the $10 gold pattern and initial dollar pattern, plus a $10 gold obverse pattern.[12] None of these galvanoes have lettering or stars around the edges but only show the central design.

These central designs of Liberty heads and eagles started out as sketches and were then put in three dimensional in clay model form three to five times the final size of the coin. After a negative plaster of Paris cast was made of the clay model and touched up to restore lost detail, a positive plaster cast was then made. This new cast was touched up to again restore lost detail and to heighten and sharpen the design detail. Sometimes this last positive plaster cast was reviewed by Linderman as shown in Morgan's letter to Linderman on March 7, 1877: "... forward you by Express a plaster cast showing the alterations I have made in the Head of Liberty according to your suggestions. I have also sketched round the Head the way in which I propose putting the Motto and date ..." This letter indicates the lettering and date were not a part of the plaster cast but just sketched onto it.

When this positive cast was satisfactory, a negative cast was made and touched up. After being dipped in hot beeswax and coated with powered copper, it was electroplated with copper as previously quoted in Morgan's letter of January 8, 1877 to Linderman: "The other head is being electroplated previous to reduction by the machine..." Electroplating began on a commercial scale around 1840-41[13] and was used to produce a positive copy of the design in copper. This positive copper shell was backed with lead to strengthen it producing a galvano, and then placed in a reducing machine which traced the design in concentric circles with a tracer point. A cutting tool at the other end of a lever arm cut out in reduced size a positive design on a hub steel cylinder. The design could be in intaglio or relief depending on the type galvano the engraver selected. However, this relief galvano reduced to a relief hub was the better method.

The positive hub of a design produced by the reduction machine had to be touched up by the engraver since the design transfer could not be accomplished in all respects at that time. Concentric marks left by the cutting tool would have had to be removed and some design edges and features sharpened. Design features to be cut down could be made on this hub, but features to be enlarged would have to be done on a die with intaglio design. Therefore, if needed and to possibly safeguard the hub, the design was transferred to a die by the hubbing process. The hub was first hardened and then forced into a pointed cylinder of annealed steel using a screw press. Several blows of the hub was required to completely transfer the design with the die being annealed after each blow to resoften the steel. Then the engraver could fill in the design where required on this die. Next a design working hub was prepared from this touched up die using the hubbing process again. The design working hub could also be touched-up as required. Simpler designs, such as wreath and ring of pearls, were likely engraved directly into a die face and a hub could then be made using the hubbing process.

Sometimes there were problems in this hubbing operation, as Morgan related to Linderman in his letter of January 22, 1877:

> *Unfortunately I have been greatly delayed lately by accidents. The working hub for the Head of Liberty... was doubled at the last blow. Another was commenced but this split when it was nearly finished... This hubbing would be done much quicker if the dies had two blows each day instead of one — one first thing in the morning and another in the afternoon thus given time during the day for softening. I should be glad if Mr. Key would assist me in lettering the dies. If I had these facilities and no accidents I feel certain I should be able to have the coins ready by Feb 14th. I beg to thank you for the criticism on the Head of Liberty. I will carefully attend to the suggestions in finishing the Hub.*

It should be noted that it was probably this design working hub of just the Liberty head where the LIBERTY letters were punched into the head band (these are incuse on the coin). This letter indicated that Mr. Key would also be involved in preparing the master dies by punching in the peripheral lettering.

The time was quite lengthy for these reduction and hubbing operations as related in Morgan's January 1, 1878 letter to Linderman about the Hayes Presidential Medal. "... Presuming that I could have the Machine at once, I could get the die finished in about four weeks, I calculate nine days for the reduction, six days finishing and nine days hubbing...". Large medals would likely have taken longer for the reduction and hubbing operations than smaller coins like the half dollar.

A completed design working hub was then used to transfer the design to a master die in a hubbing operation. The steel die cylinder started out with a cone on the end to allow for metal expansion and to reduce the possibility of die cracks. As a rule the central design was hubbed first into the cone of the die being made, after which separate design working hubs of simpler design elements such as wreath, denticles or ring of pearls could be hubbed into the outer portions of the die. Finally, the peripheral lettering, stars and date were added to the master die (usually by William Key) to complete it. Various design working hubs could be utilized in alternate combinations to produce different master dies.

After a master die was hardened it could then be used to strike specimen coins (or patterns) as Morgan related to Linderman in a letter of August 8, 1877: "... dies turned, lettered, and hardened and specimens made from them..." Sometimes Morgan forwarded to Linderman impressions in plaster or wax of the dies to save the time and effort of striking specimens.

Returning to Morgan's work early in 1877, Linderman wrote to Morgan on February 23, 1877 with some suggestions to improve the designs on the specimens sent earlier that month, including making the Liberty head larger and changing the emphasis from the hair to the cap. In that same time period, Linderman requested preparation of new reverses with shield designs. These changes required Morgan to design entirely new reverses and to modify the Liberty head plaster model again in the confines of his residence, since he was still on a six-month trial period.

Morgan forwarded to Linderman, as described in a March 7 letter,

> *... a plaster cast showing the alterations I have made in the Head of Liberty according to your suggestions.*
>
> *I have also sketched round the Head the way in which I propose putting the motto and date. Arranged in this way you will see it gives us an opportunity of making the head much larger in the circle. The date being at the back of the head looks a little strange at first. I can not call to mind any coin where it is so placed, but I can not myself see any objection to its position.*
>
> *If you do not like this arrangement I should be able to get the head larger than in the specimen coins by doing away with the inner ring of pearls and making the letters a little smaller.*
>
> *I am engraving the shield reverse. I like it very much and think it will be certainly the best reverse we have had.*

This letter shows it was Morgan's idea to move the date towards the back of the head, and he also suggested doing away with the inner ring of pearls to allow room for a larger Liberty head.

Copies of correspondence between Linderman and Morgan after the above letter until July, 1877, unfortunately have not been located. But from the available Morgan half dollar patterns, it is clear which designs he made during this time period. In order to more easily refer to the various half dollar pattern designs, the obverses will be assigned Roman numerals and the reverses letters. Thus, the first Morgan obverse design with Liberty head surrounded by a ring of pearls is I. The first reverse design (denoted as No. 2 in Morgan's letter since his No. 1 has not been reported on pattern coins), A, is the eagle with fine wing feathers encircled by a ring of pearls. The second reverse design, B, is the same design with larger wing feathers and the third reverse design, C, is the profile eagle encircled by a ring of pearls.

Apparently Linderman did not much care for the plaster cast of the Liberty head mentioned in Morgan's letter of March 7, but instead preferred Morgan's suggestion of doing away with the ring of pearls. The Morgan half dollar patterns in Judd only show one version of the Liberty head design for Nos. 1503-1510 without the ring of pearls. However, there is another similar, yet slightly different Morgan Liberty head design first pointed out by Pete Bishal which preceded the later one shown in Judd which the authors have examined on pattern coins and is shown in several books.[14,15]

This second half dollar obverse design, II, looked very similar to that eventually used on the Morgan dollar. It showed a large Liberty head without the ring of pearls and there were seven stars on the left and six on the right. E PLURIBUS UNUM was at the top in small letters with R overlapping part of a wheat stem. The second Liberty head was similar to that used in the first obverse design, I, incorporating changes suggested by Linderman. It had a larger Phrygian cap with lower part added covering more hair, right top wheat leaf folded over instead of sticking straight up, unevenly divided ear lobe instead of the previously evenly divided one, lower hair line indentation towards rear instead of near the front, and a straight neck truncation instead of curved. There are 118 denticles. Morgan probably completed the master die of this second obverse design, II, and struck specimen coins with the new shield reverse sometime in mid-Spring 1877, possibly late April or early May.

Three shield reverse designs of Morgan's pattern half dollars are shown for Judd Nos. 1503, 1504 and 1506. Once again Morgan chose to work with three design combinations. They were probably not all made and finished at the same time and there is no available correspondence suggesting their order of preparation. However, one was not finished until August 8, as shown later in a Morgan letter.

It is surmised that the shield reverse design shown in Judd 1506 was made first since it had large inscription letters with dots between words similar to the three initial reverse designs. The last shield reverse was likely that shown in Judd 1503 with a wreath below and to the sides of the shield eagle and IN GOD WE TRUST at top in the same relationship as the reverse that followed the shield reverses, very similar to the eventual Morgan dollar reverse design. This leaves the shield reverse of Judd 1504 with four-sided shield and two stars separating the letters as the middle one in the order of development.

Using this assumed order, the shield reverse design, D, had an eagle superimposed on a seven-sided shield, IN GOD WE TRUST on a ring around the shield with a small wreath around the ring, UNITED STATES OF AMERICA in large letters at the top and HALF DOLLAR at the bottom with each word separated by a dot. The upright eagle was a new design with the head turned to the left, wings outstretched with tops pointing down, and claws clutching an olive branch on the left and three arrows on the right. There were 118 denticles. The shield shape was similar to one on the Indian head cent reverse top.

The assumed next shield reverse design, E, had a slightly different eagle superimposed on a four-sided shield. This was somewhat related to the Seated Liberty series reverse design which had a four-sided shield on the breast of an eagle in the same stance as Morgan's shield eagle. Possibly Morgan was inspired to transpose the Seated Liberty reverse shield and eagle for his new shield reverse. This shield reverse, E, had the inscriptions again circling the shield but with small letters and two stars separating the lower part. IN GOD WE TRUST was on a ring around the shield with a small wreath around the ring. The eagle had a longer neck than that of the first shield reverse eagle, wider wings, longer and wider tail feathers, parallel arrow feathers and a middle arrow head on top, all more like those of the final reverse eagle. There were 118 denticles.

It must have been late Spring of 1877 when Linderman instructed Morgan to also work on a design for the $10 gold coin. This design was to have an important influence on the eventual design of the Morgan dollar reverse. In his letter to Linderman on July 14, 1877, Morgan stated, "I have nearly finished the reverses for the ten dollar and half dollar pieces. The obverse are being hubbed and will be ready about the middle of next week." That this was accomplished is indicated in Morgan's letter to Linderman on August 8, 1877, "I have the dies for the half dollar and ten dollar pieces finished and hardened ready to strike specimens... die turned, lettered, and hardened and specimens made from them." And his letter of August 11 said, "In accordance with your letter of 9th inst. I have delivered the dies to the Supr., 1 pr. dies for 10 dollar piece, 1 pr. dies for half dollar, 1 obv. for half dollar having inscription differently arranged. I beg to thank you for the instructions contained in your letter with reference to the striking of specimens. In future I will be careful to comply with them."

Apparently Linderman's letter of August 9 instructed Morgan to stop having specimens struck from pattern dies without his authorization. In the future, Morgan was to turn over the new dies to the Superintendent of the Mint who would then await instructions from Linderman on the striking of specimens. There must have been a proliferation of pattern die specimens from unauthorized strikings because there are in existence pattern half dollars of practically every combination of Morgan's obverse and reverse designs. These design combinations will be summarized later.

The half dollar pair of dies mentioned in Morgan's August 11 letter were the third obverse design, III, shown for Judd 1503, 1504, 1506 and 1508 and probably the third shield reverse design, F, for Judd 1503. The obverse die with "inscription differently arranged" was undoubtedly the fourth obverse design, IV, shown for Judd 1510.

The third Morgan half dollar obverse design, III, also had a large Liberty head without the ring of pearls similar to II design, but with some modifications to the Liberty head made at Linderman's suggestion. The motto, stars and date were the same as on design II, but with slightly different spacing, and the R in PLURIBUS was separated from the wheat stem. Liberty head changes from the II obverse included the obvious lower hair extension to back, cap with rounded lower part, curved neck truncation and the right top wheat leaf folded over high above the cap. There were now 146 denticles.

The last Morgan half dollar obverse design, IV, had the exact same Liberty head design as used in the III obverse, but with the motto divided to the left and right, seven stars at the top and six at the bottom with a small date. It also had 146 denticles.

The third shield reverse design, F, had an identical eagle as the E reverse superimposed on a slightly taller four-sided shield. IN GOD WE TRUST was on a ribbon above the shield and a wreath surrounded the shield at the bottom and sides similar to the eventual placement for the Morgan dollar reverse design. The inscription was in large letters with the lower part separated by two stars. There were 118 denticles.

Although each complete shield reverse design was different, the shields beneath all three eagles were basically identical copies of the same master shield design. The seven-sided version is nothing more than a modified copy. Also, the eagles on the E and F shield reverses are identical. This points to the conclusion that the shield and eagle portions of the design had to be on separate master partial design hubs as were the wreaths, denticles and pearl rings.

The Morgan $10 gold pattern dies mentioned in Morgan's August 11 letter, Judd 1545, used a similar arrangement for the obverse as the half dollar design, IV, with large a Liberty head, divided motto and small date, but without stars. The Liberty head was similar to that of the half dollar obverse design, III, except the cap was larger and high on the top of the head and the LIBERTY letters were much larger. The $10 gold reverse showed a spread eagle clutching an olive branch on the left and three arrows on the right, motto IN GOD WE TRUST in Gothic letters above the eagle, inscription around the eagle, and TEN DOL. denomination at the bottom. This reverse eagle design was later used for the initial Morgan dollar pattern development and the reverse looked very much like that eventually used on the Morgan silver dollar, except for the denomination and the lack of a wreath around the eagle.

A September 13, 1877 letter from Morgan to Linderman indicated he had finished another reverse design: "... I have finished the reverse for the half dollar which I mentioned in my last letter, having the eagle the same size in proportions as on the reverse of the ten dollar gold piece. I have handed over the die to the Superintendent who awaits your instructions to strike specimens. I am now engaged on the Presidential medal obverse and reverse."

This final 1877 Morgan half dollar reverse design, G, is shown in Judd 1508 and 1510. It used the same eagle as the $10 gold piece with similar design arrangements. It had the motto in Gothic letters above the eagle, inscriptions around the side, HALF DOLLAR at the bottom and stars above it. A wreath was added that surrounded the lower part of the eagle. It had 146 denticles. This reverse design G combined with obverse design III, Judd 1508, formed the basis used by Morgan to begin development of his silver dollar patterns and is very similar to the designs eventually used on the Morgan silver dollars.

The four obverse and seven reverse Morgan half dollar designs known are summarized below. *Table 5-1* shows the 17 known obverse and reverse design combinations from pattern specimens. Why some of the earlier designs were paired with later ones is not clear. Perhaps they were unauthorized strikings ordered by Morgan or struck by the coiner for pattern collectors. The design combinations using the II obverse are not listed in Judd, but patterns have been examined by the authors or have been pictured in various books and auction catalogs.

Morgan's work on the Hayes Presidential medal was interrupted by a letter of October 18, 1877, from Linderman to James Pollock, Superintendent of the Philadelphia Mint, which ordered the following:

I have to request that you will instruct Mr. Morgan to prepare without delay, dies for a silver dollar, the designs, inscriptions, and arrangement thereof to be the same as the enclosed impression for the Half Dollar and numbered '2' substituting the words 'one dollar' in place of 'half dollar,' and that you will cause six impressions to be struck in standard silver of 412 1/2 grains weight, and transmit the same to this office.

You will also instruct Mr. Barber [who was chief engraver at this time] to prepare a reverse die for a dollar with a representation of an eagle as well as the inscriptions required by law. He will select whichever of his Heads of Liberty he prefers for the obverse of the same. You will cause six pieces to be struck from these dies and forwarded with those from Mr. Morgan's dies...

The Morgan half dollar numbered '2' Linderman referred to was undoubtedly that of the Judd 1508 design with a III obverse and G reverse that were similar to the eventual silver dollar designs.

Morgan Pattern Half Dollar Obverse Design Types

I   Small Liberty head encircled by ring of 121 pearls. Six stars on left and seven on right. E PLURIBUS UNUM at top. 120 denticles. First Liberty head design showing small Phrygian cap without a lower part, small cap top, right top wheat leaf with end

Table 5-1 MORGAN PATTERN HALF DOLLAR DESIGN COMBINATIONS

Obverse	Reverse	Judd No.
I	A	1514
I	B	1516
I	C	1512
I	D	1522
I	E	1520
I	F	1518
I	G	1523a
II or III(1)	A	1509c
II or III(1)	C	1509a
II	D	Unlisted(2)
II	E	Unlisted(2)
II	F	Unlisted(3)
III	D	1506
III	E	1504
III	F	1503
III	G	1508
IV	G	1510

1. Not pictured separately in Judd. Obverse could be either II or III as they are very similar. II or III with B should also exist.
2. II obverse not pictured in Judd but authors have examined the coin.
3. II obverse not pictured in Judd but photo is Color Plate 20 in "The History of United States Coins As illustrated by the Garret Collection," by Q. David Bowers, 1979.

showing, evenly divided earlobe, lower hair indentation near front, curved neck truncation.

II Large Liberty head without ring of pearls. Seven stars on left and six on right, E PLURIBUS UNUM at top in small letters with R overlapping wheat stem. 118 denticles. Second Liberty head design similar to Morgan dollar showing large Phrygian cap with lower part below draw string, large cap top, straight back to lower part of cap, right top wheat leaf folded over low above cap, unevenly divided ear lobe, lower hair line indentation towards rear, straight neck truncation.

III Large Liberty head without ring of pearls. Stars, date and E PLURIBUS UNUM similar to II obverse except R separated from wheat stem and letters, stars and digits spaced slightly different. 146 denticles. Third Liberty head design showing large Phrygian cap with rounded back to lower part of cap, hair sticks out further at lower rear, right top wheat leaf folded over high above cap, curved neck truncation.

IV Same third Liberty head design as in III, but with inscriptions differently arranged. E PLURIBUS is on left and UNUM on right in large letters. Seven stars at top and six at bottom with small date. 146 denticles.

Morgan Pattern Half Dollar Reverse Design Types

A Eagle encircled by ring of 121 pearls. UNITED STATES OF AMERICA in large letters at top separated by two dots from HALF DOLLAR in large letters at bottom. Eagle has head turned to right with wings outstretched and lifted up with fine feathers radiating outward. Claws clutch scroll with inscription IN GOD WE TRUST with olive branch on left and three arrow heads on right. 120 denticles.

B Same as A except eagle has fewer wider-spaced and broader large wing feathers radiating outward. 120 denticles.

C Profile of eagle encircled by ring of 121 pearls. Inscriptions and denticles same as A and B. Eagle is facing to left with wings raised and tips back. Claws clutch same slightly larger scroll with inscription IN GOD WE TRUST with larger olive branch on left and three arrow heads on right. 120 denticles.

D Shield reverse with eagle superimposed on seven-sided shield. IN GOD WE TRUST on a ring around shield with small wreath around ring. UNITED STATES OF AMERICA in large letters at top and HALF DOLLAR at bottom with each word separated by a dot. Eagle is upright with head turned to left, wings outstretched with tips pointing down and claws clutching olive branch on left and three arrows on right. 118 denticles.

E Shield reverse with eagle superimposed on four-sided shield. IN GOD WE TRUST on a ring around shield with small wreath around ring. UNITED STATES OF AMERICA in small letters at top separated by two stars from HALF DOLLAR in small letters at bottom. Eagle is slightly different than that used on D with longer neck, wider wings, longer and wider tail feathers, parallel arrow feathers and a middle arrow head on top. 118 denticles.

F Shield reverse with same eagle as in E superimposed on slightly larger four-sided shield. IN GOD WE TRUST on ribbon above shield. Wreath surrounds shield at bottom and sides. UNITED STATES OF AMERICA in large letters at top separated by two stars from HALF DOLLAR in large letters at bottom. 118 denticles.

G Spread eagle same as first used on Morgan ten dollar pattern and similar to that used later on Morgan silver dollar initial pattern. IN GOD WE TRUST is in Gothic letters above eagle with wreath below and to side of eagle. UNITED STATES OF AMERICA in small letters at top separated by two stars from HALF DOLLAR in small letters at bottom. Eagle has outstretched wings with tips held up, head facing left and claws clutching olive branch on left and three arrows on right. Eagle has seven tail feathers. 146 denticles.

INITIAL DESIGN OF THE SILVER DOLLAR

The Act of Congress which proposed the coinage of silver dollars stated that there should appear on the silver dollar the devices and superscriptions provided by the Act of January 18, 1837, Section 13, which read:

That upon the coins struck at the Mint, there shall be the following devices and legends: Upon one side of each said coins, there shall be an impression emblematic of Liberty, with an inscription of the word Liberty, and the year of coinage; and upon the reverse of each of the gold and silver coins, there shall be the figure or representation of an eagle. with the inscription United States of America and a designation of the value of the coin.

Section 18 of the Coinage Act of 1873 had further provided that the coins should include the inscription "E Pluribus Unum," and that the Director of the Mint, with the approval of the Secretary of the Treasury, should also have the motto "In God We Trust" shown on coins whose size would permit such an inscription. With the overall design of the silver dollar fixed by these Acts of Congress, only the artistic details were left to the engraver.

Six silver pattern dollars of each of the designs of both Morgan and Barber were forwarded to Linderman on December 5, 1877 (see photographs in *Figures 5-1* and *5-2*).[16] In a letter regarding these pattern dollars, coiner O. C. Bosbyshell wrote to superintendent Pollock, "I also send one of the latter's [Barber's] designs in copper, in order to show clearly the work on his dies, as the silver are not as satisfactorily brought up as could have been desired". This trouble with Barber's design was to have an important bearing on Linderman's eventual choice of the design to be used. It should be noted that the old English letters used for the motto "In God We Trust" of Morgan's dollar was to make it the only U.S. coin to

Morgan Pattern Half Dollar Design Types

Obverse I
(Photo Courtesy of Bowers & Merena, Inc.)

Obverse II
(Photo Courtesy of Pete R. Bishal)

Obverse III
(Photo Courtesy of Pete R. Bishal)

Obverse IV
(Photo Courtesy of Bowers & Merena, Inc.)

Reverse A
(Photo Courtesy of Bowers & Merena, Inc.)

Reverse B
(Photo Courtesy of Bowers & Merena, Inc.)

Reverse C
(Photo Courtesy of Bowers & Merena, Inc.)

Reverse D
(Photo Courtesy of Pete R. Bishal)

Reverse E
(Photo Courtesy of Pete R. Bishal)

Reverse F
(Photo Courtesy of Coin World)

Reverse G
(Photo Courtesy of Pete R. Bishal)

Morgan Pattern Ten Dollar - Struck in Copper
(Photo Courtesy Smithsonian)

Figure 5-1 MORGAN PATTERN SILVER DOLLAR
(Seven Tail Feathers)

Figure 5-2 BARBER PATTERN SILVER DOLLAR

have old English letters in its composition and to use both upper and lower case letters. It was also at that time the only U.S. coin to have an engraver's initial (M) on both the obverse and reverse.

Another 20 each of Morgan's and Barber's pattern silver dollars were provided to Linderman in mid-December 1877.

Morgan experienced some problems with these pattern dies during the striking of additional pattern pieces in December 1877, as related in a letter to Linderman on January 1, 1878:

I have been delayed in preparing the dies for the five dollar piece, three dies have broken in striking the silver dollars, and of course I have had to prepare three others.

In the meantime, Morgan finished the model for the Hayes Presidential Medal and began to prepare the dies for this Hayes Medal and dies for the five dollar and ten dollar gold pieces. In January 1878, Morgan was also carrying out the first of many alterations to the silver dollar design. His letter to Linderman on January 30 details these alterations:

I have the working hubs for the silver dollar now finished. While making these hubs I have taken care to reduce the relief in places where from the specimens already made I found it necessary.

I have also altered the eagle cutting away the wings from the legs and making a few other minor alterations... I understand that it was your desire that I should see Col. Snowden. I found his criticism very valuable and have adopted his suggestions almost entirely.

Colonel A. Loudon Snowden was, thus, the third person besides Morgan who influenced the design of the

Figure 5-3 MORGAN PATTERN SILVER DOLLAR
(With Cut Down Wings)

dollar patterns.[17] Linderman was concerned with the progress of these alterations and wrote Pollock on January 29, February 7, and February 9 requesting that new specimens be forwarded to him when they were struck. In mid-February, Linderman made a visit to the Philadelphia Mint and instructed Morgan "to make some slight modifications in the reverse die engraved by him for the silver dollar." Linderman continued to be closely involved in the design of the dollar.

One example Morgan pattern with the eagle's wings cut away from the legs is shown in *Figure 5-3*. There are other differences from the earlier pattern of *Figure 5-1* with more of a hook on the eagle's beak, eagle's tail feathers more sharply defined though still seven in number, narrower center arrow head, wreath with a different arrangement of berries, and shorter denticles. Pete Bishal of Westport, Massachusetts has studied the denticles on the Morgan patterns and regular issue coins and has pointed out that the original dollar patterns had 151 denticles on the obverse and 148 on the reverse but the later patterns were made just the opposite: 148 denticles on the obverse and 151 on the reverse. The pattern obverse shown in *Figure 5-3* differs from that of *Figure 5-1* in that the ear helix and antihelix are the same width, LIBERTY letters are thicker, hair curl in front of the ear is straight instead of curved, the wheat stalk is mid way between "RI" instead of close to the "I", the wheat leaf is further away from the "R" and the denticles are shorter with 148 count.

Other Morgan pattern dollars exist showing still additional minor design refinements. These are changes suggested by Col. Snowden or requested by Linderman during January and February 1878. None quite match the working dies that were eventually used in the regular coinage.

In a letter to Pollock on February 21, Linderman inquired when the modifications by Morgan would be completed so that a specimen could be forwarded to his office. He also added:

... I have now to state for your information, that it is my intention, in the event of the silver bill now pending in Congress, becoming law, to request the approval by the Secretary of the Treasury, of the dies prepared by Mr. Morgan.

It is the desire of the Secretary of the Treasury, as well as my own, that if the silver bill becomes law, the coinage of silver dollars shall be commenced with the least practicable delay and carried to the full capacity of the Mints for the execution of such coinage...

It is proper to add that the specimens struck from the dies prepared by Messrs. Morgan and Barber exhibit high skill as well as artistic taste and that there is little if any difference in their merits, but that since a choice has to be made, I have selected the one having the lowest relief and requiring the lightest power to bring up the devices and inscriptions. No mention however of my preference need be made until after the receipt of the specimens herein called for and notification to you of its adoption.

Thus, Linderman preferred the Morgan's design over Barber's because of its overall lower relief and desired the least delay in commencing the silver dollar coinage once the silver bill became law.

Morgan wrote to Linderman on February 22 that the dies with alterations would be ready in a few days. He added some comments on the process of making these dies:

... I made the alterations on the working hub, which was hardened on Monday last...

These alterations make the working hub for the reverse useless as a regular working hub. I can make a specimen die from it, by cutting a part of the work in the die.

The hub for the obverse is unaltered and can be used at anytime.

I have commenced two new working hubs which I trust will be ready for use on Wednesday or Thursday next. After these hubs are finished I presume that we can make the dies for use, in from seven to ten blows each.

In making a large number of dies we cannot give more than one blow a day, so that in ten days after the working hubs are finished we could begin to coin at Philadelphia.

We can make from seven to ten dies a day. A pair of dies will average 50,000 pieces so that we shall be able to keep up a supply of dies.

It is clear from this letter and Morgan's letter of January 30, that alterations were made by cutting away the working hub, thus reducing the size and relief of the design. He could have also added and strengthened details by cutting into the master die. But for major changes, Morgan may have gone back to the design die or hub in order to make a new master die. This may have happened for the reverse in February 1878 when the eagle's tail feathers were changed from seven to eight and the number of olive leaves at the end of the branch were changed from three to nine. Production of the working dies was a slow process requiring from seven to ten blows of the working hub at the rate of one blow a day. This fact will later prove important to the story.

Both of the two reverse working hubs mentioned in the above letter were eventually used to make working dies that struck coins. As will be shown, this resulted in two minor design sub-types of the 8 tail feather reverse design.

In a letter to Linderman on February 25, Morgan wrote:

Today I delivered to Supt. Pollock an impression in silver from the Dollar dies showing the alterations which I have made under your direction.

I shall be glad to hear from you as to whether I am to make these or any other alterations on the working hubs which I have now in hand.

Thus, the design of working hubs was still not final as of that date. Soon afterward, Morgan visited Colonel Snowden for his opinion about the alterations, and on February 28 he wrote to Linderman:

Today I saw Col. Snowden with an impression of the dollar after latest alterations. Col. Snowden thinks that the alterations to the eagle's head and neck, the olive branch and arrows are improvements. He is however inclined to agree with me that the wings have been cut down a little too much, more especially at the extremities which now appear rather thin and poor compared with what they were.

On February 28, the day that Congress passed the Bland-Allison silver dollar bill, Linderman wrote to Pollock ordering that the alterations be made to the working hub:

... you will instruct Mr. Morgan to finish his new working hubs, showing the alterations, as speedily as may be practicable, and that immediately thereafter you will cause working dies to be made in sufficient quantity to commence striking pieces as soon as possible after the bill may become a law ...

On March 1, Linderman sent the following telegram to Pollock:

The specimen sent on twenty fifth ulto Morgan modified die has been approved and adopted. Conform strictly to it in making new working hubs.

In a separate telegram the same day, he ordered:

... commence at once the preparation of silver dollar blanks to your full capacity and get the working dies ready as soon as possible and commence striking. The full force of the Engravers Dept. will be applied to the preparation of silver dollar dies.

The Philadelphia Mint was, therefore, under great pressure to begin striking the new silver dollar. The approved design consisted of, in Linderman's words:

... the obverse of the coin bears a free cut head of Liberty crowned with a Phrygian cap decorated with wheat and cotton, the staples of the country, — the legend 'E Pluribus Unum,' thirteen stars and the year of coinage. On the reverse, surrounded by an olive wreath is an eagle with outspread wings bearing in his talons a branch of olive and a bundle of arrows – emblems of peace and war – the inscriptions 'United States of America' and 'One Dollar' and the motto 'In God We Trust'...

The Phrygian cap or Liberty cap originated in Phrygia and was worn by ex-Roman slaves to show they were free.

President Hayes and Secretary of the Treasury, John Sherman, had expressed to Linderman a desire to possess the first and second specimens, respectively, of the regular silver dollar coinage. In a letter to Pollock on February 28, Linderman ordered, "You will instruct the coiner to hand you the first piece struck and the second piece, with a certificate of their being the first and second pieces struck and transmit the pieces and certificates to me."

DESIGN CHANGES IN THE REGULAR COINAGE

The new working hubs were not completed until about February 28, and since the working dies required seven to ten blows at one blow per day, the first coins were not struck until two weeks after the law was passed. The initial delivery of 303 coins was sent to Linderman on March 12. The first three coins went to President Hayes, Treasury Secretary John Sherman, and Mint Director Linderman, as had been prearranged. Contemporary newspaper accounts indicates that the first dollar struck in the presses used for regular coinage of the new silver dollar was struck at 3:17 the afternoon of March 11, 1878 at the Philadelphia Mint. The Chicago Daily Tribune carried a detailed account of the event in its March 12, 1878 edition as shown on the next page.

Another contemporary newspaper account of this first striking of the Morgan silver dollar was on the front page of the March 13, 1878 issue of The Cincinnati Commercial newspaper. Pollock, Morgan and Colonel Bosbyshell were all present during this first striking according to this account (although Morgan and Bosbyshell's names were misspelled and Pollock was given the title of Governor). The account datelined Philadelphia, March 12 was as follows:

The first of the new silver dollars, the planchet or blank was dropped into the receiving tube of the coining press by Mr. Albert Downing foreman, Governor Pollock, Colonel Bosby Shell, and George E. Morgan, the designer, standing near, was caught by the nimble forks, that have shut to on many a coin before pressed quickly forward the lower die, grasped around the edge by hard steel collar, stamped heavily by the obverse die above, and, as the machine shuddered in relaxation, rolled down into the catch-box with a clunk a poor blurred and deformed silver dollar, that had to be melted over again.

Dollar No. 2 came out glittering and perfect.

'That's the veto coin, because this first piece goes to President Hayes.' These first pieces of the press are specimens for official distribution.

Dollar No. 3 fell into the box and rested by the side of the

President's keepsake.

'Here we have Secretary Sherman's little memento' whispered the Chief, as the coiner placed the pieces in two of the twelve envelopes which he held in his hand...

When the dozen coins were ready, the press was stopped, but soon started up again, steam turned on, and by 6 o'clock this evening $70,000 had been turned.

...The first of the new coin was struck off yesterday...

On page 1 of the Cincinnati Enquirer issue of March 13, 1878 was a report for March 12 stating "President Hayes, Secretary Sherman and Director of the Mint Linderman today received from Philadelphia each a sample of the new silver dollar".

The first dollar struck for regular issue that was given to President Hayes resides in the Rutherford B. Hayes Museum at Fremont, Ohio. It is a VAM 9 variety with eight tail feathers as predicted by Pete Bishal of Westport, Massachusetts. This first Morgan silver dollar came in a holder about two inches square with a center hole for the dollar and two attached flaps to cover both sides of the dollar. One flap has the numeral one embossed on the outside and the holder fits into a separate case. Unfortunately, the dollar has been heavily polished over the years in an attempt to clean it. Accompanying the dollar is an envelope with words on the outside: "His Excellency, Rutherford B. Hayes, President – First Silver Dollar Coined, Phila., 1878"

A certificate inside the envelope had the following statement with signatures of the coiner and superintendent:

Mint U.S. Philadelphia, Coiner's Department, March 11, 1878 – I hereby certify that the Silver Dollar enclosed in case No. 1, is the first one of the Dollar authorized by the Act of 1878, struck in the presses used for the regular coinage in the Mint of the United States.

O. C. Bosbyshell, Coiner
J. A. Pollock, Superintendent

The whereabouts of the number two dollar struck for Sherman and the number three dollar struck for Linderman are not presently known. As of early 1992 only four coins from the first VAM 9 dies are known to exist in presentation proof condition plus two uncirculated and two circulated business strikes. The VAM 9 die must have been retired early. *Figures 5-4* and *5-5* show examples of a first obverse and an eight tail-feather reverse hub designs. There are two different A design types with minor design differences. The A[1] reverse has a

---

THE FIRST DOLLAR
IT WAS COINED YESTERDAY AFTERNOON AT 3:17
Special Dispatch to the Tribune

PHILADELPHIA, March 11.- There had been no announcement of the time for beginning the coinage of the new silver dollars at Mint, so it was by accident that your correspondent, dropping in at 2 o'clock this afternoon was the only press representative there to see the first of the new coinage made. The dies were finished soon after noon, and the first pair was placed in the largest coining machine, used for double eagles. A little time was spent and a half dozen planchets spoiled before the dies were exactly adjusted. Then Albert Downing, foreman of the coining room, put a polished planchet under the press, and, giving the wheel a single revolution, the first dollar was stamped. It was removed by hand, and, critical examination developing flaws, the pressure was readjusted and another put in.

TEN MORE

were then coined, but the eleventh was found defective, and this, as well as the first, was once defaced and returned to the melting room. The first twelve having been struck on polished planchets, were removed by hand, to prevent indentation, and each inclosed in an envelope numbered to show the order of its coinage. The first goes to the President and the second to Secretary Sherman. The first was struck at 3:17, and at 3:35 steam was turned on and the dollars began

MERRILY CLANKING

into the box at the rate of eighty a minute. Tomorrow two more pairs of dies will be finished, and another machine put to work, so that, on Thursday when ten more will be done, turning out $150,000 of the new shiners a day. The dies for the San Francisco and Carson Mints will be ready then, and will be forwarded at once. The first delivery will be made on Thursday. The Secretary has as yet made no orders for the issue of the new coinage, but it is believed that it will be issued only for gold coin, because it will

COMMAND THE SAME PRICE READILY.

Orders are already in for millions from store-keepers who want them for advertising purposes Whatever silver finds its way into the Treasury will be promptly paid out for the purchase of bullion for coining purposes.

Article from the March 12, 1878 Chicago Daily Tribune
(Courtesy of Numismatic News)

March 13, 1878 The Cincinnati Commercial
Account of Striking of First Morgan Dollar
(Courtesy The Rutherford B. Hayes Library)

raised eagle's beak and the A² reverse has a hooked eagle's beak as illustrated in Chapter 6.

Every A¹ has extensive doubling in the wreath, peripheral lettering, olive branch leaves, and along the lower edge of the eagle's right wing. In addition, many of the denticles are either doubled or show remnants of design. The doubling is slightly different for each die, which would indicate it is not from a doubled working hub. Ongoing research by Pete Bishal has determined that the original master A¹ design was created through combining two different master reverse hub's eagles of the same basic design but of slightly different size. The A¹'s could thus be considered a single design. On the other hand, the A² reverse was only used by impressing A¹ working dies so they only exist as A²/A¹ dual hubs.

The first obverse design type exists in three minor design types. The I¹ has an incused designer's initial "M" and a thinner ear helix and antihelix with more space between them than on the I² obverse, which has a vague raised designer's initial like two vertical bars. Ongoing research of obverse doubling similar in nature to the first reverse type, but of less severity and evident on the chin, suggests the same cause.

Table 5-2 lists the coinage of the silver dollar for each week in 1878.[18] Daily coinage figures for the first few weeks when the new silver dollars were being struck are given in *Table 5-3*.[19] The dates shown are when the coins were delivered by the coiner to the Superintendent of the Mint and not the date actually coined. They were usually struck a day or two before the delivery took place. These figures will be useful in later discussions of the number of coins struck with the various design varieties.

Linderman desired that the two western mints, San Francisco and Carson City, be supplied with dies and collars as quickly as possible, so that they could help strike the large number of silver dollars (2,000,000 per month) required by law. On March 12 he instructed Pollock:

... as soon as it is ascertained that the dies for the silver dollar work satisfactorily, and that the resulting coins are equally so, you will cause to be prepared and transmitted to this office, any special instructions which may be necessary to enable the Coiners of the two Western Mints to prepare their dies in a similar manner to the mode adopted at your Mint.

I refer especially to the basining of the dies, giving the radius for each die. You will cause a careful measurement to be made of the height pile of twenty pieces, and communicate the same to this office.

It is desirable that there should be great uniformity as possible to secure in the dollars manufactured at all mints.

"Basing of the dies" was the process of polishing the field around the design of the dies after it received the required number of hub blows. The die face was held against a slowly revolving dish shaped zinc lap eight inches in diameter and one and one half inches thick. A

Obverse of
First Morgan Dollar Struck
VAM 9 Variety

Reverse of
First Morgan Dollar Struck
VAM 9 Variety

First Morgan Dollar Struck For President Hayes
(In case with accompanying certificate and envelope)

fine lens grinding compound and water on the lap did the actual polishing of the die face.

William Barber's reaction to this letter was sent to Pollack shortly thereafter:[20]

The new silver dollar dies from the new hubs will not basin on any specific basin but require three different grades... a matter of some pains and skill to us of long practice. I hesitate to put the task on the Western Mints which have not had the experience.

Because of this objection, the dies were not shipped to the western mints at that time.

Early in the second week of the silver dollar coinage (March 18 to 20), Linderman visited the Philadelphia Mint for "conference on various points." One of these points turned out to be correction of the "slight imperfections" in the dies of the silver dollar. As a result of this visit, Morgan and Barber were instructed to make new hubs and dies for both the obverse and reverse of the silver dollar. The reason for these changes were to further reduce the relief of the design and to change the reverse design slightly (the number of the eagle's tail feathers was changed from eight to seven, since all previous eagles had an odd

Figure 5-4 FIRST REVERSE DESIGN TYPE, A–8 TAIL FEATHERS

Figure 5-5 FIRST OBVERSE DESIGN TYPE, I (Evenly divided rear portion of ear)

Table 5-2 WEEKLY SILVER DOLLAR COINAGE, 1878

Week Ending	Number of Pieces	Week Ending	Number Of Pieces
3/16	233,200	8/3	382,000
3/23	416,100	8/10	194,000
3/30	352,200	8/17	162,000
4/6	422,000	8/24	276,000
4/13	480,000	8/31	266,000
4/20	458,000	9/7	230,000
4/27	470,000	9/14	268,000
5/4	314,000	9/21	174,000
5/11	156,000	9/28	254,000
5//18	168,000	10/5	200,000
5/25	234,000	10/12	248,000
6/1	170,000	10/19	238,000
6/8	154,000	10/26	114,000
6/15	360,000	11/2	60,000
6/22	418,000	11/9	60,050
6/29	102,000	11/16	250,000
7/6	none (bullion settlement)	11/23	322,000
7/13	134,000	11/30	274,000
7/20	276,000	12/7	210,000
7/27	402,000	12/14	260,000
		12/21	148,000
		12/28	94,000
		12/29-12/31	106,000
		TOTAL	10,509,550

Table 5-3 DAILY SILVER DOLLAR COINAGE, 1878 (as delivered by coiner)

Date	Number of Pieces	Date	Number of Pieces	Date	Number of Pieces
March 12	100	March 20	100,000	March 29	80,000
March 13	40,000	March 21	56,000	March 30	62,000
March 14	85,000	March 22	80,000	April 1	36,000
March 15	48,000	March 23	64,000	April 2	70,000
March 15 (Proofs)	100	March 25	50,000	April 3	74,000
March 16	60,000	March 26	50,000	April 4	62,000
March 18	56,000	March 26 (Proofs)	200	April 5	90,000
March 18 (Proofs)	100	March 27	60,000	April 6	90,000
March 19	60,000	March 28	50,000		

Figure 5-6 SECOND REVERSE DESIGN TYPE, B¹-7 TF PAF
(Long center arrow shaft)

Figure 5-7 SECOND OBVERSE DESIGN TYPE, II
(Unevenly divided rear portion of ear)

number of tail feathers, and the berries, leaves and bows of the wreath were made smaller as a result of heavy basining).

The high relief of the eight tail feather design shortened the life of the dies. "Efforts of ingenuity" were used to make the dies produce better, as Barber put it in a letter to Pollock on March 23:

I wish to report that by using what I might call 'efforts of ingenuity' we have succeeded in making our dies produce very well this last five days...

I expect to go on equally well at this Mint until the new hub is finished, when we shall stop all irregular methods and proceed as formerly.

Unfortunately, the details of these irregular methods were not given in this letter. However, Barber might have been referring to the extra steps in the basining process mentioned in his previous letter. Examination of the die varieties of the first reverse design (8 TF) indicates that working hubs and dies were individually re-engraved, adding two to three small feathers to both sides of the eagle's legs just below the bottom of the wings (see page 108). Apparently the basining process polished part of the center designs off the dies and they had to be individually touched up. Also there is evidence that the A² hub was reimpressed into some rehubbed A¹ reverse dies causing some doubling of the design. The A² reverse apparently basined better than the A¹ reverse and required less individual touch up of the dies.

Linderman was quite concerned over the slow progress in producing the working dies, since the Philadelphia Mint urgently needed them for producing in April the minimum 2,000,000 silver dollars prescribed by the Bland-Allison Act. Dies were also needed at the San Francisco and Carson City Mints so that they could begin striking silver dollars and relieve the burden on the Philadelphia Mint. The pressure to produce silver dollars was so great that coinage of all other denominations was temporarily suspended and the mint was working overtime.[21] Fortunately the stock of fractional silver coins on hand was sufficient to meet the light demands. In today's terms, 2,000,000 coins a month seems a rather small figure, but the Philadelphia Mint had previously never struck coins at that rate.

In answer to a request by Linderman to Pollock on March 23 that "Barber and Morgan report in writing their progress in making new hubs and dies," Barber replied to Pollock (on the same day):

... the new hub commenced when the Director was here will be finished on the 28 of this month and the dies therefrom I expect to ship on the 11th of April.

and Morgan replied to Pollock on Monday, March 25:

I beg to say that the new hub for reverse of silver dollar was finished and hardened today (March 25th).

New dies from this hub will be ready about 2nd of April but I can enter this hub into the dies – fifty in number made from the old hub and have these ready this week.

This letter from Morgan indicates the possibility of a dual hub reverse, an explanation of how the seven over eight tail feather reverse originated. It was to be done as a matter of expediency, in order to save more than a week in obtaining the much-needed new working dies. That this short-cut operation was indeed carried out is indicated by Morgan's letter to Linderman on March 26:

Today I have made and finished dies from the new hub for reverse of silver dollar with reference to which I reported to you yesterday. These dies are now being used in the coining room by Mr. Downing – who is most competent to judge of these things – prefers to use them for a few days before he gives an opinion as to how the dies will work.

With the dies from this hub there was no difficulty with the basins.

I am now finishing as fast as I possible can the hub referred to in Mr. Barber's report. This hub is a lower radius and the dies from this, may work better than those now used.

I shall have it finished tomorrow (27 Inst.) and will proceed to make dies at once.

We have been more successful with the hardening lately. We find this steel requires greater heat, than that used previously.

The dies for the last four or five days have made a fair average of pieces.

The second hub referred to in this letter was undoubtedly the new obverse hub.

The new second design reverse hub had the eagle's tail feathers changed from eight to seven, as shown in *Figure 5-6*. Other changes in the reverse design included: smaller wreath and olive branch leaves, the A of AMERICA touching the eagle's wing, and lower relief. The new second design obverse hub was also of lower relief and had small changes in design details, as shown in *Figure 5-7*: the letters in LIBERTY were thicker, rear portion of ear was divided unequally, and the rim was thinner.

The purpose of the detailed background which has just been given is to provide conclusive evidence of the existence of the so called seven over eight tail feather reverse and how and why it occurred. (The seven over eight tailfeather reverse is not illustrated here because each modified die was different and it was not a basic design type. They are illustrated in Chapter Eight.)

In summary, it can be concluded at this point, first of all, that the new seven tail feather, parallel arrow feather (7 TF PAF) reverse hub of lower relief was entered into some eight feather reverse dies. Presumably, since the two reverses had border lettering that differed in position with respect to the eagle, the old die lettering, including the wreath, was ground and lapped away around the edge. When the new hub was entered into the old dies, only the center part of the design had a doubled appearance (the various parts of the design that were doubled and the die varieties are discussed in Chapter Eight). Dies actually begin as cones in order to prevent the metal from spreading, cracking and chipping during each blow from the hub. Thus, in order to finish the die in one or two blows from the hub, only the outer edge of the die could be ground away.

Also shown is an exact date when the eight tail feather reverse was first used (March 11) and when the seven over eight tail feather variety was first struck (March 26). The coiner's report states that 233,200 silver dollars were struck during the week ending March 16, and that 416,100 were struck during the week ending March 23. Including the 50,000 struck on March 25, a total of at least 699,300 eight tail feather silver dollars were struck, including 300 proofs.

There is evidence that the lower relief, second design obverse hub was impressed on the old, higher relief obverse dies. These dual hub obverses have doubled stars, LIBERTY, symbol letters, and other design details (these will be discussed further and illustrated in Chapter Seven).

Some of the difficulties the mint had during March in striking silver dollars were indicated in O. C. Bosbyshell's (the coiner) letter of April 1 to superintendent Pollock:

I have the honor to report that the new dollar dies are working satisfactorily, so far as the mechanical operations are concerned - that is, they seem to be of a proper radius, our pieces bring up the work on them with ease, and the coins pile evenly, and without rocking.

The dies however, do not stand as well as could be desired - they crack and sink shortly after entering the presses. This would indicate some defect either in the hardening, or in the steel used. During the coinage of March there were used forty-six (46) dies, (32 obverse and 14 reverses), and they produced an average of 43,543 pieces per pair. Whilst this appears to be a good average it must be remembered that in order to produce the amount of coins deemed desirable, we ran many of the dies a longer time in the presses, than we ought to have done.

The average number of pieces to a pair of Trade Dollar dies, during 1877, was about 100,000.

With dies as well prepared as these seem to have been, we ought, with those at present in use, attain the same results, and so far as I am able to state the difficulty is alone in the steel, or manner of treating it.

In an effort to obtain better results in the hardening of the dies, a new foreman, S.W. Straub, was brought into the hardening department at this time.

On April 4, a proof dollar of the new coinage was sent to Linderman and a sample of 25 regular coins was sent to Pollock as representative of coins produced from the new dies. Thus, it was probably on this date that the new seven tail feather reverse dies were first used. (This is about the date estimated in Morgan's letter of March 25.) From March 26 to April 4 the dual hub reverse dies were no doubt used exclusively. According to *Table 5-2*, the coinage for this period, including April 4, was 544,000 which would be a minimum figure for the 7/8 TF reverse. Since about 50 reverse dies were modified, it is likely that they were used after April 4. On some of these dies, no doubt, the old design was probably completely removed and the eight tail feathers did not show beneath the seven tail feathers. Only 13 different dual hub B/A reverse die varieties are known. The other 37 A reverses dies may have been ground down sufficiently so that little of the original design remained. Possibly these include the 5 known B¹ 1878-P, 7 known B¹ 1878-CC and 2 known B¹ 1878-S and 8 condemned 1878-S reverse dies. In addition some of these B/A reverse dies may have been condemned at the Philadelphia Mint.

The coiner's reports of April 1 and April 30 state that the reverse dies averaged 71,535 coins for March and 67,000 coins for April. Thus, for the 13 known dual hub reverse dies a total of about 840,000 coins would have been struck. This would indicate that either the 7/8 TF reverse dies were used beyond April 4 or that their average life was 45,000 coins per die. There is evidence that the dual hub obverses were used considerably longer than the dual hub reverses, since they have appeared with later reverses and 38 varieties are known.

Since 32 obverse dies were used in March to strike 1,001,500 coins, the average number of pieces struck per die was only 31,197. The coiner's April 30 report states that 18 obverse dies were used to strike 2,010,000 coins, an average of 111,667 coins per die. Thus, there could be quite a wide variation in the number of coins per obverse die variety used at that time.

An article in the Washington, D.C. *Evening Star Newspaper* of April 6, 1878 concerning the silver dollar design change explained that the relief of both the obverse and reverse had been made lower:

Improving THE DOLLARS — A change has been made in the coinage of the silver dollar. The muchly abused eagle is there, but below the general surface of the coin. The Goddess of Liberty's head on the other side has also been depressed, to prevent constant friction and wearing away. The dies are working better now than at first, consequently the coins issued lately have a smoother appearance and are of much finer finish then those first turned out at the mint.

Linderman, however, was still not satisfied with the coins. On April 5 he wrote a letter concerning the relief of the obverse dies. Morgan replied on April 8:

... I have come to the conclusion that the head is well protected by the border when the dies do not sink or even when they sink a little but when the dies sink as many of them did during the last month the heads come much too close together, and in some coins which have been issued they would actually touch.

Today in consultation with Mr. Key and Mr. Downing I examined the coins now being made. We came to the conclusion that in respect to the devices being protected by the border they are much better than have been made and leave little to be desired.

I noticed some time ago that when the dies had settled a little as they almost invariably do – a place on the cheek which comes opposite of the wing of the eagle – did not come up satisfactorily. In the hub now being used I have cut down this part. I cannot see that it would be any advantage to reduce the relief in any other place.

I am sorry that it does not seem to be possible to tell what pressure is required to bring up the devices on the dollar. The Superintendent and the Engraver seem to be of opinion that the unfortunate breakage of the stake of one press, the center piece of another and lastly the main-arch of another have been caused by the great pressure necessary to bring up the devices of the coin.

Mr. Downing is decidedly of opinion that no more pressure than is required to bring up the Trade Dollar. That the breaking of the stakes and center pieces is no extraordinary occurrence and that the crack in the arch of press No. 7 is an unfortunate matter which is a little better than guessing to give an opinion.

I am glad to be able to report a decided improvement in the hardening of the dies. After much careful experiment we now get the dies to stand much better. During the last four or five days they have averaged about 80,000 pieces per pair of dies, which I respectfully submit to you as about as good an average as we can expect... I have lately pointed out several dies which should never have been allowed to go into the presses. This I believe you will agree with me is more a matter for the Engraver and the Foreman.

Although Mr. Barber does not appear to take any great interest in the finish of the dies himself, he has expressly forbidden Mr. Straub to receive any instructions from me.

From this letter it is apparent that Barber and Morgan were not on the best of terms, probably because of Linderman's special interest in the young Englishman and the adoption of Morgan's design for the silver dollar. The dies that Morgan believed should not have been allowed in the presses were probably some of the seven over eight tail feather reverses and the doubled LIBERTY obverses. The letter also reveals that at the time the new seven tail feather dies were first used, the hardening process had been improved so that the dies averaged 80,000 pieces.

Finally on April 8, 1878, the first shipment of dies were shipped from the Philadelphia Mint to the two western mints as reported by an April 9 letter from Linderman to Pollock:

I have rec'd your letter of the 8th inst. advising this office of the shipment to the Western Mints of 20 pairs of dies and 12 collars, for the standard silver dollar, together with suggestions as to the proper mode of treating the dies, hardening, etc...

They arrived at the Carson City Mint on the morning of April 16 as reported by the Carson City *Morning Appeal* April 17, 1878 edition as shown on the next page.

This same edition of the *Morning Appeal* also had a separate one line stating, "A few new dollars were struck off yesterday as samples." So the first Morgan dollars were struck at the Carson City Mint the first day that the dies arrived on April 16, 1878, apparently without any significant ceremonies.

Production was to begin on April 17 at the rate of 30,000 coins per day. There were two smaller coining presses and one larger press at the Carson City Mint at that time. The big 18,000 pound Ajax press could strike 90 coins per minute which would have been sufficient to coin this amount in a normal ten hour working day, allowing time for unloading the coins from the press and operator breaks.

The *Morning Appeal* writer was more than a little harsh on the Morgan dollar design which was the Type II obverse and the seven tail feather parallel arrow feather reverse, B[1]. Expressing great disgust at the dies general appearance and the wretched workmanship of the Philadelphia dollar, the poor maligned eagle was called a wide, flat, pelican – bat of the wilderness. It was wished that the Government employ a new designer to give a new die, dollar and deal and it was even suggested that a small discount on the face of the dollar should be allowed! Such words were rather strong coming from the silver production area that the Bland-Allison Act primarily served.

It was the evening of April 16, 1878 when the first shipment of Morgan dollar dies and collars arrived at the San Francisco Mint, a scant half a day later than for the Carson City Mint. Unlike the Carson City Mint first striking, Superintendent Henry Dodge of the San Francisco Mint invited the press and others to witness the ceremony of issuing the first dollar. An account of this was given in the April 18, 1878 issue of the *New Alta California*.

From this eyewitness accounting, the first dollars were struck at the San Francisco Mint at 3:30 PM on April 17, 1878, witnessed by various members of the press, Ex-Governor Low, and Mint officers. It is interesting to note that coiner Circott received the first San Francisco Morgan dollar rather than the Mint Superintendent or ex-Governor - sometimes the workers do get rewarded! This is in contrast to the first struck Philadelphia Morgan dollar which was presented to President Hayes per his desire even though he had vetoed the Bland-Allison Act. The whereabouts of the Circott first struck coin is unknown today. There is no documentation of the first Carson City struck Morgan dollar being specially presented to anyone.

After nearly one thousand coins were initially struck on April 17, the die cracked and the press was stopped at the San Francisco Mint. This was a portent of things to come for on Saturday April 20, 1878, Linderman reported to Pollock in a letter:

> Supt. Dodge telegraphs the 8 reverse and 3 obverse new silver dollar dies have been condemned.
>
> I do not know that this information is of any importance except it may indicate the propriety of forwarding say ten extra reverse dies.
>
> It will be necessary for the Engraver to get ready as soon as possible another lot of silver dollar dies for shipment to S. F.

The following Monday, April 22, Linderman fur-

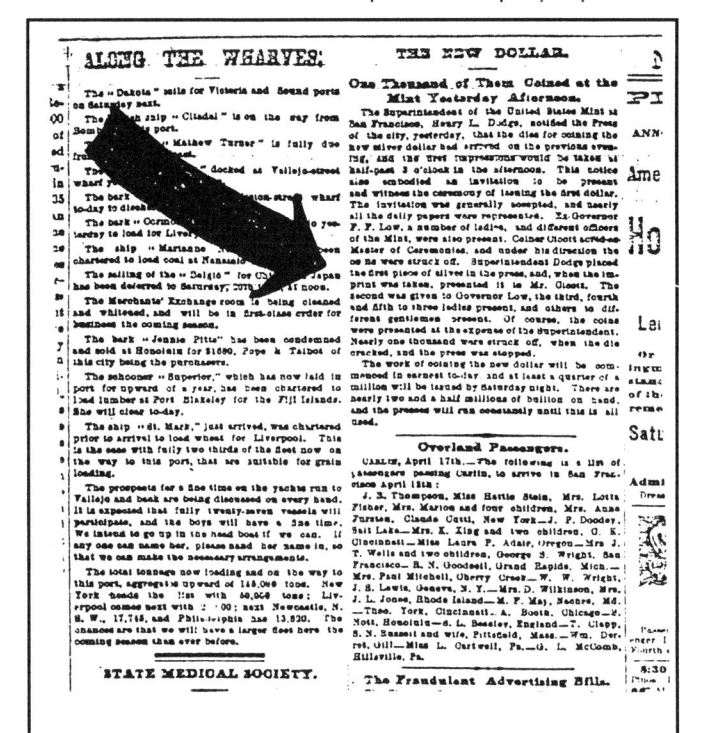

THE NEW DOLLAR
One Thousand of Them Coined at the Mint Yesterday Afternoon.

The Superintendent of the United States Mint at San Francisco, Henry L. Dodge, notified the Press of the city, yesterday, that the dies for coining the new silver dollar had arrived on the previous evening, and the first impressions would be taken at half–past 3 o'clock in the afternoon. This notice also embodied an invitation to be present and witness the ceremony of issuing the first dollar. The invitation was generally accepted, and nearly all the daily papers were represented. Ex-Governor F. F. Low, a number of ladies, and different officers of the Mint, were also present. Coiner Cicott acted as Master of Ceremonies, and under his direction the coins were struck off. Superintendent Dodge placed the first piece of silver in the press, and, when the imprint was taken, presented it to Mr. Cicott. The second was given to Governor Low, the third, fourth and fifth to three ladies present, and others to different gentlemen present. Of course, the coins were presented at the expense of the Superintendent. Nearly one thousand were struck off, when the die cracked, and the press was stopped.

The work of coining the new dollar will be commenced in earnest to-day, and at least a quarter of a million will be issued by Saturday night. There are nearly two and a half millions of bullion on hand, and the presses will run constantly until this is all used.

April 18, 1878 New Alta California Account of Striking of First Morgan Dollars at San Francisco
(Courtesy of the California State Library)

Dies at Last... Yesterday morning the new dies for the U. S. mint arrived from Philadelphia. There were ten obverse, ten reverse and six collars. The dies were hardened yesterday and the big Ajax press will start up today. There are 632,325 blanks ready for the press, and when they get to work will turn out the dollars at the rate of 30,000 per day. We have had our little say about the dollars coined in Philadelphia, and now the Coiner here is driven to follow in the footsteps, or rather the press whacks, of the concern on the Delaware. Great disgust was expressed at the general appearance of the dies. All that has been said as to the wretched workmanship of the Philadelphia dollar, will be equally true of the Carson dollar, and it can't be helped. The die represents the same wide, flat, pelican – bat of the wilderness, and will show up all the defects of the coin. The C. C. in the die is very indistinct, and looks as if it would turn out two periods. We wish it may, and that the unartistic appearance of the coin will lead the Government to employ a new designer and give us a new die, dollar and deal. The United States ought to be ashamed to issue such a piece of workmanship, and at least should allow a small discount on the face of the thing.

April 17, 1878 Carson City Morning Appeal Account of Striking of First Morgan Dollars at Carson City Mint
(Courtesy of the Nevada State Museum)

91

Figure 5-8 SECOND REVERSE DESIGN TYPE, B²-7 TF PAF
(Short center arrow shaft)

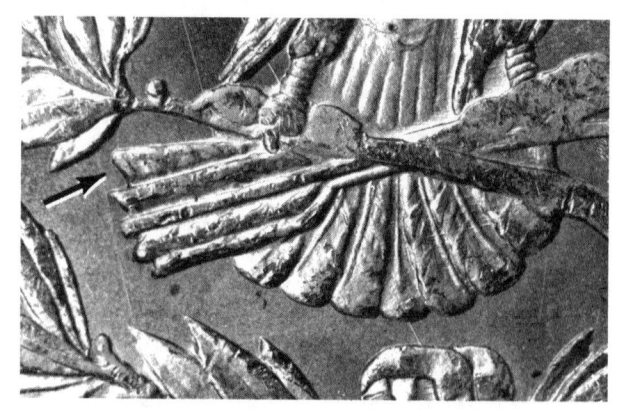

Figure 5-9 THIRD REVERSE DESIGN TYPE, C-7 TF SAF

ther instructed Pollock to continue the overtime work at the Philadelphia Mint:

Referring to my dispatch of current date in which I informed you that instructions sent you by mail in Saturday last to discontinue overtime, with certain exceptions, would not take effect until the close of this month, I have now to state that information received from Superintendent Dodge in yesterday by telegraph, indicates that we cannot depend upon any considerable amount of silver dollar coinage at S. F. from the first lot of dies; and in view of this fact it was deemed best that you should continue to run to your full capacity, with overtime until the close of the month, by which time we will be better able to determine what will be required.

Thus, by this rather lengthy sentence the burden of the Morgan dollar production of a minimum of $2,000,000 worth of silver per month continued to fall on the Philadelphia Mint. This extraordinary effort by the Philadelphia Mint in April was reported by the coiner Bosbyshell in a letter to Pollock on April 30, 1878,

I have the honor to transmit herewith a Report of the Coinage executed for the month of April 1878, showing the enormous amount of two million ten – thousand Silver Dollars (2,010,000).

This showing is exceedingly gratifying to me, as it is a greater amount of work than has ever been executed in one month at any Mint. To accomplish this pleasing result has required ceasless (sic) endeavor on the part of all persons employed in this Department, and I feel sure that you will join with me in awarding the mead (sic) of praise due, to these faithful employees...

*Very Respectfully
Your Obt. Servant
O. C. Bosbyshell
Coiner*

Chief Engraver, William Barber, in a letter to Pollock on April 11, 1878 stated that 15 pairs of dies for San Francisco and five for Carson City Mints would be shipped the middle of the following week or about April 17. They would have arrived at these mints about April 25 or 26, 1878, thus ending the initial striking crises of the Morgan dollar.

Early in April, the second design reverse hub was modified slightly by shortening the middle arrow shaft (see *Figure 5-8*).

Apparently in the haste of preparing the second design hub, the length of the middle arrow shaft had not been reduced from the 8 TF design as had the other feather ends, and the middle arrow shaft stuck out rather obviously. The B¹ hub was used in modifying all the 7/8 TF dies (this is a key point to look for in searching for the 7/8 TF reverse), and was used on some of the later 1878-P and some 1878-CC, and 1878-S.

Linderman was still not completely satisfied with the design, as indicated by his letter to Pollock on April 10:

... I note a decided improvement in the execution of the silver dollar but I think there is room for some further slight improvement. I have had some correspondence with Mr. Morgan which I suggested for his careful consideration whether the head of Liberty was still too much in relief. He says that the more recent coinage shows the head to be low enough in relief. It occurs to me that the rim or border of the coin is rather pinched - not full enough. I make no pretensions to knowledge on these technical points and would have no attempt at any alterations made unless clearly indicated as both necessary and practicable. I should think that Mr. Straub and Mr. Downing could tell us whether the rim of the coin is as it should be. I would be glad if you would quietly examine the matters herein referred to and write me the results. Of course nothing in the way of alteration must be undertaken that would in any way risk what has already been accomplished...

The personnel of the Coining and Hardening Department, Downing and Straub, commented on Linderman's inquiry in a letter to Pollock on April 12:

... The original width of border on the dies of the 412 1/2 gr. silver dollar was well designed, but new hubs were made from one pair of these dies to change the radius. As all steel enlarges during the hardening process, the hub and dies from it expanded, this increased the reeded border, and as the collar controls the diameter it decreased the plain border in width. As to what the width of that border should be is a matter in which persons will differ largely in artistic taste and judgement. Viewing it from a mechanical standpoint we are of the opinion that an increased width of border would be advantageous, as there would be a better protection for the face of the coin, less liability for abrasion, and the piles would stand more firmly with additional surface which would be given to the pieces to rest on. The variation in centering of the coins would be less perceptible in a wide border than in a narrower one.

Figure 5-10 THIRD REVERSE DESIGN TYPES
C¹ and C² (Long serif of A)   C³ (Short serif of A)

Linderman wrote to Pollock on April 15, ordering that the improvement be made:

... you express the opinion that further improvement in the new silver dollar is both practicable and desirable and the same can be accomplished without interfering with the several designs or impairing improvements already made.

The foregoing is in-accord with my own views and I desire that the proposed improvement be undertaken as soon as may be practicable and carefully conducted until accomplished ...

On April 17, Morgan wrote to Lindeman (as quoted in Shafer's article):

... in the hubs on which I am now at work, I am most carefully attending to all the points where I have noticed improvements can be made either in appearance or in the working of the coins.

When the coins were first made, the reverse border was broader and heavier than the obverse.

In the hubs now being used I tried to get the border equal in width by lessening the reverse. The hub, however, expanded more than usual in the hardening and made the reverse narrower than the obverse border.

I shall get the border equal and slightly heavier than they are now.

The reverse dies now fill up quickly while striking the coin. I am finishing this hub so that I believe this filling will be avoided.

I noticed that some places in both dies are apt to get rubbed too low in the polishing. I have softened both the original dies and deepened these places.

I notice that the part of the cheek coming opposite to the wing of the eagle is still the last to come up when the dies have sunk a little. I shall cut down both the cheek and the wing... I shall have these hubs finished next week, and we shall proceed to use them as soon as finished.

The two different coin designs caused some concern to the public. There were various inquiries to the Treasury Department and the Philadelphia Mint pointing out the design differences and the fact that they did not stack up to the same height. The main concern was whether the new design coin was genuine. Bosbyshell, the coiner, had the duty of explaining the differences, and in one letter he remarked:

... I might add that in the issuance of a new piece of money, it always requires time to perfect the designs, and the preparation of the dies. This should be done before any pieces are issued, but in the case of the new dollar it was not done, and subsequent alterations were unavoidable because found to be necessary.

The dies worked much better during April, as indicated in a letter from Bosbyshell to Pollock of April 30:

... To produce the amount of pieces reported [2,010,000] there were used eighteen (18) obverse and thirty (30) reverse dies, or twenty-four (24) pairs of dies. Hence in April each pair of dies averaged 83,750 pieces...

On May 17, Morgan reported to Linderman the progress on making the new dies:

We have made two pairs of dies from the new hubs for the silver dollar and tried them in the coining presses. I understand that you have received a piece struck from these dies.

I have to report that the reverse dies worked well both on the basin and in the presses, an improvement in both cases on those used before. You will notice that the border is now broader.

The obverse dies worked well in the presses. The failing which we have always noticed before on the cheek having in these dies entirely disappeared. The obverse dies, however, do not go on the basin satisfactorily. They could be finished by hand or put on another basin, but as there will not be any difficulty in making a slight change in the Hub so that the dies could be rubbed down on the same basin as heretofore, I have softened the hub with this view.

When hardened I propose to make two more dies and test them again.

If you think the reverse is now satisfactory in appearance we could take this hub into general use.

I beg to say that we have now in stock nearly 100 pairs of dollar dies...

The two new pairs of dies mentioned in this letter struck the first coins of the third obverse and reverse designs. The C reverse is the so called 1878-P 7 TF SAF (slanted arrow feather) type, as illustrated in *Figure 5-9*.

The new III obverse had a wider rim, more details in the cotton blossoms, and lines in the wheat leaves. It is illustrated in Chapter Six.

On May 20, Linderman wrote to Pollock about these new dies: "*... I do not deem it advisable to make any changes at present from the dies now in use ...*"

Linderman probably wanted to reduce the stockpile of dies mentioned in Morgan's letter before changing designs again.

On June 5, Morgan again reported to Linderman on his progress with the new dies:

Having still about 100 pairs of dies for the silver dollars in stock, we have had no necessity to make dies for this coin during the last two weeks.

With a view of making the work come up easier and more uniform I have made two slight alterations in depth of work and width of border.

The dies were tried in the coining presses but in neither case was the result exactly satisfactory as I wished. I am now engaged on a third attempt which I believe will give us all we want.

As soon as these dies are tried I will request to have forwarded to you some pieces which I hope will meet with your approval.

We have always had a difficulty in making hubs from dies. The metal would spread, causing the hub to be weak. After hardening little pieces would break off and then each die had to be repaired. I met this difficulty. I suggested a way to Mr. Straub which he very ably and willingly carried out. We shall not be troubled in this way again. Our tests have been entirely satisfactory...

On June 28 Morgan wrote Linderman again: "...The dies from our new hubs in the dollar are made are working very satisfactory in every way".

These new dies were basically the same as those reported by Morgan on May 17 and June 5, except for small differences in the rim width and design details. The first trial reverse dies used on about May 17 had the A in AMERICA nearly touching the eagle's wing. The bottom feather of the eagle's right wing next to the leg was rounded and not connected to the wing on the left. The rim was also rather narrow. The second trial reverse die, used on about June 5, was similar to the first one except that the bottom feather of the eagle's right wing extended to the junction of the next two feathers and a thin line was present between the eagle's leg and first feather. The final version of the third reverse design had the left serif of A in AMERICA cut down so that it was away from the wing (See *Figure 5-10*), the bottom feather of the eagle's right wing was squared off and raised, and the rim was wider.

The first trial die of the third obverse design, used about May 17, had lines in all wheat leaves and the end of the wheat leaf was well below the bottom of the R in PLURIBUS. A second obverse die used at that time was similar except for excessive polishing of the top of the die, which eliminated some of the design detail. The first and second trial obverse dies have been seen on coins in combination with the first trial reverse dies. The first trial obverse die was also used with the second trial reverse die on a proof coin. A long wheat leaf with weak lines is close to the bottom of the R in the final version of the third obverse design, and the rim is also wider. These differences in the third obverse design are illustrated in Chapter Six.

Only a few trial obverse and reverse dies of the early third design were used on May 17 and June 5. As a result, these coins are scarce. The final versions of the third design obverse and reverse dies were used only at the Philadelphia mint during 1878. The large stockpile of the second design dies was used to supply the Western mints.

The earliest date that the third design obverse and reverse dies could have been used extensively is June 28. This design was used for practically all later years of the Morgan series. Because of the large number of dies in the stockpile at that time, a number of different die mar-

riages occurred. These combinations will be discussed further in Chapter Six.

The second reverse (7 TF PAF) was first used on April 4, and the third reverse (7 TF SAF) was first used on a regular basis on June 28. On the basis of the weekly coinage report then, about 3,600,000 7 TF PAF were struck during this period (less an unknown number of 7/8 TF), and more were probably struck after June 28. As of June 5, 100 pairs of dies were available, and during June, 30 pairs of dies were sent to Carson City and 36 pairs to San Francisco. This left 34 pairs of the second design, which would have struck about 80,000 coins apiece or 2,720,000 in all. However, in April, 30 reverses were used to strike 2,010,000 coins (average of 67,000 coins), while only 18 obverses were used (average of 111,667 coins). Thus, the second obverse design dies lasted longer than the second reverse designs. From June 5, the 34 second design obverse dies could have struck about 3,800,000 coins, while the same number of reverse dies could have struck about 2,300,000 coins. Added to the approximately 2,600,000 coins struck from April 4 to June 5, this would total about 6,400,000 second design obverse and 4,900,000 second design reverse coins struck.

This would have left about 2,800,000 coins of the third obverse design (total 1878 mintage at Philadelphia, 10,500,000, minus the approximate coinage from March 12 through April 4, 1,300,000; minus 6,400,000 equals 2,800,000), and about 4,300,000 coins of the third reverse design (10,500,000 minus 1,300,000 minus 4,900,000 equals 4,300,000). The authors have seen combinations of the second obverse design with the third reverse design and some coins that have both the obverse and reverse third design for the 1878-P. This tends to confirm the trend shown in the above mintage figures.

Twelve presentation pieces were struck on the first day of Morgan dollar coinage, March 11, 1878, using the first die of VAM 9. There were 100 proof silver dollars delivered by the coiner to the Superintendent of the Mint on March 12, 1878. These were likely the eight tail feather variety VAM 14-3. Another 100 proof dollars were delivered on March 15 and another 100 on March 18. These were still the eight tail feather varieties VAM 14-3 and 14-8. On March 26, 200 more dollar proofs were delivered. Since this was the first day that the dies from the new seven tail feather hub were ready, these were probably all seven tail feather coins of variety VAM 131. Robert Julian reports an additional 50 proofs were delivered on November 8[22] and these were probably the C reverse variety VAM 215 with slanted arrow feathers.

DESIGN CHANGES AFTER 1878

The third design of the regular coinage was used until 1904, although Linderman continued to be dissatisfied with the reverse design. He wrote to Morgan on July 5, 1878:

Whilst the head on the obverse of the silver dollar is very good indeed, the eagle in the reverse looks a little as if it had been drawn from a model instead of from life, and it is evident that the Artist has suffered from a necessity of crowding so much in a limited space.

The wreath under the eagle rather unduly competes with the bird, and I think that the Old English letters might have been omitted and modern letters used in their place.

The changing of devices after a coin is once issued to any considerable extent is not good policy and for that reason I think it is doubtful whether we should sanction any change in the devices of the silver dollar, unless there should be by law, a change in the weight of the piece.

With a view to get a good eagle for the gold coins less than the double eagle, as well as for the silver coins of less denomination than the dollar, I desire that you will make a new model of an eagle and cut therefrom a new reverse for the silver dollar, omitting the wreath, and substituting the modern letters now in use at the Mint, for the Old English letters. If you should succeed in getting an entirely satisfactory representation of an eagle, it is probable that we shall adopt it at some future time. The model must be regarded as an experiment and will be submitted to me for inspection...

Linderman became ill in the fall of 1878 and died on January 27, 1879. His death was probably the reason why no further design modifications were made.

Correspondence in 1880 with the Carson City Mint about the various reverse designs used during that year fairly well summarizes the difficulties experienced in 1878. Colonel Snowden, who was then Superintendent of the Philadelphia Mint, wrote to Burchard, the new Director of the Mint (as quoted in Shafer's article):

... The first hubs were found to be so defective on account of the haste in their preparation that they were condemned on my own recommendation, although I was then not an officer of the mint.

The second hubs were prepared also under great pressure. These were also defective. The defects were pointed out to Director Linderman, but he was so anxious to have the different mints commence on the coinage, that he ordered dies from these hubs to be prepared and forwarded to the mints ...

Accompanying these dies was a letter of instruction stating their defects, acquainting the officers of the difficulties they would encounter in their use ...

To remedy the defect in these dies the Director came to Philadelphia and called me to meet him at the mint, which I did, and at his request I pointed out to the engraver the defects in the hubs, to wit: that the dies struck therefrom had too great a radii and were basined on 13 and 18, whereas they should be basined, in my judgement, on number 20 obverse and 25 reverse.

I also pointed out the necessity of cutting away enough of the ground of the hub to allow proper basining.

The third hub was made in conformity with my suggestion and the dies have proven entirely satisfactory...

In 1900, the reverse was slightly modified and used on most of the coins from that late to 1904. It is designated the C^4 reverse and has a larger space between the eagle's left wing and the eagle's neck which tended to fill up on the C^3 reverse. In addition, the center space in the I of IN was made larger, the stars were larger and the eagle's breast feathers are not as distinct.

Some of the C^3 reverses were reimpressed with the new C^4 reverse hub. The resulting C^4/C^3 dual hub dies were used for some coinage during 1900-1904. The dual hubbing shows as two olives above the olive branch with the top one being shallow, and doubled olive leaves, arrow heads, wing feathers and eagle's head.

For the last year of issue of the Morgan dollar in 1921, new obverse and reverse master dies were made. This was necessary, since in 1910, every die and hub in the Philadelphia Mint was destroyed except for those used for regular coinage denominations during that year.[23] Both the obverse and reverse designs and details are slightly different from previously used designs. Morgan made the master die in the then older way of hubbing the central main design and punching in the stars and lettering instead of using the available Janvier reducing machine and reducing the entire design and lettering. As a result, the design retained the sharpness of the 1904 and prior designs. Most of the working dies were basined because proof-like coins exist for the 1921-P, D and S mints. However, they are not as prevalent as for the earlier years of the Morgan dollar either because the dies struck larger quantities of coins or not all dies were basined.

It is not clear how Morgan developed the design for the 1921 master die. He may still have had the original clay models or he may simply used a coin to transfer the central design into a design hub. Either way the design was gone over extensively resulting in much sharper hair and wing feathers. The relief is lower and the overall look of the coin is harsher and different than previously.

The 1921 obverse, IV, differed from the type III obverse in that the lettering of the symbol and LIBERTY was slightly different as well as the finer details of the Liberty head. The 1921 reverse, D, differed from the type C reverse in that it had parallel arrow feathers, large stars, flat eagle's breast, and minor differences in the legend lettering. Two slightly different hub designs were used for the 1921 reverse. The first used on some 1921-P coins, type D^1, had 17 berries in the wreath with a shallow olive branch under the eagle's claw. The second design, D^2, was used on some 1921-P and all 1921-D and S. It had 16 berries in the wreath and a thicker olive branch under the claw.

The number of edge reeding for the Morgan dollar varied over the years and with each mint. This is discussed in detail in Chapter Seven. To briefly summarize, in general the New Orleans Mint used 176 reeds from 1879 to 1882 and 181 reeds from 1882 to 1904 for the Morgan silver dollar, the Carson City Mint used 177 and 178 reeds, the San Francisco Mint used 181 to 191 reeds over the years but stabilized at 189 in 1900 - 1904 and 1921. The Philadelphia Mint used from 157 to 194 reeds over the years but generally used 179 - 181 in 1879 - 1883, 189 - 190 in 1884 - 1900 and 189 in 1901 - 1904 and 1921. Proof coins had 179 reeds from 1879 - 1894, 189 - 190 from 1896 - 1899 and 186 from 1900 - 1904. Thus, some mints and the proofs have unique edge reeding counts.

SUMMARY

Based upon letters from Director of the Mint Linderman, Superintendent of the Philadelphia Mint Pollock, chief engraver Barber, special engraver Morgan, coiner Bosbyshell and the personnel in the Hardening and Coining Departments, Straub and Downing, the evolution of the Morgan silver dollar design was traced was traced. Among the conclusions drawn were:

1. Three different obverse designs were used during 1878 at the Philadelphia Mint. The later designs were lower in relief and the second design had a narrow rim. The first and third design had minor design type variations.
2. Three different reverse designs were used during 1878 at the Philadelphia Mint. The first was the eight tail feathers, the second was the seven tail feathers with parallel arrow feathers, and the third was the seven tail feathers with slanted arrow feathers. The later designs were lower in relief and had other small differences, including a narrow rim on the second design. There were two minor design type variations for the first design, two for the second design, and three for the third design.
3. Two persons besides Morgan contributed to the final design of the Morgan silver dollars: Linderman and Colonel Snowden.
4. The first design obverse and reverse dies were used in regular coinage from March 11, 1878, to at least March 26, 1878, at only the Philadelphia Mint. A minimum of 699,300 of this design with eight tail feathers were struck.
5. There is evidence that the second minor design type hub of the first reverse design was entered into five dies of the first minor design type of this first reverse design. The dual dies had doubling of some design features particularly the eagles lower beak and tongue.
6. The second design reverse hub (7 TF PAF) was entered into 50 eight tail feather first design dies. At least 544,000 coins from these dual hub reverse dies (7/8 TF) were struck from March 26 to April 4, 1878, and more were struck after this. Thirteen of these dual hub dies have been identified to date. Not all of these dies had the eight tail feathers showing beneath the seven tail feathers. However, the average coinage of each die variety was only about 70,000.
7. There is evidence that the second design obverse hub was entered into the first design dies (probably also 50 dies). Between 40,000 and 110,000 coins of each die variety were struck. Thirty nine of these dual hub dies have been identified to date.
8. The second design dies were used from April, 1878, to at least June 28, 1878. A few dies were probably used after this period. As many as 6,400,000 second design obverse and up to 4,900,000 second design reverse coins were struck.
9. The third design dies were used from June 28, 1878 until 1904. Possibly as many as 2,800,000 third obverse design coins and 4,300,000 third reverse design coins were struck at Philadelphia in 1878.
10. Morgan dollars were first struck at the Philadelphia Mint on March 11, 1878, at the Carson City Mint on April 16, 1878 and at the San Francisco Mint on April 17, 1878.
11. The first Morgan dollar struck in the presses used for the regular coinage was given to President Hayes and currently resides in The Rutherford B. Hayes Museum at Fremont, Ohio. It is an eight tail feather VAM 9 variety and is one of 12 presentation pieces struck.
12. 300 eight tail feather, 200 seven tail feather (parallel arrow feather) and 50 seven tail feather (slanted arrow feather) proofs were struck during 1878. Three different die varieties of the eight tail feather proofs exist and 12 presentation pieces were struck.
13. Master dies for the Morgan dollar were normally made by impressing a design hub with the central design only into the master die first. Then the wreath and denticles were hubbed into the die. And finally the peripheral lettering, stars and date were punched in by hand by Mr. Key. Changes in the design were also made by cutting away portions of hubs and dies.
14. The 1921 Morgan design is from new master dies since all hubs and dies had been destroyed in 1910.
15. The number of edge reedings varied with year and mint up until 1900 when it was standardized at 189. Some mints and proofs have unique edge reeding counts.
16. The complete date was in the working hubs in 1878 and 1921. In 1879, the 187 was in the working hub and the 9 was punched into each working die. From 1880 to 1883 the 18 was in the working hub and the last two digits were punched into the working dies. From 1884 to 1900 the entire date was punched into each working dies using a logotype.

Footnotes

[1] "The Employment of George Morgan, Mint Engraver", *The Numismatic Scrapbook Magazine*, February 1964, p. 310.
[2] Letter from Morgan to Dr. Linderman on July 27, 1876, *The Numismatic Scrapbook Magazine*, February 1964.
[3] Letter from Morgan to Dr. Linderman on September 18, 1876, Record Group 104, National Archives.
[4] *The Numismatist*, February, 1925, p. 109.
[5] Includes research and contributions on half and ten dollar pattern development by Pete R. Bishal of Massachusetts.
[6] Robert W. Julian, "History of Morgan Dollars," *Coin World*, September 26, 1984, p.1.
[7] Letter from Morgan to Dr. Linderman on November 1, 1876. Record Group 104, National Archives.
[8] "To Marry a Goddess," *The Numismatist*, May 1896.
[9] J. H. Judd, *U.S. Pattern, Experimental and Trial Pieces*, sixth Ed., Western Publishing Co.
[10] *The Numismatist*, July 1936, p. 531.
[11] *The Numismatist*, October 1913, p. 541.
[12] William S. Nawrocki, "Rare Galvanoes," *COINage*, 1984.
[13] *Encyclopedia Brittanica*, Fifteenth Edition, p. 691, "Electroplating."
[14] "Comprehensive Catalogue & Encyclopedia of U. S. Coins," *Coin World*, 1990, p. 346 No.E1180.
[15] *The History of United States Coinage as Illustrated by the Garret Collection*, by Q. David Bowers, 1979 Color Plate 20, J-1503.
[16] Barber pattern silver dollar reprinted by permission from: J.H. Judd, *United States Pattern, Experimental, and Trial Pieces*.
[17] Colonel Snowden had been Chief Coiner of the Philadelphia Mint from 1866 to 1876.
[18] Compiled from the *Reports on Coinage and Medals, 1873-1899*, Record Group 104, No.70, National Archives.
[19] Editor's Note: *The Numismatic Scrapbook Magazine*, February 1965, p. 313 (with corrections).
[20] Neil Shafer "The Morgan Silver Dollars, 1878-1921", *The Whitman Numismatic Journal*, November 1964.
[21] *Annual Director of the Mint Report, 1878*.
[22] Robert Julian, "History of the Morgan Dollar," *Coin World*, November 21, 1984.
[23] *The Numismatist*, October 1913, p. 541.

Chapter 6
Description of the Designs

This chapter describes the four reverse and four obverse major designs used for the Morgan silver dollar. Some of the design changes were minor, but they are of interest since they were made to the hubs used to make many working dies. The 1878-P seven over eight tail feather reverses, the 1878-P doubled LIBERTY obverses and the 1900 – 1904 two olive reverses are not discussed in detail in this section on design changes. They were actually a dual hub combination of the second design hub impressed over the first design in the working dies. They are treated separately as die varieties.

The Morgan silver dollar was struck during the period from 1878 to 1904 and again in 1921. Design changes were made in 1878, 1884, 1900 and 1921. A particularly notable year for design changes was 1878 since three reverse and three obverse design types were used. These alterations in 1878 were made to perfect the design and the dies used.

Photographs and a list of differences of the designs are included at the end of this chapter.

REVERSE DESIGN DESCRIPTIONS

The initial reverse, A, (8 TF) used on the coins struck at the Philadelphia Mint in 1878 had eight eagle's tail feathers, flat eagle's breast, large arrow feathers with the arrow points spread, large leaves in the branch held by the eagle's talon, and high relief. There were also slight differences from later designs in the eagle's beak, wing feathers, leg feathers, and stars. The first working hub of the 8 TF design, A^1, had a raised eagle's beak, the I of IN touched the top of the eagle's wing, and small feathers were individually engraved between the wing and leg. The second working hub, A^2, had a hooked eagle's beak, and the I of IN was away from the eagle's wing. However, because of the time pressures at the Philadelphia Mint to produce the Morgan dollars, the A^2 reverse dies were never made in the normal manner. Instead, five A^1 dies were re-impressed with the A^2 hub which produced doubling on some features of the die such as doubled eagle's lower beak and tongue. There are no known A^2 design type dies; only the dual hub A^2/A^1 types have been found to date. The A^1 and A^2/A^1 reverses were used from March 11, 1878 for the next month or so with the I and II/I obverses.

The second reverse, B, (7 TF PAF) was used on some 1878-P coins from April 4, 1878, to at least June 28, 1878, and on all 1878-S and 1878-CC coins. The relief of the coin was made lower, the rim was thinner, the number of eagle's tail feathers was changed to seven, the berries, leaves and bows on the wreath were made smaller, and the A in AMERICA touched the eagle's wing. An early version of this design, B^1, had a long center arrow shaft which appeared on some 1878-P, S, and CC coins. The later version of the design, B^2, had a short center arrow shaft and appeared on some 1878-P,CC, and S, some 1879-S, and some 1880-CC coins. A few of the dies of the first design, A, were re-impressed with the second design working hub, B^1, on March 26, 1878, and this resulted in the seven over eight tail feather design variety reverse, B/A. These dual hub dies were used from March 26 to April 4, 1878, and to a limited extent thereafter to strike some 1878-P coins. The number of the original eight tail feather ends showing varied from one to seven.

The third reverse, C, (7 TF SAF) was used on some 1878-P on a trial basis on May 17 and June 5, 1878, and was used regularly after June 28, 1878. The number of tail feathers remained at seven but the eagle's breast was rounded and the top arrow feather was slanted. In addition, the A of AMERICA no longer touched the eagle's wing, the eagle's beak was less hooked, the rim was wider, and the wing feathers near the eagle's body were slightly changed. The first two dies of this design, C^1, were used on about May 17, 1878, and had a long serif on the A next to the eagle's wing in AMERICA. The bottom feather of the eagle's right wing, next to the leg, was rounded and not connected to the wing on the left. The next trial die, C^2, was used on June 5, 1878, and was similar to C^1 except that the bottom feather was connected to the wing on both sides and a thin line was present between the eagle's leg and the first feather. The final version, C^3, was used after June 28, 1878, and had the A serif cut away from the wing and the bottom feather squared off and raised. It was used on some 1879-S, 1880-CC, 1900-P, S, 1901-P, O, S, 1902-O, 1903-O and on all others including 1879-P, CC, O, 1880-P, O, S, and from 1881 to 1889. A new minor design type reverse, C^4, was used on some 1900-S, 1901-P, O, S, 1902-P ,O, S, 1903-O, S and 1904-S and on all 1903-P and 1904-P, O. This C^4 reverse had a larger space between the edge of the eagle's left wing and the eagle's neck, a larger center space in the I of IN and less articulated eagle's breast feathers.

A few of the C^3 reverse dies were re-impressed with the C^4 reverse hub. This showed up as two olives above the olive branch with the top one being shallower compared to the normal one olive, and doubling on the olive leaves, arrow heads, wing feathers, and eagle's head. These C^4/C^3 reverses were used on some 1900-P,S, 1901-P, O, S, 1902-P, O, S, 1903-S, and 1904-S.

The fourth reverse, D, was used in 1921. The

1921 reverse type D differed from the type C reverse in that it had parallel arrow feathers and large stars, the eagle's breast was flat, the branch held by the eagle was bent and had slightly different leaves, and the letters in the legend had minor differences. This design is not the same as the old parallel arrow feather, seven tail feather design type B.

New obverse and reverse master dies were made in 1921, since in 1910, every die in the Philadelphia Mint was destroyed except for those used for regular coinage denominations during that year. There were two minor reverse design Types of the D reverse. The first design, D^1, was used for some 1921-P. It had 17 berries in the wreath as in the C^3 reverse. The top arrow feather met the olive branch at the middle talon of the eagle's right claw and the olive branch was weak and shallow under this claw. The second design, D^2, was used for some 1921-P and all 1921-D and S. It had 16 berries in the wreath instead of the normal 17 berries. One berry was missing at the top inside of the right wreath. In addition, the top arrow feather met the olive branch between the right and center talon of the eagle's right claw and the olive branch was full and raised under this claw. Apparently two slightly different master hubs were prepared and used during 1921.

In addition, the 1921 P dollars show two different types of edge reeding. The normal reeding for the 1921-P, D and S dollars showed a total of 189 reeds around the coin's edge. Some of the 1921-P with the D^1 reverse had "Infrequent Reeding" with only a total of 157 reeds around the coin's edge.

OBVERSE DESIGN DESCRIPTIONS

The first obverse design, I, was used mostly with the eight tail feather reverse and some second design reverses in 1878 at the Philadelphia Mint. It differed from the later obverse design used on most 1878 coins in that it had higher relief, a wider rim, thinner inner ear fill, shallower designer's initial M, thinner letters in LIBERTY, and a thicker, evenly divided rear portion of ear. Other small differences were no gap in the band in the lower part of the cap, less detail on the cotton tops and less hair detail.

The first working hub of the obverse design, I^1, had an incuse designer's initial, M, a thinner ear helix and antihelix with more space between them, two strands in curl in front of ear, hair strands ends below ear were separated, well defined with blunt ends away from ear, and there is an extra crease at neck and jaw junction. This I^1 obverse was used with some A^1 and B^2 reverses early in 1878. The second working hub, I^2, had a raised designer's initial, M, with two parallel vertical bars, thicker ear helix and antihelix with thin space between them, three strands in curl in front of ear, and hair strand ends below ear are not as well defined and some have pointed ends and close to ear. This I^2 obverse was used with some A^1, A^2/A^1, and B^1 reverses early in 1878.

The second obverse design, II, was used on all the 1878-S and 1878-CC. It was also used with some 1878-P 7/8 TF (after March 26, 1878), 1878-P 7 TF PAF (after April 4, 1878), and 1878-P 7 TF SAF (on June 5 and after June 28, 1878) reverses. The most obvious distinction between this design and the third obverse design used from 1878 to 1904 was that the tops of the cotton blossoms were flatter and lacked the fine detail of the later design. Other differences included the thicker letters of LIBERTY with the tail of the L slanting more, no lines on the wheat leaves, straight left wheat leaf, the less pronounced band of the lower part of the cap, unequally divided rear portion of ear, and a thinner rim. some of the dies of the first obverse design were re-impressed with the second design working hubs late in March 1878, which resulted in a dual hub, II/I. This is evidenced by doubled stars, LIBERTY, symbol letters, and other details on some coins with the eight tail feathers, seven over eight tail feathers, seven tail feathers parallel arrow feather and seven tail feathers slanted arrow feather reverses. This doubling is a die variety, since multiple coins exist with exactly the same doubling. The earlier dies were purposely re-impressed with the later design hub to lower the relief and extend the life of the dies.

The third obverse design, III, was used with some of the 1878-P TF SAF reverses on May 17, 1878, on a regular basis at the Philadelphia Mint sometime after June 28, 1878, and thereafter on all coins from 1879 to 1904. It had a wider rim, thinner letters of LIBERTY, more detail in the cotton blossoms, and lines in the wheat leaves. The first trial die of the third obverse design, III^1, was used on May 17, 1878. It had lines in all the wheat leaves, and the wheat leaf end was well below the bottom of the R in PLURIBUS. The final version, III^2, was used after June 28, 1878, and had a long wheat leaf with weak lines close to the bottom of the R.

The fourth obverse, IV, was used in 1921. This type IV differed from the type III obverse in that the lettering of the symbol and LIBERTY was different and details of the Liberty head were changed (the eyelash was missing and the nose, lips, chin, hair lines, and cotton blossoms were modified).

DESIGN COMBINATIONS

Table 6-1 shows the known obverse and reverse design combinations for the Morgan dollar. There were four basic obverse designs with two minor design changes and one dual hub obverse type. There were also four basic reverse designs with four minor design changes and three dual hub reverse types. If the infrequent reeding of the 1921-P is also included then there are a total of 26 design type combinations for the Morgan dollar!

Table 6-1 DESIGN COMBINATIONS

OBVERSE	MINT	REVERSE
I^1	some 1878-P	A^1, B^2
I^2	some 1878-P	A^1, A^2/A^1, B^1
II/I	some 1878-P	A^1, A^2/A^1, B/A, B^1, B^2, C^1, C^3
II	some 1878-P	B/A
II	some 1878-CC, few 1878-S	B^1
II	some 1878-P,CC, most 1878-S	B^2
II	some 1878-P	C^2, C^3
III^1	some 1878-P	C^1, C^2
III^2	some 1879-S, 1880-CC	B^2
III^2	some 1878-P, 1879-S, 1880-CC, 1900-P, S, 1901-P, O, S, 1902-O; all 1879-P, O, CC, 1880-P, O, S, 1881-1899, 1900-O	C^3
III^2	some 1900-P, S, 1901-P, O, S, 1902-P, O, S, 1903-S, 1904-S	C^4/C^3
III^2	some 1900-S, 1901-P, O, S; all 1902-P, O, S, 1903-S, 1904-S, all 1903-P, O, 1904-P, O	C^4
IV	some 1921-P	D^1
IV	Infrequent Reeding-some 1921-P	D^1
IV	some 1921-P; all 1921-D, S	D^2

DESIGN TYPE IDENTIFICATION SUMMARY

The following lists describe the key points for the identification of each design type. If additional descriptive detail is required, the reader is referred to the photographs and list of differences of each design at the end of this chapter.

Obverse Design Types

I   Thin letters in LIBERTY, evenly divided rear portion of ear
- I^1 Incused designer's initial M.
- I^2 Raised designer's initial M with two parallel vertical bars.

II/I   Short or very thin ear fill, evenly divided rear portion of ear, thicker letters in LIBERTY, some portions of the lettering or stars doubled.

II   Thicker letters in LIBERTY, unevenly divided rear portion of ear.

III   Thin letters in LIBERTY, unevenly divided rear portion of ear, lines in wheat leaves.
- III^1 Lines in all wheat leaves, wheat leaf end well below bottom of R in PLURIBUS. Long wheat leaf between wheat stalks.
- III^2 Long wheat leaf below R, close to bottom of R, with weak lines. Short wheat leaf between wheat stalks.

IV   Eyelash missing, hairlines more pronounced, LIBERTY letters different.

Reverse Design Types

A   Eight tail feathers.
- A^1 Raised eagle's beak.
- A^2/A^1 Hooked eagle's beak with lower beak and tongue usually doubled. Top arrow head and shaft doubled.

B/A   Long center arrow shaft, parallel arrow feathers, seven tail feathers with portions of eight tail feathers usually showing below seven tail feathers, portions of A die design around branch leaves, wreath and bow, or IN GOD WE TRUST.

B   Seven tail feathers, parallel arrow feathers, flat eagle's breast.
- B^1 Long center arrow shaft.
- B^2 Short center arrow shaft.

C   Seven tail feathers, slanted arrow feathers, round eagle's breast.
- C^1 A in AMERICA very close to eagle's wing, bottom feather of eagle's right wing next to leg is rounded and not connected to wing on left.
- C^2 A in AMERICA very close to eagle's wing, bottom feather of eagle's right wing extends to junction of next two feathers, thin line present between eagle's leg and first feather.
- C^3 Left serif of A in AMERICA cut down so it is further from wing, bottom feather of eagle's right wing squared off and raised.
- C^4/C^3 Two olives connected above olive branch with upper one shallow.
- C^4 Larger space between eagle's left wing edge and eagle's neck.

D   Parallel arrow feathers, flat eagle's breast, bent branch held by eagle's right talon.
- D^1 17 berries in wreath.
- D^2 16 berries in wreath.

I Obverse

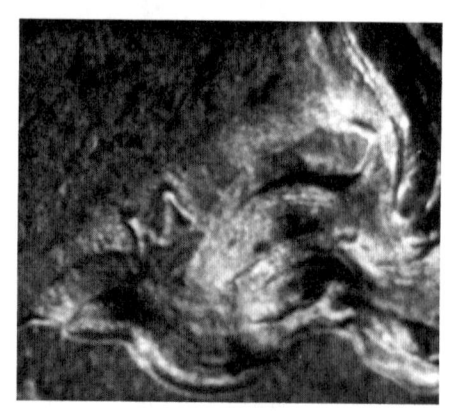

I¹ Obverse

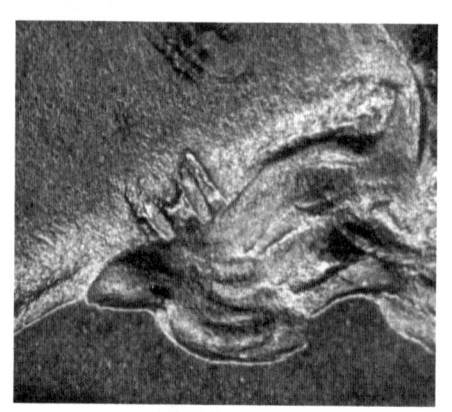

I² Obverse

I **Obverse.** Used on most 1878-P 8 TF and some 7 TF PAF. Differs from the second 1878-P obverse design in the following ways:
   a. Thicker, evenly divided rear portion of ear.
   b. Thinner LIBERTY letters (bottom of T and Y), with top of bottom leg of E slanting down at its end, and the tail of the L slanting less.
   c. Thin inner ear fill.
   d. Band in lower part of cap which has no gaps and ends at cap edge.
   e. Shallow designer's initial M.
   f. Less detail on cotton boll tops.
   g. Less hair detail.
   h. Wider rim.

Minor Design Types

I¹ **Obverse.** Incused designer's initial M, thinner ear helix and antihelix with more space between them, two strands in curls in front of ear, hair strand below ear are separated and well defined with blunt ends away from ear and there is an extra crease at neck and jaw junction.

I² **Obverse.** Raised designer's initial M, with two parallel bars, thicker ear helix and antihelix with thin space between them, three strands in curl in front of ear, hair strand ends below ear are not as well defined and some have pointed ends and are close to the ear.

A¹ Reverse

A² Reverse

A Reverse

A Reverse. Used on early 1878-P (8 TF). Differs from the second 1878-P design in the following ways:
  a. Eight eagle's tail feathers.
  b. I of IN touching or close to wing top.
  c. Arrow points spread.
  d. Large leaves on branch held by eagle's right talon.
  e. Large berries in wreath, nine on right and eight on left.
  f. Large leaves in wreath.
  g. Large loops in bows.
  h. Smaller eagle's beak with large tongue showing.
  i. Wing feathers different at ends and near body.
  j. More feathers on eagle's legs.
  k. Small stars.
  l. Wider rim.

Minor Design Types

A¹ Reverse. Raised eagle's beak, I of IN touching top of eagle's wing, two or three small feathers individually engraved on each die between bottom of wing and leg.

A² Reverse. Hooked eagle's beak, I of IN away from wing, small feathers not present on both sides of the eagle between bottom of wing and leg, wreath smaller, more space between ends of eagle's tail feathers and bow loops.

(Note: This design type was used only as a dual hub over A¹ type dies)

II Obverse. Used on all 1878-S and 1878-CC, on some 1878-P 7/8 TF, and on some 1878-P 7 TF PAF and SAF. Differs from third design in the following ways:

a. Unequally divided rear portion of ear.
b. Thicker LIBERTY letters, more slanted tail of L.
c. Less pronounced band in lower part of cap.
d. No lines on wheat leaves.
e. Straight left wheat leaf which ends at inner edge of R (later design is curved and ends near middle of R staff).
f. More staggered wheat grains in stalks.
g. Leaf between wheat stalks which leans to left.
h. Less detail on tops of cotton bolls.
i. Thick eyelash.
j. Narrow rim.

II Obverse

B Reverse. Used on some 1878-P and all 1878-S and 1878-CC (7 TF PAF) and some 1879-S and 1880-CC. Differs from third design in the following ways:

a. Parallel arrow feathers.
b. Flat eagle's breast.
c. A of AMERICA touching eagle's wing.
d. Hook on eagle's beak.
e. Narrow rim.

Minor Reverse Designs
B¹ Reverse. Long center arrow shaft.
B² Reverse. Short center arrow shaft.

B Reverse

III Obverse

III¹ Obverse  **III² Obverse**

III Obverse. Used on all coins from 1879 to 1904 and on some 1878-P 7 TF SAF. The main features of this design were:
- a. More detail in cotton blossoms bolls.
- b. Lines in wheat leaves.
- c. Thinner letters in LIBERTY.
- d. Wide rim.

Minor Design Types

III¹ Obverse. Lines in all wheat leaves, long leaf between stalks, wheat leaf end well below bottom of R, bottom of E and R run together in LIBERTY. Point of Liberty head neck in middle of denticle.

III² Obverse. Long wheat leaf below R (close to R with weak lines), short wheat leaf between wheat stalks, LIBERTY letters thinner with shorter serifs on B and R. Long lines between cotton bolls. Point of Liberty head neck between denticles.

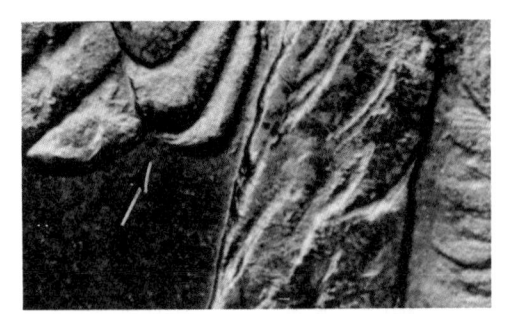

C¹ Reverse

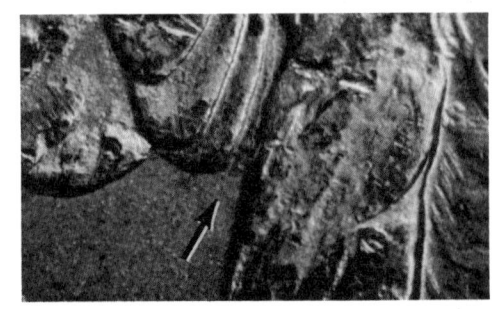

C² Reverse

C³ Reverse

C Reverse

C Reverse. Used on some 1878-P (7 TF SAF), 1879-S, and 1880-CC and on all other coins from 1879 to 1904. The main features of this design were:
  a. Seven eagle's tail feathers.
  b. Rounded eagle's breast.
  c. Slanted top arrow feather.
  d. A of AMERICA not touching eagle's wing.
  e. Wide rim.
  f. Seven berries on right and ten on left wreath.
  g. Doubled designer's initial M at top (C³ only).

Minor Design Types

C¹ Reverse. A in AMERICA nearly touching eagle's wing with bottom of left serif slanting down to left, inner side of right serif of A cut off square, bottom feather of eagle's right wing next to leg rounded and not connected to wing on left.

C² Reverse. Same as C¹ except that inner right serif of A is thinner, bottom feather of eagle's right wing extending to junction of next two feathers, thin line present between the eagle's leg and first feather.

C³ Reverse. Left serif of A cut down so it is not flat on top and is away from the wing, bottom of serif not slanting, bottom feather of eagle's right wing squared off and raised.

C⁴ Reverse. Used on some 1900-P, S, 1901-P, O, S, 1902-O, 1903-O and all 1902-P, S, 1903-P, S, and 1904. Differs from type C³ in the following ways:
a. Larger space between the eagle's left wing edge and eagle's neck.
b. Large center space in I of IN and thicker and larger upper serifs on IN.
c. Larger stars.
d. Cut down olive.
e. Center arrow shaft reduced in length.
f. Eagle's breast feathers not as articulated.

C⁴ Reverse

IV Obverse. Used on all 1921. Differs from type III in the following ways:
a. Symbol lettering different, particularly E, L, and U.
b. Eyelash missing.
c. LIBERTY Lettering different, particularly E and T.
d. Nose not engraved as deeply.
e. Upper lip different.
f. Lower lip not as raised.
g. No crease above chin.
h. Cotton bolls different.
i. Hair lines more pronounced.

IV Obverse

17 Berries
D¹ Reverse

D Reverse

Infrequent Reeding

D **Reverse.** Used on 1921. Differs from type C in the following ways:
  a. Parallel arrow feathers.
  b. Large stars.
  c. Flat eagle's breast.
  d. Bent branch held by eagle's right talon; leaves slightly different.
  e. Letters in legend slightly different, especially E and T.

Minor Design Types

D¹ Reverse. 17 berries in wreath as in C³ reverse. Top arrow feather meets olive branch at middle talon of eagle's right claw. Olive branch is weak and shallow under eagle's right claw.

D² Reverse. 16 berries in wreath with one missing at top inside of the right wreath. Top arrow feather meets olive branch between right and center talons of eagle's right claw. Olive branch is full and raised under eagle's right claw.

Infrequent Reeding. Collar with a total of 157 reeds around coin's edge instead of normal 189 reeds.

Chapter 7
Discussion of Significant Varieties

Morgan dollars had varieties and errors produced at any of the three major steps in the production of coins; fabrication of the planchets, making the dies, or striking the coins. However, the production of Morgan dollars underwent many more individual inspections by mint personnel than is customary nowadays with the more automated equipment. As a result, very few Morgan dollar planchet and striking errors were let out of the mints compared to modern coins.

Nevertheless, Morgan varieties and errors can still be classified by the Planchet-Die-striking (PDS) error identification system discussed by Alan Herbert.[1] These three categories can be defined as follows:

Planchet Errors – Any error occurring during preparation of the planchet. This includes occluded gas, clipped planchets, laminations, impure metal and split planchets. Very few Morgan dollar errors occurred in this category except for a number of laminations.

Die Errors & Varieties – Any error or variety on dies that shows up on the coins. This includes engraving touch-ups, hub breaks and cracks, die breaks and cracks, doubled dies, dual hub dies, mispositioned dates, mispositioned mint marks, double dates, double mint marks, overdates, dual mint marks, clashed dies, die gouges and scratches, and overpolished dies. There are certain other die varieties of interest to collectors such as mint mark letter variations, date digit variations, identifying marks on dies, and reeding variations on collars. Morgan dollars are particularly numerous in all of these die errors and varieties because of its large size, sharp design detail, and the many difficulties experienced in perfecting the die technology and design in the early years of production.

Striking Errors – Any error occurring during the striking of the coin. This includes die pressure adjustment pieces, misaligned dies, rotated dies, partial collar, broadstrikes, off-center strikes, multiple strikes, struck through strikes, and strike doubling. Morgan dollars had few of these striking errors because of close inspections made except for the struck-through strikes and machine doubling.

The following sections discuss the various types of varieties and errors and their causes for the Morgan dollar. Emphasis is placed on the die errors and varieties since this was the largest category for the Morgan dollar.

PLANCHET ERRORS

Occluded Gas in Planchet
One of the few types of defective planchets occurring in the Morgan dollars was the occluded gas in a planchet. Gas trapped when the ingot was cast may remain trapped when the silver strips were later rolled out.

Planchets with occluded gas when struck in the coining presses would cause raised portions in the coin to occur as the gas expanded and pushed the thin metal outward into a bump after being struck.

Clipped Planchets
Clips are planchets with missing portions that may have the form of curved, straight, or ragged sections. Curved clips result from overlapping punches on the metal strips; straight clips are caused when the punch overlaps the end of the strip. If the punch overlaps a broken area of the strip, a ragged clip results. Extremely few Morgan clips are known and these are the smaller rim clip type. Separation of defective planchets by hand at selecting tables after they were punched and cleaned, automatic weighing of the planchets with a tolerance of 1.5 grains, adjusting the weight of heavy planchets by hand, feeding the planchets into the upsetting machines and coining presses by hand and a final inspection and counting by hand after being struck eliminated practically all planchet type errors except for a few minor ones.

Laminated Planchets
Any slag, oil, grease, dust, or dirt that is within the silver strips when they are rolled may cause thin layers or laminations to form. These laminations may break off causing depressed areas in the planchets and the resultant coins. The depressed areas will not show any portions of the design. They should not be confused with struck through striking errors. These show weak and diffused portions of the design in the depressed area due to partial transfer through the top layer.

Impure Metal Streaks
Related to the laminated planchet are impure metal streaks. In these cases the impurities lie on the sur-

1879-S Occluded Gas   1888-O Occluded Gas

1921-P Rim Clip

1921-P Impure Metal Streak and Lamination

1921-S Split Planchet

1904-O Lamination

1921-P Ragged Edge Clip

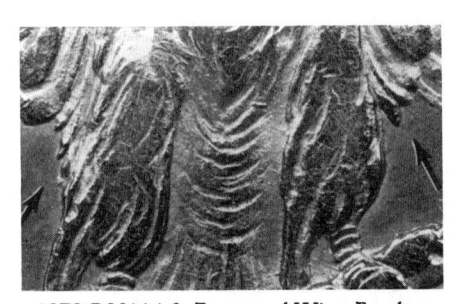

1878-P VAM 9 Engraved Wing Feather

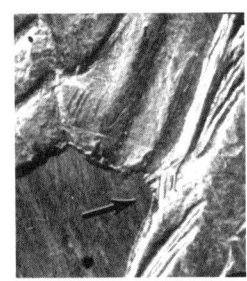

1878-S VAM 47 Engraved Wing Feather

face of the planchet causing dark rough spots or streaks. They generally lower the value of a coin and must be relatively large before they are collectable as errors.

Split Planchets

If the impurities are embedded completely through the planchet thickness, then a split planchet may result. A thin layer of impurities can cause a small separation of the metal to form a split. Few split planchets prior to 1921 are known because all Morgan dollars were given a ring test to detect defective planchets.

DIE ERRORS AND VARIETIES

Re-engraved 1878-P 8 TF Reverses

Examination of coins with the 8 TF reverse reveals that two minor design types were used. The first one, A^1, was used with the first design obverse, I. It had a raised eagle's beak and the I of IN touched the top of the eagle's wing. In addition, two or three small feathers were individually engraved on each die between the bottom of the wing and the leg. This made each die of this design unique since the details of the added small feathers differed. Apparently the center detail of the design was weakened when the dies were basined, requiring that they be re-engraved.

The second 8 TF working hub design type A^2, had a hooked eagle's beak and the I of IN was away from the wing top. The wreath was smaller, and there was more space between ends of the eagle's tail feathers and the bow loops. Some of these dies also showed one or two feathers added or partially polished away between the bottom of the wing and the leg.

Re-engraved 1878-S and 1879-S Reverses

All of the mints experienced some difficulty in basining the B reverse (7 tail feather, flat eagle's breast) dies. Often there were overpolished areas in the eagle's wings or peripheral lettering. Also the lower feathers of the wings next to the legs tended to be weak or missing. The San Francisco Mint individually touched up some of the B reverse dies used in 1878-S and 1879-S by adding a feather or strengthened a feather of the wing next to the eagle's right leg. Each of these differed slightly in the way they were touched up creating a number of minor die varieties. It was also highly unusual to have a branch mint engrave the working dies since normally they only basined and machined them to fit their own special presses. Neither the Philadelphia or Carson City Mints touched up the wing feathers on the B reverse.

Hub and Die Breaks and Cracks

Only the more prominent die breaks and cracks are considered here. Through normal use die breaks and cracks developed in every die and also in the working hubs. These occurred in many forms including hair lines between stars and the design; filled letters and numbers (especially in the motto and mint marks that were small in size); and metal between the letters in the motto. These are another means, besides the date, mint mark, or design, by which a coin can be identified. The hairline cracks, partially filled mint marks, die chips around the motto on the reverse, and die chips around date digits (such as spiked 8's) are not included in the list of die varieties since they were common as the dies wore out.

Because of the hasty preparation of the hubs and dies and the pressure to strike a large number of coins from inadequately prepared dies, many poor specimens of the dollar were struck early in 1878. As can be seen from the correspondence of that period, the dies cracked and were often run longer in the presses than they should have been.[2] (Bosbyshell's letter of April 1, 1878)

> ... the dies however, do not stand as well as could be desired – they crack and sink shortly after entering the presses... We ran many of the dies a longer time in the presses, than we ought to have done...

It is difficult to determine whether a missing portion of a design was caused by a die fill or a hub break. The best way of distinguishing between them is by the number of coins struck with the defect. The hub would, of course, have made at least a few dies showing the defect (the number of dies made dependent upon when the hub was retired). A single die usually would have struck a few tens of thousands of coins with a particular defect, since the defect would usually have occurred late in the die's lifetime.

Two defects that appear on the 1878 coins are definitely hub breaks. These are the broken R in TRUST to form "TIUST" on the reverse B²c and the broken point on the number 4 right star of the II 2 obverse. In both of these, the break was a gradual process, with some coins showing only the start of the design deterioration. The broken R reverse appears with 12 different II/I obverses, the II 1 and II 2 obverses, the 1878-S, and the 1879-S. The broken star obverse appears with many different reverses of the 1878-P and also with the 1878-S and 1878-CC. Both of these defects are fairly common (many millions of coins were struck), with the broken star the most prevalent.

The broken top of the O in GOD on the reverse B²b has been found with seven different obverses. This was probably a break in the working hub. It is also found in combination with the broken R reverse, B²c.

The II/I 8 and II/I 25 obverse dies are similar except that the latter die shows more of the bottom serifs missing from the N and M in UNUM. These two dies were probably made by a working hub just before it was retired. The breaks in the hub letters became progressively worse in making these two dies. It was not a progressive fill in the dies, since many coins show exactly the same defects and they occurred with three different reverse dies in each case.

Die defects could have produced up to about 100,000 coins with a particular defect. One interesting die flake and crack is the II/I 15 obverse, which has a flake of metal on the cheek and a line through the ear. An example of a die scratch is the reverse A¹d which has spikes on both sides of the A in STATES.

Most die breaks were unique with a particular die. However, some have appeared on coins of different years and mints, indicating that they were caused by a hub break. The best examples of this are the broken R in TRUST on some 1878 TF PAF, 1878-S, and 1879-S PAF and the filled E in WE in the years 1902-1904.

The following is a list of major hub and die breaks.

Major Hub and Die Breaks

1878-P	II 2	Broken points off number 4 star on right (hub break)
	II/I 8	Broken bottom serifs of N and M in UNUM (hub break)
	II/I 14	Line through top part of B in PLURIBUS
	II/I 15	Die crack though center ear and die flake on cheek
	II/I 25	Broken bottom serifs of N and M in UNUM (hub break)
	A¹d	Spiked A of STATES and filled E of ONE
	B¹c	Die chip on eagle's right wing next to body
	B¹e	Broken D of DOLLAR
	B²b	Filled O of GOD (hub break)
	B²c	Filled R in TRUST to form TIUST (hub break)
	B²e	Bottom of D of DOLLAR completely broken
1878-CC	II 2	Die chips on head
	II 3	Broken point off number 4 star on right (hub break)
1878-S	B²a	Die break through wreath and die chip on eagle's breast
	B²b	Filled R in TRUST to form TIUST (hub break) and die chips on eagle's wings.
1879-CC		G in GOD filled
1879-S		Broken R in TRUST to form TIUST (hub break)
1880-P		Die break in first 8
1880-CC		Dots in CC, metal in CC
1880-S		Die chip in wreath
1881-S		Die chip in wreath
1884-S		Die chip in wreath
1887-P		Die break on D of DOLLAR
1888-O		Die break between E and PLURIBUS down across face. Die crack through R in PLURIBUS
1889-P		Die break at top of eagle's right wing
1890-P		Die chip in G in GOD
1899-O		Die breaks in wreath
1900-O		Die break in date

Doubled Dies

The production of the Morgan working dies required from seven to ten blows from a working hub. Between each blow the die had to be annealed. Any misalignment between each blow from the hub could cause doubling of the die. Dies were generally carefully inspected between each blow, consequently, doubled dies are quite scarce for the Morgan dollar. The exception was the 1878-P dies early in that year when the die production processes were being perfected and time pressures forced the use of imperfect dies.

The most prominent doubled dies are the 1888-O doubled head and 1901-P shifted eagle. The 1888-O and 1901-P doubled coins pose something of a problem as to how they occurred. With a die shift as great as they show, the outer portion of the coin should also show doubling. Part of the doubled design could have been removed by polishing down the edges of these dies between impressions; the most likely explanation, however, is that the doubling of the die occurred before the last impression with the hub. An earlier impression in the die would not show the outer parts of the design. This is because the die starts as a cone and is flattened out in seven to ten blows, thus, a misalignment of an early impression would only have doubled the center portions. If the doubling of these dies had occurred at an early blow, the later ones would have smoothed the doubling.

An unusual doubled die is the 1887-O with all stars and lettering next to the rim doubled in a radial direction. This could have been caused by an excessively heated die during the annealing prior to the last hub blow.

A doubled die coin can be distinguished from a dual hub die coin, such as the 1878-P 7/8 TF variety. A doubled die will have a progressive shift of the same design across the die, while the dual hub die will have different features of the two designs brought out at various places on the die.

Many 1878-P coins have identical doubling of the design which means that the doubling actually originated in the die. The first design type reverse, A, and obverse, I, show many examples. The I 3 obverse shows a pronounced doubling of PLURIBUS - one of the largest shifts the authors have seen. This die has a misalignment between the hub and die at the top, producing a regular shift in the lettering (in contrast to the dual hub types that show intermittent doubling). Another example of a doubled reverse is the type B²d, which has a doubled motto. The following is a list of the major doubled dies.

Doubled Dies

1878-P	Doubled design (I 1-16, II 4, II 5, A¹a-m, B²d)
1878-CC	Doubled obverse, doubled LIBERTY, double cotton leaves
1878-S	Doubled LIBERTY (eight types); doubled motto (four types); doubled obverse
1879-P	Double reverse lettering
1882-CC	Double reverse lettering
1882-O	Double reverse lettering
1883-P	Sextupled stars
1883-O	Doubled stars
1886-P	Doubled arrows
1887-P	Doubled LIBERTY motto, stars and reverse lettering
1887-O	Doubled motto and stars in a radial direction
1888-P	Doubled reverse lettering, doubled eyelid and ear
1888-O	Doubled head, doubled lower reverse, doubled reverse lettering
1888-S	Doubled stars and profile
1889-P	Doubled ear
1889-O	Doubled N in UNUM
1891-P	Doubled ear
1891-S	Doubled obverse stars
1892-P	Doubled reverse lettering, doubled profile
1892-O	Doubled ear
1893-P	Doubled obverse stars
1896-P	Doubled obverse stars
1897-P	Doubled left stars
1900-P	Doubled eagle
1900-O	Doubled obverse stars
1901-P	Shifted eagle, doubled lower reverse
1902-P	Doubled ear
1902-O	Doubled reverse lettering, doubled profile
1904-O	Doubled profile
1921-P	Tripled obverse stars
1921-S	Doubled date and stars

Dual Hub Dies

Since the Morgan dollar working dies had to receive from seven to ten blows from the working hubs, two or more working hubs could have been used to produce a working die. For most of the years, only a single obverse and reverse design type was used. The few working hubs used in a year (a working hub could make up to 250 working dies) were usually made from a single master die. Thus, the design type was the same on the working hubs except for 1878 and 1900 when different design types were used.

It may have been possible for two working hubs of a given design type to have different minor shifts of the design. Slightly different master dies could have been individually touched up. Use of two working hubs with minor design differences to produce a working die would result in some shifting and doubling of the design, which may or may not be regular depending upon the design differences in the working hubs. On the other hand, misalignment between blows from the same working hub could produce a regular shift over a portion of the working die design.

It is difficult to distinguish between doubling of a die design due to hub misalignment and hubs with slight shifts of the same design types. Therefore, the paragraphs that follow will be restricted to dual hub dies of different design types. For the Morgan dollar, this occurred in three different cases for the 1878-P early in that year, two reverse combinations and one obverse combination. It also occurred in 1900 to 1904 for the reverse. In each case the dual hubbing was a deliberate modification of old dies to produce better working dies as quickly as possible without going through the lengthy process of making new dies.

Dual Hub 1878-P Reverse, B/A (7/8 TF)

Although this variety was first discovered in 1948, an explanation of the condition at the Philadelphia Mint which caused this variety was not put forth until Shafer's article in 1964.[3] Further, the exact way in which the variety was produced was not definitely established until Morgan's letter of March 25, 1878, was presented in an article entitled "1878 7/8 Tail Feather Silver Dollar: How and Why," by Leroy C. Van Allen, in the April 1965 issue of *The Numismatic Scrapbook Magazine*.

Until the discovery of this letter, the authors had spent many hours puzzling over how the defective 7/8 TF dies were made. It could not have been done by merely giving the old 8 TF reverse dies a blow from the new 7 TF reverse hub, since the border lettering positions differed. This would have resulted in doubled border lettering, which has not appeared on a single coin of this type.

Another theory was that the dies were individually re-engraved; that is, that the seven tail feather design was re-engraved over the old eight tail feather design. This theory, however, could not explain why portions of the older design sometimes showed around the olive branch and its leaves, the loops in the wreath bow, or the motto IN GOD WE TRUST above the eagle. What actually happened is herein reviewed.

The original Morgan pattern die for the silver dollar was finished in December 1877, with the eagle showing seven tail feathers shifted slightly to the left. In January and February 1878, the design in the hub was modified by reducing the relief, cutting away the wings from the legs, and making the eagle's tail feathers more symmetrical by adding an eight tail feather. Apparently Morgan was not aware that eagles in previous coins had always shown an odd number of tail feathers. In the haste of approving the design and preparing working dies, this defect was over looked.

The working dies were not finished until almost two weeks after the Bland-Allison Act authorizing the coinage of silver dollars had been passed. In an effort to meet the required minimum coinage of 2,000,000 per month, the Philadelphia Mint operation was put on an overtime basis and only silver dollars were struck.

Many problems were encountered with the first dies. They required special procedures to polish the design field before use in the presses, and the dies cracked and sank after a short time in the presses. To try to correct some of these deficiencies and "slight imperfections," Morgan was again ordered to prepare new hubs. The design relief was further reduced to help extend the die lifetime, and the number of eagle's tail feathers was changed to seven.

There was great pressure to make these hubs with the new design as quickly as possible. Satisfactory working dies were needed so that they could be forwarded to the western mints to help relieve the coining burden.

Completing the working dies, however, required from seven to ten blows from the hub at the rate of one per day. To speed up the process of making the working dies, Morgan suggested entering the new hub into some of the old design dies that were on hand. This suggestion was made in his letter of March 25 to Mint Director Linderman:

I beg to say that the new hub for reverse of silver dollar was finished and hardened today (March 25).

New dies from this hub will be ready about 2nd of April but I can enter this hub into dies — fifty in number made from the old hub and have these ready this week.

Morgan's letter of March 26 indicates that it was carried out:

Today I have made and finished dies from the new hub for reverse of silver dollar with reference to which I reported to you yesterday. These dies are now being used in the coining room...

These letters, then, indicate that some 50 8 TF reverse dies were modified ("reimpressed") using the new design hub as a matter of expediency to supply the mint with better dies as quickly as possible. Although 50 reverse dies were reimpressed with the new hub, the extra tail feathers did not show on all the dies. Some of the die modifications were carried out more expertly than others; also, some of the dies may have split or cracked in the process, making them useless. Thirteen different reimpressed reverse dies have been identified to date.

Morgan did not detail the steps used to make the reimpressed dies. To complete the die modifications in a single day, only one or two blows with the B^1 design hub could have been struck. The complete design could not have been brought out in these one or two blows. What must have happened was that the border lettering was lapped and polished away, since it would have been out of register. This would have left the central eagle design intact, resulting in a doubled appearance of the tail feather ends since this portion of the design had been changed. Many of these dies show evidence of extensive polishing to eliminate the doubling. This resulted in shallow design and lettering.

Other differences between the designs sometimes show up on the reimpressed dies, giving further proof that only the border was lapped down. Examples are the metal in the olive branch and leaves, the wreath bow, and the motto IN GOD WE TRUST. Whether these differences showed up and the number and extent of the extra tail feathers depended on how long the die had been held against the lapping wheel. Dies from both the 8 TF reverse design types were probably modified; this would account for the different lengths of the protruding feather ends.

Also in evidence are dies in which the hub and die were not in register. This resulted in doubled dies. The examples of these are the doubled legs variety, B/Ab and B/Am. Many 7/8 TF varieties show some slight doubling of the center design, but none have the obvious shift of these. Some design elements are apparent near the olive branch leaves and wreath bows, showing that the die was reimpressed. The lower portion of the design is not doubled because it was polished off.

The reverse B/Aa also shows some slight doubling. Extra tail feather lines appear to the left of the eagle's right leg, and extra talon tips are shifted to the left just below the olive branch on the left and the lower arrow shaft on the right. This variety is actually the largest shift the authors have seen over a tail feather width!

The reverse B/Ad has three tail feather ends showing, and a fourth one is sometimes evident on early strike specimens. This reimpressed reverse seems to be the commonest type of 7/8 TF, with the polished down B/Ak the next most frequent. The latter variety is a good example of tail feather ends that were partially polished off, only a thin line remains of one of the ends.

Considering the average reverse die lifetime during the period in which they were used, up to about 70,000 of each design might have been struck. There are probably more die varieties of the 7/8 TF reverses (B/A design type) than the 13 known. The authors would be interested in hearing of any new ones found.

Dual Hub 1878-P Obverses, II/I (Doubled LIBERTY)

Although the reimpressed reverse has been known since 1948, the equivalent modification for the obverse was not reported until 1965[4] – some 87 years after it took place! Obviously there is still much to be learned about our American coins.

There was good reason to modify the first design obverse dies. They struck an average of only 30,000 coins – less than half the average for the first design reverse dies. Thus, it would have been reasonable to modify the old design dies (probably 50 dies) with the new lower relief hub, so that a longer lasting die could be produced as quickly as possible.

Examination of the coins yields strong evidence that the II obverse design was impressed over the I obverse design on some Philadelphia Mint dies early in 1878. Four major points lead to this conclusion. First, 1878-P are the only coins in which the date, stars, lettering, and LIBERTY all appear doubled and in so many variations. Since the same coining presses and methods were used throughout the Morgan series, it is rather unusual for this to occur in only part of one year. Second, multiple coins exist with exactly the same doubled obverse design, which indicates a die variety. Third, the doubling has odd characteristics which suggest more than a simple misalignment between hub impressions; that is, the doubled star points have different orientations on the same coin, and the doubled letters of LIBERTY have different thicknesses. In addition, the variations in the ear details do not correspond to the LIBERTY design for a particular obverse design type (evenly divided ear of the I obverse with thick LIBERTY letters of the II obverse). Fourth, since the reverse had been reimpressed during 1878 to improve the dies, this would also have been likely for the obverse.

A detailed comparison of the I and II obverse designs shows that some stars have different orientation, that the letters in LIBERTY have different widths, and that the top of the bottom leg of E slants down at the end in the I obverse. These differences are shown in the accompanying photographs in *Figure 7-1* (the raised appearance of the lettering is an optical illusion).

The ear of the I obverse has an evenly divided rear portion of the ear, whereas the II obverse rear portion of the ear is uneven and narrower (refer to the photographs in *Figure 7-2*). The wider ear would always have predominated in the impression of a die, since it would have enlarged a deeper or wider cavity into the die face. Thus, the II/I obverses always have an evenly divided rear portion of the ear. The ear fill is of a different size and shape in the I and II obverses. In the II/I obverse, it is always shorter and thinner and varies in length with each die. This is the best indication of the II/I obverse besides the doubled LIBERTY or stars.

The authors' explanation of why the inner ear fill is shorter on the II/I obverse is as follows. When the new hub was made, the center of the ear was cut out deeper so that the ear fill could be made wider. When the II hub was impressed into the I dies, the inner part of the ear in the hub impressed into the I dies, the inner part of

Figure 7-1 LIBERTY Types

I Obverse

II Obverse

II/I Obverse

the ear in the hub did not contact that portion of the die. Metal was forced from the area around the ear into the center of the ear, but not enough metal to be formed by the hub. This reduced the size of the ear fill, depending on how hard the hub was impressed into the die and how long the die was polished (since this was a high part of the die).

Apparently most of the I obverse dies were not lapped and polished down before being reimpressed with the II obverse hub, as was the case with the B/A reverse. The reason was that the position of the lettering had not been changed, as had the reverse design. The II obverse design differed only in small details from the I obverse, and could be impressed in the old dies without the re-impression being obvious (87 years went by before what had happened was finally discovered).

The II/I obverse is apparently more plentiful than the B/A reverse, since it appears with so many reverse designs. Some 40 different reimpressed obverses are listed in this book. They have appeared with all three of the major reverse design types. Undoubtedly, other II/I

Figure 7-2 EAR TYPES

I Obverse

II Obverse

II/I Obverse

A^2/A^1 Reverse, Doubled Beak

obverse die varieties are yet to be found.

Forty examples of the dual hub obverse are known. Most of the doubling is shifted to the left, although one is shifted to the right (II/I 19) and one is shifted up (II/I 10). The authors' estimate for the number of coins struck of each variety would be 30,000 to 70,000 since that was the average life for the obverse dies of that period. Some of the obverse dies that were used extensively with many reverse dies may have struck over 100,000 coins.

Dual Hub 1878-P Reverse A^2/A^1 (Doubled Beak)

A new dual hub 1878-P reverse was discovered in early 1975. It was determined that the previously listed minor reverse design type of the eight tail feather reverse A^2, was actually a dual hub A^2/A^1. The first working hub of the 8 TF design A^1, had a raised eagle's beak, the I of IN touched the top of the eagle's wing and small feathers were individually engraved between the wing and leg. The second working hub of the 8 TF design A^2, had a hooked eagle's beak, and the I of IN was away from the eagle's wing.

Apparently the basining process (lapping of the coin's field) polished part of the center design off the A^1 reverse dies and they had to be individually touched up. The A^2 reverse design must have basined better, so to save the time in making new dies, the A^2 hub was entered into five A^1 reverse dies. The A^1 reverse dies were not first polished down on the edges as were the 7/8 TF dies since the design difference between A^1 and A^2 reverses were slight. There are no known A^2 design type dies; only the five dual hub A^2/A^1 types have been found to date. It must have been an interim expediency measure to prepare better dies until the new 7 TF hub, B, was ready.

1900-P VAM 11 C^4/C^3

113

All five A²/A¹ reverse dies have a doubled top arrow head and most also have doubled top arrow shaft on the right. Four have a doubled lower eagle's beak and two also have the upper beak doubled.

Dual Hub, C⁴/C³ (Two Olive Reverse)

In 1979 it was reported that some of the later date Morgan dollar coins had similar type of doubling on the reverse. This turned out to be due to a dual hub where some of the C³ reverse dies were reimpressed with the C⁴ reverse hub. The C⁴ reverse had a large space between the eagle's left wing and neck and a smaller olive branch. The space between the neck and the wing tended to fill up on the C³ reverse so a fair number of C³ reverse dies were reimpressed with the C⁴ hub apparently to cure this problem.

The dual hub shows up as two olives on the olive branch with the top right olive being shallower than the normal C⁴ size left olive. This is due to the larger C³ olive which remains showing. There is also various doubling of the olive leaves, arrow shafts and heads, wing feathers and eagle's head. These C⁴/C³ dual hub reverses were used on some 1900-P, S; 1901-P, O, S; 1902-P, O, S; 1903-S and 1904-S.

Date Position and Dashes

Date position of the Morgan dollars is fixed for the years 1878 through 1883. But from 1884 through 1904 there are variations in positioning of the date left or right, up or down and slanting. In addition, from 1879 through 1886, some dies have a dash index mark underneath the second digit from the right (7 or 8).

For the year 1878, three different obverse designs were used. The first obverse design, I, used primarily with the eight tail feather reverse, A, had all working dies with the same date position. The Liberty head vee was centered over a denticle and the left edge of the 1 bottom cross bar was lined up over the left edge of the third denticle from the neck vee. Also there was doubling at the top right outside of the 7 in all dies. Thus, the entire date was on the working hubs and master die.

The second obverse design, II, was used with most of the 1878-P and all of the 1878-CC and 1878-S seven tail feather parallel arrow feather reverses, B. The date position was fixed and the same as in the I obverse and the 7 had doubling on the top right side of the 7 in all dies. The dates in the II obverse were also in the working hubs and master die.

For the third obverse design, III, the Liberty head neck vee was between the denticles and the left edge of the 1 bottom cross bar was centered over the third denticle from the neck vee. This obverse was used on some later 1878-P dies and there was no variation in date position for the obverse design either for that year of use. Thus, the date in the III obverse for 1878-P were also in the working hubs and master die. None of 1878 dies show unique doubling of the date digits. Any doubling of the date digits was always in conjunction with doubling of the other parts of the design. The date digits were not punched into individual 1878 working dies.

During 1879–1883 the III obverse was used for all working dies. The position and orientation of the 18 in the date is the same in all cases including the 1878-P with this obverse. For 1879 the 187 appears to be in a fixed position. In order to change the date from 1878 to 1879, the last digit was apparently removed from the master hub by grinding it away. Then, a four digit logo type was used to punch in the 9 into each working die using the first three digits as a guide. Any shift of the logo type between blows would produce doubling of some or all of the digits as has been seen on the die varieties. There were also cases of just the 9 being punched in since some die varieties show only this digit doubled and its position varied slightly.

For 1880, both the digits on the right were removed from the master hub. Then a four digit logotype was used to punch the date into the working dies. This resulted in many doubled date varieties for this year. Also, the four digit logotype deepened the first two digits further as the last two digits were added causing uneven date digit heights on the struck coins. To eliminate this difficulty, a two digit logotype was used to add the last two digits into the working dies in some cases. From 1881 to 1883 the first two digits, 18, were on the working hubs and the last two digits were punched into each working die using either a four or two digit logotype or a single digit punch. The bottom of the third digit, 8, was centered over the tenth denticle from the neck vee.

Because of the broad round bottom of the 8, a short dash was often marked on the die just above the tenth denticle as an index mark to position the second 8 in the date. This resulted in the so-called dash dates. These were formerly thought to be the result of a faulty logotype used to punch in the date digits. However, the dashes vary in lateral and vertical positions with respect to the bottom of the second 8 but are always centered above the tenth denticle. The convincing proof is the 1885-O VAM 7 which shows a dash under the second 8 centered above the tenth denticle and a vertical die gouge centered on this tenth denticle. Apparently the die engraver counted over ten denticles from the Liberty head neck vee, made a little vertical scratch on this denticle to mark it, and then made the dash index mark above it. Basining of the working dies probably removed these shallow dashes from many of the dies. As shown in the accompanying chart, there are dash index marks under the third digit, 7 or 8, for some of the working dies from 1879 through 1886.

In 1884 the date digits were made slightly smaller and the overall date position and orientation started to vary. From 1884 to 1904 there are dates close to the Liberty head neck vee (near date), dates quite a distance from the neck vee (far dates), high and low dates and dates with a slant. There are also doubled dates of all

Date Lateral Position
(Quantities of Dies)

Date	Very Near	Near	Far	Very Far
1884-P			6	3
1884-CC			2	
1884-O			5	3
1884-S			1	1
1885-P			2	
1885-O		1	1	
1885-S			1	
1886-P		1	2	
1886-O		2	1	
1887-P		4	2	
1887-O	1	1	3	
1887-S	1	1	1	
1888-P	1	4	1	
1888-O			2	
1888-S		2		
1889-P			7	3
1889-CC			1	
1889-O			2	
1889-S			4	1
1890-P			3	1
1890-CC		1	1	1
1890-O		2	2	1
1890-S		1	1	
1891-P			1	
1891-CC		1		
1891-O		1	1	
1891-S		2	3	
1892-P		1	1	
1892-CC			1	
1892-O	1	1	2	
1892-S			1	
1893-P		1		
1893-CC			1	
1894-O	1		1	
1894-S			1	
1895-P			1	1
1895-O			2	
1896-P	4	6		
1896-O		2	6	
1896-S		1		
1897-P		2		
1897-O		2		
1897-S	1	1		
1898-P		3		
1898-O	3			
1898-S		5		
1899-O		3		
1899-S		1	1	
1900-P	2	10		
1900-O	2	9		
1900-S		3		
1901-O		1		
1901-S			1	
1902-P	1	2		
1902-O		8		
1902-S		3		
1903-P		2		
1903-O		1		
1904-O			2	
1904-S			1	

combinations of digits and direction for all years and mints. The complete dates were punched into each working die by hand using two or four digit logo type and single digit punches.

The dash index marks were used sometimes in 1884 through 1886. However, lining up the bottom of the third digit, 8, over the tenth denticle from the neck vee with the smaller date digits and narrower date resulted in the left edge of the 1 being further from the neck vee than the previous standard of over the third denticle.

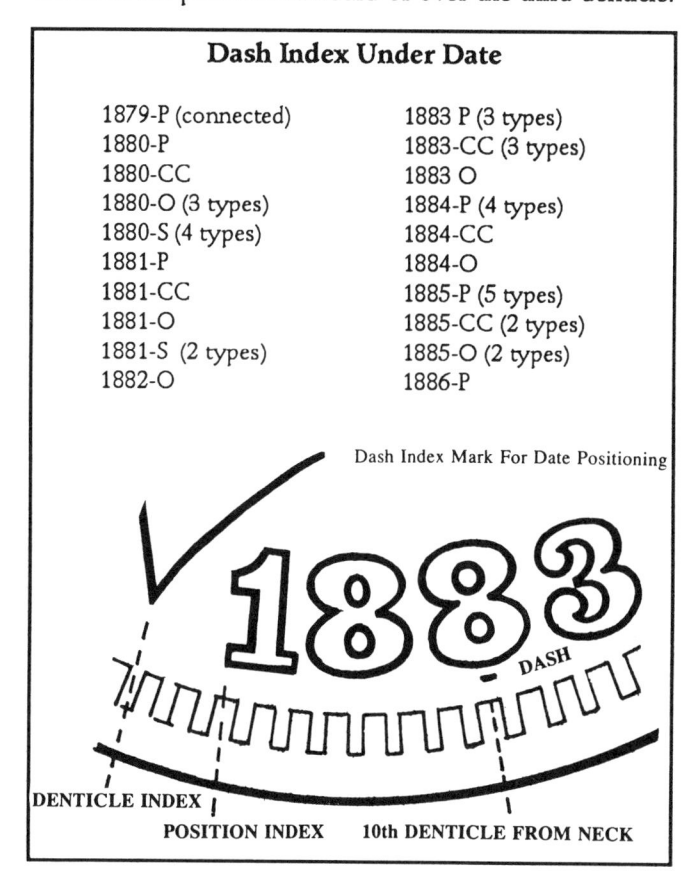

Dash Index Under Date

1879-P (connected)	1883 P (3 types)
1880-P	1883-CC (3 types)
1880-CC	1883 O
1880-O (3 types)	1884-P (4 types)
1880-S (4 types)	1884-CC
1881-P	1884-O
1881-CC	1885-P (5 types)
1881-O	1885-CC (2 types)
1881-S (2 types)	1885-O (2 types)
1882-O	1886-P

Dash Index Mark For Date Positioning

DENTICLE INDEX
POSITION INDEX 10th DENTICLE FROM NECK

Date Positions

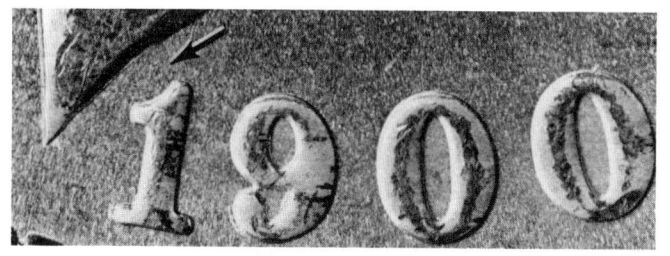

Very Near Date

Very Far Date

Use of the dash index was abandoned after 1886 and the hand punched dates varied in lateral position from very near to very far.

For 1921 the date was in the master die and all working hubs and dies. The date positions and orientation are all the same and there is slight doubling on top of both 1's for all dies.

The accompanying diagram shows the guide for the date lateral position. This applies for the dates after 1878. The left edge of one bottom crossbar is used as an index. If it fell within the third denticle from the Liberty head neck vee, then it is considered to be normal. The space between denticles on either side of the third denticle is defined as near and far. Beyond this date position is defined as very near or very far. The following listing provides the known mispositioned lateral dates.

Mispositioned Mint Marks

Since the mint marks were also punched in by hand, their placement and orientation varies. They were positioned approximately in the center of the area between the D and O of DOLLAR and the bottom of the wreath. As shown in the accompanying diagram, the normal position (for O and S mint marks) is determined to be within the box formed by horizontal lines at the bottom of the wreath and tops of D and O and the vertical lines from the middle of the right side of the D and middle of the left side of the O. CC mint marks, being wider, use vertical lines on the right inside of the D and the left inside of the O for the lateral indices.

The tilt angle guides are extensions of the lines formed by the right inside of the D and left inside of the O. If the vertical line of the mint mark falls outside these limits, it is defined as tilted.

Mint Mark Placement

1878-CC	IV CC set high, IV set high and shifted right, III CC tilted right, III CC set high
1878-S	S set high, S shifted left, S tilted right
1879-CC	CC shifted left
1879-O	O tilted right, O shifted left & right, O set low
1879-S	S tilted left, S shifted left
1880-S	Large S tilted left, small S tilted left, small S shifted left, large S tilted very far to left
1880-O	Small O set high
1880-S	Large S tilted left, S shifted left, S tilted left
1881-O	O tilted left, O tilted right, O set high, O shifted left
1881-S	S tilted left & right, S shifted left, S set high
1882-CC	CC tilted right
1882-O	O tilted left
1882-S	S tilted left
1883-CC	CC slanted left
1883-O	O tilted left and right, O shifted left
1883-S	S tilted right
1883-CC	CC tilted left
1884-O	O set high, O tilted left
1884-S	S tilted right and shifted left, S shifted left
1885-CC	CC tilted left
1885-O	O shifted right, O set high
1886-O	O tilted left, O tilted right, O set high, O shifted right
1886-S	S tilted left
1887-O	O tilted right, O shifted right
1887-S	S set high
1888-O	O set high, O set very high
1889-CC	CC shifted right
1889-O	O set high, O set high and tilted right, O set high
1889-S	S tilted left, S shifted right
1890-CC	CC tilted left (two types)
1890-O	O set high, O tilted left, O set high and shifted left, O tilted right, O shifted right
1890-S	S set high and tilted left, S set high, S tilted left and shifted left, S tilted left and shifted right, S shifted right
1891-CC	CC set high, CC tilted slightly left
1891-O	O tilted right, O set high, O shifted right
1891-S	S set high
1892-CC	CC tilted left, wide CC, dropped C
1892-O	O set high, O set high and tilted left, O tilted right
1892-S	S tilted right, S set high
1893-CC	CC tilted right and left
1893-O	O tilted right
1894-O	O tilted right, O tilted slightly left
1894-S	S tilted slightly right, S shifted right and tilted slightly right, S set high
1895-O	O tilted slightly right
1895-S	S tilted right
1896-O	O tilted slightly left, O tilted slightly right, O set high
1897-O	O tilted right, O set high, O set high and shifted left, O set high and tilted right
1897-S	S tilted right, S set high
1898-O	O set high, O tilted right
1898-S	S tilted slightly right
1899-O	Medium O tilted slightly right, small O tilted right, small O set high, medium O set high, medium O set high and tilted right, medium O set high and shifted left, O set high and tilted right
1899-S	S tilted right (two types), S set high and tilted right
1900-O	Medium O tilted slightly right, medium O tilted slightly left, small O tilted right, medium O tilted right, medium O set high.
1900-S	S set high (2 types), S shifted right
1901-O	O tilted left, O tilted right, O set high

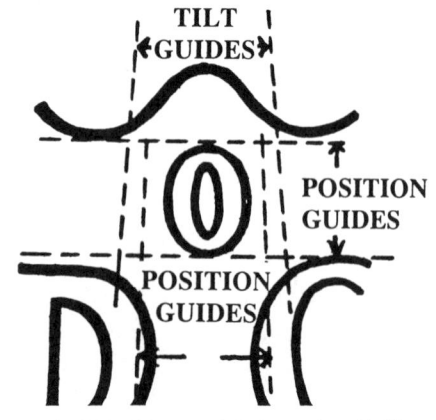

Mint Mark Position and Orientation Guides

1901-S	S set high and tilted right, S set high
1902-O	Small O tilted right, medium O tilted left and set high, medium O set high, medium O tilted left
1902-S	S tilted left
1903-O	O tilted slightly left, O shifted right and tilted left, O set high, O titled left and right
1903-S	S tilted left, S shifted right
1904-O	O tilted left, O shifted right, O set high
1904-S	S tilted right, S set high
1921-S	S shifted left

Doubled Dates

These are by far the most common die varieties. Practically every date has one or more die varieties with doubled date digit(s). In some cases, all the date digits are doubled with a regular shift indicating a logotype was used to punch all four digits into the die simultaneously. Any misalignment of the logotype between blows would cause doubling of the date digits. Others show only one or two doubled digits indicating that single digits may have also been individually punched sometimes. Because micro-doubled dates are so numerous they are not listed separately here. Only the more spectacular ones are given in the following listing.

When looking for doubled dates (or mint marks), the collector must be careful not to confuse these with a doubled die or machine doubling. The doubled die or machine doubling will always show some additional feature of the coin doubled, while the true doubled date will not. If by chance a coin has machine doubling and a doubled date from repunching, the repunched number doubling will probably not follow the machine doubling trend of the coin.

Strongly Doubled Dates

Date	VAM #
1879-P	20
1880-P	22
1880-S	7
1883-P	4
1883-CC	4
1884-CC	7
1885-P	6
1886-P	11
1887-P	5
1887-O	2
1889-P	6
1889-O	6
1890-P	4
1890-S	11
1892-S	2
1896-P	5, 6
1896-O	6, 7
1899-S	7

Doubled Mint Marks

Since the mint marks were also punched into the dies by hand, micro doubling of them was fairly common due to misalignment of the punch between blows of the mallet. The 1879-O VAM 4 has an O/O horizontal with the original O punched sideways. Also the 1895-S VAM 5 has an S/S horizontal. The following listing gives some of the more strongly doubled mint marks.

Strongly Doubled Mint Marks

Date	VAM #
1879-S	30
1880-S	18, 19
1881-S	5, 7
1882-O	7
1883-O	4
1884-O	6
1885-S	6
1887-S	2
1890-CC	5
1890-S	2, 3
1892-CC	4
1895-S	3
1896-S	3

Overdates

Overdates that have one year date punched over another year date on a die are known for two years of the Morgan series. There are a number of overdate dies of 80/79 for the 1880-P, CC, S, and O and one each 7/6 for the 1887-P and O.

The 1880 80/79 overdates were discovered during 1964-1967 and again in 1976-1977 when some additional overdates on the surface of digits were discovered. A total of 24 repunched obverse working die overdates have been identified to date making these one of the most interesting varieties of the Morgan series.

The strongest showing overdate is the 1880-CC, VAM 4 80/79 in which both the 7 and 9 numerals show clearly within the 80. The 1880-CC also has the complete 7 showing high and low within the 8 and nothing in the 0. Two working dies also show a dash below the 8 and faint remains of a 7 within or above the 8. Thus, five 1880-CC overdate dies are known. However, about one-third of existing 1880-CC are the strong overdates and another half are weak overdates, so they don't bring any premium over the normal coin at present.

The 1880-P has ten types of overdates. The strongest is VAM 6 8/7 spikes with two prominent ears above the 8 and a cross bar within the top loop that are clearly visible with the naked eye. This overdate is popular and brings a substantial premium over a normal coin. VAM 7, 8/7 cross bar and VAM 8, 8/7 ears are also prominent overdates and bring even higher premiums than VAM 6 because of their increased scarcity (only a couple uncirculated specimens are known). The weak and common VAM 9 8/7 stem and VAM 10 8/7 bit do not bring premiums. VAM 23 shows the 79 on top of the 80 digits as a check mark on the left side of upper loop of 8 and 9 loop ends on left side of 0. It is a scarce and visible that brings a substantial premium. There are three weak overdates that show a check mark on the top loop of the 8 and one faint remains of 9 loop ends on 0 that do not bring any premiums.

The 1880-O has five types of overdates. The

strongest is VAM 4, 80/79 and has faint ears above the 8, a cross bar in the upper loop of 8 and remains of 9 in upper part of 0. The second strongest VAM 5, 8/7 ear shows one faint ear above the 8 and a cross bar in the upper loop of 8. Both of these overdates bring a modest premium over the normal coin. VAM 6, 8/7 spike has a long spike ear above the 8 and horizontal spike within the top loop of 8. There are two weak overdates that show a check mark on the top loop of the 8 that do not bring a premium.

The 1880-S has four types of overdates. The strongest, VAM 8 80/79, has a faint ear above the 8 and metal in the upper loop of the 8 and part of 0. The second, VAM 10 8/7 cross bar has a faint ear above the 8 and a horizontal line within the top loop. The third, VAM 11 0/9, has metal with polishing marks within the 0. The fourth, VAM 12 8/9 spikes, has two spikes above the 8 and a small piece of metal at the top right inside of the 0. VAM 10 brings a substantial premium because of its scarcity. The only other 1880-S that brings a modest premium is VAM 11 0/9.

The 1887 overdates were discovered in 1972 and early 1973. The 1887-P has one die variety showing part of a 6 under the 7. A long curved line extends upward from the bottom right side of the bottom of the 7 and a short thick spike shows on the left side of the bottom of the 7. The 1887-O has a similar appearing 6 under the 7 except that the remaining portions of the 6 are not as thick and are a little longer in length. Both of these popular overdates bring premium prices.

The 1880 series of overdates show varying degrees of overdate strength within the 80 digits, above and below them and on their surface. This is due to the varying depths that the 80 digits were punched over the 79 digits and the degree of polishing the dies subsequently received. Each working die had the digits repunched by hand using single digit punches or two or four digit logotypes. The old 79 digits were not ground off the working dies since this would have resulted in a depression in the dies and resulted in a raised area on the coins. Welding the digits on working dies to fill then up was not performed since neither electric arc nor oxyacetylene welding techniques had yet been invented in 1880.

When the 80 digits were punched into the 79 digit cavities, the annealed die allowed the metal to flow into the voids of the 7 and 9. The plastic metal flow was three dimensional since the digits had depth as well as height and width. After the 80 digits were punched into the working die, the die face was polished or basined at each mint using a rotating horizontal iron disc with successively finer emery grit compounds mixed with oil. This polished down any raised metal or rough edges on the die field around the over dated digits and removed the 79 digit traces to various degrees. However, the 79 digits remaining on the tops of the 80 digits were not disturbed by the basining process.

The initial discovery of the 1880-P 8/7 was first

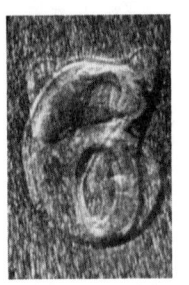

80/79 Superposition

7/6 Superposition

reported in 1964 by A. George Mallis in a pamphlet entitled *List of Die Varieties, Morgan Head Silver Dollars*. The overdate designs on top of the 80 digits were first pointed out by Anthony and Dazelle Morano in the December 1964 issue of *Numismatic Scrapbook Magazine*. They were later discussed by Tom DeLorey in the June 9, 1976 "Collectors' Clearinghouse" in *Coin World*. The plastic metal flow of 80 digits into the 79 digits was demonstrated by Leroy Van Allen in the October 27 and November 3, 1976 "Collectors' Clearinghouse" in *Coin World*, by forcing model date digits into clay molds. These demonstrations duplicated the various features of the 1880 overdates including the 79 digits on top of the 80 digits.

Dual Mint Marks

Dual mint marks are defined as a different design mint mark repunched over the original one. The different design mint mark can be of the same branch mint type or of another branch mint. Both of these kinds of dual mint marks are known for the Morgan series. Dual mint marks of different design occurred for the 1879-CC and 1900-S and dual mint marks of different branch mints occurred for the 1882-O and 1900-O. These were deliberate mint mark alterations (except for the 1900-S) and not just a simple punch misalignment between blows as was the case for doubled mint marks.

The 1879-CC, large CC over small CC, is the so-called, "capped CC." This was the first year the large CC mint mark was used, and possibly older dies were modified. The tops of the small mint mark appear to show just above the large mint mark. By scaling a drawing of the small CC used on the 1878-CC and laying it over an enlarged photograph of the 1879-CC L CC/S CC, it appears that tops of the small CC line up with the "caps" and that the bottom of the small right CC agrees with portions of the metal in the center of the large right CC. There has been some attempt to obliterate the small mint mark, as evidenced by the rough surface.

Apparently about one third of the 1879-CC coins are the L CC/S CC; out of a total of 756,000 minted, about 250,000 probably were the L CC/S CC. So far only one design variety has been apparent. The die shows progressive wear, with the rough spots gradually smoothed out. At the same time the G in GOD becomes partially and then completely filled in. This variety is the only one heavily discounted because of the messy looking mint mark.

The 1900-S dual mint mark has a narrow IV S over a wide V S mint mark. Both size mint marks were used during 1899 and 1900. Apparently a wide mint mark was punched in first and the narrow one was punched in later. Some die states do not show the remains of the wide mint mark so that portions of the die must have been polished down sometime during the dies lifetime or the remains of a large S later dislodged.

Three varieties of the 1882-O O/S exist. The first shows the S mint mark diagonal bar inside and flush with the top of the O mint mark. An earlier die state of this variety shows as a thin diagonal line. A second O/S variety shows the S mint mark diagonal bar inside and depressed below the top of the O mint mark. An earlier die state of this variety shows as a diagonal teardrop at the lower part of the O loop opening. The third O/S variety shows as a short diagonal bar at the top left side of the O mint mark opening. An earlier die state of this variety shows as a triangle dot at left side of the loop opening and a fine diagonal line in the middle.

The relative rarity ranking of the most visible, later die state O/S varieties are close to each other. The O/S depressed in most available followed by the O/S broken with the scarcest being the O/S flush. The earlier die states are generally scarcer with the die state O/S depressed as a teardrop being rare.

Five different 1900-O O/CC die varieties are known. In each of these, the CC appears in a slightly different position with respect to the O mint mark — low; centered shifted left or right; centered die chips and high shifted left or right. Since the Carson City Mint stopped striking silver dollars in 1893, why did seven years elapse before these dual mint mark dies were used at the New Orleans Mint? The answer is that on July 1, 1899, the Carson City Mint status was officially changed to an assay office. Its three coining presses, remaining coin dies, and associated machinery were shipped to the Philadelphia Mint by the middle of September 1899. In 1900 when the New Orleans Mint asked for more working dies, the Philadelphia Mint presumably was short and they sent the CC dies they had in storage after the mint marks were modified. Probably the 1882-O O/S and the 1880/79 and 1887/6 overdates were also repunched for working dies out of necessity.

The O/CC are popular dual mint marks and bring substantial premiums. VAM numbers 8, 11 and 12 are the ones usually encountered. VAM 7 is scarce and VAM 9 is extremely rare and will bring high premiums. VAM 8 is actually an O/O/CC with the O/O more evident as the die wears. The later die state of VAM 8 shows rust spots around the mint mark.

Clashed Dies

The clashed dies are evident on practically all dates of the Morgan silver dollar. It resulted when a blank planchet was not advanced in the press, allowing the obverse and reverse dies to come into contact. A portion of each die would be impressed into the other and this resulted in the extra impression being raised on the coin (as illustrated in the photographs). The clashing of the dies could occur at any time during their life; therefore, coins struck from clashed dies may number from a few to several hundred thousand. Severe clash marks were often removed from the working dies by polishing the die fields and the dies reused again.

In the accompanying line drawings the opposite side is superimposed by a dashed outline. This shows how the designs line up when the dies came together. From these drawings the clash photographs can be related to the various part of the design.

There are various degrees of clashed dies and even cases of multiple clashes out of register on the same coin. On the reverse, a light clash shows up as a sideways vee to the right of the eagle's left wing and next to the upper leaves of the wreath. This is an impression from the back of the Liberty head cap. Also on the reverse, a line extends upwards from the top of the eagle's right wing to the N of the IN in the motto. This impression is from the obverse neck line. The fact that all these impressions show up most clearly on the right side of the coin indicates that the right sides of the obverse

Design Superposition for Clashed Dies

and reverse dies must have come together first. Sometimes the cotton bolls and stems show above the arrow heads.

On more heavily clashed dies, the nose and lip profile shows up on the reverse next to the inner part of the left wreath. The Liberty head's hair can cause marks next to the eagles throat. The ultimate in clashed dies, however, occurs when part of the word LIBERTY from the obverse is impressed on the reverse. The E in LIBERTY shows tilted to the left below the eagle's tail feathers. Only three dates have been found so far with full E showing on the reverse: 1886-O, 1889-O, and 1891-O. The 1889-O is the scarcest and the 1891-O the most common. A partial E showing has been found for 1878-P VAM 84, 1880-P, 1883-O, 1884-P, 1887-P, 1888-O and 1891-O.

On the obverse part of the right wreath from the reverse shows up as a jagged line extending upward from the bottom of the cap. A line extending diagonally down from the junction of the chin and neck line is an impression from the upper part of the eagle's right wing, and lines between the lip, nose and chin come from the upper left wreath of the reverse.

Clashed die coins are generally not collectible since they are so common. The exception is when an E from LIBERTY shows on the reverse. A partial E is collected to a minor degree and generally does not command a premium. A full E is more desirable and it brings a premium depending upon its rarity.

Die Scratches and Gouges

The dies pick up scratches during normal handling; however, since most of them are minor, they are not included in this book. Every die has hairline polishing marks around and in the design from the basining process. These can be useful in identifying specific dies but again, they are not included in this book. A few long deep large gouges are included as die states. These are given in the following listing.

Clashed Obverse

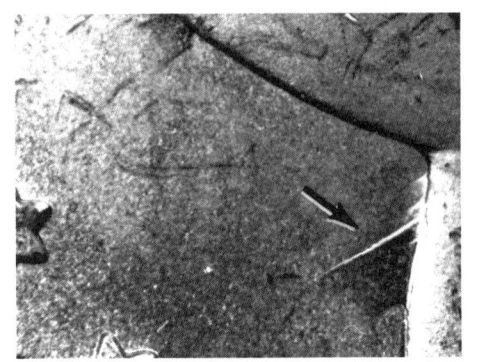

Neck

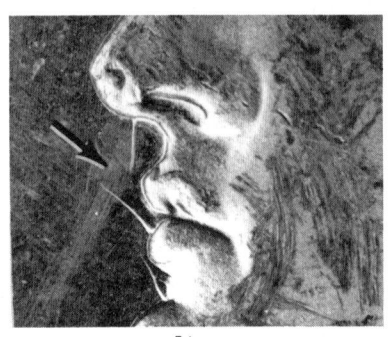

Lips

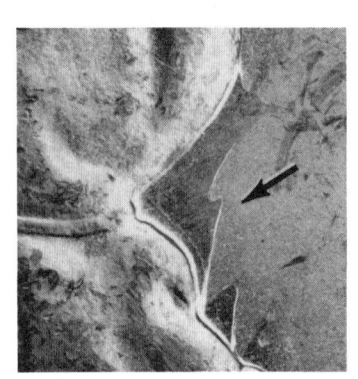

Back of Cap

Clashed Reverse

Top of Eagle's Right Wing

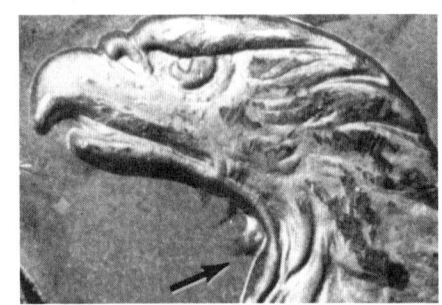

Eagle's Neck

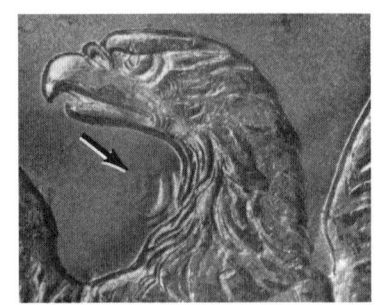

Eagle's Neck

Left Wreath

Right Wreath

120

Partial E's From Clashed Dies

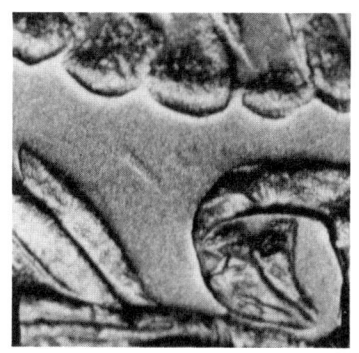

1878-P E VAM 84

1880-P E

1883-O E

1884-P E

1887-P E

1891-O E

1888-O E

Die Scratches and Gouges

1878-P	VAM 131 Scratch thru B or R in LIBERTY
	VAM 146 Line through ER-Y in LIBERTY
	VAM 195 Line through B of LIBERTY
1878-CC	Line in eye, line in IB in LIBERTY, lines in eagle, spiked lip
1878-S	Lines in eagle's tail feathers, lines in eagle, line in eagle's wing, horizontal band in cotton leaves
1879-S	Long lines in hair above forehead, broad ribbon in lower hair
1880-O	Line through eagle's neck, hangnail eagle, gouge in wreath
1881-CC	Line above arrow feathers
1881-O	Line through DO of DOLLAR
1882-S	Line in first U in PLURIBUS
1886-P	Gouge in designer's initial, M, on obverse
1887-P	Line below eagle's tail feathers
1890-O	Two diagonal bands right of date
1890-CC	Tailbar die gouge
1891-CC	Spitting eagle die gouge
1891-S	Die gouge in olive branch
1894-S	Worn line in eye
1896-P	Die gouge in 6, die gouge in 8
1896-O	Die gouge in 6
1900-O	Heavy lines around wheat stalks
1901-P	Lines around NE - DO
1921-P	Horizontal line from eagle's tail feathers eagle, vertical line from eagle's tail feathers
1921-S	Line between B and U of PLURIBUS, two horizontal bars at top of head

Overpolished Dies

Each die had to be basined (polished the field) before it could be used in the presses. Also, during their use they may have been again polished to remove clash marks or die cracks and breaks as they wore out. If an abnormal amount of design was removed during this polishing, then it is defined as an overpolished die.

One of the first part of the design to be removed from overpolishing was the bottom of the leaves in the wreath on the reverse. Some of the leaves became narrow, flat, and separated from the main wreath. It was quite common for some of the wreath leaves to be disconnected and, therefore, these cases are not included in this book. More severe overpolished dies showed missing portions of the eagle's wings on the reverse. On the obverse, portions of the hair would be missing as well as the bridge of the nose. The following listing gives the major known overpolished dies. Most of these are for 1878 when difficulties were experienced in obtaining a good basining of the dies.

Overpolished Dies

1878-P   VAM 14-2, 30, 79, 132, and 188 obverse
            VAM 18, 42, 70, 80, 81, 100, and 196 reverse
1878-S   Shallow date, missing feathers in wings, overpolished wing
1879-O   Overpolished wing
1882-O   Shallow neck, overpolished wing
1888-S   Overpolished wing

Mint Mark Variations

Four branch mints struck the Morgan silver dollars: the New Orleans Mint from 1879 to 1904, the San Francisco Mint from 1878 to 1904, the Carson City Mint from 1878 to 1885 and from 1889 to 1893, and the Denver Mint in 1921. These mints used mint marks in a variety of sizes, except for the Denver Mint, which used only a micro size D (see the accompanying list and photographs).

The New Orleans Mint used two basic O's. The first, used from 1879 to 1884, was a tall oval medium O with a narrow slit, II O. The second, used from 1884 to 1904, was a circular medium O with a wide opening, III O. The type II O was also used on some 1888 and 1889 coins. A small O, type I O, was used on some 1880, 1896, 1899, 1900, and 1902 coins; this was the mint mark size intended for use on the Seated Liberty and Barber quarters. A large oval O, type IV O, with a narrow slit was also used on some 1879 coins. This was probably an experimental size, since 1879 was the first year the Morgan silver dollar was struck at the New Orleans Mint. It may have been the size used on the eagles. Sometimes the type III O has a narrow slit opening. It can be seen on coins of a few years, and is actually the type III O mint mark with the design punched deeper than normal, thus closing the center of the O. The dates that have type III O with closed centers usually have a prominently raised mint mark indicating it was punched deeper than usual.

The San Francisco Mint used four basic types of mint marks. A small square S, III S, was used in 1878 and on some 1879 coins. A medium rounded S, IV S, was used from 1879 to 1900; and a large S with rounded top and bottom strokes, V S, was used from 1899 to 1904, since the type IV S had a tendency to fill in. A micro S, I S, was used in 1921. S mint marks of different sizes, meant for other coins, were also used. The very large S, VI S, on some 1880 coins was used on the Seated Liberty dollars, and a very small round S, type II S, found on a few 1903 coins, was used on the Barber quarters.

The Carson City Mint used two basic size mint marks. A small size CC, I-IV CC, was used in 1878 and on some in 1880; it was the same mint mark used on the Seated Liberty silver dollars and was apparently punched into the die one letter at a time, since the spacing between letters and the orientation varies. The second size was a large CC, V CC; these letters were punched simultaneously most of the time since the spacing and individual orientation show few variations.

Mint Mark Descriptions

New Orleans:

I O Small O
1880, 1896, 1899, 1900, 1902

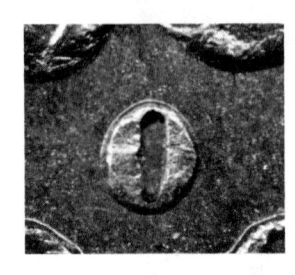

II O Tall oval medium O with narrow slit
1879-84, 1888, 1889

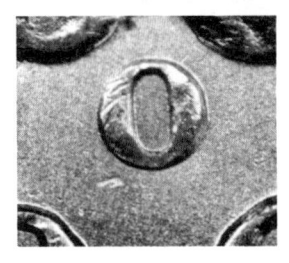

III O Circular medium O with wide opening
1884 - 1904

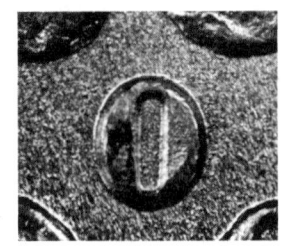

IV O Large oval O with narrow slit 1879

San Francisco:

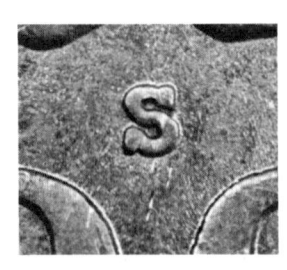

I S Micro S
1921

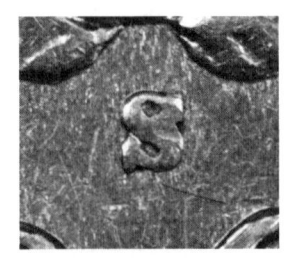

II S Small Round S
1903

122

San Francisco *continued:*

III S Small square S
1878, 1879

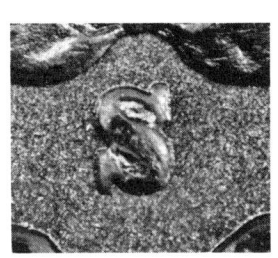

IV S Medium rounded S with pointed serifs
1879-1900

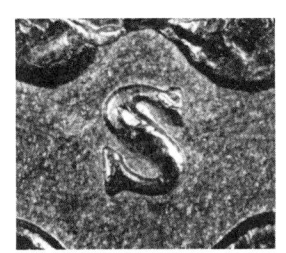

V S Large S with rounded top and bottom serifs and wider than IV S
1899-1904

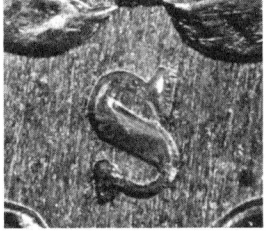

VI S Very large S with thick center shaft and top and bottom strokes at tips
1880

Carson City:

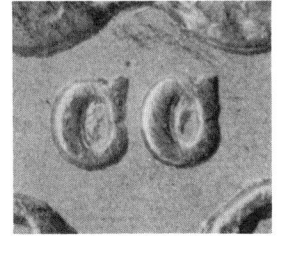

I CC Small CC, very closely spaced letters
1878, 1880

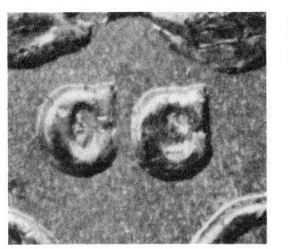

II CC Small CC, medium spacing
1878, 1880

III CC Small CC, wide spacing
1878

Carson City *continued:*

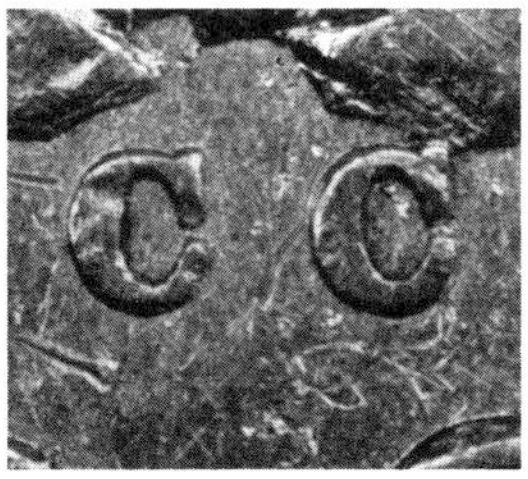

IV CC Small CC, very wide spacing
1878

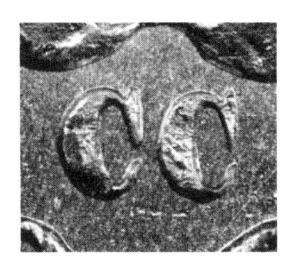

V CC Large CC, medium spacing
1879-1885, 1889-1893

Denver:

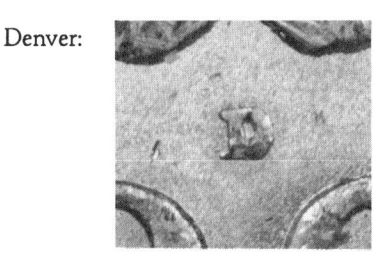

I D Micro D
1921

Date Variations

Every numeral used in the dates on the Morgan silver dollars had at least two and sometimes as many as four varieties (see accompanying list and illustrations). Most of these differences were small, but they do help in identifying each date by characteristics other than the last two digits. Most design differences can be detected only on coins of EF grade or better.

The most obvious change in date design came in 1884, when the size and width of all digits were reduced. For the 1921 coins, each digit was modified slightly. The digit 2 was apparently changed each year it was used. The 0, 1, 3, 9 digits were each changed three times.

The many different digit designs came about because each date digit punch was handmade. The last digit accounts for most of the digit varieties.

Identifying Marks on Individual Dies

Some of the silver dollars from the Philadelphia Mint in 1884 had small dots placed alongside the designer's initial M on both the obverse and reverse. In past years, small dots had been placed on coins to indicate a change of design; this was probably also the case for the 1884 silver dollar. In that year the size of the date and the width of the numbers were reduced. Apparently, the dots were to distinguish the new dies with reduced date size during the transition early in 1884, in order to prevent a mix up of the working hubs. After the transition, the raised dot on the working hub was easily ground off.

Date Variations

I 1	Wide 1	1878-1883
II 1	Narrow 1	1884-1904
III 1	Medium 1	1921
I 2	Large Openings (Open and closed)	1882
II 2	Small Openings	1892
III 2	Medium Openings	1902
IV 2	Short Lower Crossbar End	1921
I 3	Wide 3	1883
II 3	Narrow 3, Long Center (Opened and closed)	1893
III 3	Medium 3, Medium Center	1903
I 4	Long crossbar end	1884, 1894
II 4	Short crossbar end	1904
I 5	Narrow top opening	1885
II 5	Wide top opening	1895
I 6	Narrow top end (open and closed)	1886
II 6	Wide top end	1896
I 7	Long Serifs	1878, 1879
II 7	Short Serifs	1887, 1897

I 8	Wide 8	1878-1883	
II 8	Narrow 8	1884-1899	
I 9	Wide 9 (open and closed)	1879	
II 9	Narrow 9 (open and closed)	1889-1904	
III 9	Straight back to 9	1921	
I 0	Wide 0	1880	
II 0	Narrow Straight 0	1890	
III 0	Narrow Elliptical 0	1900-1904	

Two different sized dots have been found on the obverse, as shown in the Chapter Eight photographs. Their positions next to the initial M are also slightly different. Detection of the dot on the reverse requires a strong magnifying glass, and only one size has been found so far. The authors have seen the obverse and reverse dot dies used only together, never separately. On worn coins, the reverse dot is very difficult to see.

Why a dot was placed on the reverse at all is an interesting question. Since there was no design change on the reverse in that year, there was no need to identify the reverse dies.

Dots

Some of the 1921-P, D, S dies show raised circular dots first pointed out by Steve Sabella of New York in June 1979. These are different than the dots found next to the designers initial, M, on the 1884-P dies. They are found only on the D^2 reverse and on the obverse in combination with the D^2 reverse. They vary in diameter from two to eight thousands of an inch. The most prominent dot is just below the eagle's right wing on the 1921-P. Both the 1921-D and S have a dot almost as large below the eagle's wings in the field. Possibly these large dots were used to identify the D^2 reverse dies when they were first used. However, there was no need to do this for the Denver and San Francisco mints since they only used the D^2 reverses. Also, the dots are found on the obverses and there are quite a range of dot sizes.

A possible cause of some raised dots was the use of a Rockwell hardness tester on the face of the dies after they were hardened. These dots appear quite suddenly on the D^2 reverse of the 1921 Morgan dollars and are also on the 1921 through 1924 Peace dollars.

In performing a hardness test, the Rockwell tester drives the conical point of a tool into the metal. The depth of penetration produced by a given force is then related to the hardness of the metal. Different size points of the test tool and force settings produced a range in size of depressions in the metal. These depressions have circular shapes and smooth round tops.

A typical Rockwell hardness tester tool has a conical point of 0.1 mm radius with included angle of 120°. Using the RC60 scale, a 160 kg force produces a 0.2-0.4 mm diameter (8-16 thousands of an inch) depressions and a 50 kg force produces 0.07-0.13 mm diameter (2.7-5 thousands of an inch). These are the same size as the dots seen on the coins.

About 50 obverse and over 75 reverse dots have been found on the 1921 Morgan dollars. These occur in the fields, face, hair and even on the denticles of the obverse. On the reverse the dots are concentrated near the coin center in the fields and on the eagle's wings and breast feathers. Anywhere from one to five dots appear on any one coin and generally, but not always, with both sides having dots. Over 30 P, 12 S and 15 D mint die pairs with dots have been found. The P coins have two dies with 8 thousands of an inch diameter dots on reverse, one with 7 thousands, and the rest 2 to 5 thousands. The P obverse dot sizes range from 2 to 5 thousands. The D reverse has one die with a 7 thousands dot with the rest of the reverse and obverse dots 2 to 5 thousands. The S obverse has one die with a 5 thousands dot with the rest of the reverse and obverse dots 2 to 4 thousands.

It is likely that many small dots of two to four

1921-D Dot

thousands in diameter were caused by gas bubbles trapped in the steel when it was cast. The larger dots could have been special identification marks on the dies or possibly due to Rockwell hardener tests on the face of the dies.

Edge Reeding

The number of edge reeding produced by the collars varied over the years and by mint for the Morgan dollar. The lowest count is 157 total for the so-called "infrequent reeding" variety of 1921-P, 168 for an 1878-P variety and 176 through 194 for the other dates and mints. In the following chapter on listing of die varieties the edge reeding count is provided for each die variety. The edge or third side of a coin is useful as an aid to die, mint, proof and counterfeit identification through the reeding count.

In the manufacturing of collars a milling machine was first used to make grooves on the swedging tool cylinder. The operator could set the indexing space on the milling machine to obtain a certain number of reeds on the swedging tool. This tool was then forced into the collar to produce the collar reeding. One swedging tool could make quite a few collars before it wore out. In making the swedging tools, apparently the milling machine mechanical tolerance allowed variations of one reed when a group of tools were made at one time.

All collars were made at the Philadelphia Mint and shipped to the branch mints along with obverse and reverse die pairs as the need arose. Apparently, the Philadelphia Mint established certain patterns of edge reeding counts that varied over the years and with individual branch mints.

There are several methods to check the edge reeding counts. A fine lead pencil can be used to go around the edge marking off each ten and then summing the total. This requires good eyesight, a steady hand and quite a bit of time. Another method suggested by Stuart Clyde of Florida is to make a start mark on edge reed, place carbon paper on regular paper on a pane of glass, and then roll coin on edge on carbon and paper to make reed top impressions until the start mark is encountered again. The impressions on the paper can then be counted in groups of ten. This has the advantage of making a permanent impression, making it easier to see and to double check the count.

However, the quickest method, by far, requiring only a few seconds to check the total count, is to use another coin of known edge reeding count. New Orleans coins have only edge reeding count of 181 from 1883 through 1898 and the Peace and Ike dollars only have 189 count. The known and unknown count coins are laid on a flat surface on top of protective paper. The edges are pushed together so that the reedings interlock and some indexes on both coins are opposite each other (the numeral 1 in the date is convenient). Next, the two coins are rotated together keeping the reeding interlocked like gears. Several twists of the hands will bring the index marks back together or near one another. If the edge reeding counts aren't exactly the same, then the number of reeds more or less from the known one can be visually counted or the edges slid together until the indexes line up. In this method the design features of the coin are protected during rotation since the rims are higher. It is best to use uncirculated or high grade circulated coins only since worn or nicked reeding will not interlock properly at some points. Also, if the counts of the two coins differ appreciably then the reeds will tend to skip. The 181 and 189 known counts are all that is needed to check Morgan reeding count range, except for the 157 and 168 which are scarce and can be visually identified anyway when placed adjacent to another coin with higher count.

All reeding counts given in the listing of die varieties were checked by the authors. A few varieties were not available for count and hopefully will be checked in the future. *Figure 7-3* shows the reeding counts for the 1878-P varieties broken down by obverse and reverse design type combinations. This is an expansion of a chart originally provided by Fred Miller in the January, 1978 issue of the NECA Errorscope.

The normal reeding count for the 1878-P falls into three groupings: 179 and 180, 188 and 189, and 193 and 194, The first grouping was devoted to the P coins for 1878 to 1883 except for one 1878-CC variety with 179 reeds. The last grouping occurred for only the 1878-P and 1883-P. The second grouping of 188 and 189 was used by both the P and S coins throughout the Morgan series.

During 1878 there were ten coining presses at the Philadelphia Mint with six large enough to strike silver dollars. These six presses were probably used almost exclusively to strike silver dollars during 1878 from March 11 on because of the high quantity requirements. Thus, it is not surprising that different collars were used during the same time period. Also some dies and collars were probably used for a while, set aside, and then reused again later which tended to stretch out the time period when certain types were used.

The first Morgan die used, VAM 9 with eight tail feather reverse, used a collar with 193 reeds. The 193 col-

Figure 7-3 REEDING FOR 1878-P

DESIGN COMBINATIONS	168	176	177	178	179	180	188	189	193	194
$I^1 \cdot A^1$						8, 10, 14-4	14-1, 14-3	3, 14-6, 14-7, 14-8	9, 14-2, 14	
$I^2 \cdot A^1$					12	15	1	2,4,5,6,7, 14-5	6	
$II/I \cdot A^1$					16, 17					
$I^2 \cdot A^2/A^1$						23				
$II/I \cdot A^2/A^1$						18, 19, 21, 22		20		
$II/I \cdot B/A$			31		44	30,33,38,40,42,43				
$II \cdot B/A$					32,34,36,37 39,41-A,45	41				
$I^2 \cdot B^1$						70				
$II/I \cdot B^1$						79,80,81,82,83,84				
$I^1 \cdot B^2a$						100				
$II/I \cdot B^2a$				114		110, 116		116	111, 119	112,113,115,117, 118, 122
$II \cdot B^2a$					131, 132	131, 132			133	130, 131
$II/I \cdot B^2b$					142	140,143,144,145		140		141
$II \cdot B^2b$										146
$II/I \cdot B^2c$						162, 164, 165			166,168,169,170 171	160,161,163,167
$II \cdot B^2c$									185,186,187,188	
$II \cdot B^2d$					190					
$II \cdot B^2e$					195, 195-A					
$II/I \cdot B^2f$					196	197				197
$II \cdot B^2f$										200
$II/I \cdot C^1a$					200, 201					
$III^1 \cdot C^1a$						202				
$II \cdot C^2a$					210-A					210, 210B
$III^1 \cdot C^2a$		220								
$II \cdot C^3a$	222			222					221, 222	222, 223
$III^2 \cdot C^3a$									230	230

127

lar was also used for three other eight tail feather varieties.

The 188 and 189 group was used almost exclusively for the eight tail feathers varieties in March and April. Then came the 179 and 180 group used for some eight tail feathers, all 7/8 tail feathers and B^1 reverses, much of the B^2 reverses and some early C reverse experimentation in May. Within this group it is curious that the 180 reed was used almost exclusively with the II/I obverses while the 179 reed was used primarily for the II obverses. One clear trend is that all 1878-P B^1 coins have 180 reeds. For the 7/8 tail feathers, those with the II/I obverse have primarily 180 reeds and those with the II obverse have primarily 179 reeds. The A^2/A^1 reverses have primarily 180 reeds.

The 193 and 194 group was used for much of the B^2 reverses, some early C^3 reverses and most of the final C^3 reverse coins. Thus, it would appear that the II obverse and B reverse dies were used well beyond May when the early C reverse experiments were tried. Some varieties show more than one count. This can be due to a common variety with multiple dies such as the VAMs 131, 222 and 230. Or it can be due to the one unique die being used with several collars such as VAMs 6, 116, 140, 197 and 200.

A surprise is an "almost" infrequently reeded coin, VAM 222, with 168 reeds discovered by Fred Miller. It is significantly lower in number than for this and other years except for the 1921-P infrequently reeded variety with 157 reeds. Apparently, this collar was produced in error and was used with only one pair of dies.

Also, the VAM 220 with 176 reeds was probably an error or a trial case since it is the only P variety with this number of reeds used exclusively later for 1879 to 1882-O. VAM 31 with 177 reeds is a similar case of a single P use of collars meant for CC mint. VAM numbers 114 and 222 with 178 reeds are somewhat isolated cases of also using CC collars.

Figure 7-4 shows the reeding counts for the Morgan dollar by year and mint. The reeding counts for proof dollars are also indicated where known. Proof Morgan dollars had unique reeding counts of 179 from 1883 through 1894 and 186 from 1900 through 1904. Proof reeding counts are not unique for 1878 as they varied with design type and varieties. From 1879 through 1882 the reeding count was also 179 but some P business strike varieties also had this reeding count. From 1896 through 1899 the proof reeding count was 189 and 190 which was the same as some P business strikes. Still, the reeding count can be used to positively identify proofs for some years and help confirm them in other years.

As in the number of die varieties, the 1878-P has a greater number (14) of different reed counts than for any other year and mint combination. This is not surprising since much experimentation occurred during this first year of issue. It has both the lowest reeding count, 168 (except 1921) and the highest, 194.

One of the most obvious trends is the constant count for the New Orleans Mint. It is 176 for 1879 to 1881. For 1882, it is 176 and 181. From 1883 to 1904 it is a constant 181. There are a few isolated die variety exceptions in 1899-1901 and 1904 which have higher reed counts of 187-190. And one P mint variety in 1883 has a 181 count. At any rate, the counts of 176 and 181 are unique to the O mint for those years of occurrence, except for 1883.

Another constant trend is the Carson City Mint. The count is 177 and/or 178 for all years except for 1878 for which there is an additional count of 179. It also has all unique counts for the years 1879, 1881, and 1883 to 1893 and one unique count for 1880 and 1882.

The trends for the P and S mints are not nearly so clear since their counts are much more varied and with multiple counts for many years. However, the S mints are higher than all the CC and all the O mints for all years except 1899 and 1904. From 1879 to 1883 the Philadelphia Mint count is clustered around 178 to 181 with unique values of 179 and 180. The San Francisco Mint count from 1879 to 1883 varies from 181 to 189 with 182-187 unique counts for those years. From 1884 to 1899, the P and S counts were somewhat overlapping but from 1885 to 1889 the P counts were higher than the S. From 1901 to 1921 the P and S counts are 189 except for the 1921-P "Infrequent Reeding" of 157.

These trends can be helpful in detecting altered and counterfeit coins. For example, any 1889-CC, 1892-S, 1893-S, or other scarce P, CC or S with an 181 count would be an immediate suspect as an altered O coin. Or an 1895-O with a count other than 181 would be suspect. There are more subtle differences such as an added S mint mark to an 1893-P would have a wrong reed count of 189 instead of 187. But more coins need to be checked for the P and S years 1884 to 1899 to be certain of their total combination of counts and that no other overlaps exist other than those shown.

1878-P Die Marriages

A die marriage chart shows the reverse and obverse die variety combinations for coins. It can be used to indicate the sequence of die usage, the use of a die with more than one other die, and to quickly identify coin dies.

Table 7-1 is a die marriage chart for the 1878-P coin. Each line indicates a different coin type; 106 types have been discovered so far for the 1878-P. Short descriptions have been added to some die varieties to aid in identifying coins.

The die varieties listed were for a single die, except where a design was transferred from a working hub to many working dies without subsequent alterations (this goal was realized only for the second and third design types). The die varieties that definitely appeared on more than one die were: B^1a, B^2a, B^2c, C^1a; and C^3a for the reverse and II 1, II 2, and III^2 1 for the

128

Figure 7-4 MORGAN DOLLAR EDGE REEDING

Pr = Proof

NUMBER OF REEDS

YEAR	157	168	176	177	178	179	180	181	182	183	184	185	186	187	188	189	190	191	192	193	194
1878		P	P	P CC	P	P CC	P	S					S		P	Pr P					
79			O	CC	P	Pr P	P	P S	S		S	S	S	S	P S	S				P	
80			O	CC	CC P	PPr P	P	P	S	S	S	S	S	S							
81			O		CC	Pr P	P	P	S	S	S	S	S	S		P					
82			O		CC P	PPr P	P	O	S	S			S	S	P	P					
83					CC	Pr P	P	P O					S	S	P	P					
84				CC	CC			O						P S	P	P	P				
85				CC		Pr		O				S	S	S	P	P	P				
86						Pr		O					S	S	P	P	P				
87								O				S	S	S		P	P				
88								O					S	S	S	P	P S				
89								O						S	S	P	P				
90				CC	CC			O					S	S	S	P	P S				
91				CC		Pr		O					S	S	S	P	P S				
92				CC		Pr		O						S		P	P S				
93				CC	CC	Pr		O					S	S		P	P			P	
94						Pr		O					S		Pr	P S		P			
95								O				S				Pr P	Pr P				
96								O					P	S		P	P				
97								O						S	P	P Pr S	P Pr S				
98														S	S	PPr	PPr				
99								O							S O	O O P	P				
1900								O					S	POS	P	POS	PO				
01								O					Pr			POS					
02								O					Pr			P S					
03								O					Pr			P S					
04								O					Pr			POS					
21	P															PSDPr					

Table 7-1 1878-P DIE MARRIAGE CHART

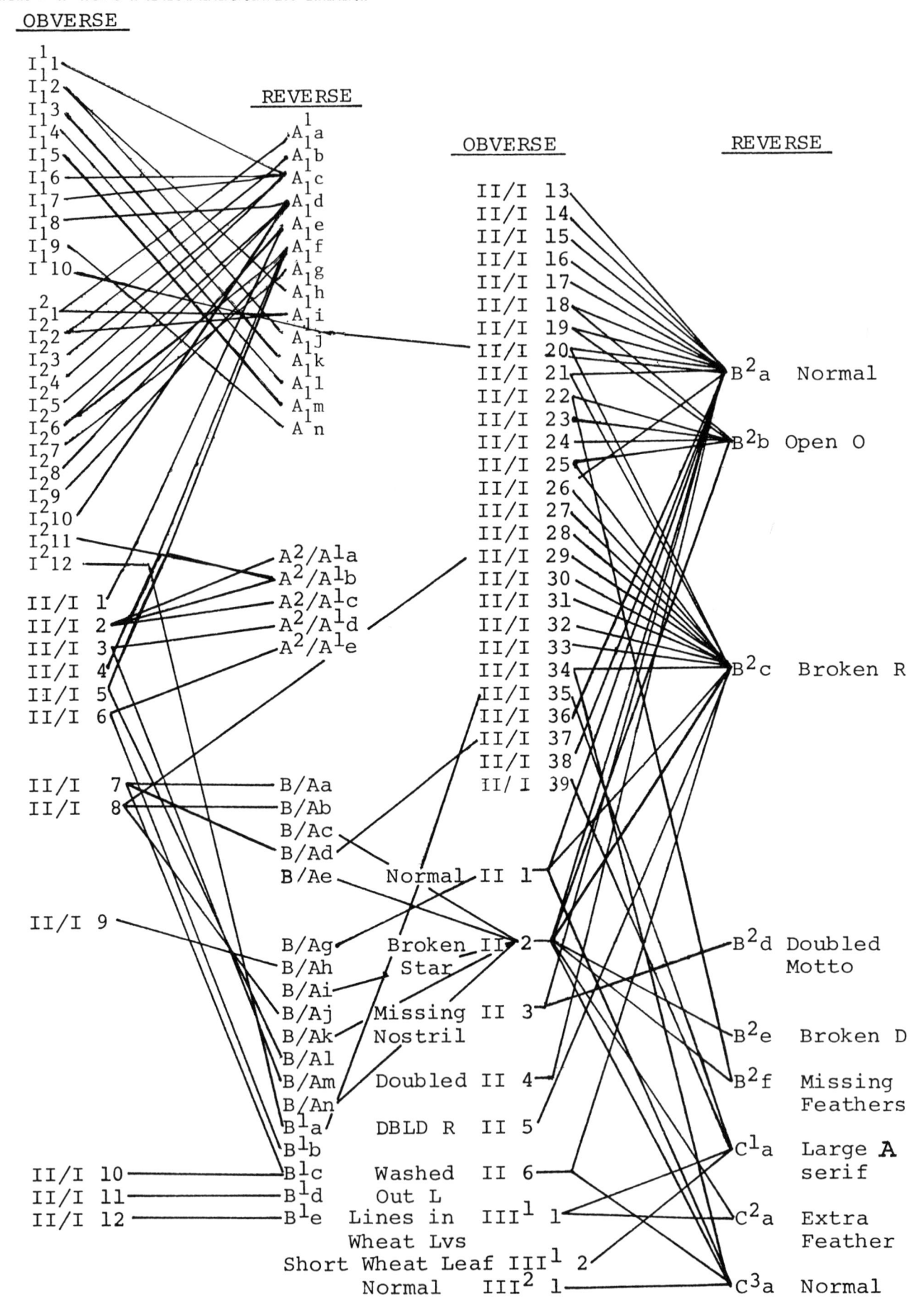

obverse.

A die would often be used in the press in combination with more than one opposite die. This could occur when a die wore out and was replaced without changing the other die. Some dies were used with as many as three different opposite dies! Proof of this are one of a kind dies (II/I 2 and II/I 7 and II/I 8) which appeared with three different identifiable reverse dies.

Master Hub and Die Doubling

There are a few cases where doubling of parts of the design shows up over a number of years and mints. This is due to the doubling of a master hub or master die. Two instances known are the III^2 obverse and C^4 reverse. The C^3 reverse also has very slight doubling at the designer's initial M.

1882-CC Doubled N in UNUM, Master Hub Doubling III^2

III^2 design is doubled on all working dies due to a doubled master hub and die. N in UNUM is doubled above diagonal crossbar.

C^4 design is doubled on all working dies due to a doubled master hub and die. Some letters in the legend are doubled including left side of OLLA in DOLLAR, bottom of crossbar of second A in AMERICA, slightly on bottom of U, E, D in UNITED, and slightly on bottom of F in OF.

1901-O Doubled A in DOLLAR Master Hub Doubling C^4

STRIKING ERRORS

The Morgan series did not have very many coins that are classified as striking errors. This was because of the many individual inspections performed on the coins at that time. There could have been multiple coins of a particular striking error but each coin would be unique in the degree of the error. The following paragraphs describe some of the known Morgan dollar striking errors.

Die Pressure Adjustment Pieces

As a die setter set up a coining press to strike the Morgan dollars, the die pressure had to be slowly increased until all of the design was brought out. As a result, a number of die adjustment pieces would be struck with a weak design. These pieces would normally be returned for remelting as defective coins but occasionally some of them apparently slipped out of the mint to the public. Light strikes have weak design detail, particularly near the edges, due to the slight convexity of the die field. The accompanying photographs show various degrees of light strikes.

Weak Strikes

During normal striking of coins, the die striking pressure may not be sufficiently high to bring up all of the coin detail. Unless quite a bit of the center or eagle detail is missing they are not considered error coins. Rather they are considered poorly struck coins and are discounted from the value of fully struck coins since they are not as desirable to collectors and investors.

Weak strikes were the result of insufficient die striking pressure and incorrect basining of the dies. Each mint basined the individual dies and apparently the basin radii varied slightly from mint to mint and over the years. Thus, typically the S mint dollars have full center detail with rounded rims whereas the O mint dollars have incomplete center detail with full square rims. Changes in the basin radii would cause the planchet metal to flow more to the coin center or to the edge. Usually the P and CC mint coins were evenly struck.

For the B reverse, the weakness in strike usually shows up as flat eagles talons and on the obverse as flat, creamy spots with planchet striations showing on the jaw. For the C reverse, the strike weakness shows as flat eagle's breast feathers and on the obverse as flat hair above the ear. Sometimes a little depression occurred in the middle of the breast resulting in the so-called 'belly button' striking error. These belly buttons were most fre-

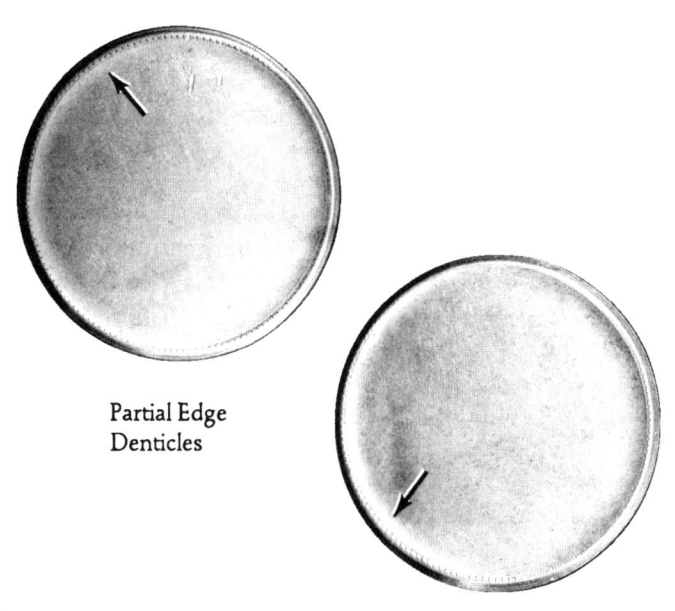

Partial Edge Denticles

1921-D Weak Strike

1880-CC Weak Strike from Out of Level Dies or Thin Planchet

1889-P Misaligned Die

1894-O Misaligned Die

1902-O Belly Button

quent for the New Orleans Mint which was also noted for weak breast feather strikes. Some known belly buttons are as follows: 1885-O, 1887-O, 1890-P, 1891-P, 1900-O, 1901-O, and 1902-O.

Misaligned Dies

Another type of die adjustment piece can be produced during the initial adjustment of the coin presses. This is the misaligned die coin which has one die off center from the other. It is a result of the initial aligning of the dies before striking the production coins.

Rotated Dies

Normally, the obverse and reverse of the silver dollar are upside down with respect to each other. However, sometimes the dies are positioned incorrectly or become loose in the press, and rotations of up to 180 degrees have been found. Rotations of 5 to 10 degrees are fairly common and are within the normal tolerance of setting up dies in a press. These are generally not collected and do not bring a premium price. Rotations of 90 degrees and 180 degrees are the most popular and bring substantial premiums. Actually either the obverse or reverse die could be loose in the coining press, but it is difficult to tell which one was rotated. They are referred to as rotated reverses because when a coin is flipped over from an upright obverse, then the reverse is not in the normal upright position.

The most commonly found rotated reverse Morgan dollar is the 1878-CC with rotation of 26 to 90 degrees clockwise. Next most common is the 1888-O with rotation of 30 degrees clockwise to 175 degrees counter clockwise. The 1886-O, 1887-P and 1890-O also have rotations in both directions. All rotated reverse dollars are very scarce however. In the following listing of known rotations, all have been checked by the authors and Jim Baxter, who has studied these errors. There are several other dates supposedly having rotated reverses (1879-CC, 1881-S, 1898-P, 1901-P, and 1901-O) but hearsay data is notoriously unreliable for this type error on the amount and direction of rotation.

Rotated Reverse Morgans

YEAR	DIE VARIETY	ROTATION	HIGHEST CONDITION AVAILABILITY
1878-CC	5	26-90° CW	BU
1883-O	1	35-75° CCW	BU
1886-O	4	15-48° CW	AU
	11	33-45° CCW	AU
1887-P	1	70-142° CW	Circulated
	1	80-140° CCW	AU
1888-O	9	30° CW to 175° CCW	BU
1889-P	1	20° CCW	BU
1889-O	1	60-105° CW	Circulated
	3	36-72° CW	AU
	9	25-46° CW	Circulated
1890-O	2	20-60° CW	BU

	8	36° CCW	Circulated
1891-O	1	50-120° CCW	Circulated
1894-O	6	25° CCW	F
1904-O	2	108° CCW	BU
	13	28-70° CCW	BU
1921-P	3	45° CCW	BU

A new device is available to precisely and easily measure the amount of die rotation of rotated reverse coins. It was designed by co-author Leroy C. Van Allen and called "Rota Flip." Rota Flip consists of a large plastic flip to securely hold and line up a coin within a circular scale plus a separate plastic overlay to measure the amount of die rotation.

A coin is inserted between the plastic, the obverse is lined up vertically, the flip with the coin is then flipped over and the plastic overlay placed on the reverse and lined up with the reverse top to show the degrees of rotation. Coins can be measured in or out of the flips, plastic or cardboard holders, grading services slabs and GSA plastic holders. It is light weight, fits in a shirt pocket and allows accurate measurements to within 1 or 2 degrees of rotation. An accompanying 5½ x 8½ inch booklet discusses in detail the value increases for rotated reverse coins, lists known die rotations for each U. S. coin type, shows how to make measurements with "Rota Flip," discusses causes of die rotation in coining presses and gives indices to properly line up all U. S. coin types.

The "Rota Flip" (with booklet) is available for

1878-CC Rotated Die 35° CW

$19.95 plus $2.00 postage and handling from Leroy C. Van Allen, P.O. Box 196, Sidney, OH., 45365.

Partial Collar

The collar acts as a third die to form the edge reeding on the dollar. If any part of the planchet edge did not fit into the collar when it was struck, then part of the edge reeding would be missing. This could have been caused by a Type I planchet without upset edges and with a larger diameter than a Type II planchet failing to fit into the collar. It could also have been caused by coining press malfunctions that did not permit proper positioning of the collar. These partial collars are also known as "railroad rims" because of their resemblance to a flanged railroad car wheel. They are fairly scarce and bring sizable premiums.

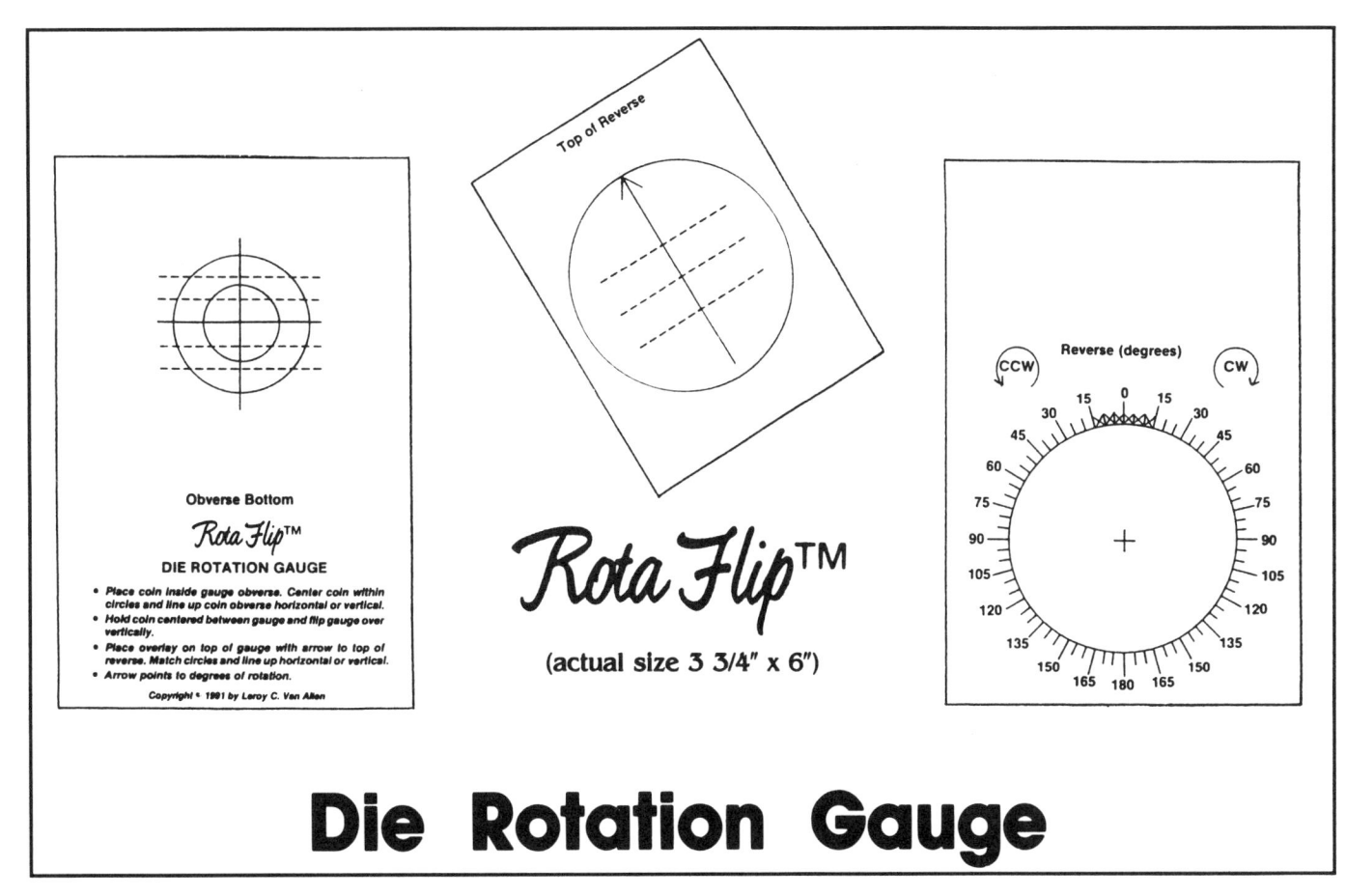

Die Rotation Gauge

Partial Collars

1879-S Wide Partial Collar

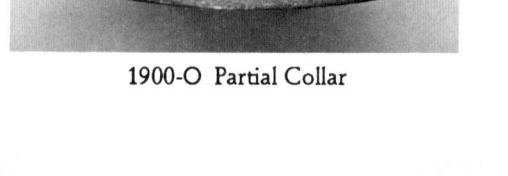

1878-S Partial Collar Narrow

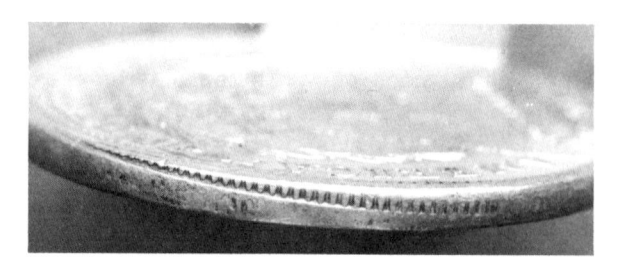

1900-O Partial Collar

1921-S Tilted Partial Collar

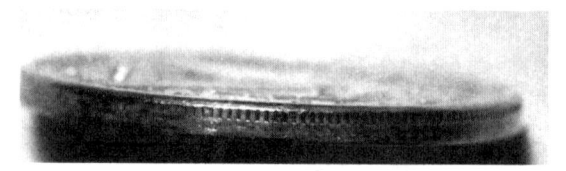

1888-P Partial Collar

1896-P Tilted Partial Collar

Broadstrikes

If the coin was struck centered but entirely out of the collar, then it would not have any reeding on the edge. It would also have a larger diameter than normal because the collar was not present to contain the expansion of the metal outwards. Not many broadstrike Morgan dollars are known and they command substantial premium prices. To be broadstruck, the rim denticles must show if the strike is not perfectly centered.

Off-Center Strikes

Off-center strikes are coins struck once outside the collar without any edge reeding and at least far enough off-center so that some rim denticles are missing. They are caused when the planchet failed to drop into the collar either because a Type I planchet without upset edges was unable to fit into the collar or because a Type II planchet was not fed properly into the collar. Off-center strikes are described by the percentage off center and the direction of the off-center portion. The direction of the design shift is commonly referred to as the K (Kolit) number of a clock system, after Michael Kolman and Dr. Litman, who devised the system in the 1950's. As an example, 30 percent off center at K 6 means the design was shifted 30 percent in the 6 o'clock direction.

The accompanying photographs show some of the known off-center strikes for Morgan dollars. Note that the K 5 and K 6 examples have raised rims and were a Type II planchet. Also note the planchet striations on the unstruck portion that was smoothed out in the struck portion of the 30 percent off center 1880-S. Off center Morgans are very rare and bring very large premiums. The 50 percent off center strikes are the most desirable and expensive, particularly if a date shows.

Multiple Strikes

Multiple strikes occurred when a coin was not fully ejected from the coin press after the first strike and was struck a second or more times. The later strikings can have only slight shifts in alignment or it can be way off center. Multiple struck Morgan dollars are exceedingly rare and command huge premiums. The 1888-O shown was struck first normally within the collar and then a second time about 55 percent off center to the right and rotated 65 degrees counter clockwise. The left side rim is slightly flattened when it probably jammed against a counting machine. Also shown is an undated Morgan that was broad struck and double struck at K 5, 80 percent off center. The spectacular 1887-P was struck a second time at K 6, 25 percent off center.

Capped Die

The only capped die Morgan coin is an 1886 in

Broad and Off Center Strikes

1879-P Broadstruck on Type I Planchet

1901-S Broadstruck on Type II Planchet

1921-P Broadstruck on Type II Planchet

1878-S 10% Off Center at K11

1889-O 15% Off Center at K5
(Photo Courtesy Phil Steiner)

1891-S 15% Off Center at K7

1880-S 15% Off Center at K2

1879-P 20% Off Center at K9

1921-P 25% Off Center at K7

1880-S 30% Off Center at K1

1921-S 50% Off Center at K6

Multiple Strikes

1888-O Double Struck

1887-P Double Struck

Broadstruck and Double Struck
(Photo Courtesy Coin World)

the Amon Carter collection. It is also the only known two headed Morgan dollar. The obverse shows a dished obverse with a normal obverse. A reversed and enlarged Liberty head is on the reverse where another struck coin was forced into the planchet. It was caused when a normally struck coin failed to eject and another planchet was fed on top of it. The two were struck together impressing the obverse image of the first struck coin into the reverse of the second planchet (brockage) and forcing the planchet edges to expand outwards and up around the top obverse die. A unique coin and worth a huge premium.

1886 Capped Die & Brockage Reverse

Struck Through Strikes

1878-S Struck Through Scrap

1897-P Struck Through Metal Piece

1896-P Embedded Wire

Struck Through Strikes

Struck through strikes occurred when objects other than blanks or coins were struck against the surface of the planchet. It was not uncommon for silver slivers to fall on top of the lower (reverse) die or planchet. This produced weak or missing portions of the design where the metal sliver was between the die and the planchet. Struck through coins can be distinguished from laminations that peel off, because laminations will have a rough surface with no design detail. Struck through coins have a smoother surface (from the normal smooth planchet surface) and will show die design transferred through the object on top of it.

Machine Doubling

Machine doubling is doubling of a portion of the coin caused by coin press mechanisms during striking. Most machine doubling for the Morgan dollar was on the reverse side. It produced a regular doubled appearance across parts of the coin design. The machine doubling was a flat outline just to the side of the design with sharp edges, shiny top surface and raised only a little above the coin's field. Each coin machine doubling would show some differences in the degree and extent of doubling even though they were from sequential strikes.

It is sometimes difficult to distinguish between machine doubling and a doubled die. In most cases the doubled die will have the tops of the design doubled where the hub entered furthermost into the die and this doubling will have rounded edges with usually dull tops. The doubled die would have produced multiple coins with exactly the same doubling extent and degree.

Machine doubling should not be confused with a mint mark doubled due to misalignment between punches of the letter. Machine doubling can include doubling of the mint mark as well as other features. When doubling of a mint mark is detected, look carefully at the adjacent wreath and letters to see if they also have the characteristics of machine doubling in the same direction with flat and shiny tops. If die doubling is present on the lower reverse around the mint mark, then any doubling of the mint mark from misalignment between punches would probably be in a different direction from the die

1880-S Struck Through Grease

1881-CC Struck Through Scrap

1881-P (?) Struck Through Grease Obverse – Normal Reverse

1921-P Date Struck Through Grease

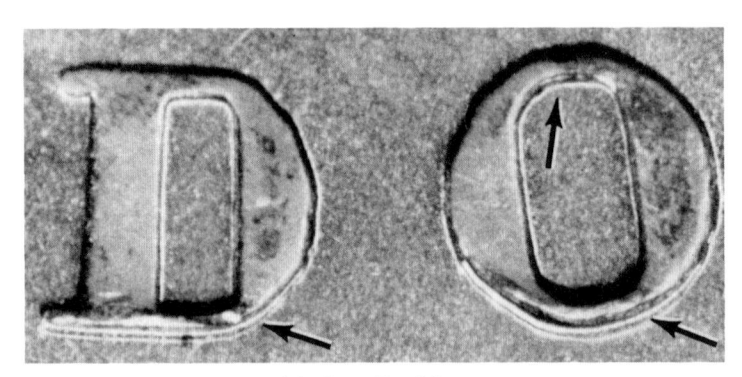

Machine Doubling

doubling since the mint mark was always punched in later.

Sometimes the obverse shows the sides of the date digits, stars and denticles pushed in part ways or slanted. This is due to the obverse die scraping the sides of the design and should not be confused with a doubled die. Examine the design sides with a strong magnifying glass to detect vertical lines from the die edges scraping and if the pushed in design sides exist for the date and other design features.

Machine doubling was due to looseness and wear of the coining press parts. This allowed the dies to move, rock back and forth, or bounce during striking of the coin. Through long usage the surfaces that the back of the working dies rested against in the presses (triangle for obverse die and die stake for reverse die) would become worn. The resulting surfaces with ridges allowed the dies to rock back and forth slightly under the coining presses. Every so often these surfaces had to be machined flat again to eliminate the die rocking. Bolts that held the triangle and die stake in place could also become loose allowing the dies to move under the striking pressures. Generally the pressure from the lower reverse die rising up one eight of an inch to force the coin out of the collar was not enough to cause appreciable doubling on the reverse of the coin even if it moved slightly sideways when it rose.

Footnotes

[1] Alan Herbert, *The Official Identification and Price Guide to Minting Varieties and Errors*, Fifth Edition, New York: House of Collectibles, 1991, p. 37.

[2] Portions of letters quoted in this chapter are excerpts from letters presented in Chapter 5.

[3] Niel Shafer, "The Morgan Silver Dollars of 1878 - 1921" *The Whitman Numismatic Journal,* November 1964, pp. 60-70.

[4] Leroy C. Van Allen, "1878 7/8 Tail Feather Silver Dollar: How and Why," *The Numismatic Scrapbook Magazine,* April 1965, pp. 948-953.

Chapter 8
Condition Analysis & List of Die Varieties

This chapter discusses the condition characteristics and lists the known die varieties for the Morgan dollar from 1878-1904 and 1921. Each die variety is designated by a number (so-called VAM number) unique to a pair of dies. This is followed by the obverse and reverse die designations, a short description of the main variety feature, number of edge reedings, and the interest and rarity numbers. Below this line is a detailed description of the obverse and/or reverse die characteristics. These descriptions are not repeated again if the particular die was used with a different combination of reverse and obverse dies. Only the die designation would be listed again.

Because the date (before 1921) and mint mark were individually punched into each working die there are many minor doubled dates and mint marks for the Morgan dollar. Also the sharp and raised design of the Morgan dollar showed the doubling quite clearly if there was any misalignment between the numerous hub blows it took to make a working die. Of the over 1,700 Morgan die varieties, the vast majority are of minor doubling and do not command any significant price premium.

The discussion for each date and mint includes general comments such as strike characteristics, availability of proof-like surfaces and other factors. Those varieties that are especially significant and scarce are also pointed out. The characteristics of the proof issues are briefly summarized. A more detailed discussion of condition availability for proofs and business coins can be found in the excellent book by Wayne Miller, *The Morgan and Peace Dollar Textbook*, 1982, Adam Smith Publishing and the later reference by John Highfill, *The Comprehensive U.S. Silver Dollar Encyclopedia*, 1992, Highfill Press.

Chapter One of this book contains a section on the relative condition availability of Morgan and Peace

Figure 8-1 DIE CLASSIFICATION SYSTEM

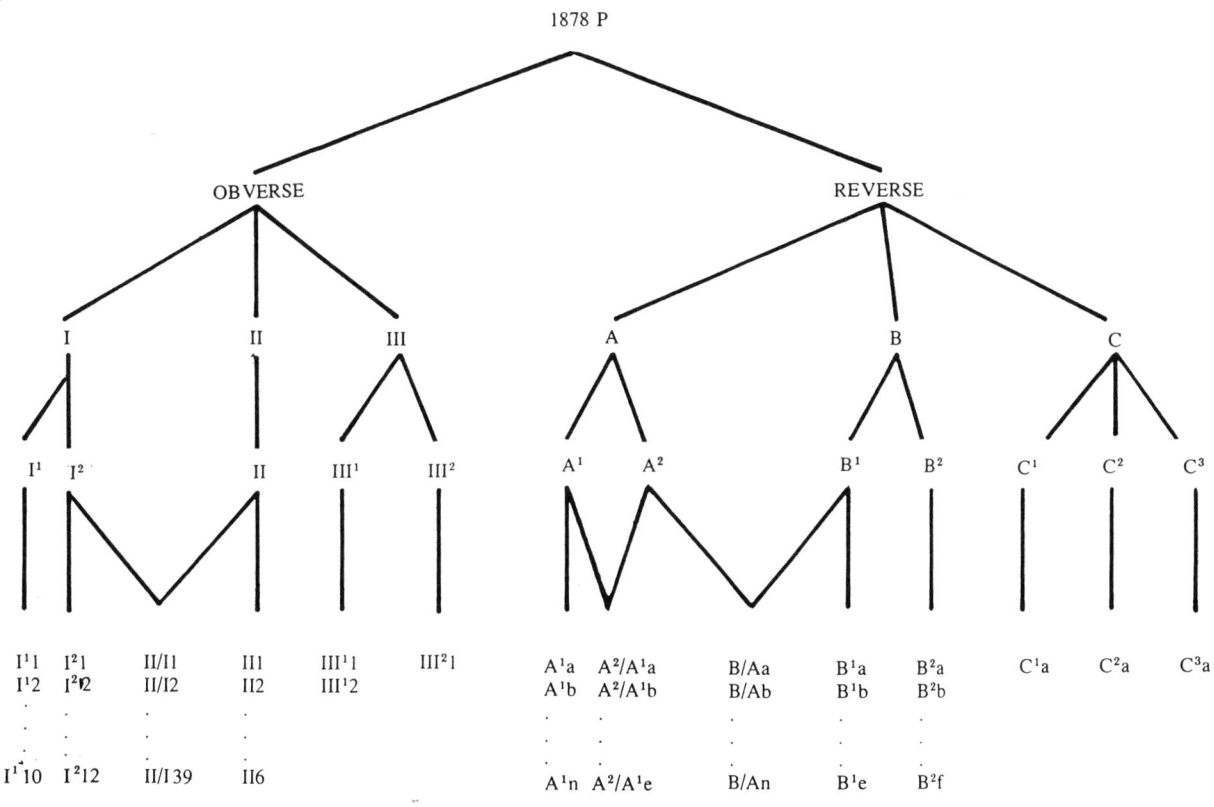

```
                                    1878 P
                        /                           \
                  OBVERSE                          REVERSE
              /      |      \                /        |        \
              I      II     III              A        B         C
            / \      |     / \             / \      / \       / | \
           I¹ I²     II  III¹ III²        A¹  A²   B¹  B²    C¹ C² C³
```

I¹1	I²1	II/I1	II1	III¹1	III²1	A¹a A²/A¹a	B/Aa	B¹a	B²a	C¹a	C²a	C³a
I¹2	I²2	II/I2	II2	III¹2		A¹b A²/A¹b	B/Ab	B¹b	B²b			
.	.	.	.	.		.	.	.	.			
I¹10	I²12	II/I39	II6			A¹n A²/A¹e	B/An	B¹e	B²f			

A   Design Types
A¹   Working Hub Designs
A¹a   Working Die Varieties

139

dollars. Included are charts that list the rank order of availability based on PCGS and NGC grading service population and census reports in grades MS63, 64, 65 and 66 plus PL and DMPL for the Morgan dollars. Also included are graphs displaying this information in visual format for quick reference.

KEY TO CLASSIFICATION

Because the obverse and reverse design types were intermixed in so many combinations during 1878, a classification system which includes both the obverse and reverse design types is required. The system used in this book is a modified version of Shafer's system of assigning numbers to the obverse and letters to the reverse design types (See *Figure 8-1*). Shafer's design designations were not used exactly since the reimpressed obverses and reverses are not considered design types because each die was different.

The design type (such as eight or seven tail feather reverse) is designated by a Roman numeral for the obverse and by a capital letter for the reverse. Minor design variations which were used in the working hubs are designated by superscript numerals on basic design type. Particular working die varieties are indicated by Arabic numerals for the obverse and by lower case letters for the reverse. As an example, II/I•A²b means that a reimpressed obverse (II design over I design type) of the number 2 die variety is in combination with the A design type reverse of the second minor variation and the b die variety.

In descriptions of obverse varieties, reference may be made to doubled stars on either side of the date. To facilitate easy reference these stars have been assigned numbers. The key is as follows:

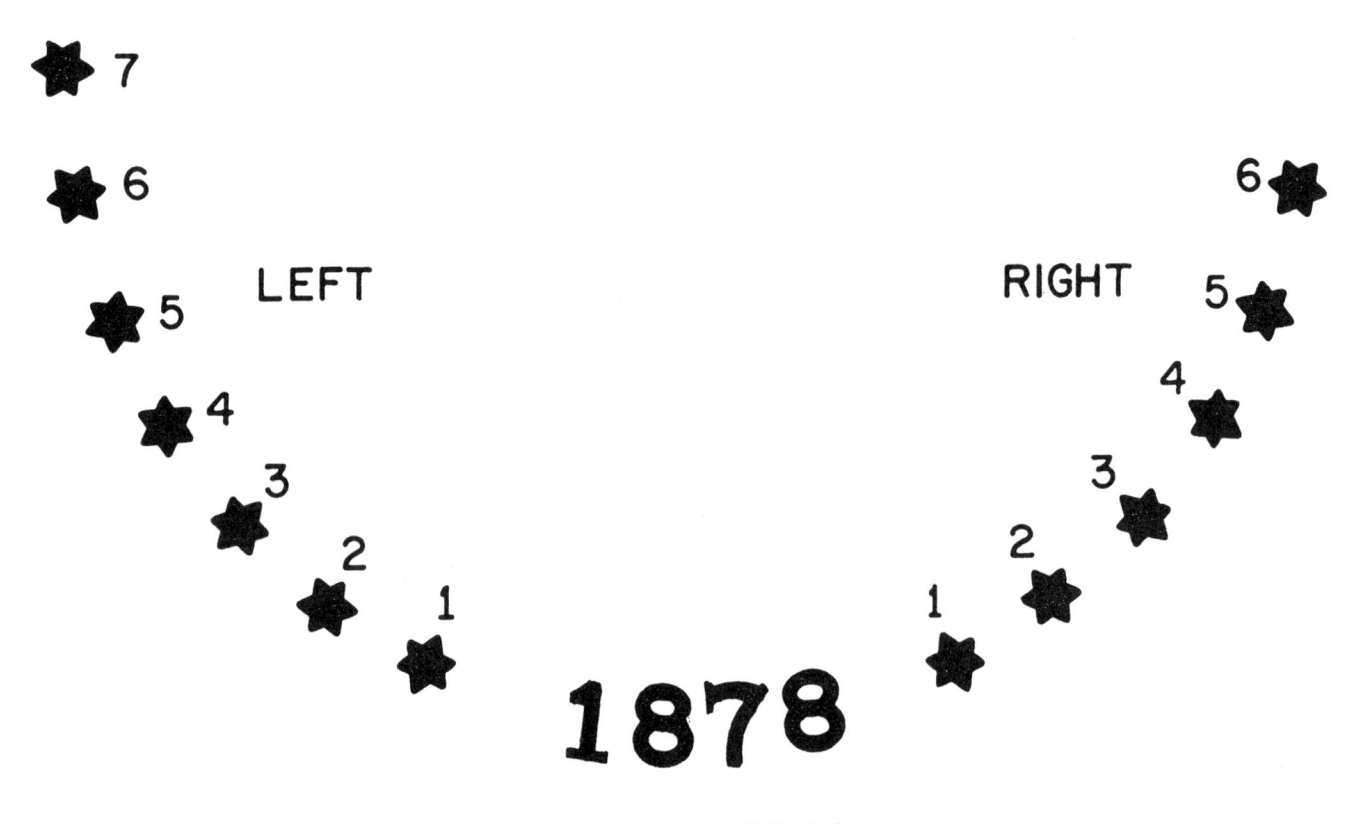

Figure 8-2 STAR NUMBERS

To aid in descriptions of the location of tail feather ends which show below the seven tail feather design on the 7/8 TF dies, numbers have been assigned to each of the seven tail feathers, as shown on the next page:

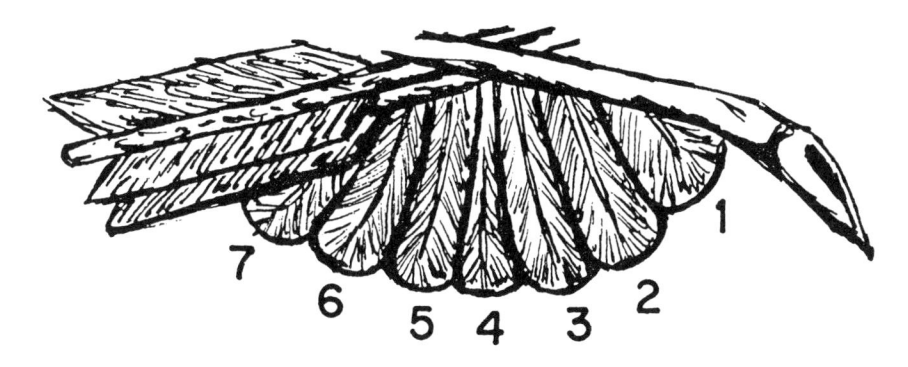

Figure 8-3 TAIL FEATHER NUMBERS

Because of the large number of die varieties for the 1878-P silver dollar, the identification of a coin can be difficult. The quickest method of identifying a particular variety is to concentrate on the reverse design first, since these changes are more obvious and collectors are more familiar with them. The following procedure is suggested:

(1) Determine the major design type of the reverse (8 TF, 7/8 TF, 7 TF PAF, or 7 TF SAF).
(2) Examine the reverse closely to identify the minor design type (raised or hooked beak of the first design, short or long center arrow shaft for the second design, and short or long serif A of AMERICA for the third design), check to see if any die breaks exist (open O in GOD, broken D in DOLLAR, broken R in TRUST), or determine the number of tail feather ends showing in the 7/8 TF reverse (compare with the photographs in later sections).
(3) Check the obverse to determine the design type.
(4) Consult the die marriage chart, page 130, to see which coins have a particular reverse die type and associated obverse die types.
(5) Compare the descriptions of these obverse dies in the list of varieties and the photographs of LIBERTY with your coin to make the final identification.

The authors would be interested in hearing of any new 1878-P found. A few more should turn up since a large number of dies were modified.

DIE DESCRIPTIONS

The following list describes the Morgan die varieties from 1878-1904 and 1921. A photograph of each die variety is also included to supplement the description. The die varieties are designated by a number, type, and a short title descriptive of the main variety feature. The number is unique to a variety for a particular year and mint. Thus, VAM 1 of 1879-P (VAM stands for Van Allen-Mallis) means the first coin variety listed for 1879-P. The type designation (such as III^{2}1 • C^{3}a) gives the design type, working hub design, and working die variety for both obverse and reverse of the coin. The authors would be interested in hearing of any new varieties found.

For the 1878-P varieties the reverse design types have been assigned blocks of numbers as shown in *Table 8-1*. This will make possible the addition of new varieties to the 1878-P list while maintaining a logical grouping of types with a proper number sequence. The unassigned numbers in each block should be sufficient to cover all new varieties found.

The number R-1-8 opposite each variety designation estimates the degree of rarity and the number I-1-5 estimates the degree of interest as defined in the Glossary of Abbreviations at the beginning of the book.

Table 8-1 ASSIGNMENT OF NUMBERS

	Number Block	Design Types Obverse Reverse
1878-P	1-14	I — A
	15-29	Other types — A
	30-69	All types — B/A
	70-78	I — B^1
	79-99	II/I — B^1
	100-109	I — B^{2}a
	110-129	II/I — B^{2}a
	130-139	II — B^{2}a
	140-159	All types — B^{2}b
	160-184	II/I — B^{2}c
	185-189	II — B^{2}c
	190-194	All types — B^{2}d
	195-199	All types — B^{2}e,f
	200-209	All types — C^1
	210-219	All types — C^2
	220-299	All types — C^3

1878-P 8 Tail Feathers

This design type was the first to be struck for the Morgan silver dollars. Pete Bishal first, correctly identified the first pair of Morgan dollar dies used, the VAM 9. Twelve proof presentation pieces were struck at the initial striking of the Morgan dollar on March 11, 1878 and given to various dignitaries. (The first Morgan struck was given to President Hayes.) These same dies of VAM 9 were used to strike business coins. However, only about four proof and four business strike VAM 9 specimens are currently known making the coins struck from the first pair of dies very rare.

Eight tail feather proofs are also known in the VAM 14-3 and 14-8 varieties with VAM 14-3 being the most common. According to the coiner's daily delivery records, 300 Morgan proofs were delivered during the time the 8 tail feather design was struck. This is fewer than the usual quoted figure of 500. All 8 tail feather proofs exhibit only moderate cameo contrast.

Many of the 8 tail feather varieties exhibit strong doubling of parts of the obverse and/or reverse design. This was due to problems experienced in preparing the new design dies. These coins are generally fully struck. Many exhibit only one sided proof-like because of the frequent changing of dies to maintain production with the short lived dies.

1878-P 7/8 Tail Feathers

A number of reverse dies were modified by impressing the newer seven eagle's tail feather design over the original eight tail feather design. This was done to save die preparation time, but many of these die varieties show some of the original eight tail feathers tips below the seven tail feathers. Only those varieties with four to seven tips showing command the price premium of the 7/8 tail feathers (TF) with VAM 41 being the most prominent one. VAM's 31 and 43 with doubled legs command a modest premium. The scarcest 7/8 TF variety is VAM 44 with only about a twenty specimens known. It commands a substantial premium. VAM's 32 and 45 are also fairly scarce.

The 7/8 TF are also generally fully struck. Fully proof-like specimens usually have only moderate cameo contrast and some of the 7/8 TF are only one sided proof-like.

1878-P 7 Tail Feathers (Flat Breast)

Numerous varieties of the seven tail feathers B reverse with flat eagle's breast and parallel arrow feathers exist. Most of these are minor with the II/I obverse although a few show large design doubling. VAM's 117 and 141 show some strongly tripled stars. None of these 7 TF varieties command a significant premium, however, because there are so many.

Only 200 7 TF flat breast proofs were struck according to the coiner's daily delivery records. All of these are the VAM 131 variety with normal dies that did not have the doubling so common with this design type. Generally these proofs have only moderate contrast and are scarce.

Some business coins show strike weakness in the eagle's talon and in the arrow shafts and olive branch. But usually they are well struck. Fully two-sided proof-likes exist but most exhibit only moderate contrast.

1878-P 7 Tail Feathers (Round Breast)

This design type uses the seven tail feather C reverse with round eagle's breast and slanted arrow feathers that was used on later years from 1879 to 1904. A few die varieties exist but none are very significant or scarce. The exceptions are VAM 220 which is rare, VAM 203 which is fairly scarce and VAM 222 – some of which have the unusually low edge reeding count of 168 (lowest of any Morgan except 1921-P Infrequent Reeding which has 157).

Only about half a dozen 1878 proofs with the round breast reverse are known . From Treasury Department records, 50 proof Morgan dollars were delivered on November 8, 1878. These would have been the round breast reverse type since the Philadelphia Mint had been using this reverse type since June of that year. It is the rarest of the Philadelphia Mint proof Morgan dollars from 1878-1904. All are VAM 215 variety. These proofs exhibit the deep mirrors and white cameos characteristic of early Morgan dollar proofs.

Business strikes with this round breast C reverse are usually fully struck. Proof-like specimens are scarcer than for the 8 TF and 7 TF flat breast type because the die life was much longer for this design type. Some proof-likes with the C reverse show very deep mirrors and excellent cameo contrast.

1878-P

(Listed in Order of Reverse Type)

1   **I²1 • A¹a (Doubled E)**   (188)   I-2   R-4
Obverse I²1 – Slightly doubled bottom letters in E PLURIBUS UNUM. First star on right doubled on left side. First five stars on left doubled slightly on right side. 187 in date slightly doubled. 1 is doubled at top of bottom crossbar. First 8 is doubled at bottom inside of lower loop. 7 doubled on left side of vertical shaft.
Reverse A¹a – First 8 TF design type used, with raised beak, small feathers between eagle's legs and bottom wings, I of IN touching top of eagle's wing. This die variety has inside of E of ONE, R of DOLLAR and last A of AMERICA strongly doubled. Letters of legend frequently have machine doubling. Two small feathers added on eagle's right side and three on eagle's left side between leg and bottom of wing.

2   **I²2 • A¹b (Doubled Reverse)**   (189)   I-2   R-4
Obverse I²2 – Doubled bottoms of E PLURIBUS and both sides of first U in UNUM. Left side of all left stars slightly doubled. Doubled 87 in date. First 8 doubled slightly at top of inside of lower loop. 7 doubled on left side and tripled on right side of vertical shaft.
Reverse A¹b – Doubled reverse mostly apparent in lower left of wreath and in lettering of UNITED, AMERICA, and ONE DOLLAR. Three small feathers added on eagle's right and two on eagle's left side between leg and bottom of wing.

3   **I¹1 • A¹c (Doubled Reverse)**   (189)   I-2   R-4
Obverse I¹1 – Slightly doubled tops of E and P of E PLURIBUS. Doubled bottom of last star on left. Doubled 87 in date. First 8 doubled slightly at bottom right outside. 7 doubled slightly on right side of vertical shaft.
Reverse A¹c – Letters in UNITED doubled strongly on top and bottom. STATES OF AMERICA letters doubled at bottom. ONE DOLLAR letters doubled at top. Left wreath strongly doubled. Three small feathers added on eagle's right and two on eagle's left side between leg and bottom of wing.

4   **I²3 • A¹c (Doubled Date)**   (189)   I-3   R-4
Obverse I²3 – Shallow doubled lower obverse, including all of date, all left and right stars, E, PLURIB and UNUM. The stars have a regular shift indicating a rotation of hub and die between blows.

5   **I²4 • A¹c (Doubled Motto)**   (189)   I-3   R-4
Obverse I²4 – Doubled motto with R, I, and B having large shifts at bottom. All stars on left slightly doubled. 78 in date slightly doubled on right outside.

6   **I²5 • A¹d (Doubled Motto)**   (189/193)   I-2   R-4
Obverse I²5 – Slightly doubled motto at bottom and all left stars on right side. Doubled date with 1 at lower left, both 8's at bottom inside of lower loop and top of both loops and 7 on left side of vertical shaft.
Reverse A¹d – Doubled reverse especially evident in left side of wreath, end leaves in the branch held in eagle's talons, stars and legend letters on side away from rim. Two small feathers added on eagle's right and three on eagle's left side between leg and bottom of wing.

7   **I²6 • A¹d (Spiked A)**   (189)   I-2   R-4
Obverse I²6 – Doubled left stars, E, PLURIBUS U, and 187 in date. A slight rotation of hub and die between blows.
Reverse A¹d – Die shows evidence of wearing out, with a scratch in the die causing spikes at the side of A in STATES and filled center of E in ONE.

8   **I²7 • A¹g (Doubled Reverse)**   (180)   I-2   R-4
Obverse I²7 – Doubled E PLUR of the motto on the left side and top of the letters. All stars on left doubled. Slightly doubled 87 in date with 8 doubled at bottom inside of lower loop and 7 doubled on left side of vertical shaft.
Reverse A¹g – Doubled left side, top and bottom including legend, wreath, star and wing tip. Top of UNITED tripled. Wreath to left of ribbon bow heavily polished with parts of leaves missing. Two small feathers added on eagle's right and one long one on eagle's left side between leg and bottom of wing.

9   **I¹2 • A¹h (Doubled Reverse)** (Some Presentation Proof pieces also)   (193)   I-2   R-7
Obverse I¹2 – Doubled E PLUR-BU and-UM of the motto at the top of the bottom serifs. First four stars on left and all of the stars on right slightly doubled on out side. First 8 doubled at top inside of upper loop. 7 in date doubled slightly on right side. First obverse die used.
Reverse A¹h – All of legend and motto doubled. Left wreath and olive leaves slightly doubled. Three small feathers added on eagle's right and two one eagle's left side between leg and bottom of wing. First reverse die used.

10   **I²8 • A¹e (Doubled Motto)**   (180)   I-3   R-4
Obverse I²8 – First six stars on left doubled on left and right sides. E PLURIB doubled on left side and at bottom. Doubled date with 1 doubled at top left, above bottom cross bar and on right side of vertical shaft. First 8 doubled at bottom left inside of lower loop and right outside of both loops. 7 doubled on right side of vertical shaft and top left serif. Second 8 doubled slightly at bottom inside and upper left outside of lower loop.
Reverse A¹e – Doubled left side including legend, wreath, and wing tip. Two small feathers added on eagle's right and left side between leg and bottom of wing. Slightly concave reverse.

1878-P

11   **I²6 • A¹f (Doubled Reverse)**   I-2   R-7

Reverse A¹f – Doubled lower and left wreath, all of legend, and stars. Three small feathers added on eagle's right and two on eagle's left side between leg and bottom of wing. Eagle's right leg and right wing doubled on outside. Olive branch leaves are doubled on outside.

12   **I²9 • A¹f (Doubled Motto)**   (179)   I-3   R-4

Obverse I²9 – Doubled bottoms of E, PL-RIB-S. First four stars on left doubled on left and right sides. Five to seven stars on left doubled on right side only. First star on right doubled on left side only. Both 8's in date doubled at top inside of upper and lower loops. 7 doubled at top right of vertical shaft.

13   **I²1 • A¹i (Concave Field)**   I-3   R-4

Reverse A¹i – Slight doubling of UNTED, TTES, and MERICA on bottom of letters toward coin rim and of ONE DOLLAR on tops of letters toward coin rim. Right star is doubled on right side. Slight doubling on outside of wreath. Three small feathers added on eagle's right and two on eagle's left side between leg and bottom of wing. Field has more curvature than any other Morgan dollar and is especially concave near rim.

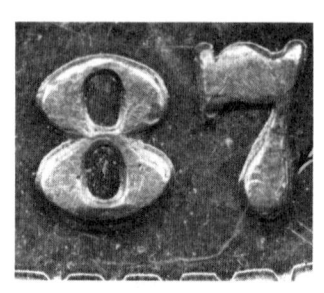

1 O I¹1

1 O I¹1

2 O I²2

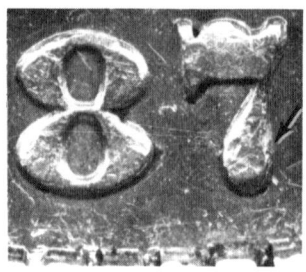

1 R A¹a

2 R A¹b

3 O I²1

4 O I²3

3 R A¹c

5 O I²4

6 O I²5

144

1878-P

6 O I²5

6 R A¹d

6 R A¹d

7 O I²6

8 O I²7

8 R A¹g

9 O I¹2

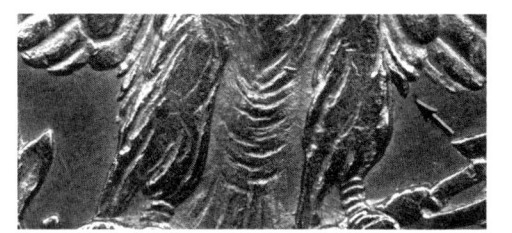

9 R A¹h

10 R A¹e

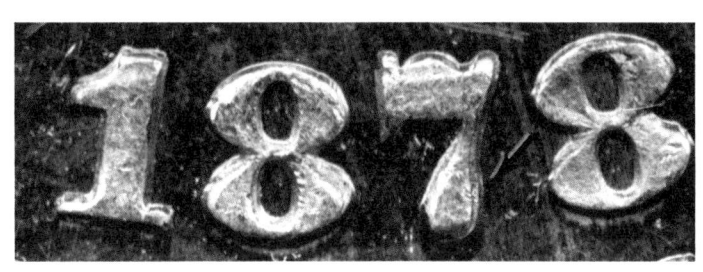

10 O I²8

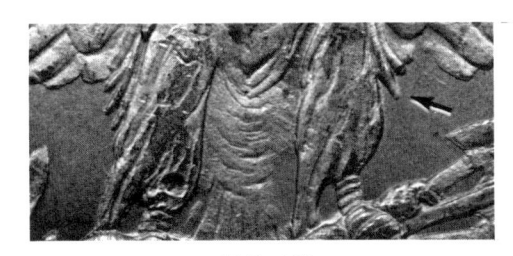

11 R A¹f

12 O I²9

12 O I²9

13 R A¹i

145

1878-P

14   I¹2 • A¹j (Doubled Motto)   (193)   I-2   R-4

Reverse A¹j – Strong doubling of ONE, UNITED, STATES, OF and IN GOD WE TRUST. Slight doubling of M, E, I and A in AMERICA, D, O, and R in DOLLAR, right star and wreath. Two small feathers added on eagle's right and one small and one long on eagle's left side between leg and bottom of wing.

14-1   I¹3 • A¹k (Normal Obverse)   (188)   I-2   R-4

Obverse I¹3 – Normal Type I obverse with no apparent die breaks or doubling except for slight doubling to top of P in PLURIBUS.

Reverse A¹k – Slight doubling of lower and left side of wreath, olive leaves and bottom of eagle's right wing. Slightly doubled bottom of UNITED STATE and top of ONE. Three small feathers added on eagle's right and two on eagle's left side between leg and bottom of wing.

14-2   I¹4 • A¹l (Polished Ear)   (193)   I-2   R-4

Obverse I¹4 – Normal I die that has been overpolished so that stars and date are shallow. Hair lines to right of ear are shallow. Inside of ear is flat with shortened inner ear fill.

Reverse A¹l – Slightly doubled bottom of AMERICA, AR in DOLLAR and right star. One long and two short feathers added on eagle's right and two on eagle's left side between leg and bottom of wing. Heavy vertical die polishing scratch above extra feathers on eagle's left wing.

14-3   I¹5 • A¹m (Doubled Reverse)   (Some Proofs)   (188)   I-2   R-4

Obverse I¹5 – All stars on right and first four stars on left doubled on lower right side. Date slightly doubled with 1 doubled below upper crossbar. First 8 doubled at top inside and lower left outside of both loops. 7 doubled at top right and below crossbar. Second 8 doubled at top inside of both loops and lower left outside of upper loop.

Reverse A¹m – Doubled UNITED STATES OF ONE DOLLAR near rim and AMERICA away from rim. Both stars and outside of wreath doubled. Three small feathers added on eagle's right and two on eagle's left side between leg and bottom of wing similar to A¹b but wings have not been polished as much.

14-4   I²2 • A¹i (Concave Field)   (180)   I-3   R-4

14-5   I²10 • A¹d (Spiked A)   (189)   I-2   R-4

Obverse I¹10 – Slightly doubled motto letters R-US, UNU, all left stars on left side, and all right stars toward rim. All digits in date doubled with 1 doubled at top of lower crossbar; both 8's doubled at lower inside of lower loop, and 7 doubled on left side of vertical stem. Die overpolished with weak nostril and lower hairlines.

Reverse A¹d – Die scratch causing spikes at sides of A in STATES.

14-6   I¹6 • A¹c (Dot on Ear)   (189)   I-3   R-5

Obverse I¹6 – Slightly doubled first three right stars and first six left stars towards rim. E doubled at bottom, and U-UNU doubled at bottom inside towards rim. Both 8's doubled slightly at top inside of both loops and 7 is doubled slightly on right side of vertical shaft. Ear is over polished with dot die break in middle of lower earlobe. Some specimens show a large radial crack next to fourth right star.

14-7   I¹7 • A¹c (Dot Next to Ear)   (189)   I-2   R-4

Obverse I¹7 – Doubled first five stars on right and first four on left towards rim. Slightly doubled below upper crossbar towards rim. Slightly doubled date with 1 doubled below upper bar, both 8's doubled at top inside of both loops, and 7 doubled below crossbar and on right side of vertical shaft. Die flake next to ear at top right outside. Radial die crack on right side of 1.

14-8   I¹8 • A¹d (Doubled Eyelid)   (189)   I-2   Proof

Obverse I¹8 – Slightly doubled top of P in PLURIBUS. Eyelid doubled in front of eye about one third down from top. All left and right stars quadrupled towards rim. Entire date doubled with 1 doubled below upper crossbar, both 8's at top inside and lower left outside of upper loop and 7 below upper crossbar and right side of vertical shaft.

14-9   I¹9 • A¹n (Tripled Eyelid)   (189)   I-2   R-5

Obverse I¹9 – Eyelid tripled in front of eye just below front of eyelid. First three stars on left slightly doubled towards rim. First three stars on right slightly tripled towards rim. Entire data doubled with 1 doubled slightly below upper crossbar, both 8's at top inside of upper loop, and 7 below crossbar and on upper right of vertical shaft.

Reverse A¹n – All legend letters and wreath leaves doubled towards rim. Bottom of eagle's right wing doubled. Two small isolated feathers added on eagle's right and two on eagle's left side between leg and bottom of wing.

14-10   I¹10 • A¹k (Doubled Hair)   (188)   I-2   R-4

Obverse I¹10 – All stars on right tripled and quadrupled on lower right side. First four stars on left doubled on lower right side. Date doubled with 1 doubled below upper crossbar. First 8 doubled at bottom outside, top inside of both loops and lower left outside of upper loop. 7 doubled at top right and below crossbar. Second 8 doubled slightly at top inside of both loops and lower left outside of upper loop. Doubled nose, lip, chin and lower hair.

1878-P

14 R A¹j

14-1 R A¹k

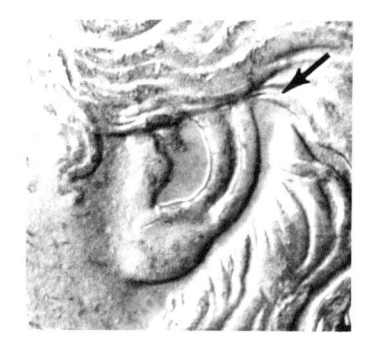

14-2 O I¹4

14-2 R A¹l

14-8 O I¹8

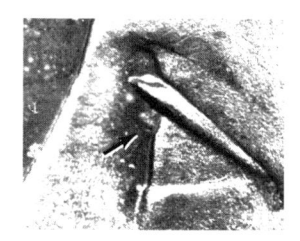

14-8 O I¹8

14-3 R A¹m

14-3 O I¹5

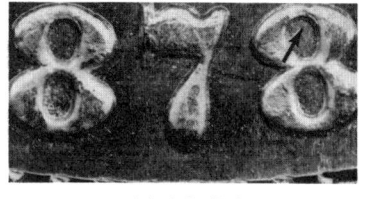

14-6 O I¹6

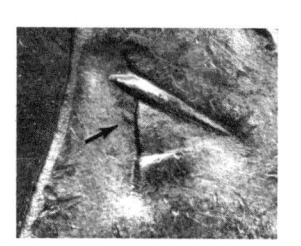

14-9 O I¹9

14-5 O I²10

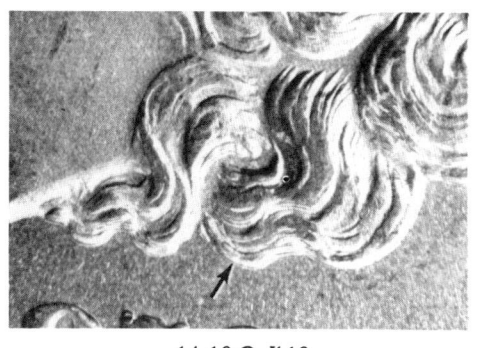

14-7 O I¹7

14-10 O I¹10
(Photo courtesy Jeff Oxman)

14-9 R A¹n

147

1878-P

15 II/I 1 • A¹e (Doubled LIBERTY) (180) I-3 R-4
  Obverse II/I 1 – Second obverse design type, II, reimpressed over first type, I. Doubled LIBERTY with large shift to left. Doubled R in PLURIBUS. All left and right stars are doubled. First 8 and 7 doubled at top.

16 II/I 4 • A¹f (Doubled LIBERTY) (179) I-3 R-4
  Obverse II/I 4 – Doubled LIBERTY shifted left. First four stars on left tripled with rest of stars on left and right doubled, some with large shifts. 1 and 7 in date doubled with 1 doubled on both sides of shaft and 7 doubled at top and left side of crossbar. Some specimens have a spike of metal between loops of first 8 in left side.

17 II/I 5 • A¹f (Doubled Reverse) (179) I-2 R-4
  Obverse II/I 5 – Slightly doubled LIBERTY shifted left. All stars on right and left doubled. Die chips in lower loop of first 8; first 8 doubled slightly at top outside and right outside of upper loop and top inside of lower loop. 7 doubled at top right and left side of upper serif.

18 II/I 2 • A²/A¹a (Doubled Date) (180) I-4 R-4
  Obverse II/I 2 – Doubled LIBERTY shifted up and left. Doubled E, P, L, U, R, S, and M in motto with large shift in date and all stars on right. All left stars tripled.
  Reverse A²/A¹a – Second 8 TF design type, A², with hooked beak and I of IN away from top of eagle's right wing reimpressed over first 8 TF design type, A¹. Doubled inside of wreath, NE of ONE and AR of DOLLAR. Two extra small feathers added on eagle's right and partial one on left side between leg and bottom of wing. Top of left wreath overpolished so that tip of leaf appears to be an extra berry on the left side but shadow of leaf remains on field of coin. (See page 149). Eagle's lower beak and tongue are doubled. Doubled strike on tops of letters on some coins. Top arrow head and shaft doubled.

19 II/I 2 • A²/A¹b (Doubled Date) (180) I-4 R-4
  Reverse A²/A¹b – Doubled inside of wreath, N of ONE, DOLLAR, and right star with AR tripled at bottom. Partial small feather added on eagle's right side between leg and bottom of wing. Top of wreath overpolished so that tip of leaf appears to be an extra berry on the left side. Eagle's lower and upper beak are doubled. Top arrow head and shaft doubled.

20 II/I 2 • A²/A¹c (Doubled Date) (189) I-3 R-4
  Reverse A²/A¹c – Doubled left lower wreath, olive branch leaves, arrow tips and bottom of eagle's wings. ON of ONE, lower parts of LLAR in DOLLAR, and U, N, and T of UNITED strongly doubled with most of other letters faintly doubled. Thin small feather added on eagle's right side between leg and bottom of wing. Top arrow head and shaft doubled.

21 II/I 3 • A²/A¹d (Doubled B) (180) I-3 R-4
  Obverse II/I 3 – Slightly doubled LIBERTY shifted left. Doubled P, U, R, and B in PLURIBUS and 1 and 2 stars on right. Nostril missing from overpolished die. First 8 doubled at top inside of upper loop and second 8 doubled at bottom outside of lower loop.
  Reverse A²/A¹d – Doubled wreath, N of ONE tripled. L, A and R of DOLLAR doubled, and bottom of UNITED doubled. Thin small feather added on eagle's right side between leg and bottom of wing. Eagle's lower beak slightly doubled on inside. Top arrow head and shaft doubled.

22 II/I 6 • A²/A¹e (Doubled ERTY) (180) I-3 R-4
  Obverse II/I 6 – Doubled last four letters of LIBERTY, shifted down. First three letters have polishing marks. Slightly doubled E PLURIBUS UNUM at left top serifs, doubled 2 and 3 stars on left, and doubled 3 and 4 stars on right. Doubled tops of wheat leaves and grains, cotton leaves and blossoms.
  Reverse A²/A¹e – Doubled A and R of DOLLAR, ERICA of AMERICA, N of ONE, and both stars, two small feathers added on eagle's right and two fine lines on eagle's left side between leg and bottom of wing. Eagle's top and lower beak slightly doubled. Top arrow head and middle arrow shaft doubled.

15 O II/I 1

16 O II/I 4

17 O II/I 5

18 O II/I 2

148

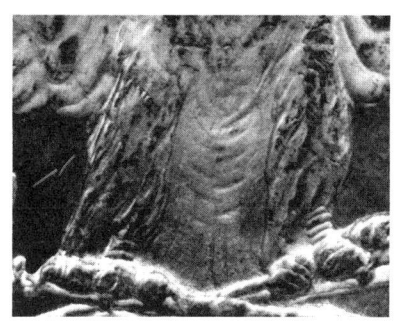

1878-P

18 R A²/A¹a

18 R A²/A¹a

19 R A²/A¹b

19 R A²/A¹b

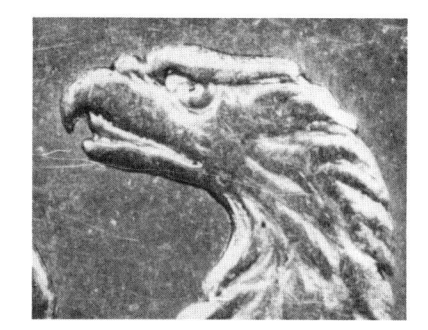

20 R A²/A¹c

20 R A²/A¹c

21 R A²/A¹d

21 R A²/A¹d

18 and 19 R
A²/A¹a and A²/A¹b
Extra Berries

20-22 R
A²/A¹c-e
Normal Berries

21 O II/I 3

22 O II/I 6

22 R A²/A¹e

149

1878-P

23   I²11 • A²/A¹b (Doubled Eagle's Beak)   (180)   I-3   R-4
   Obverse I²11 – Doubled motto letters at top with E-P showing very thin tops of letters. All stars left and right are doubled slightly near rim. Date doubled slightly at bottom with 7 doubled also on right side. Nose, lips and chin slightly doubled. LIBERTY doubled left and up and also slightly to right.

30   II/I 7 • B/Aa (Extra Talons)   (180)   I-3   R-4
   Obverse II/I 7 – Type II LIBERTY; doubled E, P, and R; doubled 187 in date with 1 doubled on left at shaft, 8 on top surface and 7 on left of top serif; all stars on left and first three stars on right doubled. Area around nose and lips overpolished. Fine diagonal polishing line through R in LIBERTY.
   Reverse B/Aa – Four talons on left and right; extra one shifted to left by width of one toe. Tail feather lines to left of eagle's right leg.

31   II/I 8 • B/Ab (Doubled Legs)   (177)   I-5   R-4
   Obverse II/I 8 – Type II LIBERTY; doubled P on left and tripled S at top right; partially broken bottom serifs of N and M in UNUM. Doubled 2, 3, 6 and 7 stars on left, and 1, 3, 4 and 5 stars on right. 1 and 7 in date doubled at top right.
   Reverse B/Ab – Extra set of legs and talons on the right; design remains in leaves of branch and above branch on right; polishing scratches across arrow feathers and eagle's right talon, and also across bow in wreath. Possible faint tail feathers between 1 and 2 TF. Die chips around R in TRUST.

32   II 2 • B/Ac (3 TF)   (179)   I-3   R-6
   Obverse II 2 – Normal type II obverse with broken point off number 4 star on right and 7 in date doubled on right side (hub defect).
   Reverse B/Ac – Three tail feather ends showing under 2, 3 and 4 TF. Design remains in leaves of branch and in bow of wreath. Die chips in IN GOD WE TRUST; doubled O, D, and W.

33   II/I 7 • B/Ad (3TF)   (180)   I-3   R-4
   Obverse II/I 7 – Some coins show die chip at left between loops of first 8.
   Reverse B/Ad – Three tail feather ends showing; a strong one under 4 TF and two faint ones between 4 and 5 TF and 5 and 6 TF. Sometimes a very faint tail feather shows under 6 TF on early strike specimens. Eagle's legs are one and a half times normal width, with the talons doubled (double set of claws). Design remains in leaves of branch and below branch on left; also some in center of wreath bow. Diagonal polishing line from 1 TF down through 4 TF.

34   II 2 • B/Ae (4 TF)   (179)   I-3   R-5
   Reverse B/Ae – Four tail feather ends showing; one between 2 and 3 TF and one under each 3, 4, and 5 TF. Design remains in leaves of branch and below branch on left, also around wreath bow. Doubled O, D, W, and E of IN GOD WE TRUST.

35   **Former VAM 35 now VAM 41 A; B/Af was polished down B/Ak.**

36   II 1 • B/Ag (4 TF)   (179)   I-4   R-4
   Obverse II 1 – Normal type II obverse with no apparent die breaks or doubling except for 7 in date slightly doubled on right side (hub defect).
   Reverse B/Ag – Four tail feather ends showing; between 2 and 3 TF and under 3, 4, and 5 TF. Design remains in leaves of branch, below branch on left, and around wreath bow. Die chips around D, W, E, and U of IN GOD WE TRUST.

37   II 2 • B/Ag (4 TF)   (179)   I-4   R-4
   Obverse II 2 – E and P have bulges at top right and B is doubled at right inside and bottom of outside of lower loop.

38   II/I 9 • B/Ah (5 TF)   (180)   I-4   R-4
   Obverse I/II 9 – Doubled LIBERTY with shift to left; largest shift of this kind known. All letters in E PLURIBUS UNUM and all left and right stars doubled. Doubled date with 1 doubled on both sides of shaft, first 8 doubled at top outside and inside right of upper loop, 7 doubled on right, second 8 doubled on inside right of upper loop.
   Reverse B/Ah – Five tail feather ends showing; between 2 and 3, 3 and 4, 4 and 5, and under 5 and 6 TF. Design remains in leaves of branch, below branch on left, and around wreath bow. Eagle's right wing separated from leg due to over polishing.

22 R A²/A¹e

30 O II/I 7

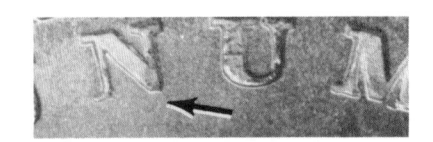

31 O II/I 8

32 O II 2

1878-P

23 O I²11

23 O I²11

30 R B/Aa Extra Talons

31 R B/Ab Doubled Legs

32 R B/Ac 3 TF

33 R B/Ad 3 TF

34 R B/Ae 4 TF

36 & 37 R B/Ag 4 TF

38 R B/Ah 5 TF

39 R B/Ai 5 TF

40 R B/Aj 5 TF

1878-P

38 O II/I 9

| 39 | **II 2 • B/Ai (5 TF)** | (179) | I-4 | R-5 |

Reverse B/Ai – Five tail feather ends showing; between 2 and 3, 3 and 4, 4 and 5, 5 and 6 and under 6 TF. Design remains in leaves of branch, below branch on left, and inside wreath bow. Die chips around R in TRUST.

| 40 | **II/I 8 • B/Aj (5 TF)** | (180) | I-4 | R-5 |

Reverse B/Aj – Five tail feather ends showing; between 2 and 3, 3 and 4, 4 and 5 and under 5 and 6. Design remains in leaves of branch, below branch on left, and inside left outside of wreath bow. Die chips around R and U in TRUST on some coins.

| 41 | **II 2 • B/Ak (7 TF)** | (180) | I-5 | R-5 |

Obverse II 2 – Fourth star on right has just part of point broken off.
Reverse B/Ak – Seven tail feather ends showing; under 2, between 2 and 3, under 3, 4, 5, 6, and faintly between 6 and 7 TF (one of the best examples of the 7/8 TF, with the ends extending halfway between the 7 TF ends and the top of the bows). Design remains in leaves of branch, below branch on left, and around wreath bow. Faint outline of arrow shafts below crossover of branch and arrow shafts. Extra feather below eagle's head. Die chips around R in TRUST. Doubled right leg and talons on eagle.

| 41A | **II 2 • B/Ak (4 TF)** | (179) | I-3 | R-4 |

Reverse B/Ak – Four tail feather ends showing; partial end between 2 and 3 TF, thin line between 3 and 4 TF, full end below 5 TF, and partial end between 5 and 6 TF. Some early strikes show a broken line below 4 TF. Design remains in leaves of branch, below branch on left, and around wreath bow. Doubled right leg and talons. Polished down version of B/Ak.

| 42 | **II/I 5 • B/Al (7 TF)** | (180) | I-4 | R-5 |

Reverse B/Al – Seven tail feather ends showing; between 1 and 2 (weak), between 2 and 3, under 3, 4, 5, and 6, and between 6 and 7 (weak). Some of the extra tail feather ends show a doubled appearance. Design remains in leaves of branch, below branch on left, and around wreath bow. Portion of extra arrow head below middle one. Die chips around E, T, R, and U in WE TRUST. Top of U in UNITED missing, polishing marks on lower half, and doubled D in GOD and T in TRUST.

| 43 | **II/I 3 • B/Am (Doubled Legs)** | (180) | I-5 | R-5 |

Reverse B/Am – Doubled legs and talons on the left; design remains in leaves of branch, at end of arrow feathers and around wreath bow. Three tail feather ends showing, faint ones between 4 and 5 TF, 5 and 6 TF and 6 and 7 TF. Die chips in IN GOD WE TRUST.

| 44 | **II/I 37 • B/Ad (3 TF)** | (179) | I-5 | R-7 |

Obverse II/I 37 – LIBERTY doubled slightly with BER showing faint shadows on right side. First star on right and number seven on left doubled. Cotton blossoms and leaves are tripled on right side.

| 45 | **II 2 • B/An (Doubled Talons)** | (179) | I-3 | R-6 |

Reverse B/An – Left leg is doubled with one and one-half normal width. Middle talon is doubled on left foot and outside talon is doubled on right foot. Olive branch is doubled above tail feathers. Die has been overpolished in eagle's wings and tail feathers. Diagonal polishing marks are in tail feathers.

| 70 | **I¹12 • B¹a (Doubled Letters)** | (180) | I-2 | R-4 |

Obverse I¹12 – Doubled motto with R, I and B having large shifts at bottom and UM tripled on right side. All stars on right tripled at bottom. 878 in date doubled. First 8 doubled at top inside of both loops and at bottom outside of lower loop. 7 doubled below upper crossbar and at bottom left and upper right of vertical shaft. Second 8 doubled at top inside and bottom outside of lower loop and tripled at lower left outside of upper loop. Nostril slightly overpolished.
Reverse B¹a – Earlier type B reverse; 7 TF parallel arrow feather, with long center arrow shaft. Die overpolished with last three leaves disconnected from olive branch and part of eagle's lower right wing missing.

| 79 | **II/I 35 • B¹a (Missing Nostril)** | (180) | I-2 | R-4 |

Obverse II/I 35 – Slightly doubled LIBERTY shifted left. Doubled 2 through 7 stars on left and first three stars on right. Lower part of Liberty head nose missing because of overpolished die.

| 80 | **II/I 6 • B¹b (Disconnected Leaves)** | (180) | I-2 | R-4 |

Reverse B¹b – Die overpolished with last three leaves disconnected from olive branch. Diagonal polishing lines below tail feathers. Small die chip on eagle's right wing at top next to body.

| 81 | **II/I 7 • B¹c (Spiked P)** | (180) | I-2 | R-4 |

Reverse B¹c – Die overpolished with last three leaves disconnected from olive branch and blank spots in middle of both eagle's wings. Die chip on eagle's right wing in middle next to body.

1878-P

41 R B/Ak 7 TF

41A R B/Ak (Polished) 4 TF

42 R B/Al 7 TF

43 R B/Am Doubled Legs

44 O II/I 37

45 R B/An Doubled Talons

70 O I²12

70 O I²12

81 R B¹c

70 R B¹a

79 O II/I 35

80 R B¹b

153

1878-P

82	II/I 10 • B¹c (Doubled LIBERTY)	(180)		I-3	R-4

Obverse II/I 10 – Doubled LIBERTY shifted up. Doubled E, P, R, B, S, U, and N in motto. Doubled 1, 2, 3 and 5 stars on right with first one very strong; doubled 1, 2, 4, and 5 on left. Doubled 1 on right side, both 8's doubled over center of top loop.

83	II/I 11 • B¹d (High 1)	(180)		I-3	R-4

Obverse II/I 11 – Doubled LIBERTY shifted left; all letters in E PLURIBUS UNUM doubled. Doubled 1, 2, 5 and 6 stars on left and 1, 2, 3, and 4 stars on right. 1 in date doubled on right side and set high. First 8 doubled at top right outside and left outside of upper loop and bottom inside of lower loop. 7 doubled slightly on left side of left top serif and right side on left lower serif.

Reverse B¹d – B¹ type reverse with no apparent defects except for slight overpolishing in middle of eagle's wing.

84	II/I 12 • B¹e (Washed-out L)	(180)		I-2	R-4

Obverse II/I 12 – Slightly doubled LIBERTY shifted left, with surface around L flat and detail not brought out. Missing nostril. Doubled E, P, L, U, R, B and S in E PLURIBUS. Doubled 1, 2, 3, 4, 6, and 7 stars on left and all stars on right. Slanted dash below first 8 and die chip at top left inside of first 8 upper loop.

Reverse B¹e – D of DOLLAR broken at bottom with just two lines remaining. Die chip on eagle's right wing, 6th feather down and also next to body. Die overpolished with blank areas in eagle's left wing and tail feathers. Clash marks with faint remains of E of LIBERTY below tail feathers.

100	I¹10 • B²a (Doubled Letters)	(180)		I-2	R-4

Obverse I¹10 – Doubled top of E PLURIBUS UNUM and some stars toward rim.

Reverse B²a – Later type B reverse, with shorter center arrow shaft and die chips around R and U of TRUST. The eagle's wings show at least 6 different states of overpolishing where the field shows through.

110	II/I 8 • B²a (Broken N and M)	(180)		1-3	R-4
111	II/I 13 • B2a (Dropped R)	(193)		I-2	R-4

Obverse II/I 13 – Slightly doubled LIBERTY (L, I, and B only). Doubled U and R in PLURIBUS, with the R dropped down. Doubled 7 star on left and 1 star on right.

112	II/I 14 • B2a (Line in B)	(194)		I-2	R-4

Obverse II/I 14 – Type II LIBERTY. Extra vertical line in top loop and extra horizontal lines in bottom loop of B of PLURIBUS. Doubled 2 and 3 stars on left and 1 and 3 stars on right. 1 in date doubled at top right.

113	II/I 15 • B²a (Flake on Cheek)	(194)		I-2	R-4

Obverse II/I 15 – Type II LIBERTY; doubled N, U, M in UNUM; doubled 2 star on left and 1, 2 and 5 stars on right. Both 8's in date doubled. Die break through center ear, and large die flake on cheek.

114	II/I 16 • B²a (Doubled R)	(178)		I-2	R-4

Obverse II/I 16 – Slightly doubled LIBERTY. Doubled P, R and B in PLURIBUS. Doubled first six stars on left and first four on right. Die overpolished in hair above date on some specimens.

Reverse B²a – Die slightly overpolished with flat spot in middle of eagle's left wing and right wing slightly separated from the leg.

115	II/I 17 • B²a (Doubled Date)	(194)		I-3	R-4

Obverse II/I 17 – Doubled I, B, E, R, T, and Y in LIBERTY, shifted left with R, T, and Y having large shifts. Doubled N, U, and M in UNUM and doubled date. All stars on right and left doubled, some with large shifts.

116	II/I 18 • B²a (Doubled P)	(180, 179)		I-2	R-4

Obverse II/I 18 – Type II LIBERTY; doubled P, L, R, and B in PLURIBUS and doubled 1, 3 and 4 stars on left and 1, 2, 3 and 4 on right. 1 in date doubled on top right. Lower part of nostril missing. Die flake near hairline behind eye with die crack leading to hair.

117	II/I 19 • B²a (Tripled Star)	(194)		I-4	R-4

Obverse II/I 9 – Doubled LIBERTY shifted right; doubled E, P and R in E PLURIBUS. Doubled 2, 3, and 4 stars on left and doubled 1 – 5 stars on right (number 2 is tripled and is one of the best examples of a tripled star). 1 in date is doubled on left side of stem. Incomplete band in cap.

82 O II/I 10

83 O II/I 11

1878-P

83 O II/I 11

84 O Dash Below First 8

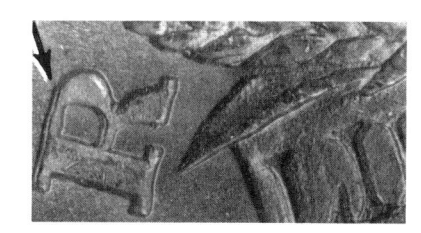

100 O I¹ 10

84 O II/I 12

111 O II/I 13

112 O II/I 14

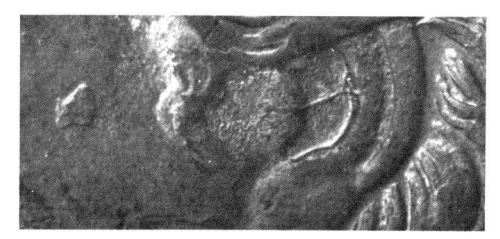

113 O II/I 15

114 O II/I 16

115 O II/I 17

116 O II/I 18

117 O II/I 19

118 O II/I 20

155

1878-P

118	II/I 20 • B²a (Shifted P)		(194)	I-2	R-4

Obverse II/I 20 – Type II LIBERTY. Doubled bottom serif of P; metal on top of serif in U of PLURIBUS. Doubled 3, 4, and 7 stars on left; doubled 1 and 2 stars on right.

119	II/I 21 • B²a (Shifted E)		(193)	I-2	R-4

Obverse II/I 20 – Slightly doubled LIBERTY, shifted left and up. E in motto doubled on top and bottom right outside. All left stars are doubled. Ear is doubled on the inside.

120	II/I 31 • B²a (Doubled P)		(I-2)	R-4

Obverse II/I 31 – Type II LIBERTY. Doubled bottom serifs of P and metal on R of PLURIBUS. Metal on right side of U in UNUM. All stars on left and first three on right doubled.

121	II/I 38 • B²a (Doubled Motto)			I-3	R-4

Obverse II/I 38 – LIBERT in LIBERTY doubled slightly on left side. Strongly doubled 1 and 3 stars on right. E, P, U and R in E PLURIBUS strongly doubled.

122	II/I 36 • B²a (Doubled Motto)		(194)	I-3	R-4

Obverse II/I 36 – Type I LIBERTY doubled slightly to left. Type II ear. Motto letters all doubled with PLURI particularly strong. All left stars doubled slightly on left side. Doubled 1, 4, 5 and 6 stars on right with number one having a large shift.

130	II 1. B²a (Normal)		(194)	I-1	R-2
131	II 2 • B²a (Normal)	(Some Proofs)	(179, 180, 194)	I-1	R-2

Obverse II 2 – Some specimens show die chip on hair below LIBERTY, or diagonal die scratch through B or through R and top of T in LIBERTY.

132	II 3 • B²a (Missing Nostril)		(179, 180)	I-2	R-4

Obverse II 3 – Same as II 2 but die has been overpolished so that nostril is missing.

133	II 4 • B²a (Doubled)		(193)	I-2	R-4

Obverse II 4 – Same as II 2, but with slightly doubled LIBERTY, doubled letters in E PLURIBUS UNUM, and metal in P.

140	II/I 18 • B²b (Partially Open O)		(180, 189)	I-2	R-4

Reverse B²b – Same as B²a, but with hub break fill which leaves open the upper part of O in GOD (this example is only partially open).

141	II/ 19 • B²b (Tripled Star)		(194)	I-4	R-4
142	II/I 22 • B²b (Doubled 878)		(179)	I-3	R-4

Obverse II/I 22 – Doubled LIBERTY shifted left; doubled P, R, U, U, and M in PLURIBUS UNUM; doubled top of 878 in date and right side of 7 vertical shaft. All left and right stars slightly doubled.

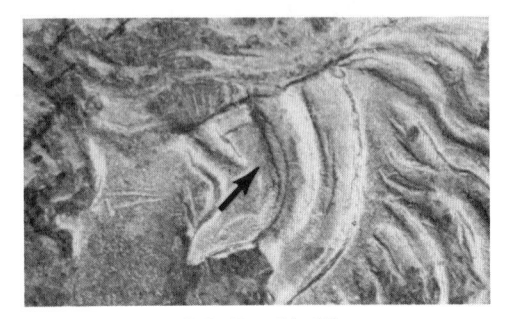

119 O Doubled Ear

119 O II/I 21

120 O II/I 31

121 O II/I 38

1878-P

121 O II/I 38

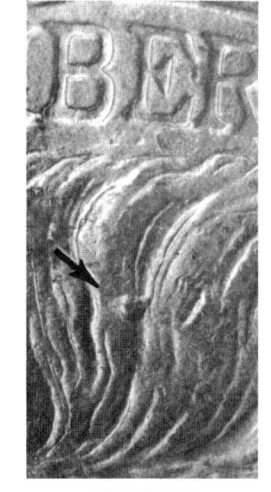

131 O II 2

131 O II 2

131 O II 2

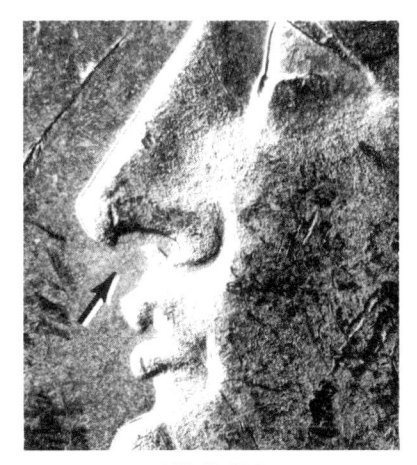

132 O II 3

133 O II 4

142 O II/I 22

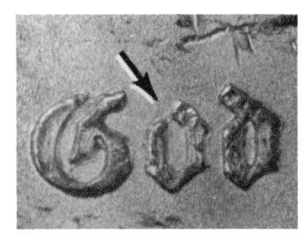

140 R B²b

143 O II/I 23

| 143 | II/I 23 • B²b (Doubled 8) | (180) | I-2 | R-4 |

Obverse II/I 23 – Doubled LIBERTY shifted left; doubled R in PLURIBUS. Doubled 2, 6, and 7 stars on left. Doubled top of first 8 in date.

| 144 | II/I 24 • B²b (Doubled LIBERTY) | (180) | I-2 | R-4 |

Obverse II/I 24 – All letters slightly doubled in LIBERTY with shift to left. Metal at top right of E; slightly doubled R.

| 145 | II/I 25 • B²b (Broken N and M) | (180) | I-2 | R-4 |

Obverse II/1 25 – Type II LIBERTY, doubled U and R in PLURIBUS; broken bottom serifs of N and M, with bottom right serif of M completely gone. Doubled 3 star on left and 5 star on right. 1 and 7 in date doubled on right side with 1 slanted to left.

| 146 | II 2 • B²b (Line in E, R, Y) | (194) | I-2 | R-3 |

Obverse II 2 – Same as II 2, but with diagonal die gouge through bottom of E, two through top of R and one through middle of Y in LIBERTY.

1878-P

144 O II/I 24

145 O II/I 25

146 O II 2
Line in E, R, Y

160 **II/I 20 • B²c (Shifted P)** (194) I-2 R-4
Reverse B²c – Same as B²a, but with die fill on the arm of R in TRUST which results in TIUST. This is a break in the hub, since the variety appears on many dies (some of the 1878-P 7 TF, 1878-S, and 1879-S).

161 **II/I 21 • B²c (Shifted E)** (194) I-2 R-4

162 **II/I 25 • B²c (Broken N and M)** (180) I-2 R-4

163 **II/I 26 • B²c (Shifted U)** (194) I-3 R-4
Obverse II/I 26 – Slightly doubled LIBERTY (L, I, B, and T only) shifted to left. Doubled E, U, R, and M in E PLURIBUS UNUM (U and M are particularly large shifts). Doubled 7 star on left. Doubled 18 in date.

164 **II/I 27 • B²c (Broken R)** (180) I-2 R-4
Obverse II/I 27 – Slightly doubled LIBERTY (I, B, and T only) shifted to left. Metal on P, and broken upper part of R in PLURIBUS. Doubled 1, 3, and 4 stars on right.

165 **II/I 28 • B²c (Spiked P)** (180) I-2 R-4
Obverse II/I 28 – Type II LIBERTY. Metal on E, P, L, U, R, and S in E PLURIBUS UNUM. Doubled 2, 3, and 5 stars on left and 1, 3, and 5 stars on right.

166 **II/I 29 • B²c (Spiked P)** (193) I-2 R-4
Obverse II/I 29 – Type II LIBERTY. Metal on E, P, U, and R of E PLURIBUS. All stars on left and first star on right doubled.

167 **II/I 30 • B²c Spiked P)** (194) I-2 R-4
Obverse II/I 30 – Type II LIBERTY. Metal bottom left side of P; shifted U and doubled bottom of R in PLURIBUS. Slightly doubled right side of 7 in date.

168 **II/I 31 • B²c (Doubled P)** (193) I-2 R-4

169 **II/I 32 • B²c (Quadrupled Stars)** (193) I-3 R-4
Obverse II/I 32 – Doubled LIBERTY shifted to left, E, PLUR-R doubled on left side, S doubled at bottom; UNUM doubled at top. First five stars on left quadrupled with 2-4 having very large shifts. 6 and 7 stars on left tripled. 1-3 nd 5 stars on right doubled 4 tripled. Doubled date with 1 doubled at top right and 878 doubled on surface at bottom of loops and crossbar.

170 **II/I 33 • B²c (Doubled Date)** (193) I-3 R-4
Obverse II/I 33 – Doubled LIBERTY shifted slightly to left; doubled P, U, and R. All stars on left slightly doubled; all stars on right doubled. Date doubled, with tops of 1878 showing the greatest shift.

171 **II/I 34 • B²c (Tripled R)** (193) I-3 R-4
Obverse II/I 34 – Doubled LIBERTY with no shift (good example of perfect register with thicker type II LIBERTY letters). Doubled P and U, tripled R in PLURIBUS. Doubled 1 and 3 stars on left and 1, 3 and 4 stars on right.

185 **II 1 • B²c (Broken R)** (193 I-2 R-3

186 **II 2 • B²c (Broken R)** (193) I-2 R-3
Reverse B²c – (Some also with open O and some with overpolished reverse.)

1878-P

160 R B²c

163 O II/I 26

163 O II/I 26

164 O II/I 27

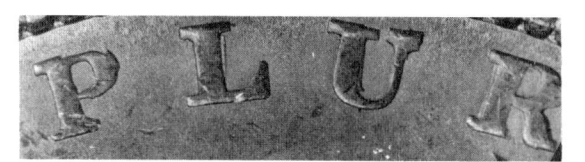

165 O II/I 28

166 O II/I 29

167 O II/I 30

169 O II/I 32

170 O II/I 33

171 O II/I 34

187 O II 5

188 O II 6

190 O B²d

1878-P

187	II 5 • B²c (Doubled R)	(193)		I-2	R-4

Obverse II 5 – Same as II 1, except letters L, U, R, and B in PLURIBUS and UN in UNUM are doubled. R is doubled strongly at top, middle and lower right side. Bottom serif of U is doubled strongly at top left.

188	II 6 • B²c (Washed Out L)	(193)		I-2	R-4

Obverse II 6 – Same as II 1, except that die is polished down so that L of LIBERTY is weak and wheat leaf above L is shortened.

190	II 3 • B²d (Doubled Motto)	(179)		I-2	R-4

Reverse B²d – Same as reverse B²a but with doubled GOD and WE to right, eagle's left wing feathers at top and top edge of eagle's right. Wings are overpolished in center.

195	II 2 • B²e (Broken D)	(179)		I-2	R-3

Obverse II 2 – Diagonal line through B in LIBERTY.
Reverse B²e – Bottom of D of DOLLAR completely broken.

195A	II 2 • B²e (Broken D)	(179)		I-2	R-3

Obverse II 2 – Diagonal line through R and top of T in LIBERTY.
Reverse B²e – Same as reverse B²a, but with partially broken bottom of D of DOLLAR.

196	II/I 22 • B²f (Doubled 878)	(179)		I-3	R-4

Reverse B²f – Die overpolished with part of eagle's lower right wing missing next to leg.

197	II 2 • B²f (Missing Feathers)	(180, 194)		I-2	R-4
198	II/I 2 • B²f (Doubled Date)	(194)		I-3	R-4
199	II/I 27 • B²f (Broken) R)	(180)		I-2	R-4
200	II/I 39 • C¹a (Broken N and M)	(179, 194)		I-2	R-6

Obverse II/I 39 – Serifs of N and M in UNUM broken similar to II/I 25. Type II LIBERTY. First six stars on left and first three stars on right doubled. 1 doubled at top right.
Reverse C¹a – Serif of A of AMERICA almost touches eagle's wing, with bottom of letter serifs slanting down and to left. Inner side of right serif of A is cut off square. Bottom feather of eagle's right wing next to leg is rounded and not connected to wing on left. Leaves of right wreath doubled on outside and inside of legend letters doubled towards rim.

201	II/I 35 • C¹a (Thick Letters)	(179)		I-2	R-6
202	III¹ 1 • C¹a (Lines in Wheat Leaves)	(180)		I-3	R-5

Obverse III¹ 1 – Lines in all wheat leaves, with more detail in cotton blossom tops than type II obverse. Thin letters in LIBERTY. Complete line at bottom of cap. Date slightly doubled at top inside of upper and lower loops of 8's and left sides of 1 and 7 shafts; all left and right stars doubled.

203	III¹ 2 • C¹a (Short Wheat Leaf)	(179)		I-2	R-6

Obverse III¹ 2 – Same as III1 1, but with heavy die polishing at top. Wheat leaf below R is short, well below the R, and contains lines. Wheat grains are well separated, with a long wheat leaf between the stalks. Bottom serifs are thin in motto. Bottom of E and R run together in LIBERTY.

210	II 2 • C²a (Extra Feather)	(194)		I-2	R-4

Reverse C²a – Same as C¹a, except that inner serif of A is thinner. Bottom feather of eagle's right wing extends to junction of next two feathers, and a thin line is present between eagle's leg and first feather.

210A	II 2 • C²a (Line Through R)	(179)		I-2	R-5

Obverse II 2 – Diagonal line through R and top of T in LIBERTY.

210B	II 2 • C²a (Line Through IB)	(194)		I-2	R-5

Obverse II 2 – Diagonal line through the middle of I and lower part of B in LIBERTY and curving downwards from B into hair and extending up from I across wheat leaf.

215	III¹1 • C²a (Extra Feather)			I-2	Proof
220	II/I 34 • C³a (Triple R)	(176)		I-3	R-7

Reverse C³a – Left serif of A is cut down so it is not flat on top and is away from wing. Bottom of serif is not slanting. Bottom feather of eagle's right wing is squared off and raised. This is normal reverse design used for most of the Morgan silver dollar series.

221	II 1 • C³a (Cut Down A)	(193)		I-1	R-3
222	II 2 • C³a (Cut Down A)	(168, 178, 193, 194)		I-1	R-2

160

1878-P / 1878-CC

| 223 | II 6 • C³a (Washed Out L) | (194) | I-2 | R-6 |
| 230 | III²1 • C³a (Normal) | (193, 194) | I-1 | R-2 |

Obverse III²1 – Long wheat leaf below R, close to R, with weak lines. Short wheat leaf between wheat stalks. Thicker bottom serifs in motto letters. LIBERTY letters are thinner, with shorter serifs on B and R. This is the normal obverse design for most of the Morgan silver dollar series.

195 R B²e

196 R B²f

202 O III²1

203 O III¹2

210B O Lines in IB

221 O II 1

1878-CC

All 1878-CC have the B reverse with flat breast eagle and parallel arrow feathers. The minor design types B¹ with long center arrow shaft and B² with short center arrow shaft are about equally available. VAM's 6, 18 and 24 have doubled cotton leaves and bolls and are worth a modest price premium. VAM's 11 and 14 have heavy die polishing lines in the eagle's wing and while interesting, bring only a slight premium. The CC mint marks vary in position and spacing since they were punched in by hand into each die.

Although the center portions of the design are well struck on 1878-CC, the B reverse did cause weak strike problems. On the obverse, occasionally planchet striations will show on the jaw along with a creamy color of the original planchet surface. Planchet striations are caused by rough edges of the draw benches used to obtain the final thickness of the silver strips. Weakly struck coins did not smooth out these planchet striations where planchet contact against the die was weak. On the reverse, weakly struck 1878-CC will show on the eagle's legs and talons and on the arrows.

Proof-like surfaces are available although not as high a proportion as for later lower mintage years of 1879-1885-CC. The dies were used longer for the 1878-CC to achieve the higher mintage thus resulting in a lower percentage of early strike proof-like specimens. Extremely deep mirror white cameos are available but quite scarce. The average 1878-CC proof-like has fairly good contrast.

1878-CC

1   **II 1 • B¹a (Normal Die)**   I-1   R-3
Obverse II 1 – Normal die of 1878-P type II with the 7 in date doubled slightly on right side (a hub defect).
Reverse B¹a – Normal die of 1878-P type B¹ with a long center arrow shaft. Medium spaced small mint marks, II CC, at medium height.

1A   **II 1 • B¹a (Line in Eye)**   (179)   I-2   R-4
Obverse II 1 – Same as Obverse II 1 except a die scratch which shows as a thin line through the bottom of the R in LIBERTY, a thick line extending down from the middle of the eye lash, a thin line in the bottom corner of the eye, and a thick line at the rear of the nostril.

IB   **II 1 • B¹a (Line in IB)**   I-2   R-3
Obverse II 1 – Slanted die gouge in top of I and bottom of B in LIBERTY. Date is doubled.

2   **II 2 • B¹ a (Doubled LIBERTY)**   I-2   R-3
Obverse II 2 – LIBERTY slightly doubled shifted left. Some specimens show die chip on nostril. Some also show die chip on front of forehead and top of eyelid or between loops of 8 on left.
Reverse B¹a – Normal die of type B¹ with medium mint marks, II CC, at medium height with die chips in the center of both C's.

3   **II 1 • B¹b (Very Wide CC)**   I-3   R-3
Obverse II 1 – Line in eye variety.
Reverse B¹b – Normal die of type B¹ with very widely spaced mint marks, IV CC, set high and touching wreath.

4   **II 3 • B¹c (Close CC)**   (177)   I-2   R-3
Obverse II 3 – Normal die of 1878-P type II with broken point off number 4 star on right (a hub chip).
Reverse B¹c – Normal die of type B¹ with closely spaced mint marks, I CC, at medium height. Die chips show in center of both C's.

5   **II 3 • B¹d (Wide CC)**   I-2   R-3
Reverse B¹d – Normal die of type B¹ with widely spaced mint marks, III CC, at medium height.

6   **II 4 • B¹b (Doubled Obverse)**   (178)   I-3   R-4
Obverse II 4 – Doubled ear and cotton blossom leaves on the right edges, date, all stars on right and left on bottom edges.

7   **II 1 • B²a (Medium CC)**   (177)   I-2   R-3
Reverse B² a – Normal die of 1878-P type B² with a short center arrow shaft. Medium spaced mint mark, II CC, at medium height.

8   **II 1 • B²b (Wide CC)**   (177)   I-2   R-3
Reverse B²b – Normal die of type B² with widely paced mint marks, II CC, at medium height tilted slightly to right. Some specimens show die polishing lines in eagle's left wing and across breast.

9   **II 3 • B²c (CC Tilted Right)**   (177)   I-2   R-3
Reverse B² c – Normal die of type B² with widely spaced mint marks, III CC, set high and slanted right.

10   **II 3 • B²d (Wide CC)**   I-2   R-3
Reverse B² d – Normal die of type B² with widely spaced mint marks, III CC, at medium height.

11   **II 3 • B²b (Lines in Eagle)**   I-3   R-5
Reverse B²b – Die polishing marks strongly evident as heavy lines at the bottom of the eagle's right wing and in the middle left wing. III CC mint mark at medium height and tilted slightly to right.

12   **II 3 • B²e (Very Wide CC)**   (177)   I-2   R-3
Reverse B²e – Normal die of type B² with very widely spaced mint marks, IV CC, at medium height.

1 O Doubled 7

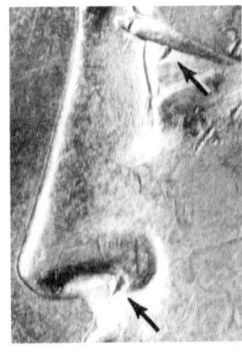

1A O Line in Eye

1B O Line in IB

1878-CC

| 13 | II 5 • B²a (Doubled Date) | | I-3 | R-4 |

Obverse II 5 – Same as II 4 obverse except cotton blossom leaves are not doubled.

| 14 | II 2 • B²b (Doubled LIBERTY) | (178) | I-2 | R-3 |
| 15 | II 3 • B²f (Spiked Lip) | | I-2 | R-4 |

Obverse II 3 – Vertical die gouge from lower lip to chin and die gouge running through IB of LIBERTY up to wheat leaf.
Reverse B²f – Normal die of type B² with widely spaced mint marks, III CC, at medium height. Left C is doubled at left inside and right C has diagonal spike at left inside.

| 16 | II 1 • B¹e (Doubled CC) | | I-3 | R-4 |

Reverse B¹e – Normal die of type B¹ with very widely spaced mint marks, IV CC, set high with right one touching wreath and doubled inside at top.

| 17 | II 1 • B¹e (Doubled CC) | (179) | I-3 | R-4 |

Obverse II 1 – Line in Eye variety.

| 18 | II 4 • B¹c (Doubled Obverse) | | I-3 | R-4 |
| 19 | II 1 • B¹f (Wide CC With Dot) | (179) | I-2 | R-3 |

Reverse B¹f – Normal die of B¹ with widely spaced mint marks, III CC at medium height. Left mint mark C has die chip in center and is punched deeper in die than right C.

| 20 | II 1 • B¹g (Medium CC with Dot) | | I-2 | R-3 |

Obverse II 1 – Line in eye variety.
Reverse B¹g – Normal die of type B¹ with medium spaced mint marks, II CC at medium height. Left mint mark C has die chip in center.

| 21 | II 4 • B²a (Doubled Obverse) | (179) | I-3 | R-4 |

Obverse II 4 – Late die state with die cracks in date, stars, and letters.

| 22 | II 3 • B¹a (Die Chips in CC) | (177) | I-2 | R-3 |

Reverse B¹a – Closed II CC's with die chip inside.

| 23 | II 1 • B¹c (Close CC) | (177) | I-2 | R-3 |
| 24 | II 6 • B¹f (Doubled Cotton Leaves) | (179) | I-3 | R-4 |

Obverse II 6 – Doubled cotton leaves and bolls on right side. Eyelash doubled at top.

2 O Doubled LIBERTY

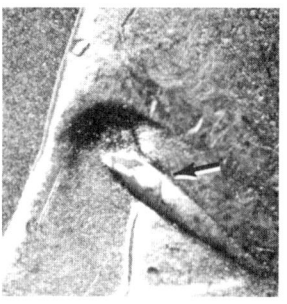

2 O Die Chips

2 O Die Chip

2 R Die chips in C's

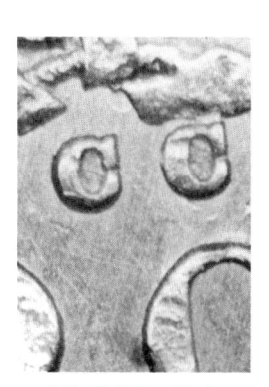

3 R CC Set High

6 O Doubled Date

1878-CC / 1878-S

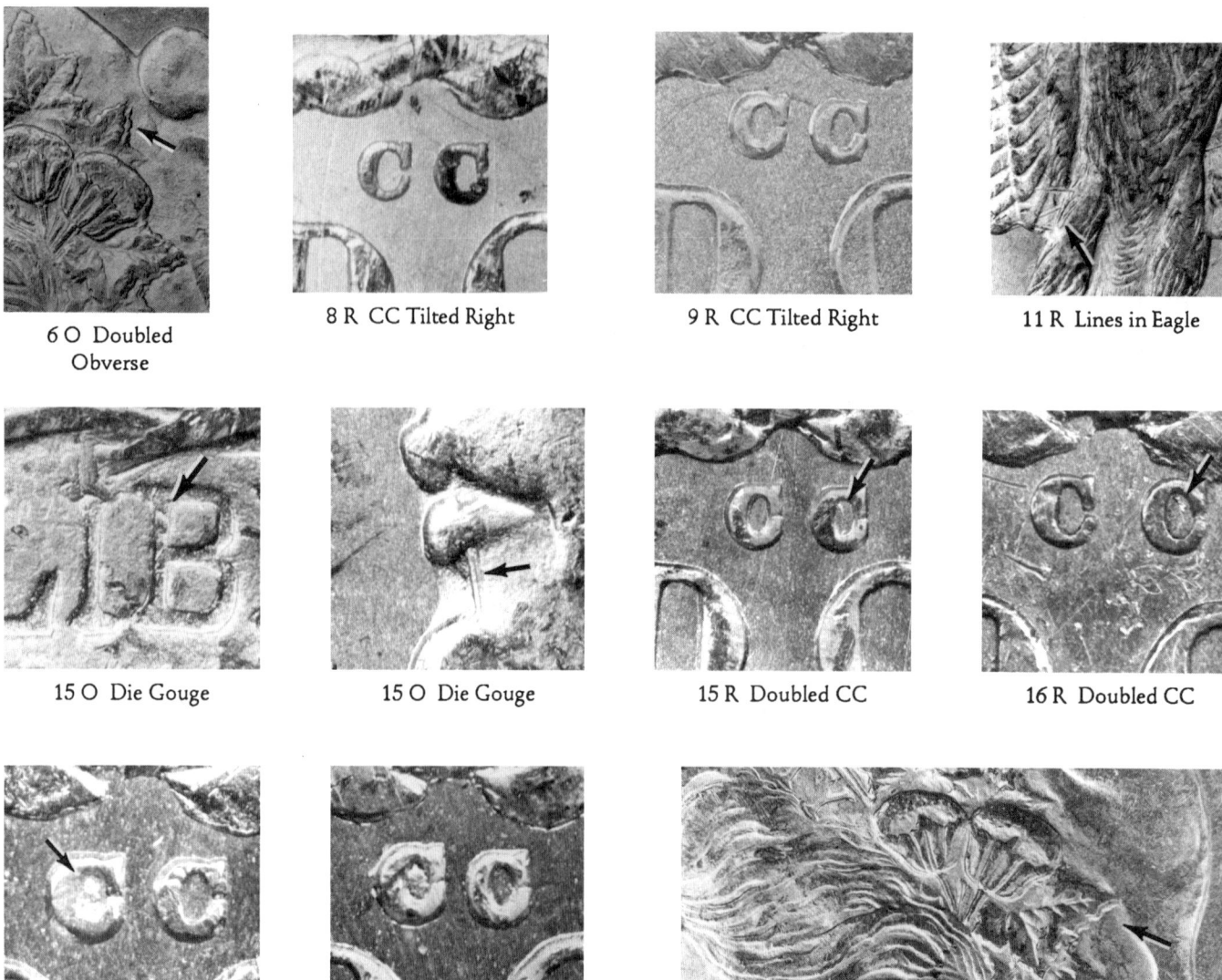

6 O Doubled Obverse

8 R CC Tilted Right

9 R CC Tilted Right

11 R Lines in Eagle

15 O Die Gouge

15 O Die Gouge

15 R Doubled CC

16 R Doubled CC

19 R Wide CC With Dot

20 R Die Chip in CC

24 O Doubled Cotton Leaves

1878-S

The 1878-S also comes in only the B reverse with flat breast and parallel arrow feathers. However, practically all are the B^2 reverse with short center arrow shaft. About a dozen B^1 reverse with long center arrow shaft are known and they are all circulated. VAM's 26 and 27 with B^1 reverse command substantial premiums and were from the first dies used at that mint. Many of the 1878-S reverse dies were individually touched up at that mint to add feathers between the eagle's right wing and leg. This area tended to be overpolished by the die basining. Although these touched up dies by the branch mint are unique in the Morgan series (along with some 1879-S flat breast), the many touched up dies makes them common with no price premium. There are also many slightly doubled design dies for the 1878-S but they command only modest price premiums to collectors.

As with the 1878-CC, the 1878-S had some striking problems because of the B reverse. Planchet striations on the jaw occasionally show as well as weak eagle's legs and talons and arrows. Unless very noticeable and distracting they will not lower the coin's value significantly.

Proof-like 1878-S are fairly common but most have brilliant devices with low contrast. There are a lot of one-sided proof-like 1878-S due to the frequent changing of dies during this first year of striking and use of the B reverse. Buyers of this date should always check to see that proof-likes purchased are reflective on both sides because the excellent luster of this year can be deceptive. Some extraordinary deep mirror white cameo exist for this date but are quite rare.

1878-S

1 II 1 • B² a (Normal Die) (184) I-1 R-2
  Obverse II 1 – Normal die of 1878-P type II with broken point off number 4 star on right and 7 in date doubled slightly on right side (a hub defect). Some specimens show a die gouge through IB of LIBERTY
  Reverse B² a – Normal die of 1878-P type B² with small III S mint mark. Some specimens show diagonal polishing marks in eagle's tail feathers and through first top berry in left wreath or long horizontal polishing lines through neck and eagle's right wing.

1A II 1 • B² a (Die Scratch on Wing) I-2 R-4
  Reverse B² a – Vertical die scratch through lower part of eagle's right wing with a die chip in the middle of eagle's breast similar to VAM 16.

1B II 1 • B²a (Pitted Tail Feathers) (184) I-2 R-4
  Reverse B²a – Pitted die from rust in eagle's tail feathers and lower right wreath. Two dies chips in lower part of eagle's right wing.

2 II 1 • B² b (Broken R) (184) I-2 R-2
  Reverse B² b – Same as B² a, but with die fill on the arm of R in TRUST which results in TIUST. (A hub break since it also appears on some 1878-P 7 TF and 1879-S.) Some specimens show a die fill on the top of G in GOD separating the loop from the stem. Some specimens show a die break through the berry and leaf in wreath under N in UNITED.

3 II 2 • B² a (Doubled LIBERTY Right) I-2 R-3
  Obverse II 2 – LIBERTY slightly doubled to right.

4 II 3 • B² a (Doubled Date) (184) I-2 R-4
  Obverse II 3 – Date doubled at bottom. In addition, both 8's are doubled at the top left inside the upper loop. The 7 is doubled at the top and upper right side. Broken 4 star on right. All letters of LIBERTY slightly doubled on right side. Nostril and eyelid are slightly doubled.

1 R Line in Tail Feathers

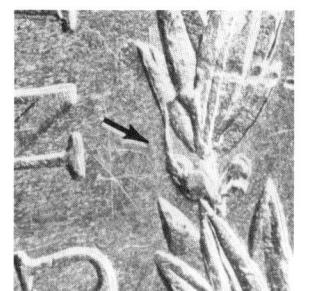

1 R Die Break in Wreath

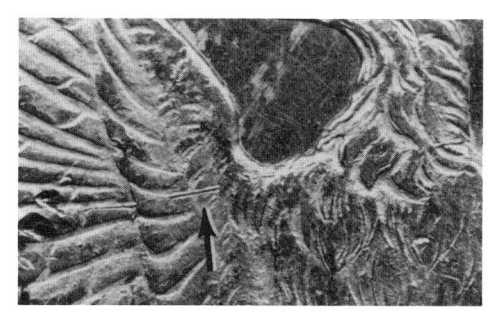

1 R Die Gouge in Eagle

1 O Die Gouge through B

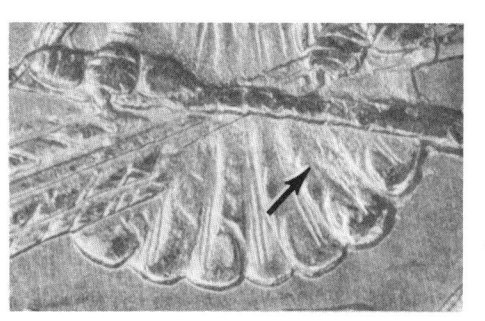

1B R Pitted Tail Feathers

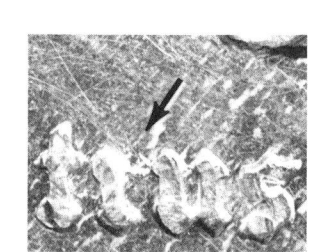

2 R Broken R

2 R Open G

3 O Doubled LIBERTY Right

1878-S

5	**II 4 • B² i (Doubled 878)**		I-2	R-4

Obverse II 4 – Both 8's are doubled on the right side of the upper loop opening. Crossbar of the 7 is doubled at top and right side. S of PLURIBUS and UNU of UNUM slightly doubled right side. All letters of LIBERTY doubled with shift down. Lower hair slightly doubled. Nostril, lips and chin doubled.
Reverse B² i – Feather engraved between eagle's right wing and leg. R in TRUST broken.

6	**II 5 • B² j (Doubled Motto)**	(184)	I-2	R-3

Obverse II 5 – Motto letters doubled on top surface. Doubled 6 and 7 stars on left and 4, 5, and 6 stars on right. Doubled LIBERTY shifted left and up. Point on number 4 star on right is not broken off.
Reverse B² j – Feather engraved between eagle's right wing and leg. R in TRUST broken.

7	**II 6 • B² i (Doubled LIBERTY Down)**	(184)	I-3	R-3

Obverse II 6 – All letters of LIBERTY doubled with shift down. Point on number 4 star on right is broken off. Both 8's in date doubled at top right of upper loop opening and 7 is doubled on right and at top. Doubled nose, lips, chin, and neck.

8	**II 7 • B² k (Doubled LIBERTY Left)**	(184)	I-2	R-3

Obverse II 7 – LIBERTY slightly doubled to left and also right on IB-R-Y. Point on number 4 star on right is broken.
Reverse B² k – Feather engraved between eagle's right wing and leg. R in TRUST not broken.

9	**II 7 • B² l (Doubled LIBERTY Left)**		I-2	R-3

Reverse B² l – Feather engraved between eagle's right wing and leg. R in TRUST broken.

10	**II 8 • B² b (Doubled Motto)**		I-2	R-3

Obverse II 8 – LURIB of PLURIBUS doubled with LU doubled at top and RIB doubled at bottom.

11	**II 9 • B² b (Doubled Motto)**		I-3	R-3

Obverse II 9 – All motto letters doubled strongly. All left stars doubled on left side with 6 and 7 also doubled on right. Doubled 1, 2, 4, 5, and 6 right stars. 1 and 7 in date doubled at top right. First 8 doubled on lower left outside of upper loop. Second 8 tripled at left inside of upper loop.

12	**II 10 • B² b (Doubled Motto)**		I-2	R-4

Obverse II 10 – Motto letters doubled slightly on lower portion of top surface. Broken 4 star on right.

13	**II 7 • B² c (Doubled LIBERTY Left)**		I-2	R-3

Reverse B² c – Small III S mint mark set slightly high and to right.

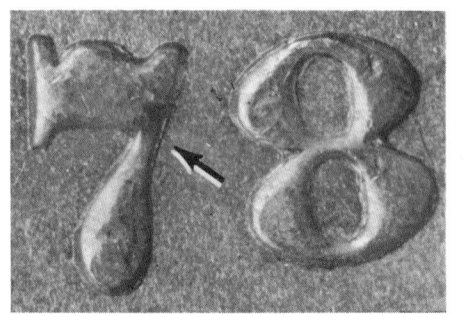

4 O Doubled Date

5 O Doubled 878

5 and 7 R Engraved Feather

6 R Engraved Feather

6 R Doubled Motto

7 O Doubled LIBERTY

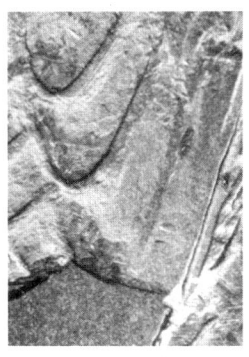

1878-S

8 R Engraved Feather

8 O Doubled LIBERTY

11 O Doubled Motto

9 R Engraved Feather

10 O Doubled Motto

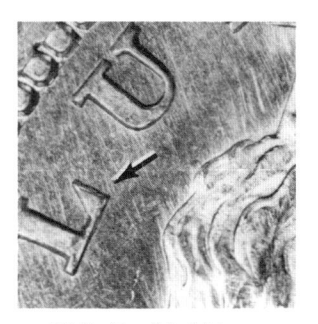

12 O Doubled Motto

13 R S Set High

14 R Engraved Feather

14 O Doubled LIBERTY

14 O Doubled P-R

14 O Doubled P-R

15 R Engraved Feather

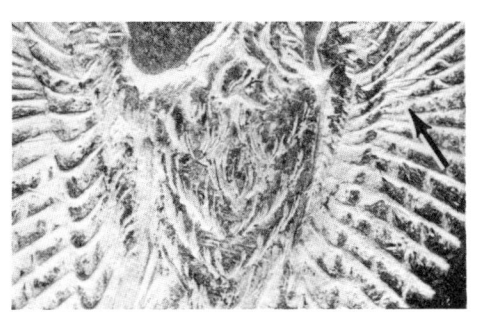

15 R Lines in Eagle

1878-S

14   II 11 • B² m (Doubled LIBERTY Left)   (181)   I-2   R-3
Reverse B²m – Portions of eagle's wings over polished in middle. Feather engraved between eagle's right wing and leg. R in TRUST not broken.

15   II 11 • B² n (Lines in Eagle)   I-2   R-3
Obverse II 11 – LIBERTY slightly doubled to left. P in PLURIBUS has bulge at top right outside, R is doubled slightly on left side and bottom crossbar of B is thin. 7 in date doubled at top and right side.
Reverse B²n – Die polishing marks are strongly evident as heavy lines in middle of both wings and two diagonal lines between eagle's legs. Feathers engraved between eagle's right wing and leg. R in TRUST partially broken.

16   II 12 • B² o (Die Scratch on Wing)   (184)   I-2   R-4
Obverse II 12 – E PLURIB letters in motto doubled on right side and some on bottom. 18-8 in date doubled slightly on bottom. Number 3 stars doubled on right and left. LIBERTY doubled slightly to left.
Reverse B²o – Vertical die scratch through lower part of eagle's right wing. Some specimens show a die chip in middle of eagle's breast. Feather engraved between eagle's right wing and leg. R in TRUST not broken.

17   II 13 • B² d (Doubled D)   (184)   I-2   R-4
Obverse II 13 – Bottom of die overpolished with shallow date and missing portions of lower hairline. First 8 in date has small die chip on right side between loops. 7 has raised slanted dash at very bottom on some specimens.
Reverse B² d – D in DOLLAR doubled at left top outside and at left and right bottom outside. R in TRUST not broken.

18   II 1 • B² e (Extra Wing in Feathers)   (184)   I-3   R-4
Obverse II 1 – Point of number four star on right only partially broken.
Reverse B²e – Fine engraving lines in middle of both eagle's wings where die was overpolished due to incorrect basining.

19   II 14 • B² b (Doubled Motto, Die Gouge)   (181)   I-3   R-4
Obverse II 14 – LIBERTY slightly doubled with shift up. Point on number 4 star on right is broken off. Nostril and eyelid doubled. Letters of E PL-R-BUS and U of motto doubled. Thick broad horizontal die gouge across wheat leaves and top cotton leaf. Field is slightly concave.
Reverse B²b – Arm of R completely missing in TRUST with open G in God. Die extremely overpolished with letters of UNITED STATES very shallow and a number of leaves disconnected in the wreath. Small dots of metal all over eagle.

20   II 15 • B² o (Concave Obverse)   (184)   I-2   R-3
Obverse II 15 – Field slightly concave, especially near the rim. Point of number 4 star on right broken off. Die chips on surface of E.

21   II 16 • B²f (Concave Obverse, Doubled Reverse)   I-3   R-3
Obverse II 16 – Field slightly concave, especially near the rim. Point of number 4 star on right broken off. LIBERTY doubled slightly to left. E, P and B in E PLURIBUS slightly doubled at top with B also doubled and broken at bottom.
Reverse B²f – Left wreath and lower part of right wreath doubled towards rim. UNITED STATES, ONE DOLLAR and left star doubled towards rim. Feather engraved between eagles right wing and leg.

22   II 19 • B²g (Doubled Motto, S Set Left)   I-3   R-3
Reverse B²g – Small III S mint mark set left and slightly high. R in TRUST not broken.

23   II 1 • B²h (S/S Left)   I-3   R-3
Reverse B²h – III S mint mark doubled with short diagonal line at top middle inside of upper loop and curved line within lower loop. R of TRUST is partially broken. Eagle's left wing slightly overpolished in center.

24   II 6 • B²a (Doubled LIBERTY Down)   (185)   I-3   R-3
Reverse B²a – Portions of eagle's left wing overpolished in middle.

16, 20, and 28 R
Engraved Feather

16 R Line in Eagle's
Wing

16 R Die Chip

1878-S

16 O Doubled Motto

17 O Dash 7, Overpolished Die

18 R Extra Wing Feathers

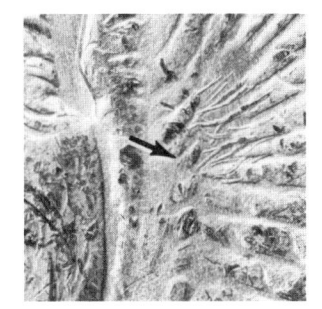

18 R Extra Wing Feathers

17 R Doubled D

20 O Die Chips on E

19 R Shallow Letters

19 O Die Gouge

19 O Doubled Motto

21 O Doubled B

22 R S Set Left

23 R S/S Left

21 R Engraved Feather

169

1878-S

| 25 | II 1 • B²e (S Set High and Right) | (184) | I-2 | R-3 |

| 26 | II 1 • B¹a (Long Center Arrow Shaft) | (186) | I-3 | R-7 |

Reverse B¹a – Normal die of 1878-P type B¹ with long center arrow shaft. Small III S mint mark set slightly to right with slight tilt to left.

| 27 | II 1 • B¹b (Long Center Arrow Shaft) | (185) | I-3 | R-7 |

Reverse B¹b – Small III S mint mark centered and upright.

| 28 | II 1 • B²o (Die Scratch on Wing) | (184) | I-2 | R-4 |

| 29 | II 17 • B²q Tripled LIBERTY) | (184) | I-2 | R-4 |

Obverse II 17 – LIBERTY tripled with images to left and right. Doubled eyelid and nostril.
Reverse B²q – Feather engraved between eagle's right wing and leg. R in TRUST not broken.

| 30 | II 18 • B²r (Quadrupled LIBERTY) | (185) | I-2 | R-3 |

Obverse II 18 – LIBERTY quadrupled with images to left, right and above.
Reverse B² r – Feather engraved between eagle's right wing and leg. R in TRUST not broken. Portions of eagle's left wing overpolished in middle.

| 31 | II 1 • B²s (Engraved Wing Feather) | (184) | I-2 | R-3 |

Reverse B²s – Feather engraved between eagle's right wing and leg. R in TRUST not broken.

| 32 | II 1 • B²t (Engraved Wing Feather) | (184) | I-2 | R-3 |

Reverse B²t – Feather engraved between eagle's right wing and leg. R in TRUST not broken.

| 33 | II 1 • B²u (Engraved Wing Feather) | (184) | I-2 | R-3 |

Reverse B²u – Feather engraved between eagle's right wing and leg. R in TRUST not broken.

| 34 | II 1 • B²v (Engraved Wing Feather) | (184) | I-2 | R-3 |

Reverse B²v – Feather engraved between eagle's right wing and leg. R in TRUST not broken. UNITED STATES OF doubled slightly towards rim.

| 35 | II 1 • B²w (Engraved Wing Feather) | (181) | I-2 | R-3 |

Reverse B²w – Feather engraved between eagle's right wing and leg. R in TRUST broken.

26 R B¹ Reverse, Tilted S

27 R B¹ Reverse

29 R Engraved Feather

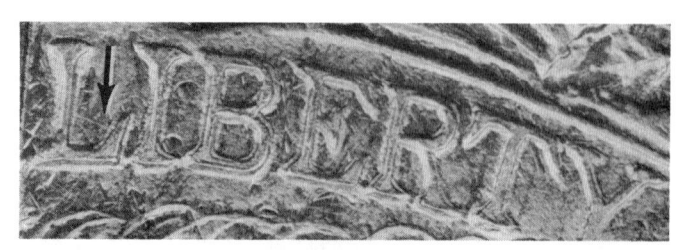

29 O Doubled LIBERTY

30 O Doubled LIBERTY

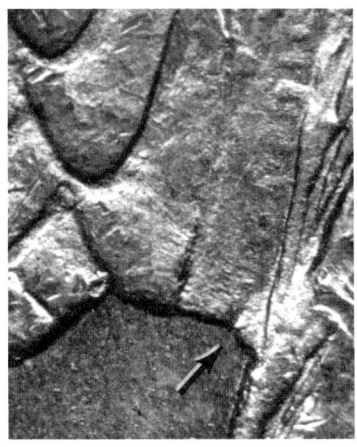

1878-S

30 R Engraved Feather

31 R Engraved Feather

32 R Engraved Feather

33 R Engraved Feather

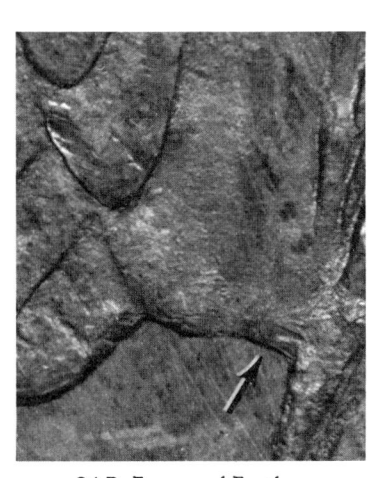

34 R Engraved Feather

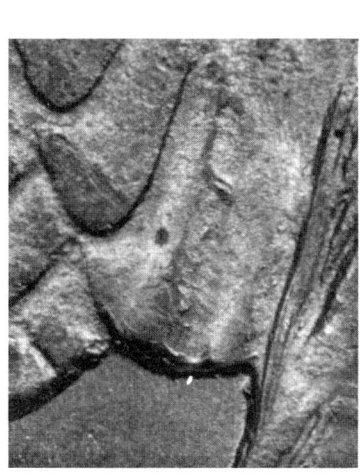

35 R Engraved Feather

36 R Engraved Feather

36 R Engraved Feathers
Left Wing

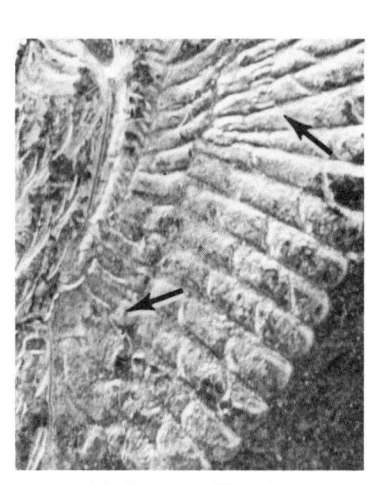

36 R Engraved Feathers
Right Wing

1878-S

36 II 1 • B²x (Engraved Wing Feathers) (184) I-2 R-3
Reverse B²x – Feather engraved between eagle's right wing and leg plus portions of feathers engraved in center of wings and next to body on eagle's left wing. R in TRUST broken.

37 II 1 • B²y (Engraved Wing Feather) (184) I-2 R-3
Reverse B²y – Feather engraved between eagle's right wing and leg. R in TRUST broken.

38 II 1 • B²z (Engraved Wing Feather) (184) I-2 R-3
Reverse B²z – Feather engraved between eagle's right wing and leg. R in TRUST broken.

39 II 1 • B²aa (Engraved Wing Feather) (181) I-2 R-3
Reverse B²aa – Feather engraved between eagle's right wing and leg. R in TRUST broken.

40 II 1 • B²ab (Engraved Wing Feather) (184) I-2 R-3
Reverse B²ab – Feather engraved between eagle's right wing and leg. R in TRUST broken.

41 II 19 • B²a (Doubled LIBERTY Up) (184) I-2 R-3
Obverse II 19 – LIBERTY doubled up.
Reverse B²a – Heavy vertical polishing lines in eagle's right wing.

42 II 20 • B²ac (Engraved Wing Feather) (184) I-2 R-3
Obverse II 20 – Doubled L-R-B U in Motto. Broken 4 star on right.
Reverse B²ac – Feather engraved between eagle's right wing and leg. R in TRUST not broken.

43 II 1 • B²r (Engraved Wing feather) (185) I-2 R-3

44 II 1 • B²j (Engraved Wing Feather) (184) I-2 R-3

45 II 1 • B²ad (Engraved Wing Feather) (184) I-2 R-3
Obverse II 1 – Small die chips below eyelid, on nose, behind eye and on cheek.
Reverse B²ad – Feather engraved between eagle's right wing and leg. R in TRUST slightly broken.

46 II 1 • B²i (Engraved Wing Feather) (184) I-2 R-3

47 II 1 • B²ae (Engraved Wing Feather) (184) I-2 R-3
Reverse B²ae – Feather engraved between eagle's right wing and leg. R in TRUST broken. Slightly doubled bottom inside of ITED STATES F and tops of IN GOD W.

48 II 1 • B²af (Engraved Wing Feather, S Tilted Right) (184) I-2 R-3
Obverse II 1 – Slight doubling of B in PLURIBUS.
Reverse B²af – Feather engraved between eagle's right wing and leg. R in TRUST partially broken. III S mint mark set slightly high with tilt to right.

49 II 1 • B²ag (Engraved Wing Feather) (184) I-2 R-3
Reverse B²ag – Feather engraved between eagle's right wing and leg and extending up towards body.

50 II 21 • B²ah (Tripled Eyelid, Engraved Wing Feather) (184) I-2 R-3
Obverse II 21 – Eyelid tripled in front of eye just below front of eyelid. 7 doubled on right side of vertical shaft. Broken 4th star on right.
Reverse B²ah – Feather engraved between eagle's right wing and leg extending upwards to top of wing with dots on surface.

37 R Engraved Feather

38 R Engraved Feather

39 R Engraved Feather

1878-S

40 R Engraved Feather

41 R Gouges in Wing

42 R Engraved Feather

41 O Doubled LIBERTY

42 O Doubled B

45 R Engraved Feather

47 R Engraved Feather

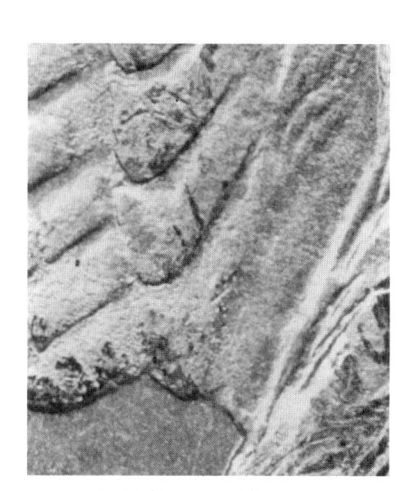

48 R Engraved Feather

48 R S Tilted Right

| 51 | II 1 • B²ai (Engraved Wing Feather) | (184) | I-2 | R-3 |

Reverse B²ai – Feather engraved between eagle's right wing and leg.

| 52 | II 1 • B²aj (Engraved Wing Feather) | (184) | I-2 | R-3 |

Reverse B²aj – Feather engraved between eagle's right wing and leg. R in TRUST broken.

| 53 | II 1 • B²ak (Engraved Wing Feather) | (184) | I-2 | R-3 |

Reverse B²ak – Feather engraved between eagle's right wing and leg. R in TRUST not broken.

1878-S

54   II 22 • B²a (Doubled Profile)   (181)   I-2   R-3
Obverse II 22 – Liberty head profile doubled on nose, lips and chin. First four stars on left doubled towards rim. LIBERTY doubled slightly on left.

55   II 1 • B²aj (Engraved Wing Feather)   (181)   I-2   R-3
Reverse B²aj – Feather engraved between eagle's right wing and leg. R in TRUST not broken.

56   III 1 • B¹c (Long Center Arrow Shaft)   (184)   I-3   R-7
Reverse B¹c – Small III S mint mark set high, slightly to left and upright.

49 R Engraved Feather

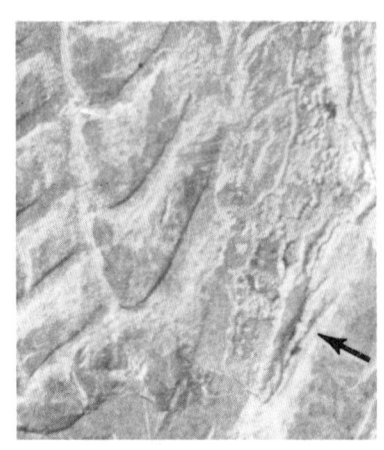

50 R Engraved Feather

51 R Engraved Feather

52 R Engraved Feather

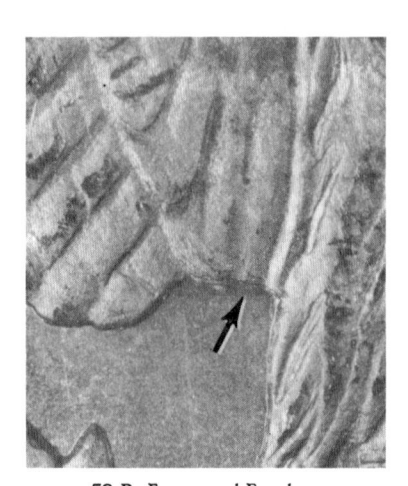

53 R Engraved Feather

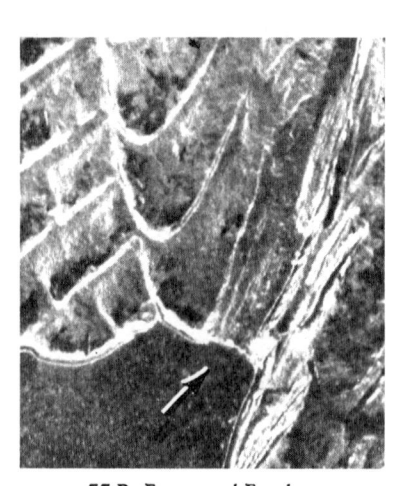

55 R Engraved Feather

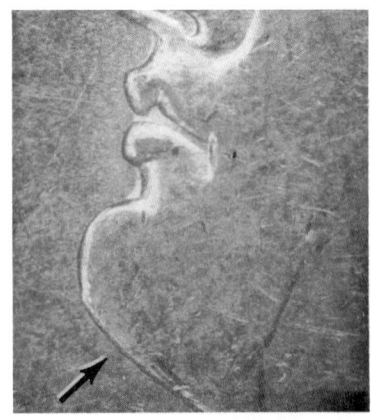

54 O Doubled Profile

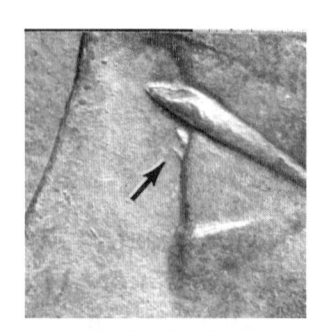

50 O Tripled Eyelid

1879-P

This was the first year that the C³ reverse with round breast and slanted arrow feathers was used exclusively. Usually this date is fully struck. Luster is average because of long use of dies to achieve high mintage. Quite a number of minor die varieties exist but none command significant premiums.

Fully proof-like specimens are fairly scarce for this date and the later 1880-1884-P mints. Deep mirror cameos exist for some of the proof-likes. Proofs are usually much better than the 1878-P proofs with deep mirrors and excellent contrast.

1	III² 1 • C³ a (Closed 9)		I-1	R-1

Obverse III² 1 – Normal die of III² type with closed 9 in date. Knob of 9 touches body.
Reverse C³ a – Normal die of C³ type.

1A	III²1 • C³ a (Pitted Reverse)	(180)	I-2	R-3

Reverse C³ a – Pitted die to right of wreath bow and on right side of eagle's tail feathers.

2	III²2 • C³ a (Open 9)		I-1	R-2

Obverse III²2 – Normal die with open 9 in date. Knob of 9 does not touch body.

3	III²3 • C³ a (Doubled 879)	(181)	I-2	R-4

Obverse III² 3 – Doubled 879 in date. Slight doubling on right outside of both loops of 8. 7 doubled on lower right side and at top with dash below shaft. Both loops of 9 doubled on outside left. Closed and open 9 varieties.

4	III²4 • C³ a (Doubled 187)	(180)	I-2	R-4

Obverse III²4 – Doubled 187 in date. 1 is doubled strongly at bottom right and on right side of lower crossbar. 8 is doubled slightly at top right outside of both loops. 7 is doubled on right side and at top right. Open 9.

5	III²5 • C³ a (Doubled Date)		I-2	R-4

Obverse III² 5 – Date doubled at top with all numbers doubled at top outside. Open 9 variety.

6	III²6 • C³ a (Doubled 79)		I-2	R-4

Obverse III² 6 – Doubled 79 in date. Seven is doubled to the left with two points at the lower left of the top crossbar and a doubled stem. The 9 is doubled outside and inside at ten o'clock. Open 9 variety. Some specimens show a die chip between the loops of the 8 on the left side.

7	III²7 • C³ a (Doubled 9)	(179)	I-2	R-3

Obverse III²7 – Upper left outside of 9 is doubled. Some specimens show a die chip between the loops of the 8 on the left side. Open 9 variety.

1A R Pitted Wreath

3 O Doubled 879

7 O Doubled 9

4 O Doubled 187

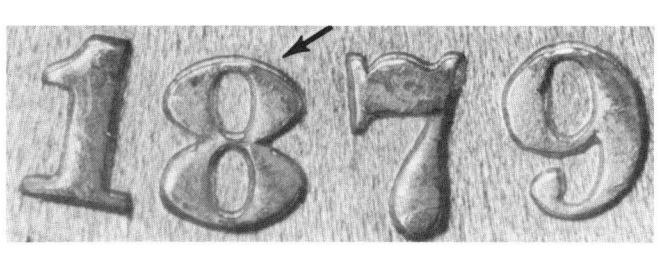

5 O Doubled Date

1879-P

8 III²8 • C³a (Doubled 1-79) (179) I-2 R-3
Obverse III²8 – Doubled 1-79 in date. The right side of stem of the 1 and 7 are doubled. The lower left side of upper loop of the 9 is doubled.

9 III²9 • C¹a (Doubled 8-9) I-2 R-3
Obverse III²9 – Doubled 8-9 in date. 8 is doubled slightly on lower left outside of upper loop and bottom right outside of lower loop. 9 doubled strongly on left side of upper loop. Closed 9.

10 III²10 • C³a (Doubled 1) I-2 R-3
Obverse III²10 – 1 in date is doubled at top left of upper serif and on top left and right of bottom crossbar. Open 9 variety.

11 III²11 • C³a (Doubled 7) I-2 R-3
Obverse III²11 – 7 is doubled on left side of upper left serif and on right side of lower left serif. Closed 9.

12 III²12 • C³a (Doubled Date, Tripled 1) I-2 R-4
Obverse III²12 – Entire date doubled. 1 doubled on right and left sides of vertical shaft, on lower surface of top crossbar and is tripled on middle and right bottom of lower crossbar. 8 doubled on surface of right side of lower loop and top left of lower loop opening. 7 doubled strongly on lower right side of vertical shaft. Lower left outside of upper loop of 9 is doubled. Open 9 variety.

13 III²13 • C³a (Doubled 18-9) (179) I-2 R-3
Obverse III²13 – Doubled 18-9 in date. 1 is doubled slightly at top left point, on surface of top crossbar and strongly at top left and right of bottom crossbar. The arc shows at top inside of lower loop of 8. 9 is doubled slightly at left outside of upper loop. Closed 9 variety.

14 III²14 • C³a (Doubled 879) I-2 R-3
Obverse III²14 – Doubled 879 in date. 8 is doubled at top inside of lower loop. 7 is doubled on right side of lower serif. 9 is doubled on left outside of upper loop. Closed 9 variety.

15 III²15 • C³a (Doubled Date) (180) I-2 R-3
Obverse III²15 – All digits in the date are doubled. 1 is doubled slightly on the lower surface of the upper crossbar. 8 doubled at bottom right outside of lower loop. 7 doubled slightly at right of lower serif and strongly at bottom right of shaft. 9 doubled on left outside of both loops. Open 9 variety.

16 III²16 • C³a (Doubled Date) (180) I-2 R-3
Obverse III²16 – All digits in date are doubled. 1 is doubled at upper left as vertical step on side of serif. 8 is slightly doubled on lower left outside of upper loop with die chip between loops on left side. Right side of 7 lower serif is doubled with bottom of crossbar slightly doubled. Loops of 9 are both slightly doubled on left outside. Open 9 variety.

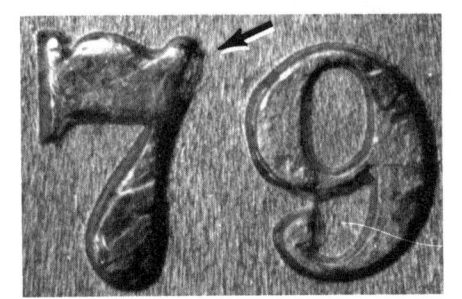

6 O Doubled 79

10 O Doubled 1

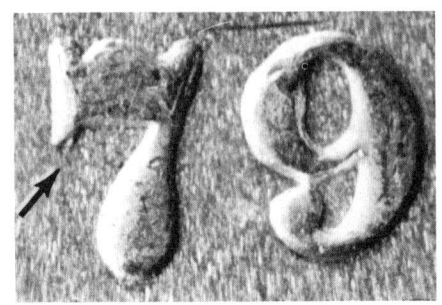

11 O Doubled 7

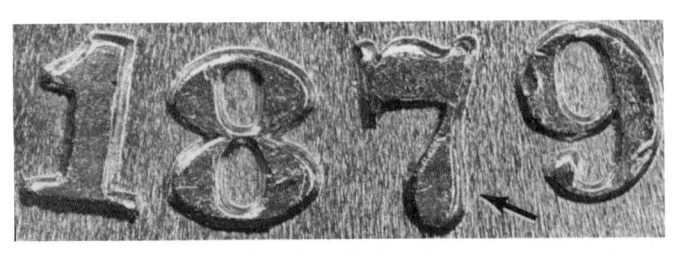

8 O Doubled 1-79

9 O Doubled 8-9

1879-P

17   III²17 • C³b (Doubled Date)   (179)   I-3   R-4

Obverse III²17 – Entire date is strongly doubled at 10 o'clock. 1 is doubled at top left and on left side of vertical shaft. 8 is doubled at left outside and right inside of both loops with slight doubling at bottom right outside of lower loop. 7 doubled at very top, on left side of crossbar, at top left vertical shaft and faintly at bottom right. 9 doubled at left outside and right inside of both loops.

Reverse C³b – Centers of both eagle's wings overpolished with fine diagonal polishing lines on eagle's left wing.

12 O Tripled 1, Doubled Date

13 O Doubled 18-9

14 O Doubled 8-9

15 O Doubled Date

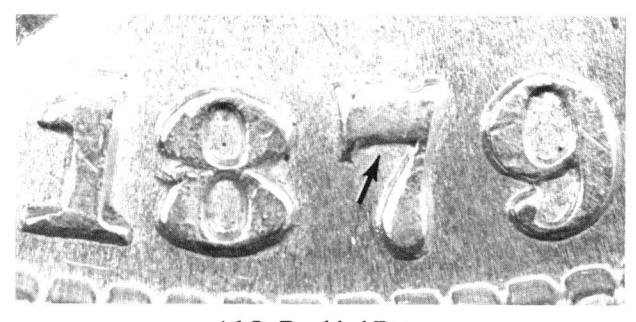

16 O Doubled Date

17 O Doubled Date

17 R Overpolished Wing

18 O Doubled 187

177

1879-P

18   III²18 • C³a (Doubled 187)   (180)   I-2   R-3
Obverse III²18 – Doubled 187 in date at top. 1 doubled at top and left corners as two steps. 8 doubled at top outside and bottom inside of upper loop. 7 doubled slightly on right side of top serif. Open 9 variety.

19   III²19 • C³a (Doubled Date)   (180)   I-2   R-3
Obverse III²19 – All digits in date are doubled. 1 is doubled above lower crossbar and slightly at top of upper crossbar. 8 doubled slightly at bottom left outside of lower loop. 7 doubled all across very top of crossbar. 9 doubled slightly at bottom left outside of lower loop. Heavy vertical polishing lines inside of ear and in hair.

20   III²20 • C³a (Doubled Date)   (179)   I-3   R-4
Obverse III²20 – Entire date strongly doubled. 1 doubled at very top, on top right of vertical shaft and at top on both sides of bottom crossbar. 8 doubled at top and lower left outside of upper loop and at right inside of both loops. 7 doubled at very top, on left side of crossbar and at top left on right side of vertical shaft. 9 doubled on left outside of both loops and at right inside of lower loop. First three stars on left doubled towards rim.

21   III²21 • C³a (Doubled Date)   (178)   I-2   R-3
Obverse III²21 – Entire date slightly doubled. 1 doubled at lower right side of vertical shaft and at bottom and right side of lower crossbar. 8 doubled slightly at left inside and lower right outside of lower loop. 7 doubled across very top and right side of vertical shaft. 9 doubled at left outside of both loops.

22   III²22 • C³a (Doubled Date)   (179)   I-2   R-3
Obverse III²22 – Entire date is slightly doubled. 1 doubled at top and left corner as two steps. 8 doubled at lower left outside of upper loop and bottom right outside of lower loop. 7 doubled at top left and right. 9 doubled at left outside of both loops.

23   III²23 • C³b (Doubled Date and Olive Leaves)   (181)   I-2   R-3
Obverse III²23 – Entire date is doubled. 1 doubled slightly at lower left of base. 8 doubled at left inside and right outside of both loops. 7 doubled slightly at top outside and strongly at lower right side of vertical shaft. 9 doubled at left outside of both loops.
Reverse C³b – Top olive leaves are doubled on left side as thin lines.

24   III²24 • C³a (Doubled 1-9)   (179)   I-2   R-3
Obverse III²24 – Doubled 1-9 in date. 1 doubled slightly below bottom of crossbar. 9 doubled at left outside of both loops. Open 9 variety. Number 4 – 7 left stars doubled slightly towards rim.

25   III²25 • C³a (Doubled Date)   (180)   I-2   R-3
Obverse III²25 – Entire date is doubled. 1 doubled slightly below upper crossbar. 8 doubled strongly on lower right outside of lower loop. 7 doubled at right of lower serif and strongly on lower right of vertical shaft. 9 doubled at left outside of both loops.

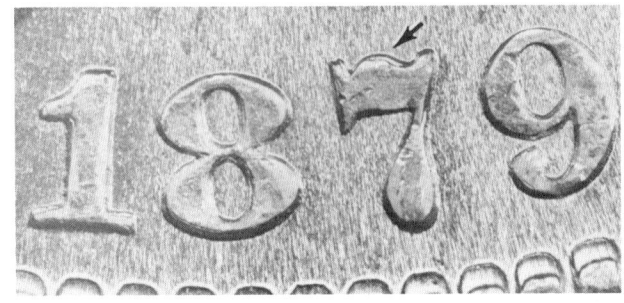

19 O Doubled Date

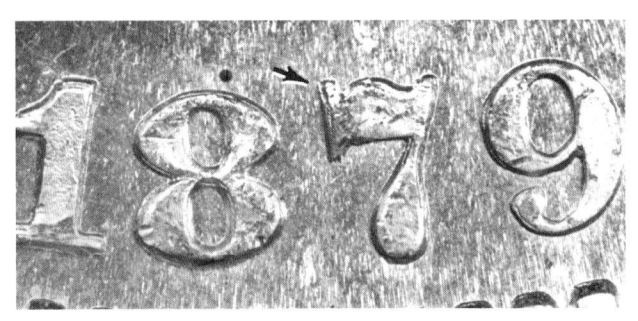

20 O Doubled Date

21 O Doubled Date

22 O Doubled Date

1879-P

23 O Doubled Date

23 R Doubled Olive Leaves

24 O Doubled 1-9

25 O Doubled Date

26   **III² 26 • C³ a (Doubled Date)**   (181)   I-2   R-3
Obverse III² 26 – Entire date is doubled. 1 doubled slightly at top right of vertical shaft. 8 is doubled strongly at right outside of lower loop. 7 doubled on left side of crossbar and strongly on lower right of vertical shaft with dash below shaft. 9 doubled slightly on left outside of upper loop.

27   **III² 27 • C³ a (Doubled 879)**   (179)   I-2   R-3
Obverse III² 27 – Doubled 878 in date. 8 doubled slightly at left inside and lower right outside of lower loop. 7 doubled at lower right of vertical shaft. 9 doubled at left outside of lower loop.

28   **III² 28 • C³ a (Doubled 8-9)**   (180)   I-2   R-3
Obverse III² 28 – Doubled 8-9 in date. 8 doubled slightly at bottom right outside of lower loop. 9 doubled at left outside of both loops.

29   **III² 23 • C³ a (Doubled Date)**   (179)   I-2   R-3
Obverse III² 23 – Die has been lightly polished with some missing lower hair detail.
Reverse C³ a – Die has been lightly polished with some disconnected wreath leaves.

30   **III² 29 • C³ a (Doubled 879)**   (179)   I-2   R-3
Obverse III² 29 – Double 879 in date. 8 doubled slightly at left inside and both loops. 7 doubled on right side of vertical shaft on surface. 9 doubled on left outside of both loops.

31   **III² 1 • C³ c (Double Reverse)**   (179)   I-2   Proof
Reverse C³ c – Doubled UNIT, ES OF, AMERICA, and ONE DOLLAR toward rim. TED, O, ERICA, ONE DOLL also doubled on side toward coin center, left and right wreaths doubled at top outside.

32   **III² 30 • C³ a (Doubled 1-79)**   (179)   I-2   R-3
Obverse III² 30 – 1-79 in date. 1 doubled below upper crossbar as a notch, on lower right side of vertical shaft and below lower crossbar as notch on left side and notch on right end. 7 doubled slightly on lower right side of vertical shaft. 9 doubled on left outside of upper loop.

33   **III² 31 • C³ a (Doubled 8-9, Pitted Left Wreath)**   (179)   I-2   R-3
Obverse III² 31 – Doubled 8-9 in date. 8 doubled on left inside of upper loop. 9 doubled on left outside of both loops.
Reverse C³ a – Pitted die from rust in lower left wreath and above D of DOLLAR.

34   **III² 7 • C³ d (Doubled 9 and Reverse Lettering)**   (179)   I-2   R-3
Reverse C³ d – Doubled UNITED STATES OF AMERICA, ONE DOLLAR, stars and IN GOD WE TRUST on sides and top outside of left wreath.

1879-P

26 O Doubled Date

27 O Doubled 879

28 O Doubled 8-9

30 O Doubled 879

Proof 31 R Doubled Legend

32 O Doubled 1-79

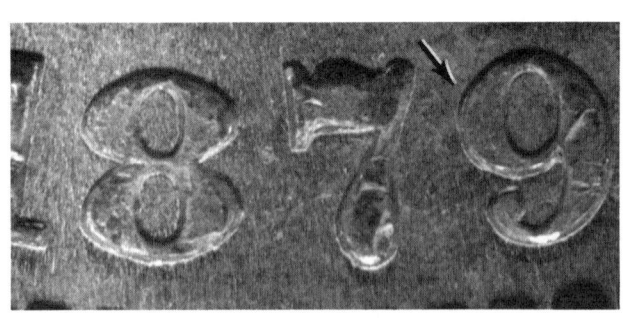

33 O Doubled 8-9

33 R Pitted Wreath

34 R Doubled Reverse Lettering

35   III²32 • C³a (Doubled Date and Stars)   (179)   I-3   R-3
   Obverse III²32 – Entire date is doubled. 1 doubled below top and bottom crossbar. 8 doubled at lower left outside of upper loop and right inside and bottom outside of lower. 7 doubled slightly at bottom of stem. 9 doubled at left outside of upper loop. All left and right stars doubled towards rim. Liberty head profile of forehead, nose, lips and chin slightly doubled.

35 O Doubled Date

1879-CC

This is the first of the more expensive key date Morgan dollars. Not many die varieties are known for this date. The most prominent is VAM 3 with a large CC over small CC, the so-called capped CC variety. This is the only major die variety in the Morgan series that is price discounted. Apparently the large CC was punched over the small CC of the type used for the 1878-CC and attempts were made to obliterate the small CC remains with engraving tools. The result is a messy looking CC which in the past was mistaken for a counterfeit CC.

Generally this issue is strongly struck although some slightly weak strikes exist. Although scarce in uncirculated condition, a fairly large percentage of these are full proof-like with average to good contrast. But deep mirror cameos are quite rare.

1   III²1 • C³a (Closed 9)   I-1   R-3
   Obverse III²1 – Normal die of III² type with closed 9 in date.
   Reverse C³a – Normal die of C³ type with V CC mint mark shifted to the left.

2   III²2 • C³b (Open 9)   (177)   I-1   R-3
   Obverse III²2 – Normal die with open 9 in date.
   Reverse C³b – Normal die with V CC mint mark shifted slightly and tilted to the left. Bottom of G in GOD partially filled.

3   III²3 • C³c (Large Over Small CC)   I-3   R-3
   Obverse III²3 – 18 in date doubled strongly at top. Open 9 doubled slightly at bottom.
   Reverse C³c – Metal above and within the CC mint mark, a large over small mint mark. G in GOD filled on some specimens.

4   III²1 • C³d (Doubled C)   (178)   I-2   R-3
   Obverse III²1 – Die chip on the left between the loops of the first 8 in date. Closed 9 variety.
   Reverse C³d – V CC mint mark shifted to left with large spacing between C's. Right C is doubled on left inside.

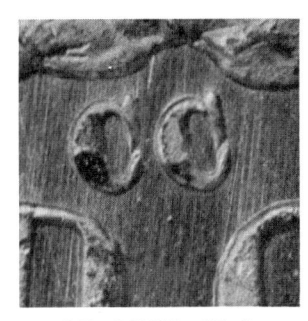

3 O Doubled 18

2 R CC Tilted Left 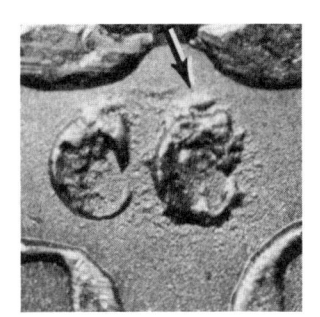   3 R Large Over Small CC   4 R Doubled C

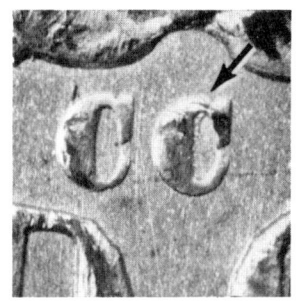

181

1879-O

The first issue for the New Orleans Morgan dollar is usually characterized by a strong strike and good luster. Some soft strikes with slightly weak hair over the ear and breast feathers exist, however. Although a number of minor varieties exist the only major one for this date is VAM 4 O/O horizontal which is possibly a tripled O. The remains of a horizontal O shows within the normal O mint mark and it brings some price premium. There are also two size mint marks but both are common and do not bring any premium.

Proof-likes are fairly scarce for this issue but some deep mirror cameos exist. Many coins of this issue were lightly circulated and then put back into storage vaults. Always carefully examine purported uncirculated specimens for gray areas and traces of wear.

Twelve branch mint proofs were struck for this date to commemorate the reopening of the New Orleans Mint. Four proofs are known to have survived and two of these are very deep mirror cameos.

1   III²1 • C³a (Closed 9)   (176)   I-1   R-2
Obverse III²1 – Normal die of III² type with closed 9. Some specimens show die chip between loops of 8 on left side.
Reverse C³a – Normal die of C³ type with tall, oval medium mint mark centered and upright.

2   III²2 • C³a (Open 9)   (176)   I-1   R-2
Obverse III²2 – Normal die of III² type with open 9 in date.

3   III²3 • C³b (Large O)   (176)   I-1   R-2
Obverse III²3 – The loop of the 9 is doubled to the left. Closed and open 9 varieties.
Reverse C³b – Normal die of C³ type with large, IV O centered mint mark.

4   III²4 • C³c (O/O horizontal)   (176)   I-3   R-5
Obverse III²4 – 9 in date has the upper loop strongly doubled to the left. Open 9 variety.
Reverse C³c – Medium II O centered mint mark over horizontal O. The horizontal O shows as lines at the top and bottom of the opening. Possibly triple O with first two punches high and low.

5   III²5 • C³a (Doubled 9)   (176)   I-2   R-3
Obverse III²5 – 9 in date is doubled at bottom lower left. Open 9 variety.

6   III²5 • C³d (O Tilted Right)   (176)   I-2   R-3
Reverse C³d – Centered II O mint mark tilted right.

7   III²2 • C³e (O Tilted Left)   (176)   I-2   R-3
Reverse C³e – Centered II O mint mark tilted slightly left.

1A O Die Chips in Date

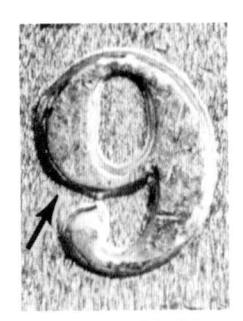

3 O Doubled 9

4 O Doubled 9

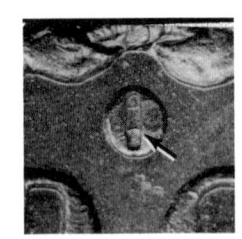

4 R O/O Horizontal

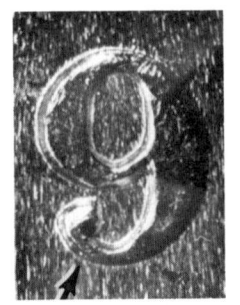

5 O Doubled 9

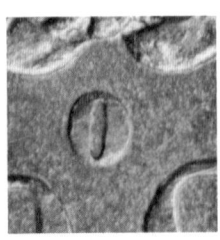

6 R O Tilted Right

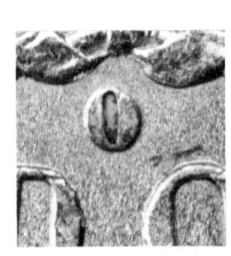

7 R O Tilted Left

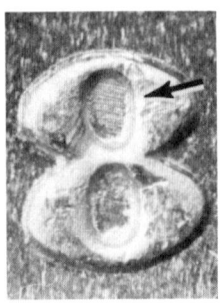

8A O Die Chips in 8

11 R O Set Left

1879-O

| 8 | III²2 • C³b (Large O) | (176) | I-1 | R-2 |

| 8A | III²2 • C³b (Die Chips in 8) | (176) | I-1 | R-3 |

Obverse III²2 – Die chips with horizontal polishing marks inside upper loop of 8 and at top and bottom inside of lower loop.

| 9 | III²5 • C³b (Doubled 9) | (176) | I-2 | R-3 |

| 10 | III²6 • C³b (Doubled 8-9) | (176) | I-2 | R-3 |

Obverse III²6 – Doubled 8-9 in date. 8 doubled at left and top inside of lower loop with polishing marks inside of lower loop and lower right inside of upper loop. 9 doubled on top surface of left outside of lower loop.

| 11 | III²6 • C³f (Doubled 8-9) | (176) | I-2 | R-3 |

Reverse C³f – IV O mint mark set left and tilted slightly right.

| 12 | III²7 • C³b (Doubled 87) | (176) | I-2 | R-4 |

Obverse III²7 – Doubled 87 in date. 8 doubled slightly on lower outside of lower loop and slightly at top inside of upper loop. 7 doubled on right side and slightly at bottom of crossbar.

| 13 | III²8 • C³e (Doubled Date) | (176) | I-2 | R-3 |

Obverse III²8 – Entire date is doubled. 1 doubled at very top. 8 doubled slightly at very top and right outside of upper loop and very slightly on right outside of lower loop. 7 doubled slightly on right side of left serif, top outside of crossbar and right outside of vertical stem. 9 doubled on left outside of upper loop.

| 14 | III²9 • C³b (Doubled 879) | (176) | I-2 | R-3 |

Obverse III²9 – Doubled 879 in date. 8 doubled at top right inside of lower loop. 7 doubled at right side below crossbar and as a short spike on right side of lower serif. 9 doubled slightly on surface at left outside of both loops.

| 15 | III²10 • C³b (Doubled Date) | (176) | I-2 | R-3 |

Obverse III²10 – Entire date doubled slightly on top surface. 1 doubled at very top and half of loop at left side of bottom crossbar. Right outside of upper loop of 8 is slightly doubled. Bottom of 7 crossbar is doubled. Upper and lower loops of 9 are doubled on left outside.

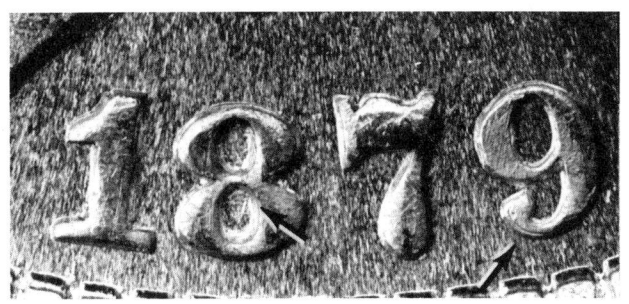

10 O Doubled 8-9

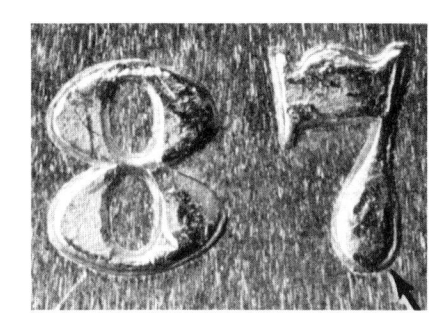

12 O Doubled 87

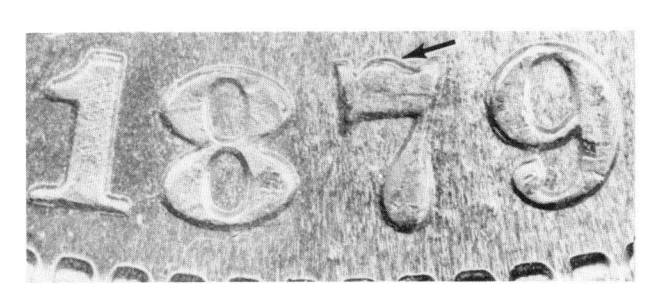

13 O Doubled Date

14 O Doubled 879

15 O Doubled Date

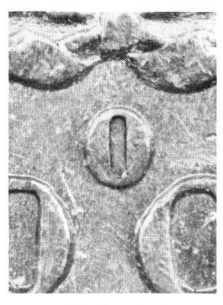

16 R Low O

1879-O

16 III²3 • C³g (Doubled 9, Low O Set Right) (176) I-2 R-3
Reverse C³g – IV O mint mark set low, upright and slightly to the right.

17 III²11 • C³a (Doubled 87) (176) I-2 R-4
Obverse III²11 – Doubled 87 in date. 8 doubled slightly at the top outside and left inside of lower loop. 7 doubled on right side of vertical stem.

18 III²12 • C³h (Doubled 8-9, Low O) (176) I-2 R-3
Obverse III²12 – Doubled 8-9 in date. 8 doubled at bottom of lower loop. 9 doubled at left outside of both loops. Open 9 variety.
Reverse C³h – IV O mint mark set low, upright and centered.

19 III²13 • C³a (Doubled 87) (176) I-2 R-3
Obverse III²13 – Doubled 87 in date. 8 doubled slightly at bottom left outside of both loops. 7 doubled below crossbar. Open 9 variety.

20 III²7 • C³a (Doubled 87) (176) I-2 R-4

21 III²14 • C³a (Doubled 187) (176) I-2 R-3
Obverse III²14 – Doubled 187 in date. 1 slightly doubled below both crossbars. 8 doubled at lower left outside of upper loop and at bottom outside of lower loop. 7 doubled slightly below upper crossbar.

22 III²15 • C³a (Doubled 8-9) (176) I-2 R-3
Obverse III²15 – Doubled 8-9 in date. 8 doubled slightly at top outside of upper loop. 9 doubled on left outside of both loops.

23 III²16 • C³a (Tripled 8, Doubled 9) (176) I-2 R-3
Obverse III²16 – 8 tripled at left inside of upper loop. 9 doubled slightly on left outside of upper loop.

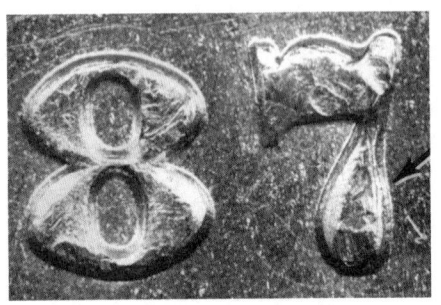

17 O Doubled 87

18 O Doubled 8-9

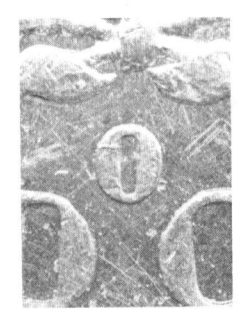

18 R O Set Low

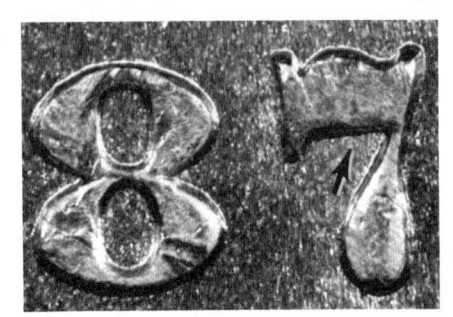

19 O Doubled 87

21 O Doubled 187

22 O Doubled 8-9

23 O Tripled 8, Doubled 9

1879-O / 1879-S

24   III² 17 • C³h (Doubled Date, Low O)   (176)   I-2   R-3

Obverse III² 17 – All digits in date are slightly doubled. 1 doubled at very bottom of base. 8 doubled at bottom outside of lower loop. 7 doubled on lower right of vertical shaft. 9 doubled on left outside of both loops. Open 9 variety.

25   III² 18 • C³b (Doubled Date)   (176)   I-2   R-3

Obverse III² 18 – All digits slightly doubled in date. 1 doubled slightly on right side of vertical shaft. 8 doubled slightly at top outside of upper loop and top right inside of lower loop. 7 doubled at very top and slightly on lower right side of vertical shaft. 9 doubled at left outside of both loops.

26   III² 3 • C²a (Doubled 9, Die Chips in Date)   (176)   I-2   R-3

Obverse III² 3 – Both loops of 9 are doubled on left outside. Die chips with polishing marks in upper part of lower loop of 8 and 9. Closed 9 variety.

27   III² 19 • C³a (Doubled 18)   (176)   I-2   R-3

Obverse III² 19 – Doubled 18 in date. 1 doubled at top left and at top left and right of bottom crossbar. First 8 doubled at top outside of upper loop.

24 O Doubled Date

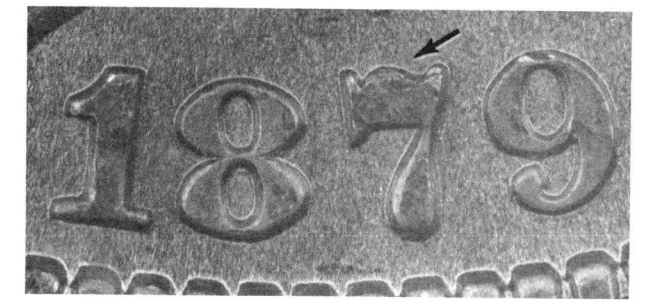

25 O Doubled Date

26 O Doubled 9

27 O Doubled 18

1879-S

This issue is usually fully struck as are most of the other common date S mints from 1880 to 1882. Occasionally a slightly weak strike will surface, however. A number of minor die varieties exist that do not command any premium. The one major variety is the B reverse with flat eagle's breast and it commands a substantial premium in all grades. Most of these flat breast reverse of 1879 have engraved wing feathers like the 1878-S. Although a number of the dies were engraved at the San Francisco Mint they do not bring any additional premium over the usual flat breast variety.

Proof-like 1879-S are available although somewhat scarcer than those of 1880-S and 1881-S. A few exhibit deep mirror cameo on both sides. Some 1879-S are only one sided proof-like and command only a slight premium over a non proof-like. Proof-like 1879-S flat breast reverse of 1878 are very scarce for the high uncirculated grades.

1   III² 1 • C³a (Closed 9)   (183)   I-1   R-2

Obverse III² 1 – Normal die of the III² type with closed 9.
Reverse C³a – Normal die of C³ type with medium IV S mint mark centered and upright.

1A   III² 1 • C³a (Polished 8)   I-1   R-3

Obverse III² 1 – 8 in date has polishing lines within loops. There are also polishing lines in lower hair.

1879-S

1B	III²1 • C²a (Hair Ribbon)	(185)	I-2	R-3

Obverse III²1 – Horizontal die gauge through lower hair.

2	III²2 • C³a (Open 9)	(185)	I-1	R-2

Obverse III²2 – Normal die of III² type with open 9.

3	III²3 • C³b (Doubled 9)	(185)	I-2	R-3

Obverse III²3 – 9 in date doubled on left side. On some specimens 8 has spike of metal on left side between loops. Open 9 variety.
Reverse C³b – Centered IV S mint mark tilted to left.

4	III²2 • B²a (PAF Reverse)	(184)	I-4	R-5

Reverse B²a – PAF reverse of B² type with small III S mint mark. R in TRUST not broken.

5	III²1 • B²b (Broken R)	(184)	I-4	R-4

Reverse B²b – PAF reverse of B² type with small III S mint mark. Broken R in TRUST with upper serif partially missing

6	III²2 • B²c (TIUST)	(184)	I-4	R-4

Reverse B²c – PAF reverse of B² type with small III S mint mark tilted slightly to the left. Broken R in TRUST to form TIUST with upper serif completely missing. Feather engraved between eagles right wing and leg.

7	III²1 • B²d (S/S Up)		I-4	R-4

Reverse B²d – Small III S mint mark doubled at bottom. PAF reverse of B² type with R in TRUST not broken.

7A	III²1 • B²d (S/S Up)	(184)	I-4	R-4

Reverse B²d – R in TRUST partially broken.

8	III²4 • B²e (Doubled 9)		I-4	R-4

Obverse III²4 – 9 in date doubled in left inside and left outside of both loops.
Reverse B²e – Feather engraved between eagle's right wing and leg. R in TRUST is partially broken.

9	III²5 • B²e (Doubled 9)	(184)	I-4	R-4

Obverse III²5 – Closed 9 in date doubled on left outside of lower loop.

10	III²6 • B²b (Doubled 79)		I-4	R-4

Obverse III²6 – 7 in date doubled at bottom of upper crossbar. Closed 9 with some showing a die flake at top left outside showing as a short arc.

11	III²1 • C³c (S/S Left)	(182)	I-3	R-3

Reverse C³c – IV S mint mark doubled with a short vertical line within the upper loop on right inside and curved line on right inside of lower loop.

12	III²7 • C³c (S/S Left)	(182)	I-3	R-3

Obverse III²7 – 7 in date slightly doubled on surface on right side of vertical shaft and on right side of bottom serif.

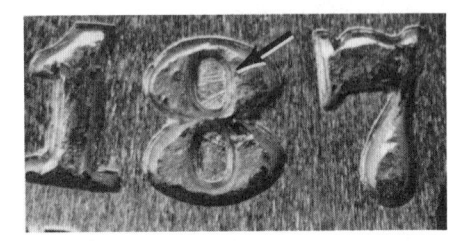

1A O Polished 8

1B O Hair Ribbon, Die Gouge

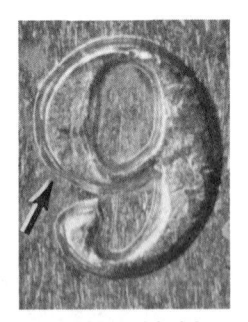

3 O Doubled 9

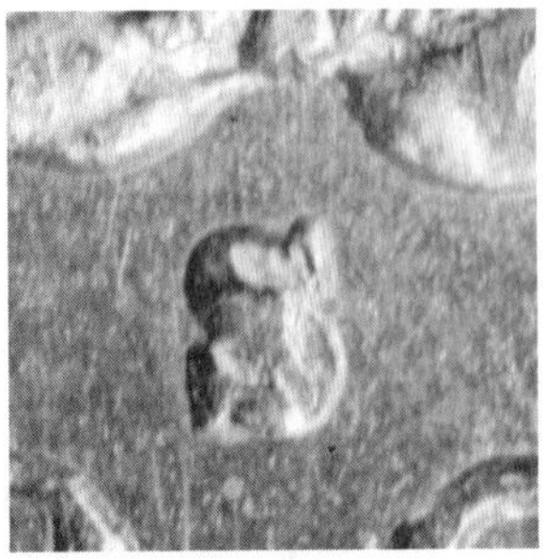

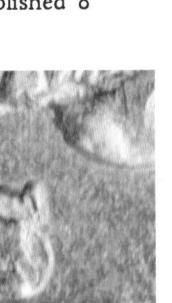

3 R S Tilted Left

5 R Broken r

6 R TIUST

1879-S

6 R Engraved Feather

7 R S/S Up

8 O Doubled 9

9 O Doubled 9

9 R Engraved Feather

10 O Doubled 79

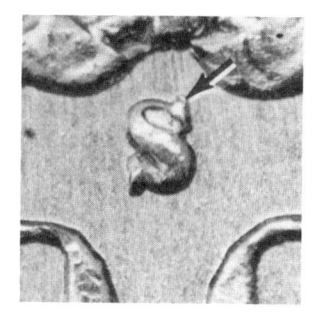

11 R S/S Left

12 O Doubled 7

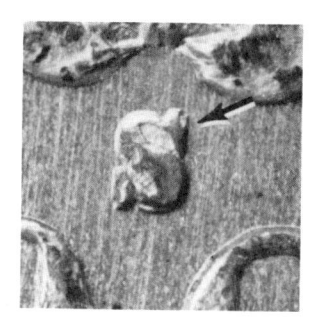

13 R S/S Right

13   III²2 • C³d (S/S Right)   (184)   I-2   R-3
       Reverse C²d – IV S mint mark doubled on all of right side of upper serif.

14   III²3 • C³e (S/S Middle)   (184)   I-2   R-3
       Reverse C³e – IV S mint mark doubled at bottom of upper loop opening as thick slanted bar and in middle of lower loop opening as a curved line.

15   III²8 • C³f (Doubled 18 and S/S)   (185)   I-2   R-3
       Obverse III²8 – 1 in date doubled at top left and right of lower crossbar. First 8 doubled at top right inside of lower loop. Open 9 variety.
       Reverse C³f – Filled IV S mint mark with top serif doubled on lower right side and slightly at very bottom.

16   III²3 • C³a (Doubled 9)   (182)   I-2   R-3

16A   III²3 • C³a (Doubled 9, Gouge in Bow)   I-2   R-4
       Reverse C³a – Triangular die gouge from lower right end towards mint mark.

17   III²9 • C³f (Doubled Date)   (185)   I-2   R-3

1879-S

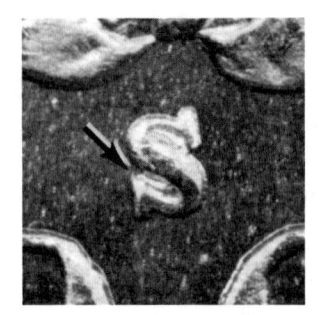

14 R S/S Middle

15 O Doubled 1

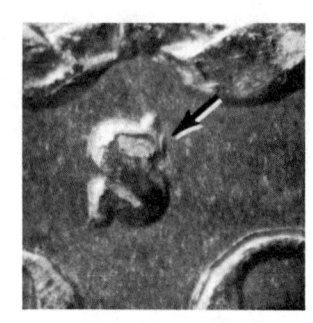

15 R Doubled S

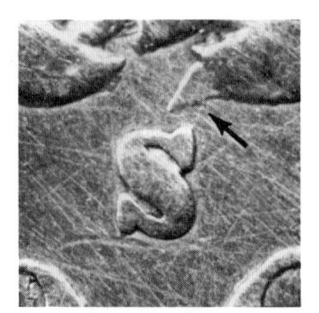

16A R Gouge in Bow

18 O Doubled Date

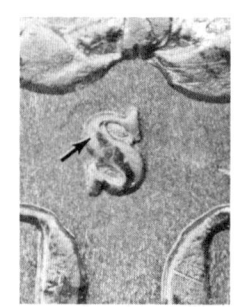

19 R S/S Tilted Left

| 18 | III²9 • C³b (Doubled Date) | | I-2 | R-3 |

Obverse III²9 – Entire date slightly doubled on surface. 1 doubled at top right. 8 doubled at bottom right outside. 7 doubled on bottom of upper serif and right side of shaft plus very bottom. 9 is doubled at left outside of both loops.

| 19 | III²1 • C³g (S/S Tilted Left) | (184) | I-2 | R-3 |

Obverse III²1 – With polishing lines in 8.
Reverse C³g – IV S mint mark doubled on left side of top loop with tilt to left.

| 20 | III²8 • C³a (Doubled 1) | (185) | I-2 | R-3 |
| 21 | III²10 • C³h (Doubled Date, S/S High) | (184) | I-3 | R-3 |

Obverse III²10 – Entire date is doubled. 1 is doubled at bottom of lower crossbar in middle. 8 doubled slightly at left inside and right outside of lower loop. 7 doubled strongly at very top and slightly on right side of vertical shaft. 9 doubled slightly at left outside of both loops.
Reverse C³h – IV S mint mark doubled with curved diagonal line in middle of upper loop opening and a diagonal line at top of lower loop opening.

| 22 | III²11 • C³b (Doubled Date) | (183) | I-2 | R-3 |

Obverse III²11 – Entire date is doubled. 1 is doubled at very top and top right of vertical shaft. 8 is doubled at top outside of upper loop and bottom right outside of lower loop. 7 is doubled below crossbar and on right side of vertical shaft. 9 is doubled on left outside of both loops.

23	III²4 • B²a (PAF Reverse, Doubled 9)		I-4	R-4
24	III²5 • B²a (PAF Reverse, Doubled 9)		I-4	R-4
25	III²6 • B²a (PAF Reverse, Doubled 7)	(184)	I-4	R-4

Obverse III²6 – Top of 9 not broken away to form arc. Some specimens show raised dots on feathers from rusted die.

| 26 | III²12 • C³a (Doubled 879) | (184) | I-2 | R-3 |

Obverse III²12 – Doubled 879 in date. 8 doubled slightly at lower left outside of upper loop and top inside of lower loop with spike of metal between loops on left of some specimens. 7 doubled in middle at top and on lower right side of shaft. 9 doubled strongly on left outside and slightly on inside of upper loop and slightly on left outside of lower loop.

| 27 | III²13 • C³b (Doubled Date) | (185) | I-2 | R-3 |

Obverse III²13 – Entire date is doubled. 1 is doubled below upper crossbar. 8 doubled at top inside of lower loop, doubled slightly at lower left outside of upper loop, and has a notch on the left outside of the upper loop. 7 doubled below upper crossbar and at very bottom of stem. 9 doubled slightly at lower left outside of both loops.

1879-S

28   III²14 • C³a (Doubled 1-9)   (185)   I-2   R-3
     Obverse III²14 – Doubled 1-9 in date. 1 doubled below upper crossbar. 9 doubled slightly on left outside of both loops.

29   III²15 • C³a (Doubled 9 and Right Obverse)   (185)   I-3   R-4
     Obverse III²15 – 9 in date doubled at left outside of upper loop. Right side doubled towards rim on wheat grain, top leaf, back of Liberty cap, BUS UNUM and 3 to 6 stars on right. Long diagonal die gouge in hair above eye.

30   III²1 • C³i (S/S Far Left)   (182)   I-3   R-3
     Reverse C³i – IV S mint mark doubled with short vertical spike at top middle of upper loop opening and curved line in middle of lower loop opening. S mint mark set slightly to right with slight tilt to left.

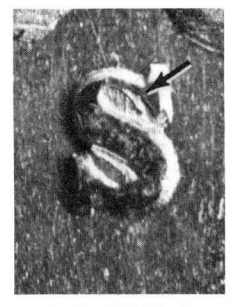

21 R S/S High	21 O Doubled Date	25 O Doubled 7
22 O Doubled Date		26 O Doubled 879
27 O Doubled Date		28 O Doubled 1-9
29 O Die Gouge	29 O Doubled Obverse	30 R S/S Far Left

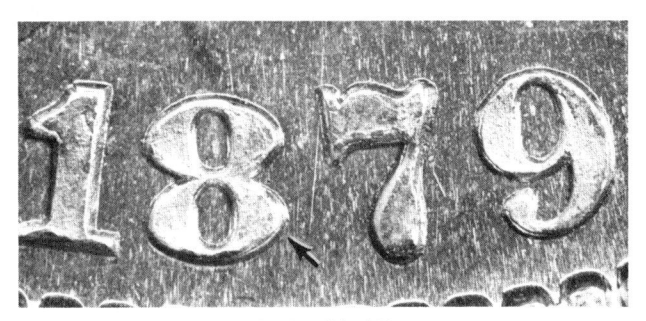

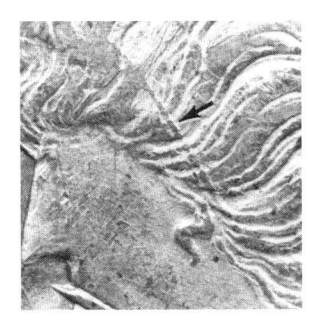

1879-S

31 III²16 • C³j (Doubled 879, S Set Left) (182) I-2 R-3
Obverse III²16 – Doubled 879 in date. 8 tripled at bottom right outside of lower loop. 7 doubled slightly below crossbar. 9 doubled at left outside of upper loop.
Reverse C³j – Medium IV S mint mark set to left and upright.

32 III²5 • C³a (Doubled 9) (184) I-2 R-3

33 III²17 • C³k (Doubled 18-9, S Set Right) (181) I-2 R-3
Obverse III²17 – Doubled 18-9 in date. 1 doubled at below lower crossbar. 8 doubled at lower outside of lower loop. 9 doubled slightly at left outside of lower loop.
Reverse C³k – Medium IV S mint mark upright and set to right.

34 III²5 • B²f (PAF, Engraved Wing Feather) (181) I-4 R-4
Reverse B²f – Feather engraved between eagle's right wing and leg. R in TRUST broken with upper serif almost completely missing.

35 III²5 • B²g (PAF, Engraved Wing feather) (181) I-4 R-4
Reverse B²g – Feather engraved between eagle's right wing and leg. R in TRUST partially broken.

36 III²1 • C³b (Polished 8, S Tilted Left) (184) I-2 R-3
Obverse III²1 – Polishing lines within loops of 8.

37 III²1 • C³l (S/S Line) (184) I-2 R-3
Reverse C³l – Medium IV S mint mark doubled with a long thin line on right side of upper loop opening and a curved line on right side of lower loop opening. S mint mark centered and upright.

38 III²18 • C³a (Doubled 879) (185) I-2 R-3
Obverse III²18 – Doubled 879 in date. 8 doubled at top right outside and lower left outside of upper loop. 7 doubled at top of crossbar and lower right of vertical shaft. 9 doubled on left outside of both loops.
Reverse C³a – Polishing lines in upper loop of IV S mint mark.

39 III²1 • B²g (PAF, Engraved Wing Feather) (183) I-4 R-4

40 III²19 • C³a (Doubled 18-9) (185) I-2 R-3
Obverse III²19 – Doubled 18-9 in date. 1 doubled in middle of lower crossbar on ends. 8 doubled at top right outside of upper loop. 9 doubled outside of both loops.

41 III²20 • C³a (Doubled Stars and Date) (185) I-2 R-3
Obverse III²20 – All left and right stars doubled towards rim. All digits in date slightly doubled. 1 is doubled at very bottom. 8 doubled slightly at lower left outside of upper loop. 7 doubled at top outside and below crossbar. 9 doubled slightly at left outside of lower loop.

31 O Doubled 879

33 O Doubled 18-9

31 R S Set Left

33 R S Set Right

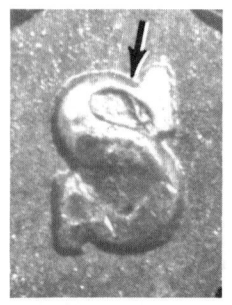

37 R S/S Line

1879-S / 1880-P

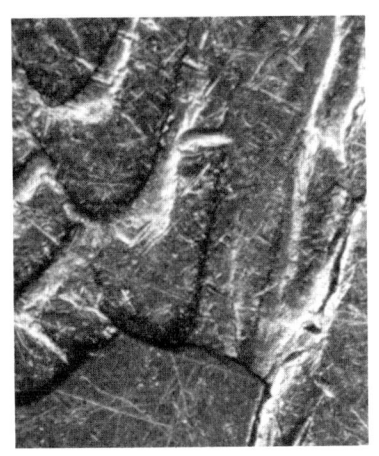

34 R Engraved Feather

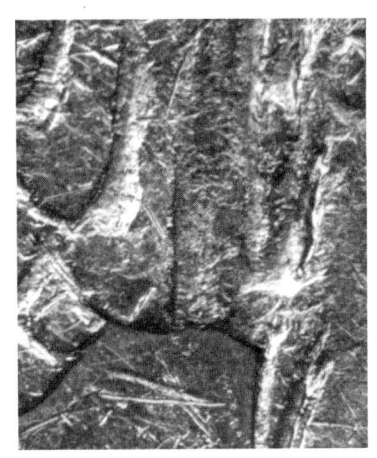

35 R Engraved Feather

38 O Doubled 879

40 O Doubled 18-9

41 O Doubled Date and Stars

1880-P

The strike for 1880-P is average for the series with most fairly well struck. But quite a few show a touch of weakness in the hair over the ear. This date contains its share of slightly doubled dates because of its fairly high mintage. It does have a number of interesting and scarce overdates however. The most prominent are VAM's 6, 7 and 8 with remains of the 7 within and above the 8. These command sizeable premiums in any grade. Only a few uncirculated specimens of VAM 7 and 8 are known, they are rare in all grades, however, and they are worth large premiums. VAM's 2, 9, 10, 11, 16, 25 and 29 are weaker overdates and not as scarce so they command little premium. VAM 23 shows the remains of the 79 on top of the 80 digits. It is quite scarce and brings a substantial premium.

Proof-like coins as with most early P mints are fairly scarce. Some deep mirror cameos do exist. The proof issue is one of the most available and generally has excellent contrast.

1   III^2 1 • C^3 a (Normal Die)   I-1   R-1
    Obverse III^2 1 – Normal die of III^2 type.
    Reverse C^3 a – Normal die of C^3 type.

1880-P

1A	III²1 • C³a (Broken 8)		I-2	R-5

Obverse III²1 – First 8 has a vertical die crack on the right side showing as a line below and a large knob of metal at top with line continuing up into hair and neck.

1B	III¹1 • C³a (Lines in 8)		I-2	R-4

Obverse III¹1 – Second 8 has diagonal polishing lines at top right inside of lower loop.

2	III²2 • C³a (Doubled 0, 8/7)		I-3	R-4

Obverse III²2 – 0 in date doubled at top inside showing as a thin arc with a dot on right side below arc. Remains of 7 shows on surface of left side of upper loop of second 8 in form of check mark.

3	III²12 • C³a (Doubled 80 and Dash)	(180)	I-2	R-4

Obverse III²12 – 80 in date is doubled. The second 8 is doubled slightly at the very bottom, on lower left outside of upper loop and at the top on the left and right sides. It also has a faint long dash well below the bottom. The 0 is strongly doubled at top left and right outside and inside of lower left.

4	III²3 • C³3 (Doubled 0 and Dash)		I-2	R-3

Obverse III²3 – 0 in date is strongly doubled at top left and right bottom inside left side. A dash appears below the 8 in the date.

5	III²4 • C³a (Doubled Date)	(180)	I-2	R-3

Obverse III²4 – Entire date doubled. 1 doubled on right side of vertical shaft and below bottom of crossbar. First 8 doubled slightly on left inside of loops and bottom right outside of lower loop. Second 8 is doubled on lower left side of upper loop. The 0 is doubled on top left and right and on left inside. Some specimens show a large vertical die crack through 0 extending from hair down to the rim.

6	III²5 • C³a (8/7 Spikes)	(180)	I-5	R-5

Obverse III²5 – 8 repunched over 7 in date. Two serifs of 7 are clearly visible above second 8 as two short spikes and crossbar of 7 is visible inside the upper loop of the 8. There is a slight bulge on left side of the 0 where original 9 was punched. 1 is tripled at the very bottom. First 8 is doubled slightly at bottom outside of lower loop. Second 8 is doubled slightly at lower left outside of upper loop. 0 is doubled at left inside. Fine die chips show on right inside of first 8 lower loop.

7	III²6 • C³(8/7 Crossbar)		I-5	R-7

Obverse III²6 – 8 repunched over 7 in date different than III²5 obverse. There are no ears above the 8 but the crossbar of the 7 is clearly visible in the upper loop with a straight lower edge. In the lower loop of the 8 remains the shaft of the 7 shows as two short lines. The 9 does not show in the 0. 1 doubled at very bottom left.

8	III²7 • C³a (8/7 Ears)	(179)	I-4	R-6

Obverse III²7 – Second 8 has two short ears at top. A small piece of metal is on the right side of the upper loop opening. The 9 does not show in 0.

1A O Broken 8

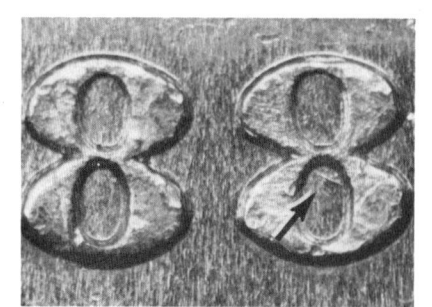

1B O Lines in 8

2 O Doubled 0

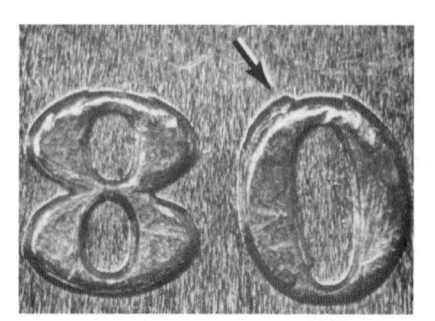

3 O Doubled 80 and Dash

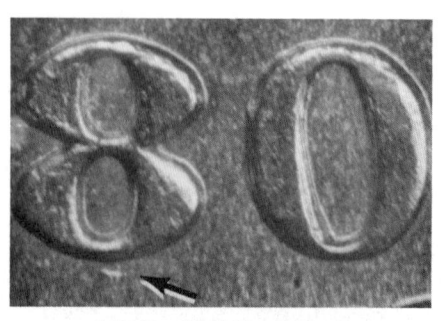

4 O Doubled 0 and Dash

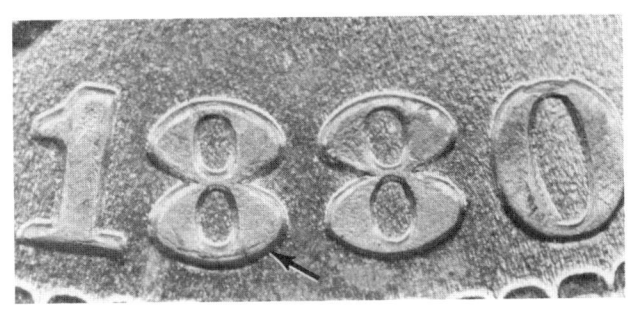

1880-P

5 O Doubled Date

6 O 8/7 Spikes, Doubled Date

6 O 8/7 Spikes

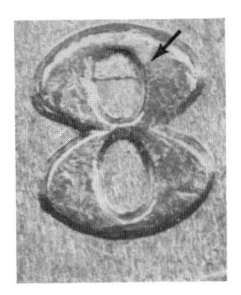

7 O 8/7 Crossbar

8 O 8/7 Ears

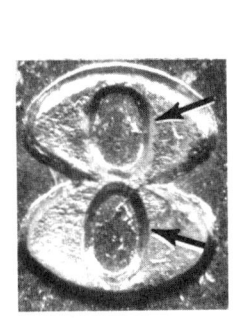

9 O 8/7 Stem

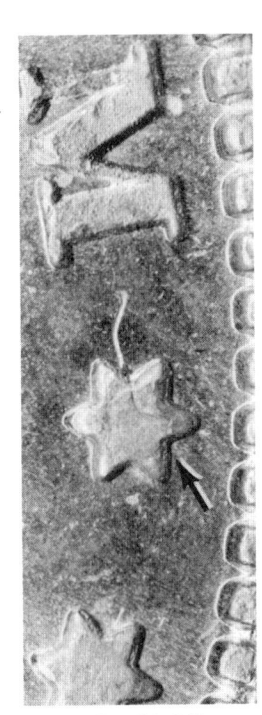

9 O 8/7 Stem

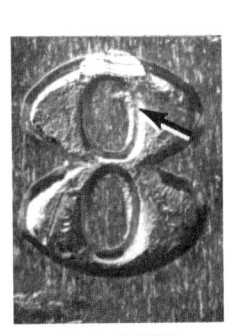

10 O 8/7 Bit

9 O Doubled Stars

9 III² 8 • C³ a (8/7 Stem) (179) I-3 R-5

Obverse III² 8 – Second 8 has small piece of metal on right side of upper loop. Bottom loop has stem of 7 showing as a faint outline and metal inside. The 9 does not show in 0 but a bulge shows at 10 o'clock. 1 is doubled at very bottom. First 8 doubled at lower loop left outside of both loops. Second 8 tripled at lower left outside of upper loop. 0 doubled at left and right top outside and lower inside. All left stars and motto letters doubled near rim and all right stars tripled near rim.

10 III² 9 • C³ a (8/7 Bit) (180) I-3 R-4

Obverse III² 9 – Second 8 has two spikes on right inside of upper loop and metal on top of right of lower loop. Some specimens have one spike in upper loop. Possible 8/7 but evidence is not conclusive. 0 doubled at top left inside.

193

1880-P

11   **III² 10 • C³ a (Doubled 880, 8/7)**   (179)   I-3   R-4
Obverse III² 10 – Doubled 880 in date. Bottom outside and lower loop and top inside of lower loop of first 8 is doubled. Lower left outside of upper loop on second 8 is doubled. 0 is doubled at top left outside and top inside. Die chip to left between loops of first 8. Remains of 7 shows on surface of the left side of upper loop of second 8 in form of check mark.

12   **III² 11 • C³ a (Doubled 1-80)**   (181)   I-2   R-4
Obverse III² 11 – 1-80 in date is doubled. The 1 is doubled above the bottom crossbar. The 0 is doubled on the inside right and is faintly doubled at top left and right outside. Second 8 is doubled at bottom left outside of upper loop.

13   **III² 13 • C³ e (Doubled 1)**   I-2   Proof
Obverse III² 13 – 1 in date is doubled at top left of upper crossbar and slightly at top left of bottom crossbar.

14   **III² 14 • C³ e (Doubled First 8)**   (180)   I-3   R-4
Obverse III² 14 – First 8 in date doubled strongly at very bottom right outside.

15   **III² 15 • C³ a (Doubled Second 8)**   (179)   I-2   R-3
Obverse III² 15 – Second 8 in date doubled at top on right and left outside.

16   **III² 16 • C³ a (Doubled 80, 8/7)**   (179)   I-3   R-4
Obverse III² 16 – 80 in date doubled. Second 8 is doubled on lower left outside of upper loop. The 0 is doubled at top left and right outside. Remains of 7 shows on surface of left side of upper loop of second 8 in the form of a check mark.

17   **III² 17 • C³ a (Doubled 18-0)**   I-3   R-4
Obverse III² 17 – 18-0 in date doubled. 1 doubled slightly at bottom. First 8 doubled very strongly at bottom outside and is doubled at top inside of both loops and bottom right outside of upper loop. 0 doubled slightly on lower left inside of loop.

18   **III² 18 • C³ a (Doubled 1-80)**   (178)   I-2   R-3
Obverse III² 18 – 1-80 in date is doubled. The 1 is doubled below upper crossbar. The second 8 is doubled on the lower left outside of the upper loop and right outside of lower loop. The 0 is doubled at the top left and right outside and on the lower left inside.

19   **III² 19 • C³ a (Tripled 8, Doubled 1-80)**   I-3   R-4
Obverse III² 19 – 1 doubled slightly below crossbar. First 8 is tripled at bottom right outside of both loops. Second 8 and 0 are doubled slightly at top left and right outside. 0 is tripled slightly on left inside.

20   **III² 20 • C³ a (Doubled Date)**   (181)   I-2   R-4
Obverse III² 20 – Entire date is slightly doubled. 1 is doubled at bottom edge of crossbar. First 8 is doubled on bottom right outside and with a short spike between loops on right. Second 8 is doubled on top left and right and left outside of lower loop with short dash below lower loop. 0 is doubled on top left and right outside.

21   **III² 21 • C³ a (Doubled Date)**   I-2   R-4
Obverse III² 21 – Entire date is doubled. 1 is doubled slightly below the upper crossbar and at bottom. First 8 is doubled on bottom outside and with a short spike between loops on right. Second 8 is doubled slightly on lower left outside of upper loop. 0 is doubled on left inside and slightly on right inside of opening. Left and right stars slightly doubled towards rim.

22   **III² 22 • C³ a (Doubled Date)**   I-3   R-4
Obverse III² 22 – Entire date is doubled. The 1 is faintly doubled below top crossbar and at left bottom of lower crossbar. First 8 is faintly doubled at top left side of both loops. Second 8 is strongly doubled all across bottom and faintly at top inside of lower loop and bottom outside on right and left sides of upper loop. 0 is tripled at bottom at left and right sides of bottom next to field and at top surface on left.

11 O 8/7
Check Mark

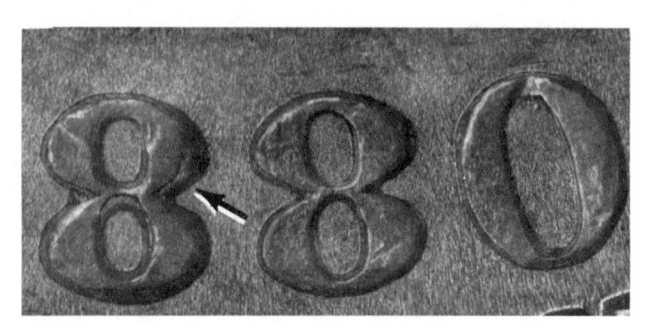

11 O Doubled 880

1880-P

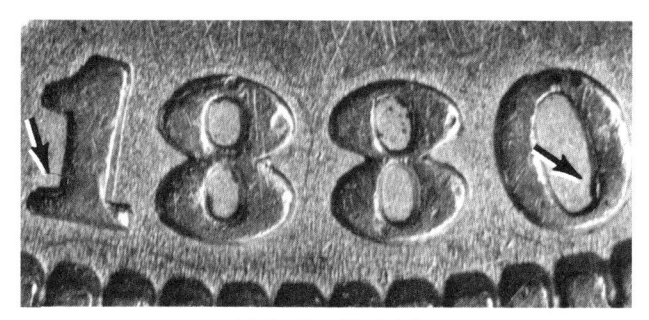

12 O Doubled 1-0

13 O Doubled 1

14 O Doubled First 8

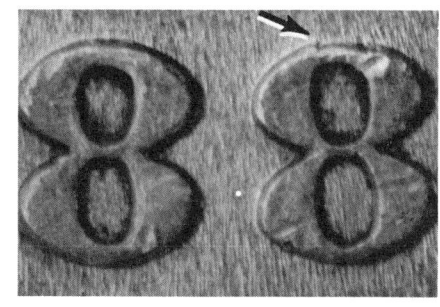

15 O Second 8 Doubled

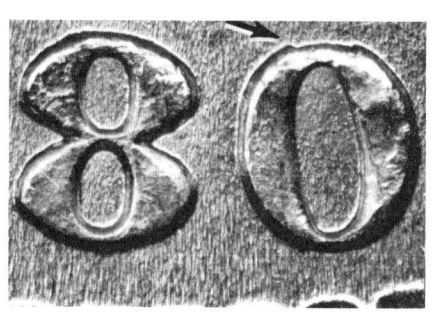

16 O Doubled 80

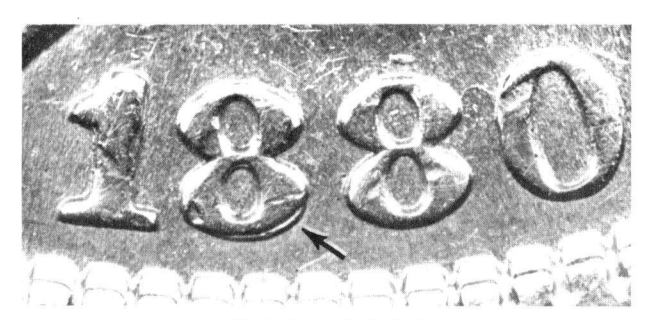

17 O Doubled 18-0

18 O Doubled 1-80

19 O Tripled 8, Doubled 80

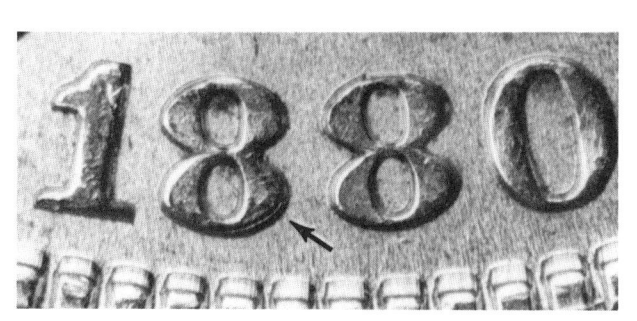

20 O Doubled Date

1880-P

21 O Doubled Date

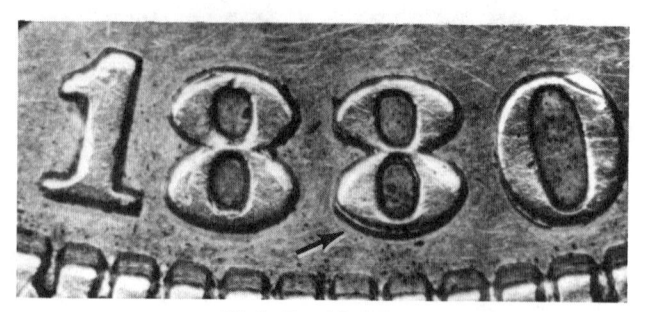

22 O Doubled Date

23   III² 23 • C³ a (80/79)   I-4   R-6

Obverse III² 23 – 80 repunched over 79 in date. Remains of 7 shows on top of 8 as check mark on left side of upper loop and a vertical line on right side of upper loop extending down to top of lower loop and up to short spike on field at top right outside of upper loop. Remains of 9 shows on top of 0 as raised metal on upper left side ending diagonally at middle left side, dot on lower left that was end of 9 loop, vertical bar on middle right side. 1 doubled below bottom crossbar and slightly below upper crossbar, first 8 doubled slightly on surface of upper loop and outside and tripled below bottom loop.

24   III² 24 • C³ a (Doubled 1-80)   (179)   I-2   R-3

Obverse III² 24 – 1-80 in date doubled. 1 doubled slightly at top left of lower crossbar. Second 8 is doubled on the lower left outside of upper loop. 0 doubled at top left and right outside and slightly on lower left inside. Die chips at top inside at upper loop of second 8 and 0.

25   III² 25 • C³ a (0/9)   (180)   I-3   R-5

Obverse III² 25 – Faint remains of 9 on top of 0 showing as raised metal on lower left side of 0. Lower crossbar of 1 doubled at very bottom. Second 8 doubled slightly at lower left outside of upper loop. Upper inside of loop of 0 doubled strongly.

26   III² 26 • C³ a (Doubled Date, Tripled 8)   I-3   R-4

Obverse III² 26 – Entire date is doubled. 1 is doubled slightly above crossbar and strongly above bottom crossbar on both sides. First 8 is strongly doubled at top left outside and bottom inside of lower loop. Second 8 is tripled at top inside of both loops. 0 is doubled at top left and right outside plus lower right inside.

27   III² 27 • C³ a (Doubled 1-80)   I-2   R-3

Obverse III² 27 – Doubled 1-80 in date. 1 doubled slightly above lower crossbar on left side and at very left bottom. Second 8 doubled at top inside of both loops and at bottom left outside of both loops. 0 doubled slightly at bottom outside and left and right top outside.

28   III² • C³ a (Doubled 1-8, Tripled 0)   (181)   I-2   R-3

Obverse III² 28 – Doubled 1-8 in date. 1 doubled slightly below upper crossbar and on left side of crossbar. Second 8 doubled at left outside and bottom inside of upper loop. 0 tripled at lower left inside and doubled at top inside and left and right top outside.

29   III² 29 • C³ a (Doubled 80, 8/7)   I-3   R-3

Obverse III² 29 – Doubled 80 in date and 8/7 checkmark similar to VAM 16. Second 8 is doubled on the lower left outside of upper loop. The 0 is doubled at the top left and right outside but not as strong as VAM 16. First 8 has die chip on upper left inside of lower loop. Remains of 7 show on surface of left side of upper loop of second 8 in the form of a check mark. Right side of check mark is more curved than VAM 16.

30   III² 30 • C³ a (Doubled 1-80)   (181)   I-2   R-3

Obverse III² 30 – Doubled 1-80 in date. 1 doubled slightly below lower crossbar. Second 8 doubled slightly at bottom left outside of upper loop. 0 doubled slightly at left and right inside. Some specimens show large die flakes around R in date and 7th star on left.

31   III² 31 • C³ a (Doubled Date)   (180)   I-2   R-3

Obverse III² 31 – Entire date doubled slightly. 1 doubled on surface at top of upper crossbar and above bottom crossbar on left side. First 8 doubled slightly at right inside of lower loop. Second 8 doubled slightly at lower left outside of upper loop. 0 doubled slightly at left inside.

32   III² 32 • C³ a (Doubled Date)   (178)   I-2   R-3

Obverse III² 32 – Entire date doubled slightly. 1 doubled slightly above lower crossbar. First 8 doubled at top left inside of both loops and tripled at bottom outside at lower loop. Second 8 doubled at lower left outside of upper loop. 0 doubled slightly at top left and right outside and tripled at lower left inside. Slightly doubled Liberty head profile on lips, chin and nose.

1880-P

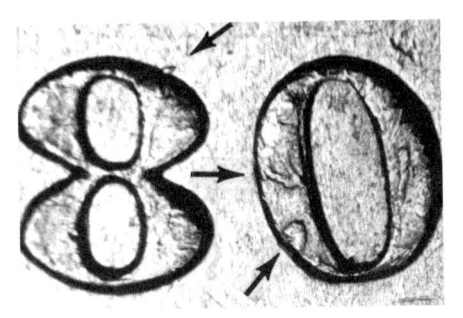

23 O 80/79

24 O Doubled 80

25 O 0/9

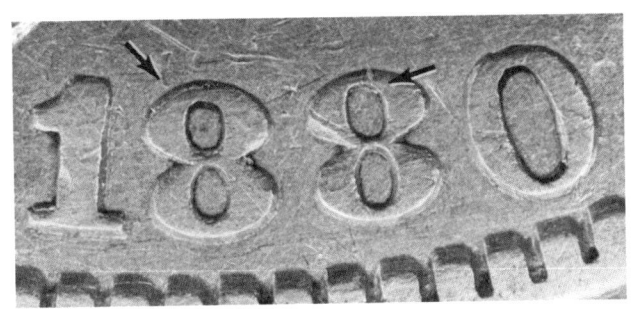

26 O Doubled Date, Tipled 8

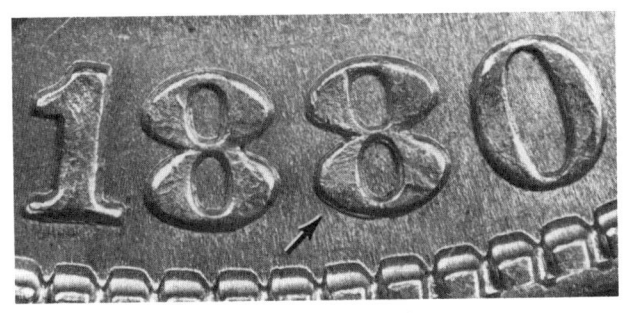

27 O Doubled 1-80

28 O Doubled 1-8, Tripled 0

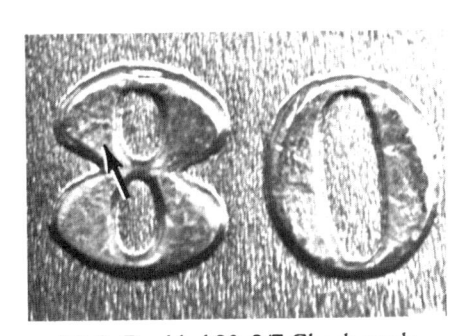

29 O Doubled 80, 8/7 Check mark

30 O Doubled 1-80

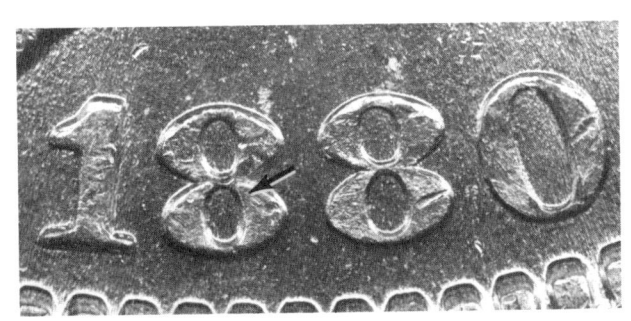

31 O Doubled Date

1880-P

| 33 | III²33 • C³a (Doubled Date) | (180) | 1-2 | R-3 |

Obverse III²33 – Entire date doubled. 1 is doubled strongly at top of upper crossbar. First 8 doubled on surface at bottom right outside of lower loop. Second 8 doubled at lower loop, 0 doubled on left and right bottom outside.

| 34 | III²34 • C³a (Doubled 188, Doubled Obverse) | (180) | I-2 | R-3 |

Obverse III²34 – Doubled 188 in date. 1 doubled below upper and lower crossbars. First 8 doubled on bottom left outside of lower loop. Second 8 doubled slightly on lower left outside of upper loop. All stars and legend letters doubled at top towards rim.

| 35 | III²35 • C³a (Doubled 1-80) | (180) | I-2 | R-3 |

Obverse III²35 – Doubled 1-80 in date. 1 doubled slightly below bottom crossbar. Second 8 doubled on lower left outside of upper loop. 0 doubled at upper left and lower right inside. First 8 shows die chips in lower loop on some specimens.

| 36 | III² • C³a (Doubled Date) | (180) | I-2 | R-3 |

Obverse III²36 – Entire date doubled slightly 1 doubled above lower crossbar on left and right. First 8 doubled on surface at right inside of lower loop. Second 8 doubled slightly at lower left outside of upper loop. 0 doubled at lower right inside with die chip at lower left outside.

| 37 | III²37 • C³a (Doubled Date) | (180) | 1-2 | R-3 |

Obverse III²37 – Entire date is doubled. 1 doubled at lower right of vertical stem. First 8 doubled on left inside of lower loop. Second 8 doubled on lower left outside of upper loop. 0 doubled at top left and right outside.

| 38 | III²38 • C³a (Doubled Date) | (181) | 1-2 | R-3 |

Obverse III² 38 – Entire date is doubled. 1 doubled on left of top and bottom crossbars. First 8 doubled on surface at top and right inside and bottom of lower loop. Second 8 doubled slightly at lower left outside of upper loop. 0 doubled slightly at top left and right outside and lower left outside. 0 set lower than rest of date digits.

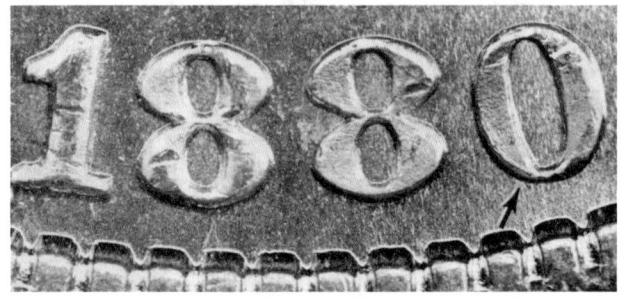

32 O Doubled Date

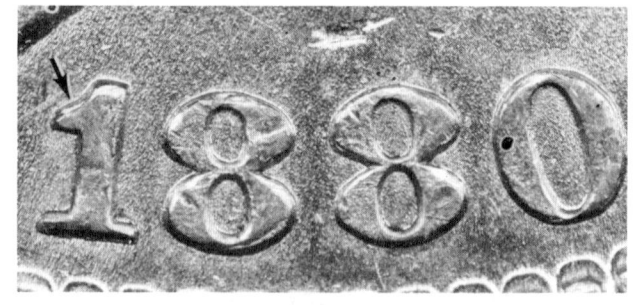

33 O Doubled Date

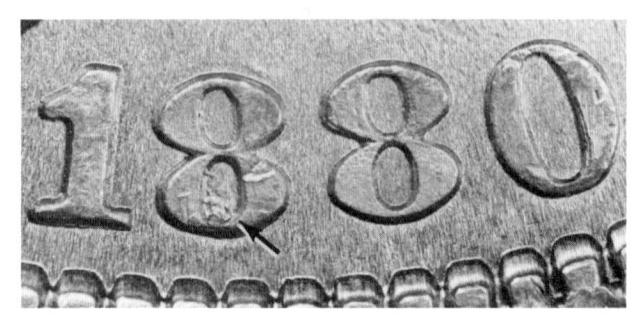

35 O Doubled 18-0

36 O Doubled Date

37 O Doubled Date

38 O Doubled Date

1880-P / 1880-CC

34 O Doubled 188

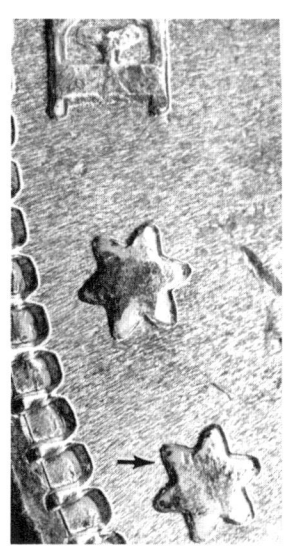

34 O
Doubled Stars and Letters

1880-CC

This issue was beset by numerous problems. To begin with, the Annual Assay Commission discovered early in 1881 that some of the issues were defective with low fineness (less silver content than normal). As a result 96, 000 of the 1880-CC dollars were melted in 1881 decreasing the net mintage to 495,000. The strike is quite variable with an even distribution from well struck to quite weak. Many of the coins have cloudy surfaces probably due to storage contamination. Planchet striations sometimes are evident in the hair above the ear and on the eagle's breast feathers. Locating a problem free high grade specimen can be quite a challenge.

Normal dies without varieties do not exist. Some B reverse dies with flat breast were used but they are not scarce for the issue and only bring a modest premium. Most of the varieties are overdates. VAM's 4, 5 and 6 are the most prominent overdates of the entire Morgan series with complete 79 digits showing under the 80. However, they make up a sizeable percentage of this issue as well as a couple other less prominent overdates and do not bring any premium.

Proof-likes make up a good percentage of the issue but it is difficult to locate a problem free specimen with minimal abrasions.

1   III²1 • C³a (SAF Large CC)   **Normal die does not exist**
     Obverse III²1 – Normal die of III² type.
     Reverse C³a – Normal die of C³ type with large V CC mint mark and slanted arrow feathers.

2   III²1 • B²a (PAF Small CC)   **Normal die does not exist**
     Reverse B²a – Normal die of B² type with centered small II CC mint mark and parallel arrow feathers.

3   III²2 • C³b (Dash Under 8)   I-2   R-3
     Obverse III²2 – First 8 is doubled at top inside of lower loop and upper loop has polishing marks. A high set dash appears just below the second 8 with upper loop doubled on left outside. 0 is doubled at the top left and right. First stars on left and right have die chips.
     Reverse C³b – Normal die of C³ type with centered large V CC mint mark. There are die chips at the top inside of the loop of each C of the mint mark and at top left of O in DOLLAR.

4   III²3 • B²a (80/79)   (178)   I-5   R-4
     Obverse III²3 – 80 repunched over the 79 in date. The two serifs of the 7 show above the 8, the bottom of the crossbar shows in the top of the upper loop and the stem show on the right side of the lower loop. The 9 shows within the 0 in the top left and bottom and a bulge shows outside at 10 o'clock. 1 has die chip at top right of shaft. First 8 has vertical polishing marks inside partially filled loops.

1880-CC

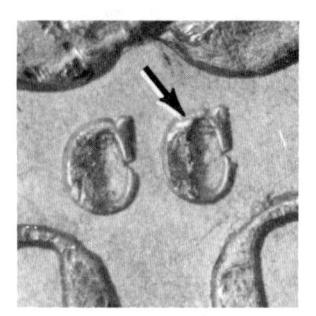

3 R Doubled CC

3 O Dash

4 O 80/79

5   III² 4 • C³ c (8/7 High)   (177)   I-5   R-4
Obverse III² 4 – 8 repunched over the 7 in the date with the original 7 punched high. There are prominent ears above the 8, a crossbar in the upper loop, the stem of the 7 shows on the right side of the lower loop, and the bottom of the 7 stem shows just below the 8.
Reverse C³c – Normal die of C³ type with slanted arrow feathers and small II CC mint mark with slight tilt to right. Vertical die gouge below arrow feathers and olive branch.

6   III2 5 • C³ d (8/7 Low)   (177)   I-5   R-4
Obverse III²5 – 8 repunched over 7 in date with the original 7 punched low. The ears are faint above the 8 and the crossbar and stem of the 7 show strongly. The bottom of the 7's stem shows well below the 8. A small piece of metal with polishing marks shows at the bottom inside the 0. First 8 has diagonal polishing marks inside partially filled loops.
Reverse C³d – Normal die of C³ type with centered small I CC mint mark and slanted arrow feathers. CC has a dot of metal in center of each C. Die scratch through M of AMERICA, bottom of eagle's right wing and inside of eagle's left wing.

7   III² 6 • B² a (8/7 Dash)   I-3   R-4
Obverse III² 6 – 8 repunched over 7. A short ear shows at the left at top of the second 8. Bottom of stem shows as low dash below 8. Bottom loop of 8 shows two diagonal polishing marks and die chips on the right side and top. The 0 shows no part of the 9 but has a slight bulge on outside at 10 o'clock. First 8 is doubled at top inside of lower loop and has die chips inside upper loop.

8   III2 6 • C³ d (8/7 Dash)   (177)   I-3   R-3
Obverse III² 6 – Same as III² 6 but has been further polished down after receiving heavy clash marks. A vertical polishing mark shows on right outside between loops of second 8.

9   III² 6 • C³ a (8/7 Dash)   I-3   R-5

10   III² 7 • C³ c (8/7 Dash and Doubled 8)   (177)   I-3   R-4
Obverse III² 7 – First 8 has horizontal polishing lines on right side of upper loop and is doubled at top inside of lower loop. Second 8 has a short dash just below bottom and is doubled at lower left outside of upper loop.

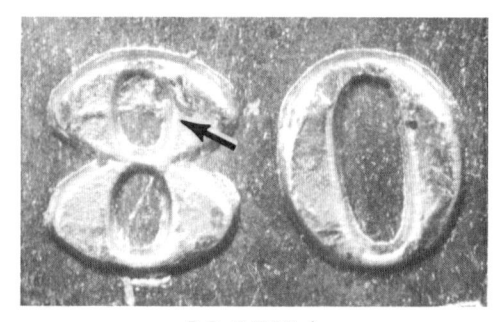

5 O 8/7 High

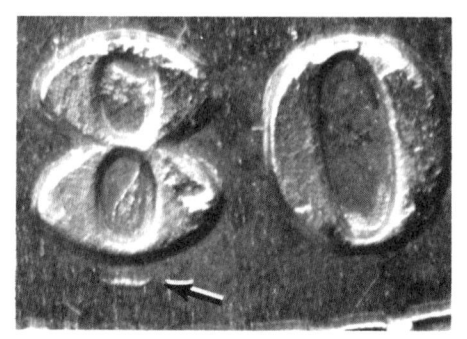

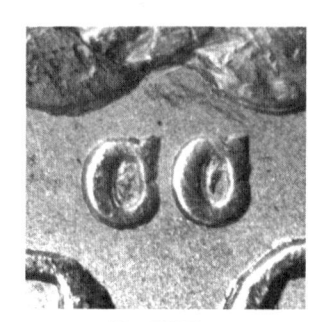

6 O 8/7 Low

6 R CC Dots

200

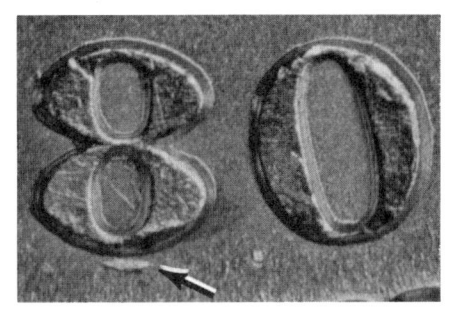

1880-CC / 1880-O

7 O 8/7 Dash 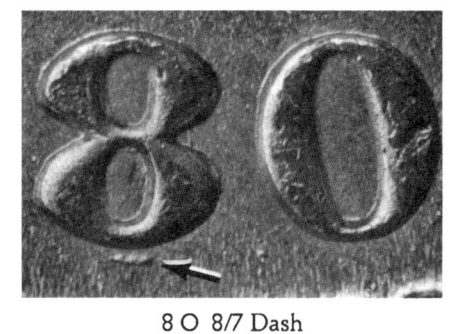   8 O 8/7 Dash 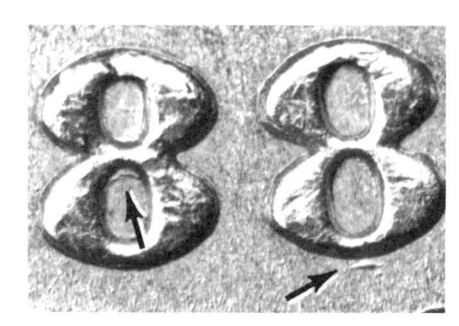   10 O Doubled 8 and 8/7 Dash

1880-O

The 1880-O is similar to the 1879-O with strong strike usual, some soft strikes exist, and many coins exist that have been lightly circulated. Proof-likes are fairly scarce and some deep mirror cameos exist.

This issue has numerous varieties, but most are minor. Two size O mint marks were used but both are readily available and do not bring any premium. Quite a few overdate die varieties exist with VAM's 4 and 5 fairly prominent but commanding only a modest premium because of their availability. The other overdates are less prominent and do not bring much of a premium except for VAM 6B because of its rarity.

1   III^{2}1 • C^{3}a (Small O)   (176)   1-1   R-2
    Obverse III^{2}1 – Normal die of III^2 type.
    Reverse C^{3}a – Normal die of C^3 type with small, round I O mint mark centered and upright.

1A III^{2}1 • C^{3}a (Hangnail Eagle)   (176)   1-2   R-5
    Reverse C^{3}a – Die gouge through the eagle's left tail feather and lower arrow feather.

2   III^{2}1 • C^{3}b (Medium O)   (176)   I-2   R-2
    Reverse C^{3}b – Normal die of C^3 type with medium, tall, oval shaped, II O mint mark centered and upright.

2A III^{2}1 • C^{3}b (Impaled Eagle)   (176)   I-2   R-4
    Reverse C^{3}b – Horizontal spike of metal through eagle's neck due to die scratch. II O mint mark.

3   III^{2}2 • C^{3}b (Dash Under 8, Doubled 80)   (176)   I-2   R-3
    Obverse III^{2}2 – A thin dash appears well below the second 8. Second 8 also doubled slightly at bottom left outside of upper loop. 0 doubled slightly at bottom left inside and slightly at top left and right outside.

1A R Hangnail Eagle    2A R Impaled Eagle 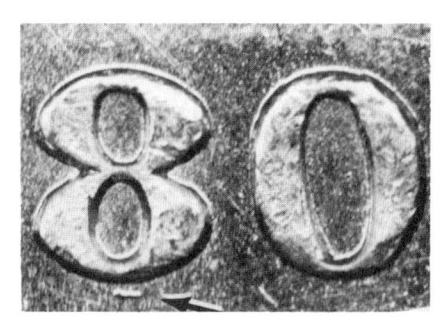   3 O Dash Under 8, Doubled 80

201

1880-O

4 III² 3 • C³ a (80/79) (176) I-4 R-4
Obverse III² 3 – 80 repunched over 79 in date. Faint ears appear above the 8 and metal is at the top within the upper loop. The 0 has metal inside the upper part of the loop. 1 doubled on right side of vertical shaft. First 8 doubled on left inside and right outside of lower loop. Second 8 doubled at left outside of both loops.

5 III² 4 • C³ b (8/7 Ear) (176) I-4 R-5
Obverse III² 4 – 8 repunched over 7 in date. Metal in top loop of second 8 but different than III² 3. Faint ear above 8 on left. No metal in 0.
Reverse C³ b – Die scratch below wreath center, within mint mark opening, below the arrow shaft, and a spike of metal from the right wing to the eagle's neck.

6 III² 5 • C³ a (8/7 Spike) (176) I-4 R-5
Obverse III² 5 – 8 repunched over 7 in date. A long spike extends from the top left side of the second 8. Small horizontal spike on right inside of upper loop of second 8. Die clash marks are evident on some specimens.
Reverse C³ a – Heavy die clash marks are evident on some specimens.

6A III² 5 • C³ a (8/7 Spike) (176) I-4 R-5
Reverse C³ a – Die gouge on left side of left wreath.

6B III² 5 • C³ a (Hangnail Eagle) (176) I-4 R-6

7 III² 1 • C³ c (O/O) (176) I-2 R-4
Obverse III² 1 – Date has die chips at top and left side of 1, on the right of first 8 upper loop, and below 0.
Reverse C³ c – I O mint mark is doubled on right and left side of top surface.

8 III² 1 • C³ d (High O) (176) I-2 R-3
Reverse C³ d – I O mint mark set high.

9 III² 6 • C³ a (Doubled 0) (176) I-2 R-4
Obverse III² 6 – 0 in date is doubled strongly at top right and left outside and on lower left of the opening.

10 III² 7 • C³ b (Doubled 1-8) (176) I-2 R-3
Obverse III² 7 – 1-8 doubled in date. 1 doubled slightly below upper crossbar and lower right side of shaft. Second 8 doubled slightly at lower outside of upper loop. 0 has three patches of shallow die chips inside. Lower part of hair has heavy polishing marks.

11 III² 8 • C³ a (Dash Under 8, Doubled 188) (176) I-2 R-3
Obverse III² 1 – A faint dash appears below the second 8 and the upper loop is doubled slightly at bottom left outside. 1 is doubled on top serif surface. First 8 is doubled on lower loop surface at bottom right.

12 III² 9 • C³ a (Doubled 1-80) (176) I-2 R-3
Obverse III² 9 – 1-80 doubled in date. 1 doubled on surface at top right of vertical shaft. Second 8 is doubled at lower left outside of upper loop. 0 is doubled at top left and right outside and at top left of opening.

13 III² 10 • C³ a (Doubled 80) (176) I-3 R-4
Obverse III² 10 – Doubled 80 in date. Second 8 is doubled on lower left outside of upper loop. 0 is doubled strongly at top left outside and tripled at top right outside. It is also tripled on lower left inside and doubled almost entirely up the left inside.

14 III² 11 • C³ a (Doubled 80) (176) I-2 R-3
Obverse III² 11 – Doubled 80 in date. Second 8 is doubled slightly at outside top left and right. 0 is doubled slightly at top left outside.

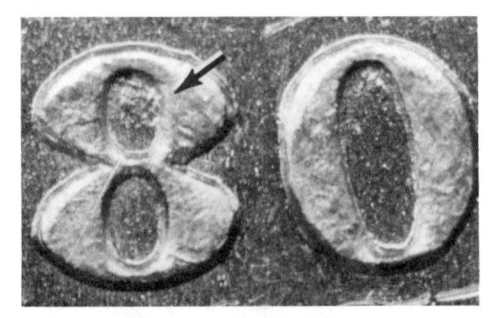

4 O 80/79 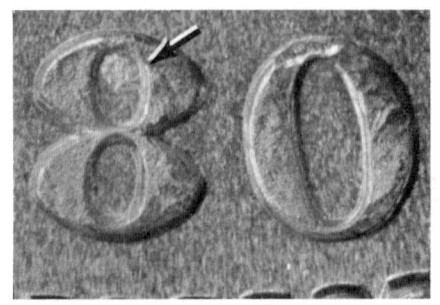 | 5 O 8/7 Ear 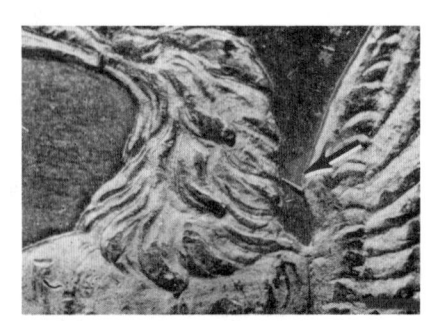 | 5 R Die Scratches

1880-O

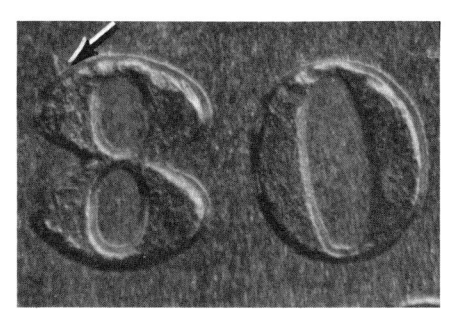

6 O 8/7 Spike

7 O Die Chips

6A R Die Gouge

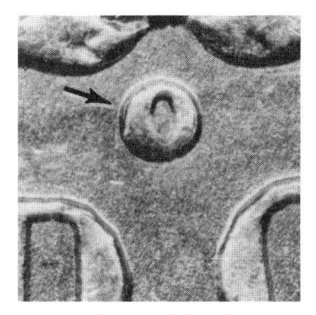

7 R Doubled O

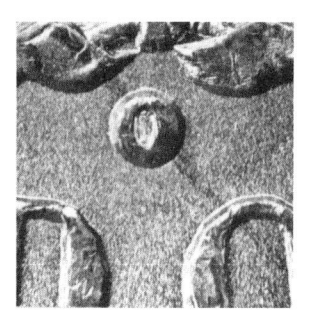

8 R O Set High

9 O Doubled 0

11 O Dash Under 8

10 O Doubled 1-8

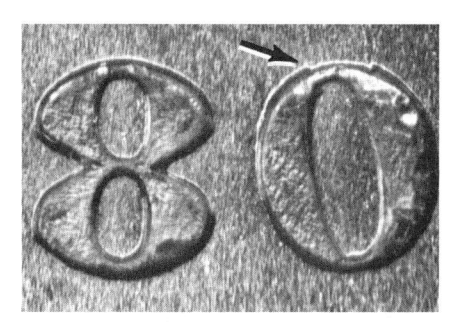

12 O Doubled 80

1880-O

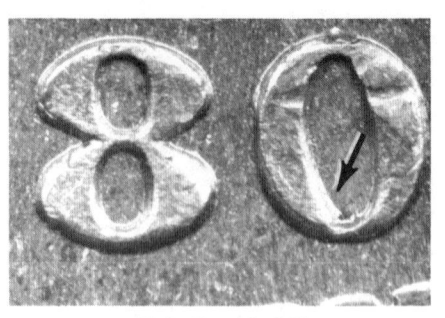

13 O Doubled 80   14 O Doubled 80   15 O Doubled 80

| 15 | III²12 • C³b (Doubled 80) | (176) | I-2 | R-3 |

Obverse III² 12 – Doubled 80 in date. Second 8 doubled slightly at lower left outside of upper loop. 0 double strongly at lower left inside and lower left outside surface.
Reverse C³ b – Letters of UNITED STATES OF AMERICA have die chips and breaks at top. II O mint mark.

| 16 | III²13 • C³a (8/7 Check Mark) | | I-3 | R-5 |

Obverse III² 13 – 8 repunched over 7 in date. Remains of 7 shows on surface of left side of upper loop of second 8 in the form of a check mark. Short vertical bar on surface at right side of junction of 8 loops extending down into side of top of lower loop opening. Second 8 is doubled on lower left side of upper loop.

| 17 | III²13 • C³b (8/7 Check Mark) | | I-3 | R-5 |

| 18 | III²14 • C³a (Doubled 1-8) | (176) | I-2 | R-3 |

Obverse III² 14 – 1 tripled on top left outside of upper crossbar and doubled to top left and right and slightly below bottom crossbar. Second 8 doubled slightly at lower left outside of upper loop.

| 19 | III²15 • C³a (Doubled 188) | | I-2 | R-3 |

Obverse III² 15 – 188 in date slightly doubled. 1 doubled above and below and to right of bottom crossbar. Both 8's doubled slightly at bottom inside of loops. Second 8 doubled at lower left outside of upper loop. Some specimens show die chips at lower left outside of lower loop of both 8's.

| 20 | III²1 • C³e (O/O Right) | | I-2 | R-4 |

Reverse C³ e – II O mint mark repunched with original showing as a bar in the middle and top right of opening and ending in a thin line curving to left at bottom of loop opening.

| 21 | III²16 • C³a (8/7 Check Mark, Ear) | | I-3 | R-4 |

Obverse III² 16 – 8 repunched over 7 in date. Remains of 7 shows on surface of the left side of upper loop of second 8 in the form of a faint check mark set high. Vertical line on side of lower loop opening at upper right. Short ear at top right outside of loop. First 8 is doubled at right inside of lower loop. 0 doubled at lower left inside.

| 22 | III²17 • C³f (Doubled 880, O/O Low) | (176) | I-2 | R-3 |

Obverse III² 17 – Doubled 880 in date. First 8 doubled at top inside of upper loop as a thin curved line. Second 8 doubled slightly at lower left outside of upper loop. 0 doubled on surface at lower right inside.
Reverse C³ f – II O mint mark doubled at lower right outside as a short thin line.

| 23 | III²17 • C³a (Doubled Date) | (176) | I-2 | R-3 |

Obverse III² 17 – Entire date is doubled. 1 and first 8 doubled slightly at very bottom outside. Second 8 doubled at lower left outside of upper loop. 0 doubled slightly at top left and right outside and at bottom outside on surface.

| 24 | III²18 • C³a (Doubled 880) | (176) | I-2 | R-3 |

Obverse III² 18 – Doubled 880 in date. First 8 doubled at top and right inside of lower loop. Second 8 doubled at top left and right outside of upper loop. 0 doubled slightly at lower right inside.

| 25 | III²5 • C³g (8/7 Spike, High O Set Right) | (176) | I-4 | R-5 |

Reverse C³ g – I O mint mark set high and to right.

| 26 | III²19 • C³a (Doubled 80) | (176) | I-2 | R-3 |

Obverse III² 19 – 80 in date doubled. Second 8 doubled at lower left outside of upper loop. 0 doubled at top left inside on surface.
Reverse C³ a – Die overpolished with surface roughness around wreath, eagles tail feathers, olive leaves and UNIT ONE.

| 27 | III²20 – C³a (Doubled 80) | (176) | I-2 | R-3 |

Obverse III² 20 – 80 in date slightly doubled. Second 8 doubled at lower left outside of upper loop. 0 doubled at lower left inside and at top right inside.

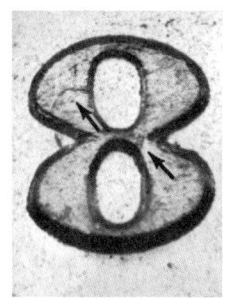

1880-O

16 O
8/7 Check mark

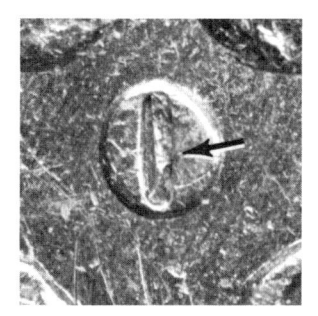

20 R O/O Right

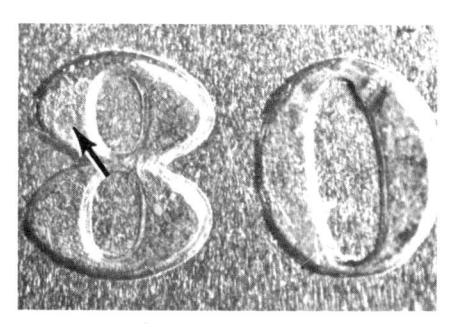

21 R 8/7 Check mark

18 O Doubled 1-8

19 O Doubled 188

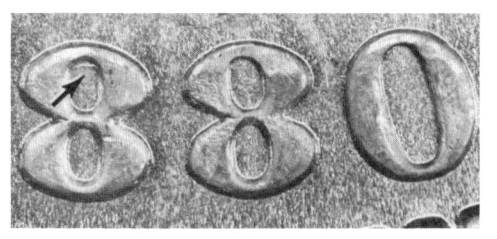

22 O Doubled 880

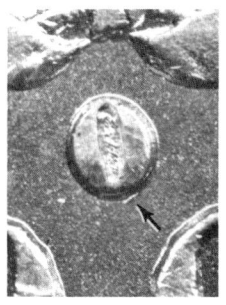

22 R O/O Low

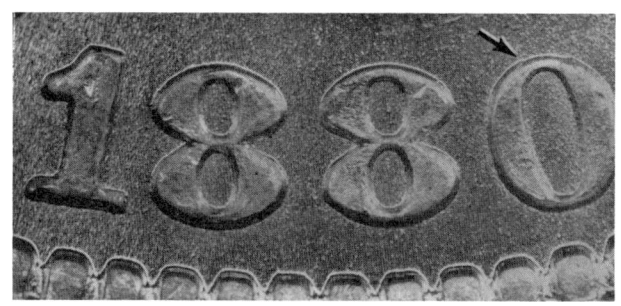

23 O Doubled Date

24 O Doubled 880

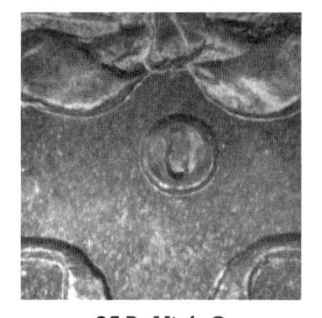

25 R High O

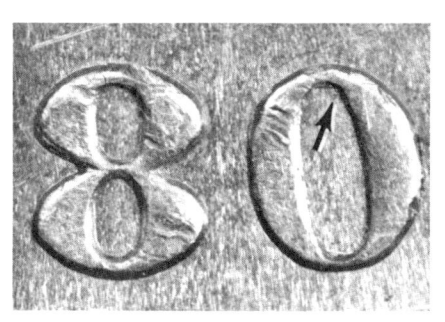

27 O Doubled 80

26 O Doubled 80

205

1880-O

28	III² 21 • C³ c (Doubled 188, High O Set Right)	(176)	1-2	R-3
29	III² 21 • C³ c (Doubled 188, O/O)	(176)	I-2	R-3

Obverse III² 21 – 188 in date doubled. 1 doubled slightly at top left. First 8 doubled at left inside of upper loop and right outside of lower loop. Second 8 doubled at lower left outside of upper loop.

30	III² 22 • C³ a (Doubled 880)	(176)	I-2	R-3

Obverse III² 22 – Doubled 880 in date. First 8 doubled at top right inside and bottom outside of lower loop. Second 8 doubled at lower left outside. 0 doubled slightly at top left and right outside.

31	III² 18 • C³ b (Doubled 880)	(176)	I-2	R-3
32	III² 23 • C³ a (Doubled 18-0)	(176)	I-2	R-3

Obverse III² 23 – Doubled 18-0 in date. 1 and first 8 doubled slightly at bottom outside. 0 doubled at lower left inside.

33	III² 24 • C³ a (Doubled 80)	(176)	I-2	R-3

Obverse III² 24 – Doubled 80 in date. Second 8 doubled slightly at top left and right outside. 0 also doubled slightly at top and right outside plus lower left inside.

34	III² 25 • C³ b (Doubled 188)	(176)	I-2	R-3

Obverse III² 25 – Doubled 188 in date. 1 doubled on lower right side of vertical shaft. First 8 doubled on left inside of lower loop. Second 8 doubled slightly on lower left outside of upper loop.

35	III² 21 • C³ b (Doubled 188)	(176)	I-2	R-3
36	III² 26 • C³ b (Doubled 1-80)	(176)	I-2	R-3

Obverse III² 26 – Doubled 1-80 in date. 1 doubled slightly at top right of lower crossbar. Second 8 doubled at lower left outside of upper loop. 0 doubled slightly at lower right inside.

37	III² 2 • C³ a (Dash Under 8, Doubled 80)	(176)	I-2	R-3
38	III² 27 • C³ b (Doubled 18)	(176)	I-2	R-3

Obverse III² 27 – Doubled 18 in date. 1 doubled at top of upper serif. First 8 doubled slightly at top left outside of upper loop and on surface at bottom right outside of lower loop.

39	III² 28 • C³ h (Doubled 1-8, O Tilted Right)	(176)	1-2	R-3

Obverse III² 28 – Doubled 1-8 in date. 1 doubled at top left and right of lower crossbar. Second 8 doubled slightly at lower left outside of upper loop. Ear has die flake in middle.
Reverse C³ h – Small I O mint mark set slightly high and tilted right.

40	III² 29 • C³ a (Doubled 880, Dash Under 8)	(176)	I-2	R-3

Obverse III² 29 – Doubled 880 in date. First 8 doubled slightly at right inside and bottom right outside of lower loop. A very thin horizontal dash appears just below the second 8. 0 tripled at lower left inside and doubled at top right inside.

41	III² 30 • C³ b (Doubled 1-80)	(176)	I-2	R-3

Obverse III² 30 – Doubled 1-80 in date, 1 doubled slightly below upper crossbar. Second 8 doubled slightly at lower left outside of upper loop. 0 tripled at lower left outside surface and doubled at lower left inside.

42	III² 31 • C³ a (Doubled 80)	(176)	I-2	R-3

Obverse III² 31 – Second 8 doubled slightly at lower left outside of upper loop. 0 doubled slightly at lower left inside.

43	III² 32 • C³ i (Doubled Ear, O/O Center)	(176)	I-3	R-3

Obverse III² 32 – Ear doubled on right side of inner ear fill and outside. Hair line above ear slightly doubled as is eyelid and lower cotton leaf edge. Second 8 in date doubled at lower left outside of upper loop.
Reverse C³ i – II O mint mark doubled inside as thin vertical line in middle of opening.

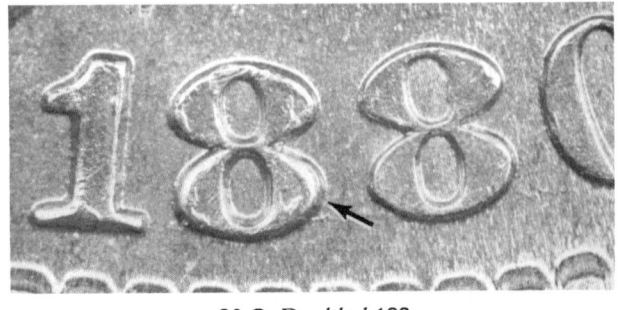

29 O Doubled 188

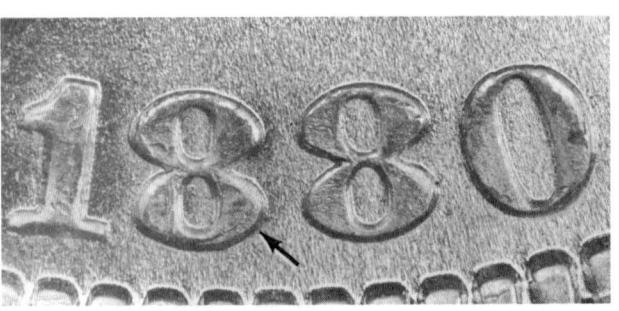

30 O Doubled 880

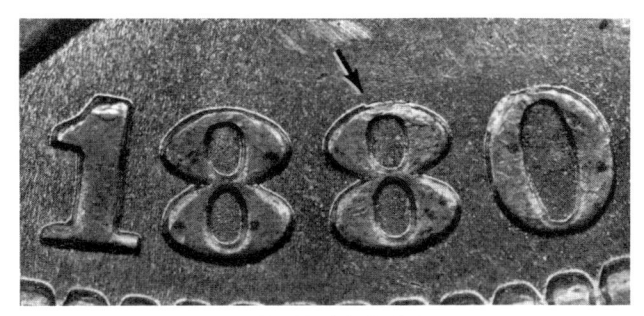

1880-O

32 O Doubled 18-0

33 O Doubled 80

34 O Doubled 188

36 O Doubled 1-80

38 O Doubled 18

39 O Doubled 1-8

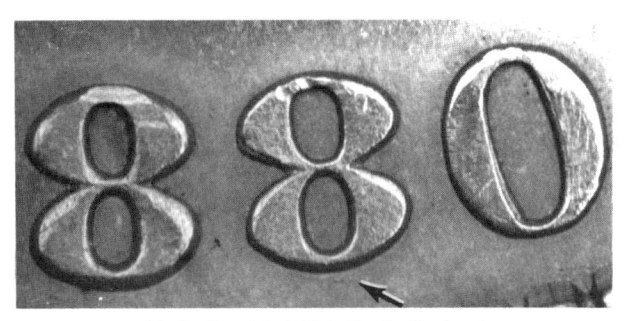

40 O Doubled 880, Dash Under 8

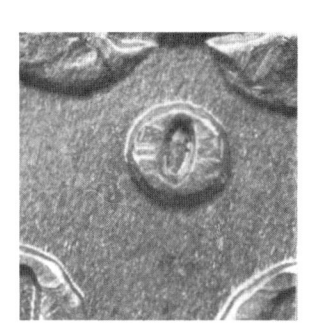

39 R O Tilted Right

207

1880-O / 1880-S

44   III²33 • C³a (Doubled Date)   (176)   I-2   R-3
   Obverse III²33 – Entire date is doubled. 1 doubled at top left of top and bottom crossbar. First 8 doubled on surface of right inside of lower loop. Second 8 doubled at top left and right outside of upper loop and slightly at left inside of lower loop. 0 slightly doubled at right and lower left inside.

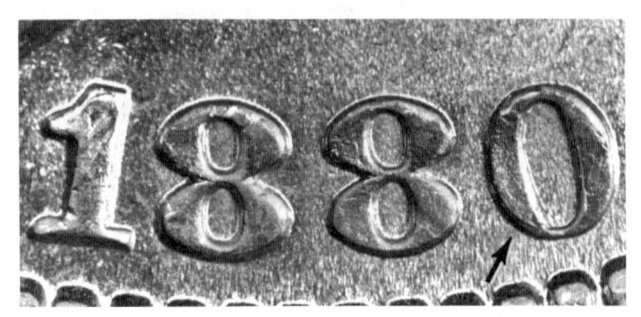

41 O Doubled 1-80

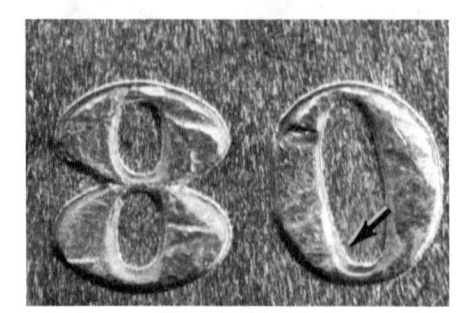

42 O Doubled 80

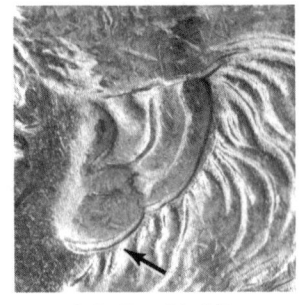

43 O Doubled Ear

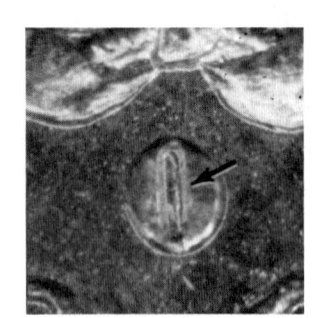

43 R O/O

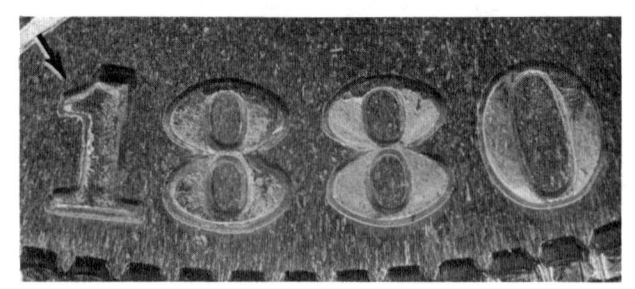

44 O Doubled Date

1880-S

The 1880-S is usually fully struck with good luster. Some slightly weak strikes do exist. It is the most readily available Morgan dollar in proof-like condition with good cameo contrast.

There are a large number of die varieties for the 1880-S but the majority are minor doubled dates and mint marks. Five overdate die varieties are known. VAM 8, 9 80/79 and VAM 11 0/9 bring a modest premium and VAM 10 brings a substantial premium because of its rarity. The other overdate, VAM 12, is not very prominent and fairly common with little price premium. There are two size mint marks but both are common and do not bring any premium.

1   III²1 • C³a (Medium S)   (186)   I-1   R-2
   Obverse III²1 – Normal die of III² type.
   Reverse C³a – Normal die of C³ type with medium IV S mint mark.

2   III²1 • C³b (Large S)   (186)   I-1   R-2
   Reverse C³b – Normal die of C³ type with a very large centered and upright VI S mint mark.

3   III²1 • C³c (S Tilted Left)   I-2   R-3
   Reverse C³c – Normal die of C³ type with very large centered mint mark tilted left.

4   III²2 • C³a (Doubled Date)   I-2   R-3
   Obverse III²2 – Entire date is doubled. 1 doubled at the bottom. First 8 is doubled on bottom surface of lower loop. Second 8 is doubled on lower left outside of upper loop. 0 is doubled at top left and right outside.

5   III²3 • C³a (Doubled 0)   (185)   I-2   R-3
   Obverse III²3 – 0 in date is doubled at top outside at left and right. Some specimens show a die crack through B of Liberty.

6   III²3 • C³c (Doubled 0)   (188)   I-2   R-3

1880-S

7   III² 4 • C³ d (Doubled Date)   (188)   I-3   R-4
Obverse III² 4 – All digits in date doubled. The 1 is doubled below the top and bottom crossbars The first 8 is doubled at top and bottom outside and on surface at top inside of lower loop. Second 8 is doubled on the lower left outside of the upper loop. The 0 is doubled at the bottom outside and top outside left and right.
Reverse C³ d – Normal die with IV S mint mark tilted left and partially filled.

8   III² 5 • C³ a (80/79 Ear)   (186)   I-4   R-3
Obverse III² 5 – 80 repunched over 79 in date. Second 8 has metal in upper loop, faint spike at top left and faint line at bottom. The 0 has a small piece of metal at the top right inside.

9   III² 5 • C³ e (80/79 Ear)   (185)   I-4   R-4
Reverse C³ e – VI S mint mark repunched with original showing as a spike to left top serif.

10   III² 6 • C³ q – (8/7 Crossbar)   (186)   I-4   R-6
Obverse III² 6 – 8 repunched over 7 in date. Second 8 has a few small dots of metal at top within upper loop. A horizontal line shows at bottom of upper loop curving slightly up on the left side. An additional small amount of metal shows on the right inside of the upper loop. No metal in 0.
Reverse C³ q – All legend letters doubled slightly in radial direction. Motto letter doubled at top. Right and left wreath doubled slightly towards rim. Very large centered VI S mint mark tilted left.

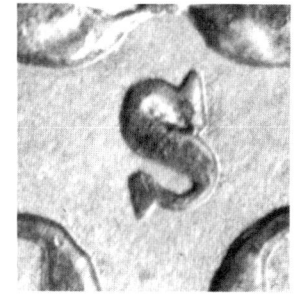

3 R S Tilted Left

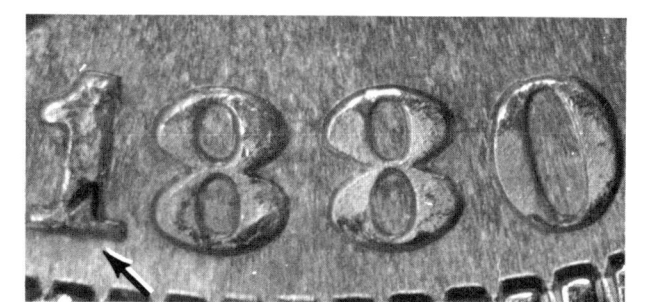

4 O Doubled 1-0

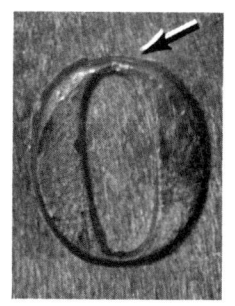

5 O Doubled 0

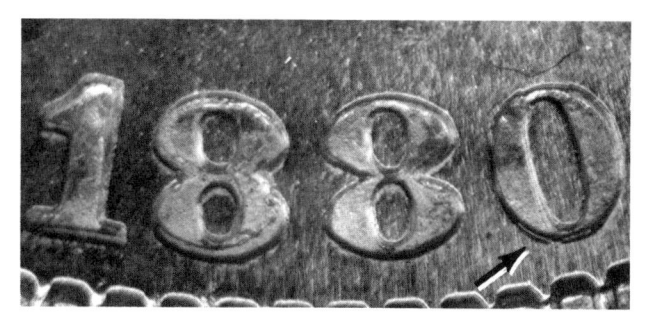

7 O Doubled Date

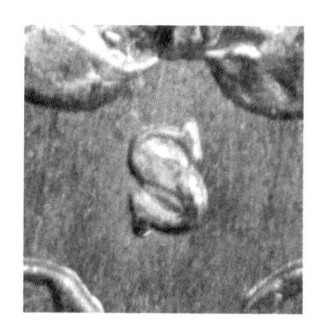

7 R IV S Tilted Left

8 O 80/79

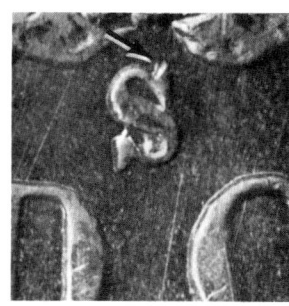

9 R S/S

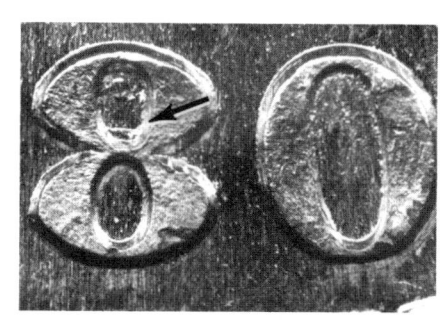

10 O 8/7 Crossbar

1880-S

11 III²7 • C³f (O/9) (184) I-4 R-3

Obverse III²7 – Metal with polishing marks in the remains of the 9 within the top of the opening in 0 of the date. There is a bulge on the outside of the 0 at 10 o'clock. The top loop of the second 8 has a few dots of metal on the right outside of lower loop. 1 doubled on right side of shaft and below upper crossbar. Second 8 doubled on lower outside of upper loop.

Reverse C³f – IV S mint mark set high and repunched with short vertical spike extending downwards from middle of top loop opening and curved line in middle inside of lower loop opening.

12 III²8 • C³d (8/7 Spikes, Doubled 188) (183) I-4 R-3

Obverse III²8 – 80 repunched over 79 in date. Second 8 has a check mark on top of left side of upper loop, a thin diagonal line at top left outside, a faint vertical line at top right outside, a slight bulge of metal at top right inside of upper loop, a diagonal pointed dash attached to bottom outside of lower loop and is doubled at bottom left outside of upper loop. 0 has a small piece of metal at top right inside and a slight bulge at top left outside. 1 is doubled slightly on surface at right side. First 8 doubled at top left inside and on right inside on surface of lower loop.

13 III²9 • C³a (Dash Under 8, Doubled Date) I-2 R-4

Obverse III²9 – A high set and thin dash appears just below the second 8 in date. The second 8 is also slightly doubled at bottom left outside of upper loop. The 0 is doubled on the lower right inside. 1 is doubled at top right of vertical shaft. First 8 doubled on top and right inside of lower loop.

14 III²10 • C³a (Dash Under 8) (185) I-2 R-4

Obverse III²10 – A high set and thin dash appears just below and angles slightly down to the right of the second 8. A small dot of metal is at top inside of upper loop of second 8 and upper loop is doubled at lower left outside. 0 is doubled slightly at top and bottom left side of opening.

15 III²11 • C³g (S/S Right, Dash Under 8) (183) I-3 R-4

Obverse III²11 – Second 8 in date doubled at bottom left side as a thin curved line; a thin dash is set well below the bottom and the bottom left outside of the upper loop is slightly doubled.

Reverse C³g – IV S mint mark repunched with original showing as a short vertical line at top right of upper loop opening and as a vertical curved line at very right side of lower loop opening. Mint mark set slightly left.

16 III²12 • C³a (Doubled 8) (188) I-2 R-3

Obverse III²12 – Die chip on right between the loops of the first 8 of the date. Second 8 is doubled on left bottom outside of upper loop.

17 III²12 • C³c (Doubled 8) (186) I-2 R-3

18 III²3 • C³h (S/S, Doubled 0) I-3 R-4

Reverse C³h – Mint mark repunched with original showing as a curved line centered inside upper loop. IV S mint mark is partially filled.

19 III²3 • C³i (S/S Tripled, Doubled 0) (185) I-3 R-4

Obverse III²3 – Doubled 0 same as VAM 5 but with horizontal die gouge in upper loop of first 8 and several die chips at top right of upper loop of second 8.

Reverse C³i – IV S mint mark tripled with original showing as short and long vertical bars to right of upper serif.

20 III²13 • C³h (Tripled 0) I-2 R-4

Obverse III²13 – 188 in date is doubled and 0 is tripled. 1 is doubled slightly below upper serif and first 8 is doubled slightly at top of upper loop opening. Second 8 doubled slightly at lower left outside of upper loop. 0 in date is tripled strongly on lower left outside and is raised well above the surface of the original 0. The 0 is also doubled at very bottom left inside of opening.

Reverse C³h – Eagle's right wing has a die chip near the tip of the wreath in addition to repunched mint mark.

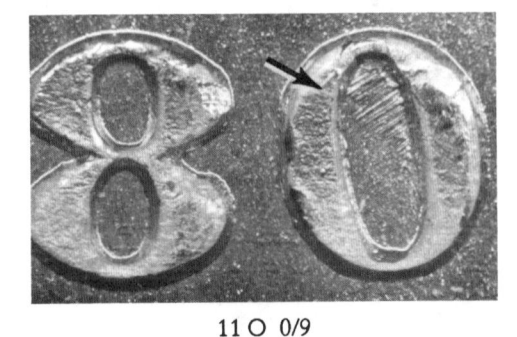

11 O O/9   11 R S/S   12 O 8/7 Spikes

1880-S

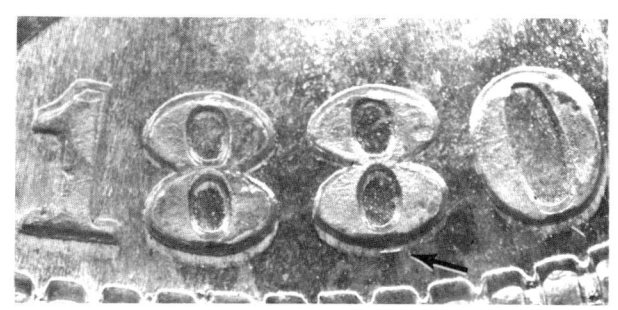

13 O Dash Under 8, Doubled Date

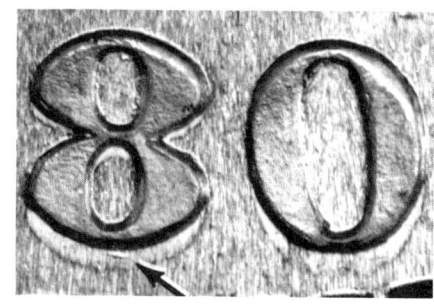

14 O Dash Under 8

15 O Dash Under 8

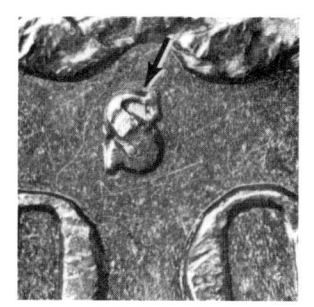

15 R S/S

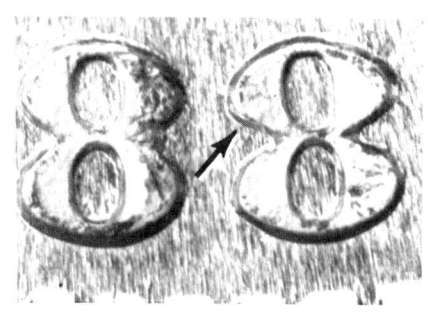

16 O Doubled 8

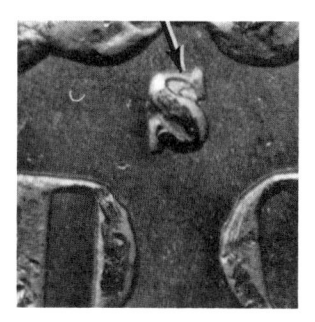

18 R S/S

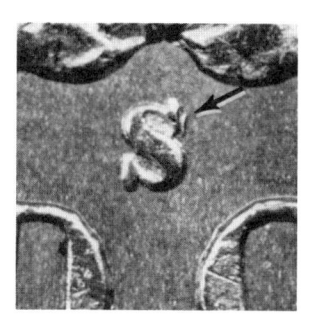

19 R S/S

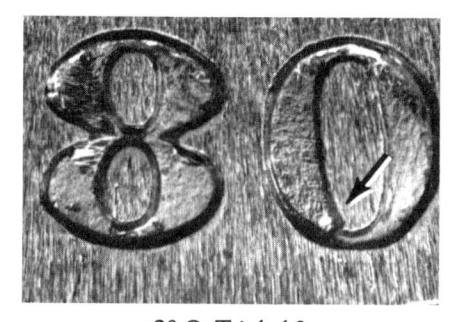

20 O Tripled 0

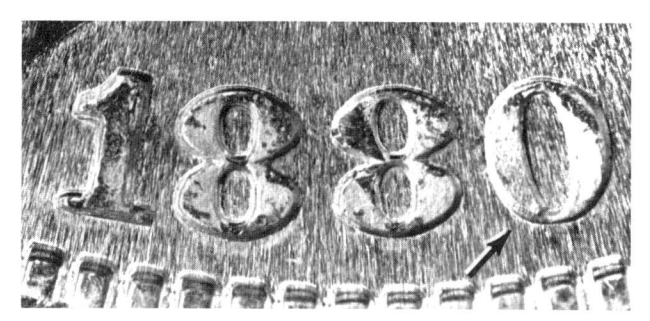

20 O Doubled 18, Tripled 0

20 R Die Chip

1880-S

21	III² 14 • C³ j (Doubled 80)	(185)	I-2	R-3

Obverse III² 14 – 80 doubled in date. Second 8 has top loop doubled on the outside at bottom on both sides and inside as a thin line at top and bottom. Lower loop is doubled as a thin line at the top inside. 0 doubled at top on left and right sides.
Reverse C³ j – IV S mint mark with top loop filled and diagonal shaft doubled inside lower loop.

22	III² 14 • C³ c (Doubled 80)	(188)	I-2	R-3
23	III² 15 • C³ e (S/S Top, Doubled 80)		I-2	R-4

Obverse III² 15 – Doubled 80 in date. Second 8 is doubled on lower left outside of upper loop. 0 is doubled on right inside.

24	III² 16 • C³ k (Doubled 80, Die Chip 8)		I-3	R-3

Obverse III² 16 – 80 in date is slightly doubled. First 8 has a small die chip in top inside of upper loop. Second 8 is doubled slightly on lower left outside of upper loop. 0 is doubled at top left and right outside.
Reverse C³ k – Slight doubling of legend letters in radial direction plus motto and wreath leaves on outside. Very large VI S mint mark tilted left.

25	III² 17 • C³ a (Doubled 880)	(187)	I-2	R-4

Obverse III² 17 – 880 in date is doubled. First 8 is doubled at bottom right outside of lower loop. Second 8 slightly doubled at lower left outside of upper loop. 0 is doubled strongly on lower left side and is raised well above the surface of the original 0. The 0 is also doubled at very bottom left inside of opening similar to III² 13 obverse. Some specimens show die chip on right side of first 8.

26	III² 18 • C³ a (Doubled 880)	(184)	I-2	R-3

Obverse III² 18 – Doubled 880 in date. First 8 is doubled at bottom and has die chip between loops on left side. Second 8 slightly doubled at lower left outside of upper loop. 0 doubled at top left and right outside and slightly at lower left and right outside.

27	III² 18 • C³ j (Doubled 880)		I-2	R-4
28	III² 19 • C³ a (Doubled 880)		I-2	R-3

Obverse III² 19 – Doubled 880 in date. First 8 is doubled on top surface at bottom right outside and top left inside of lower loop. Second 8 doubled at lower left outside of upper loop. 0 doubled slightly at lower left inside.

29	III² 19 • C³ c (Doubled 880)	(187)	I-2	R-3
30	III² 20 • C³ h (S/S and Doubled Date)	(187)	I-3	R-3

Obverse III² 20 – Entire date doubled. 1 doubled faintly on right surface of vertical shaft. First 8 doubled on surface at top inside and right outside of lower loop. Second 8 doubled at left outside of upper loop. 0 doubled faintly on right inside.

31	III² 21 • C³ c (Doubled Date)	(187)	I-2	R-4

Obverse III² 21 – Entire doubled faintly at very bottom right. First 8 doubled strongly on surface at bottom of lower loop. Second 8 doubled at lower left outside of upper loop. 0 doubled on left and right outside at top and bottom.

32	III² 21 • C³ h (S/S and Doubled Date)	(187)	I-3	R-3

Reverse C³ h – No dot on eagle's wing.

33	III² 22 • C³ l (Doubled Date)	(184)	I-2	R-3

Obverse III² 22 – Entire date is doubled. 1 is doubled on left side of vertical shaft. First 8 is doubled on top surface at bottom of lower loop with a die chip between loops on right side. Second 8 is doubled at lower left outside of upper loop. 0 is doubled slightly at lower left inside.
Reverse C³ l – VI S mint mark tilted left and doubled with short diagonal spike on left inside of upper loop and a long diagonal line within lower loop.

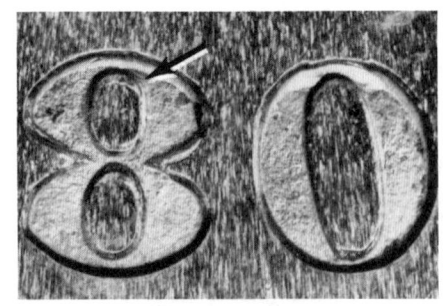

21 O Doubled 80    21 R Doubled S    24 O Doubled 80, Die Chip in 8

1880-S

23 O Doubled 80

25 O Doubled 880

26 O Doubled 880

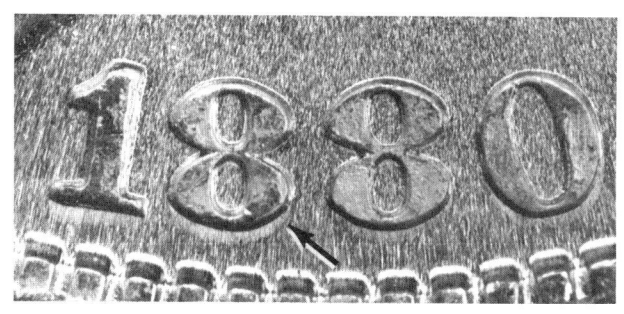

31 O DOubled Date

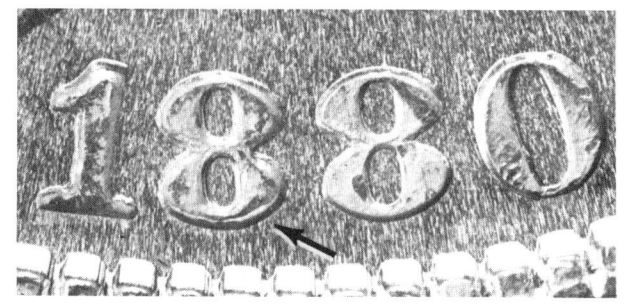

32 O Doubled Date

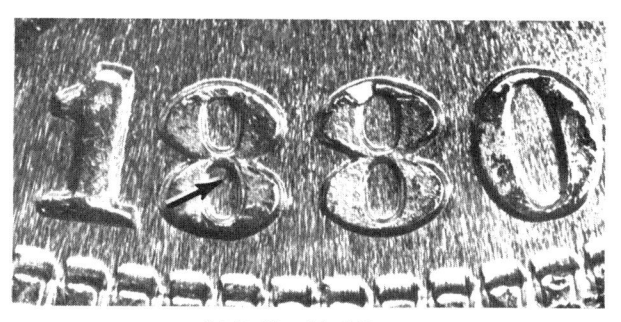

34 O Doubled Date

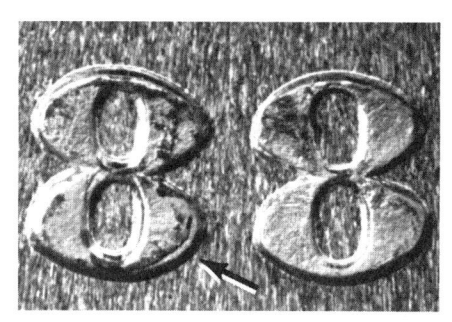

28 O DOubled 880

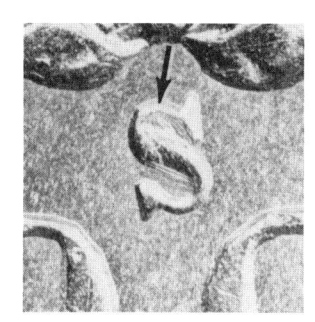

33 R Doubled S

33 O Doubled Date

213

1880-S

34 III²23 • C³m (Doubled Date) I-2 R-3
Obverse III²23 – Entire date is doubled slightly. 1 is doubled faintly below top crossbar and above bottom crossbar. First 8 is doubled on right inside of lower loop and slightly on bottom outside. Second 8 is doubled at bottom left outside of upper loop. 0 is doubled on top surface at left inside and slightly on lower right inside.
Reverse C³m – IV S mint mark set to left.

35 III²24 • C³n (Doubled Date) (188) I-3 R-3
Obverse III²24 – Entire date slightly doubled. 1 is doubled faintly at bottom of top crossbar. First 8 is doubled at top inside of upper loop. Second 8 is doubled at bottom left outside of upper loop. 0 is doubled at top left and right outside and faintly at top right inside.
Reverse C³n – VI S mint mark tilted very far to left.

36 III²4 • C³o of (Doubled Date, S/S Right) (188) I-2 R-4
Reverse C³o – IV S mint mark repunched with the original showing as a curved line at top and left inside of loop, a curved line in middle of lower loop, and a short vertical line to middle right of upper serif.

37 III²25 • C³a (Doubled 80) (188) I-2 R-3
Obverse III²25 – Doubled 80 in date. Second 8 doubled faintly at left bottom outside of upper loop. 0 doubled faintly at left and right outside.

38 III²12 • C³g (Doubled 8, S/S Right) I-2 R-4
Obverse III²12 – No die chip between first 8 loops.

39 III²25 • C³g (Doubled 80, Large S) I-2 R-3

40 III²26 • C³a (Doubled 80, S Tilted Left) I-2 R-3
Obverse III²26 – Doubled 80 in date. Second 8 doubled faintly at left bottom outside of upper loop. 0 doubled faintly at bottom left outside on top surface.

41 III²27 • C³a (Doubled 1-80) I-2 R-3
Obverse III²27 – Doubled 1-80 in date. 1 doubled as a notch at the top left of lower crossbar. Second 8 doubled at left bottom outside of upper loop. 0 doubled at left inside and strongly at top left and right outside.

42 III²21 • C³a (Doubled Date) I-2 R-4
Reverse C³a – Some specimens show a large die chip on wreath leaf opposite NI of UNITED and a smaller die chip on field next to I of UNITED.

43 III²28 • C³p (Doubled 1-80, S/S) I-2 R-3
Obverse III²28 – 1-80 doubled in date. 1 doubled slightly at top of bottom serif on both sides. Second 8 doubled slightly at lower left outside of upper loop. 0 doubled at left and right inside.
Reverse C³p – VI S mint mark doubled with curved line at top inside of upper loop and a thin diagonal line at top inside of lower loop.

44 III²29 • C³a (Doubled Date) (186) I-2 R-3
Obverse III²29 – Entire date is doubled. 1 is doubled on surface at top left of upper crossbar, top left and right of lower crossbar and at lower left of vertical shaft. First 8 doubled on surface at top inside and right outside of lower loop. Second 8 doubled at lower left outside of upper loop. 0 doubled slightly at top left and right outside.

45 III²30 • C³r (Doubled Date, S/S Up) (188) I-2 R-3
Obverse III²30 – Entire date is doubled. 1 is doubled on surface at lower right side of vertical shaft top right of lower crossbar. First 8 doubled on surface at left inside of lower loop. Second 8 doubled at lower left outside of upper loop. 0 doubled at top left and right outside and on surface at lower right inside.
Reverse C³r – IV S mint mark repunched with original showing as a carved bulge at bottom inside of upper loop and a horizontal curved line within middle of lower loop.

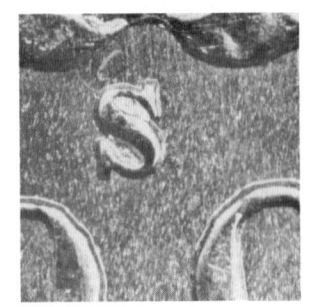

34 R S Set Left

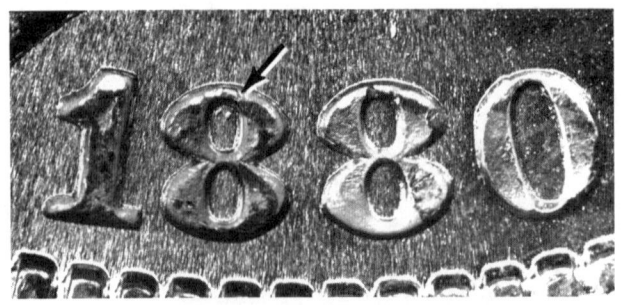

35 O Doubled Date

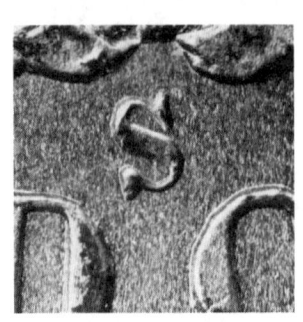

35 R S Tilted Left

1880-S

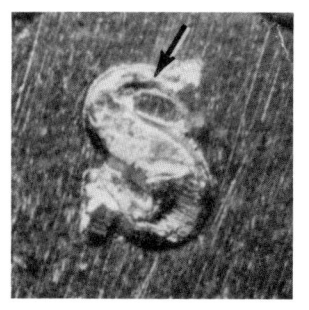

36 R S/S Right

37 O Doubled 80

40 O Doubled 80

41 O Doubled 1-80

43 O Doubled 1-80

44 O Doubled Date

45 O Doubled Date

42 R Die Chip in Wreath

43 R S/S

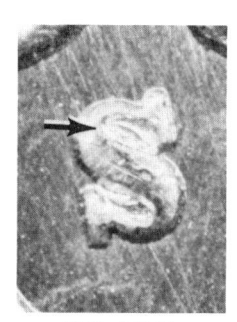

45 R S/S Up

215

1880-S

| 46 | III²31 • C³b (Dash Under 8, Doubled 80) | (183) | I-2 | R-3 |

Obverse III²31 – A high set and short dash appears just below the second 8. Second 8 is also doubled at lower left outside of upper loop. 0 is doubled at top left and right outside.

| 47 | III²32 • C³a (Doubled Date) | (188) | I-2 | R-3 |

Obverse III²32 – Entire date is doubled. 1 is doubled on surface at lower right side of vertical shaft and top right of lower crossbar. First 8 doubled on surface at left inside of both loops and on right outside of lower loop. Second 8 doubled at lower left outside of upper loop. 0 doubled strongly at top left outside and faintly on top right outside.

| 48 | III²33 • C³c (Doubled Date, S Tilted Left) | (186) | I-2 | R-3 |

Obverse III²33 – Entire date is doubled. 1 is doubled on surface at top left of upper crossbar and at top left and right of lower crossbar. First 8 doubled on surface at lower left outside of upper loop and at bottom outside of lower loop. Second 8 doubled slightly at lower left outside of upper loop. 0 doubled slightly at lower left inside and outside.

| 49 | III²29 • C³r (Doubled Date, S/S Up) | (186) | I-2 | R-3 |
| 50 | III²13 • C³s (Tripled 0, S/S Down) | (185) | I-2 | R-3 |

Reverse C³s – IV S mint mark repunched showing as a horizontal line within the middle of the upper loop opening and a diagonal line at top of lower loop opening.

51	III²18 • C³r (Doubled 880, S/S Up)	(186)	I-2	R-3
52	III²20 • C³a (Doubled Date)	(185)	I-2	R-3
53	III²27 • C³c (Doubled 1-80, S Tilted Left)	(187)	I-2	R-3
54	III²15 • C³a (Doubled 80)		I-2	R-3
55	III²34 • C³a (Doubled 80, Die Chip Wreath)	(189)	1-2	R-3

Obverse III²34 – Doubled 80 in date. Second 8 doubled slightly on lower left outside of upper loop. 0 doubled at left and right outside at top and bottom.

Reverse C³a – Large die chip on wreath leaf opposite NI of UNITED and a smaller die chip in field next to I of UNITED as in VAM 42.

| 56 | III²35 • C³a (Doubled Date) | (188) | I-2 | R-3 |

Obverse III²35 – Entire date doubled. 1 doubled at top right of vertical shaft. First 8 doubled strongly at top inside and bottom outside of lower loop. Second 8 doubled slightly at lower loop. 0 doubled slightly at lower left inside.

| 57 | III²24 • C³c (Doubled Date) | (186) | I-2 | R-3 |
| 58 | III²36 • C³c (Doubled 88, S Tilted Left) | (184) | I-2 | R-3 |

Obverse III²36 – Doubled 88 in date. First 8 doubled at right inside and slightly at bottom outside of lower loop. Second 8 doubled slightly at lower left outside of upper loop.

| 59 | III²36 • C³d (Doubled Date, S Tilted Left) | (182) | I-2 | R-3 |
| 60 | III²33 • C³t (Doubled Date, S/S) | (187) | I-2 | R 3 |

Reverse C³t – IV S mint mark repunched showing as a curved diagonal line in middle of upper loop opening.

61	III²33 • C³d (Doubled Date, S Tilted left)	(187)	I-2	R-3
62	III²12 • C³b (Doubled 8)	(183)	I-2	R-3
63	III²37 • C³b (Doubled Date)	(188)	I-2	R-3

Obverse III²37 – Entire date is doubled. 1 doubled slightly below upper crossbar. First 8 doubled on surface at lower right outside of upper and lower loops and at top right inside of lower loop. Second 8 doubled at lower left of upper loop. 0 doubled at left and right outside at top and bottom.

46 O Doubled 80, Dash 8   50 R S/S Down   55 O Doubled 80

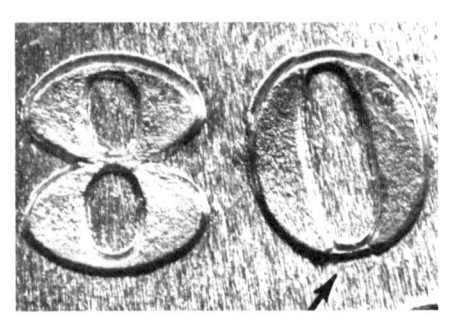

1880-S

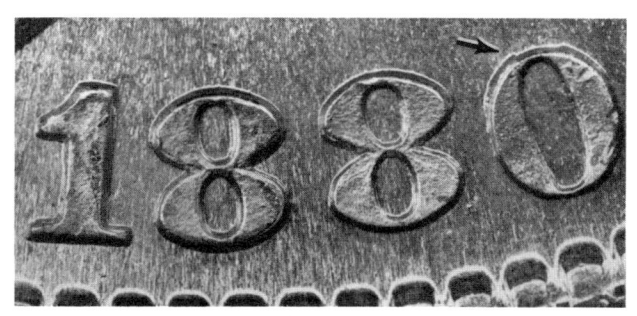

47 O Doubled Date

48 O Doubled Date

56 O Doubled Date

58 O Doubled 88

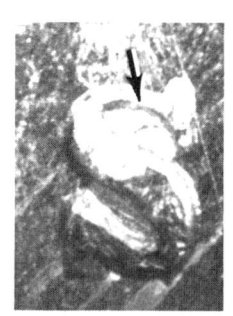

60 R S/S

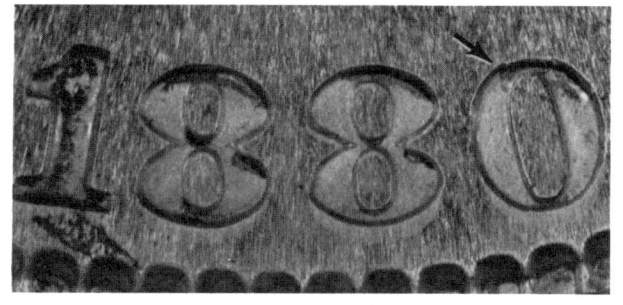

63 O Doubled Date

64 O Doubled Date

64   **III²38 • C³u (Doubled Date, S/S)**   (188)   I-2   R-3

Obverse III²38 – Entire date is doubled. 1 doubled slightly on right side of vertical shaft. First 8 doubled at top inside of lower loop. Second 8 doubled at lower left outside of upper loop. 0 doubled at left and right top outside.

Reverse C³u – IV S mint mark is doubled with diagonal line at top of upper loop opening and a short horizontal line on right inside of lower loop. Mint mark is set slightly left with slight tilt to right.

65   **III²30 • C³c (Doubled Date, S Tilted Left)**   (188)   I-2   R-3

66   **III²24 • C³a (Doubled Date)**   (185)   I-2   R-3

67   **III²39 • C³a (Doubled Date)**   (188)   I-2   R-3

Obverse III²39 – Entire date is doubled. 1 doubled as a notch on left side of lower crossbar. First 8 doubled on surface at left and right of lower loop. Second 8 doubled at lower left outside of upper loop. 0 doubled top left and right outside and lower left inside.

68   **III²31 • C³j (Doubled Date, S/S)**   (188)   I-2   R-3

69   **III²15 • C³v (Doubled 80 and Reverse)**   (186)   I-2   R-3

Reverse C³v – Doubled left wreath, UNITED STATES OF AMERICA, and left star towards rim. VI S mint mark centered and tilted slightly left.

70   **III²22 • C³b (Doubled Date)**   (184)   I-2   R-3

64 R S/S

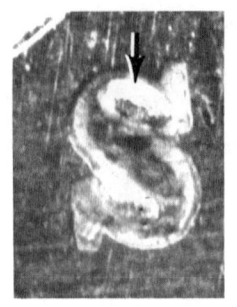

67 O Doubled Date

69 R Doubled Wreath and Lettering

1881-P

A full strike is typical for this date but weak strikes do exist. Luster is variable however and many are dull because of the high mintage. A few minor die varieties exist but none are significant enough to command a price premium.

Proof-like coins are fairly scarce and are a little more difficult to find than other early P mints. Proofs tend to have excellent contrast and nice ones are somewhat available.

1   III^{2}1 • C^{3}a (Normal Die)   I-1   R-2
Obverse III^{2}1 – Normal die of III^2 type. Some specimens show a die chip between the loops of the first 8 or a small die gouge at bottom of Y in LIBERTY.
Reverse C^{3}a – Normal die of C^3 type.

1A   III^{2}1 • C^{3}a (Die Chips in 8)   (180)   I-2   R-3
Obverse III^{2}1 – Short die chip at top left inside of upper loop of first 8. In some specimens, second 8 has die chips in middle of both loops. Some specimens show die chip at top inside of both loops.

2   III^{2}2 • C^{3}a (Dash Under 8)   I-2   R-3
Obverse III^{2}2 – A dash appears below the second 8 in the date.

3   III^{2}3 • C^{3}a (Doubled 1)   I-2   R-3
Obverse III^{2}3 – Second 1 in date doubled at top.

4   III^{2}4 • C^{3}a (Doubled 1 Left)   I-2   R-3
Obverse III^{2}4 – Second 1 in date doubled at top on left side only. First 8 has a spike of metal between loops on right.

5   III^{2}5 • C^{3}a (Doubled 8)   (180)   I-2   R-3
Obverse III^{2}5 – First 8 in date doubled at right inside of upper loop.

6   III^{2}6 • C^{3}a (Tripled 8)   (179)   I-2   R-4
Obverse III^{2}6 – First 8 in date is tripled strongly at bottom right outside of upper and lower loops and at top left inside of lower loop. Upper loop of first 8 is also doubled at top left inside.

7   III^{2}7 • C^{3}a (Doubled 1, Tripled 8)   (180)   I-2   R-3
Obverse III^{2}7 – First 1 doubled at bottom of lower crossbar. First 8 tripled at bottom outside of lower loop and doubled at top inside of upper and lower loop with short spike at top left inside of upper loop. All left and right stars doubled faintly towards rim.

8   III^{2}8 • C^{3}a (Doubled 18-1)   (181)   I-2   Proof
Obverse III^{2}8 – 18-1 in date doubled. First 1 is doubled slightly at top right of vertical shaft. First 8 is doubled on surface at top right inside lower loop. Second 1 is doubled at top left.

1881-P

9   **III²9 • C³a (Doubled 18-1)**   (180)   I-2   R-4
    Obverse III²9 – 18-1 in date doubled. First 1 doubled slightly above crossbar on right. First 8 is doubled strongly on surface of lower right inside of both loops and at top right outside of upper loop with die chip between loops on right side. Second 1 is doubled at top left.

10 **III²10 • C³a (Doubled 18-1)**   (181)   I-2   R-4
    Obverse III²10 – 18-1 in date doubled. First 1 is doubled slightly at top right of vertical shaft. First 8 is doubled at top inside of upper loop with die chip at top left inside of upper loop, doubled at top and right inside of lower loop and doubled at bottom outside of lower loop. Second 1 is doubled slightly at top left. Faint dash just under second 8 in some specimens.

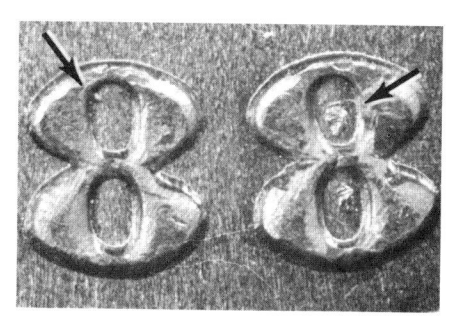

1A O Die Chip in 8s

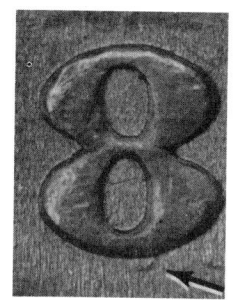

2 O Dash

3 O Doubled 1

5 O Doubled 8

4 O Doubled 1 Left

6 O Tripled 8

7 O Doubled 1, Tripled 8

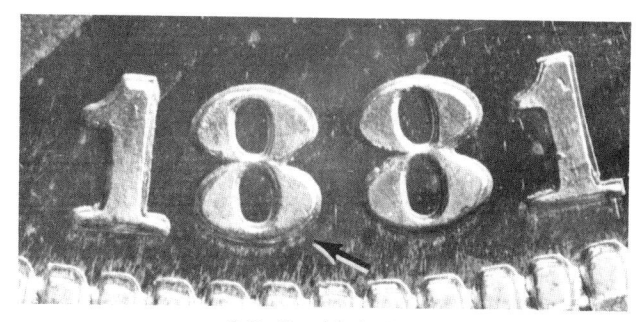

8 O Doubled 18-1

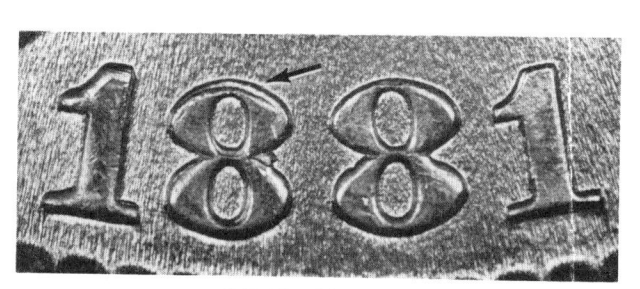

9 O Doubled 18-1

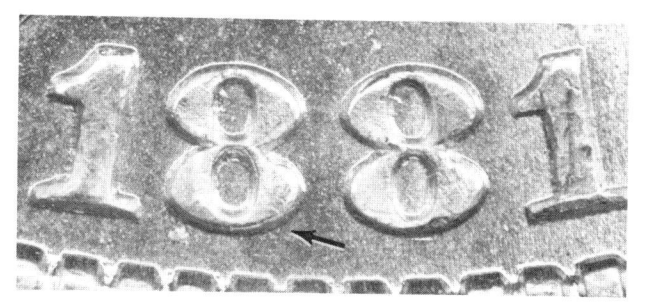

10 O Doubled 18-1

11 O Doubled 8-1

219

1881-P

| 11 | III² 11 – C³ a (Doubled 8-1) | (180) | I-2 | R-3 |

Obverse III² 11 – Doubled 8-1 in date. First 8 doubled on surface at top outside of upper loop. Second 1 has a notch at lower left of vertical shaft.

| 12 | III² 12 • C³ a (Doubled 1-1) | (179) | I-2 | R-3 |

Obverse III² 12 – Both 1's in date are doubled below upper crossbar. Short die chip at top left inside of first 8.

| 13 | III² 13 • C³ a (Doubled 18) | (181) | I-2 | R-3 |

Obverse III² 13 – 18 doubled on surface at very bottom outside. First 8 has die chip at left inside of upper loop.

| 14 | III² 14 • C³ a (Doubled 18-1) | (180) | I-2 | R-3 |

Obverse III² 14 – Doubled 18-1 in date. First 1 doubled slightly on top right of vertical shaft. First 8 doubled at top right outside and on right outside surface of upper loop. Second 1 doubled all across very top.

| 15 | III² 15 • C³ a (Doubled Second 1) | (181) | 1-2 | R-3 |

Obverse III² 15 – Second 1 doubled below upper crossbar. First 8 has short die chip at top left inside of upper loop.

| 16 | III² 16 • C³ a (Doubled 18 and Stars) | (180) | I-3 | R-3 |

Obverse III² 16 – All left and right stars tripled towards rim. First 1 doubled at top inside of both loops and tripled at bottom outside of lower loop plus a short die chip at top left inside of upper loop.

12 O Doubled 1-1

13 O Doubled 18

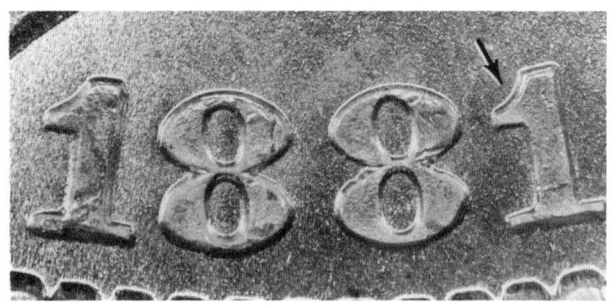

14 O Doubled 18-1

15 O Second 1 Doubled

16 O Doubled 18 and Stars

1881-CC

Half the mintage was released as uncirculated coins during the 1973-74 and 1980 GSA sales, so BU coins are not scarce. The strike is generally full and the luster excellent because of the low number of coins struck by the dies. The overall quality is the highest for the Carson City Mint. No significant die varieties exist.

A considerable percentage of the issue are proof-likes because of the low die mintages. A significant number of these have very deep mirrors with cameo devices.

1   **III²1 • C³a (Normal Die)**   I-1   R-3
Obverse III²1 – Normal die of III² type.
Reverse C³a – Normal die of C³ type with large V CC mint mark.

2   **III²2 • C³a (Doubled 88)**   I-2   R-4
Obverse III²2 – Both 8's in date doubled. First 8 has die chip on left inside of top loop and is doubled as a thin line at the top inside of the lower loop. Second 8 has die chips in a band across middle inside of upper loop and is doubled on the right inside of lower loop.
Reverse C³a – Thin line die scratch from olive branch to leaves just above the arrow feathers.

3   **III²3 • C³a (Dash Under 8)**   (178)   I-2   R-4
Obverse III²3 – The second 8 in the date has a thin dash below the bottom loop. The first 1 is doubled on the surface of the vertical shaft on the right side. The first 8 is doubled on the surface at the top inside and bottom right outside of both inside of upper loops.

4   **III²4 • C³a (Doubled 18)**   I-2   R-3
Obverse III²4 – Doubled 18 in date. 1 doubled slightly on right side of vertical bar. First 8 doubled on surface on left inside and lower right outside of both loops.

5   **III²1 • C³b (CC Tilted Left)**   (178)   I-2   R-3
Reverse C³b – V CC mint mark centered and tilted slightly to left.

6   **III²3 • C³b (Doubled 18, CC Tilted Left)**   (178)   I-2   R-3
Obverse III²3 – There is no dash under the second 8.

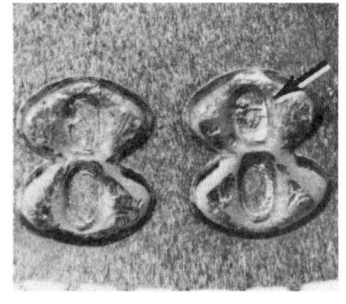

2 O Doubled 88

2 R Die Scratch

3 O Dash 8, Doubled 18

4 O Doubled 18

5 R CC Tilted Left

1881-O

Most coins of this date are fully struck but the luster tends to be subdued because of long use of the dies to achieve high mintages. Slider coins are fairly common although not as much as 1879-O and 1880-O. Numerous minor die varieties exist but none are significant.

Proof-likes are not especially scarce but many have little or dull contrast.

1 III² 1 • C³ a (Normal Die) (176) I-1 R-2
Obverse III² 1 – Normal die of III² type.
Reverse C³ a – Normal die of C³ type with tall oval medium II O mint mark, centered and upright.

1A III² 1 • C³ a (Spike in 8) (176) I-2 R-3
Obverse III² 1 – First 8 had a short die chip at top left inside of upper loop.

2 III² 1 • C³ b (O/O Low) (176) I-2 R-4
Reverse C³ b – Mint mark tilted to left and repunched with original showing at bottom of opening.

2A III² 1 • C³ b (O/O Low, Spike in 8) (176) I-2 R-3
Obverse III² 1 – First 8 has a short die chip spike at top left inside of upper loop.

3 III² 2 • C³ a (Doubled 18) (176) I-2 R-3
Obverse III² 2 – Doubled 18 in date. The 1 has a doubled vertical bar on the right side. The upper and lower loops of the first 8 are doubled on the left inside.

4 III² 3 • C³ a (Doubled 1) (176) I-2 R-3
Obverse III² 3 – Last 1 in date doubled at top and on lower right side of vertical bar.

5 III² 3 • C³ c (O/O Right, Doubled 1) (176) I-2 R-3
Reverse C³ c – II O mint mark doubled on right inside with a shallow thin diagonal bar (die gouge) two-thirds way up in opening.

6 III² 1 • C³ d (O Tilted Left) (176) I-2 R-3
Reverse C³ d – II O mint mark centered and tilted left.

6A III² 1 • C³ d (Spike in 8) (176) I-2 R-3

7 III² 1 • C³ e (O Set High) (176) I-2 R-3
Reverse C³ e – II O mint mark centered and set high.

8 III² 1 • C³ f (O Tilted Right) (176) I-2 R-3
Reverse C³ f – O mint mark centered and tilted slightly to right.

9 III² 4 • C³ g (Bar O, Doubled 8) (176) I-2 R-3
Obverse III² 4 – First 8 in date doubled at top inside of upper and lower loops and on surface at bottom outside of lower loop.
Reverse C³ g – Short die chip at lower right inside of II O mint mark.

10 III² 5 • C³ h (O/O Top Right, Tripled 18-1) (176) I-3 R-4
Obverse III² 5 – Tripled 18-1 in date. First 1 tripled at bottom of top and bottom crossbars. 8 tripled at top inside of both loops, lower left outside of top loop and bottom outside of lower loop. Second 1 is doubled slightly at bottom of crossbar and on right side of vertical bar.
Reverse C³ h – II O mint mark doubled on middle and top right side of opening.

11 III² 1 • C³ i (O/O Left) (176) I-3 R-3
Obverse III² 1 – Spike in 8 same as 1A.
Reverse C³ i – II O mint mark doubled slightly on the left side of opening as a thin vertical line.

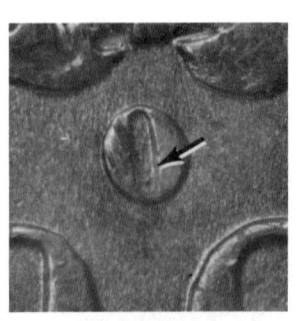

1A O Spike in 8

2 R O/O Low

3 O Doubled 18

1881-O

4 O Doubled 1

5 R O/O Right

6 R O Tilted Left

7 R O Set High

8 R O Titled Right

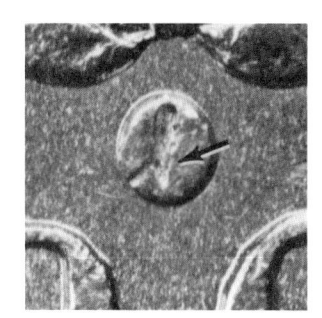

9 R Bar O

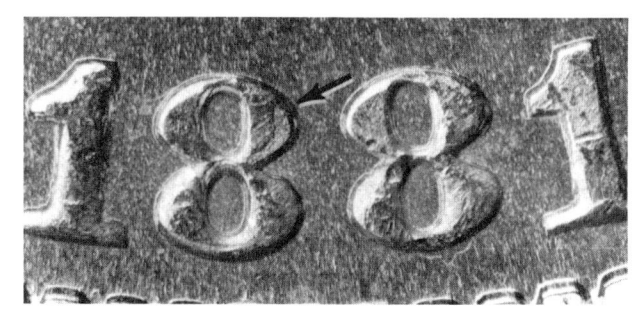

10 O Tripled 18-1

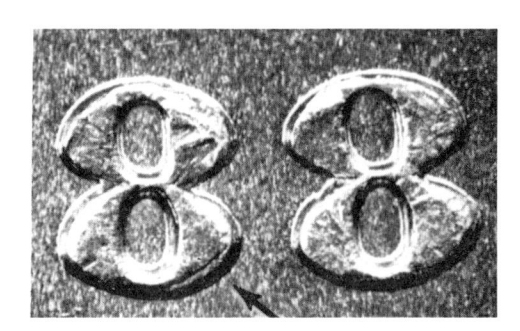

9 O Doubled 8

10 O Tripled 18-1

10 R O/O Top Right

11 R O/O Left

12 R O/O Lower Right

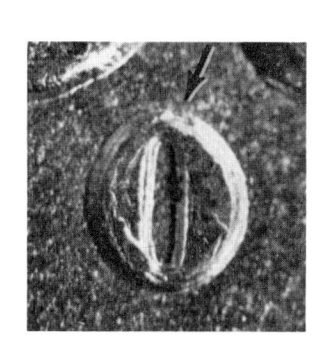

13 R O/O High

1881-O

| 12 | III²1 • C³i (O/O Lower Right) | (176) | I-2 | R-4 |

Reverse C³i – Centered II O mint mark doubled right inside of opening as a thin vertical bar curving to left at bottom of opening.

| 13 | III²4 • C³k (Doubled 8, O/O High) | (176) | I-3 | R-3 |

Reverse C³k – II O mint mark doubled strongly at top left and right outside.

| 14 | III²6 • C³a (Doubled First 8, Die Gouge DO) | (176) | I-2 | R-3 |

Obverse III²6 – Spike in first 8 as in 1A. First 8 is doubled on surface at bottom right outside of lower loop.
Reverse C³a – Doubled die gouge through DO in Dollar.

| 15 | III²7 • C³a (Doubled 1) | (176) | I-2 | R-3 |

Obverse III²7 – Second 1 doubled slightly at top left of upper crossbar and as a notch on the lower right side of vertical shaft. Spike in first 8 as in 1A.

| 16 | III²8 • C³a (Doubled 1) | (176) | I-2 | R-3 |

Obverse III²8 – First 1 doubled slightly at bottom of upper crossbar and at top right of vertical shaft. First 8 has a short die chip in top left inside of upper loop.

| 17 | III²9 • C³a (Dash Under 8) | (176) | I-2 | R-3 |

Obverse III²9 – Second 8 in date has a thin dash just below the bottom loop. First 8 has a short die chip in top left inside of upper loop.

| 18 | III²10 • C³a (Doubled 18) | (176) | I-2 | R-3 |

Obverse III²10 – Doubled 18 in date. 1 doubled below upper crossbar. First 8 doubled at top left inside of lower loop and has a short die chip spike at top left inside of upper loop.
Reverse C³a – A long thin die gouge runs from D through O to L in DOLLAR.

| 19 | III²11 • C³a (Doubled 1-1) | (176) | I-2 | R-3 |

Obverse III²11 – Doubled 1-1 in date. First 1 doubled strongly below upper crossbar. Second 1 also doubled faintly below upper crossbar. First 8 has a short die chip spike at top left inside of upper loop.

| 20 | III²12 • C³a (Doubled 18) | (176) | I-2 | R-3 |

Obverse III²12 – Doubled 18 in date. First 1 doubled slightly at top right of vertical shaft. First 8 doubled at top and right inside and bottom outside of lower loop with die chip at top left inside of upper loop.

| 21 | III²1 • C³h (O/O Top Right) | (176) | I-2 | R-3 |

| 22 | III²13 • C³d (Doubled 1-1, O Tilted Left) | (176) | I-2 | R-3 |

Obverse III²13 – Doubled 1-1 in date. First 1 doubled at top right of vertical shaft as a notch. Second 1 doubled at top of upper serif and on lower left side of vertical shaft.

| 23 | III²1 • C³k (O Set Left) | (176) | I-2 | R-3 |

Obverse III²1 – First 8 has a short die chip at top left inside of upper loop.
Reverse C³k – II O mint mark centered, upright and set to left. Eagle's right wing is overpolished on some specimens.

| 24 | III²14 • C³a (Doubled Second 1) | (176) | I-2 | R-3 |

Obverse III²14 – Second 1 doubled at lower left side on vertical shaft as a notch.

| 25 | III²1 • C³l (O/O Right) | (176) | I-2 | R-3 |

Reverse C³l – II O mint mark centered and tilted left with doubling on right inside and die chips on lower right outside. Eagle's right wing and left wreath are overpolished.

| 26 | III²15 • C³a (Doubled 18) | (176) | I-2 | R-3 |

Obverse C³a – Doubled 18 in date. First 1 doubled slightly at top right of vertical shaft. First 8 doubled at top outside, left inside and right outside of upper loop.

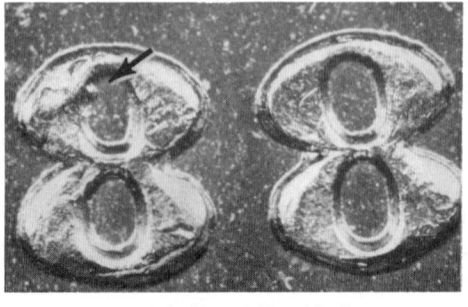

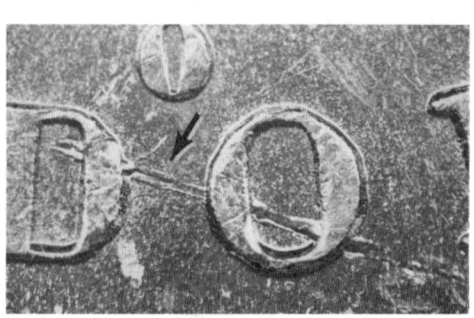

14 O First 8 Doubled

14 R Die Gouges

1881-O

15 O Doubled 1

16 O Doubled 1

(Photo Not Available)

17 O Dash Under 8

(Photo Not Available)

20 O Doubled 18

18 O Doubled 18

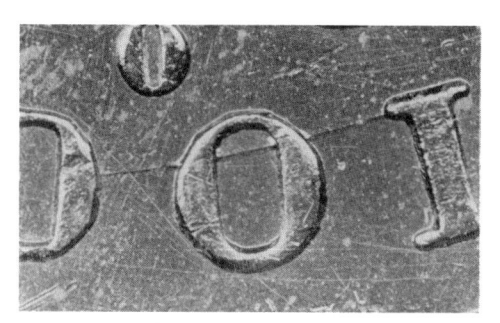

18 R Die Gouge DOL

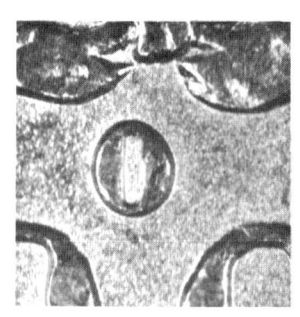

23 R O Set Left

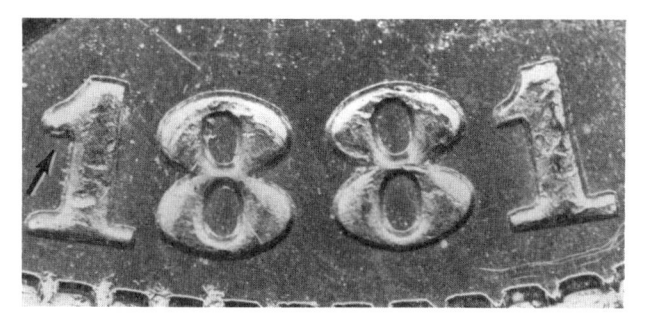

19 O Doubled 1-1

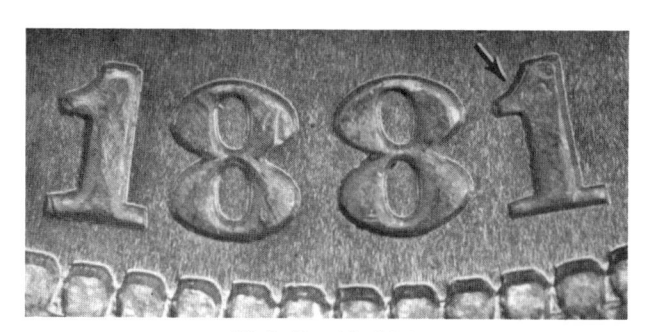

22 O Doubled 1-1

24 O Second 1 Doubled

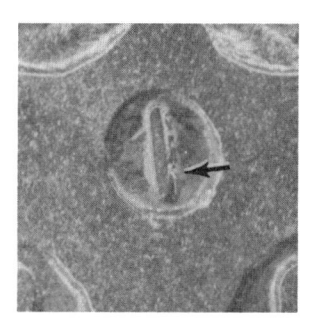

25 R O/O

26 O Doubled 18

225

1881-S

The typical 1881-S is fully struck with outstanding luster. Even though it was a high mintage issue the average number of coins per die pair struck was fairly low so not many coins were struck with worn dies. Apparently this issue escaped significant melting during 1918-1920 and were not mishandled or shipped all over the country. Thus, they are the most plentiful Morgan dollars in nice condition. Numerous die varieties exist but none are particularly significant.

It is readily available in proof-like condition although most are brilliant with little contrast. Many are semi-proof-like or one sided proof-like. The excellent luster of the issue can give proof-like appearance and the coins should be checked to see if clear mirrors exist on both sides when purchasing proof-like specimens. Two-sided cameo proof-likes are scarcer for this date than any other early S mint.

1   III^{2}1 • C^{3}a (Normal Die)   (189)   I-1   R-1
    Obverse III^{2}1 – Normal die of III^2 type. Some specimens show die chips between loops on both sides of first 8.
    Reverse C^{3}a – Normal die of C^3 type with a medium IV S mint mark centered and upright.

1A   III^{2}1 • C^{3}a (Spike in 8's)   (186, 189)   I-2   R-4
    Obverse III^{2}1 – First 8 has a short die chip inside the upper loop at 11 o'clock. Second 8 has die flakes in lower loop. Some specimens also show a short die chip inside the upper loop at 11 o'clock on the second 8 and die flakes at top inside of lower loop of first 8.

2   III^{2}2 • C^{3}a (Doubled 8)   (184)   I-2   R-3
    Obverse III^{2}2 – The first 8 in the date is doubled inside and below the lower loop.

3   III^{2}3 • C^{3}a (Dash Under 8)   I-2   R-3
    Obverse III^{2}3 – The second 8 in the date has a dash under 8.

4   III^{2}4 • C^{3}a (Doubled 18-1)   (185)   I-2   R-3
    Obverse III^{2}4 – Die chip between the loops on the right of the first 8 with a short die chip at top left inside of upper loop, surface doubling on bottom outside of lower loop and tripled on top left inside of lower loop. First 1 doubled slightly below upper crossbar. Second 1 doubled slightly on left side of vertical shaft.

5   III^{2}1 • C^{3}b (S/S Left)   (186)   I-3   R-4
    Obverse III^{2}1 – Spike in first 8 upper loop.
    Reverse C^{3}b – Mint mark is repunched and tilted slightly to left with original showing as a long vertical spike within the middle of the upper loop opening and an arc to the right of the lower loop opening.

6   III^{2}4 • C^{3}b (S/S Left)   (186)   I-3   R-4

7   III^{2}5 • C^{3}c (S/S Left and Up, Doubled Date)   (187)   I-3   R-4
    Obverse III^{2}5 – Top of lower crossbar of both 1's and inside bottom of both loops in both 8's slightly doubled.
    Reverse C^{3}c – Mint mark is repunched with original showing as a short vertical spike to the right of the upper loop opening and an arc within the middle of the lower loop opening.

8   III^{2}1 • C^{3}d (S/S Right)   1-2   R-4
    Reverse C^{3}d – Mint mark is repunched with original showing as a vertical bar to right of top serif. Loops of mint mark filled.

8A   III^{2}1 • C^{3}d (S/S Right)   (183)   I-2   R-4
    Obverse III^{2}1 – First 8 has a short die chip inside the upper loop at 11 o'clock. Second 8 has die chips in lower loop. A spiked die chip is also at top left outside of second 8.

9   III^{2}6 • C^{3}a (Doubled and Spiked 8's)   I-2   R-4
    Obverse III^{2}6 – First 8 has a short die chip inside the upper loop at 11 o'clock and spike die chip between the loops on the right. Second 8 has short spike of metal inside the upper loop at 11 o'clock and strongly doubled at bottom right inside.

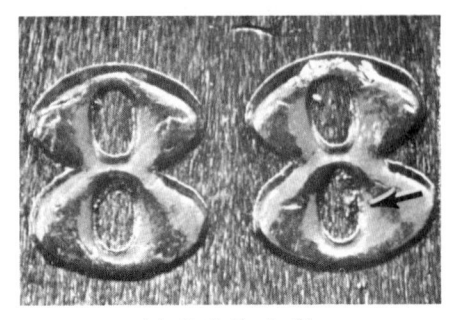

1A O Spike in 8's 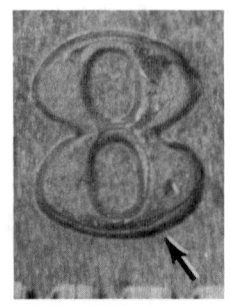   2 O Doubled 8 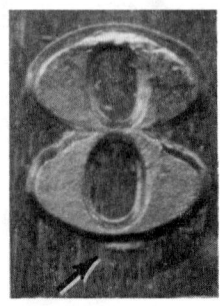   3 O Dash

1881-S

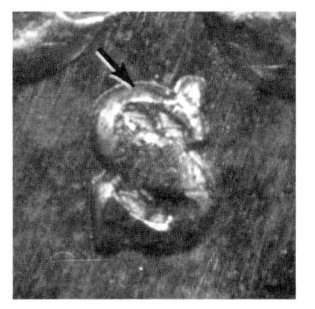

5 R S/S Left

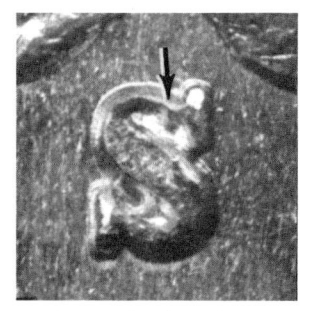

7 R S/S Left and Up

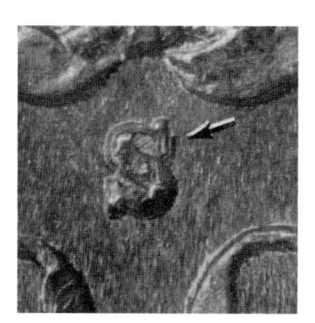

8 R S/S Right

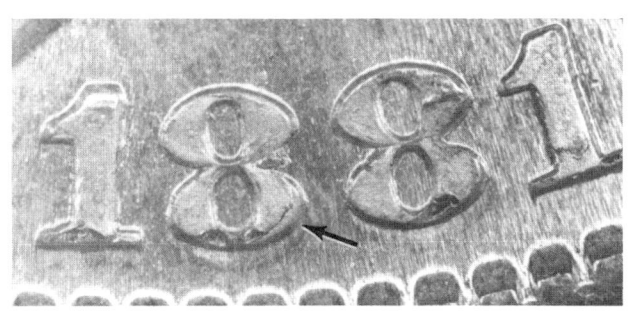

4 O Doubled 18-1

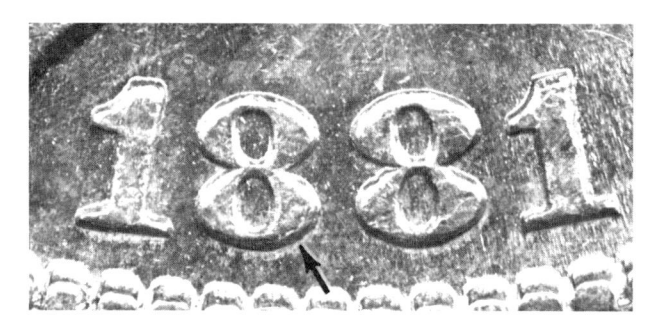

7 O Doubled Date

8A O Spike 8

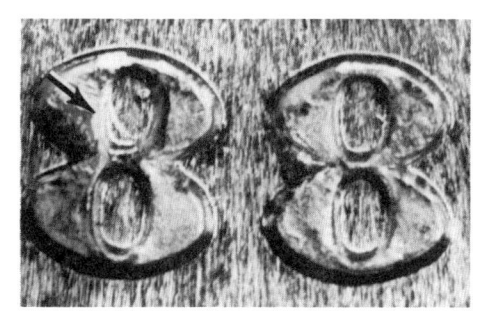

9 O Doubled 8's

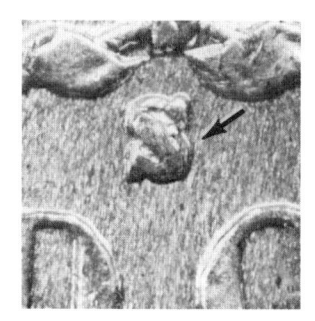

12 R S/S Surface

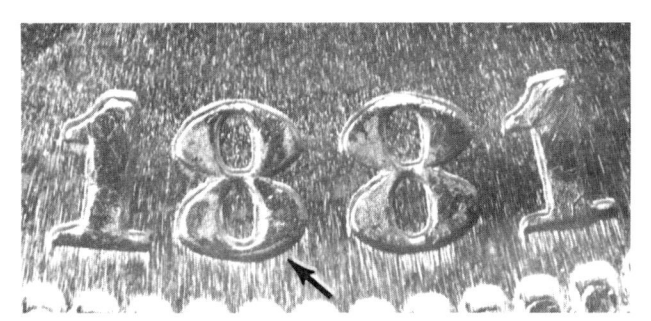

11 O Doubled 18-1

13 R S/S Left

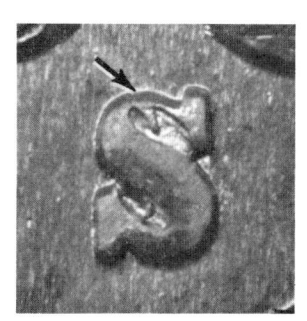

14 R S/S Far Left

1881-S

#	Varieties	(Ref)	I	R
10	III² 6 • C³ b (S/S Left)		I-3	R-4
11	III² 7 • C³ a (Doubled 18-1)	(184)	I-2	R-3

Obverse III² 7 – 18-1 in date doubled slightly at very top. In addition, first 8 is doubled on surface at top left inside and lower right outside of upper loop and right inside and bottom outside of lower loop.

| 12 | III² 1 • C³ e (S/S Surface) | (184) | I-2 | R-4 |

Obverse III² 1 – Die chips in 8's.
Reverse C³ e – Mint mark is repunched with surface doubling on right side of upper serif and lower loop.

| 13 | III² 1 • C³ f (S/S Left) | (186) | I-3 | R-4 |

Obverse III² 1 – Spike die chip in upper loop on second 8 barely shows.
Reverse C³ f – Mint mark is repunched with original showing as a spike at left of upper loop opening and an arc in the middle of lower loop opening. Loops are partially filled.

| 14 | III² 1 • C³ g (S/S Far Left) | | I-3 | R-4 |

Reverse C³ g – Mint mark is repunched with original showing as a short spike at far left inside of upper loop opening.

| 15 | III² 8 • C³ g (Doubled 88, S/S Far Left) | (185) | I-3 | R-3 |

Obverse III² 8 – Doubled 88 in date. First 8 doubled on top surface inside and bottom outside of lower loop and left inside and right outside of top loop. Second 8 has a bulge at top left outside of lower loop.

| 16 | III² 8 • C³ a (Die Chip in Leaves) | | I-2 | R-4 |

Reverse C³ a – Large die chip on wreath leaf opposite NI of UNITED on some specimens.

| 17 | III² 9 • C³ h (Doubled 18-1, S/S Down) | (187) | I-3 | R-4 |

Obverse III² 9 – Doubled 18-1 in date. First 1 doubled slightly at very bottom. First 8 doubled on surface at bottom outside of lower loop with die chip in left inside of upper loop. Second 1 doubled at lower left of vertical shaft with two vees at bottom of vertical shaft.
Reverse C³ h – Mint mark is repunched with original showing as thin horizontal line in middle of upper loop and faint diagonal line at top inside of lower loop.

| 18 | III² 4 • C³ i (S/S Down) | | I-3 | R-4 |

Reverse C³ i – Mint mark is repunched with original showing as a thin line diagonal line curved at top in middle of upper loop and faint diagonal line at top inside of lower loop.

| 19 | III² 10 • C³ f (Doubled Date, S/S Left) | (186) | I-3 | R-4 |

Obverse III² 10 – All digits in date slightly doubled. First 1 doubled at very top and on surface at bottom of upper crossbar. First 8 doubled slightly at very top and tripled at bottom outside of lower loop. Second 8 doubled very slightly at lower left outside of upper loop and at bottom outside of lower loop. Second 1 doubled at bottom of left vertical shaft.

| 20 | III² 20 • C³ j (S/S Up) | (185) | I-2 | R-4 |

Reverse C³ j – Mint mark is repunched with curved line at bottom inside of lower loop. Partially filled loops of mint marks. Small dots of metal all over eagle.

| 21 | III² 8 • C³ k (Doubled 88, S Tilted Right) | (183) | I-2 | R-3 |

Reverse C³ k – Medium IV S mint mark centered and tilted right with loops partially filled.

| 22 | III² 11 • C³ l (Slanted Date, S Set Left) | (185) | I-2 | R-3 |

Obverse III² 11 – Date slanted with first 1 close to rim.
Reverse C³ l – IV S mint mark set left with slight tilt to right.

| 23 | III² 12 • C³ k (Doubled 18, S Tilted Right) | (183) | I-2 | R-3 |

Obverse III² 12 – Doubled 18 in date. First 1 doubled on right side. First 8 tripled at bottom surface and edge of lower loop, doubled at top inside of lower loop, and doubled at top inside and lower left outside of upper loop. Second 8 has a bulge at top left outside of lower loop.

| 24 | III² 13 • C³ c (Doubled 18-1, S/S Left and Up) | (185) | I-3 | R-4 |

Obverse III² 13 – Doubled 18-1 in date. 1 doubled slightly at top left of lower crossbar, bottom left and top right of vertical shaft. First 8 doubled strongly on surface at top and right inside and bottom outside of lower loop. Second 1 doubled slightly at top left of upper crossbar.

| 25 | III² 12 – C³ a (Doubled 18) | (184) | I-2 | R-3 |

Obverse III² 12 – Die polished down somewhat.

| 26 | III² 10 • C³ c (Doubled Date, S/S Left and Up) | (186) | I-3 | R-4 |

1881-S

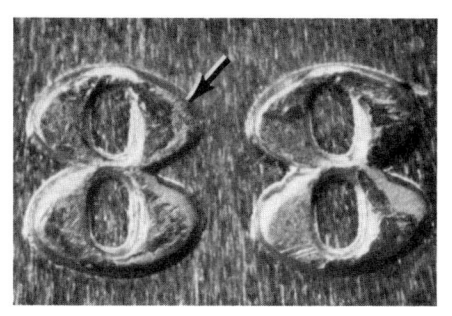

15 O Doubled 88

16 R Die Chip in Leaves

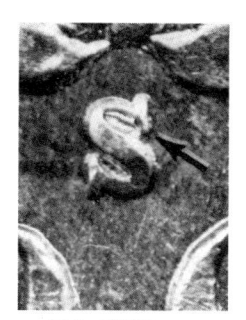

17 R S/S Down

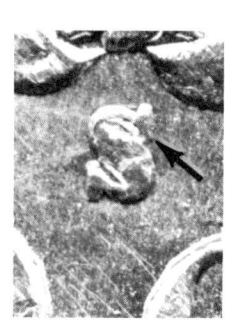

18 R S/S Down

17 O Doubled 18-1

19 O Doubled Date

20 R S/S Up

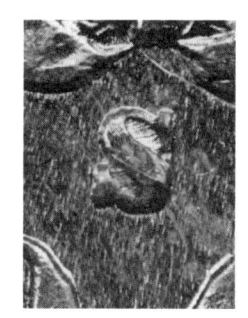

21 R S Tilted Right

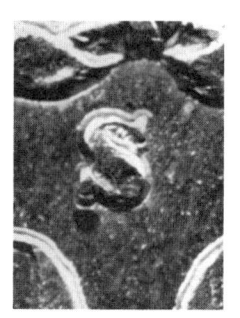

22 R S Set Left

23 O Doubled 18

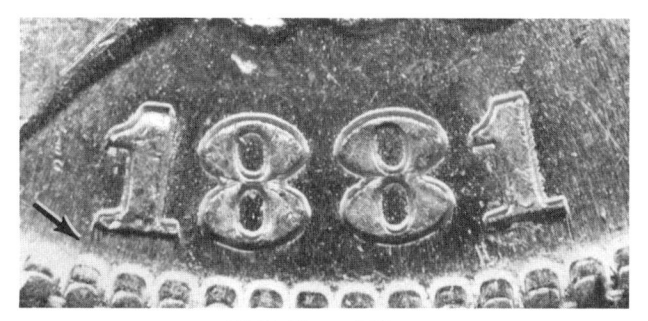

22 O Slanted Date

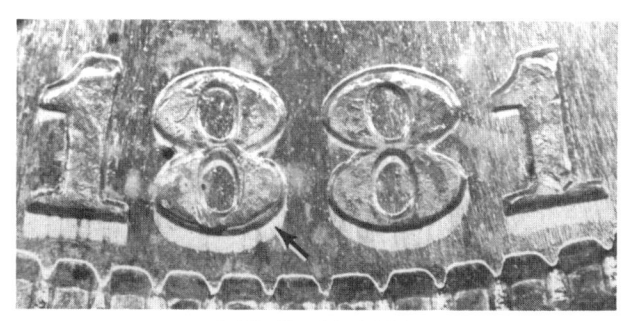

24 O Doubled 18-1

229

1881-S

27 III² 14 • C³ a (Doubled 18-1) (185) I-2 R-3
Obverse III² 14 – Doubled 18-1 in date. First 1 doubled slightly at top right of vertical shaft and at top left and right of bottom crossbar. First 8 is doubled slightly at top inside and strongly at bottom outside of lower loop. Upper loop of first 8 has spike at left inside. Second 1 doubled slightly at lower left side of vertical shaft.

28 III² 15 • C³ m (Doubled 1-1, S/S Left) (186) I-3 R-4
Obverse III² 15 – Doubled 1-1 in date. First 1 doubled below upper crossbar and on right side of vertical shaft. Second 1 doubled at lower left of vertical shaft.
Reverse C³ m – Mint mark is repunched with original showing as a diagonal line at right of upper loop opening and an arc at the right of the lower loop opening. IV S mint mark is set high.

29 III² 16 • C³ a (Doubled First 8) (186) I-2 R-3
Obverse III² 16 – First 8 is doubled on surface at right inside of both loops. Both 8's show short die chip inside upper loop at 11 o'clock.

30 III² 1 • C³ c (S/S Left and Up) (187) I-3 R-4

31 III² 17 • C³ a (Doubled 18) (185) I-2 R-3
Obverse III² 17 – Doubled 18 in date. First 1 doubled on surface of right side of shaft. First 8 doubled faintly on right inside and lower right outside of bottom loop. First 8 has a short die chip in upper loop at 11 o'clock.

32 III² 8 • C³ n (Doubled 88, S Set Left) (184) I-2 R-3
Reverse C³ n – IV S mint mark set left with slight tilt to left. TED, TATES, AMERICA, motto and right wreath tip slightly doubled towards rim.

33 III² 18 • C³ o (Doubled 8, High S) (186) I-2 R-3
Obverse III² 18 – Doubled first 8 on lower right inside of upper loop and right inside of lower loop. Both 8's have a die chip at top left inside of upper loop.
Reverse C³ o – Medium IV S mint mark centered and set high.

34 III² 19 • C³ 9 (Doubled 188, S/S Far Left) (185) I-2 R-3
Obverse III² 19 – Doubled 188 in date. 1 doubled slightly at top right of vertical shaft. First 8 doubled at left inside and on surface at right outside of upper loop and top inside and bottom outside of lower loop. Second 8 tripled at top inside of upper loop.

35 III² 20 • C³ a (Doubled 18) (185) I-2 R-3
Obverse III² 20 – Doubled 18 in date. 1 doubled on left top of base. First 8 doubled strongly on surface at right outside of upper loop, top and right inside and bottom outside of lower loop. First 8 has short die chip at top left inside of upper loop.

36 III² 1 • C³ k (S Tilted Right) (184) I-2 R-3

37 III² 14 • C³ p (Doubled 18-1, S Tilted Left) (186) I-2 R-3
Reverse C³ p – Medium IV S mint mark centered and tilted slightly left.

38 III² 6 • C³ o (Doubled 18-1, Spiked 8's, High S) (186) I-2 R-4

39 III² 21 • C³ a (Doubled 18-1, Dash Under 8) (186) I-2 R-3
Obverse III² 21 – Doubled 18-1 in date. First 1 doubled at top right. First 8 doubled at top inside of lower loop with short die chip inside upper loop at 11 o'clock. Second 1 doubled at left side of vertical shaft. Second 1 doubled at left side of vertical shaft. Second 8 has dash just below lower loop.

40 III² 22 • C³ m (Doubled 18-1, S/S Left) (185) I-2 R-3
Obverse III² 22 – Doubled 18-1 in date. First 1 doubled slightly at upper right of vertical shaft. First 8 doubled at top left inside of both loops and slightly at bottom right outside of lower loop. Second 1 doubled at very top and slightly at lower left side of vertical shaft.

27 O Doubled 18-1   28 O Doubled 1-1

1881-S

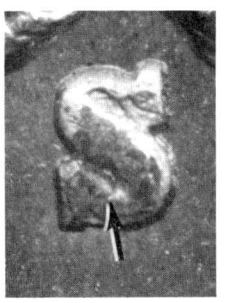

28 R S/S

29 O First 8 Doubled

31 O Doubled 18

32 R S Set Left

33 O First 8 Doubled

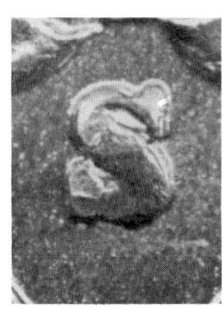

33 R High S

34 O Doubled 188

35 O Doubled 18

37 R S Tilted Left

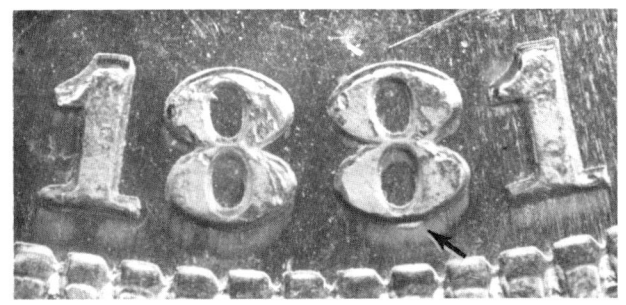

39 O Doubled 18-1, Dash Under 8

40 O Doubled 18-1

1881-S

41	III² 23 • C³ q (Doubled 8-1, S/S Line)	(184)		I-2	R-3

Obverse III² 23 – Doubled 8-1 in date. First 8 doubled on surface at lower right outside of upper loop and top inside of lower loop. Second 1 doubled slightly and left side of vertical shaft.
Reverse C³ q – Mint mark is repunched with original showing as a thin diagonal line at right of upper loop opening and an arc at right of lower loop opening. IV S mint mark set slightly high.

42	III² 1 • C³ p (S Tilted Left)	(186)		1-2	R-3

Obverse III² 1 – Short die chip inside upper loop of first 8 at 11 o'clock.

43	III² 1 • C³ r (S/S Curve)	(182)		I-2	R-3

Reverse C³ r – IV S mint mark repunched slightly as curved line at right inside of lower loop. Some specimens show die chip in wreath leaf opposite U of UNITED.

44	III² 24 • C³ p (Tripled 8, S Tilted Left)	(189)		I-2	R-3

Obverse III² 24 – First 8 tripled on lower right outside of both loops, tripled at top left inside of upper loop and doubled at top inside of lower loop. Upper loop has a spike of metal at top left inside.

45	III² 25 • C³ s (Doubled 18, S/S)	(185)		I-2	R-3

Obverse III² 25 – Doubled 18 in date. 1 doubled at top left and right of lower crossbar. First 8 doubled at top right inside of lower loop and on lower right surface of upper loop.
Reverse C³ s – IV S mint mark doubled at lower left of lower serif.

46	III² 2 • C³ o (Doubled First 8, S Set High)	(184)		I-2	R-3
47	III² 26 • C³ a (Doubled 18)	(184)		I-2	R-3

Obverse III² 26 – Doubled 18 in date. 1 doubled slightly at top right of vertical shaft. First 8 doubled at upper left inside and right outside of upper loop and right inside and bottom right outside of lower loop.

48	III² 23 • C³ a (Doubled 8-1)	(184)		1-2	R-3
49	III² 26 • C³ l (Doubled 18, S Set Left)	(184)		1-2	R-3
50	III² 27 • C³ t (Doubled 18, S/S)	(186)		I-2	R-3

Obverse III² 27 – Doubled 18 in date. 1 doubled at top right of vertical shaft. First 8 doubled on surface of right outside of both loops.
Reverse C³ t – IV S mint mark repunched with top serif doubled on right outside and lower serif doubled as a notch on lower left outside.

51	III² 26 • C³ p (Doubled 18, S Tilted Left)	(184)		I-2	R-3

41 O Doubled 8-1

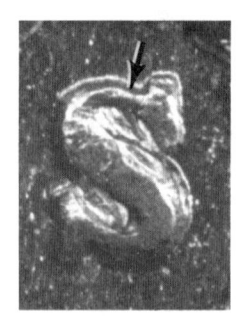

41 R S/S Line

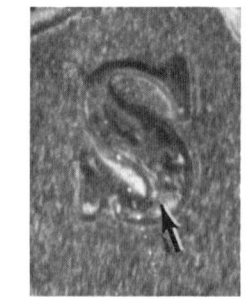

43 R S/S

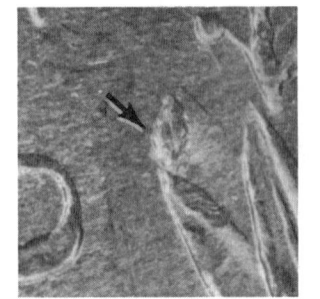

43 R Die Chips in Wreath

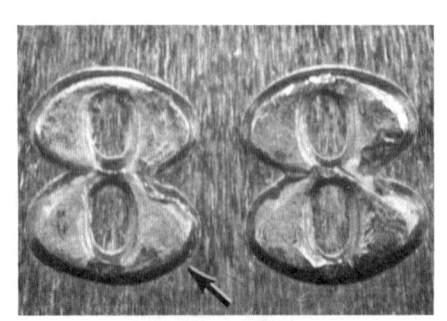

44 O Tripled 8

45 O Doubled 18

1881-S / 1882-P

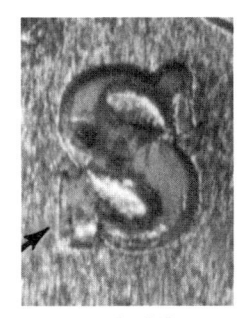

45 R S/S

47 O Doubled 18

50 O Doubled 18

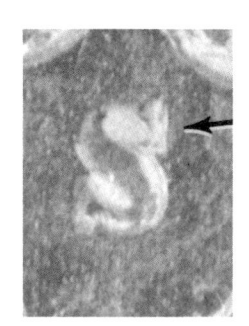

50 R S/S

1882-P

Full strike specimens are available although slightly weakly struck examples exist. Luster is generally better than earlier P mint coins and some show nice frosted devices. A fair number of minor die varieties exist but none are significant.

As with all early P mints proof-like specimens are fairly scarce. Some cameo proof-likes exist however. Most proofs show good cameo contrast and nice ones are available.

1	III²1 • C³a (Closed 2)	(180)	I-1	R-1

Obverse III²1 – Normal die of III² type with thick 1 in date. The top knob and serif of the tail almost touch the curve of the 2. Some specimens show die chip between loops on left of first 8.
Reverse C³a – Normal die of C³ type.

1A	III²1 • C³a (Dot 2)	(179)	I-2	R-4

Obverse III²1 – Small dot of metal on surface in middle of bottom crossbar.

1B	III²1 • C³a (Metal in 2)	(180)	I-2	R-3

Obverse III²1 – Both loops of 2 have die chips and diagonal polishing marks.

1C	III²1 • C³a (Metal in Date)	(180)	I-2	R-3

Obverse III²1 – Metal in both 8's and the 2 in the date caused by die flaking, chipping and insufficient polishing. Some specimens only have metal in the 2.

1D	III²1 • C³a (Metal in 82)	(180)	I-2	R-3

Obverse III²1 – Second 8 has die chip in bottom right inside of lower loop. Both loops of 2 are filled with shallow metal from die chips and flakes with horizontal polishing marks.
Reverse C³a – Some specimens show die rust pits around E of ONE.

2	III²2 • C³a (Open 2)		I-1	R-2

Obverse III²2 – Normal die of III² type with thin 2. Knob and serif of tail do not touch body of 2.

3	III²3 • C³a (Doubled 8)		I-2	R-3

Obverse III²3 – Second 8 in date is doubled on top left. Open 2 variety.

4	III²4 • C³a (Doubled 2)		I-2	R-3

Obverse III²4 – 2 is doubled slightly on right side of the ball at top. Upper loop of 2 is filled with shallow metal from die chips with horizontal polishing marks.

1882-P

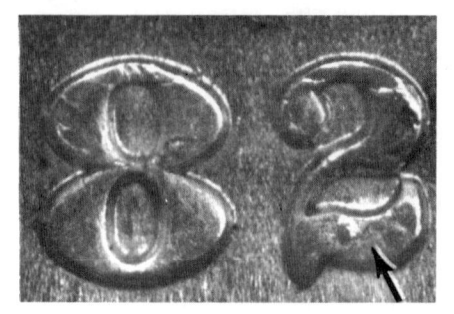

1A O Dot 2

1B O Metal in 2

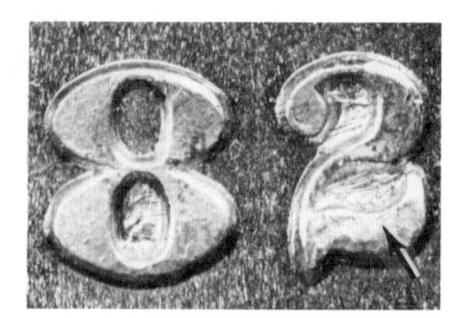

1D O Metal in 82

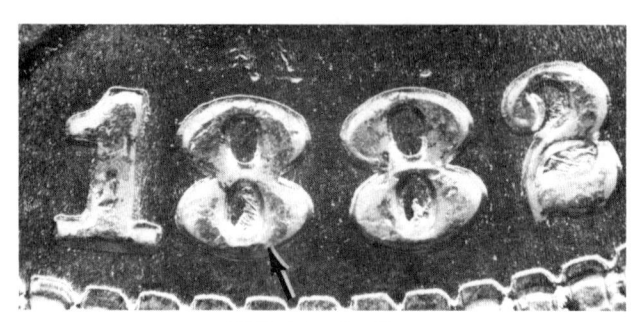

1C O Metal in Date

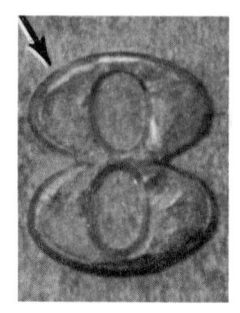

3 O Doubled 8

1D R Pitted Die

5   **III² 5 • C³ a (Doubled 1)**   (180)   I-2   R-3
     Obverse III² 5 – 1 in date doubled at top right of the stem. The 882 is partially filled at top and bottom. Closed 2 variety.

6   **III² 6 • C³ a (Doubled 18)**   I-2   R-4
     Obverse III² 6 – 18 in date doubled. 1 is doubled at top right of the stem. Upper loop of first 8 is doubled on left. Open 2 variety.

7   **III² 7 • C³ a (Doubled 1-82)**   (178)   I-2   R-4
     Obverse III² 7 – 1-82 in date slightly doubled. 1 is doubled at the top right of the stem. Second 8 doubled on left side of upper loop and right side of lower loop. 2 doubled on left side of upper loop.

8   **III² 8 • C³ a (Doubled 2)**   I-2   R-4
     Obverse III² 8 – 2 in date doubled strongly at top inside of upper loop.

9   **III² 9 • C³ a (Doubled 82)**   (180)   I-2   R-3
     Obverse III² 9 – 82 in date doubled. Second 8 is doubled slightly on left outside of upper loop and bottom outside of lower loop. 2 doubled slightly at top and right outside of upper loop. First 8 has die chip on left side between loops.

10   **III² 10 • C³ a (Doubled 82)**   I-2   Proof
     Obverse III² 10 – 82 in date is doubled. Second 8 is doubled strongly on left outside of upper loop. 2 is doubled slightly on left side of shaft.

11   **III² 11 • C³ a (Doubled Date)**   (180)   I-2   R-4
     Obverse III² 11 – Entire date is slightly doubled. 1 is doubled slightly at bottom of upper crossbar. First 8 is doubled slightly at right inside and left outside on upper loop. Second 8 is doubled at top outside of upper loop and doubled slightly on left outside of lower loop. 2 is doubled slightly at top left outside of upper loop.

12   **III² 12 • C³ a (Doubled Date)**   (181)   I-2   R-3
     Obverse III² 12 – Entire date is doubled. 1 is doubled slightly at very bottom. First 8 is doubled slightly at right outside of upper loop. Second 8 is doubled strongly at left outside of upper loop and slightly at bottom outside of lower loop. 2 is doubled slightly at left outside of upper loop.

13   **III² 13 • C³ a (Doubled 188)**   (181)   I-2   R-3
     Obverse III² 13 – 188 in date is doubled. 1 is doubled faintly below top crossbar. First 8 is doubled faintly at bottom left outside and top left inside of upper loop and at bottom right outside of lower loop. Second 8 doubled at left outside of upper loop and faintly at bottom outside of lower loop.

14   **III² 14 • C³ a (Doubled 882)**   (180)   I-2   R-3
     Obverse III² 14 – Faintly doubled 882 in date. First 8 doubled at left inside of upper loop. Second 8 doubled at left outside of both loops. 2 doubled on right side of upper loop.

1882-P

4 O Doubled 2

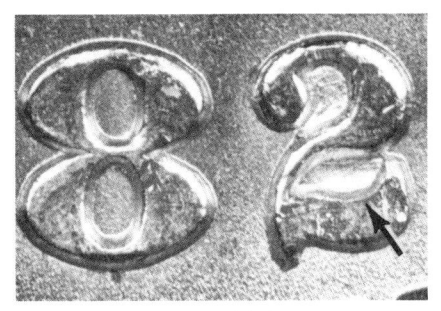

5 O Doubled 1

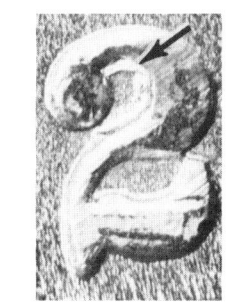

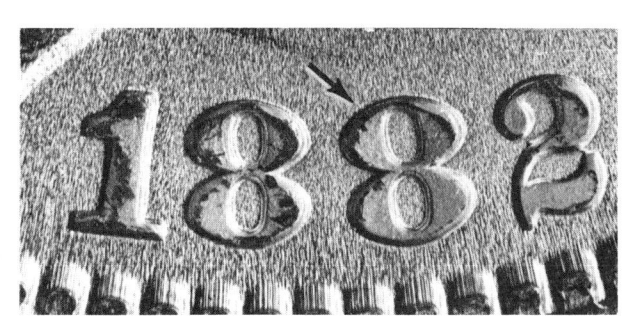

(Photo Not Available)

6 O

8 O Doubled 2

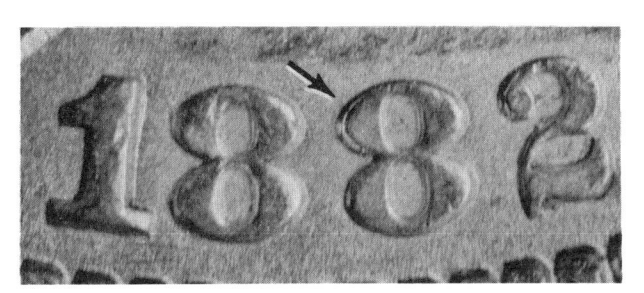

7 O Doubled 1-82

11 O Doubled Date

9 O Doubled 82

10 O Doubled 82

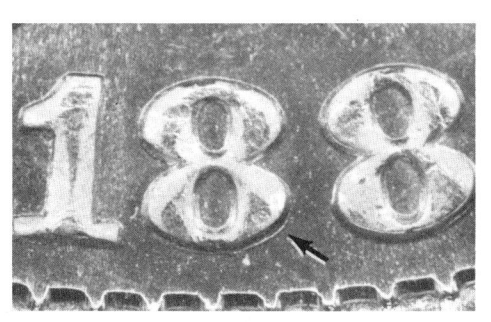

13 O Doubled 188

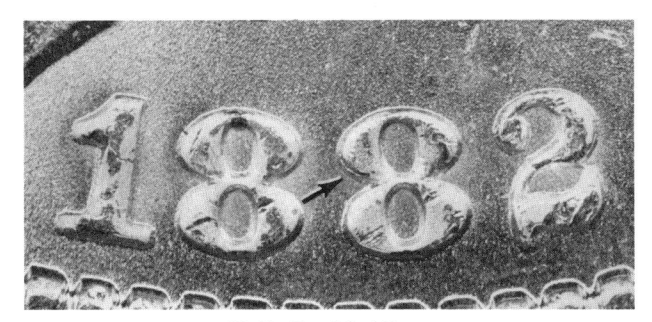

12 O Doubled Date

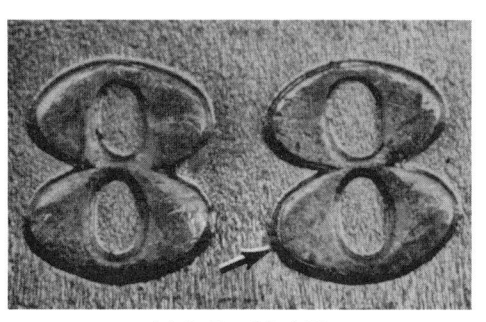

14 O Doubled 88

1882-P

| 15 | III² 15 • C³ a (Doubled 8-2) | (179) | I-2 | R-3 |

Obverse III² 15 – Doubled 8-2 in date. First 8 doubled at left outside and right inside of upper loop. Upper ball of 2 doubled on right side.

| 16 | III² 16 • C³ a (Doubled Date) | (180) | I-2 | R-3 |

Obverse III² 16 – Entire date doubled. 1 doubled slightly at top right of vertical shaft. First 8 doubled slightly at lower left outside of upper loop. Second 8 doubled strongly on left outside of upper loop and at bottom left of lower loop. 2 doubled at left and right outside of upper loop.

| 17 | III² 17 C³ a (Doubled Date) | (179) | I-2 | R-3 |

Obverse III² 17 – Entire date is doubled. 1 doubled below upper serif. First 8 doubled slightly at right inside and left outside of upper loop. Second 8 is doubled strongly at top outside of upper loop and slightly at left outside of lower loop. 2 doubled strongly at top outside of upper loop and on right side of ball, upper loop, shaft and serif.

| 18 | III² 18 • C³ a (Doubled Date) | (179) | I-2 | R-3 |

Obverse III² 18 – Entire date is doubled. 1 doubled slightly on upper right surface of vertical shaft. First 8 doubled at left outside of upper loop. Second 8 doubled at top outside of upper loop and upper left outside of lower loop. 2 doubled at top outside of upper loop.

| 19 | III² 19 • C³ a (Doubled Date) | (181) | I-2 | R-3 |

Obverse III² 19 – Entire date is doubled. 1 doubled slightly below upper crossbar. First 8 tripled at top inside and lower left outside of upper loop and doubled slightly at bottom outside of lower loop. Second 8 doubled strongly at left outside of upper loop and at bottom outside of lower loop. 2 doubled slightly on right side of ball and right outside of upper loop.

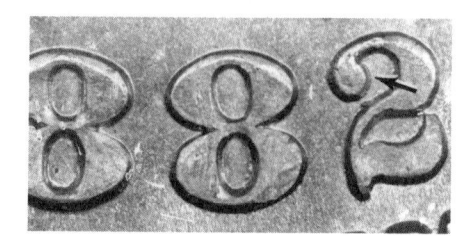

15 O Doubled 8-2

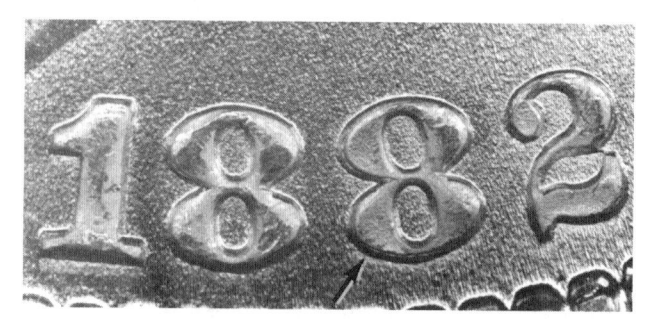

16 O Doubled Date

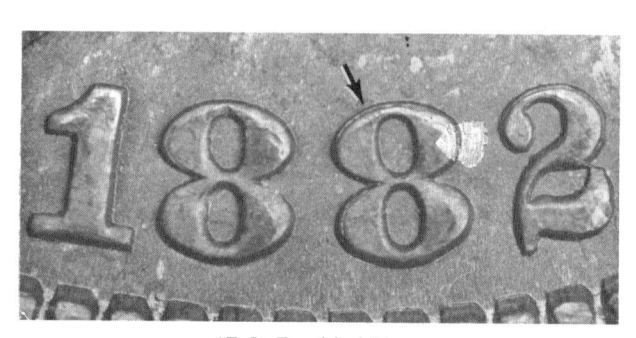

17 O Doubled Date

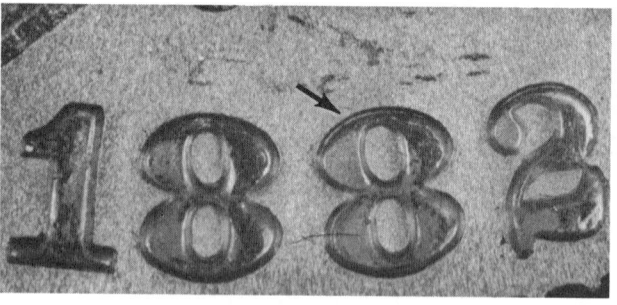

18 O Doubled Date

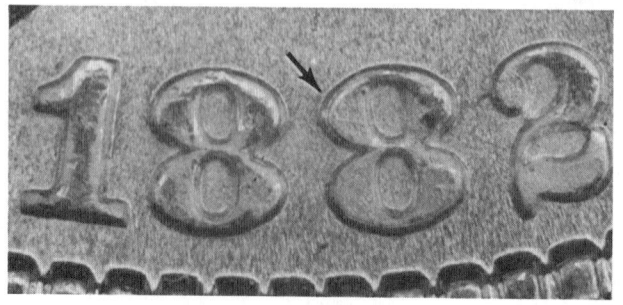

19 O Doubled Date

1882-CC

Half the mintage was in the GSA sales so BU specimens are readily available. Usually the strike is full and luster good. Several die varieties exist but none are significant.

A significant number of proof-like specimens exist and some have very deep mirrors with cameo contrast.

1 III²1 • C³a (Open 2) I-1 R-2
   Obverse III²1 – Normal die of III² type with open 2 at top.
   Reverse C³a – Normal die of C³ type with large open V CC mint mark.

2 III²2 • C³b (Doubled 882 and Reverse) (177, 178) I-2 R-3
   Obverse III²2 – Doubled 882 in date. First 8 doubled slightly at right outside of upper loop and left inside of lower loop. Second 8 doubled strongly on left outside of upper loop and slightly on bottom outside of lower loop. 2 doubled slightly at top outside of upper loop. Some specimens show first two stars on right with fine polishing marks below them and a heavy diagonal polishing mark below the first 8 on later die states.
   Reverse C³b – All legend letters and stars doubled near rim.

3 III²3 • C³c (Doubled 1-82) (177) I-2 R-3
   Obverse III²3 – 1 doubled below bottom crossbar on some specimens. Second 8 and 2 slightly doubled at top and upper left side. Date set low close to rim. Some specimens show die chip between loops of second 8 on right. Open 2 variety.
   Reverse C³c – Right C of mint mark set low.

4 III²4 • C³a (Closed 2) I-1 R-3
   Obverse III²4 – Normal die of III² type with closed 2.

5 III²5 • C3a (Doubled 882) (178) I-2 R-3
   Obverse III²5 – 882 doubled in date. First 8 doubled slightly on right outside with dot at top inside of upper loop. Second 8 doubled slightly at top outside and lower left outside of upper loop and on right outside of lower loop. 2 doubled at top outside and inside of upper loop plus right outside of upper loop. Closed 2 variety.

6 III²6 • C³a (Doubled Date) (178) I-2 R-3
   Obverse III²6 – Entire date is doubled. 1 is slightly doubled at top left of lower crossbar. First 8 is doubled at top outside and right inside of upper loop and on right outside of lower loop. Second 8 is doubled at top and outside of upper loop and right outside of lower loop. 2 doubled at top and right outside of upper loop.

2 O Doubled 882

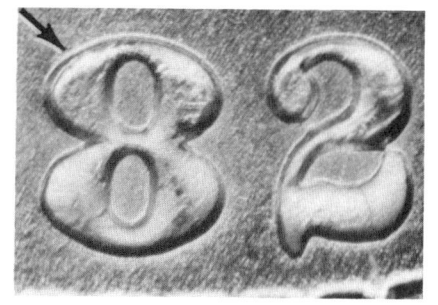

3 O Doubled 82

2 R Doubled Legend

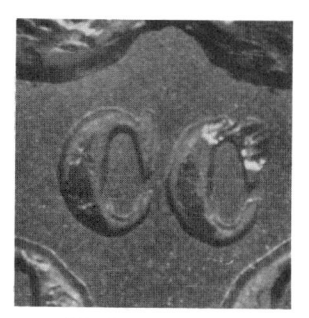

3 R Low Right C

5 O Doubled 882

237

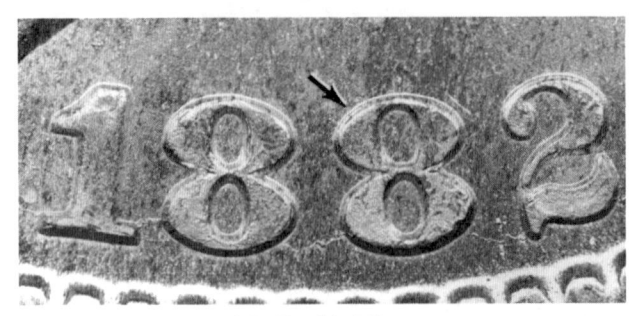

6 O Doubled Date

1882-O

Like the 1881-O, the 1882-O tends to be fully struck but with subdued luster. The reverse tends to be weaker struck more often however. Slider coins are are also fairly common. A large number of die varieties exist and a few are significant. Three very visible O/S mint marks (VAM's 3, 4 and 5) are fairly scarce and command substantial premiums in higher grades. Earlier die states of O/S exist but are not as visible. The O/S reverses show raised dots due to rusted dies and proof-likes are unknown. A very strongly doubled O mint mark of VAM 7 is visible below and within the O and carries a modest premium.

Proof-likes are fairly available and quite a few have cameo contrast.

1   III²1 • C³a (Open 2)   (181)   I-1   R-2
     Obverse III²1 – Normal Die of III² type with open 2 at top. The open 2 is more common than the closed 2.
     Reverse C³a – Normal die of C³ type with tall oval medium II O mint mark centered and upright.

2   III²2 • C³a (Closed 2)   (181)   I-1   R-2
     Obverse III²2 – Normal die of III² type with closed 2.

3   III²3 – C³b (O/S Flush)   (181)   I-5   R-3/4
     Obverse III²3 – Second 8 in date doubled on lower left outside of upper loop and bottom outside of lower loop. 2 doubled on right outside of upper loop. Polishing marks inside ear with area around neck overpolished. Open 2 variety.
     Reverse C³b – O over S variety with the center shaft of the S flush within the O. Small dots of metal all over eagle probably due to rusted die. An earlier die state shows a thin diagonal line (formerly VAM 6)

4   III²4 • C³c (O/S Depressed)   (181)   I-5   R-3
     Obverse III²4 – Polishing marks inside ear. Second 8 doubled at left outside of both loops. 2 doubled on right outside of upper loop. Small dots of metal all over the Liberty Head. Open 2 variety.
     Reverse C³c – O over S variety with the center shaft of the S depressed within the O. Small dots of metal all over eagle and wreath. An earlier die state shows as a diagonal tear drop at lower part of opening.

5   III²5 • C³d (O/S Broken)   (181)   I-4   R-3
     Obverse III²5 – Second 8 in date doubled on left side of loop. 2 doubled faintly at top outside. Die chip between loops on left side of first 8. Polishing marks inside ear. Open 2 variety.
     Reverse C³d – O over S variety with the center shaft of the S broken within the O. Small dots of metal all over eagle and wreath. An earlier die state shows as a triangular dot at left side of loop opening and as a fine line in the middle.

6*   III²2 • C³e (O Tilted Left)   (181)   1-2   R-3
     Reverse C³e – II O mint mark, tilted left and some have a heavy horizontal die scratch at the bottom of the opening.
     VAM 6 was formerly O/S line

7   III²6 • C³f (O/O Low)   (176)   I-4   R-4
     Obverse III²6 – 882 in date is slightly doubled. First 8 doubled at right inside and outside of upper loop. Loops of second 8 doubled on left outside. 2 doubled at top outside. Open 2 variety.
     Reverse C³f – Mint mark repunched with the original showing below and inside.

8   III²1 • C³g (O/O Right)   I-2   R-4
     Reverse C³g – Mint mark repunched with the original showing on the right side and top of the opening.

1882-O

3 O Doubled 82

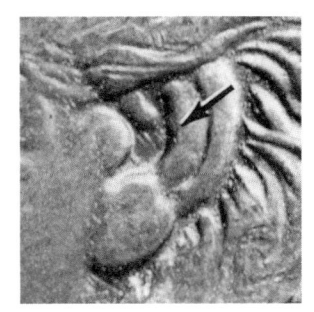

3 O Polishing Marks

3 R O/S Flush

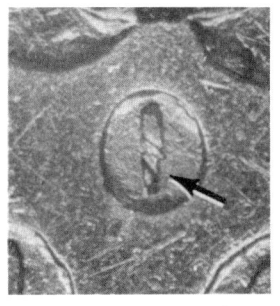

4 R O/S Depressed

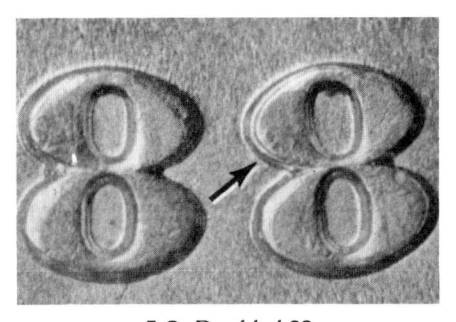

5 O Doubled 82

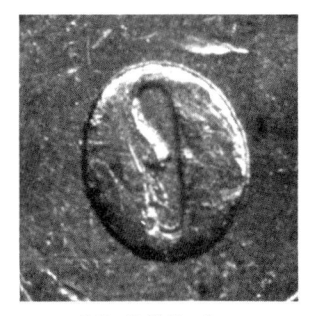

5 R O/S Broken

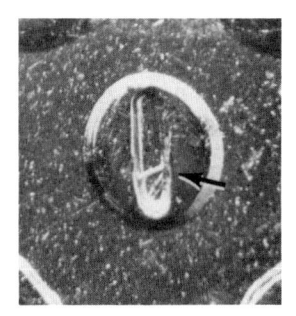

6 R Die Scratch in O

7 O Doubled 882

7 R O/O Low

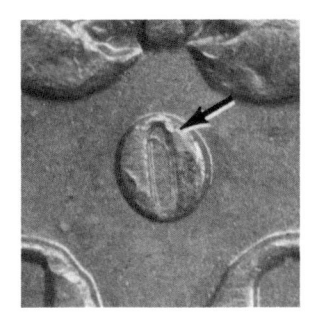

8 R O/O Right

9 R O/O Left

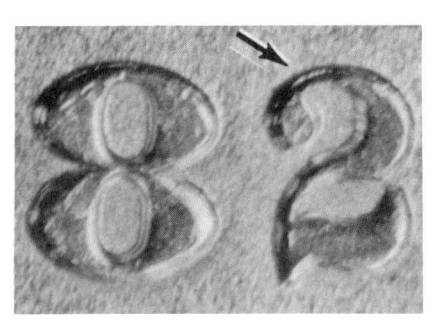

10 O Doubled 82

10 O Doubled 18, Filled Date

239

1882-O

9 III²10 • C³a (Doubled 18) I-2 R-4
Obverse III²10 – Metal in 882. Both 8's have die flakes on right side of lower loop opening. 2 has die flakes in upper loop with curved horizontal step at lower left side of loop opening. Lower loop of 2 is also filled and has heavy horizontal polishing marks. In addition, 1 doubled slightly at top right outside and first 8 is doubled slightly at top inside of loops.

10 III²7 • C³a (Doubled 82) (176) I-2 R-3
Obverse III²7 – 82 in date is doubled. Top loop of second 8 is doubled at top and bottom loop at top right. 2 is doubled faintly at top. Short die chips between loops of first 8 on left and some coins show both sides. Open and closed 2 variety.

11 III²8 • C³a (Doubled 8) I-2 R-3
Obverse III²8 – Second 8 in date doubled on left side of upper loop. Open 2 variety.

12 III²2 • C³f (O/O Low) I-4 R-4

13 III²9 • C³h (O/O Lower Left, Doubled 2) I-2 R-4
Obverse III²9 – 2 in date is doubled with a horizontal curved line just above bottom crossbar.
Reverse C³h – Mint mark repunched with the original showing on the lower left side of opening.

14 III²10 • C³h (O/O Lower Left, Doubled 18) (181) I-2 R-4

15 III²2 • C³i (O/O Left) (181) I-2 R-4
Reverse C³i – II O Mint mark repunched with original showing as a vertical bar on left side of loop opening and die chips with polishing marks at bottom inside of loop.

16 III²8 • C³e (O Tilted Left) I-2 R-3
Obverse III²8 – With closed 2.

17 III²10 • C³e (Metal in 882, O tilted Left) (181) I-2 R-4
Obverse III²10 – Die has a long horizontal die crack above date and first three stars on left.

18 III²11 • C³a (Doubled 882 Left) (176) I-2 R-3
Obverse III²11 – 882 in date doubled. First 8 doubled slightly at lower left outside of upper loop and right outside of lower loop. Top loop of second 8 doubled at top left and bottom loop doubled on left side and faintly at bottom. 2 doubled all across the very top and right side of lower serif.

19 III²12 • C³a (Doubled 82) (176) I-2 R-3
Obverse III²12 – 82 in date is doubled. Second 8 is doubled at top and left outside of upper loop. 2 is doubled at top and left outside of upper loop and slightly on right side of lower left serif.
Reverse C³a – Some specimens show overpolished die with field showing through eagle's right wing.

20 III²13 • C³a (Doubled 1-8) (181) I-2 R-3
Obverse III²13 – Doubled 1-8 in date. 1 is doubled on top right side of shaft. First 8 has die chip with polishing mark at top right inside of upper loop, at bottom inside of lower loop, and a small mark on left outside of upper loop. Second 8 is doubled slightly at top inside of upper loop. Both loops of 2 have die chips at lower inside.

21 III²14 • C³a (Doubled 882) (176) I-2 R-4
Obverse III²14 – Doubled 882 in date. First 8 doubled slightly on right outside of upper loop. Second 8 doubled at top left outside of upper loop and slightly at bottom right of lower loop. 2 doubled strongly on left outside of upper loop and on right side of lower left serif.

22 III²11 • C³j (Doubled 82 and Reverse) (176) I-3 R-3
Reverse C³j – Outer portion doubled with letters doubled outward in a radial direction for UN-ED, STATES OF AMERICA, R of DOLLAR, both stars, motto, tip of eagle's right wing, top outside of right wreath. Die overpolishing with disconnected leaves in the wreath and field showing through eagle's left wing.

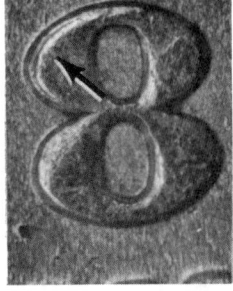

11 O Doubled 8 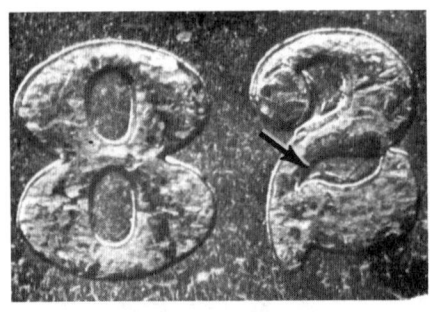   13 O Doubled 2 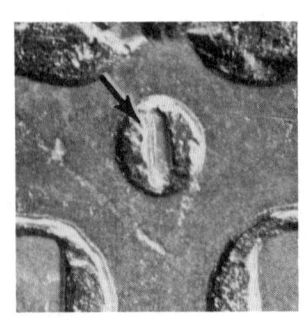   15 O O/O Left

1882-O

16 O O Tilted Left

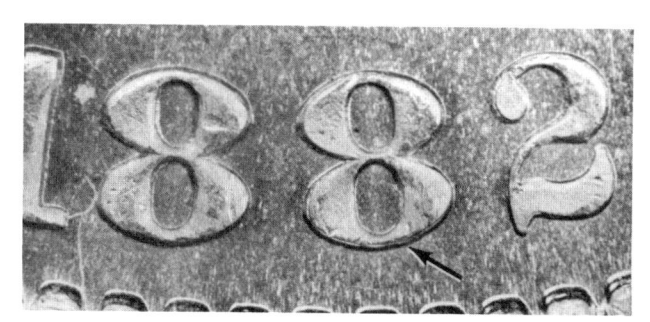

18 O Doubled 82 Left

19 O
Overpolished Wing

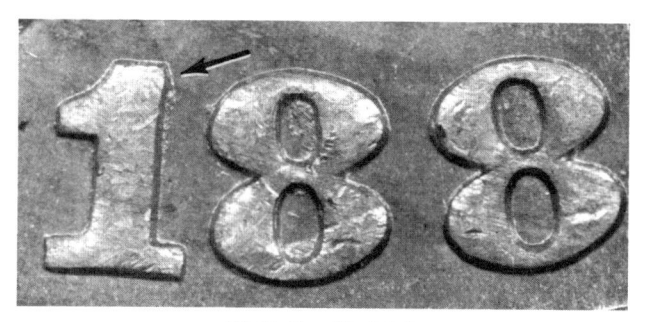

20 O Doubled 1-8

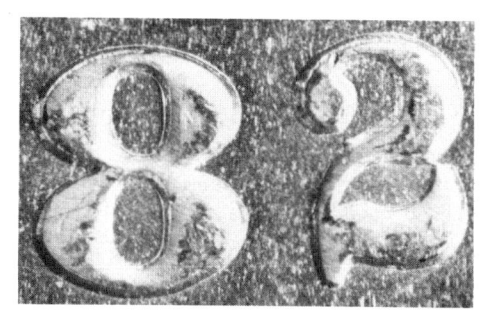

19 O Doubled 82

21 O Doubled 882

22 R Doubled Reverse

23 O Doubled 18

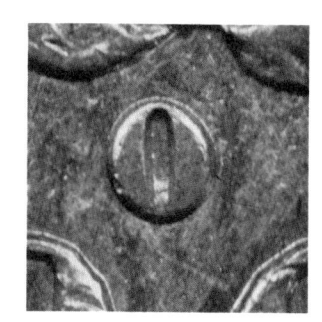

23 R O Tilted Left

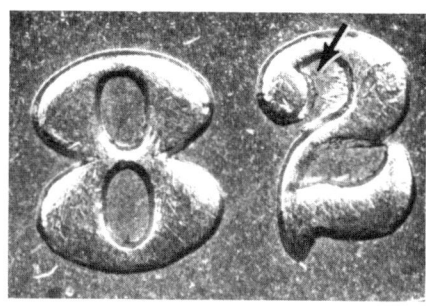

24 O Doubled 2

241

1882-O

23 III²15 • C³k (Doubled 18, O Tilted Left) (181) I-2 R-3
Obverse III²15 – Doubled 18 in date. 1 doubled below upper crossbar at top right of vertical shaft. First 8 doubled at top right inside of lower loop.
Reverse C³k – II O mint mark set left and tilted left.

24 III²16 • C³k (Doubled 2, O Tilted Left) (181) I-2 R-3
Obverse III²16 – 2 in date doubled on right side of knob. Die chips and polishing lines in upper loop and at bottom of lower loop of 2.

25 III²16 • C³l (Doubled 2, O/O Left) (181) I-2 R-3
Reverse C³l – II O mint mark repunched with original showing as a vertical bar on left side of loop opening but slightly more pronounced then C³i with diagonal polishing lines on right side of opening. Heavy horizontal polishing lines in eagle's tail feathers and in wreath bow.

26 III²17 • C³a (Doubled 2) (181) I-2 R-3
Obverse III²17 – 2 in date doubled on right side of knob but slightly stronger than VAM 24. Lower loop has horizontal line at top inside.

27 III²18 • C³e (Doubled 1-82) (181) 1-2 R-3
Obverse III²18 – Doubled 1-82 in date. 1 doubled slightly below upper crossbar. Second 8 doubled at left outside of upper loop. 2 doubled slightly at right outside of upper loop.

28 III²19 • C³e (Doubled Date and Stars) I-3 R-3
Obverse III²19 – Entire date is doubled. 18 doubled slightly at very bottom. Second 8 doubled at left outside of upper loop. 2 doubled slightly at right outside of upper loop. All left and right stars doubled towards rim. Tops of E PLUR doubled towards rim and right lower serif of M doubled at top.

29 III²20 • C³a (Doubled Date) (181) I-2 R-3
Obverse III²20 – Entire date is doubled. 1 is doubled at top right vertical shaft. First 8 is doubled at top inside of lower loop. Second 8 is doubled at left outside of both loops. 2 is doubled at top right outside of upper loop.

30 III²21 • C³g (Doubled 1-2, Dash, O/O Right) (181) I-2 R-4
Obverse III²21 – Doubled 1-2 in date. 1 doubled strongly below upper crossbar. 2 doubled slightly on right side of upper ball. Second 8 has a faint dash below lower loop.

31 III²22 • C³a (Doubled Date) (181) I-2 R-3
Obverse III²22 – Entire date doubled. 1 doubled at top right of vertical shaft. First 8 doubled at top inside of upper loop. Second 8 doubled at left outside of upper loop. 2 doubled at left outside and right inside of upper loop.

32 III²23 • C³a (Doubled 882) (181) I-2 R-3
Obverse III²23 – Doubled 882 in date. First 8 doubled at right inside of upper loop. Second 8 doubled at left outside of both loops. 2 doubled at left outside and right inside of upper loop.

33 III²24 • C³a (Doubled 882) (181) I-2 R-3
Obverse III²24 – Doubled 882 in date. First 8 doubled slightly at bottom outside of upper loop. Second 8 doubled at left outside of upper loop. 2 doubled strongly at right outside of upper loop and slightly at right side of upper ball.

34 III²25 • C³a (Double Date) (181) I-2 R-3
Obverse III²25 – All digits in date are doubled. 1 doubled slightly below upper crossbar and at top of lower crossbar. First 8 doubled slightly at lower left outside of upper loop. Second 8 doubled at top and left outside of upper loop. 2 doubled at top and left and right outside of upper loop and on right side of lower serif.

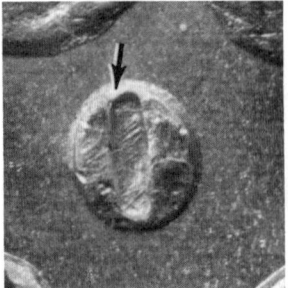

25 R O/O Left 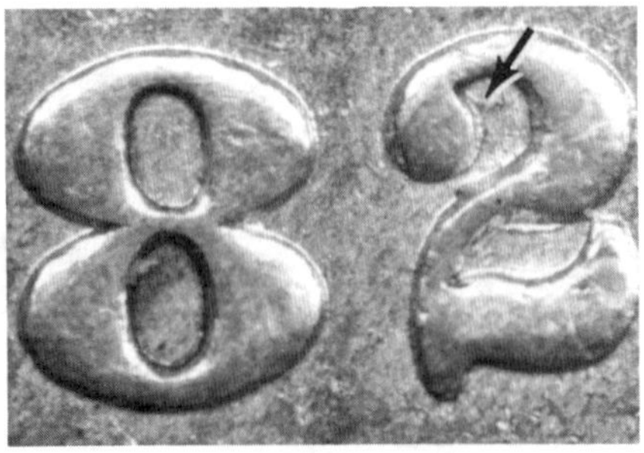   26 O Doubled 2 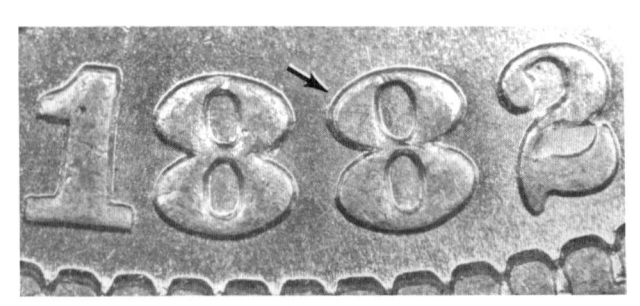   27 O Doubled 1-82

1882-O

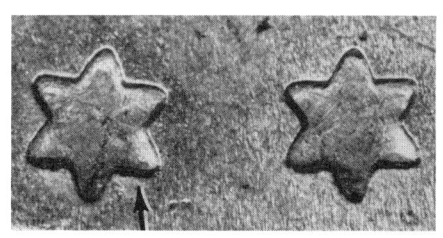

28 O Doubled Stars

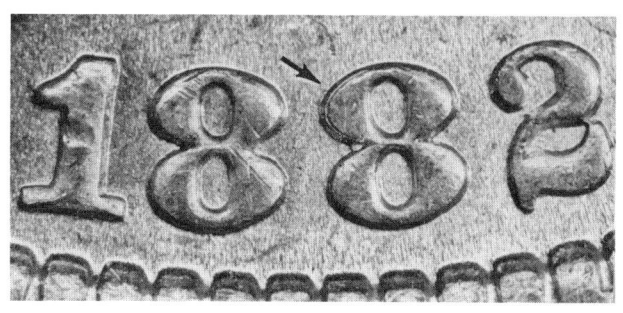

28 O Doubled Date

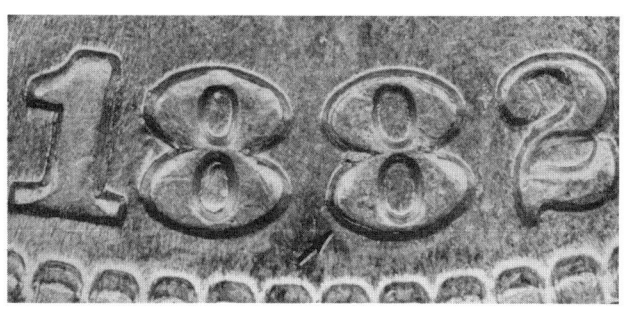

29 O Doubled Date

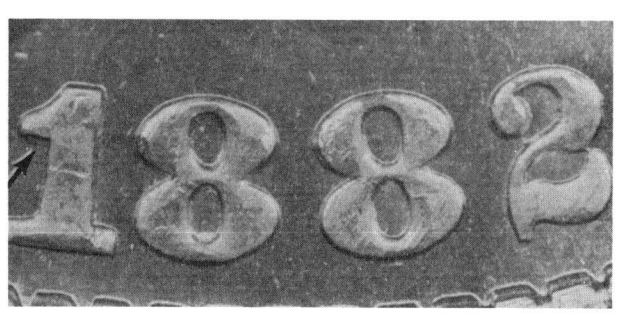

30 O Doubled 1-2, Dash Under 8

31 O Doubled Date

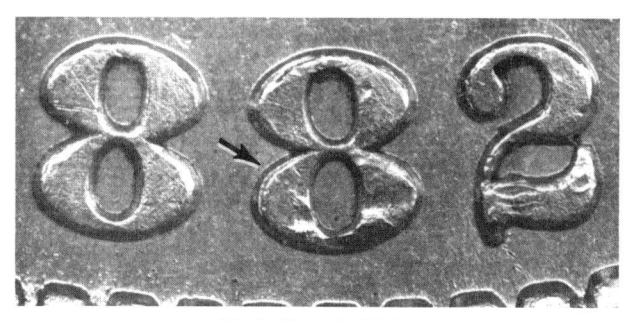

32 O Doubled 882

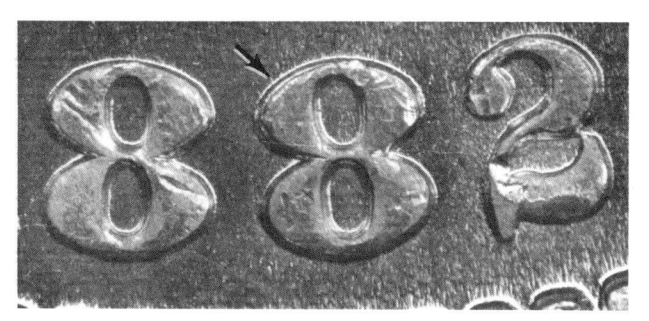

33 O Doubled 882

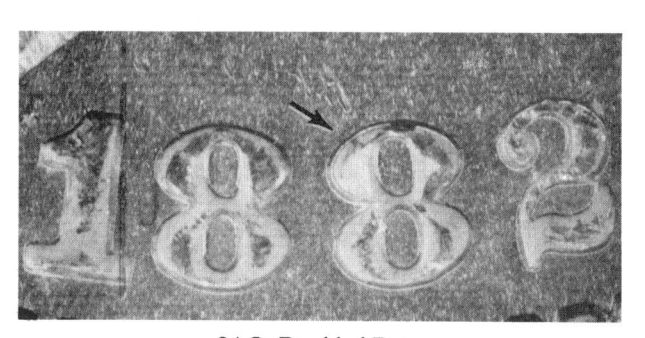

34 O Doubled Date

1882-S

1882-S

Most specimens are fully struck although a few exist with slight weakness. Luster is usually excellent. This last year of the four common date S mint years, 1879-1882, is fairly available in nice condition although not quite as much as 1880-S and 1881-S. Quite a few minor die varieties exist but none are significant. VAM 20 has one of the farthest tilted S mint mark to the left known.

Proof-likes are fairly available but not quite as much as earlier S mints. Most tend to be brilliant and many are one-sided proof-like. Two-sided cameo proof-likes are fairly scarce like that for 1881-S.

1   III² 1 • C³ a (Open 2)   (187)   I-1   R-2
    Obverse III² 1 – Normal die of III² type with open 2 in which tail does not touch body of 2. Some specimens show die chips between loops of both 8's on right side or on first 8 right side and second 8 left side.
    Reverse C³ a – Normal die of C³ type with a medium IV S mint mark centered and upright.

2   III² 2 • C³ a (Doubled 882)   (183)   I-2   R-3
    Obverse III² 2 – Doubled 882 in date. First 8 doubled at left and top outside and right inside of upper loop and right outside of lower loop. Second 8 doubled strongly at left outside and faintly at top outside of upper loop and at bottom and right outside of lower loop. 2 doubled at top and right outside and top inside of upper loop.

3   III² 3 • C³ b (Doubled 82)   (187)   I-2   R-3
    Obverse III² 3 – 82 in date doubled slightly at top. Die chip on right side of first 8 and on left side of second 8 between loops. Open 2 variety.
    Reverse C³ b – IV S mint mark is filled and titled left.

4   III² 4 • C³ a (Doubled 88)   (187)   I-2   R-3
    Obverse III² 4 – Doubled 88 in date. The first 8 is doubled on the left inside of the upper loop. The second 8 is doubled on the left outside of the upper loop. Both open and closed 2 varieties.

5   III² 5 • C³ a (Doubled 882)   (186)   I-2   R-3
    Obverse III² 5 – Doubled 882 in date. The first 8 is doubled on the right outside of both loops. Second 8 doubled at top and top right of lower loop. The 2 is doubled at top right.

6   III² 1 • C³ c (S/S)   I-3   R-4
    Reverse C³ c – IV S mint mark repunched with original showing as a thin diagonal line on right side of upper loop and curved line at right inside of lower loop with tilt to far left.

7   III² 6 • C³ a (Doubled 82)   I-2   R-3
    Obverse III² 6 – Doubled 82 in date. Second 8 is doubled slightly on left inside of upper loop. 2 is doubled very slightly on right outside of upper loop. Both 8's have die chips between loops an left and right sides.

8   III² 7 • C³ a (Doubled 8-2)   (187)   I-2   R-3
    Obverse III² 7 – Doubled 8-2 in date. First 8 doubled on inside of upper loop. 2 doubled slightly at top outside. 82 in date very shallow due to over polished die.

9   III² 8 • C³ a (Doubled 18-2)   I-2   R-3
    Obverse III² 8 – Doubled 18-2 in date. 1 is doubled slightly on surface of right side of vertical shaft. First 8 is doubled on right outside of upper loop. 2 is doubled at top and right outside of upper loop and has die chip at left inside of lower loop.

10   III² 9 • C³ a (Doubled 1-82)   (187)   I-2   R-3
    Obverse III² 9 – Doubled 1-82 in date. 1 is doubled on top right side of shaft. First 8 has die chip at top inside of upper loop, at bottom inside of lower loop with polishing marks and a small mark on left outside of upper loop. Second 8 and 2 are doubled slightly on right outside of upper loop.

2 O Doubled 882 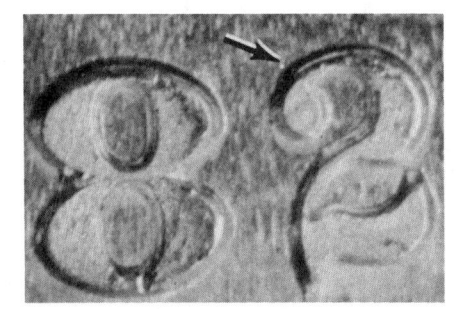   3 O Doubled 82 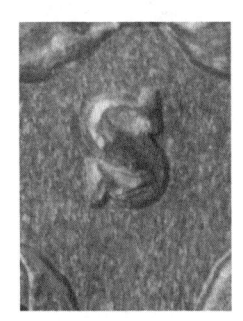   3 R S Filled, Tilted Left

1882-S

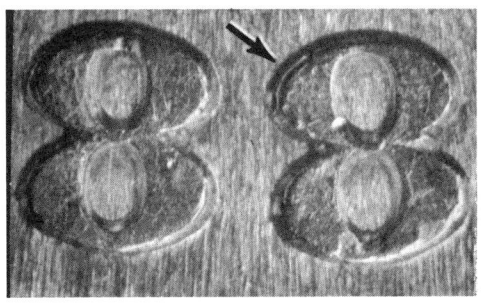

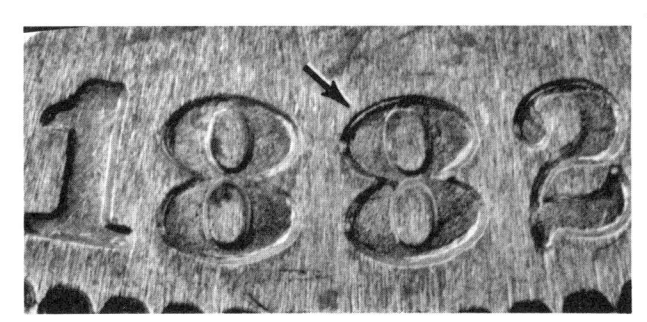

4 O Doubled 88

5 O Doubled 882

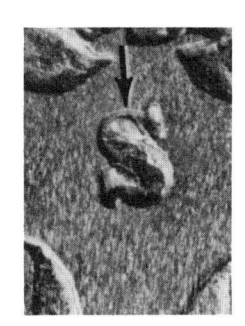

6 R S/S

7 O Doubled 82

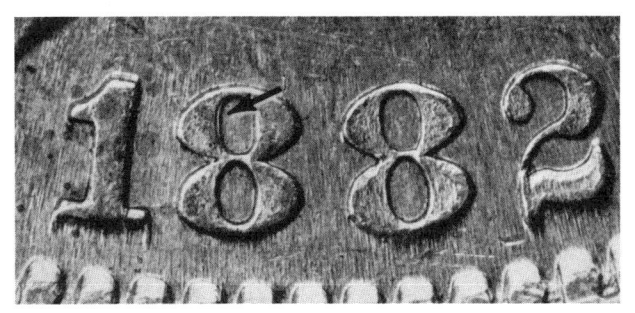

8 O Doubled 8-2

9 O Doubled 18-2

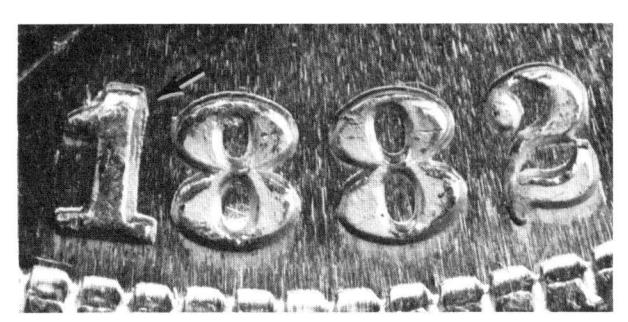

10 O Doubled 1-82

11 O Doubled 882

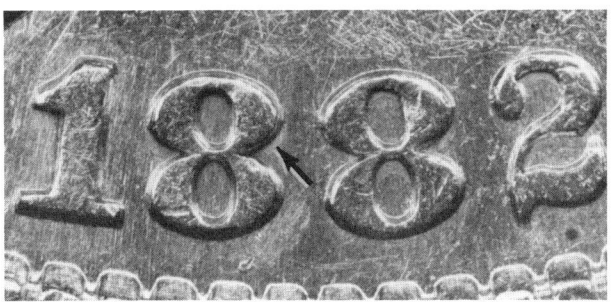

12 O Doubled 882

1882-S

11 III² 10 • C³ b (Doubled 882) (187) I-2 R-4
  Obverse III² 10 – Doubled 882 in date. First 8 is doubled strongly on left inside and slightly on right outside of upper loop with spikes of metal between loops on both sides. Second 8 is doubled strongly on left outside of upper loop, slightly at bottom outside of lower loop and has a die chip between loops on right side. 2 is doubled on left side of upper loop.

12 III² 11 • C³ a (Doubled 882) I-2 R-3
  Obverse III² 11 – Doubled 882 in date. First 8 is doubled slightly on lower right outside and lower left inside of upper loop. Second 8 doubled slightly on top left outside of upper loop and right outside of lower loop. 2 doubled on right outside. First U in PLURIBUS has shallow die gouge showing as a diagonal line in bottom inside of U.

13 III² 12 • C³ a (Doubled Date) (186) I-2 R-3
  Obverse III² 12 – 1 in date doubled slightly on right side of vertical shaft and top right of lower crossbar. The first 8 is doubled on the left outside of the top loop. The second 8 is doubled on the bottom inside of the top loop and the bottom and right side of the lower loop. Closed 2 variety with upper loop doubled slightly at top left outside.

13A III² 12 • C³ a (Doubled Date) (186) I-2 R-3
  Reverse C³ a – Die break below uppermost berries in left wreath.

14 III² 13 • C³ a (Doubled Date) (185) I-2 R-4
  Obverse III² 13 – Entire date doubled. 1 doubled on right side of vertical shaft. First 8 strongly doubled on left inside and right outside of both loops. Second 8 doubled strongly at very top and left outside of top loop and is doubled slightly at bottom left outside and top right outside of lower loop. 2 doubled at top and right outside of upper loop and on right side of bottom serif.

15 III² 14 • C³ a (Doubled 882) I-2 R-4
  Obverse III² 14 – Doubled 882 in date. First 8 is doubled slightly on surface at bottom right of lower loop and lower left inside of upper loop. Second 8 is tripled at top outside of upper loop and doubled on right outside of lower loop. 2 is doubled at very top outside.

16 III² 15 • C³ a (Doubled Date) (186) I-2 R-4
  Obverse III² 15 – Entire date doubled. 1 doubled at top left of lower crossbar. First 8 doubled on right outside of both loops with die chip between loops on right side. Second 8 is doubled at top outside of upper loop and right outside of lower loop. 2 is doubled at top and right outside of upper loop and has a die chip on surface on right of lower crossbar. Open 2 variety.

17 III² 5 • C³ c (Doubled 882, S/S) I-3 R-4

18 III² 13 • C³ b (Doubled Date, S Tilted Left) (186) I-2 R-4

19 III² 16 • C³ d (Doubled Date, S/S) I-2 R-3
  Obverse III² 16 – Entire date doubled. 1 doubled at top of lower crossbar on both sides and as a fine horizontal line well below the upper crossbar. First 8 doubled at top left outside of upper loop and at right outside of lower loop. Second 8 doubled at top left outside of upper loop and at bottom and right outside of lower loop. 2 doubled at top and right outside of upper loop.
  Reverse C³ d – IV S mint mark slightly doubled at bottom outside of lower loop.

20 III² 17 • C³ e (Doubled Date, S Tilted Far Left) (186) I-2 R-3
  Obverse III² 17 – Entire date doubled. 1 doubled slightly on top right side of vertical shaft. First 8 doubled slightly on right outside of lower loop. Second 8 doubled slightly on left inside and strongly on right outside of upper loop. 2 doubled strongly on right outside of upper loop.
  Reverse C³ e – IV S mint mark tilted far to left and shifted slightly to left. One of the farthest S tilts known.

12 O Die Gouge

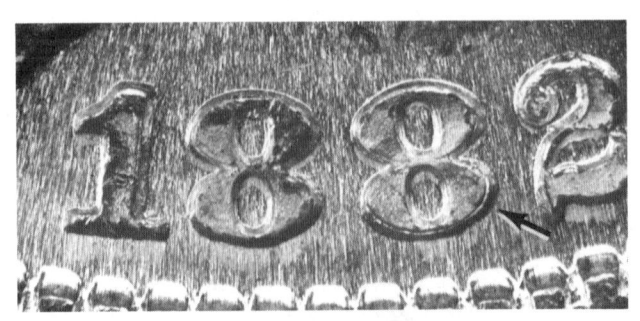

13 O Doubled Date

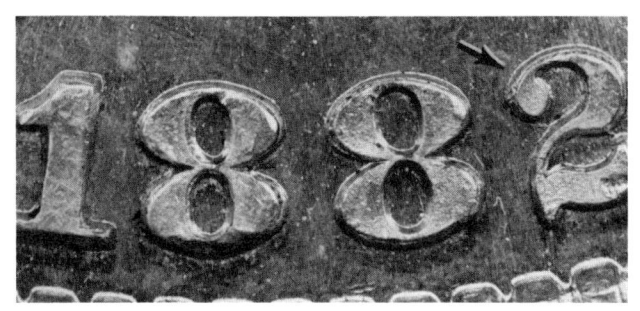

1882-S

14 O Doubled Date

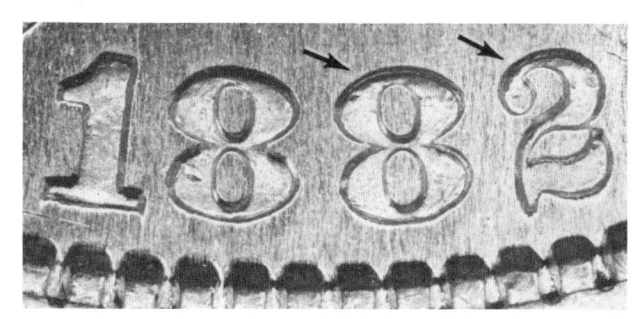

15 O Doubled 882

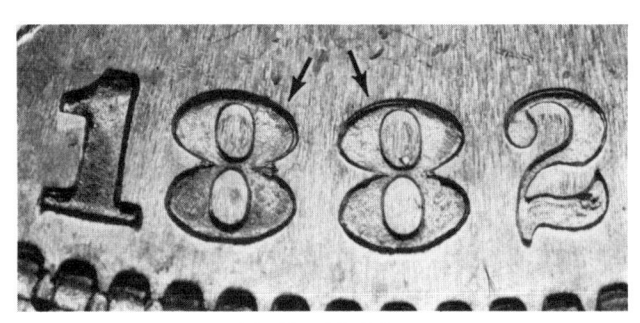

16 O Doubled Date

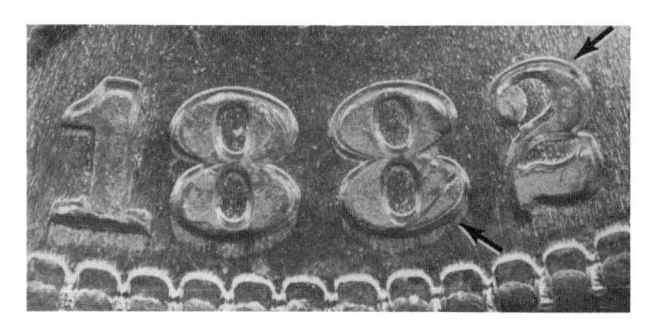

19 O Doubled 882

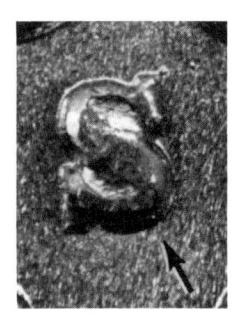

19 R S/S

20 O Doubled Date

20 R S Tilted Left

| 21 | III²18 • C³b (Doubled 882) | (187) | 1-2 | R-3 |

Obverse III² 18 – Doubled 882 in date. First 8 doubled slightly at left outside and right inside of upper loop and right outside of lower loop. Second 8 doubled strongly at left outside of upper loop and right and bottom outside of lower loop. 2 doubled at top outside of upper loop.

22	III²10 • C³a (Doubled 882)	(186)	I-2	R-4
23	III²9 • C³b (Doubled 1-82, S Tilted Left)	(186)	I-2	R-3
24	III²19 • C³a (Doubled Date)	(187)	I-2	R-3

Obverse III² 19 – Entire date is doubled. 1 is doubled slightly on surface at top right of shaft. First 8 doubled on right outside and slightly on lower left inside of upper loop. Second 8 doubled on left outside of upper loop with die chip between loops on right side. 2 doubled on right outside of upper loop and slightly on right side of lower serif.

25	III²15 • C³b (Doubled Date, S Tilted Left)	(186)	I-2	R-3
26	III²18 • C³a (Doubled 882)	(185)	I-2	R-3
27	III²17 • C³a (Doubled Date)	(187)	I-2	R-3

1882-S / 1883-P

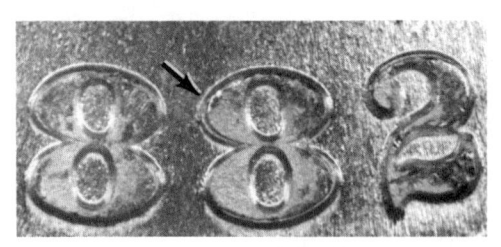

21 O Doubled 882

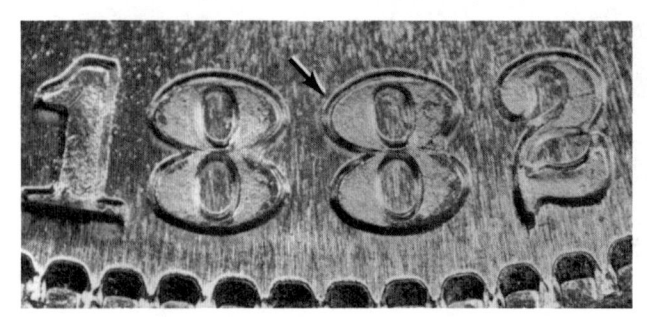

24 O Doubled Date

1883-P

This issue generally is fully struck although slightly weak struck examples exist, particularly on the reverse. Luster is usually fairly good. Some specimens exhibit a surface roughness on the devices which are fine raised dots due to rusted dies. A number of minor die varieties exist but two are unusually interesting. VAM 4 has strong doubling above the 83 and VAM 10 has all left and right stars quadrupled to sextupled towards the rim.

It is the most available 1879-1884-P proof-like but is still fairly scarce. Most have fairly good contrast and a number have very deep mirrors with cameo devices on both sides. The proofs have fairly good contrast but generally not as good as the 1880-1882 years and are more difficult to obtain in nice condition.

1   III² 1 • C³ a (Normal)   (180)   I-1   R-1
    Obverse III² 1 – Normal die of III² type. Some specimens show a die chip between the loops of the first 8 on left.
    Reverse C² a – Normal die of C³ type.
    Note: Some specimens show rusted obverse and reverse dies with fine pits over Liberty head and eagle.

2   III² 2 • C³ a (Low Dash Under 8)   (193)   I-2   R-3
    Obverse III² 2 – Normal die with a dash well below the second 8.

3   III² 3 • C³ a (High Dash Under 8, Doubled 8-3)   I-2   R-3
    Obverse III² 3 – Normal die with a dash just below the second 8. First 8 doubled at bottom outside of lower loop. 3 doubled at bottom inside of lower loop.

4   III² 4 • C³ a (Doubled 1-83)   (180)   I-3   R-3
    Obverse III² 4 – Doubled 1-83 in date. 1 is doubled below top crossbar and at top right. 83 is doubled strongly at top left and right outside. In addition, the lower loop of second 8 is doubled at top right outside. Also, the top of the lower serif of the 3 is doubled and the lower loop has a notch at lower left.

5   III² 5 • C³ a (Doubled 1-3, High 8)   (180)   I-2   R-3
    Obverse III² 5 – 1 doubled at left end of lower crossbar. 3 in date doubled at bottom inside of lower loop and shows as a notch in loop. Second 8 set higher than other numerals. A short, shallow dash set low shows between the 1 and first 8.

6   III² 6 • C³ a (Low 3, Doubled 1-3)   (180)   I-2   R-3
    Obverse III² 6 – 3 set lower than the rest of the date. 1 doubled as notch on left side of lower crossbar. 3 doubled at bottom inside of lower loop.

7   III² 7 • C³ a (Doubled 18-3)   (180)   I-2   R-3
    Obverse III² 7 – Doubled 18-3 in date. 1 doubled slightly at top right outside of vertical shaft. First 8 doubled at top inside of upper loop. 3 doubled slightly at bottom of lower loop.

8   III² 8 • C³ a (Doubled 18-3)   (180)   I-2   R-3
    Obverse III² 8 – Doubled 18-3 in date. 1 is doubled on left of upper serif and base. First 8 is doubled at top inside of lower loop. 3 is doubled on right side of upper serif.

9   III² 9 • C³ a (Doubled 18-3, Stars and Motto)   (180)   I-3   R-4
    Obverse III² 9 – Doubled 18-3 in date. 1 doubled at bottom of upper crossbar and base plus left side of vertical shaft. First 8 doubled at left inside of both loops and at bottom outside of lower loop. 3 is doubled slightly at bottom inside of lower loop. All stars and motto letters are doubled next to rim in radial direction.

1883-P

2 O Low Dash

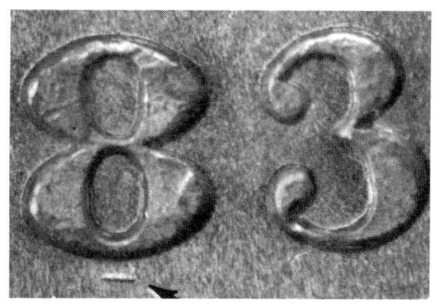

3 O High Dash

5 O Doubled 3, High 8

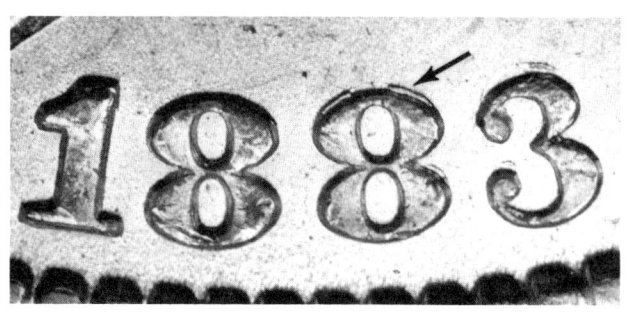

4 O Doubled 83

5 O High 8

6 O Low 3

8 O Doubled 18-3

7 O First Doubled 8

9 O Doubled Stars, Motto

1883-P

| 10 | III² 10 • C³ a (Doubled Date, Dash 8, Sextupled Stars) | (180) | I-3 | R-4 |

Obverse III² 10 – Entire date is doubled. 1 doubled strongly below upper and lower crossbars. First 8 doubled strongly below lower loop. Second 8 doubled below lower loop as a thin line in middle. 3 doubled slightly at bottom left inside of lower loop. Second 8 has a long curved dash set well below lower loop. All left and right stars and tops of UNUM letters quadrupled to sextupled towards rim with first five stars on right having large shifts.

| 11 | III² 11 • C³ a (Doubled 18-3) | (188) | I-2 | R-3 |

Obverse III² 11 – Doubled 18-3 in date. 1 doubled on surface at bottom of upper crossbar and base. First 8 doubled faintly on lower inside of both loops. 3 doubled faintly at top inside of upper loop and at bottom inside of lower loop.

| 12 | III² 12 • C³ a (Doubled 18) | (188) | I-2 | R-3 |

Obverse III² 12 – Doubled 18 in date. 1 doubled on surface on right side of vertical shaft. First 8 doubled on surface on left inside of lower loop.

| 13 | III² 13 • C³ a (Slanted Date, Doubled 1-3) | (192) | I-2 | R-3 |

Obverse III² 13 – Date slanted with 83 high above rim. 1 doubled below bottom crossbar. 3 doubled at bottom inside of lower loop.

| 14 | III² 14 • C³ a (Doubled 18-3) | (188) | I-2 | R-3 |

Obverse III² 14 – Doubled 18-3 in date. 1 doubled at top right of vertical shaft. First 8 doubled at top left inside of both loops. 3 doubled slightly at bottom right outside of lower loop.

| 15 | III² 15 • C³ a (Doubled 8-3) | (181) | I-2 | R-3 |

Obverse III² 15 – Doubled 8-3 in date. First 8 doubled slightly on right outside of lower loop. 3 doubled slightly at bottom inside of lower loop.

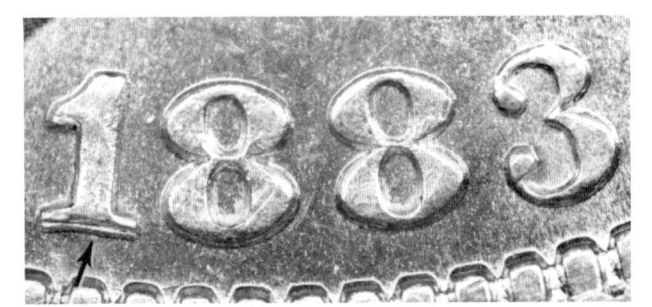

9 O Doubled 18-3

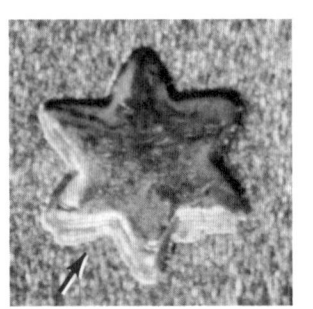

10 O Sextupled Stars

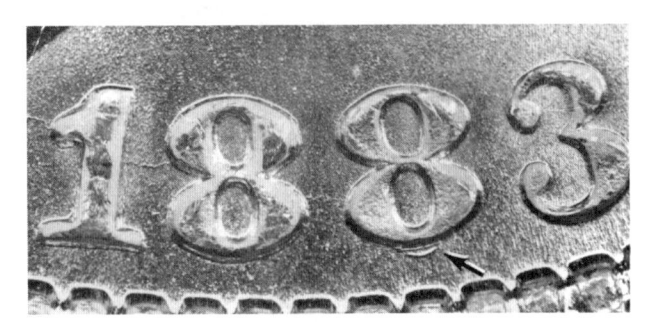

10 O Doubled Date

11 O Doubled 18-3

12 O Doubled 18

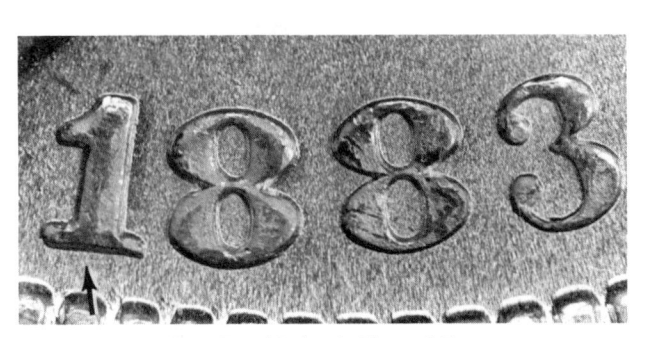

13 O Doubled 1-3, Slanted Date

14 O Doubled 18-3

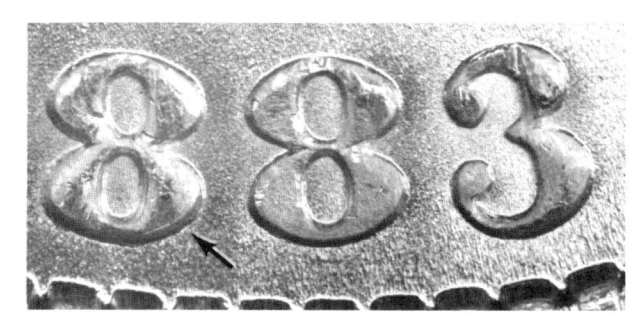

15 O Doubled 8-3

1883-CC

Over half the mintage was in the GSA sale so BU specimens are readily available. Usually the strike is full and the luster good. A few die varieties exist but the only significant one is VAM 4 with an unusually strong doubled date.

A fair proportion of this issue are deep mirror proof-likes with good contrast. A sizeable number are cameo proof-likes.

1   III²1 • C³a (Normal Die)   I-1   R-2
   Obverse III²1 – Normal die of III² type. Some specimens show die chip between loops of first 8 on right.
   Reverse C³a – Normal die of C³a type with large centered V CC mint mark.

2   III²1 • C³b (Slanted CC)   (178)   1-2   R-3
   Reverse C³b – Large V CC slanted with left C set high. Both C's have polishing marks inside.

3   III²3 • C³b (Dash Under 8)   (178)   I-2   R-3
   Obverse III²3 – Dash under second 8 in date. First 8 doubled at top inside of lower loop. Some specimens show only a dot left of the dash.

4   III²4 • C³c (Doubled Date, Dash Under 8)   (178)   I-3   R-3
   Obverse III²4 – All digits in date are doubled. The 1 is doubled on the right side of the vertical bar and above the bottom right serif. First 8 is doubled at the top inside of the upper loop and metal is on the left outside. Second 8 is doubled at top and a short dash appears well below the bottom loop. The 3 is doubled at top and metal is also at top and right and just above the end of the lower loop.
   Reverse C³c – First C has diagonal line at top inside of loop and metal within it. Second C has metal at bottom inside of loop and short line at very top inside of loop.

5   III²5 • C³a (Doubled 18-3)   (178)   I-2   R-3
   Obverse III²5 – Doubled 18-3 in date. 1 doubled on surface on lower part of upper crossbar, on right side of vertical shaft and on top of right side of lower crossbar. First 8 doubled on left inside of lower loop. 3 doubled at bottom inside of lower loop.

6   III²6 • C³a (Doubled 18, Dash 8)   (178)   1-2   R-3
   Obverse III²6 – Doubled 18 in date. 1 doubled on surface at right side of vertical shaft. First 8 doubled on surface at left inside of both loops. A very short dot dash appears under second 8 on some specimens.

7   III²7 • C³d (Doubled Date, CC/CC)   (178)   1-2   R-3
   Obverse III²7 – Entire date is slightly doubled. 1 is doubled on surface at bottom of upper crossbar, on right side of vertical shaft and at top of bottom crossbar. First 8 doubled on surface at left inside of both loops. Second 8 doubled slightly at top right outside of lower loop. 3 doubled slightly on right side of upper ball and at bottom inside of lower loop.
   Reverse C³d – First C in mint mark is doubled at bottom inside. Second C is doubled slightly at lower left of upper serif.

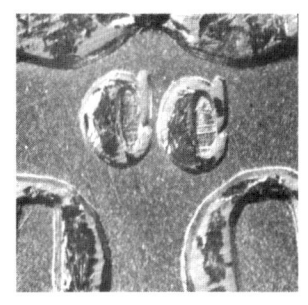

2 R Slanted CC Left

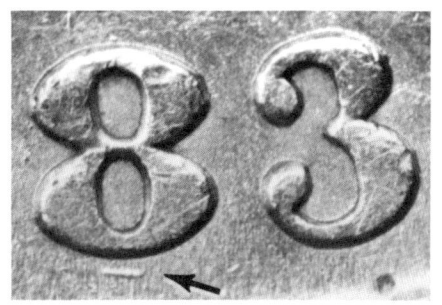

3 O Dash

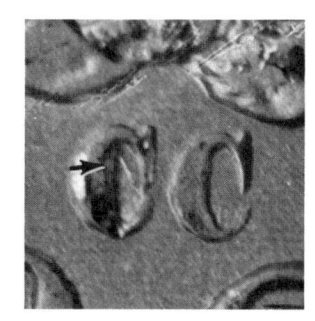

4 R Doubled CC

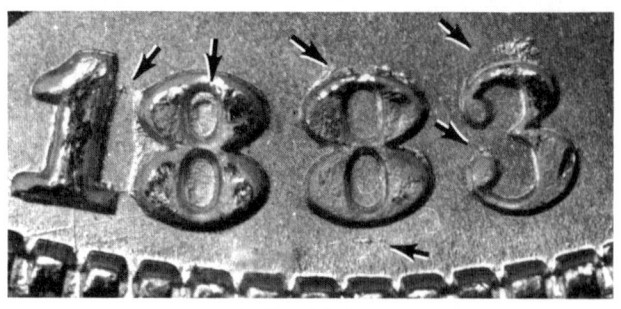

1883-CC / 1883-O

4 O Doubled Date

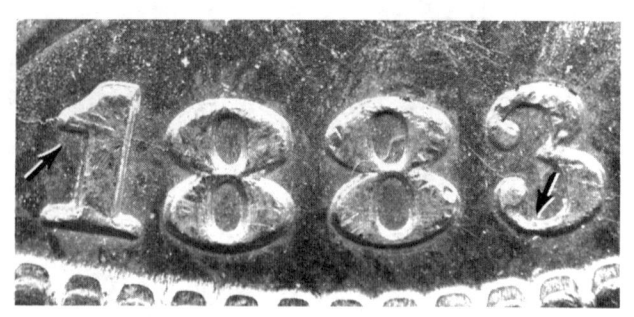

5 O Doubled Date

6 O Doubled 18, Dash 8

7 O Doubled Date

7 R CC/CC

1883-O

The first of the common date O mints, the strike runs the gamut from extremely flat to razor sharp. However, full strikes are fairly easy to locate. Luster is generally good but can be dull on some coins from dies that were used in the coining presses a long time. This issue is not plagued by an abundance of sliders as the earlier O mint issues were. Although numerous die varieties exist, only VAM 4 with a doubled O mint mark below the O is very significant.

Proof-likes are available but not as readily as the early S mints. Generally the contrast is fairly good and very deep mirror cameos can occasionally be found. Twelve branch mint proofs were reported struck and two are known.

| 1 | III²1 • C³a (Normal Die) | (181) | I-1 | R-2 |

Obverse III²1 – Normal die of III² type. Some specimens show a die chip between loops of first 8 on left.
Reverse C³a – Normal die of C³ type with tall oval medium II O mint mark centered and upright.

| 1A | III²1 • C³a (Die Flake in 8) | (181) | I-2 | R-4 |

Obverse III²1 – Die flake in lower loop of first 8 and under loop on lower right outside.

| 1B | III²1 • C³a (Gouge In 8) | (181) | I-2 | R-4 |

Obverse III²1 – Diagonal die gouge on top left inside of lower loop of first 8.

| 2 | III²2 • C³a (Dash Under 8) | (181) | I-2 | R-3 |

Obverse III²2 – Dash under second 8 in date. Some specimens show 1 doubled well below upper crossbar as a short spike.

| 3 | III²9 • C³b (O/O Right) | (181) | I-2 | R-3 |

Obverse III²9 – 1 doubled at bottom of crossbar and on left top side of vertical shaft.
Reverse C³b – Mint mark repunched with the original showing on the right side of the opening.

| 4 | III²3 • C³c (O/O Down, Doubled 1) | (181) | I-2 | R-3 |

Obverse III²3 – 1 in date doubled slightly at top left and on top right of stem plus at bottom of lower crossbar. Second 8 is set high. Date shallow from overpolished die.
Reverse C³c – II O mint mark repunched with the original showing at the top of the opening and below at left and right sides.

| 5 | III²1 • C³d (O/O Right and High) | (181) | I-2 | R-3 |

Reverse C³d – Mint mark repunched with the original showing at the top and right side of the opening.

| 6 | III²1 • C³e (O/O High) | (181) | I-2 | R-4 |

Reverse C³e – Mint mark repunched with the original showing at the top of the opening.

1883-O

7   III²4 • C³a (Doubled 18-3)   (181)   I-2   R-3
Obverse III²4 – Doubled 18-3 in date. 1 doubled slightly at top left. First 8 doubled at bottom outside of lower loop. 3 doubled at bottom left inside of lower loop.

8   III²1 • C³f (O Tilted Far Right)   (181)   I-2   R-3
Reverse C³f – Normal die with II O mint mark tilted far to right.

9   III²5 • C³e (High 8, O/O High)   (181)   I-2   R-4
Obverse III²5 – Second 8 in date set higher than first 8 and 3. Faint doubling at bottom of 1 and at bottom inside of 3 lower loop.

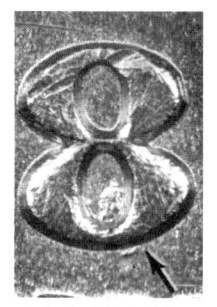

1A O Die Flake In First 8

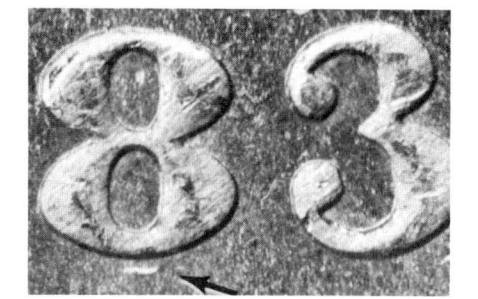

2 O Dash

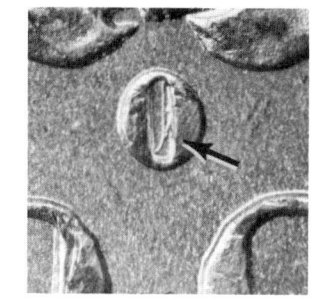

3 R O/O Right

1B O Gouge in 8

3 O Doubled 1

4 O Doubled 1

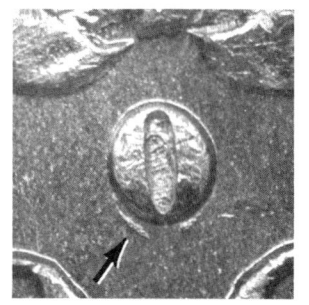

4 R O/O Down

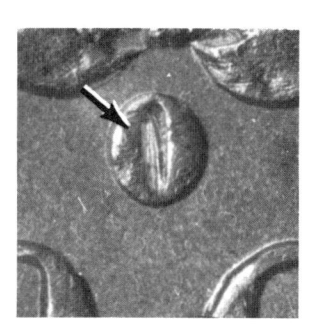

5 R O/O Right

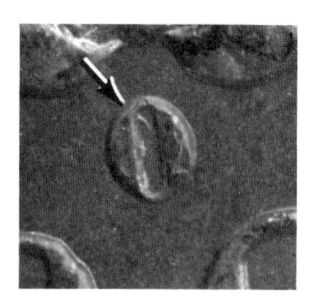

6 R O/O High

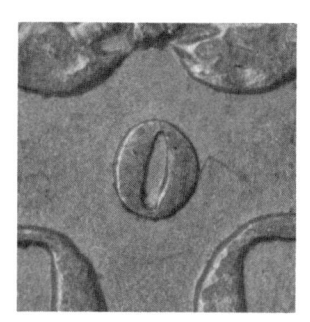

8 R O Tilted Right

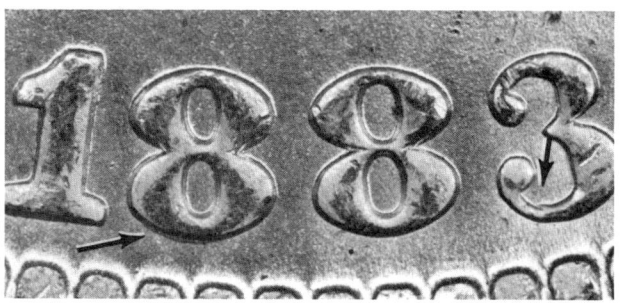

7 O Doubled 18-3

9 O High 8

253

1883-O

10	III²5 • C³g (High 8, O/O Low)	(181)	I-2	R-3

Reverse C³g – II O mint mark repunched with original showing as a diagonal line at bottom of loop opening.

11	III²5 • C³h (O Tilted Slightly Right, High 8)	(181)	I-2	R-3

Reverse C³h – II O mint mark centered and tilted slightly right.

12	III²1 • C³i (O Set Left)	(181)	I-2	R-3

Reverse C³i – II O mint mark set slightly to left.

13	III²1 • C³j (O/O Right and Down)	(181)	I-2	R-3

Reverse C³j – II O mint mark repunched with the original showing at top inside and lower right outside.

14	III²6 • C³a (Doubled 1-3)	(181)	I-2	R-3

Obverse III²6 – 1 in date doubled at bottom of crossbar and on top left side of shaft. 3 doubled slightly at bottom left inside of lower loop.

15	III²7 • C³a (Slanted Date)	(181)	I-2	R-3

Obverse III²7 – Date slanted with 83 higher than normal.

16	III²5 • C³k (O/O Line)	(181)	I-3	R-4

Reverse C³k – High upright II O mint mark repunched with the original showing as a high raised line in the center of the opening and curving to the left at top.

17	III²8 • C³l (Low 3, O Tilted Left)	(181)	I-2	R-3

Obverse III²8 – 3 in date punched low with bottom close to rim.
Reverse C³l – II O mint mark tilted slightly to the left.

18	III²5 • C³a (High 8)	(181)	I-2	R-4

Reverse C³a – II O mint mark has fine diagonal polishing line at bottom of opening.

19	III²9 • C³1 (Doubled 1)	(181)	I-2	R-3

Obverse III²9 – 1 doubled slightly at top left and at top right of stem.

20	III²10 • C³f (Doubled 3, O Tilted Right)	(181)	I-2	R-3

Obverse III²10 – 3 in date doubled slightly at bottom left inside of lower loop.

21	III²11 • C³a (Doubled 18)	(181)	I-2	R-3

Obverse III²11 – Doubled 18 in date. 1 doubled on surface to top right of vertical shaft. First 8 doubled slightly at lower left inside of upper loop.

22	III²3 • C³a (Doubled 1)	(181)	I-2	R-3

Reverse C³a – Some specimens show an E die clash below eagle's tail feathers.

23	III²12 • C³a (Doubled 1)	(181)	I-2	R-3

Obverse III²12 – 1 doubled on surface at top right of vertical shaft. Slight slant to date with 1 closest to rim.

24	III²1 • C³m (Doubled Reverse)	(181)	I-2	R-3

Reverse C³m – Middle leaves in clusters of left and right wreaths doubled towards rim. Top inside of wreath bow and designer's initial, M, doubled.

25	III²10 • C³i (Doubled 3, O Set Left)	(181)	I-2	R-3
26	III²4 • C³i (Doubled 18-3, O Set Left)	(181)	I-2	R-3
27	III²12 • C³n (Doubled 1, O/O Surface)	(181)	I-2	R-3

Reverse C³n – II O mint mark repunched with doubling on surface at lower left and right sides.

10 R O/O Low

11 R O Tilted Slightly Right

12 R O Set Left

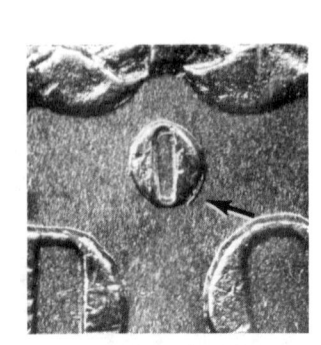

13 R O/O Right 4 Down

1883-O

14 O Doubled 1

15 O Slanted Date

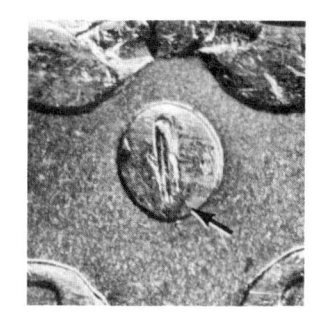

16 O O/O Line

17 O Low 3

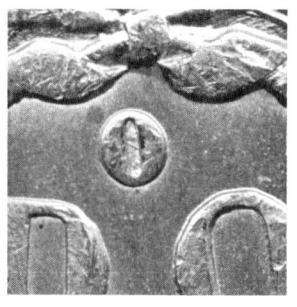

17 R O Tilted Left

19 O Doubled 1

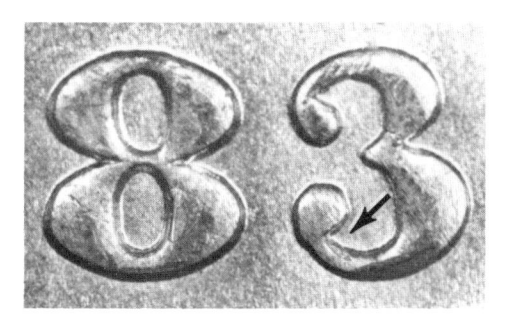

20 O Doubled 3

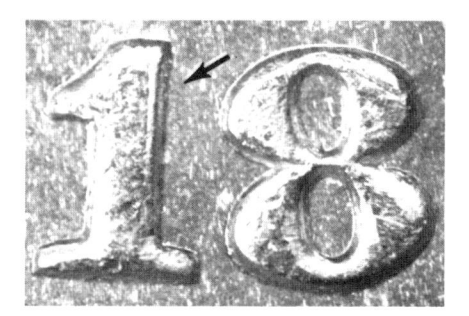

21 O Doubled 18

23 O Doubled 1

24 O Doubled Wreath

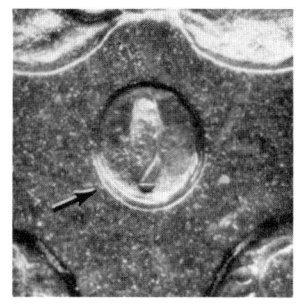

27 R O/O

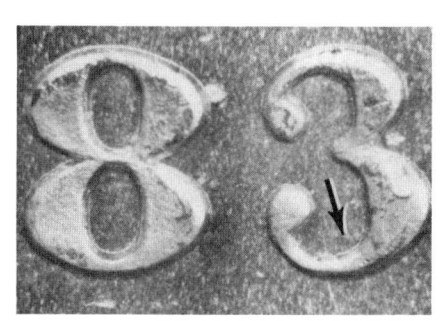

28 O Doubled 3

255

1883-O

28 III² 14 • C³ a (Doubled 3) (181) I-2 R-3
Obverse III² 14 – 3 doubled at bottom left inside of lower loop.

29 III² 14 • C³ o (Doubled 3, O/O) (181) I-2 R-3
Reverse C³ o – II O mint mark repunched with doubling at lower right inside.

30 III² 2 • C³ h (Dash Under 8, O Tilted Slightly Right) (181) I-2 R-3

31 III² 15 • C³ a (Doubled 18-3) (181) I-2 R-3
Obverse III² 15 – Doubled 18-3 in date. 1 doubled slightly below bottom crossbar. First 8 doubled slightly at top inside of upper loop. 3 doubled at bottom left inside of lower loop.

32 III² 16 • C³ a (Dash Under 8) (181) I-2 R-3
Obverse III² 16 – Long thin dash under second 8 in date. Some specimens show weakly struck periphery of stars and letters.

33 III² 10 • C³ p (Doubled 3, O/O Right) (181) I-2 R-3
Obverse III² 10 – Also shows diagonal die gouge at top left inside of lower loop of first 8.
Reverse C³ p – II O mint mark repunched with doubling at right inside and polishing line at top inside.

34 III² 17 • C³ j (Doubled 18-3, O/O Right and Down) (181) I-2 R-3
Obverse III² 17 – Doubled 18-3 in date. 1 doubled as line on top left of lower crossbar. First 8 doubled at left inside of both loops. 3 doubled at bottom inside of lower loop.

35 III² 18 • C³ a (Doubled 18 and Stars) (181) I-2 R-3
Obverse III² 18 – Doubled 18 in date. 1 doubled below upper crossbar and on surface at top and right of vertical shaft. First 8 doubled slightly at top inside of both loops and bottom left outside of upper loop. All right stars, first left star and UNUM strongly doubled towards rim.

36 III² 19 • C³ a Doubled 18-3) (181) I-2 R-3
Obverse III² 19 – Doubled 18-3 in date. 1 doubled at top left of upper crossbar as two notches and at bottom of lower crossbar with a notch at right. First 8 doubled slightly at top inside of upper loop. 3 doubled slightly in middle bottom inside of lower loop.
Reverse C³ a – Some specimens show a partial die clash E below eagle's tail feathers.

37 III² 20 • C³ a (Doubled 8-3) (181) I-2 R-3
Obverse III² 20 – Doubled 8-3 in date. First 8 doubled slightly at lower left inside of both loops. 3 doubled at top outside of upper loop and right outside and bottom inside of lower loop.

38 III² 21 • C³ a (Doubled 18-3) (181) I-2 R-3
Obverse III² 21 – Doubled 18-1 in date. 1 doubled below upper crossbar and on right side of vertical shaft. First 8 doubled at left inside of both loops. 3 doubled at bottom inside of lower loop.

29 R O/O

31 O Doubled 18-3

32 O Dash Under 8

33 R O/O Right

34 O Doubled 18-3

35 O Doubled 18

1883-O / 1883-S

35 O Doubled Stars, M

36 O Doubled 18-3

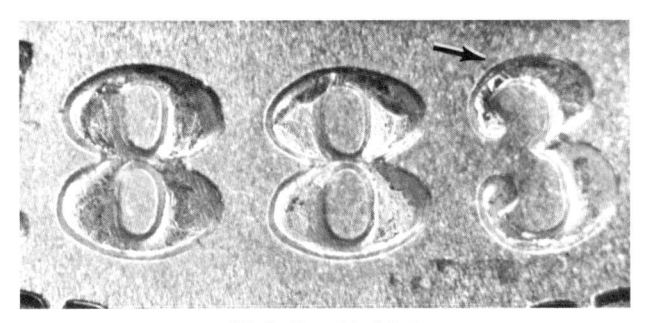

37 O Doubled 8-3

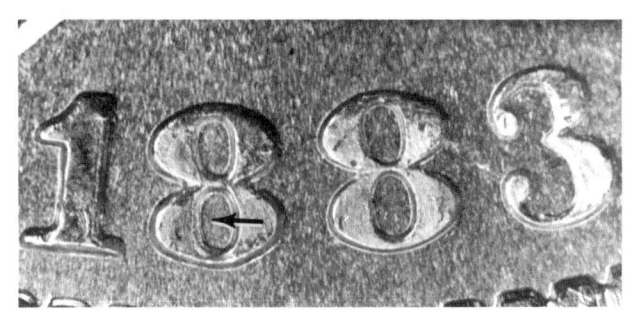

38 O Doubled 18-3

1883-S

This year is the beginning of the scarcer uncirculated S mints. Apparently this and some of the later S mints were extensively melted during 1918-1920 thus making uncirculated specimens scarce while circulated specimens are common. As with the earlier S mints, the 1883-S generally has a full strike and good luster. A few die varieties exist but none are significant. Proof-likes on both sides are difficult to locate and most tend to be brilliant although some cameos are known. Beware of one sided proof-likes or coins with good luster being passed off as fully proof-like.

1   III² 1 • C³ a (Normal Die)   (187)   I-1   R-2
  Obverse III² 1 – Normal die of III² type. Some specimens show a die chip between loops of second 8 on right.
  Reverse C³ a – Normal die of C³ type with medium IV S mint mark centered and upright.

2   III² 1 • C³ b (S Tilted Right)   I-2   R-3
  Reverse C³ b – Normal die with IV S mint mark tilted slightly to right.

3   III² 2 • C³ a. (Doubled 18)   (186)   I-2   R-3
  Obverse III² 2 – Doubled 18 in date. 1 is doubled at top left of upper crossbar as two notches at bottom of upper crossbar and top left of vertical shaft. First 8 doubled on left inside of upper loop.

4   III² 3 • C³ a (Doubled 1-3)   (186)   I-2   R-3
  Obverse III² 3 – Doubled 1-3 in date. 1 doubled slightly below upper crossbar and strongly at upper right of vertical shaft with a triangular projection sticking out on the field. 3 doubled at bottom left inside of lower loop. First 8 has horizontal polishing marks at right inside of upper loop.

5   III² 4 • C³ a (Doubled 18)   (186)   I-2   R-3
  Obverse III² 4 – Doubled 18 in date. 1 doubled on surface at bottom of upper crossbar and left and right sides of vertical shaft. First 8 doubled on surface at left inside of upper loop with die chips on left and right side of upper loop.

6   III² 5 • C³ a (Doubled 18-3)   (187)   I-2   R-3
  Obverse III² 5 – Doubled 18-3 in date. 1 doubled on surface at top and right side of shaft. First 8 doubled at top inside of upper loop and left inside of lower loop. 3 doubled slightly at bottom inside of lower loop.

7   III² 6 • C³ a (Tripled First 8, Doubled 1-3)   (187)   I-2   R-3
  Obverse III² 6 – First 8 tripled on left inside of both loops and doubled at top inside of lower loop. 1 doubled on top right of vertical shaft and at top right of lower crossbar. 3 doubled slightly at bottom inside of lower loop.

1883-S

8   III²7 • C³a (Doubled 8-3)   (187)   I-2   R-3

Obverse III²7 – Doubled 8-3 in date. First 8 doubled on left inside of both loops. 3 doubled at bottom inside of lower loop and ball of lower loop. 1 has die chip on vertical shaft.

Reverse C³a – Some specimens show die chip in wreath opposite N of UNITED.

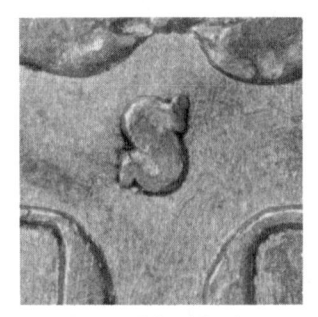

2 R S Tilted Right

3 O Doubled 18

5 O Doubled 18

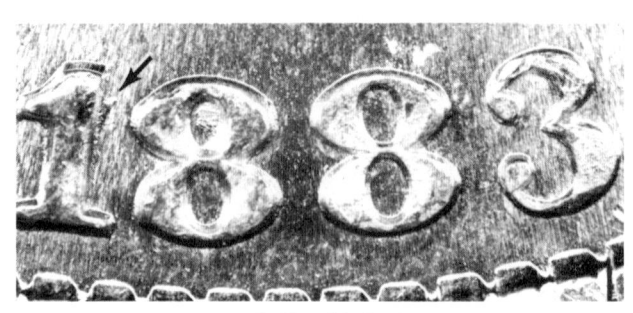

4 O Doubled 1-3

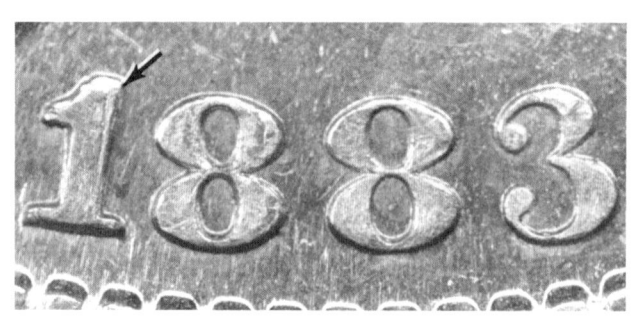

6 O Doubled 18-3

7 O Doubled 18-3

8 O Doubled 8-3

8 R Die Chip in Wreath

258

1884-P

This date is usually fairly well struck although slightly weak strikes occasionally surface. Luster can be good to slightly below average in keeping with its high mintage. A few varieties exist. The one significant variety shows a small dot next to the designer's initial, M, on obverse and reverse in two different sizes. These dots were to identify working dies when the date was made smaller in 1884. The dot variety brings a moderate premium.

Proof-likes are quite scarce and are usually brilliant. Some very deep mirror cameos exist however. Proofs have fairly good contrast and are available with few hairlines.

1   III² 1 • C³ a (Normal Die) (187, 189) I-1 R-1
    Obverse III² 1 – Normal die of III² type
    Reverse C³ a – Normal die of C³ type.

2   III² 2 • C³ a (Dash Under 8) (188) I-2 R-3
    Obverse III² 2 – Dash under second 8 in date. Date set further right than normal.
    Reverse C³ a – Some specimens show a partial E under the eagle's tail feathers.

3   III² 3 • C³ b (Large Dot) (188) I-4 R-4
    Obverse III² 3 – Large dot after the engraver's initial M. Date set further right than normal.
    Reverse C³ b – Small dot after engraver's initial M.

4   III² 4 • C³ b (Small Dot) (189) I-4 R-4
    Obverse III² 4 – Small dot after engraver's initial M. Date set further right than normal.
    Reverse C³ b – Dot is in slightly different position than in VAM 3.

5   III² 5 • C³ a (Doubled 18) (188) I-3 R-3
    Obverse III² 5 – Doubled 18 in date. 1 is doubled slightly at top left. First 8 is doubled at top left and right outside. Ear doubled on left inside and right outside.

6   III² 6 • C³ a (Low Dash Under 8) (189) I-2 R-4
    Obverse III² 6 – Thin dash set very low below second 8. Date set further right than normal.

7   III² 7 • C³ a (Slanted Dash Under 8) I-2 R-4
    Obverse III² 7 – Slanted dash set left of center below second 8. Date set very much further right than normal.

8   III² 8 • C³ a (Far Date) (189) I-2 R-3
    Obverse III² 8 – Date set further right than normal.

9   III² 9 • C³ a (Very Far Date) I-2 R-3
    Obverse III² 9 – Date set much further right than normal. Second 8 has a big dot on surface of right side of upper loop.

10 III² 10 • C³ a (Doubled 188 and Stars) (187) I-2 R-3
    Obverse III² 10 – Doubled 188 in date with digits doubled at very top outside. All left stars, first two on right and E – P doubled at 12 o'clock. Lips and chin of Liberty head slightly doubled. Date set much further right than normal.

11 III² 12 • C³ a (Low Dash Under 8) (188) I-2 R-3
    Obverse III² 12 – Long dash set well below second 8 and centered. Date set further right than normal.

12 III² 1 • C³ c (Doubled Motto) (187) I-2 R-3
    Reverse C³ c – Doubled tops of IN GOD WE TRUST letters. Tops of lower serifs of TATES OF AM also doubled at top right of right wreath.

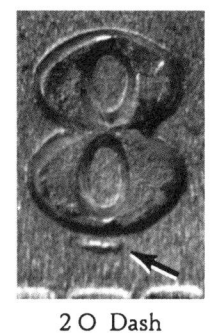

2 O Dash

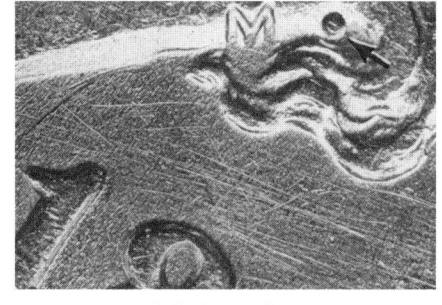

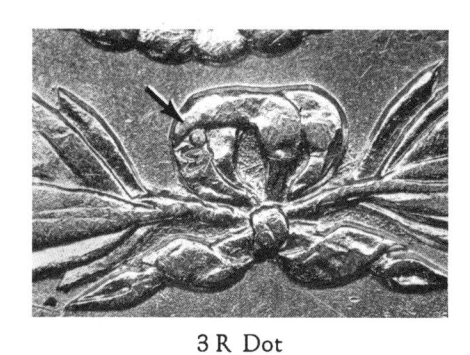

3 O Large Dot

3 R Dot

1884-P

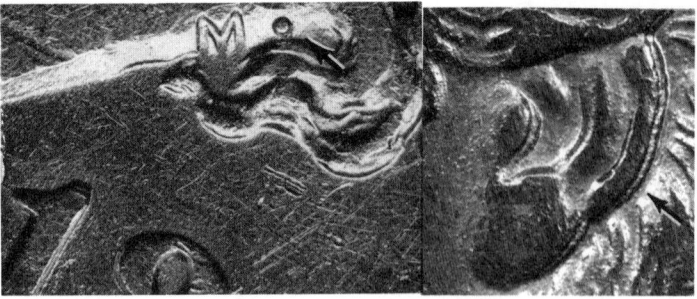

4 O Small Dot

5 O Doubled Ear

5 O Doubled 18

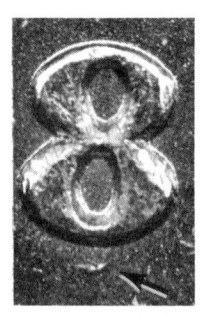

6 O Low Dash Under 8

7 O Slanted Dash Under 8

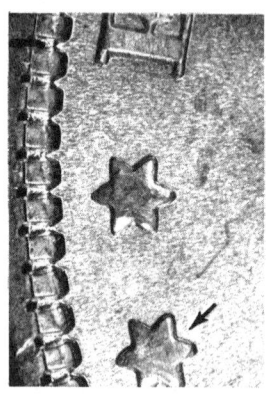

10 O Doubled Stars and E

9 O Very Far Date, Dot 8

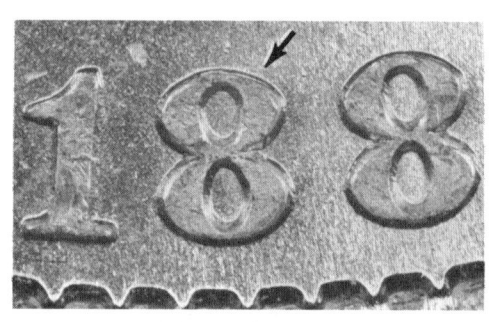

10 O Doubled 188

11 O Far Date, Partial Dash Under 8

12 R Doubled Motto

260

1884-CC

Eighty-five percent of the mintage was in the GSA sales resulting in general availability of BU specimens. Generally the strike is full and luster good, but some slightly weakly struck specimens exist. A few minor die varieties exist but none command a premium.

Like the 1882-CC and 1883-CC a fair proportion are proof-like with good contrast and some are very deep mirror cameos.

1 III²1 • C³a (Normal Die) I-1 R-3
Obverse III²1 – Normal die of III² type.
Reverse C³a – Normal die of C³ type with large V CC mint mark.

2 III²2 • C³b (Doubled 18 Top) (177) I-2 R-3
Obverse III²2 – Doubled 18 in date. The 1 is a wide curved vertical spike above the top point and is doubled slightly above the bottom crossbar. The left outside of the loops of the first 8 are doubled. Some specimens show a thick die break through the bottom of the date digits.
Reverse C³b – First C of mint mark is doubled on the left inside.

3 III²3 • C³a (Doubled 18 Left) (177) I-2 R-3
Obverse III²3 – Doubled 18 in date. 1 doubled below top crossbar and to the left of bottom crossbar. The inside right of the top and bottom loops of the first 8 have die chips and right outside of upper loop is slightly doubled. Some specimens show a die break through the bottom of the date digits.

4 III²4 • C³a (Spiked Date) (177) I-2 R-4
Obverse III²4 – There is a vertical spike of metal from the top of the 1 in the date. Some specimens show a horizontal spike to the left of the lower loop of the first 8. A thin die break line shows below the designer's initial M. The third star on the left has a hook at the bottom point due to a die chip.
Reverse C³a – Some specimens show a horizontal die gouge through E in STATES.

5 III²5 • C³c (CC/CC) (177) I-2 R-4
Obverse III²5 – Doubled 18 in date. 1 is doubled to left showing as horizontal lines from upper and lower crossbars. The first 8 is doubled at the top left side of both loops and the upper right inside of lower loop. Date set further right than normal.
Reverse C³c – Mint mark doubled with first C doubled at top inside and bottom left outside and second C doubled at right inside.

6 III²6 • C³b (Doubled First 8) I-2 R-4
Obverse III²6 – First 8 is doubled on the right side of the lower loop and at top right outside of upper loop.

7 III²7 • C³a (Doubled 18 Bottom) (177) I-3 R-4
Obverse III²7 – Doubled 18 in date. 1 is doubled at bottom and a spike of metal extends to left from left side of the bottom crossbar. The first 8 is doubled strongly all along the bottom and on the bottom left of the upper loop.

8 III²1 • C³d (CC Tilted Left) I-2 R-3
Reverse C³d – Large V CC mint mark tilted left.

9 III²8 • C³a (Dash Under 8) I-2 R-4
Obverse III²8 – Dash under second 8 in date.

10 III²9 • C³d (Far Date, CC Tilted Left) (178) I-2 R-3
Obverse III²9 – Date set further right than normal.

11 III²10 • C³a (Doubled 18) (177) I-2 R-3
Obverse III²10 – Doubled 18 in date. 1 doubled at top as a as a notch on left side of lower crossbar. First 8 doubled on top left outside of lower loop with die chips on right inside of both loops.

2 O Doubled 18 Top    2 R Doubled C    3 O Doubled 18 Left

1884-CC / 1884-O

12   III² 8 • C³ d (Dash Under 8, CC Tilted Left)   (178)   I-2   R-3

4 O Spiked Date

5 O Doubled Date

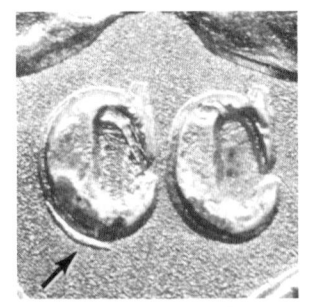

5 R Doubled CC

6 O Doubled First 8

7 O Doubled 18 Bottom

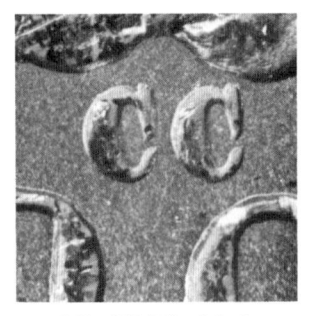

8 R CC Tilted Left

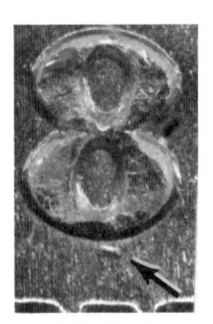

9 O Dash Under 8

11 O Doubled 18

1884-O

This O mint has a wide variation in strike from flat to full. Full strike specimens are fairly easy to locate, however. Luster is average but can range from very good to dull. Numerous die varieties exist but only VAM 6 with doubling on the left outside and inside of the O mint mark is very significant and commands a modest premium.

Proof-likes are somewhat available like the 1883-O and 1885-O and have fairly good contrast. Very deep mirror cameos can occasionally be found.

1   III² 1 • C³ a (Oval O)   (181)   I-1   R-2
    Obverse III² 1 – Normal die of III² type.
    Reverse C³ a – Normal die of C³ type with a tall oval medium II O mint mark centered and upright.

2   III² 1 • C³ b (Round O)   (181)   I-1   R-2
    Reverse C³ b – Normal die of C³ type with circular III O mint mark with narrow slit.

262

1884-O

3	**III²2 • C³r (Doubled 1, O/O Line on Left)**	(181)		I-2	R-3

Obverse III²2 – The top of the 1 is doubled to left. Date set further right than normal.
Reverse C³r – II O mint mark doubled on left inside as a line and at top inside as a diagonal line.

4	**III²3 • C³a (Doubled 18)**	(181)		I-2	R-3

Obverse III²3 – Doubled 18 in date. 1 shows a curved vertical spike at top left and a short horizontal spike to left of bottom crossbar. First 8 is slightly doubled on left outside of lower loop and has a large bulge to right outside lower loop. Entire head is covered with dots of metal from a pitted die.

5	**III²4 • C³a (Far Date)**	(181)		I-2	R-3

Obverse III²4 – Date set further right than normal.
Reverse C³a – II O mint mark. Opening filled almost flush on some specimens.

6	**III²4 • C³c (O/O Left and Down)**	(181)		I-3	R-4

Reverse C³c – II O mint mark repunched with original showing on left side of opening, a spike below the O and line outside the lower left.

7	**III²4 • C³d (O/O Tilted Left)**	(181)		I-2	R-3

Reverse C³d – II O mint mark repunched with original showing diagonally within opening. Right wreath doubled on outside and TATES OF AMERICA doubled at bottom.

8	**III²5 • C³e (O/O Center)**	(181)		I-2	R-3

Obverse III²5 – Date set much further right than normal.
Reverse C³e – II O mint mark repunched with original showing upright within all but extreme left of opening.

9	**III²1 • C³f (O/O Right)**	(181)		I-2	R-3

Reverse C³f – II O mint mark repunched with original showing upright within half of opening.

10	**III²4 • C³g (O/O Left)**	(181)		I-2	R-3

Reverse C³g – II O mint mark repunched with original showing as a wavy vertical line within left side of opening. So-called O/CC variety.

11	**III²3 • C³f (Doubled 18, O/O Right)**	(181)		I-2	R-3

Obverse III²3 – 1 doubled as dot to left of the bottom of the crossbar and at very top. First 8 doubled at left outside of top loop and right outside of bottom loop.

12	**III²1 • C³h (O/O Line)**	(181)		I-2	R-3

Reverse C³h – II O mint mark repunched with original showing as a thin vertical line on left side of opening.

13	**III²1 • C³i (O/O Centered High)**	(181)		I-2	R-3

Reverse C³i – II O mint mark repunched with original showing as curved line centered at top of opening.

14	**III²4 • C³j (O/O Right High)**	(181)		I-2	R-3

Reverse C³j – II O mint mark repunched with original showing as a curved line at top of opening shifted slightly to the right.

15	**III²5 • C³k (O/O Far Right)**	(181)		I-2	R-3

Reverse C³k – II O mint mark repunched with original showing as a thin vertical line curved slightly at top and on inside and upper right side of opening.

16	**III²5 • C³a (Very Far Date)**	(181)		I-2	R-3

17	**III²1 • C³l (O/O Far Left)**	(181)		I-2	R-3

Reverse C³l – II O mint mark repunched with original showing as a vertical bar in middle and right side of opening and very thin space on left side.

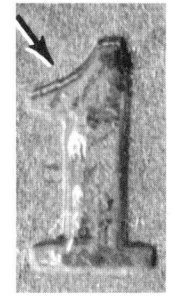

3 O Doubled 1 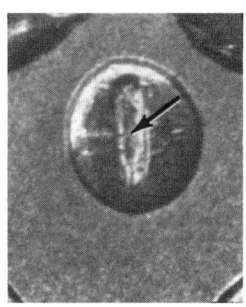   3 R O/O Line    4 O Doubled 18 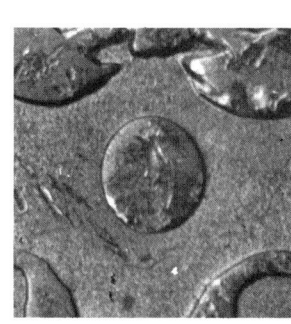   5 R Filled O

1884-O

18   III²6 • C³b (Dash Under 8)   (181)   I-2   R-3
Obverse III²6 – Dash under second 8 in date with date set further right than normal.

19   III²7 • C³a (Doubled 18)   (181)   I-2   R-3
Obverse III²7 – Doubled 18 in date. Top of 1 doubled faintly as a thin line starting at. middle of upper curve to almost the right side. First 8 doubled faintly at top left outside. Date set much further right than normal.

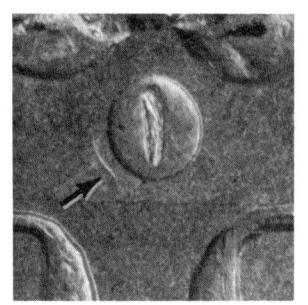

6 R O/O Left and Down

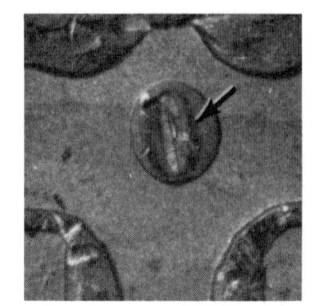

7 R O/O Tilted Left

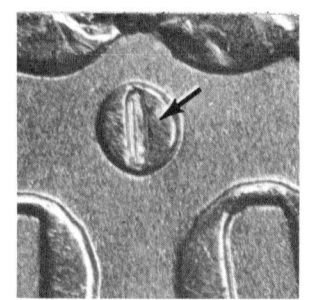

8 R O/O Center

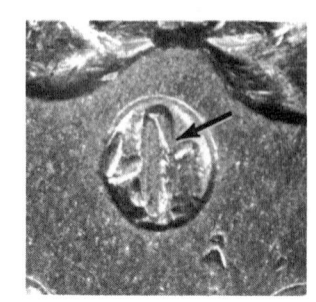

9 R O/O Right

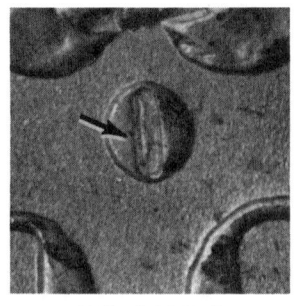

10 R O/O Left

11 O Doubled 18

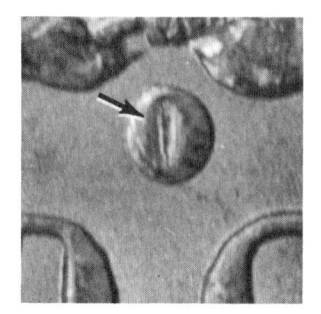

12 R O/O Line

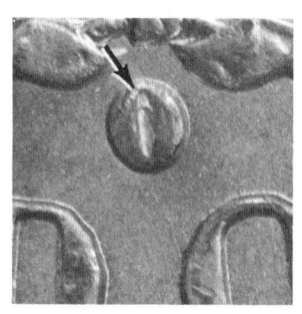

13 R O/O Centered High

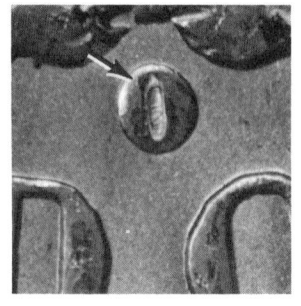

14 R O/O Right High

15 R O/O Far Right

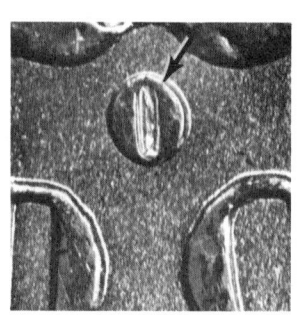

17 R O/O Far Left

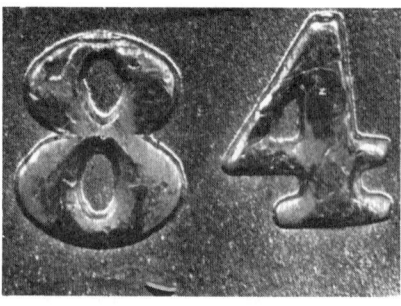

18 O Dash Under 8

19 O Doubled 1

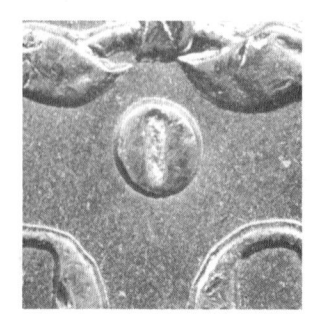

20 R High O

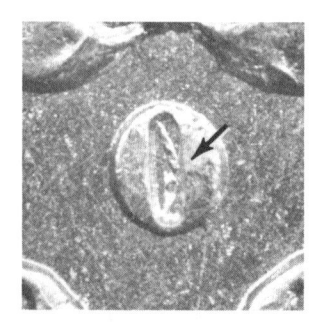

21 R O/O Curved

1884-O

20	III²2 • C³m (Doubled 1, High O)	(181)		I-2	R-3

Reverse C³m – II O mint mark set high and upright.

| 21 | III²5 • C³n (Very Far Date, O/O Curved) | (181) | | I-2 | R-3 |

Reverse C³n – II O mint mark repunched with original showing as a raised curved line in middle of opening.

| 22 | III²8 • C³o (Slanted Low Date, O/O Tilted) | (181) | | I-2 | R-3 |

Obverse III²8 – Date set much further right than normal and slanted with 1 very close to rim.
Reverse C³o – II O mint mark repunched with original showing as a vertical bar in right half of opening. Mint mark centered and tilted to left.

| 23 | III²9 • C³a (Doubled 1-4) | (181) | | I-2 | R-4 |

Obverse III²9 – 1 and 4 in date doubled at very top. Date set further right than normal.

| 24 | III²10 • C³a (Doubled 18) | (181) | | I-2 | R-3 |

Obverse III²10 – 1 doubled as a slanted line to left of lower crossbar. First 8 doubled at top left and right outside of upper loop.

| 25 | III²1 • C³p (O/O Centered Low) | (181) | | I-2 | R-3 |

Reverse C³p – II O mint mark tilted left, repunched with original showing as a curved line centered at bottom of opening.

| 26 | III²11 • C³a (Doubled 18) | (181) | | I-2 | R-3 |

Obverse III²11 – Doubled 18 in date. 1 is doubled at top of upper crossbar. First 8 doubled at top outside of upper loop as a broken line and as a vertical bar at top of loop.

27	III²4 • C³b (Far Date)	(181)		I-2	R-3
28	III²6 • C³a (Dash Under 8)	(181)		I-2	R-4
29	III²4 • C³i (O/O Centered High)	(181)		I-2	R-3
30	III²11 • C³q (Tripled 1, O/O Bar)	(181)		I-2	R-3

Obverse III²11 – 1 tripled at very top. Date set further right than normal.
Reverse C³q – II O mint mark doubled with original showing as a raised band on left inside of opening.

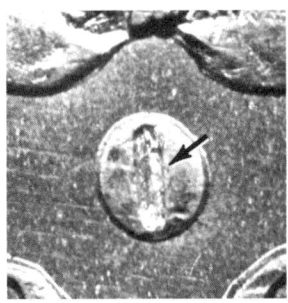

22 O Slanted Date

22 R O/O Tilted

23 O Doubled 4

24 O Doubled First 8

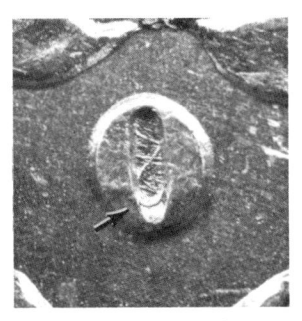

25 R O/O Centered Low

26 O Doubled 18

265

1884-O / 1884-S

31	III²5 • C³s (Very Far Date, O/O Line On Right)	(181)	I-2	R-3

Reverse C³s – II O mint mark doubled on right inside as a thin shaft curved slightly left at very top.

32	III²5 • C³t (Very Far Date, O Tilted Left)	(181)	I-2	R-3
33	III²7 • C³t (Doubled 18, O Tilted Left)	(181)	I-2	R-3
34	III²12 • C³a (Doubled 18)	(181)	I-2	R-3

Obverse III² 12 – Doubled 18 in date. 1 doubled at top left and right of upper crossbar. First 8 doubled at top right outside of upper loop and left inside of lower loop as a short hook.

35	III²13 • C³u (Doubled Eyelid, Reverse)	(181)	I-2	R-3

Obverse III² 13 – Eyelid doubled at lower edge and eye in front. Date set further right than normal.
Reverse C³u – TATES AMER and top of right wreath doubled towards rim.

36	III²3 • C³a (Doubled 18)	(181)	I-2	R-3

30 O Tripled 1

30 R O/O Bar

31 R O/O Line on Right

32 R O Tilted Left

34 O Doubled 18

1884-S

The 1884-S is a rarity in uncirculated condition although it is fairly common in the circulated grades. There are quite a few sliders around and some bring substantial premiums because of the large uncirculated price increases. A few higher grade MS65 specimens are known. Generally the strike is fairly good but some have slight weakness on the reverse. Luster is typically good. A few die varieties exist but none are significant.

Proof-like uncirculated 1884-S are extremely rare with only a couple known. Some with semi-proof-like on one side and proof-like on the other are known. Some fully proof-like AU specimens exist.

1	III²1 • C³a (Normal Die)		I-1	R-2

Obverse III² 1 – Normal die of III² type.
Reverse C³a – Normal die of C³ type with medium IV S mint mark centered and upright.

2	III²1 • C³b (S Tilted Right)	(187)	I-2	R-3

Reverse C³b – Normal die of C³ die with IV S mint mark shifted left and tilted right.

1884-S / 1885-P

| 3 | III²2 • C³c (S/S Left) | | I-3 | R-3 |

Obverse III²2 – Date set further right than normal.
Reverse C³c – IV S mint mark is repunched with original showing as a short spike of metal at top of upper loop opening and a vertical spike of metal at left of the lower loop opening.

| 4 | III²2 • C³a (Far Date) | (187) | I-2 | R-3 |
| 4A | III²2 • C³a (Far Date) | | I-2 | R-3 |

Reverse C³a – Die chip at very top of right wreath.

| 5 | III²3 • C³a (Very Far Date) | (187) | I-2 | R-3 |

Obverse III²3 – Date set much further right than normal.

| 6 | III²2 • C³d (Far Date, S Set Left) | (187) | I-2 | R-3 |

Reverse C³d – IV S mint mark upright and set to left with loops filled.

| 7 | III²3 • C³e (S/S High, Very Far Date) | (187) | I-2 | R-3 |

Reverse C³e – IV S mint mark doubled with diagonal line in upper loop and curved line in lower loop.

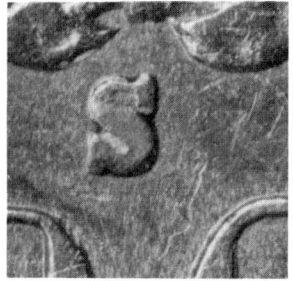

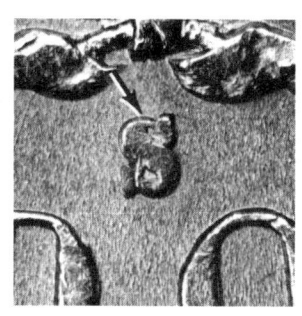

2 R S Tilted Right

3 R S/S Left

4A R Die Chip in Wreath

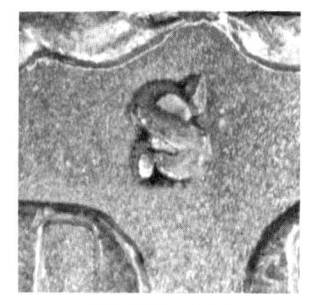

6 R S Set Left

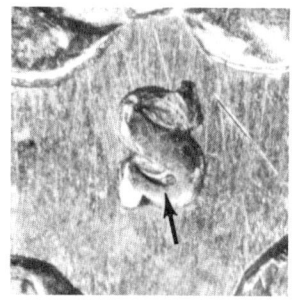

7 R S/S

1885-P

This is the first so-called common P mint from 1885 to 1887. The strike is generally good as is the luster. A number of minor die varieties exist. VAM 6 is significant with strongly doubled date digits at top and brings a modest premium.

Proof-likes are fairly available and a high percentage of them are very deep mirror frosted or cameos. Proofs usually have average contrast and are plagued by hairlines.

| 1 | III²1 • C³a (Normal Die) | | I-1 | R-1 |

Obverse III²1 – Normal die of III² type.
Reverse C³a – Normal die of C³ type.

| 1A | III²1 • C³a (Pitted Reverse) | | I-2 | R-3 |

Reverse C³a – Die is pitted below left wreath around ONE D.

| 1B | III²1 • C³a (Pitted Reverse) | (189) | I-2 | R-3 |

Reverse C³a – Die is pitted around DOL of DOLLAR.

1885-P

2	III² 2 • C³ a (Doubled 5)	(189)		I-2	R-3

Obverse III² 2 – 5 in date doubled all across the top. Some specimens show a faint dash well below the second 8. Date set on right side of normal position tolerance.

3	III² 3 • C³ a (High Dash Under 8)	(188)	I-2	R-3

Obverse III² 3 – 5 in date doubled all across the top. Short dash under and touching second 8.

4	III² 4 • C³ a (Low Dash Under 8)	(188)	I-2	R-3

Obverse III² 4 – Dash well below second 8 shifted right.

5	III² 5 • C³ a (Doubled 85)	(188)	I-2	R-3

Obverse III² 5 – 85 in date doubled at bottom. Date set further right than normal.

6	III² 6 • C³ a (Doubled Date)	(189)	I-4	R-4

Obverse III² 6 – All numerals in date doubled at very top with large shift.

7	III² 7 • C³ a (Low Dash Under 8)	(189)	I-2	R-3

Obverse III2 7 – Dash well below second 8 shifted left.

8	III² 8 • C³ a (Thick Dash Under 8)		I-2	R-4

Obverse III² 8 – Thick dash under and touching second 8.

9	III² 9 • C³ a (Far Date)	(188)	I-2	R-3

Obverse III² 9 – Date set further right than normal.

10	III² 10 • C³ a (Doubled 5)		I-2	R-3

Obverse III² 10 – 5 in date doubled all across the top. Date set in middle of normal position tolerance. There is a small vertical mark on tenth denticle from point of Liberty Head neck.

11	III² 11 • C³ a (Tripled 5)		I-2	R-3

Obverse III² 11 – 5 in date is tripled all across the top. Date set on left side of normal position tolerance.

12	III² 12 • C³ a (Doubled 5)	(188)	I-2	R-3

Obverse III² 12 – 5 in date is doubled at top outside as a thin line set well above top of 5.

13	III² 13 • C³ a (Doubled 5)	(189)	I-2	R-3

Obverse III² 13 – 5 in date is doubled all across the top outside with doubling slightly stronger on right side.

14	III² 14 • C³ a (Doubled 5)	(188)	I-2	R-3

Obverse III² 14 – 5 in date is doubled at top outside as a thin broken line set very far above top of 5.

15	III² 15 • C³ a (Doubled 18-5)	(188)	I-3	R-4

Obverse III² 15 – 18-5 doubled in date. 1 doubled at very top as a thin curved line. First 8 doubled strongly at bottom inside of lower loop as a thick bar. 5 doubled slightly at very top as a thin line.

16	III² 6 • C³ a (Doubled First 8)	(189)	I-2	R-3

Obverse III² 16 – First 8 in date doubled at top inside of upper loop.

17	III² 17 • C³ a (Slanted Date)	(188)	I-2	R-3

Obverse III² 17 – Date slanted with 1 closer to rim.

18	III² 18 • C³ a (High Dash Under 8)	(188)	I-2	R-3

Obverse III² 18 – Short dash just under and against bottom outside of second 8 lower loop.

1A R Pitted Reverse

1B R Pitted Reverse

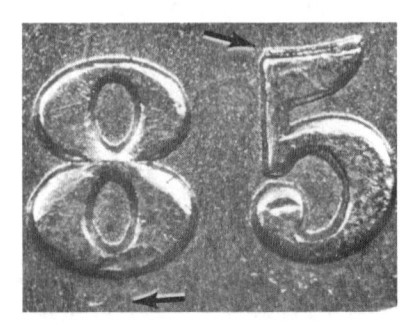

2 O Dash Under 8, Doubled 5

1885-P

3 O Dash Doubled 5

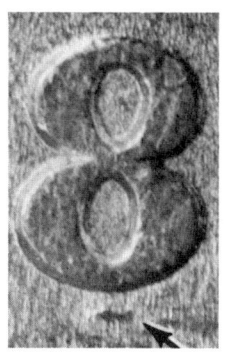

4 O Low Dash

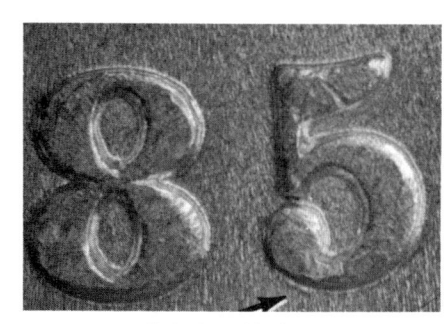

5 O Doubled 85

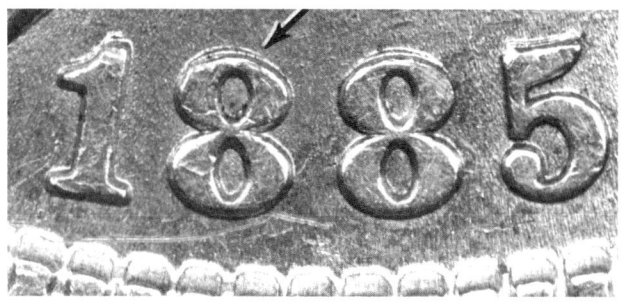

6 O Doubled Date

7 O Low Dash Under 8

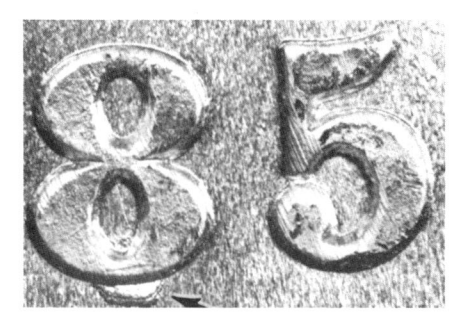

8 O Thick Dash Under 8

10 O Doubled 5

11 O Tripled 5

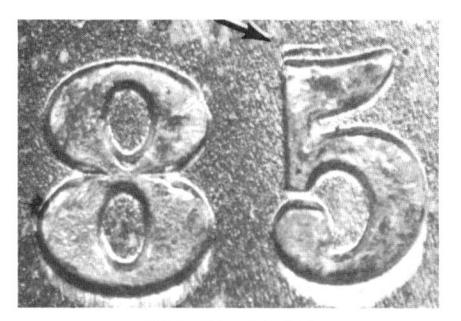

12 O Doubled 5

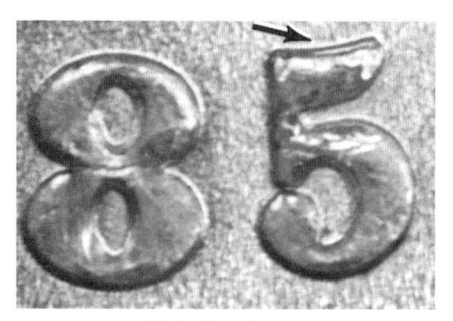

13 O Doubled 5

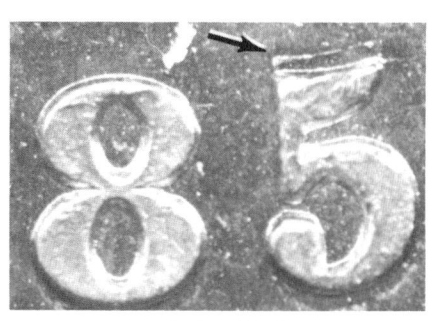

14 O Doubled 5

1885-P / 1885-CC

| 19 | III²19 • C³a (Doubled First 8) | (189) | I-2 | R-3 |

Obverse III²19 – First 8 doubled inside lower loop as an arc at top and line at left.

| 20 | III²20 • C³a (Low Dash Set Right) | (188) | I-2 | R-3 |

Obverse III²20 – Faint short dash set well below second 8 and to the right over 10th denticle.

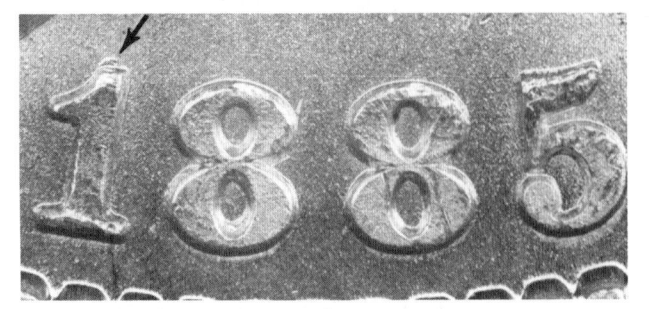

15 O Doubled 18-5

17 O Slanted Date

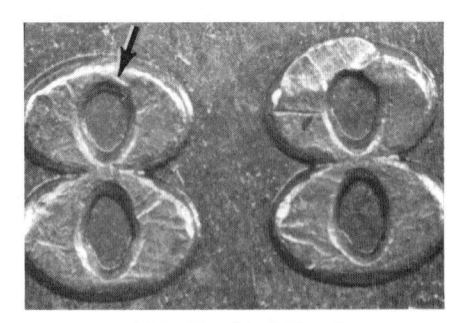

16 O Doubled First 8

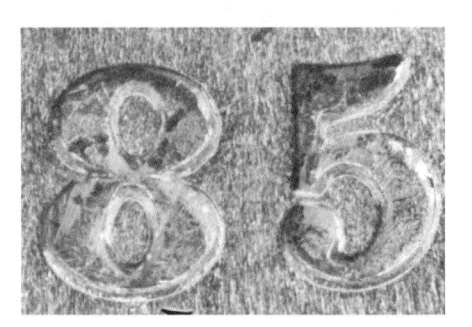

18 O High Dash Under 8

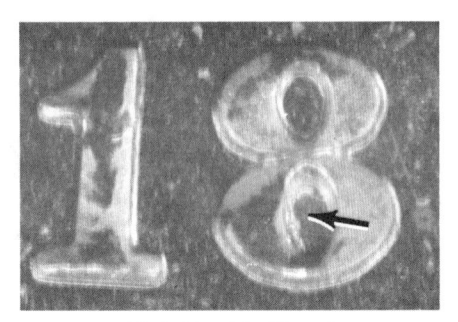

19 O Doubled First 8

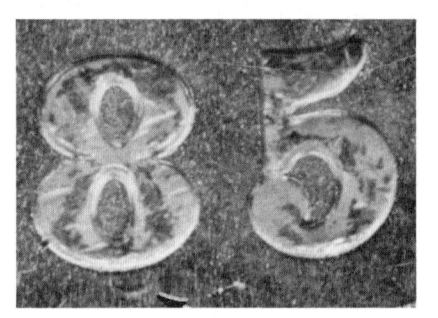

20 O Low Dash Set Right

1885-CC

Over half the mintage was in the GSA sales. So even though it has the third lowest mintage (excluding non-available 1895-P business strike) it is readily available in BU. It is quite rare in circulated grades however. The strike is generally full although there are some slightly weakly struck with planchet striations in the hair above the ear. Only a couple of minor die varieties are known. One has a very thick dash below the second 8, but it does not command any premium. As with the 1881-CC a considerable percentage are proof-likes and quite a few of these are deep mirror cameos.

| 1 | III²1 • C³a (Normal Die) | | I-1 | R-3 |

Obverse III²1 – Normal die of III² type.
Reverse C³a – Normal die of C³ type with large V CC mint mark.

270

1885-CC / 1885-O

2 III²2 • C³a (Dash Under 8)   I-2   R-3
   Obverse III²2 – 5 in date doubled slightly at bottom for about half the curve. Dash under second 8.

3 III²1 • C³b (CC Tilted Left)   I-2   R-4
   Reverse C³b – Large V CC mint mark tilted left with right C almost touching wreath.

4 III²3 • C³a (Thick Dash Under 8)   I-2   R-4
   Obverse III²3 – Thick dash under and touching second 8 with die chips at bottom inside of lower loop. Bottom of dash is faintly doubled. One of the largest dashes known.
   Reverse C³a – Die chips within both mint mark C's.

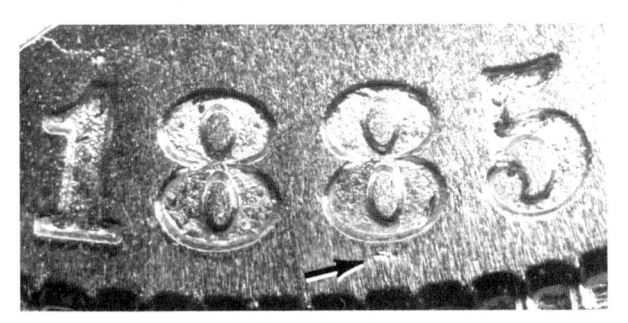

2 O Dash Doubled 5 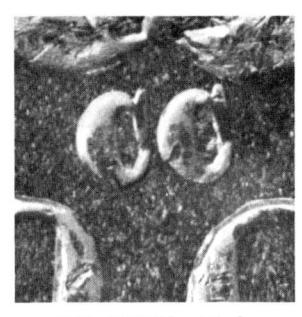   3 R CC Tilted Left    4 O Thick Dash Under 8

1885-O

This is another common date O mint that has wide variations in strike although fully struck specimens are available. The luster can also vary considerably. A number of minor die varieties exist and the most interesting is VAM 9 which has a moderate shift in a doubled date. Proof-likes are somewhat available but many have a shallow depth. Deep mirror cameos are fairly scarce.

1   III²1 • C³a (Normal Die)   (181)   I-1   R-2
    Obverse III²1 – Normal die of III² type.
    Reverse C³a – Normal die of C³ type with circular medium III O mint mark centered and upright.

1A III²1 • C³a (Rusted Wing)   (181)   I-2   R-4
    Reverse C³a – Top of eagle's left wing and neck covered with raised spots due to rusted die.

2   III²2 • C³a (Doubled 5)   (181)   I-2   R-3
    Obverse III²2 – 5 in date doubled at top.

3   III²3 • C³a (Doubled 18)   (181)   I-2   R-3
    Obverse III²3 – 1 in date doubled below the top bar. First 8 doubled slightly at top right inside of upper loop.

4   III²4 • C³a (Doubled 18)   (181)   I-2   R-3
    Obverse III²4 – 18 in date doubled. Bottom crossbar of 1 doubled at top and appears as a short spike on the left and a slight bulge to the right of the stem. Inside lower loop of first 8 doubled at bottom and left.

5   III²5 • C³a (Slanted Date)   (181)   I-2   R-3
    Obverse III²5 – Date set high and slanted to make 5 higher than 1. Date set further left than normal.

6   III²6 • C³a (Low Date)   (181)   I-2   R-3
    Obverse III²6 – Date set low with slight slant down to right so that 5 is very close to rim.

7   III²7 • C³a (Dash Under 8)   (181)   I-2   R-4
    Obverse III²7 – Small short dash well below second 8 with vertical mark on denticle underneath 8.

8   III²1 • C³b (O Shifted Right)   (181)   I-2   R-3
    Reverse C³b – Normal die with III O mint mark shifted to the right.

9   III²8 • C³a (Doubled 885)   (181)   I-3   R-3
    Obverse III²8 – Large vertical shift in 885 in date. Both 8's show a curved spike slanting down to left from middle right inside of lower loop. 5 has a faint horizontal curved line at lower inside of loop, and a vertical bar at left outside of loop opening.

1885-O

10 III²9 • C³a (Dash Under 8, Bar Ear) (181) I-2 R-3

Obverse III²9 – Small short dash just under second 8. Vertical die gouge in front of ear.

1A R Rusted Wing and Neck

2 O Doubled 5

3 O Doubled 18

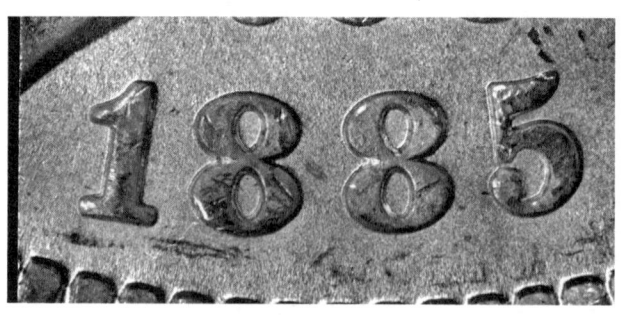

5 O Slanted Date

6 O Low Date

4 O Doubled 18

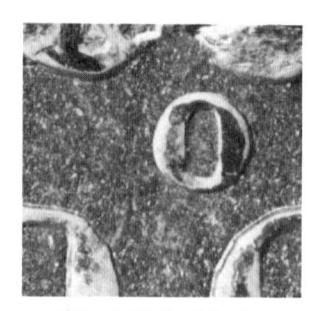

8 R O Shifted Right

10 O Dash Under 8

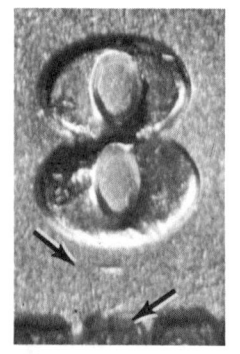

7 O Dash Under 8

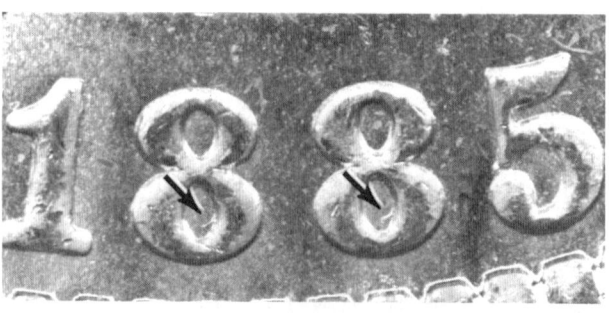

9 O Doubled 885

10 O Bar Ear

272

1885-O / 1885-S

| 11 | III²10 • C³c (Far Date, High O) | (181) | I-2 | R-3 |

Obverse III²10 – Date set farther right than normal.
Reverse C³c – Normal die with III O mint mark set high.

| 12 | III²1 • C³d (O/O Left) | (181) | I-2 | R-4 |

Reverse C³d – III O mint mark repunched with original showing as a vertical bar on left side of loop opening.

| 13 | III²10 • C³a (Far Date) | (181) | I-2 | R-3 |
| 14 | III²7 • C³b (Dash Under 8, O Shifted right) | (181) | I-2 | R-3 |

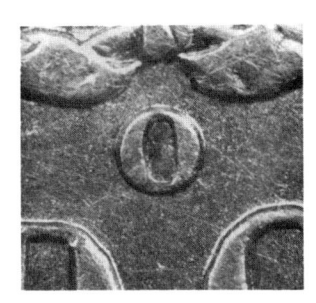

11 R High O

12 R O/O Left

1885-S

The typical strike has a touch of weakness and some are fairly flat on the reverse. Bold strikes can be found however. The luster tends to be good. Several minor die varieties exist but VAM 6 has significant doubling of the S mint mark on the left side.

Proof-likes are quite scarce and a few deep mirror cameos exist. Quite a number of one sided proof-likes are available and the reflection depth should be checked on both sides when buying proof-likes.

| 1 | III²1 • C³a (Normal Die) | (185, 187) | I-1 | R-2 |

Obverse III²1 – Normal die of III² type.
Reverse C³a – Normal die of C³ type with a medium IV S mint mark centered and upright.

| 1A | III²1 • C³a (Die Flake in Wreath) | (187) | I-2 | R-3 |

Reverse C³a – Large die flake in wreath leaves opposite NI of UNITED. Same as VAM 7.

| 2 | III²2 • C³a (Doubled 5) | | I-2 | R-3 |

Obverse III²2 – 5 in date doubled at top appearing as two short dashes on the left and right side.

| 3 | III²3 • C³a (Doubled 8) | | I-2 | R-3 |

Obverse III²3 – Second 8 in date doubled faintly at the top and lower loop doubled on the top left.

| 4 | III²4 • C³a (Doubled 18) | (185) | I-2 | R-4 |

Obverse III²4 – Doubled 18 in date. 1 doubled slightly below upper crossbar and on left and right side of lower crossbar. First 8 doubled strongly on left outside of upper loop and lower left outside of lower loop.

| 5 | III²5 • C³a (Far Date) | (187) | I-2 | R-3 |

Obverse III²5 – Date set further right than normal.

| 6 | III²1 • C³b (S/S) | | I-3 | R-4 |

Reverse C³b – IV S mint mark strongly doubled with original showing as vertical spike to left of lower serif, a thin diagonal line to left of upper loop, a curved line on right inside of lower loop, and a thin diagonal line on right inside of upper loop.

| 7 | III²6 • C³a (Doubled Date) | (187) | I-2 | R-3 |

Obverse III²6 – Entire date doubled slightly at very top of digits.
Reverse C³a – Some specimens show a large die flake in wreath leaves opposite NI of UNITED.

1885-S / 1886-P

2 O Doubled 5

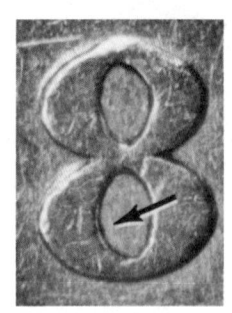

3 O Doubled 8

4 O Doubled 18

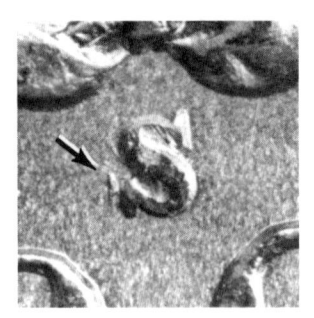

6 R S/S

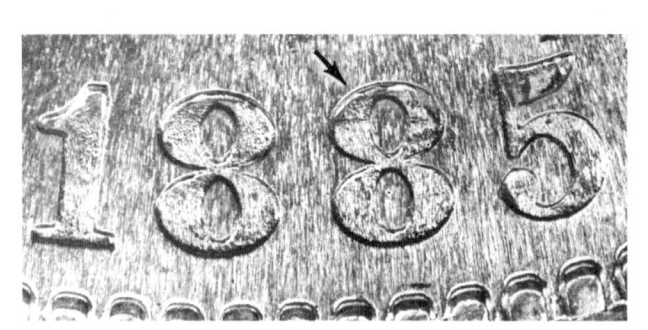

7 O Doubled Date

7 R Die Break in Leaves

1886-P

The usual strike on this issue is full although there are some specimens with a touch of weakness. Luster is generally good but a sizeable proportion are dull due to worn dies. These coins exhibit surface roughness and radial flow lines in the fields due to die erosion by the planchet metal moving against the die surfaces when struck. This dull luster from worn dies is common for the 1886-1891-P mint coins. A fair number of minor die varieties exist with doubled dates but none are very significant.

Proof-likes are somewhat available but most have only moderate mirror depth and light frosted contrast. Some very deep mirror cameos do exist however. Proofs have adequate but not striking contrast and many coins are plagued with hairlines.

| 1 | III²1 • C³a (Closed 6) | (189) | I-1 | R-1 |

Obverse III²1 – Normal die of III² type with closed 6. Upper knob touches lower loop. Some specimens show die chip between loops of first 8 on left side and some show die chips in upper loop of 6.
Reverse C³a – Normal die of C³ type.

| 1A | III²1 • C³a (Line in 6) | | I-2 | R-4 |

Obverse III²1 – Thick horizontal line curving down at right end in lower part of upper loop of 6.

| 1B | III²1 • C³a (Die Gouge in M) | | I-2 | R-4 |

Obverse III²1 – Die gouge in designer's initial M at base of neck showing as a horizontal curved line.

| 2 | III²2 • C³a (Open 6) | (189) | I-1 | R-2 |

Obverse III²2 – Normal die of C³ type with open 6. Upper knob distinctly separate from lower loop.

| 3 | III²3 • C³a (Doubled 1 Weak) | | I-2 | R-3 |

Obverse III²3 – 1 in date doubled below the crossbar. Closed 6 variety. Some specimens show a thin dash well below second 8.

| 4 | III²4 • C³a (Doubled 18 Strong) | (190) | I-3 | R-3 |

Obverse III²4 – 18 in date doubled. 1 doubled below top crossbar. First 8 doubled at top inside of upper loop and slightly at right outside of lower loop. Doubling more pronounced than III²3 obverse. Closed 6 variety.

1886-P

1 O   Die Chips in 6

1A O   Line in 6

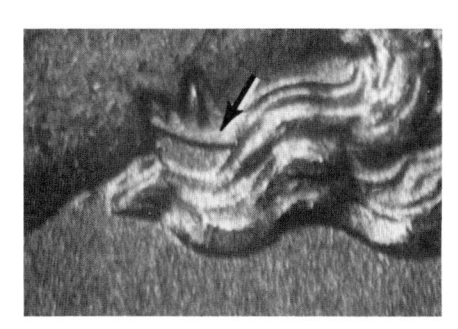

1B O   Die Gouge in M

3 O   Doubled 1 Weak

4 O   Doubled 1 Strong

5 O   Doubled 18

| 5 | III² 5 • C³ a (Doubled 18) | (190) | I-3 | R-3 |

Obverse III² 5 – 18 in date doubled. Doubling of the 1 appears as a line under the top crossbar and projecting out from the stem. Loops of the 8 are doubled inside at top. Closed 6 variety.

| 6 | III² 6 • C³ a (High 6) | (188) | I-2 | R-3 |

Obverse III² 6 – 6 in date punched higher than normal.

| 7 | III² 7 • C³ a (High Date) | (190) | I-2 | R-3 |

Obverse III² 7 – Entire date set higher than normal. Open and closed 6 varieties.

| 8 | III² 8 • C³ a (Far Date, High 6) | | I-2 | R-3 |

Obverse III² 8 – Date set further right than normal with closed 6 set slightly high.

| 9 | III² 9 • C³ a (Doubled 1-6) | (189) | I-3 | R-4 |

Obverse III² 9 – 1-6 doubled strongly. 1 is doubled strongly at very bottom. Closed 6 is doubled strongly at top. Date set further right than normal.

| 10 | III² 10 • C³ a (Doubled 18) | | I-2 | R-3 |

Obverse III² 10 – 18 in date doubled. 1 doubled well below as a thin line. First 8 doubled at bottom and on right side of lower loop as a thin line. High 6 in date.

| 11 | III² 11 • C³ a (Doubled 188) | | I-3 | R-4 |

Obverse III² 11 – 188 in date doubled. 1 is doubled strongly below crossbar. First 8 doubled at upper right inside of upper loop and at bottom right outside. Second 8 doubled on lower left inside of bottom loop.

| 12 | III² 12 • C³ a (Doubled Date) | (189) | I-2 | R-4 |

Obverse III² 12 – Entire date doubled. 1 has short horizontal spike just below upper crossbar. First 8 is slightly doubled on left bottom outside of upper loop showing as a thin curved line. Second 8 is doubled slightly at top inside of upper loop. Both loops of the 6 are doubled inside at the top left with the top one being strong and ending bluntly on the right side.

| 13 | III² 13 • C³ a (Near Date) | (189) | I-2 | R-4 |

Obverse III² 13 – Date set further left than normal with closed 6. Second with horizontal die chip at top inside of upper loop of second 8.

| 14 | III² 14 • C³ a (Dash Under 8) | (189) | I-2 | R-4 |

Obverse III² 14 – Faint dash under second 8 in date.

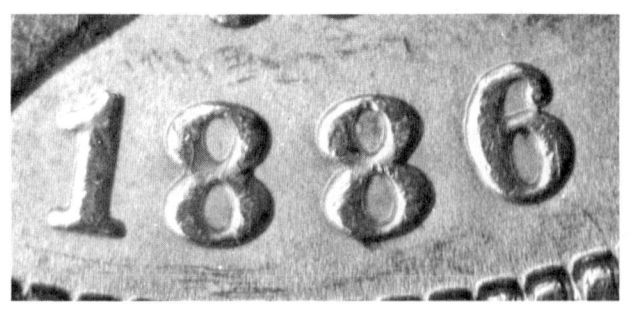

1886-P

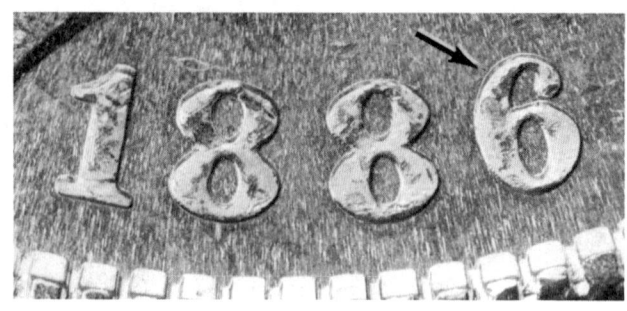

6 O High 6

7 O High Date

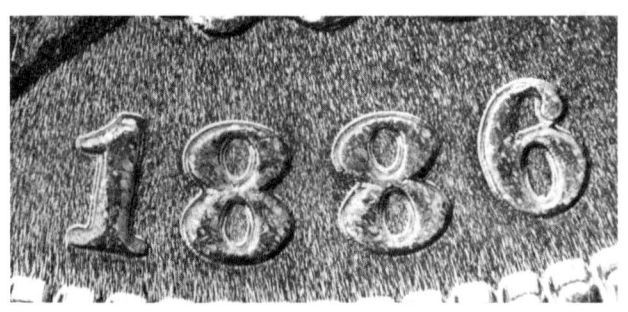

8 O High 6

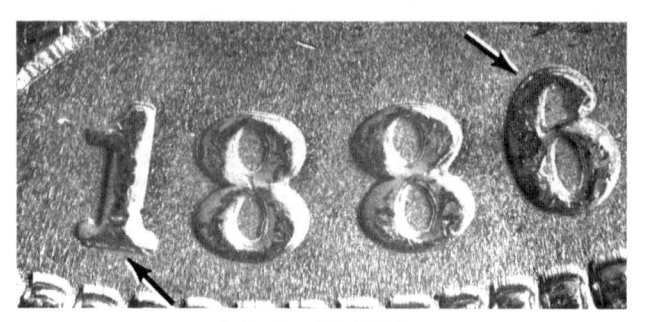

9 O Doubled 1-6

10 O Doubled 18

13 O Near Date, Bar 8

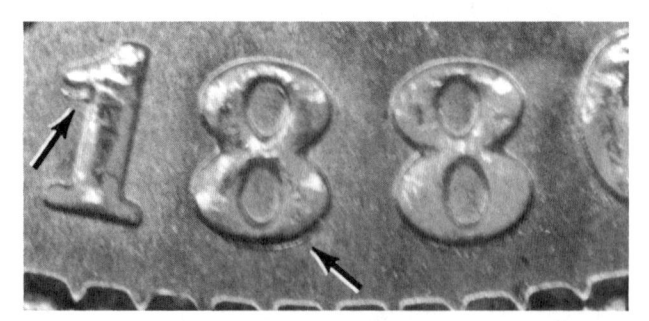

11 O Doubled 188

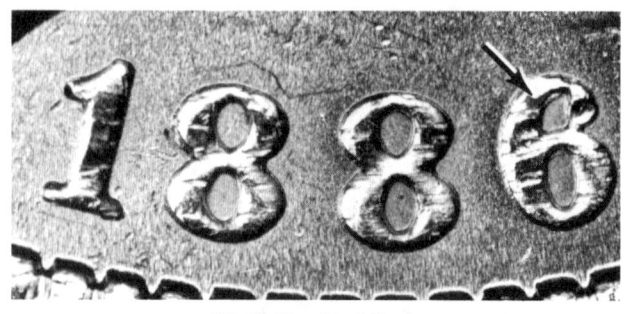

12 O Doubled Date

276

1886-P / 1886-O

15   III² 15 • C³ a (Doubled 18-6, Dash 8)   (179)   I-2   Proof
Obverse III² 15 – Doubled 18-6 in date. 1 doubled below upper crossbar as a thin line and slightly below bottom crossbar. First 8 doubled at top inside of upper loop and bottom outside of lower loop. 6 doubled slightly at bottom outside of lower loop. Second 8 has a thick dash adjacent to bottom of lower loop.

16   III² 15 • C³ a (Doubled 1)   (189)   I-2   R-3
Obverse III² 15 – 1 doubled at bottom of base.

17   III² 1 • C³ b (Doubled Arrows)   (190)   I-2   R-3
Reverse C³ b – Lower three arrow feathers doubled at bottom, wreath bow doubled at top inside, and olive branch doubled at far left.

18   III² 16 • C³ a (Doubled 6)   (189)   I-2   R-3
Obverse III² 16 – 6 doubled at very top outside as a curved line.

14 O Dash Under 8

16 O Doubled 1

18 O Doubled 6

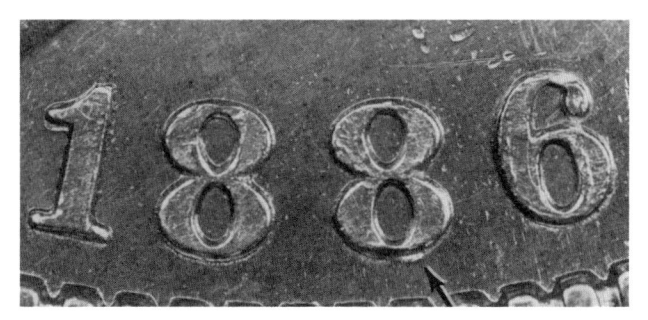

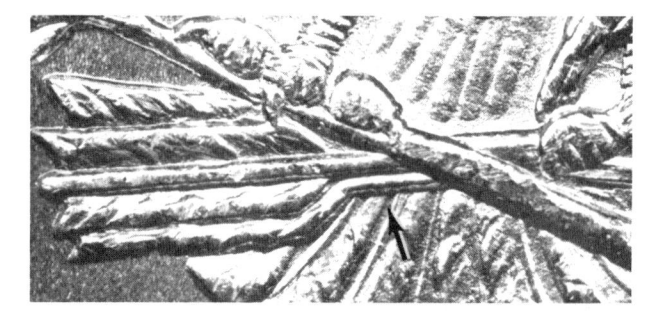

Proof 15 O Doubled 18-6, Dash Under 8

17 R Doubled Arrows

1886-O

This issue is typically fairly well struck but some weak strikes are around and sliders are plentiful. Luster is usually average but can vary considerably. A number of die varieties exist. The only significant one is VAM 1A with an "E" under the eagle's tail feathers due to clashed dies. It is fairly scarce in circulated grades and quite rare in uncirculated condition. Higher grade circulated and uncirculated VAM 1A specimens command some price premiums. Fully prooflike specimens in general are extremely rare and vary considerably in strike and contrast. However, what many consider to be the most spectacular Morgan dollar in terms of depth of mirror, cameo contrast, lack of abrasions and rarity is the 1886-O formerly in the Wayne Miller collection.

1   III² 1 • C3 a (Normal Die)   (181)   I-1   R-2
Obverse III² 1 – Normal die of III² type with closed 6.
Reverse C² a – Normal die of C³ type with circular medium III O mint mark centered and upright.

1A   III² 1 • C³ a (E on Reverse)   (181)   I-4   R-4
Reverse C³ a – Clashed die with full E under eagle's tail feathers on left side.

2   III² 2 • C³ a (High 6)   (181)   I-2   R-3
Obverse III² 2 – Normal die with high 6 in date.

1886-O

3	III²6 • C³a (Open 6)	(181)	I-2	R-3

Obverse III²6 – Normal die of III² type with open 6.

4	III²1 • C³b (O Tilted Left)	(181)	I-2	R-3

Reverse C³b – Normal die with III O mint mark tilted to the left.

5	III²3 • C³a (Doubled 18)	(181)	I-2	R-3

Obverse III²3 – 18 in date doubled. Short stem of original 1 projects below bottom crossbar of new 1. First 8 is doubled to the lower left just below bottom loop. Closed 6 variety.

6	III²4 • C³c (Doubled 1)	(181)	I-2	R-3

Obverse III²4 – 1 in date doubled at top. Closed 6 variety.
Reverse C³c – Normal die with III O mint mark tilted to the right.

7	III²1 • C³d (O/O Down)	(181)	I-3	R-4

Reverse C³d – Mint mark repunched with original showing as two arcs at bottom.

8	III²2 • C³e (O Set High)	(181)	I-2	R-3

Reverse C³e – III O mint mark set high.

9	III²5 • C³a (Doubled 6)	(181)	I-2	R-4

Obverse III²5 – 6 in date doubled at top outside as a thin curved line.

10	III²6 • C³e (Doubled 18-6)	(181)	I-3	R-4

Obverse III²6 – Doubled 18-6 in date. 1 doubled as a thin line on right side below lower crossbar. First 8 doubled below lower loop. 6 doubled at top outside of upper loop.

11	III²7 • C³e (Near Date, O Set High)	(181)	I-2	R-3

Obverse III²7 – Date set further left than normal and set slightly high.

12	III²8 • C³a (Doubled 6)	(181)	I-2	R-3

Obverse III²8 – 6 doubled at top inside of upper loop. Date set further left than normal.

13	III²9 • C³a (Doubled 1)	(181)	I-2	R-3

Obverse III²9 – 1 doubled slightly below upper crossbar.

14	III²10 • C³a (Far Date)	(181)	I-2	R-3

Obverse III²10 – Date set further right than normal.

15	III²1 • C³f (O Set Right)	(181)	I-2	R-3

Reverse C³f – Medium III O mint mark upright and set slightly to right.

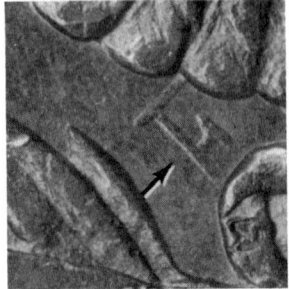

1A R E

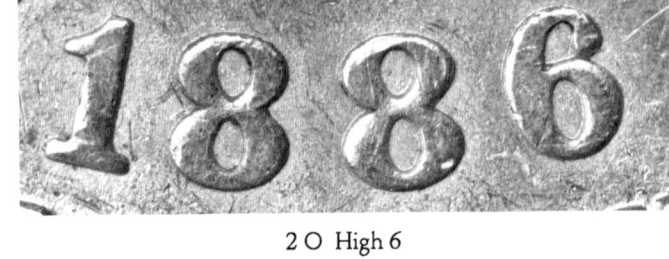

2 O High 6

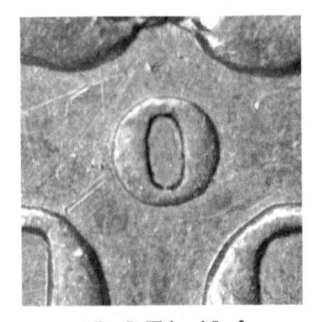

4 R O Tilted Left

5 O Doubled 18

6 O Doubled 1

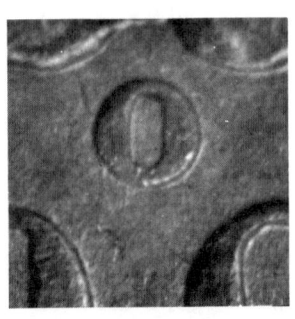

6 R O Tilted Right

278

1886-O / 1886-S

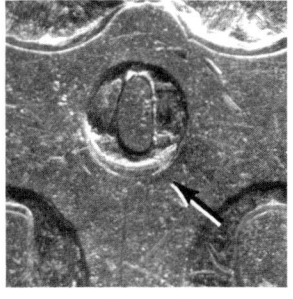

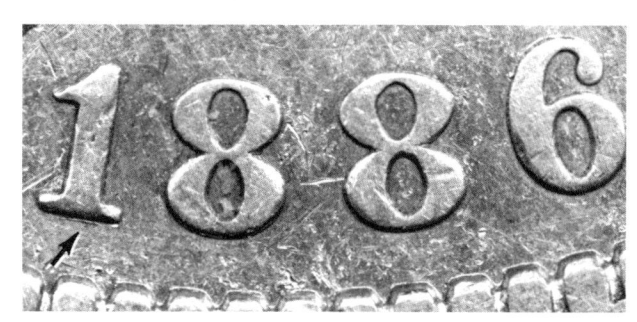

7 R O/O

8 R O Set High

10 O Doubled 18-6

9 O Doubled 6 *Photo Not Available*

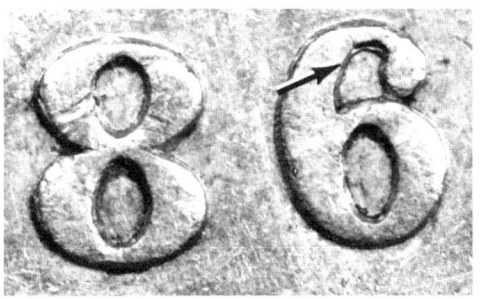

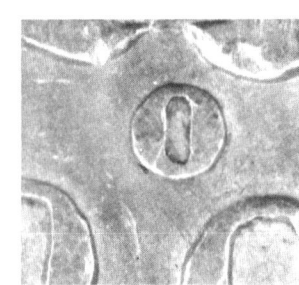

12 O Doubled 6

13 O Doubled 1

15 R O Set Right

1886-S

The 1886-S usually comes fully struck with good luster. Because of the fairly low mintage, many semi proof-like specimens exist. Full proof-likes are somewhat available with a few of these being deep mirror cameos. Only a couple minor die varieties exist.

| 1 | III²1 • C³a (Normal Die) | | I-1 | R-3 |

Obverse III²1 – Normal die of III² type with closed 6.
Reverse C³a – Normal die of C³ type with a medium IV S mint mark centered and upright.
Note: Some specimens show die chips in bottom of top loop of 6 and in I, G and E of IN GOD WE and O of OF on the reverse.

| 1A | III²1 • C³a (Lines in 6) | (187) | I-2 | R-3 |

Obverse III²1 – 6 in date has horizontal polishing lines in lower loop.

| 2 | III²1 • C³b (S/S) | (187) | I-2 | R-4 |

Obverse III²1 – Some specimens have die chips in 6 all across opening of top loop and in the upper part of the lower loop.
Reverse C³b – Doubled IV S mint mark tilted left with thin vertical line to right of top serif and metal at top left side of bottom serif.

| 3 | III²2 • C³c (Doubled 18-6, S Tilted Left) | (187) | I-2 | R-3 |

Obverse III²2 – 18-6 in date doubled. 1 and first 8 are doubled at very bottom next to field. 6 is doubled slightly at very top outside of upper loop next to field. 6 also shows die chips in lower part of upper loop.
Reverse C³c – IV S mint mark centered with slight tilt to left and doubled on outside of upper and lower serifs.

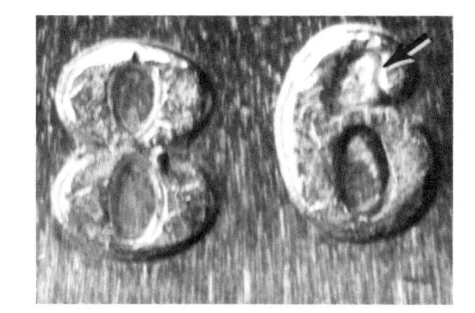

1 O Die Chips in 6

1A O Lines in 6

2 O Die Chips in 6

1886-S / 1887-P

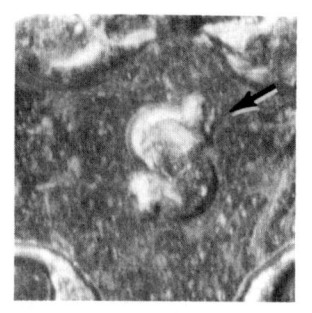

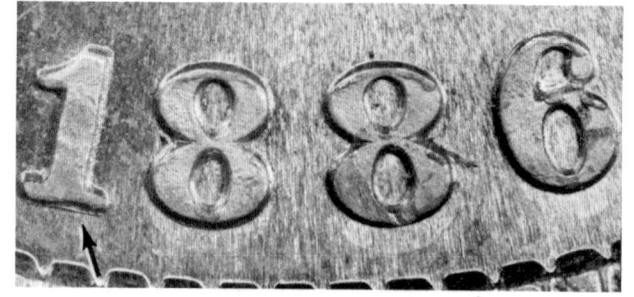

2 R S/S

3 O Doubled 18-6

3 R S Tilted Left

1887-P

On the average this issue is not quite as fully struck nor is the luster as good as the 1886-P. However, because of the high mintage fully struck lustrous specimens can be found. The 1887-P frequently has indentations in the jaw and neck area due to grease and debris having collected in the deepest recesses of the die cavity. If large and distracting, these indentations can lower the value of an otherwise high grade BU coin. A fair number of minor die varieties exist with most of these being doubled date digits. How ever, VAM 2 7/6 overdate has remains of the 6 showing as curved lines on either side of the bottom of the 7 and brings a substantial premium in all grades.

Proof-like are somewhat available as for the 1886-P, but the contrast tends to be less. A few deep mirror cameos are available. Proofs have adequate but not striking contrast.

1   III²1 • C³a (Normal Die)   (190)   I-1   R-1
Obverse III²1 – Normal die of III² type. Some specimens show die chips between loops of 8's in various combinations such as on both sides of first 8, on left side of second 8, on left side of first 8 and on both sides of second 8, on right side of both 8's, on left side of first 8 and on right side of second 8, on right side of first 8 and both sides of second 8.
Reverse C³a – Normal die of C³ type.

1A   III²1 • C³a (D With Tail)   I-2   R-6
Reverse C³a – Die break on D in DOLLAR to form tail.

2   III²2 • C³a (7/6)   (189)   I-5   R-4
Obverse III²2 – 7 repunched over 6 in date. The bottom loop of the 6 shows as a long curved line starting up slightly from the lower right bottom of the 7 and extending upwards one-third the digit height. On the left side of the stem, a short spike slants upwards at a point one-third the way up on the stem height. A short vertical spike shows at the very top of the 7 crossbar in the middle. A short spike also slants upwards from the middle right side of the crossbar.

3   III²3 • C³a (Doubled 1-7)   (189)   I-3   R-4
Obverse III²3 – 1-7 in date doubled. 1 is doubled below upper crossbar. 7 is doubled strongly at very top. Entire date is set further left than normal. Some specimens show a die chip between loops of first 8 on left and second 8 on right.

4   III²4 • C³a (Doubled 18-7)   (190)   I-2   R-4
Obverse III²4 – Doubled 18 and 7 in date. The 1 and 8 are doubled slightly at bottom. First 8 also doubled at top inside of lower loop. 7 is doubled all across the top and there is a vertical spike above the top left serif. Date set further left than normal.

5   III²5 • C³a (Doubled Date)   (190)   I-4   R-4
Obverse III²5 – Entire date doubled. The 1 is doubled slightly on top left side of lower crossbar. First 8 is doubled at top inside of upper loop and die chip is between the loops on the left side. Second 8 is doubled strongly at top inside of upper loop and die chips between the loops on both sides. The 7 is doubled below the crossbar and on the right side. Date set further left than normal.

6   III²6 • C³a (Spiked Tail Feather, Low Date)   (189)   I-2   R-3
Obverse III²6 – Entire date set lower and further right than normal with die chip between loops of first 8 on left side.
Reverse C³a – Third tail feather has a die gouge under it showing as a thin horizontal line.

7   III²7 • C³a (Doubled 18 Weak)   (190)   I-2   R-3
Obverse III²7 – 18 in date doubled slightly at bottom. Date set further left than normal.

8*   III²8• C³a (Far Slanted Date)   (190)   I-2   R-3
Obverse III²8 – Date set further right than normal and slanted with 1 closest to rim.
* The former VAM 8 is the same as VAM 11.

1887-P

| 9 | III²9 • C³a (Doubled 18 Strong) | (189) | I-3 | R-4 |

Obverse III²9 – 18 in date doubled strongly all across bottom.

| 10 | III²10 • C³a (Doubled 18) | (189) | I-2 | R-3 |

Obverse III²10 – 1 doubled weakly at bottom. First 8 in date doubled at bottom with die chip to left of loops on some specimens.

1A R D with Tail

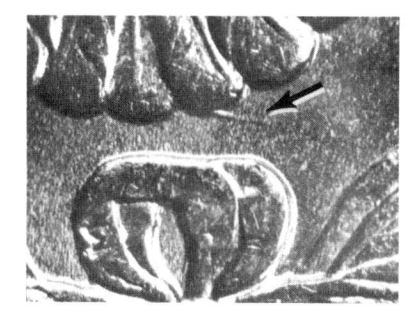

2 O 7/6

6 R Die Gouge

3 O Doubled 1-7

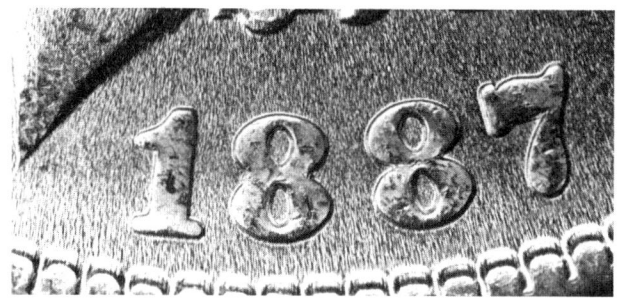

6 O Low and Far Date

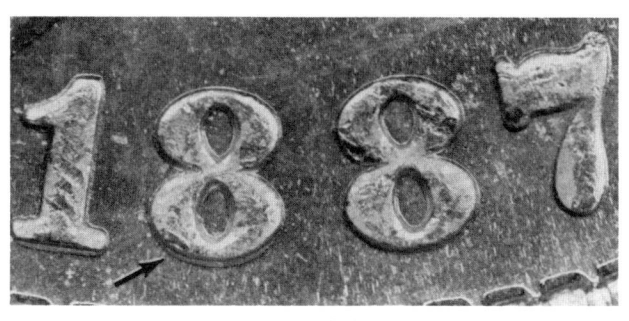

4 O Doubled 18-7

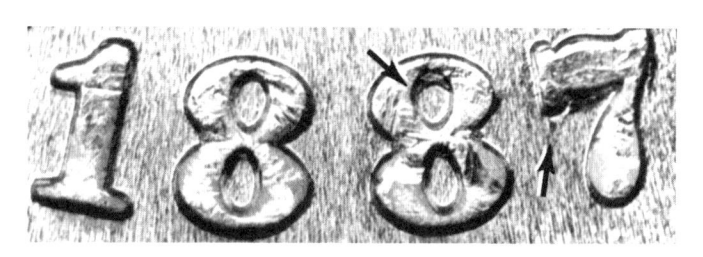

5 O Doubled Date

7 O Doubled 18 Weak

9 O Doubled 18 Strong

10 O Doubled 18

1887-P

11   III² 11 • C³ a (Doubled 18-7)   (189)   I-3   R-4
Obverse III² 11 – Doubled 18 and 7 in date. The 1 and first 8 are doubled all across the bottom. 7 doubled at top. The first 8 has a die chip between the loops on the left in some specimens.

12   III² 12 • C³ a (Doubled LIBERTY)   (190)   I-2   R-3
Obverse III² 12 – Stars on each side of the date are doubled at bottom. Letters PLURIB are doubled at top. LIBERTY is doubled to the right.

13   III² 13 • C³ a (Doubled Stars)   (190)   I-3   R-4
Obverse III² 13 – First four stars on right and first two stars on left doubled at bottom with first two on right showing strong shifts.

14   III² 14 • C³ a (Near Date)   (189)   I-2   R-3
Obverse III² 14 – Date set further left than normal.

15   III² 15 • C³ a (Doubled Stars and Motto)   (189)   I-3   R-4
Obverse III² 15 – First three stars on right, all stars on left and motto letters RIB doubled towards rim. Front of eye doubled and LIBERTY slightly doubled on right side.

16   III² 1 • C³ b (Doubled Reverse Legend)   (190)   I-2   R-3
Reverse C³ b – Doubled ITED STATES OF AMERICA AR, right star towards rim and some outer edges or right wreath leaves.

8 O   Far Slanted Date

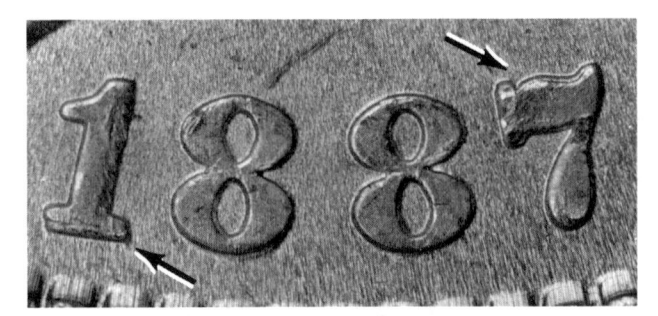

11 O   Doubled 18-7

12 O   Doubled LIBERTY

13 O   Doubled Stars

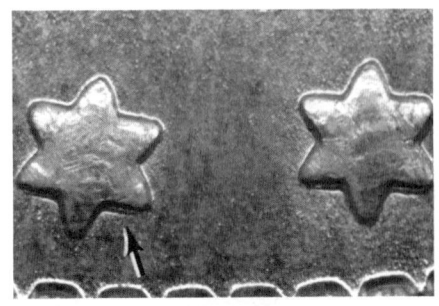

15 O   Doubled Stars

16 R   Doubled AMERICA

1887-O

Strike on this issue ranges from very weak to full with most coins having some trace of weakness. Luster is quite variable as well. Because of the high mintage lustrous fully struck specimens can be located however. Like the 1887-P there is one die variety, VAM 3, with the 7/6 overdate. The curved lines of the 6 base is not quite as prominent at the bottom of the 7 however. It is a little scarcer in most grades than the 1887-P 7/6 overdate but rare in MS64 and above. Most of the 1887-O 7/6 are slightly weakly struck and some later die states are very weak. Fully proof-like overdates are unknown in contrast to the P mint overdate where some are fully proof-like. A number of other die varieties exist but all are minor except VAM 2. This variety shows remains of the 1-7 first punch way to the left of the date which is the largest shift of date doubling in the Morgan dollar series.

Proof-likes are somewhat available but they tend to have soft strikes. A fair proportion are deep mirror cameos exist. According to Wayne Miller, the Amon Carter, Jr. collection had a branch mint 1887-O which is the only one known.

1   III^2 1 • C^3 a (Normal Die)   (181)   I-1   R-1
    Obverse III^2 1 – Normal die of III^2 type. Some specimens show die chips between loops on both sides of first 8.
    Reverse C^3 a – Normal die of C^3 type with circular medium III O mint mark centered and upright.

2   III^2 2 • C^3 a (Doubled 1, Tripled 7)   (181)   I-5   R-4
    Obverse III^2 2 – The entire date has been doubled with shift to the right. The top point of the original 1 is visible to the left of the new 1 with dot of metal at top. The 7 is tripled with doubling at the top and a dot of metal to the left of the crossbar and metal at the extreme lower left. One of the largest shifts of date doubling known.

3   III^2 3 • C^3 a (7/6)   (181)   I-5   R-4
    Obverse III^2 3 – 7 repunched over 6 in date. The bottom loop of the 6 shows as a long curved line starting from the lower right bottom of the stem of the 7 and extending upwards almost half the digit height. On the left side of the stem, a short spike curves to the left and then up at a point one third the way up on the stem height.
    Reverse C^3 a – Some specimens show depression in eagle's breast due to weak strike.

4   III^2 4 • C^3 a (Doubled 1-7)   (181)   I-2   R-3
    Obverse III^2 4 – Doubled 1-7 in date. The 1 is doubled at the top and the 7 is doubled at the bottom.

5   III^2 5 • C^3 a (Doubled Stars and Motto)   (181)   I-5   R-5
    Obverse III^2 5 – A doubled die in the radial direction causing all stars and lettering to be doubled next to rim. Denticles are filled below and to the left of date. Die chips between loops of first 8 on left and second 8 on right.

6   III^2 6 • C^3 a (Doubled 188)   (181)   I-3   R-3
    Obverse III^2 6 – 1 in date doubled all across very bottom. Both 8's doubled at bottom inside at lower loop.

7   III^2 7 • C^3 a (Doubled 18)   (181)   I-2   R-3
    Obverse III^2 7 – 1 and 8 in date doubled slightly all the way across very bottom.

8   III^2 8 • C^3 a (Doubled 87)   (181)   I-2   R-4
    Obverse III^2 8 – 87 in date doubled at bottom. Second 8 has thin curved line at bottom left side. The 7 has a short diagonal line well below bottom also on the left side. The first 8 has a die chip between the loops on the left side.

9   III^2 9 • C^3 a (Doubled 1-7 Top)   (181)   I-2   R-4
    Obverse III^2 9 – Doubled 1-7 in date. The 1 is doubled strongly at bottom of upper serif and 7 is doubled slightly all across the top.

10   III^2 10 • C^3 a (Doubled 87)   (181)   I-2   R-3
    Obverse III^2 10 – Doubled 87 in date. Second 8 doubled at lower left outside. 7 doubled slightly at very top. Die chips between loops of first 8 on left and right and on second 8 on right.

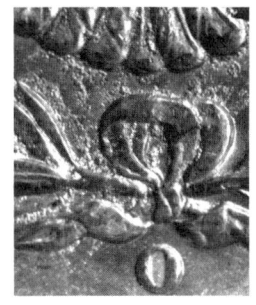

1A R   Pitted Reverse   2 O   Doubled 1, Tripled 7

1887-O

3 O 7/6

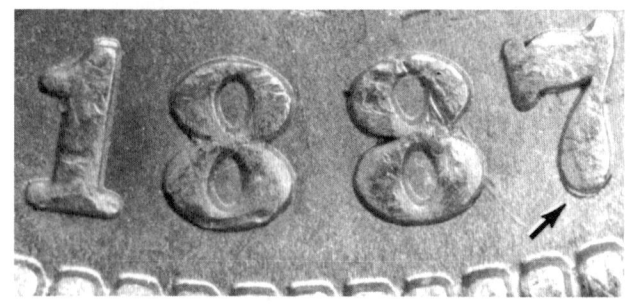

4 O Doubled 1-7

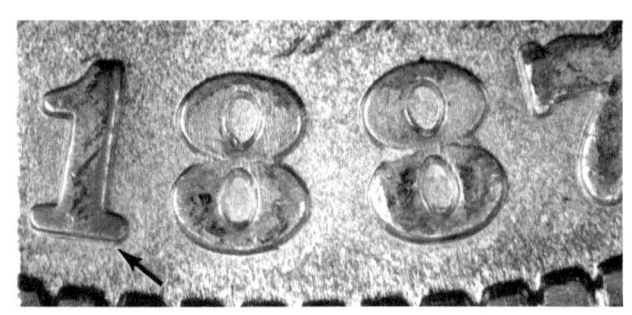

6 O Doubled 188

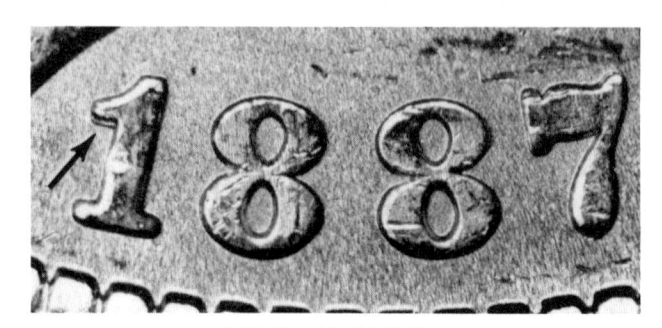

9 O Doubled 1-7 Top

5 O Doubled Stars and Motto

7 O Doubled 18

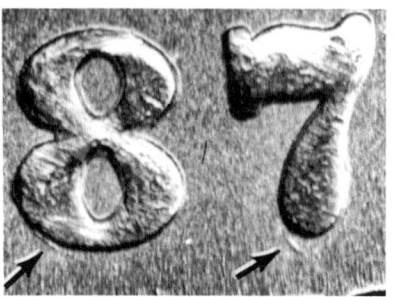

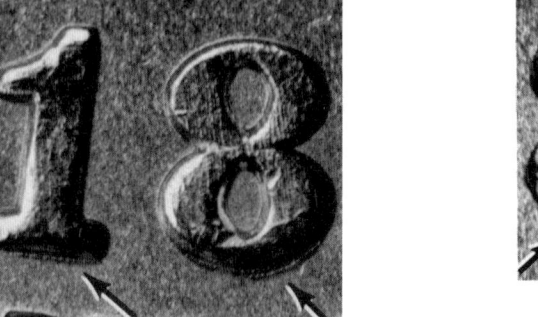

8 O Doubled 87

10 O Doubled 87

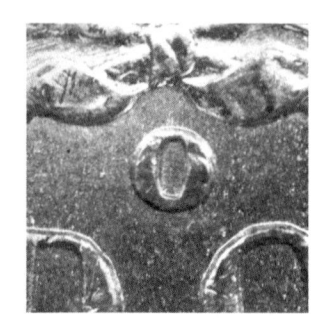

13 R O Set Right

11	III² 11 • C³ a (Near Date)	(181)	I-2	R-3
	Obverse III² 11 – Date set further left than normal.			
12	III² 12 • C³ a (Far Date)	(181)	I-2	R-3
	Obverse III² 12 – Date set further right than normal.			
13	III² 13 • C³ b (Near Date, O Shifted Right)	(181)	I-2	R-3
	Reverse C³ b – Normal die with III O mint mark shifted slightly left.			

1887-O

| 14 | III²13 • C³a (Low Date) | (181) | I-2 | R-3 |

Obverse III² 13 – Date set further left than normal with 1 close to rim.

| 15 | III²14 • C³a (Doubled 1-87) | (181) | I-2 | R-3 |

Obverse III² 14 – Doubled 1-87 in date. 1 doubled at top left of lower crossbar. 8 doubled faintly at top outside of upper loop. 7 doubled strongly all across very top. Date set much further left than normal.

| 16 | III²15 • C³a (Doubled 1) | (181) | I-2 | R-3 |

Obverse III² 15 – 1 doubled slightly below upper crossbar. Date set further right than normal.

| 17 | III²16 • C³a (Doubled 8-7) | (181) | I-2 | R-3 |

Obverse III² 16 – Doubled 8-7 in date. First 8 doubled slightly on bottom right outside of lower loop. 7 doubled about upper serif. Date set further right than normal.

18	III²8 • C³b (Far Date, O Shifted Right)	(181)	I-2	R-3
19	III²1 • C³b (O Shifted Right)	(181)	I-2	R-3
20	III²17 • C³a (Doubled 88)	(181)	I-2	R-3

Obverse III² 17 – Doubled 88 in date. First 8 doubled at bottom outside of lower loop. Second 8 doubled very slightly also at bottom outside of lower loop.

| 21 | III²1 • C³c (O Tilted Right) | (181) | I-2 | R-3 |

Reverse C³c – III O mint mark centered and tilted slightly to right.

| 22 | III²18 • C³a (Doubled Eyelid & Stars, Pitted Reverse) | (181) | I-3 | R-3 |

Obverse III² 18 – All left stars doubled towards rim and eyelid doubled underneath.
Reverse C³a – Pitted die below eagle's tail feathers.

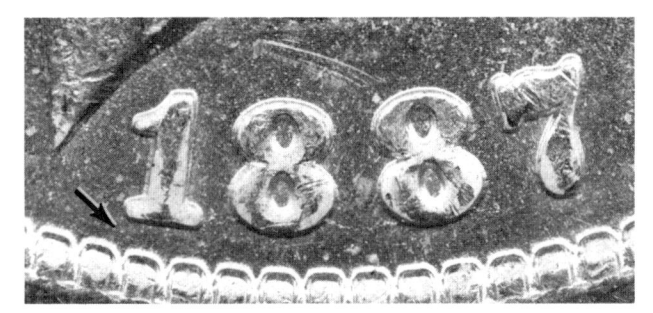

14 O Low Date

15 O Doubled 1-87

16 O Doubled 1, Far Date

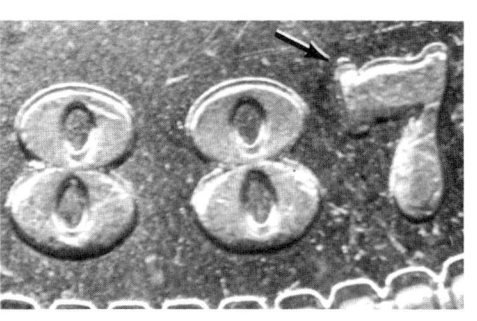

17 O Doubled 8-7

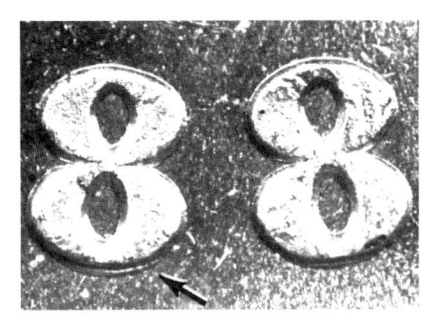

20 O Doubled 88

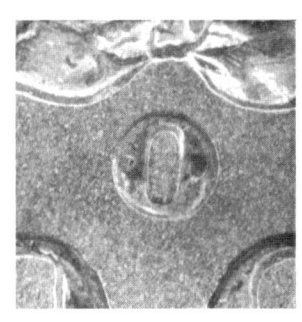

21 R O Tilted Right

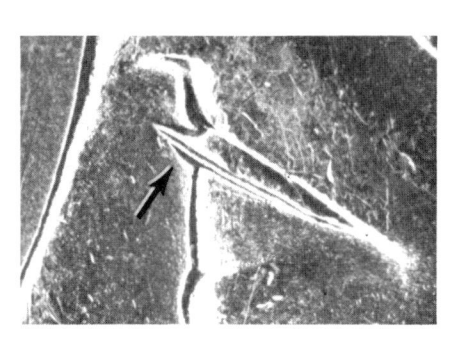

22 O Doubled Eyelid

1887-S

1887-S

Typically the strike is good as well as the luster for this issue. It is difficult, however, to find specimens without excessive bag marks. A few die varieties exist but all are fairly minor. Proof-likes are fairly scarce and some are cameos. One sided proof-likes are not uncommon.

1   III²1 • C³a (Normal Die)   (185)   I-1   R-2
         Obverse III²1 – Normal die of III² type. Some specimens show die chips between the loops of the first 8 on the left side and second 8 on the right side.
         Reverse C³a – Normal die of C³ type with a medium IV S mint mark, centered and upright.

2   III²1 • C³b (S/S Left)   (187)   I-3   R-4
         Obverse III²1 – Some specimens show die chip between loops of second 8 on the right side.
         Reverse C³b – Mint mark repunched with original showing arcs within the top and bottom loops.

3   III²2 • C³a (Slanted Date, Doubled 7)   (187)   I-2   R-3
         Obverse III²2 – Both 8's have die chips between loops on left side. 7 is doubled at bottom of crossbar. Date set high with right side slanted up.

4   III²3 • C³a (Doubled 1-7)   I-3   R-3
         Obverse III²3 – Doubled 1 and 7 in date. The 1 is doubled at top left as two curved lines well away from 1. The 7 has a dot and short vertical line to left of top left serif. Liberty head profile slightly doubled. Date set further left than normal.

5   III²4 • C³a (Near Date)   I-2   R-3
         Obverse III²4 – Date set further left than normal with die chip between loops of first 8 on left.

6   III²5 • C³a (Very Near Date)   (186)   I-2   R-3
         Obverse III²5 – Date set much further left than normal.

7   III²1 • C³c (High S)   (185)   I-2   R-3
         Reverse C³c – IV S mint mark set high.

8   III²6 • C³a (Far Date)   (186)   I-2   R-3
         Obverse III²6 – Date set further right than normal.

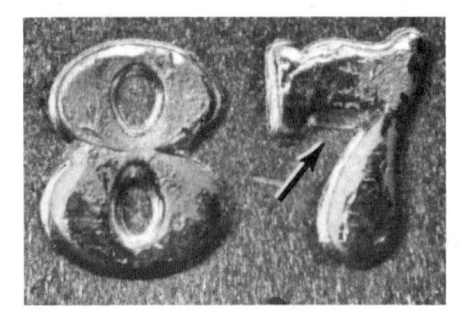

3 O Doubled 7

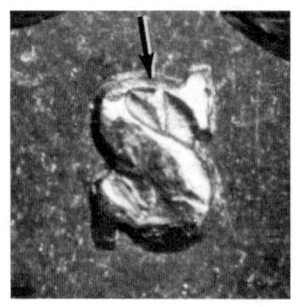

2 R S/S Left

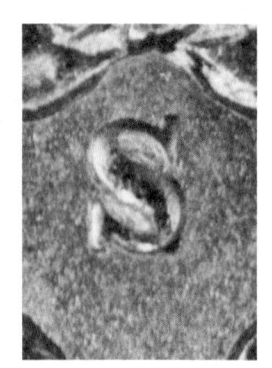

7 R High S

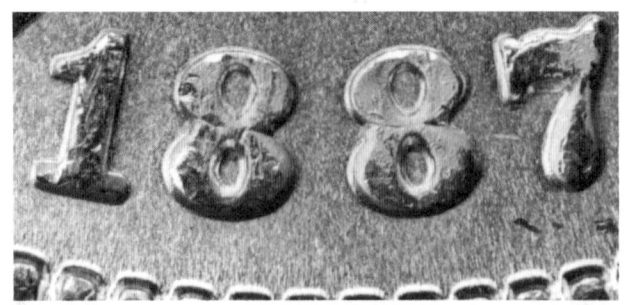

3 O Slanted Date

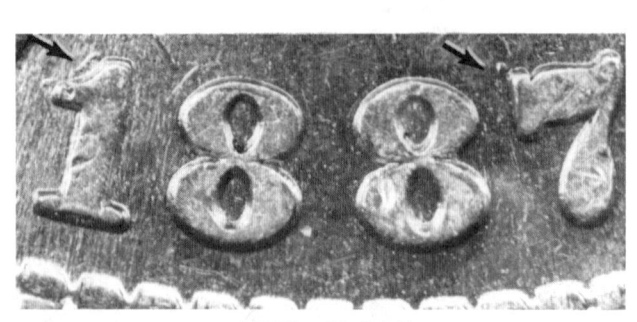

4 O Doubled 1-7

1888-P

An average strike is typical for this issue although a number of weak strikes are around. Luster tends to be fairly good. Nice fully struck specimens with good luster can be located with some searching. A number of minor die varieties exist but none are very significant. Proof-likes are fairly scarce and most have only moderate contrast. Proofs have fairly good contrast but a number have slight weakness in strike in the hair over the ear.

1 III²1 • C³a (Normal Die)   (188, 190)   I-1   R-1
Obverse III²1 – Normal die of III² type. Some specimens show die chip between loops of first 8 on right side.
Reverse C³a – Normal die of C³ type.

2 III²2 • C³a (Near and High Date)   (190)   I-2   R-3
Obverse III²2 – Date set further left and higher than normal.

3 III²3 • C³a (Very Near Date)   (190)   I-2   R-3
Obverse III²3 – Date set much further left than normal.

4 III²1 • C³b (Doubled Reverse)   I-3   R-4
Obverse III²1 – Die crack through bottom of date with die chip on lower left bottom of first 8.
Reverse C³b – Outer portion doubled with lower inside of lettering doubled in UNITED STATES OF AMERICA and top inside of NE-OL-AR. Outside of eagles right wing, motto, upper part of left wreath on outside and lower outside of right wreath slightly doubled.

5 III²4 • C³a (Doubled 1)   (190)   I-2   R-3
Obverse III²4 – 1 doubled at top as thin, short, curved line.

6 III²1 • C³c (Doubled Reverse)   I-3   R-4
Reverse C³c – Outer portion doubled with letters doubled in outward direction in UNITED STATES, F, ONE, D-LAR and left star. IN GOD WE and left wreath slightly doubled.

2 O Near and High Date

4 R Doubled Legend

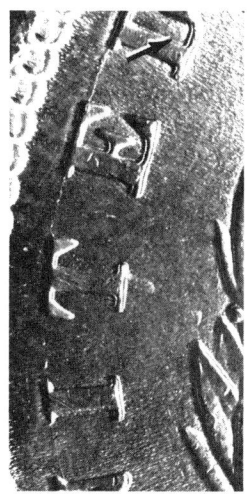

4 R Doubled Legend

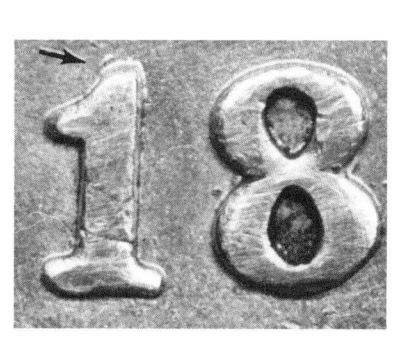

5 O Doubled 1

6 R Doubled Reverse

1888-P

7	III²5 • C³d (Near Slanted Date, Doubled Reverse)		I-3	R-4

Obverse III²5 – Date set further left than normal and slanted with 1 close to rim.
Reverse C³d – Top left doubled with NITED doubled towards rim and STATES OF AMERIC and motto doubled towards the left. Outside edge of eagle's right wing, left middle outside of eagle's left wing, top of eagle's beak, and upper left outside of left wreath slightly doubled. Upper left field is rough with polishing lines and fine die chips. Large long horizontal polishing lines across eagle's tail feathers and arrow shafts.

8	III²6 • C³a (Near Slanted Date)	(190)	I-2	R-3

Obverse III²6 – Date set further left than normal and slanted with last 8 far from rim. Date set higher than VAM 7.

9	III²7 • C³a (High Date)	(190)	I-2	R-2

Obverse III²7 – Date set higher than normal.

10	III²8 • C³a (Slanted Date)	(190)	I-2	R-3

Obverse III²8 – Date slanted with last 8 far from rim. Date lateral position is normal.

11	III²9 • C³a (Doubled Ear)		I-3	R-4

Obverse III²9 – Ear strongly doubled on right outside of large lobe and on right side of small inner lobe. Hairline just above ear is slightly doubled.

12	III²7 • C³e (High Date, Doubled Reverse)	(190)	I-2	R-3

Reverse C³e – Lower inside of letters doubled in U-TED STATES OF AMERICA, right wreath top inside of LLAR and right star towards rim. Left and right wreath doubled towards rim. W-RUST in motto doubled at top.

13	III²10 • C³a (Far Date)	(190)	I-2	R-3

Obverse III²10 – Date set further right than normal.

14	III²11 • C³a (Doubled Stars, Near Date)	(190)	I-2	R-3

Obverse III²11 – All left and right stars doubled towards rim. Lower parts of UNUM doubled towards rim. Date set further left than normal.

15	III²12 • C³a (Doubled Last 8)	(190)	I-3	R-4

Obverse III²12 – Last 8 in date doubled in lower loop as two thick vertical lines.

16	III²13 • C³f (Doubled 1, Doubled Lower Reverse)	(190)	I-2	R-3

Obverse III²13 – 1 doubled slightly below upper crossbar.
Reverse C³f – Lower reverse doubled including lower wreath and bow, bottom arrow shaft and NE DOL-AR.

17	III²1 • C³g (Die Chips in 8's, Doubled Reverse)	(189)	I-2	R-3

Obverse III²1 – Die chips in lower loops of first and third 8's.
Reverse C³g – Doubled outside of left and right wreaths, IN GOD WE TRUST, MERICA and E-AR.

7 O Near Slanted Date

7 R Doubled Reverse

7 R Doubled Reverse

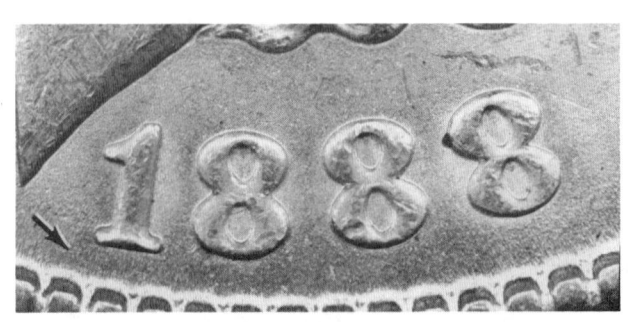

8 O Near Slanted Date

11 O Doubled Ear

1888-P

| 18 | III² 14 • C³ a (Doubled Eyelid) | (188) | I-2 | R-3 |

Obverse III² 14 – Eyelid strongly doubled. Hair above ear and bottom edge of lower cotton leaf are slightly doubled.

| 19 | III² 15 • C³ a (Doubled Left Stars) | (188) | I-2 | R-3 |

Obverse III² 15 – All left stars doubled towards rim.

9 O High Date

10 O Slanted Date

12 R Doubled Letters

14 O Doubled Stars

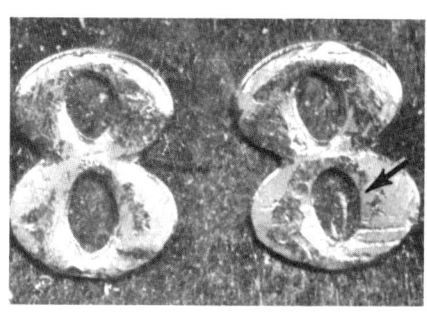

15 O Doubled Last 8

16 R Doubled Wreath

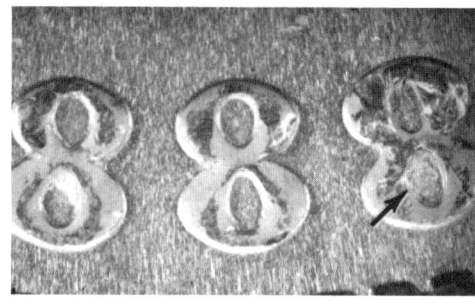

17 O Die Chips in 8's

17 R Doubled Wreath

16 O Doubled 1

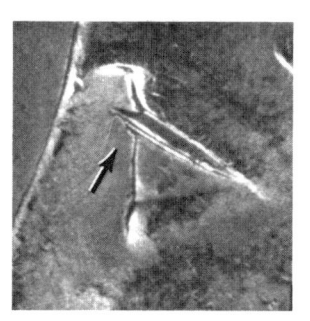

18 O Doubled Eyelid

289

1888-O

1888-O

Typically this issue is slightly weakly struck although because of the large mintage the strike can range from very flat to very sharp. Luster is average to good. A number of die varieties exist but only two are significant. VAM 1B has a long diagonal die break from between "E" and "P" down across the Liberty head, face and neck on late die stages. It is the largest die break in the Morgan dollar series, is fairly scarce and commands a significant premium. VAM 4 has strongly doubled lips, chin, nose and cotton leaves easily visible to the naked eye. It is the strongest doubled obverse of the Morgan dollar series and commands a large premium. It is usually weakly struck and is unknown in uncirculated grades and is scarce in AU. Proof-likes are somewhat difficult to locate and generally only have average contrast. A few deep mirror cameos are known however.

1   III^{2}1 • C^{3}a (Round O)   (181)   I-1   R-I
       Obverse III^{2}1 – Normal die of III^2 type.
       Reverse C^{3}a – Normal die of C^3 type with centered circular medium III O mint mark with narrow slit, centered and upright.

1A   III^{2}1 • C^{3}a (E on Reverse)   (181)   I-3   R-5
       Obverse III^{2}1 – Large die vertical die crack through R in PLURIBUS.
       Reverse C^{3}a – Centered, circular, medium II O mint mark. Clashed die with almost full E under eagles tail feathers on left side.

1B   III^{2}1 • C^{3}a (Die Break on Face)   (181)   I-4   R-6
       Obverse III^{2}1 – Large diagonal die break extending from rim between E and P across the Liberty Head nose, cheek, neck and lower curls. Early die states show just a line from denticles to dot.

2   III^{2}1 • C^{3}b (Oval O)   (181)   I-1   R-2
       Reverse C^{3}b – Normal die of C^3 type with tall oval medium II O mint mark set high.

3   III^{2}2 • C^{3}a (Doubled 18-8)   (181)   I-3   R-4
       Obverse III^{2}2 – Doubled 18-8 in date. 1 doubled strongly at top left and on entire left side. First 8 has upper loop doubled strongly at top outside and lower loop doubled at top left outside and lower inside. Lower loop of third 8 doubled strongly at bottom.

4   III^{2}3 • C^{3}a (Doubled Head)   (181)   I-5   R-5
       Obverse III^{2}3 – Doubled Liberty head variety with two complete sets of lips, chin and nose clearly visible. Hair is filled and also lower parts of ERT in LIBERTY. The wheat and cotton leaves above LIBERTY are doubled strongly to the right.

5   III^{2}4 • C^{3}b (Doubled 1)   (181)   I-2   R-3
       Obverse III^{2}4 – 1 in date doubled below upper crossbar. There is a faint doubling of the upper lip and nose of the Liberty head.

6   III^{2}5 • C^{3}b (Doubled 8)   (181)   I-2   R-3
       Obverse III^{2}5 – Last 8 in date doubled faintly at top.

7   III^{2}1 • C^{3}c (O Set High)   I-2   R-3
       Reverse C^{3}c – III O mint mark set high.

8   III^{2}1 • C^{3}d (O Set Very High)   (181)   I-3   R-3
       Reverse C^{3}d – III O mint mark set very high and to right so it almost touches the wreath.

1A R Die Crack

1B O Die Break Dot

1B O Die Crack

1888-O

9   **III²1 • C³e (Doubled Wreath)**   (181)   I-3   R-5

Reverse C³e – Doubled lower reverse with middle outside of right wreath strongly doubled. Top inside of ONE DOLLAR and bottom inside of ERICA letters doubled. Right star doubled on left side. Bottom of eagle's tail feathers, arrow shafts and olive leaves slightly doubled. III O mint mark.

10   **III²6 • C³a (Slanted Date)**   (181)   I-2   R-3

Obverse III²6 – Date slanted with 1 close to rim.

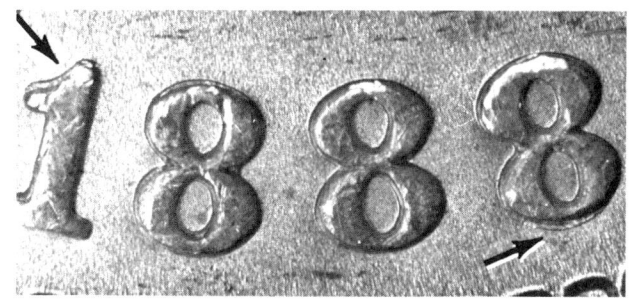

3 O Doubled 18-8

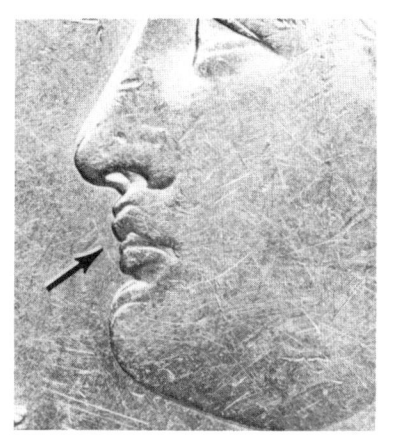

2 R High O

4 O Doubled Head

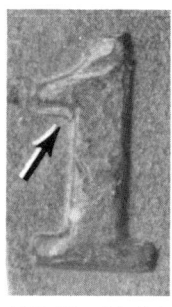

5 O Doubled 1

4 O Doubled Head

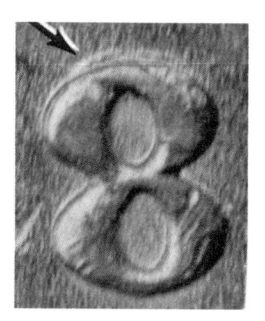

6 O Doubled 8

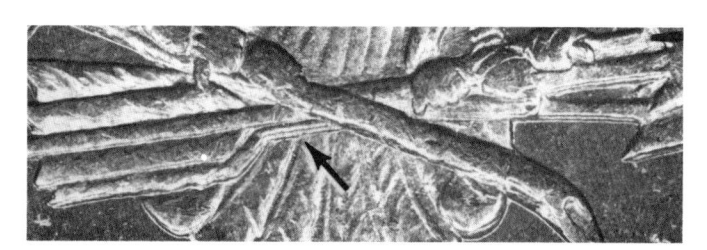

9 R Doubled Arrows

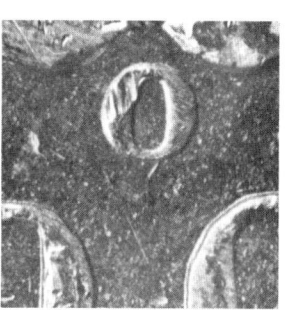

7 R O Set High

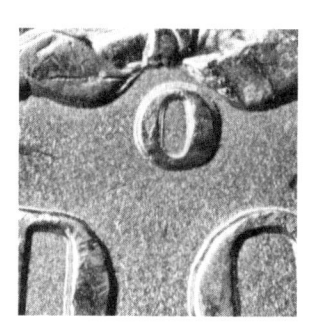

8 R O Set Very High

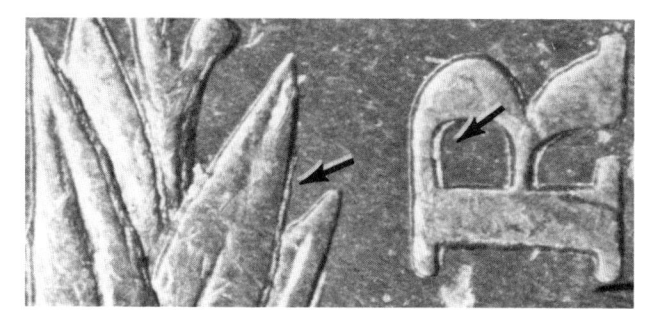

9 R Doubled Wreath

10 O Slanted Date

291

1888-O

11	III²7 • C³a (Doubled 1)	(181)	I-2	R-3

Obverse III²7 – 1 doubled slightly below upper crossbar.

12	III²6 • C³f (Slanted Date, Doubled Legend)	(181)	I-2	R-3

Reverse C³f – Doubled bottom of letters towards rim in TES OF AMERICA, tops and sides in G-D WE TRUST, right side of right star and right side of top leaves in right wreath. Centered III O mint mark.

13	III²8 • C³a (Doubled 88)	(181)	I-2	R-3

Obverse III²8 – First and second 8's in date doubled slightly at bottom outside of lower loops.

14	III²9 • C³a (High Near Date)	(181)	I-2	R-3

Obverse III²9 – Date set high and further left than normal.

15	III²1 • C³g (O/O Low, Doubled Legend)	(181)	I-3	R-4

Reverse C³g – III O mint mark doubled well below the bottom outside. Doubled right wreath and eagle's left wing edge towards rim. F-AMERICA-AR, right star and TRUST strongly doubled towards the rim.

16	III²10 • C³c (Doubled Second 8, Far Date, O Set High)	(181)	I-2	R-3

Obverse III²10 – Second 8 doubled slightly at bottom outside of lower loop. Date set further right than normal.

17	III²11 • C³b (Near Date, Oval O)	(181)	I-3	R-3

Obverse III²11 – Date set further left than normal.

11 O Doubled 1

12 O Doubled Letters

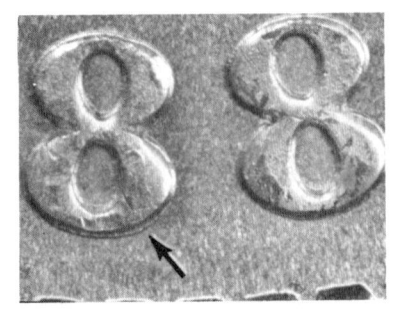

13 O Doubled First and Second 8's

14 O High Near Date

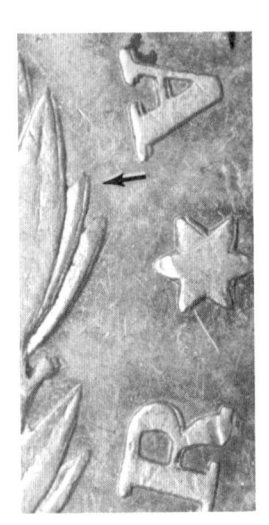

15 R Doubled Wreath and Letters

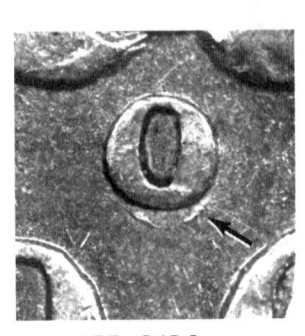

15 R O/O Low

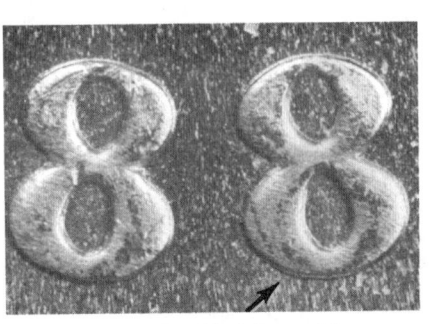

16 O Doubled Second 8

1888-S

The 1888-S generally has an average strike but numerous weakly struck specimens are on the market. Luster is generally good. A few minor die varieties exist but none are significant. As with most S mint issues one sided proof-likes and semi proof-likes are fairly common. Full two-sided proof-likes are fairly scarce and some deep mirror cameos exist.

1	III²1 • C³a (Normal Die)		(186)	I-1	R-3

Obverse III²1 – Normal die of III² type.
Reverse C³a – Normal die of C³ type with a medium IV S mint mark centered and upright.

1A	III²1 • C³a (Extra Claws)		(187)	I-3	R-4

Reverse C³a – Heavy die gouges below eagles right talon, between legs and on the eagle's lower right wing.

2	III²1 • C³b (S/S)		(186)	I-2	R-4

Reverse C³b – IV S mint mark repunched with original showing as a thin curved line on left side of upper loop opening.

3	III²2 • C³a (Doubled 8)			I-2	R-4

Obverse III²2 – Last 8 doubled all across top outside. Date set further left than normal.

4	III²1 • C³c (Overpolished Wing)		(187)	I-2	R-3

Reverse C³c – Eagle's right wing is overpolished with field showing in middle and fine diagonal polishing lines throughout wing.

5	III²3 • C³a (Slanted Date)		(186)	I-2	R-3

Obverse III²3 – Date is slanted with last 8 high above rim.

6	III²4 • C³d (Doubled Date, S/S)		(187)	I-2	R-3

Obverse III²4 – Entire date is doubled. 1 is doubled above top crossbar. All 8's doubled slightly at top outside of upper loop and at top left outside of lower loop.
Reverse C³d – IV S mint mark repunched with original showing as a slanted bar in lower portion of upper loop opening and a short curved line on right side of lower loop opening.

7	III²5 • C³a (Doubled 18-8)		(187)	I-2	R-3

Obverse III²5 – Doubled 18-8 in date. 1 and first 8 slightly doubled at very bottom outside. Last 8 doubled at top outside of upper loop.

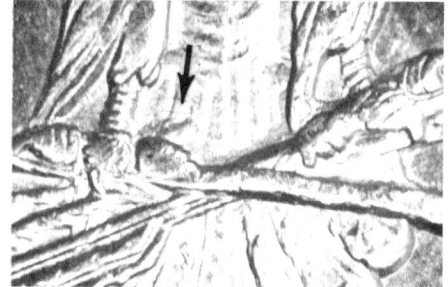

1A R Die Gouges

2 R S/S

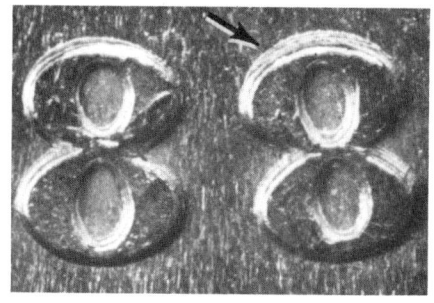

3 O Doubled 8

4 R Overpolished Wing

5 O Slanted Date

1888-S / 1889-P

8   III²6 • C³e (Doubled Stars, S/S)   (187)   I-2   R-3
Obverse III²6 – All left and right stars plus E PL-R doubled towards rim. Liberty head profile is also doubled. Date set further left than normal.
Reverse C³e – IV S mint mark repunched with original showing as a horizontal curved line within middle of upper loop opening and lower loop is doubled at top inside. Top serif is doubled on the right side.

9   III²5 • C³b (Doubled 18, S/S)   (186)   I-2   R-3

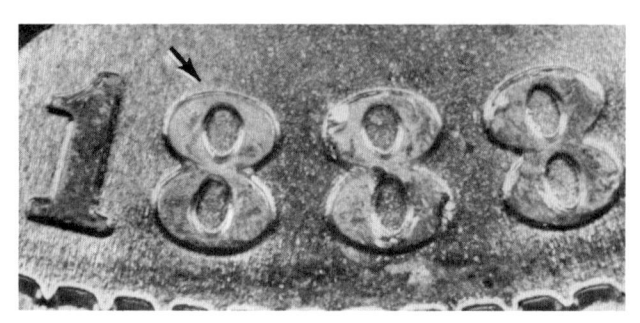

6 O Doubled Date

7 O Doubled 18-8

6 R S/S

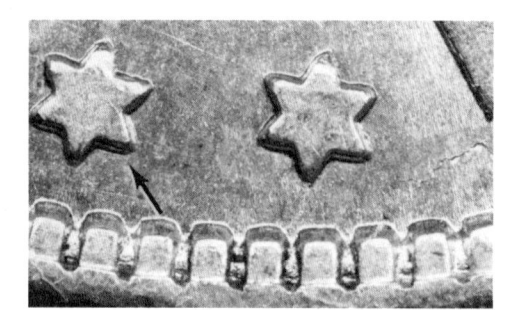

8 O Doubled Stars

8 R S/S

1889-P

    This large mintage issue generally has a slightly weak strike although extremes of strike can readily be found. The main problem with this issue is the generally dull luster caused by extended use of dies to produce the high mintages. The majority of these coins have rough fields due to worn dies causing the dull luster. A number of minor die varieties exist but none are very significant.

    Proof-likes are quite scarce and exhibit only slight contrast. It is among the scarcest of all 1880's P mint proof-likes. Proofs have fairly good contrast but a few exhibit slight weakness in the strike.

1   III²1 • C³a (Closed 9)   (189)   I-1   R-1
Obverse III²1 – Normal die of III² type with tail of 9 touching body. Some specimens show die chips between loops of second 8 on right, both 8's on right, or first 8 on right and second 8 on both sides.
Reverse C³a – Normal die of C³ type.

2   III²2 • C³a (Open 9)   (190)   I-1   R-1
Obverse III²2 – Normal die with tail of 9 not touching body.

3   III²3 • C³a (Doubled 189)   I-2   R-3
Obverse III²3 – 1 in date doubled below upper and lower crossbar. Bottom of first 8 and 9 doubled faintly. All right stars doubled slightly towards rim. Closed 9 variety. Date set further right than normal.

4   III²4 • C³a (Very Far Date)   I-2   R-3
Obverse III²4 – Die chip between loops of first 8 on right. Open 9 variety. Date set much further right than normal.

5   III²5 • C³a (Far Date)   (190)   I-2   R-3
Obverse III²5 – Date set further right than normal. Closed and open 9 varieties.

1889-P

| 5A | III²5 • C³a (Bar Wing) | (190) | I-2 | R-4 |

Reverse C³a – Die break on to of eagle's right wing showing as a short parallel bar.

| 6 | III²6 • C³a (Doubled 1-9) | (190) | I-3 | R-4 |

Obverse III²6 – 1-9 in date doubled. 1 doubled at bottom and below upper crossbar. 9 doubled strongly at top outside. Closed 9 variety. Some specimens have a die chip between loops of first 8 on right. Date set further right than normal.

| 7 | III²7 • C³a (High 9) | (190) | I-2 | R-3 |

Obverse III²7 – 9 in date is set higher than rest of numerals by about 20 percent. Some specimens show die chip between loops of second 8 on right.

| 8 | III²8 • C³a (Very Far Date, High 9) | | 1-2 | R-3 |

Obverse III²8 – Date set much further right than normal. Open 9. High 9. Both 8's have die chips at top inside of lower loop. 9 has die chips at bottom inside of upper loop and top right inside of upper loop.

| 9 | III²9 • C³a (Slanted Date) | (190) | I-2 | R-3 |

Obverse III²9 – Date slanted with 9 higher than 1 and set further right than normal. Open 9.

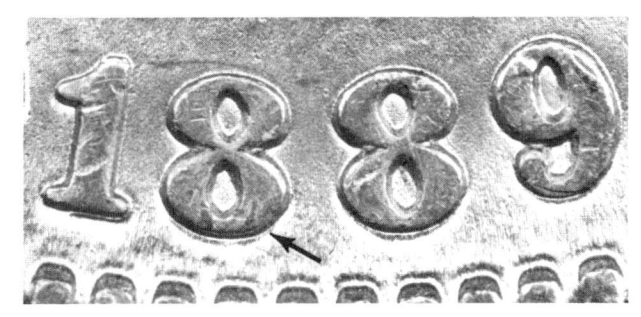

3 O Doubled 18-9

5A R Bar Wing

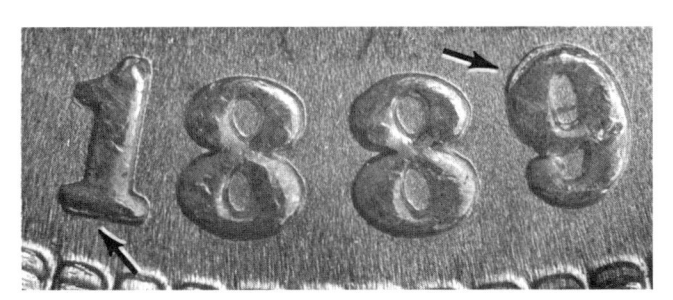

6 O Doubled 1-9

7 O High 9

8 O Very Far Date, High 9

9 O Slanted Date

1889-P

| 10 | III² 10 • C³ a (Doubled First 8) | | I-2 | R-3 |

Obverse III² 10 – Date set further right than normal and first 8 is doubled at very top outside as a thin arc.

| 11 | III² 11 • C³ a (Doubled 18) | | I-3 | R-4 |

Obverse III² 11 – 1 in date doubled very strongly at top. First 8 doubled slightly at top outside center. Date slanted with 9 higher than 1. Open 9 variety.

| 12 | III² 12 • C³ a (Doubled 1) | (190) | I-2 | R-3 |

Obverse III² 12 – 1 doubled slightly below upper crossbar. Date set further right than normal with 9 set high.

| 13 | III² 13 • C³ a (Very Far Slanted Date) | (190) | I-2 | R-3 |

Obverse III² 13 – Date slanted with 1 close to rim and 9 far from rim and set much further right than normal. Closed 9 variety.

| 14 | III² 14 • C³ a (Doubled 1-9) | (190) | I-2 | R-3 |

Obverse III² 14 – Doubled 1-9 in date. 1 doubled at lower right bottom crossbar. 9 doubled slightly at top outside of upper loop. Some specimens show a die chip between the loops of first 8 on right.

| 15 | III² 15 • C³ a (Doubled 889) | (190) | I-2 | R-3 |

Obverse III² 15 – Doubled 889 in date. First 8 doubled at top inside of lower loop. Second 8 doubled slightly at top inside of upper loop. 9 doubled at top inside of upper loop and at right top inside of lower loop.

| 16 | III² 16 • C³ a (Doubled Ear) | (189) | I-3 | R-3 |

Obverse III² 16 – Ear is doubled on lower left outside and left inside. Hair above ear is doubled on lower edge. Right stars doubled towards rim. Date set further right than normal.

| 17 | III² 17 • C³ a (Doubled 18) | (189) | I-2 | R-3 |

Obverse III² 17 – 18 doubled in date. 1 doubled as a short horizontal spike below upper crossbar. First 8 doubled at top inside of upper loop. Date set further right than normal.

| 18 | III² 18 • C³ a (Doubled Ear) | (190) | I-2 | R-3 |

Obverse III² 18 – Ear is doubled on right outside and right side of inner ear fill or concha. Hair above ear is doubled on lower edge. Lower edge of cotton leaves are doubled. Date is set much further right than normal with slight slant so 1 is further from rim than rest of date.

| 19 | III² 1 • C³ b (Doubled Reverse) | (190) | I-2 | R-3 |

Reverse C³ b – Doubled left wreath leaves, TED, and IN GOD WE TRUST toward rim.

| 20 | III² 19 • C³ a (Doubled Ear) | (190) | I-2 | R-3 |

Obverse III² 19 – Ear is doubled on right outside and right side of inner ear fill or concha. Hair above ear is doubled on lower edge. Doubled forehead. Date is in normal position.

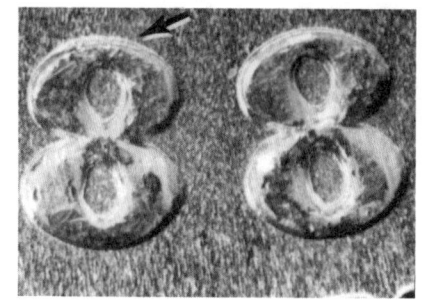

10 O Doubled First 8

11 O Doubled 18

12 O Doubled 1

12 O Far Date and High 9

13 O Very Far Slanted Date

1889-P / 1889-CC

21   III²20 • C³a (Doubled Ear)   (190)   I-2   R-3
Obverse III²20 – Ear is doubled on right outside. Hair above ear is doubled on lower right edge. Date is set further right than normal.

14 O Doubled 1-9

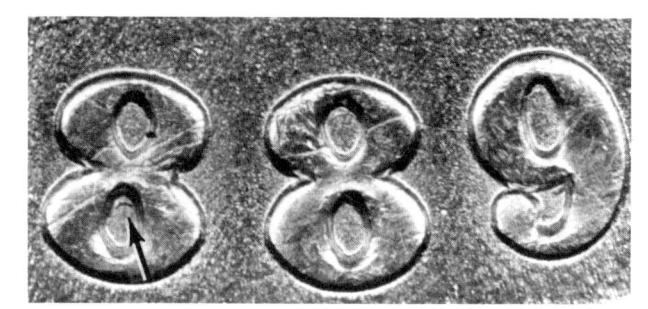

15 O Doubled 889

16 O Doubled Ear

17 O Doubled 18

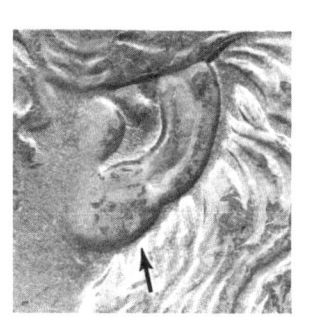

18 O Doubled Ear

19 R Doubled Wreath

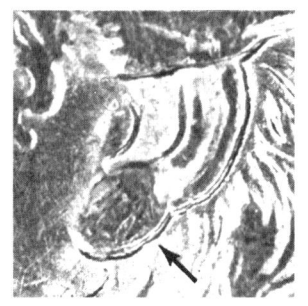

20 O Doubled Ear

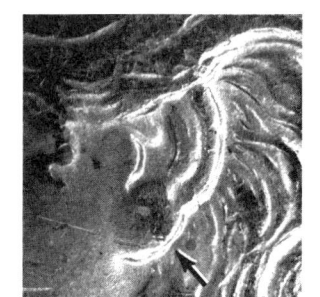

21 O Doubled Ear

1889-CC

This rarest of the Carson City dollars is generally well struck with good luster because of the low mintage. The few dies used did not have to strike an excessive number of coins to achieve the mintage. A significant percentage of the issue are proof-likes and most have good contrast. Only a couple minor die varieties are known.

1   III²1 • C³a (Normal Die)   I-1   R-3
Obverse III²1 – Normal die of III² type.
Reverse C³a – Normal die of C³ type with large centered V CC mint mark.

2   III²2 • C³b (High 9, Doubled 1)   (177)   I-2   R-4
Obverse III²2 – 9 in date higher than rest of numerals by about 15 percent. 1 doubled below upper crossbar.
Reverse C³b – V CC mint mark set slightly to right.

3   III²3 • C³c (Far Date)   I-2   R-4
Obverse III²3 – Date set further right than normal.
Reverse C³c – V CC mint mark tilted slightly to left.

1889-CC / 1889-O

2 O High 9

2 O Doubled 1

2 R CC Set Right

3 R CC Tilted Left
(Photo courtesy F.C.I.)

1889-O

The typical 1889-O has a weak strike with fairly good luster although full struck specimens do exist as well as ones with dull luster. A number of minor die varieties exist but two are significant. VAM 1A shows the "E" of LIBERTY below the eagle's tail feathers as in the 1886-O and 1891-O, but it is much scarcer than for those two dates and only one BU specimen is known. VAM 6 has a strongly doubled date below the 1 and above the 9 and is worth a modest premium.

Proof-likes are fairly scarce but have fairly good contrast.

1   III^2 1 • C^3 a (Round O)   (181)   I-1   R-1
      Obverse III^2 1 – Normal die of III^2 type. Open 9. Some specimens show die chips between loops of second 8 on left, both 8's on right side and both 8's on both sides.
      Reverse C^3 a – Normal die of C^3 type with circular medium III O mint mark centered and upright.

1A   III^2 1 • C^3 a (E on Reverse)   (181)   I-4   R-7
      Reverse C^3 a – Centered, circular medium III O mint mark. Clashed die with full E under eagle's tail feathers on left side.

2   III^2 8 • C^3 b (Oval O)   (181)   I-2   R-3
      Obverse III^2 8 – Some specimens show die chip between loops of first 8 on right. Date set further right than normal.
      Reverse C^3 b – Normal die of C^3 type with high set, tall, oval, medium II O mint mark, centered and upright.

3   III^2 8 • C^3 c (O/O Top Left)   (181)   I-2   R-4
      Reverse C^3 c – Centered, circular medium III O mint mark, doubled at top left.

4   III^2 1 • C^3 d (O/O Top Right)   (181)   I-2   R-4
      Obverse III^2 1 – Die chip between loops of second 8 on right.
      Reverse C^3 d – III O mint mark set high and doubled slightly on left top surface and at top right outside.

5   III^2 2 • C^3 a Doubled 18)   (181)   I-2   R-3
      Obverse III^2 2 – 18 in date doubled at bottom.

1889-O

6   III²3 • C³a (Doubled 18-9)   (181)   I-4   R-5
Obverse III²3 – 18 in date doubled strongly at bottom. 9 in date doubled slightly at top and strongly at bottom inside of lower loop. Sometimes a spike shows below the top crossbar of the 1.

7   III²4 • C³a (Doubled 1-89)   (181)   I-2   R-3
Obverse III²4 – Date doubled with clockwise shift about the first 8. Upper crossbar of 1 doubled at bottom. The upper loop of the second 8 and 9 are doubled at top.

8   III²5 • C³e (O Set High, Tilted Right)   (181)   I-2   R-3
Obverse III²5 – Normal die of III² type. Closed 9.
Reverse C³e – III O mint mark set high and tilted slightly to right.

9   III²1 • C³f (O Set High)   (181)   I-2   R-3
Obverse III²1 – Some specimens show die chip between loops of both 8's on right side.
Reverse C³f – III O mint mark set upright and high.

1A R E

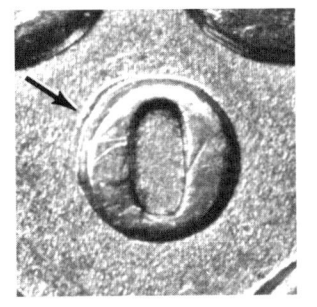

3 R O/O

4 R O/O Top Right

5 O Doubled 18

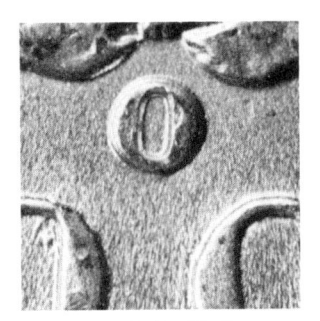

8 R O Set High, Tilted Right

9 R O Set High

6 O Doubled 18-9

7 O Doubled 1-89

1889-O / 1889-S

10	III²6 • C³f (Wide Date)	(181)		I-2	R-4

Obverse III²6 – 6-9 in date further to the right of the rest of date than normal.

11	III²6 • C³a (Wide Date)	(181)		I-2	R-4
12	III²7 • C³a (Doubled 1, Far Date)	(181)		I-2	R-4

Obverse III²7 – 1 in date is doubled below upper crossbar. First 8 has die chips between loops on both sides. N in UNUM is doubled at top of diagonal bar. Date set further right than normal. Closed 9.

13	III²8 • C³a (Far Date)	(181)		I-2	R-3

Obverse III²8 – Date set further right than normal. Some specimens show die chips between loops of first 8 on left and right.

14	III²9 • C³a (Doubled 9)	(181)		I-2	R-3

Obverse III²9 – 9 doubled slightly at top left outside of upper loop.

15	III²10 • C³a (Doubled 88, Tripled 9)	(181)		I-2	R-3

Obverse III²10 – Both 8's doubled slightly at top outside of upper loop. 9 tripled at top outside of upper loop.

16	III²8 • C³f (Far Date, High O)	(181)		I-2	R-3
17	III²8 • C³g (Far Date, High O)	(181)		I-2	R-4

Reverse C³g – Oval medium II O mint mark and set very high.

10 O Wide Date

12 O Doubled 1

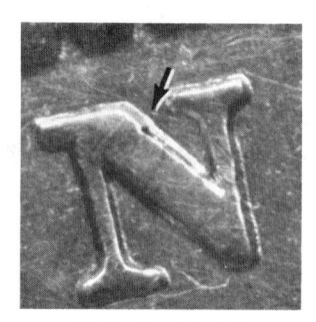

12 O Doubled N

14 O Doubled 9

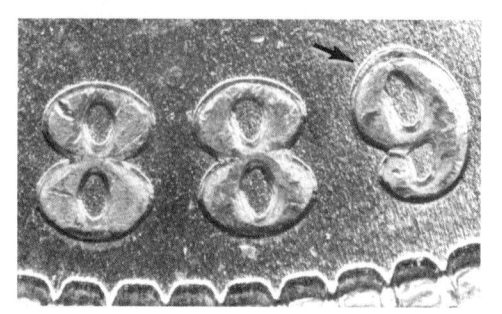

15 O Doubled 88, Tripled 9

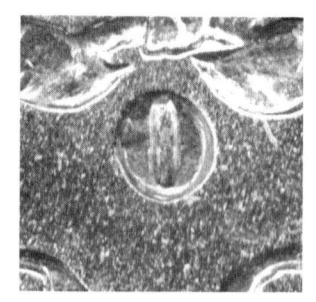

17 R High O

1889-S

This date is generally well struck with good luster. A few die varieties exist but none are particularly significant. Semi proof-like specimens are fairly common but fully proof-like ones are scarce and some of these are cameos.

1	III²1 • C³a (Normal Die)			I-1	R-3

Obverse III²1 – Normal die of III² type with closed 9. Some specimens show a die chip between loops of first 8 on left.
Reverse C³a – Normal die of C³ type with a medium IV S mint mark centered and upright.

2	III²2 • C³b (S Tilted Left)	(188)		I-2	R-3

Obverse III²2 – Date set further right than normal. Closed and open 9.
Reverse C³b – IV S mint mark centered and tilted to the left.

3	III²2 • C³a (Far Date)	(187)		I-2	R-3

300

1889-S

| 4 | III²2 • C³c (S/S Down) | | I-2 | R-4 |

Obverse III²2 – Die chip between first 8 loops on right.
Reverse C³c – IV S mint mark doubled on right side and bottom of lower loop and at bottom of lower serif. Filled loops.

| 5 | III²3 • C³a (High 9) | (184) | I-2 | R-4 |

Obverse III²3 – 9 in date set higher than rest of date numerals and doubled on right side and bottom of lower loop. Later specimens show die chip between loops of first 8 on right. Date set further right than normal.

| 6 | III²4 • C³a (Doubled 9) | | I-2 | R-4 |

Obverse III²4 – 9 in date is doubled just above the top loop a thin curved line at top left. Liberty head profile slightly doubled.

| 7 | III²1 • C³d (S/S Middle) | (187) | I-2 | R-4 |

Reverse C³d – IV S mint mark repunched with original showing as a curved horizontal line within middle of upper loop opening.

| 8 | III²5 • C³a (Doubled 1, Far Slanted Date) | (187) | I-2 | R-3 |

Obverse III²5 – 1 is doubled slightly below base. Date set further right than normal with 9 far from rim.

| 9 | III²6 • C³a (Far Slanted Date) | (184) | I-2 | R-3 |

Obverse III²6 – Date set further right than normal and slanted with 9 farther from rim than 1.

2 R S Tilted Left

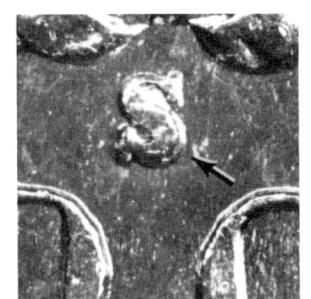

4 R S/S Down

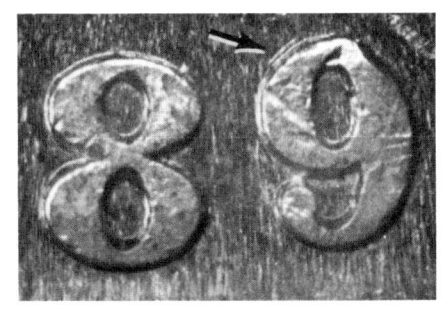

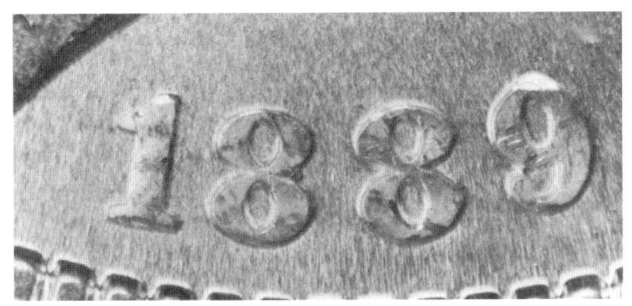

6 O Doubled 9

5 O High 9

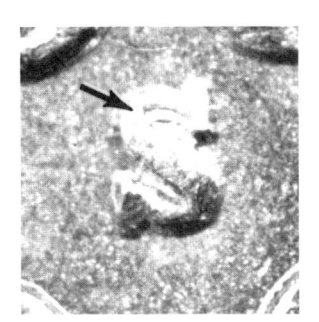

7 R S/S Middle

8 O Doubled 1

9 O Far Slanted Date

8 O Far Slanted Date

1889-S / 1890-P

10 III²7 • C³e (Doubled Profile, S Set Right) (187) I-2 R-3
   Obverse III²7 – Nose, lips and chin profile slightly doubled.
   Reverse C³e – IV S mint mark centered, upright and set slightly to right.

11 III²8 • C³a (Very Far Date) (184) I-2 R-3
   Obverse III²8 – Date set much further right than normal.

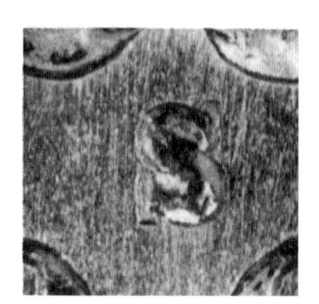

10 R S Set Right

10 O Doubled Profile

1890-P

Coins of this date tend to have a touch of weakness in the strike. Like the 1889-P, the 1890-P generally has dull luster from dies used longer than usual. Some minor die varieties exist. VAM 4 is strongly doubled at the top of 90 and is fairly significant.

Proof-likes are fairly scarce and tend to be dull with little contrast although a few cameos are known. Proofs are fairly scarce because of the low mintage but they have good contrast and are generally fully struck.

1 III²1 • C³a (Closed 9) I-1 R-1
   Obverse III²1 – Normal die of III² type with closed 9.
   Reverse C³a – Normal die of C³ type.

2 III²2 • C³a (Open 9) I-1 R-2
   Obverse III²2 – Normal die of III² type with open 9.

3 III²3 • C³a (Doubled 1) (191) I-2 R-3
   Obverse III²3 – 1 in date doubled with short spike below top crossbar.

4 III²4 • C³a (Doubled 1-90) (189) I-3 R-4
   Obverse III²4 – 1-90 in date doubled. 1 is doubled below upper crossbar as short horizontal spike. 9 doubled strongly at very top outside. 0 doubled as a long arc at top left outside.

5 III²5 • C³a (Doubled 1-90) I-3 R-5
   Obverse III²5 – 1-90 in date doubled at top. In addition, the bottom crossbar of the 1 is doubled at top.

6 III²6 • C³a (Doubled 0) I-2 R-3
   Obverse III²6 – 0 in date doubled at top.

7 III²7 • C³a (Slanted Date) (190) I-2 R-3
   Obverse III²7 – Date slanted with 0 higher than 1. Closed 9. Date set further right than normal.

8 III²8 • C³a (Doubled 1-90) I-2 R-4
   Obverse III²8 – 1-90 in date doubled. 1 is doubled below upper crossbar as a short horizontal spike. Closed 9 is slightly doubled at bottom inside of both loops, on left and right to outside of upper loop and at top left outside of lower loop. 0 is slightly doubled at bottom inside and at very top left outside with an additional arc well above on top outside.

1890-P

9   III²9 • C³a (Doubled 89)   I-2   R-3
Obverse III²9 – 8 and 9 are both doubled at bottom inside of lower loop. Closed 9.
Reverse C³a – G in GOD has die chip at top inside.

10   III²10 • C³a (Doubled 90, Far Date)   (190)   I-2   R-3
Obverse III²10 – 90 in date doubled. 9 doubled at top outside of upper loop. 0 doubled slightly as faint broken arc at top left outside. Date set further right than normal. Closed 9.

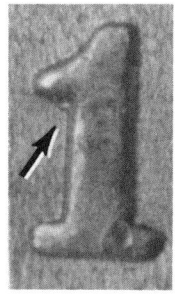

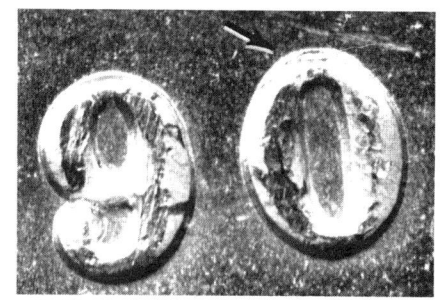

3 O Doubled 1

4 O Doubled 1-90

6 O Doubled 0

7 O Slanted Date

8 O Doubled 1-90

(Photo Not Available)

5 O

9 O Doubled 89

9 R Die Chip in G

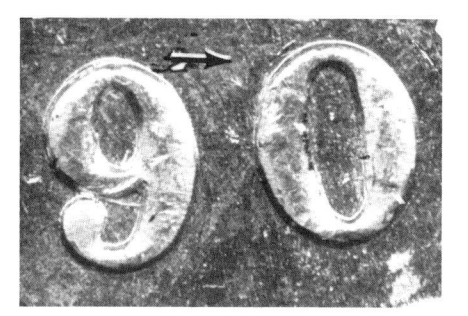

10 O Doubled 90

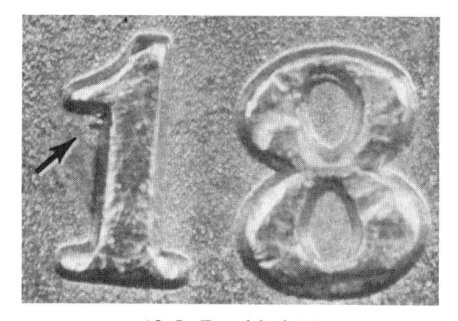

12 O Doubled 18

303

1890-P / 1890-CC

| 11 | III² 11 • C³ a (Near Date) | (189) | I-2 | R-3 |

Obverse III² 11 – Date set further left than normal.

| 12 | III² 12 • C³ a (Doubled 18) | | I-2 | R-3 |

Obverse III² 12 – 18 in date doubled. 1 has short spike below top crossbar. 8 doubled at top inside of upper loop.

| 13 | III² 13 • C³ a (Far Date) | (190) | I-2 | R-3 |

Obverse III² 13 – Date set further right than normal.

| 14 | III² 14 • C³ a (Doubled Profile, Slanted Date) | (190) | I-2 | R-3 |

Obverse III² 14 – Liberty head profile slightly doubled on nose, lips and chin. Date slanted with 1 closest to rim.

14 O Slanted Date

1890-CC

This high mintage CC issue is usually fairly well struck although some coins can be quite flat. Luster is usually good. A few minor die varieties exist and VAM 3 has a significantly doubled 90 at the bottom. The most significant die variety is VAM 4, Tail bar, that has a wide die gouge extending vertically between the eagle's tail feathers and left wreath. This die variety brings a moderate premium in all grades. Proof-likes are fairly available and quite a few are very deep mirror cameos.

| 1 | III² 1 • C³ a (Normal Die) | | I-1 | R-2 |

Obverse III² 1 – Normal die of III² type.
Reverse C³ a – Normal die of C³ type with large centered, V CC mint mark.

| 2 | III² 1 • C³ b (CC Tilted Left) | | I-2 | R-3 |

Reverse C³ b – Normal die with large V CC mint mark leaning to the left with top of second C touching wreath.

| 3 | III² 2 • C³ c (Doubled 90) | (178) | I-4 | R-4 |

Obverse III² 2 – 90 in date doubled. 9 doubled strongly at bottom and to lower left of top loop. 0 doubled strongly to lower left. Date is set much further right than normal. Some specimens are polished with only doubling on lower left outside of 9 showing.
Reverse C³ c – Normal die with centered V CC mint mark tilted to the left.

| 4 | III² 3 • C³ d (Tail Bar) | (178) | I-5 | R-5 |

Obverse III² 3 – Date set further right than normal. Diagonal die gouge in back of eye.
Reverse C³ d – Die gouge from junction of eagle's tail feathers down to wreath. Centered V CC mint mark tilted to right with vertical spikes of metal at the top of both C's just to the left of the serif.

| 5 | III² 1 • C³ e (Doubled CC Top) | | I-3 | R-4 |

Obverse III² 1 – Some specimens show die wear at top of lower loops of 8 and 9.
Reverse C³ e – Doubled mint mark. First C doubled at left inside with short spike at top. Second C doubled strongly at lower inside. Some specimens only show right C doubled.

| 6 | III² 4 • C³ f (Doubled 18) | | I-3 | R-4 |

Obverse III² 4 – Doubled 18 in date. 1 is doubled strongly all across the top. First 8 is doubled slightly at top.
Reverse C³ f – First C in mint mark doubled with vertical spike just to left of top serif and a short curved line at lower left inside of opening.

1890-CC

| 7 | III²1 • C³g (Doubled CC Inside) | | I-3 | R-3 |

Reverse C³g – Doubled mint mark. First C doubled strongly on lower left inside of loop. Second C tilted slightly to right and doubled slightly on lower left inside of loop.

| 8 | III²3 • C³a (Far Date) | | I-2 | R-3 |

Reverse C³a – Both C's of mint mark show polishing marks within opening on some coins.

| 9 | III²5 • C³a (Near Date) | (177) | I-2 | R-3 |

Obverse III²5 – Date set further left than normal. Die chips on lower inside of upper loop and on upper inside of lower loop of 8 plus right inside of lower loop of 9.

| 10 | III²6 • C³a (Doubled 18) | (178) | I-2 | R-3 |

Obverse III²6 – Doubled 18 in date. 1 doubled at very bottom and on surface at right of vertical shaft. 8 doubled at top outside of both loops.

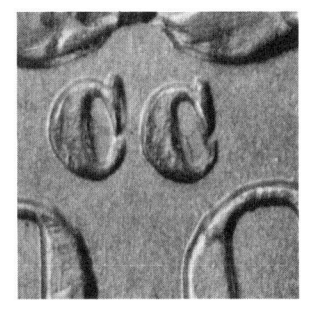

2 R CC Tilted Left

3 O Doubled 90

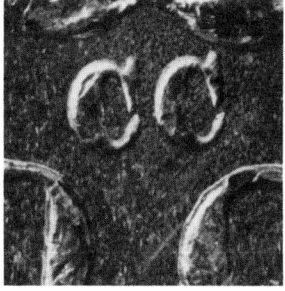

3 R CC Tilted Left

4 R Tail Bar

4 R Doubled CC

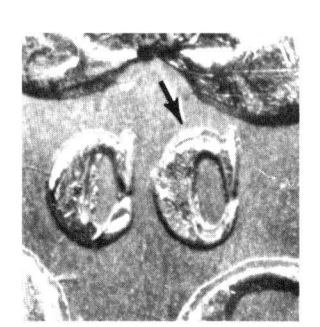

5 R Doubled CC Top

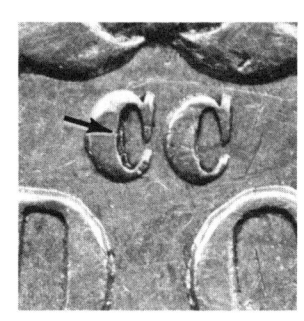

7 R Doubled CC Inside

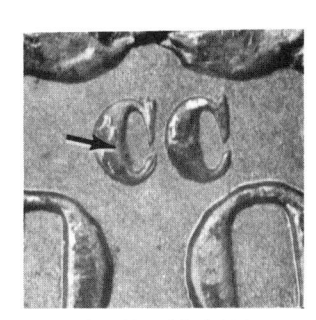

6 O Doubled 18

6 R Doubled CC

10 O Doubled 18

305

1890-CC / 1890-O

11	III²3 • C³b (Far Date, CC Tilted Left)	(178)	I-2	R-3
12	III²3 • C³h (Far Date, Doubled C)	(178)	I-2	R-3

Obverse III²3 – Diagonal die gouge in back of eye.
Reverse C³h – Left C mint mark doubled at top inside.

13	III²7 • C³a (Doubled 1)	(178)	I-2	R-3

Obverse III²7 – 1 doubled at top left and right of lower crossbar. Date set further right than normal.

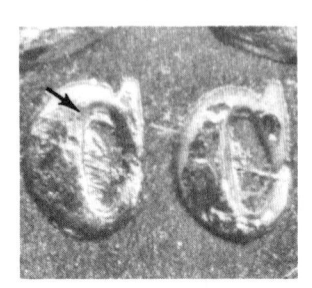

12 O Line in Eye

12 R Doubled Left C

13 O Doubled 1

1890-O

The usual strike for this date is fairly weak but with good luster. Fully struck specimens can be located because of the high mintage. Some minor die varieties exist and the most significant is VAM 10 with two diagonal die gouges just to the right of the date. Proof-likes are fairly available and usually have good contrast. However, the strike is often weak.

1	III²1 • C³a (Normal Die)	(181)	I-1	R-1

Obverse III²1 – Normal die of III² type.
Reverse C³a – Normal die of C³ type with medium III O mint mark centered and upright.

1A	III²1 • C³b (High O, Die Gouge in E)	(181)	I-2	R-3

Reverse C³b – Diagonal die gouge above and through lower part of E in ONE.

2	III²1 • C³b (High O)	(181)	I-2	R-3

Reverse C³b – Normal die with III O mint mark set high and upright.

3	III²1 • C³c (O Tilted Left)	(181)	I-2	R-3

Reverse C³c – Normal die with III O mint mark set high and tilted slightly to the left.

4	III²2 • C³a (Doubled 0)	(181)	I-2	R-4

Obverse III²2 – 0 in date doubled at top.

5	III²3 • C³a (Doubled 9)	(181)	I-3	R-4

Obverse III²3 – Doubled 9 in date showing as a thick arc above left and thin line at above right. A thin line shows at bottom of upper loop opening.

6	III²1 • C³d (O Set High and Left)	(181)	I-2	R-3

Reverse C³d – III O mint mark set high and left.

7	III²4 • C³b (Slanted Date)	(181)	I-2	R-3

Obverse III²4 – Date slanted with 0 set higher than 1.

8	III²1 • C³e (O Tilted Right)	(181)	I-2	R-3

Reverse C³e – Normal die with III O mint mark at normal height and tilted right.

9	III²5 • C³d (Far Date)	(181)	I-2	R-3

Obverse III²5 – Date set further right than normal.

10	III²6 • C³a (Near Date with Bar)	(181)	I-3	R-4

Obverse III²6 – Date set further left than normal. A wide die gouge down with striations extends diagonally from the 0 in the date down to the right to the rim. A second die gouge also extends diagonally from rim under first star on right.

1890-O

| 11 | III²6 • C³d (Near Date, O Set High and Left) | (181) | I-2 | R-3 |

Obverse III²6 – Date not quite as far left as VAM 10 and does not have die gouge near date.

| 12 | III²1 • C³f (O/O Down) | (181) | I-2 | R-3 |

Reverse C³f – III O mint mark doubled with original showing at top inside and bottom outside.

13	III²6 • C³b (Near Date, High O)	(181)	I-2	R-3
14	III²5 • C³b (Far Date, High O)	(181)	I-2	R-3
15	III²7 • C³g (High Date, O Set Right)	(181)	I-2	R-3

Obverse III²7 – Date set high and further right than normal.
Reverse C³g – III O mint mark at normal height with slight shift to right.

1A R Die Gouge in E

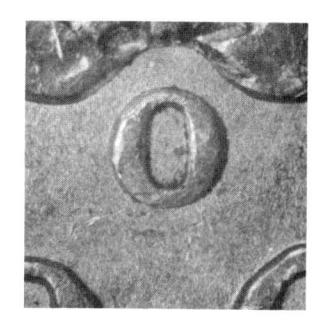

2 R High O

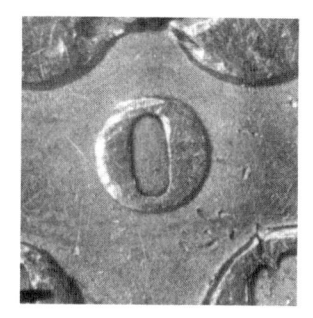

3 R O Tilted Left

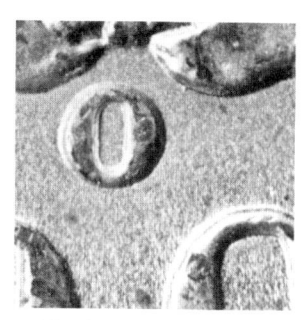

6 R O Set High and Left

4 O Doubled 0

5 O Doubled 9

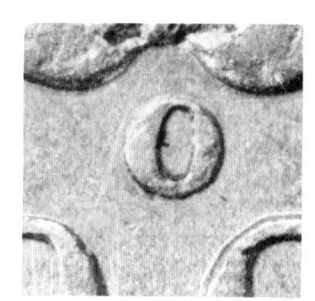

8 R O Tilted Right

7 O Slanted Date

10 O Near Date With Bar

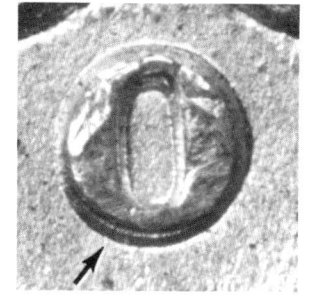

12 R O/O Down

15 O High Far Date

15 R O Set Right

1890-O / 1890-S

16   III²1 • C³g (O Set Right)   (181)   I-2   R-3

17   III²8 • C³b (Very Far Date, High O)   (181)   I-2   R-3
     Obverse III²8 – Date set much further right than normal.

18   III²1 • C³h (Doubled Wreath)   (181)   I-2   R-3
     Reverse C³h – III O mint mark set high. Left and right wreaths doubled slightly towards rim. N-G-W-U slightly doubled.

19   III²2 • C³i (Doubled O, O/O Inside)   (181)   I-3   R-3
     Reverse C³i – III O mint mark doubled as thick broken line at top inside. Raised dots around NE of ONE and R of DOLLAR and lower wreath from rusted die.

18 R Doubled Wreath

19 R Pitted Reverse

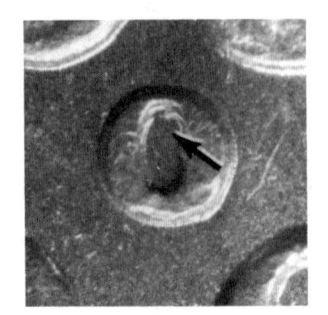

19 R O/O Inside

1890-S

The strike for this issue is usually strong and luster excellent. Sometimes cloudy spots are on the surface, probably due to storage contamination. A fair number of minor die varieties exist but only VAM 12 is significant with strongly doubled 90 at top. VAM 17 has one of the farthest S mint marks tilted to the left. Semi proof-likes and one sided proof-likes are frequently encountered. Two sided mirror proof-likes are fairly scarce and exhibit moderate to good contrast.

1   III²1 • C³a (Normal Die)   (188)   I-1   R-2
     Obverse III²1 – Normal die of III² type.
     Reverse C³a – Normal die of C³ type with medium IV S mint mark centered and upright.

2   III²1 • C³b (S/S Left)   (188)   I-3   R-4
     Reverse C³b – Mint mark repunched with original showing as a broken arc within the upper loop and a complete arc within the lower loop.

3   III²1 • C³c (S/S Down)   I-3   R-4
     Reverse C³c – IV S mint mark repunched with original showing as a horizontal curved thin line at lower right of upper loop opening.

4   III²2 • C³c (S/S Right, Doubled 1-9)   (188)   I-3   R-4
     Obverse III²2 – Doubled 1 in date shows as a short horizontal spike just below upper crossbar. Some specimens show faint doubling at top outside of 9.

5   III²1 • C³d (S/S Right)   I-2   R-4
     Reverse C³d – IV S mint mark repunched with original showing to right of upper serif.

6   III²1 • C³e (S Set High)   (190)   I-2   R-3
     Reverse C³e – IV S mint mark set upright and high.

7   III²1 • C³f (S Tilted and Shifted Left)   (187)   I-2   R-3
     Reverse C³f – IV S mint mark tilted left and shifted slightly to left.

8   III²1 • C³g (S Tilted Left and Shifted Right)   (190)   I-2   R-3
     Reverse C³g – IV S mint mark tilted left and shifted slightly to right.

1890-S

| 9 | III²3 • C³h (Far Date) | | I-3 | R-3 |

Obverse III²3 – Date set further right than normal.
Reverse C³h – IV S mint mark very close to wreath and tilted slightly to left.

| 10 | III²3 • C³a (Far Date) | (190) | I-2 | R-3 |

Reverse C³a – Some specimens show die break in left wreath opposite I in UNITED.

| 11 | III²4 • C³a (Near Date) | (190) | I-2 | R-3 |

Obverse III²4 – Date set further left than normal.

| 12 | III²5 • C³a (Doubled 1-90) | (190) | I-4 | R-4 |

Obverse III²5 – 1-90 doubled strongly in date. 1 is doubled below upper serif. 9 doubled at top outside. 0 doubled strongly at top left outside showing as a thick arc.

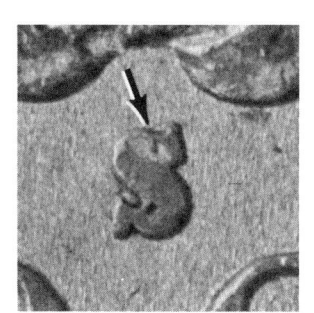

2 R S/S Left

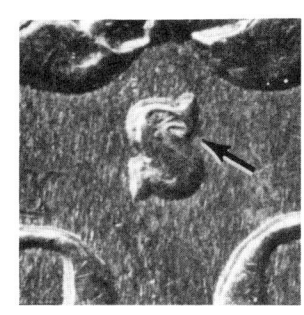

3 R S/S Down

4 O Doubled 1-9

5 R S/S Right

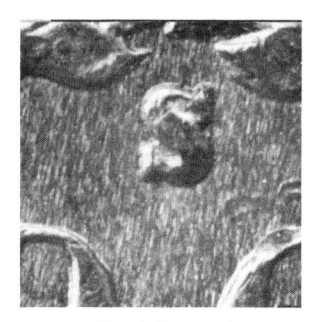

6 R S Set High

7 R S Tilted and Shifted Left

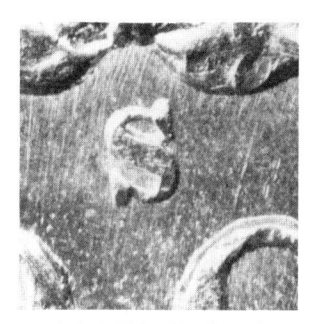

8 R S Tilted Left and Shifted Right

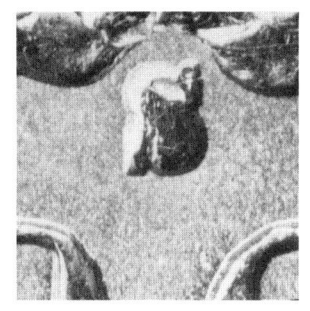

9 R Set High and Titled Left

12 O Doubled 1-90

309

1890-S

13	III²6 • C³e (Doubled 18)		I-3	R-4

Obverse III²6 – Strongly doubled 18 in date. 1 doubled below upper crossbar showing as short spike ending in fine line. 8 doubled strongly at top of upper and lower loop openings plus at lower left outside of upper loop.
Reverse C³e – Loops of S mint mark are filled in addition to being set high.

14	III²7 • C³i (Doubled 0, S Set High and Tilted Left)	(188)	I-2	R-3

Obverse III²7 – 0 doubled slightly at top left outside.
Reverse C³i – IV S mint mark set high and tilted to left with filled loops.

15	III²3 • C³f (Far Date, S Tilted and Shifted Left)	(188)	I-2	R-3
16	III²3 • C³c (S/S Down, Far Date)	(191)	I-3	R-4
17	III²3 • C³j (Far Date, S Tilted Left)	(190)	I-2	R-3

Reverse C³j – IV S mint mark tilted to left. One of the farthest tilts to the left.

18	III²1 • C³k (Doubled Reverse)	(191)	I-2	R-3

Reverse C³k – Letters of legend and motto doubled slightly towards rim. Outside wreath leaves also doubled towards rim.

19	III²3 • C³k (Far Date, Doubled Reverse)	(191)	I-2	R-3
20	III²1 • C³l (S/S and Doubled Arrows)	(190)	I-2	R-3

Reverse C³l – IV S mint mark repunched with original showing to right of upper serif and diagonal line below middle bar. Arrow shafts and feathers doubled at bottom.

21	III²1 • C³j (S Tilted Left)	(187)	I-2	R-3
22	III²3 • C³m (Far Date, S Set Right)	(190)	I-2	R-3

Reverse C³m – IV S mint mark set right and is upright.

23	III²3 • C³i (Far Date, S Set High and Tilted Left)	(190)	I-2	R-3
24	III²8 • C³a (Doubled Profile)	(189)	I-2	R-3

Obverse III²8 – Slightly doubled nose, lips, chin and neck of Liberty head profile.

25	III²1 • C³n (S/S High)	(190)	I-2	R-3

Reverse C³n – IV S mint mark doubled as a shadow outline at very top outside, doubled top serif at top left, and a diagonal line in middle of lower loop.

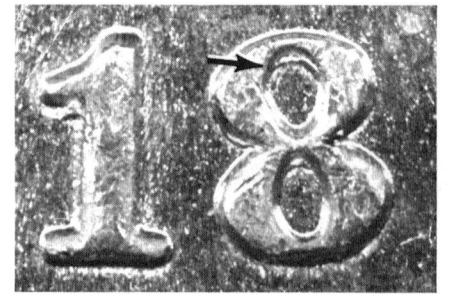

13 O Doubled 18

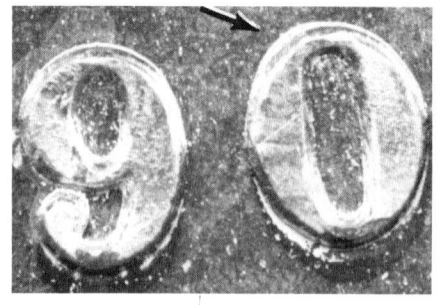

14 O Doubled 0

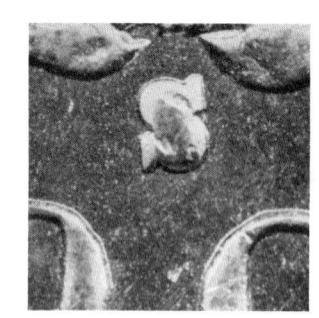

14 R S Set High

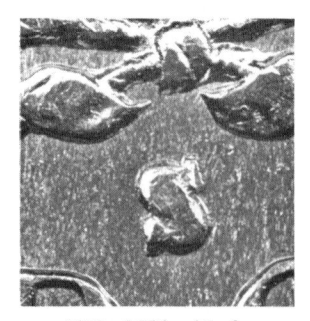

17 R S Tilted Left

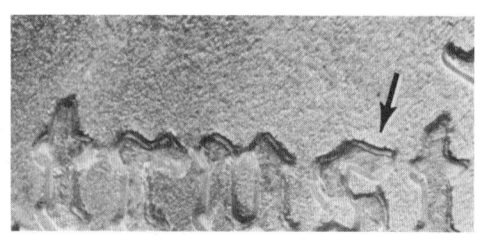

18 R Doubled Reverse

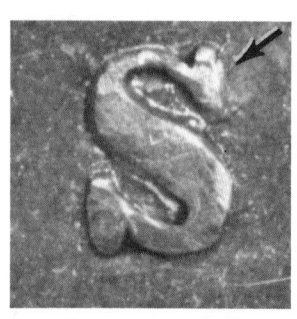

20 R Doubled S

310

20 R Doubled Arrow Shafts and Feathers

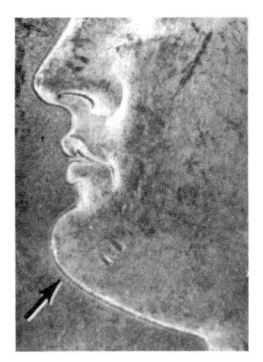

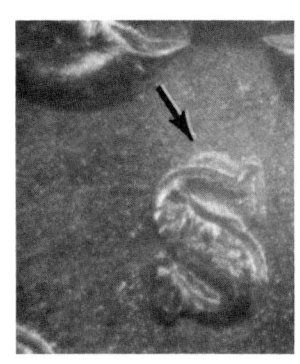

24 O Doubled Profile

25 R S/S High

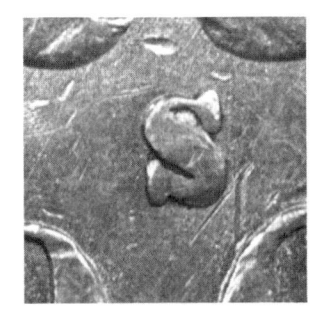

22 R S Set Right

1891-P

The typical 1891-P has a slightly weak strike and dull luster as for the previous two P mint years. A few die varieties exist but none are significant. Full proof-likes are quite scarce and even semi-proof-likes with good luster are very difficult to locate. Proofs have good contrast but often have a touch of weakness in the strike.

| 1 | III²1 • C³a (Normal Die) | (190) | I-1 | R-2 |

Obverse III²1 – Normal die of III² type.
Reverse C³a – Normal die of C³ type.

| 1A | III²1 • C³a (Die Chip on Forehead) | (190) | I-2 | R-4 |

Obverse III²1 – Die chip on forehead above eye.

| 2 | III²2 • C³a (Doubled Ear) | (189) | I-3 | R-4 |

Obverse III²2 – Ear strongly doubled at bottom and halfway up side. Hair strongly doubled just above the ear. Small die chip on forehead just in front of the hairline.

| 2A | III²2 • C³a (Doubled Ear, Mustache) | | I-3 | R-5 |

Obverse III²2 – Die break in front of upper lip.

| 3 | III²3 • C³a (Far Date) | | I-2 | R-3 |

Obverse III²3 – Date set further right than normal with slight slant so that second 1 is higher than first 1.

| 4 | III²4 • C³a (Doubled 1) | (190) | I-2 | R-3 |

Obverse III²4 – Second 1 doubled at top outside.

| 5 | III²5 • C³a (Doubled 1-1) | (190) | I-2 | R-3 |

Obverse III²5 – Doubled 1-1 in date. First 1 is doubled as a line below upper crossbar. Second 1 is doubled slightly at top outside.

| 6 | III²6 • C³a (Slanted Date) | (189) | I-2 | R-3 |

Obverse III²6 – Date slanted in normal lateral position with 1 closest to rim.

| 7 | III²7 • C³a (Doubled 91) | (190) | I-2 | R-3 |

Obverse III²7 – Doubled 91 in date. 9 doubled as thin curved line at bottom inside of both loops. 1 doubled as thin horizontal line above left side of lower crossbar.

1891-P / 1891-CC

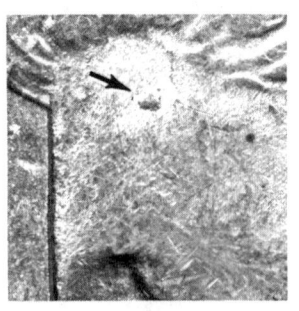

1A O Die Chip on Forehead

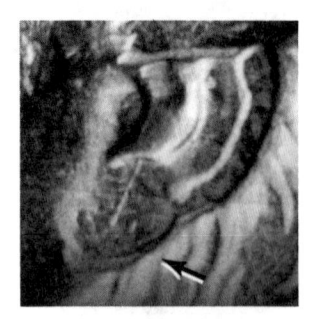

2 O Doubled Ear

2A O Die Break on Lip

4 O Doubled Last 1

3 O Slanted Date

5 O Doubled 1-1

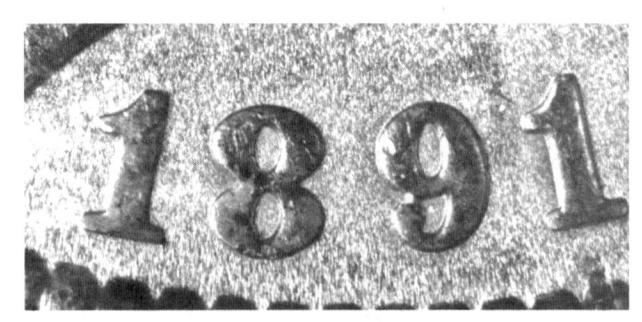

6 O Slanted Date

7 O Doubled 91

1891-CC

This issue is usually fairly well struck although quite a few have a touch of weakness and some are quite flat. Luster is usually good. A couple minor die varieties exist and one is rather unusual. It is VAM 3, spitting eagle, with a small die gouge in front of the eagle's beak. Proof-likes are fairly hard to locate and deep mirrors are scarcer than for 1890-CC. However, their depth of mirror and contrast tend to be only moderate.

1   III²1 • C³a (Normal Die)   I-1   R-2
      Obverse III²1 – Normal die of III² type.
      Reverse C³a – Normal die of C³ type with V CC mint mark letters set apart with a slight tilt to the left.

2   III²1 – C³b (High CC)   (177)   I-2   R-3
      Reverse C³b – Normal die with V CC mint mark letters close together and set high to the right so that second C almost touches wreath.

1891-CC / 1891-O

3   **III²1 • C³c (CC/CC Top and Spitting Eagle)**   I-2   R-4
Reverse C³c – Mint mark set wide apart with a slight tilt to the left. The first C is doubled strongly at the top and lower left inside. Second C doubled slightly at top. Later die states show only the left C doubled and a die gouge shows below the eagle's beak as a spitting eagle.

4   **III²2 • C³d (C/C Right)**   I-2   R-4
Obverse III²2 – Date set further left than normal.
Reverse C³d – Both C's in mint mark tilted slightly left. Left C has horizontal polishing marks within the loop and is doubled slightly on right side of top serif.

5   **III²2 • C³a (Near Date)**   (177)   I-2   R-3

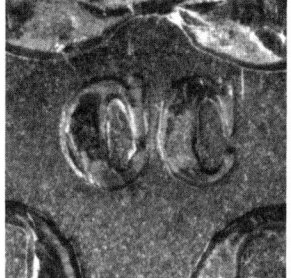

2 R High CC    3 R CC/CC 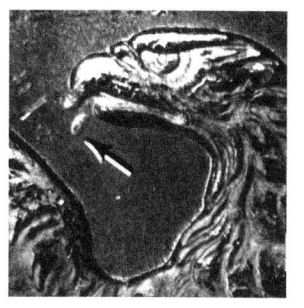   3 R Spitting Eagle 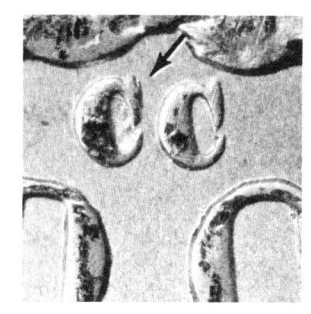   4 R C/C Right

1891-O

The strike for the 1891-O is usually fairly weak for the hair over the ear and the eagle's breast feathers. But it can vary from bold to very washed out. Luster is usually fairly dull. A few minor die varieties exist but one significant one, VAM 1A, shows an "E" from LIBERTY below the eagle's tail feathers due to clashed dies. It is readily available in lower circulated grades, but scarcer in AU and quite rare in uncirculated. VAM 3 sometimes shows a partial E die clash but in a different position than VAM 1A. Only the 1886-O, 1889-O and 1891-O show a full "E" die clash.

Proof-likes are very scarce for this issue and generally do not have much contrast although some cameos exist.

1   **III²1 • C³a (Closed 9)**   (181)   I-1   R-2
Obverse III²1 – Normal die of III² type with closed 9 in date.
Reverse C³a – Normal die of C³ type with medium III O mint mark centered and upright.

1A   **III²1 • C³a (E on Reverse)**   (181)   I-4   R-3
Reverse C³a – Clashed die with full E under eagle's tail feathers on left side.

2   **III²2 • C³a (Open 9)**   (181)   I-1   R-2
Obverse III²2 – Normal die of III² type with open 9 in date.

3   **III²1 • C³b (O Tilted Right)**   (181)   I-2   R-3
Reverse C³b – III O mint mark tilted right. Partial E under eagle's tail feathers on left side.

4   **III²2 • C³b (O Tilted Right)**   (181)   I-2   R-3

5   **III²1 • C³c (O/O Top)**   (181)   I-2   R-3
Reverse C³c – III O mint mark repunched with original showing as curved line just above top.

6   **III²1 • C³d (O/O Down)**   (181)   I-3   R-4
Reverse C³d – III O mint mark repunched with original showing fine line well below and to left.

7   **III²3 • C³b (Doubled 9)**   (181)   I-2   R-3
Obverse III²3 – Open 9 in date doubled at top.

8   **III²1 • C³e (O Set High)**   (181)   I-2   R-3
Reverse C³e – III O mint mark set high and upright.

9   **III²4 • C³e (Far Date, High O)**   (181)   I-2   R-3
Obverse III²4 – Date set further right than normal.

1891-O

| 10 | III²5 • C³e (Slanted Date, O Set High) | (181) | I-2 | R-3 |

Obverse III²5 – Date slanted with left 1 set closer to rim.

| 11 | III²6 • C³g (Near Date, O Set Right) | (181) | I-2 | R-3 |

Obverse III²6 – Date set further left than normal.
Reverse C³g – III O mint mark is centered, upright and set slightly to right.

1A R E

3 R O Tilted Right

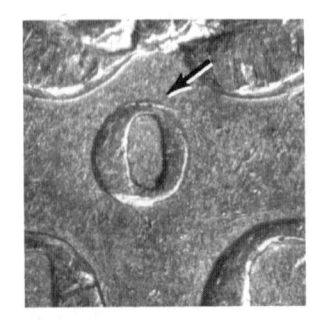

5 R O/O Top

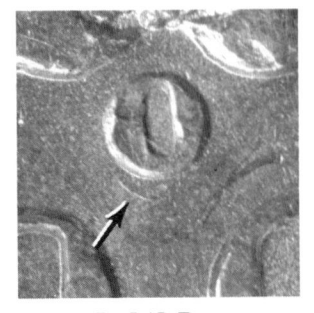

6 R O/O Down

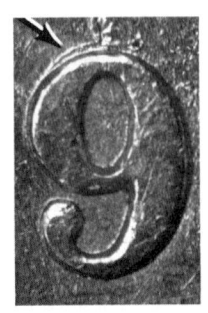

7 O Doubled 9

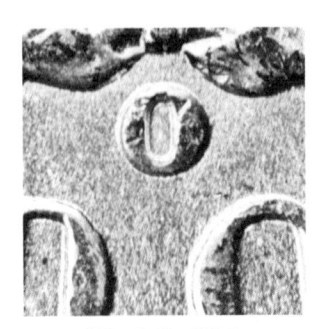

8 R O Set High

10 O Slanted Date

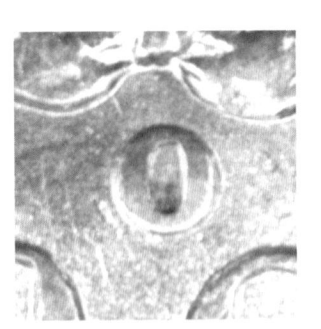

11 R O Set High

314

1891-S

The 1891-S, like the 1890-S, is usually fully struck and lustrous. It is also plagued by cloudy spots due to storage contamination. A few minor die varieties exist but none are significant. One sided proof-likes and semi proof-likes are fairly common. But two sided proof-likes are fairly scarce, about the same as 1890-S. Some deep mirror cameos exist but these are usually plagued by many bag marks.

1	III²1 • C³a (Normal Die)		I-1	R-2

Obverse III²1 – Normal die of III² type.
Reverse C³a – Normal die of C³ type with IV S mint mark centered and upright.

1A	III²1 • C³a (Die Gouge in Olive Branch)		I-2	R-5

Reverse C³a – Die gouge in ends of leaves of olive branch and first adjacent leaf in the wreath.

1B	III²1 • C³a (Die Gouge Arrow Feathers)		I-2	R-4

Reverse C³a – Long thin die gouge from olive branch diagonally down to top arrow feather. Fine pit marks all over eagle.

2	III²1 • C³b (S/S Down)		I-3	R-4

Reverse C³b – Mint mark repunched with original showing as a short arc within the upper loop and the lower loop is doubled at the bottom.

3	III²2 • C³a (Doubled Stars)		I-3	R-4

Obverse III²2 – All stars on left are doubled on side next to rim and eyelid is doubled. Date set further left than normal.

4	III²3 • C³a (Near Date)	(190)	I-2	R-3

Obverse III²3 – Date set further left than normal.

5	III²4 • C³a (Far Date)	(190)	I-2	R-3

Obverse III²4 – Date set further right than normal.

5A	III²4 • C³a (Far Date)	(190)	I-2	R-3

Reverse C³a – Short die break on right side of upper berry cluster of left wreath.

1A R Die Gouge in Olive Branch

1B R Die Gouge Arrow Feathers

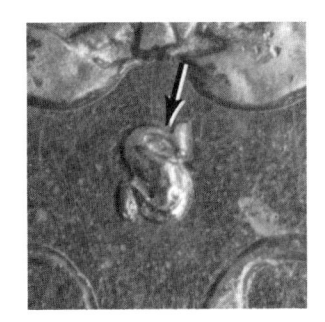

2 R S/S Down

3 O Doubled Stars

5A R Die Break in Wreath

315

1891-S / 1892-P

6   III²5 • C³a (Doubled 1-1)   (190)   I-2   R-3
Obverse III²5 – Doubled 1-1 in date. First 1 is doubled below upper crossbar as a short horizontal line. Second 1 doubled at top left outside of upper crossbar.

7   III²6 • C³a (Far Slanted Date)   (190)   I-2   R-3
Obverse III²6 – Date set further right than normal with second 1 further from rim than first 1.

8   III²7 • C³a (Doubled Stars)   (185)   I-2   R-3
Obverse III²7 – All stars on left are slightly doubled on side next to rim. Date in normal position.

9   III²8 • C³a (Doubled Stars, Far Date)   (191)   I-2   R-3
Obverse III²8 – All stars on left are slightly doubled on side next to rim. Date set further right than normal.

10   III²4 • C³c (Far Date, High S Mint Mark)   (190)   I-2   R-3
Reverse C³c – IV S mint mark set high.

6 O Doubled 1-1

7 O Far Slanted Date

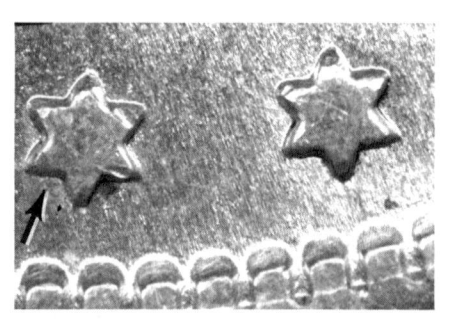

8 O Doubled Stars

9 O Doubled Stars

1892-P

    Usually the 1892-P has a fairly weak strike although full strikes are available. Luster can range from good to fairly dull. A few die varieties exist but none are significant. Fully proof-like specimens are quite rare although a few deep mirror cameos are known. Proofs generally have good contrast but quite a few show some weakness in the strike.

1   III²1 • C³a (Normal Die)   I-1   R-2
Obverse III²1 – Normal die of III² type.
Reverse C³a – Normal die of C³ type.

2   III²2 • C³a (Doubled 1-2)   I-2   R-4
Obverse III²2 – 1-2 in date doubled. 1 is doubled under upper crossbar as a horizontal line. 2 is doubled as a thin line across very top. Open 9. Date set further right than normal.

3   III²3 • C³b (Doubled Reverse)   (190)   I-3   R-4
Obverse III²3 – Lower part of upper crossbar of 1 slightly doubled. Stars on right doubled and stars on left tripled towards rim.
Reverse C³b – Outer portion doubled with lower inside of letters doubled in UNITED STATES OF AMERICA and top inside of ONE DOLLAR. Motto doubled at top. Upper part of left wreath doubled on outside and lower part of right wreath doubled slightly on outside.

| 4 | III²4 • C³a (Near Date) | (190) | I-2 | R-3 |

Obverse III²4 – Date set further left than normal.

| 5 | III²5 • C³a (Doubled Profile, Tripled Motto) | (190) | I-2 | R-3 |

Obverse III²5 – Doubled Liberty head profile including forehead, nose, lips and chin. Tripled bottom inside of letters E PLURIBUS.

| 6 | III²2 • C³b (Doubled 1-2 and Reverse) | (190) | I-3 | R-4 |

| 7 | III²6 • C³a (Doubled Stars, Tripled UNUM) | (190) | I-2 | R-3 |

Obverse III²6 – All left and right stars doubled towards rim. Tops of UNUM letters tripled towards rim.

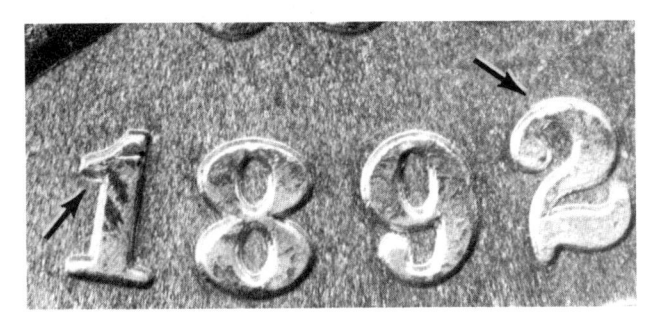

2 O Doubled 1-2

3 R Doubled Motto

3 O Doubled 1

5 O Doubled Profile

7 O Doubled Stars and Letters

1892-CC

The strike is usually fairly good for this date although some specimens can be quite weak. The luster is usually good. Only a few die varieties exist and none are very significant. Proof-likes are scarce but they can be found with deep mirror cameos.

| 1 | III²1 • C³a (Normal Die) | (177) | I-1 | R-2 |

Obverse III²1 – Normal die of III² type with open 2. Some specimens have base of 2 filled in.
Reverse C³a – Normal die of C³ type with V CC mint mark.

| 2 | III²1 • C³b (CC Tilted Left) | | I-2 | R-3 |

Reverse C³b – V CC mint mark tilted to left with second C touching wreath.

| 3 | III²2 • C³a (Doubled 2) | | I-2 | R-3 |

Obverse III²2 – 2 in date doubled at top.

| 4 | III²1 • C³c (CC/CC Down) | (177) | I-3 | R-4 |

Reverse C³c – First C of V CC mint mark doubled slightly at inside top. Second C doubled strongly at outside left and bottom and in the top inside.

| 5 | III²3 • C³d (Wide CC) | | I-2 | R-4 |

Obverse III²3 – Normal die of III² type with closed 2.
Reverse C³d – V CC mint mark set at medium height but with wider spacing than normal.

1892-CC / 1892-O

| 6 | III²1 • C³e (Dropped C) | | I-2 | R-3 |

Reverse C³e – Right C of V CC mint mark set lower than left C.

| 7 | III²4 • C³a (Slanted Date) | | I-2 | R-3 |

Obverse III²4 – Date slanted with open 2 appreciably higher than 1.

| 8 | III²5 • C³a (Far Date) | (177) | I-2 | R-3 |

Obverse III²5 – Date set further right than normal. 8 and 9 show die chips in lower loops.

| 9 | III²5 • C³b (Far Date, CC Tilted Left) | (177) | I-2 | R-3 |

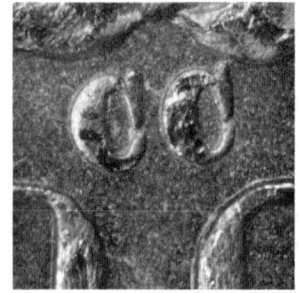

2 R CC Tilted Left

3 O Doubled 2

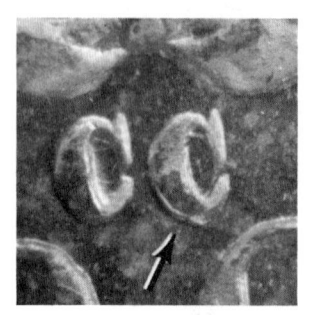

4 R CC/CC

5 R Wide CC

6 R Dropped C

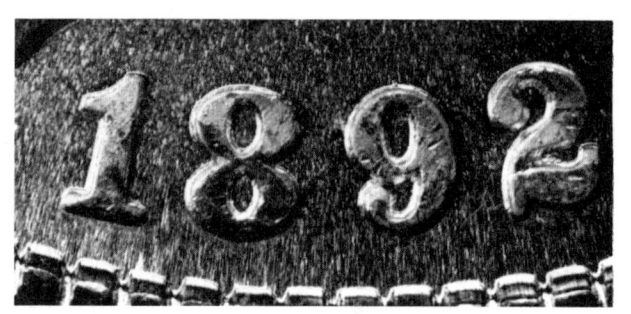

7 O Slanted Date

1892-O

This is probably the most consistently flat struck date of the entire Morgan series. A small number of full strikes exist however. A few die varieties exist but none are significant. Full proof-likes are extremely rare and usually have little contrast. It is among the rarest of Morgan dollars in proof-like.

| 1 | III²1 • C³a (Normal Die) | (181) | I-1 | R-2 |

Obverse III²1 – Normal die of III² type with open 9.
Reverse C³a – Normal die of C³ type with medium III O mint mark centered and upright.

| 2 | III²2 • C³b (Doubled 2) | (181) | I-2 | R-3 |

Obverse III²2 – 2 in date doubled at top. Closed 9 variety. Date set further right than normal with slight slant with 1 closer to rim.
Reverse C³b – Medium III O mint mark set high.

| 3 | III²3 • C³a (Closed 9) | (181) | I-1 | R-2 |

Obverse III²3 – Normal die of III² type with closed 9.

| 4 | III²3 • C³b (High O) | (181) | I-2 | R-3 |

318

1892-O / 1892-S

5   III²4 • C³c (Doubled Date)   (181)   I-3   R-4
Obverse III²4 – Entire date doubled. 1 doubled at top left of upper crossbar and top right of lower crossbar. 8 doubled at bottom inside of both loops, at top outside of upper loop and right outside of lower loop. 9 doubled at bottom inside of both loops and at top right outside of upper loop. 2 doubled above lower crossbar, on left inside of upper loop, and at top outside of upper loop. Date set much further left than normal. First two stars on right doubled on right side.
Reverse C³c – Medium III O mint mark set high and tilted slightly to left.

6   III²5 • C³b (Near Date)   (181)   I-2   R-3
Obverse III²5 – Date set further left than normal. Open 9 variety.

7   III²6 • C³d (Doubled Ear, O/O)   (181)   I-3   R-3
Obverse III²6 – Ear strongly doubled on right outside of large lobe and on right side of small inner lobe. Date set much further left than normal.
Reverse C³d – Medium III O mint mark set high and doubled at top left outside.

8   III²7 • C³a (Doubled 1-2)   (181)   I-2   R-3
Obverse III²7 – Doubled 1-2 in date. 1 doubled slightly below upper crossbar as a thin line next to vertical shaft. 2 doubled slightly at top outside.

9   III²8 • C³e (Far Slanted Date, O/O Left)   (181)   I-2   R-3
Obverse III²8 – Date set further right than normal with slant to make 1 closer to rim.
Reverse C³e – Medium III O mint mark set high and doubled on top left outside and top right inside.

2 O Doubled 2

4 R High O

5 O Doubled Date

7 O Doubled Ear

7 R O/O

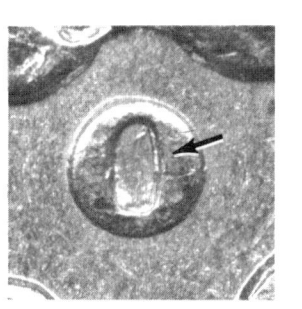

9 R O/O Left

5 R High O, Tilted Left

8 O Doubled 1-2

9 O Far Slanted Date

1892-O / 1892-S

10   III² 9 • C³ f (Doubled 92, O Tilted Right)   (181)   I-2   R-3
     Obverse III² 9 – Doubled 92 in date. 9 doubled at bottom inside of upper loop. 2 doubled at top outside.
     Reverse C³ f – Medium III O mint mark set right and tilted right.

11   III² 10 • C³ g (Doubled Profile)   (181)   I-2   R-3
     Obverse III² 10 – Liberty head profile doubled slightly on nose, lips and chin.
     Reverse C³ g – UNITED and left wreath doubled slightly towards rim.

10 O Doubled 92 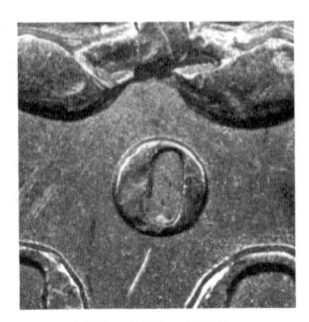   10 R O Set Right, Tilted Right    11 R Doubled UNITED

1892-S

Although quite rare in mint state, the 1892-S is usually fully struck and lustrous. Lower grade circulated specimens are quite common. A few die varieties exist and only VAM 2 is significant because of the unusually strongly doubled date and rarity. Proof-like specimens make up a fair proportion of the scarce mint state population, but they are still extremely scarce and generally show little contrast.

1   III² 1 • C³ a (Normal Die)   (190)   I-1   R-2
     Obverse III² 1 – Normal die of III² type. Some specimens have base of 2 filled in.
     Reverse C³ a – Normal die of C³ type with a medium IV S mint mark centered and upright.

2   III² 2 • C³ a (Doubled Date)   (190)   I-4   R-5
     Obverse III² 2 – All digits of date are doubled. 1 doubled at top left. Loops of 8 doubled strongly at top inside and upper loop doubled at lower right. Upper loop of 9 doubled at bottom as thin line in lower loop. 2 doubled below upper knob as triangular patch.

3   III² 3 • C³ a (Far Date)   I-2   R-3
     Obverse III² 3 – Date set further right than normal.
     Reverse C³ a – Medium IV S mint mark centered and upright with shallow filled upper loop and horizontal polishing mark through upper loop.

4   III² 1 • C³ b (S Tilted Right)   I-2   R-3
     Reverse C³ b – IV S mint mark centered and tilted slightly to right.

5   III² 1 • C³ c (S/S Right)   (190)   I-2   R-3
     Reverse C³ c – IV S Mint mark doubled as a curved line in the upper loop, line to the lower right outside of upper serif and line to the right of the bottom of the lower serif.

6   III² 1 • C³ d (High S)   (190)   I-2   R-3
     Reverse C³ d – IV S mint mark set high with slight tilt to right.

7   III² 2 • C³ b (Doubled 892, S Tilted Right)   (190)   I-3   R-4
     Obverse III² 2 – Die has been polished down with only a thin diagonal curved line within upper loops of 8 and 9 and notch on right inside of 2 loop.

1892-S / 1893-P

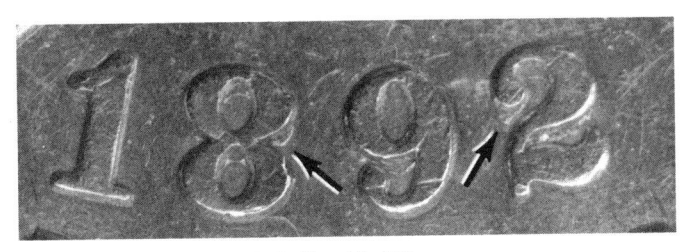

2 O Doubled Date

7 O Doubled 892

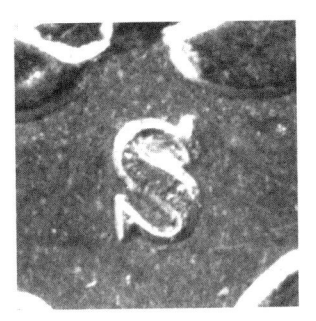

3 R Filled S

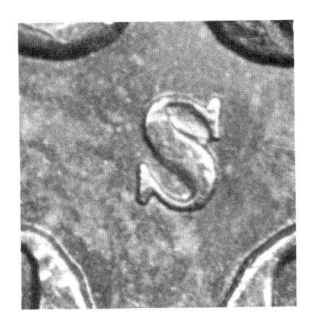

4 R S Tilted Left

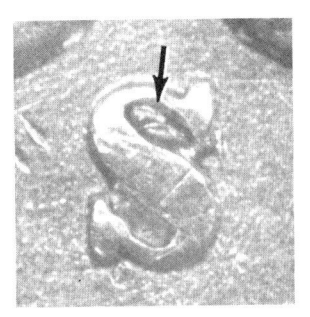

5 R S/S Right

6 R High S, Tilted Right

1893-P

Fully struck specimens with good luster is typical of this issue no doubt due to less extended use of dies to achieve the low mintage. A couple minor die varieties exist. Two of them have the 3 doubled at the top which is not present on 1893-S and is an indication of a counterfeit if seen on the 1893-S. Proof-likes are extremely rare and the few known have little contrast. Proofs generally are fairly weakly struck and are the most poorly struck Morgan proofs. Their contrast ranges from moderate to good.

1   **III² 1 • C³ a (Normal Die)**   I-1   R-3
    Obverse III² 1 – Normal die of III² type with open 3. Upper loop not touching center bar.
    Reverse C³ a – Normal die of C³ type.

2   **III² 2 • C³ a (Doubled 3 Low)**   I-3   R-4
    Obverse III² 2 – 3 in date doubled at top and shows as an arc above the 3. Open 3 variety.

3   **III² 3 • C³ a (Doubled 3 High)**   (189)   I-3   R-4
    Obverse III² 3 – 3 in date doubled at top. Closed 3 variety. The original 3 was punched above the new 3 very high. Die chip to right between loops of 3.

4   **III² 4 • C³ a (Doubled Stars)**   I-3   R-4
    Obverse III² 4 – All stars on right and left doubled at bottom. Lower portions of E PL-R-B and first U in UNUM doubled. Closed 9 in date.

5   **III² 5 • C³ a (Near Date)**   I-2   R-3
    Obverse III² 5 – Date set further left than normal. Closed 9 in date.

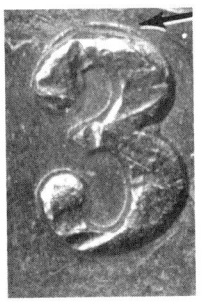

2 O Doubled 3 Low

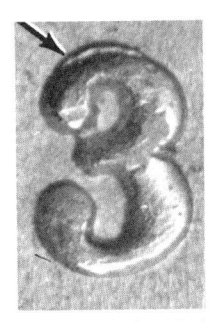

3 O Doubled 3 High

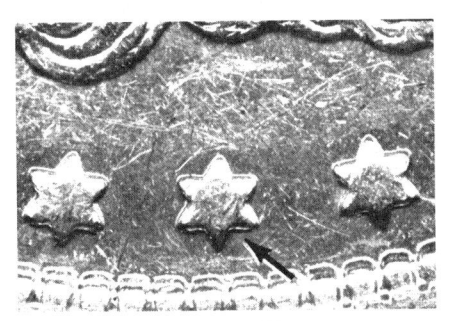

4 O Doubled Stars

1893-CC

1893-CC

A fair proportion of this issue is quite weakly struck with flat hair above the ear and no feather definition on the eagle's breast. Fully struck specimens with good luster are available however. A few die varieties exist but none are significant. Proof-likes are quite rare and are generally weakly struck. Twelve branch mint proofs were struck of this date to commemorate the closing of the Carson City Mint in 1893. Four proof specimens are known and they generally have very-deep mirrors, good contrast and sharp strike.

1   III²1 • C³a (Normal Die)   I-1   R-3
Obverse III²1 – Normal die of III² type with closed 3.
Reverse C³a – Normal die of C³ type with centered V CC mint mark.

2   III²1 • C³b (CC Tilted Right)   I-2   R-3
Obverse III²1 – Some specimens show die chip in 3 on right side between loops.
Reverse C³b – V CC mint mark tilted to right.

3   III²2 • C³a (Doubled 3)   I-2   R-3
Obverse III²2 – 3 in date doubled all across very top and has die chip between loops on right.

4   III²3 • C³c (Doubled 3, Far Date, CC Tilted Left)   (178)   I-2   R-3
Obverse III²3 – 3 in date doubled at top left outside of upper loop. Date set further right than normal.
Reverse C³c – V CC tilted slightly to left with left C having largest tilt.

5   III²4 • C³a (Doubled Profile)   (178)   I-2   R-3
Obverse III²4 – Doubled Liberty head profile in forehead, nose, lips, chin and front of eye.

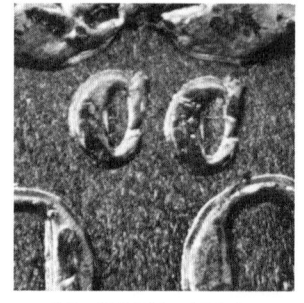

2 R CC Tilted RIght

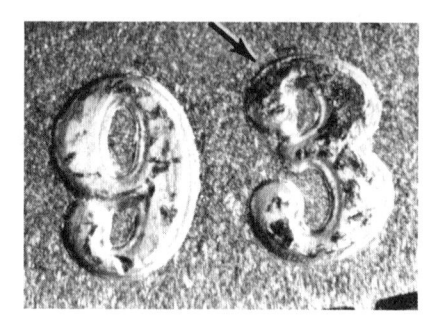

3 O Doubled 3

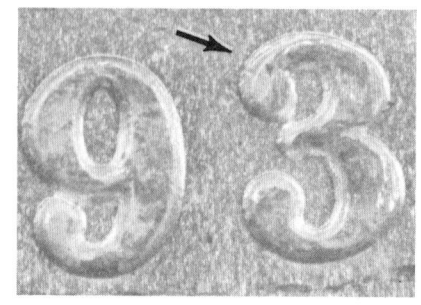

4 O Doubled 3

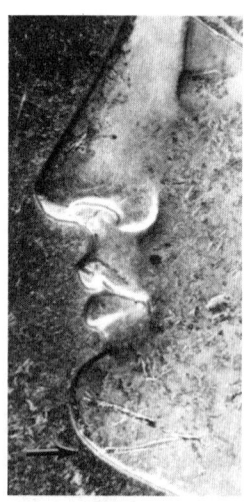

5 O Doubled Profile

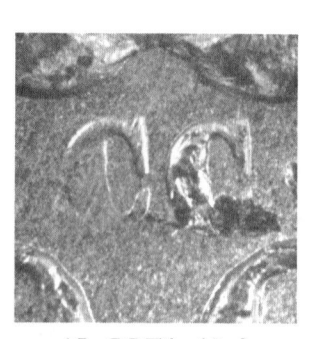

4 R CC Tilted Left

322

1893-O

Generally this issue is fairly weakly struck although fully struck as well as very flat specimens exist. Luster is generally good because of the low mintage. Only five minor die varieties exist. Full proof-likes on both sides are rare.

1   III²1 • C³a (Normal Die)   (181)   I-1   R-3
Obverse III²1 – Normal die of III² type.
Reverse C³a – Normal die of C³ type with centered medium III O mint mark centered and upright.

2   III²1 • C³b (O Tilted Right)   (181)   I-2   R-3
Reverse C³b – III O mint mark tilted to the right.

3   III²2 • C³a (Slanted Date)   (181)   I-2   R-3
Obverse III²2 – Date slanted with 3 set higher than 1.

4   III²3 • C³b (Doubled 1)   (181)   I-2   R-3
Obverse III²3 – 1 doubled slightly below upper crossbar.

5   III²2 • C³b (Slanted Date, O Tilted Right)   (181)   I-2   R-3

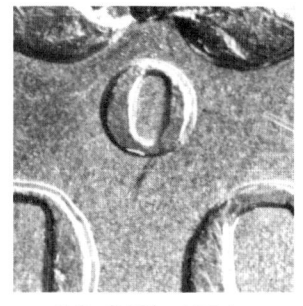

2 R O Tilted Right   3 O Slanted Date   4 O Doubled 1

1893-S

This issue is the lowest mintage and rarest in all grades. It is typically fully struck with good luster. Only one die variety is known and it has a small raised, diagonal die polishing line in the top of T in LIBERTY. This polishing line is diagnostic for a genuine 1893-S. Numerous counterfeits exist with some having added S mint marks to 1893-P or altered 8 to a 3 in an 1898-S. Fully proof-like specimens are extremely rare.

1   III²1 • C³a (Normal Die)   (187)   I-1   R-3
Obverse III²1 – Normal die of III² type with slightly raised 3. Small diagonal polishing mark in top of T in LIBERTY.
Reverse C³a – Normal die of C³ type with a medium IV S mint mark centered and upright.

1894-P

This second lowest mintage issue is generally well struck with good luster. Although the mintage is only 10,000 more than the scarce 1893-S it is more available in all grades. Only two dies varieties are known for this issue. Circulated 1894-P have been counterfeited by removing the O mint mark from 1894-O. Always carefully check the mint mark area for tooling marks and polishing.

Fully proof-like specimens are extremely rare and only a few are known in the uncirculated grade. Proofs are generally nice with full strikes and good contrast. They command a premium over other proofs because of the scarcity of high grade uncirculated business strikes.

1   III²1 • C³a (Normal Die)   (189)   I-1   R-3
Obverse III²1 – Normal die of III² type.
Reverse C³a – Normal die of C³ type.

2   III²2 • C³a (Far Date)   (179)   I-2   Proof
Obverse III²2 – Date set further right than normal.

1894-O

Generally this issue is weakly struck but with good luster. Fully struck specimens exist but are almost invariably heavily bag marked. A few minor die varieties exist but none are significant. Fully proof-likes are extremely rare and unknown in high grade uncirculated condition.

1	III²1 • C³a (Normal Die)	(181)	I-1	R-2

Obverse III²1 – Normal die of III² type.
Reverse C³a – Normal die of C³ type with medium III O mint mark centered and upright.

2	III²1 • C³b (O Tilted Right)	(181)	I-2	R-3

Reverse C³b – III O mint mark tilted to the right.

3	III²1 • C³c (O Tilted Left)	(181)	I-2	R-3

Reverse C³c – III O mint mark tilted slightly to the left.

4	III²2 • C³a (Doubled 1-4)	(181)	I-3	R-4

Obverse III²2 – 1 and 4 in date doubled. The upper crossbar of the 1 is doubled at bottom. The 4 is doubled at the top left.

5	III²3 • C³a (Doubled 1)	(181)	I-2	R-3

Obverse III²3 – 1 in date doubled slightly below top crossbar.

6	III²4 • C³a (Very Near Date)	(181)	I-2	R-3

Obverse III²4 – Date set much further left than normal.

7	III²3 • C³b (Doubled 1)	(181)	I-2	R-4
8	III²5 • C³b (Far Date, O Tilted Right)	(181)	I-2	R-3

Obverse III²5 – Date set further right than normal.

2 R O Tilted Right

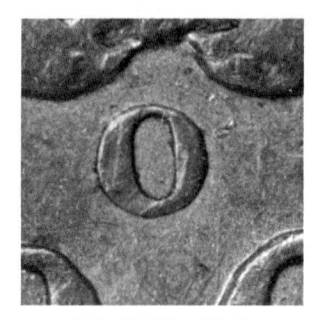

3 R O Tilted Left

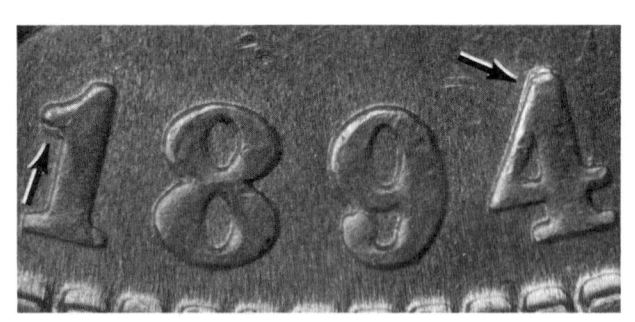

4 O Doubled 1-4

5 O Doubled 1

1894-S

This date is well struck with good luster. Some specimens show extensive die polishing lines in the fields. Proof-likes are scarce and exhibit moderate to good contrast. They are the most available proof-like by far for the years 1893 to 1895.

1	III²1 • C³a (Normal Die)		I-1	R-2

Obverse III²1 – Normal die of III² type.
Reverse C³a – Normal die of C³ type with a medium IV S mint mark, centered and upright.

1A	III²1 • C³a (Worm Eye)	(186)	I-2	R-3

Obverse III²1 – Die polishing line in front of eye as well as lines in back of cap and in hair.

2	III²1 • C³b (S Tilted and Set Right)		I-2	R-3

Reverse C³b – IV S mint mark, set right and tilted slightly to the right and doubled at left inside of upper loop.

3	III²1 • C³c (S Tilted Right)	(185)	I-2	R-3

Reverse C³c – IV S mint mark centered and tilted slightly to right.

4	III²2 • C³a (Far Date)	(186)	I-2	R-3

Obverse III²2 – Date set further right than normal.

5	III²3 • C³d (Doubled 1, High S)	(190)	I-2	R-3

Obverse III²3 – 1 in date doubled below upper crossbar.
Reverse C³d – Medium III O mint mark set high and upright.

6	III²1 • C³d (High S)	(185)	I-2	R-3

1A O Die Scratch in Eye

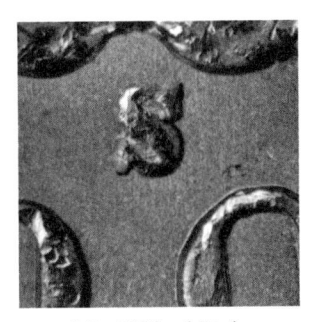

2 R S Tilted Right

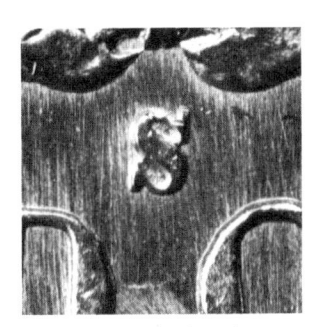

3 R S Tilted Right

5 O Doubled 1

5 R S Set High

325

1895-P

No fully documented and authenticated business strikes are known. All of the 12,000 business strikes were apparently melted in the 1918-20 melts. Proofs are fairly available and a fair proportion of these are in top condition with minimal hairlines and good contrast. Three die varieties of the proof are known according to date position.

1	III²1 • C³a (Proof Die)		I-1	Proof

Obverse III²1 – Proof die of III² type. Only 1895-P proof specimens are known to exist.
Reverse C³a – Proof die of C³ type.

2	III²2 • C³a (Far Date)		I-2	Proof

Obverse III²2 – Date set further right than normal.

3	III²3 • C³a (Very Far Date)		I-2	Proof

Obverse III²3 – Date set much further right than normal.

1895-O

The strike for this issue is generally a little weak although fully struck specimens exist. Luster is usually fairly good because of the low mintage. A high grade uncirculated specimen is an extreme rarity for this issue. A couple die varieties exist but none are significant. Proof-likes are known but are extremely rare.

1	III²1 • C³a (Normal Die)	(181)	I-1	R-3

Obverse III²1 – Normal die of III² type.
Reverse C³a – Normal die of C³ type with medium III O mint mark centered and upright.

2	III²1 • C³b (O Tilted Right)	(181)	I-2	R-3

Reverse C³b – Normal die with III O mint mark tilted slightly to the right.

3	III²2 • C³a (Doubled 5)	(181)	I-2	R-4

Obverse III²2 – 5 in date doubled at top. Date set further right than normal.

4	III²3 • C³a (Far Date)	(181)	I-2	R-3

Obverse III²3 – Date set further right than normal.

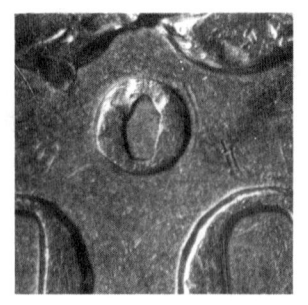

2 R O Tilted Right

3 O Doubled 5

1895-S

A full strike and good luster is typical for this date. Some specimens show extensive die polishing lines in the fields, particularly on semi and full proof-likes. Only four die varieties are known and two are quite significant. VAM 3 has a repunched S mint mark showing well to the left of the upper loop. It is the largest shift of doubled "S" mint mark known for the Morgan dollar. VAM 4 has a "S" mint mark repunched over a horizontal "S" mint mark. However, because the 1895-S is relatively expensive in all grades, these two interesting die varieties command only modest premiums. Proof-likes are fairly scarce although they make up a significant proportion of this low mintage issue. Most proof-likes have little contrast although some deep mirror cameos are known. Semi proof-likes are abundant in the issue.

1	III²1 • C³a (Normal Die)	(185)	I-1	R-3

Obverse III²1 – Normal die of III² type.
Reverse C³a – Normal die of C³ type with a medium IV S mint mark centered and upright.

1895-S / 1896-P

2   III²1 • C³b (S Tilted Right)   I-2   R-2
       Reverse C³b – Normal die with IV S mint mark tilted to the right.

3   III²1 • C³c (S/S)   I-5   R-5
       Reverse C³c – IV S mint mark tilted to right and repunched. Original mint mark shows as a curved vertical dash at left outside of upper loop, a short spike at top outside of upper loop and a curved line in center of lower loop. Largest shift of S mint mark known for Morgan dollars.

4   III²2 • C³d (S Over Horizontal S)   (188)   I-5   R-4
       Obverse III²2 – 9 doubled at top left inside of upper loop.
       Reverse C³d – IV S mint mark repunched over a horizontal S. Original S shows as a triangular raised metal to left outside of upright S and as a diagonal line through top and bottom loops of S.

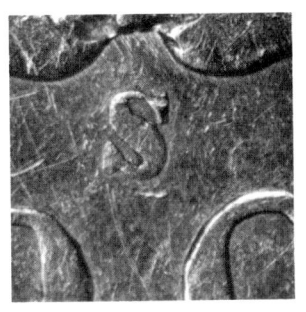

2 R   S Tilted Right 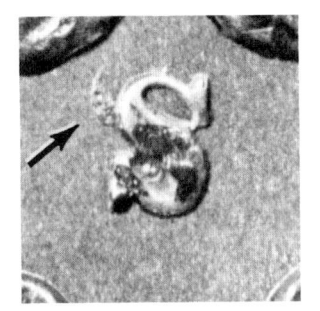   3 R   S/S

4 O   Doubled 9    4 R   S Over Horizontal S    4 R   S Over Horizontal S

1896-P

     The strike is usually full and luster good for this issue. A number of minor die varieties exist but only VAM 5 with strongly doubled 1 and 6 is really very significant. Proof-likes are not very scarce but most have only light to moderate contrast. Proofs generally have excellent contrast and are fully struck making them among the best Morgan proofs available.

1   III²1 • C³a (Normal Die)   (189)   I-1   R-2
       Obverse III²1 – Normal die of III² type.
       Reverse C³a – Normal die of C³ type.

1A   III²1 • C³a (Bar 6)   (190)   I-2   R-5
       Obverse III²1 – 6 in date has vertical die gouge as bar on right inside of lower loop and a short tip at right inside of the upper loop.

1B   III²1 • C³a (Pitted Reverse)   I-2   R-3
       Reverse C³a – Rust die pits around D and L of DOLLAR.

2   III²2 • C³a (Doubled 6)   (186)   I-2   R-3
       Obverse III²2 – 6 in date doubled at top. Date set much further left than normal.

1896-P

3   III²3 • C³a (Doubled 89)   (190)   I-3   R-4
Obverse III²3 – 89 in date is doubled with large shift to right within lower loops. The 8 has vertical shaft at top left inside of lower loop. The 9 has a dot to right of lower loop end.

4   III²4 • C³a (Doubled Stars and 6)   (191)   I-4   R-5
Obverse III²4 – All stars right and left doubled with first two on both sides having large shifts. 6 in date doubled on lower left inside of lower loop and at top center of upper loop. Date set low and much further left than normal.

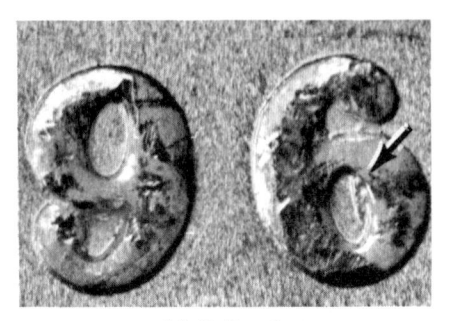

1A O Bar 6

1B R Pitted Reverse

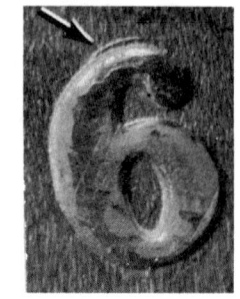

2 O Doubled 6

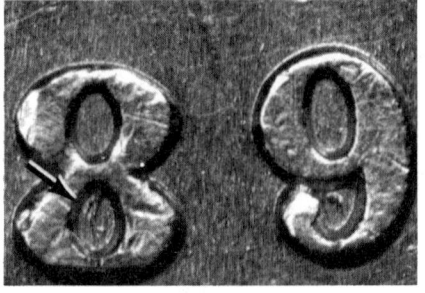

3 O Doubled 89

4 O Doubled 6

4 O Doubled Stars

4 O Doubled Stars

6 O Doubled 6

7 O Doubled 1

4 O Very Low Near Date

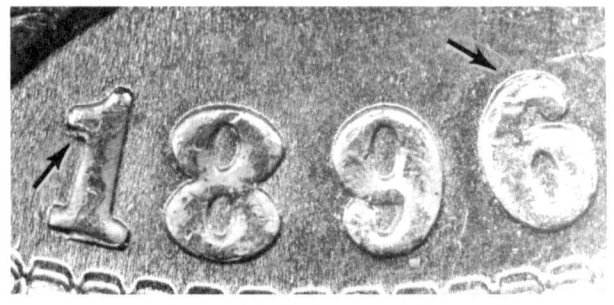

5 O Doubled 18-6

1896-P

5 III² 5 • C³ a (Doubled 18-6)   I-4   R-4
Obverse III² 5 – 18-6 in date doubled strongly. 1 is doubled strongly below upper serif and at lower right of bottom crossbar. 8 is doubled slightly at top inside and lower left outside of upper loop plus at bottom outside of lower loop. 6 is doubled at top outside of upper loop and at top right outside of lower loop.

6 III² 6 • C³ a (Doubled 6)   (190)   I-3   R-4
Obverse III² 6 – 6 in date doubled at top outside of upper loop as thick curved line and at top outside of lower loop as a short thin line. Doubling is set higher and is thicker than VAM 2. Date set further left than normal.

7 III² 7 • C³ 3 (Doubled 1)   I-2   R-3
Obverse III² 7 – 1 in date doubled at top left as short spike and slightly just below upper crossbar. Date set further left than normal.

8 III² 8 • C³ a (Doubled 1-6)   (189)   I-2   R-3
Obverse III² 8 – Doubled 1-6 in date. 1 doubled slightly below top crossbar. 6 doubled at top outside showing as a flat curved line next to top loop.

9 III² 9 • C³ a (Doubled 96)   (186)   I-2   R-3
Obverse III² 9 – Doubled 96 in date. 9 doubled as a faint curved line just above the top loop. 6 doubled as a long curved line and short segment well above top loop.

10 III² 10 • C³ a (Doubled 6, Low Date)   I-2   R-3
Obverse III² 10 – 6 in date doubled just above top outside of upper loop as thin curved segment and dot on right. Date set close to rim.

11 III² 11 • C³ a (Near Date)   (190)   I-2   R-3
Obverse III² 11 – Date set further left than normal.

11A III² 11 • C³ a (Gouged 8)   I-2   R-4
Obverse III² 11 – Vertical die gouge in left top inside of lower loop of 8.

12 III² 12 • C³ a (Near Slanted Date)   (190)   I-2   R-3
Obverse III² 12 – Date set further left than normal and slanted with 1 close to rim.

13 III² 13 • C³ a (Doubled 1)   (190)   I-2   R-3
Obverse III² 13 – 1 in date doubled below upper crossbar. Date set further left than normal.

8 O Doubled 1-6

10 O Doubled 6, Low Date

9 O Doubled 96

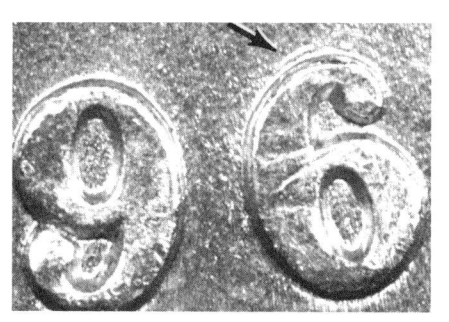

10 O Doubled 6, Low Date

11A O Gouged 8

1896-P / 1896-O

| 14 | III² 14 • C³ a (Doubled 6) | (190) | I-2 | R-3 |

Obverse III² 14 – 6 in date doubled just above top outside of upper loop as a dot on left and thin curved line joining top of loop and doubled slightly at bottom outside of lower loop.

| 15 | III² 15 • C³ a (Doubled 1-9, Tripled 6) | (191) | I-2 | R-3 |

Obverse III² 15 – 1 doubled below upper crossbar. 9 doubled faintly at top outside of upper loop. 6 tripled at top outside of upper loop.

| 16 | III² 16 • C³ a (Doubled 6, Very Low Date) | (191) | I-2 | R-3 |

Obverse III² 16 – 6 doubled at lower left inside of lower loop. Date set much further left than normal and very close to rim. One of the lowest dates in Morgan series.

| 17 | III² 17 • C³ a (Doubled 6, Near Date) | (190) | I-2 | R-3 |

Obverse III² 17 – 6 doubled slightly at top outside. Date set further left than normal.

| 18 | III² 18 • C³ a (Very Near Date) | (189) | I-2 | Proof |

Obverse III² 18 – Date set much further left than normal.

11 O Near Date

12 O Near Slanted Date

13 O Doubled 1

14 O Doubled 6

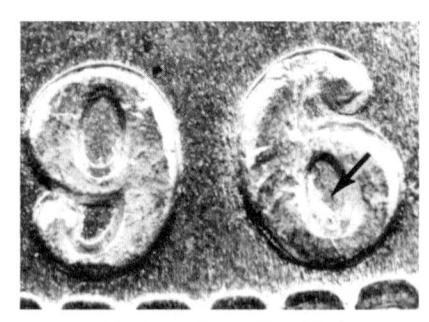

16 O Low Date, Doubled 6

15 O Doubled 1-9, Tripled 6

16 O Low Date, Doubled 6

330

17 O Doubled 6

1896-O

Typical strike is fairly weak and the luster fairly dull. High grade specimens are quite rare despite the relatively high mintage. Apparently most of the issue was released into circulation after four years of low New Orleans mintages. A number of minor die varieties exist. VAM 7 shows strong doubling below 96 and is worth a modest premium. VAM 4 has a small O mint mark readily detected but is extremely scarce and only known in low circulated grades. Proof-like specimens are extremely rare and generally have little contrast.

1   III² 1 • C³ a (Normal Die)   (181)   I-1   R-2
Obverse III² 1 – Normal die of III² type.
Reverse C³ a – Normal die of C³ type with medium III O mint mark, centered and upright.

1A   III² 1 • C³ a (Gouged Date)   (181)   I-2   R-5
Obverse III² 1 – Heavy die gouges in date. The 8 has die chips at bottom of upper loop opening and a thick horizontal bar die gouge at top of lower loop opening. The 6 has a thick vertical bar die gouge extending from middle of lower loop opening to its top. The upper loop opening of the 6 has a die chip at the very bottom. The 1 has a short horizontal line to the left of bottom of upper serif. There are polishing lines throughout the lower part of the Liberty's head and within LIBERTY.

2   III² 1 • C³ b (O Tilted Left)   (181)   I-2   R-3
Reverse C³ b – Normal die with medium III O mint mark, tilted slightly left.

3   III² 1 • C³ c (O Tilted Right)   (181)   I-2   R-3
Reverse C³ c – Normal die with medium centered III O mint mark tilted slightly right.

4   III² 1 • C³ d (Small O)   I-4   R-6
Reverse C³ d – Normal die with small I O mint mark, centered and tilted to right

5   III² 2 • C³ a (Doubled 1-6)   (181)   I-2   R-3
Obverse III² 2 – 1-6 in date doubled. 1 doubled slightly on surface below upper crossbar. 6 doubled at top outside.

6   III² 3 • C³ c (Doubled 1-6)   (181)   I-3   R-4
Obverse III² 3 – 1-6 in date doubled. 1 is doubled to the top left. 6 is doubled strongly below and to the left. Date set further right than normal.

7   III² 4 • C³ c (Doubled 96)   (181)   I-4   R-4
Obverse III² 4 – 96 in date doubled strongly at bottom. Date set further left than normal.

1A O Gouged Date    2 R O Tilted Left 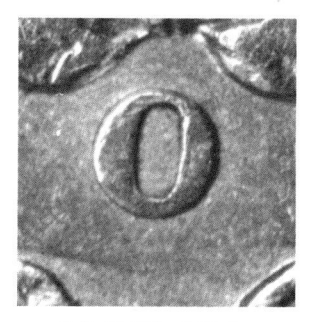   3 R O Tilted Right

1896-O

5 O Doubled 1-6

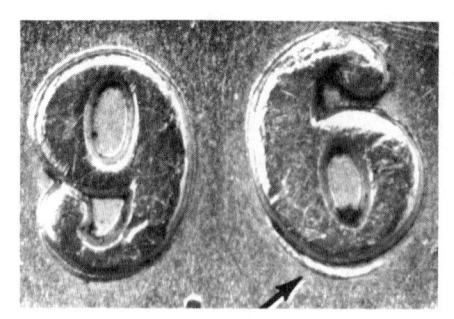

7 O Doubled 96

8 R Oval O

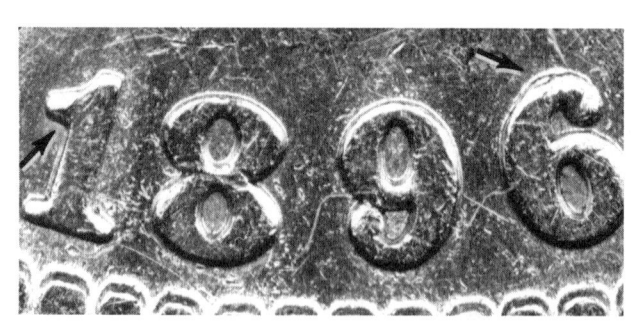

5 O Doubled 1-6

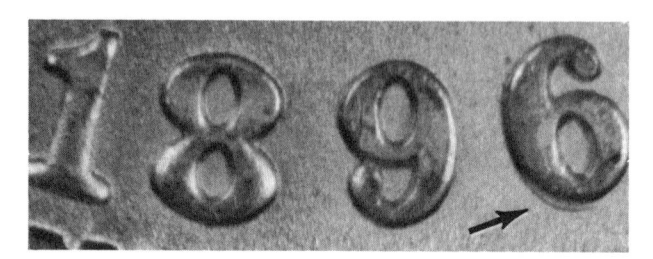

6 O Doubled 1-6

| 8 | III²1 • C³e (Oval O) | (181) | I-3 | R-5 |

Reverse C³e – Normal die of C³ type with an oval II O mint mark.

| 9 | III²5 • C³a (Doubled 1) | (181) | I-2 | R-3 |

Obverse III²5 – 1 doubled at top left as a short curved bar and at left end of top crossbar as a shallow dot.

| 10 | III²6 • C³a (Doubled l) | (181) | I-2 | R-3 |

Obverse III²6 – 1 in date doubled slightly below upper crossbar.

| 11 | III²7 • C³a (Doubled 18) | (181) | I-2 | R-4 |

Obverse III²7 – 18 in date doubled. 1 is doubled strongly at bottom outside of lower loop. 8 is doubled slightly at bottom left outside.

| 12 | III²8 • C³a (Doubled 18-6) | (181) | I-3 | R-4 |

Obverse III²8 – 18-6 doubled in date. 1 doubled strongly below bottom crossbar and slightly below upper crossbar. 8 doubled at bottom left outside of lower loop. 6 doubled strongly on right outside of upper loop and shows as a curved teardrop well away from loop. Date set further left than normal.

| 13 | III²10 • C³f (Near Date, High O) | (181) | I-2 | R-3 |

Obverse III²10 – Date set further left than normal.
Reverse C³f – III O mint mark set slightly high.

| 14 | III²11 • C³c (Doubled 6, O Tilted Right) | (181) | I-2 | R-3 |

Obverse III²11 – 6 doubled slightly at top outside. Date set further left than normal.

| 15 | III²12 • C³c (Doubled 96, O Tilted Right) | (181) | I-2 | R-3 |

Obverse III²12 – 96 doubled very slightly at top outside. Date set further left than normal.

| 16 | III²12 • C³a (Doubled 1, Near Date) | (181) | I-2 | R-3 |

Obverse III²12 – 1 doubled below upper crossbar. Date set further left than normal.

| 17 | III²10 • C³c (Near Date, O Tilted Right) | (181) | I-2 | R-3 |
| 18 | III²10 • C³f (High O) | (181) | I-2 | R-3 |

1896-O / 1896-S

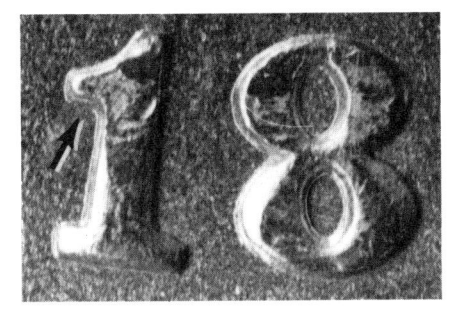

9 O Doubled 1

10 O Doubled 1

11 O Doubled 18

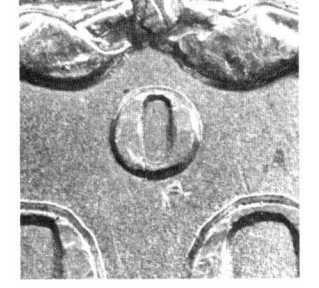

12 O Doubled 18-6

13 R High O

14 O Doubled 6 Top

15 O Doubled 96 Top Slight

16 O Doubled 1

1896-S

Usually this issue has a touch of weakness in the strike although it can vary from full to moderately weak. Luster is generally good. High grade uncirculated specimens with full strike are quite scarce for this relatively high mintage issue and apparently most were released into circulation like the 1896-O after four years of low mintages. A few minor die varieties exist but none are significant except VAM 5 showing S/S with a large shift to the northeast. Proof-likes are very rare with little contrast.

1   **III² 1 • C³ a (Normal Die)**   (186)   I-1   R-2
    Obverse III² 1 – Normal die of III² type.
    Reverse C³ a – Normal die of C³ type with a medium IV S mint mark, centered and upright.

2   **III² 2 • C³ d (Doubled 1-6)**   1-2   R-4
    Obverse III² 2 – Doubled 1-6 in date. 1 doubled below upper crossbar. 6 doubled at top as a curved thin line just above very top.
    Reverse C³ d – IV S mint mark doubled to left of upper serif.

3   **III² 3 • C³ b (S/S)**   I-3   R-4
    Obverse III² 3 – 8 has vertical spike die gouge within center of lower loop and 9 has dot in center of lower loop.
    Reverse C³ b – IV S mint mark repunched with original showing as a thin diagonal line on right side of upper loop opening and as an arc on right side of lower loop opening.

1896-S

| 4 | III²4 • C³a (Near Date) | | I-2 | R-3 |

Obverse III²4 – Date set further left than normal.

| 5 | III²1 • C³c (S/S Right and Up) | (188) | I-3 | R-4 |

Reverse C³c – IV S mint mark repunched with original showing as a short spike above top loop, vertical serif to top right of top serif, curved arc to right of lower loop and vertical serif within lower loop opening.

| 6 | III²5 • C³d (Doubled 1, S/S Center) | (188) | I-3 | R-3 |

Obverse III²5 – 1 doubled slightly below upper crossbar.
Reverse C³d – IV S mint mark repunched with original showing as a curved arc at top of upper loop opening.

| 7 | III²6 • C³a (Doubled 6) | (186) | I-2 | R-3 |

Obverse III²6 – 6 in date doubled at top outside of upper loop.

| 8 | III²6 • C³e (Doubled 6, S/S Down) | (186) | I-2 | R-3 |

Reverse C³e – IV S mint mark repunched with original showing as two thin arcs at left side of upper loop opening and middle shaft doubled at bottom.

2 O Doubled 1-6

2 R S/S

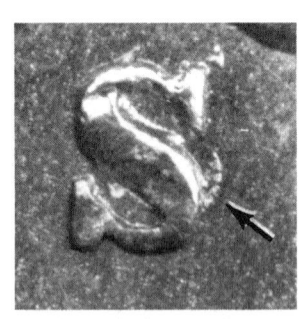

5 R S/S Right and Up

3 O Die Gouge

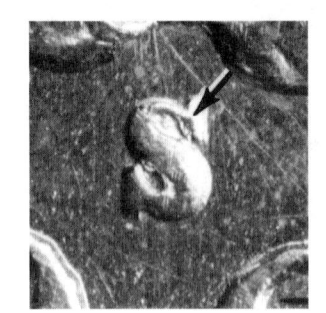

3 R S/S

6 O Doubled 1

7 O Doubled 6

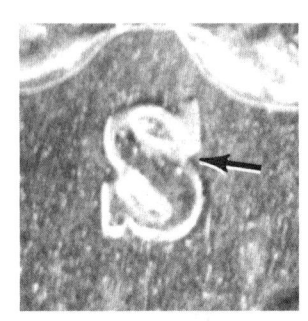

8 R S/S

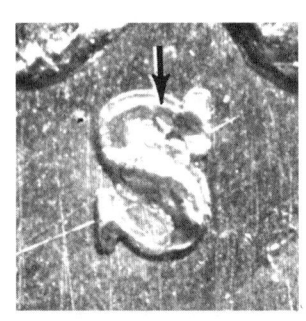

6 R S/S

334

1897-P

A full strike and good luster is typical for this date. A few minor die varieties exist but none are significant. Proof-likes are fairly scarce and generally have little contrast. Proofs have excellent contrast and are fully struck.

1   III²1 • C³a (Normal Die)   (189)   I-1   R-2
Obverse III²1 – Normal die of III² type.
Reverse C³a – Normal die of C³ type.

1A   III²1 • C³a (Pitted Reverse)   (190)   I-2   R-5
Reverse C³a – Die is pitted to left below the eagle's tail feathers and in the lower left wreath.

2   III²2 • C³a (Doubled 18)   (190)   I-2   R-3
Obverse III²2 – Doubled 18 in date. 1 doubled as thin line well below base. 8 in date doubled strongly at bottom outside and top inside of lower loop. Date set further left than normal.

3   III²3 • C³a (Doubled 1)   (190)   I-2   R-3
Obverse III²3 – 1 in date doubled below top crossbar.

4   III²4 • C³a (Doubled 7)   I-2   R-3
Obverse III²4 – 7 is doubled at top left serif and as a fine line just above top of 7.

5   III²5 • C³a (Doubled 18)   (188)   I-2   R-3
Obverse III²5 – 18 in date doubled. 1 is doubled as a short horizontal spike just below the upper crossbar. 8 doubled slightly at top inside of both loops.

6   III²6 • C³a (Near Date)   I-2   R-3
Obverse III²6 – Date set further left than normal.

6A   III²6 • C³a (Near Date, Pitted Reverse)   (190)   I-2   R-3
Reverse C³a – Pitted die below eagle's tail feathers as in VAM 1A.

7   III²7 • C³a (Slanted Date)   I-2   R-3
Obverse III²7 – Date slanted with 1 very close to rim.

8   III²8 • C³a (Doubled Left Stars)   I-3   R-4
Obverse III²8 – Normal date. All left stars doubled strongly towards rim.

1A R Pitted Reverse

2 O Doubled 18

3 O Doubled 1

4 O Doubled 7

5 O Doubled 18

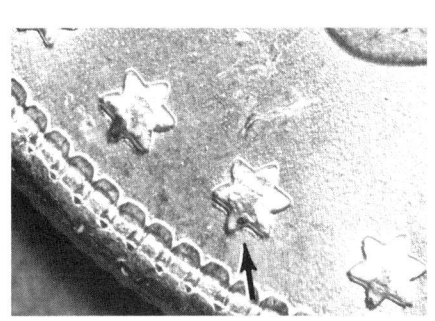

8 O Doubled Stars

1897-P / 1897-O

7 O Slanted Date

1897-O

A touch of weakness in the strike is typical for this issue although specimens can be found with flat strikes and full strikes. Luster is generally dull. A few die varieties exist but none are significant. Proof-likes are extremely rare comparable to the rarity of the 1896-O. Generally the contrast is light although a few cameos are known.

1   III²1 • C³a (Normal Die)   (181)   I-1   R-2
Obverse III²1 – Normal die of III² type.
Reverse C³a – Normal die of C³ type with medium III O mint mark centered and upright.

2   III²1 • C³b (O Tilted Right)   (181)   I-2   R-3
Reverse C³b – Normal die of C³ type with III O mint mark set high and tilted right.

3   III²1 • C³c (O Set High)   (181)   I-2   R-3
Reverse C³c – Normal die with III O mint mark set upright and high.

4   III²2 • C³b (Doubled 7)   (181)   I-2   R-4
Obverse III²2 – 7 in date doubled at very bottom. Date set further left than normal.

5   III²1 • C³d (O Set High and Left)   (181)   I-2   R-3
Reverse C³d – Normal die with III O mint mark set high and to left.

6   III²3 • C³e (Near Date)   (181)   I-2   R-3
Obverse III²3 – Date set further left than normal.
Reverse C³e – Normal die with III O mint mark set high and slightly left with tilt to right.

7   III²3 • C³c (Near Date, High O)   (181)   I-2   R-3

2 R O Tilted Right    3 R O Set High    4 O Doubled 7

5 R O Set High and Left    6 R O Set High, Tilted Right

1897-S

The strike is usually full and the luster good. A few minor die varieties exist and only VAM 4 with the doubled 1-7 is of some significance because of the large separation in the doubling. Proof-likes are fairly available and usually have good cameo contrast.

1   III²1 • C³a (Normal Die)   (190)   I-1   R-2
Obverse III²1 – Normal die of III² type.
Reverse C³a – Normal die of C³ type with a medium IV S mint mark centered and upright.

2   III²2 • C³a (Doubled 18)   I-2   R-4
Obverse III²2 – 18 in date doubled. The 1 has a short spike just below the top crossbar. The 8 is doubled inside the top loop.

3   III²1 • C³b (S Tilted Right)   I-2   R-3
Reverse C³b – IV S mint mark centered and tilted slightly to right.

4   III²3 • C³a (Doubled 1-7)   (186)   I-3   R-4
Obverse III²3 – 1-7 in date doubled. The 1 has a long horizontal line well below the top crossbar. 7 is doubled at top and shows as a thin broken line.

5   III²4 • C³a (Doubled 1)   (187)   I-2   R-3
Obverse III²4 – 1 doubled slightly at bottom of upper crossbar.

6   III²4 • C³b (Doubled 1)   I-2   R-3

7   III²5 • C³a (Doubled 1, Tilted 7)   I-3   R-4
Obverse III²5 – 1 doubled at very top on surface. 7 tilted to left. Date set much further left than normal.

8   III²1 • C³c (S Set High)   (190)   I-2   R-3
Reverse C³c – IV S mint mark set slightly high.

9   III²6 • C³a (Near Date)   (190)   I-2   R-3
Obverse III²6 – Date set further left than normal.

10   III²6 • C³b (Near Date, S Tilted Right)   (190)   I-2   R-3

11   III²7 • C³a (Doubled 1-9)   (190)   I-2   R-3
Obverse III²7 – Doubled 1-9 in date. 1 doubled slightly just below upper crossbar. 9 doubled at top inside of upper loop.

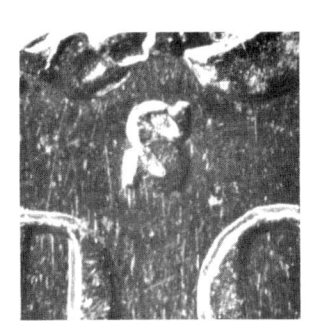

2 O Doubled 18

3 R S Tilted Right

5 O Doubled 1

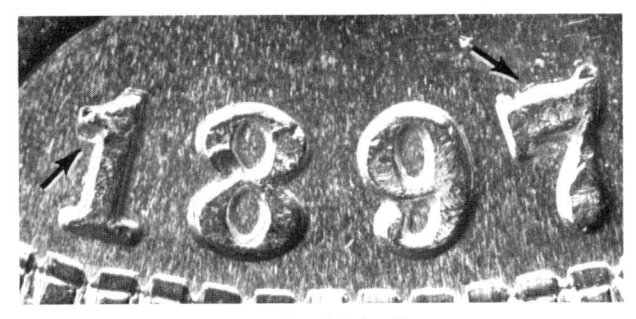

4 O Doubled 1-7

7 O Near Date, Tilted 7

1897-S / 1898-P

7 O Doubled 1

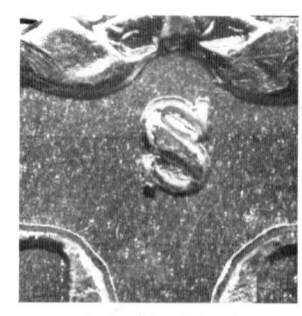

8 R S Set High

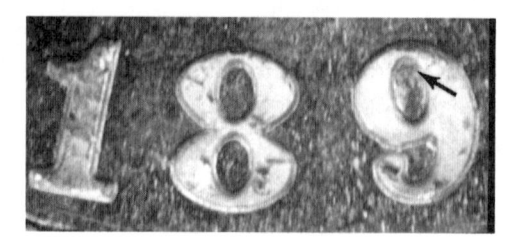

11 O Doubled 1-9

1898-P

This issue has a good strike and good luster. A few die varieties exist but none are significant. Proof-likes are fairly available but generally have little contrast. Proofs are generally of high quality with full strike and very deep cameos.

1   III²1 • C³a (Open 9)   (189)   I-1   R-2
     Obverse III²1 – Normal die of III² type with open 9.
     Reverse C³a – Normal die of C³ type.

2   III²2 • C³a (Closed 9)   I-1   R-2
     Obverse III²2 – Normal die of III² type with closed 9.

3   III²3 • C³a (Near Date)   (190)   1-2   R-3
     Obverse III²3 – Date set further left than normal. Open and closed 9's.

4   III²4 • C³a (Doubled 8)   I-2   R-4
     Obverse III²4 – Second 8 in date doubled strongly at bottom left outside. Date set further left than normal. Closed 9.

5   III²5 • C³a (Doubled 8)   (189)   I-2   R-3
     Obverse III²5 – Second 8 in date doubled at top inside of both loops and on lower right outside of upper loop.

6   III²6 • C³a (Doubled First 8)   (189)   I-2   R-3
     Obverse III²6 – First 8 in date doubled slightly at bottom left outside of lower loop as a thin curved line on field.

7   III²7 • C³a (Doubled Date)   (189)   I-2   R-3
     Obverse III²7 – Entire date is doubled. 1 doubled at top left and right of bottom crossbar. 898 all doubled at bottom inside of both loops and top outside of upper loops.

8   III²8 • C³a (Doubled 1)   (190)   I-2   R-3
     Obverse III²8 – 1 doubled below upper crossbar.

9   III²9 – C³a (Slanted Date)   (189)   I-2   R-3
     Obverse III²9 – Date slanted with 1 closest to rim.

10   III²10 • C³a (Near Date, Doubled Second 8)   (189)   I-2   R-3
     Obverse III²10 – Second 8 in date doubled at top inside and lower right inside of both loops. Date set further left than normal.

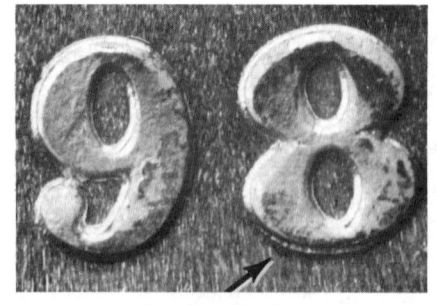

4 O Doubled 8

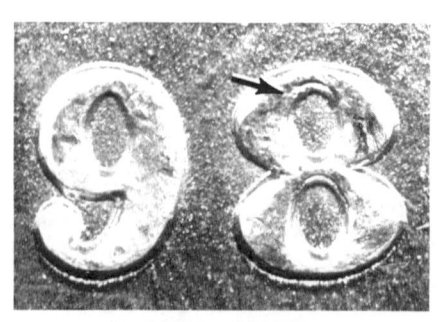

5 O Doubled 8

6 O Doubled First 8

338

7 O Doubled Date

8 O Doubled 1

9 O Slanted Date

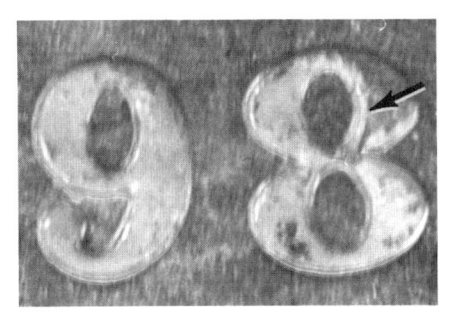

10 O Doubled Second 8

1898-O

Generally the strike is fairly full although it is not uncommon to find slightly weak and weak struck specimens. Luster is generally good. Many thousands of uncirculated bags of 1898-O to 1904-O mint were released by the Treasury in 1962-1964 of these formerly scarce to rare dates. The 1898-O is slightly less available now than the 1904-O which were the two dates released in largest quantities. A number of minor die varieties exist but none are significant. Proof-likes are fairly available and most have little to moderate contrast although a few fairly contrasty proof-likes are known.

1	III²1 • C³a (Normal Die)	(181)	I-1	R-2

Obverse III²1 – Normal die of III² type with open 9.
Reverse C³a – Normal die of C³ type with medium III O mint mark centered and upright.

2	III²2 • C³a (Doubled 8 Bottom)	(181)	I-2	R-3

Obverse III²2 – Second 8 in date doubled slightly at top and right inside of upper loop and top inside and bottom right outside of lower loop. Date set much further left than normal.

3	III²3 • C³a Doubled 18 Top)	(181)	I-2	R-3

Obverse III²3 – 18 in date doubled. 1 doubled at very top as notch. Second 8 in date doubled slightly at top left and bottom right inside of upper loop.

4	III²1 • C³b (O Set High)	(181)	I-2	R-3

Reverse C³b – III O mint mark set high and upright.

5	III²1 • C³c (O Tilted Right)	(181)	1-2	R-3

Reverse C³c – III O mint mark centered and tilted to the right.

6	III²4 • C³a (Near Date)	(181)	I-2	R-3

Obverse III²4 – Date set further left than normal.

7	III²4 • C³b (Near Date)	(181)	I-2	R-3
8	III²4 • C³c (Near Date)	(181)	I-2	R-3

1898-O

9   III² 5 • C³ a (Doubled 8)   (181)   I-2   R-3
Obverse III² 5 – Near date not as close as III² 4 obverse with second 8 doubled slightly at top left outside of upper loop and top inside of lower loop.

10   III² 5 • C³ d (Doubled 8)   (181)   I-2   R-3
Reverse C³ d – III O mint mark set high and tilted very far to right.

11   III² 6 • C³ d (Doubled 898)   (181)   I-2   R-3
Obverse III² 6 – Near date not as close as III² 4 obverse. Doubled 898 in date. 89 doubled slightly at bottom outside of lower loops. Second 8 doubled slightly on right inside of upper loop and top inside and bottom right outside of lower loop.

12   III² 7 • C³ b (Doubled 8)   (181)   I-2   R-3
Obverse III² 7 – Second 8 in date doubled slightly at top outside of upper loop and strongly on bottom inside of upper loop as thick crescent.

13   III² 8 • C³ b (Very Near Date)   (181)   I-2   R-3
Obverse III² 8 – Date set much further left than normal. Second 8 tripled slightly at top right inside of lower loop.

2 O Doubled 8 Bottom

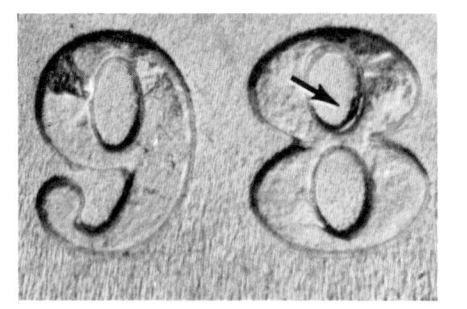

3 O Doubled 8 Top

4 R O Set High

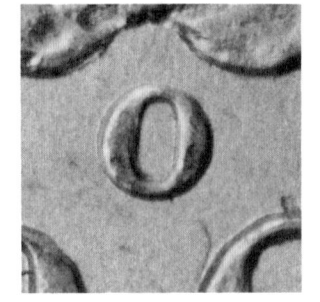

5 R O Tilted Right

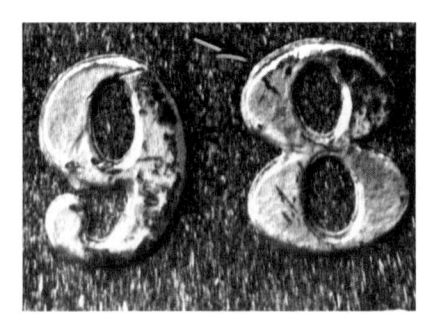

9 O Doubled 8

11 O Doubled 898

10 R O Set High Tilted Right

12 O Doubled 8

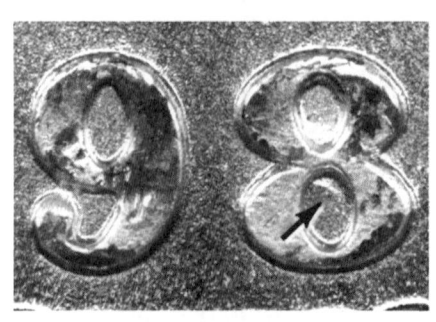

13 O Tripled Second 8

14	**III² 9 • C³ a (Doubled First 8)**	(181)	I-2	R-3

Obverse III² 9 – Date set very near with first 8 doubled slightly on bottom right outside of lower loop.

15	**III² 10 • C³ b (Doubled 1-8, O Set High)**	(181)	I-2	R-3

Obverse III² 10 – Doubled 1-8 in date. 1 doubled on surface at very top. Second 8 doubled at top and right inside of upper loop and top inside of lower loop. Top of 18 shallow.

16	**III² 11 • C³ b (Doubled Second 8, O Set High)**	(181)	I-2	R-3

Obverse III² 11 – Second 8 in date doubled at bottom inside of upper loop.

17	**III² 12 • C³ b (Doubled Second 8, O Set High)**	(181)	I-2	R-3

Obverse III² 12 – Second 8 in date doubled at top right inside of upper loop and top inside and bottom right outside of lower loop. Date at left side of normal position.

18	**III² 13 • C³ a (Doubled First 8)**	(181)	I-2	R-3

Obverse III² 13 – First 8 doubled slightly at top inside of both loops.

19	**III² 9 • C³ c (Doubled First 8, O Tilted Right)**	(181)	I-2	R-3

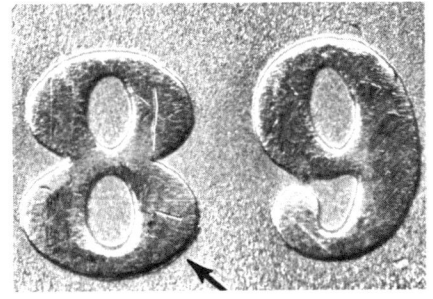

14 O Doubled First 8

15 O Doubled 1-8

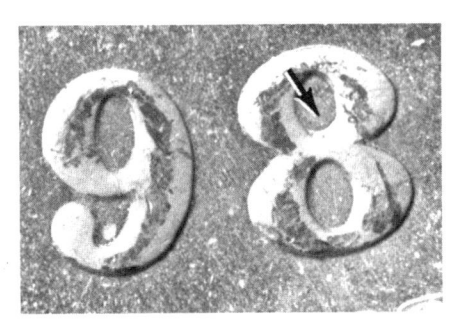

16 O Doubled Second 8

17 O Doubled Second 8

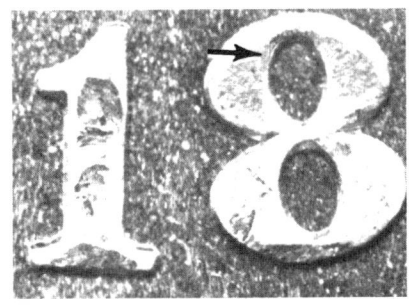

18 O Doubled First 8

1898-S

The strike for this issue is generally fairly full but weakly struck specimens may also be encountered. Luster is generally excellent. A few minor die varieties exist but only VAM 6 with a fairly strongly doubled "S" mint mark with quite a bit of separation downward is of some significance. Proof-likes are fairly scarce and generally have little contrast although a few cameos are known to exist.

1	**III² 1 • C³ a (Closed 9)**		I-1	R-2

Obverse III² 1 – Normal die of III² type with closed 9. The bottom loop of the 9 touches the upper loop.
Reverse C³ a – Normal die of C³ type with a medium IV S mint mark, centered and upright.

2	**III² 2 • C³ a (Open 9)**		I-1	R-3

Obverse III² 2 – Normal die with open 9. The lower loop of the 9 does not touch the upper loop.

3	**III² 5 • C³ b (S/S Center, Doubled 1)**		I-2	R-3

Obverse III² 5 – 1 in date doubled below upper crossbar.
Reverse C³ b – IV S mint mark doubled below center shaft.

341

1898-S

4	III²1 • C³c (S/S Right)	(187)		I-3	R-4

Reverse C³c – IV S mint mark doubled to right of top serif and below bottom serif.

5	III²3 • C³d (Doubled 1)	(188)		I-2	R-3

Obverse III²3 – 1 in date doubled slightly just below crossbar. Closed 9.
Reverse C³d – IV S mint mark tilted slightly to the right.

6	III²4 • C³e (Doubled Date, S/S Down)	(187)		I-3	R-4

Obverse III²4 – Entire date is doubled. 1 is slightly doubled below upper crossbar. 898 are doubled at top inside of upper loops. Date set further left than normal. Closed 9.
Reverse C³e – IV S mint mark doubled down with original showing as a curved horizontal line in center of upper loop, slanting line below center shaft and curved horizontal line below lower loop, ending in an extended part of the lower loop on the right and doubled lower serif.

7	III²1 • C³f (S/S Upright)	(188)		I-3	R-4

Reverse C³f – IV S mint mark doubled to right of top serif and below bottom serif but more centered and upright than VAM 4.

8	III²5 • C³d (Near Date, S Tilted Right)	(188)		I-2	R-3

Obverse III²5 – Date set further left than normal.

8A	III²5 • C³d, (Near Date, S Tilted Right)	(187)		I-2	R-4

Reverse C³d – Two thick die gouges through wreath bow loop.

9	III²6 • C³d (Doubled 8, S Tilted Right)	(187)		I-2	R-4

Obverse III²6 – Second 8 doubled at top outside of upper loop. Date set further left than normal.
Reverse C³d – Two thick die gouges through wreath bow loop.

10	III²7 • C³g (Near Slanted Date, S Tilted Far Right)	(187)		I-3	R-4

Obverse III²7 – Near date with slight slant with 1 closest to rim.
Reverse C³g – Medium IV S mint mark centered and tilted very far to the right.

11	III²7 • C³a (Near Slanted Date)	(187)		I-2	R-3
12	III²8 • C³h (Doubled Second 8, S/S High)	(186)		I-2	R-3

Obverse III²8 – Second 8 doubled at top inside of lower loop. Date set further left than normal.
Reverse C³h – IV S mint mark set high and doubled to right of top serif and left side of bottom serif.

13	III²1 • C³d (S Tilted Right)	(187)		I-2	R-3

3 R S/S Center   4 R S/S Right   5 O Doubled 1   5 R S Tilted Right

6 O Doubled Date   6 R S/S Down   7 R S/S Upright

342

1898-S / 1899-P

8A R Die Gouge in Bow

9 O Doubled Second 8

10 O Near Slanted Date

10 R S Slanted Far Right

1899-P

The strike is usually fairly good although slightly weakly struck specimens are around. Luster is generally good. Although a low mintage issue, it is not exceptionally scarce. Apparently it escaped being significantly melted. It is highly unlikely that the date continued to be struck into 1900 as it has always been the policy, as required by law, for business strike dies to be dated the year used. Only a few die varieties are known which tend to confirm only a few dies were used for a low total mintage. None of the die varieties are significant however. Proof-likes are fairly scarce and most have moderate contrast although a few very deep mirror cameos are known. Proofs have fairly good contrast but not as much as the few preceding dates.

1   III²1 • C³a (Normal Die)   I-1   R-3
    Obverse III²1 – Normal die of III² type with open 9's.
    Reverse C³a – Normal die of C³ type.

2   III²2 • C³a (Doubled 9)   I-2   R-4
    Obverse III²2 – Second 9 in date doubled at top.

3   III²3 • C³a (Closed 9's)   I-1   R-3
    Obverse III²3 – Normal die with closed 9's.

4   III²4 • C³a (Doubled 189)   (189)   I-2   R-3
    Obverse III²4 – Doubled 189 in date. 1 is doubled slightly below base. 8 is doubled on right outside of both loops as a thin arc to the right of the upper loop and a thin line to the lower right of the lower loop. First 9 doubled faintly on inside of lower loop.

5   III²5 • C³a (Doubled 18-9)   (188)   I-2   R-3
    Obverse III²5 – Doubled 18-9 in date. 1 doubled as a short horizontal line below upper crossbar. 8 doubled at top inside of upper loop and at bottom outside of lower loop. Second 9 doubled at top outside of upper loop.

6   III²6 • C³a (Open and Closed 9's)   (190)   I-2   R-3
    Obverse III²6 – First 9 closed and second 9 open lower loop.

1899-P / 1899-O

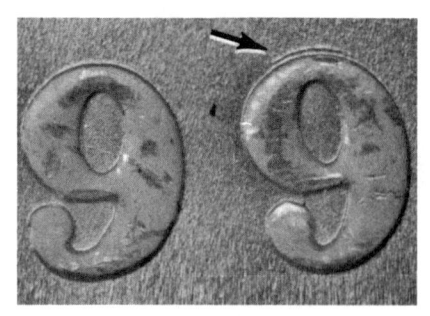

2 O Doubled 9

4 O Doubled 189

5 O Doubled 18-9

6 O Open and Closed 9's

1899-O

Generally the 1899-O is well struck. Some weak strikes are around because of the large mintage and some dies were not basined as well as others or the striking pressure was not adequately high in the coining presses. Luster tends to be very good. Quite a few minor die varieties exist. VAM's 4, 5 and 6 have a small "O" mint mark and are quite scarce in any grade and command a significant premium. Only a few uncirculated small "O" specimens are known. Proof-likes are fairly scarce and usually have little contrast although a few very deep mirror cameos exist.

1	III² 1 • C³ a (Open 9's)		I-1	R-2

Obverse III² 1 – Normal die of III² type with open 9's in date.
Reverse C³ a – Normal die of C³ type with medium III O mint mark centered and upright.

2	III² 2 • C³ b (Closed 9's)		I-1	R-2

Obverse III² 2 – Normal die with closed 9's.
Reverse C³ b – Normal die with III O mint mark tilted slightly to the right and set slightly high.

2A	III² 2 • C³ b (Closed 9's)	(181)	I-1	R-2

Reverse C³ b – Two large die breaks in second leaf cluster from top of left wreath.

3	III² 1 • C³ b (O Tilted Right)		I-2	R-3

4	III² 2 • C³ c (Small O Tilted Right)		I-3	R-4

Obverse III² 2 – Some specimens show die chips in lower loop of second 9.
Reverse C³ c – Normal die with small I O mint mark tilted to the right and set slightly high and to right.

5	III² 2 • C³ d (Small O Set Upright)		I-3	R-4

Reverse C³ d – Normal die with small I O mint mark set high with slight tilt to right.

6	III² 3 • C³ c (Near Date, Small O)	(181)	I-3	R-4

Obverse III² 3 – Date set further left than normal.

7	III² 1 • C³ e (High O)		I-2	R-3

Obverse III² 1 – Some specimens show die chips in lower loop of second 9.
Reverse C³ e – III O mint mark set upright and very high.

1899-O

| 8 | III²4 • C³a (Slanted Date) | | I-2 | R-3 |

Obverse III²4 – Date slanted with second 9 higher than 1. Closed 9's.

| 9 | III²4 • C³b (Slanted Date) | | I-2 | R-3 |
| 10 | III²4 • C³f (Slanted Date) | (188) | I-2 | R-3 |

Reverse C³f – III O mint mark set high and tilted very far to right.

| 11 | III²5 • C³b (Doubled 1) | | I-2 | R-3 |

Obverse III²5 – 1 in date is doubled slightly at bottom of upper crossbar. Open 9's.

| 12 | III²6 • C³b (Doubled 18-9) | | I-2 | R-4 |

Obverse III²6 – 18-9 in date doubled. The 1 is doubled at the bottom on the middle and right side. The 8 is doubled all across the bottom and slightly at the top of both loop openings. Second 9 is doubled as a thin curved line at bottom left inside of top loop opening.

| 13 | III²7 • C³g (Doubled 899, O/O) | | I-2 | R-4 |

Obverse III²7 – Slightly doubled 899 in date. First 8 has hook of curved metal on right inside of lower loop. Lower ball of first 9 doubled slightly on left side of some specimens. Second 9 shows fine curved line on lower right outside of lower loop.
Reverse C³g – Centered III O mint mark doubled slightly on right inside.

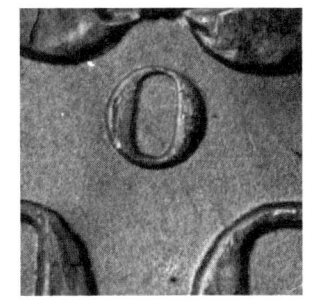

2 R O Tilted Right

4 R O Tilted Right

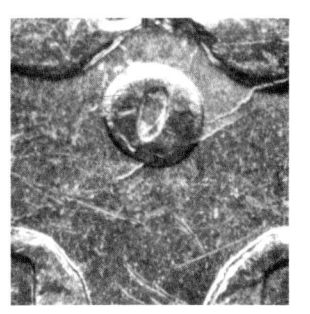

5 R High O

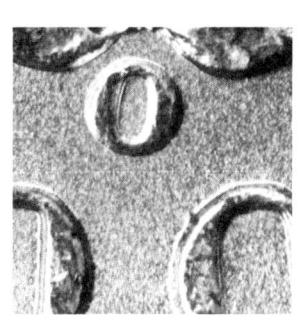

7 R High O

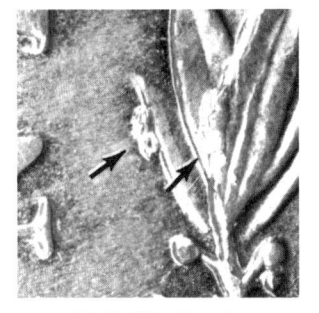

2A R Die Breaks in Wreath

8 O Slanted Date

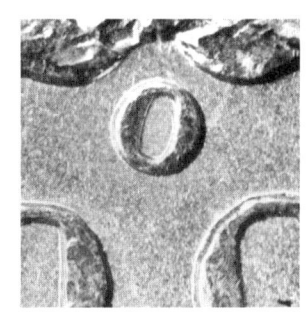

10 R High O Tilted Right

11 O Doubled 1

12 O Doubled 18-9

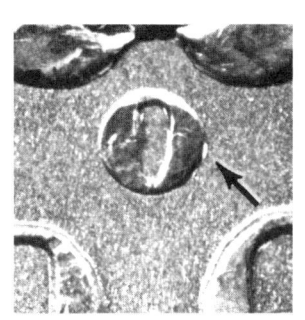

13 R O/O

1899-O

14   III²8 • C³h (Doubled 89, High O)   I-2   R-3
   Obverse III²8 – Slightly doubled 89 in date. 8 and first 9 doubled slightly at top inside of upper loop.
   Reverse C³h – Upright III O mint mark set high and shifted slightly to left.

15   III²9 • C³i (Doubled 1-9, High O)   I-3   R-4
   Obverse III²9 – Doubled 1-9 in date. 1 doubled slightly below upper crossbar. Second 9 doubled strongly at top outside as thin curved arc and at bottom left inside of upper loop. Date set further left than normal.
   Reverse C³i – Upright III O mint mark, set high and shifted slightly to right.

16   III²10 • C³a (Doubled First 9)   I-2   R-3
   Obverse III²10 – First 9 doubled at right side and slightly at left outside of lower loop.

17   III²3 • C³e (Near Date, High O)   (181)   I-2   R-3

18   III²1 • C³f (High O Tilted Right)   (181)   I-2   R-3

19   III²11 • C³b (Slanted Date)   (181)   I-2   R-3
   Obverse III²11 – Date slanted with second 9 higher than 1 but set further left than III²4. Open 9's.

20   III²5 • C³j (Doubled 1 and Reverse)   (189)   I-3   R-3
   Obverse III²5 – First 9 is closed.
   Reverse C³j – III O mint mark set high and tilted to right. Doubled UNITED STATES OF AMERI and motto letters towards rim.

21   III²4 • C³e (Slanted Date, High O)   (181)   I-2   R-3

22   III²12 • C³e (Doubled 899, High O)   (181)   I-2   R-3
   Obverse III²12 – Doubled 899 in date. 8 and first 9 doubled slightly at bottom outside of lower loop. Second 9 doubled slightly at top outside of upper loop. Date set further left than normal.

23   III²2 • C³a (Closed 9's)   (189)   I-2   R-2

24   III²13 • C³e (Doubled 9, High O)   (181)   I-2   R-3
   Obverse III²13 – Second 9 doubled as a thin line above top loop.

25   III²14 • C³a (Doubled 189)   (188)   I-2   R-3
   Obverse III²14 – Doubled 189 in date. 1 doubled slightly below base. 8 doubled at right inside of upper and lower loops. First 9 doubled at right inside of lower loop.

26   III²1 • C³k (Doubled Reverse)   (181)   I-2   R-3
   Reverse C³k – Legend and motto letters doubled towards rim along with wreath outside edge. III O mint mark set slightly high and upright.

27   III²15 • C³f (Doubled 9)   (181)   I-2   R-3
   Obverse III²15 – Second 9 doubled at lower left outside of upper loop as a thin line.

28   III²16 • C³e (Doubled 1-9, High O)   (181)   I-2   R-3
   Obverse III²16 – Doubled 1-9 in date. 1 doubled below upper crossbar. Second 9 doubled slightly at very top outside of upper loops. Date set on left side of normal position.

29   III²17 • C³a (Doubled Second 9)   (181)   I-2   R-3
   Obverse III²17 – Second 9 doubled on top inside of upper loop.

13 O Doubled 889

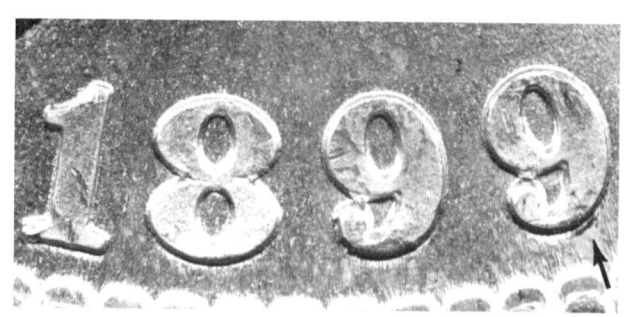

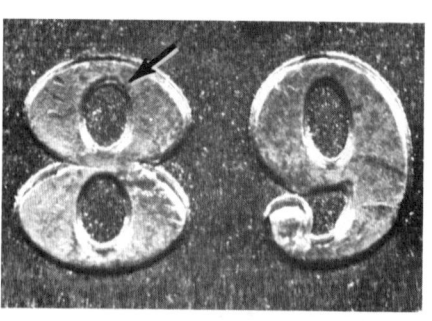

14 O Doubled 89

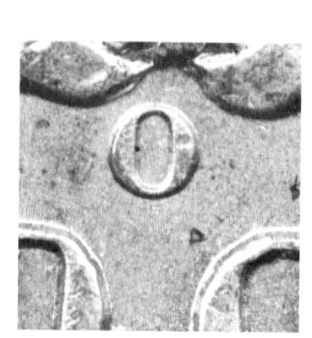

14 R High O Shifted Left

1899-O

15 O Doubled 1-9

15 R High O Shifted Right

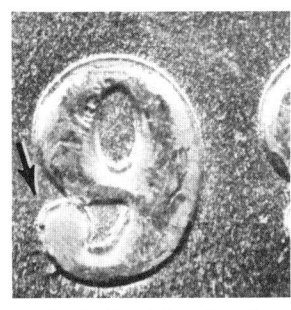

16 O Doubled First 9

19 O Slanted Date

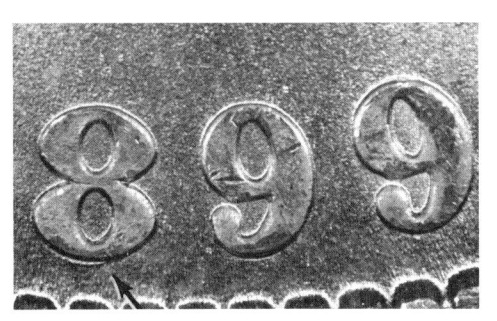

22 O Doubled 889

20 R Doubled Legend

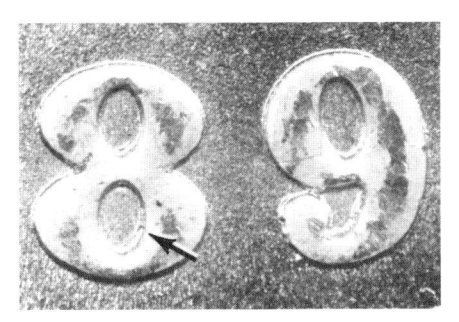

25 O Doubled 89

26 R Doubled Legend Letters

24 O Doubled 9

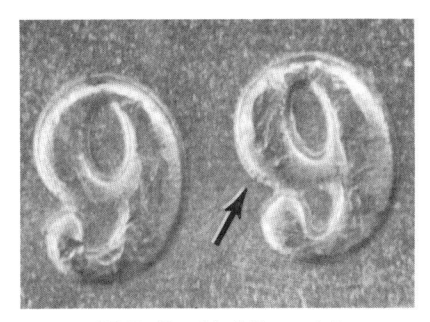

27 O Doubled Second 9

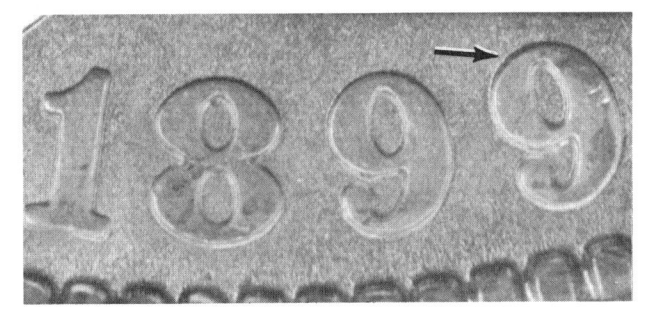

28 O Doubled 1-9

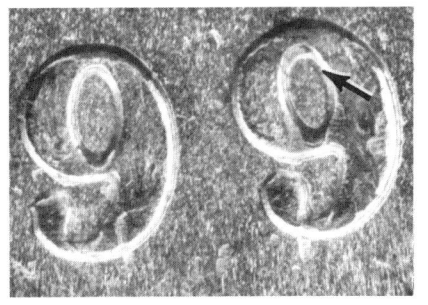

29 O Doubled Second 9

1899-S

A full strike and good luster is typical for the 1899-S. A few minor die varieties exist but the only significant one is VAM 7 with a strongly doubled 1-99. Proof-likes make up a fair proportion of the issue but they have little contrast.

1 III²1 • C³a (Narrow S) — I-1 R-2
Obverse III²1 – Normal die of III² type with open 9's.
Reverse C³a – Normal Die of C³ type with narrow, medium IV S mint mark, centered and upright.

2 III²1 • C³b (Wide S) — I-1 R-2
Reverse C³b – Normal die with wide, large V S mint mark centered.

3 III²1 • C³c (S/S Center) — I-2 R-4
Reverse C³c – Normal die with IV S mint mark tilted to the right and slightly doubled below upper loop.

4 III²1 • C³d (Spiked S) — I-2 R-4
Reverse C³d – Normal die with IV S mint mark tilted to the right with a wide spike at top.

5 III²1 • C³e (S Tilted Right) (186) — I-2 R-3
Reverse C³e – Normal die with IV S mint mark centered and tilted right.

6 III²2 • C³d (Doubled 99) (188) — I-2 R-3
Obverse III²2 – 99 in date doubled. First 9 doubled at bottom right. Second 9 doubled inside the lower loop. Open 9's.

7 III²3 • C³a (Doubled 1-99) — I-3 R-5
Obverse III²3 – Doubled 1-99 in date. 1 is doubled below upper serif. First and second 9 are both strongly doubled, shifted right and show as spot to right of lower loop end, vertical curved line on left side of upper loop opening and horizontal curved line at top right outside.

8 III²4 • C³b (Doubled 9) — I-2 R-3
Obverse III²4 – First 9 doubled showing as a thin broken and curved line on right inside of lower loop.

9 III²5 • C³f (Wide S Tilted Right) — I-2 R-3
Obverse III²5 – Normal die of III² type with closed 9's.
Reverse C³f – V S mint mark centered and tilted right.

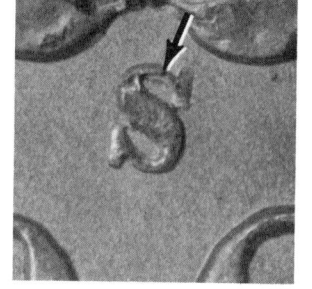

3 R S/S Center

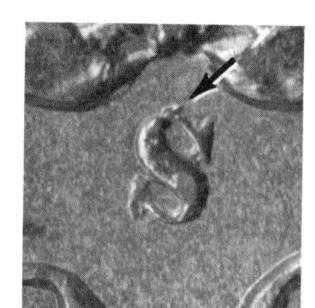

4 R Spiked S

5 R S Tilted Right

6 O Doubled 99

7 O Doubled 1-99

8 O Doubled 9

9 R Tilted S

10	III²1 • C³g (S/S Top Serif)		I-2	R-4

Reverse C³g – Normal die with IV S mint mark set slightly high and tilted right with top serif doubled as a vertical line at top left side and spike inside of lower loop.

11	III²6 • C³e (Near Date, S Tilted Right)		I-2	R-3

Obverse III²6 – Date set further left than normal.

12	III²1 • C³h (High S, Tilted Right)	(184)	I-2	R-3

Reverse C³h – IV S mint mark set high and tilted to right. Some specimens show die chip in wreath opposite NI of UNITED.

13	III²7 • C³a (Far Date)	(187)	I-2	R-3

Obverse III²7 – Date set further right than normal.

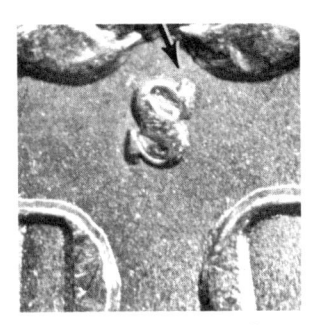

10 R S/S Top Serif

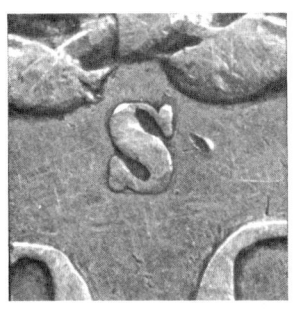

12 R High S Tilted Right

1900-P

The usual strike on this issue is slightly weak and fully struck specimens are fairly difficult to locate. Luster is usually fairly good but can be dull. Quite a few minor die varieties exist but only VAM 11 with slightly doubled bottom of eagle's wings and tail feathers plus arrow shafts is very significant. In this year a slightly modified reverse design type, C⁴, was introduced with less articulated eagle's breast feathers and other minor differences. It was used on some 1900-P, S, 1901-P, O, S, 1902-O and all 1902-P, S, 1903 and 1904. Proof-likes are fairly scarce and are invariably brilliant with little contrast. Some of these show noticeable die polishing lines in the fields. Proofs generally have good contrast but not all of them.

1	III²1 • C³a (Normal Die)	(189)	I-1	R-2

Obverse III²1 – Normal die of III² type.
Reverse C³a – Normal die of C³ type.

2	III²1 • C⁴a (Normal Die)		I-1	R-2

Reverse C⁴a – Normal die of C⁴ type.

3	III²2 • C³a (Doubled Date)		I-2	R-3

Obverse III²2 – Entire date doubled to ten o'clock.

4	III²3 • C³a (Low Date)		I-2	R-3

Obverse III²3 – 1 in date closer to rim than normal.

3 O Doubled Date

4 O Low Date

1900-P

5 III²4 • C³a (Near Date) (187, 188, 189) I-2 R-3
Obverse III²4 – Date set further left than normal. Open 9.

6 III²5 • C³a (Near Date Set Low) (189) I-2 R-3
Obverse III²5 – Date set further left than normal with 1 closer to rim than normal.

7 III²6 • C³a (Very Near Date Set Low) (189) I-2 R-3
Obverse III²6 – Date set very much further left than normal with numerals set low next to rim.

8 III²7 • C³a (Doubled 1) (189) I-2 R-3
Obverse III²7 – 1 in date doubled below upper crossbar, slightly below lower crossbar and on lower left side of vertical shaft. Closed 9.

9 III²8 • C³a (Doubled 1-0) (187) I-2 R-3
Obverse III²8 – Doubled 1-0 in date. 1 doubled at bottom of upper crossbar. First 0 doubled at top outside. Open 9 variety. Date set further left than normal.

10 III²9 • C³a (Doubled 1-00) I-2 R-4
Obverse III²9 – 1-00 in date doubled. 1 is doubled strongly at bottom of upper crossbar and bottom crossbar is slightly doubled at bottom right and top left and right. First 0 is doubled slightly at top right outside. Second 0 is tripled slightly at top left and right outside and is doubled all across top outside. Open 9 variety. Date set further left than normal.

11 III²1 • C⁴/C³a (Doubled Eagle, 2 Olive Reverse) (189) I-4 R-5
Reverse C⁴/C³a – Extra olive to right of olive connected to olive branch. Doubling on right side of olive leaves in top cluster and first two leaves in the lower cluster, bottom of arrow feathers, shaft and arrow heads, first four tail feather ends, feathers on lower part of eagle's right wing, all of eagle's left wing, eagle's nostril and eye, bottom of top leaves on right wreath and right side of GOD WE-TRU.

12 III²10 • C³a (Doubled Date) I-3 R-4
Obverse III²10 – All date digits strongly doubled to twelve o'clock. 1 doubled at top of upper and lower crossbar. 9 doubled at top outside of upper loop and bottom inside of both upper and lower loops. Both 0's doubled at top outside and bottom inside. Date set much further left than normal.

13 III²11 • C³a (Doubled 1-0) (188) I-2 R-3
Obverse III²11 – Doubled 1-0 in date. 1 is doubled slightly at bottom of base. First 0 doubled slightly at bottom outside. Date set further left than normal and slanted with 1 close to rim.

14 III²12 • C³a (Near Slanted Date) (189) I-2 R-3
Obverse III²12 – Date set further left than normal and slanted with 1 close to rim.

15 III²13 • C³a (Slanted Date) (189) I-2 R-3
Obverse III²13 – Date in normal lateral position but slanted with 1 next to rim.

16 III²1 • C⁴/C³b (2 Olive Reverse) (189) I-3 R-3
Reverse C⁴/C³b – Extra olive to right of olive connected to olive branch. Doubling at base of left olive leaf cluster, back of lower arrow head, right side of eagle's nostril and eye, and upper feathers of eagle's left wing. Pitting about eagle's neck.

17 III²14 • C³a (Near Date, Doubled Last 0) (189) I-2 R-3
Obverse III²14 – Second 0 doubled slightly at top outside. Date set further left than normal.

18 III²1 • C⁴/C³c (2 Olive Reverse) (189) I-3 R-3
Reverse C⁴/C³c – Extra olive to right of olive connected to olive branch. Doubling at base of all three olive leaf clusters, top of second arrow feather from top, back of lower arrow head, on right of two innermost right wing feathers next to leg, right side of eagle's nostril and eye, and upper feathers of eagle's left wing.

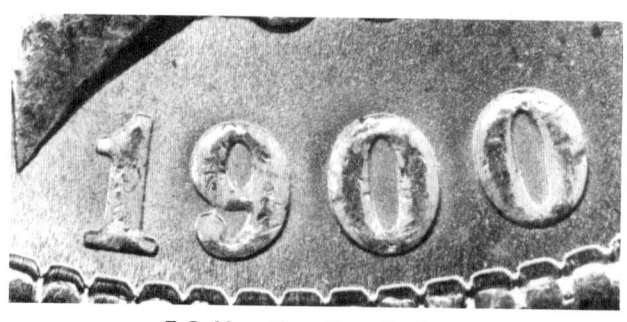

6 O Near Date Set Low

7 O Very Near Date Set Low

1900-P

8 O Doubled 1

9 O Doubled 1-0

11 R C⁴/C³

10 O Doubled 1-00

11 R Doubled Eagle

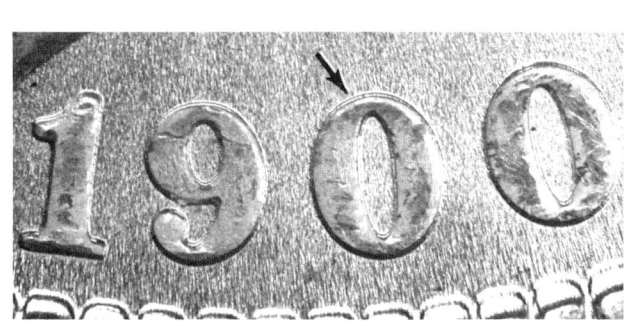

12 O Doubled Date

11 R C⁴/C³

13 O Doubled 1-0

16 R C⁴/C³

17 O Doubled O

14 O Near Slanted Date

15 O Slanted Date

351

1900-P

| 19 | III²1 • C⁴/C³ d (2 Olive Reverse) | (189) | I-2 | R-3 |

Reverse C⁴/C³ d – Extra olive to right of olive connected to olive branch. Doubling at base of left and lower olive leaf clusters, back of lower arrow head, and on right of two innermost right wing feathers next to leg.

| 20 | III²15 • C³a (Near Date, Doubled First 0) | (190) | I-2 | R-3 |

Obverse III² 15 – First 0 in date doubled at lower inside as a curved thick bar. Date set further left than normal.

| 21 | III²16 • C³a (Doubled 900) | (190) | I-2 | R-3 |

Obverse III² 16 – Doubled 900 in date. 9 doubled faintly at very bottom right outside. Both 0's doubled at lower right inside.

| 22 | III²17 • C³a (Doubled 19) | (187) | I-2 | R-3 |

Obverse III² 17 – Doubled 19 in date. 1 doubled faintly at bottom right of lower crossbar. 9 doubled at lower left outside of upper loop and at bottom outside of lower loop. Date set further left than normal.

| 23 | III²18 • C³a (Doubled Stars) | (188) | I-2 | R-3 |

Obverse III² 18 – First two stars on left and right doubled towards rim. Date set low and further left than normal.

18 R 2 Olive Reverse

19 R 2 Olive Reverse

20 O Doubled First 0

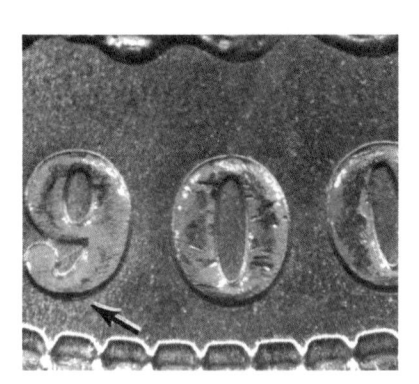

21 O Doubled 900

22 O Doubled 19

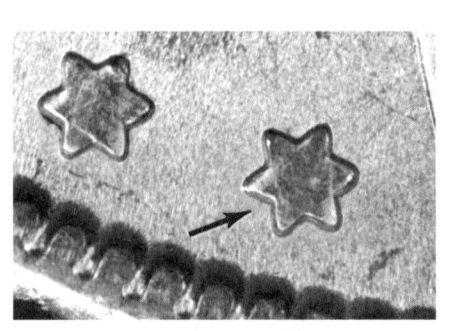

23 O Doubled Stars

1900-O

Generally the strike on this issue is fairly strong but weakly struck specimens are also around because of the high mintage. The luster is usually good. Quite a few minor die varieties exist. The most significant are the O/CC mint marks, VAM's 7-12. Five CC reverse dies left over from the Carson City mint when it closed in 1893 were modified in 1900 by punching the O mint mark over the CC mint mark. Various amounts of the CC remnants show from two low curved lines to the entire "C" s. All O/CC coins command a significant premium and VAM 9 is particularly scarce while VAM's 8, 11 and 12 are the most frequently encountered. VAM 29A has a very large high die break from 19 to the rim and is very scarce and significant. VAM 5 has a small "O" mint mark and is a significant die variety. However, it is very scarce and known only in low circulated grades. Proof-likes are fairly scarce and have little contrast. The O/CC are unknown in full proof-like. Many proof-likes show fine die polishing lines in the fields.

1   III²1 • C³a (Closed 9)   I-1   R-2
     Obverse III²1 – Normal die of III² type with closed 9.
     Reverse C³a – Normal die of C³ type with medium III O mint mark centered and upright.

2   III²2 • C³a (Open 9)   I-1   R-2
     Obverse III²2 – Normal die of with open 9.

2A   III²2 • C³a (Polished Wheat)   (187)   I-3   R-3
     Obverse III²2 – Heavy die polishing lines around wheat stalks.

3   III²5 • C³c (O Tilted Right)   (181)   I-2   R-3
     Obverse III²5 – Date set further left than normal.
     Reverse C³c – Normal die with III O mint mark tilted slightly to the right.

4   III²5 • C³c (O Tilted Left)   I-2   R-3
     Reverse C³c – Normal die with III O mint mark tilted slightly to the left.

5   III²3 • C³d (Small O)   (181)   I-3   R-5
     Obverse III²3 – Date set much further left than normal. Open 9.
     Reverse C³d – Normal die of C³ type with small I O mint mark, tilted to right.

6   III²6 • C³b (O Tilted Right)   (189)   I-2   R-3

7   III²4 • C³e (O/CC Low)   (181)   I-4   R-7
     Obverse III²4 – First 0 in date doubled slightly at bottom left.
     Reverse C³c – Normal die with III O mint mark, centered and upright punched over CC. The CC mint mark shows as curved lines on the left and right at the bottom of the O.

8   III²5 • C³f (O/O/CC Centered Shifted Left)   (181)   I-5   R-4/5
     Reverse C³f – Normal die with III O mint mark, centered and upright, with doubled O punched over CC. O is doubled at top left outside with notch missing at 11 o'clock in doubling and doubled at bottom inside of opening as a thin curved line. The CC mint mark is centered and shifted left under the O and shows as a thin broken curve on the left and two thick projections on the right connected to the O.

8A   III²5 – C³f (O/O/CC Centered, Shifted Left with Rust Spots)   I-5   R-4
     Obverse III²5 – Die clash marks are evident.
     Reverse C³f – Die rust spots are evident around the mint mark area. Some specimens show clash marks and die polishing in central area.

2A O Polished Wheat 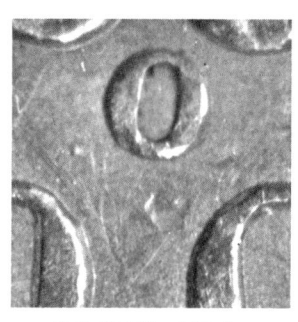   3 R O Tilted Right 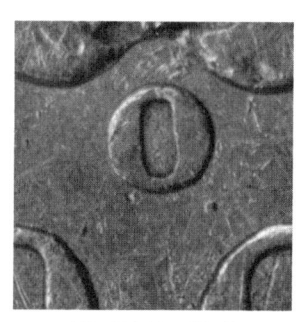   4 R O Tilted Left

1900-O

9   III² 6 • C³ g (O/CC Centered Shifted Right)   (181)   I-4   R-7
Obverse III² 6 – Doubled 900 in date. 9 doubled at top inside of upper loop. Both 0's doubled at top inside. Date set further left than normal and slanted with 0's higher than 1.
Reverse C³ g – Normal die with III O mint mark, centered and upright, punched over CC. The CC mint mark is centered and shifted right under the O and shows as a thin broken curve on the left and two faint projections on the right.

10   III² 5 • C³ e (O/CC Low)   (181)   I-4   R-4/5
Obverse III² 5 – With open 9.

11   III² 3 • C³ i (O/CC High Shifted Left)   (181)   I-4   R-4
Reverse C³ i – III O mint mark, centered and upright, punched over CC. The CC mint mark is high and shifted left under the O and shows as a broad curve on the left and one thick projection on the right connected to the O.

12   III² 5 • C³ j (O/CC High, Shifted Right)   (181)   I-5   R-4/5
Reverse C³ j – III O mint mark centered and upright, punched over CC. The CC mint mark is high and shifted right under the O and shows as a complete thin C high on the left and complete C ends as two thick projections on the right. Heavy horizontal polishing marks are around the wreath bow area.

13   III² 7 • C³ k (Doubled 19-0)   (181)   I-3   R-4
Obverse III² 7 – 19-0 in date doubled. 1 shows short horizontal spike below crossbar. 9 is doubled at top inside of upper loop and slightly at bottom outside. Second 0 doubled strongly at bottom outside. Date set further left than normal. Closed 9.
Reverse C³ k – III O mint mark tilted to the right and set right.

14   III² 8 • C³ l (Doubled 00 Top)   (181)   I-2   R-4
Obverse III² 8 First 0 doubled slightly at bottom outside. Last 0 in date is doubled at top. Open 9 variety. Date is set further left than normal.
Reverse C³ l – Normal die with III O mint mark set high.

15   III² 9 • C³ m (Doubled 00 and Stars)   (189)   I-3   R-4
Obverse III² 9 – Doubled 00 in date. The first 0 is doubled on the lower left inside and lower right outside. Second 0 doubled slightly on lower left inside. First two stars on right doubled at bottom. Closed 9 variety. Date set further left than normal.
Reverse C³ m – III O mint mark set high, upright and shifted slightly left.

16   III² 10 • C³ b (Doubled 1)   (189)   I-2   R-4
Obverse III² 10 – 1 is doubled below upper serif.

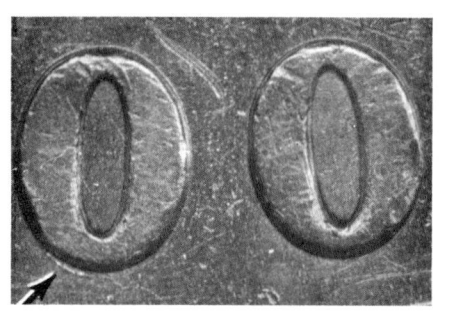

7 O Doubled O

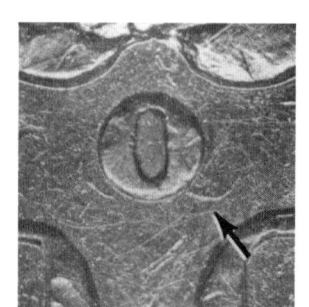

7 R O/CC Low

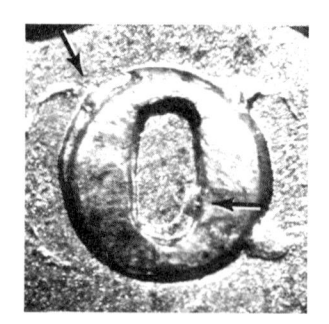

8 R O/O/CC Centered Shifted Left

8A R O/CC Centered Die Chips

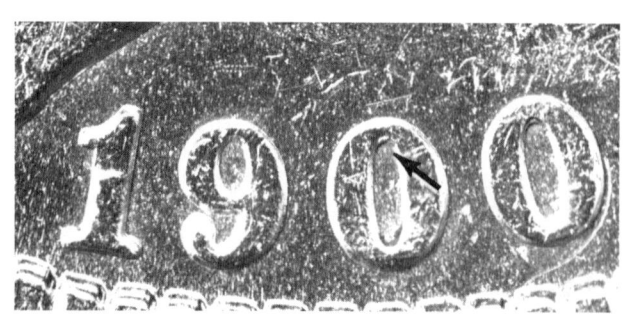

9 O Doubled 900

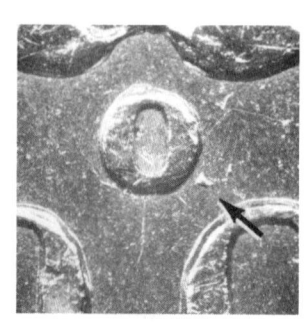

9 R O/CC Centered Shifted Right

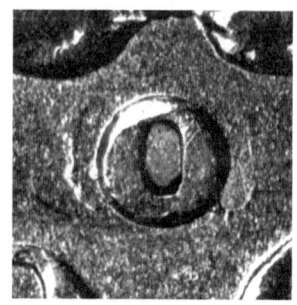

11 R O/CC High Shifted Left

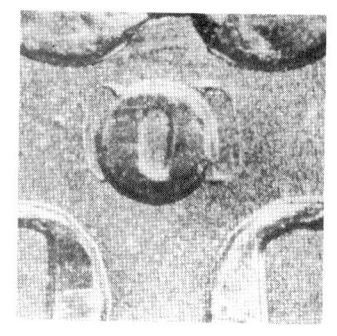

1900-O

12 R O/CC High Shifted Left

13 O Doubled 19-0

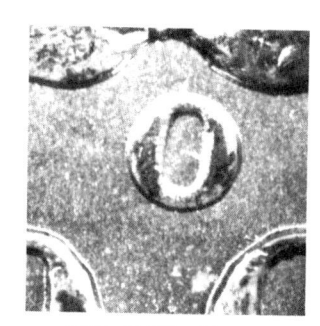

13 R O Tilted Right

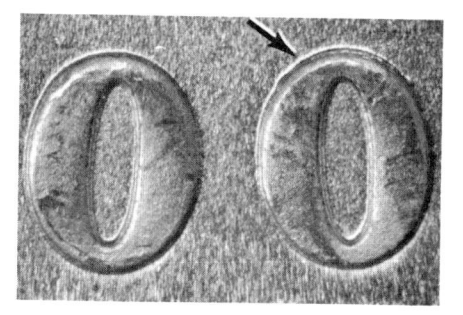

14 O Doubled 0

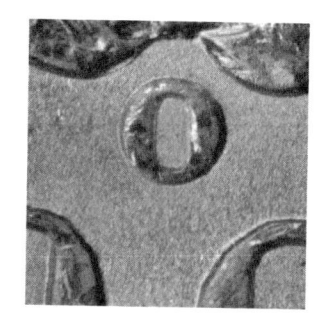

14 R O Set High

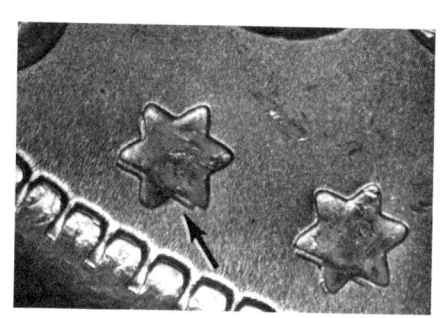

15 O Doubled Stars

16 O Doubled 1

15 O Doubled 00

15 R O Set High Shifted Left

17 O Doubled 9

18 O Doubled 19

19 O Doubled 190

355

1900-O

17   III² 11 • C³ 1 (Doubled 9)   I-2   R-4
Obverse III² 11 – 9 in date doubled as thin curved line below bottom loop and to lower left and bottom outside of upper loop. Date set further left than normal and slanted with 0's higher than 1. Open 9.

18   III² 12 • C³ a (Doubled 19)   I-3   R-3
Obverse III² 12 – Doubled 19 in date. 1 is doubled as thin horizontal line below bottom crossbar. 9 is doubled as thin curved line below bottom loop and to left bottom outside of upper loop. Date set further left than normal.

19   III² 13 • C³ a (Doubled 190)   I-2   R-4
Obverse III² 13 – Doubled 190 in date. 1 is doubled slightly to left of bottom crossbar. 9 is doubled to left outside of lower loop as thin curved arc and on right inside of lower loop as a thin vertical line. 0 is doubled slightly at lower left outside as short spike. Date is set much further left than normal and slanted with 0's higher than 1. Closed 9.

20   III² 14 • C³ 1 (Doubled 900)   I-2   R-4
Obverse III² 14 – Slightly doubled 900 in date. 9 doubled very slightly on lower right outside of lower loop. First 0 doubled slightly at bottom outside. Second 0 doubled slightly at top outside. Open 9.

21   III² 5 • C³ 1 (Near Date, High O)   (190)   I-2   R-3
Reverse C³ 1 – Some specimens show high die crack through tops of ED STATES OF.

22   III² 3 • C³ a (Very Near Date)   (190)   I-2   R-3

23   III² 15 • C³ 1 (Slanted Date   I-2   R-4
Obverse III² 15 – Date set further left than normal and slanted with 1 very close to rim.

24   III² 5 • C³ n (O/O Left)   I-2   R-3
Reverse C³ n – III O mint mark set high and doubled on left inside. Mint mark punched very deep into die with narrow center opening.

25   III² 5 • C³ o (O/O Down)   I-2   R-4
Reverse C³ o – III O mint mark doubled at top inside and bottom outside. Mint mark punched very deep into die with narrow center opening.

26   III² 5 • C³ p (O/O Left and Down)   I-2   R-3
Reverse C³ p – III O mint mark set high and doubled on left inside and lower right outside.

27   III² 16 • C³ 1 (Doubled 190 Left)   I-3   R-3
Obverse III² 16 – Doubled 190 in date. 1 doubled at top left of lower crossbar. 9 doubled at lower left outside of bottom loop as thin curved line. 0 doubled at lower left outside as long thin curved line.

28   III² 17 • C³ 1 (Doubled 190 Down)   I-2   R-3
Obverse III² 17 – Doubled 190 in date. 1 doubled strongly below upper crossbar and slightly below bottom crossbar. 9 doubled at top inside of upper loop on surface and at bottom outside of upper and lower loops. First 0 doubled slightly at top inside of loop on surface. Open 9 variety.

29   III² 8 • C³ b (Doubled 00)   I-2   R-3

29A   III² 8 • C³ b (Die Break in Date)   I-4   R-7
Obverse III² 8 – Spectacular large die break through bottom of 190 to rim below vee of neck. Break is as high as date digits above field.

30   III² 18 • C³ b (Doubled 1-0)   I-2   R-4
Obverse III² 18 – Doubled 1-0 in date. 1 is strongly doubled below upper and lower crossbars. Second 0 is doubled at bottom inside and slightly at top right outside. Closed 9 variety.

19 O Slanted Date   20 O Doubled 900

1900-O

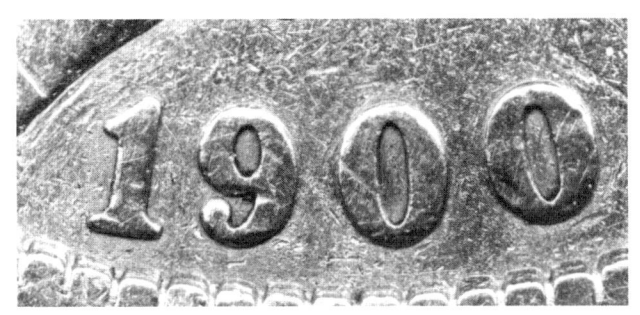

23 O Slanted Date

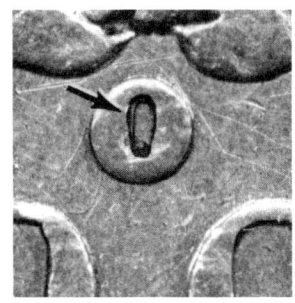

24 R O/O Left

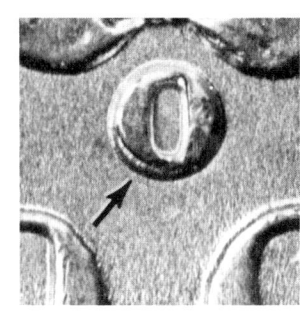

25 R O/O Down

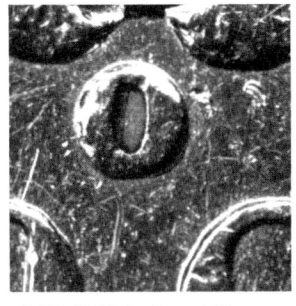

26 R O/O Left and Down

27 O Doubled 190 Left

34 R O Set High, Tilted Right

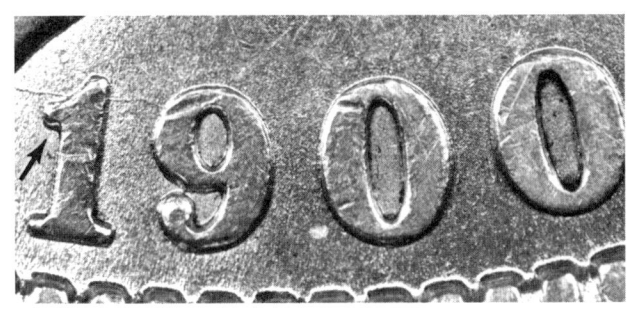

28 O Doubled 190 Down

30 O Doubled 1-0

29A O Die Break

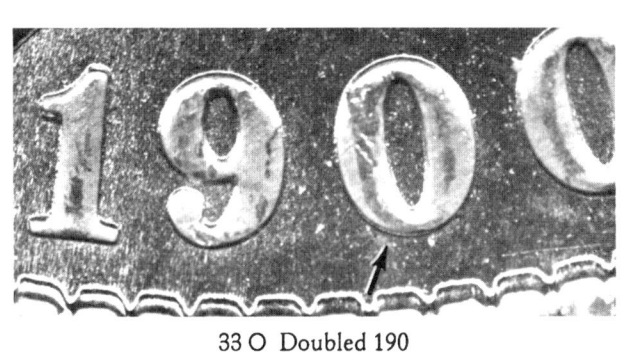

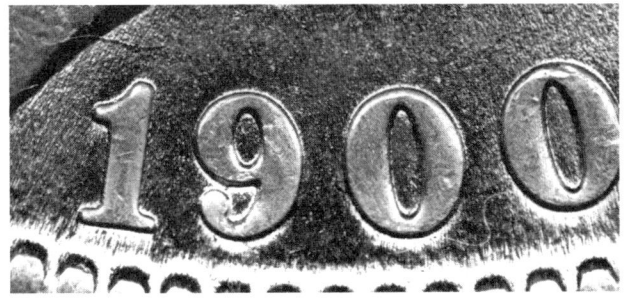

33 O Doubled 190

31 O Slanted Date

34 O Low Date

357

1900-O / 1900-S

31 III² 19 • C³ 1 (Slanted Date) (181) I-2 R-3
Obverse III² 19 – Date in normal position and slanted with 1 very close to rim.

32 III² 2 • C³ 1 (O Set High) (189) I-2 R-3

33 III² 20 • C³ k (Doubled 190, O Tilted and Shifted Right) (189) I-2 R-3
Obverse III² 20 – Doubled 190 in date. 1 doubled below upper crossbar. 9 doubled at top inside of upper loop. 0 doubled at lower left outside.

34 III² 21 • C³ q (Low Date, O Set High and Tilted Right) (181) I-2 R-3
Obverse III² 21 – Date set low to rim and further left than normal.
Reverse C³ q – Medium III O mint mark set high and tilted to right.

35 III² 22 • C³ 1 (Doubled 900, High 0) (181) I-2 R-3
Obverse III² 22 – Doubled 900 in date. 9 doubled slightly at top inside of upper loop. Both 0's doubled at top inside. Date set further left than normal.

36 III² 23 • C³ a (Doubled 00) (181) I-2 R-3
Obverse III² 23 – Doubled 00 in date. First 0 slightly doubled at lower left outside. Second 0 doubled at top inside as a short arc.

37 III² 5 • C³ r (Near Date, O/O Left) (189) I-2 R-3
Reverse C³ r – III O mint mark doubled with large shift to left and showing as a bar in middle of opening and crescent on left outside.

38 III² 24 • C³ a (Slanted Date) (187) I-2 R-3
Obverse III² 24 – Date set towards left side of normal position and slanted with 1 closer to rim.

35 O Doubled 900

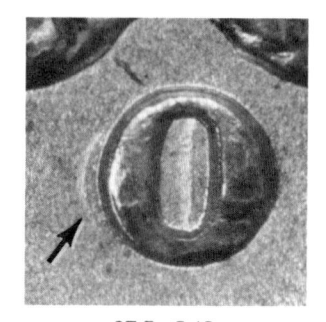

36 O Doubled 00

37 R O/O

38 O Slanted Date

1900-S

The usual strike is full but it can vary to very flat. Luster is usually good. A number of die varieties exist but only VAM 3A with wide over narrow "S" mint mark is significant. A slightly wider "S" mint mark was used on some 1899-S and 1900-S and on all 1901-S, 1902-S, 1903-S and 1904-S. Apparently only one die was modified with larger "S" punched on top of narrower "S" (similar to 1879-CC with large CC over small CC). Proof-likes are fairly scarce and have little contrast.

1 III² 1 • C³ a (Narrow S) (189) I-1 R-2
Obverse III² 1 – Normal die of III² type with open 9.
Reverse C³ a – Normal die of C³ type with narrow IV S mint mark.

1900-S

2	III²1 • C³b (Wide S)	(189)	I-1	R-2

Reverse C³b – Normal die with wide V S mint mark.

2A	III²1 • C³b (Extra Arrow Feather)	(189)	I-2	R-3

Reverse C³b – Heavy die gouge just above top arrow feather.

3	III²2 • C³c (S/S Right)		I-3	R-4

Obverse III²2 – Date set further left than normal.
Reverse C³c – IV S mint mark repunched with original showing as a short vertical spike to right of upper serif.

3A	III²2 • C³c (Wide Over Narrow S)		I-5	R-5

Reverse C³c – Same die as VAM 3 (identical die cracks) except narrow IV S mint mark was repunched with a wide V S mint mark and shows as a thin vertical line on left outside of upper loop and a thick spike on right outside of lower loop.

4	III²3 • C³d (Doubled 00)		I-2	R-4

Obverse III²3 – Both O's in date an doubled all across top outside.
Reverse C³d – V S mint mark set high.

5	III²2 • C³a (Near Date)	(189)	I-2	R-3

Reverse C³a – Normal die of C³ type with wide V S mint mark.

6	III²2 • C³d (Near Date)	(189)	I-2	R-3

7	III²4 • C³e (Doubled O, S/S Right)	(189)	I-2	R-3

Obverse III²4 – Second 0 doubled at top outside. Seventh star on left has two short spikes.
Reverse C³e – IV S mint mark doubled slightly on upper right of top serif and set slightly high and to right.

8	III²5 • C³b (Doubled 190)	(189)	I-2	R-3

Obverse III²5 – Doubled 190 in date. 1 has a spike at top in middle of curve. 9 has a short spike at top left outside and top right inside of upper loop. First 0 has a long curve of metal at top left outside. Date set further left than normal.

9	III²2 • C³f (Near Date, S/S Serifs)	(187)	I-2	R-3

Obverse III²2 – Seventh star on the left has two short spikes.
Reverse C³f – IV S mint mark doubled on lower right of top serif and bottom left of lower serif. S set high and centered.

10	III²2 • C³g (Near Date, High S)	(187)	I-2	R-3

Reverse C³g – IV S mint mark set high.

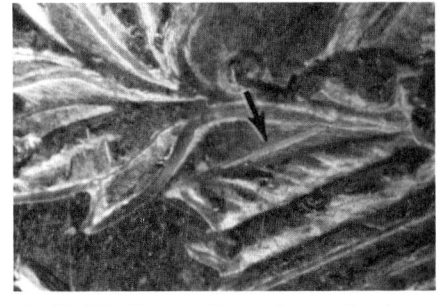

1A R Die Gouge Above Arrow Feathers

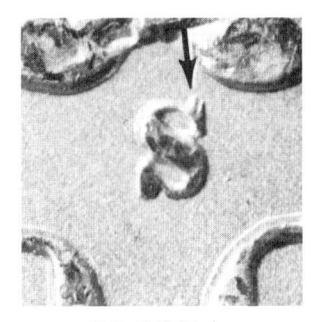

3 R S/S Right

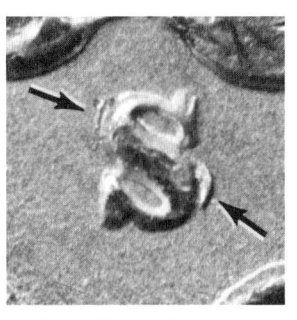

3A R Wide/Narrow S

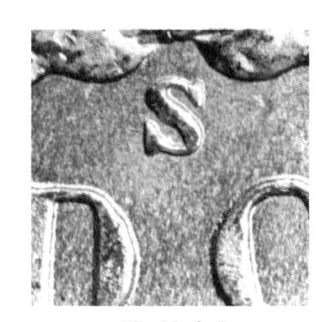

4 R High S

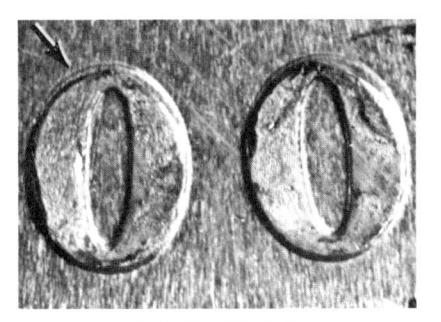

4 O Doubled 00

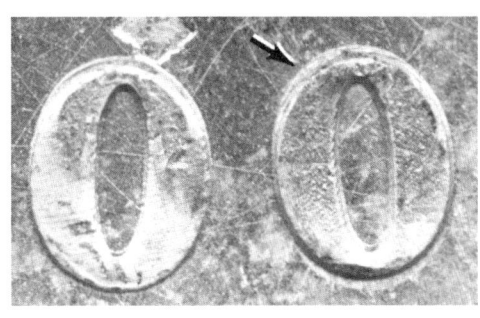

7 O Doubled Second 0

7 R S/S Right

1900-S

| 11 | III²6 • C³b (Doubled 190) | (189) | I-2 | R-3 |

Obverse III²6 – Doubled 90 in date. 1 doubled below upper serif. 9 doubled at top inside of upper loop. First 0 doubled at top outside. Date set further left than normal.

| 12 | III²7 • C³b (Slanted Date) | (189) | I-2 | R-3 |

Obverse III²7 – Slight slant to date with 1 closest to rim.

| 13 | III²8 • C³b (Doubled 9, Tripled 0) | (189) | I-2 | R-3 |

Obverse III²8 – 9 doubled slightly at bottom right inside of lower loop. Second 0 tripled at top inside.

| 14 | III²9 • C³d (Doubled 900, High S) | (189) | I-2 | R-3 |

Obverse III²9 – Doubled 900 in date. 9 doubled at lower inside of lower loop. First 0 doubled slightly at lower inside. Second 0 tripled at top inside and doubled at lower inside.

| 15 | III²1 • C³h (S Set Right) | | I-2 | R-3 |

Reverse C³h – V S mint mark set upright and shifted slightly to right.

| 16 | III²2 • C⁴/C³a (Near Date, 2 Olive Reverse) | (189) | I-3 | R-4 |

Reverse C⁴/C³a – Wide V S mint mark centered and upright. Shallow extra olive to right of olive connected to olive branch. Slight doubling at base of left olive leaf cluster and back of lower arrow head.

| 17 | III²2 • C³e (Near Date, S/S Right) | (189) | I-2 | R-3 |

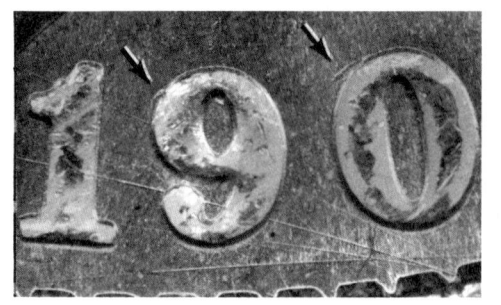

8 O Doubled 190

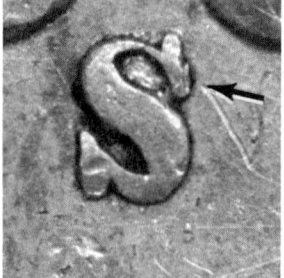

9 R S/S

11 O Doubled 190

12 O Slanted Date

13 O Doubled 9, Tripled Second 0

14 O Doubled 900

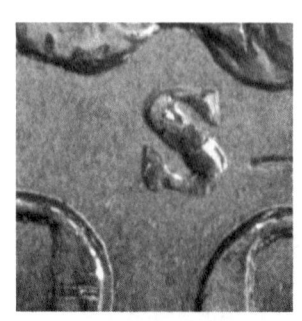

15 R S Set Right

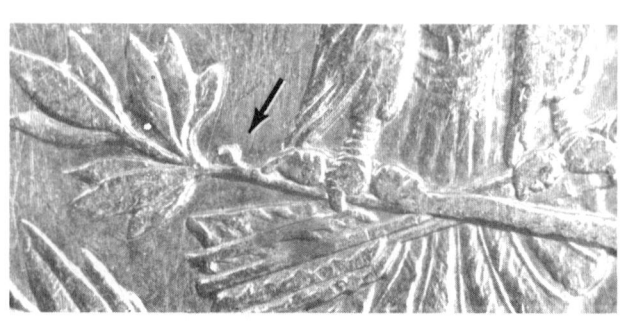

16 R 2 Olive Reverse

1901-P

This issue seems to be split between specimens with a fairly good strike with C^3 reverse and those with a fairly weak strike with C^4 reverse. Luster is usually dull. Lustrous fully struck specimens with minimal bag marks are truly very rare. A few die varieties exist. One of significance is VAM 3 with shifted eagle. It is the strongest doubled reverse die of the Morgan series and shows pronounced doubling of the bottom of the eagle's wings and tail feathers, olive branch and arrow shafts. It commands a large premium in all grades and only two are known in uncirculated. Prooflikes are virtually unknown except for a couple of pieces. The proofs have only moderate contrast. This is probably due to new master dies prepared in 1900 with C^4 reverse having less contrast because of modification of working hubs with less contrast than the original master die. The Philadelphia mint also changed from wood to gas annealing furnaces for planchets in 1901 which may have affected their luster.

1   III²1 • C³a (Normal Die)   (189)   I-1   R-2
   Obverse III²1 – Normal die of III² type with closed 9.
   Reverse C³a – Normal die of C³ type.

2   III²1 • C⁴a (Normal Die)   I-1   R-3
   Reverse C⁴a – Normal die of C⁴ type.

2A   III²1 • C⁴a (Reverse Die Gouges)   (189)   I-2   R-3
   Reverse C⁴a – Diagonal die scratches and gouges around NE of ONE and DO of DOLLAR.

3   III²1 • C⁴b (Shifted Eagle)   (189)   I-5   R-5
   Reverse C⁴b – Shifted Eagle variety. Eagle has been shifted to twelve o'clock so that the lower part of the eagle's wings, tail feathers, olive branch and leaves, arrow shafts and arrowheads and eagle's lower beak are strongly doubled. Letters OD and W are doubled below and within the motto IN GOD WE TRUST. The doubling was caused by a misalignment between the hub and die in one of the early blows.

4   III²1 • C⁴c (Doubled Reverse)   (186)   I-4   Proof
   Reverse C⁴c – Doubled lower reverse. UNITED, ONE DOLLAR, MERICA, both stars and wreath are doubled towards rim.

5   III²2 • C⁴/C³a (Doubled Ear, 2 Olive Reverse)   (189)   I-3   R-3
   Obverse III²2 – Inner ear lobe, bottom outside of ear lobe, hair above ear, eyelid and lower edge of cotton leaves are slightly doubled.
   Reverse C⁴/C³a – Faint shallow extra olive to right of olive connected to olive branch. Back of lower arrow head, upper feathers of eagle's left wing and right sides of eagle's nostril are slightly doubled.

2A R Die Gouges

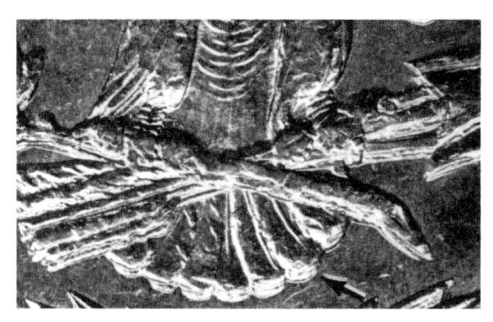

3 R Shifted Eagle

4 R Doubled Reverse

5 O Doubled Ear

5 R C⁴/C³

1901-P

6   III²1 • C⁴/C³ b (2 Olive Reverse)   (189)   I-3   R-3
Reverse C⁴/C³ b – Extra olive to right of olive connected to olive branch. Doubling at base of top and left olive leaf clusters and back of lower arrow head.

7   III²1 • C⁴/C³ c (Doubled Wing and Arrows)   (189)   I-3   R-4
Reverse C⁴/C³ c – Faint shallow extra olive to right of olive connected to olive branch. Eagle's left wing strongly doubled at middle and bottom, arrow heads and eagle's left claws doubled on left side, top of olive branch doubled at bottom, and two innermost eagle's right wing feathers are doubled next to leg.

8   III²3 • C³ a (Doubled Second 1)   (189)   I-2   R-3
Obverse III²3 – Second 1 in date doubled slightly below base.

9   III²1 • C⁴/C³ d (2 Olive Reverse)   (189)   I-3   R-3
Reverse C⁴/C³ d – Extra olive to right of olive connected to olive branch. Doubling on top of olive branch at right of olives, at base of top and left olive leaf cluster, at bottom of leaves of middle and lower olive leaf clusters, eagle's middle talon of right claw, middle of eagle's left wing, right side of eagle's nostril and eye, and on right of two innermost right wing feathers next to leg.

10   III²4 • C⁴ a (Slanted Date)   (189)   I-2   R-3
Obverse III²4 – Date slanted with first 1 closest to rim.

6 R C⁴/C³

7 R Doubled Wing and Arrows

8 O Doubled Second 1

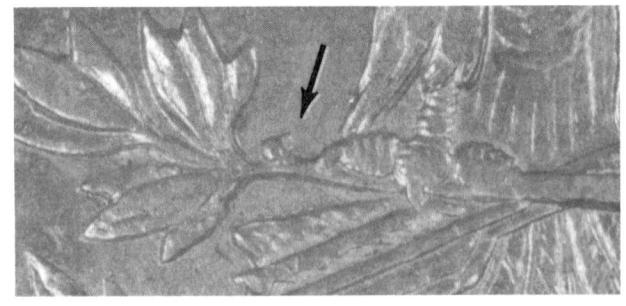

9 R C⁴/C³

10 O Slanted Date

1901-O

A fairly weak strike is typical for this issue although because of the large mintage fully struck specimens can be located. Luster is generally good. Quite a few minor die varieties are known but none are significant. Proof-likes are somewhat scarce but have little contrast.

1   **III²1 • C³a (Normal Die)**   (181)   I-1   R-2
  Obverse III²1 – Normal die of III² type with closed 9.
  Reverse C³a – Normal die of C³ type with medium III O mint mark centered and upright.

2   **III²2 • C⁴a (Normal Die)**   (181)   I-1   R-1
  Reverse C⁴a – Normal die of C⁴ type with III O mint mark.

3   **III²2 • C⁴/C³j (Doubled 1-01, 2 Olive Reverse)**   (181)   I-3   R-3
  Obverse III²2 – 1-01 in date doubled. First 1 doubled below top and bottom crossbars. Lower inside of 0 is doubled. Last 1 doubled at top, above bottom crossbar, and on lower right side of stem.
  Reverse C⁴/C³j – Extra olive to right of olive connected to olive branch. Doubling on top of olive branch at right of olives, at base of olive leaf clusters, top of upper arrow feathers, back of lower arrow head, on right of two innermost right wing feathers next to leg, and right side of eagle's nostril and eye.

4   **III²1 • C⁴b (O Tilted Left)**   I-2   R-3
  Reverse C⁴b – III O mint mark tilted left.

5   **III²1 • C⁴c (O Tilted Right)**   I-2   R-3
  Reverse C⁴c – III O mint mark set high and tilted right.

6   **III²1 • C⁴d (High O)**   I-2   R-3
  Reverse C⁴d – III O set high and to right.

7   **III²3 • C⁴a (Double 90)**   I-2   R-3
  Obverse III²3 – Bottom of 9 slightly doubled. 0 doubled at bottom left outside. Closed 9.

8   **III²4 • C⁴a (Doubled 1-01)**   I-3   R-3
  Obverse III²4 – 1-01 doubled in date. First 1 is doubled slightly at very top left. 0 doubled at lower left and bottom outside. Second 1 doubled strongly below upper crossbar. Closed 9.

9   **III²1 • C³b (O Tilted Right)**   (181)   I-2   R-3
  Reverse C³b – III O mint mark set high with slight tilt to right.

3 R C⁴/C³

3 O Doubled 1-01

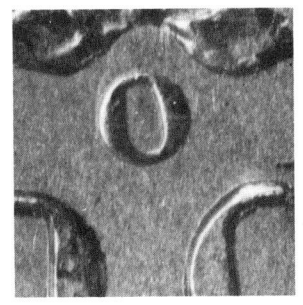

4 R O Tilted Left

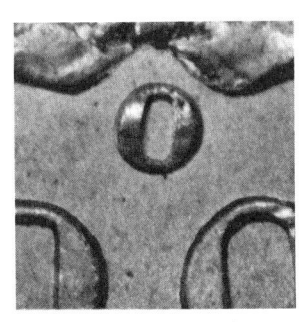

5 R O Tilted Right

6 R High O

1901-O

10	III²5 • C⁴e (Far Date, High O)		I-2	R-3

Obverse III²5 – Date set further right than normal.
Reverse C⁴e – III O set high and centered.

11	III²6 • C⁴b (Slanted Date)	(189)	I-2	R-3
12	III²1 • C⁴/C³a (2 Olive Reverse)	(181)	I-3	R-3

Reverse C⁴/C³a – Shallow extra olive to right of olive connected to olive branch. Doubling on top of olive branch at right of olives, at base of top and left olive leaf cluster, faintly on end of second arrow feather next to olive branch, back of lower arrow head, right side of eagle's nostril and eye and on right of two innermost right wing feathers next to leg. III O mint mark set slightly to right.

13	III²6 • C⁴/C³b (Slanted Date, 2 Olive Reverse)	(181)	I-3	R-3

Reverse C⁴/C³b – Faint shallow extra olive to right of olive connected to olive branch. Doubling on right of eagle's nostril, eye, point of beak, two feathers adjacent to eagle's right leg and back of lower arrow head. III O mint mark set high with tilt to left.

14	III²7 • C⁴/C³c (Near Date, 2 Olive Reverse)	(181)	I-3	R-3

Obverse III²7 – Date set further left than normal.
Reverse C⁴/C³c – Extra olive to right of olive connected to olive branch. Doubling at base of top and left olive leaf cluster, on right of eagle's nostril, and back of lower arrow head. III O mint mark upright and slightly high.

15	III²1 • C⁴/C³d (2 Olive Reverse)	(181)	I-3	R-3

Reverse C⁴/C³d – Extra olive to right of olive connected to olive branch. Doubling at base of top olive leaf cluster and back of lower arrow head. III O mint mark tilted left.

16	III²1 • C⁴/C³e (2 Olive Reverse)	(181)	I-3	R-3

Obverse III²1 – Strong diagonal polishing line through R of LIBERTY.
Reverse C⁴/C³e – Faint shallow extra olive to right of olive connected to olive branch. Doubling at base of left olive leaf cluster, faintly on end of second arrow feather next to olive branch, right of eagle's nostril, eye and beak end, two feathers adjacent to eagle's right leg and back of lower arrow head. III O mint mark set high, upright, and set slightly to right.

17	III²1 • C⁴/C³f (2 Olive Reverse)	(181)	I-3	R-3

Reverse C⁴/C³f – Extra olive to right of olive connected to olive branch. Doubling on top of olive branch at right of olives, at base of top and left olive leaf cluster, back of lower arrow head, and right side of eagle's nostril and eye. III O mint mark set slightly high and to left with slight tilt to left.

18	III²1 • C⁴/C³g (2 Olive Reverse)	(181)	I-3	R-3

Reverse C⁴/C³g – Extra olive to right of olive connected to olive branch. Doubling at base of left olive leaf cluster, back of lower arrow head, feathers at top of eagle's left wing and right side of eagle's nostril. III O mint mark set high, upright and centered.

19	III²1 • C⁴/C³h (2 Olive Reverse)	(181)	I-3	R-3

Reverse C⁴/C³h – Extra olive to right of olive connected to olive branch. Doubling at lower edge of lower olive leaves, some leaves at wreath center, and bottom arrow feather plus back of lower arrow head. III O mint mark set high, upright and centered. Gap between the neck and wing appears to be a C³ narrow type but with outline of C⁴ type at edge of wing,

20	III²8 • C³a (Doubled 0, Bar Ear)	(189)	I-2	R-3

Obverse III²8 – 0 is doubled slightly at bottom right outside. Closed 9. Diagonal die gouge in lower part of ear opening.

21	III²5 • C³a (Far Date)	(181)	I-2	R-3
22	III² • C³c (High O)	(181)	I-2	R-3

Reverse C³c -III O set high.

7 O Doubled 0

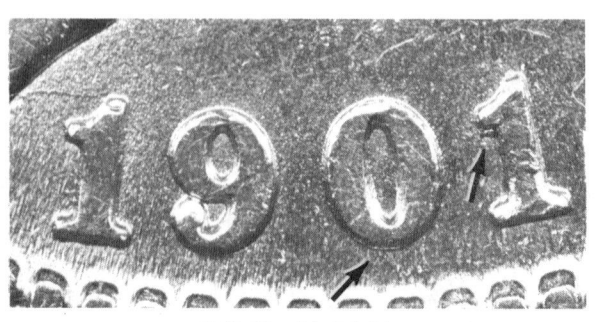

8 O Doubled 1-01

364

1901-O

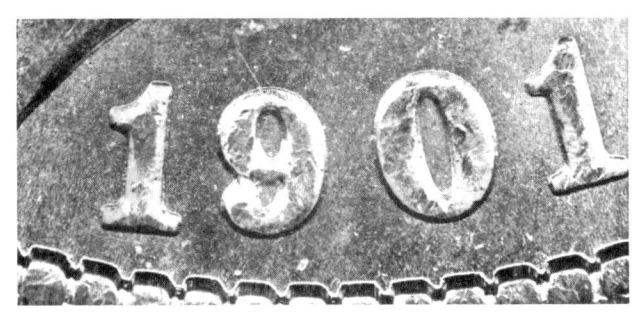

11 O Slanted Date

12 R C⁴/C³

9 R High O Tilted Right

13 R C⁴/C³

14 R C⁴/C³

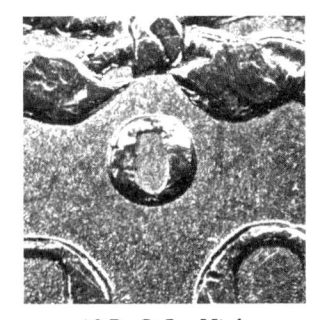

10 R O Set High

15 R C⁴/C³

16 R C⁴/C³

17 R C⁴/C³

18 R C⁴/C³

20 O Die Gouge in Ear

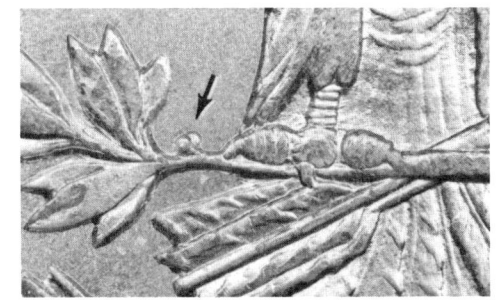

19 R C⁴/C³

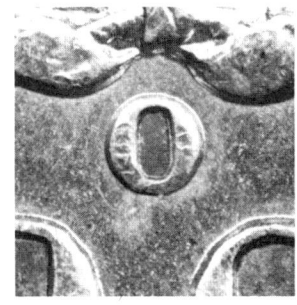

22 R High O

20 O Doubled 0

365

1901-O

23	III²1 • C⁴/C³i (2 Olive Reverse)		(181)	I-3	R-3

Obverse III²1 – Vertical polishing lines in Liberty head nose and mouth.
Reverse C⁴/C³i – Extra olive to right of olive connected to olive branch. Doubling at base of left and lower olive leaf cluster, top of upper arrow feather, back of lower arrow head, upper middle feathers of eagle's left wing, and right side of eagle's nostril and eye. III O mint mark centered and upright with slight shift to right.

24	III²8 • C³c (Low Date, High O)		(181)	I-2	R-3

Obverse III²8 – Date set low close to rim.

25	III²6 • C³a (Slanted Date)		(181)	I-2	R-3
26	III²9 • C³a (Doubled Profile)		(181)	I-2	R-3

Obverse III²9 – Liberty head profile is doubled all along forehead, nose, lips and chin.

27	III²10 • C⁴/C³k (Doubled 01, 2 Olive Reverse)		(181)	I-3	R-4

Obverse III²10 – Doubled 01 in date. 0 doubled strongly at bottom outside. 1 doubled at top right corner of vertical shaft. Date set at left side of normal position. Slightly doubled Liberty head profile.
Reverse C⁴/C³k – Extra olive to right of olive connected to olive branch. Doubling at base of left olive leaf cluster, back of lower arrow head, upper part of eagle's left wing, and right side of eagle's nostril and eye. Centered and upright III O mint mark.

28	III²11 • C⁴/C³g (Doubled Ear, 2 Olive Reverse)		(181)	I-3	R-3

Obverse III²11 – Ear slightly doubled at very top below hairline and below inner ear fill. Date set in normal position and slanted with first 1 closest to rim.

29	III²5 • C³c (Far Date, High O)		(181)	I-2	R-3
30	III²1 • C³d (O Set Right)		(181)	I-2	R-3

Reverse C³d – III O mint mark upright and set slightly to right.

31	III²6 • C³b (Slanted Date, O Tilted Right)		(181)	I-2	R-3
32	III²9 • C³c (Doubled Profile, High O)		(181)	I-2	R-3

23 R C⁴/C³

24 O Low Date

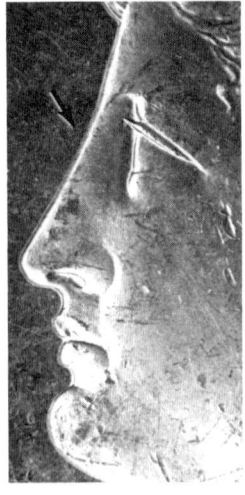

26 O Doubled Profile

27 O Doubled 01

27 R C⁴/C³

28 O Doubled Ear

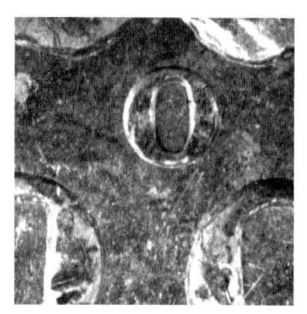

30 R O Set Right

1901-S

Typically the 1901-S is weakly struck although sharply struck specimens exist. Often on weakly struck coins, planchet striations will show in areas not fully struck up against the dies on both obverse and reverse. A few minor die varieties exist but none are significant. Proof-likes are extremely rare and have little contrast.

1	III²1 • C³a (Normal Die)	(189)	I-1	R-2

Obverse III²1 – Normal die of III² type with closed 9.
Reverse C³a – Normal die of C³ type with large V S mint mark centered and upright.

2	III²1 • C⁴a (Normal Die)	(189)	I-1	R-2

Reverse C⁴a – Normal die of C⁴ type with upright V S mint mark.

3	III²1 • C³b (High S Tilted Right)		I-2	R-3

Reverse C³b – V S mint mark set high and tilted slightly to the right.

4	III²1 • C⁴b (High S)		I-2	R-3

Reverse C⁴b – V S mint mark set high.

5	III²1 • C⁴/C³a (2 Olive Reverse)	(189)	I-3	R-3

Reverse C⁴/C³a – Faint shallow extra olive to right of olive connected to olive branch. Doubling at base of top and left olive leaf clusters, right of eagle's nostril, three feathers adjacent to eagle's right leg and back of lower arrow head.

6	III²2 • C⁴/C³b (2 Olive Reverse, Far Date)	(189)	I-3	R-3

Obverse III²2 – Date set further right than normal.
Reverse C⁴/C³b – Shallow extra olive to right of olive connected to olive branch. First lower leaf on left wreath doubled at bottom. Reverse overpolished with weak tail feathers and many leaves in wreath disconnected. Gap between the neck and wing appears to be a C³ narrow type but with outline of C⁴ type at edge of wing. A in DOLLAR and right star doubled as in C⁴ type.

7	III²1 • C⁴/C³c (2 Olive Reverse)	(189)	I-3	R-3

Reverse C⁴/C³c – Extra olive to right of olive connected to olive branch. Doubling at base of middle olive cluster, top of second arrow feather from top, feathers of upper middle part of eagle's left wing, right side of eagle's nostril and back of lower arrow head. Large V S mint mark set high and upright.

8	III²1 • C⁴/C³b (2 Olive Reverse)	(189)	I-3	R-3
9	III²1 • C⁴/C³d (2 Olive Reverse)	(189)	I-3	R-3

Reverse C⁴/C³d – Shallow extra olive to right of olive connected to olive branch. Doubling on top of olive branch at right of olives, at base of middle and lower olive leaf clusters, at bottom of lower arrow feathers, at bottom of bow ends, back of lower arrowhead, right side of eagle's nostril and top feathers of eagle's left wing. Large V S mint mark set slightly high and upright.

1901-S / 1902-P

3 R High S Tilted Right

4 R High S

5 R C⁴/C³

6 R C⁴/C³

7 R C⁴/C³

9 R C⁴/C³

1902-P

The strike is usually good for this issue. Luster is usually some what subdued and can be satiny and brilliant, again probably due to the introduction of gas annealing furnaces at that mint in 1901. A few minor die varieties exist but none are significant. Proof-likes are fairly scarce and generally have little contrast with brilliant surfaces. Proofs also have little contrast.

1	III²1 • C⁴a Normal Die)	I-1	R-2

Obverse III²1 – Normal die of III² type with closed 9.
Reverse C⁴a – Normal die of C⁴ type.

2	III²2 • C⁴a (Near Date)	I-2	Proof and Regular

Obverse III²2 – Date set further left than normal. Closed 9.

3	III²3 • C⁴a (Very Near Date)	I-2	R-3

Obverse III²3 – Date set much further left than normal. Closed 9 variety.

4	III²4 • C⁴a (Doubled Ear)	I-3	R-5

Obverse III²4 – Ear strongly doubled at right outside and left inside hairline doubled just above ear, and Liberty head profile is doubled along nose, lips and chin.

1902-P

5   **III²5 • C⁴a (Doubled Profile)**   (189)   I-2   R-3
Obverse III²5 – Liberty head profile is doubled along forehead, nose, lips and chin.

6   **III²2 • C⁴/C³a (Near Date, 2 Olive Reverse)**   (189)   I-3   R-3
Reverse C⁴/C³a – Extra olive to right of olive connected to olive branch. Doubling on top of olive branch at right of olives, at base of top and left olive leaf clusters, tops of arrow feathers, back of lower arrow head, outside of lower leaf on first cluster on right side of wreath, outside of lower large leaf on second cluster on left side of wreath and letters N-TAT-OF towards rim.

7   **III²2 • C⁴/C³b (Near Date, 2 Olive Reverse)**   (189)   I-3   R-3
Reverse C⁴/C³b – Shallow extra olive to right of olive connected to olive branch. Doubling at base of top and left olive leaf clusters, faintly on second arrow feather next to olive branch, right of eagle's nostril and eye, and back of lower arrow head.

8   **III²1 • C⁴/C³c (2 Olive Reverse)**   (189)   I-3   R-3
Reverse C⁴/C³c – Extra olive to right of olive connected to olive branch. Doubling at base of all three olive leaf clusters, back of lower arrow head, feathers at top of eagle's left wing, and right side of eagle's nostril and eye.

4 O Doubled Ear

4 O Doubled Profile

5 O Doubled Profile

6 R C⁴/C³

7 R C⁴/C³

8 R C⁴/C³

9 O Doubled 1

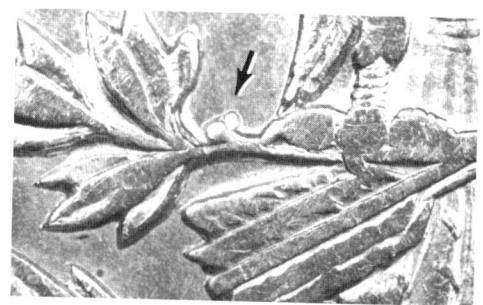

9 R C⁴/C³

369

1902-P / 1902-O

9   III² 5 • C⁴/C³ d (Doubled 1, 2 Olive Reverse)   (189)   I-3   R-3
Obverse III² 5 – 1 doubled below crossbar. Date set further left than normal.
Reverse C⁴/C³ d – Extra olive to right of olive connected to olive branch. Doubling on top of olive branch at right of olives, at base of all three olive leaf clusters, on end of second arrow feather next to olive branch, back of lower arrow head, on right of two innermost right wing feathers next to leg, feathers at top of eagle's left wing, right side of eagle's nostril and eye, top leaf of second leaf cluster of left wreath and UNITED STATES OF towards rim.

10   III² 1 • C⁴/C³ e (2 Olive Reverse)   (189)   I-3   R-3
Reverse C⁴/C³ e – Shallow extra olive to right of olive connected to olive branch. Doubling on top of olive branch at right of olives, at base of all three olive leaf clusters, on top of upper two leaves in lower olive leaf cluster, at top of all arrow feathers, back of lower arrow head, feathers at top of eagle's left wing and right side of eagle's nostril.

11   III² 2 • C⁴/C³ f (2 Olive Reverse)   (186)   I-3   Proof
Reverse C⁴/C³ f – Shallow extra olive to right of olive connected to olive branch. Doubling on top of olive branch at right of olives at base of all three olive leaf clusters, on top of upper leaf in lower olive leaf cluster, at top of lower three arrow feathers, back of lower arrow head, feathers in upper middle of eagle's left wing, and right side of eagle's nostril.

10 R C⁴/C³   Proof 11 R C⁴/C³

1902-O

This issue has a strike that ranges from slightly weak to very flat. Luster is usually good. Fully struck (full hair over ear) pieces that are lustrous with minimal bag marks are difficult to locate for this common "O" mint. Numerous minor die varieties exist but only one is very significant, VAM 3, with small "O". It is very scarce and is known only in low circulated condition. Proof-likes are somewhat scarce but have little contrast. However, proof-likes and semi proof-likes tend to be fully struck quite a bit of the time.

1   III² 1 • C⁴ a (Closed 9)   I-1   R-2
Obverse III² 1 • Normal die of III² type with closed 9. Some specimens show base of 2 filled in.
Reverse C⁴ a – Normal die of C⁴ type with medium III O mint mark, centered and upright.

2   III² 2 • C⁴ a (Open 9)   I-1   R-2
Obverse III² 2 – Normal die with open 9. Ball of 9 does not touch body of 9.

3   III² 1 • C³ a (Small O)   (181)   I-3   R-5
Reverse C³ a – Normal die of C³ type with small I O mint mark tilted to the right.

4   III² 3 • C⁴ a (Near Date)   (181)   I-2   R-3
Obverse III² 3 – Date set further left than normal. Closed 9.

5   III² 3 • C⁴ b (Near Date, High O)   (181)   I-2   R-3
Reverse C⁴ b – III O mint mark set high and upright.

6   III² 1 • C⁴ c (O Tilted Left)   (181)   I-2   R-3
Obverse III² 1 – Some specimens show base of 2 filled in. Closed 9.
Reverse C⁴ c – III O mint mark set high and tilted to left.

7   III² 3 • C⁴ d (Near Date, High O Tilted Left, Bar O)   I-2   R-3
Reverse C⁴ d – III O mint mark, set high to right and tilted slightly left. Some specimens show die break at top inside showing as a horizontal bar.

1902-O

| 8 | III²3 • C⁴/C³k (2 Olive Reverse, O/O Down) | (181) | I-3 | R-4 |

Reverse C⁴/C³k – III O mint mark repunched with original showing as a thin curved line at lower left outside and as a thin vertical line with a curve at top on right inside. Extra olive to right of olive connected to olive branch. Doubling on top of olive branch at right of olives, at base of olive leaf clusters, on end of second arrow feather next to olive branch, middle talon on eagle's right leg, on right side of two innermost right wing feathers next to leg, right of eagle's nostril and eye, and back of lower arrow head. UNI-ED TAT OF doubled faintly towards rim.

| 9 | III²4 • C⁴g (Doubled 1) | | I-2 | R-3 |

Obverse III²4 – 1 in date doubled just below upper crossbar as a thin horizontal line. Profile of Liberty head doubled on forward hair line, forehead, nose, lips and chin. E PLU and all of left stars doubled slightly towards rim.
Reverse C⁴g – Legend and motto letters doubled towards rim

| 10 | III²5 • C⁴f (Doubled 1) | | I-2 | R-3 |

Obverse III²5 – 1 in date doubled slightly at bottom of lower crossbar. Closed 9:
Reverse C⁴f – III O mint mark set slightly to right.

| 11 | III²1 • C⁴h (Doubled Reverse) | | I-3 | R-3 |

Reverse C⁴h – Outer portion doubled with letters doubled outward in radial direction for all legend letters, stars, tops of motto letters and outside edge of right wreath.

| 12 | III²6 • C⁴/C³a (Doubled Profile, 2 Olive Reverse) | (181) | I-3 | R-3 |

Obverse III²6 – Double nose, lips, chin and neck on Liberty head profile. All stars on left doubled slightly near rim. E-PLURIBUS UNUM doubled slightly on lower portions of letters towards rim. Date set low and further left than normal.
Reverse C⁴/C³a – III O mint mark doubled slightly at top right inside. Shallow extra olive to right of olive connected to olive branch. Doubling on top of arrow feathers, base of left olive leaf cluster, on top of olive branch at right of olives, and back of lower arrow head. OD WE TRUS doubled at top.

1 O Filled 2    5 R High O 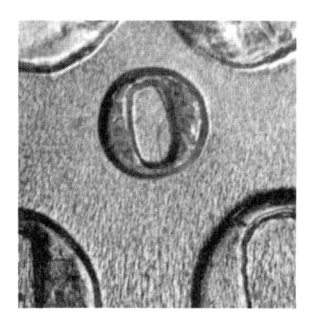   6 R O Tilted Left 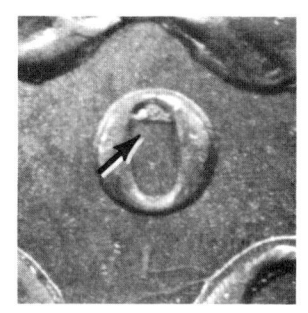   7 R Bar O

8 R O/O Down    8 R C⁴/C³   9 O Doubled 1

10 O Doubled 1    10 R O Set Right 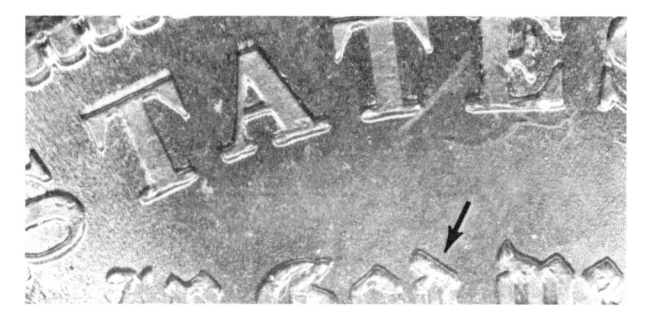   11 R Doubled Reverse

12 O Low Date

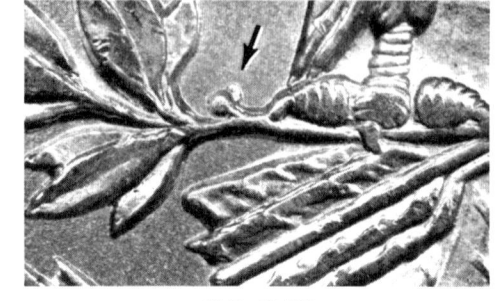

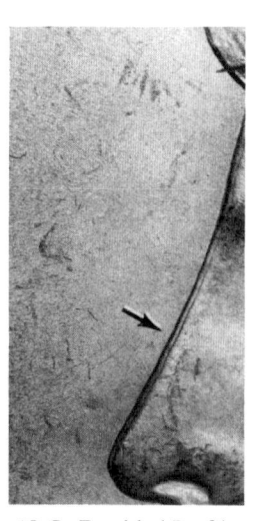

12 R O/O

12 R C⁴/C³

12 O Doubled Profile

| 13 | III²7 • C⁴a (Doubled 1-02) | (181) | I-2 | R-3 |

Obverse III²7 – Doubled 1-02 in date. 1 doubled strongly at bottom of lower crossbar at mid height. 02 doubled at very bottom as a line on the field. Date set further left than normal.

| 14 | III²8 • C⁴i (Doubled Profile and Reverse Lettering) | (181) | I-2 | R-3 |

Obverse III²8 – Doubled nose, lips, chin and neck on Liberty head profile.
Reverse C⁴i – Slightly doubled UNITED STATES OF AMERICA and right star in a radial direction.

| 15 | III²8 • C⁴/C³b (Doubled Profile, 2 Olive Reverse) | (181) | I-3 | R-3 |

Reverse C⁴/C³b – Extra olive to right of olive connected to branch. Doubled tops of arrow feathers, olive leaves, olive branch to right of olives, eagle's right leg and middle talon, top arrow shaft, and on right of two innermost right wing feathers next to leg. Slightly doubled lower inside of GOD W-U.

| 16 | III²9 • C⁴/C³c (Doubled Ear, 2 Olive Reverse) | (181) | I-3 | R-3 |

Obverse III²9 – Ear doubled slightly at lower outside. Date set further left than normal with base of 2 filled in. Closed 9.
Reverse C⁴/C³c – III O mint mark set high and slightly to right. Extra olive to right of olive connected to olive branch. Doubling on top of olive branch at right of olives, at base of left olive leaf cluster, faintly on end of second arrow feather next to olive branch, back of lower arrow head, back of eagle's nostril and right two innermost right wing feathers next to leg. W in WE doubled on right side.

| 17 | III²10 • C⁴/C³d (Doubled Ear, 2 Olive Reverse) | (181) | I-3 | R-3 |

Obverse III²10 – Ear doubled slightly at very bottom outside. Date set further left than normal. Closed 9.
Reverse C⁴/C³d – III O mint mark set high, upright and centered. Extra olive to right of olive connected to olive branch. Doubled tops of arrow feathers, top of olive branch at right of olives, at base of left olive leaf clusters, and back of lower arrow head. IN GOD WE TRUST doubled at top. UNITED STATES OF doubled towards rim.

| 18 | III²3 • C⁴/C³e (Near Date, 2 Olive Reverse) | (181) | I-3 | R-3 |

Reverse C⁴/C³e – Extra olive to right of olive connected to olive branch. Doubling at base of left olive leaf cluster and back of lower arrow head. Pitting in D of DOLLAR and below second leaf cluster of left wreath.

| 19 | III²11 • C⁴/C³f (Doubled Profile, 2 Olive Reverse) | (181) | I-3 | R-3 |

Obverse III²11 – Doubled front hairline, forehead, nose, lips, and chin on Liberty head. Date set much further left than normal. Closed 9.
Reverse C⁴/C³f – Extra olive to right of olive connected to olive branch. Doubling at base of top and left olive leaf clusters, top of lower leaf in top olive leaf cluster, top of middle leaf in left olive leaf cluster, top of olive branch at right of olives, middle claw of eagle's right leg, at end of second arrow feather next to olive branch, at top of second leaf cluster of left wreath, next to designer's initial M in bow and right two innermost right wing feathers next to leg .

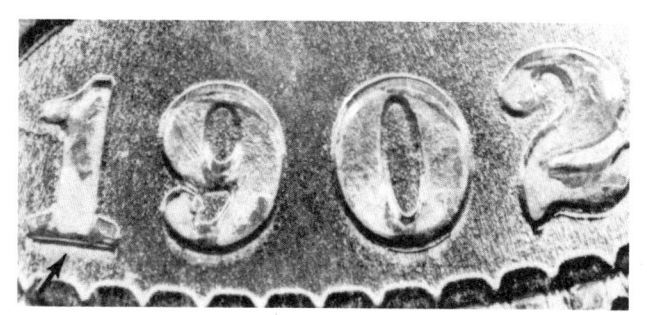

1902-O

13 O Doubled 1-02

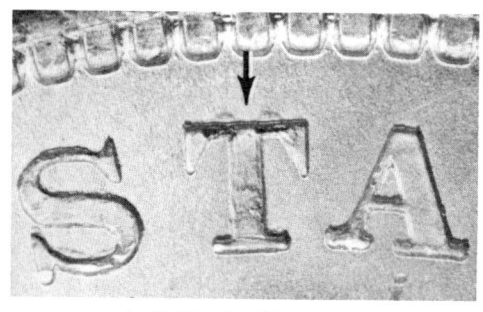

14 R Doubled Lettering

15 R C⁴/C³

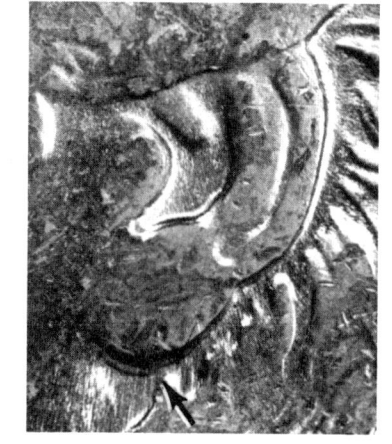

16 R C⁴/C³

16 O Doubled Ear

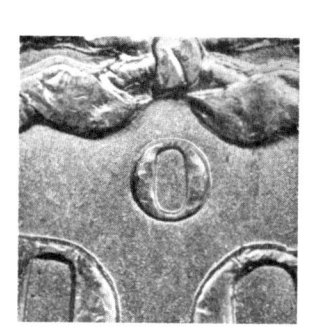

16 R O Set High and Right

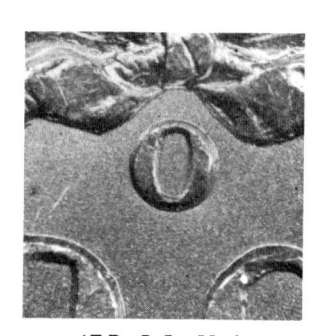

17 R O Set High

17 R C⁴/C³

17 O Doubled Ear

18 R C⁴/C³

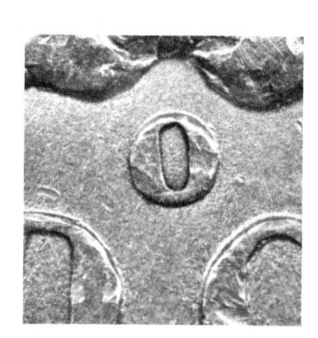

20 R O Tilted Left

19 R C⁴/C³

373

1902-O

20   **III² 8 • C⁴/C³ g (Doubled Profile, 2 Olive Reverse)**   (181)   I-3   R-3

Reverse C⁴/C³ g – III O mint mark set slightly high, to right, and tilted to left. Extra olive to right of olive connected to olive branch. Doubling at base of top and left olive leaf clusters, top of lower leaf in top olive leaf cluster, top of middle leaf in left olive leaf cluster, top of top leaf in lower olive leaf cluster, top of olive branch at right of olives, tops of arrow feathers, back of lower arrow head, faintly on right side of two innermost right wing feathers next to leg, and right of eagle's nostril and eye. IN GOD WE TRUST and NITED STATES OF doubled towards rim.

21   **III² 12 • C⁴/C³ h (Tripled Profile, 2 Olive Reverse)**   (181)   I-3   R-3

Obverse III² 12 – Tripled front hairline, tip of nose, chin and cap back of Liberty head plus E PLUR lower portions towards rim. Doubled nose, lips, neck, cap top of Liberty head plus left stars and S-UNUM towards rim.

Reverse C⁴/C³ h – Extra olive to right of olive connected to olive branch. Doubling at base of top and left leaf clusters, tops of bottom leaf in top clusters and top leaf in bottom cluster, top of upper 3 arrow feathers, right side of middle talon on eagle's right leg, top of upper arrow head and shaft, and back of lower arrow head.

22   **III² 3 • C⁴ j (Near Date, O Tilted Left)**   (181)   I-2   R-3

Obverse III² 3 – Base of 2 filled in.

Reverse C⁴ j – III O mint mark tilted to left at normal height.

23   **III² 13 • C⁴/C³ i (Doubled Ear, 2 Olive Reverse)**   (181)   I-3   R-3

Obverse III² 13 – Ear doubled on inner right side. Date set further left than normal.

Reverse C⁴/C³ i – III O mint mark set slightly high, centered and upright. Extra olive to right of olive connected to olive branch. Doubling on top of olive branch at right of olives, at base of top and left olive leaf clusters, top of middle leaf in left olive leaf cluster, top of top leaf in lower olive leaf cluster, tops of arrow feathers, back of lower arrow head, middle top of eagle's left wing, and back of eagle's nostril and eye. NI-E TATE O doubled faintly towards rim.

24   **III² 1 • C⁴ k (O Set High and Right)**   (181)   I-2   R-3

Reverse C⁴ k – III O mint mark set high, upright, and slightly to right.

25   **III² 14 • C⁴/C³ j (Doubled Obverse, 2 Olive Reverse)**   (181)   I-3   R-3

Obverse III² 14 – Outside of ear doubled on right, hairline above ear doubled at bottom and eyelid doubled underneath. Date at left edge of normal position.

Reverse C⁴/C³ j – III O mint mark set slightly high and to right with slight tilt to left. Extra olive to right of olive connected to olive branch. Doubling on top of olive branch at right of olives, at base of top and left olive leaf clusters, on end of second arrow feather next to olive branch, middle talon on eagle's right leg, right of eagle's nostril and eye and back of lower arrow head. UNI-ED TAT OF doubled faintly toward rim.

26   **III² 15 • C⁴ l (Doubled Profile and Reverse Lettering)**   (181)   I-3   R-3

Obverse III² 15 – Doubled nose, lips, and chin on Liberty head profile. Date set further left than normal.

Reverse C⁴ l – Slightly doubled UNITED STATES OF ER-C in a radial direction, doubled upper right and left wreath towards rim, and IN GOD WE RUST doubled at top. III O mint mark set slightly high and tilted left.

27   **III² 1 • C⁴/C³ l (2 Olive Reverse)**   (181)   I-3   R-3

Reverse C⁴/C³ l – III O mint mark set slightly high and set slightly to right with slight tilt to right. Extra olive to right of olive connected to olive branch. Doubling on top of olive branch at right of olives, at base of olive leaf clusters, at top of middle leaf in olive leaf clusters, at top of upper leaves in lower olive leaf cluster, top of arrow feathers and sheaves, top of eagle's right claw on right talon, back of lower arrow head, and top feathers in eagle's left wing.

28   **III² 15 • C⁴/C³ m (Doubled Profile, 2 Olive Reverse)**   (181)   I-3   R-3

Reverse C⁴/C³ m – III O mint mark set slightly high with slight tilt to left. Extra olive to right of olive connected to olive branch. Doubling on top of olive branch at right of olives, at base of olive leaf clusters, at top of upper leaf in lower olive leaf cluster, back of lower arrow head, middle feathers in eagle's left wing, and eagle's nostril. Polishing lines between olive branch and arrow feather and around eagle's legs.

20 R C⁴/C³   21 R C⁴/C³

1902-O

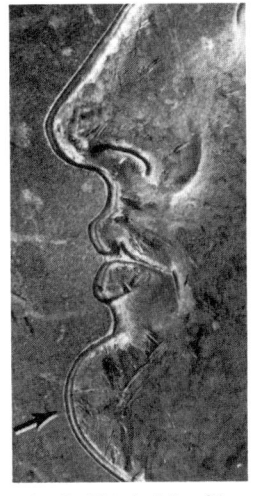

21 O Tripled Profile

23 O Doubled Ear

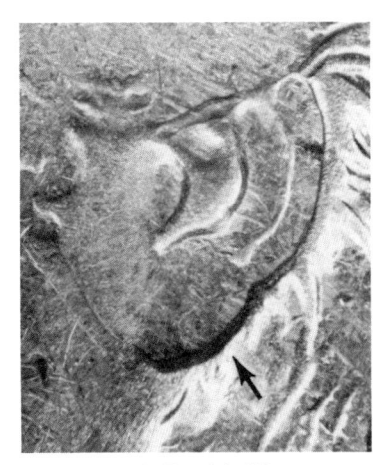

25 O Doubled Ear

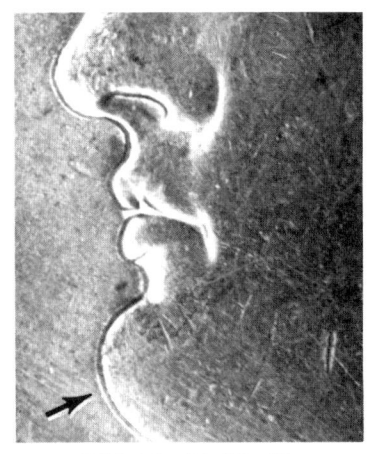

26 O Doubled Profile

23 R C⁴/C³

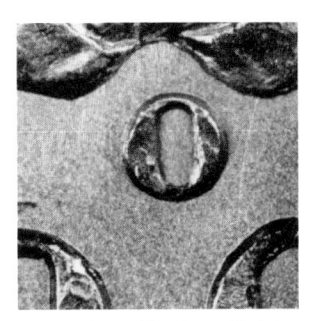

24 R O Set High and Right

25 R C⁴/C³

26 R Doubled Letters

27 R C⁴/C³

28 R C⁴/C³

29 R C⁴/C³

375

1902-O

29   III² 16 • C⁴/C³ n (Doubled Ear, 2 Olive Reverse)   (181)   I-3   R-3
  Obverse III² 16 – Ear doubled slightly at middle outside. Liberty head profile slightly doubled on nose, lips, chin and neck. First U in PLURIBUS has horizontal die gouge on right side.
  Reverse C⁴/C³ n – III O mint mark set slightly high, upright and tilted slightly to right. Extra olive to right of olive connected to olive branch. Doubling on very top of olive branch at right of olives, at base of left and bottom olive leaf clusters, around tops of leaves in top olive leaf cluster, back of lower arrow head, upper middle feathers of eagle's left wing, right side of eagle's nostril and eye, and eagle's beak.

30   III² 15 • C⁴/C³ o (Doubled Profile, 2 Olive Reverse)   (181)   I-3   R-3
  Reverse C⁴/C³ o – III O mint mark set slightly high, upright and slightly to right. Extra olive to right of olive connected to olive branch. Doubling on top of olive branch at right of olives, at base of olive leaf clusters, around upper leaf in top olive leaf cluster, at top of upper leaf in lower olive leaf cluster, on end of second arrow feather next to olive branch, back lower arrow head, faintly on right two innermost right wing feathers next to leg, upper middle feathers of eagle's left wing, right side of eagle's nostril and eye, eagle's beak, and top of eagle's right wing. Slight doubling of NT-ED STA-E towards rim and D, W-T in motto on right side.

31   III² 3 • C⁴/C³ p (Near Date, 2 Olive Reverse)   (181)   I-3   R-3
  Obverse III² 3 – Some specimens show base of 2 filled in.
  Reverse C⁴/C³ p – III O mint mark set slightly high and set slightly to right. Extra olive to right of olive connected to olive branch. Doubling on top of olive branch at right of olives, at base of left olive leaf cluster, on end of second arrow feather next to olive branch, back of lower arrow head, right of eagle's nostril and eye, and top middle feathers of eagle's left wing.

32   III² 1 • C⁴/C³ q (2 Olive Reverse)   (181)   I-3   R-3
  Obverse III² 1 – Base of 2 filled in.
  Reverse C⁴/C³ q – III O mint mark set slightly high, centered, and tilted slightly to left. Extra olive to right of olive connected to olive branch. Doubling at back of lower arrow head, right of eagle's nostril and eye and top feathers of eagle's left wing. UNITED STATE OF doubled faintly toward rim.

33   III² 8 • C⁴ b (Doubled Profile, High O)   I-2   R-3

34   III² 3 • C⁴/C³ r (Near Date, 2 Olive Reverse)   (181)   I-3   R-3
  Reverse C⁴/C³ r – III O mint mark set high and tilted left. Extra olive to right of olive connected to olive branch. Doubling on top of olive branch at right of olives, at base of olive leaf clusters, top of upper leaf in bottom olive leaf cluster, tops of arrow feathers, back of lower arrow head, middle feathers of eagle's left wing and right of eagle's nostril and eye.

35   III² 6 • C⁴ j (Doubled Profile, O Tilted Left)   (181)   I-2   R-3

36   III² 9 • C⁴ b (Doubled Ear, High O)   (181)   I-2   R-3

37   III² 1 • C⁴ b (High O)   (181)   I-2   R-3

38   III² 8 • C⁴/C³ s (Doubled Profile, 2 Olive Reverse)   (181)   I-3   R-3
  Reverse C⁴/C³ s – III O mint mark centered and upright with slight shift to right. Extra olive to right of olive connected to olive branch. Doubling on top of olive branch at right of olives, at base of olive leaf clusters, top of upper two leaves in bottom olive leaf cluster, tops of arrow feathers and middle of shafts, back of lower arrow head, middle feathers of eagle's left wing and right of eagle's nostril and eye.

39   III² 1 • C⁴/C³ t (2 Olive Reverse)   (181)   I-2   R-3
  Reverse C⁴/C³ t – III O mint mark set slightly high, centered and upright. Extra olive to right of olive connected to olive branch. Doubling on top of olive branch at right of olives, at base of all olive leaf clusters, edge of top olive leaf clusters, top leaf of lower olive lead cluster, tops of arrow feathers, back of lower arrow head, middle top of eagle's left wing, right side of two innermost wing feathers next to leg and right of eagle's nostril and eye.

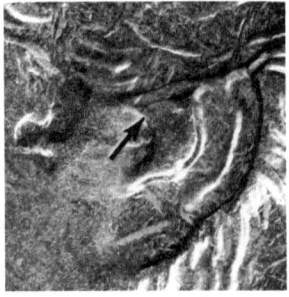

29 O Doubled Ear    30 R C⁴/C³   31 R C⁴/C³

1902-O / 1902-S

| 40 | III²15 • C⁴a (Doubled Profile, Near Date) | (181) | I-2 | R-3 |
| 41 | III²17 • C⁴a (Doubled 1, Near Date) | (181) | I-2 | R-3 |

Obverse III²17 – 1 in date doubled slightly below upper crossbar. Date set further left than normal.

32 R C⁴/C³

34 R C⁴/C³

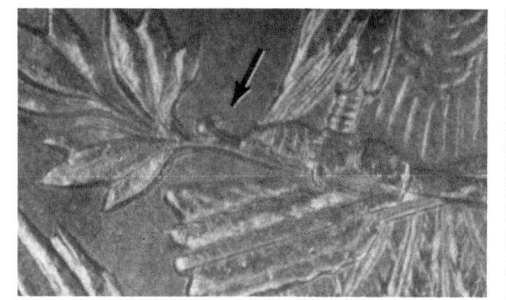

38 R C⁴/C³

39 R C⁴/C³

41 O Doubled 1

1902-S

Very weakly struck is the norm for this issue with heavy planchet striations across the head, eagle and parts of the fields showing quite often. Full strikes are occasionally seen however. Luster is usually good. A few minor die varieties exist but none are significant. Proof-likes are quite rare and have little contrast.

| 1 | III²1 • C⁴a (Normal Die) | | I-1 | R-2 |

Obverse III²1 – Normal die of III² type with closed 9. Some specimens show base of 2 filled in.
Reverse C⁴a – Normal die of C⁴ type with large V S mint mark centered and upright.

| 2 | III²2 • C⁴a (Near Date) | (189) | I-2 | R-3 |

Obverse III²2 – Date set further left than normal.

| 3 | III²3 • C⁴/C³a (Doubled 02, 2 Olive Reverse) | (189) | I-3 | R-3 |

Obverse III²3 – Doubled 02 in date. 0 doubled slightly on top right outside. 2 tripled at top outside.
Reverse C⁴/C³a – Extra olive to right of olive connected to olive branch. Doubling at base of left olive leaf cluster, top of olive branch at right of olives and back of lower arrow head. Slight doubling of E STAT-F towards rim.

| 4 | III²1 • C⁴b (S Tilted Left) | | I-2 | R-3 |

Reverse C⁴b – V S mint mark centered tilted left.

| 5 | III²4 • C⁴/C³b (Doubled 19, 2 Olive Reverse) | (189) | I-3 | R-3 |

Obverse III²4 – Doubled 19 in date. 1 doubled below upper crossbar on field surface and at top left and right of lower crossbar on surface of digit. 9 doubled slightly at lower left inside of lower loop. Date set further left than normal.
Reverse C⁴/C³b – Extra olive to right of olive connected to olive branch. Doubling at base of top and left olive leaf cluster, below bottom leaf in left and lower leaf cluster, top of olive branch at right of olives, slightly on top of arrow feathers, back of lower arrow head, and faintly on right of two innermost right wing feathers next to leg. STATES OF doubled faintly towards rim.

1902-S

6   **III²5 • C⁴/C³ c (Doubled Profile, 2 Olive Reverse)**   (189)   I-3   R-3
    Obverse III²5 – Slightly doubled nose, lips, and chin of Liberty head profile.
    Reverse C⁴/C³ c – V S mint mark tilted left. Extra olive to right of olive connected to olive branch. Doubling on top of olive branch at right of olives, at base of top and left olive leaf clusters, at top of top leaf in lower olive leaf cluster, on end of second arrow feather next to olive branch, right of eagle's nostril and eye, and back of lower arrow head.

7   **III²6 • C⁴/C³ d (Doubled Profile, 2 Olive Reverse)**   (189)   I-3   R-3
    Obverse III²6 – Slightly doubled nose, lips and chin on Liberty head profile. Date set further left than normal with base of 2 filled in.
    Reverse C⁴/C³ d – Extra olive to right of olive connected to olive branch. Doubling at top of olive branch at right of olives, base of left olive leaf cluster, slightly on top of arrow feathers, back of lower arrow head, upper feathers of eagle's left wing, right of eagle's nostril and faintly on right of two innermost right wing feathers next to leg. UNITED STATES OF doubled faintly towards rim.

8   **III²5 • C⁴/C³ b (Doubled Profile, 2 Olive Reverse)**   (189)   I-3   R-3

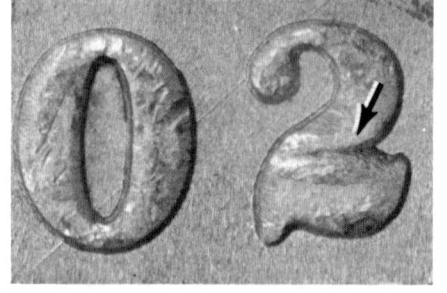

1 O Filled 2

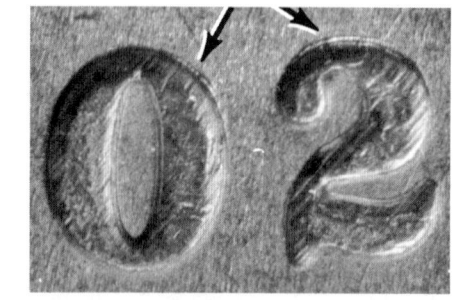

3 O Doubled 02

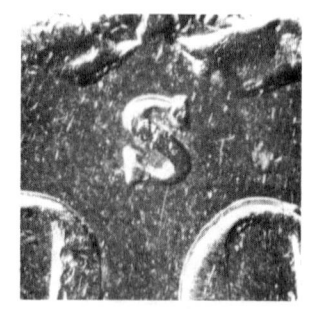

4 R S Tilted Left

5 O Doubled 19

3 R C⁴/C³

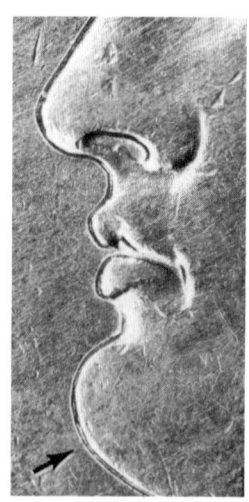

6 O Doubled Profile

5 R C⁴/C³

6 R C⁴/C³

7 R C⁴/C³

378

1903-P

Full strike is the general rule for this issue. Luster is seldom very flashy, but tends to be brilliant and subdued. This gives it a sameness look over the devices and field. In terms of full strike and minimal bag marks, the 1903-P is the most generally available in nice condition for the later P mints. A surprisingly few number of minor die varieties exist and none are significant. Proof-likes are fairly scarce and have little contrast. Some proof-likes have numerous fine die polishing lines in the fields. Sliders of this issue are often hard to differentiate from uncirculated specimens because of the brilliant and subdued luster. Proofs have little contrast.

1	III²1 • C⁴a (Closed 9)		I-1	R-2

Obverse III²1 – Normal die of III² type with closed 9.
Reverse C⁴a – Normal die of C⁴ type.

2	III²2 • C⁴a (Open 9)		I-1	R-2

Obverse III²2 – Normal die with open 9.

3	III²3 • C⁴a (Doubled 3)	(189)	I-2	R-3

Obverse III²3 – 3 in date doubled slightly at top inside of upper loop. Closed 9.

4	III²4 • C⁴a • (Near Date)		I-2	R-3

Obverse III²4 – Date set further left than normal.

5	III²5 • C⁴a (Doubled Profile, Near Date)	(189)	I-2	R-3

Obverse III²5 – Slightly doubled lower front hairline, nose, lips, and chin on Liberty head profile. Date set further left than normal.

3 O Doubled 3

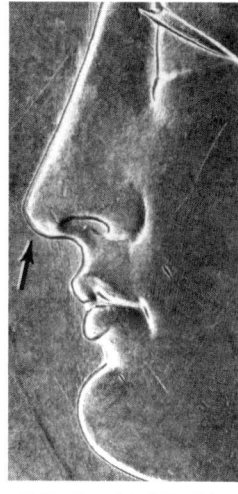

5 O Doubled Profile

1903-O

This issue usually has a good strike and good luster. Only a few minor die varieties exist and none are significant. Proof-likes are very scarce and have little to some light contrast. Semi proof-like are more available but should not be mistaken for full proof-likes.

1	III²1 • C⁴a (Normal Die)		I-1	R-2

Obverse III²1 – Normal die of III² type with open 9.
Reverse C⁴a – Normal die of C⁴ type with medium III O mint mark, centered and upright.

2	III²1 • C⁴b (O Tilted Left)	(181)	I-2	R-3

Reverse C⁴b – Centered III O mint mark tilted slightly to left and set slightly high.

3	III²2 • C⁴c (O Set Right, Tilted Left)		I-2	R-3

Obverse III²2 – Normal die of III² type with closed 9.
Reverse C⁴c – III O set right and tilted left.

1903-O / 1903-S

4	III²3 • C⁴c (Doubled 3, O Set Right, Tilted Left)	(181)	I-2	R-4

Obverse III²3 – 3 in date doubled at top outside as thin curved arc. Closed 9. Slight doubling of Liberty head profile including nose, lips and chin.

5	III²3 • C⁴a (Doubled 3)	(189)	I-2	R-4
6	III²1 • C⁴d (High O)	(181)	I-2	R-3

Reverse C⁴d – III O mint mark set high, centered and upright

7	III²4 • C⁴d (Near Date, High O)	(181)	I-2	R-3

Obverse III²4 – Date set further left than normal.

8	III²1 • C⁴e (High O Set Right)	(181)	I-2	R-3

Reverse C⁴e – III O mint mark set high and to right with slight tilt to left.

9	III²5 • C⁴b (Doubled 1, O Tilted Left)	(181)	I-2	R-3

Obverse III²5 – 1 in date doubled slightly at lower right outside of base as a thin line. Liberty head profile slightly doubled along forehead, nose, lips and chin.

10	III²1 • C⁴f (O Tilted Right)	(181)	I-2	R-3

Reverse C⁴f – III O mint mark centered and tilted slightly to right.

11	III²2 • C³a (High O)	(181)	I-2	R-5

Reverse C³a – Normal die of C³ type with medium O mint mark, set slightly high, centered and upright.

2 R O Tilted Left

3 R O Set Right, Tilted Left

6 R High O

8 R High O Set Right

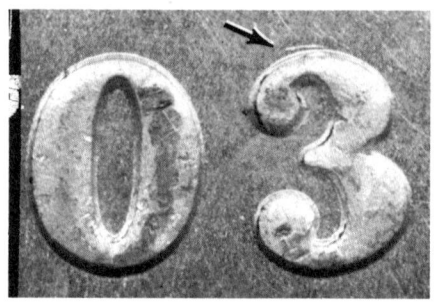

4 O Doubled 3

9 O Doubled 1

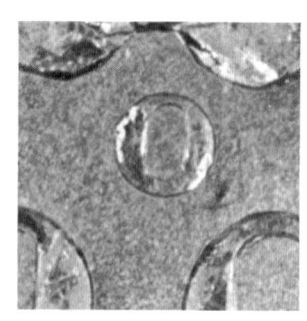

10 R O Tilted Right

1903-S

The strike on this issue is full and the luster very good. Although scarce in mint state, the quality is generally high. A few minor die varieties exist. However, a significant and scarce variety is VAM 2 with a small "S" mint mark of the size used on Barber quarters. The highest grade for this small "S" variety is a slider AU and it is rare above EF grades. Proof-likes are extremely rare and when encountered, have little contrast.

1	III²1 • C⁴a (Normal Die)		I-1	R-2

Obverse III²1 – Normal die of III² type with open 9.
Reverse C⁴a – Normal die of C⁴ type with large V S mint mark centered and upright.

380

1903-S

2   III²1 • C⁴b (Small S)   (189)   I-4   R-4
Reverse C⁴b – Normal die with small II S mint mark centered and upright.

3   III²1 • C⁴c (S Tilted Left)   (189)   I-2   R-3
Reverse C⁴c – Centered V S mint mark tilted to the left.

4   III²1 • C⁴/C³a (2 Olive Reverse)   (189)   I-3   R-3
Reverse C⁴/C³a – Extra olive to right of olive connected to olive branch. Doubling at base of left olive leaf cluster, top of top leaf in lower leaf cluster, top of olive branch at right of olives, tops of arrow feathers, top feathers of eagle's left wing, right of eagle's nostril and back of lower arrow head. Centered V S mint mark tilted to left.

5   III²2 • C⁴/C³b (Slanted Date, 2 Olive Reverse)   (189)   I-3   R-3
Obverse III²2 – Slight slant to date with 1 closest to rim.
Reverse C⁴/C³b – Faint shallow extra olive to right of olive connected to olive branch. Doubling at base of top and left olive leaf clusters, right of eagle's nostril and eye, and back of lower arrow head. V S mint mark set upright and slightly high.

6   III²1 • C⁴/C³c (2 Olive Reverse)   (189)   I-3   R-3
Reverse C⁴/C³c – Faint shallow extra olive to right of olive connected to olive branch. Doubling at back of lower arrow head. V S mint mark is centered and upright.

7   III²2 • C⁴c (Slanted Date, S Tilted Left)   (189)   I-2   R-3

8   III²1 • C⁴/C³d (2 Olive Reverse)   (189)   I-3   R-3
Reverse C⁴/C³d – Faint shallow extra olive to right of olive connected to olive branch. Doubling at base of top and left olive leaf cluster, back of lower arrow head, upper part of eagle's left wing, and right side of eagle's nostril and eye. Centered V S mint mark with slight tilt to right.

9   III²1 • C⁴d (S Set Right)   (189)   I-2   R-3
Reverse C⁴d – V S mint mark set slightly to right and upright.

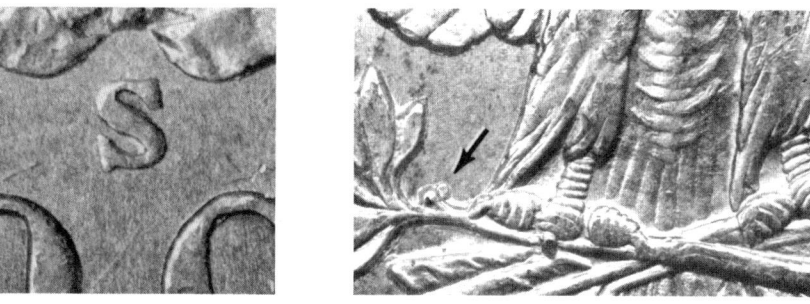

3 R S Tilted Left

4 R C⁴/C³

5 R C⁴/C³

5 O Slanted Date

6 R C⁴/C³

8 R C⁴/C³

1904-P

1904-P

Generally the strike has a touch of weakness although full strikes are available. Luster is generally dull and subdued. A few minor die varieties exist but none are significant. Full proof-likes with deep mirrors are very rare and the few known specimens exhibited little contrast. Proofs have little contrast like the two previous issues and most are marred by hairlines and dull luster.

1 III²1 • C⁴a (Normal Die)　　　　　　　　　　　　　　　　　　　　　　　　I-1　　R-2
   Obverse III²1 – Normal die of III² type with closed 9.
   Reverse C⁴a – Normal die of C⁴ type.

1A III²1 • C⁴a (Pitted Reverse)　　　　　　　　　　　　　　　　　　　　　　I-2　　R-3
   Reverse C⁴a – Reverse pitted around D in DOLLAR.

2 III²2 • C⁴a (Doubled 1-4)　　　　　　　　　　　　　　　　　　　　　　　　I-2　　R-3
   Obverse III²2 – 1 and 4 in date doubled slightly above the bottom crossbars.

3 III²3 • C⁴a (Spiked 1, Doubled 4)　　　　　　　　　　　　　　　　　　　　I-2　　R-3
   Obverse III²3 – 1 in date has short vertical spike above bottom crossbar on right side. 4 is doubled at bottom of both crossbars. Liberty head profile slightly doubled.

4 III²4 • C⁴a (Doubled 9-4)　　　　　　　　　　(181)　　　　　　　　　　　I-2　　R-3
   Obverse III²4 – Doubled 9-4 in date. 1 has a spike of metal projecting up from right side of base. 9 is doubled strongly at bottom outside of both loops. 4 is doubled slightly at left bottom of crossbar. Liberty head profile slightly doubled.

5 III²5 • C⁴a (Doubled Profile)　　　　　　　　　(189)　　　　　　　　　　　I-2　　R-3
   Obverse III²5 – Slightly doubled profile of Liberty head including forehead, nose, lips and chin.

2 O Doubled 1-4

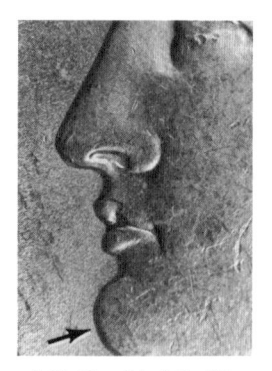

5 O Doubled Profile

3 O Spiked 1, Doubled 4

4 O Doubled 9-4

1904-O

The strike is usually slightly weak although quantities of fully struck as well as flat strikes can be encountered because of the large mintage. Luster is generally good. Many hundreds of original mint bags were released by the Treasury in 1962-64 making the 1904-O the most available BU O mint after the 1885-O. Quite a few minor die varieties exist but none are particularly significant. Proof-likes are fairly available but generally have little contrast. A few deep mirrors with some light contrast are known.

1   III²1 • C⁴a (Normal Die)   I-1   R-2
Obverse III²1 – Normal die of III² type with closed 9.
Reverse C⁴a – Normal die of C⁴ type with medium III O mint mark centered and upright.

1A   III²1 • C⁴a (Polishing Lines on Reverse)   (181)   I-2   R-3
Reverse C⁴a – Heavy vertical polishing lines in eagle's wings and horizontal polishing lines in eagle's tail feathers and arrow feathers.

2   III²1 • C⁴b • (O Tilted Left)   I-2   R-3
Reverse C⁴b – Normal die with III 0 mint mark tilted to the left.

3   III²2 • C⁴a (Doubled 19)   I-2   R-3
Obverse III²2 – Doubled 19 in date. 1 doubled below upper crossbar and slightly at bottom. 9 doubled strongly at bottom. Closed 9 variety.

4   III²3 • C⁴a (Doubled Date)   I-2   R-3
Obverse III²3 – Entire date is doubled. 1 doubled at top right of bottom crossbar as vertical line with hooks on end. Doubled 9 in date on lower left outside and top inside of upper loop. 0 doubled slightly at bottom outside and 4 at top left outside. Closed 9. Some specimens have a filled 4.

4A   III²3 • C⁴a (Doubled Date)   I-2   R-3
Reverse C⁴a – Pitted reverse and polishing marks as in 5A reverse.

5   III²4 • C⁴a (Doubled 1-4)   I-2   R-3
Obverse III²4 – Doubled 1-4 in date. 1 doubled at bottom of top crossbar. Lower crossbar of 4 doubled at top right. Closed 9. Profile of Liberty head is slightly doubled.

5A   III²4 • C⁴a (Doubled 1-4)   I-2   R-3
Reverse C⁴a – Reverse pitted around OL in DOLLAR. Heavy polishing marks in eagle's wings and tail feathers plus wreath bow.

6   III²4 • C⁴b (Doubled 1-4)   (181)   I-2   R-3
Obverse III²4 – Some have a filled 4.
Reverse C⁴b – Heavy polishing marks on eagle and in wreath bow.

7   III²1 • C⁴c (O Set Right)   I-2   R-3
Reverse C⁴c – III O mint mark set high and slightly to right.

8   III²5 • C⁴a (Far Date)   I-2   R-3
Obverse III²5 – Date set further right than normal. Closed 9.

9   III²6 • C⁴d (Low Date)   I-2   R-3
Obverse III²6 – Date set lower than normal. Closed 9.
Reverse C⁴d – III O mint mark set right and tilted left.

10   III²1 – C⁴e (O/O)   I-2   R-3
Reverse C⁴e – III O mint mark set high and tilted to left with short curved segment at bottom right outside. Polishing lines in wreath center, olive branch leaves, eagle's tail feathers and wings.

1A R Polishing Lines in TF 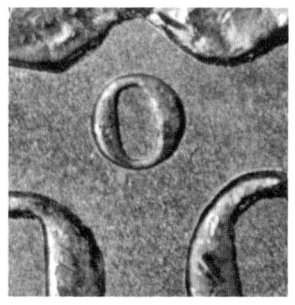   2 R O Tilted Left 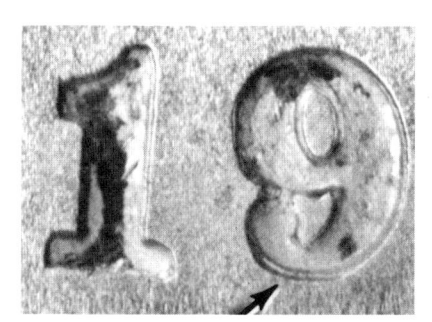   3 O Doubled 19

1904-O

4 O Doubled Date

4 O Filled 4

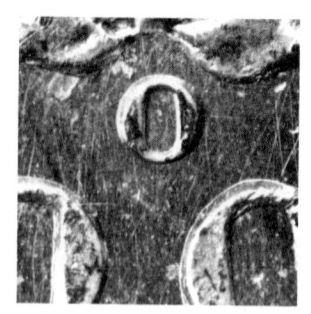

7 R O Set Right

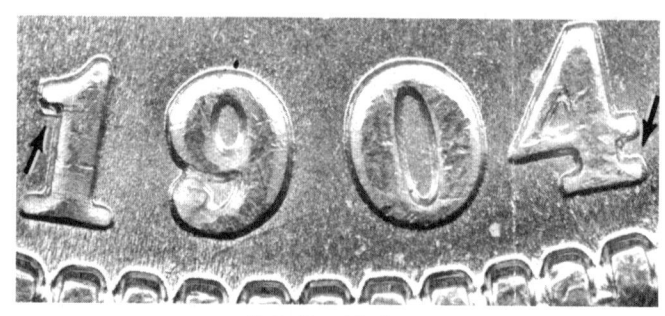

5 O Doubled 1-4

5A R Pitted Reverse

9 O Low Date

10 R O/O

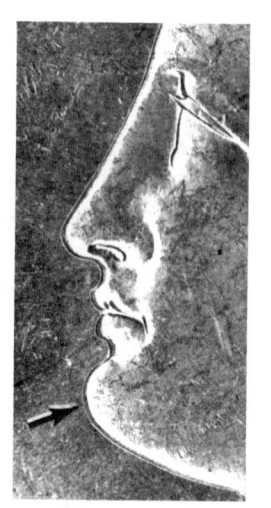

11 O Doubled Profile

11	III²7 • C⁴a (Doubled Profile)	(189)	I-2	R-3

Obverse III²7 – Profile of Liberty head is doubled in forward hairline, forehead, nose, lips and chin.

12	III²8 • C⁴b (Doubled 9-4)	(189)	I-2	R-3

Obverse III²8 – Doubled 9-4 in date. 9 doubled on bottom outside of both loops. 4 doubled slightly on left side of lower half of vertical shaft.

13	III²1 • C⁴f (High O)	(181)	I-2	R-3

Reverse C⁴f – III O mint mark set high, centered and upright. Some show heavy polishing lines in eagle's wings, neck and tail feathers plus wreath center and right side.

14	III²2 • C⁴f (Double 19, High O)	(181)	I-2	R-3
15	III²1 • C⁴g (High O Tilted Left)	(189)	I-2	R-3

Reverse C⁴g – III O mint mark set high and slightly to right with slant to left. Fine polishing lines in eagle's tail feathers and wings.

16	III²9 • C⁴a (Slanted Date)	(181)	I-2	R-3

Obverse III²9 – Slight slant to date with 1 closest to rim.

17	III²4 • C⁴b (Doubled 1-4)	(181)	I-2	R-3

Reverse C⁴b – Heavy polishing marks on eagle and in wreath bow on some specimens.

1904-O

| 18 | III²7 • C⁴f (Doubled Profile, High O) | (181) | I-2 | R-3 |

Reverse C⁴f – Not all specimens have polishing lines in eagle.

| 19 | III²10 • C⁴f (Doubled 9, High O) | (189) | I-2 | R-3 |

Obverse III²10 – 9 doubled at lower left outside of upper and lower loops.
Reverse C⁴f – Polishing lines in eagle and wreath like VAM 13.

| 20 | III²1 • C⁴h (High O Tilted Left) | (189) | I-2 | R-3 |

Reverse C⁴h – III O mint mark set high and slightly to left with slant to left.

| 21 | III²11 • C⁴f (Doubled O, High O) | (189) | I-2 | R-3 |

Obverse III²11 – III O mint mark doubled at top outside.

22	III²7 • C⁴b (Doubled Profile, O Tilted Left)	(189)	I-2	R-3
23	III²5 • C⁴f (Far Date, High O)	(181)	I-2	R-3
24	III²12 • C⁴a (Doubled 9-4)	(181)	I-2	R-4

Obverse III²12 – Doubled 9-4 in date. 9 doubled at top right inside of lower loop as short spike. 4 doubled at very top as short horizontal line.

12 O Doubled 9-4

13 R Polishing Lines

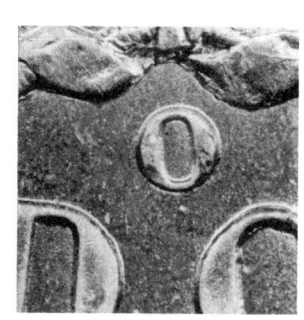

15 R High O, Tilted Left

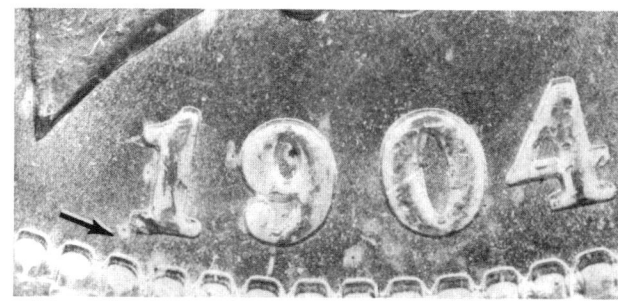

16 O Slanted Date

19 O Doubled 9

20 R High O, Tilted Left

21 O Doubled 0

24 O Doubled 9-4

385

1904-O / 1904-S

25   III² 13 • C⁴ b (Doubled Profile and 9, O Tilted Left)   (181)   I-2   R-3
Obverse III² 13 – Profile of Liberty head is doubled in nose, lips and chin. 9 doubled slightly on lower left outside of bottom loop. Date set on left side of normal position.

26   III² 14 • C⁴ h (Doubled 19 and Profile, High O Tilted Left)   (181)   I-2   R-3
Obverse III² 14 – 1 doubled slightly below upper crossbar. 9 doubled slightly at lower left outside of upper loop. Profile of Liberty head doubled from hair down to neck. Date set further right than normal.

27   III² 1 • C⁴ i (Doubled AR)   (181)   I-2   R-3
Reverse C⁴ i – AR in DOLLAR doubled slightly at very bottom. III O mint mark tilted slightly left.

28   III² 1 • C⁴ j (Doubled Reverse Legend)   (189)   I-2   R-3
Reverse C⁴ j – UNITED STATES OF AMERICA and IN GOD WE TRUST doubled and tripled slightly towards rim.

25 O Doubled 9

26 O Doubled 19

27 R Doubled AR

28 R Doubled Legend

1904-S

Most specimens of this issue have a touch of weakness in the strike although full strikes can be located. Luster is good. A few minor die varieties exist but none are very significant. Proof-likes are extremely rare and are seldom encountered in the market. Those known have little contrast.

1   III² 1 • C⁴ a (Normal Die)   I-1   R-2
Obverse III² 1 – Normal die of III² type with closed 9.
Reverse C⁴ a – Normal die of C⁴ type with large V S mint mark centered and upright.

1A   III² 1 – C⁴ a (Die Gouge in STATES)   (189)   I-2   R-3
Reverse C⁴ a – Diagonal die gouge through A in STATES.

1B   III² 1 • C⁴ a (Filled 4)   (189)   I-2   R-4
Obverse III² 1 – Die chips in 4 to almost fill upper part.

2   III² 2 • C⁴ a (Doubled Profile)   (189)   I-2   R-3
Obverse III² 2 – Profile of Liberty head is doubled on forward hairline, forehead, nose, lips and chin. E PLURI U-UM doubled slightly on lower portions of letters towards rim. Date set further right than normal.

1904-S

3   III²3 • C⁴/C³ a (Slanted Date, 2 Olive Reverse)   (189)   I-3   R-3
Obverse III²3 – Slight slant to date with 2 closest to rim.
Reverse C⁴/C³ a – Extra Olive to right of olive connected to olive branch. Doubling at base of top and left olive leaf clusters, right of eagle's nostril and eye, and back of lower arrow head. GOD WE doubled on right side.

4   III²1 • C⁴/C³ b (2 Olive Reverse)   (189)   I-3   R-3
Reverse C⁴/C³ b – Shallow extra olive to right olive connected to olive branch. Doubling at base of all three olive clusters, back of lower arrow head, feathers at top of eagle's left wing, right side of eagle's nostril and eye, and lower right of OD WE TR. V S mint mark centered and tilted right.

5   III²4 • C⁴ b (Doubled 4, High S)   (189)   I-2   R-3
Obverse III²4 – 4 doubled slightly below crossbar and base.
Reverse C⁴ b – Large V S mint mark set high and upright.

6   III²5 • C⁴ a (Doubled 4)   (189)   I-2   R-3
Obverse III²5 – 4 doubled slightly at bottom inside of opening and at top right of bottom crossbar.

1A R Die Gouge in A
(Photo courtesy of Goldfreed)

3 R C⁴/C³

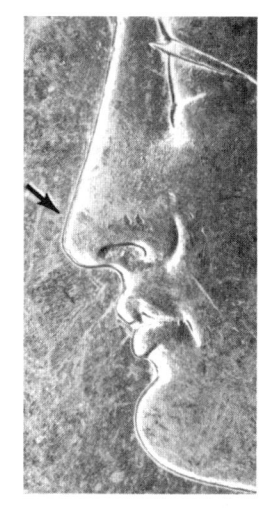

2 O Doubled Profile

1B O Filled 4

4 R C⁴/C³

6 O Doubled 4

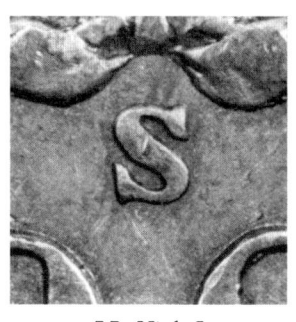

5 R High S

5 O Doubled 4

387

1921-P

A slight touch of weakness is usually evident in the lower wreath leaves on the reverse. Fully struck coins with all wreath leaves detailed are somewhat difficult to locate. Luster is usually average but many are dull due to long use of dies with metal flow evident on die extremities. Occasionally some specimens show exceptional luster with quite a bit of frosting on the devices. The design of the 1921 Morgan is slightly different than the previous issues. In 1910 all master dies and hubs were destroyed at the Philadelphia mint except for those in current production. Thus, new master dies had a slightly flatter and coarser look. The central relief is lower, the hair details and eagle's wing feathers are coarser and more deeply outlined. The eagle's breast is flat and the feathers have little detail. Aesthetically, the 1921 design is not as pleasing to most people.

Because of the large mintage, a number of minor die varieties exist. Two minor design types are known for the 1921-P. The initial design had 17 berries in the right reverse wreath and shallow middle part of the olive branch. The later design which was also used on all 1921-S and D had 16 berries in the right wreath and full olive branches. Both design types are common for the 1921-P. Some of the first design type had edge reeding with a very low count of 157 (instead of normal 189) and are known as VAM 2 "infrequent reeding". Seven different obverse/reverse die combinations are known so this edge variety is not particularly scarce. One of the infrequent reeding varieties, VAM 4, has N of IN on the reverse repunched with strong doubling. VAM 1B has the heaviest die polishing lines known for the Morgan series.

A curious phenomena shows up on some of the second design 1921-P, D and S coins. Small circular dots show on various portions of the obverse and reverse dies. These may have been used to identify some of the first dies of the second 1921 design and some may also be marks from Rockwell hardness tests on dies. The most prominent dots visible to the naked eye are VAM's 8 and 9 which have a small circular raised dot on the field below eagle's right wing and on field between eagle's left wing and top arrow head point respectively. Smaller dots are on a number of other dies but most are not significant and were probably caused by gas bubbles trapped in the die steel melts.

Proof-likes are fairly scarce and only have little to light contrast. Proof-likes exist for both design types as well as for all seven die varieties with infrequent reeding edge. A fair number of the proof-likes exhibit cloudy spots due to storage contamination. It is very difficult to find nice proof-likes with deep mirrors, fully struck, spot free, some contrast and with minimal bag marks. Because of a large mintage and high survival rate, proof-likes should ordinarily be fairly available. Apparently at some point in 1921, all three mints discarded the practice of basining working dies. Since 1916, silver coins had designs not intended to be basined. With all three mints working to capacity in 1921 to replace the dollars melted in 1918-20, short cuts were probably taken in production. Without the basining step the design was not usually struck up completely in the wreath area.

Two types of proofs exist. A regular proof issue of 12 pieces was produced, known as Chapman proofs, because Henry Chapman of Philadelphia persuaded the Philadelphia mint to strike them. They have very deep mirrors and light contrast similar to the 1902-1904 proofs. They are the rarest of the Morgan proofs. A second 1921 proof type is the so-called Zerbe proof. These lack the depth of mirror and contrast of the Chapman proofs and are more correctly termed presentation pieces. It is estimated that 20-200 pieces were produced to appease Farran Zerbe because of the delay in the production of the new Peace dollars. Zerbe proofs can be identified by a small die scratch from the second U in UNUM to the denticles.

1 IV • D¹a (17 Berries) I-2 R-3
Obverse IV 1 – Normal die of IV type with open 9. Both 1's in date are doubled at top left side. Some specimens show a small dot after first 1.
Reverse D¹a – Extra berry inside of the right wreath opposite top berry to give a total of 17 berries rather than normal 16 for type D² reverse. TED of UNITED, ST-T-S of STATES are slightly doubled to three o'clock.

1A IV 1 • D¹a (Pitted Reverse) I-3 R-4
Reverse D¹a – 17 berry reverse with pitted die around eagle's tail feathers and center of wreath and many hundreds of fine polishing marks on lower part of die.

1B IV 1 • D¹a (Polished Reverse) (189) I-3 R-3
Reverse D¹a – Die excessively polished with heavy raised lines all over field of coins.

1C IV 1 • D¹a (Wreath Die Gouge) (189) I-2 R-4
Reverse D¹a – Thin vertical die gouge from eagle's tail feathers down through wreath bow.

2 IV 1 • D¹a (Infrequent Reeding) (157) I-5 R-3
Edge – This edge is infrequently reeded having about 34 reeds per linear inch.

2A IV 1 – D¹a (Infrequent Reeding, Reverse Die Gouges) (157) I-5 R-3
Reverse D¹a – Two short vertical die gouges down from denticles above S and T in STATES. Edge Infrequent Reeding.

1921-P

1 O Doubled 1-1

1 O Dot Date

1 R Extra Berry

1A R Pitted Reverse

1C R Die Gouge

1B R Die Polishing Lines

1 R Doubled Letters

3	IV 1 • D²a (16 Berries)		I-1	R-1

Reverse D²a – Normal die of D² type with 16 berries in wreath. There is a spike gouge above the bottom crossbar on right side of F in OF for all die varieties.

3A	IV 1 • D²a (Spike Tail Feathers)		I-2	R-5

Reverse D²a – Horizontal die gouge extending to right from number 3 tail feather.

3B	IV 1 • D²a (Pitted Reverse)		I-2	R-4

Reverse D²a – 16 berries reverse with pitted die to right of wreath bow above and inside D of DOLLAR.

3C	IV 1 • D²a (Pitted Reverse)	(189)	I-2	R-4

Reverse D²a – Pitted die around LL of DOLLAR.

3D	IV 1 • D²a (Overpolished Wing)	(189)	I-2	R-3

Reverse D²a – Eagle's left wing overpolished near body as are tail feathers next to eagle's right leg with many fine polishing lines present.

3E	IV 1 • D²a (Pitted Reverse)	(189)	I-2	R-4

Reverse D²a – Pitted die around arrow feathers.

3F	IV 1 • D²a (Pitted Reverse)	(189)	I-2	R-4

Reverse D²a – Pitted die around lower right wreath and AR in DOLLAR.

1921-P

2A R Die Gouges

3A R Spiked Tail Feathers

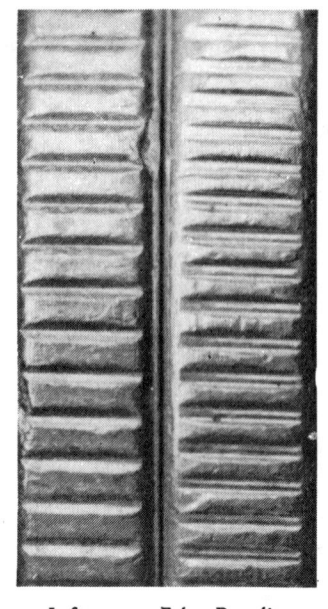

Infrequent Edge Reeding

3B R Pitted

3C R Pitted Reverse

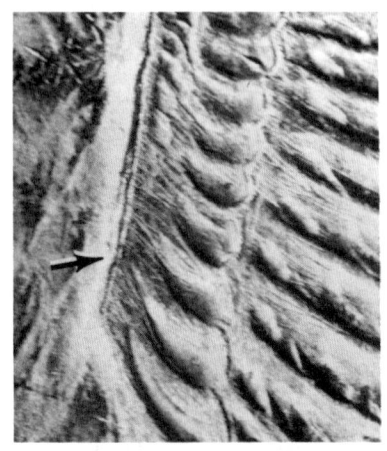

3D R Overpolished Wing

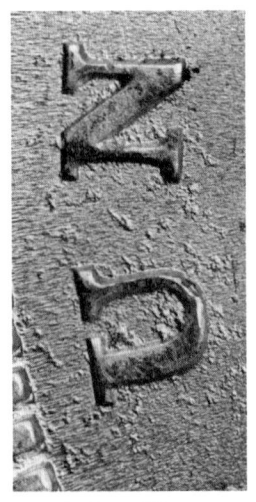

3E R Pitted Reverse

3F R Pitted Reverse

3G R Pitted Reverse

3H R Die Gouge in Olive Leaves

4 R Doubled N

390

1921-P

3G	IV 1 • D²a (Pitted Reverse)	(189)	I-2	R-4

Reverse D²a – Pitted die around UN of UNITED.

3H	IV 1 • D²a (Die Gouge Olive Leaves)	(189)	I-2	R-4

Reverse D²a – Long thick horizontal die gouge through upper olive leaf cluster.

4	IV 1 – D¹b (Infrequent Reeding, Doubled N)	(157)	I-5	R-3

Reverse D¹b – N of IN set low and doubled above serifs and at very top. Edge is infrequently reeded.

5	IV 2 • D²a (Doubled Date, Tripled Stars)	(189)	I-2	R-3

Obverse IV 2 – Entire date is doubled with tops of all digits doubled and left side of diagonal shaft of 2 also doubled. All left and right stars plus E-PL slightly tripled towards rim, with 4-7 stars on the left tripled the strongest.

Reverse D²a – Eagle's left wing is overpolished near body.

6	IV 3 – D²a (Doubled Date and Stars)	(189)	I-2	R-3

Obverse IV 3 – Outline of all date digits are doubled towards rim as are first three stars on left, all stars on right and tops of NUM.

7	IV 1 • D¹c (Tripled Reverse)	(189)	I-2	R-3

Reverse D¹c – Tripled ITED-T on left side, doubled U-E at bottom inside and doubled L-R at bottom outside.

8	IV 4 • D²b (Dot Next to Wing)	(189)	I-4	R-3

Obverse VI 4 – Very small circular raised dot to left of M in UNUM.
Reverse D²b – Small circular raised dot on field next to eagle's right wing. Possibly used to identify first dies of D² reverse.

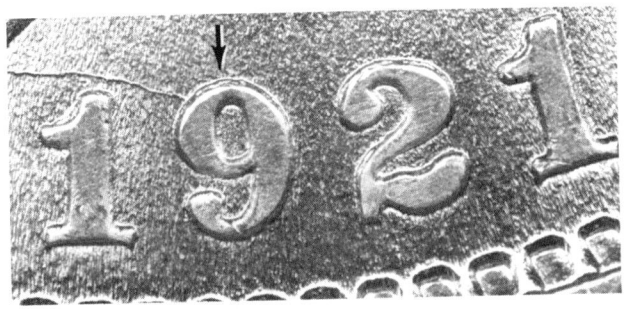

5 O Doubled Date

6 O Doubled Date

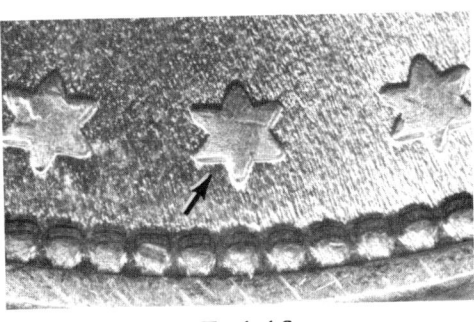

5 O Tripled Stars

5 R Tripled ITED

8 O Dot

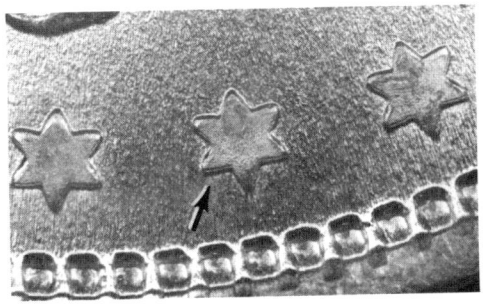

6 O Doubled Stars

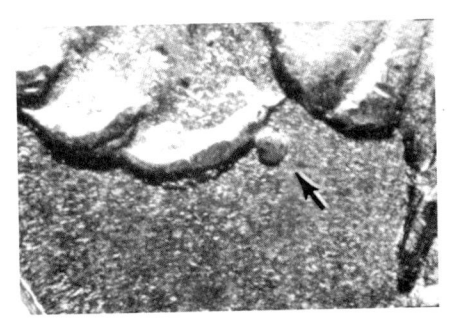

8 R Dot

9 O Dot

391

1921-P

| 9 | IV 5 • D²c (Dot Below Wing) | (189) | I-4 | R-3 |

Obverse IV 5 – Small circular raised dot above B in PLURIBUS, and below first star on right.
Reverse D²c – Small circular raised dot on field between eagle's left wing and top arrow head point, between two top arrow feathers, and above S in TRUST.

| 10 | IV 6 • D²a (Doubled Date and Stars) | (189) | I-3 | R-3 |

Obverse IV 6 – Outline of all date digits are doubled towards rim as are all right and left stars.

| 11 | IV 3 • D²d (Doubled Date and Stars, Doubled Reverse) | (189) | I-2 | R-3 |

Reverse D²d – Doubled right star and U-TED STATES OF A-ERICA and LL-R towards center, bottom right of G of GOD, and bottom of eagle's lower beak.

| 12 | IV 7 • D¹a (Tripled Stars) | (189) | I-2 | R-3 |

Obverse IV 7 – All stars on right and 4 to 7 stars on left are tripled towards rim with first three left stars slightly doubled.
Reverse D¹a – Horizontal polishing lines in all tail feathers.

| 13 | IV 8 • D¹a (Doubled Stars and Date) | (189) | I-2 | R-3 |

Obverse IV 8 – All left and right stars, date digits and E PLURIBUS UNUM doubled slightly towards rim.
Edge – Infrequent reeding variety.

| 14 | IV 9 • D²a (Tripled Stars) | (189) | I-2 | R-3 |

Obverse IV 9 – Left stars and E-PL tripled towards rim with date digits and right stars very slightly doubled towards rim.

NOTE: In the 1921-P series there appear numerous raised dots on various locations on both the obverse and reverse sides. It was first thought that these raised dots were put there by the mint workmen for some presently unknown reason. Current thought however is that these dots are the result of imperfect die steel and not the result of being deliberately put there. Therefore, these are not listed as die varieties at this time.

9 R Dot

11 O Doubled Stars and Letters

12 O Tripled Stars

13 O Doubled Stars

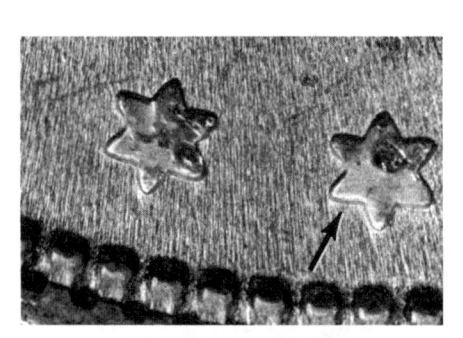

14 O Doubled Stars

1921-D

The strike on this issue is invariably slightly weak to quite weak on the wreath leaves. Fully struck specimens with all wreath leaves full are very difficult to locate. Luster is usually average but varies from fairly frosty to dull because of the high mintage and long use of the dies. A few die varieties exist. VAM 3 is significant with a dot just below eagle's right wing that can be seen with the naked eye. Full proof-likes are very scarce and have only a little contrast. A number of semi proof-like pieces exist with frosty devices but these should not be mistaken for full proof-likes.

1   **IV 1 • D²a (Normal Die)**   I-1   R-1
Obverse IV 1 – Normal die of IV type.
Reverse D²a – Normal die of D² type with small centered I D mint mark There is a spike above the bottom crossbar on the right side of F in OF for all die varieties. Both 1's in date are doubled at top left.

1A   **IV 1 • D²a (TRUT)**   I-2   R-4
Reverse D²a – Die fill in S of TRUST to form TRUT.

1B   **IV 1 • D²a (Capped R Die Chip)**   (189)   I-3   R-5
Reverse D²a – Heavily die cracked with die chip above R in AMERICA.

2   **IV 2 • D²a (Doubled Date)**   I-2   R-3
Obverse IV 2 – Entire date doubled. The doubling is to the upper left of all numbers.
Reverse D²a – Some specimens show diagonal die gouge through upper part of D in DOLLAR.

2A   **IV 2 • D²a (Doubled Date, Die Gouge in O)**   (189)   I-2   R-3
Reverse D²a – Die gouge at top right inside of O in DOLLAR.

3   **IV 3 • D²b (Dot Next to Wing)**   (189)   I-4   R-3
Obverse IV 3 – Small circular raised dot below eye and two in hair between ear and date.
Reverse D²b – Small circular raised dot on field next to eagle's right wing, in middle of eagle's left wing next to body, in upper loop of S in STAT, in middle of sixth tail feather, and above and below stem to right of first berry in left wreath.

4   **IV 1 • D²c (Dots on Reverse)**   (189)   I-3   R-3
Reverse D²c – Small circular raised dot on field above left olive leaf cluster with smaller dot just to left of it. Additional very small dots at junction of eagle's right wing and neck, on lower middle of eagle's right wing, in middle of eagle's sixth tail feather, and to left of arrow feather ends on field.

5   **IV 4 • D²a (Tripled Date and Stars)**   (189)   I-2   R-3
Obverse IV 4 – Date tripled with doubling at very top outside and below serifs and loops towards rim. Left stars tripled and right stars doubled towards rim.

NOTE: As in the 1921-P series, in the D series there appear numerous raised dots on various locations on both the obverse and reverse sides. It was first thought that these raised dots were put there by the mint workmen for some presently unknown reason. Current thought however is that these dots are the result of imperfect die steel and not the result of being deliberately put there. Therefore, these are not listed as die varieties at this time.

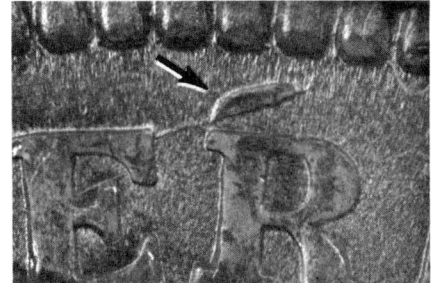

1A R
TRUT

1B R Die Chip Above R

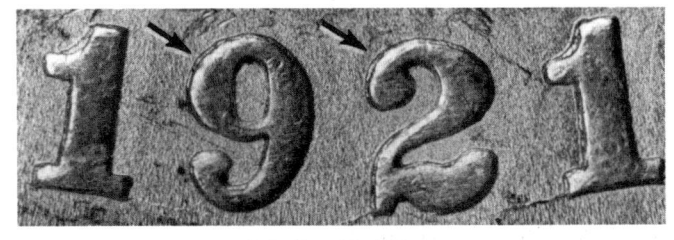

2 O Doubled Date

1921-D / 1921-S

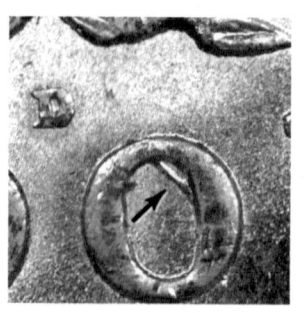

2A R Die Gouge in O

3 O Dot

3 R Die Crack in Wing

3 R Dot

4 R Dot

5 O Tripled Date

5 O Tripled Stars

1921-S

Most specimens of this issue were not fully struck. They show weakness in the wreath leaves and a mushy appearance on the cheek, hair and eagle's breast due the planchet roughness not being smoothed out by the dies. Luster is generally dull, either because of strike weakness on cheek and eagle's breast and/or die wear in fields. A fully struck piece with good luster is very rare. Only a few die varieties exist. VAM 4 has a dot below the eagle's left wing and although not as large as the largest dots for the 1921-P and D, it is still barely visible to the naked eye. VAM 1B has two prominent diagonal die gouges at the top of the Liberty head.

Full proof-likes are extremely rare and the few known specimen have little contrast. Even semi proof-like coins are very scarce. Apparently the working dies were not basined and polished at this mint except in a couple isolated cases to repair the dies.

Twenty-four branch mint proofs were reported struck for Farren Zerbe supposedly to compliment the Philadelphia proofs also struck for him. Less than half a dozen specimens are known and the one piece Wayne Miller has examined had little contrast.

1921-S

1	**IV 1 • D²a (Normal Die)**		I-1	R-1

Obverse IV 1 – Normal die of IV type.
Reverse D²a – Normal die of D² type with small centered I S mint mark. There is a spike above the bottom crossbar on the right side of F in OF for all die varieties. Both 1's in date are doubled at top left.

1A	**IV 1 • D²a (Die Scratch)**		I-2	R-3

Obverse IV 1 – Diagonal die scratch connecting B and U in PLURIBUS.

1B	**IV 1 • D²a (Thorn Head)**	(189)	I-3	R-4

Obverse IV 1 – Two large horizontal die gouges at top of head with upper one appearing as a thorn from the top wheat leaf and the lower one as a band on the right of the top cotton leaf.

1C	**IV 1 • D²a (Pitted Reverse)**	(189)	I-2	R-3

Reverse D²a – Pitted die around arrow heads.

2	**IV 1 • D²b (S Shifted Left)**		I-2	R-3

Reverse D²b – Small I S mint mark shifted left.

3	**IV 2 • D²a (Doubled Date and Stars)**	(189)	I-2	R-3

Obverse IV 2 – Outline of all date digits is doubled towards rim as are all left and right stars. Some specimens show a die chip in lower loop of 2.

4	**IV 2 • D²c (Dot Below Wing)**	(189)	I-3	R-3

Reverse D²c – Very small circular raised dot on field between eagle's left wing and arrow shafts and under eagle's jaw.

NOTE: As in the 1921-P series, in the S series there appear numerous raised dots on various locations on both the obverse and reverse sides. It was first thought that these raised dots were put there by the mint workmen for some presently unknown reason. Current thought however is that these dots are the result of imperfect die steel and not the result of being deliberately put there. Therefore, these are not listed as die varieties at this time.

1A O Die Scratch

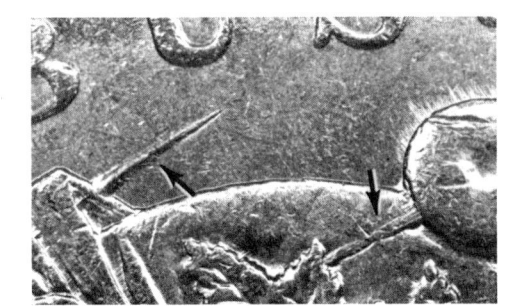

1B O Die Gouges

2 R S Shifted Left

1C R Pitted Reverse

3 O Doubled Date

1921-S

3 O Doubled Stars

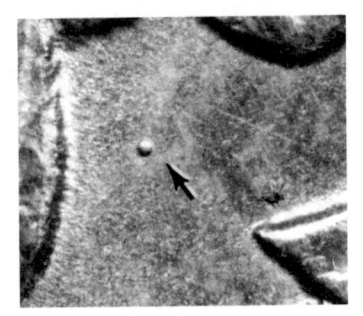

4 R Dot

Chapter 9
GSA Sale of Carson City Dollars

During late 1972 through 1974 and again in 1980 the General Services Administration of the U. S. Government conducted seven mail order sales of some three million Morgan Carson City silver dollars. With total gross sales of $107 million, this was the largest sale of a U. S. coin series in numismatic history.

BACKGROUND OF THE SALES

Ever since the Morgan dollars were first struck, the Treasury, mints and the Federal Reserve banks held huge stocks of Morgan and Peace dollars. The silver dollar was not widely accepted for public use which caused millions of these dollars to be stored for many years in uncirculated condition. Then the release of previously scarce New Orleans mint Morgans (1898, 1902, 1903, and 1904) during 1962 and 1963 from the Federal Reserve Banks stimulated collector and speculator interest.

The Treasury holdings of silver dollars in Washington, D.C.. dwindled from 180 million in January 1960 to 28 million on January 1, 1964. As the Treasury stocks of these dollars became low, word circulated that the older Morgan dollars were also being passed out in addition to the common Peace dollars. A run on the Treasury resulted in March 1964 as collectors, dealers and speculators scrambled to get these remaining silver dollars at face value.

Before the Treasury completely ran out of these dollars, the General Accounting Office made an audit of the Treasury's remaining silver dollars. Nearly three million were discovered to be uncirculated Carson City silver dollars of special numismatic value. These three million silver dollars were set aside and were withheld from public distribution when the silver dollar sales were halted by the Treasury on March 26, 1964.

The problem of how to equitably dispose of these scarce Carson City dollars was turned over to the Joint Committee on the Coinage. In its report to Congress, the Commission recommended the mail bid procedure for disposing of the coins with pre-established minimum prices.

Section 205(a) of the Bank Holding Company Act Amendments (Public Law 91-607) of December 1970 authorized the General Services Administration to sell these dollars. In July 1971, Congress provided an appropriation of $10 million for the GSA to develop and implement the dollar disposal program. A small group of GSA staff was assembled in Washington, D.C. on November 1971, to arrange for the coin inspecting, sorting, ordering, packaging and mailing details.

More than thirty forms, cards and letters and labels were designed and produced. Millions of brochures and 100,000 posters were printed and distributed to the 40,000 U. S. Post Offices and nearly 60,000 banks, savings and loans and credit unions in a massive advertising campaign.[1] Several special documentary movies were produced and shown on television. Three hundred and ninety two special coin displays of one each of ten different Carson City dollar years for sale were fabricated. They were sent to various banks on a rotational basis and were used at important coin shows for the GSA display.

TRANSFER OF DOLLARS

On December 6, 1971, the GSA took possession of the dollars from the Treasury Department. The 2.9 million dollars weighing 77 tons were transferred from the Treasury vaults in Washington, D.C. to the U. S. Bullion Depository at West Point, New York, where the various inspection and packaging operations were to be carried out. Seven heavily-guarded semi-trailer trucks were used to haul the valuable cargo and by January 1972, all of the dollars were at West Point.[2]

The bag count of silver dollars was verified by Treasury and GSA representatives and the bags of dollars were placed in ten bins in one vault of the Depository. There were separate bins for each of those years with substantial quantities of Carson City dollars, namely, 1878 and 1880 through 1885. Another bin held the years with only a few thousand Carson City dollars; 1879, 1890 and 1891. The last two bins were for the mixed circulated late non-Carson City dollars and the mixed circulated dollars. All bins had a wooden plank flooring above the concrete floor so the canvas bags would not pick up any moisture from the floor.

INITIAL SORTING

Late in March 1972, a special team of noted numismatists examined a separate group of fifty coins with varying degree of toning and tarnish to establish grading standards for the silver dollars. Members of this team were John J. Pittman, President of the American Numismatic Association, Rochester, New York; Amon Carter, Jr. a member of the Joint Commission on the Coinage, Fort Worth, Texas; Henry Grunthal, curator of European and Modern Coins for the American Numismatic Society, New York, New York; Clifford Mishler, editor of *Coins* and *Numismatic News Weekly*, Iola, Wisconsin; and Margo Russell, editor of *Coin World*, Sidney, Ohio.[3] The fifty coins were divided into two groups; twenty two that fell below acceptable standards and twenty eight that were acceptable. These coins were permanently mounted in two clear plastic cases to be used as standards in the sorting process.

Then began the long process of sorting the coins. Initially an automatic scanning machine was considered for use for sorting. This machine could automatically scan both the obverse and reverse sides of the coin and determine the date and mint mark by comparison with standard designs. However, use of this machine was rejected because it was apt to add more scratches and nicks. Furthermore, it could not discriminate the more subtle grading requirements such as tarnish, scratches and errors. In the end, reliance had to be made on the eyes of the trained inspectors.

Hand sorting of the 2.9 million coins was performed by six white gloved women with four to five supervisors. Each coin was first segregate by date and mint mark. Then within this group the coins were further sorted into one of three categories: (1) uncirculated that met the grading standards, (2) Tarnished or slightly scratched, and (3) errors (such as off center strikes, laminations and filled dies) or rejects (gouged or badly scratched).

The Bank Holding Company Act Amendments which were signed by President Nixon on December 31, 1970, authorizing the sale of the dollars by GSA did not permit error or variety coins to be sold separately from the normal coins. Thus, they were mixed in at random with the two categories of coins sold; those that met the grading standards and those that fell below the grading standard to be sold at a reduced cost. Also at the suggestion of various coin collectors, the GSA rejected the idea of cleaning the tarnished coins. It was felt that this would introduce controversy on the condition of the coins.

As the coins were sorted they were packed into special wooden boxes with sliding masonite tops. Tolerances of the boxes were such that not one coin more than fifty stacks of twenty coins could fit into a box. Each box of a thousand had a seal and was recorded in the log book. This sorting operation took most of the remainder of 1972.

GSA HOLDINGS OF SILVER DOLLARS

As a result of the sorting operations, the GSA had five categories of silver dollars: (1) uncirculated CC, (2) mixed CC, (3) mixed uncirculated (of other mints), (4) mixed circulated, and (5) unsalable (due to severe gouge or badly worn). *Table 9-1* shows the quantities of coins in each category.[4] Note that the mixed CC category included uncirculated CC dollars that were tarnished and scratched and were therefore to be sold at reduced prices. Also note that this mixed CC category also included one each of the uncirculated 1889-CC, 1892-CC and the 1893-CC. These were put in this category since there was not enough to include as separate bid categories of the uncirculated CC.

Since the uncirculated 1878-CC were sold at the same price ($15), the culled (tarnished/scratched) 1878-CC had to be sold at a lower price. All 13,426 culled 1878-CC were put in the mixed circulated category and sold for $3 each.

Table 9-2 shows a further breakdown of the GSA sorting categories for the CC dollars. The rejects/errors consisted of 2 to 5 percent of the total coins of each year. The scratched/tarnished consisted of 10 to 30 percent of the total coins with the years 1878, 1882, 1883, and 1884 particularly high. The initial sorting culled out 72,000 1882-CC, 78,000 1883-CC, and 77,000 1884-CC as scratched/tarnished. Later, additional coins were added to this category for these three years.

1880-CC Storage Bin

Storage Box for 1000 Coins

Table 9-1 ORIGINAL GSA HOLDINGS FOR SALE

Year	Uncirc. CC	Mixed CC	Mixed Uncirc.	Mixed Circ.	Unsalable	Total
1878 CC	47,567			13,426 (culled)		60,993
1879 CC	3,633	490				4,123
1880 CC	114,942	16,587				131,529
1881 CC	122,709	24,776				147,485
1882 CC	382,913	222,116				605,029
1883 CC	523,853	231,665				755,518
1884 CC	788,630	174,008				962,638
1885 CC	130,823	17,462				148,285
1889 CC		1				1
1890 CC	3,610	339				3,949
1891 CC	5,177	510				5,687
1892 CC		1				1
1893 CC		1				1
Various P,O,S			27,980			27,980
Various				84,165	311	84,476
Totals	2,123,857	687,956	27,980	97,591	311	2,937,695

Table 9-2 GSA CARSON CITY SILVER DOLLAR CATEGORIES

CC Year	Unc.	Scratched/ Tarnished	Combined	Rejects/ Errors	Unc. Overdates	Tarnished Overdates	% Mixed CC	% Mixed Circ.	% Total Minted
1878	47,567	— 13,426 —						14	2.7
1879	3,633	— 490 —					.07		.5
1880	114,942	12,087		4,500	(45,000)	(5,000)	2.41		22.1
1881	122,709	16,776		8,000			3.60		49.6
1882	382,913	216,116		6,000			32.29		44.6
1883	523,853	221,665		10,000			33.67		62.7
1884	788,630	159,008		15,000			25.29		84.6
1885	130,823	11,462		6,000			2.54		64.9
1890	3,610	325		14			.05		.1
1891	5,177	423		87			.08		.3

Early in 1973 it was noted that some of the 1880-CC dollars in the GSA displays were of the strong overdates. At the request of members of the numismatic hobby, the GSA further segregated the 1880-CC strong overdates into separate boxes in the spring of 1973. These were examined by numismatists (Van Allen and Mallis) for varieties early in May 1973. Sampling of the various dates of Carson City dollars revealed numerous minor varieties for each date such as doubled dates and mint marks. Of special importance were the strong overdates of the 1880-CC; VAM 4 (80/79), VAM 5 (8/7 High), and VAM 6 (8/7 Low). From the sampling it was estimated that 15,000 VAM 4, 13,000 VAM 5, and 10,000 VAM 6 were in the uncirculated category, while 1,600 VAM 4, 1,900 VAM 5 and 1,000 VAM 6 were in the mixed category. Totals of these overdates sold by the GSA were about 16,000 VAM 4, 15,000 VAM 5 and 11,000 VAM 6.

There were 27,980 mixed non-CC uncirculated coins. Anywhere from one to five bags existed for 1879-S, 1880-S, 1881-S, 1882-S, 1883-P, 1883-O, 1884-O, 1885-P, 1885-O, and 1887-O. The remaining were common date 1922 and 1923-P Peace dollars.

Some 84,000 mixed circulated coins also were for sale. They consisted of many different dates from all mints. Their condition was mostly VF to AU with a few F. The culls of damaged and mutilated coins were removed by the GSA.

For the mixed CC category the 1882, 1883 and 1884 years constituted 81 percent of the total amount. The 1880, 1881, and 1885 each constituted 2 to 4 percent with 1879, 1890 and 1891 comprising much less than a percent each. The 1878-CC comprised 14 percent of the

Table 9-3 GSA DOLLAR SALES

Year	1972-1974 Min. Bid ($)	Oct. '72 Mar. '73	June '73 July '73	Oct. '73	Feb. '74	April '74 June '74	February 1980 Prices ($)	February 1980 Quantity	July 1980 Min Bid $180	Mixed CC 2nd, 5th & 6th Sales
1878 CC	15		47,556							
1879 CC	300				3,608					512
1880 CC	60			73,856		36,794			4,281	16,588
1881 CC	60			70,865		32,826			18,975	24,814
1882 CC	30	291,494	55,597			35,689				222,261
1883 CC	30	257,391	40,391			30,320	60	195,745		231,780
1884 CC	30	267,733	64,384			28,349	65	428,152		174,068
1885 CC	60			67,782		31,470			31,564	17,463
1889 CC										1
1890 CC	30		3,589							357
1891 CC	30		5,157							525
1892 CC										1
1893 CC										1
Mixed CC	15		170,299			218,666	45	299,390		
Mixed Unc.	5		27,949							
Mixed Circ.*	3		97,563							
Totals	3	816,618	512,585	212,503	3,608	414,114		923,290	54,820	688,371

* Includes 13,426 tarnished/scratched/error 1878-CC.

total mixed circulated category.

For some of the years the GSA holdings were a sizeable percentage of the total amounts minted. About 85 percent of 1884 mintage was held while approximately 60 percent for 1883 and 1885 and 50 percent for 1881 and 1882 were held. The dumping of such large quantities of coins of a given year on the market would naturally have a depressing effect on prices. To minimize such an effect, the GSA established minimum bid prices for each category and year CC based on the current market values. It was only natural that some categories would not be sold out at these minimum bid prices as the free market prices dropped.

PACKAGING THE COINS

All the uncirculated CC and other mint silver dollars were packaged into plastic holders for single coins. The CC dollars were then placed in a special velvet lined presentation case. Circulated Morgan and Peace silver dollars were placed individually in a mylar display packet and enclosed in a carrying envelope.

Packaging of the silver dollars commenced in mid-fall of 1972 at the West Point Depository and was completed in mid-summer 1973. Two complete assembly lines for packaging the coins were installed there. Each line employed 22 women plus several supervisors and helpers. Their salaries were a major cost of the sale of the silver dollars.

During the packaging operations the women workers all wore cotton gloves and handling of the coins was at a minimum. The coin was placed in a hole in the black plastic insert. The inscription on this insert stated Carson City Uncirculated Silver Dollar, Carson City Silver Dollar, or Silver Dollar depending on the category of the coin.

Next, the plastic insert with coin was placed into a two-piece, clear plastic holder. These two halves were fused together by a sonic sealer. All CC dollars were placed in a special presentation case along with a card describing the background of the Carson City dollars. A special card was added to the 1880-CC boxes to alert the recipient of possible overdates. The box was then placed in a mailing carton with the coin date or category stamped on the outside.

GSA SALES

The GSA conducted a total of seven sales; five between 1972 and 19774 and two in 1980. The first five sales generated net revenues of about $55.3 million with expenses of $7.8 million. Net revenues from the last two 1980 sales were $52 million with expenses close to $2 million.

Terms of the first five sales were those recommended by the Joint Commission on Coinage. Coins were sold by public mail bid with pre-established minimum prices. They were to be sold to the highest bidder with a limit of one coin per category per bidder. If there were less bidders than coins then the coins were to be awarded to all bidders at the minimum price. Only U.S. citizens could bid on the coins.

From October 1972 to March 1973 the first sales were conducted for the 1882-CC, 1883-CC and 1884-CC categories at a minimum bid of $30 each. This was somewhat below the then current market price of $35 to $40 a

GSA Presentation Case

coin for these dates. As shown in *Table 9-3* only 250,000 to 290,000 of each date were sold. Since none of the dates were sold out they all went for $30 each.

The second sale from June to July 1973 featured 1878-CC, 1882-CC, 1883-CC, 1884-CC, 1890-CC 1891-CC, mixed CC, mixed uncirculated, and mixed circulated. All but the 1882-CC, 1883-CC, 1884-CC and mixed CC were sold out with an average price of $16.55 for the 1878-CC, $58.22 for the 1890-CC, $53.85 for the 1891-CC and $5.55 for the mixed uncirculated.

In the third sale of October 1973 the 1880-CC, 1881-CC, and 1885-CC were offered at $60 each. With a 1973 market price of around $65 to $70 each, response to this sale was slow with only one-half to two-thirds of the coins selling at the minimum bid price.

The fourth sale in February 1974 featured the 1879-CC with only 3,608 coins available at $300 each minimum bid. All were sold at an average of $478.39 per coin.

All of the dates not previously sold were again offered in the fifth sale, April to June 1974. Only the 1882-CC sold out at an average price of $33.08 each. By this time the market was pretty well saturated and sales had fallen off. There still remained 195,724 1883-CC, 428,128 1884-CC, 4,261 1880-CC, 18,960 1881-CC, 31,548 1882-CC and 298,968 mixed CC. The Carson City dollar sales had stimulated the overall silver dollar market but predictably the market value of the dates with substantial offerings had dropped.

After the fifth sale the GSA determined it was not feasible to offer the remaining 978,000 coins under the same terms and conditions because of the saturated market. Public Law 96-2, enacted on March 7, 1979, amended the Bank Holding Company Act of 1970 and authorized selling the remaining coins at such prices and terms and conditions deemed proper by the Administration.

On November 13, 1979 the GSA announced the sale plan for the remaining coins. There were to be two sales. The first running February 8, 1980 through April 8, 1980 would offer the 1883-CC at $42 each, 1884-CC at $40 each and the mixed CC at $20 each. There would be no limit per order but orders per category would initially be filled with 500 coins. A second sale was to be held in July 1980 and would offer the 1880-CC, 1881-CC and 1885-CC in a sealed-bid auction with the minimum prices of $180 per coin. Orders were limited to five coins of each category.

When these two last sales were announced on November 13, 1979 the spot price for silver was $16 per ounce. As the date for the first sale approached the price of silver was rapidly increasing. By January 4, 1980 it had reached $36 an ounce. On January 7, 1980 the GSA suspended the prices announced in November since at that point the mixed CC category coins each contained $28 worth of silver compared to the $20 selling price. The GSA decided to announce prices on the date the sale opened, February 8, 1980. Because of this, 17 million brochures, 60,000 posters and 750,000 mail order folders with the old prices worth $341,000 had to be scrapped. Prices on the day of the sale would be available via toll-free telephone and notices in 55 major daily newspapers and weekly numismatic publications.

Prices set on the day of the sale on February 8, 1980 were 1883-CC at $65 each, 1884-CC at $60 each and mixed CC at $45 each. By that time silver prices had dropped from a high of $50 per ounce to about $38 per ounce. Uncirculated 1883-CC and 1884-CC dollars were trading around $70-$75 in the open market and the coin market was at the height of the bull market frenzy. As a result, the public interest in the sale was far greater than envisioned by the GSA. During the first 10 days 350,000 orders were received and an additional 150,000 during the remainder of the sale.

The GSA chose a limit of 10 coins per order for the 1883-CC, 20 for the 1884-CC, and five for the mixed CC. It had reserved the right to reduce the limits in the terms and conditions of the sale. Only orders received during the first ten days would be selected since it was projected that no more than 350,000 orders could be processed within its budget. However, only 181,814 orders actually received any coins-roughly one-third of the total orders. There were many customer complaints about not receiving any coins, the lengthy time for status notification and the lengthy time it took to receive the returned orders, refund checks and finally the coins. A lower coin limit per order could have been set to provide a greater percentage of orders with at least some coins.

The last sale held on July 1980 for the 1880-CC, 1881-CC and 1885-CC was also sold out with approximately 18,000 bids received. This last sale was conducted without any major problems, unlike the previous sales.

Overall, the sales of the Carson City silver dollars was financially successful to the Government with net receipts of close to $100 million for about 3 million coins. But it took a lengthy time from the date the CC dollars were first put aside in 1964 until they were first offered for sale in 1972. And it was 16 years by the time the final sale was conducted. The sixth sale left many customers bitter because of not receiving any coins and long delays in processing their orders and receiving their coins.

It helped stimulate the silver dollar market in the mid-1970's and again in 1980. Although the market for many of the Carson City dollars dropped somewhat in value after the 1972 to 1974 sales, their prices rebounded a few years later. By 1984 the CC dollars were selling from two to over ten times the 1972-74 GSA selling prices in grades MS 60 to MS 65. They are still a very popular numismatic item because of the magic of the CC mint mark.

Footnotes

[1] U.S. General Services Administration, News Release #5954, October 31, 1972.

[2] Ibid.

[3] GSA News Release #5952, October 31, 1972.

[4] All dollar quantities given in this Chapter were obtained directly from GSA in Washington, D.C.

Chapter 10
Redfield Hoard and Continental-Illinois Bank Hoard

REDFIELD HOARD

Certainly no other private hoard of United States coins in recent history has received so much publicity or created such interest as the so-called Redfield hoard. It was of prime interest to silver dollar collectors and investors since the hoard contained over 400,000 Morgan and Peace silver dollars. Although not nearly as large a quantity as the General Services Administration sales that had almost three million Carson City silver dollars or the Continental-Illinois Bank hoard of about one and one-half million Morgan dollars, it still had a major impact on the dollar market.

Other hoards of hundreds of bags of silver dollars existed (and may still exist) after nearly all of the hundred of thousands of silver bags were finally released to the public in the mid-1960's. Many gambling casinos in Nevada, for example, had large stocks of silver dollars on hand for a while. But none of these hoards had the publicity, so many scarcer dates, or were sold in such a large single transaction of $7.3 million up until the mid-1970's.

Much of the details of the Redfield hoard are clothed in secrecy. Little is known of the life of the man who accumulated the hoard, LaVere Redfield. The quantities of dates and mint marks of the coins were never publicly released and were open to much speculation. Many court cases resulted from the intrigue surrounding the disbursements of the Redfield fortune. This chapter attempts to unravel some of the mystery of the Redfield hoard.

Accumulation Of The Hoard

Born on October 29, 1897, in Ogden, Utah, LaVere Redfield grew up in poverty. When he was twenty four years old he married a woman named Nell who was then twenty eight years old.

LaVere Redfield began to accumulate his fortune as a young man when he moved with his wife to Los Angeles. During the depression he speculated in land and oil stocks. He bought land at tax sales and stocks at deflated prices. He always practiced thrift as a result of a childhood of poverty.

At the age of thirty seven, after making many millions of dollars, he moved to Nevada in 1935. There he bought a large farm and lived the life of a farmer. He continued to invest in real estate in Nevada and at one time owned over eighty square miles in Washaw County where Reno is located. Many of the people farming the land that Redfield owned were eventually given the land with just a promise without any formal deeds. Later he bought a three story stone chateau in Reno from an unsuccessful gubernatorial candidate where he lived for the rest of his life with his wife, Nell.

LaVere Redfield
(Photo Courtesy Paramount Coin Corp.)

Redfield never gave the appearance of being a multi-millionaire. He would walk around Reno in old denims and shirts like any other farmer. To save money he would buy cases of bent unlabeled cans of food because they were cheaper. His car was an old pick-up truck which he would roll down the hill from his house in the morning to save the battery. But on the other hand he carried large amounts of cash on his person. At one real estate auction in Reno after being the successful bidder at fifty thousand dollars, he paid off the amount in cash from a shopping bag he had with him.

Redfield distrusted the government and the banks and preferred hard currency. For several decades he accumulated silver coins in his basement. Most of these were silver dollars. Employee friends at the bank would alert him whenever unusual bags of silver dollars were in the banks and Redfield would trade paper money for silver dollars at face

Paramount Redfield Dollar

403

Redfield Mansion
(Photo Courtesy Paramount Coin Corp.)

value. These he would dump down a coal chute to the basement of his house, where they sat for many years. He was not a collector in the usual sense, but more an accumulator of hard assets.

As a hoarder and accumulator, Redfield did not go through the coins and pick out the best ones. So the bags of silver dollars were the usual mixture of various grades including uncirculated. But he learned which dates commanded some premiums and would obtain these from the banks in favor of the more common date dollars. Thus his accumulation was mostly S mint Morgan and Peace dollars with some Carson City and Philadelphia Mints. Apparently Redfield did some limited trading and selling of silver dollars when to his advantage. But primarily he just preferred to put his extra money into hard assets that some day would bring premium prices.

Not very much is known of Redfield's personal life. He occasionally went on gambling sprees and played blackjack at the Reno casinos for very high stakes. He did not smoke and drank only sparingly with dinner. His world travelling was done in a modest fashion in keeping with his character around Reno.

Redfield received national publicity when his house was robbed in 1952. Burglars removed a four hundred pound safe in a robbery involving jewels, negotiable securities and about one and one half million dollars in cash. A female friend masterminded the burglary and Redfield was reluctantly forced to testify in the case after fleeing to California to avoid it.

In 1963 another burglary took place in which about one hundred thousand silver dollars were taken. That case has never been solved.

Because of his attempts to conceal his wealth, he came under increasing surveillance by the Internal Revenue Service. In 1960, acting as his own lawyer, he was convicted of a $350,000 income tax evasion charge. He was sentenced to serve five years at Terminal Island, but in 1962 was paroled after serving eighteen months. While in jail, he received a free gall bladder operation.

Redfield died on September 6, 1974 in Reno at the age of seventy six. His wife died later in April of 1981. Labeled an eccentric multimillionaire by the press, this frugal and wise investor amassed a fortune estimated between seventy million to two hundred million dollars. At the time of his death, authorities in charge of the estate, and the Internal Revenue Service found 680 bags of precious metals, mostly silver and gold coins, hidden in the basement of his home. Behind false walls constructed of cardboard boxes and concrete under enormous piles of trash were 407,283 Morgan and Peace silver dollars, 351,259 of which were uncirculated. A note found with the hoard to the beneficiary of Redfield's will read "The government can't tax wealth that can`t be located. Burn this and tell no one. Carry on as though no coin or currency was left." Ironically, it was the Internal Revenue Authorities who found this note.

Also left by Redfield were uncashed dividend checks dating back to 1959, three containers of stamps, nineteen thousand sets of bronze coins, paper money and huge land holdings. The silver dollars were just a small portion of his huge estate.

Aquisition Of The Dollars From The Estate

Court battles began immediately after Redfield's death. There were two wills found. The first dated October 10, 1972 was a hand written document leaving half of his estate to his widow and half to a niece in Idaho Falls. A second will dated May 1974, also hand written, left most of the estate to the University of Nevada, The City of Reno, Nevada, Nevada State Prison and Reno's Veteran's Hospital. However, a handwriting expert's testimony proved the second will to be a forgery, so the estate went to his widow and niece.

From October 1974 through April 1975, Stack's of New York, was retained to undertake an appraisal of the numismatic items of the estate. It is doubtful if every item in the estate was examined and listed because of the time and effort it would have taken to physically examine over four hundred thousand coins. Samples were probably taken of the circulated coins and an estimated

Bags of Silver Dollars from Redfield Hoard
(Photo Courtesy Paramount Coin Corp.)

value given. Also samples were probably only taken of the various uncirculated bags to verify the dates and mint marks. Many silver dollars were found loose in the basement of the Redfield house and these were shoveled into bags (to the chagrin of numismatists) prior to inventoried. This mixed up some of the dates and as a result probably precluded a completely accurate inventory by Stacks. This was borne out later by some silver rolls from the Redfield estate containing a few odd dates.

Stack's appraised the portion of the Redfield collection that was later sold to A-Mark for five million, two hundred thousand dollars. They advised the three executrices that disclosure of the coin inventory might depress the market price.

A suit for seven hundred and thirty thousand dollars plus damages was filed by Stack's later in 1976 against the executrices of the estate and their attorney, Gerald C. Smith for their appraisal fee. Stack's alleged that a one thousand dollars per day appraisal services fee had been agreed upon even though it was not in writing and that this appraisal fee would be waived in lieu of a ten percent commission of the gross sales amount of the collection, if the estate utilized the advice and assistance it received from Stack's. Also, the fee would be waived if Stack's handled the liquidation, but as it later turned out, Stack's did not handle the liquidation.

Early in 1975, Steve Markoff, Chairman, and Gary Gordon, President of A- Mark Coins Company of Beverly Hills, California, heard a rumor of a large coin collection in an estate in Reno, Nevada. Contact with the court house in Reno revealed it was the LaVere Redfield estate and the name of the attorney handling the estate. It took six months of talking and interviews with attorneys, judges of court, bankers and accountants before the estate thought A-Mark was serious. Finally after signing a non-disclosure agreement that the nature of the collection could not be revealed under severe financial penalties, A-Mark examined the collection.

On November 4, 1975, the probate court entered an order authorizing the executrices to sell the coins at private sale. A-Mark signed an agreement on December 17, 1975 to purchase a portion of the Redfield collection for approximately five million, nine hundred thousand dollars, to be consummated on January 19, 1976.

Meanwhile, Joel Rettew, a fifty percent owner of Rare Coin Galleries learned of the existence of the Redfield hoard in September 1975 from a Reno physician who was also a coin collector. Rettew contracted one of the executrices, Luana Miles, who advised him to employ Nevada counsel and seek an opportunity to bid on the coins. Rare Coin Galleries did not have sufficient funds to purchase the Redfield coin hoard so they formed a joint venture agreement with Bowers and Ruddy on December 23, 1975. Bowers and Ruddy was a majority owned subsidiary of General Mills who would provide the actual funds for the purchase of the hoard. Although the joint venture contacted the estate they could not obtain any information on the Redfield hoard.

On December 22, 1975 Rettew contracted Stack's and although he did not obtain any information on the hoard, he did learn of a dispute between Stack's and the estate of the two hundred and fifty thousand dollar appraisal fee claimed by Stack's. On December 31, 1975 the joint venture provided a letter agreement to Stack's stating they would pay Stack's a consulting fee of two hundred and fifty thousand dollars for providing an opinion of the value and method of evaluation of the Redfield coins if they ended up buying the estate coins. Stack's then provided Rare Coin Galleries Bowers and Ruddy information on the hoard which they had not provided to anyone else. Bowers and Ruddy used this information to authorize a funding bid for the Redfield hoard from General Mills.

On January 9, 1976 the joint venture filed a bid in the amount of $6,501,156 accompanied by a bank check in that amount. General Mills had authorized Bowers and Ruddy to commit up to seven million dollars of General Mills funds to purchase the Redfield coins. Because of this bid, the probate court found that the November 4, 1975 order for a private sale was erroneously entered because it would result in the sale of the estate assets at less than the best possible price obtainable. Since the coins and title had not yet passed to A-Mark nor had the coins been paid for, the court declared the December 17, 1975 purchase agreement between A-Mark and the estate to be void. The probate court then ordered a public sale to be held on January 27, 1976. A-Mark naturally appealed the probate court's order but the Supreme Court of Nevada affirmed the order.

This public sale of the Redfield hoard took place in the probate court on January 27, 1976. Besides A-Mark and the joint venture of Rare Coin Galleries and Bowers and Merena, other coin dealers present with intention of bidding for the hoard included Leon Hendrickson of Indiana, Jules Karp of New York, John Love of Montana and Carl White. However, the court refused to disclose the official inventory so only A-Mark knew the exact hoard contents and Rare Coin Galleries and Bowers and Ruddy joint venture only had an opinion of the hoard value and a method of evaluation provided by Stack's.

Bidding began at $6.7 million dollars and progressed at one hundred thousand dollar increments between A-Mark and the joint venture. A-Mark won with a bid of seven million, three hundred thousand dollars, the largest single transaction by far for coins up to that time. At the next raise A-Mark would have had to recess and discuss it.

A-Marks primary financing was supplied by Girard Trust Bank of Philadelphia. However, Jules Karp and Leon Hendrickson each advanced A-Mark three hundred and fifty thousand dollars for a total of seven hundred thousand dollars in a joint agreement which was also used to purchase the Redfield hoard. A dispute arose between A-Mark and Karp and Hendrickson. A-Mark contended that the advance was in the nature of a sixty day loan, while Karp and Hendrickson contended that it was for the purchase of a proportionate interest in the Redfield collection. A compromise settlement was reached in which Karp and Hendrickson received seven hundred thousand dollars plus one hundred and fifty 1879-CC MS-60 silver dollars, fourteen thousand common uncirculated silver dollars dated prior to 1904 and seven thousand circulated silver dollars. They also agreed not to disclose any information concerning the value of the coins of the Redfield collection.

A-Mark brought suit against the Redfield estate seeking a reduction in the price of the coins of one million four hundred thousand dollars, the difference between the original agreement and the later bid price. They alleged they already had contractual rights to the property. However, the Supreme Court of Nevada affirmed the probate court's power to annul its order for a private sale and direct, instead, a public sale. A probate court has jurisdiction to vacate a prior order upon learning that it was entered into through mistake.

A suit was also brought by A-Mark against General Mills, Bowers & Ruddy, Rare Coin Galleries, James Ruddy, David Bowers and Joel Rettew, alleging intentional interference with a contractual relationship with an advantageous business relationship. However, the trial court concluded in the case, which dragged on until 1983, that A-Mark never had a valid contract with the Redfield estate for the purchase of the Redfield collection with which the defendants could have interfered and that the conduct of the defendants in seeking to bid on the coins was not a wrong act against A-Mark.

Dispersion Of The Hoard

A-Mark took physical possession of the coins in Reno, Nevada. Transporting 407,596 silver dollars in 441 bags weighing twelve and one half tons and worth at least $7.3 million was not a simple task. A Brinks semi-trailer truck, lined with sixteen inches of foam rubber was used to transport the coins over a secret route escorted by the State Highway patrol. While the bags of coins were being loaded into the truck at Reno in a very secret operation, someone driving by saw a man holding a shot gun and thought the bank was being robbed. Shortly after the police, newspaper and television people showed up. The coins had to be locked up again until the circus died down.

The large loan A-Mark had used to purchase the coins had to be repaid as quickly as possible to minimize the interest charges. But such a large quantity of silver dollars, with supposedly 351,259 grading uncirculated, could not be dumped onto the market all at one time without depressing their prices. A-Mark enacted a three year marketing plan for most of the dollars with planned distribution well into the 1980's.

Three coin firms consisting of Paramount International Coin, Robert L Hughes and John Love were designated as primary distributors and each received major portions of the Redfield hoard from A-Mark. They had to sign agreements which stipulated the dispersal plan and that the contents of the hoard would not be disclosed. Paramount and Hughes did aggressive marketing with full page ads in numismatic newspapers and magazines plus flyers. Paramount packaged the dollars in sonically sealed plastic holders identifying each coin's grade and that it was from the Redfield collection. Hughes placed the dollars in a custom holder with a certificate identifying it as a Redfield dollar plus a photo of the front page of the *Coin World* article on the Redfield hoard sale. All of the dollars were heavily promoted as being part of the Redfield hoard.

Although the exact quantity of dates and mints of the Redfield dollars has not been disclosed, Redfield dates are known through the extensive advertising. The Redfield dates are listed in *Table 10-1* (with estimated quantities of bags indicated taken from John Highfill's book *The Comprehensive U.S. Silver Dollar Encyclopedia*).

The hoard contained virtually no scarcer date O Mints and relatively few P Mints, being heavy in S Mints. As expected in a hoard of this size, many of the dollars were of very high quality while many were also dirty or spotted and heavily bagmarked.

Through clever promotion strategy, the market reacted positively to the availability of the Redfield dollars. Overall, the market was stimulated by new collectors of dollars being added because of their availability. Specific Redfield dates did not have any uniform pattern of price changes in the late 1970s when they were heavily marketed. Some dates were up in grade MS-65 but down in grade MS-60, such as the 1886-S, 1888-S, 1889-S and 1895-S. Overall the Redfield Peace dollar dates moved up with the market. The later date Morgan S Mints carried the stigma of a Redfield date for many years with relatively slow price appreciation except for the 1901-S which was

Table 10-1 REDFIELD HOARD DATES

Estimated Quantities of Bags					
1878-S	Dozens	1889-S	3-5	1898-S	Under 1
1879-CC	½	1890-P	Many	1899-S	Under 1
1879-S	Dozens	1890-S	Many	1900-S	Few
1879-S		1891-CC	3-5	1902-S	1
Rev. '78	3	1891-S	Many	1903-P	Under 1
1880-S	Dozens	1892-P	1-2	1921-S	Under 1
1881-S	Dozens	1892-CC	2-4	1922-S	Few
(Most common)		1893-P	1-3	1923-S	Few
1882-S	Dozens	1893-CC	Few	1924-S	Under 1
1883-S	¼	1895-S	¼	1925-S	3-4
1885-CC	1	1896-P	Couple Dozen	1926-S	Many
1886-S	Several	1896-S	Under 1	1927-S	3-5
1887-S	Many	1897-P	Couple Dozen	1928-S	Several
1888-S	2	1897-S	Couple Dozen	1935-S	Under 1
1889-P	Many	1898-P	Couple Dozen		

not a Redfield date. It was not until 1982 and 1983 that the 1890-S and 1891-S had the Redfield stigma lifted and made exceptionally rapid advances in price. The common date early S mints followed the general market advances of 1979 through 1984 because the Redfield quantities of those dates were rather small with little market impact compared to the thousands of bags of these dates widely available throughout the country.

The Redfield hoard had the greatest market impact on the scarcer S Mint dates because of the significant quantities of uncirculated specimens suddenly available. In general, it had a slightly depressing effect on their price advances over the years coupled later with a slow market on the more expensive coins in the early and mid-1980s. But within ten years of the Redfield hoard making its first splash on the dollar market, the stimulus or stigma of these dollars had all but faded away.

CONTINENTAL-ILLINOIS BANK HOARD

This hoard of Morgan silver dollars was clothed in secrecy until the publishing of some details about it in John Highfill's book, *The Comprehensive U.S. Silver Dollar Encyclopedia*. It was the largest single, private hoard of U.S. silver dollars to be released into the coin market since the final dispersal of silver dollars by the Treasury Department in the early 1960's.

During the final rush for silver dollars from the Treasury Department in 1962 and 1963, many millions of Morgan and Peace silver dollars were purchased at face value. These were resold in the open market in the mid-60's at slightly over face value. Many private individuals accumulated hoards of these cartwheels from tens to hundreds of bags. The Redfield hoard was probably the largest hoard of a single individual that was held for many years. A number of coin dealers handled hundreds of bags of silver dollars but these generally were turned over and resold as quickly as possible so they really weren't considered hoards. The casinos in Nevada kept considerable stocks of silver for use in gambling. But these disappeared when the price of silver rose above $1.29 per ounce in 1967 and the bullion content of a silver dollar became worth more than one dollar.

Some banks accumulated hoards of silver dollars as collateral for loans. Most of the bank hoards were probably bags of coins left over from the early 1960s when silver dollars traded freely in commerce and most banks had some stock of silver dollars as well as other coins. The banks ceased to give silver dollars out shortly after the Treasury Department exhausted their supply in 1964 and they traded at over face value on the open market.

The Continental-Illinois Bank of Chicago released the largest known hoard of about 1,500 bags of Morgan silver dollars to the coin market in 1982-84. Because of financial problems, the bank was forced to sell its hoard of silver dollars at that time. Ed Milas of RARCOA, in Chicago, purchased all of the bags of silver dollars sold by the bank. The purchase price or details of the transaction have never been made public. But estimates have put the value of the transaction at around fifty million dollars.

The recession of 1982-83 and tumble of bullion prices from the 1980 peak had depressed the coin market. Coin prices had fallen severely and activity was slow. With these economic conditions, RARCOA and two other firms, SilverTowne of Winchester, Indiana, and Colonial Coins of Houston, Texas, were selected to help disperse the hoard of silver dollars. The coins were marketed in a quiet and controlled way. The deal was kept in secrecy and over a year was taken to disperse the silver dollars. Most of the employees of these three firms were not aware of the size or details of the hoard. This was done to not adversely affect the coin market.

Exact quantities of the silver dollars by date and mint in this hoard have not been released. What has been published to date reveals that there were about 1,000 bags of a thousand coins each of uncirculated coins and about 500 bags of circulated coins. The Brilliant Uncirculated coins dated from 1878-1904 with most of them being 1878-1888 with a lot of common S Mint coins. The quality of these BU coins were very high, since most of them came from the bank in the original mint canvas bags. Because of the long-term storage in canvas bags, many of the coins had beautiful toning on them. The AU coins were 1878-1885 with most of them being 1879-1882 O-Mint coins.

Of the known primary hoard distribution, SilverTowne handled at least 350 BU bags and 500 AU bags. Colonial Coins handled about 500 BU bags which were primarily 1879-1882 S-Mint coins, 1883-1885 O-Mint coins, and 1885-1887 P-Mint coins. The exceptional quality of these common date coins was, in general, far superior to those of the Redfield hoard. They were stored in the original mint bags and carefully handled by the distributors. In contrast, the Redfield bags of coins were thrown down a chute to his basement. Some of these bags broke open and the coins were later shoveled up. Some were supposedly contaminated with peach juice from ruptured cans that were stored in his basement.

During the release of the Continental-Illinois Bank hoard, late in 1982 through 1984, the coin market picked up again. The demand for nice silver dollars was high and their availability actually fueled the increased activity. Through careful marketing and an overall rising coin market, this large hoard of silver dollars was readily absorbed and prices actually increased substantially for quality coins.

Part III
The Peace Silver Dollar

Chapter 11
Development of the Design

The minting of the Peace silver dollar was first suggested by Farren Zerbe of San Francisco, California, a veteran numismatist and the official historian of the American Numismatic Association (ANA), at the Chicago ANA Convention in August, 1920. Zerbe presented a paper at this convention entitled, "Commemorate the Peace with a Coin for Circulation," which proposed that a new coin be issued by the U. S. Government commemorating the signing of the peace treaty between the United States and Germany at the end of World War I. The paper stated that "our Peace coin should be of good size for art effects, and if it be one for popular use by all the people, the half dollar...would be a common choice. But should we resume the coinage of the silver dollar, that coin should be a consideration."[1]

The ANA recommended that the dollar be a commemorative coin and be issued for general circulation. However, it was pointed out that the commemorative coins had never been issued for general circulation, but were usually sold at a premium to raise funds for expositions or memorial projects, which prevented them from reaching general circulation.[2]

The ANA appointed a five-member committee under the chairmanship of Judson Brenner of Youngstown, Ohio, to propose the bill to Congress. Members of the committee, besides Zerbe, were Dr. J. M. Henderson of Columbus, Ohio; Congressman William A. Ashbrook of Jamestown, Ohio; and Howland Wood of New York City. During December 1920, the committee met with Congressman Albert H. Vestal, Chairman of the House Committee on Coinage, Weights and Measures. As a result, a joint resolution was presented to Congress on May 9, 1921, proposing that a coin be struck commemorating the end of the war.[3] This was the same day that coinage of the Morgan silver dollar was resumed. This joint resolution stated:[4]

To Provide for the Coinage of Peace Dollars

RESOLVED by the Senate and House of Representatives of the United States of America in Congress assembled, That as soon as practicable after the passage of this resolution, all standard silver dollars coined under the provisions of Section 2 of the Act entitled 'An Act to conserve the gold supply of the United States; to provide silver for subsidiary coinages and for commercial use; to assist foreign Governments at war with the enemies of the United States; and for the above purposes to stabilize the price and encourage the production of silver,' approved April 23, 1918 [Pittman Act], shall be of an appropriate design commemorative of the terminations of the war between the Imperial German Government and the people of the United States.

Such design shall be selected by the Director of the Mint with the approval of the Secretary of the Treasury. Each standard silver dollar of such design shall be known as the 'Peace Dollar.'

The joint resolution encountered no difficulties until Congressman Vestal asked permission to have it placed on the unanimous consent calendar, which would have assured its passage. A member of the House objected to this procedure, and the resolution was placed on the regular calendar. Later debate on the resolution showed that the Congressmen were reluctant to recommend a silver dollar coinage. Congress eventually adjourned without voting on the resolution.[5]

Later the coin was authorized without Congressional action, under the provisions of the Pittman Act of April 23, 1918. The Secretary of the Treasury, Andrew W. Mellon, gave approval to change the design of the silver dollar. The Morgan design had existed for 43 years; and the 1890 Act only prevented design changes more often than every 25 years.

Under an executive order by President Harding on July 28, 1921, all essential matters relating to the design of medals, insignia, and coins produced by the executive departments were to be submitted, for advice on the merit of such designs, to the executive officer of the Commission of Fine Arts.[6]

INITIAL DESIGN

The Commission of Fine Arts held a contest for the design. Invitations to eight leading sculptors of the U.S. to submit designs for the new standard dollar were sent on November 23, 1921. Those submitting sketches

Farran Zerbe

1921
Peace Dollar

were: Robert Aitken, Chester Beach, Victor D. Brenner, Anthony De Francisci, John Flanagan, Henry Hering, Hermon A. MacNeil, and Adolf Weinman. The winner was to receive a prize of $1,500 upon completion of a finished model and the others were to receive $100 each. The eventual winner, De Francisci of New York City, submitted two sets of sketches on December 13, 1921. He had two ideas and wanted to present them both.

Anthony De Francisci came from Italy and served under Weinman and was also an apprentice to James E. Fraser, designer of the Indian Head - Buffalo nickel and Herman MacNeil, designer of the Standing Liberty quarter. He only had three weeks to submit his sketches and was 33 at that time. In developing the design of the Liberty Head, he utilized his new bride of 22, Teresa Cafarelli (also from Italy), as a model in their Manhattan studio. He stated that "I was unable, owing to the shortness of time, to engage in the search of a model akin to my mind's picture – that is, a professional model. I do derive some help from the features of Mrs. De Francisci, but generally the Liberty head as it stands is a composite one.[7] De Francisci described how he used Teresa as a model.[8] "I opened the window of my studio and let the wind blow on her hair while she was posing for me... The nose, the fullness of the eye and the mouth are much like my wife's, although the whole face has been elongated." He went on to say in remarks reported on January 12, 1922 by the Minneapolis Tribune.[9] "You will see that the Liberty is not a photograph of Mrs. De Francisci. It is a composite face and in that way typifies something of America. I did not try to execute an 'American type' or a picture of any woman. I wanted the Liberty to express something of the spirit of the country – the intellectual speed and vigor and vitality America has, as well as its youth..."

Each of the two reverse designs originally submitted by De Francisci showed an eagle with a broken sword to symbolize disarmament. One showed the eagle standing on the sword, literally breaking it with its beak. The second showed the eagle clutching a broken sword with olive branches over its head. James E. Fraser, a sculptor member of the Commission of Fine Arts, and De Francisci visited the Director of the Mint in Washington, D. C. on December 15 and again on December 19 to make some alterations in the models and in connection with their submission for approval to the Secretary of the Treasury. The initial reverse approved on December 19 showed the eagle clutching a broken sword.

Reaction to the description of this approved design as published on December 19 was critical of the broken sword, however, as related by O'Reilly of the Bureau of the Mint:[10]

The accepted model for the reverse of the standard dollar bears at its base of the eagle a device representing a broken sword. As a result of published description of the model numerous protests against use of this device are being received.

Mr. Fraser, the sculptor member of the Fine Arts Commission has suggested in a telegram received this morning that the broken sword be removed from the model.

Mr. Charles Moore, Chairman of the F.A.C. has also suggested that the broken be not used as part of the design.

As a result of these protests an olive branch was substituted for the broken sword and the revised models were submitted to the Secretary of the Treasury on December 23 for his approval.[11] Mr. De Francisci visited the Philadelphia Mint on December 21, 22, 23, and 28 for consultation in changes in the reverse model design and master hub preparation.[12]

Teresa De Francisci

The modified design was approved on December 24 and the dies were ready for coinage on December 29, 1921, just a scant three days from years end, as related by acting Mint Director O'Reilly:[13]

The Sec., Under Sec., Moore, Fraser all approve design without sword. Your telegram today completes authority. Francisci at Phil today to supervise preparation of hub. Dies will be ready for coinage 29th. Under Sec. does not wish to give publicity to change hence issued newspaper notice your name stating sword which appeared upon one of the models submitted does not appear on coin. Very widespread protest against use of broken sword...

From December 29 to 31, 1921, a total of 1,006,473 pieces in high relief were struck. At least five matte proofs and perhaps two dozen or so satin proofs were struck at this time. The first specimen of the Peace silver dollar went by special messenger on January 3, 1922 to President Harding; others were delivered to the Secretary of the Treasury and to the Director the Mint, Washington, D.C.[14] The new dollars were released into general circulation on the same day.

The obverse of the coin shows a classic Liberty Head with a tiara of rays of light above her head. The word LIBERTY appears around the top of the head and IN GOD WE TRUST is inscribed at either side of the neck. The date is at the bottom.

On the reverse, a bald eagle is shown perched on a mountain crag with rays emanating from the lower right of the coin. Although the sun does not show, the rays shine as a token of the dawn of a new era, symbolic of the abolishment of war and the perpetuation of peace. The eagle holds an olive branch in its talons. In a semicircle at the top of the coin are the inscriptions UNITED STATES OF AMERICA, and below this, E PLURIBUS UNUM. In the lower half appear the words ONE DOLLAR, with PEACE at the very bottom of the coin.

Reaction to the new silver dollars was mixed. The Liberty head was criticized as having a startled or unkempt look. *The Wall Street Journal* had an article entitled "Our Flapper Silver Dollar."[15] There was also talk that the high relief of the design prevented the coins from stacking well. But perhaps their greatest shortcoming was the weak, flat strikes with central details of the coin not being brought out – particularly the central hairlines of the Liberty Head.

At that time, George T. Morgan was the Chief Engraver of the Mint. Thus, there was again a similar set of circumstances reminiscent of the problems encountered in 1878 on the Morgan silver dollar when Morgan was a special engraver. He was under time pressure to perfect the Morgan silver dollar dies in 1878 – the main problem being too high relief causing the dies to break and to wear out rapidly. Forty three years later, Morgan was again under time pressure to produce a new silver dollar design. The final design models were not approved until December 23, 1921, which left only a week to prepare the working dies and to strike coins before the end of the year. As a result, the dies produced were not completely satisfactory for striking production coins - the problem being too high relief.

DESIGN CHANGES IN OF THE REGULAR COINAGE

George Morgan wrote De Francisci early in January 1922 about changing the design relief of the new Peace dollar. He stated:[16]

I know you will be disappointed but the pressure necessary to bring up the work was so destructive to the dies that we got tired of putting new dies in.

A January 10, 1922 letter from the Acting Director of the Mint, O'Reilly to the Superintendent of the Philadelphia Mint reiterated the difficulties with the high relief 1921 design:

Request you to discontinue all work on preparation of dies for 1922 silver dollars.

It is understood from your letter of Jan. 6, 1922, that the relief of model from which dies were prepared for 21 coins is too great, and its distribution and areas not wisely planned; that the highest relief on each side is in the center of the coin and to attempt to drive the metal into this part of the coin brings a fin to the outer edge and breaks the die, and that this results in a decided difference in thickness which mars the appearance of the coin and interferes with stacking. It is also understood that the change is necessary to bring the model nearer to coin relief, and that such changes could be made at the mint without changing design, after consulting with its designer.

In accordance with your suggestion over the telephone it has been decided to take the matter up with the FAC with a view to procuring from Mr. Francisci a new model of lower relief. In doing this it is understood no change will be made in the design of the coin...

The same day O'Reilly sent a letter to the Director of the Mint, Baker, who was out West at the time:[17]

Experiments with 1922 dies like those sent Denver and San Francisco show relief still too high. Absolutely necessary have new model made by Francisci lowering relief to get coin to stack. No change whatever in design. Have today wired Denver and S.F. not to start dollar coinage until further instructed. Taking up matter with F.A.C. tomorrow.

This letter indicates that high relief coins with 1922 date were struck at Philadelphia Mint early in January in 1922, but were undoubtedly destroyed since they were experimental. High relief dies had been sent to the Denver Mint on January 6 but were returned on January 12.[18]

In mid-January 1922, Morgan slightly modified the design by adding two short rays in front on the obverse, and strengthened the letters, the details of hair, the feathers, and the mountain. At least five trial pieces were struck in matte proof of these slightly modified but still high relief 1922 dollars.[19]

Confirming telephone communications requesting that trial pieces, about 5 in number, struck from dies of new dollars now being prepared, be sent to Mr. Jones E. Fraser, Sculptor member of F.A.C. for inspection and report. I have also to request that at lease 2 pieces be sent from the same experimental strike to Director of Mint. It is understood that these trial pieces are to be returned to you by Mr. Fraser, and by this Bureau.

Apparently the Bureau of the Mint did not destroy these trial pieces as Breen reports five pieces known of the high relief 1922 Peace dollar.[20] Since their design differed from subsequent 1922 coins, these trial pieces in matte proof are among the rarest of silver dollar types.

This high relief 1922 design was still not satisfactory for striking regular coins. So later in January 1922, De Francisci was called to the Philadelphia Mint to supervise the production of the new master die by the Janvier engraving machine.[21] The relief of the design was made lower which De Francisci was understandably unhappy about but which he also realized had to be done. Further changes to the design detail were made without the knowledge or consent of De Francisci by George Morgan.[22] Concave fields were made flat, and small changes were made in the olive branches, rays, hairlines, feathers, and mountains.

Several proof satin finish dollars of the lower relief design were struck.[23, 24] Regular business strikes were produced by all three mints, Philadelphia, Denver, and San Francisco. But these initial 1922 low relief dies were still not completely satisfactory. Many of these early low relief design coins show a weakness in strike in the hair over the ear and on the eagle's wing feathers above the leg. This initial 1922 low relief design shows a detached olive branch from the eagle's foot and two hills to the right of the mountain crag. Only one or two dies of this initial low relief design was used at the Philadelphia Mint making them fairly scarce for that large issue of coins. About one-third of the 1922 Denver Mint coins and about one-half of the 1922 San Francisco Mint coins were of this design. It is well known that 1922-S coins are typically weakly struck.

Some minor design changes to the reverse were made shortly after the introduction of the lower relief design in 1922. The olive branch was made to go up against the eagle's right foot, a third hill was added to the right of the other two, the talon was connected to the toe of the eagle's left claw, and the rays around DOLLAR were strengthened. The obverse design was not changed. The field radius of the master obverse and reverse dies were probably changed to allow fuller striking of the design.

The low relief design was used for the remaining years of the Peace dollar series. Only a couple of very minor changes to the obverse design was made when the coinage resumed in 1935. The 1935-S was also struck with a design showing an added fourth ray below ONE and a seventh ray added below the eagle's tail. This was apparently a left over experimental die made during 1922.[25]

Footnotes

[1] Walter Breen, "The 1922 Type of 1921 Peace Dollar," *The Numismatic Scrapbook Magazine*, July 1961, p. 1723.
[2] "New U. S. Silver Dollar to Employ Controversial Peace Coin Design," *Coin World*, August 19, 1964, p. 3.
[3] Ibid.
[4] Breen, p. 1724.
[5] Ibid.
[6] *Coin World*, August 19, 1964, p. 3.
[7] Ibid.
[8] Don Taxay, *The U.S. Mint and Coinage*, 1966, Arco Publishing.
[9] Ibid.
[10] Memo for Under Secretary by O'Reilly, Bureau of the Mint, December 23, 1921.
[11] Letter from Raymond T. Baker, Director of the Mint, to Secretary of the Treasury, December 23, 1921.
[12] Letter from Baker to Superintendent U.S. Mint Philadelphia, January 28, 1922.
[13] Telegram from Acting Dir. of Mint to Baker, c/o U. S. Mint San Francisco, December 24, 1921.
[14] Breen, p. 1725.
[15] Joseph Moss, "Peace Dollar," *The Numismatist*, July, 1942.
[16] Ed Reiter, "The Lady on the Dollar," *COINage*, 1978.
[17] Letter from O'Reilly to Baker c/o Checkline Banking & Trust Co., Reno, Nevada, January 10, 1922.
[18] Letter from Baker to Superintendent U.S. Mint Denver, February 27, 1922.
[19] Letter O'Reilly to Superintendent U.S. Mint Philadelphia, January 14, 1922.
[20] Walter Breen, *Encyclopedia of U.S. and Colonial Proof Coins: 1722–1977*, F.C.I. Press, Inc., New York 1977, p. 220.
[21] Breen, "The 1922 Type of 1921 Peace Dollar," p. 1726.
[22] Ibid
[23] Walter Breen, *Encyclopedia of U.S. and Colonial Proof Coins: 1722–1977*, 1977 F.C.I. Press, p. 221.
[24] Wayne, Miller, *The Morgan and Peace Dollar Textbook*, Adam Smith Publishing, 1983.
[25] T.W. Voetter, *The Numismatist*, October, 1940.

Chapter 12
Description of the Designs

The Peace silver dollar had several design changes, three for the obverse and four for the reverse. The first changes of the design were made in 1922 to correct some of the difficulties experienced with the high relief 1921 design. This high relief caused the dies to wear rapidly, the full design could not always be brought out (particularly the hairlines on the obverse), and the coins did not stack well. Further changes were made in 1934 and 1935 after a lapse from the 1928 of silver dollar coinage. A list of differences with accompanying photographs of the designs are included at the end of this chapter.

REVERSE DESIGN DESCRIPTIONS

The initial reverse design, A, was used on all coins struck at the Philadelphia Mint late in 1921 and for a few proof coins. The major characteristic of this design was the very high relief.

The second reverse design, B, was used on all 1922 to 1928, 1934, 1935-P, and some 1935-S coins. The relief of the design was considerably reduced, minor changes were made on the eagle, and the number of light rays was reduced. There are two versions of this B reverse. The first, B^1, has a detached olive branch from the eagle's foot, only two hills to the right of the mountain crag, a detached talon from the toe at the rear of the eagle's left claw, and weakness in some of the rays where they meet the tops of D–AR. This was discovered by Robert Maxey of Baltimore, MD and reported by Herbert P. Hicks in the January and February 1981 issues of the *Error–Variety News*. The B^1 reverse appears on a few of the 1922-P, about one third of the 1922-D and about one half of the 1922-S.

Since the B^1 reverse tended to result in weakly struck coins, it was modified early in 1922 to a B^2 reverse. The field curvature was changed to provide more fully struck coins and a number of minor design improvements and corrections were made. The olive branch was extended to meet the eagle's foot, a third hill was added to the right of the other two and some lines were added to strengthen their detail, the tail of R in DOLLAR was made slightly longer and extends past the vertical ray, the talon was attached to the toe at the rear of the eagle's left claw, and the rays intersect the DOLLAR letters in full relief.

The third reverse design C, was used on only a few 1935-S coins. Thus, we have the unusual situation that a design change was made for, or at, only one branch mint!. This reverse is the same as the previous reverse except for two small additions: a fourth ray was added below ONE, and a seventh ray was added below the eagle's tail.

These added rays are in approximately the same position as the extra rays used in the 1921 reverse. This variety was discovered by Mr. Berghli of San Diego, California, and was reported by T.W. Voetter in the May 1939, *The Numismatist*.

A possible explanation of the cause of this die variety was given by Voetter in a later article in the October 1940, issue of *The Numismatist*. In 1922 two different reverse hubs may have been made but one of them was unsatisfactory and was destroyed after making only a few working dies. One of these dies was later sent to the San Francisco Mint and was not used for coinage until 1935.

Since the coins struck at the Philadelphia Mint in 1935 were all of the second reverse type, this extra rays reverse design was only used at the San Francisco Mint. Only about one fourth to one third of the 1935-S coins have the added rays, which indicates that only one of the dies used had these extra rays (about 2 million 1935-S dollars were struck, and one Peace dollar die could strike up to half a million dollars before being retired).

OBVERSE DESIGN DESCRIPTIONS

The first obverse design, I, was also used on all coins struck at the Philadelphia Mint late in 1921 and for a few 1922 proof coins. It, too, had a very high relief as well as a slightly concave field.

The second obverse design, II, was used during 1922 to 1928. The relief was greatly reduced and the field was made much flatter. Changes in design detail included thinner letters and numbers, three additional short rays at the front of the cap, and a second line in the head band.

When the minting of the Peace dollar was resumed in 1934, slight obverse design changes were again made. In the third obverse design, III, the motto lettering was made thinner and the tail of the R in TRUST was straightened. Why the motto lettering was changed is a mystery, since the Liberty head design was not changed. Perhaps a new master die was made using the original Galvano with the basic design and the motto was added separately. However, the dies and hubs used in 1928 should have still been available in 1934; they obviously were available for the reverse, since it was not changed in 1934.

DESIGN COMBINATIONS

Table 12-1 shows the design combinations for the Peace silver dollar. Although three different designs are known for both the obverse and reverse, only four separate combinations exist.

I Obverse. Used in 1921 only. Differs from later design in following ways:
  a. Higher relief and concave field.
  b. Letters and numbers thicker.
  c. Rays from cap thicker, first three short rays missing on left.
  d. Only one line in head band.

A Reverse. Used in 1921 only. Differs from the later design in following ways:
  a. Higher relief.
  b. Less curved eagle's beak.
  c. Earlier division of branch at eagle's feet and different shaped leaves.
  d. Eagle's right ankle thinner.
  e. Eagle's left ankle showing.
  f. Mountain ranges different; only two peaks show instead of three.
  g. Four rays below ONE instead of three.
  h. Eight rays below eagle's tail instead of six.
  i. Twenty-one rays below eagle's wing instead of nineteen and one half, some rays shorter.

II Obverse. Used During 1922 to 1928.

B Reverse. Used for all 1922 to 1928, 1934, 1935-P, and some 1935-S.

Table 12-1 DESIGN COMBINATIONS FOR PEACE DOLLAR

Obverse	Mint	Reverse
I	all 1921 & some 1922 proofs	A
II	some 1922-P,D,S and some 1922 proofs	B¹
II	some 1922-P,D,S; all 1923 to 1928	B²
III	all 1934, 1935-P, and some 1935-S	B²
III	some 1935-S	C

MINOR DESIGN TYPES:

B¹ Reverse. Detached olive branch from eagle's foot, two hills to right of mountain crag, detached talon from toe at rear of eagle's left claw, R in DOLLAR is short, and rays are weak where they meet the tops of D–AR.

B² Reverse. Olive branch connected to eagle's foot, third hill added to right of mountain crag, talon connected to toe at rear of eagle's left claw, R in DOLLAR is slightly longer and extends past the vertical ray, and rays intersect DOLLAR letters in full relief.

B¹ Reverse. Detached olive branch

B² Reverse. Connected olive branch

B¹ Reverse. Two hills

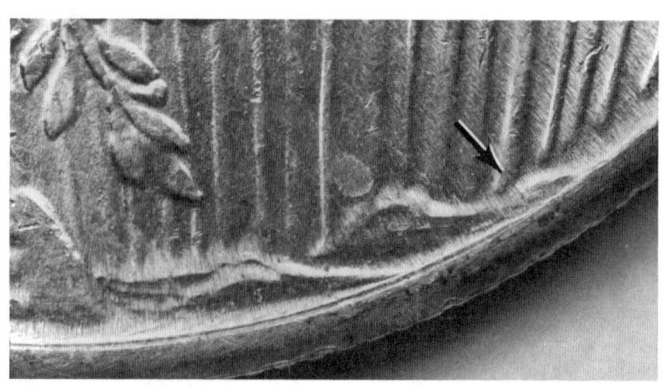

B² Reverse. Three Hills

III Obverse. Used in 1934 and 1935. Differs from earlier design in following ways:
   a. IN GOD WE TRUST lettering thinner.
   b. Straight tail on R in TRUST.

C Reverse. Used for some 1935-S. Differs from earlier design in following ways:
   a. Added fourth ray below ONE.
   b. Added seventh ray below eagle's tail.

Chapter 13
Discussion of Significant Varieties

MINT MARK VARIATIONS

Two branch mints struck the Peace silver dollar. The San Francisco Mint struck them from 1922 to 1928 and again in 1934 and 1935. Only one size mint mark was used – a micro S. The Denver Mint struck Peace dollars in 1922, 1923, 1926, 1927, and 1934. A micro D was used in all these years; in addition, a medium size D was used on some 1934 coins. The following is a list and description of various mint marks used:

San Francisco:
I S   Micro S: 1922–1928, 1934, and 1935

Denver:
I D   Micro D: 1922, 1923, 1926, 1927 and some 1934

II D   Medium D: some 1934

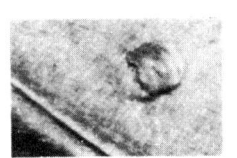

MINT MARK PLACEMENT

Only a few die variations are known of the mint mark placement for the Peace dollar series. The following is the short list of this variety. The 1935-S listed is of the type B reverse.

1926-D	D tilted right	1934-D	High D
1926-S	Medium high S	1934-D	D tilted right
1926-S	High S	1934-S	S tilted left
1927-S	High S	1935-S	S tilted left
1928-S	Medium high S		

DATE VARIATIONS

There were small differences in the numbers used for the date each year. Five different 1's were used and four different 2's. The fact that there were so many different design 1's and 2's on the Peace silver dollar indicates that the complete date was changed for almost every year on the master die using a logotype.

I 1	Thick 1	1921
II 1	Rounded top 1	1922, 1925 – 1928 
III 1	Pointed top 1	1923 
IV 1	Tall large top 1	1924 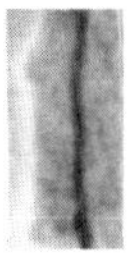
V 1	Small top 1	1934, 1935 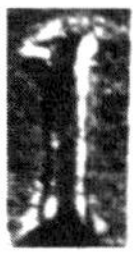
I 2	Thick 2	1921 
II 2	Straight bottom 2, rounded end	1922, 1924, 1926-1928 
III 2	Large end 2	1923 
IV 2	End of 2 slanting upwards	1925 
I 3	Small closed 3	1923 
II 3	Large open 3	1934, 1935 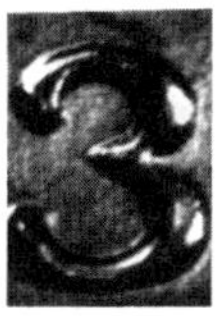
I 4	Small 4	1924 

II 4	Large 4	1934
I 5	Small 5	1925
II 5	Large 5	1935
I 6		1926
I 7		1927
I 8		1928
I 9	Wide 9	1921
II 9	Thin 9, circular opening	1922–1928
III 9	Thin 9, oblong opening	1934, 1935

CLASHED DIES

As in the case of the Morgan silver dollars, clashed dies were common with the Peace silver dollars. The clashed reverse shows as an extra line extending up from the top of the eagle's right wing (an impression from the back of Liberty's neck), a vee above the eagle's left wing (from the junction of the neck and chin of the Liberty head), a raised bump or short curved vertical line above LL in DOLLAR (from the end of the headband), and a horizontal line extending from the branches below DOLLAR (from the top of the Liberty head below the R.

The clashed obverse shows as an extra line extending down from the chin and neck junction to the top of the E in WE (an impression of the second ray from the top of the left wing – in this case the obverse line is incused rather than raised, since it is incused in the reverse die), an incused vertical line at the end of the head band (from the rays above DOLLAR on the reverse), and a short vertical line between the rays to the right of E in LIBERTY (from the branches on the reverse).

MACHINE DOUBLING

Press machine doubling is another common Peace dollar variety. On the Peace silver dollar, most doubled coins are only doubled on the obverse. This suggests that they are due to machine doubling since there would be an equal likelihood of doubled obverse and reverse dies. A 1923-P doubled obverse is definitely from machine doubling since it was the only doubled coin in a mint sealed bag of coins (all 1923-P dates) examined by the authors. In addition, of the several doubled 1922, 1923, and 1925-P coins known for each date, none are identical, which indicates that they are from machine doubling.

It was noted in the discussion of the Morgan silver dollars that one side, the reverse, was predominantly doubled from mechanical play in the press during striking. For the Peace dollar, it was the obverse and it was not the result of a repunched date, since other features were usually doubled.

Looseness in the press die holder and other parts caused the dies to move or shift during the striking process. This resulted in the shelf-like machine doubling. This doubling is slightly different for each coin. Because they are so common, they do not command any price premium.

DIE BREAKS

The Peace dollar dies were generally used longer in striking coins than the Morgan dollar dies. There were also less inspections of the coins so that more errors and die breaks on coins were released. The Peace dollar series has some very spectacular die breaks showing on the coins.

Since the die breaks occurred near the end of the die's lifetime, relatively fewer coins were struck with the defect. Also the die break would begin as a small hairline crack showing on some coins and would progress to a longer die break on later coins as the die continued to deteriorate and chip away.

Small hairline cracks are fairly common on Peace dollars although not as frequent as they were on the Morgan dollars. They are not listed because of this and command no premium to collectors. Die breaks that are readily visible to the naked eye with significant chips out of the die are collectable and do command a premium price. The following is a list of major die breaks:

Major Die Breaks
VAM
1922-P 2A - Break from ear down to neck.
    2B - Break from nose to upper lip.
    2C Vertical break at the back of hair.

Clashed Obverse

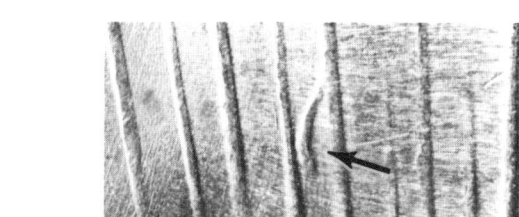

Clashed Reverse

VAM
   2D - Break below eagle's wing in field.
   2E - Horizontal break on eagle's back.
1923-P 1A - Break on back of jaw.
   1B - Slanting break at back of hair.
1923-P 1C - Diagonal break from O in Dollar.
   1D - Vertical break on cheek.
   1E - Diagonal break across eagle's back.
1924-P 1B - Break in middle of wing.
   1C - Back of hair.

DOUBLED DIES

It took several blows of the working hub to transfer the design to a working die. Any misalignment of the hub and die during the later blows could cause doubling of some of the design.

There are some significant doubled dies of the Peace dollar series that are visible to the naked eye. The strongest is the 1934-D with strongly doubled Liberty head profile and rear rays in the tiara. There are also doubled rays on the tiara of a 1923-P die that are very visible. A number of other dates have less prominent doubling on the obverse and reverse. The following is a listing of known doubled dies. There also have been reported, which the authors have not seen, a 1927-P doubled obverse and doubled reverses for 1925-P, 1927-S and 1934-D.

List of Double Dies

VAM
1921-P 2 Doubled PEACE letters on left side.
1922-P 3 Doubled leg feather and olive leaves.
   4 Doubled motto and designer's initials.
   5 Tripled olive leaves and leg feathers.
1922-D 3 Doubled olive branch.
1923-P 2 Doubled tiara rays, designer's initials, TRUST, and lower hair curl.
   3 Doubled lower reverse olive leaves.
1924-P 2 Doubled rays above ONE and eagle's back and rear feather of leg.
1925-S 2 Doubled olive branches, leaves, rays and leg feathers.
1926-P 2 Doubled olive branches, leaves, rays and leg feathers.
1928-S 3 Doubled rear rays in tiara, designer's initials, motto and back of hair.
1934-D 3,4 Doubled profile, designer's initials, rear tiara rays, and TRUST.

DOTS

A number of the Peace dollars have round raised dots on their surfaces similar to those found on the 1921 P, D, and S Morgan dollars. These are from tiny gas bubbles trapped in the steel when it was cast. The dots are not from the use of a Rockwell hardness tester of the face of the dies after they were hardened. The size of the dots ranged from two to seven thousands of an inch in diameter and are considered too small and numerous to have been made by a Rockwell hardness tester.

The dates occurred from 1921 through 1924 and no coins show these raised dots from 1925 and afterwards. Presumably the steel for the dies was better made without gas bubbles or from a different source in 1925 and later years so the dots did not show up on the coins.

Some coins only show a single dot on either the obverse or reverse. Some dates show multiple dots scattered over various parts of the coin. The 1924-P has several varieties that show over thirty dots of various sizes on the obverse!

The following is a list of currently known Peace dollar dot coins. Undoubtedly other dot coin varieties exist.
1921-P One dot below ONE on reverse.
1922-P Two varieties with single dots.
1922-D One dot in O of ONE.
1923-P Three varieties with single dots.
1923-D One dot below N of IN.
1924-P 12 varieties with up to over 30 dots on the obverse of a single variety.
1924-S One dot below E in WE.

ROTATED DIES

As with the Morgan dollar, the Peace dollar normally has the obverse and reverse upside down with respect to each other. Some rotations have been found from this position due to the dies positioned incorrectly or working loose in the press. The following is a list of the currently known rotations in degrees:

Year	Rotation
1921-P	20° CCW
1922-P	100° CCW
1922-D	45° – 53° CW
1923-P	25° – 100° CW
1927-D	15° CW

OTHER ERRORS

Some examples of other Peace dollar errors are shown in the accompanying photographs. Several different types of planchet errors are illustrated. The 1922-P

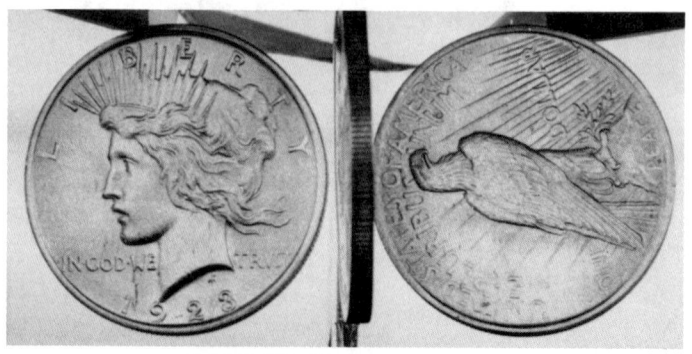

1923-P 75° Clockwise Rotation

422

has a long split in the planchet from the date to the ear. The 1924-P has a split below the ear. It was caused by impurities lying within the whole thickness of the planchet. A related error is the 1923-P with obverse and reverse laminations. In these cases, the rolling of the silver strip caused the slag impurities to be rolled out in a thin layer just under the surface of the planchet resulting in large laminations.

There are a number of spectacular striking errors in the Peace dollar series. The 1922-P shows a strike through on the reverse, also caused by a strip of metal between the die and planchet. A weak strike is illustrated on the 1924-P. It shows a smooth surface in the hair over the ear.

The Peace dollar series has a relatively greater number of rim clips than the pre-1921 Morgan dollar series. Some examples are shown in the accompanying photos. The clips do not extend much beyond the coin rim. Large clips are extremely rare for silver dollars because of the weight check of the coins at the mints. The 1923-P shows three small clips. Multiple clips are quite rare on silver dollars. The more usual is a single clip like the 1922-P example shown.

Another striking error is the 1923-S partial collar with only part of the edge reeding showing. This so-called "railroad rim" effect was caused by the planchet being partially within the collar when it was struck by the dies.

A related error is the broadstruck 1922-S dollar shown in the accompanying photos. This was caused when the planchet was struck entirely out of the collar by the dies. As a result, the coin has a larger diameter than normal without edge reeding. The authors have also seen a nice 1921-P and 1922-D broadstruck dollars.

Double struck Peace dollars are extremely rare. One example is the 1921-P shown in the accompanying photo. It failed to be ejected from the press after being struck the first time. It was struck a second time after rotating about 10 degrees CW. This second strike obliterated all of the first strike design except for part of the date numeral 1, IN and L of LIBERTY on the obverse and UNITED and ONE on the reverse. The edge of the coin shows two sets of reeding where the coin did not fully drop or was not completely pushed back into the collar.

Another example of a double struck Peace dollar is the illustrated 1922-S. It is one of the more spectacular striking errors of the Peace dollars. This one was struck a second time about 180 degrees rotated from the first strike. The bottom of the obverse shows E and R of LIBERTY from the first strike adjacent to the date numbers. The original strike design was almost completely obliterated from the reverse except for faint rays at 11 o'clock. The second strike was not completely in the collar as shown by the collar's top markings on the lower obverse. Since the first striking of the coin would not fit easily back into the collar, the coin ended up with the lower obverse sitting on top of the collar. As a result, the lower obverse die did not obliterate the first strike design of that part of the coin held up on top of the collar.

The double struck 1923-P is different with a vertical shift between strikings of half a coin width. Also shown is a 1922-S that was struck about 10 percent off center. These two types of striking errors are very rare for Peace dollars and they command large premium prices.

1922-S Broadstuck

1923-S Tilted Partial Collar

1923-P Lamination

1924-P Obverse
Weakly Struck

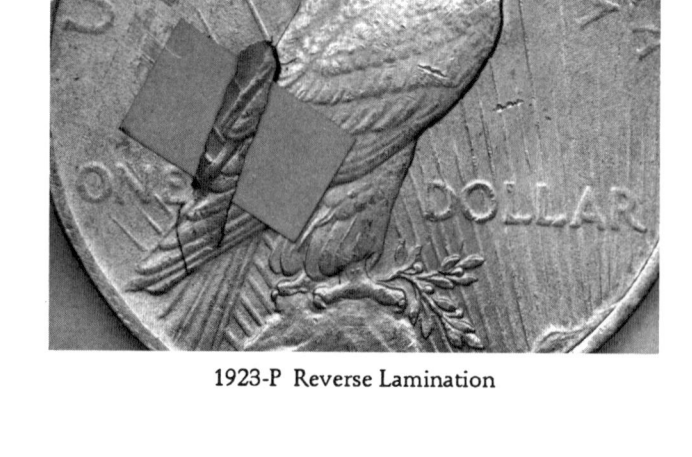

1922-P Rim Clip

1924-P Split Planchet

1922-P Split Planchet

1923-P Reverse Lamination

1922-P Reverse Struck Through

1923-P Triple Clip
(Photo Courtesy of Natalie Halpern)

1921-P Double Struck

1921-P Double Struck,
Double Reeding

1922-S Double Struck, Rotated 180°

1923-P Double Struck

1922-S Struck 10% Off-Center

Chapter 14
Condition Analysis and List Of Die Varieties

The following is a discussion of condition availability and listing of die varieties for the Peace dollar from 1921 – 1928 and 1934 and 1935. The die varieties are designated by a number, type, and a short description of the main variety feature. There are fewer Peace dollar varieties than Morgan dollar varieties because only one-third as many coins were minted, they were minted for a fewer number of years, and the die making technology was more advanced. This last factor allowed the dies to strike more coins and the date did not have to be punched into each individual working die. Also, the edge reeding in the collar was standardized for all issues at 189.

Nonetheless, the Peace dollar has large variations in quantity minted, fullness of strike, luster, frostiness, and die wear from year to year and mint to mint. It is not as popular with collectors and investors as the Morgan dollar by a wide margin. Many factors contribute to this reduced popularity including more rounded and less sharply detailed design, lack of proof-likes, less frostiness or contrast of the devices, generally a higher percentage of coins with excessive die wear evidenced by "orange peel" or surface roughness, a more modern design which lacks the strength of the more classic Morgan design, and the coins are not as old. Assembling a nice set of Peace dollars can be challenging, but considerably easier and less costly than trying to put together a comparable quality Morgan dollar set.

1921-P

The first year of issue of the Peace dollar is of high relief design. They were struck during the last three days of 1921. Because of the high relief and rushed production, most coins of this date show a weak strike with detail lacking in the hair over the ear on the obverse and lack of detail on the wing feathers over the eagle's right leg on reverse. This lack of high point detail should not be mistaken for coin wear however. A slightly circulated coin will show some wear on the cheek and upper parts of the eagle's wing.

Sliders are common for this date and a coin should always be carefully examined to determine if any wear exists. Tilt the coin under a strong light to see if grayish areas or hairlines exist on the cheek and eagle or in the fields. Its availability from the grading services in MS64-66 is just slightly under the median. That is, it is neither very common nor very scarce in these grades compared with other Peace dollars.

One minor variety shows slight doubling of PEACE.

1   **I 1 • Aa (Normal Die)**   I–1   R–2
     Obverse I 1 – Normal die of I type. Detail of hair around ear usually missing even on BU specimens, due to weak strike.
     Reverse Aa – Normal die of A type.

2   **I 1 • Ab (Doubled PEACE)**   I–2   R–3
     Reverse Ab – Letters in PEACE doubled slightly on left side.

1922-P

Because of the difficulty of striking the high relief design late in 1921, the design relief was made shallower early in 1922. The initial attempt was not entirely satisfactory with the B^1 reverse resulting in slight weakness in the hair over the ear and eagle's wing above the leg. Only a few dies of the B^1 reverse were used at the Philadelphia Mint however, so they are only a small fraction of the large 1922-P mintage. A later modification of the design changed some of the details and the field radius of curvature which allowed more fully struck coins. As a result, weakness of strike is generally not a problem for this year.

Despite the enormous mintage, the 1922-P is more difficult to locate in MS65 condition than the other high mintage date, the 1923-P. It also has a problem with the so-called water spots probably caused by improper washing and drying of the planchets, or later washing and rebagging of contaminated coins.

Its availability from the grading services in MS64 is among the most common, just under that for the 1923-P. In MS65 it is the third most common

1921-P 2 R Doubled PEACE

and in MS66 it is at about the top one-third point in overall availability.

This date has some fairly large die breaks as some dies were used well beyond their normal service retirement point. The very visible die breaks command a significant price premium and are popular collector's items. The 1922-P also has several minor doubled dies and a nice visible die gouge in the high rays below "E" of LIBERTY. These minor varieties are worth only a small premium in price.

1   **II 1 • B^{1}a (Early Design)**   I–3   R–3
    Obverse II 1 – Normal die of II type.
    Reverse B^{1}a – Normal die of B^1 type.

2   **II 1 • B^{2}a (Normal Die)**   I–1   R–1
    Reverse B^{2}a – Normal die of B^2 type.

2A **II 1 • B^{2}a (Ear Ringed)**   I–3   R–6
    Obverse II 1 – Die break causing shaft of metal from ear down to neck.

2B **II 1 • B^{2}a (Moustache)**   I–3   R–6
    Obverse II 1 – Die break from nose to back of upper lip of Liberty Head.

2C **II 1 • B^{2}a (Extra Hair)**   I–3   R–6
    Obverse II 1 – Curved sliver of metal at back of hair due to die break.

2D **II 1 • B^{2}a (Reverse Field Die Break)**   I–3   R–6
    Reverse B^{2}a – Die break in field above DOLLAR causing diagonal sliver of metal.

2E **II 1 • B^{2}a (Reverse Wing Die Break)**   I–3   R–6
    Reverse B^{2}a – Die break on eagle's back causing a raised tear drop of metal.

2F **II 1 • B^{2}a (Die Gouge in Rays)**   I–3   R–3
    Obverse II 1 – Horizontal die gouge in rays below E of LIBERTY.

3   **II 1 • B^{2}c (Doubled Leg Feathers)**   I–3   R–3
    Reverse B^{2}c – Lower leg feathers doubled on left side as are left olive leaves and couple of feathers on left edge of eagle's middle left side.

4   **II 4 • B^{2}a (Doubled Motto)**   I–2   R–3
    Obverse II 4 – Slightly doubled bottom of WE TR, designer's initials, date digits and lower hair strands.

1922-P 2A O Ear-Ringed Die Break

1922-P 2B O Moustache Die Break

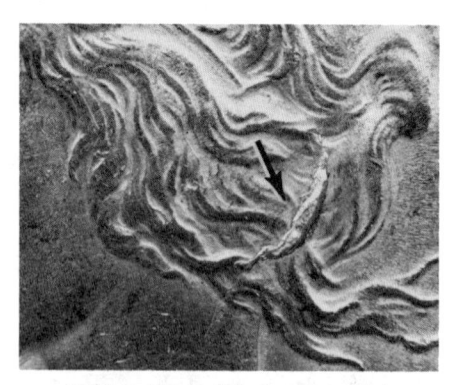

1922-P 2C O Die Break in Hair

1922-P 2D R Die Break in Field

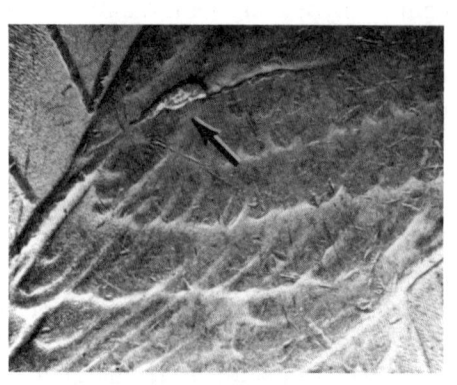

1922-P 2E R Die Break on Eagle

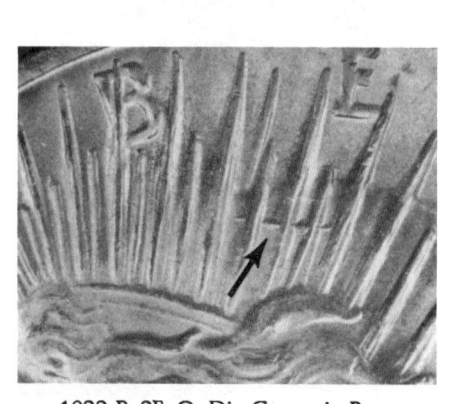

1922-P 2F O Die Gouge in Rays

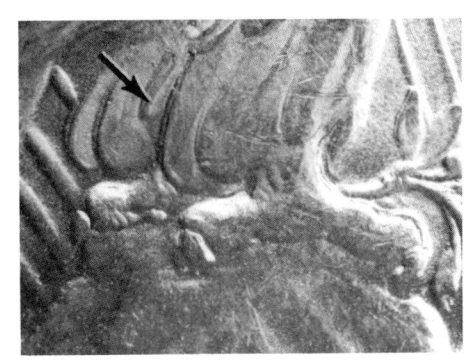

1922-P 3 R Doubled Leg Feathers

1922-P 4 O Doubled Motto, Designer's Initials

1922-P 5 R Tripled Olive Leaves
(Photo courtesy of Jeff Oxman)

1922-D

About one-third of the date was struck using the earlier B^1 reverse. These coins are typically weakly struck. Those coins with the later B^2 reverse usually are much better struck.

The fairly high mintage for this branch mint meant some dies were in service excessively long. As a result, the 1922-D shows an above average amount of die cracks and roughness in the field or "orange peel" appearance due to worn dies. The die cracks appear around the periphery and across the neck. They do not affect the value in most cases. It is at about the top one-third point in overall availability from the grading services in MS64-66.

There is only one known minor variety for this date that has small doubling of the olive branch.

1   **II 1 • B^1a (Early Design)**   I–2   R–2
     Obverse II 1 – Normal die of II type.
     Reverse B^1a – Normal die of B^1 type.

2   **II 1 • B^2a (Normal Die)**   I–1   R–1
     Reverse B^2a – Normal die of B^2 type.

3   **II 1 • B^2c (Doubled Olive Branch)**   I–3   R–3
     Reverse B^2c – Doubled lower reverse including left side of olive branch and leaves, rear of leg feathers and rays above olive branch.

1922-D 3 R Doubled Olive Branch

1922-S

This date is difficult to locate in fully struck MS65 condition. The reason is that about one-half were struck with the earlier B^1 reverse. Although it has a large mintage, apparently large quantities were released into circulation for this first year of issue of the Peace dollar by the San Francisco Mint. Its availability in grades MS64-66 from the grading services is at about the one-third point from the scarcest date.

1   **II 1 • B^1a (Early Design)**   I–1   R–1
     Obverse II 1 – Normal die of II type.
     Reverse B^1a – Normal die of B^1 type.

2   **II 1 • B^2a (Normal Die)**   I–1   R–1
     Reverse B^2a – Normal die of B^2 type.

1923-P

This date is the most readily available Peace dollar in mint state even though it has a lower mintage than the 1922-P. It is the most readily available in MS64 and MS65 from the grading services and about on par with the 1925-P in MS66 as the most available for the grade. The problem in finding minimum bag marked Peace dollars is the large and high relief wing of the eagle. It is much more vulnerable to visible bag marks than the more shallow and detailed Morgan dollar eagle.

Some of the early strike 1923-P exhibit frosting in the hair of the Liberty Head and frosting in the feathers of the eagle. When combined with the usual full strike and with a minimum of bag marks, these can be among the most attractive of the Peace dollars. As with the 1922-P, some of the 1923-P show the so-called water spots which can decrease the coin's value depending upon their extent and location.

The 1923-P also has some spectacular large die breaks like the 1922-P. It also has a large but shallow die gouge extending vertically down from the chin. There are two known doubled dies. One doubled die is the second strongest doubled die of the entire Peace dollar series showing doubled rear rays of light in the tiara. This is visible to the naked eye and commands a significant premium but is difficult to locate. The common 1923-P thus has some very interesting varieties.

1	II 1 • B^{2}a (Normal Die)	I–1	R–1

Obverse II 1 – Normal die of II type
Reverse B^{2}a – Normal die of B^2 type

1A	II 1 • B^{2}a (Whisker Jaw)	I–3	R–6

Obverse II 1 – Extra sliver of metal from jaw to neck due to die break.

1B	II 1 • B^{2}a (Extra Hair)	I–3	R–4

Obverse II 1 – Sliver of metal at back of hair due to die break. Several variations of this type die break exist with the metal positioned at various places on the LIBERTY head hair.

1C	II 1 • B^{2}a (Tail on O)	I–2	R–4

Reverse B^{2}a – Die break from lower part of O in DOLLAR extending diagonally down to left.

1D	II 1 • B^{2}a (Whisker Cheek)	I–3	R–6

Obverse II 1 – Sliver of metal on cheek due to die break.

1E	II 1 • B^{2}a (Die Break on Eagle's Back)	I–2	R–4

Reverse B^{2}a – Die break from top left of eagle's wing down across back to middle right wing.

1F	II 1 • B^{2}a (Chin Bar)	I–2	R–3

Obverse II 1 – Vertical bar of shallow raised metal from chin down right side of D motto to top of 1 due to die gouge.

2	II 4 • B^{2}a (Doubled Rays)	I–4	R–4

Obverse II 4 – Rays of light in tiara are doubled on left side with those in rear having strongest doubling. Tops of TR in TRUST, lower back hair curl, rear of neck, and right side of designer's initials are slightly doubled.

3	II 1 • B^{2}b (Doubled Lower Reverse)	I–3	R–4

Reverse B^{2}b – Doubled lower reverse including rays, back of feathers on legs, and olive leaves.

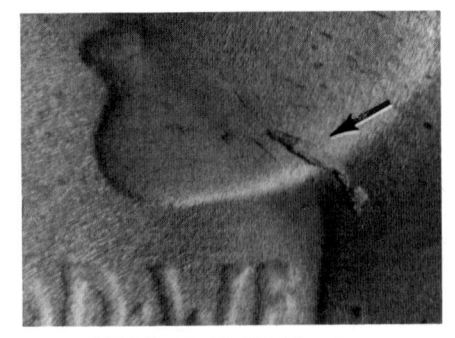

1923-P 1A O Whisker Jaw

1923-P 1C R Tail on O

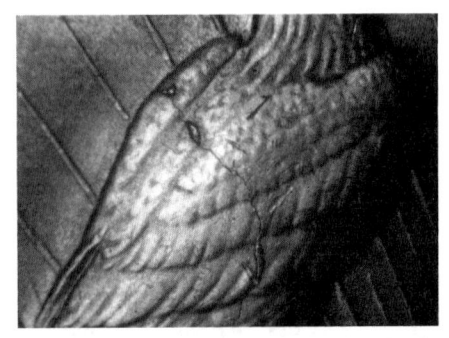

1923-P 1E R Die Break on Eagle's Beak
(Photo courtesy of Bill Fivaz)

1923-P 1B O Extra Hair 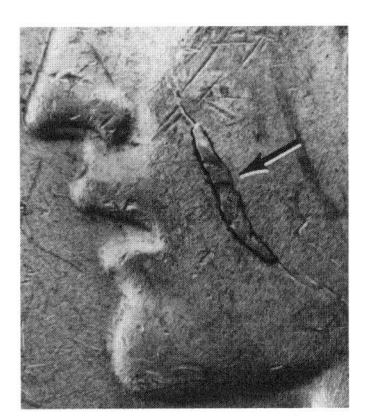
1923-P 1D O Whisker Cheek 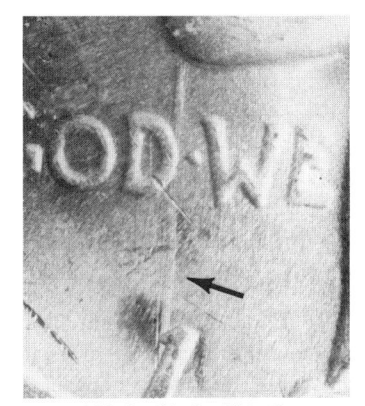
1923-P 1F O Chin Bar

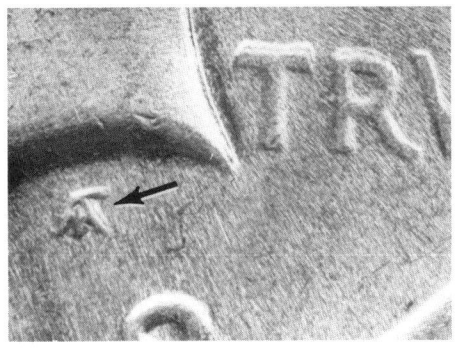

1923-P 2 O Doubled Rays, Motto & Hair
1923-P 3 R Doubled Lower Reverse 

1923-D

Locating full strike specimens is not a problem with this date. But is difficult to locate minimum bag marked MS65 pieces. As with the 1922-D, many of the dies were used beyond their normal service life and peripheral die cracks and ones across the base of the neck are common. It is at about the median point in MS64 and 65 availability from the grading services and among the scarcest in MS66.

1   II 1 • B²a (Normal Die)   I-1   R-2
    Obverse II 1 – Normal die of II type.
    Reverse B²a – Normal die of B² type with micro I D mint mark.

1923-S

A notoriously difficult date to find fully struck with minimum bag marks. Although the B² reverse was used to strike the entire issue of this date, apparently the strike pressure was very seldom set high enough to bring up the full design detail in the hair over the ear or feathers over the leg. The lower striking pressure extended the die life time for the large mintage. The 1923-S ranks with the 1928-S and 1925-S as the most difficult Peace dollar dates to find of the lower relief design with full strikes. Its availability from the grading services in MS64-66 approaches that of the scarcest dates in these grades.

Only one minor die variety is known with the doubled mint mark on the left side.

1   II 1 • B²a (Normal Die)   I-1   R-1
    Obverse II 1 – Normal die of II type.
    Reverse B²a – Normal die of B² type with micro I S mint mark.

2   II 1 • B²a (S/S Left)   I-2   R-4
    Reverse B²b – Micro I S doubled on left side.

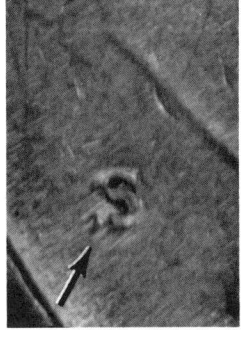

1923-S 2 R
Doubled S

1924-P

This date has a problem with worn dies showing excessive "orange peel" appearance over the fields and devices. Coins struck with worn dies exhibit dull luster and roughness in the otherwise smooth fields. There exist nice fully struck early strike specimens, so locating MS65 coins is not too difficult. This date is about the fourth most commonly available in grades MS64 and 65 from the grading services and about the third most available in MS66.

The 1924-P has some very interesting die varieties. A shallow die gouge exists from the left side of the D in the motto down to 1. There is also a very large die break in the center of the wing. A doubled die reverse shows doubled rays above ONE and top of the eagle's back.

| 1 | II 1 • B^{2}a (Normal Die) | I–1 | R–1 |

Obverse II 1 – Normal die of II type.
Reverse B^{2}a – Normal die of B^2 type.

| 1A | II 1 • B^{2}a (Bar D) | I–2 | R–4 |

Obverse II 1 – Vertical bar of shallow metal from left side of "D" in motto down to left side of 1 due to die gouge.

| 1B | II 1 • B^{2}a (Die Break on Wing) | I–3 | R–4 |

Reverse B^{2}a – Large circular die break in center of wing.

| 1C | II 1 • B^{2}a (Die Breaks in Hair) | I–3 | R–4 |

Obverse II 1 – Two vertical die breaks at back of hair.

| 2 | II 1 • B^{2}i (Doubled Reverse) | I–3 | R–3 |

Reverse B^{2}i – Rays above ONE and eagle's back and rear feathers of leg are doubled.

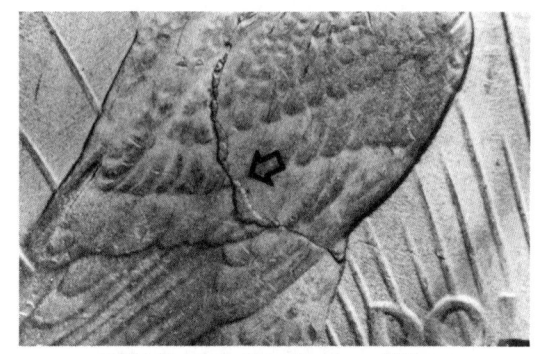

1924-P 1B R Die Break on Wing

1924-P 1A O Bar D

1924-P 1C O Die Breaks in Hair

1924-P 2 R Doubled Reverse

1924-S

A low mintage date which is for the most part weakly struck. Locating a true MS65 coin is very difficult because of excessive bag marks and weak strike problems. It is about fifth or sixth scarcest in MS64-66 from the grading services.

| 1 | II 1 • B^{2}a (Normal Die) | I–2 | R–2 |

Obverse II 1 – Normal die of II type.
Reverse B^{2}a – Normal die of type with micro I S mint mark.

1925-P

In general, this date is fully struck with brilliant fields and nice luster. Many 1925-P's have light golden toning on both sides which was probably caused by some contaminant in their storage area at the Philadelphia Mint. In contrast with the 1924-P, the 1925-P seldom exhibits surface roughness due to worn dies. In MS64 it is about the third most available from the grading services; in MS65, the second most available behind the 1923-P and in MS66 about on par with the 1923-P as the most available.

1   II 1 • B^2a (Normal Die)   I-1   R-1
Obverse II 1 – Normal die of II type.
Reverse B^2a – Normal die of B^2 type.

1925-S

Another San Francisco Mint coin that is typically weakly struck with excessive bag marks. Therefore, MS65 pieces are difficult to locate. This date is at about the lower one-third point in availability from the grading services in MS65 and among the scarcest in MS65 and 66. There is a doubled die reverse with doubled olive branches, rays and leg feathers.

1   II 1 • B^2a (Normal Die)   I-1   R-2
Obverse II 1 – Normal die of II type.
Reverse B^2a – Normal die of B^2 type with micro I S mint mark.

2   II 1 • B^2b (Doubled Olive Branches)   I-3   R-3
Reverse B^2b – Doubled olive branches and leaves on left side, rear feathers of eagle's legs and rays below olive branches, behind legs and above and below ONE on left side.

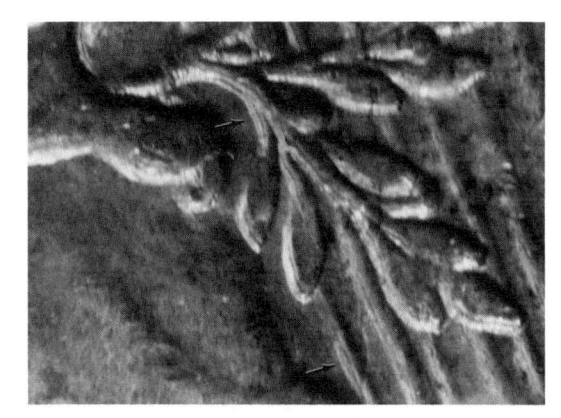

1925-S 2 R Doubled Olive Branches, Rays

1926-P 2 R Doubled Rays & Feathers

1926-P

A relatively low mintage coin which makes MS65 condition fairly scarce. As with the 1925-P, this date typically shows a full strike with good luster and brilliant fields. Some even exhibit the two-sided light golden toning so desirable on the 1925-P. It is at about the top one-third point in availability from the grading services in MS64-66. There is a doubled die reverse with doubled olive branches, rays and leg feathers.

1   II 1 • B^2a (Normal Die)   I-1   R-2
Obverse II 1 – Normal die of II type
Reverse B^2a – Normal die of B^2 type.

2   II 1 • B^2b (Doubled Olive Branches)   I-3   R-3
Reverse B^2b – Doubled olive branches and leaves on left side, rear feathers of eagle's legs and rays below ONE on left side.

1926-D

This date is one of the easiest mint mark Peace dollars to find in nice MS65 condition. Most show a full strike with nice luster. Very few show die cracks like the 1922-D and 1923-D due to excessive die usage. It is at about the top one-third point in availability from the grading services in MS64 and 65 and slightly more available in MS66.

A minor die variety shows a D mint mark tilted to the right.

1   II 1 • B²a (Normal Die)   I-1   R-2
     Obverse I 1 – Normal die of II type.
     Reverse B²a – Normal die of B² type with micro I D mint mark.

2   II 1 • B²b (D Tilted Right)   I-3   R-3
     Reverse B²b – Normal die of B² type with micro I D mint mark tilted to right at normal height.

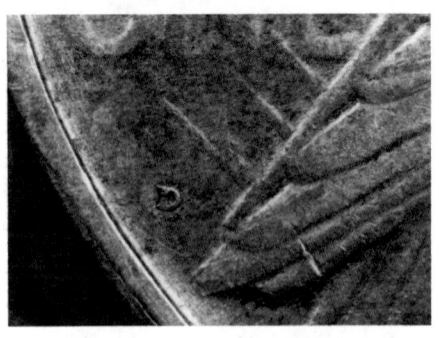

1926-D 2 R D Tilted Right

1926-S

Among the best struck of the San Francisco minted coins, this date is not too difficult to locate in MS65 condition. This date is at about the mid-point in availability in MS64-66 from the grading services. Two minor die varieties exist with different placement of the S mint mark.

1   II 1 • B²a (Normal Die)   I-1   R-2
     Obverse II 1 – Normal die of II type.
     Reverse B²a – Normal die of B² type with micro I S mint mark.

2   II 1 • B²b (High S)   I-3   R-3
     Reverse B²b – Normal die of B² type with micro I S mint mark set high.

3   II 1 • B²c (Medium High S)   I-2   R-3
     Reverse B²c – Normal die of B² type with micro I S mint mark set medium high and tilted slightly left.

1926-S 1 R Normal S
(Photo courtesy of Coin World)

1926-S 2 R High S
(Photo courtesy of Coin World)

1926-S 3 R Medium High S

1927-P

This low mintage date is usually fully struck with good luster and brilliant fields. Because of the low mintage many AU specimens have been saved. Beware of sliders being passed off as BU. Always examine the high points and fields for grayish cast due to wear or hairlines. It is at about the lower one-third point in availability from the grading services in MS64-66.

1   II 1 • B²a (Normal Die)   I-1   R-3
     Obverse II 1 – Normal die of II type.
     Reverse B²a – Normal die of B² type.

1927-D

Very difficult to locate in MS65 condition, but this issue usually is fully struck with good luster. As a scarce date, many sliders are around and the buyer must be careful when buying BU coins. This date is among the scarcest from the grading services in grades MS64-66.

1   II 1 • B²a (Normal Die)   I–1   R–2
Obverse II 1 – Normal die of II type.
Reverse B²a – Normal die of B² type with micro I D mint mark.

1927-S

This date has the typically somewhat weak San Francisco Mint strike although fully struck pieces occasionally can be found. The Redfield hoard contained nice specimens of the 1927-S, making them temporarily available in quantity in the late 1970s. This date is also among the scarcest from the grading services in grades MS64-66.

There is only one variety for this date – an S mint mark set high.

1   II 1 • B²a (Normal Die)   I–1   R–3
Obverse II 1 – Normal die of II type.
Reverse B²a – Normal die of B² type with micro I S mint mark.

2   II 1 • B²b (High S)   I–2   R–3
Reverse B²b – Normal die of B² type with micro I S mint mark set high.

1928-P

Because this is the lowest mintage Peace dollar, it was saved extensively in all grades. The main problem with mint state specimens is a slight weakness in strike for some of them. As with any scarce Peace dollar, sliders abound and the buyer must always carefully examine any offered as mint state to determine if any wear exists on high points or in fields. It is just below the median in availability in grades MS64 and 65 from the grading services and among the scarcest in MS66.

1   II 1 • B²a (Normal Die)   I–1   R–3
Obverse 1 – Normal die of II type.
Reverse B²a – Normal die of B² type.

1928-S

It is extremely difficult to locate a fully struck MS65 specimen similar to the 1923-S, 1924-S and 1925-S if not more so. Consistently weak strikes are the major problem of this date. This date is among the scarcest in availability in grades MS64-66 from the grading services.

There are two die varieties of the 1928-S — an S mint mark set slightly high and one with slightly doubled right obverse.

1   II 1 • B²a (Normal Die)   I–1   R–2
Obverse II 1 – Normal die of II type.
Reverse B²a – Normal die of B² with micro I S mint mark.

2   II 1 • B²b (Medium High S)   I–2   R–3
Reverse B²b – Normal die of B² type with micro I S mint mark set at medium high.

3   II 2 • B²a (Doubled Motto)   I–3   R–4
Obverse II 2 – OD, WE, TR and designer's initials are doubled on right side. Back of neck, back of hair, and right side of rear light rays in tiara are slightly doubled.

1928-S 3 O Doubled Rays   1928-S 3 O Doubled Motto & Designer's Initials

1928-S 2 R Medium High S

1934-P

A relatively low mintage date that is usually well struck. Nice MS65 specimens can be located with enough searching. It is at about the median point in availability from the grading services in MS64-66.

1	**III 1 • B²a (Normal Die)**		I-1	R-3

Obverse III 1 – Normal die of III type.
Reverse B²a – Normal die of B² type.

1934-D

A good portion of this date was apparently released into circulation because of the first date of reissue after a lapse of some seven years. Mint state specimens have excessive bag marks so MS65 specimens are fairly scarce. Weak strikes are not a problem with this date. This date is among the scarcest in MS64 in availability from the grading services, at about the median point in MS65 and a little more available than the median point in MS66.

The 1934-D has the most spectacular die variety of the entire Peace dollar series, the doubled obverse. It is very visible to the naked eye with doubled Liberty head facial features, date, motto letters, and the rear light rays of the tiara. This variety is fairly scarce but still readily collectable.

There are two size D mint marks for this date with the larger one being slightly scarcer. Two die varieties show the smaller D mint mark set high and the other with a smaller mint mark tilted to the right.

1	**III 1 • B²a (Normal Die)**		I-1	R-2

Obverse III 1 – Normal die of III type.
Reverse B²a – Normal die of B² with micro I D mint mark.

2	**III 1 • B²b (Medium D)**		I-2	R-3

Reverse B²b – Normal die of B² type with medium II D mint mark.

3	**III 2 • B²b (Doubled Obverse)**		I-4	R-4

Obverse III 2 – Doubled forehead, eyelids, nose, lips, and chin on Liberty Head. Motto letters and date digits doubled slightly on right side with WE having large shifts. Rays of light in tiara from midway between B and E back are doubled on lift side with last three having very distinct separate images.
Reverse B²b – Medium II D mint mark is filled.

4	**III 2 • B²a (Doubled Obverse, Micro D)**		I-4	R-5
5	**III 1 • B²c (High D)**		I-2	R-3

Reverse B²c – Micro I D mint mark set high.

6	**III 1 • B²d (D Tilted Right)**		I-2	R-3

Reverse B²d – Micro I D mint mark set at normal height and tilted to right.

1934-D 3 O Doubled Rays

1934-D 5 R High D

1934-D 3 O Doubled Nose & Lips

1934-S

This date was also almost all released into circulation like the 1934-D. Mint state specimens are the scarcest and highest priced of all Peace dollars. When located, the 1934-S tends to be well struck for an S mint coin, and nice MS65 specimens can be found. This was the only Peace dollar S mint not in the Redfield hoard. It is about the scarcest in availability in MS64 from the grading services and among the scarcest in MS65 and 66.

The only known die variety shows the S mint mark tilted to the left.

1   **III 1 • B²a (Normal Die)**   I–1   R–2
Obverse III 1 – Normal die of III type.
Reverse B²a – Normal die of B² with micro I S mint mark.

2   **III 1 • B²b (S Leaning Left)**   I–2   R–3
Reverse B²b – Micro I S mint mark leaning left.

1934-D 6 R D Tilted Right

1935-P

This date does not have any particular problems with weak strike or excessive bag marks. Even though mint state specimens are fairly scarce, really nice MS65 coins can be located. It is at about the top one-third point in availability in MS64-66 from the grading services.

1   **III 1 • B²a (Normal Die)**   I–1   R–2
Obverse III 1 – Normal die of III type.
Reverse B²a – Normal die of B² type.

1935-S

The strike is usually above average in fullness for an S mint and bag marks are not excessive for the date. This last date in the series is at about the median point in availability in MS64-66 from the grading services.

One die variety shows an added fourth ray below ONE and a seventh added below the eagle's tail feathers. Apparently this was a left over die from 1922 when the design underwent several changes. About one-third of this date show the added rays so it is not a scarce variety and generally commands no premium in price.

Another die variety shows a high micro S mint mark leaning to the left.

1   **III 1 • B²a (Normal Die)**   I–1   R–2
Obverse III 1 – Normal die of III type.
Reverse B²a – Normal die of B² type.

2   **III 1 • B²b (S Leaning Left)**   I–2   R–3
Reverse B²b – High micro I S mint mark leaning left.

3   **III 1 • Ca (Extra Ray)**   I–2   R–3
Reverse Ca – Normal die of C type with micro I S mint mark. Some specimens show a filled I S mint mark.

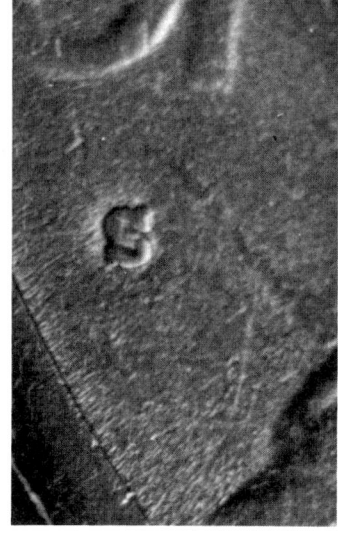

1935-S 2 R High S

Part IV
Working With The Coins

Chapter 15
Detecting Counterfeits

Counterfeit coins can be defined as any coin produced or altered outside the mint. Silver dollars have been counterfeited in the past years for two purposes:
(1) Common date coins were made for general circulation.
(2) Scarce coins were made for sale to coin collectors and or dealers.

Of course there is an underlying motive of the counterfeiter; to realize a profit. Hopefully this chapter will better prepare both the dealer and the collector to detect counterfeit silver dollars.

The older counterfeiting purpose was to inexpensively produce a counterfeit coin that would readily pass for general circulation, since the counterfeiter's profit is the difference between the cost to produce the counterfeit coin and the circulation value of one dollar. In as much as silver dollars are no longer in circulation, this counterfeiting purpose is no longer applicable. In the past, however, a number of common date coins were counterfeited and may still be around. Some of these coins were made of debased metal which produced a soft metal coin that was easily scratched and had many design imperfections. Some common date silver dollars were made of high purity silver when the price of silver was very low during the 1930's.

Since silver dollar coin collecting has only become widespread in relatively recent times (for example, after the initial Morgan silver dollar series was completed in 1904), counterfeit coins of numismatic value is a more recent problem. And specifically, altered coins are the primary counterfeiting threat faced by the collector today. The counterfeiter makes his profit from the difference between the cost to produce and the selling price to a coin dealer or collector. Thus, the scarcer and higher priced coins, such as 1889-CC and 1893-S, are more frequently counterfeited to realize a bigger profit.

GENERAL DETECTION METHODS

Table 15-1 is a guide for counterfeit detection. It summarizes the characteristics to look for in the coin's physical makeup, design, field, and edge. Counterfeiting methods fall into three general categories:
(1) Cast Coins
(2) False Dies
(3) Coin Alteration

CASTING COINS has been a favorite method of making counterfeit silver dollars because it is relatively simple and the cost is low. Most cast coins have many surface defects such as weak detail and extra lumps of metal. All cast coins have a different crystalline structure than a struck coin and can be positively identified by X-ray diffraction or microscopic examination.

FALSE DIES can be used to duplicate the mint operations and genuine coins which have been melted can provide the correct metal ingredients. The test for the counterfeiter is then to make as nearly perfect a die as possible. Of all the known methods for making false dies, the cast process is potentially the most perfect. The best cast process consists of casting a ceramic mold directly from a genuine coin which is used to cast a hub, and in turn, is used to make a working die. Little design detail is lost in the metal to metal design transfer from hub to dies. Modern materials and methods allow very good ceramic molds to be made which produce nearly perfect hubs. Counterfeit coins made from the resultant dies can be very difficult to detect. Close examination of the entire coin surface for imperfections is the best detection method.

ALTERATIONS of a genuine coin into one of greater value is another common counterfeiting method and the biggest threat to collectors today. Mint marks can be either added or eliminated; dates can be changed; cuts, scratches, or worn designs can be touched up; and furthermore, two common coins can be mated to produce a scarce coin. All coin alterations depend upon the skill and patience of the counterfeiter. If skillfully done, coin alterations can be very difficult to detect. The close examination of suspect areas with a magnifying glass or microscope is the best method of detection.

The general procedure for detecting counterfeit silver dollars is one of examination in finer and finer detail until all tests of the examiner are passed satisfactorily. Often some small detail of a coin will initially arouse suspicion that the coin is a counterfeit. The coin should then be carefully examined in detail for confirmation that the coin is either counterfeit or genuine.

The following general steps are suggested for the collector in checking their coins:
(1) **Look at the general obverse, reverse, and edge appearance** of the coin with the naked eye to spot any obvious defects such as weak design, large scratches, and extra metal. Many crude cast coins or coins prepared from poorly made false dies can be detected by this initial quick examination. Know the general design features of the coin and compare them with a genuine coin.
(2) **Examine the date digits, mint mark, or mint mark areas** closely with a 10 to 15 power magnify-

Table 15-1 GUIDE FOR COUNTERFEIT DETECTION

COUNTERFEITING METHOD		PHYSICAL	DESIGN	FIELD	EDGE
CAST COINS	Sand Mold / Lost Wax, Ceramic, and Plastic Processes	Often made of debased metal; Weight and size often not within tolerances; Crystal structure not same as struck coin and can be positively identified by X-ray diffraction or microscopic examination	Very poor detail; Usually fine detail lost and sharp edges rounded	Lumps, streaks, spots, and scratches are frequent defects	Weak detail, incorrect number of reeds, overlapping reeds, reeds missing
FALSE DIES	Hand Cut	Can match genuine coin	Obvious design differences exist	Can be perfect	Can match genuine coin
	Machine Engraving	Can match genuine coin	Some general loss of detail and some engraving marks	Fine engraving marks usually in circular pattern	Can match genuine coin
	Impact	Can match genuine coin	Portions of design are weak, broadened and doubled; usually near edge	Can be perfect	Can match genuine coin
	Spark Erosion	Can match genuine coin	Slight weakening of design details and uniform tiny pits	Uniform tiny pits in some cases	Can match genuine coin
	Electrochemical Machining	Can match genuine coin	General loss of detail	Can be perfect	Can match genuine coin
	Powdered Metal	About 5% undersize	General loss of detail and some crushing of design	Some surface roughness	Can match genuine coin
	Cast	Can match genuine coin	Loss of some detail and rounding of sharp corners. Nearly perfect with use of hub	Lumps, dots, lines, etc. Nearly perfect with use of hub.	Can match genuine coin
COIN ALTERATION	Mint Mark / Date	Perfect if genuine coins used	May not match specific year design	May be rough, raised, or shallow around alteration	Perfect if genuine coins used
	Surface		Altered area generally shallow with polishing marks	Altered area generally shallow with polishing marks	
	Split Coin	May be off weight, debased metal core or copper shell	Perfect if genuine coins used	Perfect if genuine coins used	Fine line somewhere on edge

ing glass. Many of the altered coins can be detected from scratches, polishing marks, and extra metal around these areas or incorrect design date digits or mint mark letters. Compare with a genuine coin or the photographs of date and mint mark types in this book.

(3) **Examine the obverse and reverse design** with a magnifying glass for obvious defects such as lumps of extra metal, weak design, rounded corners where design meets the field, uniform tiny pits, engraving lines in a pattern, excessive polishing, random doubling of design, etc. Again compare with a known genuine coin of same or similar design year. The best detection weapon is detailed comparison.

(4) **Examine the coin edge** with a magnifying glass to see if it has even and distinct reeding. Counterfeit coins often have reeding that is uneven, weak, or overlapping. Split coins usually have portions of the seam which is apparent somewhere on the coin's edge.

(5) **Test the coin's ring.** Balance the center of the coin on the end of a finger and gently tap the edge with a hard object. It should have a clear ring of the correct pitch (basic frequency) and timbre (overtones). Compare the ring with a known genuine coin. Counterfeit coins of incorrect size, debased metal, or split parts will not have a proper ring.

In addition to the above steps, the following are more sophisticated detection techniques which the collector can use for confirmation. Weigh the coin on a balance scale to see if it is within tolerance (412.5 +/- 1.5 grains). Check the coin size (1.5 inches diameter and 0.114 inches thickness). The U.S. Secret Service recommends a simple acid test for silver coins.[1] The acid will blacken a scraped or cut portion of a debased metal counterfeit coin, but will not discolor a genuine silver coin. The acid formula consists of:

Silver nitrate	10 grams
Nitric acid	1 cc
Distilled water	30 cc

These ingredients are available at any drugstore.

If the collector is not completely satisfied as to a coin's authenticity, several courses of action remain. The coin can be presented to a collector friend for an opinion. However, this is not usually satisfactory for a cleverly made counterfeit, since one is apt to receive varied opinions which will still not resolve the issue. Most dealers will also give an opinion on a coin's authenticity if it is presented to them in person. And since the backgrounds of the dealers are varied, one can still receive varied opinions.

The next step is to send the coin to a professional authenticator who will give a written statement of the coin's authenticity for a nominal fee. The American Numismatic Association provides a coin authentication service. Write to the following address for further details on service charges and procedures for sending coins:

ANA Certification Service
818 North Cascade Avenue
Colorado Springs, CO 80903

Alternatively, the coin can be presented at one of the 70 U.S. Secret Service field offices or sent to the main office at the following address:

U. S. Secret Service
1800 G Street, N. W.
Suite 239
Washington, D. C. 20006
c/o Counterfeiting Office

There is no charge for the Secret Service examination. However, two to three months should be allowed for the examination. If the coin is adjudged to be counterfeit, it will be seized without compensation since possession of a counterfeit coin is unlawful. There will be no prosecution however, unless there was an attempt to knowingly defraud someone. The U.S. Secret Service has the use of several laboratories for examining coins, one of which is located in the Treasury Building in Washington, D. C. Although sophisticated testing techniques are available (such as X-ray diffraction testing), these laboratories rely on detailed examination and comparison of the coin's design for most assessments.

The following sections discuss each counterfeiting methods in more detail. Some photographs are included, which in the authors' opinions, represent some of the counterfeit silver dollar types.

CAST COINS

Cast coins are counterfeit coins made by introducing molten metal into a mold containing the desired design features. After the metal has cooled, it permanently retains the design and shape of the mold. The mold can be made of various materials such as fine sand, plastics, or ceramics.

The primary advantage of cast coins for the counterfeiter is their relative ease of production. The process eliminates the need for large presses, die fabrication, and planchet production. All that is needed is the basic metal (white metal, lead base, or common genuine coins), a means to melt the metal and the mold materials.

Modern materials and production techniques allow counterfeiting high quality cast coins. They can be made of the correct metallic content, proper density, good design detail, clear and smooth surfaces, sharp reeded edges, normal vibration ring, etc. Although the appearances of modern cast coins can be made to closely approach that of a genuine coin, its physical makeup will differ. The metal crystalline structure of a struck coin is disturbed by the flow of metal when it is struck. The metal crystalline structure of cast coins is not disturbed by the cooling process.[2] Thus, a nearly perfect cast coin can be positively identified by comparing its crystalline structure with a known genuine coin. Either X-ray diffractometry or metallographic (binocular) microscope examination can be used for this comparison.[3] These are sophisticated equipment only available at special laboratories. However, the great majority of cast coins can be identified by their size, weight, and design defects.

Mold halves from different coins can be paired to produce rare obverse and reverse combinations without actually possessing the rare coin. For example, an 1890-CC reverse mold could be paired with a 1889-P obverse mold to produce the scarce 1889-CC. New varieties can be created by pairing various design obverse and reverse molds.

Known cast counterfeit coins are listed below. Some of them had weights as low as 286 grains and some were within the weight tolerance of 412.5 ± 1.5 grains.

1878-P, S	1885-P	1901-P
1879-S	1888-O	1902-P
1880-O	1889-P, O (2)	1903-P
1881-P, S	1892-O	1904-S
1883-P, S	1899-O	1921-D, S
	1900 P	1922-D

The following subsections discuss the older methods of making cast coins using sand molds and the newer methods using the lost wax, ceramic, and plastic processes.

Sand Molds

One of the oldest methods of making counterfeit silver dollars is to use a sand mold. This is done by pressing a genuine coin into a container of fine casting sand to imprint the design into the sand. The same procedure is repeated to make the other half of the mold using the other side of the coin (or another coin if desired). The two mold halves are then placed together after passageways have been impressed in the molds to allow the molten metal to enter and allow gases to escape.[4]

Any of several metals can be melted and poured into the molds. After cooling the molds are separated and the extra metal in the passageways are cut and polished off. The seam (formed where the two molds meet) must also be smoothed, and the reeding on the coin edge must be touched up using files or a milling machine.

Since until recently most counterfeits were meant for circulation, the profit margin for the counterfeiter was small for each coin. Therefore, most of the cast counterfeits from sand molds used debased metals such as white metal or a lead base metal. These metals were similar in appearance to silver thus allowing the counterfeit coins to be passed when they were only given cursory examination.

A sand mold produces counterfeit coins with many defects. Since casting sand is relatively coarse in texture, the resulting coin has much design detail lost and a rough surface. The coin's edge will have weak and uneven reeding if touched up by hand. If the reeding was added by using a milling machine, often times the reeding will be overlapping at the start-finish junction. The softness of the debased metal will cause it to have an unusually large number of nicks, scratches, and gouges for its apparent time in circulation. The debased metal will also cause the coin's ring to be dull and low pitched. The contraction of the metal as it cools in the mold will result in the counterfeit coin having a slightly reduced diameter than normal. The light weight of the white and lead base metals will cause the coin to weigh less than standard.

Because of all of these defects, the cast mold is seldom used nowadays to make coins of numismatic value. However, the collector may still come across some of these counterfeit types when examining common date coins.

An example of a cast counterfeit 1883 P silver dollar made from sand molds is shown in the accompanying photographs. Readily apparent is the poor design detail, rough surface, and large gouges on the surface and edges. The debased metal from which it was made causes it to have a very dull ring when compared with a genuine coin.

Modern Processes

Modern cast counterfeit coins can be much more deceptive than those made with a sand mold because of the use of better materials and procedures. One of these more modern processes is known as the lost wax method.[5] A rubber mold is first made of a genuine coin. From that rubber mold several wax replicas of the coin are made. Plaster of Paris molds are made from the wax replicas. After they have dried, molten metal is injected to cast the coin and at the same time vaporize the wax replica. The fine texture of the plaster plus using centrifugal force to inject the molten metal into all parts of the mold produces a counterfeit coin with less surface defects. The first mold of rubber transfers more detail of the genuine coin than casting sand. However, the rubber will not withstand the high temperatures of molten metal necessitating manufacture of the wax core to make the plaster molds.

Other materials may be used in basically the same process as just described above to give even better detail. The initial mold can be made out of plastics or high quality plaster rather than rubber.[6] These molds are then used to make plastic replicas of the coin giving better detail than wax. These replicas are encased in plaster or ceramic material to make the negative mold to cast the

1883 Cast Counterfeit

metal. The molten metal can vaporize the plastic core just as in the lost wax process.

These modern processes can produce cast counterfeit coins with very good design detail, proper metallic content, strong reeding on the edges, normal vibration ring, etc. They must be examined closely to detect any defects. Some of the fine detail is usually lost in the three transfer steps. One should look for rounding of sharp edges in the design; fine lines missing in the hair, eagles wings and wreath; defects in the edge reeding; and bits of extra metal where chips broke off the molds when they were parted from the core. In addition, the coin diameter may be slightly less than normal due to metal shrinkage during the cooling process. As a last resort, crystalline structure examination with an X-ray diffractometry machine or metallographic (binocular) microscope will reveal whether the coin was cast or struck.

The accompanying photographs show a counterfeit 1921-S Morgan dollar made by modern casting processes. The design is shallow, particularly on the obverse. Much of the design detail around the cotton blossoms is missing, and the inner ear fill and part of the ear are also missing. The date digits are rounded where they meet the field instead of meeting at a sharp angle as in a genuine struck coin. The reverse has a large V S mint mark and slanted arrow feathers used on the C⁴ reverse rather than the micro I S mint mark and parallel arrow feathers on the reverse used in 1921. Note also the rounding of the wreath design and letters on the reverse where they meet the field and the numerous dark blemishes on the coin's surface. The edge has overlapping reeding as discussed and illustrated later in the section on the coin edges. In addition, the coin's diameter is slightly less than normal and the thickness is slightly greater than normal, thus producing a higher pitched ring than that of a genuine coin.

FALSE DIES

False dies can be broadly defined as any die of U.S. coins that is not an official product of the mint. For the Morgan and Peace silver dollars, of concern is the fabrication of false dies outside the mint for the purpose of illegally producing coins. These false dies can be made by hand cutting the coin design into the die or by transferring the design from a legal coin to the die using mechanical or electrical means.

There are a number of advantages of false dies to a counterfeiter. The most obvious one is that the false die allows production of numerous counterfeit coins of the same design – more so than the casting method. But perhaps the greatest advantage to the counterfeiter is that false dies can allow almost exact duplication of the mint coin production process thus making counterfeit coin detection very difficult.

The use of false dies allows a coin of the exact

1921-S Cast Counterfeit

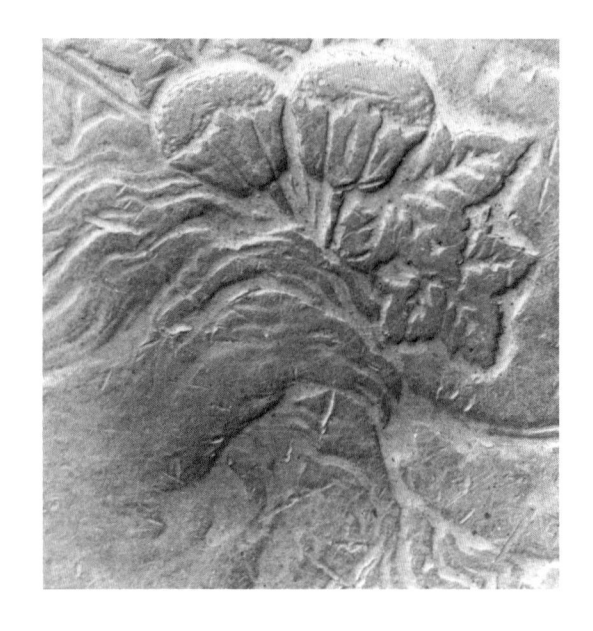

size, weight, metallic content, design, and crystal structure to be produced.[7]

Careful production of the false dies can duplicate almost perfectly the legal coin design. Then, planchets can be made of the proper size, weight, and metallic content. Next, the planchets can be annealed, polished, cleaned, and a raised edge formed on them just as does the mint. These planchets can then be struck from the false dies in presses with a collar forming the reeded edge. In other words, the forger can, with enough attention to detail and with proper equipment, duplicate almost exactly the Treasury process of minting coins.

These false dies also allow counterfeiting of the various mint errors. Off-center strikes, rotated reverses, multiple strikes, clipped planchets, "railroad" rims, thick and thin planchets, etc. can all be counterfeited by duplicating the procedures that caused the mint to accidently produce them.

Additionally, false dies allow the forger to counterfeit rare coins without possessing one. The obverse of one coin can be paired with the reverse of another to make false dies and strike rare or new combinations. For both the Morgan and Peace dollars, the mint marks appear on the opposite side from the date. Consequently, the rare combinations can be counterfeited using common coins. However, unless the forger is careful to select the proper design obverse and reverse from the various Morgan and Peace dollar designs, improper design pairings will readily allow counterfeit detection.

The following subsections discuss the various methods of making false dies and the characteristics that aid in counterfeit detection.[8]

Hand Cut Dies

A straightforward method of producing false dies is to use various hand engraving tools to cut the coin design directly onto the face of the die. The exactness of the copied design depends upon the patience, skill and the tools of the engraver. Because the design of hand cut dies is inexact, the counterfeit coins produced by this method are among the easiest to detect. Detection is merely a matter of comparing the design features with a genuine coin and noting the differences.

The accompanying photographs show an example of a coin from 1890-O hand cut dies. On the obverse, the most obvious difference in the design are the large numerals in the date, elongated 0 in the date, the pointed chin, and the sagging jaw line. On the reverse, the bottom of the eagle's wings curve downward too much, the wing tops are too narrow, the tail feather ends are too far separated and the wreath bow has too large a loop.

The 1888-O counterfeit from hand cut dies is unusual in that it also shows doubling of the motto lettering and date. This is due to the striking process because the doubling shows lines and striations on the doubled portion from the rough edge of the die where it slid across the coin face. Most collectors can immediately spot a fake from hand cut dies because its overall appearance has a slightly strange impression. Closer examination of lettering will reveal roughness and non-standard design detail.

Machine Engraving

The design of a coin can also be transferred to a die by an engraving machine or pantograph. A tracing tool travels over the coin surface guiding a drill over the face of the die at the same time to duplicate the design. This process is similar to the mint use of the Hill portrait lathe and the Janvier reducing machine as described in Chapter 3. Machine engraving allows more accurate transfer of the design than hand cut dies.

Because the forger transfers the coin design to a false die on a one to one basis, some of the detail is lost in the process. This problem is avoided at the mint by using a large scale model giving a reduction of three to eight times in the transfer process. This reduction allows the required design to be transferred.

Unless the machine engraved false die is carefully polished, fine engraving marks will remain. These will show on the counterfeit coins as spiral marks or some other type of tracing pattern. The other identification feature is the loss of design detail through the rounding of the design edges and general elimination of the finer features of the design.

The accompanying photographs show an example of a coin from 1900-O from machine engraved false dies. There is much detail lacking on the obverse, particularly in the hairlines and cotton blossoms for a coin with this much relief remaining. The machine lines are difficult to show in a photograph of the whole coin, but do show faintly at the top in the field as concentric circles. The detail on the reverse is sharper, but is still lacking somewhat on the wings and lettering.

Impact

In the impact method of producing false dies, the coin to be copied is driven into the die face with sufficient kinetic energy to imprint the design. Various methods can be used to drive the coin into the die face. One method is to use an explosive charge against the outside face of the coin with the inside face placed next to the die. Another method is to mount the coin to be copied on the end of a pivot bar. The bar is then rotated at high speed driving the coin into the heated die face.

False dies produced by impacting a coin have many imperfections. A large coin such as the silver dollar does not impact evenly across the entire die face which results in some portions of the design being weaker than others. The impact tends to spread the coin (especially coins of soft metal like silver) thus broadening some

1890-O Counterfeit Coin
From Hand Cut Dies

1888-O
Counterfeit from Hand-Cut Dies (also shows strike doubling)

design details in the false die, usually in an outward direction.[9] Attempts can be made to touch up these defects by hand engraving. However, careful inspection of the coin design will reveal the imperfections of impact made false dies.

The accompanying photographs show an example of a coin from 1889-CC impact produced false dies. The design is sharp in the center on both the obverse and reverse. However, there is some doubling evident halfway to the coin's edge. Some of the letters and stars are weak with broad shadowy outlines.

1888-O
Counterfeit Showing Hand Engraved Date
(also with strike doubling)

Spark Erosion

Electrical sparks can be used to transfer the coin design to a false die. The coin to be copied is placed close to the die face with a dielectric or nonconductor fluid flowing between them acting both as a coolant and to wash away the metal as the die face is eroded away. Electrical connections are made to the coin and die to cause sparks to pass between them. The sparks jump between the closest points of the coin and die removing metal from the die with each spark. As the metal is removed from the die, the sparks move to the next shortest distance, thus eventually transferring the complete design. Since metal is also removed from the coin by each spark (although at a lower rate), several coins must be used during the production of one die to maintain the design detail.

Since each spark removes metal from the die in the form of a tiny pit, the resultant die face is uniformly covered by these pits. Low amperage and high frequency sparks minimize the size of these pits. Some of these pits can be removed by polishing, particularly on the field of the die. However, the design can be polished only minimally because it will lose the design detail. Thus, high magnification of the coin design will reveal these tiny pits left in a false die made by spark erosion.

Electromechanical Machining

Metal can also be removed from a die face by etching using electricity, the reverse of electroplating. The coin is placed close to the die face in an electrolyte or conductive fluid. Electrical connections to the coin and die cause a direct current to pass from the die to the coin and slowly remove metal from the die face. The electrolyte serves as a conductor between the two surfaces and to wash away the dissolved metal. The current and thus the amount of metal removed depends upon the dis-

1900-O Counterfeit from
Machine Engraved Dies

tance between the two surfaces. Because of this, the flow of current will vary across the die face until the complete design is etched out making the distances between the coin and die face equal at all places.

Unlike the spark erosion process which removes metal at the small spark juncture, the electrochemical machining removes metal over a larger area because of the current diffusion through the electrolyte. Thus, the fine design details tend to be lost in the transfer process even though the coin is brought very close to the die face.

Powered Metal

A coin design can be copied directly using powdered metal. The coin is placed in a metal cylinder and powdered metal is added covering the coin design. A plunger in the cylinder is pushed by a hydraulic press compacting the powdered metal. The compacted metal is withdrawn and heated fusing the metal in a sintering process. The false die is thus formed out of the fused metal with the coin design on the end.

Because of the shrinkage during sintering, the resultant false die is approximately five percent undersize. Additionally, the high pressure that is necessary to compact the powdered metal crushes some of the coin design because of the softness of silver. The false dies produced from powdered metal therefore have many imperfections.

Cast

False dies can also be made by casting metal into a mold having the coin design. In the past, cast false dies have been made by using three casting steps. First a wax or plaster intaglio of the coin is made. A transfer is made to a plaster or ceramic positive mold. Molten metal is then poured into this mold to make the cast die.

A more recent method of making cast false dies uses two casting steps and one metal-to-metal transfer step. The refractory ceramic slurry is applied directly onto the coin face. After hardening, the ceramic mold is used to cast a hub (design is raised). After the hub is hardened it is directly impressed into the die face. This method of using a highly accurate metal-to-metal design transfer step replaces a less accurate coin-to-wax or coin-to-plaster step. Better clay materials and methods of using them allows the ceramic mold to be made directly from the coin. It does require a press, however, to transfer the design from the hub to the die.

The older process of making cast false dies using three casting steps usually results in imperfections during the first two soft transfers. The flaking off of plaster or ceramic particles during mold separation causes extraneous raised metal on the coin in the form of dots, lines, etc. In addition, these first two soft transfers lose some of the design detail, particularly the sharp corners and fine lines.

The later method of making cast false dies eliminates a soft transfer step lessening the chances of mold flaking and improving the design detail through the use of a metal-to-metal transfer.

EDGES

The coin edge is, in effect, the third side of the coin and has frequently been neglected by counterfeiters. The collar is used like a third die in producing the reeds on the coin's edge during mint striking operations. If the counterfeiter used false dies, a collar can also be made with the correct number and design reeds by using an automatic gear cutting or milling machine. This will allow the mint operations to be duplicated thus producing a more nearly perfect counterfeit coin. However, the counterfeiter must have access to large presses, milling machines, ovens, etc.; he must obtain the basic materials of steel, silver, mold ingredients, etc.; and he must be knowledgeable in the details of the minting process.

An alternative method of putting reeds on the coin edge is to add them after the coin has been struck. In this case the dies impress the design onto an oversize planchet which is then trimmed to size. The coin is placed into a special machine in which a tool rotates around the coins edge impressing the reeds individually. The difficulties with this method are in obtaining the correct number of reeds, in merging the start and end of the machining, and in setting the machining pressure so as not to cause the coin's edge to be too thick or the coin's diameter too small.

The accompanying photograph shows an example of a 1921-S silver dollar with machined reeding. Clearly evident is the overlapping of the reeding where the machining did not merge together, but rather, it ended up interwoven. This is easily seen by following the reeds in one direction and noticing that they fade out between the reeds of the other direction. The edge of

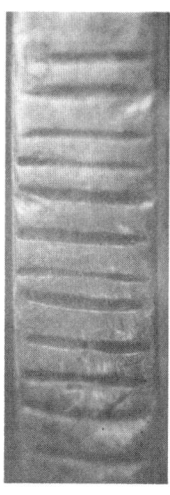

1889-O Counterfeit
Hand Milled Reeding

1921-S Counterfeit
Overlapping Reeding

1889-CC Counterfeit from Impact Dies

this 1921-S silver dollar was also slightly thicker than normal and the coin's diameter was less than normal.

The edge of a cast coin presents the counterfeiter with a problem. To cast a coin, ports are needed in the mold to inject the molten metal and to let gases escape. After the metal has cooled and solidified, these ports contain metal which must be removed from the coin. Since the area where the port has been removed is likely to be rough, uneven, or polished, the ports are usually placed in an inconspicuous area such as the coin's edge. The two halves of the mold also produce a line on the coin's edge where they meet. Thus, a cast coin's edge has usually been touched up by hand at some point. This is frequently detectable from the unevenness of the reeds, varying spacing and depth and roughness of the area.

COIN ALTERATIONS

Counterfeit silver dollars can be made by altering common date genuine coins into scarcer ones. This is an individual coin operation requiring a skillful craftsman and special tools. However, it eliminates the need for the metallurgical knowledge and extensive work required for the preparation of cast coins or false dies. The following subsections briefly describe some of the coin alteration methods.

Mint Mark

Mint marks can be added or removed from silver dollars to increase their worth. This alteration is performed on a lower priced coin of the year of the desired counterfeit coin. The classic example of the Morgan series is to remove the mint mark of an 1895-O to make a counterfeit 1895-P. Some collectors do this just to have something to fill that hole in their coin boards without wanting to make a profit from the sale of the coin. Other common examples are an 1894-O converted to 1894-P, 1901-O to 1901-P and 1928-S to 1928-P. In any case the mint mark can be removed by grinding or cutting it away with jeweler's tools. The area is then polished to remove any tool marks. Close examination of a suspect coin area, where a mint mark was removed, will usually reveal the polishing or tool mark evidence.

Mint marks can also be added to a common date Philadelphia minted coin to increase its value. The desired mint mark is removed from a low-priced branch mint coin and glued or soldered to a coin to be altered. The artistry of the counterfeiter reflects, to a large degree, how much evidence remains of the mint mark addition. Rough edges around the field at the base of the mint mark may remain from the cutting out or soldering steps.[10] A genuine mint mark has sharp corners at this base merging into a smooth flat field. Since there are many different designs of each branch mint mark, sometimes the counterfeiter will attach the wrong mint mark design to a certain year. In some cases a slight prying of a glued mint mark will cause it to fall off.

Mint marks can also be added by cutting away part of the coin's field to form the desired letter(s). In this case the field is lowered around the mint mark and the added mint mark design will not conform precisely to a genuine one. Tool marks may also be evident around the letter(s).

Another method to add a mint mark to a coin is to drill a hole at the mint mark position and insert a plug containing the desired mint mark. The plug is then brazed into place and the seam polished. Usually the plug hole goes completely through the coin. Close examination of the area around a suspect coin mint mark and on the opposite side will usually reveal the seam or polishing marks. The Morgan dollar is hard to plug in this manner since the side opposite the mint mark is within the wheat leaves making it difficult to polish the seam on the obverse.

One of the most common of altered silver dollars is the 1893-S. Many are made by adding the S to an 1893 P by any of the various methods discussed. Other counterfeit 1893-S coins are altered dates as discussed in the next subsection. Mint marks have also been added to the P mint coins to make altered 1889-CC, 1892-S, 1895-S, 1896-S, 1903-S, 1904-S, and 1934-S. Before purchasing any expensive branch mint coin, the mint mark should be closely examined for any tell-tale irregularities.

By far the most serious threat to collectors including those specializing in varieties are the added-on mint marks. The 1896-S shown was certified by ANACS as having an added mint mark. For variety collectors this mint mark should immediately pop out as having a strange shape. It does not conform to the IV S mint mark normal for that date or any of the other known Morgan mint mark designs (I, II, III, or V). Obviously, the counterfeiter fabricated their own mint mark and added it on.

The 1903-S shown is a much more difficult case. Here the mint mark is a type IV S with the proper shape, size and design. The problem is that only V S mint marks were used from 1901 to 1904. So is this a new variety or is it a fake? The field around the mint mark does not have any evidence of tooling marks. Then, the next step

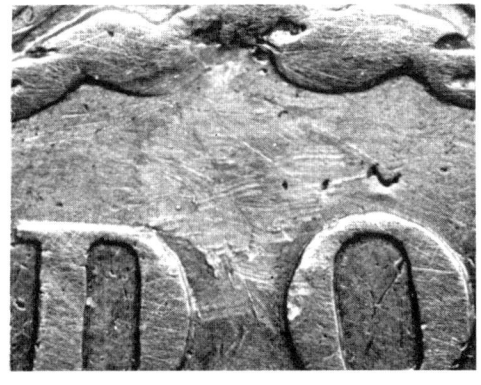

1895 (?) Altered Mint Mark

is to carefully examine all around the edge of the mint mark where it meets the field. There should be a smooth flow of metal from the side of the mint mark down into the coin field. As the microscope photo shows, this 1903-S mint mark has a line where it meets the field along with ragged edges; the sure sign of an added on mint mark.

In examining the edge of mint marks where they meet the field, a hand held magnifying glass of 10 to 15 power will sometimes reveal the edge lines or ragged edges. On more carefully altered coins, a stereo microscope of 20 to 45 power may reveal these details. Sometimes going to a 100 power microscope is necessary. When examining the mint mark, the coin should be held at an angle under the glass or microscope so that the light is reflected off the edge of the mint mark and the vision is aimed directly at the field and mint mark junction. Usually, this requires tilting the coin so its field is at a 45 degree angle to the line of sight. If there is any doubt about the mint mark or date appearance, the coin should be sent to a certification service such as ANACS.

Date

The various altering methods discussed for mint marks also apply to date digits. A digit can be removed from one coin and another digit soldered into place from a second coin. The digit can also be added in the form of a plug. One of the most common methods of date alteration, however, is to cut away portions of a digit to form another one.

Altered dates pose a threat to collectors but fortunately few of these are done skillfully enough to fool those familiar with the dollar date digit designs. The 1893-S shown was altered from an 1898-S and was certified thus by ANACS. The immediate tip-off is the thin center bar of the 3 which is not thick with a blunt end like the normal 1893 "3". This was due to the thin center area of the 8 from which it was made. In addition note that the balls at the top and bottom of the 3 are smaller and do not come together as close as the normal 3. This particular coin had a S/S Right mint mark of the 1898-S VAM 4, further confirming that is was altered from the 1898-S. Variety collectors who recognize unique doubled dates and mint marks have an edge on the normal collector for identifying coins and spotting fakes.

Counterfeit 1889-CC coins have been made by transplanting the "88" from any 1884 to 1889 coin onto an 1879-CC. The date digits are larger for the 1879-CC since they were reduced in size in 1884 for the Morgan series. Therefore, comparison of the "1" and "9" digit size with any 1889 coin will reveal the altered 1889-CC. Similarly, the 1892-S can be fabricated by transplanting a "9" onto an 1882-S. Here again some of the digit sizes will be incorrect. The 1895-S can be made by transplanting a "9" from the 1885-S. Although digits are the same size for the two years, the "5"s are of slightly different design.

Therefore, for any suspect digit transfer coin, check to see if the correct digit size and design are on the coin. Examine closely around the base of the digits where they join the field for any evidence of soldering. There should be sharp corners at the base of the digits merging into a smooth and flat field.

Surface

Strictly speaking, the surface alteration of a coin may not be counterfeiting in its true sense. In most cases surface alteration is performed to upgrade a coin by removing scratches and bag marks or by reducing the apparent wear. The coin will thus bring a better price. Or in some cases the field of the coin will be polished in the hopes of passing it off as a proof coin. Thus, for these

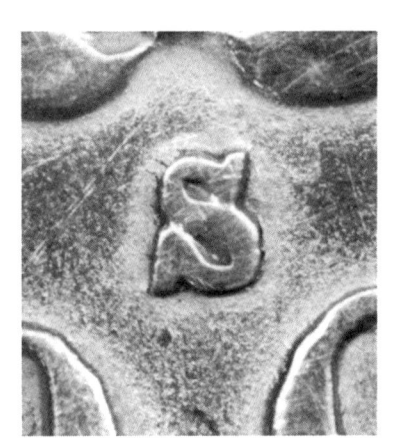

1896-S
Added S
Mint Mark
to 1896-P

1903-S
IV S Mint
Mark Added
to 1903-P

1893-S
Altered Date From 1898-S

cases the collector may be deceived about the coin's condition but not as to year or mint mark.

The various tools useful for surface alteration include engraving, jewelers, and honing types. In all cases, the tools must be used by a skillful artisan for best results. Engraving and jewelers tools can be used to work and polish metal around deep scratches to remove them. Honing can make the coin's surface change shape without removal of metal. This process is known as jet, vapor, or wet honing and consists of an air jet blowing a liquid containing tiny grit.[11] Spherical glass beads is a very effective grit for smoothing a coin's surface.

Split Coin

A scarce coin can be fabricated by joining the obverse and reverse of common coins together. Since genuine designs are used for both obverse and reverse, the coin can appear to be perfect. However, as with other types of counterfeits, the key to detection is knowing what to look for from knowledge of the counterfeiting methods.

Fabrication of a split coin consists of machining or filing down the surface of two genuine coins until their combined thickness is within the required tolerance. The desired date and mint mark (or lack of one) from these two coin halves are combined by soldering. A seam appears on the coin rim which the counterfeiter must attempt to hide by filing and polishing. The milled edges of the Morgan and Peace dollars makes this difficult to achieve.

A variation of the split coin is to hollow out one coin and drop in a different design. The two parts are soldered together with the seam not in the center of the reeding, but at the edge making it more difficult to spot.

Split coins can also be fabricated from electrotype shells. The obverse and reverse shells are made of thin copper built up by an electrolytic process from genuine coins.[12] The design is thus reproduced accurately for both the obverse and reverse. These two shells are placed over a whole metal core or a ground down genuine coin of correct thickness and weight. For counterfeit silver dollars, the copper shells are silver plated. The coin rim still poses a problem for the counterfeiter since at least one seam must be somehow hidden. Variations of the electrotype counterfeit include using a genuine coin for one side and an electrotype shell for the other.

Since all split coins have a seam where the parts were joined together, examination of the coin's edge will usually reveal portions of the seam line. In some cases careful plating and polishing can make this seam difficult to detect. One sure test of a split coin is to listen to the coin's ring. Balance the center of the coin on a finger and gently tap the coin's edge with a hard object. Split coins will not ring at the correct pitch (basic frequency) or have the same timbre (set of overtones) as a genuine silver dollar. It usually helps to compare the suspect coin's ring with that of a known genuine coin of the denomination.

Selected Bibliography

1. Taxay, Don. *Counterfeit, Mis-struck and Unofficial U.S. Coins*. New York: Arco Publishing Company, 1963. (A comprehensive guide on counterfeiting methods and their detection.)
2. Newman, Eric P. "Hobby Must Regulate Its Own Field, Expose Fakes." *Coin World*, March 24, 1965, p. 18. (Discusses counterfeiting methods and their detection. Presented at Professional Numismatists Guild educational forum, Chicago, 1965.)
3. Taxay, Don. "Modern Counterfeiters Directing Activity Toward Faking Rare Coins." *Coin World*, April 7, 1965, p. 65. (Describes various counterfeiting methods. Presented at Professional Numismatists Guild education forum, Chicago, 1965.)
4. Ford, John J., Jr. "Knowledge Only Effective Weapon Against Counterfeits." *Coin World*, April 7, 1965, p. 24. (Discusses some frequently counterfeited coins and methods used to produce them. Presented at Professional Numismatists Guild educational forum, Chicago, 1965.)
5. Welsh, David E., "Skill Applied to Altering Coins Requires Exact Knowledge of Methods." *Coin World*, April 21, 1965, p. 76. (Describes methods of altering coins.)
6. Newman, Eric P., "Numismatics Faces Major Problem as Coin Forgery Nears Perfection." *Coin World*, November 15, 1967, p. 34. (Describes various methods for producing counterfeit coins. Presented at the International Numismatic Congress, Copenhagen, Denmark, August 28, 1967.)

Footnotes

[1] U.S. Department of the Treasury, U.S. Secret Service, *Know Your Money*, 1966, p. 11.

[2] Eric P. Newman, "Eric P. Newman says Hobby Must Regulate its Own Field, Expose Fakes," *Coin World*, March 24, 1965, p.18.

[3] Don Taxay, *Counterfeit, Mis-struck, and Unofficial U. S. Coins*, Arco Publishing Co., New York, 1963, pp. 53 and 56.

[4] Ibid., p.32.

[5] Ibid., p. 33.

[6] Newman, *Coin World*, March 24, 1965, p. 18.

[7] Eric P. Newman, "Numismatics Faces Major Problems as Coin Forgery Nears Perfection," *Coin World*, November 15, 1967.

[8] The principal source consulted on the preparation of the various types of false dies was Newman's article in the November 15, 1967 issue of *Coin World*.

[9] Taxay, p. 48.

[10] David W. Walsh, "Skill Applied to Altering Requires Exact Knowledge of Methods," *Coin World*, April 21, 1965, p. 76.

[11] Newman, *Coin World*, November 15, 1967, p. 34.

[12] Taxay, p. 48.

Chapter 16
Silver Dollar Preservation And Storage

Silver dollars over the years have been subjected to all sorts of use and abuse. Business strikes were, of course, meant to be used in commerce and little care was taken to preserve them over their 50 to 100 years existence by Government workers or the general public. After being struck at the various mints they were all placed in canvas bags of 1,000 coins to be weighed, accounted for, and shipped. During handling and shipment the coins jostled against one another picking up scratches, digs and slide marks (so called bag marks). Just picture bags of dollars being banged around in stiffly sprung stage coaches or wagons over pot-holed and rutted trails of the nineteenth century and the poor dollars at the bottom of a 60 pound bag! Or being tossed around onto platforms and into vaults. It is a wonder *any* survived in MS 65 condition.

The cloth of the canvas bags contained sulphur compounds which would readily tarnish any silver coins that were against the canvas for any length of time. Over many decades in a bag, dirt and dust could seep through the canvas to coat the coins. So just because coins have come directly from a mint sealed bag does not mean they will all be in a state of preservation just as they were struck from the mint press.

Once the bags were opened for commerce at a bank or by individuals their fate could take many turns. They may have been piled loosely in a cashier's drawer or in someone's desk to pick up more nicks and scratches. Many were placed into 20 coin rolls with wrappers of paper. The sulphur in the paper could cause toning of the coin edge or coin obverse or reverse if it was against the paper.

Fortunately most of the Morgan and Peace dollars remained in bags of 1,000 coins until recent times, mid-1960's and onward. Silver dollars were for the most part disliked and unused by the public. These coins generally received a minimum of surface damage and contaminants. Many coins, however, reached circulation where handling, bouncing in pockets and purses, and sliding on gambling tables and the like wore the coin. There are even dollars with a hole in the middle from a bullet!

It was not until the collector/dealer/investor acquired the coins that any thought and effort for their preservation was given.

HANDLING SILVER DOLLARS

The preservation of silver dollars begins with the proper handling of the coins. Ideally they should be handled using cotton or polyethylene gloves by only their edges. Wearing gloves is not very practical for most people and are awkward to use by many. They are really only needed as an extra safety precaution when handling the most expensive or delicate proof coins.

Silver dollars like other numismatic coins should only be handled by the reeded edges where contaminants and toning are not very noticeable. Grasping the coin carefully between the thumb and forefinger is the accepted method for holding a coin for examination and transfer between viewers. Care should be taken that the coin is not accidently dropped on a table top or floor as a rim dent will likely result.

Above all, do *not* hold or even brush the thumb and forefinger against the obverse and reverse surfaces. The oils in the fingers when left on the coin's surface will etch a series of parallel white lines otherwise known as a finger print. No amount of later cleaning will remove the finger print since the metal will have been permanently etched. Buyers generally shun dollars with visible finger prints which of course lowers their value.

Avoid coughing or sneezing on the dollars since the particles from the mouth can cause permanent spots on the surface. Also, tobacco smoke has undesirable chemicals in the particles and smoke should not be directed towards a coin.

REMOVAL OF CONTAMINANTS

Before silver dollars are stored, one has to consider whether any surface contaminants should be removed. When in doubt, it is best *not* to remove any surface contamination or clean the dollar. Improper cleaning of a coin can be worse than no cleaning at all in most cases and can result in a drastic reduction in value. One of the worse cases of Morgan dollar abuse in a cleaning attempt was the very first Morgan dollar business strike of the President Hayes' specimen. It was struck from brand new dies on a polished planchet. But over the years the family members or museum curators in a well meaning attempt to remove tarnish caused by the coin resting in a cardboard and felt-lined holder stamped No. 1 have unmercifully polished the surfaces until this pedigreed coin is now in AU condition!

Which leads to the first rule of cleaning, never use anything abrasive such as silver polish or other things such as baking soda to polish silver dollars. Removal of contaminants does not mean to also polish or disturb the silver surface.

Dirt

But what kind of surface contaminants are there

on uncirculated silver dollars? The most common is *dirt* and *grease*. Usually this is in the form of a light coating on uncirculated coins. Generally, this will not pose any further damage to the coin since the surface will have probably oxidized and stabilized. Occasionally, the dirt coating may be fairly heavy or spotty detracting from the appearance of the coin. It may also be likely to cause some form of corrosion or pitting. This coating should be removed from the coin to improve its preservation and appearance.

The safest way to remove this from the silver dollar is with a neutralizing solvent that will not attack the silver-copper mixture of the dollar. One such solvent is Trichlorotrifloroethane marketed by E & T Kointainer Co. Another is marketed under TEST-N-SAFE brand. Acetone is another dirt and grease solvent. It is not as safe as the above mentioned products as it may leave some residue if the coin is not rinsed thoroughly after application of the acetone. However, it is readily available as finger nail polish remover.

If the coin is entirely coated with dirt and grease it will have to be dipped in the above solutions following the kit instructions. If the contaminant is localized then a cotton swab on a stick or Q-tip swab can be gently used to clean a small area.

Toning

Toning is the second most common contaminant. It can appear as a small crescent, only on the edge, or over all of one or both sides. It may be a very light delicate shade, multicolored or dark. Generally, the light or colored shades are attractive and desirable. The grey, spotted or dark toning are usually not attractive and therefore can lower the coin's value. Toning is usually a thin film of oxidized silver in combination with another compound, usually sulphur. The thin film results in light interference layers that produce various colors. Other types of toning have colors of the compounds of the oxidized layer. Light attractive toning will usually not further alter the oxidized surface and should not be removed in most cases. Heavily, unattractive toning can pose a danger to the surface and in many cases it is better to remove it for safer coin preservation and to increase its value.

Neutralizing solvents in many cases will not remove toning, particularly the dark and heavy. The oxidized layer has to be removed. This requires a light acid bath that chemically removes the oxidized layer. There are many silver dips on the market. They consist of a chemical, thioura and small amounts of sulfuric or nitric acid. Obviously, this solution can react with the silver-copper metal as well as the oxide layer. So, these silver dips have to be used carefully. The coin should be immersed in the solution only a few seconds and immediately thoroughly rinsed in water. This can be followed by using a neutralizing solvent to be sure the surface is completely clean of all chemical residue.

If a neutralizing solvent is not used, then the water must be removed from the coin surface or water spots can result if the coin is left to dry on its own. The best way to dry the coin is to use a hair dryer to quickly evaporate the water. Or a clean soft towel can be used by gently patting the coin surface (do not rub as hairlines may result).

Carbon Spots

Another contaminant is the so-called carbon spots. These appear as black or dark grey spots with usually a dark core and lighter toned rings surrounding the core. The core is usually a small spot of impurity that is imbedded or etched into the coin's surface. Some of these spots are due to a speck of impurity in the metal when the silver ingots were cast. Others are a contaminant that got between the die and planchet when the coins were struck. And some are contaminants that got on the coin surface after it was struck. They generally have the characteristic of reacting with the silver-copper coin metal and growing in size over a period of time.

These carbon spots can sometimes be removed by dipping in a neutralizing or silver dip. If that does not work then a cotton swab or wooden toothpick can be used to dislodge the impurity. However, it may leave a pit in the surface, but at least this should not be active and growing. If this still fails then there is not much that the average collector can do to remove the spots. At least the dip may have removed the toned ring around the spot but this may appear again in time.

Impure Metal Streaks

Another form of contaminant is the impure metal streak. It appears as a dark rough area on the coin's surface. This impurity is the melt slag that had become trapped in the cast silver ingot. During the preparation of the melt in a furnace, graphite, lamp black or charcoal was placed on top of the molten metal while it was being heated and mixed. This was to protect the melt surface from the oxygen in the atmosphere. The lighter impurities also rose to the surface of a melt. When the melt was poured into an ingot mold, most of these impurities and charcoal (known as slag) remained in the bottom of the melt crucible. Some impurities were poured into the ingot mold where they again rose to the surface or end of the ingot which later got cut off. However, at times small amounts of this melt slag became trapped inside the ingot. When the ingot was later rolled out into a strip, these slag spots become flattened and elongated to become impure metal streaks. If they were on the coin's surface then they would be visible as dark areas. If they were just below the surface of the coin metal then sometimes they would cause a thin layer of metal to be detached or loose in the form of a metal lamination.

Since the impure metal was in place of the silver-copper metal, the black area is imbedded in the coin's surface. These impurities cannot usually be removed very easily. Dips will not phase them since they are a thick layer of impurities. Besides, if the impurities were removed, then what would be left would be a rough depression. This is not very desirable since it has an artificial looking appearance. It is best to just leave the impurities since nothing much can be done with them.

Wood

Occasionally little flecks of wood will be found embedded in the surface of the coin. This seems to be more prevalent for O Mint coins. Most of the time they can be dislodged using a cotton swab dipped in solvent or a wooden toothpick. However, their removal will leave a depression in the coin's surface since these chips were struck between the planchet and die. The chips came from the planchets being dried in a revolving riddle with sawdust after they had been whitened or cleaned in a weak sulfuric acid bath and rinsed in boiling water. Again, most of the time it is best to leave the coin alone and not try to remove the wood flecks.

Circulation Grime

Circulated coins, of course, are coated to varying degrees with dirt and grease or grime. Removal of all of this coating will result in an unnatural appearing coin which is instantly recognized as being cleaned. The best advice is to leave the coin in its natural state and not to clean it. There are a couple of exceptions to this rule however. If the coin is exceptionally dirty and dark looking, then it may help to remove just part of the dirt coating. This must be done evenly so as to not give the coin an unnatural cleaned look. In this case a quick immersion in a neutralizing solution or silver dip will remove some of the dirt coating. This should be followed by a thorough rinse in warm water followed by carefully drying. The slightly cleaned coin will be more natural looking, plus more sanitary and pleasant to handle. Alternately, a cotton swab with acetone can be used to remove some of the excessive dirt and grease.

Another reason to remove the dirt and grease is to study and identify die varieties. To detect many of the coin varieties such as doubled dates and mint marks, the areas must be free of most dirt and grease. For example, it takes only a thin dirt coating to hide the fine details of the 1900-O/CC. Some details caused by a doubled or dual hub die, such as doubled stars and letters, are almost impossible to detect under the normal circulation grime. In these cases it is best to remove some of the grim in local areas around the date, mint mark, stars or lettering using a Q-tip or cotton swab that has been saturated with acetone. A few light passes with the Q-tip will remove much of the grime to allow close examination with a magnifying glass.

Proofs

Proof Morgan dollars were sold by the Philadelphia Mint in paper envelopes via the mail or over the counter. Probably over 90 percent of Morgan proofs with original uncleaned surfaces are toned because of storage in these paper envelopes. Most of this toning consists of light shades of various colors on the coin's delicate surfaces. The toning is usually very attractive and should not be disturbed. Unfortunately, the majority of Morgan proof dollars have had their surfaces slightly scratched, rubbed or cleaned in some way. This shows up as hairline scratches or shiny high points on the coin. Their owners, in a well meaning attempt to remove toning, may have lightly rubbed the coin with a cloth which inevitably produced hairlines. Also, the insertion, removal, or sliding around in paper envelopes could produce hairline scratches on the frosted mark-free devices and smooth mirror fields. It only takes the slightest touch or rubbing to make hairline marks on the delicate proof surface.

Since Morgan proofs are normally naturally toned from being stored in mint paper envelopes, an untoned proof is the exception. Therefore, the toning on proofs should not be removed using silver dips. They should be left toned. In some rare instances, obvious surface contaminants should be removed using only a neutralizing solvent.

Storage

Methods for storing silver dollars have changed considerably over the years. Most of the uncirculated Morgan and Peace silver dollars spent the majority of their existence in mint and bank canvas bags of 1,000 coins. It is only since the early to mid-1960s that many of these bags were opened and dispersed. Coins in these bags were relatively safely stored as long as the bags were not moved and as long as the coin was not against the canvas. Of course, dirt and moisture could easily permeate the canvas.

Nineteenth and early twentieth century collectors most often kept their collections in paper envelopes with notations on the outside. The sulphur in these envelopes inevitably toned the silver dollars, especially if they were uncirculated. Those collectors who could afford it kept their collection in wooden cabinets with trays lined in velvet, felt or pure cotton. The coins were left exposed to the airborne contaminants of the atmosphere. The coin was free to slide on the cloth when the drawer was opened or closed which could introduce slight wear or "cabinet friction" on the coin's high points.

Early collectors also had available "anti-tarnish tissue" which was free of sulphur as well as sulphur free paper envelopes. A dollar wrapped in this tissue paper and placed in a paper envelope would still be somewhat open to the atmosphere and if the tissue rubbed against the coin surfaces it would produce hairline scratches.

Bulk Storage

Silver dollars stored in canvas bags should be removed and stored in rolls of 20 or in individual holders. This is to prevent further tarnishing and accumulations of bag marks on the coins.

Rolls were originally wrapped in paper sized for that purpose. But the paper could add tarnish and did not seal the coins from the atmosphere. The plastic tube became available in the early 1960's which was airtight and made of inert polystyrene plastic.

Early tubes were rather thin which could crack and the lids did not always lock tightly in place. More recent tubes have thicker plastic with secure screw type lids. The safest and most secure tubes are square and made of a white opaque polyethylene. They are chemically inert and will not crack easily.

The coins should not be loose in the tube where they can bounce against one another. The tube should have polyethylene material such as a polyethylene envelope or a piece of saran wrap placed on top of the roll to act as a spacer against the top coin and lid.

Holders

Paper envelopes used by early collectors hid the coin. Every time the coin was to be examined it had to be removed from the envelope which was inconvenient and exposed the coin to handling and rubbing against the envelope. In the 1950's 2 x 2 inch cardboard holders lined with thin mylar or cellophane windows became available. The two halves were folded over the coin and stapled together to enclose the coin. The windows allowed both obverse and reverse sides to be visible. However, for silver dollars there was not much cardboard area to make notations. Unless the staples were crimped flat with pliers they could tear the windows and scratch the adjacent coins when inserted or removed from boxes. In addition, the paper dust particles from the cardboard tended to stick to the windows because of static electricity and be pressed against the coin when the holder was stapled shut. These particles could cause local corrosion spots and toning on the coin surface. These holders are not airtight and dollars tend to tone around the edges if they are stored in them for any length of time. Cardboard holders are not recommended and fortunately, their use has fallen off in recent years.

Over the years various types of holder designs made of inert polystyrene have been available. One type consisted of a recessed round central ring to hold the coin and a square sliding window to enclose the coin. A paper ring surrounded the enclosed coin for notations. It was not completely airtight and one had to be careful not to scrape the coin high points when closing the window. It is not generally available at present. Another polystyrene holder still available consists of two halves that snap together. It is not airtight and notations can only be made using stick on labels. A recently introduced polystyrene holder under the market name "Air-Tite" consists of two round halves that snap together and an inner black neoprene rubber seal. It is safe but has no area for notations and is somewhat difficult to get apart.

Acrylic or lucite holders have been available for some time, both for individual coin holders and albums. It is a safe inert plastic and usually consists of a center section with a cutout for the coin and two outside square windows. The three sections screw together to provide an airtight holder. It is somewhat bulky with raised screws on some brands. Again notations must be on separate labels or cards.

In the mid-1960's the so-called 2 x 2 flip became available. It consisted of two pockets joined together made out of polyvinyl chloride plastic. The coin was inserted in one pocket and a card with notations in the other pocket. When folded over the coin was visible through the clear plastic, no staples were needed, and it was free from cardboard dust. Although not airtight, it was convenient and compact for storing individual coins and became the most popular type of holder.

Much has been written in recent years about the unsafe properties of polyvinyl-chloride or PVC plastic. The stabilizer and softener chemicals in PVC can be

Roll Tubes for Silver Dollars

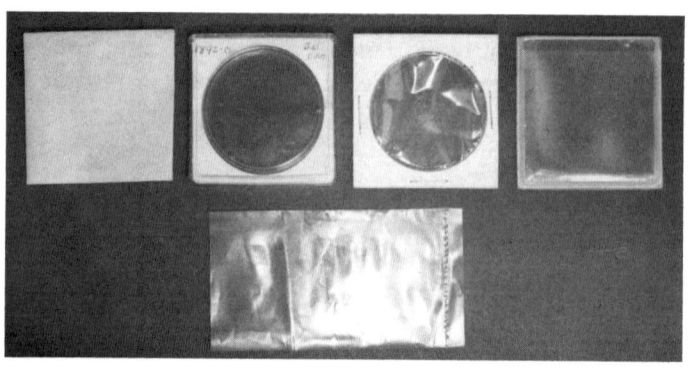

| Paper Envelopes | Plastic with Slide Cover | Cardboard 2 X 2 | Vinyl Flip |

Polyethylene Envelope

released over time and under the right heat and humidity conditions. This can coat the coin and leach out the copper in the alloy to form a so-called green slime. In addition, as the PVC breaks down with time hydrogen chloride gas is released which, under humid conditions, forms hydrochloric acid and etches the coin's surfaces. Silver dollars have been stored for ten years or more in vinyl flips with no visible damage. On the other hand, a green coating can develop on the coins in less than a year. Vinyl flips are manufactured in various chemical formulations and some are safer for coin storage than others. However, to be on the safe side, silver dollars should not be stored alone in vinyl flips for long periods of time.

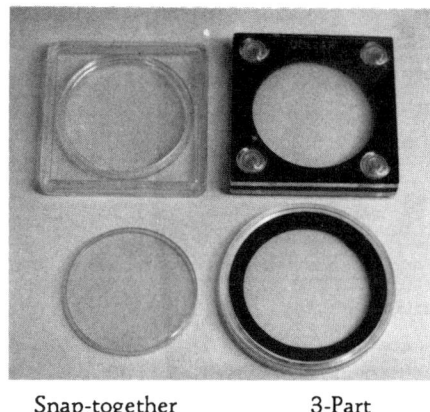

Flips made out of an inert mylar (a polyethylene derivative), under the trade name "Saflip", became readily available in the early 1980's. They are somewhat more expensive than vinyl flips. Their stiffness makes them harder to handle in displaying and stacking coins. Also, the plastic scratches and splits easily as the coins are inserted or removed from the flip. They are, of course not airtight but the plastic will not chemically damage the coin. The hardness of the plastic does pose a greater potential for physical damage to the coin from the plastic edge and from the coin sliding about inside the pocket.

There are several ways to encapsulate the coin in safe materials before placing it in a flip. Polyethylene envelopes that are chemically inert have been available for many years. Once the coin has been inserted into the envelope, the top can be folded over to make it relatively airtight. The envelope can be stapled to a paper envelope with notations which was a fairly common storage method years ago. Unfortunately, the polyethylene envelopes are somewhat cloudy and thin, thus not providing as clear a view of the coin as the crystal clear vinyl flips nor as much mechanical protection.

The coin in a polyethylene envelope can be inserted into a flip pocket to give it greater mechanical protection and ease of handling. But the folded polyethylene envelope is somewhat difficult to insert and withdraw from the flip and the multilayered and wrinkled polyethylene envelope hides much of the coin detail, so it must be withdrawn from both the flip and envelope to be examined. This can unduly expose the coin to physical mishandling and to contaminants.

Another way to encapsulate the coin that has been available since the 1950's, (only heavily promoted since late 1970's) is cast triacetate holders in the form of coin shells. These are marketed under the trade name "Kointain" and consist of two round halves that fit together giving an airtight seal and are snug against the coin edge. The two halves are slightly convex so that they do not touch the coin's surfaces. The plastic is inert and rigid giving good coin protection and safe storage. The two halves are somewhat cumbersome to fit together and pull apart. Also, the plastic has a slight grayish cast which subdues the silver dollar luster and proof-like qualities. Still, for long term storage, a silver dollar in a "Kointain" holder and placed in a mylar or vinyl flip is very convenient and safe.

Individual flips can be best stored in either single row or double row boxes available for the 2 x 2 inch holder. Double row boxes hold about 200 flips while single row boxes can be obtained in various sizes that hold from 30 to 100 coins. When transporting flips in these boxes the flips should be tightly packed together so the coins will not slide around inside the flips as the boxes are jostled and handled. Spacers of foam rubber or crumpled paper can be used to fill up partial rows of flips.

Small stacks of flips can be bound together for physical security using rubber bands. This is safe for only short time periods for a few days or less. The sulphur in the rubber bands can leach through the porous flip layer and produce a dark toned band across the coin's surface. This band may or may not be removed by using a silver dip. It is best to turn the top flip over so the paper card insert is between the rubber band and the coin. Long term storage of coins in flips should not be with rubber bands around or near the coins because of severe toning danger they cause.

Silver dollars have also been encapsulated in plastic holders that were sonically sealed. The coin could only be removed from these holders by cracking and breaking them apart.

The first plastic holders used to encapsulate silver dollars were those produced by the General Services Administration. They were relatively large in size and were sold by the GSA in 1972-74 and again in 1980. Almost three million uncirculated Carson City Morgan silver dollars were encapsulated in these holders. The plastic is inert and the coins are safe in these holders.

Paramount International Coin Corp. placed many of the Morgan and Peace silver dollars from the Redfield hoard in small sonically sealed plastic holders. These holders were the first to include the coin's grade and also identified that it was from the Redfield collection. They were marketed for three to five years beginning in 1976.

In 1986 the Professional Coin Grading Service began grading coins and placing them in sonically sealed plastic holders about the same size as the Paramount International Coin Corp. Redfield dollar holders. The card insert included the coin year and mint designation, overall grade number and coin identifying number. The encapsulated coin was safe in the inert plastic. Within a few years, several other coin grading services also encapsulated graded coins in similar size holders. Coins in the grading services holders are safe from handling and contamination dangers plus remain positively identified for each grading service's grade designation. However, the coins can not be handled separately for examination or photographing.

Albums

The earliest albums for displaying a silver dollar collection consisted of cardboard with cut-outs for the coin and the year and mint below this opening. A paper layer on the back of the board prevented the coin from falling out the rear but not the front. This type of coin album, while providing some measure of physical security because it held the coins separately, was very dangerous. The coin surfaces were exposed to the atmosphere. Further, the cardboard tended to tone the coin edges and the paper backing toned the coin reverses. Cardboard dust was present which could settle on the coin's surfaces. These inexpensive coin albums are not recommended for display of uncirculated silver dollars.

Later albums were somewhat improved by providing sliding windows of cellulose triacetate strips for the front and back of the coin openings in the board. This encapsulated the coin, better protecting it. The plastic in the windows was inert and clear to show the coin. However, the cardboard around the coin edges could still introduce some toning depending on how sulphur free the cardboard was and if cardboard dust would be present. But the new problem introduced by this type of album was the potential and real danger of the window slide edges scraping across the coin obverse high points as the slide was pushed into the page. This could cause fine parallel scratch lines in a horizontal direction in the hair and cheek area of the dollars. Albums with sliding windows are not recommended because of this danger.

For the past ten years or so, the all plastic album has been available. They were originally made of PVC plastic sheets with insert plastic holders, most also of PVC plastic. While they were clear and displayed the coins nicely with good physical security, they were extremely dangerous chemically. As with PVC flips, the plastic was unstable and generally broke down coating the coins, in some cases in less than a year. Later plastic album used an inert plastic holder to slide into a soft PVC plastic page. This at least eliminated the direct contact of the coin with the PVC plastic. But since the coins were still not in airtight holders, the PVC chemicals could still migrate to the coin surfaces. One safer alternative is to put each coin in a safe holder such as a "Kointain" that is airtight and then put them into the plastic album pages.

Albums made of three layers of plexiglas or lucite with cutouts in the center layer for the coins have been available since the 1960's. The three sections screwed together making a relatively airtight holder that displayed the coins in very clear and inert plastic. These albums are relatively expensive and bulky but provide excellent physical and chemical protection while displaying the coins nicely.

Recently available albums use chemically inert and airtight individual coin holders such as mylar, plexiglas or lucite. These are mounted in various ways in the page with some albums using pins to secure the holder, allowing it to be rotated so both coin sides can be viewed.

In evaluating individual holders and albums to house coins three factors need to be considered:

1. Material
2. Construction
3. Contamination of materials

The material immediately surrounding and in contact with the coin should be chemically stable and inert under normal storage conditions. Construction of the holder or album should protect the coin physically and be airtight. Contact should preferably be only on the coin edge or rim. If contact is made on the coin obverse or reverse surface, it should be with a relatively soft substance that will not abrade the surface. The coin should be held mechanically secure so it will not move around and it should not be exposed to sharp sliding edges. The holder or album should not be contaminated with potentially damaging paper dust or other foreign particles when it was manufactured or shipped.

Chapter 17
Grading

GRADING EVOLUTION

Over the past years there has been much in the coin newspapers and journals on silver dollar grading. Grading has undergone a tremendous evolution in recent decades. This section will examine the Morgan and Peace silver dollar grading changes (and things unchanged) over the years, what makes a coin eye appealing, the condition availability and the effects of the grading evolution.

Early Development

Before the late 1960's the major grading concern was whether a coin was circulated or uncirculated. Rolls and bags of dollars were readily available from banks, Federal Reserve and the U.S. Treasury. Relatively few people collected or invested in these common coins. Then came the great silver dollar rush on the Treasury in 1964 when most of the remaining Morgan and Peace dollars were finally permanently released to the public. That meant the prices of these series would start the march upward.

Interest in these series increased with this sudden influx into the market of an attractive, large sized, silver coin. The standard grading reference used in the 1960's was Brown and Dunn. Coverage in circulated grades was fairly detailed but uncirculated was not described although several grades were mentioned in the introduction.

Still, knowledgeable dealers and collectors could tell some coins were more desirable and sold better than others. So, gradually in the late 60's and early 70's various terms evolved to describe uncirculated dollars. Most used terms such as BU, Choice, and Gem BU to describe increasingly desirable uncirculated coin grades and these were priced accordingly. The premium of a Gem coin usually was not that much over a BU or Choice. This was due to the large supply of rolls and bags for many dates.

But as the dollars were dispersed and the number of collectors and investors increased, supply and demand forced prices upward. Uncirculated grading terms became more and more complex. By the mid 70's well over 30 terms were routinely used to describe uncirculated dollars in the various publications. How was a collector/dealer/investor to know if BU Gem was any better than Choice Superb? Grading terminology was chaotic for uncirculated dollars.

Out of this confusion grew the ANA grading guide. When released in 1977, it recognized three levels of uncirculated or BU dollars with numerical grades based on the Sheldon numbering system. In practice this was reduced to MS60 and MS65 since MS70 was, in reality, nonexistent for dollars. Red book and other price guides plus many ads used these two MS grades in the late 1970's.

As the market prices for dollars continued to rise, the price differences between MS60 and MS65 became larger and larger in many instances. Actual pricing by many dealers and collectors developed to fall between and above these grades depending on how nice the coin's condition.

The 1980's

In October 1980, the *Coin Dealer Newsletter* (so called Grey Sheet) pricing guide added MS63 prices for dollars to reflect the widening gap of price between MS60 and MS65. The ANA grading guide added the intermediate grades of MS63 and MS67 in the Second Edition released late in 1981.

In March, 1985, the *Coin Dealer Newsletter* added the MS64 grade for silver dollars to fill the wide price gap that had developed between the MS63 and MS65 grades. By this time there were well over a dozen grading services following the pioneering of ANACS and INS in the mid-1970's. Collectors, investors and dealers actively traded certified graded coins by a number of these grading services. However, it was perceived that not all of the grading services used the same standards. There were also problems of self-serving interests when a grading service was also associated with a particular coin firm.

So, in the mid-1980's, grading was still chaotic and confusing for silver dollars. Many investors and collectors were being mislead and losing money when their certified graded coins didn't hold the value paid for them. Often coins certified by certain grading services were deeply discounted by dealers when buying them because the coins failed to meet their own grading standards. And there was confusion with the practices of split two-sided grading versus a single grade number.

To attempt to overcome these problems in coin grading, the Professional Coin Grading Service was formed in 1986. Coins graded by them were encapsulated in inert plastic with a label inside that specified the coin's overall grade and identification of date/mint. A group of dealers formed a trading network that would buy and sell PCGS graded coins on a sight unseen basis over electronic trading networks. The PCGS coin grading standards were adequately conservative so the coins traded at established price levels for the grades.

In a short time PCGS graded coins soon dominated the certified and graded coin market. Also, the perceived grading standards used by PCGS became the primary accepted one used by the coin industry. Most everyone began examining raw coins with the object of what grade would PCGS give it. Resubmittal of PCGS graded coins also became popular for those borderline graded coins with the hopes of achieving a higher grade. There were also perceived grading changes in PCGS graded coins over the years but these were small compared to the vast difference in grading standards used previously by the various grading services.

PCGS had introduced the eleven point grading for uncirculated coins in early 1986. The Third Edition of the ANA grading guide, released in 1987, added these eleven points and also utilized coin photographs rather than line drawings. The bid sheets summarizing the prices of the electronic trading network, American Numismatic Exchange, utilized these eleven point grade prices. These bid sheets soon became the dominant pricing guide for dealers as the encapsulated coins were traded similar to commodities. *The Certified Coin Dealer Newsletter* was added as a pricing guide using the eleven point grading. As could be expected, the coin prices became more volatile because of the instantaneous price reporting of the electronic trading network and the leverage that could be exercised by the market makers on these networks.

Other coin grading services soon followed the PCGS lead in encapsulating graded coins. But only a few grading services gained wide acceptance of their so-called slabbed coins – PCGS, NGC and ANACS. Grading standards were much more stable from 1986 onward than in the immediate previous years. But prices became the big variable instead, which is the way it should be in a free market economy.

Coin Grading Machines

The earliest claimed coin grading machine which the authors saw demonstrated was that of Dr. Sidney Auerback, in May 1985 at New York City. It had been demonstrated over the previous few years to several coin dealers. It consisted of a video camera, display terminal, analyzer and disc drive storage. Details revealed of the system were sketchy, but apparently it operated by integrating the light intensity in a horizontal line across the coin and displaying the horizontal line intensities as a profile with vertical distance. The machine could not provide a coin grade and was not very accurate in showing correlations among scanned coins and photos.

In August of 1986, the authors visited the Milton Roy Company in Rochester, NY, to view and participate in a coin grading machine demonstration by Henry Merton. Milton Roy Co. were leaders in image analysis. A demonstration using their Omnicon 3500 and its successor 1101 was made on coins. The system consisted of a high resolution video camera whose output went through shading correction, detection, digital analysis, storage and display. After some initial adjustments of the machine through interactive tests of coin scanning by the authors, the machine demonstrated the capability to detect and display grading characteristics of abrasions, fullness of strike and loss of luster from wear. It could not at that time, provide a coin grading number. Henry Merton pursued the development of a grading machine and in February 1991, the announcement was made that a company he was associated with, CompuGrade, had starting grading coins using computer grading.

Meanwhile, in November 1986, Amos Press commissioned Battelle Memorial Institute of Columbus, Ohio, to determine the feasibility and practicality of using equipment to grade coins. By August 1987, Battelle reported that it was technically feasible to grade coins using various types of equipment such as laser scanning, optical scanning, high-resolution video imaging, holography and computerized image analysis. A working engineering model was subsequently developed which could demonstrate measuring various coin characteristics and computer software was worked on to analyze and display the measured data. In the summer of 1990, Amos Press bought the ANACS grading service of the ANA. The utilization of their computerized grading machine had not yet been announced by early 1992.

In May of 1990, after more than two years of development, PCGS demonstrated a coin grading machine called "PCGS Expert" and stated they had begun using it to grade coins. The "PCGS Expert" consisted of a single color video camera with sequenced lights around it. A stage automatically positioned the coins relative to the camera. Strike was measured on the obverse for Morgan dollars by counting the number of lines in the hair above the ear and on the reverse by the eagle's breast and claws. Luster was determined by measuring the amount of light scattered vertically from the coin to the camera from a low angle light. Abrasions were determined by sequencing lights to get various angle reflections. A marks analysis was performed for primary regions of interest which were the cheek, neck and left and right fields for the obverse. For these marks, histograms versus intensity were the basic analysis tool for comparisons of major characteristics. Then the characteristics of areas of interest were summed using various weighting factors to give the overall MS grade. This number could be modified considering the strength of strike, luster and eye appeal plus any minor characteristics.

Computer machine grading has thus arrived and promises to give consistent grading. However, the accuracy and consistency compared to traditional consensus grading by human graders depends a great deal on the parameters used to determine grades that are input to the machine and the various weighting factors that are used in analyzing the camera input data. Over a period of time, the grading machines will constantly be refined with improved accuracy and consistency. The number of coin series capable of being graded will be expanded from the initial ones of silver dollars. Ultimately the improved grading capabilities offered by computerized grading machines will lead to more consistent grading and to the betterment of the hobby.

GRADING FACTORS

Coin Value, that is what it is all about. A coin grade is translated into value by the collector/dealer/investor using various price grades. The grade in the coin examiner's mind may be a numerical one, descriptive term or just how nice the condition appears. The question is, what factors determine how nice a coin is (meaning value or price).

What makes a dollar eye appealing? It will of course depend upon the beholder (like beauty). But over the years five factors have become generally used:

1. Abrasion or wear
2. Strike
3. Luster
4. Color
5. Proof-like

Abrasions are scratches, scuff marks and contact marks in general on a coin's surface. Morgan and Peace dollars struck for circulation were all put into canvas bags of 1,000 coins by each mint. This was to facilitate the accounting and shipping of them. Transporting a bag of 1,000 dollars weighing 60 pounds caused abrasions on virtually every one of them. Of course fewer abrasions on a coin makes it more desirable. But the complication is what size, how many and where can these abrasions be to affect the coin's value. These are subjective judgments in many instances. Over the years, some accepted guidelines have evolved on these abrasions or bag marks. For the Morgan dollar the cheek area is the first, second and third most important area to look for these bag marks. It is a large raised area on the Liberty Head that was open and most vulnerable to abrasions. A relatively clean cheek is required for an eye appealing Morgan dollar but abrasions in other areas that are noticeable can also downgrade a coin. For the Peace dollar the cheek area is smaller but the Liberty Head neck and eagle's wing are more vulnerable to bag marks and thus important areas in grading.

Strike refers to the fullness of the design detail. Weak areas make the coin less attractive or valuable. For the Morgan dollar a weakness in strike typically shows up first in the hair above the Liberty Head ear and the eagle's breast feathers. For the Peace dollar it shows first in the hair over the Liberty Head ear and the eagle's wing feathers over the legs.

Luster refers to the frostiness of the design devices and the brilliance of the field. This is determined primarily by die wear. New dies used to strike coins will strike coins with frosty devices and brilliant fields. As the dies wear from striking thousands of coins, the frostiness is gradually polished away to give a more brilliant look and the fields become rough, producing a dull appearance. The coins are more attractive and valuable when there is frosting on the devices and brilliant fields producing a nice contrast. Luster of a coin can also be affected by coatings or contaminants on the surface.

Color is anything other than natural silver brilliance. It can be natural or artificial toning or dirt/grease coating. Natural toning occurs when silver oxidizes from being in contact or near canvas bags or paper with high sulfur content. It can be multicolored or a solid color and its attractiveness is very much a personal thing. Very dark tones or spotty toning is generally considered to be undesirable. Light dirt or grease coating picked up from many years storage in a bag does not affect the value but a heavy coating can decrease the value.

Proof-like refers to the degree of reflection in the coin's field. Basining of the Morgan dies to obtain a slight curvature for the field for better striking of the coins resulted in polished and smooth fields of the die. This in turn resulted in smooth mirror-like fields of the coins when they were struck. As the dies were used and wore, the field surface would become rough, gradually losing their reflective quality. Only the first five to ten thousand coins struck from a new Morgan die would result in proof-like (PL) coins unless it was again polished during its life to remove clash marks, for example. The greater the degree of reflectance, the more valuable the coin. A clear reflectance of at least three inches is required for a full PL and a deep mirror is one beyond about four to five inches. Both sides of a coin must be PL for a coin to be valued as a full PL. There are no PL Peace dollars because Peace dollar dies were not basined or polished except for some rare instances to repair a die that was badly clashed.

The most desirable and eye appealing coins with the highest value will therefore have a minimum of distracting bag marks, full strike with sharp detail, a cameo-type luster on the devices, with or without attractive toning and very deep mirrors. The state of these factors will determine the relative value of a coin.

CONDITION AVAILABILITY SPECTRUM

One of the most fascinating and frustrating things about Morgan and Peace dollars is the fact that the dates and mints are not equally available with the same eye appealing factors of abrasions, strike, luster, color, and proof-like. There can be no such thing as a matched series of Morgan or Peace dollars. Differences in the basining of the dies, planchet preparation, striking of the coins, coin storage and transportation, and the survival percentage preclude identical looking coins for all dates and mints.

For mint state coins there can be approximated curves of the relative number of surviving coins within the various coinages of the five grading factors.

For example, under abrasions, years like 81-S or 03-P tend to have a higher percentage of coins available with a minimum of bag marks as compared to a 78-CC or 95-S which tend to be bag marked or "baggy" as they say. This can be illustrated in a chart in *Figure 17-1* which shows the degree of abrasions on a horizontal axis versus the relative surviving number in mint state on a vertical axis.

The distribution of abrasions for other dates and mint would have curves somewhere between these two extremes. When translated into a grade number, this same chart shown in *Figure 17-2* would show a higher proportion of coins falling into the MS65 range for the 81-S and the 03-P than the 78-CC or 95-S. Note that, within say, the MS65 grade, there is a definite range of surviving number of coins from slightly better than average number of abrasions to a number approaching the minimum number of abrasions. This shows that even within a grade number "some are better than others." There will be some MS65 coins just approaching the minimum number of abrasions for MS67 and others that have a number of approaching that for MS63. In other words, the continuous distribution curve for MS63, 65 and 67 results in ranges for each grade and not just a single point on the distribution curve.

Similar curves of the relative number of surviving mint state can also be shown for strike as illustrated in *Figure 17-3*. Again, certain dates will show distribution curves skewed at one extreme or the other such as the 81 S which normally are fully struck and 02-O which are normally slightly weakly struck. These differences were caused by the different die basining and strike pressures used by the various mints.

A chart illustrating the variances in luster is shown in *Figure 17-4*. In this case, the later P mints of 1901 to 1904 tend to mostly have brilliant surfaces on the devices while some years like the 80-S have a fairly high percentage of coins with significant frosting. These differences were caused by the state of frostiness of the master hub and dies in use at the time, the number of coins struck while the die was in service, and the manufacturing process used at each mint for the planchets.

Proof-likes can also be charted to show the relative surviving number in mint state as shown in *Figure 17-5*. Certain Morgan dollar dates like the 81-S have a high percentage of PL and DMPL coins while others like an 01-P are extremely scarce in PL. This was due to the length of service of the dies which tended to be longer in later years of the Morgan series and the coin melts in 1917 and 1918 which destroyed about half of the Morgan dollars minted.

MINT STATE GRADING CHANGE EFFECTS

Back in the late 1970's when there were but two practical MS grades of MS60 and MS65, they each covered a wide spectrum of the MS coin condition. This is illustrated in *Figure 17-6*. Some dates like the 81-S had a fairly high proportion of MS65 coins in comparison to others such as the 80-O which had a relatively small proportion in that grade. But many MS65's were better or lower than the average because of the wide grade spectrum.

Then in October 1980 the addition of MS63 to the Grey Sheet pricing guide changed the coverage of MS60 and MS65. MS67 was also added but not listed in the Grey Sheet because of the limited availability and market for that grade. The addition of these two grades narrowed the surviving spectrum average for MS60 and MS65 as shown in *Figure 17-7*.

That is, the better MS65's prior to October 1980 became MS67's and the lower MS65's became part of the MS63 spectrum. Also the better MS60's became part of the new MS63 grade. This is illustrated in *Figure 17-8*.

The shaded area shows the grading spectrums absorbed from the old MS60 and MS65 into the new MS63 and MS67 grades. This had the effect of tightening up the MS65 grading spectrum with the more baggy or weakly struck old MS65 becoming MS63. So the MS65 grade encompassed fewer coins of the MS spectrum and they tended to be of better average condition. That is because coins that became MS67 were much fewer than those that became MS63.

Those people who bought coins with a condition at the lower end of the old MS65 spectrum but at full MS65 price suddenly found that their MS65 coins had changed to MS63 grade and price with a loss in value. But, if they had paid a price below the standard MS65 price, then the true value of the coin probably had not changed much even though the grade fell from the low end of the old MS65 to the upper part of the new MS63 spectrum.

Another effect on the coin grading and value is the condition of the coin market. In a rising or hot market, demand is ahead of the supply and the full spectrum of coins in say, the MS65 grade can be bought and sold. In a slow or receding market the supply outstrips the demand. This has the effect of the buyer demanding the upper part of the spectrum of a grade and a general tightening of grading for coins traded.

So, during 1980 through 1982 there were two effects of the tightening of the MS65 grading; the narrowing of the MS65 condition spectrum range with the addition of MS63 and MS67, and the slow market where buyers demanded the better coins within a grade range. This was the result of the grading evolution process and not a grading revolution.

The addition of the MS64 grade in March 1965 and the eleven point grading early in 1986 further narrowed the spread of each grade. Dominance of encapsulated graded coins after their introduction by PCGS early in 1986 established a coin grade, except by resubmittal. In a slow market, such as 1990-1991, the buyers could still be choosy and pick out the upper end coins in a particular grade.

But why do we need all of the MS grades and their complexity? Can a MS65 coin be accurately graded

Figure 17-1 **ABRASIONS DISTRIBUTION**

78 CC, 95 S   81 S, 03 P

Relative Surviving # in M.S.

Excessive — Avg. — Minimum — None
Bag marks, scratches, scuff marks

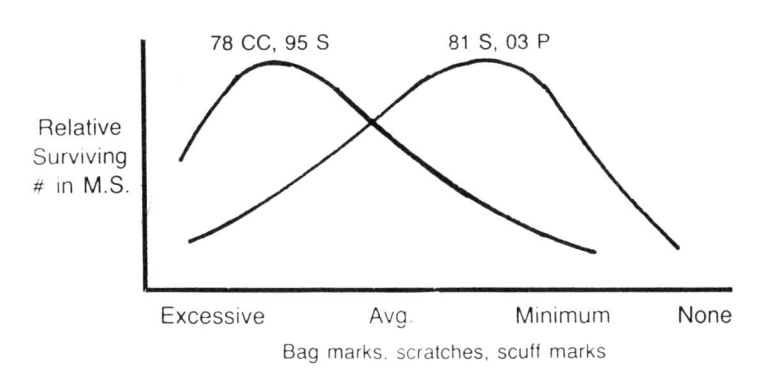

Figure 17-2
ABRASIONS DISTRIBUTIONS WITH GRADE

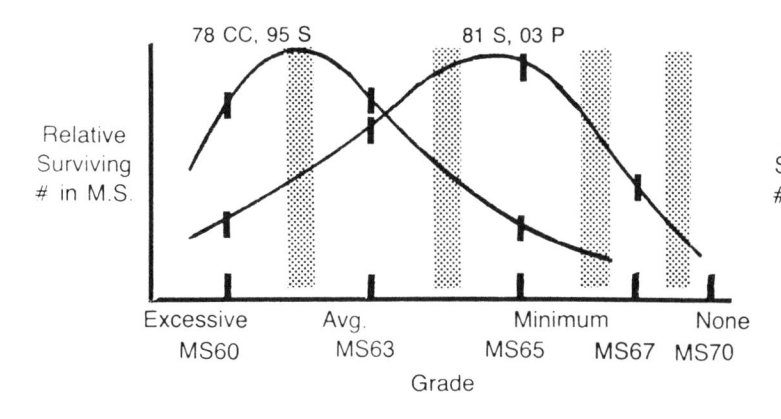

78 CC, 95 S   81 S, 03 P

Relative Surviving # in M.S.

Excessive / MS60 — Avg. / MS63 — Minimum / MS65 — MS67 — None / MS70
Grade

Figure 17-3 **STRIKE**

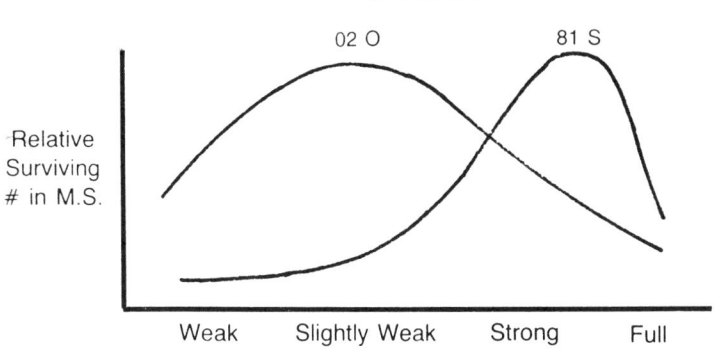

02 O   81 S

Relative Surviving # in M.S.

Weak — Slightly Weak — Strong — Full

Figure 17-4 **LUSTER**

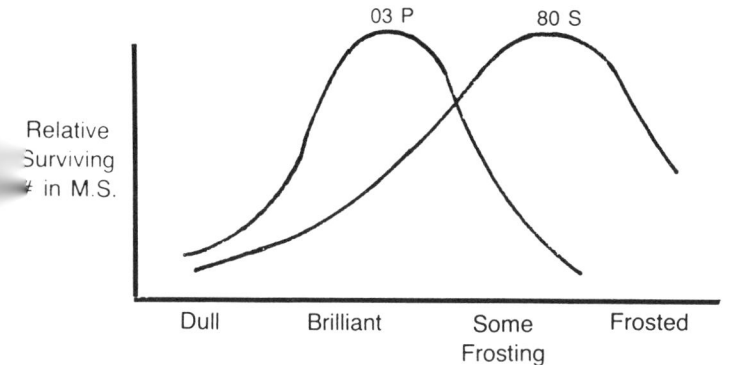

03 P   80 S

Relative Surviving # in M.S.

Dull — Brilliant — Some Frosting — Frosted

Figure 17-5 **PROOF-LIKE**

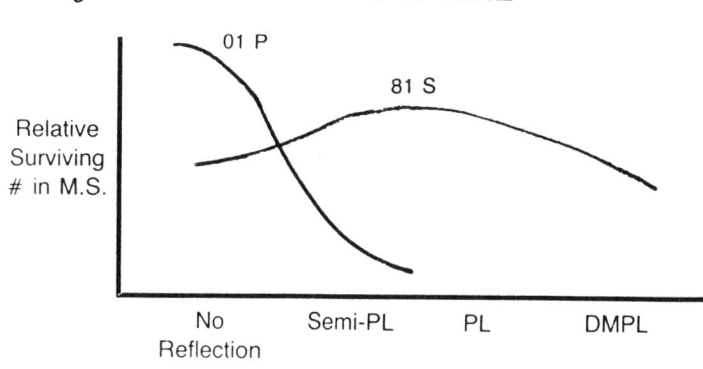

01 P   81 S

Relative Surviving # in M.S.

No Reflection — Semi-PL — PL — DMPL

Figure 17-6 **THREE MS GRADE DISTRIBUTIONS**

80 O   81 S

Relative Surviving # in M.S.

MS60 — MS65 — MS70

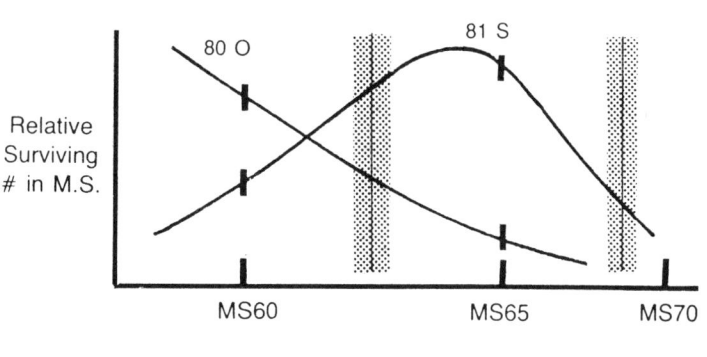

Figure 17-7 **FIVE MS GRADE DISTRIBUTIONS**

80 O   81 S

Relative Surviving # in M.S.

MS60 — MS63 — MS65 — MS67 — MS70

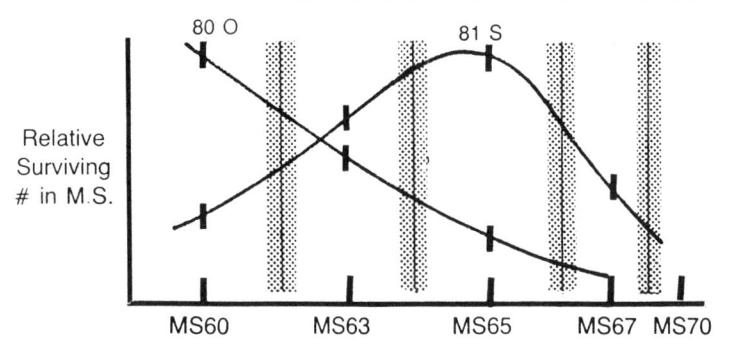

Figure 17-8 **GRADING CHANGES**

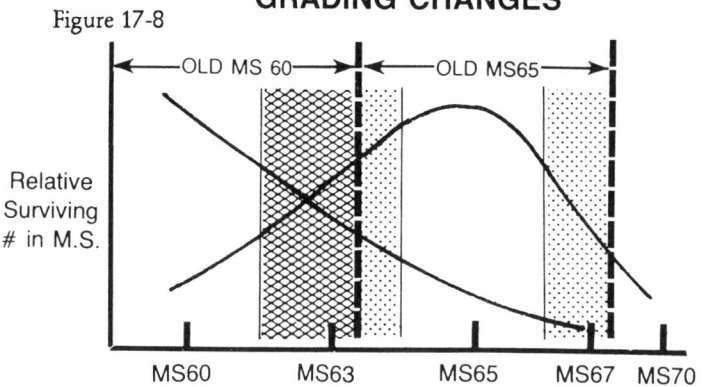

←—— OLD MS 60 ——→ ←—— OLD MS65 ——→

Relative Surviving # in M.S.

MS60 — MS63 — MS65 — MS67 — MS70

and differentiated from a MS64? Yes – but only with experience. It is the areas of the condition spectrum where one grade merges into another such as MS64 merges into MS63 and MS64 into MS65 that is the hardest to grade. Valuewise it is probably easier to get some agreement. But to assign a specific grading number is still, after all, an opinion with much subjective input. The idealized grading areas with a fine line dividing as shown in the charts in reality become grading areas with overlaps and wide dividing bars because of differing opinions.

GRADING SCALE

A grading scale describes the various conditions of a coin in uncirculated and circulated condition. This scale can be one using adjectives or numbers. Up until the late 1970's, adjectives were used exclusively to denote the condition grade of silver dollars. These adjectives were fairly well standardized for the circulated grades. The uncirculated grades generally used BU, Choice and Gem to denote the increasingly higher uncirculated grades. But many other adjectives were also used for uncirculated silver dollars such as select and superb, plus their various combinations.

With the publishing of the ANA grading guide in 1977 a numerical scale as well as adjectives was introduced for grading silver dollars. It was based on the scale used in Dr. William Sheldon's book, *Penny Whimsy*. This was a scale from 1 to 70 and originally reflected the change of value with condition for large cents. The coin market has since changed to make the Sheldon scale inaccurate for determining the value of large cents for each condition. But the Sheldon scale gained popularity and was adapted for indicating the grading condition for other series. Incorporation into the ANA grading guide for all U.S. series gave the Sheldon grading scale a basis for widespread use.

The current most popular U.S. coin pricing guide, the *Coin Dealer Newsletter* or "Grey Sheet," uses adjectives to describe circulated grades and Sheldon numbers for the uncirculated or mint state grades. In addition, most collectors, dealers, and investors use adjectives to refer to circulated grades and in the uncirculated grade designations, the Sheldon numbers in eleven points from MS60 to MS70. A few still use the old adjectives of Typical, Select, Choice and Gem and others use the older terms of Choice, Gem and Superb Gem or a host of other terms to designate uncirculated grades. The authors support the ANA grading guide and numerical scale designations because it is the most widely used grading reference.

The quantitative grading numbers of the ANA grading guide range from 1 which is the basal state of a barely recognizable silver dollar to mint state 70 for a coin in perfect state, just as it left the dies. Silver dollars below condition 7, very good, are not generally collectable except for the rarest years and mints. Business strikes do not exist in MS70 since they were all placed in bags of 1,000 coins for transportation where they picked up abrasions.

The following sections discuss and illustrate the coin examination procedures and the various grading factors of abrasions/wear, strike, luster, color and proof-like.

EXAMINING SILVER DOLLARS

Collectors, dealers and investors of Morgan and Peace silver dollars will need to examine them for two reasons: (1) to determine their grade and thus value, and (2) to identify error coins or die varieties. The first reason is by far the most frequent need for most people.

Grading Examination

The grading of silver dollars requires experience, experience and more experience! There are many factors in grading dollars as discussed later in this chapter. This section will briefly examined some of the techniques and mechanics of examining and grading coins.

First, there must be adequate lighting to examine the coin's surface. Most dealers at coin shows and coin stores have moveable incandescent lamps. It is best to be within several feet of the lamp to obtain bright enough light. Overhead lighting at coin shows and in coin stores may not be bright or numerous enough to provide sufficient lighting on the coin. Also, the type of lighting may be different than normal. This can cause an emphasis on the frosted device. For example, the cameo proof-like (PL) you bought at a show may be just a nice frosted coin when re-examined at home under more usual lighting! Or worse yet, hairline scratches or scuff marks may suddenly appear later under better light and you then get a sinking feeling of having overpaid for the coin.

Lighting for grading at your normal working area, whether at home or at the office, should be from a desk lamp. It can be either a fixed or movable incandescent lamp. Fluorescent type lights should be avoided because they are too long and the light is too diffused to detect hairlines. Personal preference and space will dictate the type. All that is required is that the incandescent lamp provide relatively close and bright enough light. A small spot of light such as that provided by Tensor-type lights is generally not recommended since a point source of light will cause too many bright and dark spots on the coin's surface. But these are suited for detecting hairlines.

It is best to examine the coins out of a holder. This may not always be possible if the coin is in a sealed, encapsulated, stapled or screw holder. The plastic film of the flip or cardboard holder should be clear enough so it does not mask, cloud or distort the appearance of the coin's surface. If in doubt about some part or feature of a coin, ask the dealer or person for permission **first** before removing the coin from a holder. It is only common courtesy. The coin was put in a holder for protection. Most owner's of coins will provide a tray or cloth so the coins can be removed from the holder and placed on a soft surface for examination without dropping it on a hard surface. You would not want to be embarrassed and have to buy a coin you dropped on the floor or case. A silver dollar dropped at a coin show causes considerable noise and undesirable attention!

Always handle a coin by the **edges**. When passing a coin to another person be sure they have a tight grip on the edge before you release your grip. As a precaution, place your free hand under the coin when passing it as this is the most likely time a coin could be accidentally dropped.

Most of the time, examination of silver dollars can be satisfactorily performed in currently available flips. Searching through a double row box of coins can be done without taking each holder out of the box. Simply make sure there is enough room in the row to flip the coins toward you so you can see the obverse clearly. This may require that some holders be temporarily removed from the back of the row to give adequate room. In this way the date, mint and condition of interest can be spotted while flipping through the holders in a box.

When a coin of interest is found you should take the holder out of the box and examine both obverse and reverse. Look first for any signs of wear to see if the coin is circulated or uncirculated. Be careful of AU and sliders as they can be deceptive! Tilt the coin to see if there are any grey areas on the high points of the design or in the field that indicate wear.

Grading a circulated coin is a matter of determining the degree of wear as specified hereafter. Grading an uncirculated coin requires consideration of bag marks, strike, luster, color, proof-like and overall eye appeal. This is more complex and requires practice and experience.

It usually helps if the coin is held of to the side so that the light is not directly reflected in a straight line from the coin to your eye. The bag marks and scratches will show up better with this side lighting on the coin surface. **Tilt** the coin back and forth to get optimum lighting to show up these bag marks and scratches. With a little practice, this technique will become second nature.

Most people can grade dollars with the naked eye. Others use a variety of magnifying glasses to show up the nicks, scratches or strength of strike. These can be 3x wide angle glass with or without a built-in light. Others use a 7x or 10x glass to examine clearly the coin detail. It all depends on how good your eyes are, experience and what you are used to.

It is difficult to detect hairline polishing, faint scuff marks or a fine scratch with just the naked eye. Tilt the coin carefully at various angles to the light to catch any of these defects on a coin's surface. A magnifying glass may be required to really confirm their presence.

Be particularly wary of toned coins! They may be hiding these defects or a weak strike. Look through the toning at the coin's surface to detect bag marks, hairlines and scratches. Unfortunately, coins may be artificially toned to hide surface defects. It is best to stay clear of toned coins until experience in grading brilliant coins is obtained or they are purchased from a reliable dealer/collector.

When examining loose coins from a roll be careful to not let the coins slide against one another. The roll owner will not appreciate you adding more marks to the coins! Either place the stack of coins on a stable surface and examine them one by one or hold the roll securely in one hand and remove single pieces or groups of coins carefully with the other hand. Do not let the coins bang against one another or drop them!

Variety Examination

The large size of the silver dollar makes it relatively easier to examine than the smaller denomination coins for several reasons: (1) they are easier to handle, (2) the design, lettering, date, and mint marks are considerably larger, and (3) any variations in design are more evident, sometimes even to the naked eye.

Another important factor is that a great many of the available coins in this series are either in uncirculated condition or at least in a high grade which makes for easier examination.

On the other hand, being larger in size, they have more area to examine and the serious collector will want to look for doubling and other details even more carefully than on other denomination of coins. The use of a good magnifying glass or stereo microscope is highly recommended for a comprehensive study of this series.

A comfortable straight backed chair and a flat top with ample working space make long sessions of examining coins easier and more efficient. A cloth or paper placed on top of the table will protect the uncirculated coins and also protect the table top from dirty circulated coins.

Before examining circulated or badly tarnished uncirculated coins, they may have to be selectively cleaned using the procedures outlined in the chapter on silver dollar preservation and storage. It can be very frustrating trying to decide if the material around the date or mint mark is due to doubling or just dirt. Excessively dirty coins can have much of the fine coin detail hidden while heavily tarnished coins often have poor surface contrast which makes it difficult to discern specific coin details.

Lighting

Proper lighting is also very important in order to be able to examine small variety details of a coin. Incandescent table lamps, and small high intensity lamps are all satisfactory and the choice depends on one's personal preference and what is available. The important thing is to have the working area well lighted and to adjust the lamp so it does not present any glare.

Lighting at coin shows can be variable – from excellent to practically nonexistent. More than one collector (or cherry picker) has thought they had found a nice variety at a show only to have it somehow disappear when reexamined at home. Most of the time this is due to poor lighting.

The standard lighting at a coin show is movable incandescent light. But you need to get at least within a few feet of the light to clearly see the minor varieties. Some dealers may not have lights at their tables. In such a case, ask the dealer if you can examine the coin at a nearby table that has proper lighting. Most ceiling lights at coin shows do not provide adequate lighting for close examination of coins.

At home you should have either a movable or fixed incandescent desk lamp. You cannot rely on overhead or floor lamps to provide enough light for close up studying of coins. The Tensor type lights should be avoided as too much of a point source of light will cause a mixture of bright and dark spots on the coin. The movable feature of the lamp allows the light to be moved to the best position while remaining comfortably seated and not bending over or causing back strain.

When examining a coin, it should be tilted and rotated in relation to the light to bring out the desired detail. Low angle viewing is also very often effective.

Magnifying Glass

Magnifying glasses are required in most cases for examining the coin detail to identify die varieties. Most of the planchet and striking errors can be identified with the naked eye although one may want to examine some of the finer detail with a lens to confirm the cause or to detect counterfeits. Shown in the photograph are some typical hand held lens and choices of wide and narrow fields in these lens are generally available. The more expensive lens usually have less distortion at the field edges and coated glass for better light transmission.

The 7 to 10x hand held magnifying glass are the most useful in identifying varieties. The 7x can aid in determining the more prominent varieties but 10x is needed on some of the more minor doubling. 16x is used by some collectors for detailed study. Most of the time and for most general use, the 10x glass is more than sufficient.

As in most things, there are various quality magnifying glasses. A single lens is useful up to about 3x. To study varieties at least a doublet is required which is a glass with two lens. Cost for these is relatively inexpensive, generally in the ten dollar or less range. Such double lens glass are available up to about 16x. The two lens, except in the more expensive types, cannot correct distortion at the edge of the field. This effectively narrows the usable field down. It also puts added strain on the eyes due to the distortion. Some people get use to the doublets and have used them for many years.

The best hand held glasses are the Hastings Triplet design type. With three lens, the field can be distortion free from edge to edge. If you ever start using a Triplet type glass you will never want to revert back to the doublet type. The coin detail will be much clearer with little distortion once things are in focus. A 10x Triplet is sufficient to pick out most varieties and identify them.

The main disadvantage of Triplet glasses is their price. Generally, they cost $20-30. But if you really want to study the coins the price is well worth it in the saved time and eye strain. Various brands are available but Bausch and Lomb is very popular. A wide range of powers can be had from 3 to 25x. Just do not forget and leave them behind on the table at shows!

Stereo Microscope

A stereo microscope is best for showing detail clearly and at high power. However, it has some disadvantages being bulky in even the smallest models, making them difficult to bring and use at coin shows. Only die hards are seen using stereo microscopes at coin shows! These instruments are best used at home.

It also takes some time to place the coin under the microscope and to adjust the lighting and focus. A hand held magnifying glass is usually much quicker for examination unless one is systematically examining a large number of coins for varieties. Focusing and tilting the coin for best lighting effect soon becomes second nature and takes just a few seconds.

The stereo microscope should generally be reserved for examining those coins that are more difficult to VAM because of weaker detail needing higher magnification of 20 to 60x. It is also useful to blow up the coin detail if unusual doubling, die breaks or design needs to be checked and a hand held glass just does not provide the clarity

Hand-Held Lenses

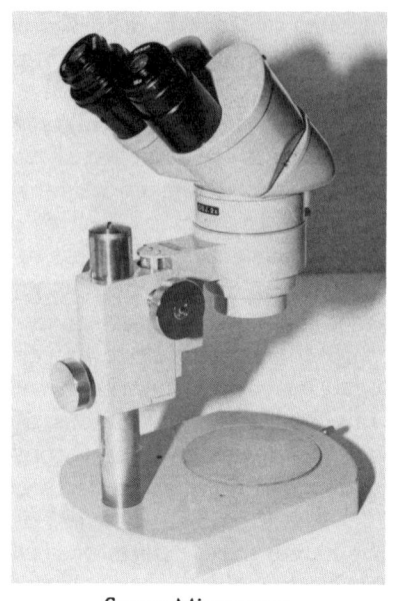

Stereo Microscope

needed.

There are many stereo microscopes on the market. The photograph shows a quality instrument. Cost of such an instrument is about $300 or greater to get quality optics. Lower priced instruments will have greater distortion - particularly in the edge of the field and dimmer edges. This will make it more difficult to focus and will tire the eyes more quickly. Stage illumination is not necessary since the spot lights provided are poor for coin lighting. They cause too many bright spots and dark areas. A broader lamp that is adjustable and provides a more diffuse light is better. One or more Tensor type lamps usually will work well.

You may also want to consider getting a camera attachment for one of the eyepieces. Excellent pictures can be obtained using a 35 mm SLR. At least make sure that the adapter is available for the microscope if you have any photographic inclination and might decide to pursue it in the future.

It is also very handy to have a turret on the microscope to change magnification powers quickly. With this feature you can quickly switch from 20x to 40 or 60x to double check a feature. Otherwise you will need to switch eyepieces (or objective lens which is even harder).

The 15x to 45x is the most useful magnifying range and a wide field of view is recommended. Sloping eyepieces make viewing coins somewhat easier but this feature is not necessary. For the serious variety collector, the stereo microscope will soon pay for itself many times over both in the ease of examining coins and in the greater accuracy made possible in studying the coin's detail.

Identifying Varieties

78-P - Starting with the date with the largest number of die varieties, here the key is the reverse, to quickly narrow down the possibilities. First, determine which of the four basic reverse types the coin has - 8 TF, 7/8 TF, 7 TF PAF or 7 TF SAF. These are easily identified and a magnifying glass is not needed except for the weaker 7/8 TF varieties. The next step is to identify the sub-type of the reverse - the A^1 or A^2/A^1 8 TF, the particular 7/8 TF die variety, the B^1 or B^2 7 TF PAF, and the C^1, C^2 or C^3 7 TF SAF. From this point, several different paths can be taken depending upon one's preference and experience.

For the 8 TF, check with a magnifying glass the added feathers between the eagle's wings and legs against the VAM book photographs. Each A^1 die was touched up in this area and the added feathers are unique. The A^2/A^1 dies have unique doubling on the eagle's beak which is fairly easy to identify for a specific die variety. Some 8 TF reverse dies were with a number of obverse dies. These can be narrowed down by checking the specific doubled obverse areas against the VAM book photos and descriptions. With experience and study, certain doubled areas can be used as diagnostic for a given die variety. Some collectors even make detailed reference notes on obverse and reverse coin outline drawings of the key doubled areas.

7/8 TF dies are fairly easy to identify by determining the number of tail feather ends showing and comparing them with the book photos. Of course, the VAM 44 is easy to spot (but hard to find) by the unique doubling of the cotton bolls and leaves of the obverse.

The 7 TF PAF varieties are the hardest to identify of the 78-P series because there are so many die varieties and many are very similar. First, narrow down the sub type of the reverse, i.e., B^1a, B^1b, B^2a, B^2b, etc. Then, check the obverse to see if it is of the II/I type. If it is, then look at LIBERTY or other doubled features and compare with book photographs. Some II/I and II varieties are very close and require careful comparison of book description and coin features. Other varieties have distinctive features such as a tripled star or broken letters which allow for quick identification.

Narrowing down the C reverse varieties is a similar process as the B reverses. After the reverse sub type is identified, then check the obverse for II/I, II, or III specific varieties.

78-S - This date has many different doubled date and design varieties. The B^1 (long center arrow shaft) variety is of course easy to identify, but much scarcer than the B^2 (short center arrow shaft) variety. The hard part is to identify the engraved wing feather varieties. These have a re-engraved feather between the eagle's right wing and leg which are very similar looking. It requires careful study of the bottom curvature of this feather and other details to identify the specific variety out of about 25 known. The 79-S also has this engraved feather variety but fewer in number (about 10).

Overdates and Over Mint Mark - The two years of overdates (1880, 1887) and over mint marks (1882, 1900) are for the most part easily identifiable varieties. The major 80-P overdates (VAM's 6-9) are each very distinctive. The minor 80-P overdates with 8/7 checkmark can be distinguished by other doubling of the date.

80-CC overdates are easy to identify by the strong 80/79 and 8/7 varieties or the reverse type of the 8/7 dash varieties.

80-O overdates VAM's 4,5, and 6 are easily distinguishable. The VAM 6, 6A, and 6B can be identified by the reverse die gouge in left wreath or hangnail eagle. The VAM's checkmark can be identified by doubling of the date or reverse mint mark.

80-S overdates are also easily distinguishable using the book photographs. The 87-P and 87-O 7/6 overdates are no problem with but one overdate each.

82-O -O/S over mint mark VAM's 3,4 and 5 are easy to tell apart. The various die states require careful examination with a 10x glass to separate one from another.

469

00-O -O/CC VAM's 7-12 are fairly easy to identify using the VAM book photographs. Do not confuse VAM 7 with VAM 9 (detached short right loop of C).

2 Olive Reverse - These are dual hub C^4/C^3 varieties which occur on the 00-P, 01-P, 01-O, 01-S, 02-P, 02-O, 02-S, 03-S and 04-S. Unless the variety has some unique doubled date, ear or mint mark feature, these are very difficult to distinguish apart. The 01-O has over ten and the 02-O has over seventeen, 2 olive reverses making them a real challenge to identify. The doubled features are similar for all these varieties and sometimes they can be best resolved by die polishing lines next to the eagle's legs or mint mark position.

Other - Most of the other dates have only doubled dates and mint marks with an occasional doubled die feature elsewhere on the coin. Minor doubled dates and mint mark and their combinations can be a bear to identify. It is not unusual to get stuck on some of these minor varieties and take 20-30 minutes tracing one down. This is particularly true of 80-S, 82-S and other dates with a large number of varieties. It requires careful study of the doubling of each date digit and mint mark doubling plus the combination of obverse and reverse dies to finally pin down a particular minor variety.

One should start with a quick examination of the date and mint mark to see if they have any unique doubling features. For the S and O mints, it is sometimes easier to determine the particular mint mark doubling variety and then narrow down the obverse combinations.

ABRASION/WEAR

Abrasions are one of the major factors in determining the grade of a mint state of an uncirculated silver dollar. Wear is the grading criteria for circulated silver dollars and is described and illustrated in later sections for the Morgan and Peace dollars.

Abrasions can take many forms on a dollar. The most common are the so-called **bag marks**. These are surface indentations, scuff areas, scratches, and scrapes caused by the dollars coming in contact with one another during the minting process, counting, bagging and transportation. Immediately after the striking of the silver dollar in the minting press, the lower die rose to push the coin up out of the collar. Then the press feed fingers pushed the coin off the lower die back towards the rear of the press into a chute where the coin dropped into a collection box. Naturally coins dropping on top of one another caused contact marks. Next, the full box of Morgan dollars was taken to the reviewing room to be inspected for flaws and counted. The Morgan dollars were dumped onto tables where more abrasions were imparted. After counting, the dollars were dropped into canvas bags of 1,000 coins again causing more marks. For the Peace dollar, the box of coins from the presses were dumped into bins and run through counting machines where they dropped into the canvas bags of 1,000 coins collecting many abrasions in this process.

Typical Scrapes of MS60

All business strike Morgan and Peace silver dollars ended up in canvas bags of 1,000 coins. This was the standard shipping and value container. They were sealed at the mint with a weight tolerance of two hundredths of an ounce total. Thereafter the bag of coins was carried, thrown, and dropped from place to place and transported via stagecoach, wagon, railroad car, boat, automobile and truck to various bank destinations. During this process, the coins shifted and jostled within the bag picking up more bag marks. Their large size and the nearly 60 pounds weight of a bag caused many marks on most silver dollars even though they may never have been placed into circulation. Not all bags were subjected to the same movements, so abrasions on the coins in bags will vary among bags of a given date and among those from various mints and years. And within a given bag, coins will exhibit a full spectrum of bag marks from minimum to excessive.

The placement and extent of a bag mark on the coin will affect how attractive the coin is and therefore its grade and value. The first place most people notice and examine on a silver dollar is the large open cheek area. A bag mark in the center of the cheek will be more noticeable than one in the hair or side of the field. Also, a light scuff or frost break is less noticeable than a deep cut or scrape. The extent and placement of bag marks for the various MS grades is illustrated and described in a later section. Large scrapes, typical of a MS60 coins are shown in the accompanying photograph.

Rim Dents and nicks are another form of abrasions. Rim nicks are a form of bag marks and are caused by coins contacting one another in uncirculated grade. In circulated grade the rim nicks are caused by the coin contacting various surfaces. A rim dent is a flattened area on the edge of the coin usually caused by dropping the coin on a hard floor. Large and noticeable rim dents can lower the grade of a coin one full grade step.

Hairlines are another form of abrasions and are fine parallel lines scratched into the coin's surface. They are generally caused when the coin was accidentally or intentionally brushed against cloth or other similar object. Some well meaning non-numismatists will use a cloth to rub a coin to remove dirt or toning to give a coin a shiny "new" look. Unfortunately, the cloth texture causes hairline scratches on both uncirculated and circulated coins.

Rim Dent

1921-S Hairlines in FIeld

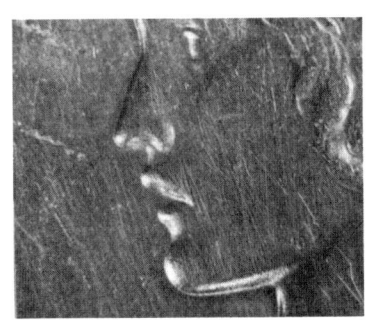

1928-P Slider AU Hairlines

Polished Coin

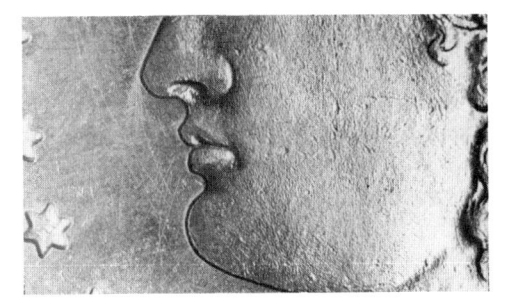

Whizzed Coin

Sometimes the hairlines will show up only on the front of the cheek or on areas of the field. Hairlines can be detected by tilting the coin under a strong light or using a 3 to 7 power magnifying glass. A couple of light hairlines will generally not lower a coin's grade. But large spots or areas can lower it one grade point. If the hairlines are extensive over the whole coin's surface, the grade may be reduced to AU. See the accompanying photographs of hairlines in the field of a 1921-S which lowers the grade one point and also a photograph of a 1928-P with extensive hairlines grading as a slider AU.

A **polished** coin is somewhat related to hairlines, except the rubbing is more severe on the coin's surface. Repeated rubbing of the surface will remove the coin's luster producing an overall shiny appearance with rounded edges of the design detail. Silver polish has also been used on silver dollars producing an even, shiny, polished look. The extreme is a whizzed coin which has been held against a buffing wheel. This buffing wheel may be cloth with polish or a fine wire wheel. The latter produces many fine scratches all over the surface giving an unnatural satiny appearance. Such severely polished or whizzed coins generally reduce their value to below that of EF or to junk uncollectible coins. Both uncirculated and circulated coins should never be subjected to polishing of any sort as it disturbs the luster of an uncirculated coin and creates an unnatural shiny look to even a circulated coin. The accompanying photograph shows an example of a polished coin. The most heartbreaking example of a polished coin that the author's have seen is the first Morgan dollar struck, the Hayes' specimen which has unfortunately been polished repeatedly over the years giving this unique proof dollar a shiny polished look.

STRIKE

Missing design detail on a coin is usually due to a weak strike. Insufficient striking pressure will cause some areas of a planchet not being forced into contact with all parts of the die design cavities. This results in some of the design detail missing on the coin and parts of the design with lower than normal relief. Usually the missing and flat design is at the deepest part of the large die cavities - the center of the Liberty Head or eagle. Sometimes the peripheral lettering and stars will show weaknesses from insufficient striking pressure. A coin with missing detail is not as attractive and is worth less in value.

Striking of silver dollars was under the control of the die setters and press operators at each of the mints. The die setters would install and align the dies and then adjust the **striking pressure** to bring up the proper detail on the struck coins. The press operator, supervisors and inspectors would examine the coins during production to detect any striking defects. If any defects were noted, then the die setter was called in to adjust the press operation. Striking pressure was a compromise between using a high enough pressure to bring out all of the design detail but low enough to not get excessive finning or metal flow between the dies and collars at the rim. Also, the lower the striking pressure the less wear and strain on the dies so they could strike more coins per die pair before they wore out. Each mint and die setter established their own standards of compromise in striking pressure between adequate design detail on the coins and die service life.

Certain dates and mints are notorious for having produced coins from weak strikes. The New Orleans Mint struck many dates showing weak strikes such as 1883-1885, 1887-1897 and 1904. But not all coins of these years show weak strikes. On the other hand, the Philadelphia Mint generally produced well struck coins. But occasionally some Philadelphia Mint coins will be weakly struck such as 1888, 1921 and 1922. The San Francisco Mint produced many years with fully struck coins. But also some S mint show weak strikes for 1894, 1921, 1922, 1923, 1925, and 1928 years. The Carson City Mint was also not immune to producing weak strikes which occurred in 1885 and 1892. Virtually every year and mint will have at least a few weakly struck coins. Conversely, years and dates notorious for weak strikes will have some fully struck coins.

For the Morgan dollar, another variable was present that affected the strength of the strike at each mint. Pre-1921 Morgan dies were all individually **basined** at each mint. This gave a clear definition between the devices and field and produced a radius of curvature of the field so the design would be optimally brought up all over the coin surface with a minimum of striking pressure. Each mint used a revolving disk with polishing compound to polish the field to a given radius. Tolerances in the disk surfaces, its wear, and the care of the workman resulted in differences in the field radius of curvature of the dies at each mint and from year to year. Dies not optimally basined combined with inadequate striking pressure resulted in inadequately struck coins. This explains why the New Orleans Mint produced many weakly struck coins - it was from improperly basined dies. It also explains why some coins have less rim detail then others since the field radius of curvature determines whether the metal flows evenly across the coin or whether it flows more to the central devices or to the rim.

Dies also sank sometimes during use. The high striking pressures occasionally caused the surface of the die to distort and become uneven resulting in coins with wavy fields.

Some examples of weakly struck Morgan dollar obverses are shown in the accompanying photographs. A slightly weak strike will show a few hair strands missing just above the ear. This would not lower the value or grade of an otherwise MS63 or MS65 coin, but would be unacceptable for a MS66 coin. Obvious flatness of the hair above the ear and some flatness in the ear detail would be unacceptable for MS65 grades. Coins showing some weakness in the peripheral lettering, outer design details, and denticles did not happen as often as weak central detail and does not affect the grade as much.

Also shown are some examples of weakly struck Morgan dollar reverses. A slightly weak struck reverse will lack clear definition of the central breast feathers of the eagle. Obvious weakness on the leg feathers and talons would be unacceptable for an MS65 coin. Extremely weak strikes will show flat areas on the wing feathers, arrow shafts and feathers, and the eagle's claws. Some of the New Orleans Mint dollars with weak strikes show a dimple or depression in the lower breast area which is called "belly button." This is sought after by some variety collectors.

It should be noted that the 1878 coins and some 1879-S and 1880-CC coins show a flat eagle's breast but with feather detail instead of the round breast detail (except 1878-P reverse of 1879). Also, the 1921 Morgans have this earlier flat breast design but with less articulated feathers. Weakly struck 1921 Morgans typically show weakness in the lower wreath and roughness in the cheek area (a common problem with 1921-S).

The Peace dollar dies were not basined. From 1916 onwards the Philadelphia Mint produced all the working dies from hubs and master dies directly from the sculptured models without retouching with a graver or adding the inscriptions.[1] This preserved the detail of the original sculptor's work better and eliminated the die basining step. Thus, the weak strikes of Peace dollars are due to the original design defects or to inadequate striking pressure. The accompanying photographs show the typically weak struck hair over the ear and weak wing feathers over the legs for the 1921 Peace dollar. This was due to the difficulty in striking the coins with the initial high relief design. The first reverse design, B^1, of the 1922 with lower relief was also difficult to strike with full central detail as shown for the 1922-S.

A related weak strike problem is **planchet striations**. These show as parallel lines on the cheek of 1878-S with whiteness of the original planchet surface visible between these lines. They also appear on some Carson City issues. Planchet striations are due to weak strikes that do not fully force the planchet against all of the die cavity. The lines on the planchet were caused by rough edges of the jaws of the draw benches used to obtain the final planchet strip thickness in pre-1921 Morgan dollar production (except after 1901 at Philadelphia Mint when they were no longer used).

During the striking of coins, extraneous material sometimes came between the planchet and dies. This caused indentations in the resulting coin. The extraneous material was usually slivers or chips of silver, grease with dirt present in the presses or wood chips from the planchet drying operations.

Excessive polishing of the Morgan dies during the basining process sometimes removed part of the design. The missing design would be near the coin's field rather than the design high points for a weak strike. On

Morgan Flat Ear    Flat Eagle's Breast    Weak Struck Reverse with Belly Button   Belly Button Reverse

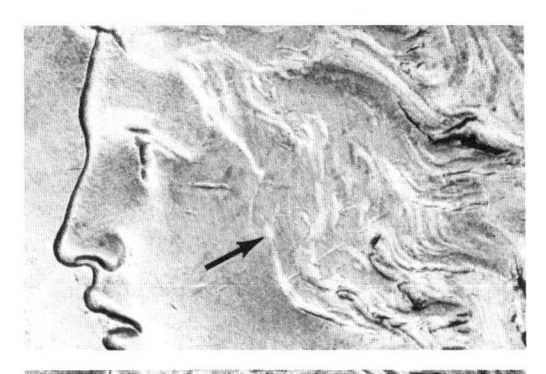

1921-P Peace Weak Hair and Eagle's Wing Feathers

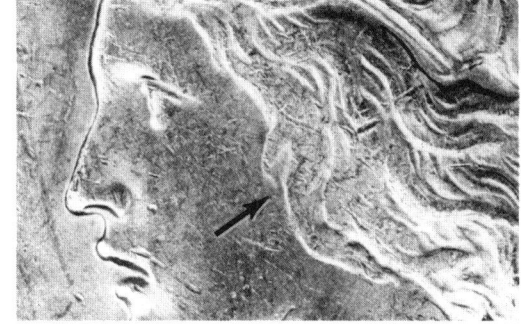

1922-S Weak Hair and Eagle's Wing Feathers

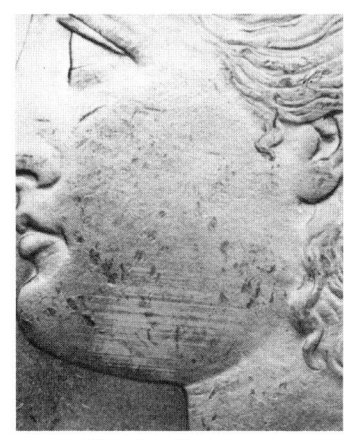

Planchet Striations    Planchet Striations    Strike Through

the obverse this shows as shallow stars and lettering or missing portions of the lower hair. On the reverse, some of the leaves became disconnected in the wreath or feathers were missing in the wing center.

LUSTER

Luster is the appearance of the original surfaces of an uncirculated coin. It varies by date, mint and even at a given mint for a particular year. For that matter it even varies within an original bag of 1,000 dollars since

Typical S-Mint Rounded Rim

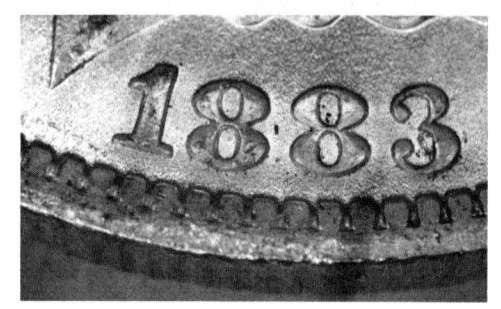

Typical O-Mint Square Rim

in making up a bag, it was common practice to mix heavy and light weight tolerance coins from different press strikings to obtain the total bag weight tolerance of two hundredths of an ounce.

New Morgan dies had polished fields due to basining and a texture on the surfaces on the devices from the reducing lathe and subsequent touch-up by the engraver. It is this polished field that gives a clear definition between the devices and field. Since silver is the most reflective of all metals, the fields of the Morgan dollar have a mirror appearance on early strikes of new dies. There was some variance from year to year and mint to mint on the degree of reflectivity of the field due to how carefully the workman basined the dies and how fine a polishing compound was used in the last basining step.

As the dies wore from striking the coins, the polished field surface became dull. The mirror surface soon disappeared, replaced by brilliant non-reflective surfaces. Through continued wear the edges of the field became rough with parallel radial microscopic grooves in the die from constant planchet metal flow against the die surfaces out towards the rim.

Near the end of the die life, die chips appeared around the stars and outer lettering and die cracks often showed up through this outer lettering. Thus the fields of Morgan coins have a varied appearance depending upon at what point they were struck during a die's lifetime. A small percentage show mirror or proof-like fields. Low mintage dates tended to have predominantly brilliant field coins while high mintage dates tended to have mostly rough fields because of the lengthy use of the dies to achieve the high mintages.

There were exceptions to this however. For example, the Philadelphia Mint struck around 20 million Morgan dollars each year from 1885 through 1890. But about 50% more dies were used in the earlier years of 1885 to 1887 than 1888 to 1890. So the coins of 1888 to 1890 tend to have a greater proportion with rough dull fields. On the other hand, the early San Francisco coins of 1878 through 1882 had mintages of half the 1888 to 1890-P using almost twice as many dies! So these early S mint coins have mostly brilliant fields with a larger proportion of proof-likes. As an average number of coins struck per die pair for the entire Morgan series, the Philadelphia Mint had the highest average with over 210,000; the New Orleans Mint the next highest with about 150,000; San Francisco Mint had 121,000; and the Carson City Mint had the lowest with 64,000. From this it is obvious why the CC and S Morgan dollars tend to have more brilliant fields than the P mint dollars.

The luster on the Liberty Head and eagle varied from deep frosted to brilliant. This depended not only upon the state of the working die, but also upon the amount of wear on the working hubs and master die. Through wear the devices of a working die would normally change from a frosted look to one with dull spots. Eventually most of the frosting would give way to a brilliant look over most of the device surface from the die wearing smooth. Some heavily worn dies would even show rough areas at the edges of the devices such as neck and chin of the Liberty Head and wing tips of the eagle.

Throughout the years the master die and working hubs also accumulated wear on the devices which reduced their frostiness. Since the working hubs had to be replaced every year or two, the working dies made from them showed considerable variance in the frostiness of the devices. For example, the 1879-S and 1880-S coins are fairly common with deep cameo devices whereas the 1881-S cameo is fairly scarce. Apparently most of the 1881-S working dies were made from a worn hub with brilliant devices whereas the 1879-S and 1880-S came from new hubs. There are a few 1881-S with deep cameo devices that must have been from another new working hub.

Over the years the master die lost most of its frostiness of the devices. By the late 1890's, the device frostiness was considerably less than that of the early S mint coins. And by the turn of the century only a little frosting remained. By 1903 and 1904, virtually all of the device frosting was gone so that the proof-like and even the proof coins had little contrast between the devices and fields with mostly brilliant surfaces on the devices.

Original coin luster is best seen by tilting the coin under a light. A radial bright bar will sweep around the coin as it is tilted. This is the so called "cartwheel" effect and is caused by light being reflected off the original surface texture. A worn polished coin with smooth surfaces will not show as pronounced a cartwheel effect since the surface texture will have been changed. This is an easy and almost automatic test used by experienced collectors and dealers to tell if there is any wear on the

Cameo   Frosted   Some Frosting

Brilliant   Some Frosting   Brilliant

Deep Frosting with
Dark Patches

Worn Die

coin's surface. Any wear on the high points or in the fields will show up as dull areas with little luster or cartwheel effect.

To most people the heavy frosted devices combined with brilliant proof-like fields have the most desirable appearance. This produces a cameo effect with the design standing out in contrast to the fields. The frostiness of the devices and brilliance of the fields varies with the year and mint and even within a given year and mint. There is a continuous spectrum of frostiness from cameo to deep frosted to some frosting to brilliant of the devices for most years and mints. The fields varied from brilliant to dull to rough looking. Early Morgan dollars tend to show the whole range of luster spectrum of the devices and fields. Later year Morgan dollars and high mintage years have fewer examples of frosted devices and brilliant fields. Occasionally there are examples of such deep frosted devices that light and dark patches can be seen to appear across the Liberty head as the coin is tilted (evident on some 79-S and 80-S). But on the other hand, the deep frosted devices tend to show the bag marks and frost breaks more prominent than brilliant devices.

Peace dollars in general have much less frosting on the devices and less brilliance in the fields than the Morgan dollar. The entire design including peripheral lettering was reduced from the Galvano to the master die. The master die was not retooled or touched up to preserve the exact quality and texture of the original sculptor's work.[2] Thus, the surfaces of the Peace design devices and lettering tended to be smoothed out and rounded off because of the reducing lathe design transfer step. The Morgan design, on the other hand, was extensively touched up on the master die and hub causing a rougher texture which resulted in more frostiness. The lettering, stars, date and wreath were punched separately into the master die resulting in rough surfaces for tops of these parts of the design and much sharper corners and detail.

The Peace dollar die fields were not basined so their fields were rougher in texture than the Morgan fields which were basined for each working die. Also, the Peace dollar dies struck more coins per die than the average Morgan dollar die so the Peace dollar coins in most cases show more roughness in the field and on the devices due to die wear. There are however, some Peace dollar coins that show quite a bit of frosting in the hair and on the eagle with fairly brilliant fields from early strikes of the dies.

In recent years, artificial cameo Morgan dollars have surfaced on the market. These have deep frosted Liberty Heads and in some cases the eagle. To most experienced collectors and dealers they are unnatural looking and can generally be easily spotted. There are several known methods to produce an artificial frosting on the coin surface. The crudest looking is one that has had a silvery white paint applied to the surface. It produces a thick looking and even appearance. There are usually areas of paint applied to the field or missing on the devices causing the frosting to not exactly follow the devices outline. Of course, the bag marks, scrapes, and frost breaks are also covered in this artificial frosting process producing a "cleaner" looking coin. But since these abrasions occurred after the coin was struck, they should always have shiny contact surfaces on untampered coins. Original frosting always has some degree of change across the Liberty Head surfaces becoming less pronounced closer to the coin's rim. In most cases the painted on frost will easily rub off or dissolve readily with denatured alcohol.

Another method to create artificial frosting is to silver plate the surfaces. This leaves excess silver in the

Die Polishing Lines in Field

crevices of the design, and of course, also creates frosted bag marks. A third method is to lightly sandblast the surface with a very fine abrasive to create the surface roughness. It produces an even texture with again frosted bag marks. If in doubt about a deep frosted coin, always examine the surface with a magnifying glass to see if the scratches, bag marks, scrapes and scuff marks have frosting within them.

In some cases the coins show fine raised dots of metal all over the Liberty Head and/or eagle. This is particularly common for 1883-P and 1883-O. It is due to rusted dies. The rust can occur during the storage of the die if the steel face is not protected (generally petroleum jelly is applied to die faces). Rust causes pits in the die resulting in raised spots on the coin. It gives a slightly rough texture and appearance to the coin. In some instances the rust spots may appear only on a small localized area. Coins struck from rusted dies are in most cases unchanged in value compared to those struck from normal dies as the overall appearance is little changed.

Sometimes fine hairlines are present on the fields. These can be from die polishing lines or from polishing lines or scratches put on the coin after it was minted. Die polishing lines appear as raised lines on the coins and they run up to the edges of the devices and through the middle of the lettering since the field was the high point of the dies. Polishing lines on the coin however, usually do not go up to the edges of the devices and lettering since these areas were protected from any cloth or other wiping material by the raised design. Polishing lines are best detected by tilting the coin under a light to show their presence at the proper reflecting angle. Die polishing lines usually do not affect the coin's grade or value but coin hairlines do, as previously discussed under abrasions. However, obvious die polishing lines in prooflike fields may cause it to only grade semi-PL instead of full PL.

COLOR

Color of a silver dollar refers to anything other than the natural silver brilliance. A coating on the coin surface can take the form of natural or artificial toning, dirt, grease, carbon spots, impure metal streaks, so-called water spots, cloudiness and even finger prints. Most people prefer the natural brilliance of silver. Attractive toning can enhance the beauty of a silver dollar to some people and thus its value. But the other surface coatings and imperfections can decrease the value of a coin if it is noticeable and distracting to the eye.

Toning is a color on the surface of the coin that can be localized in one area or cover an entire side or both sides. It is most often caused by chemical reactions of sulfur and silver to produce a thin film of tarnish on the coin's surface. The thin film results in various colors through a phenomenon called thin film interference. The incoming light wave is reflected off the toned surface and again below the surface on the silver coin. These two reflected waves of light then set up interference light waves to create the various colors depending on the thickness of the thin film coating.

Sulfur that tones silver dollars was present in the canvas bags that the mints and banks used to store them in. Over a period of many years, the coins against the canvas would become toned. Usually this toning would be one-sided or in crescent shapes if the coins overlapped others. The toning would be varied depending upon the thickness of the tarnish film and can be one solid color such as light golden or russet. Most often there would be several colors on one coin such as golden, rose, green, and blue. Occasionally, beautiful rainbow bands or crescents can also be found.

Sulfur was also present in the paper used to wrap rolls and in individual coin envelopes. The latter often caused toning on both sides of the coin. A roll of 20 coins wrapped in paper could cause the end coins to be toned on one side in a segmented fashion due to the overlapped folded paper. The middle coins in a roll sometimes ended up with light peripheral toning.

Toning can enhance the value of a coin if it is an attractive rainbow, vivid bands or light delicate shades. Grey or very dark toning is generally considered undesirable and can decrease the value of a coin. The desirability of toned coins is very much a personal preference and not all collectors and dealers like them.

Buyers of toned coins have to be particularly careful that the toning is not hiding excessive abrasions, weak strikes, hairlines or other defects. A toned coin should be carefully examined to determine its true grade in terms of abrasions, strike, luster and any proof-like tendencies. A magnifying glass can be helpful in trying to look through the toning to the coin's surface. Tilting the coin under a good light is also very helpful for the examination.

Toning can also be artificially applied to coins by various means. Artificial toning means any treatment of the coin's surface that creates toning in a few seconds to a few days. So-called natural toning generally takes many months or many years to create the delicate colors from coin contact with the canvas bags, roll wrappers and paper envelopes. The tarnishing of silver can be speeded up by subjecting the coin to hot humid weather, storage in a polluted city or near factory atmospheres, exposure to sunlight, or exposure to atmospheres with high sulphur or sulfate content. Such abuse of coins may be accidental or intentional – one would generally never

Toned Dollar

Carbon Spots

Impure Metal Streak

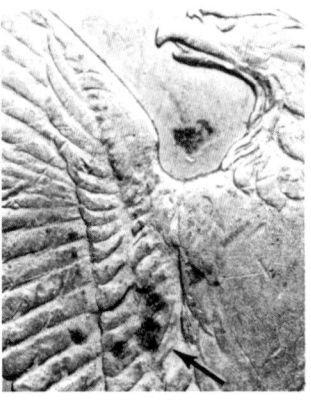

Impure Metal Streak

know which was the case.

There are chemical baths that the coin can be immersed in to cause tarnish coatings within seconds or minutes. Of course such treatment causes both sides of the coin to be toned. Or, the solution can be brushed on to only one side. Generally, the resultant toning has a thick splotchy look that is usually easy to tell from the more delicate and even natural toning. There have even been cases of paints applied to the surfaces but their thick texture causes a very unnatural look. Also, the tars in cigarette smoke can impart a light coating. On a naturally toned coin, however, the coin's luster always shines through the toning.

Because of the long term storage of many of the Morgan and Peace dollars and their transportation all over the country by various means, they are frequently coated with **dirt, dust and grease**. The canvas storage bags were not airtight. In addition, many millions of the coins were re-bagged from time to time as their original bags rotted or split. Such dirt and grease coatings can be easily seen by simply placing the coin upright under a light on a plain piece of white paper. By looking at the coin any coating on its surface will be apparent as areas darker than the normal silver luster. A light dirt or grease coating does not affect the coin's value, but a heavy coating that is distracting in appearance can lower the coin's value.

Small roundish dark areas on a coin's surface are commonly called **carbon spots**. These are localized corrosion and tarnished areas. Usually they are due to an impurity speck imbedded in the coin's surface which causes an active corrosive spot surrounded by toned rings. This impurity speck can be from impurities present in the silver melt which end up near or on the coin's surface. Or, foreign particles such as dust, tobacco, paper specks and airborne contaminants can become lodged against a coin's surface and cause a corrosive action to take place. Some carbon spots are very active and continue to grow with time. Others are stable and do not change size. Sometimes careful removal of the surface contaminant followed by local application of tarnish removal solution will completely remove a carbon spot.

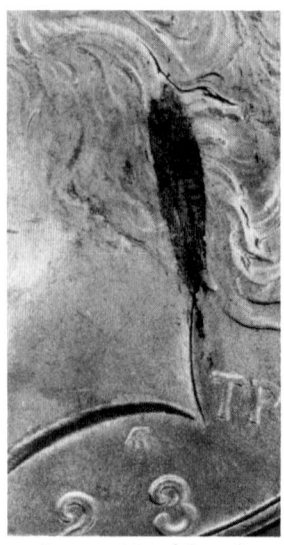

If the impurity is imbedded into the surface, then it is likely that the tarnish spot will reappear within weeks or months after its removal. Also, removal of the imbedded impurity will leave a small cavity in the surface.

Small carbon spots that require a magnifying glass to detect do not affect the value of a coin. But if there are many of these microscopic spots or the carbon spots are readily visible to the naked eye, then the coin's value is decreased. Most collectors, dealers and investors shun coins with obvious large carbon spots which reduces their value considerably.

Related to carbon spots are the **impure metal streaks**. These are due to slag trapped in the silver ingots. Slag is melt impurities that float to the top of the melt with the flux and charcoal (used to coat the top of the melt and reduce exposure to the atmospheric oxygen). The flux with impurities was supposed to have been skimmed off each melt before its pouring. Also, in pouring the melt into the ingot mold, any flux and charcoal should have floated to the top within the end gate which was later trimmed off. But, occasionally, some flux and charcoal material get trapped within the ingot. When this ingot was later rolled into strips, the impurity became flattened and elongated into a streak. If this streak was on the planchet surface the struck coin would show an elongated dark area.

Since the impure metal streak is made up of impurities imbedded in the coin metal there is no known method to remove these impurities without leaving a rough depressed area. Commercial dips will not affect an impure metal streak except perhaps remove any peripheral toning. Large unsightly impure metal streaks can make a coin very difficult to sell, thus greatly lowering its value. In general, coins with distracting impure metal streaks should be avoided or only purchased at reduced prices.

Water Spots are light whitish areas that appear on some of the early Peace dollars. These whitish areas are not simply surface coatings, but are etched into the coin's surface. Thus, the commercial coin dips have no effect on them. A possible cause of these spots could be inadequate rinsing and drying of the planchets after their being whitened in a mild sulfuric acid bath following the planchet annealing operation. Again, the presence of

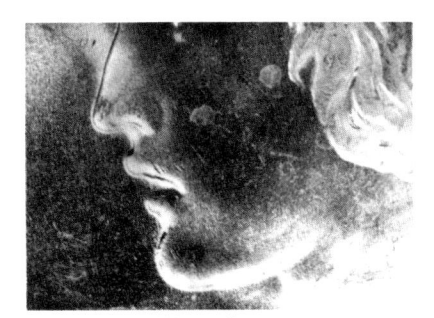

Water Spots

large distracting water spot areas can lower a coin's value whereas a couple of small insignificant spots may not.

Occasionally, a coin may have a slight **cloudiness** on one or both sides of a coin which dulls the luster. Upon close examination with a magnifying glass light white to yellow streaks and spots can be seen. Generally, this cloudiness is embedded in the coin's surface and commercial coin dips will not move it. The exact cause of the cloudiness is not known but could be due to the inadequate rinsing of the planchets, PVC from soft plastic holders or the results of severe tarnishing of the coins. The reduction in the coin's value depends on how severe the original surface luster has been subdued.

Through the mishandling of coins, **fingerprints** get imparted on them. Perspiration from the fingers contain acids which, if left on the coin, can cause the fingerprint pattern to be permanently etched into the coin's surface. This leaves a series of white parallel lines on the coin which cannot be removed by any commercial dip. Fresh fingerprints of a few months or less can sometimes be successfully removed by these dips, however. The location and extent of the fingerprints will determine how distracting they are and thus the effect on the coin's value. Of course, to avoid fingerprints on coins, they should only be handled by their edges.

PROOF-LIKE COINS

The term proof-like refers to the degree of reflection that can be seen in the field of a business strike coin. Since the nineteenth century proof coins and the early and late twentieth century proof coins had highly reflective fields, the similarity in appearance of business strike coins with reflective fields gave rise to the term proof-like.

Although the degree of reflection in a coin's field required for the term proof-like to apply has not been standardized, it is common practice to require a clear reflection of at least two to four inches. That is a distance at which an object in front of the coin can be clearly discerned in the coin's field.

Many methods are used for the reflectance test including a finger tip, eyeball, and printed matter. These methods do not provide a very standardized test so the authors have devised a Morgan Dollar Proof-Like Guide. This Guide has pairs of resolution lines running the length of a card for the distance of eight inches with various terms along the length of the lines. These terms are between pairs of lines running cross-wise on the Guide to define the Semi Proof-Like (SPL), Proof-Like (PL), and Deep Mirror Proof-Like (DMPL) distances. SPL has been defined as a reflection of one to two inches. Any reflection less than one inch is deemed not sufficient to be defined as SPL. PL is a reflection of two to four inches. DMPL is a reflection of four inches to the card's end of eight inches. Clear reflection beyond eight inches is sometimes referred to as Very Deep Mirror PL, Super DMPL, Ultra DMPL, incredible DMPL, mile mirrors, or some other superlatives. Since silver is the most reflective of all metals, the surfaces of the silver dollar fields can in rare instances have virtually a perfect mirror that one can see their face at practically any distance!

To be graded and valued as a proof-like, the Morgan silver dollar has to be proof-like on both sides. There are many examples of one-sided proof-likes. They are valued as non proof-likes or only slightly higher if the obverse is proof-like. Often the bright luster of the early S mint dollars will appear to be proof-like, but in actuality, will have little or no reflection in the fields. Before purchasing proof-like dollars at their premium prices, the degree of reflection should be tested for both sides of the coin.

As discussed under the luster section, the degree of frosting for proof-like dollars can range from deep cameo, to frosted, to some frosting, to brilliant. The degree of frosting and depth of the mirror come in all combinations but not for all years. This is because the frostiness of the devices depended upon the state of frostiness of the master die and working hubs as well as the working dies. The degree of proof-like of the fields depended upon the degree of mirror initially imparted during the basining of each Morgan working die as well as the degree of wear of each working die. Thus, as pointed out in the section on luster, the master die had lost much of its frostiness by the turn of the century and Morgan dollars after 1900 exhibit primarily only light frosting. But these last few years of the Morgan dollar can have very deep mirrored fields.

The early years of the Morgan dollars tended to have a higher percentage of deep mirrored cameos; especially for some of the low mintage years of the CC and S mints. But even these early years show weak PL's with light frosting and deep mirrors with light frosting. Those years with low numbers of coins struck per dies had a higher proportion of PL coins. Thus, the early S and CC coins have quite a few PL coins available. Some higher mintage years like 84-P, 89-P, and 90-P are relatively scarce in proof-like. Other years like 84-S, 93-O, 94-P, and 01-P are very scarce or virtually unknown in mint state PL which may be due to a high percentage of these coins being melted or released into circulation.

The **value** of a proof-like dollar depends upon its eye appeal. Generally, the deeper the frosting with the

S. PL Rev.　　　　　　　　　　PL Rev.　　　　　　　　　　D.M.PL Rev.

proof-like fields, the more contrast will be present and the higher the value. Of course the number and placement of the bag marks as well as the sharpness of the strike will affect the value of proof-like dollars. Deep mirrored cameos with full strikes and minimal marks are the most valued of Morgan dollars. But each proof-like Morgan has to be evaluated on its own merits of bag marks, strike, luster, color and depth of proof-like.

The **cause** of proof-like Morgan dollars was due to the polishing of the working dies during the initial basining process or later to polish out die clash marks. The condition of the planchet surfaces had virtually no effect on the degree of reflection in the coin's surface since during striking of the coin the planchet metal deformed and flowed into the die cavities, recesses and indentations. Business dies did not have the almost flawless mirrored fields of the proof Morgan dies. Striking of Morgan proof coins required polished and selected planchets to minimize any slight surface imperfections that might result from nicks and scratches on the planchets. But for the imperfect business die fields, the condition of the planchet surface from individual planchet polishing, smoothness of the strip rollers, or condition of the drawing bench jaws would have no effect on the degree of mirrors on the coin's field. Rough planchet surfaces could, on occasion, cause some imperfections in the form of pits or lines in the coin fields, however. Also, the constant friction of the planchet metal flow against the die surfaces gradually wore the die surfaces. But since the metal flow is generally in an outward radial direction, the die wear took the form of radial flow lines. Planchet friction against the die fields did not produce even polished die surfaces.

The sculptured models of the U.S. designs for silver coins from 1916 onwards were prepared with no intention of basining the working dies.[3] Master dies for silver coins struck prior to 1916 were lower in relief and had much greater sharpness in detail by re-engraving. In addition, they were prepared with a basined field that was polished to a perfect radius on a revolving disc.

Since the 1921 Morgan dollar was similar to the design used until 1904, it was also struck from basined working dies. Thus, there are proof-like 1921-P Morgan dollars. However, there are relatively few proof-like 1921-D and 1921-S Morgans even though they have large mintages. At some point in 1921 the mints at Philadelphia, Denver and San Francisco apparently discarded the basining step for the working dies. For the Morgan design this resulted in less than optimum striking of the coin as evidenced by many 1921-D and 1921-S with weakly struck wreath and other details. All three mints operated at full capacity in 1921 to replace as quickly as possible the silver dollars melted in 1918 and 1919 under the Pittman Act. So production shortcuts were apparently taken to achieve the highest possible production.

Basining of the Morgan dollar working dies was performed at each mint just prior to their being placed into the presses. It consisted of putting the dies upright in a fixture which held the die face against a slightly dished disc. As this disc revolved with polishing compound, it polished the die face making it slightly concave. The radius of this curvature varied with each mint and caused the planchet metal to flow more towards the coin rim or coin center in the extreme cases. The depth of the mirror on the die field was a function of how fine a compound was used during the basining process and also if a final buffing of the die face was performed. Thus, the degree of mirror initially on the working die field varied from mint to mint over the years and at a particular mint with time because of the different workmen and practices enforced.

As the basined and polished working die struck coins, the friction of the planchet metal moving against the die field would wear the die surfaces making them dull. The mirror field surfaces would gradually become less and less reflective until it became semi proof-like and finally dull with no reflection. Proof dies that are not chrome plated can strike around 2,000 coins before they are discarded with too many dull areas on the field for proof coins. So it is estimated that a proof-like Morgan working die could have struck around 5,000 to 10,000 fully proof-like coins before it became semi-proof-like or nonreflective. This represents 2 to 15% of the average production of a Morgan working die.

Morgan working dies were also occasionally polished during their lifetime to remove severe die clash marks. If the obverse and reverse dies accidently came together without a planchet between them, a portion of the design from both dies would transfer to one another. Polishing the dies to remove these clash marks resulted in mirror fields again on the dies. If the dies clashed early in the die's lifetime, some frosting may still have been present on the devices. Polishing the dies late in their lifetimes would result in proof-likes with brilliant devices.

In rare instances the Peace dollar dies were also polished to remove clash marks. This resulted in the few known weak proof-like Peace dollars with semi-proof-like and weak proof-like fields of two to three inches for the 1922-D, 1925-P, 1927-S, 1935-D, 1935-S. In practically all cases of proof-like Peace dollars the coins show evidence of die polishing lines and usually only part of the fields have any degree of reflection. As mentioned above, the Peace dollar design was not intended to utilize basined dies. But the Peace dollars frequently have die clash marks just as the Morgan dollars commonly show them. However, the Peace dollar clash marks are not as evident or severe perhaps due to the more rounded design next to the fields.

There have surfaced in recent times some dollars with artificial polished fields. These coins at first glance appear to be proof-like. But, upon closer examination, the fields do not have the same depth of mirror within the letters or near the edge of the devices. This is due to the difficulty of polishing the coin's field near the raised design. To most experienced collectors and dealers, these artificial proof-like coins are easily detected.

PROOF VERSUS PROOF-LIKE COINS

Another grading area that the buyer should beware of is a proof-like Morgan dollar being passed off as a genuine proof coin. Only 500 to 1,000 genuine Morgan proof coins were struck each year by the Philadelphia Mint (except for 1921 when about 25 were struck). A few proofs were also struck by the branch mints to commemorate special events, namely, 12 1879-O, 12 1883-O, 12 1893-CC and 24 1921-S.

All proof coins were struck under special conditions to produce an exceptional coin. New dies with fields polished to mirror finish were used. The coin planchets were also polished on both sides. These planchets were then struck twice under higher than normal pressures to produce proof coins with perfect mirror fields and exceptionally sharp detail. These proof coins were always handled separately by hand after being struck to prevent accumulating nicks and scratches.

Proof-like coins may have part or all of one side and/or both sides with a mirror-like field. Working dies for the normal Morgan dollar production had polished fields that produced coins with mirror-like fields. These dies were not as carefully polished as dies for striking proof coins. Also, the planchets did not receive special polishing. The struck coins were not individually handled by hand after injection from the dies, but instead, they fell into the hopper with other coins and were later put into canvas bags of one thousand coins. This resulted in nicks, scratches and bag marks appearing on virtually all coins. In addition, the planchet was struck only once under normal striking pressure so that the detail is not as sharp as a proof coin.

The accompanying photographs show details of the lower reverses of a proof and an exceptionally nice proof-like Morgan dollar. Note the difference in the field appearances – the proof coin has a nearly perfect mirror field with only a few die polishing marks. The proof-like field has many small blemishes, scratches and nicks. Also, the letters of the proof coin has square edges and flat tops whereas the proof-like coin has rounded edges and small dents on top. The most obvious difference is the square proof rim with no scratches, dents or abrasions and the proof-like rim rounded on the outside with many small dents. Chapter Seven notes that most Morgan proofs have unique edge reeding counts.

Proof-like fields on a coin do not change the grade of a coin. Their presence makes the coin more desirable to many collectors and thus tend to command premium prices.

GRADING PROOF SILVER DOLLARS

Grading criteria for proof Morgan and Peace silver dollars is different than that for business strike silver dollars. The proof silver dollars were individually handled by hand in removing them from the striking presses (either screw or hydraulic) and placed into envelopes. Thus, they did not accumulate bag marks like the business strikes, unless they were mishandled. Instead, the types of abrasions seen on proof dollars are tiny hairlines on the devices and/or fields, and rubbing on the high points of the devices. These are due to rubbing of the delicate surfaces by the envelope paper or rubbing with cloth by well meaning owners to remove tarnish and toning.

The strike and luster criteria apply to proof dollars as well as the business strikes. Most proof dollars were well struck and are deeply frosted or cameo. This is because they were struck twice on either a screw or hydraulic press at higher pressures than the business strikes. Also, generally less than 1,000 proof pieces were struck so the dies were new with frosting on the devices. The exceptions are the 1902 - 1904 proofs which have brilliant rather than cameo devices. Possibly, this was due to the change from wood to gas annealing furnaces for the planchets in 1901 or the master die had lost most of its frosting by that date.

A good percentage of proof dollars are toned because of their initial storage in paper envelopes. The almost perfect mirror fields were very susceptible to picking up thin tarnish films which show up as delicate toning shades. In general, toning on proof dollars does not affect the value because toning on them is so common. Exceptionally delicate and eye appealing toning can enhance the value and likewise, dark unattractive toning can lessen the value. One has to be especially careful on toned proof dollars to examine the surfaces under the toning for hairlines and rubbing.

All of the Morgan proof dollars have deep, almost perfect mirrored fields. The exception is the 1921 Zerbe proofs which do not have very deep mirrored fields. The 1921 and 1922 Peace dollar proofs do not exhibit the deep mirrored fields. Instead, they are matte or satin finish proofs with exceptionally strong strikes and sharp detail for the Peace design. Morgan proofs show full frosted hair and eagle (except 1902-1904) with very sharp hairline, cotton boll tops and eagle's feathers. Letters, stars, and date are sharp with squared edges. Rim is square and raised above sharp denticles.

Detail of Proof Reverse
Mirror field with only fine die polishing marks. Square flat-top letters and rim with no scratches, dents or abrasions.

Detail of BU Proof-Like Reverse
Mirror field has small blemishes, scratches and nicks. Letters and rim have small dents and rounded edges.

PROOF MS67 OR 68 – A virtually flawless coin with no hairlines, marks or rubbing and fully struck with outstanding luster or frosting. May have light attractive toning. Only a few proof silver dollars have survived in this condition.

PROOF MS66 – Almost flawless with only a maximum of a couple of hairlines visible under magnification on the devices or in the fields. May have barely discernable frost breaks on very high points of devices. Must have full strike and outstanding frosting and luster for date. May have light attractive toning.

PROOF MS65 – A few hairlines in fields and/or on devices and may have noticeable frost breaks on high points of devices. Sharply struck with attractive frosting and luster for date. May have attractive toning.

PROOF MS63 – Numerous hairlines in fields and/or on devices in large areas with obvious frost breaks on high points of devices. A few marks or scratches may be evident. Strike may be weak and frosting and luster may be noticeably subdued for date. May have toning that is very heavy, splotchy, dark or otherwise unattractive.

Proof Obverse and Reverse

PROOF MS60 – Excessive hairlines and polishing over most of coin surfaces. Distracting marks or scratches may be present. Strike may be weak and frosting and luster may be dull for date. May have unattractive toning.

PROOF CIRCULATED – A few proof silver dollars managed to get into circulation. In describing their grades the term proof is added before the circulated grade designation and the wear characteristics for business strike circulated grades are utilized.

GRADING MORGAN SILVER DOLLARS

Each of the grading criteria of abrasions, strike, luster, color and proof-like must be considered when grading uncirculated Morgan silver dollars. Wear is the primary grading criteria when grading circulated dollars.

For the Morgan dollar the cheek area of the Liberty Head is the most critical area for examining for abrasions since it is a flat open area in the center of the obverse. The eagle on the reverse is less likely to show abrasions because of the feather detail. Coins with distracting large abrasions on the cheek will never grade above MS63. Likewise, coins with obvious missing hair detail above the Liberty Head ear and very weak detail on the eagle's breast feathers will not grade above MS63. Any toning or proof-like tendencies should be added to the grade description.

A grading number can be assigned to both sides of the coin. However, a single number or adjective designation is more widely used and most price guides use a single number/designation. If the two sides grade differently, then the lower grade is assigned as the overall coin grade. However, usually emphasis is on the obverse grade.

MS70 – A flawless coin just as it came out of the press with full strike and outstanding luster. No known Morgan business strike coins meet this criteria.

MS66 – No bag marks or other abrasions on Liberty Head cheek visible to naked eye and only a few small abrasions elsewhere. Fully struck with exceptional luster and brilliant fields to give an overall exceptional appearance. Emphasis is on obverse.

MS65 – Only a few small, non-distracting bag marks or other abrasions on cheek visible to the naked eye with no large scratches, digs or scuff marks elsewhere. Sharply struck on both sides with good luster and bright to brilliant fields to give over all pleasing appearance. Emphasis is on obverse.

MS64 – May have a couple of small, somewhat distracting bag marks on the cheek visible to the naked eye. May show slight weakness in the strike. Luster is average or better with good overall appearance. Emphasis still on obverse.

MS63 – Some obvious bag marks, scratches, or scuff marks on cheek and in fields and design areas. May be weakly struck and darkly toned or have dull luster or dull fields due to worn dies. Appearance is still fairly good with emphasis on obverse.

MS66

MS65

MS63

MS60

MS60 – Significant and numerous bag marks, scratches, or scuff marks on cheek and elsewhere. Other characteristics such as weak strike, dull luster, unsightly toning, or other problems may detract from coin's appearance.

50 ABOUT UNCIRCULATED (AU)

Note: Slight but continuous wear in front areas of Liberty Head cheek and neck, center of obverse and reverse fields. Most of mint luster is present.

AU Obverse

I & II Obv.	Traces of wear on hair above ear, edges of cotton leaves, tops of cotton bolls, top of cap.
III Obv.	Traces of wear on hair above ear, edges of cotton leaves and top of cap; half of detail on cotton boll tops gone.
IV Obv.	Traces of wear on hair above and below ear and on top of cap; one third of detail on cotton boll tops gone.

AU Reverse

A, B, D Rev.	Trace of wear on eagle's breast, wing tips and on lines on top of eagle's legs; detail on eagle's talons smooth.
C Rev.	Center feathers on eagle's breast worn smooth; trace of wear on wing tips and on lines on top of eagle's legs; details on talons smooth.

40 EXTREMELY FINE (EF or XF)

EF Obverse
All Obv. Slight worn spots on hair above date, ear and below LIBERTY; little detail left on cotton boll tops; slight flat spots on very edges of cotton leaves. Light wear on cheek. Partial mint luster should be present.

EF Reverse
A, B, D Rev. Only a few feathers remain across the eagle's breast; top of eagle's legs smooth; talons slightly flat; top leaves of wreath have traces of wear; feathers on eagle's head and neck slightly worn; wing tips show flat spots.

C rev. Same as above except eagle's breast show feathers only at the side. Partial mint luster still present.

20-30 VERY FINE (VF)

VF Obverse
All Obv. Smooth spots on all hair from forehead to ear; lower and upper cotton leaves smooth but all are separated; wear on wheat stalk grains; cross lines on cotton bolls have smooth areas.

VF Reverse
All Rev. Smooth parts on eagle's wing; breast smooth; few feathers show on neck; talons are flat; cross point of the olive branch and arrow shafts still distinct; some of leaves in wreath are worn flat.

12-15 FINE (F)

7, 8, 10 VERY GOOD (VG)

F Obverse

All Obv.   Hair above forehead mostly smooth but outlined; lower two cotton leaves worn together but distinct from cap; some wheat stalk grains smooth; cotton bolls flat but two lines from stem show.

VG Obverse

All Obv.   All the design and the inscriptions will be very clear. Fine detail in hair lacking; hair merges with face above ear; cotton leaves flat and two lower ones merge with cap; abrasions. cotton bolls show no detail; rim still distinct.

F Reverse

All Rev.   One-quarter of eagle's right wing and edge of left wing smooth; eagle's head, neck and breast flat and joined; cross point of olive branch and arrow shafts not distinct; tail feathers show slight wear; all top leaves in wreath are flat.

VG Reverse

All Rev.   One-half of eagle's right wing and one third of left wing smooth; leaves in wreath are all worn; olive branch and arrow shafts are flat; rim still distinct.

4, 5, 6 GOOD (G)
The date, all of the letters and devices will have clear outlines. All of Liberty's hair and most of the detail on the eagle worn smooth. Rim will be worn down to tops of letters and will be flat to field of coin in a few places.

3 ABOUT GOOD (AG)
Date will be clear and most all of the design outline of the coin will be clearly legible although some faint areas will be present. Coin as a whole will be worn nearly smooth with rim flat and merging into field in many places.

2 FAIR (FR)
Date and more than half of the legend and inscription will be readable. Rim will be worn flat in most places.

1 BASAL STATE - POOR
Identifiable as a silver dollar but badly worn with only a portion of the legend or inscription legible. Partial date and no mutilation.

GRADING PEACE SILVER DOLLARS

The grading criteria of abrasions, strike, luster and color are also used to grade uncirculated Peace silver dollars. Proof-like is normally not used since any Peace dollars with proof-like tendencies are extremely rare. Wear is also the primary criteria when grading circulated dollars.

For the Peace dollar, the cheek area is also the most important area for examining for abrasions. But it is a smaller area than that of the Morgan dollar whereas the neck area is much larger and about the same size as the cheek area. So, for the Peace dollar, the cheek and neck area both have to be examined first for abrasions.

On the Peace dollar reverse, the eagle's right wing comprises a large area. The feather detail is not as articulated as that on the Morgan dollar wings and thus show bag marks, scrapes, and scratches more easily. The eagle's wing on the Peace dollar is therefore an important area to examine for abrasions; more so than the Morgan dollar eagle.

The more rounded design with less detail of the Peace dollar makes it more difficult to detect any wear on the high points. The high points of the hair, cheek, and neck on the obverse and the upper part of the eagle's right wing and head on the reverse should be carefully examined for dullness or hairlines indicating wear. Tilting the coin under a strong light and using a magnifying glass for close examination is often necessary to detect light circulation wear.

Weak strikes show as flat and rough texture on the hair over the Liberty Head ear and on the eagle's upper leg feathers and the wing feathers just above the legs. Obvious weakness in these areas will preclude a Peace dollar from grading MS65. The majority of high relief 1921 Peace design coins are weakly struck.

Many Peace dollars show dull luster due to a granular surface texture. This is caused by excessive die wear from extended use of the dies. Peace dollars with brilliant fields and some frosting in the hair and on the eagle from early strikes of the dies are more attractive and thus more desirable and valuable.

MS70 – A flawless coin just as it came out of the press with full strike and outstanding luster. No known Peace business strike coins meet this condition.

MS66 – No bag marks or other abrasions on Liberty Head cheek and neck visible to naked eye and only a few small abrasions elsewhere. Fully struck with exceptional luster and brilliant fields to give an overall exceptional appearance. Emphasis is on obverse.

MS65 – Only a few small bag marks or other abrasions on cheek, neck and eagle's wing visible to naked eye with no large scratches, digs or scuff marks elsewhere. Sharply struck on both sides with good luster and bright to brilliant fields to give overall pleasing appearance. Emphasis is on obverse.

MS64 – May have a couple of small, somewhat distracting bag marks on the cheek visible to the naked eye. May show slight weakness in the strike. Luster is average or better with good overall appearance. Emphasis still on obverse.

MS63 – Some obvious bag marks, scratches, or scuff marks on cheek, neck, eagle's wing and in fields and design areas. May be weakly struck and darkly toned or have dull luster or dull fields due to worn dies. Appearance is still fairly good with emphasis on obverse.

MS60 – Significant and numerous bag marks, scratches, or scuff marks an cheek, and elsewhere. Other characteristics such as weak strike, dull luster, unsightly toning, or other problems may detract from coin's appearance.

50 ABOUT UNCIRCULATED (AU)

MS66

MS65

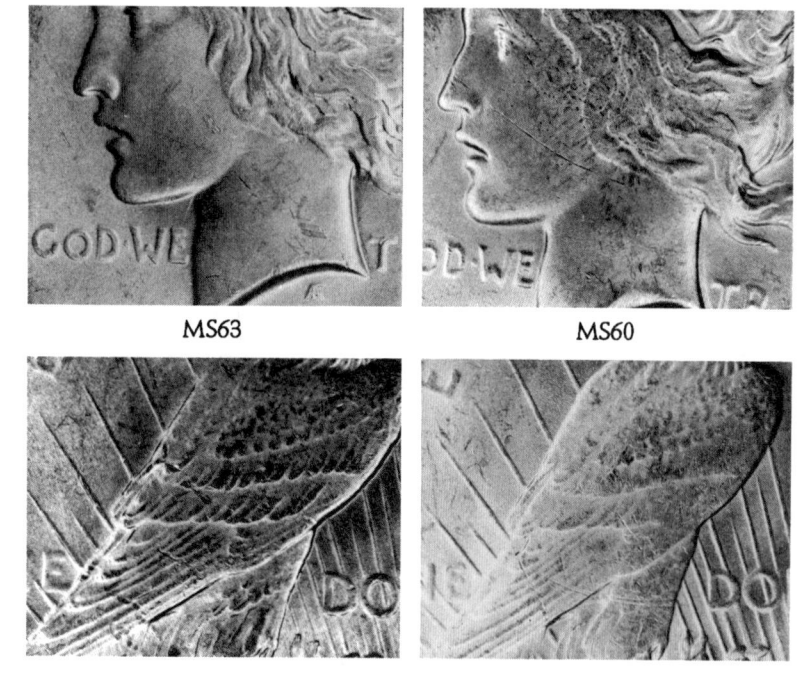

MS63

MS60

AU Obverse

I Obv.   Hair detail lacking over ear, even on uncirculated specimens; slight wear evident on hair above forehead.

II Obv.   Trace of wear on hair over ear and above forehead.

AU Reverse

All Rev.   Trace of wear on top and outside edge of eagle's right wing.

Note: Slight but continuous wear in front areas of Liberty Head cheek and neck, center of obverse and reverse fields. Most of mint luster is present.

40 EXTREMELY FINE (EF or XF)

EF Obverse

All Obv. Wear on all hair around the face, but many fine hair strands still show around the ear and head band. Light wear on cheek and neck. Partial mint luster still present.

EF Reverse

All Rev. Slight wear on eagle's right wing and legs; trace of wear on eagle's head behind the eye and on top of the neck. Partial mint luster present.

20-30 VERY FINE (VF)

VF Obverse

All Obv. Very little hair detail left around the face; front curl slightly worn.

VF Reverse

All Rev. Much feather detail missing on right wing, but the three horizontal lines of feather layers still show, wear on neck and leg feathers; trace of wear on E PLURIBUS lettering.

12-15 FINE (F)

F Obverse

All Obv. All hair around the face is smooth; slight wear on hair at the back of head and on the cap, trace of wear on the rays.

F Reverse

All Rev. All of lower horizontal line of feather layers still show, but others weak or missing; no feather detail on right leg and only lower third of neck feathers show; portion of PEACE and E PLURIBUS weak.

7, 8, 10 VERY GOOD (VG)

VG Obverse

All Rev. Hair is flattened and rays have flat spots, portions of IN GOD weak.

VG Reverse

All Rev. No horizontal line of feather layers remain; flat spots on right leg, wing and upper neck and head; few feathers on lower neck show; portions of rays, PEACE and E PLURIBUS missing.

4, 5-6 GOOD (G)
The date, Liberty Head, and eagle outline will be clear. Portions of IN GOD, PEACE and E PLURIBUS will be missing. Rim will be worn to top of letters and will be flat to field of coin in a few places.

3 ABOUT GOOD (AG)
Date will be clear and most all of the design outline of coin will be clearly legible although faint areas will be present. Coin as a whole will be worn nearly smooth, with rim flat and merging into the field in many places.

2 FAIR (FR)
Date will be weak and at least half of the legend and inscription will be readable. Rim will be worn flat to the field in most places.

1 BASAL STATE – POOR
Identifiable as a silver dollar but badly worn with only a portion of legend or inscription legible. Partial date and no mutilation.

Footnotes

[1] Nellie Tayloe Ross, Director of the Mint, "The 1936 Proof Coins," *The Numismatist*, July 1936, p. 531.

[2] Ibid.

[3] Ibid.

Chapter 18
Photographing Silver Dollars

The dollar collectors may want to photograph their coins for a variety of reasons. Particularly valuable specimens may need full coin photographs for positive identification in case of theft through the unique scratches, bag marks, and polishing lines on each coin. Enlargement photographs of the date, mint mark, or other areas may be needed to send to other collectors or authenticators to verify particular varieties. Special photographs may also be needed to publish in periodicals or books. Rather than have these photographs taken by a commercial photographer, excellent photographs can be made by most anyone using suitable amateur photographic equipment.

CAMERAS

The modern Single Lens Reflex (SLR) 35 mm camera is by far the most suitable camera available to the average collector for taking extreme close-up pictures of coins. In recent years this type camera has become readily available at moderate prices to the amateur photographer. Modern lens, films, and photographic papers allow date and mint mark pictures taken by 35 mm cameras to be enlarged to 8 x 10 inch size with little loss of detail. The modern SLR 35 mm camera boasts of such features as through the lens viewing, ground glass focusing, through the lens metering, interchangeable lens, and a wide range of lens and accessories readily available. These features make it easier to obtain good close-up pictures.

Other types of cameras such as the 35 mm range finder and 120 twin lens reflex can also take close-up pictures, but they are not as convenient as the 35 mm SLR. These other type cameras are more difficult to focus and obtain correct exposures. Taking good pictures with them takes longer, requires experimentation, and results in some wasted film frames. So this chapter will concentrate in using the SLR 35 mm camera.

There are many good makes and models of the SLR 35 mm camera on the market. The very cheapest should be avoided because of poor construction, reliability and lens quality. Likewise, an expensive one is not required. A moderately priced camera with interchangeable lens and through the lens metering would be adequate. It is the selection of the lens and other equipment for close-up photography that poses the greatest challenge.

LENS

This section surveys the various lens and equipment that can be used for close-up photography of coins. Hopefully this will enable the reader to buy items specifically suited to their purpose and thus avoid buying useless, inferior, or expensive lens and equipment through hit or miss and experimentation techniques.

Generally, coin photography falls into two categories; whole coin photos and extreme close-up photos of just a portion of a coin. Whole coin photos require a coin image size on a 35 mm film negative of up to about 1/2 times life size for a silver dollar and up to about 1-1/2 times life size for smaller coins. Extreme close-ups begin at about 2 times life size and can go to 25 times life size or more.

Lens and equipment combinations for coin photography can be categorized as follows:

- Normal and macro lens unassisted
- Supplementing normal lens
- Extending normal lens
- Reversing normal lens
- Special flat field lens
- Microscopes

An excellent pamphlet on this subject is *Close Up Photography* by William J. Owens as part of the Petersen Photo Publishing Group that is available at most photography stores. Although the treatment is general in nature, most of the discussion can be applied to coin photography.

The following sub-sections survey the performance of lens and associated equipments for close-up photography. There are two sets of photographs showing the test results of each combination of lens and equipment. One set shows the size of a silver dollar in an actual 35 mm negative size. The other set shows the enlarged photographs of the U.S. Air Force test photo charts to show any distortion. All test photographs were shot at an aperture of f/8.

Normal and Macro Lens

Most normal focal length lens for the Single Lens Reflex (SLR) 35 mm camera are about 50 to 55 mm and can focus down to about 18 inches from the subject. At this distance, a silver dollar appears about 1/5 life size on the 35 mm film negative. This is hardly large enough to obtain detailed full size coin prints and certainly not of sufficient size to obtain detailed close-ups of a date or mint mark.

A macro lens can be focused closer than a normal lens to permit about 1/2 life size of the film negative. It can take normal pictures and snap shots in addition to close-up shots. Extended focusing of the lens enables the macro lens to achieve this versatility. It can thus take excellent whole coin shots but is lacking the capability to take extreme close-ups of dates and mint marks. Macro lens are not cheap and can run $75 – $100 and upwards.

Supplementing Normal Lens

An easy and inexpensive way to enable a normal camera lens to focus closer is to use supplementary close-up lenses. These are single lens that screw in the front of the normal lens. They can be obtained in varying strengths usually expressed in diopters from +1 to +10 or +20. The diopter rating is the reciprocal of the focal length in meters.

Usually the close-up lenses come in sets of 3 in +1, +2, and +4 diopters. They can be used singly or in combinations with the highest strength put next to the normal camera lens. There are also available variable close-up lens that have a range of 1/5 to 1/2 life size on the 35 mm negative.

The accompanying diagram and photos show some typical results of photographing silver dollars with close-up lens. Using the +1, +2 and +4 close-up lens in combination, the silver dollar just fills the 35 mm negative. However, because of the multiple lens surfaces, flare became a problem (reduced contrast due to multiple light reflections off the various lens surfaces). The +10 close-up lens was 1/1.3 life-size but introduced some edge distortion. Distortion was severe at the edges for the +20 close-up lens. Flare and distortion was much less severe for the variable close-up lens.

Close-up lens are thus useful for making whole coin photos and coin close-ups showing about ½ to ¼ of a silver dollar. Flare can be a problem when using combinations of close-up lens. The stronger close-up lens of +10 and +20 have distortion at the edges because of curvature of the field and are only useful at the center part of the negative.

Extending Normal Lens

Increased magnification can be obtained by extending the normal lens further away from the camera body. It creates a larger image at the film plane and also enables focusing down to a shorter distance. The extension device is merely a light tight tube between the camera body and the normal camera lens. They are available in two convenient forms, the extension tubes and bellows.

Since no lens elements are added, flare is not increased over that of the normal lens. At higher magnification distortion can become a problem. However, the exposure must be increased as the extension becomes greater because the effective "f-number" of the lens is made greater. An "f-number" is the ratio of the lens diaphragm opening size and the lens focal length. The length of the extension plus the lens original focal length becomes the new effective focal length. Thus, a 50 mm focal length lens set at f/8 will have an aperture diameter of 1/8 of 50 mm or 6.25 mm. Adding 50 mm extension tube length will change the "f-number" to f/16 (6.25/100).

Extension tubes normally are available in sets of three of varying lengths with a total length when combined of about 50 mm. Longer individual extension tubes are also available. Unless a double cable release is used the full aperture focusing with stopped down exposure feature of the modern SLR is lost. Exposures are taken in the camera's stopped down mode (this requires matching the exposure needle in the view finder to an index mark). Unless the extension tube set is specifically

T Adapter   T-Flange    Extension Tubes    Variable Close-up Lens

+1, +2, +4 Close-up Lens    +20, +10 Close-up Lens    Flat Field Lens 35, 75, 150mm

NORMAL CAMERA

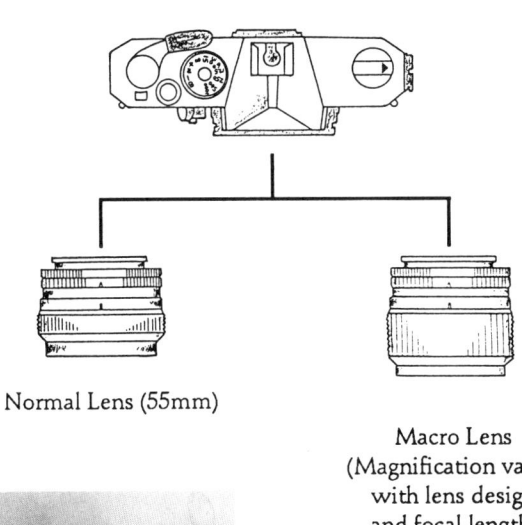

Normal Lens (55mm)

Macro Lens
(Magnification varies
with lens design
and focal length)

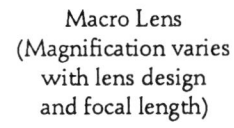

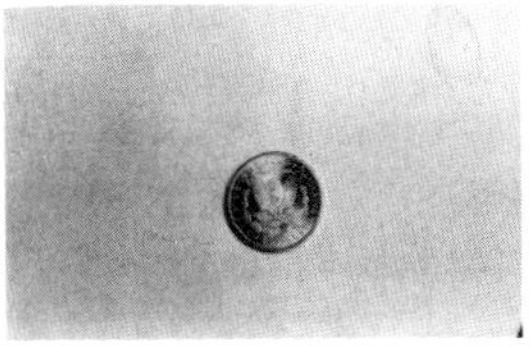

Normal Lens
0.18X (1/5.6 Life Size)

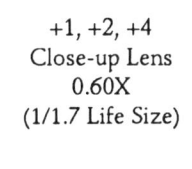

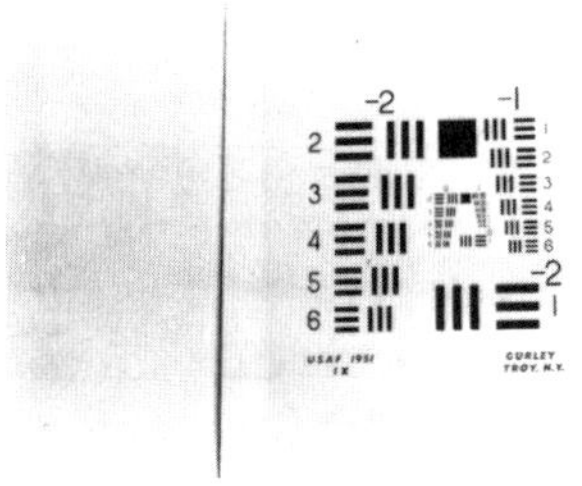

+10 Close-up Lens
0.80X (1/1.3 Life Size)

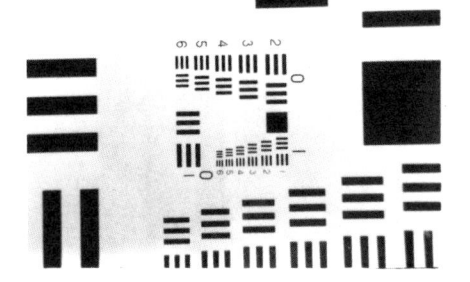

(Note edge distortion)

SUPPLEMENTING NORMAL LENS

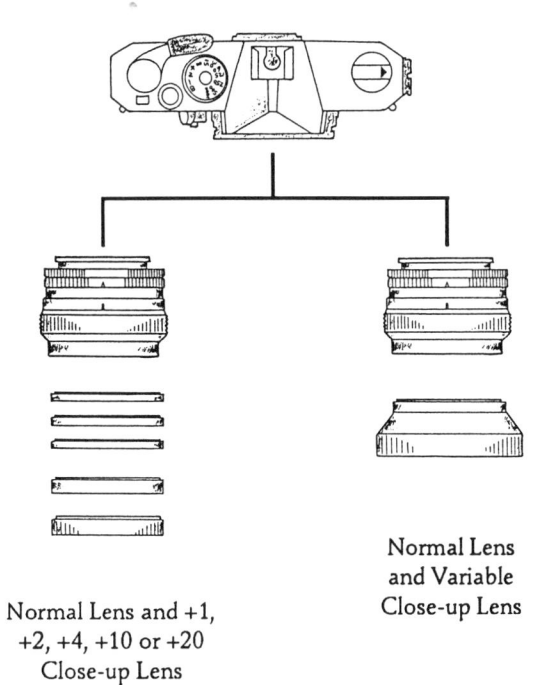

Normal Lens and +1,
+2, +4, +10 or +20
Close-up Lens

Normal Lens
and Variable
Close-up Lens

+1, +2, +4
Close-up Lens
0.60X
(1/1.7 Life Size)

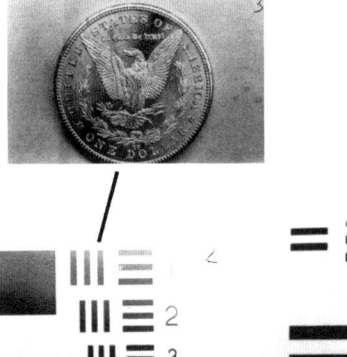

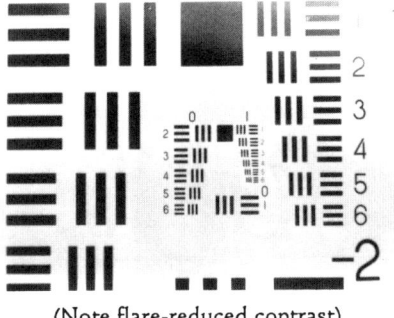

Variable Close-up Lens
0.56X (1/1.8 Life Size)

(Note flare-reduced contrast)

+20 Close-up Lens
1.9X Life Size

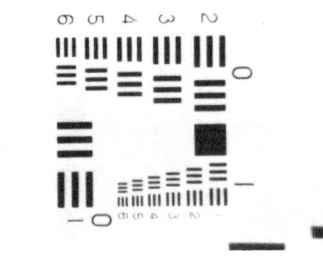

(Note extreme distortion at edges)

made for a particular brand camera, a "T" adapter will be required to match the camera body to the extension tube set (usually a standard "T" mount size). A "T" flange will usually be required to match the extension tube to the camera lens (male "T" mount to equivalent camera body female mount fitting).

A bellows can be considered a variable extension tube. The disadvantage of an extension tube set is that the magnification obtained is governed by their fixed length which may not always match the photo needs. Bellows cost more than an extension tube set but are much more versatile. Some have a separate focusing rail to achieve focusing without changing the magnification. They also need a "T" flange and "T" adapter unless made specifically for the brand of camera. Double cable releases allow viewing at full aperture. Extension tubes can be used in conjunction with bellows to achieve even greater extension lengths and magnifications.

The accompanying photos show the magnification achieved with typical extension tubes and bellows. Extension tubes can achieve about 3 times life size on the 35 mm film negative. Bellows give up to about 6 times and the combination of the two give up to about 8 times life size. This is sufficient magnification for detailed blow-ups of individual Morgan dollar mint marks.

However, note that there is introduced some edge distortion at these extreme close-ups. This is because the normal camera lens was designed to give best resolution when focused at infinity. They were not designed to give best performance when the distance to the subject (coin) is less than the effective focal length (or about 1:1 reproduction ratio).

Reversing Normal Lens

Most camera manufacturers recommend reversing the normal camera lens if reproduction ratios of greater than 1:1 are to be used. This changes the geometry of the optics back to the designed relationships of greater distance for the lens front than the rear. In addition to giving better sharpness and resolution, the focusing field is flatter, better matching the flat coin surface.

Instead of using a "T" flange to attach the normal camera lens to the extension tubes and bellows, a reversing ring adapter is used. Other than that change, the same extension tubes and bellows and their combinations can be used as for extending the normal lens as previously discussed.

The accompanying photos show the magnification and definition achieved using the normal camera lens in the reversed position. Without extension tubes or bellows, the reversed lens can give magnification of about ½ life size. However, note that there is quite a bit of edge distortion. This is due to the front of the lens being closer to the film plane than the lens rear to the subject, in contradiction to the intent of the lens design.

The normal lens in the reversed position should be used only with extension tubes or bellows in order to give good resolution and definition across the entire film frame width. Extension tubes can give about 3 times magnification using the typical set of three. Bellows can give about 6 times magnification and their combination about 8 times. The definition is quite good even at the frame edges.

Camera Body, T Adapter, Extension Tubes, Normal Lens

Camera Body, T Adapter, Extension Tubes, Reverse Ring, Normal Lens (Reversed)

Camera Body, T Adapter, Extension Tubes, Flat Field Lens

EXTENDING NORMAL LENS

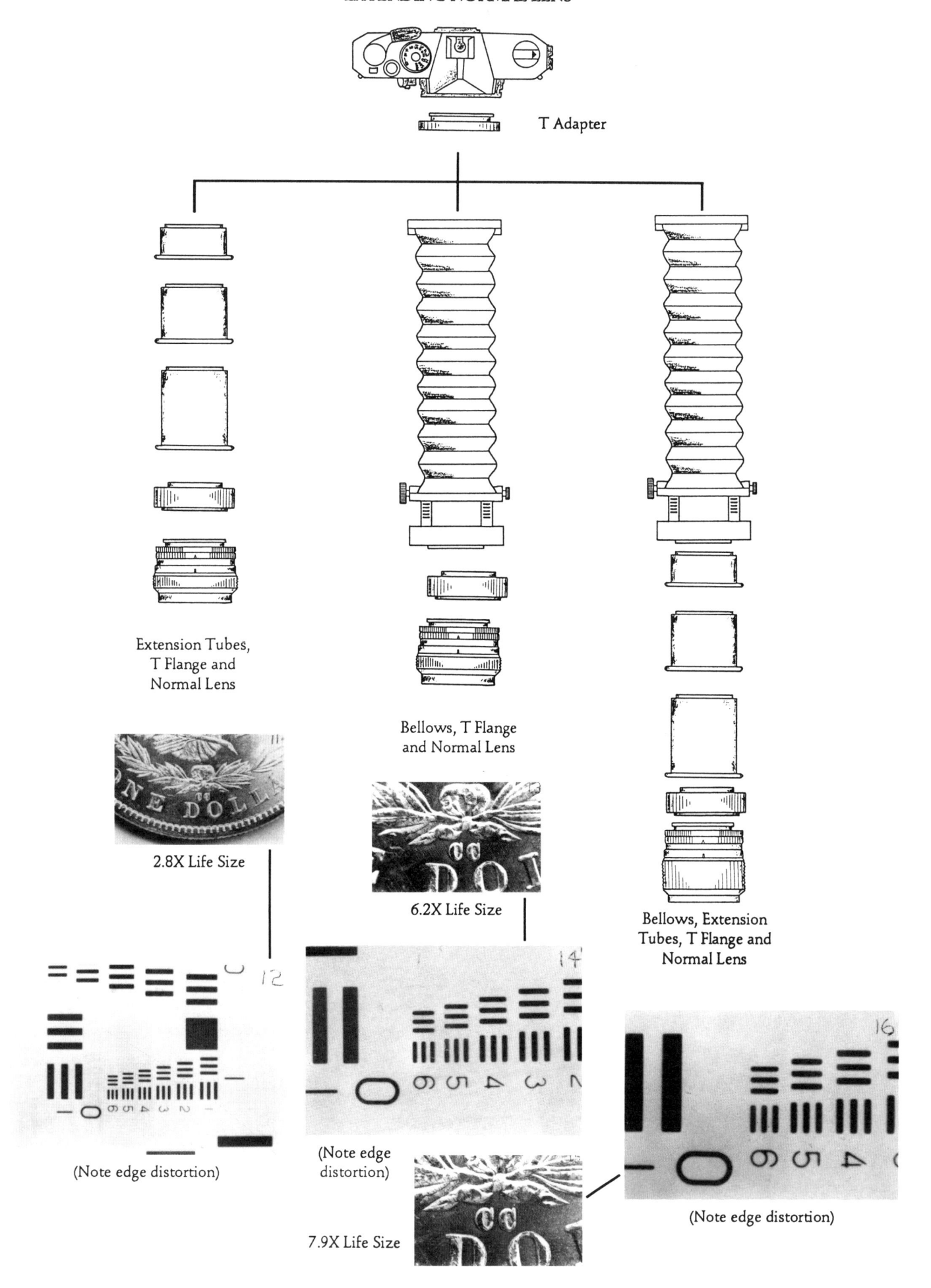

T Adapter

Extension Tubes,
T Flange and
Normal Lens

2.8X Life Size

Bellows, T Flange
and Normal Lens

6.2X Life Size

Bellows, Extension
Tubes, T Flange and
Normal Lens

(Note edge distortion)

(Note edge distortion)

7.9X Life Size

(Note edge distortion)

REVERSING NORMAL LENS

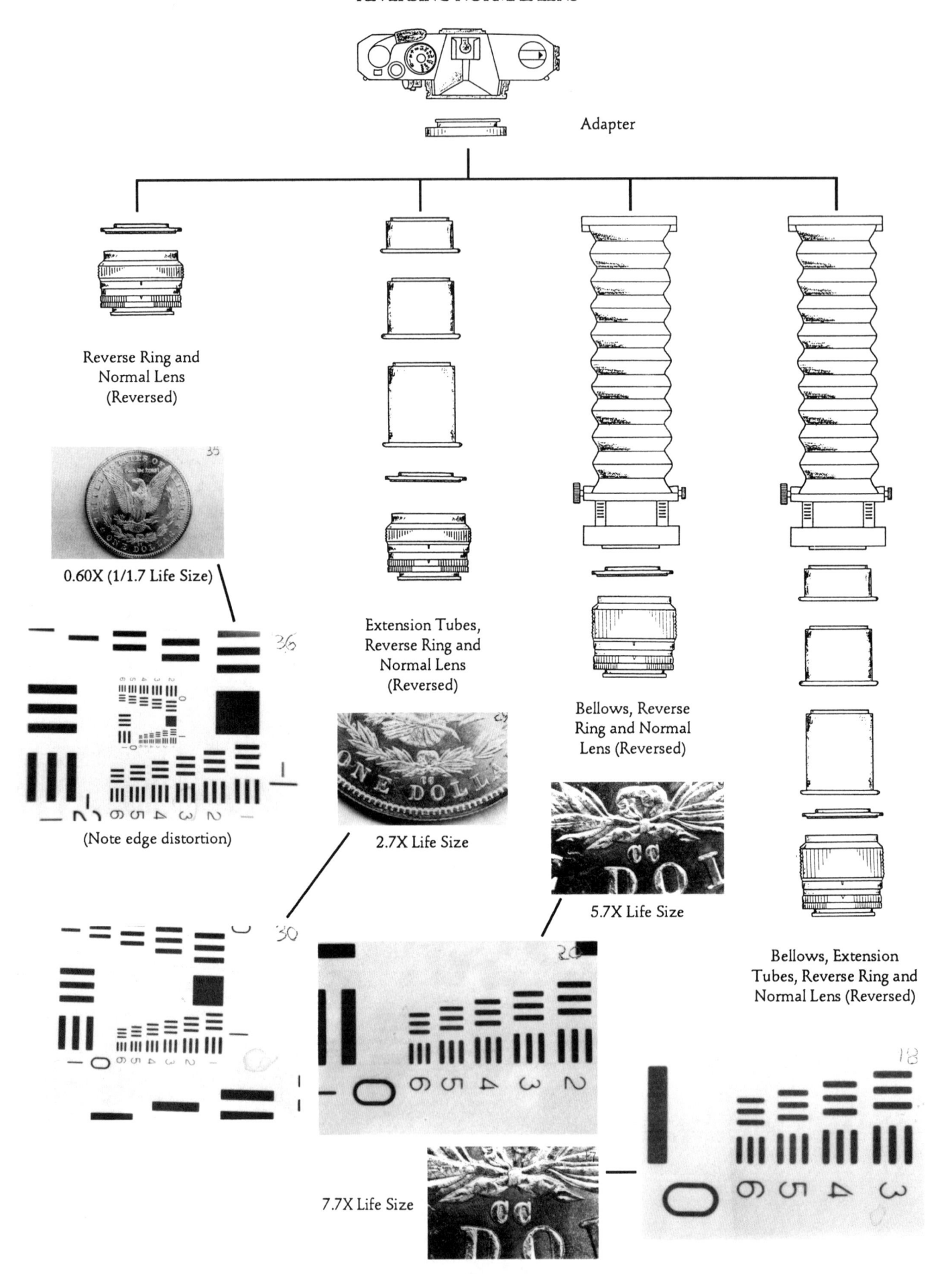

Adapter

Reverse Ring and Normal Lens (Reversed)

0.60X (1/1.7 Life Size)

(Note edge distortion)

Extension Tubes, Reverse Ring and Normal Lens (Reversed)

2.7X Life Size

Bellows, Reverse Ring and Normal Lens (Reversed)

5.7X Life Size

Bellows, Extension Tubes, Reverse Ring and Normal Lens (Reversed)

7.7X Life Size

Special Flat Field Lens

Flat field lens are designed to photograph flat subjects such as coins. Thus, they are better suited to take whole coins or extreme close-ups of mint marks than even the reversed normal lens. Flat field lens are available in a variety of focal lengths at modest cost compared to most SLR camera lens. They normally do not have a focusing capability and do not have very fast lens. The average enlarger lens is a good example of a flat field lens and they can be obtained for as low as about $20.

The accompanying photos show the magnification and definition obtained with an enlarger lens of 35 mm focal length. Using the lens without extension gives a magnification of ½. Various combinations of extension tubes and bellows can give magnification of up to 12 times. This can provide really large blow-ups of just the mint mark of the Morgan dollar. With a flat field capability, these lens provide good definition from edge to edge of the film frame.

Special 2X Converter

An interesting supplementary lens is the 2x T-converter. It is used in conjunction with extension tubes and/or bellows to provide an increased magnification. A side benefit is that it also enables the reversed normal lens or flat field lens to be further away from the subject (coin). This allows greater freedom in providing direct lighting over the coin. However, it does introduce some edge distortion.

MICROSCOPES

Even greater magnification can be achieved by using the SLR camera with microscopes. A "T" adapter is required along with a microscope adapter. Magnifications of 25 time or greater can be achieved. However, as the magnifications become greater, the depth of field becomes less so that the entire mint mark cannot be in focus at the same time. Either the top surface or the surrounding field can only be in focus.

Using the SLR with a stereo microscope can be convenient since as the coins are examined, any points of interest can be easily photographed. The greater depth of field and wider angle of the stereo microscope than the usual mono microscope makes it more suitable for coin photography.

SETTING UP THE CAMERA

Typically, the SLR camera in combination with a bellows and normal lens or a flat field lens is mounted on a copy stand. This gives a convenient method to raise and lower the whole combination over a flat surface onto which to place the coin. A tripod can also be used to mount the combination but it must be angled over the edge of a table and it is more difficult to raise and lower.

A "T" adapter is used to attach the camera body (either bayonet or threaded) to the threaded top of the bellows extension. A dual track bellow extension is preferable for stability and it should have a locking knob to secure the end of the bellows to the track. A separate focusing track where the bellows extension attaches to the copy stand allows focusing without changing the magnification but it is not necessary. A reverse ring adapter connects the outside of the camera lens to the end of the bellows. The camera lens attaches to the bellows in the reverse position. A normal focal length camera lens of about 50 mm is used. Most flat field lens will fit directly onto the bellows or extension tubes without ring adapters. The cable release is necessary to take vibration free shots.

The coin is laid on a protective cloth on the copy stand base or near the edge of a table if a tripod is used. The camera film plane must be parallel to the coin surface to prevent distortion.

If only some portion of the coin is to be photographed then the color of the background cloth or paper does not matter. Photographs of the full coin will show the background. For publications, usually only the coin is to be shown so a white background is used for black and white prints or just the coin is cut out of the print. A black background is sometimes used to sharpen the coin contrast (by reducing the flare in the camera lens) or to make a silver coin stand out more. For color slides or prints, a harmonizing or contrasting color background is used.

Plastic holders are available to hold the coin on its edge to take photographs of railroad rims. Special holders are also available or can be made with two mirrors at right angles to photograph coins with rotated reverses. In this case, the coin is placed on its edge between the vee formed by the two mirrors. The negative must be placed upside down in the enlarger to show the proper left-right relationship in the print for the rotated reverse taken with mirrors.

TAKING THE PICTURE

Before the coin is placed under the camera for close-up photographs, it should first be examined with a hand held magnifying glass to fix in one's mind the exact features to be captured in the photographs. The type and extent of doubling, orientation of the mint mark and date, or other feature details should be checked so it can later be detected through the camera view finder as the coin orientation and lighting is adjusted.

Next, the coin is placed under the camera in the approximate position for taking the picture. The camera lens "f stop" is adjusted to obtain a fairly bright image, usually about f/4 or /5.6. Then the copy stand height and bellows extension position is adjusted to bring the coin into focus on the ground glass or other type focusing screen in the SLR camera view finder. The coin is moved until the portion of the coin to be photographed comes

SPECIAL FLAT FIELD LENS

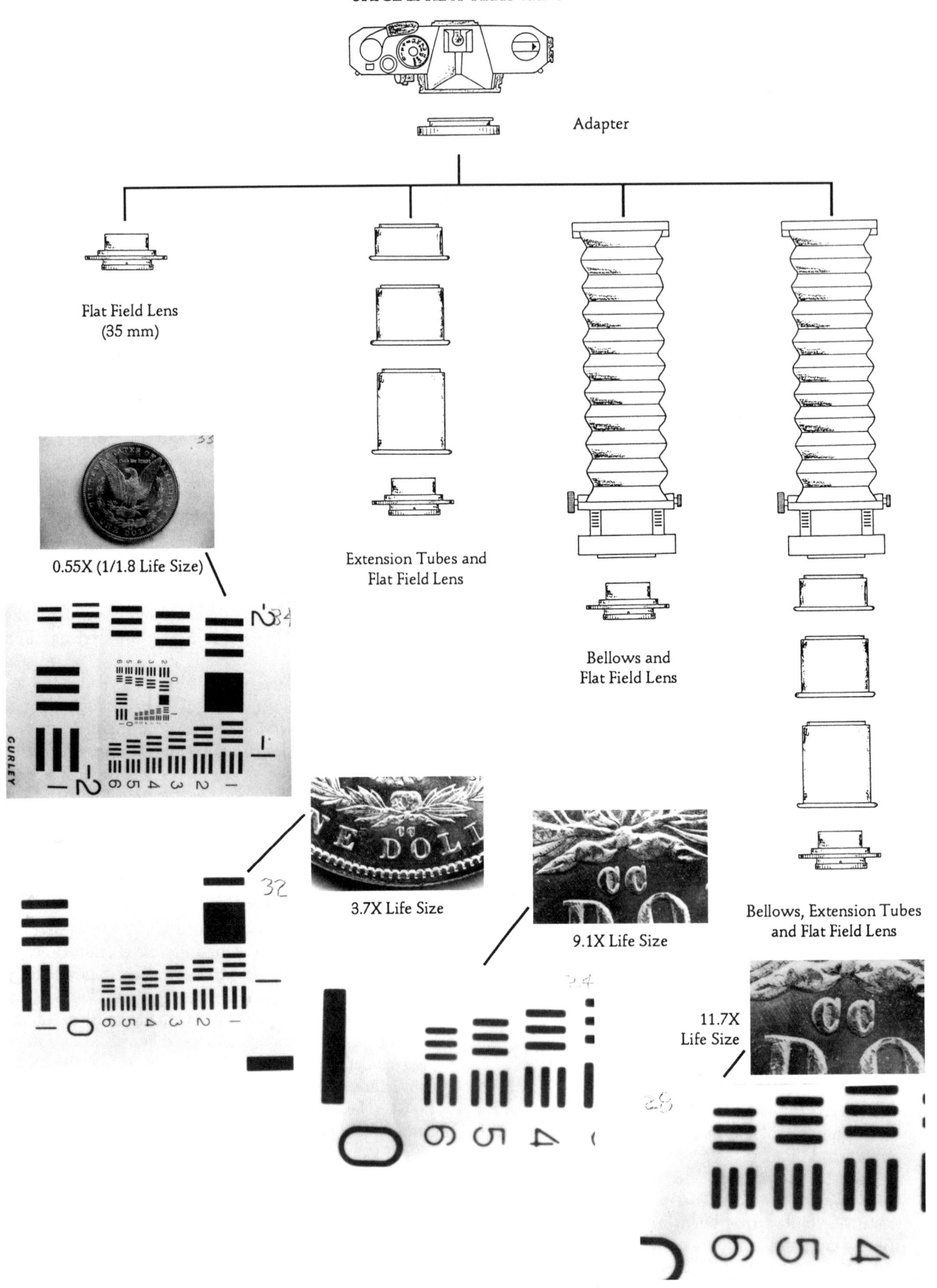

Adapter

Flat Field Lens (35 mm)

0.55X (1/1.8 Life Size)

Extension Tubes and Flat Field Lens

Bellows and Flat Field Lens

3.7X Life Size

9.1X Life Size

Bellows, Extension Tubes and Flat Field Lens

11.7X Life Size

PHOTOMICROGRAPHY

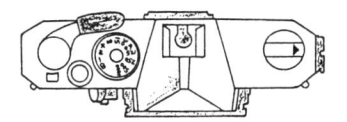

Camera Body

Adapter

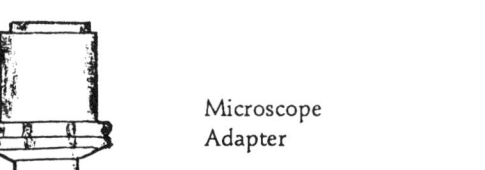

Microscope Adapter

Stereo or Mono Microscope

Microscope Adapter

26X Life Size

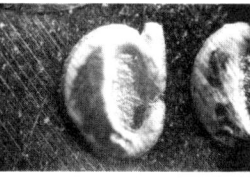

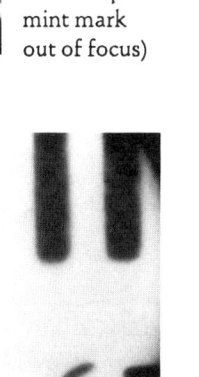

(Note extremely shallow depth of field – top of mint mark out of focus)

2X T-CONVERTER

7.7X Life Size
(With bellows, reverse ring and normal lens reversed)

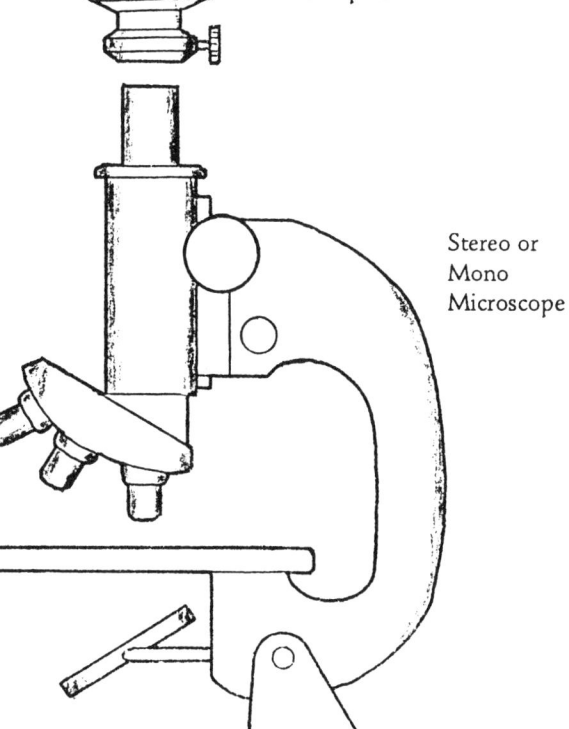

(Note some edge distortion)

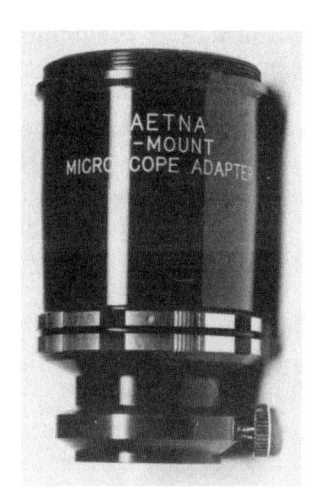

2X T-Converter

Camera Body, T-Adapter, Bellows, Extension Tubes, Flat Field Lens

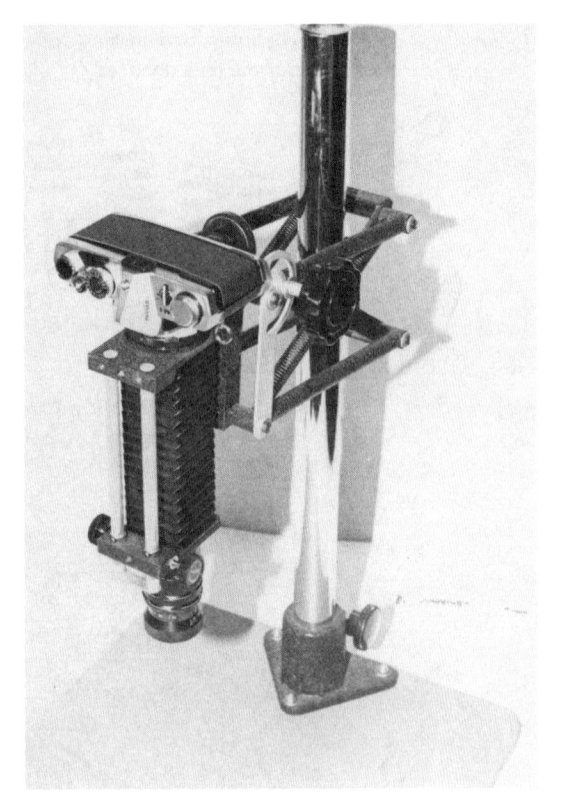

Camera with Bellows on Copy Stand

Camera and Bellows Extension
Left to right: SLR 35mm Camera Body, T-Adapter, Bellows Extension, Ring Adapter, Camera Lens (Reversed); Bottom: Cable Release

into view. An advantage of the SLR 35 mm camera is that the view finder shows exactly what will be taken by the film. Since focusing is also accomplished on the picture image coming through the camera lens, focusing is relatively easy.

Usually on the first try the coin image will not be of proper size. Either not all of the desired portion of the coin will be shown or it will be within only a small portion of the view-finder. The objective is to have the feature to be photographed cover most of the view-finder area and include some surrounding details to aid in the orientation or placement on the coin. The extension of the bellows and the copy stand height (or separate bellows camera track if available) are alternately adjusted until the desired portion of the coin fills the view-finder and is in focus. The bellows and copy stand are now locked in this position.

If photographs of the complete silver dollar are desired, several methods can be used. A normal camera lens in combination with a variable close-up supplemental lens will produce good results. A macro lens is most convenient with a wide range of focusing distance and yields excellent photographs. The normal camera lens can be reversed but is not recommended because of edge distortion introduced. Extension tubes can be used with the normal camera lens as long as the extension tube is not more than about half the lens focal length. Alternately, an inexpensive flat-field (enlarger) lens can be used. A 35 mm flat-field lens will allow about 0.5 life-size negatives but with a fixed focus it will provide only one size and the camera body must be moved to achieve correct focus on the coin. A longer focal length flat-field lens of 50 mm or 75 mm can be used with bellows to allow easier focusing.

A critical phase of photographing coins is adjusting the lighting. It is assumed that the coins have been cleaned if necessary. The lighting must now be adjusted to bring out the details desired; overall coin design, doubled details, or special details. This can be a very frustrating and time consuming job; and if it is not done properly a very unsatisfactory photograph will be produced even though the focusing and exposure were correct.

The light source is first placed near the bellows up high to give direct vertical lighting. This produces an even light over all the coin surface without shadows or strong reflected light spots. Usually this position will produce the best lighting results. The light source should be varied around the camera and in height and lateral position until the optimum combination is found. Doubled letters and designs are best shown with nearly vertical lighting to eliminate the strong shadows and bright spots.

The camera lens is now stepped down to f-8 or f-11. This increases the depth of the field so that all of the coin is in focus from the center to the edge of the frame and from the coin field to the tops of the coin design. In addition, the camera lens resolution is usually best in the range of f-5.6 to f-11.

Finally, the camera shutter speed must be set for the correct film exposure. Films such as Kodak Plus X for general purpose medium size prints and Kodak Pantatomic-X for extreme size enlargements produce satisfactory results. With film speed ratings of ASA 125 and 64, respectively, the exposure times for close-up pictures will be about ¼ to 1 second. The modern SLR 35 mm camera with built-in through the lens exposure metering system makes getting the correct film exposure for every frame very easy. Depending on the brand camera, the metering needle or indicator is set to the stopped down mark. Consult your particular camera manual on instructions for obtaining correct exposures for manual or stopped down exposure operation. To achieve the correct exposure indication, the shutter speed is adjusted in combination with the aperture setting (f-5.6 to f-11 in one half stops).

Colored 35 mm slides or prints of your coins can also be easily made with the SLR 35 mm camera. If outdoor film is used then it is best to take the photographs outdoors in direct sunlight. Filters are available to convert outdoor film to indoor lighting but the film speed is reduced by a factor of 2 to 3. This requires very long exposure times with most types of indoor lighting which may be outside the range of some camera metering systems.

A record of each exposure should be made by identifying the frame number, particular coin, and the detail of interest. The camera aperture and shutter setting may also want to be recorded; especially for the first few rolls of film shot of the coins. This allows a later appraisal of the correctness of the exposure and corrections to be made in subsequent rolls of film.

Use of camera types other than the SLR is much more difficult. The range finder type cameras have focusing indicators and metering systems that are separate from the camera lens. With close-up lens attached to the normal camera lens, focusing can be achieved by setting the camera lens to coin distance recommended for the particular close-up lens used. Alternatively, the back of the camera can be opened (before loading the film) and a piece of ground glass or waxed paper placed at the normal film very position. Then, with the shutter open in the time setting, the focusing adjustment can be made. The external exposure metering system will give an approximate exposure setting. This setting should be bracketed by higher and lower exposure settings for the first few rolls until the metering system suitability is established.

Modern twin lens reflex camera can also be used with close-up lens to take pictures of coins. Extreme close-up photographs with this type camera or the range finder type camera are not generally possible. The coin is placed under the viewing lens, with the camera set exactly parallel to the surface supporting the coin. With the close-up lens attached to the viewing lens, the camera focus and distance to the coin are adjusted to make the ground glass image sharp. If the camera had a built in exposure system, then it can be used to set the camera exposure. The coin is then centered in front of the main camera lens and the close-up lens attached to this lens.

PROCESSING THE FILM

The simplest way for film processing is to have it developed and prints made by a commercial firm. Alternatively, the film can be easily developed at home to save processing costs, obtain the developed film quicker, or to ensure consistently good results.

For film development at home all that is needed is a light tight roll film developing tank plus the developer, stop bath, and fixer solutions. All these items are inexpensive. A fine grain developer such as Microdol should be used, following the manufacturer's instructions. The film can be loaded into the developing tank in a closet or a closed room at night if a photographic dark room is not available.

If only a few frames of a roll have been exposed, then this part of a roll can be cut off in a suitable darkened room for immediate development at home. The end of the remaining unexposed portion of the film can be rethreaded into the camera's take-up spool after the leading edge is cut in half with scissors to form a leader. If many pictures of coins are to be made, it is usually cheaper to buy the film in bulk cans and load your own rolls.

MAKING YOUR OWN PRINTS

With access to a photographic enlarger, prints of the coins can also be made quite easily. Standard printing procedures and chemicals are used. A glossy white paper will give the best definition, but other textures can be used to suit one's preference. Single weight paper is satisfactory for most applications. If the print is to be published, a glossy white paper is preferred. Double weight paper minimizes the curling of the print edges, but single weight RC (resin coated) paper is acceptable nowadays for most publications.

The contrast of coins is very low since there is not the change of materials or reflectance found in the normal camera subjects. Thus, best prints are obtained if a slightly contrasting paper is used, about No. 3 paper.

This will show greater tone variation across the coin making the details more noticeable. If the print is to be published however, a slightly light print is desirable since the publishing process usually darkens the picture.

The record of the exposures taken for the roll being printed will have to be referred to in the darkroom. Most of the time, only a portion of the frame will need to be printed. Therefore, one must know what portion of the date or other coin area to print by referring to the exposure record and noting the detail of interest.

One standard darkroom technique that can be very useful in making coin prints is dodging. Often times, the lighting may not be even across the whole coin surface. This can be easily corrected in the printing process by dodging in the darker areas to lighten them (by interposing one's hand briefly over the photographic paper to block excess light in a particular area).

Index

Abbreviations, Glossary of Abbreviations, viii
Abrasions, 463, 470
Adjusting, 51
Annealing, 52
Appearance, 12
Assaying, 44
    cupellation, 44
    humid, 44
Availability, 3
    (See also Condition availability)
"Belly button", 132
Bibliographies, 36, 64, 453
Bland-Allison Act, 4, 36, 37
Bowers, 67
Bullion deposit, 42
    melting, 42
    weighing, 42
Bullion refining, 45
    electrolytic process, 47
    melt, 45
    nitric acid process, 45
    parting, 45
    sulfuric acid process, 46
Camera lens, 493
    converter 2x, 499
    extensions, 494
    flat field, 499
    normal, 493
    reversing, 496
    supplemental, 494
Cameras, 493
    film, 503
    lens, 493
    setting up, 499
    taking pictures, 499
    with microscopes, 499
CARMICHAEL, 65
CARTER, 69
Cast coins, 439, 441
    modern process, 442
    sand mold, 442
CLARK, 67
Clashed dies
    Morgan dollar, 119
    Peace dollar, 420
Cleaning coins, 455
Cleaning planchets, 52
Coin alteration, 439, 451
    date, 452
    mint mark, 451
    split coin, 453
    surface, 452
Coin presses, 62
Coinage Act of 1965, 35
Coinage authorities, 36
Coinage operations, 59
Coining costs, 26
Coin Investor's Report, 69

Coins
    cleaning, 455
    counting, 62
    examination, 141, 466, 467, 469
    photographing, 493
    striking, 61
    ringing, 62
    testing, 62
    weighing, 62
Collars, 59
Color, 463, 477
Condition availability, 12, 463
    Morgan dollar, 14, 17-19, 141
    Peace dollar, 15, 18, 427
Contaminants, 455
    carbon spots, 456
    circulation grime, 457
    dirt, 456, 478
    fingerprints, 479
    impure metal streaks, 456, 478
    toning, 456, 477
    water spots, 478
    wood, 457
Continental-Illinois Bank hoard, 407
Counterfeit detection, 439, 440
Counting, 62
Crime of '73, 21
Dash under date, 114
Date numerals
    Morgan dollar, 123, 124
    Peace dollar, 419
    position, Morgan, 114
DE FRANCISCI, 410
DELOREY, 67
Deposit melting, 42
Deposit payment, 45
Deposit weighing, 42
Design
    combinations
        Morgan dollar, 99
        Peace dollar, 416
    descriptions
        Morgan dollar, 97
        Peace dollar, 413
    evolution
        Morgan dollar, 73
        Peace dollar, 409
    identification, 98, 413
Die
    average pieces struck, 60
    basining, 86, 95, 481
    breaks, 89, 108, 420
    clashed
        Morgan dollar, 119
        Peace dollar, 420
    classification, 139
    design preparation, 54
    design reduction, 55

Die, *continued*
- dots, 125, 422
- doubled
  - Morgan dollar, 109
  - Peace dollar, 422
- dual hub, 86, 89, 110
- false (see false dies)
- identifying marks, 123
- hub hardening, 56
- marriages, 1878-P, 128, 130
- master hub and die doubling, 131
- master die preparation, 52
- overpolished, 121
- preparation, 52
- production, 59, 60
- re-engraved, 108
- rotated, 132, 422
- scratches and gouges, 120
- variety descriptions
  - Morgan dollar, 141
  - Peace dollar, 427
- working dies preparation, 57

Doubled LIBERTY, 89, 96, 112, 148-160
Draw benches, 50
DROST, 66
Dual hub, 110
Dual mint mark, 118, 469
Edge reeding, 95, 126
Edges, 449
Electrolytic process, 47
False dies, 439, 444
- cast, 449
- electrochemical machining, 449
- hand cut, 445
- impact, 447
- machine engraving, 445
- powdered metal, 449
- spark erosion, 447

"Far date", 115
Fineness, 44-48, 63
FOX, 68
General minting operations, 39
Grading, 461
- 1980's, 461
- coin grading machines, 462
- early development, 461
- examination, 466
- factors, 463
  - Morgan dollar, 483
  - Peace dollar, 487
- proofs, 482
- scale, 466

GSA, 397
- Carson City dollar sales, 397, 400
- dollar holdings, 398, 399
- packaging dollars, 400
- survey of dollars, 399

HAGER, 69
Hairlines, 470
HALPERN, 69
"Hangnail" eagle, 201
Hayes specimen silver dollar, 86

HERBERT, 68
HIGHFILL, 69, 139, 407
HOWARD, 69
HOWE, 69
Hub preparation, 56, 76
HURLBUT, 65
Important events affecting silver dollars, 37
Ingot preparation, 47
- assays, 49
- melts, 48

Interest factor, viii, 141
IVY, 69
JULIAN, 68
KLAES, 66
Legend, ix
Legislation of August 3, 1964, 35
LEMKE, 68
Lighting, 466, 467
Light strike, 131, 471
LUDWIG, 68
Luster, 463, 474
Magnifying glass, 568
MALLIS, 66, 118, 399
MARGOLIS, 61
McILVAINE, 65
Melted dollars, 33
Microscope, 468, 499
MILLER, 68, 139
Mint mark
- description
  - Morgan dollar, 122
  - Peace dollar, 419
- doubled, 117
- dual, 118
- mispositioned
  - Morgan dollar, 116
  - Peace dollar, 419

Mint organization, 42
Mintages, 22, 23, 27
Minting operations, 39
MORGAN, George, 73-93, 411
- design changes after 1878, 94
- half dollar patterns, 75-81
- initial silver dollar design, 80-84
- regular silver dollar design, 84-94

MORANO, 66
Motto, ix
"Near date" 115
Nitric acid process, 45
NEWCOMB, 65
Obverse, 98, 413
OSBON, 67
Overdates, 117, 469
Over mint marks, 118, 469
Parting, 45
Patterns, 75-83
Photographing coins, 493, 499
- lighting, 502
- making prints, 503
- processing film, 503

Pittman Act, 30, 36, 37
Planchets, 51

Planchets, *continued*
    adjusting, 51
    annealing, 52
    cleaning, 52
    cutting, 51
    errors, 107
    upsetting, 52
    weighing, 51
Polished, 471
Popularity, 3
Preparation of ingot strips, 47
Preparing bullion melt, 45
Preservation, 455
    handling, 455
    removal of contaminants, 455
    storage, 457
Price, 4
Price history, 5
Price trends, 6-11
    boom and bust of 1980's, 8
    common date, 10
    M2 growth, 11
    roll, 9
    retail sales growth, 11
    silver bullion, 9, 24
    scarcer dates, 10
Production of planchets, 51
Proof-like, 463, 479, 481
Proofs, 84, 87, 94, 96, 411, 481, 482
Public Law 88-36 of 1963, 35
Rarity scale, viii, 141
Receipt of bullion, 42
Redfield hoard, 403
REED, 69
Reeding, 95, 126
Remaining quantities, 3, 4
Reverse, 97, 413
Rim dents, 470
Rolling of strips, 49
Rotated dies (See Die, rotated)
ROUSSO, 68
Seven over eight tail feathers, 89, 96, 111, 150-153
SHAFFER, 6 6
Sherman Silver Purchase Act, 27, 36, 37
"Shifted" eagle, 110, 361
Silver
    price 9, 24
    Purchase Act, 34, 37
    sources, 41
    strips, 49
    annealing, 49
    rolling, 49

Silver dollar coinage
    daily, 1878, 87
    first dollars struck, 84-86, 90, 91, 411
    weekly, 1878, 87
Silver dollars in circulation, 4
Size and design, 12
SMITH, 6 9
SPADONE, 67
SPEER, 68
Storage, 455, 457
    albums, 460
    bulk, 458
    holders, 458
Strike, 463, 471
Striking errors, 131
    broadstrikes, 132, 423
    capped die, 136
    die pressure adjustment pieces, 131
    machine doubling, 137, 420
    misaligned dies, 132
    multiple strikes, 134, 423
    off-center strikes, 134
    partial collar, 133, 423
    rotated dies, 132, 422
    struck through strikes, 136, 423
    weak strikes, 131
    Sulfuric acid process, 46
Summary of events affecting silver dollars, 37
Symbol, ix
"Tailbar", 1890CC, 121, 304
Thomas Amendments, 34, 37
Toning, 456, 47 7
Treasury release, 3
Upsetting, 52
VAM number, vi, 141
VAN ALLEN, 66, 111, 112, 399
Varieties
    causes, 107
    examination 141, 467
    identification, 469
    literature, 65
WALLACE, 6 5
Weak strikes, 131, 471
Wear, 4 7 0
Weighing, 42, 51, 62
WOODRUFF, 6 9
Working dies preparation, 57
Zink, 69

NEW VARIETIES SINCE 1991
December 1, 1997

1878 P

14-11 I^{1}11 • A^{1}c (Doubled Eyelid) (189?) I-3 R-7
  Obverse I^{1}11– Eyelid doubled as short, thick and blunt spike just below eyelid plus a long thin spike angled downward in front of lower part of eye. E and P of E PLURIBUS doubled in clockwise direction. Raised metal in first 8 in date. Ear over polished. Strong doubling along top edges of many obverse stars.

14-12 I^{1}12 • A^{1}c (Doubled Date) (189?) I-3 R-7
  Obverse I^{1}12– Thin spike below eyelid. Slightly doubled date. 1 doubled below upper crossbar, first 8 doubled at top inside of both loops and bottom left outside of upper loop, 7 doubled below crossbar and right side of vertical shaft, second 8 doubled at top inside and bottom left outside of upper loop.
  Reverse A^{1}c– Die further polished down.

14-13 I^{1}13 • A^{1}n (Bar Eyelid) (189) I-3 R-7
  Obverse I^{1}13– Extra metal in front of eye as thick bar just below front of eyelid. Date tripled with 1 slightly tripled at lower left outside and top inside of upper loop. 7 slightly tripled below crossbar and doubled at top right. Second 8 slightly tripled at lower left outside of upper loop. All right stars very slightly doubled towards rim.

14-14 I^{1}14 • A^{1}c (Doubled LIBERTY) (189) I-3 R-7
  Obverse I^{1}14– Slightly doubled LIBERTY on right side, E PLURIB at top outside, tops of cotton leaves, bottom of nostril and nose and right side of 7. All left stars doubled towards rim and first 3 right stars tripled and 4-6 right stars doubled towards rim. Spike below eyelid and small die chip in front of lower eye. Horizontal and vertical die cracks through second 8.

14-15 I^{1}2 • A^{1}l (Doubled Motto) (193) I-3 R-7

199-1 II/I 17 • B^{2}f (Tripled Cotton Bolls) (194) I-3 R-6

1878 S

26 II 23 • B^{1}a (Long Center Arrow Shaft, S Tilted Left) (186) I-3 R-7
  Obverse II 23– Eyelid doubled at bottom front and short spikes at eye bottom front and lower part of eye socket.
  Reverse B^{1}a– Normal die of 1878 P B1 type with long center arrow shaft. Small III S mint mark set slightly to right with slight tilt to left.

27 II 1 • B^{1}b (Long Center Arrow Shaft) (185) I-3 R-7
  Reverse B^{1}b– Small III S mint mark centered and upright.

56 II 24 • B^{1}c (Long Center Arrow Shaft, S Set High) (184) I-3 R-7
  Obverse II 24– Two horizontal bars out from front of eye. L of LIBERTY slightly doubled on lower left serif.
  Reverse B^{1}c– Small III S mint mark set high, slightly to left and upright.

57 II 23 • B^{1}d (Long Center Arrow Shaft, S Set Left) (?) I-3 R-7
  Reverse B^{1}d– Small III S mint mark set slightly left well below wreath, with slight tilt to left. Die chip in G of GOD.

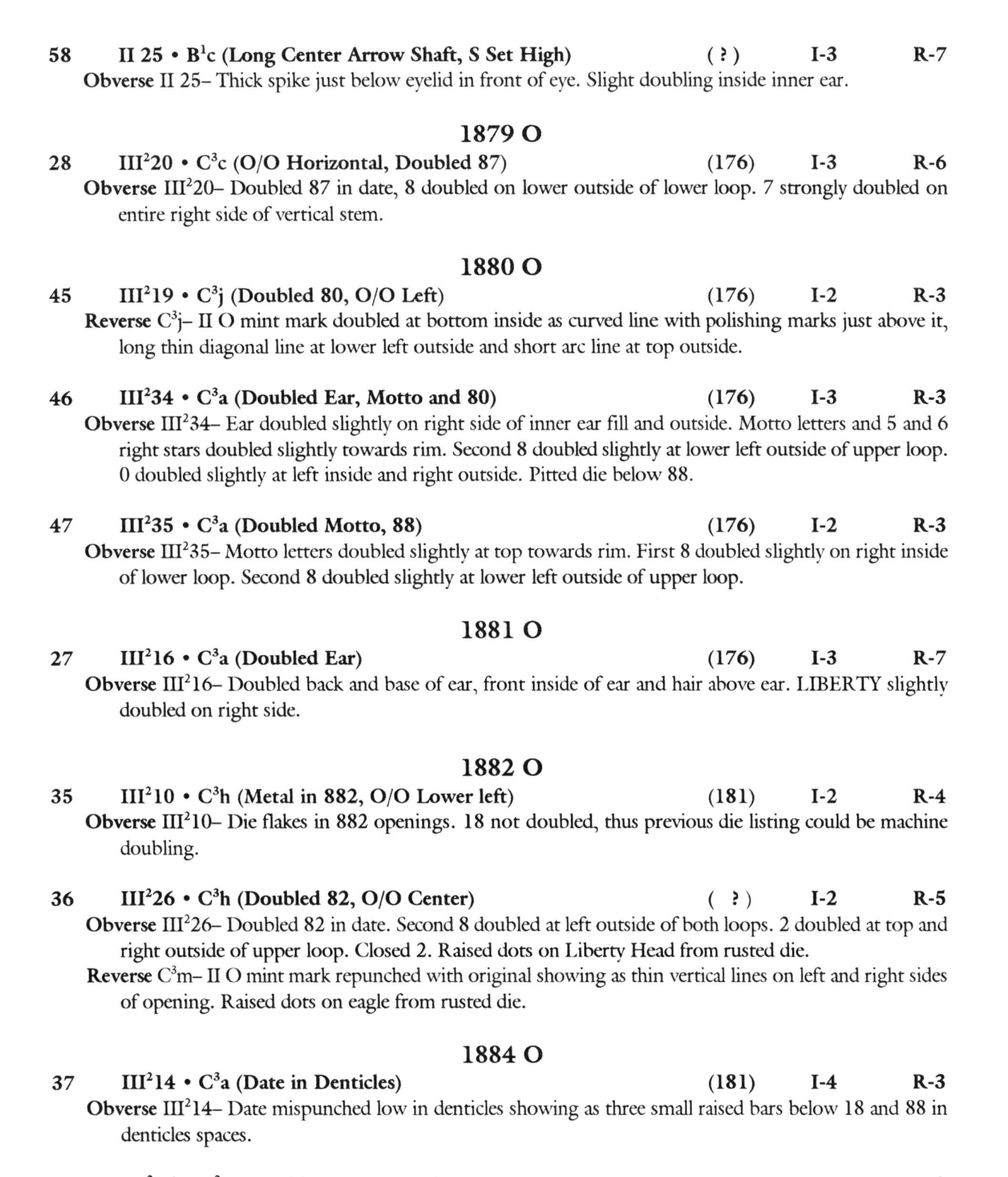

58   II 25 • B¹c (Long Center Arrow Shaft, S Set High)   (?)   I-3   R-7
      Obverse II 25– Thick spike just below eyelid in front of eye. Slight doubling inside inner ear.

1879 O

28   III²20 • C³c (O/O Horizontal, Doubled 87)   (176)   I-3   R-6
      Obverse III²20– Doubled 87 in date, 8 doubled on lower outside of lower loop. 7 strongly doubled on
      entire right side of vertical stem.

1880 O

45   III²19 • C³j (Doubled 80, O/O Left)   (176)   I-2   R-3
      Reverse C³j– II O mint mark doubled at bottom inside as curved line with polishing marks just above it,
      long thin diagonal line at lower left outside and short arc line at top outside.

46   III²34 • C³a (Doubled Ear, Motto and 80)   (176)   I-3   R-3
      Obverse III²34– Ear doubled slightly on right side of inner ear fill and outside. Motto letters and 5 and 6
      right stars doubled slightly towards rim. Second 8 doubled slightly at lower left outside of upper loop.
      0 doubled slightly at left inside and right outside. Pitted die below 88.

47   III²35 • C³a (Doubled Motto, 88)   (176)   I-2   R-3
      Obverse III²35– Motto letters doubled slightly at top towards rim. First 8 doubled slightly on right inside
      of lower loop. Second 8 doubled slightly at lower left outside of upper loop.

1881 O

27   III²16 • C³a (Doubled Ear)   (176)   I-3   R-7
      Obverse III²16– Doubled back and base of ear, front inside of ear and hair above ear. LIBERTY slightly
      doubled on right side.

1882 O

35   III²10 • C³h (Metal in 882, O/O Lower left)   (181)   I-2   R-4
      Obverse III²10– Die flakes in 882 openings. 18 not doubled, thus previous die listing could be machine
      doubling.

36   III²26 • C³h (Doubled 82, O/O Center)   (?)   I-2   R-5
      Obverse III²26– Doubled 82 in date. Second 8 doubled at left outside of both loops. 2 doubled at top and
      right outside of upper loop. Closed 2. Raised dots on Liberty Head from rusted die.
      Reverse C³m– II O mint mark repunched with original showing as thin vertical lines on left and right sides
      of opening. Raised dots on eagle from rusted die.

1884 O

37   III²14 • C³a (Date in Denticles)   (181)   I-4   R-3
      Obverse III²14– Date mispunched low in denticles showing as three small raised bars below 18 and 88 in
      denticles spaces.

38   III²15 • C³a (Possible ES in Denticles)   (181)   I-4   R-3
      Obverse III²15– Raised curved line in denticle space below first 8 and raised curved bar with straight top
      below second 8. Possible ES in STATES from reverse hub impressed in denticle spacing below 88.
      Perhaps used to position second 8 of date on vertical center line above E impression.

1885 P

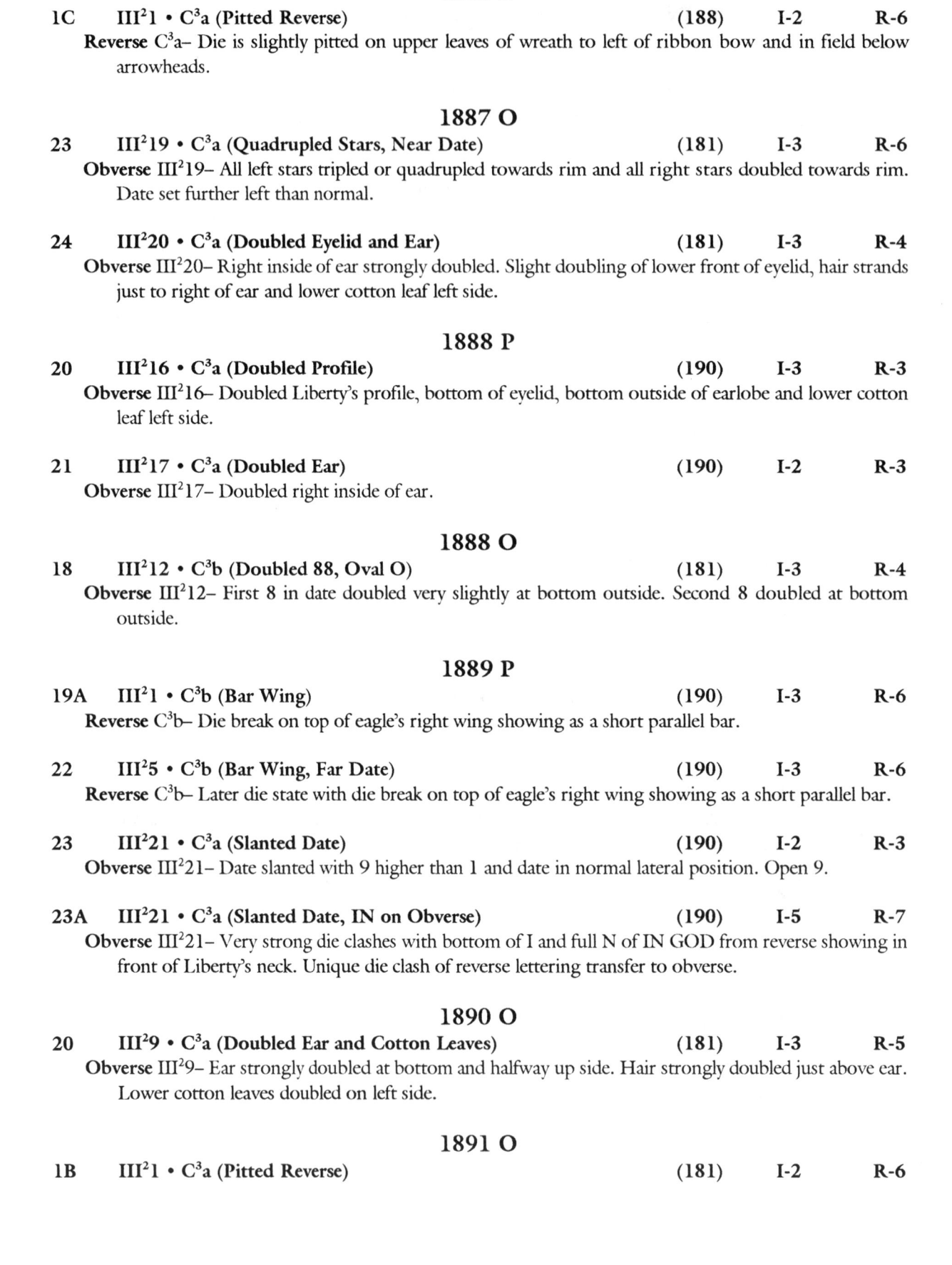

1C   III^{2}1 • C^{3}a (Pitted Reverse)   (188)   I-2   R-6

Reverse C^{3}a– Die is slightly pitted on upper leaves of wreath to left of ribbon bow and in field below arrowheads.

1887 O

23   III^{2}19 • C^{3}a (Quadrupled Stars, Near Date)   (181)   I-3   R-6

Obverse III^{2}19– All left stars tripled or quadrupled towards rim and all right stars doubled towards rim. Date set further left than normal.

24   III^{2}20 • C^{3}a (Doubled Eyelid and Ear)   (181)   I-3   R-4

Obverse III^{2}20– Right inside of ear strongly doubled. Slight doubling of lower front of eyelid, hair strands just to right of ear and lower cotton leaf left side.

1888 P

20   III^{2}16 • C^{3}a (Doubled Profile)   (190)   I-3   R-3

Obverse III^{2}16– Doubled Liberty's profile, bottom of eyelid, bottom outside of earlobe and lower cotton leaf left side.

21   III^{2}17 • C^{3}a (Doubled Ear)   (190)   I-2   R-3

Obverse III^{2}17– Doubled right inside of ear.

1888 O

18   III^{2}12 • C^{3}b (Doubled 88, Oval O)   (181)   I-3   R-4

Obverse III^{2}12– First 8 in date doubled very slightly at bottom outside. Second 8 doubled at bottom outside.

1889 P

19A   III^{2}1 • C^{3}b (Bar Wing)   (190)   I-3   R-6

Reverse C^{3}b– Die break on top of eagle's right wing showing as a short parallel bar.

22   III^{2}5 • C^{3}b (Bar Wing, Far Date)   (190)   I-3   R-6

Reverse C^{3}b– Later die state with die break on top of eagle's right wing showing as a short parallel bar.

23   III^{2}21 • C^{3}a (Slanted Date)   (190)   I-2   R-3

Obverse III^{2}21– Date slanted with 9 higher than 1 and date in normal lateral position. Open 9.

23A   III^{2}21 • C^{3}a (Slanted Date, IN on Obverse)   (190)   I-5   R-7

Obverse III^{2}21– Very strong die clashes with bottom of I and full N of IN GOD from reverse showing in front of Liberty's neck. Unique die clash of reverse lettering transfer to obverse.

1890 O

20   III^{2}9 • C^{3}a (Doubled Ear and Cotton Leaves)   (181)   I-3   R-5

Obverse III^{2}9– Ear strongly doubled at bottom and halfway up side. Hair strongly doubled just above ear. Lower cotton leaves doubled on left side.

1891 O

1B   III^{2}1 • C^{3}a (Pitted Reverse)   (181)   I-2   R-6

Reverse C³a– Die is pitted on lower left of wreath extending down to E on ONE and from N of ONE down into denticles.

1896 P

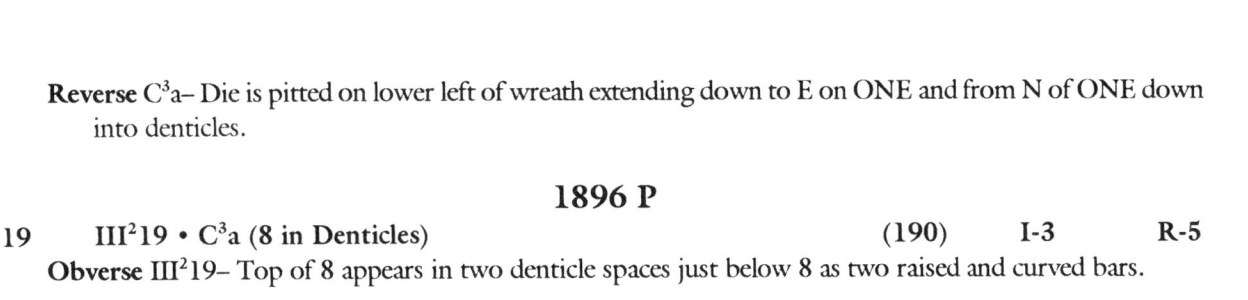

19   III²19 • C³a (8 in Denticles)   (190)   I-3   R-5
   Obverse III²19– Top of 8 appears in two denticle spaces just below 8 as two raised and curved bars.

1899 O

30   III²18 • C³b (Doubled 189, High O Tilted Right)   (?)   I-2   R-5
   Obverse III²18– Doubled 189 in date. 1 is doubled slightly at bottom. 8 is doubled as thin lines well separated from right outside of upper loop and bottom right and right outside of lower loop. 9 is doubled as short thin vertical line in middle of upper loop.

1900 P

24   III²19 • C⁴/C³a (Doubled Eagle, Quintupled Stars)   (189)   I-4   R-5
   Obverse III²19– All right stars and 1 and 2 left stars very slightly quintupled towards rim. Remainder of left stars doubled and tripled as are tops of NUM.

1901 P

11   III²5 • C⁴/C³? (Doubled Hair Above Ear)   (189)   I-3   R-5
   Obverse III²5– Hair above ear doubled as well as forehead and profile with slight spike below eyelid.

1903 O

12   III²6 • C⁴g (O/O Down)   (?)   I-3   R-3
   Obverse III²6– Very slightly doubled nose, lips and chin of Liberty head profile. Closed 9.
   Reverse C⁴g– III O mint mark repunched with original showing as a thin curved line at lower left outside and slight short horizontal line next to top right outside.

1922 P

2G   II 1 • B²a (Scar Cheek)   I-3   R-6
   Obverse II 1– Vertical die break and large die chip just behind Liberty's mouth.

6   II 1 • B²d (Doubled Reverse)   I-3   R-3
   Reverse B²d– Doubled bottom of olive leaves, berries and stems, back of leg feathers, lower rays, base of DOLLAR and E of E PLURIBUS.

7   II 1 • B²e (Doubled Wing)   I-3   R-3
   Reverse B²e– Strong doubling on eagle's right wing and down right edge and slightly doubled stems and bottoms of top olive leaves.

1922 D

4   II 2 • B²c (Doubled TRUST)   I-3   R-3
   Obverse II 2– TRUST, de Francisci's monogram and date doubled towards rim with slight doubling along bottom of neck and WE.
   Reverse B²c– Doubled bottom edge of right leaves, left edge of eagle's left leg feathers and rays below leg feathers.

1922 S

3   II 1 • B²b (Tripled Reverse)   I-3   R-3

Reverse B²b– Tripled front edge of eagle's right wing, doubled top of eagle's head, top inside of upper beak, throat and right edge of neck feathers, tripled rays below, thru and above ONE, doubled back of leg feathers, slightly doubled right side of rays thru DOLLAR, slightly tripled lower olive leaves and doubled top olive leaf on left side.

1925 S

3   II 1 • B²c (Doubled Wing)   I-3   R-3

Reverse B²c– Doubled outside edge of eagle's right wing from shoulder down to right talon, bottoms of eagle's right leg feathers and bottom edges of top olive leaves.

1926 P

3   II 2 • B²c (Doubled 6)   I-3   R-3

Obverse II 2– Doubled tip of 6 in date, designer's initial and T in TRUST.

1878 P 14-11 O I^{1}11

1878 P 14-12 O I1 ^{1}2

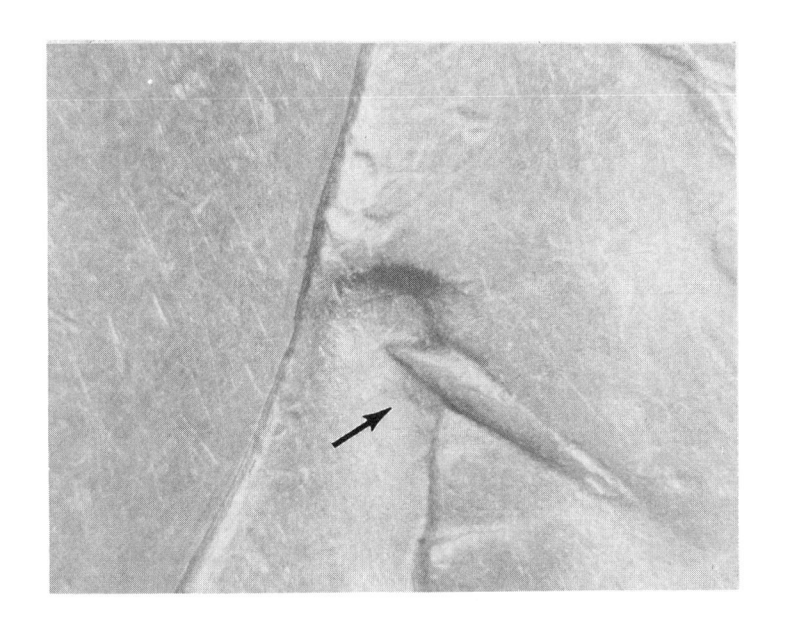

1878 P 14-13 O I^1 13

1878 P 14-14 O I^1 14

1878 S 26 O II 23

1878 S 56 O II 24

1878 S 56 R B¹c

1878 S 57 R B¹d

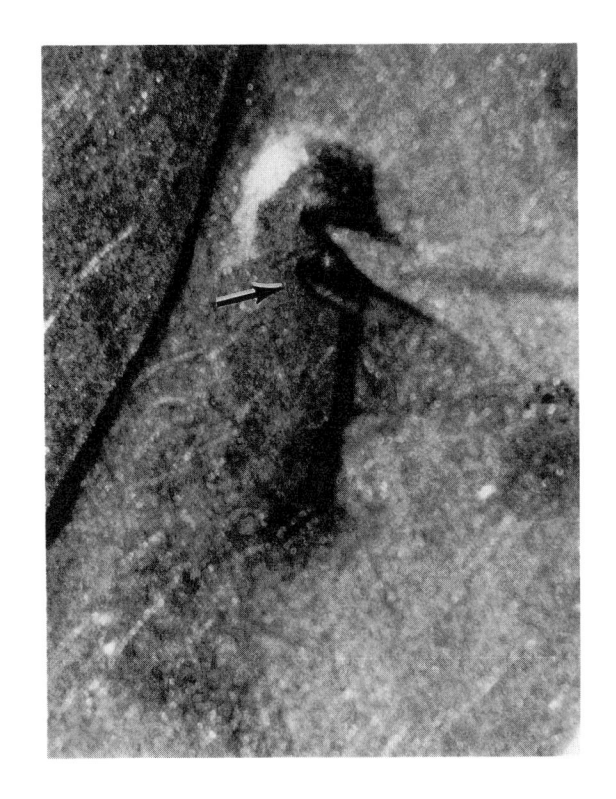

1878 S 58 O   II 25

1879 O
Doubled 87
28 O   III^2 20

1880 O
O/O Left
45 R C^{3}j

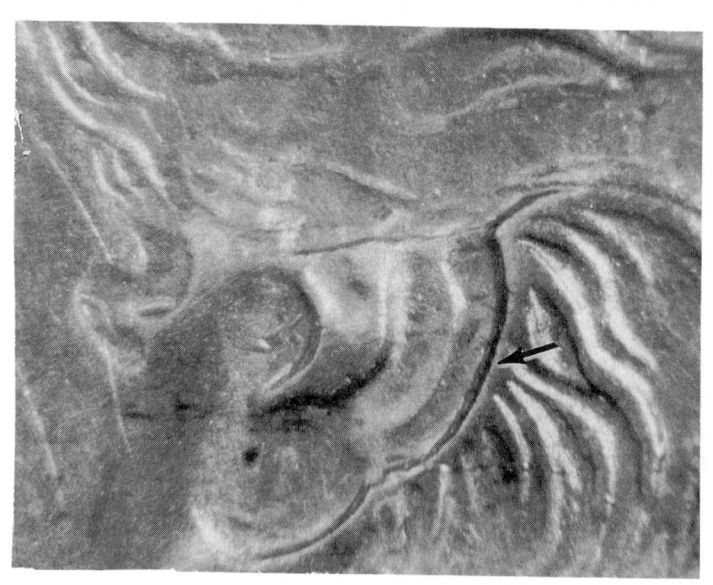

1880 Doubled ear
46 O III^2 34

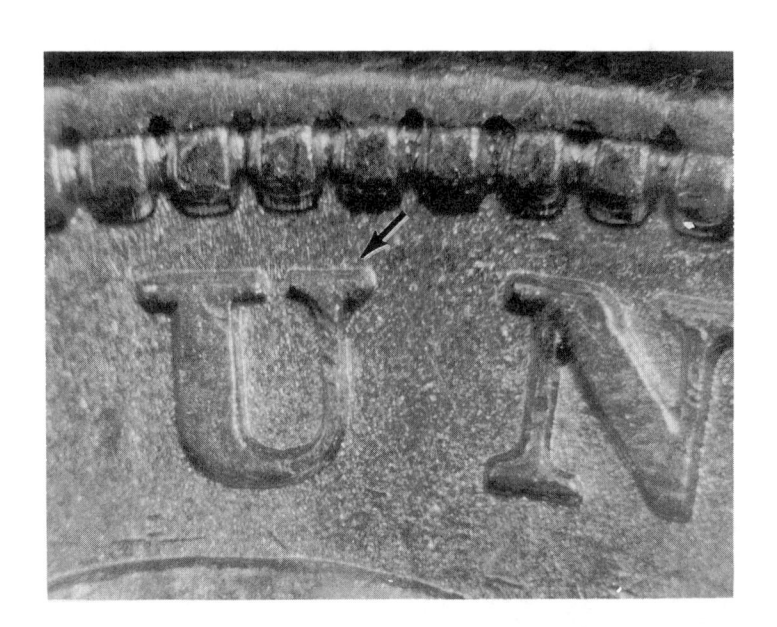

1880 O
Doubled motto, 88
47 O III^2 35

1881 O
Doubled ear
27 O III^2 16

1882 O
Dobuled 82
36 O III^2 26

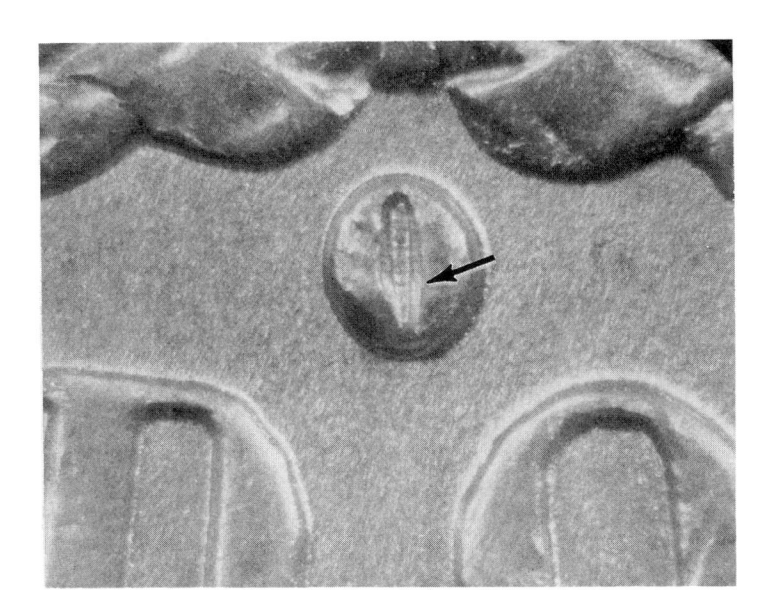

1882 O
O/O Center
36 R C^{3}h

1884 O
Date in denticles
37 O III^2 14

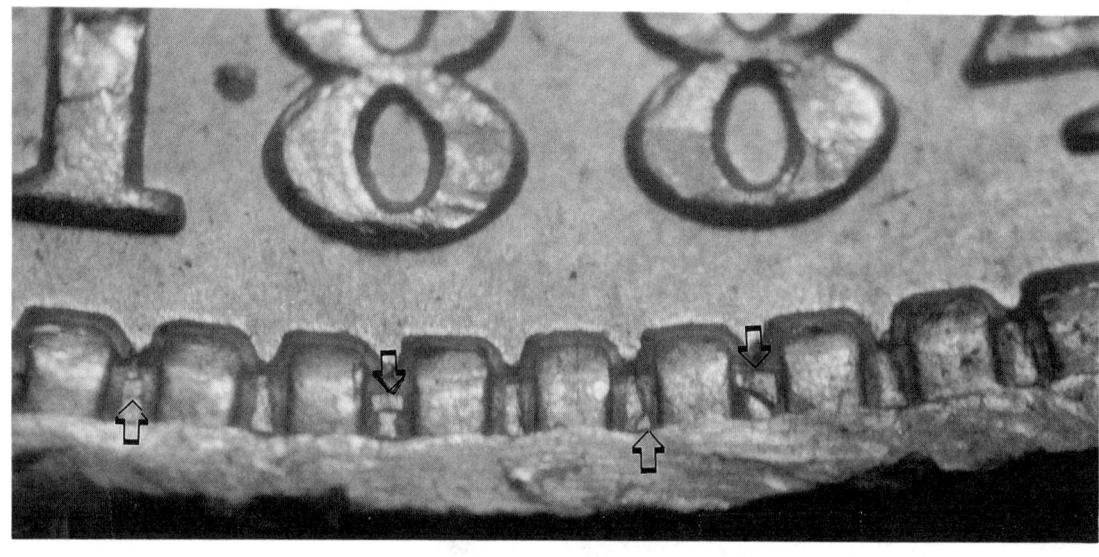

1884 O
ES in Denticles
38 O III^{2}15

1885 P
Pitted Reverse
1C R C^{3}a

1887 O
Doubled ear
24 O III^2 20

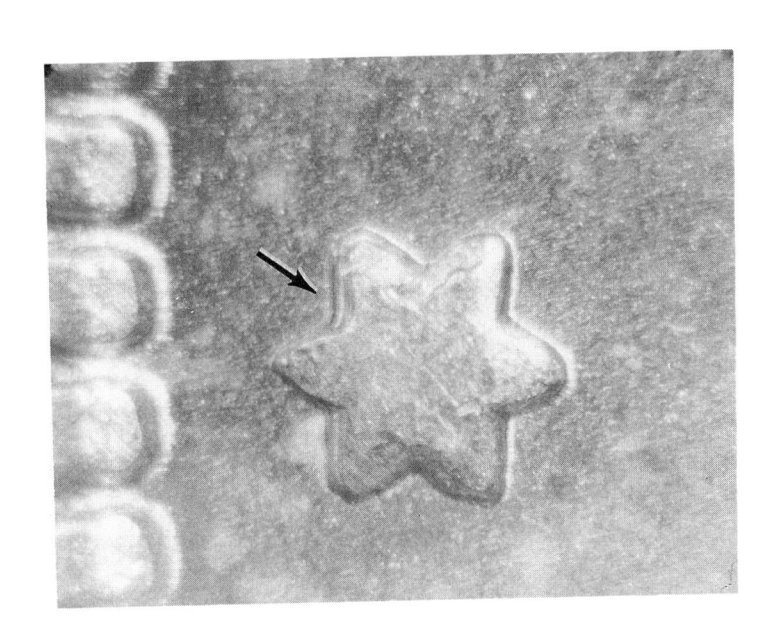

1887 O
Quadrupled stars
23 O III^2 19

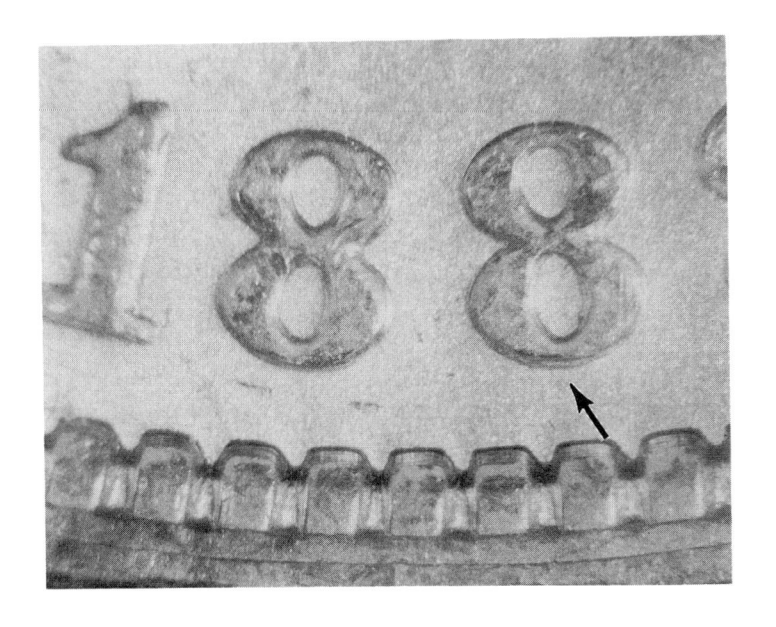

1888 O
Doubled 88
18 O III^2 12

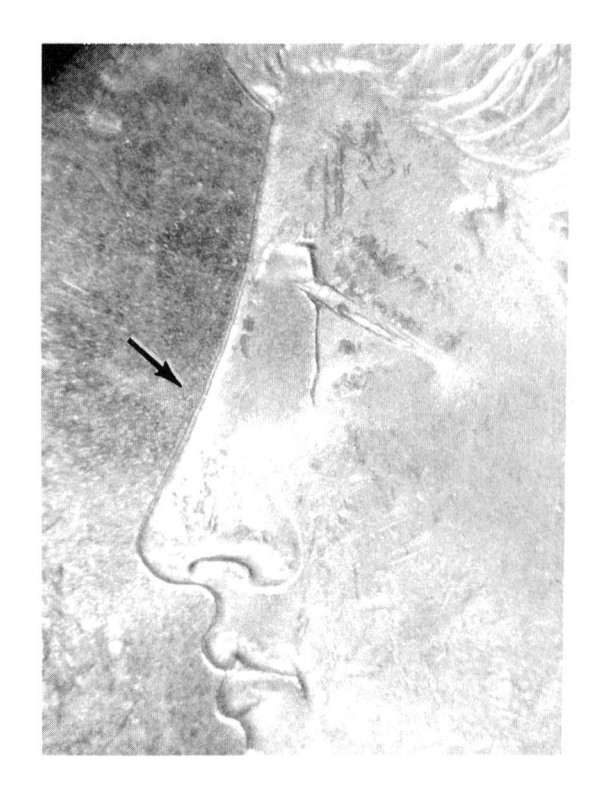

1888 P
Doubled Profile
20 O III^2 16

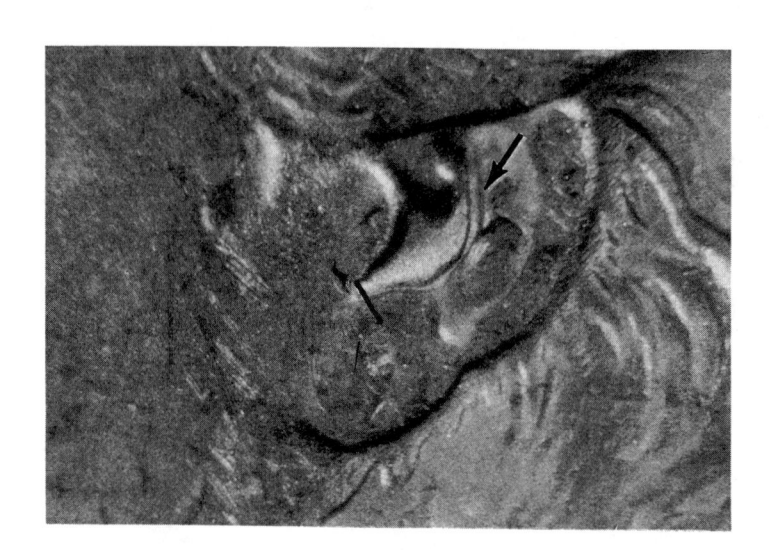

1888 P
Doubled ear
21 O III^2 17

1889 P
Slanted date
23 O III^2 21

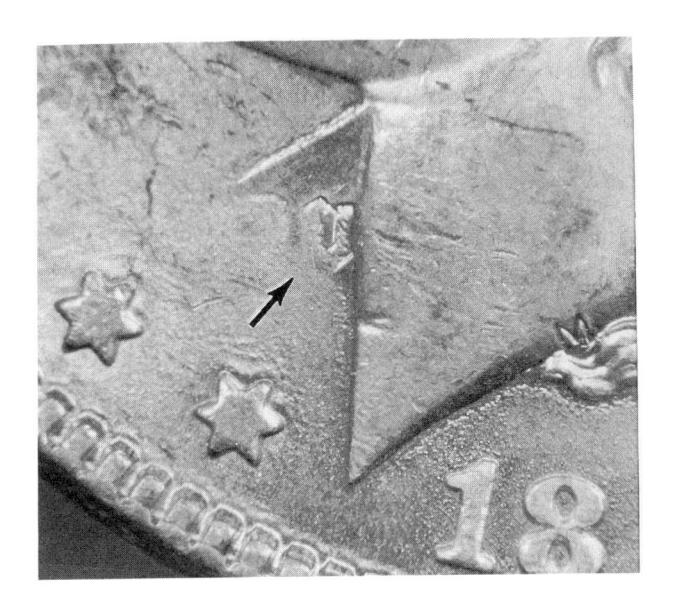

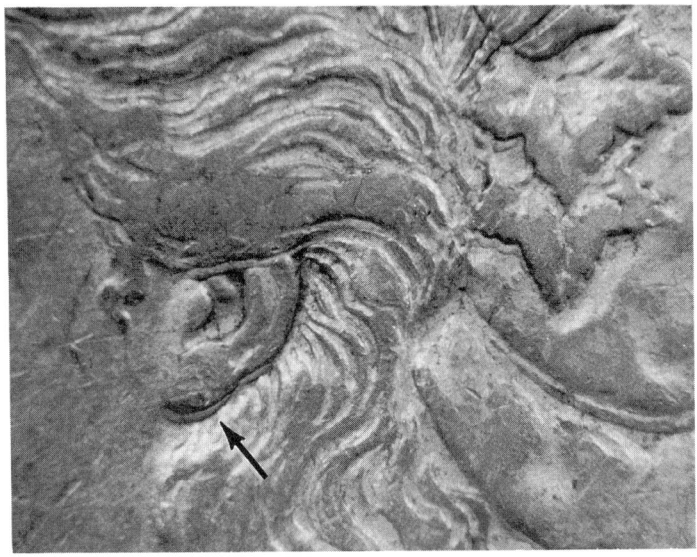

1889 P
In on Obverse
23 A O III^2 21

1890 O
Doubled ear
20 O III^2 9

1891 O
Pitted Reverse
1 B O III^2 1

1896 P
8 In Denticles
19 O   III^2 19

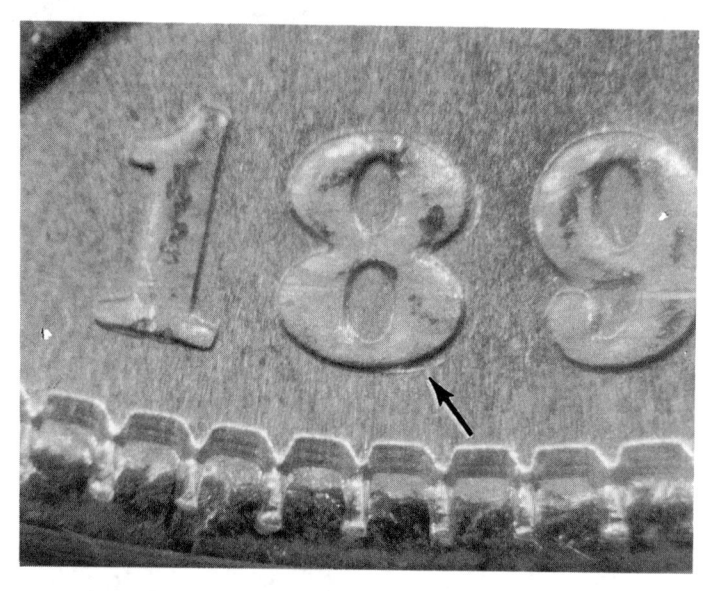

1899 O
Doubled 189
30 O   III^2 18

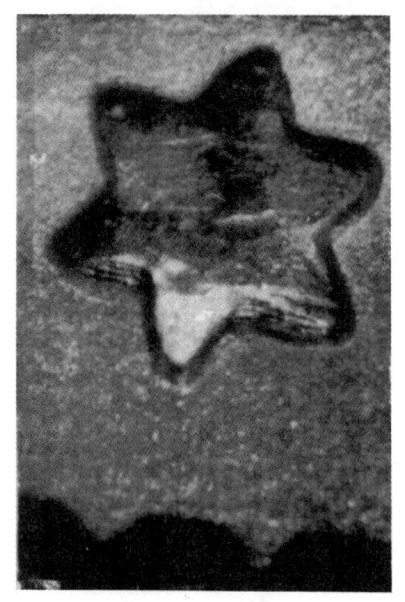

1903 O
O/O Down
12 R   C^4 g

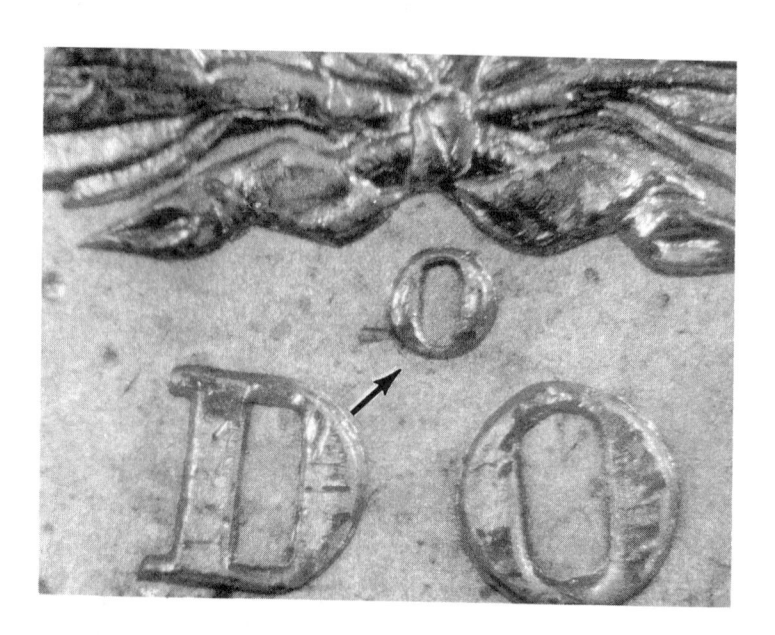

1900 P
Quintupled stars
24 O   III^2 19

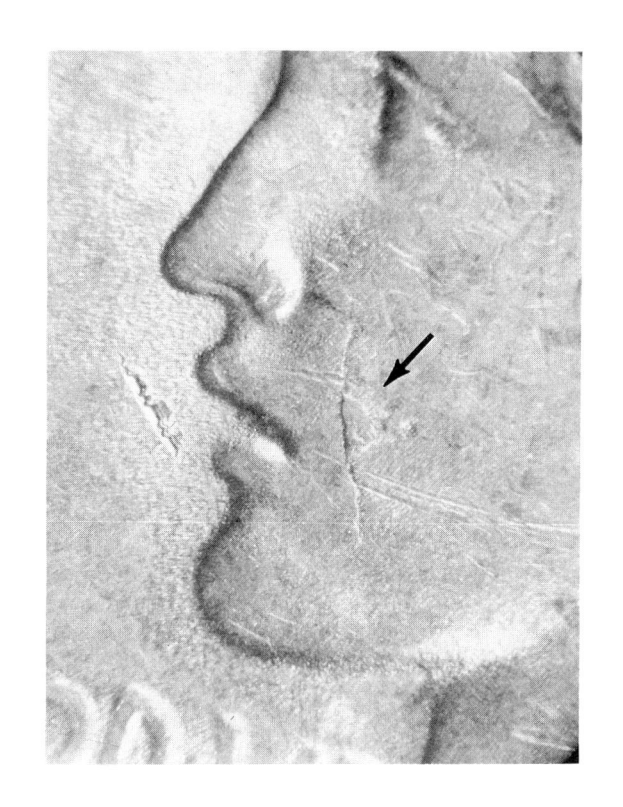

1922 P
Scar cheek
2 G O   II 1

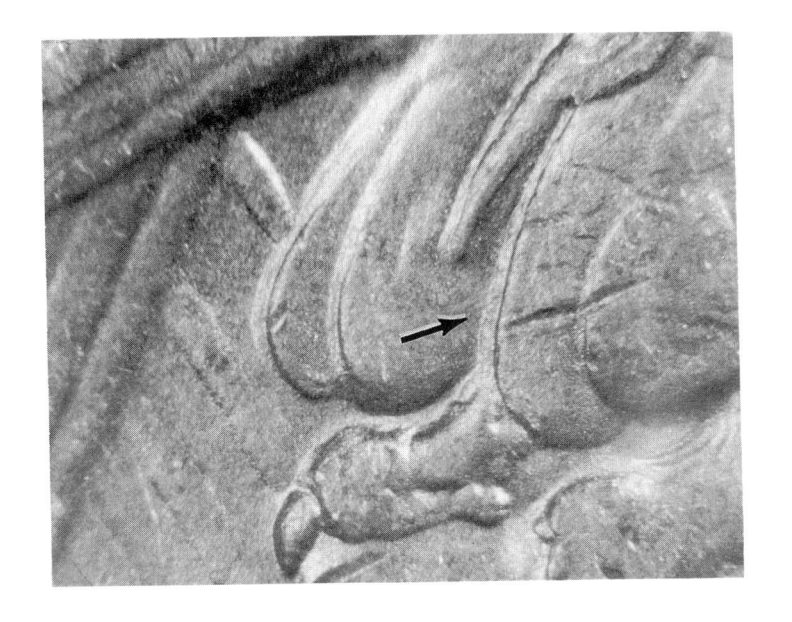

1922 S
Tripled Reverse
3 R B^2 b

1992 VAM BOOK ERRATA LIST

October 24, 1997

Page	VAM #	
85	--	in *Chicago Daily Tribune* letter, insert "at" between "was...once" second line below heading "TEN MORE"
90	--	Morgan April 8 letter, next to last para, last line– change "and" to "than" and "Foreman" to "foreman"
146	14-5	$I^1 10$ should be $I^2 10$
	14-7	Delete "slightly doubled below...towards rim"
	14-9	3rd line– "data" should be "date"
	14-10	change $I^1 10$ to $I^1 5$. Delete entire obverse description
152	44	change "blossoms" to "bolls"
154	115	change R-4 to R-6. Add at end of obverse description "Tripled right edges of cotton bolls and leaves."
160	202	change "blossoms" to "bolls"
168	22	II 19 should be II 9
162	6	delete "blossom"
174	56	III 1 should be II 24
202	5	last line– change "the right" to "eagle's left"
204	23	$III^2 17$ should be $III^2 36$
214	45	reverse description, "carved" should be "curved"
220	16	"doubled" in title should be "tripled". Add after "first 1 doubled"-- "below top and bottom crossbars. First 8 doubled."
	16 O	in photo caption, change "Doubled" to "Tripled"
222	7	$C^3 c$ should be $C^3 e$
224	12	$C^3 i$ should be $C^3 j$
	23	$C^3 k$ should be $C^3 l$
	25	$C^3 l$ should be $C^3 m$
	26	Obverse $C^3 a$ should be Obverse $III^2 15$
227	9 O	photo reversed
228	20	$III^2 20$ should be $III^2 4$
230	34	$C^3 9$ should be $C^3 g$
	38	18-1 should be "and"
239	9 R	O/O Left should be 13 R O/O Lower Left
	10 O	10 O should be 9 O
240	17	"tilted" should be "Tilted" in the title
	15 O	photo title should be 15 R O/O Left
241	16 O	photo title should be 16 R O Tilted Left
	19 O	photo title should be 19 R Over Polished Wing
242	34	title should be "Doubled Date"
251	2	III2 1 should be $III^2 1$
	7	$III^2 7$ should be $III^2 2$
252	3	$III^2 9$ should be $III^2 13$
254	19	$C^3 1$ should be $C^3 l$
255	24 O	24 O should be 24 R
256	38	"Doubled 18-1" should be "Doubled 18-3" in description
259	11	$III^2 12$ should be $III^2 11$
277	16	$III^2 15$ should be $III^2 16$
	18	$III^2 16$ should be $III^2 17$

283	1A R	photo number should be 22 R
284	13	"left" should be "right" end of last line
285	18	III^28 should be III^212
314	11	$C\ ^3g$ should be C^3f
319	–	delete /1892 S at top right
325	5	III O should be IV S
329	7	C^33 should be C^3a
353	3	C^3c should be C^3b
364	22	III^2 should be III^21
388	1	IV should be IV 1
412	–	3RD line "Jones" should be "James"
428	3	B^2c should be B^2b
	4	II 4 should be II 2
429	5	description was left out for 1922 P, add:

    5 II 1 • B^2c (Tripled Olive Leaves)   I-3   R-3

Reverse B^2c– Tripled bottom of olive leaves, back of leg feathers, base of right talon and on left rays above tail feathers.

	3	B^2c should be B^2b for 1922 D
430	2	II 4 should be II 2
431	–	1923 D description, first line, insert "it" between "But" and "is"
432	2	B^2i should be B^2b
503	–	3rd para, 7th line, "modem" should be "modern"

Problem Coins Now Graded

FREE VARIETY VERIFICATION!!

*Why pay an extra fee to have the variety attribution of your coin placed on the holder? ANACS provides this variety verification service **FOR FREE** when you request our grading service.*

VAM Numbers – FREE
Overton Numbers – FREE
Fivaz-Stanton Varieties – FREE
Sheldon and Newcomb Numbers – FREE
Cohen, Bolender, Breen and More – FREE
Flynn, Snow and More – FREE

Simply list the variety number to be verified in the space provided on the ANACS submission form. The ANACS graders will verify the attribution, and the variety designation, if correct, will be placed on the ANACS Cache.

Would you like the ANACS staff to determine the variety for you? From an extensive list of varieties, ANACS will research the standard references for you and place the correct variety designation on the holder for a small fee.

Contact ANACS at 1 (800) 888-1861 for submission forms and current pricing.

ANACS

"The Collector's Choice"®
P.O. Box 182141, Columbus, OH 43218-2141
1 (800) 888-1861

Participate In The Most Advanced Way To Buy And Sell Certified Coins.

Teletrade Auctions.

Teletrade auctions are exciting because they are real. Anyone can buy and anyone can sell. No reserve bids. No minimum orders. No mail bids. No sales calls. All you pay is a 3%-9% commission fee on purchases or sales.

Teletrade auctions are fun, easy and economical. Every coin offered is certified by PCGS, NGC or ANACS and is backed by a no-questions-asked return privilege.

Bidding is done over toll-free "800" lines. By simply entering the lot number you are interested in, you can hear the current bid or become the bidder yourself. Winners are announced 15 minutes after each auction.

Call 800-232-1132 or fill out the coupon below to receive your free introductory kit containing your first Teletrade auction. No obligation.

VISIT OUR WEB SITE!
http://www.teletrade.com

Our web site is packed with our full auction catalogs, high quality color images of actual items in upcoming auctions, prices realized and more.

Teletrade Auctions
"The Certified Coin Marketplace"

27 Main Street, Kingston, New York 12401
Phone: 800-232-1132 Fax: 914-339-6279

NOTES

NOTES

NOTES

NOTES

NOTES

NOTES